McGraw-Hill
networks™
A Social Studies Learning System

CHOOSE how you want to teach

- All print
- All digital
- Your own custom print and digital mix

MEETS YOU ANYWHERE — TAKES YOU EVERYWHERE

McGraw-Hill
networks™

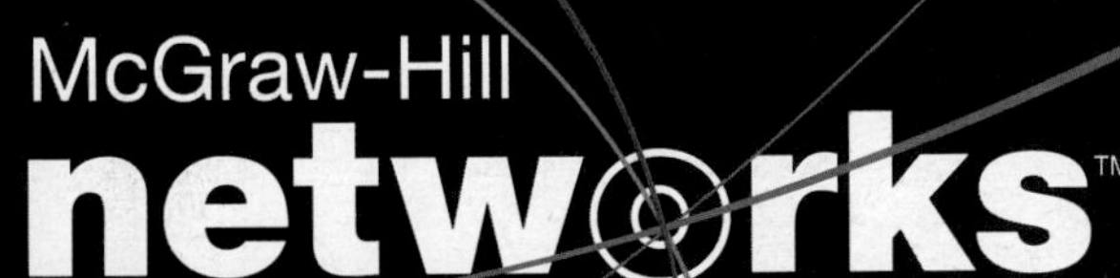

MEETS YOU ANYWHERE — TAKES YOU EVERYWHERE

MANAGE your classroom anytime

- Use prepared model lessons
- Clear pathway through critical content
- Quick, targeted instruction

From anywhere

- Plan instruction
- Create presentations
- Differentiate instruction

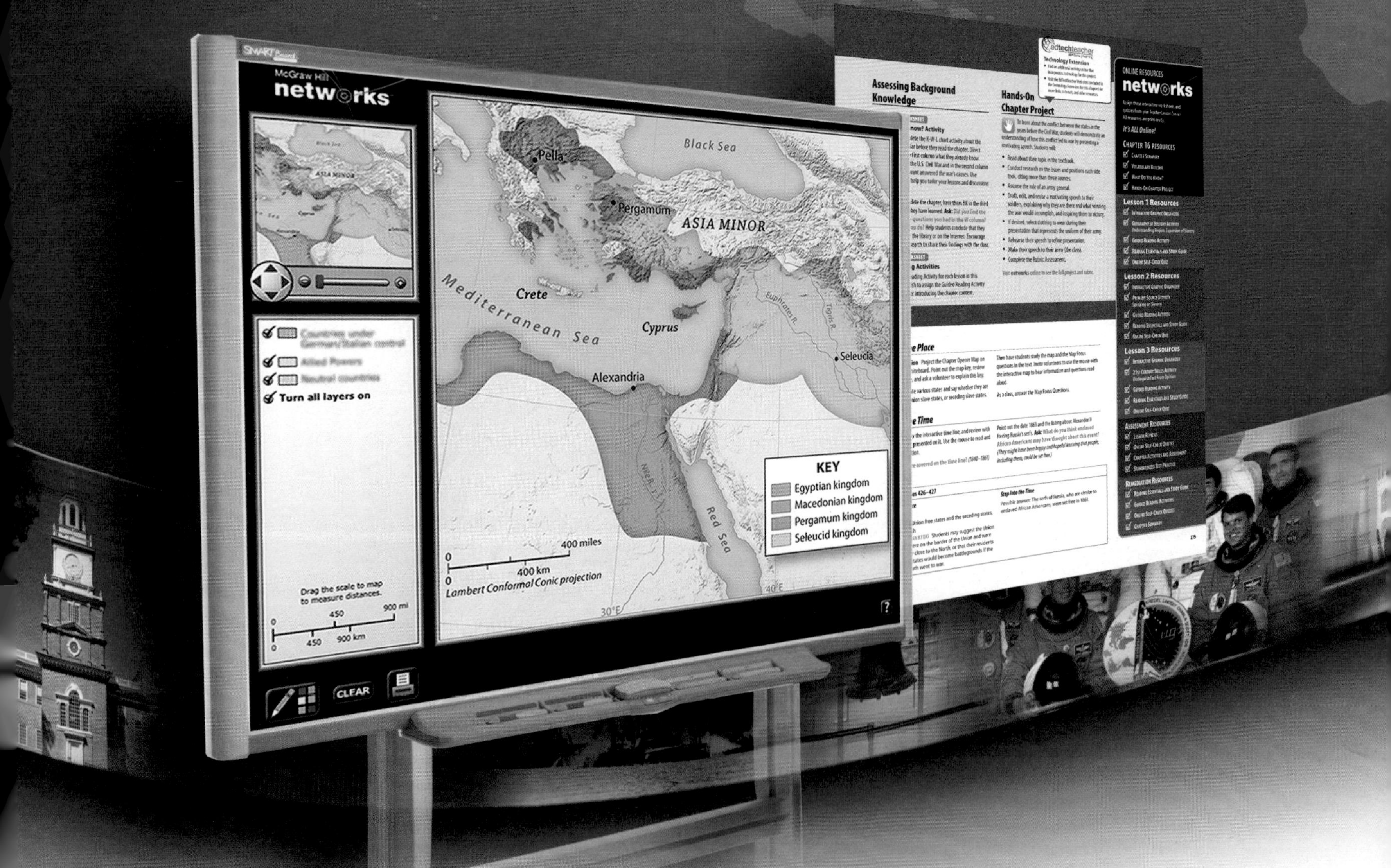

ORGANIZE with everything in one place

- Upload personal resources
- Search Resource Library
- Create class rosters
- File and Save

start networking

McGraw-Hill
networks™

MEETS YOU ANYWHERE — TAKES YOU EVERYWHERE

CUSTOMIZE everything for your students – easy, quick, and efficient

- Personalize lessons
- Create tests
- Modify assignments

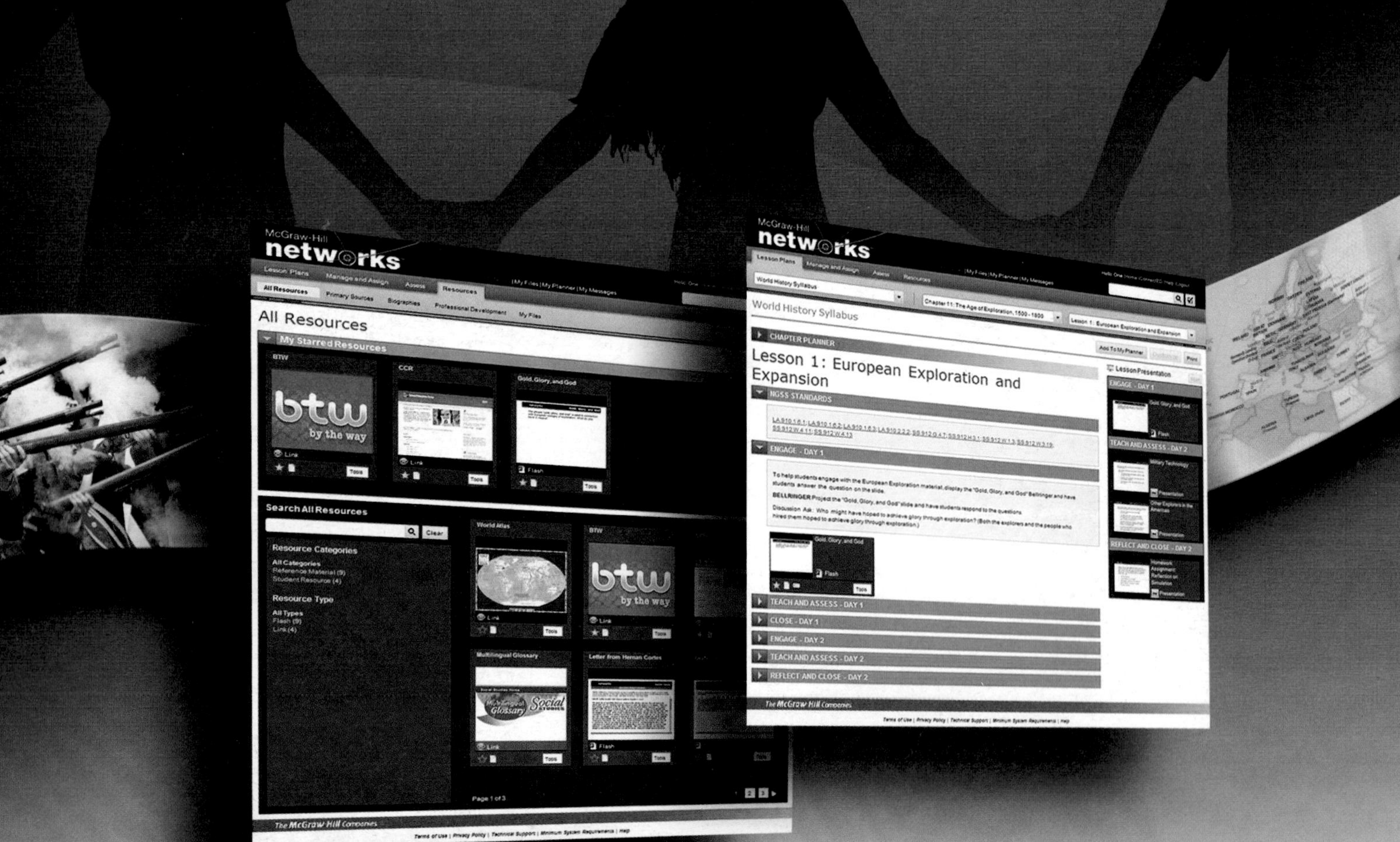

DIFFERENTIATE instruction to meet the needs of all your students

- Assign different reading levels
- Access full audio
- Use PDFs or modify worksheets
- Print or assign online

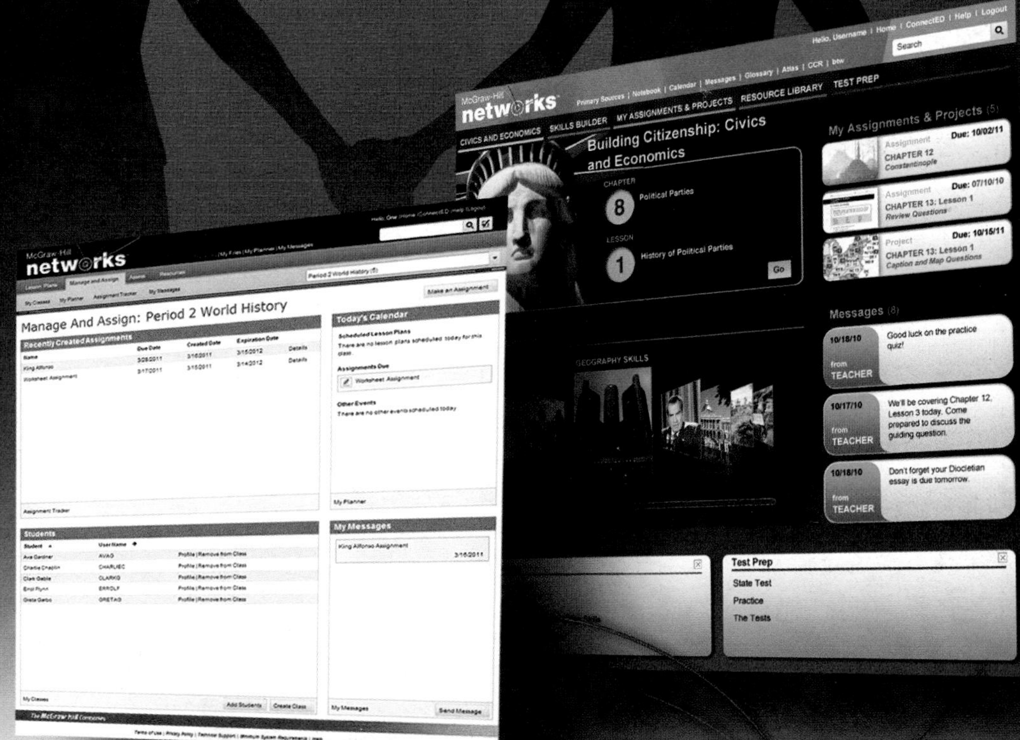

start networking

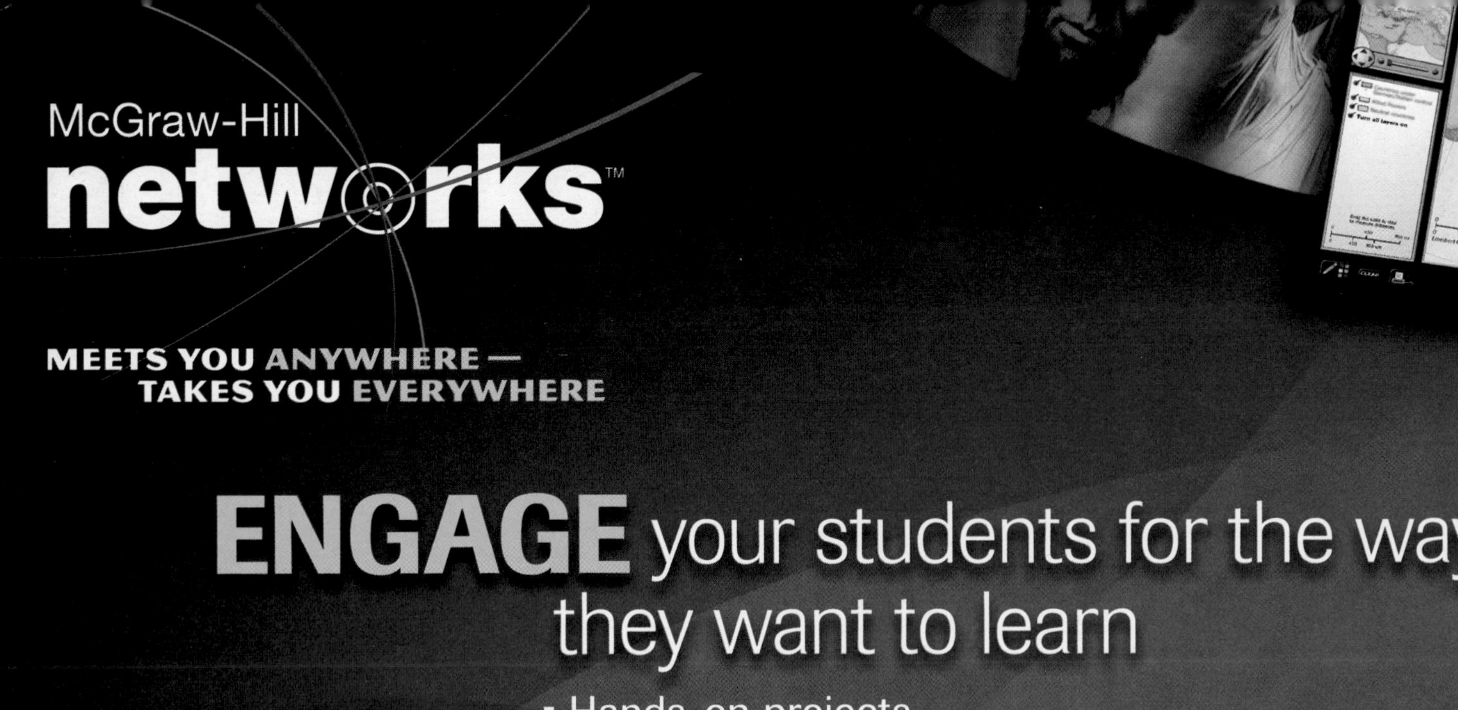

McGraw-Hill
networks
MEETS YOU ANYWHERE —
TAKES YOU EVERYWHERE

ENGAGE your students for the way they want to learn

- Hands-on projects
- Interactive maps, presentations, and primary sources
- Streaming video and games

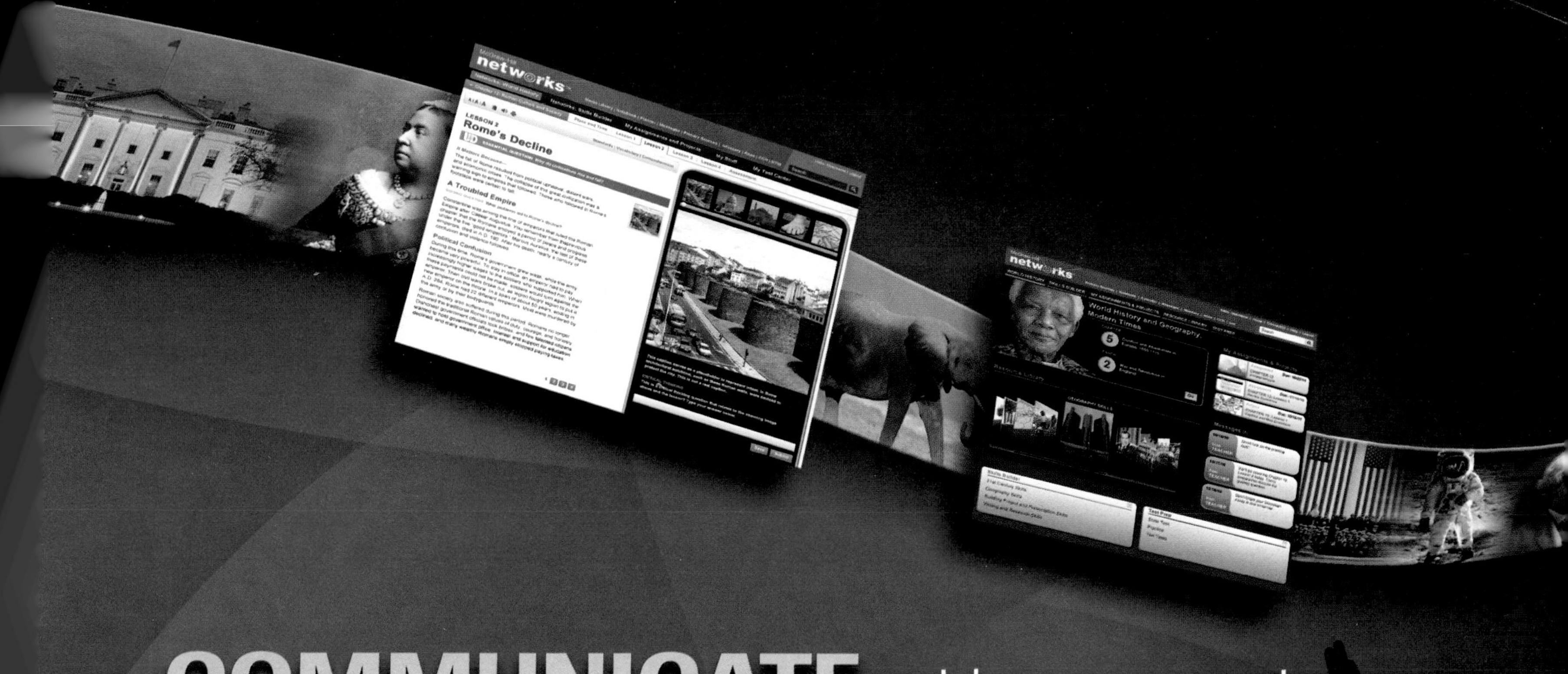

COMMUNICATE with your students

- Assign homework and tests
- Send messages
- Track and print student results

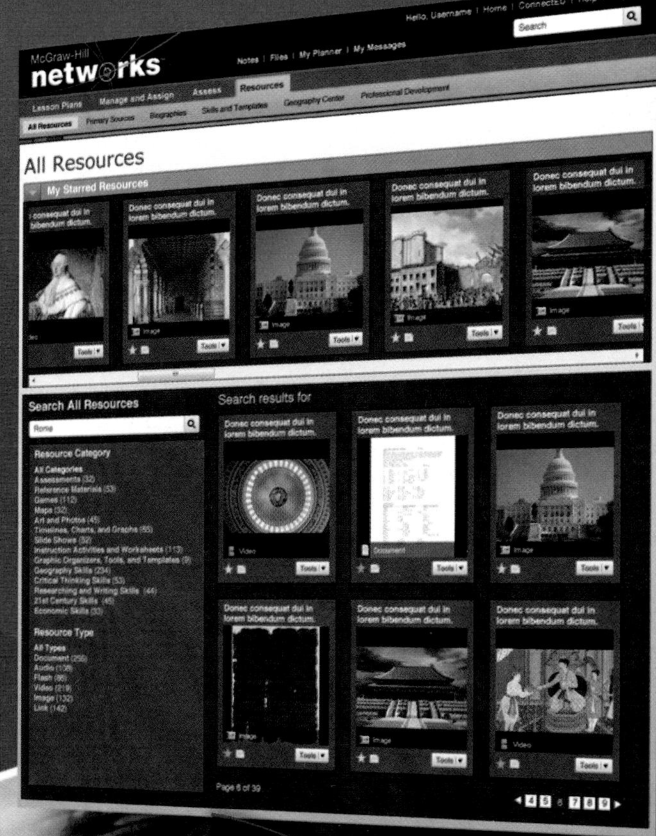

start networking

McGraw-Hill
networks™

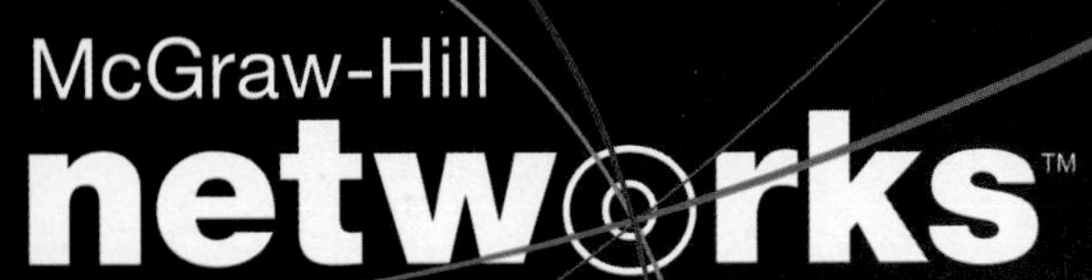

MEETS YOU ANYWHERE —
TAKES YOU EVERYWHERE

CONNECT with colleagues, students, experts, and content

1. Log on to the Internet and go to ***connected.mcgraw-hill.com***.
2. Enter User Name and Password.
3. Click on your **Networks** book.
4. Select your chapter and lesson.

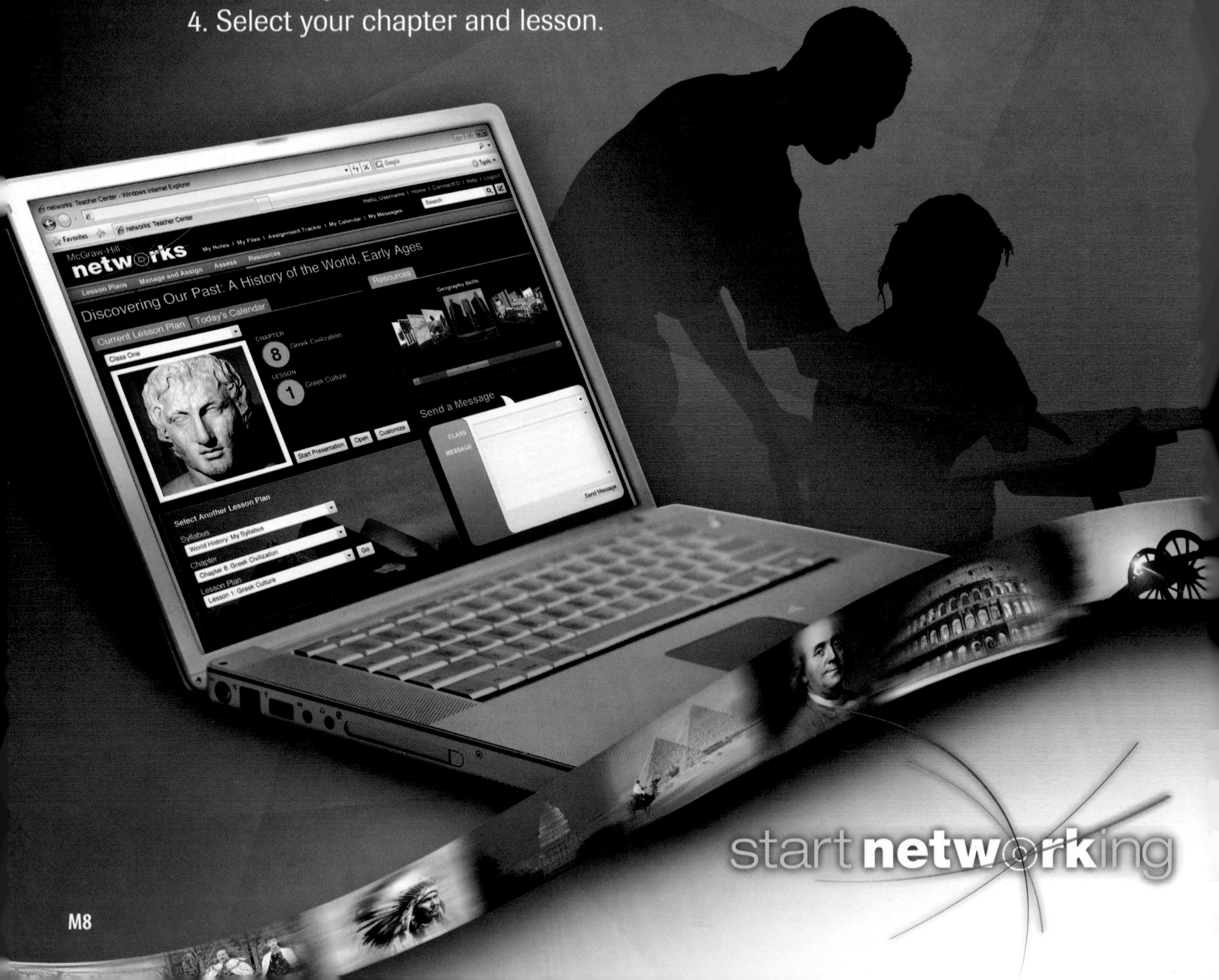

start **networking**

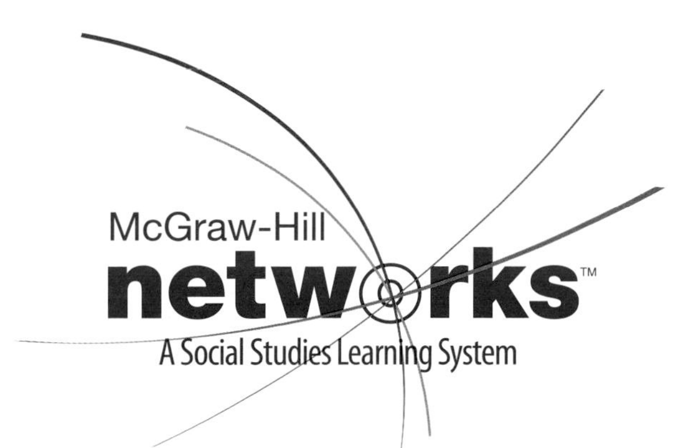

Teacher Edition

DISCOVERING OUR PAST

A HISTORY of the WORLD

Early Ages

Jackson J. Spielvogel, Ph.D.

Bothell, WA • Chicago, IL • Columbus, OH • New York, NY

AUTHOR

Jackson J. Spielvogel is Associate Professor of History Emeritus at The Pennsylvania State University. He received his Ph.D. from The Ohio State University, where he specialized in Reformation history under Harold J. Grimm. His work has been supported by fellowships from the Fulbright Foundation and the Foundation for Reformation Research. At Penn State, Spielvogel helped inaugurate the Western civilization courses, as well as a popular course on Nazi Germany. His book, *Hitler and Nazi Germany,* was published in 1987 (sixth edition, 2010). He is also the author of *Western Civilization,* published in 1991 (eighth edition, 2012). Spielvogel is the coauthor (with William Duiker) of *World History,* first published in 1998 (sixth edition, 2010). Spielvogel has won five major university-wide teaching awards. In 1988–1989, he held the Penn State Teaching Fellowship, the university's most prestigious teaching award. He won the Dean Arthur Ray Warnock Award for Outstanding Faculty Member in 1996 and the Schreyer Honors College Excellence in Teaching Award in 2000.

Cover credits:
(Main image) Emperor Charlemagne, The Gallery Collection/Corbis; (thumbnails l to r, t to b) Renaud Visage/Photographer's Choice/Getty Images, Burke/Triolo/Brand X Pictures/Jupiterimages, The McGraw-Hill Companies, Glen Allison/Photodisc/Getty Images, Library of Congress Prints and Photographs Division (LC-USZC2-2870), C. Sherburne/PhotoLink/Getty Images, Royalty-Free/CORBIS, Fernando Fernandez/age Fotostock, Photographer's Choice RF/Getty Images, Pixtal/age Fotostock, Melba Photo Agency/PunchStock, John Wang/Photodisc/Getty Images, Photodisc/Getty Images, Pixtal/age Fotostock, The McGraw-Hill Companies, Inc./Barry Barker, photographer, Author's Image/PunchStock, Ingram Publishing/SuperStock, Pixtal/age Fotostock.

National Council for the Social Studies, *National Curriculum Standards for Social Studies: A Framework for Teaching, Learning, and Assessment (Silver Spring, MD: NCSS, 2010).*

www.mheonline.com/networks

Send all inquiries to:
McGraw-Hill Education
8787 Orion Place
Columbus, OH 43240

Teacher Edition
ISBN: 978-0-07-659474-0
MHID: 0-07-659474-2

Student Edition
ISBN: 978-0-07-892714-0
MHID: 0-07-892714-5

Printed in the United States of America.

3 4 5 6 7 8 9 RMN 16 15 14 13 12

The McGraw·Hill Companies

AUTHORS, CONSULTANTS, AND REVIEWERS

Contributing Authors

Jay McTighe has published articles in a number of leading educational journals and has coauthored 10 books, including the best-selling *Understanding by Design* series with Grant Wiggins. McTighe also has an extensive background in professional development and is a featured speaker at national, state, and district conferences and workshops. He received his undergraduate degree from The College of William and Mary, earned a master's degree from the University of Maryland, and completed post-graduate studies at the Johns Hopkins University.

Dinah Zike, M.Ed., is an award-winning author, educator, and inventor recognized for designing three-dimensional, hands-on manipulatives and graphic organizers known as Foldables®. Foldables are used nationally and internationally by parents, teachers, and other professionals in the education field. Zike has developed more than 150 supplemental educational books and materials. Her two latest books, *Notebook Foldables®* and *Foldables®, Notebook Foldables®, & VKV®s for Spelling and Vocabulary 4th–12th* were each awarded *Learning Magazine's* Teachers' Choice Award for 2011. In 2004, Zike was honored with the CESI Science Advocacy Award. She received her M.Ed. from Texas A&M, College Station, Texas.

Doug Fisher Ph.D. and Nancy Frey Ph.D. are professors in the School of Teacher Education at San Diego State University. Fisher's focus is on literacy and language, with an emphasis on students who are English Learners. Frey's focus is on literacy and learning, with a concentration in how students acquire content knowledge. Both teach elementary and secondary teacher preparation courses, in addition to their work with graduate and doctoral programs. Their shared interests include supporting students with diverse learning needs, instructional design, and curriculum development. Fisher and Frey are coauthors of numerous articles and books, including *Better Learning Through Structured Teaching, and Checking for Understanding, Background Knowledge*, and *Improving Adolescent Literacy*. They are coeditors (with Diane Lapp) of the NCTE journal *Voices From the Middle*.

ACADEMIC CONSULTANTS

David Berger, Ph.D.
Ruth and I. Lewis Gordon Professor of Jewish History
Dean, Bernard Revel Graduate School
Yeshiva University
New York, New York

Albert S. Broussard, Ph.D.
Professor of History
Texas A & M University
College Station, Texas

Sheilah F. Clarke-Ekong, Ph.D.
Associate Professor, Cultural Anthropology
University of Missouri–St. Louis
St. Louis, Missouri

Tom Daccord
Educational Technology Specialist
Co-Director, EdTechTeacher
Boston, Massachusetts

Dr. Kenji Oshiro
Professor Emeritus of Geography
Wright State University
Dayton, Ohio

Justin Reich
Educational Technology Specialist
Co-Director, EdTechTeacher
Boston, Massachusetts

Joseph Rosenbloom, Ph.D.
Adjunct Professor, Jewish and Middle East Studies
Washington University
St. Louis, Missouri

TEACHER REVIEWERS

Mary Kathryn Bishop
Fairhope Middle School
Fairhope, Alabama

Janine Brown
Social Studies Department Chairperson
Discovery Middle School
Orlando, Florida

Carl M. Brownell
Social Studies Department Chairperson
Maine East High School
Park Ridge, Illinois

James Hauf
Berkeley Middle School
St. Louis, Missouri

Amy Kanuck
Morgan Village Middle School
Camden, New Jersey

Kim J. Lapple
Grades 6–12 Social Studies Chairperson
H.C. Crittenden Middle School
Armonk, New York

CONTENTS

There's More Online!

CHAPTER 5 Ancient Egypt and Kush 62

CHAPTER 6 The Israelites 86

CHAPTER 7 The Ancient Greeks 106

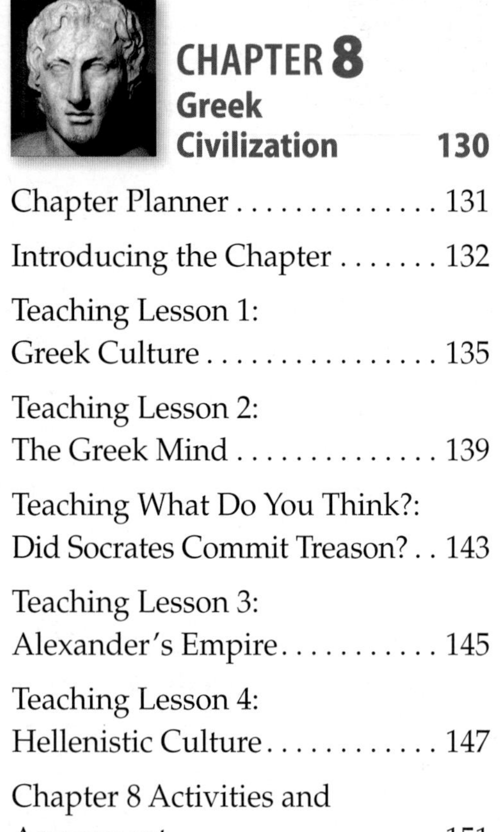

CHAPTER 8 Greek Civilization 130

CHAPTER 9 Ancient India 152

CHAPTER 10 Early China 172

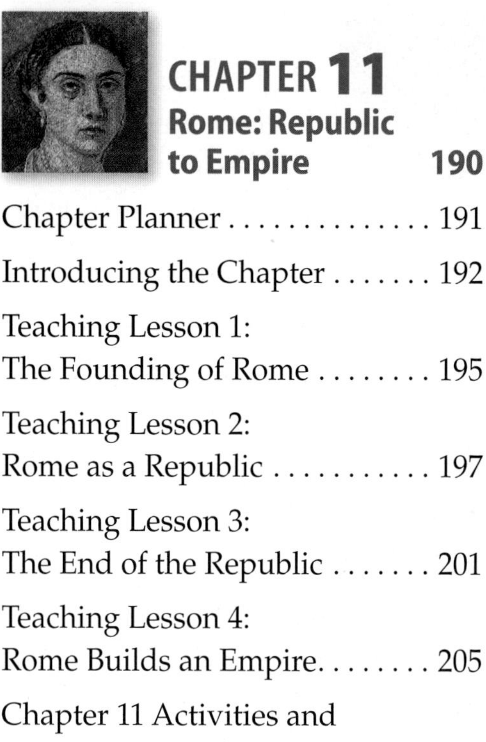

CHAPTER 11 Rome: Republic to Empire 190

CHAPTER 12 Roman Civilization 210

CHAPTER 13 The Rise of Christianity 230

CHAPTER 14 Islamic Civilization 246

CHAPTER 15 African Civilizations 262

CONTENTS

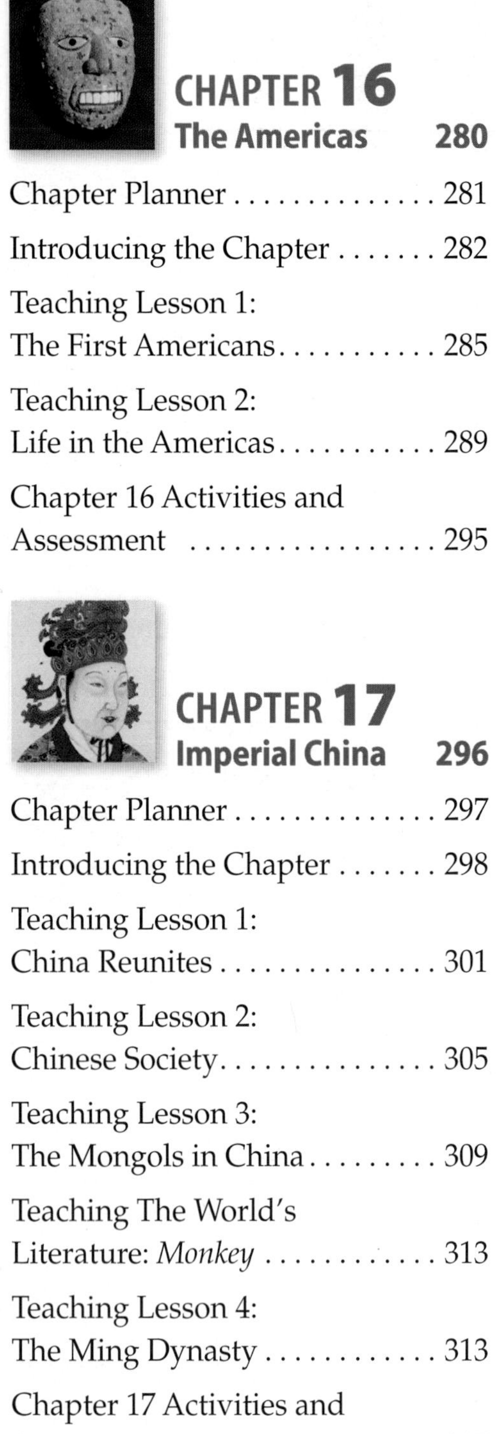

CHAPTER 16 The Americas 280

CHAPTER 17 Imperial China 296

CHAPTER 18 Civilizations of Korea, Japan, and Southeast Asia 318

CHAPTER 19 Medieval Europe 336

(l to r t to b) Werner Forman/Art Resource, NY, Max Paddler/Flickr/Getty Images, Peter Willi/SuperStock/Getty Images, The British Library/Heritage/Age fotostock.

CHAPTER 20 Renaissance and Reformation 360

CHAPTER 21 Age of Exploration and Trade 382

CHAPTER 22 The Scientific Revolution and the Enlightenment 398

CHAPTER 23 Political and Industrial Revolutions 412

TO TEACHERS Welcome to the McGraw-Hill **networks** Teacher Edition—a new approach to the Teacher Edition based on the principles of *Understanding by Design®*.

Getting Started

Author Note

Each chapter begins with a letter giving the author's perspective on the key concepts of the chapter.

Chapter Planner

The chapter planner uses the framework developed by Jay McTighe, co-author of *Understanding by Design®*.

- The goal is to focus on the desired results before planning each chapter's instruction.
- Students are guided by **Essential Questions** to the **Enduring Understanding**.
- Objectives highlight what **students will know** and what **students will be able to do** after completing the chapter.
- **Predictable misunderstandings** help you to anticipate common student misconceptions.
- **Assessment options** provide evidence of student understanding.

NCSS Standards

A complete list of the National Council for the Social Studies standards covered in this chapter

ONLINE RESOURCES
networks

There's More Online!

- INTERACTIVE WORKSHEETS
- BIOGRAPHIES
- CHARTS/GRAPHS
- GAMES
- GRAPHIC ORGANIZERS
- IMAGES
- MAPS
- PRIMARY SOURCES
- SLIDE SHOWS
- TIME LINE
- LECTURE SLIDES
- INTERACTIVE WHITEBOARD ACTIVITIES
- ASSESSMENTS
- VIDEOS

Ancient Greece: Farmers and Daily Life

Famous People, Incredible Lives: Alexander the Great

Alexander the Great's Empire

Chapter **8**

Greek Civilization

Dear World History Teacher,

Ancient Greek civilization was the fountainhead of Western culture. Socrates, Plato, and Aristotle established the foundations of Western philosophy. Herodotus and Thucydides created the discipline of history. Our Western literary forms are derived from Greek poetry and drama. Greek notions of harmony and proportion have remained the standards for Western art and architecture. A rational method of inquiry was conceived in ancient Greece. During the Classical period, the Greeks debated fundamental questions, such as the purpose of human existence, that have concerned Western thinkers since.

Despite these achievements, an element of tragedy remains. The Greeks were unable to rise above rivalries that caused them to fight and undermine their own civilization.

Although the independent Greek city-states were conquered by the Macedonians, Greek culture did not die. Under Alexander the Great, Macedonians and Greeks invaded and conquered the Persian Empire. Greeks and non-Greeks came together during the time known as the Hellenistic Era. Greek culture survived, but in a new form, mixed with the local cultures conquered by Alexander.

Jackson J. Spielvogel

More Media Resources

Current Events Online

Visit McGraw-Hill's current events Web site for high-interest news stories and activities for your students. Access the site through the Student or Teacher Center in **networks.**

Reading List

Grade 6 reading level:
Everyday Life in the Ancient World, by Sally Tagholm, Julie Ferris, Jonathan Stroud, and Sue Nicholson

Grade 7 reading level:
Alexander the Great: The Legend of a Warrior King, by Peter Chrisp

Grade 8 reading level:
The Library of Alexandria, by Kelly Trumble

At the MOVIES

Watch clips of popular culture films about Ancient Greece, such as *Jason and the Argonauts* or *Barefoot in Athens*. Or view documentaries about the civilization, such as *The Greeks: Crucible of Civilization.*

Discuss: Can fictional movies capture historical events accurately?

NOTE: Be sure to preview any clips to ensure they are age-appropriate.

Search for more videos online in the **networks** Resource Library.

130

CHAPTER **8 Planner**

UNDERSTANDING BY DESIGN®

Enduring Understandings

- *Cultures are held together by shared beliefs and common practices and values.*
- *People, places, and ideas change over time.* • *Leaders can bring about change in society.*

Essential Questions

- *What makes a culture unique?* • *How do new ideas change the way people live?*
- *What are the characteristics of a leader?*

Students will know:

- *how the ancient Greeks honored gods and goddesses*
- *the ideas that the ancient Greeks expressed in their literature, drama, art, and architecture*
- *ancient Greek beliefs about history and science*
- *how successful Alexander was in achieving his goals*
- *how Hellenistic kingdoms spread Greek culture*
- *ideas developed during the Hellenistic Era*

Students will be able to:

- **analyze** images of Greek gods and goddesses
- **organize** information about Greek gods and goddesses
- **write** a paragraph about a god or goddess
- **compare** ancient and modern Greek beliefs
- **describe** ancient Greek philosophy
- **explain** the philosophy of Socrates
- **discuss** the life of Socrates
- **compare and contrast** Socrates, Plato, and Aristotle
- **interpret** ancient Greek philosophical ideas
- **compare and contrast** the qualities of a great military leader and an effective ruler
- **categorize** Alexander's leadership qualities and military achievements
- **analyze** images of culture from the Hellenistic Era
- **explain** the meaning of *Hellenistic*
- **identify** contributions from the Hellenistic Era
- **write** a newspaper article describing an idea or a discovery from the Hellenistic Era
- **illustrate** an idea from the Hellenistic Era

Predictable Misunderstandings

Students may think:

- The Greeks and Greek culture remained in a remote area.
- There is little or no connection between the Greeks and life in the United States today.
- The Greeks excelled mostly in the arts and not in math and science.

Assessment Evidence

Performance Task

- Hands-On Chapter Project

Other Evidence

- Answers to class discussion comparing beliefs
- Discussion answers about ancient Greek thinkers
- Participation in small-group activity
- Newspaper article on idea of Hellenistic Era
- Economics of History Activity
- 21st Century Skills Activity
- Booklet on philosophical ideas
- Primary Source Activity
- Geography and History Activities
- Lesson Reviews
- Graphic organizer activities
- Interactive Whiteboard Activity responses

Pacing Guide

Introducing the Chapter	1 day
Lesson 1 Greek Culture	1 day
Lesson 2 The Greek Mind	1 day
What Do You Think?	1 day
Lesson 3 Alexander's Empire	1 day
Lesson 4 Hellenistic Culture	1 day
Chapter Activities and Assessment	1 day
TOTAL TIME	**7 Days**

Differentiated Instruction

These lesson plans are written to address the needs of your On Level students. Discussion and activities that are well-suited to your Approaching Grade Level learners, Beyond Grade Level learners, as well as your English Language Learners, are coded as follows:

AL **Approaching Grade Level**
BL **Beyond Grade Level**
ELL **English Language Learner**

NCSS Standards covered in "Greek Civilization"

Learners will understand

1 CULTURE

1. "Culture" refers to the socially transmitted behaviors, beliefs, values, traditions, institutions, and ways of living together for a group of people
2. Concepts such as beliefs, values, institutions, cohesion, diversity, accommodation, adaptation, assimilation, and dissonance
3. How culture influences the ways in which human groups solve the problems of daily living
4. That the beliefs, values, and behaviors of a culture form an integrated system that helps shape the activities and ways of life that define a culture
8. That language, behaviors, and beliefs of different cultures can both contribute to and pose barriers to cross-cultural understanding

2 TIME, CONTINUITY, AND CHANGE

2. Concepts such as: chronology, causality, change, conflict, complexity, multiple perspectives, primary and secondary sources, and cause and effect
3. That learning about the past requires the interpretation of sources, and that using varied sources provides the potential for a more balanced interpretive record of the past
4. That historical interpretations of the same event may differ on the basis of such factors as conflicting evidence from varied sources, national or cultural perspectives, and the point of view of the researcher
5. Key historical periods and patterns of change within and across cultures (e.g., the rise and fall of ancient civilizations, the development of technology, the rise of modern nation-states, and the establishment and breakdown of colonial systems)
7. The contributions of key persons, groups, and events from the past and their influence on the present

Greek Civilization 131

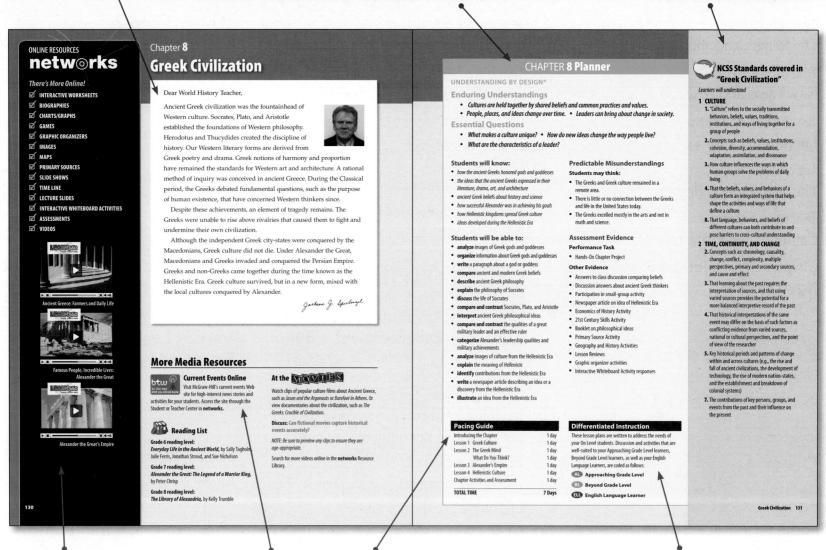

Lesson Videos

Videos available for the lessons in this chapter

More Media Resources

Books, videos, and a link to *btw*—McGraw-Hill's online current events Web site

Pacing Guide

Suggestions for how to pace the content based on your curriculum and number of school days

Differentiated Instruction

Activities are designed to meet the needs of students who are

Approaching Level

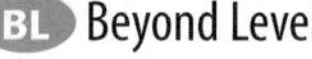

Beyond Level

ELL English Language Learners

networks

Don't forget! You can customize all your Lesson Plans online.

The Story Matters
To engage students, every chapter begins with a connection to the chapter content.

Interactive Guided Reading
This icon indicates that a worksheet is available to help students understand what they are reading. Worksheets can be printed or used online.

Assessing Background Knowledge
Pre-assessment activities for use before beginning the chapter

Hands-On Chapter Project
Cumulative projects bring world history to life and reveal student understanding through performance assessment.

Technology Extension
Available online for every Chapter Project

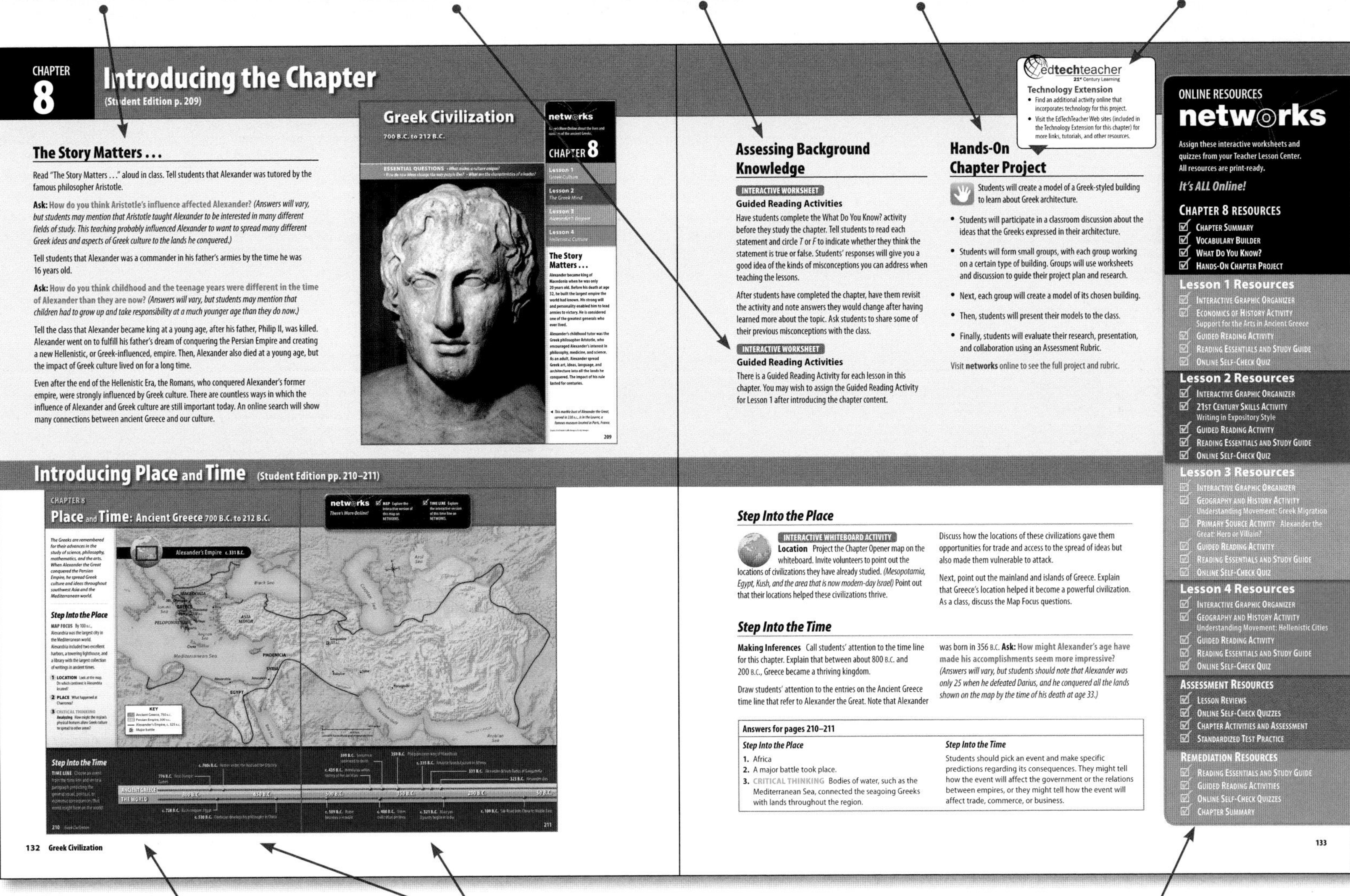

CHAPTER 8

Introducing the Chapter
(Student Edition p. 209)

The Story Matters . . .

Read "The Story Matters . . ." aloud in class. Tell students that Alexander was tutored by the famous philosopher Aristotle.

Ask: **How do you think Aristotle's influence affected Alexander?** *(Answers will vary, but students may mention that Aristotle taught Alexander to be interested in many different fields of study. This teaching probably influenced Alexander to want to spread many different Greek ideas and aspects of Greek culture to the lands he conquered.)*

Tell students that Alexander was a commander in his father's armies by the time he was 16 years old.

Ask: **How do you think childhood and the teenage years were different in the time of Alexander than they are now?** *(Answers will vary, but students may mention that children had to grow up and take responsibility at a much younger age than they do now.)*

Tell the class that Alexander became king at a young age, after his father, Philip II, was killed. Alexander went on to fulfill his father's dream of conquering the Persian Empire and creating a new Hellenistic, or Greek-influenced, empire. Then, Alexander also died at a young age, but the impact of Greek culture lived on for a long time.

Even after the end of the Hellenistic Era, the Romans, who conquered Alexander's former empire, were strongly influenced by Greek culture. There are countless ways in which the influence of Alexander and Greek culture are still important today. An online search will show many connections between ancient Greece and our culture.

Greek Civilization
700 B.C. to 212 B.C.

Assessing Background Knowledge

INTERACTIVE WORKSHEET
Guided Reading Activities
Have students complete the What Do You Know? activity before they study the chapter. Tell students to read each statement and circle *T* or *F* to indicate whether they think the statement is true or false. Students' responses will give you a good idea of the kinds of misconceptions you can address when teaching the lessons.

After students have completed the chapter, have them revisit the activity and note answers they would change after having learned more about the topic. Ask students to share some of their previous misconceptions with the class.

INTERACTIVE WORKSHEET
Guided Reading Activities
There is a Guided Reading Activity for each lesson in this chapter. You may wish to assign the Guided Reading Activity for Lesson 1 after introducing the chapter content.

edtechteacher
21st Century Learning
Technology Extension
- Find an additional activity online that incorporates technology for this project.
- Visit the EdTechTeacher Web sites (included in the Technology Extension for this chapter) for more links, tutorials, and other resources.

Hands-On Chapter Project

Students will create a model of a Greek-styled building to learn about Greek architecture.

- Students will participate in a classroom discussion about the ideas that the Greeks expressed in their architecture.
- Students will form small groups, with each group working on a certain type of building. Groups will use worksheets and discussion to guide their project plan and research.
- Next, each group will create a model of its chosen building.
- Then, students will present their models to the class.
- Finally, students will evaluate their research, presentation, and collaboration using an Assessment Rubric.

Visit **networks** online to see the full project and rubric.

ONLINE RESOURCES
networks
Assign these interactive worksheets and quizzes from your Teacher Lesson Center. All resources are print-ready.
It's ALL Online!

Chapter 8 Resources
- Chapter Summary
- Vocabulary Builder
- What Do You Know?
- Hands-On Chapter Project

Lesson 1 Resources
- Interactive Graphic Organizer
- Economics of History Activity: Support for the Arts in Ancient Greece
- Guided Reading Activity
- Reading Essentials and Study Guide
- Online Self-Check Quiz

Lesson 2 Resources
- Interactive Graphic Organizer
- 21st Century Skills Activity: Writing in Expository Style
- Guided Reading Activity
- Reading Essentials and Study Guide
- Online Self-Check Quiz

Lesson 3 Resources
- Interactive Graphic Organizer
- Geography and History Activity: Understanding Movement: Greek Migration
- Primary Source Activity: Alexander the Great: Hero or Villain?
- Guided Reading Activity
- Reading Essentials and Study Guide
- Online Self-Check Quiz

Lesson 4 Resources
- Interactive Graphic Organizer
- Geography and History Activity: Understanding Movement: Hellenistic Cities
- Guided Reading Activity
- Reading Essentials and Study Guide
- Online Self-Check Quiz

Assessment Resources
- Lesson Reviews
- Online Self-Check Quizzes
- Chapter Activities and Assessment
- Standardized Test Practice

Remediation Resources
- Reading Essentials and Study Guide
- Guided Reading Activities
- Online Self-Check Quizzes
- Chapter Summary

Introducing Place and Time
(Student Edition pp. 210–211)

CHAPTER 8
Place and Time: Ancient Greece 700 B.C. to 212 B.C.

Step Into the Place

INTERACTIVE WHITEBOARD ACTIVITY
Location Project the Chapter Opener map on the whiteboard. Invite volunteers to point out the locations of civilizations they have already studied. *(Mesopotamia, Egypt, Kush, and the area that is now modern-day Israel)* Point out that their locations helped these civilizations thrive.

Discuss how the locations of these civilizations gave them opportunities for trade and access to the spread of ideas but also made them vulnerable to attack.

Next, point out the mainland and islands of Greece. Explain that Greece's location helped it become a powerful civilization. As a class, discuss the Map Focus questions.

Step Into the Time

Making Inferences Call students' attention to the time line for this chapter. Explain that between about 800 B.C. and 200 B.C., Greece became a thriving kingdom.

Draw students' attention to the entries on the Ancient Greece time line that refer to Alexander the Great. Note that Alexander was born in 356 B.C. **Ask:** **How might Alexander's age have made his accomplishments seem more impressive?** *(Answers will vary, but students should note that Alexander was only 25 when he defeated Darius, and he conquered all the lands shown on the map by the time of his death at age 33.)*

Answers for pages 210–211

Step Into the Place
1. Africa
2. A major battle took place.
3. CRITICAL THINKING Bodies of water, such as the Mediterranean Sea, connected the seagoing Greeks with lands throughout the region.

Step Into the Time
Students should pick an event and make specific predictions regarding its consequences. They might tell how the event will affect the government or the relations between empires, or they might tell how the event will affect trade, commerce, or business.

132 Greek Civilization

133

Introducing Place and Time
- Students can step into the place and time using primary source quotes, a map or image, and a time line of the era.
- The Teacher Edition contains activities and discussion questions for these features.

Reduced SE pages
Reduced pages from the Student Edition on the left align to the accompanying teaching materials and lesson plans on the right.

There's More Online
A wide range of resources and worksheets are available online for each lesson.

Using the Lesson Plans

Lesson Plans

Complete lesson plans are provided for each chapter. Each lesson plan includes:

- lecture notes
- discussion questions
- suggested activities
- references to the lesson's projectable resources and the fully editable and printable worksheets

All resources and worksheets are available online at the **Networks Teacher Center.**

Engage

Every lesson plan begins with an Engage activity designed to motivate students and focus their attention on the lesson topic.

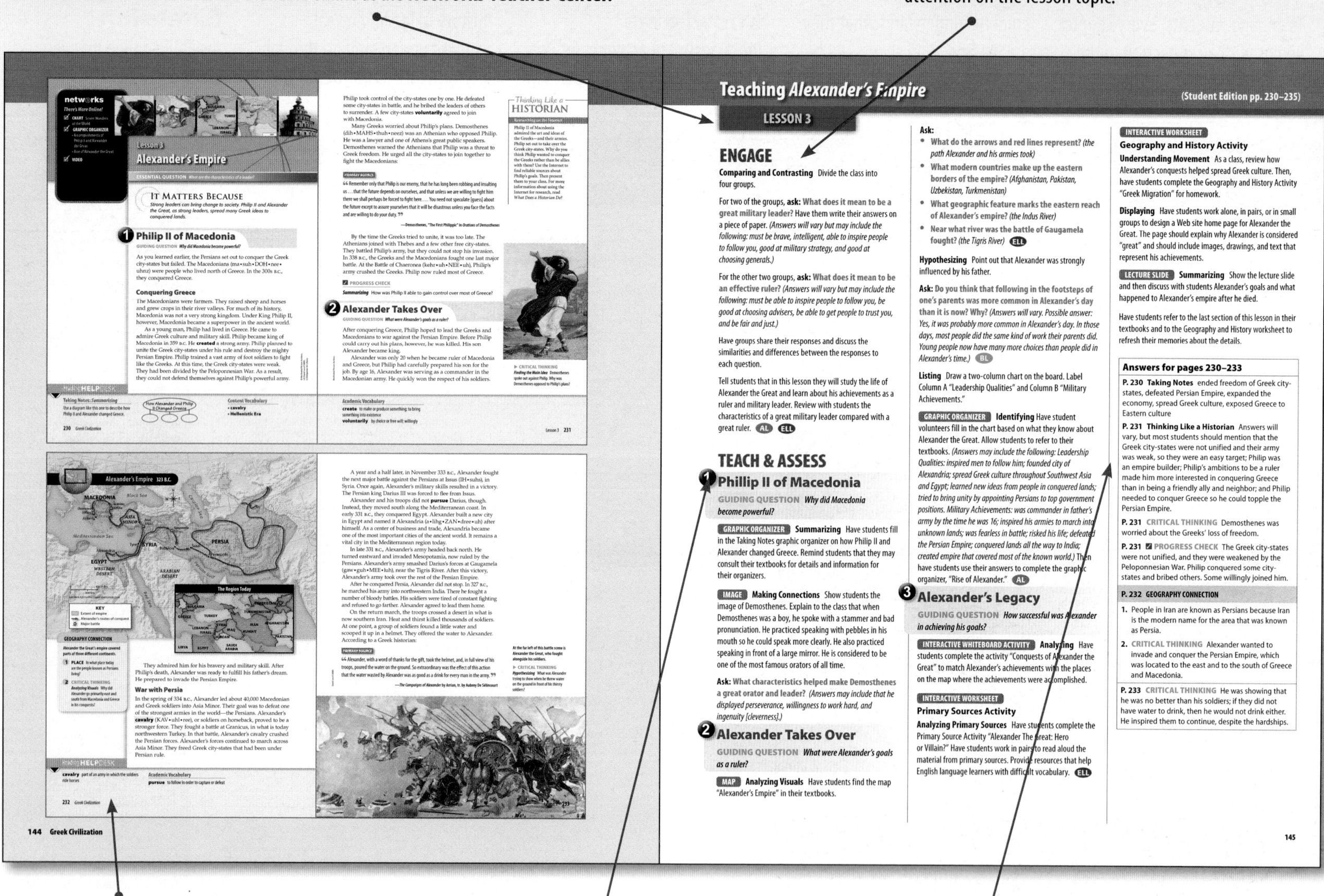

Teaching *Alexander's Empire* (Student Edition pp. 230–235)

LESSON 3

ENGAGE

Comparing and Contrasting Divide the class into four groups.

For two of the groups, **ask: What does it mean to be a great military leader?** Have them write their answers on a piece of paper. *(Answers will vary but may include the following: must be brave, intelligent, able to inspire people to follow you, good at military strategy, and good at choosing generals.)*

For the other two groups, **ask: What does it mean to be an effective ruler?** *(Answers will vary but may include the following: must be able to inspire people to follow you, be good at choosing advisers, be able to get people to trust you, and be fair and just.)*

Have groups share their responses and discuss the similarities and differences between the responses to each question.

Tell students that in this lesson they will study the life of Alexander the Great and learn about his achievements as a ruler and military leader. Review with students the characteristics of a great military leader compared with a great ruler. AL ELL

TEACH & ASSESS

1 Phillip II of Macedonia

GUIDING QUESTION *Why did Macedonia become powerful?*

GRAPHIC ORGANIZER **Summarizing** Have students fill in the Taking Notes graphic organizer on how Philip II and Alexander changed Greece. Remind students that they may consult their textbooks for details and information for their organizers.

IMAGE **Making Connections** Show students the image of Demosthenes. Explain to the class that when Demosthenes was a boy, he spoke with a stammer and bad pronunciation. He practiced speaking with pebbles in his mouth so he could speak more clearly. He also practiced speaking in front of a large mirror. He is considered to be one of the most famous orators of all time.

Ask: What characteristics helped make Demosthenes a great orator and leader? *(Answers may include that he displayed perseverance, willingness to work hard, and ingenuity [cleverness].)*

2 Alexander Takes Over

GUIDING QUESTION *What were Alexander's goals as a ruler?*

MAP **Analyzing Visuals** Have students find the map "Alexander's Empire" in their textbooks.

Ask:

- **What do the arrows and red lines represent?** *(the path Alexander and his armies took)*
- **What modern countries make up the eastern borders of the empire?** *(Afghanistan, Pakistan, Uzbekistan, Turkmenistan)*
- **What geographic feature marks the eastern reach of Alexander's empire?** *(the Indus River)*
- **Near what river was the battle of Gaugamela fought?** *(the Tigris River)* ELL

Hypothesizing Point out that Alexander was strongly influenced by his father.

Ask: Do you think that following in the footsteps of one's parents was more common in Alexander's day than it is now? Why? *(Answers will vary. Possible answer: Yes, it was probably more common in Alexander's day. In those days, most people did the same kind of work their parents did. Young people now have many more choices than people did in Alexander's time.)* BL

Listing Draw a two-column chart on the board. Label Column A "Leadership Qualities" and Column B "Military Achievements."

GRAPHIC ORGANIZER **Identifying** Have student volunteers fill in the chart based on what they know about Alexander the Great. Allow students to refer to their textbooks. *(Answers may include the following: Leadership Qualities: inspired men to follow him; founded city of Alexandria; spread Greek culture throughout Southwest Asia and Egypt; learned new ideas from people in conquered lands; tried to bring unity by appointing Persians to top government positions. Military Achievements: was commander in father's army by the time he was 16; inspired his armies to march into unknown lands; was fearless in battle; risked his life; defeated the Persian Empire; conquered lands all the way to India; created empire that covered most of the known world.)* Then have students use their answers to complete the graphic organizer, "Rise of Alexander." AL

3 Alexander's Legacy

GUIDING QUESTION *How successful was Alexander in achieving his goals?*

INTERACTIVE WHITEBOARD ACTIVITY **Analyzing** Have students complete the activity "Conquests of Alexander the Great" to match Alexander's achievements with the places on the map where the achievements were accomplished.

INTERACTIVE WORKSHEET

Primary Sources Activity

Analyzing Primary Sources Have students complete the Primary Source Activity "Alexander the Great: Hero or Villain?" Have students work in pairs to read aloud the material from primary sources. Provide resources that help English language learners with difficult vocabulary. ELL

INTERACTIVE WORKSHEET

Geography and History Activity

Understanding Movement As a class, review how Alexander's conquests helped spread Greek culture. Then, have students complete the Geography and History Activity "Greek Migration" for homework.

Displaying Have students work alone, in pairs, or in small groups to design a Web site home page for Alexander the Great. The page should explain why Alexander is considered "great" and should include images, drawings, and text that represent his achievements.

LECTURE SLIDE **Summarizing** Show the lecture slide and then discuss with students Alexander's goals and what happened to Alexander's empire after he died.

Have students refer to the last section of this lesson in their textbooks and to the Geography and History worksheet to refresh their memories about the details.

Answers for pages 230–233

P. 230 Taking Notes ended freedom of Greek city-states, defeated Persian Empire, expanded the economy, spread Greek culture, exposed Greece to Eastern culture

P. 231 Thinking Like a Historian Answers will vary, but most students should mention that the Greek city-states were not unified and their army was weak, so they were an easy target; Philip was an empire builder; Philip's ambitions to be a ruler made him more interested in conquering Greece than in being a friendly ally and neighbor; and Philip needed to conquer Greece so he could topple the Persian Empire.

P. 231 CRITICAL THINKING Demosthenes was worried about the Greeks' loss of freedom.

P. 231 PROGRESS CHECK The Greek city-states were not unified, and they were weakened by the Peloponnesian War. Philip conquered some city-states and bribed others. Some willingly joined him.

P. 232 GEOGRAPHY CONNECTION

1. People in Iran are known as Persians because Iran is the modern name for the area that was known as Persia.
2. CRITICAL THINKING Alexander wanted to invade and conquer the Persian Empire, which was located to the east and to the south of Greece and Macedonia.

P. 233 CRITICAL THINKING He was showing that he was no better than his soldiers; if they did not have water to drink, then he would not drink either. He inspired them to continue, despite the hardships.

144 Greek Civilization | 145

Reading Help Desk

This feature appears in each lesson in the Student Edition to assist students as they read. Includes:

- content and academic vocabulary
- note-taking activities and graphic organizers
- reading strategies

Teach & Assess

Teach and Assess is the core of the lesson plan. It contains the activities, lecture notes, background information, and discussion questions needed to teach the lesson.

Answers

Answers to the questions and activities in the Student Edition

networks

Don't forget! You can customize all your Lesson Plans online.

Interactive Activities

These icons indicate that there are interactive whiteboard activities, worksheets, videos, maps, images, and lecture slides online at the Teacher Center. They can be projected or used on your classroom interactive whiteboard. Worksheets can be edited and printed or assigned online.

Close & Reflect

Each lesson ends with activities designed to help students reflect on their learning and performance.

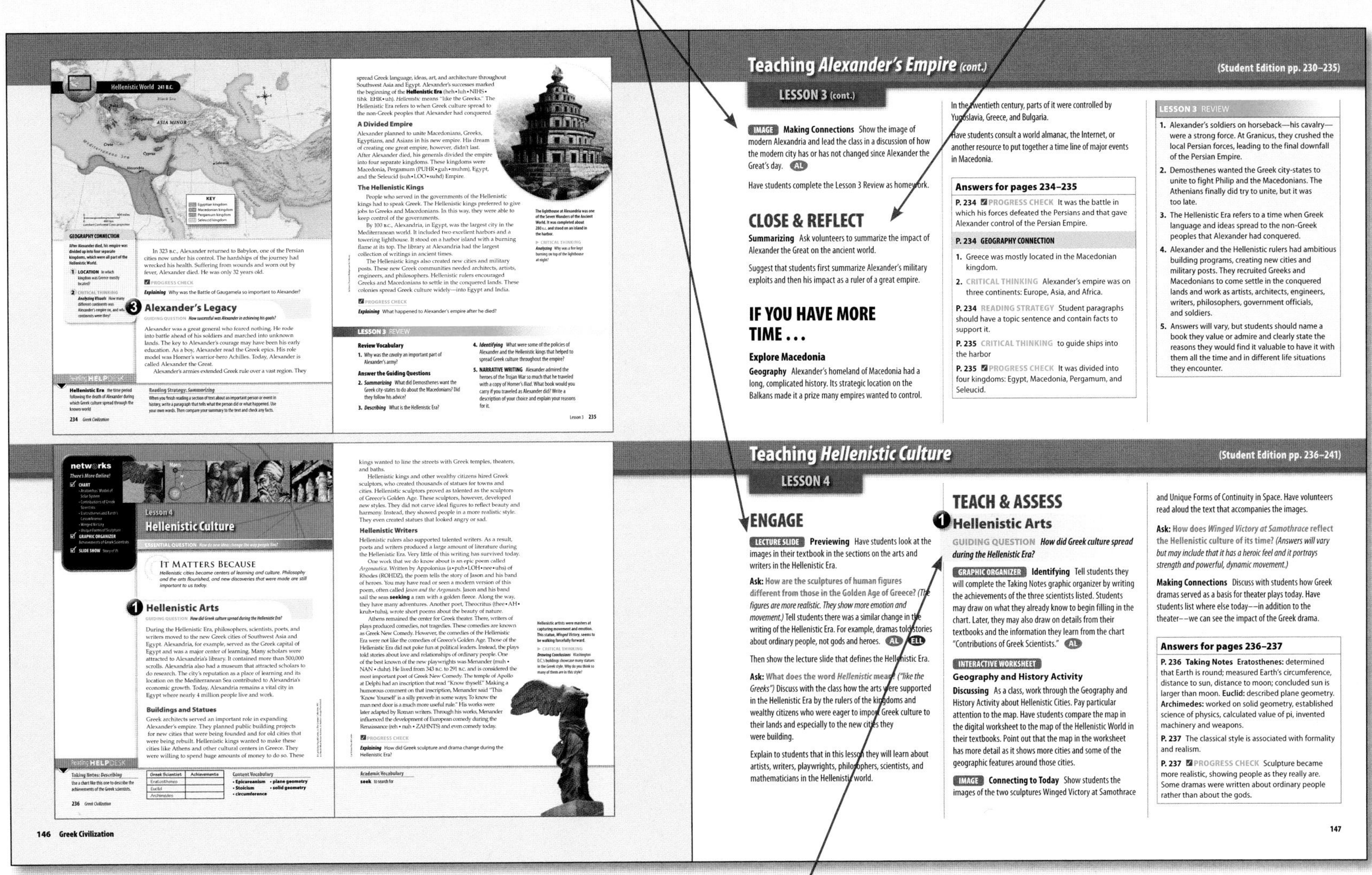

Teaching *Alexander's Empire* (cont.) (Student Edition pp. 230–235)

LESSON 3 (cont.)

IMAGE **Making Connections** Show the image of modern Alexandria and lead the class in a discussion of how the modern city has or has not changed since Alexander the Great's day. AL

Have students complete the Lesson 3 Review as homework.

CLOSE & REFLECT

Summarizing Ask volunteers to summarize the impact of Alexander the Great on the ancient world.

Suggest that students first summarize Alexander's military exploits and then his impact as a ruler of a great empire.

IF YOU HAVE MORE TIME . . .

Explore Macedonia

Geography Alexander's homeland of Macedonia had a long, complicated history. Its strategic location on the Balkans made it a prize many empires wanted to control. In the twentieth century, parts of it were controlled by Yugoslavia, Greece, and Bulgaria.

Have students consult a world almanac, the Internet, or another resource to put together a time line of major events in Macedonia.

Answers for pages 234–235

P. 234 PROGRESS CHECK It was the battle in which his forces defeated the Persians and that gave Alexander control of the Persian Empire.

P. 234 GEOGRAPHY CONNECTION

1. Greece was mostly located in the Macedonian kingdom.
2. CRITICAL THINKING Alexander's empire was on three continents: Europe, Asia, and Africa.

P. 234 READING STRATEGY Student paragraphs should have a topic sentence and contain facts to support it.

P. 235 CRITICAL THINKING to guide ships into the harbor

P. 235 PROGRESS CHECK It was divided into four kingdoms: Egypt, Macedonia, Pergamum, and Seleucid.

LESSON 3 REVIEW

1. Alexander's soldiers on horseback—his cavalry—were a strong force. At Granicus, they crushed the local Persian forces, leading to the final downfall of the Persian Empire.
2. Demosthenes wanted the Greek city-states to unite to fight Philip and the Macedonians. The Athenians finally did try to unite, but it was too late.
3. The Hellenistic Era refers to a time when Greek language and ideas spread to the non-Greek peoples that Alexander had conquered.
4. Alexander and the Hellenistic rulers had ambitious building programs, creating new cities and military posts. They recruited Greeks and Macedonians to come settle in the conquered lands and work as artists, architects, engineers, writers, philosophers, government officials, and soldiers.
5. Answers will vary, but students should name a book they value or admire and clearly state the reasons they would find it valuable to have it with them all the time and in different life situations they encounter.

Teaching *Hellenistic Culture* (Student Edition pp. 236–241)

LESSON 4

ENGAGE

LECTURE SLIDE **Previewing** Have students look at the images in their textbook in the sections on the arts and writers in the Hellenistic Era.

Ask: How are the sculptures of human figures different from those in the Golden Age of Greece? *(The figures are more realistic. They show more emotion and movement.)* Tell students there was a similar change in the writing of the Hellenistic Era. For example, dramas told stories about ordinary people, not gods and heroes. AL ELL

Then show the lecture slide that defines the Hellenistic Era.

Ask: What does the word *Hellenistic* mean? *("like the Greeks")* Discuss with the class how the arts were supported in the Hellenistic Era by the rulers of the kingdoms and wealthy citizens who were eager to impose Greek culture to their lands and especially to the new cities they were building.

Explain to students that in this lesson they will learn about artists, writers, playwrights, philosophers, scientists, and mathematicians in the Hellenistic world.

TEACH & ASSESS

1 Hellenistic Arts

GUIDING QUESTION *How did Greek culture spread during the Hellenistic Era?*

GRAPHIC ORGANIZER **Identifying** Tell students they will complete the Taking Notes graphic organizer by writing the achievements of the three scientists listed. Students may draw on what they already know to begin filling in the chart. Later, they may also draw on details from their textbooks and the information they learn from the chart "Contributions of Greek Scientists." AL

INTERACTIVE WORKSHEET

Geography and History Activity

Discussing As a class, work through the Geography and History Activity about Hellenistic Cities. Pay particular attention to the map. Have students compare the map in the digital worksheet to the map of the Hellenistic World in their textbooks. Point out that the map in the worksheet has more detail as it shows more cities and some of the geographic features around those cities.

IMAGE **Connecting to Today** Show students the images of the two sculptures Winged Victory at Samothrace and Unique Forms of Continuity in Space. Have volunteers read aloud the text that accompanies the images.

Ask: How does *Winged Victory at Samothrace* reflect the Hellenistic culture of its time? *(Answers will vary but may include that it has a heroic feel and it portrays strength and powerful, dynamic movement.)*

Making Connections Discuss with students how Greek dramas served as a basis for theater plays today. Have students list where else today—in addition to the theater—we can see the impact of the Greek drama.

Answers for pages 236–237

P. 236 Taking Notes Eratosthenes: determined that Earth is round; measured Earth's circumference, distance to sun, distance to moon; concluded sun is larger than moon. **Euclid:** described plane geometry. **Archimedes:** worked on solid geometry, established science of physics, calculated value of pi, invented machinery and weapons.

P. 237 The classical style is associated with formality and realism.

P. 237 PROGRESS CHECK Sculpture became more realistic, showing people as they really are. Some dramas were written about ordinary people rather than about the gods.

146 Greek Civilization

147

Guiding Questions

Questions focus on key knowledge that students need to understand the Essential Questions.

Using the Lesson Plans *(continued)*

SPECIAL FEATURES

The Student Edition contains numerous images, charts, graphs, and special features designed to engage student interest and focus attention on key individuals and events in history.

Special features include:

- What Do You Think?
- Biographies
- Thinking Like a Historian
- Connections to Today
- The World's Literature

1-Day and 2-Day Lesson Plans

Lesson Plans are paced to help you plan for each day's classes. Online Lesson Plans are fully customizable to meet your needs and the needs of your students.

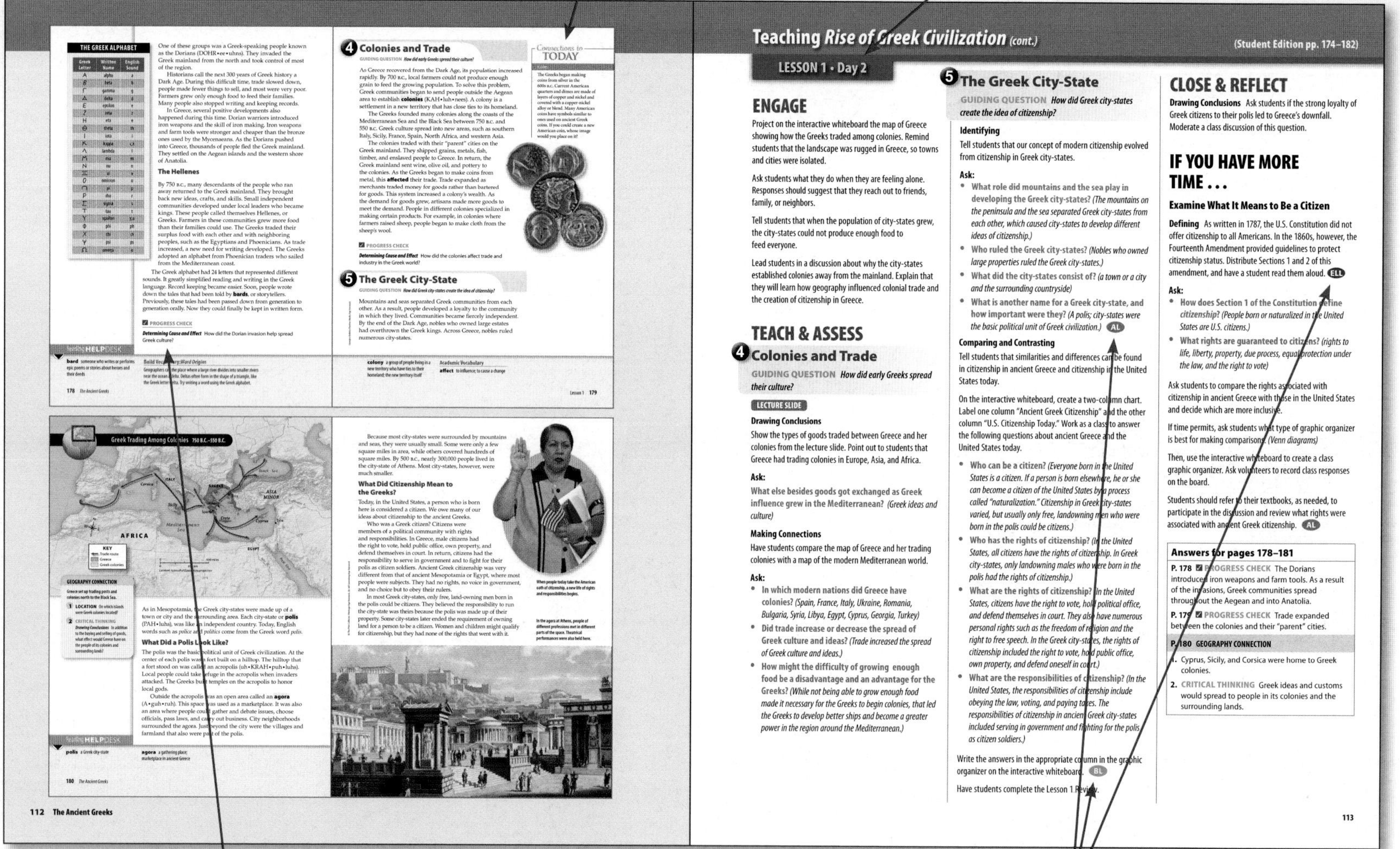

THE GREEK ALPHABET
The Hellenes
4 Colonies and Trade
CONNECTIONS TO TODAY
5 The Greek City-State
What Did Citizenship Mean to the Greeks?
What Did a Polis Look Like?
Greek Trading Among Colonies 750 B.C.–550 B.C.
AFRICA
178 The Ancient Greeks
Lesson 1 179
180 The Ancient Greeks
112 The Ancient Greeks
Teaching Rise of Greek Civilization (cont.)
(Student Edition pp. 174–182)
LESSON 1 • Day 2
ENGAGE
Project on the interactive whiteboard the map of Greece showing how the Greeks traded among colonies. Remind students that the landscape was rugged in Greece, so towns and cities were isolated.
Ask students what they do when they are feeling alone. Responses should suggest that they reach out to friends, family, or neighbors.
Tell students that when the population of city-states grew, the city-states could not produce enough food to feed everyone.
Lead students in a discussion about why the city-states established colonies away from the mainland. Explain that they will learn how geography influenced colonial trade and the creation of citizenship in Greece.
TEACH & ASSESS
4 Colonies and Trade
GUIDING QUESTION How did early Greeks spread their culture?
LECTURE SLIDE
Drawing Conclusions
Show the types of goods traded between Greece and her colonies from the lecture slide. Point out to students that Greece had trading colonies in Europe, Asia, and Africa.
Ask:
What else besides goods got exchanged as Greek influence grew in the Mediterranean? (Greek ideas and culture)
Making Connections
Have students compare the map of Greece and her trading colonies with a map of the modern Mediterranean world.
Ask:
In which modern nations did Greece have colonies? (Spain, France, Italy, Ukraine, Romania, Bulgaria, Syria, Libya, Egypt, Cyprus, Georgia, Turkey)
Did trade increase or decrease the spread of Greek culture and ideas? (Trade increased the spread of Greek culture and ideas.)
How might the difficulty of growing enough food be a disadvantage and an advantage for the Greeks? (While not being able to grow enough food made it necessary for the Greeks to begin colonies, that led the Greeks to develop better ships and become a greater power in the region around the Mediterranean.)
5 The Greek City-State
GUIDING QUESTION How did Greek city-states create the idea of citizenship?
Identifying
Tell students that our concept of modern citizenship evolved from citizenship in Greek city-states.
Ask:
What role did mountains and the sea play in developing the Greek city-states? (The mountains on the peninsula and the sea separated Greek city-states from each other, which caused city-states to develop different ideas of citizenship.)
Who ruled the Greek city-states? (Nobles who owned large properties ruled the Greek city-states.)
What did the city-states consist of? (a town or a city and the surrounding countryside)
What is another name for a Greek city-state, and how important were they? (A polis; city-states were the basic political unit of Greek civilization.) AL
Comparing and Contrasting
Tell students that similarities and differences can be found in citizenship in ancient Greece and citizenship in the United States today.
On the interactive whiteboard, create a two-column chart. Label one column "Ancient Greek Citizenship" and the other column "U.S. Citizenship Today." Work as a class to answer the following questions about ancient Greece and the United States today.
Who can be a citizen? (Everyone born in the United States is a citizen. If a person is born elsewhere, he or she can become a citizen of the United States by a process called "naturalization." Citizenship in Greek city-states varied, but usually only free, landowning men who were born in the polis could be citizens.)
Who has the rights of citizenship? (In the United States, all citizens have the rights of citizenship. In Greek city-states, only landowning males who were born in the polis had the rights of citizenship.)
What are the rights of citizenship? (In the United States, citizens have the right to vote, hold political office, and defend themselves in court. They also have numerous personal rights such as the freedom of religion and the right to free speech. In the Greek city-states, the rights of citizenship included the right to vote, hold public office, own property, and defend oneself in court.)
What are the responsibilities of citizenship? (In the United States, the responsibilities of citizenship include obeying the law, voting, and paying taxes. The responsibilities of citizenship in ancient Greek city-states included serving in government and fighting for the polis as citizen soldiers.)
Write the answers in the appropriate column in the graphic organizer on the interactive whiteboard. BL
Have students complete the Lesson 1 Review.
CLOSE & REFLECT
Drawing Conclusions Ask students if the strong loyalty of Greek citizens to their polis led to Greece's downfall. Moderate a class discussion of this question.
IF YOU HAVE MORE TIME . . .
Examine What It Means to Be a Citizen
Defining As written in 1787, the U.S. Constitution did not offer citizenship to all Americans. In the 1860s, however, the Fourteenth Amendment provided guidelines to protect citizenship status. Distribute Sections 1 and 2 of this amendment, and have a student read them aloud. ELL
Ask:
How does Section 1 of the Constitution define citizenship? (People born or naturalized in the United States are U.S. citizens.)
What rights are guaranteed to citizens? (rights to life, liberty, property, due process, equal protection under the law, and the right to vote)
Ask students to compare the rights associated with citizenship in ancient Greece with those in the United States and decide which are more inclusive.
If time permits, ask students what type of graphic organizer is best for making comparisons. (Venn diagrams)
Then, use the interactive whiteboard to create a class graphic organizer. Ask volunteers to record class responses on the board.
Students should refer to their textbooks, as needed, to participate in the discussion and review what rights were associated with ancient Greek citizenship. AL
Answers for pages 178–181
P. 178 PROGRESS CHECK The Dorians introduced iron weapons and farm tools. As a result of the invasions, Greek communities spread throughout the Aegean and into Anatolia.
P. 179 PROGRESS CHECK Trade expanded between the colonies and their "parent" cities.
P. 180 GEOGRAPHY CONNECTION
1. Cyprus, Sicily, and Corsica were home to Greek colonies.
2. CRITICAL THINKING Greek ideas and customs would spread to people in its colonies and the surrounding lands.
113

Progress Check

A progress check question appears at the end of each topic in the Student Edition to help gauge reading comprehension.

Differentiated Instruction

Activities are designed to meet the needs of students who are

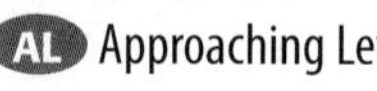

- AL Approaching Level
- BL Beyond Level
- ELL English Language Learners

networks

Don't forget! You can customize all your Lesson Plans online.

Assessment

Chapter Activities

- Exploring the Essential Question
- 21st Century Skills
- Thinking Like a Historian
- Geography Activity

Chapter Assessment

- Review of each lesson's Guiding Questions
- Document-based questions
- Short-response questions
- Extended-response questions

Activities and Assessment Answers

Answers to the Chapter Activities and Assessment questions

CHAPTER 8 Activities

CHAPTER 8 Assessment

CHAPTER 8 Assessment (continued)

NOTES

150 Greek Civilization

Chapter 8 Activities and Assessment

(Student Edition pp. 242–244)

REFLECT, REVIEW, & REMEDIATE

INTERACTIVE WORKSHEET

Chapter Summary

Provide students with the Chapter Summary worksheet to help review the chapter and prepare for assessment.

Reviewing the Enduring Understandings

Review this chapter's Enduring Understandings with students:

- Cultures are held together by shared beliefs and common practices and values.
- People, places, and ideas change over time.
- Leaders can bring about change in society.

INTERACTIVE WHITEBOARD ACTIVITY Have a student volunteer create a three-column chart on the interactive whiteboard and write "Golden Age" in one column and "Hellenistic Era" in the other. Then lead a discussion that allows students to recall philosophers, writers and playwrights, and scientists from each period and what their main accomplishments were. The student volunteer should record names of the Greek thinkers in the chart.

	Golden Age	Hellenistic Era
Philosophers		
Writers and playwrights		
Scientists		

ACTIVITIES ANSWERS

Exploring the Essential Question

1. Students should note the ideas of some of the Greek philosophers and the discoveries of some of the Greek astronomers and mathematicians. There should be mention of Greek theater, writing, art, and sculpture. Their answer should discuss the importance that gods and goddesses played in the lives of Greek citizens. Lasting influences could include art, architecture, and political ideas.

21st Century Skills

2. The blog entry should include photos and written descriptions that illustrate the way statues of the human form were idealized in the Golden Age and became more realistic and emotional in the Hellenistic Era. The illustration and description of architecture could show the evolution of styles of columns and the same changes in human figures as part of friezes and bas-reliefs that occurred in statues. The blog entry should also include the writer's opinions and preferences. The visuals should be compelling and match the print copy.

Thinking Like a Historian

3. Students should identify places and explain why the historical and modern maps do not exactly correspond (for example, where an area that used to be one country is now two countries). They also should give some general commentary on the changes that have taken place, noting whether there have been many changes or just a few, for instance.

Locating Places

4. Letters should match the correct geographic locations.
1. D; **2.** C; **3.** F; **4.** G **5.** A

ASSESSMENT ANSWERS

Review the Guiding Questions

1. C Zeus was the head of all the gods and goddesses and the most powerful. The Olympic Games were held to honor him, so C is the correct answer. Other gods and goddesses were honored in ceremonies, but the Olympics were always held in honor of Zeus.

2. F Socrates was sentenced to death because many Athenians thought he was encouraging the youth to rebel. As a result, they thought his teachings were dangerous. Thus, the answer is F. The Sophists did not believe in absolute right and wrong. The Sophists also accepted money for their teaching, but Socrates did not. Socrates did not teach about philosopher-kings; Plato did.

3. B Aristotle taught his students the principle of the golden mean—that a person should live moderately and avoid extremes in behavior. Choice B is the correct answer.

4. G After Alexander the Great's death, his generals divided the empire among themselves. Thus, choice G is the correct answer. Much of Alexander's empire was eventually conquered by Romans and others, but those takeovers took place many years after the empire was established. Alexander's troops threatened to rebel during the general's lifetime; their threats, however, did not cause the breakup of the empire.

5. C By the time of the Hellenistic Era, sculptors were carving the human figure more realistically and even depicting strong emotions. Thus, the answer is C. Sculptures showing the beauty and harmony of the ideal human were from the Golden Age of Greece.

6. I Archimedes first calculated the value of *pi*. Aristarchus claimed the sun was the center of the solar system, Eratosthenes discovered that Earth was round, and Hypatia lived after the Hellenistic Era.

Document-Based Questions

7. C Choice C is the correct answer. Demosthenes told the Athenians they need not speculate about the future, that the future was certain "unless they were willing to fight him there," and that they should not wait until he comes to Athens.

8. I Choice I is the correct answer. Demosthenes says "the future . . . will be disastrous" if the Athenians don't "do [their] duty" and conquer Philip.

Short Response

9. Students' responses should mention that the lake provided freshwater for drinking and watering crops, and the harbor made the city a major port for ships sailing on the Mediterranean Sea.

10. Students should note that Alexandria was able to thrive and grow because the Hellenistic Era (following Alexander's death) was a flourishing time for commerce and trade, the arts, building, science, and scholarship. Alexandria's location and the library, museum, and lighthouse made it a main center in that region of the world.

Extended Response

11. Students' reports should contain a description of an ideal city that reflects the values of Hellenistic culture. They should include some specific details about how they would plan the city's layout and buildings. Students may say they would encourage people to live there by paying them to come work on building the city (for example, architects and sculptors) and by providing good library facilities, support for the arts, and beautiful, open public spaces.

151

Reflect, Review, & Remediate

Each chapter ends with activities to help reinforce the chapter's content and evaluate comprehension of the Essential Questions and Enduring Understandings.

Correlation of

Discovering Our Past, A History of the World, Early Ages to the Revised NCSS Thematic Strands

The revised standards continue to be focused on ten themes, like the original standards. They represent a way of categorizing knowledge about the human experience, and they constitute the organizing strands that should thread through a social studies program.

Theme and Learning Expectation	Student Edition Chapter/Lesson
1. Culture	
1. "Culture" refers to the socially transmitted behaviors, beliefs, values, traditions, institutions, and ways of living together for a group of people	**Ch 2** L1; **Ch 8** L1, L4; **Ch 9** L3; **Ch 15** L3; **Ch 16** L2; **Ch 18** L1, L2
2. Concepts such as beliefs, values, institutions, cohesion, diversity, accommodation, adaptation, assimilation, and dissonance	**Ch 2** L1; **Ch 8** L1; **Ch 10** L2; **Ch 11** L1; **Ch 18** L1, L2
3. How culture influences the ways in which human groups solve the problems of daily living	**Ch 3** L1; **Ch 8** L4; **Ch 12** L2; **Ch 16** L2; **Ch 19** L2
4. That the beliefs, values, and behaviors of a culture form an integrated system that helps shape the activities and ways of life that define a culture	**Ch 2** L1; **Ch 3** L1; **Ch 5** L2, L3; **Ch 6** L1, L3; **Ch 8** L1, L2; **Ch 10** L2; **Ch 11** L1; **Ch 12** L2, L3; **Ch 13** L1; **Ch 14** L1; **Ch 15** L3; **Ch 16** L2; **Ch 17** L1; **Ch 18** L1, L2, L3; **Ch 19** L2
5. How individuals learn the elements of their culture through interactions with others, and how individuals learn of other cultures through communication and study	**Ch 3** L1, L2; **Ch 5** L3; **Ch 6** L1, L3; **Ch 9** L2; **Ch 10** L2; **Ch 12** L2; **Ch 18** L1
6. That culture may change in response to changing needs, concerns, social, political, and geographic conditions	**Ch 3** L1; **Ch 11** L1; **Ch 12** L3; **Ch 13** L2; **Ch 17** L4; **Ch 19** L2
7. How people from different cultures develop different values and ways of interpreting experience	**Ch 7** L2; **Ch 16** L2; **Ch 17** L1; **Ch 18** L2, L3
8. That language, behaviors, and beliefs of different cultures can both contribute to and pose barriers to cross-cultural understanding	**Ch 8** L3; **Ch 10** L3; **Ch 14** L1, L2; **Ch 17** L1; **Ch 18** L2, L3
2. Time, Continuity, and Change	
1. The study of the past provides representation of the history of communities, nations, and the world	**Ch 1** L1, L2
2. Concepts such as: chronology, causality, change, conflict, complexity, multiple perspectives, primary and secondary sources, and cause and effect	**Ch 1** L2, L3; **Ch 8** L2; **Ch 11** L3

Theme and Learning Expectation	Student Edition Chapter/Lesson
3. That learning about the past requires the interpretation of sources, and that using varied sources provides the potential for a more balanced interpretive record of the past	**Ch 1** L2, L3; **Ch 8** L2; **Ch 9** L2
4. That historical interpretations of the same event may differ on the basis of such factors as conflicting evidence from varied sources, national or cultural perspectives, and the point of view of the researcher	**Ch 1** L2, L3; **Ch 8** L2
5. Key historical periods and patterns of change within and across cultures (e.g., the rise and fall of ancient civilizations, the development of technology, the rise of modern nation-states, and the establishment and breakdown of colonial systems)	**Ch 3** L1, L2; **Ch 8** L3; **Ch 9** L3; **Ch 11** L3, L4; **Ch 17** L4; **Ch 18** L3; **Ch 20** L1; **Ch 21** L1; **Ch 22** L1, L2; **Ch 23** L2, L3, L4
6. The origins and influences of social, cultural, political, and economic systems	**Ch 3** L1, L2; **Ch 4** L1; **Ch 7** L1; **Ch 9** L1, L3; **Ch 10** L2; **Ch 12** L1; **Ch 13** L2; **Ch 15** L2; **Ch 18** L2, L3; **Ch 19** L2, L3; **Ch 22** L2
7. The contributions of key persons, groups, and events from the past and their influence on the present	**Ch 6** L1, L2; **Ch 8** L2, L3; **Ch 11** L3, L4; **Ch 12** L2, L3; **Ch 13** L1, L2, L3; **Ch 14** L1, L3; **Ch 15** L2; **Ch 17** L3; **Ch 18** L3; **Ch 19** L1, L3, L4; **Ch 20** L2, L3, L4; **Ch 21** L1; **Ch 22** L1, L2; **Ch 23** L3, L4
8. The history of democratic ideals and principles, and how they are represented in documents, artifacts and symbols	**Ch 19** L3; **Ch 22** L2
9. The influences of social, geographic, economic, and cultural factors on the history of local areas, states, nations, and the world	**Ch 10** L1; **Ch 15** L2; **Ch 19** L1, L3
3. People, Places, and Environments	
1. The theme of people, places, and environments involves the study of the relationships between human populations in different locations and geographic phenomena such as climate, vegetation, and natural resources	**Ch 2** L1; **Ch 4** L1; **Ch 5** L1; **Ch 7** L1; **Ch 9** L1; **Ch 10** L1; **Ch 11** L1; **Ch 15** L1; **Ch 16** L1
2. Concepts such as: location, region, place, migration, as well as human and physical systems	**Ch 2** L1; **Ch 4** L1; **Ch 9** L1; **Ch 15** L1; **Ch 16** L1; **Ch 18** L1, L2

Theme and Learning Expectation	Student Edition Chapter/Lesson
3. Past and present changes in physical systems, such as seasons, climate, and weather, and the water cycle, in both national and global contexts	**Ch 3** L1
4. The roles of different kinds of population centers in a region or nation	**Ch 16** L1; **Ch 18** L3; **Ch 19** L1; **Ch 20** L2; **Ch 21** L1; **Ch 23** L5
5. The concept of regions identifies links between people in different locations according to specific criteria (e.g., physical, economic, social, cultural, or religious)	**Ch 10** L1; **Ch 15** L1, L3; **Ch 16** L1, L2; **Ch 18** L1, L2; **Ch 19** L1
6. Patterns of demographic and political change, and cultural diffusion in the past and present (e.g., changing national boundaries, migration, and settlement, and the diffusion of and changes in customs and ideas)	**Ch 9** L3; **Ch 10** L3; **Ch 18** L1, L2; **Ch 20** L2; **Ch 23** L5
7. Human modifications of the environment	**Ch 3** L2; **Ch 4** L1; **Ch 5** L1; **Ch 16** L2; **Ch 23** L5
8. Factors that contribute to cooperation and conflict among peoples of the nation and world, including language, religion, and political beliefs	**Ch 6** L2, L4; **Ch 7** L3; **Ch 10** L3; **Ch 13** L1, L2; **Ch 14** L2; **Ch 17** L1, L4; **Ch 18** L1; **Ch 19** L4; **Ch 20** L2, L4; **Ch 23** L1, L3
9. The use of a variety of maps, globes, graphic representations, and geospatial technologies to help investigate the relationships among people, places, and environments	**Ch 2** L1
4. Individual Development and Identity	
1. The study of individual development and identity helps us know that individuals change physically, cognitively, and emotionally over time	**Ch 22** L2
2. Concepts such as: development, change, personality, learning, individual, family, groups, motivation, and perception	**Ch 3** L1; **Ch 10** L2
3. How factors such as physical endowment, interests, capabilities, learning, motivation, personality, perception, and beliefs influence individual development and identity	**Ch 5** L2; **Ch 13** L1; **Ch 14** L3
4. How personal, social, cultural, and environmental factors contribute to the development and the growth of personal identity	**Ch 9** L2; **Ch 10** L2, L3; **Ch 13** L1; **Ch 14** L1, L3

Theme and Learning Expectation	Student Edition Chapter/Lesson
5. That individuals' choices influence identity and development	**Ch 22** L2
6. That perceptions are interpretations of information about individuals and events, and can be influenced by bias and stereotypes	**Ch 1** L2, L3; **Ch 9** L1
5. Individuals, Groups, and Institutions	
1. This theme helps us know how individuals are members of groups and institutions, and influence and shape those groups and institutions	**Ch 9** L1; **Ch 19** L5
2. Concepts such as: mores, norms, status, role, socialization, ethnocentrism, cultural diffusion, competition, cooperation, conflict, race, ethnicity, and gender	**Ch 4** L2; **Ch 9** L1; **Ch 14** L2, L3
3. Institutions are created to respond to changing individual and group needs	**Ch 3** L2; **Ch 13** L2
4. That ways in which young people are socialized include similarities as well as differences across cultures	**Ch 23** L2
5. That groups and institutions change over time	**Ch 3** L2; **Ch 13** L3; **Ch 19** L1, L5; **Ch 20** L3, L4; **Ch 23** L1, L2
6. That cultural diffusion occurs when groups migrate	**Ch 2** L1; **Ch 9** L1, L2; **Ch 13** L2; **Ch 14** L1, L2; **Ch 18** L1; **Ch 20** L2; **Ch 21** L2; **Ch 23** L5
7. That institutions may promote or undermine social conformity	**Ch 5** L2; **Ch 9** L1; **Ch 10** L2; **Ch 18** L3; **Ch 19** L1, L2, L4; **Ch 23** L2
8. That when two or more groups with differing norms and beliefs interact, accommodation or conflict may result	**Ch 4** L2; **Ch 6** L2, L4; **Ch 7** L3; **Ch 11** L2; **Ch 13** L3; **Ch 20** L3, L4; **Ch 21** L2; **Ch 23** L1, L2, L5
9. That groups and institutions influence culture in a variety of ways	**Ch 5** L2; **Ch 7** L2; **Ch 14** L1; **Ch 17** L3, L4; **Ch 19** L1, L2, L4, L5

Theme and Learning Expectation	Student Edition Chapter/Lesson
6. Power, Authority, and Governance	
1. Rights are guaranteed in the U.S. Constitution, the supreme law of the land	**Ch 23** L1
2. Fundamental ideas that are the foundation of American constitutional democracy (including those of the U.S. Constitution, popular sovereignty, the rule of law, separation of powers, checks and balances, minority rights, the separation of church and state, and Federalism)	**Ch 11** L2; **Ch 12** L1, L2; **Ch 19** L3; **Ch 22** L2; **Ch 23** L1
3. Fundamental values of constitutional democracy (e.g., the common good, liberty, justice, equality, and individual dignity)	**Ch 7** L2, L4; **Ch 19** L3; **Ch 22** L2; **Ch 23** L1, L2
4. The ideologies and structures of political systems that differ from those of the United States	**Ch 7** L2; **Ch 19** L3; **Ch 22** L2
5. The ways in which governments meet the needs and wants of citizens, manage conflict, and establish order and society	**Ch 3** L2; **Ch 4** L1, L2; **Ch 10** L1; **Ch 11** L2, L3; **Ch 12** L1, L2, L3; **Ch 15** L2; **Ch 19** L2, L5; **Ch 22** L2; **Ch 23** L2
7. Production, Distribution, and Consumption	
1. Individuals, government, and society experience scarcity because human wants and needs exceed what can be produced from available resources	**Ch 2** L2; **Ch 10** L3; **Ch 11** L3; **Ch 15** L1, L3; **Ch 17** L2; **Ch 21** L1, L3; **Ch 23** L1
2. How choices involve trading off the expected value of one opportunity gained against the expected value of the best alternative	**Ch 2** L2; **Ch 23** L4
3. The economic choices that people make have both present and future consequences	**Ch 11** L3; **Ch 15** L3; **Ch 21** L1; **Ch 23** L4
4. Economic incentives affect people's behavior and may be regulated by rules or laws	**Ch 19** L2; **Ch 20** L2; **Ch 23** L1
5. That banks and other financial institutions channel funds from savers to borrowers and investors	**Ch 21** L3
6. The economic gains that result from specialization and exchange as well as the trade-offs	**Ch 3** L2; **Ch 4** L1; **Ch 15** L1; **Ch 21** L1, L3; **Ch 23** L1
7. How markets bring buyers and sellers together to exchange goods and services	**Ch 2** L2; **Ch 15** L1, L3; **Ch 20** L2; **Ch 21** L1, L3

Theme and Learning Expectation	Student Edition Chapter/Lesson
8. How goods and services are allocated in a market economy through the influence of prices on decisions about production and consumption	**Ch 2** L2
9. How the overall levels of income, employment, and prices are determined by the interaction of households, firms, and the government	**Ch 2** L2
8. Science, Technology, and Society	
1. Science is a result of empirical study of the natural world, and technology is the application of knowledge to accomplish tasks	**Ch 3** L1; **Ch 22** L1; **Ch 23** L4
2. Society often turns to science and technology to solve problems	**Ch 4** L1; **Ch 5** L1; **Ch 17** L2; **Ch 20** L2; **Ch 21** L1; **Ch 22** L1; **Ch 23** L4
3. Our lives today are media and technology dependent	**Ch 1** L3; **Ch 23** L4
4. Science and technology have had both positive and negative impacts upon individuals, societies, and the environment in the past and present	**Ch 3** L2; **Ch 5** L4; **Ch 17** L2; **Ch 22** L1; **Ch 23** L4, L5
5. Science and technology have changed peoples' perceptions of the social and natural world, as well as their relationship to the land, economy and trade, their concept of security, and their major daily activities	**Ch 3** L2; **Ch 5** L4; **Ch 17** L2; **Ch 20** L2; **Ch 21** L1; **Ch 22** L1; **Ch 23** L5
6. Values, beliefs, and attitudes that have been influenced by new scientific and technological knowledge (e.g., invention of the printing press, conceptions of the universe, applications of atomic energy, and genetic discoveries)	**Ch 14** L3; **Ch 20** L2; **Ch 22** L1; **Ch 23** L5
7. How media are created and received depends upon cultural contexts	**Ch 1** L2
8. Science and technology sometimes create ethical issues that test our standards and values	**Ch 22** L1; **Ch 23** L5
9. The need for laws and policies to govern scientific and technological applications	**Ch 23** L5
10. That there are gaps in access to science and technology around the world	**Ch 2** L2

Theme and Learning Expectation	Student Edition Chapter/Lesson
9. Global Connections	
1. Global connections have existed in the past and increased rapidly in current times	**Ch 2** L2
2. Global factors such as cultural, economic, and political connections are changing the places in which people live (e.g., through trade, migration, increased travel, and communication)	**Ch 2** L1, L2
3. Spatial relationships that relate to ongoing global issues (e.g., pollution, poverty, disease, and conflict) affect the health and well-being of Earth and its inhabitants	**Ch 15** L3, What Do You Think?
4. Global problems and possibilities are not generally caused or developed by any one nation	**Ch 15** L3, What Do You Think?
5. Global connections may make cultures more alike or increase their sense of distinctiveness	**Ch 21** L1, L2, L3
6. Universal human rights cut across cultures but are not necessarily understood in the same way in all cultures	**Ch 23** L2, What Do You Think?
10. Civic Ideals and Practices	
1. The theme of civic ideals and practices helps us to learn about and know how to work for the betterment of society	**Ch 7** L2, L4; **Ch 11** L2
2. Concepts and ideals such as: individual dignity, liberty, justice, equality, individual rights, responsibility, majority and minority rights, and civil dissent	**Ch 2** L3; **Ch 7** L1, L2, L4; **Ch 11** L2
3. Key practices involving the rights and responsibilities of citizenship and the exercise of citizenship (e.g., respecting the rule of law and due process, voting, serving on a jury, researching issues, making informed judgments, expressing views on issues, and collaborating with others to take civic action)	**Ch 7** L1, L4; **Ch 11** L2
4. The common good, and the rule of law	**Ch 7** L2, L4; **Ch 10** L2; **Ch 11** L2
5. Key documents and excerpts from key sources that define and support democratic ideals and practices (e.g., the U.S. Declaration of Independence, the U.S. Constitution, the Gettysburg Address, the Letter from Birmingham Jail; and international documents such as the Declaration of the Rights of Man, and the Universal Declaration of the Rights of Children)	**Ch 23** L1, L2

Theme and Learning Expectation	Student Edition Chapter/Lesson
6. The origins and function of major institutions and practices developed to support democratic ideals and practices	**Ch 2** L3
7. Key past and present issues involving democratic ideals and practices, as well as the perspectives of various stakeholders in proposing possible solutions to these issues	**Ch 11** L2
8. The importance of becoming informed in order to make positive civic contributions	**Ch 2** L3

Discovering Our Past: A History of the World, Early Ages

Correlated to Common Core State Standards, Grades 6–8

Common Core State Standards for Literacy in History/Social Studies, Science, and Technical Subjects, Grades 6–8	
College and Career Readiness Anchor Standards for Reading	
Key Ideas and Details	
1. Read closely to determine what the text says explicitly and to make logical inferences from it; cite specific textual evidence when writing or speaking to support conclusions drawn from the text.	**Student Edition:** *Reading HELPDESK: Taking Notes: Categorizing* 4, 312, 482, 642; *Analyzing* 278; *Finding Main Idea* 18, 154, 436; *Identifying* 28, 62, 76, 86, 100, 190, 198, 220, 265, 286, 328, 340, 372, 422, 474, 510, 516, 528, 540, 582, 618, 650; *Describing* 38, 236, 257, 398, 589; *Organizing* 108, 120, 350, 411, 430, 459, 564, 682; *Listing* 148, 360, 362, 380, 386, 628; *Summarizing* 404, 450, 548, 624; *Finding the Main Idea* 436; *Sequencing* 489, 556, 672, 690; *Determine Cause and Effect* 498, 598, 606, 664; *Sharing Relationships* 520; *Explaining* 696 *Lesson Review: Answer the Guiding Questions* 9, 15, 21, 37, 43, 47, 61, 69, 83, 93, 107, 119, 127, 133, 147, 153, 159, 167, 182, 189, 197, 205, 219, 227, 235, 241, 256, 264, 271, 285, 291, 299, 311, 319, 327, 333, 347, 357, 365, 379, 385, 391, 403, 410, 415, 429, 435, 441, 458, 467, 481, 488, 495, 503, 515, 519, 527, 533, 547, 555, 563, 569, 575, 588, 595, 605, 611, 623, 627, 635, 649, 657, 671, 679, 689, 695, 703 *Drawing Conclusions* 14, 15, 34, 45, 47, 50, 52, 100, 123, 133, 136, 170, 180, 218, 241, 254, 264, 274, 332, 333, 336, 338, 346, 351, 354, 365, 373, 374, 394, 401, 407, 437, 446, 467, 506, 514, 519, 529, 532, 538, 546, 555, 583, 602, 616, 620, 653, 660, 671, 673, 685, 706 *Chapter Assessment: Review the Guiding Questions* 23, 49, 71, 99, 135, 169, 207, 243, 273, 301, 335, 367, 393, 417, 445, 470, 506, 536, 578, 614, 660, 706 *Chapter Assessment: Document-Based Questions* 24, 50, 72, 100, 136, 170, 208, 244, 274, 302, 336, 368, 394, 418, 446, 471, 507, 537, 579, 615, 661 *Making Inferences* 37, 47, 67, 69, 74, 78, 89, 136, 151, 175, 191, 201, 219, 244, 246, 251, 343, 249, 359, 362, 364, 385, 391, 394, 402, 415, 423, 429, 446, 455, 461, 483, 506, 531, 543, 568, 578, 595, 605, 608, 611, 614, 626, 627, 638, 652, 681, 684, 702 *Thinking Like A Historian: Making Inferences* 67; *Drawing Conclusions* 587 *Reading HELPDESK: Reading Strategy: Listing* 440; *Making Inferences* 702 *Chapter Assessment: Extended Response, Outlining a Reference Article* 578 **Teacher Edition:** **SITT: DC** 35, 175, 193, 283; **MI** 49, 89, 133, 155, 213, 265, 363, 401 **ENGAGE: MI** 53, 119, 327 **TEACH & ASSESS: A** 29, 167, 203, 271, 289, 305, 309; **CAC** 37, 57, 67, 95, 103, 121, 125, 293, 345, 375, 391; **MI** 41, 53, 95, 99, 101, 125, 203, 205, 225, 235, 255, 291, 305, 325, 329; **DC** 57, 91, 95, 113, 143, 157, 159, 185, 195, 219, 221, 225, 239, 267, 271, 273, 313, 323, 327; **D** 67, 161, 163, 199, 387; **I** 71, 73, 91, 147, 165, 271, 289, 309, 341; **MG** 81; **C** 91, 159, 285, 291, 303; **E** 93; **P** 97; **FTMI** 101; **MC** 135; **L** 145, 349; **OI** 195; **HS** 219; **P** 275; **IW** 365 **CLOSE & REFLECT: DC** 41, 113, 127, 323; **I** 81; **A** 203; **MI** 275, 371; **CAC** 291, 349; **S** 327 **IYHMT: R** 51; **CAC** 51, 179, 289, 293; **E** 51; **MI** 59, 161; **D** 97; **HS** 111; **A** 121; **DC** 409

Codes used for the Teacher Edition pages are the initial caps of headings on that page.

Key Ideas and Details	
2. Determine central ideas or themes of a text and analyze their development; summarize the key supporting details and ideas.	**Student Edition:** *Connections to Today* 9, 12, 32, 47, 89, 122, 145, 157, 166, 168, 179, 189, 195, 240, 259, 271, 287, 293, 319, 324, 355, 413, 441, 460, 475, 481, 531, 655, 674 *Reading HELPDESK: Reading Strategy: Summarizing* 34, 234, 342, 478, 570; *Finding the Main Idea* 117, 594; *Paraphrasing* 376 *Finding the Main Idea* 37, 43, 47, 50, 231 *Summarizing* 43, 61, 127, 147, 170, 182, 235, 256, 311, 319, 327, 336, 357, 415, 418, 435, 458, 495, 503, 515, 533, 547, 555, 578, 614, 631, 649, 657, 752, 753, 579 *The World's Literature* 84–85, 348–349, 596–597 *Chapter Activities: Exploring the Essential Question, Expository Writing, Write a Summary* 366 *Reading HELPDESK: Taking Notes: Summarizing* 404, 450, 548, 624; *Finding the Main Idea* 436, 594 *Thinking Like a Historian: Researching on the Internet* 427 *Chapter Activities: 21st Century Skills: Summarizing* 444 **Teacher Edition:** **ENGAGE: S** 199 **TEACH & ASSESS: S** 11, 23, 93, 119, 145, 159, 165, 167, 177, 197, 199, 219, 227, 235, 239, 243, 251, 271, 277, 285, 291, 301, 305, 313, 315, 341, 345, 357, 393, 405, 407, 419, 421, 425; **FTMI** 21, 269, 275, 403; **IWA** 21; **MC** 91, 143; **D** 139, 163, 267; **I** 199, 207, 325; **TPS** 205; **E** 205; **HS** 219; **ICI** 367, 417, 419; **R** 425 **CLOSE & REFLECT: S** 23, 95, 97, 137, 147, 187, 217, 307, 367, 373, 379, 391, 393; **HS** 111; **I** 135, 269; **TC** 167; **C** 327; **FTMI** 375 **IYHMT: PTS** 25; **P** 39; **S** 59; **A** 121; **S** 259, 409; **SI** 333; **ICI** 343; **FTMI** 423; **C** 435

Codes used for the Teacher Edition pages are the initial caps of headings on that page.

Key Ideas and Details	
3. Analyze how and why individuals, events, or ideas develop and interact over the course of a text.	**Student Edition:** *The Story Matters* 1, 25, 51, 73, 97, 137, 171, 209, 245, 275, 303, 337, 369, 395, 419, 447, 471, 507, 537, 579, 615, 639, 661 *Step Into the Time* 2–3, 26–27, 52–53, 74–75, 98–99, 138–139, 172–173, 210–211, 246–247, 276–277, 304–305, 338–339, 370–371, 396–397, 420–421, 448–449, 472–473, 508–509, 538–539, 580–581, 616–617, 640–641, 662–663 *Biography* 8, 35, 66, 87, 123, 142, 162, 188, 201, 222, 260, 295, 326, 343, 362, 374, 377, 401, 410, 435, 464, 476, 492, 526, 574, 594, 610, 626, 646, 675, 695, 702 *Thinking Like A Historian* 20, 41, 67, 83, 102, 161, 177, 231, 252, 282, 308, 342, 403, 427, 467, 485, 555, 587, 623 *Determining/Identifying Cause and Effect* 42, 61, 69, 175, 178, 189, 197, 205, 259, 271, 298, 299, 327, 365, 391, 396, 403, 410, 425, 435, 475, 481, 483, 492, 512, 527, 534, 555, 561, 563, 575, 587, 595, 603, 605, 620, 625, 630, 630, 632, 634, 669, 689, 694, 695, 703 *The World's Literature* 84–85, 348–349, 496–497, 596–597 *Reading HELPDESK: Reading Strategy: Understanding Cause and Effect* 126, 532; *Formulating Questions* 400; *Identifying Cause and Effect* 630 *Chapter Activities: 21st Century Skills, Determining Cause and Effect* 366 *Chapter Activities: Exploring the Essential Question, Expository Writing* 444 *Chapter Activities: Thinking Like a Historian, Geography and Civilization* 444 **Teacher Edition:** **TSM:** 2, 18, 34, 48, 64, 88, 108, 132, 154, 174, 192, 212, 232, 248, 264, 282, 298, 320, 338, 362, 384, 400, 414 **HOCP:** 3, 19, 35, 49, 65, 89, 109, 133, 155, 175, 193, 213, 233, 249, 265, 283, 299, 321, 339, 363, 385, 401, 415 **SITT: E** 441 **ENGAGE: P** 41, 57, 113, 139, 219, 221; **I** 95, 111, 257, 375; **D** 95, 167, 201; **MC** 99, 101, 181, 187, 273, 429; **DS** 117; **TPS** 205; **C** 223; **M** 253; **L** 269; **MG** 355; **SS** 403 **TEACH & ASSESS: E** 5, 25, 69, 97, 101, 103, 111, 115, 117, 205, 207, 225, 253, 255, 271, 275, 301, 305, 323, 369, 417, 419, 425, 435; **A** 27, 91, 97, 157, 159, 163, 177, 203, 271, 315, 357, 371, 375, 379, 427; **MC** 41, 57, 73, 81, 91, 113, 123, 145, 163, 187, 195, 199, 221, 251, 275, 325; **D** 51, 79, 91, 111, 135, 139, 163, 185, 187, 195, 207, 235, 251, 253, 271, 273, 343, 387; **LS** 51, 69; **DC** 57; **IW** 57, 365; **DCAE** 67, 69, 77, 91, 95, 117, 127, 185, 187, 203, 221, 241, 305, 323, 333, 345, 349, 351, 355, 375, 387, 393, 419, 425, 429; **CAC** 79, 139, 141, 149, 169, 217, 257, 323, 333, 421, 433; **PS** 95, 377; **IPOV** 97, 309; **C** 99, 259, 323; **I** 101, 137, 139, 257, 289, 293, 343, 387, 407; **SS** 111, 305; **S** 139, 149, 159, 185, 227, 269, 285, 393; **L** 195, 207, 389; **P** 201; **J** 217; **UCAE** 225; **O** 239, 365, 431; **MG** 275, 309, 353, 373, 379; **GO** 365; **FTMI** 403; **MP** 403 **CLOSE & REFLECT: MC** 91, 165, 207, 239, 273, 377; **DCAE** 99, 181; **C** 137; **S** 147, 199; **E** 161; **MP** 253; **LS** 259; **MG** 285, 435; **LS** 301; **CAC** 333; **AI** 357; **E** 423, 431; **HS** 433 **IYHMT: E** 83, 207, 325; **S** 93; **DCAE** 103, 287; **AG** 115; **CAC** 121, 237; **A** 121; **MAGO** 179; **MC** 205, 289; **D** 259, 301, 311; **L** 315; **UCAE** 343; **TCAE** 395

Codes used for the Teacher Edition pages are the initial caps of headings on that page.

Craft and Structure	
4. Interpret words and phrases as they are used in a text, including determining technical, connotative, and figurative meanings, and analyze how specific word choices shape meaning or tone.	**Student Edition:** *Reading HELPDESK: Content Vocabulary* 4, 10, 18, 28, 29, 38, 39, 44, 45, 54, 62, 76, 85, 86, 100, 108, 120, 128, 140, 148, 154, 160, 174, 183, 190, 198, 212, 220, 230, 236, 248, 257, 265, 278, 286, 292, 306, 312, 320, 328, 340, 350, 360, 372, 380, 386, 398, 404, 411, 422, 430, 436, 450, 459, 474, 482, 489, 498, 510, 516, 520, 528, 540, 548, 556, 564, 570, 582, 589, 598, 606, 618, 624, 628, 642, 643, 650, 665, 672, 682, 690, 696 *Reading HELPDESK: Academic Vocabulary* 5, 6, 11, 14, 20, 30, 32, 35, 41, 46, 56, 58, 64, 65, 77, 80, 82, 87, 90, 101, 102, 106, 109, 110, 111, 112, 115, 116, 118, 124, 125, 126, 129, 130, 145, 146, 150, 151, 152, 155, 156, 157, 161, 162, 163, 164, 166, 175, 176, 177, 179, 184, 185, 186, 187, 188, 191, 194, 196, 200, 202, 203, 214, 218, 221, 222, 224, 231, 232, 237, 238, 239, 252, 254, 258, 260, 261, 262, 266, 268, 269, 270, 279, 280, 281, 287, 289, 293, 295, 297, 298, 307, 308, 309, 310, 313, 315, 316, 322, 324, 326, 329, 330, 331, 332, 342, 344, 352, 362, 374, 375, 381, 382, 387, 399, 400, 407, 408, 413, 414, 423, 424, 431, 432, 434, 437, 438, 440, 452, 454, 456, 460, 462, 464, 476, 480, 484, 490, 494, 502, 512, 517, 518, 522, 530, 532, 541, 544, 549, 550, 558, 560, 562, 565, 566, 570, 572, 586, 590, 592, 598, 602, 604, 608, 619, 620, 622, 625, 626, 629, 630, 633, 634, 643, 644, 648, 653, 656, 666, 670, 673, 674, 678, 686, 688, 692, 698, 700 *Reading HELPDESK: Reading Strategy: Context Clues* 6 *Reading HELPDESK: Build Vocabulary: Word Parts* 8; *Multiple Meanings* 193, 325; *Word Forms* 116, 250; *Word Origins*, 178, 361, 390, 558; *Suffixes* 262, 683; *Prefixes* 457 *Lesson Review: Review Vocabulary* 9, 15, 21, 37, 43, 47, 61, 69, 83, 93, 107, 119, 127, 133, 147, 153, 159, 167, 182, 189, 197, 205, 219, 227, 235, 241, 256, 264, 271, 285, 291, 299, 311, 319, 327, 333, 347, 357, 365, 379, 385, 391, 403, 410, 415, 429, 435, 441, 458, 467, 481, 488, 495, 503, 515, 519, 527, 533, 547, 555, 563, 569, 575, 588, 595, 605, 611, 623, 627, 635, 649, 657, 671, 679, 689, 695, 703 *Reading HELPDESK: Visual Vocabulary* 57, 89, 142, 239, 249, 296, 332, 345, 465, 526 *Chapter Assessment: Extended Response, Expository Writing* 536 **Teacher Edition:** **SITP:** 19 **ENGAGE: D** 29, 135, 181, 341, 417, 425; **MC** 81, 169; **AS** 115; **LS** 115; **LS** 123; **CAC** 145, 161; **P** 147, 203; **A** 405; **C** 421; **S** 427 **TEACH & ASSESS: D** 5, 13, 41, 67, 93, 119, 163, 277, 345, 373, 393, 407, 421, 425; **MC** 5, 37, 127, 135, 139; **CAC** 5, 113, 141, 345, 433; **LS** 7, 51, 53, 55; **L** 21, 255; **E** 29, 195, 273, 277, 327, 369; **C** 29, 37, 117, 159, 223, 313, 345, 365, 375; **B** 53; **MG** 73; **I** 113, 117, 291; **A** 117, 369, 433; **I** 119, 207, 235; **DCAE** 127; **S** 137, 165, 197, 393; **APS** 145, 203; **MD** 203; **P** 367; **W** 373; **VIW** 391; **M** 191; **R** 425, 435 **CLOSE & REFLECT: E** 101, 427; **C** 137 **IYHMT: PTS** 25; **D** 59, 113, 427; **UCC** 103; **CAC** 149; **MC** 183; **A** 259; **S** 301; **TCAE** 395; **UGO** 395

Codes used for the Teacher Edition pages are the initial caps of headings on that page.

Craft and Structure	
5. Analyze the structure of texts, including how specific sentences, paragraphs, and larger portions of the text (e.g., a section, chapter, scene, or stanza) relate to each other and the whole.	**Student Edition:** *Reading HELPDESK: Taking Notes: Categorizing* 4, 312, 482, 642; *Analyzing* 278; *Finding the Main Idea* 18, 154, 436; *Identifying* 28, 62, 76, 86, 100, 190, 198, 220, 265, 286, 328, 340, 372, 422, 474, 510, 516, 528, 540, 582, 618, 650; *Describing* 38, 236, 257, 398, 589; *Organizing* 108, 120, 350, 411, 430, 459, 564, 682; *Listing* 148, 360, 362, 380, 386, 628; *Summarizing* 404, 450, 548, 624; *Finding the Main Idea* 436; *Sequencing* 489, 556, 672, 690; *Determine Cause and Effect* 498, 598, 606, 664; *Sharing Relationships* 520; *Explaining* 696 *The World's Literature* 84–85, 348–349, 496–497, 596–597 *Reading HELPDESK: Reading Strategy: Listing* 440 **Teacher Edition:** **TEACH & ASSESS: S** 81; **CAC** 349
6. Assess how point of view or purpose shapes the content and style of a text.	**Student Edition:** *What Is Point of View?* 12 *What Do You Think?* 16–17, 228–229, 358–359, 442–443, 680–681 *Primary Source* 16, 17, 58, 85, 101, 111, 131, 146, 149, 150, 153, 156, 158, 167, 182, 185, 193, 195, 203, 216, 226, 228, 229, 231, 233, 240, 254, 258, 267, 287, 298, 308, 319, 324, 331, 356, 362, 374, 400, 401, 414, 427, 431, 434, 439, 479, 480, 486, 487, 488, 495, 497, 501, 521, 526, 531, 543, 549, 558, 574, 588, 593, 597, 601, 611, 653, 655, 666, 673, 680, 681, 683, 694, 700 *Chapter Assessment: Document-Based Questions: Identifying Point of View* 24 *Thinking Like A Historian: Analyzing Primary Sources* 41; *Analyzing Primary and Secondary Sources* 177, 308; *Analyzing Sources* 282; *Researching on the Internet* 427; *Identifying Points of View* 704 *What Do You Think? DBQ, Describing* 359 *Critical Thinking: Identifying Points of View* 479, 557, 689 *The World's Literature: Analyzing Literature, DBQ* 597 *Chapter Assessment: Extended Response, Descriptive Writing* 660 **Teacher Edition:** **HOCP:** 415 **ENGAGE: R** 143; **D** 389 **TEACH & ASSESS: S** 11; **MC** 91, 125, 139; **IPOV** 95, 143, 181, 183, 197, 277, 301, 309, 351, 375, 417; **C** 97; **MI** 99; **E** 101, 203; **APS** 103, 203; **I** 121, 159, 199; **A** 139; **PSA** 167; **E** 239, 303; **VIW** 391 **CLOSE & REFLECT: IPOV** 53, 221, 369 **IYHMT: PTS** 25; **D** 113, 303; **A** 121; **APOV** 199

Codes used for the Teacher Edition pages are the initial caps of headings on that page.

Integration of Knowledge and Ideas	
7. Integrate and evaluate content presented in diverse formats and media, including visually and quantitatively, as well as in words.	**Student Edition:** *Step Into the Place* 2–3, 26–27, 52–53, 74–75, 98–99, 138–139, 172–173, 210–211, 246–247, 276–277, 304–305, 338–339, 370–371, 396–397, 420–421, 448–449, 472–473, 508–509, 538–539, 580–581, 616–617, 640–641, 662–663 *Map* 12, 29, 30, 31, 34, 37, 60, 63, 68, 78, 89, 90, 101, 106, 124, 131, 151, 161, 164, 175, 180, 184, 191, 194, 204, 232, 234, 249, 253, 266, 269, 279, 281, 284, 294, 298, 314, 317, 332, 346, 354, 364, 381, 388, 399, 405, 408, 423, 426, 433, 437, 440, 451, 453, 455, 466, 468, 475, 477, 490, 491, 499, 501, 504, 511, 513, 517, 529, 534, 541, 545, 559, 561, 562, 571, 573, 576, 583, 602, 608, 612, 620, 625, 632, 634, 656, 658, 665, 678, 685, 687, 691, 704 *Infographics* 7, 39, 41, 42, 45, 114, 116, 143, 145, 200, 201, 213, 218, 224, 251, 255, 288, 290, 331, 341, 355, 375, 384, 390, 424, 428, 477, 552, 621, 630, 647, 693 *Using Charts, Graphs, and Diagrams* 35–36 *Chapter Activities: Reading Maps* 48; *Geography Activity* 70, 134, 168, 206, 242, 272, 300, 334, 366, 392, 416, 444, 468, 504, 534, 576, 612, 636, 658, 704; *Using Latitude and Longitude* 534 *Chapter Assessment: Document-Based Questions* 72, 170 *Reading HELPDESK: Reading Strategy: Reading a Map* 131 *Reading HELPDESK: Reading in the Content Area: Content Area* 145; *Charts* 354; *Pie Chart or Pie Graph* 432 *Chart* 152, 178, 239, 406, 649 *Chapter Activities: 21st Century Skills: Analyzing News Media* 300; *Analyzing Images* 392; *Communication* 658 *Chapter Activities: Thinking Like a Historian: Comparing and Contrasting* 392; *Sequencing, Create a Time Line* 468, 612 *Thinking Like a Historian: Using a Time Line, Sequence Events* 403, 416 *Analyzing Visuals* 456, 554, 561, 566, 572, 595, 656, 677 *Photographs (with questions)* 512, 565, 667, 694 **Teacher Edition:** **MMR: CEO Ch** 1, 16, 32, 46, 62, 86, 106, 130, 152, 172, 190, 210, 230, 246, 262, 280, 296, 318, 336, 360, 382, 398, 412; **ATM** 32, 46, 62, 86, 106, 130, 152, 172, 190, 210, 230, 262, 318, 336, 382, 398, 412 **HOCP:** 19, 49, 109, 133, 155, 213, 233, 249, 265, 299, 385, 415 **SITT:** 3 **ENGAGE: AV** 37, 77, 111, 177, 185, 225, 271, 343, 365, 433; **M** 55, 253; **C** 67; **I** 91, 149, 157, 267, 309, 375, 435; **P** 91, 113, 135, 147, 161, 199, 241, 285, 289; **MC** 119, 169, 331, 429; **CAC** 161; **SS** 185, 351, 403; **E** 235, 325; **A** 277, 323; **D** 313, 345, 353; **MG** 355 **TEACH & ASSESS: E** 5, 99, 101, 117, 251, 257, 369, 387; **L** 21, 199, 349, 369; **CAC** 21, 167; **A** 21, 91, 93, 145, 149, 157, 163, 293; **MC** 23, 51, 113, 147, 159, 221; **G** 25; **C** 29, 291; **D** 51, 95, 147, 157, 163, 167, 207, 239, 251, 253, 317; **SS** 53, 111, 137, 301, 305; **MG** 77, 371; **I** 77, 121, 149, 159, 167, 195, 201, 243, 327, 329, 331, 387, 389, 427; **AV** 95, 101, 125, 145, 157, 181, 205, 221, 239, 267, 285, 291, 293, 331, 365, 377, 391, 427; **S** 119, 177, 199, 271, 341; **V** 121; **LS** 137; **CTT** 147; **DC** 157; **IWA** 157, 391; **AS** 223; **C** 253; **S** 269, 271, 323, 345; **AVI** 285; **O** 365 **CLOSE & REFLECT: MC** 21; **L** 77; **I** 269 **IYHMT: ALL** 23; **OLL** 23; **BLL** 23; **CAC** 41; **C** 59, 123; **A** 69; **MC** 93, 123; **AG** 115; **I** 121, 311, 419; **AV** 165; **UV** 183; **L** 253; **AVI** 287; **HS** 301; **D** 307; **E** 315; **R** 347, 369

Codes used for the Teacher Edition pages are the initial caps of headings on that page.

Integration of Knowledge and Ideas	
8. Delineate and evaluate the argument and specific claims in a text, including the validity of the reasoning as well as the relevance and sufficiency of the evidence.	**Student Edition:** *Reliable Sources* 11–12 *What Do You Think?* 16–17, 228–229, 358–359, 442–443, 680–681 *Thinking Like A Historian* 20, 41, 67, 83, 102, 161, 177, 231, 252, 282, 308, 403, 427, 467, 485, 555, 587, 623 *Reading HELPDESK: Taking Notes: Listing arguments for and against* 386 *Chapter Assessment: Extended Response, Descriptive Writing* 660 **Teacher Edition:** **ENGAGE: P** 57; **R** 143; **A** 425 **TEACH & ASSESS: E** 7, 277, 407, 421; **DC** 57; **MI** 99; **MC** 139; **IPOV** 143; **C** 199, 241; **APS** 203; **E** 203; **AS** 223; **CAC** 225; **R** 425; **D** 425 **CLOSE & REFLECT: MC** 57; **HS** 143; **E** 277; **R** 405 **IYHMT: D** 57, 141, 417; **E** 141; **HACD** 347
9. Analyze how two or more texts address similar themes or topics in order to build knowledge or to compare the approaches the authors take.	**Student Edition:** *What Do You Think?* 16–17, 228–229, 358–359, 442–443, 680–681 *Document-Based Questions* 17, 229 *Thinking Like A Historian: Classifying and Categorizing Information* 83 *Reading HELPDESK: Taking Notes, Contrasting* 110, 160; *Comparing* 174, 183, 292; *Comparing and Contrasting* 806 *Infographic: Greek Philosophers* 224; *Chinese Philosophers* 288 *Chart: The First Four Caliphs, Critical Thinking, Contrasting* 406 **Teacher Edition:** **TEACH & ASSESS: E** 7, 195, 277; **S** 11; **I** 139; **A** 139; **IPOV** 143, 417; **PSA** 167; **MC** 197; **C** 235; **CAC** 349, 407 **CLOSE & REFLECT: HS** 143; **E** 277 **IYHMT: D** 113
Range of Reading and Level of Text Complexity	
10. Read and comprehend complex literary and informational texts independently and proficiently.	**Student Edition:** *Biography* 8, 35, 66, 87, 123, 142, 162, 188, 201, 222, 260, 295, 326, 343, 362, 374, 377, 401, 410, 435, 464, 476, 492, 526, 574, 594, 610, 626, 646, 675, 695, 702 *Primary Source* 16, 17, 58, 85, 101, 111, 131, 146, 149, 150, 153, 156, 158, 167, 182, 185, 193, 195, 203, 216, 226, 228, 229, 231, 233, 240, 254, 258, 267, 287, 298, 308, 319, 324, 331, 356, 362, 374, 400, 401, 414, 427, 431, 434, 439, 479, 480, 486, 487, 488, 495, 497, 501, 521, 526, 531, 543, 549, 558, 574, 588, 593, 597, 601, 611, 653, 655, 666, 673, 680, 681, 683, 694, 700 *Thinking Like A Historian* 20, 41, 67, 83, 102, 161, 177, 231, 252, 282, 308, 342, 403, 427, 555, 467, 485, 555, 587, 623 *The World's Literature* 84–85, 348–349, 496–497, 596–597 *Chapter Activities: 21st Century Skills: Recognize Quality Sources* 416 *Chapter Assessment: Document-Based Questions, Myth* 470 **Teacher Edition:** **MMR: RL Ch** 1, 16, 32, 46, 62, 86, 106, 130, 152, 172, 190, 210, 230, 246, 262, 280, 296, 318, 336, 360, 382, 398, 412 **HOCP:** 3, 19, 35, 49, 65, 89, 109, 133, 155, 175, 193, 213, 233, 249, 265, 283, 299, 321, 339, 363, 385, 401, 415 **ENGAGE: R** 219; **A** 219; **D** 389 **TEACH & ASSESS: E** 7, 203, 305; **APS** 93, 97, 103; **PS** 127; **MC** 135; **D** 135, 167, 207; **A** 139; **CAC** 139, 349; **I** 163, 199; **A** 219; **HS** 219 **CLOSE & REFLECT: HS** 143 **IYHMT: R** 51, 347, 369; **CAC** 83; **MC** 93, 307; **MI** 161; **HS** 301

Codes used for the Teacher Edition pages are the initial caps of headings on that page.

College and Career Readiness Anchor Standards for Writing	
Text Types and Purposes	
1. Write arguments to support claims in an analysis of substantive topics or texts using valid reasoning and relevant and sufficient evidence.	**Student Edition:** *Lesson Review: Persuasive Writing* 21, 69, 83, 93, 127, 133, 167, 197, 227, 291, 311, 357, 365, 415, 481, 503, 519, 605, 649, 657, 671 *Chapter Assessment: Extended Response, Persuasive Writing* 50, 274, 706 *Chapter Activities: Exploring the Essential Question, Persuasive Writing* 334 *Chapter Activities: 21st Century Skills: Debating* 468 **Teacher Edition:** **ENGAGE: MG** 77 **TEACH & ASSESS: DC** 143; **D** 357 **CLOSE & REFLECT: IW** 55; **C** 119; **MC** 181; **S** 183 **IYHMT: I** 227, 419
2. Write informative/explanatory texts to examine and convey complex ideas and information clearly and accurately through the effective selection, organization, and analysis of content.	**Student Edition:** *Lesson Review: Expository Writing* 9, 15, 37, 43, 107, 119, 147, 159, 182, 205, 219, 241, 256, 264, 285, 299, 319, 333, 347, 379, 410, 435, 458, 488, 495, 547, 555, 563, 569, 588, 595, 627, 679, 689, 695 *Lesson Review: Descriptive Writing* 47, 189, 271, 391, 533 *Chapter Activities: Exploring the Essential Question, Descriptive Writing* 48, 612; *Expository Writing* 70, 98, 134, 168, 206, 242, 300, 366, 416, 444, 468, 504, 534, 576, 636, 658, 704 *Chapter Assessment: Extended Response, Comparative Writing* 170; *Expository Writing* 208, 302, 446, 506; *Descriptive Writing* 244, 368, 638; *Outlining a Reference Article* 578 *Thinking Like a Historian: Comparing and Contrasting* 242; *Researching on the Internet* 427 *Step Into the Time: Time Line, Write a Paragraph* 338, 396, 616, *Chapter Activities: 21st Century Skills: Analyzing Images* 392; *Creating a Blog* 636; *Communication* 658 *What Do You Think? DBQ, Read to Write, Personal* 443 **Teacher Edition:** **HOCP:** 3, 19, 35, 49, 65, 89, 193, 233, 249, 321, 363, 401 **TEACH & ASSESS: D** 29; **A** 79; **DCAE** 127; **E** 135, 255; **MC** 139; **S** 149, 305; **I** 159; **DS** 351; **WAR** 405 **CLOSE & REFLECT: S** 97, 117, 199, 379; **E** 141, 427; **MC** 225, 227; **TAS** 243 **IYHMT: C** 59, 435; **D** 83, 405; **I** 99, 419; **AG** 115; **AV** 165; **HS** 301; **MC** 307; **COR** 329; **SI** 333; **R** 347, 435
3. Write narratives to develop real or imagined experiences or events using effective technique, well-chosen details and well-structured event sequences.	**Student Edition:** *Chapter Assessment: Extended Response, Personal Writing* 24, 72; *Descriptive Writing* 136, 394, 418, 470, 614 *Lesson Review: Personal Writing* 61, 153, 327, 385, 429, 441, 575, 611, 703; *Narrative Writing* 235, 403, 467, 527; *Creative Writing* 392, 623, 635; *Descriptive Writing* 515, 660 *Chapter Activities: Exploring the Essential Question, Descriptive Writing* 272 **Teacher Edition:** **HOCP:** 175, 265, 283, 339 **TEACH & ASSESS: D** 73 **CLOSE & REFLECT: E** 197, 235 **IYHMT: CP** 75; **D** 303, 429; **I** 311

Codes used for the Teacher Edition pages are the initial caps of headings on that page.

Production and Distribution of Writing	
4. Produce clear and coherent writing in which the development, organization, and style are appropriate to task, purpose, and audience.	**Student Edition:** *Lesson Review: Expository Writing* 9, 15, 37, 43, 107, 119, 147, 159, 182, 205, 219, 241, 256, 264, 285, 299, 319, 333, 347, 379, 410, 435, 458, 488, 495, 547, 555, 563, 569, 588, 595, 627, 679, 689, 695 *Lesson Review: Persuasive Writing* 21, 69, 83, 93, 127, 133, 167, 197, 227, 291, 311, 357, 365, 415, 481, 503, 519, 605, 649, 657, 671 *Lesson Review: Descriptive Writing* 47, 189, 271, 391, 515, 533, 660; *Personal Writing* 61, 153, 327, 385, 429, 441, 575, 611, 703; *Narrative Writing* 235, 403, 467, 527; *Creative Writing* 392, 623, 635; *Chapter Activities: Exploring the Essential Question, Descriptive Writing* 48, 272, 612; *Expository Writing* 70, 98, 134, 168, 206, 242, 300, 366, 416, 444, 468, 504, 534, 576, 636, 658, 704; *Persuasive Writing* 334 *Chapter Assessment: Extended Response, Personal Writing* 24, 72; *Descriptive Writing* 136, 394, 418, 470, 614; *Persuasive Writing* 50, 274, 706; *Comparative Writing* 170; *Expository Writing* 208, 302, 446, 506; *Descriptive Writing* 244, 368, 638; *Outlining a Reference Article* 578 *Thinking Like a Historian: Comparing and Contrasting* 242; *Researching on the Internet* 427 *Step Into the Time: Time Line, Write a Paragraph* 338, 396, 616, *Chapter Activities: 21st Century Skills: Analyzing Images* 392; *Creating a Blog* 636; *Communication* 658 *What Do You Think? DBQ, Read to Write, Personal* 443 *Chapter Activities: 21st Century Skills: Debating* 468 **Teacher Edition:** **HOCP:** 3, 19, 35, 49, 65, 89, 109, 133, 155, 175, 193, 213, 233, 249, 265, 283, 299, 321, 339, 363, 385, 401, 415 **ENGAGE: MG** 77 **TEACH & ASSESS: D** 29, 73, 357; **A** 79; **DCAE** 127; **E** 135, 255; **MC** 139; **DC** 143; **S** 149, 305; **I** 159; **DS** 351; **WAR** 405 **CLOSE & REFLECT: IW** 55; **S** 97, 117, 183, 199, 379; **C** 119; **E** 141, 197, 235, 427; **MC** 181, 225, 227; **TAS** 243 **IYHMT: C** 59, 435; **CP** 75; **D** 83, 405; **I** 99, 227, 311, 419; **AG** 115; **AV** 165; **HS** 301; **D** 303, 429; **MC** 307; **COR** 329; **SI** 333; **R** 347, 435
5. Develop and strengthen writing as needed by planning, revising, editing, rewriting, or trying a new approach.	**Student Edition:** *Chapter Activities: 21st Century Skills* 22, 48, 70, 98, 134, 168, 206, 242, 272, 300, 334, 366, 392, 416, 444, 469, 505, 535, 577, 613, 636, 659, 705 *Chapter Assessment: Extended Response* 24, 50, 72, 100, 136, 170, 208, 244, 274, 302, 336, 368, 394, 418, 446, 471, 507, 537, 579, 615, 638, 661 **Teacher Edition:** **HOCP:** 3, 19, 35, 49, 65, 89, 109, 133, 155, 175, 193, 213, 233, 249, 265, 283, 299, 321, 339, 363, 385, 401, 415 **ENGAGE: MC** 197, 217; **I** 225; **M** 253 **TEACH & ASSESS: MC** 139; **A** 169; **DS** 351 **IYHMT: E** 207; **CABA** 241; **CAC** 289; **SI** 333

Codes used for the Teacher Edition pages are the initial caps of headings on that page.

Production and Distribution of Writing	
6. Use technology, including the Internet, to produce and publish writing and to interact and collaborate with others.	**Student Edition:** *Researching on the Internet* 19–20 *Thinking Like A Historian: Internet Tips* 41; *Researching on the Internet* 102, 161, 231, 252, 342, 427, 555; *Predicting Consequences* 623 *Chapter Activities: 21st Century Skills: Apply Technology Effectively* 242; *Recognize Quality Sources* 416; *Creating a Blog* 636; *Communication* 658; *Build a Web Site* 704 *Chapter Activities: 21st Century Skills: Sequence Events Using Presentation Software* 504; *Analyzing Images, Create a PowerPoint™ Presentation* 612 **Teacher Edition:** **MMR: CEO Ch** 1, 1, 16, 32, 46, 62, 86, 106, 130, 152, 172, 190, 210, 230, 246, 262, 280, 296, 318, 336, 360, 382, 398, 412, 438, 460, 486 **HOCP:** 3, 19, 35, 49, 65, 89, 109, 133, 155, 175, 193, 213, 233, 249, 265, 283, 299, 321, 339, 363, 385, 401, 415 **TEACH & ASSESS: D** 13; **E** 181, 431; **SS** 217 **IYHMT: E** 75, 207; **CAC** 83; **MC** 123, 307; **AV** 165; **HS** 301; **COR** 329; **R** 331, 347, 369, 435; **HACD** 347
Research to Build and Present Knowledge	
7. Conduct short as well as more sustained research projects based on focused questions, demonstrating understanding of the subject under investigation.	**Student Edition:** *Focusing Research* 14 *Researching History* 18–21 *Thinking Like A Historian: Internet Tips* 41; *Researching on the Internet* 102, 161, 231, 252, 342, 427, 555; *Predicting Consequences* 623 *Chapter Activities: 21st Century Skills: Analyze and Interpret Media* 22; *Collaborate With Others* 334; *Analyzing Images* 392; *Recognize Quality Sources* 416; *Using Latitude and Longitude, Research* 534; *Communication* 658 **Teacher Edition:** **HOCP: Ch** 1, 3, 19, 35, 49, 65, 89, 109, 133, 155, 175, 193, 213, 233, 249, 265, 283, 299, 321, 339, 363, 385, 401, 415 **TEACH & ASSESS: DS** 351; **E** 431; **S** 435 **IYHMT: R** 51, 331, 347, 369, 435; **C** 59; **V** 75; **E** 75, 207, 405; **CAC** 83; **MC** 93, 123, 307; **I** 99; **AG** 115; **MI** 161; **AV** 165; **HS** 301; **COR** 329; **HACD** 347; **D** 405, 429; **S** 409

Codes used for the Teacher Edition pages are the initial caps of headings on that page.

Research to Build and Present Knowledge	
8. Gather relevant information from multiple print and digital sources, assess the credibility and accuracy of each source, and integrate the information while avoiding plagiarism.	**Student Edition:** *Focusing Research* 14 *Researching History* 18–21 *Thinking Like A Historian: Internet Tips* 41; *Researching on the Internet* 102, 161, 231, 252, 342, 427, 555; *Predicting Consequences* 623 *Chapter Activities: 21st Century Skills: Analyze and Interpret Media* 22; *Collaborate With Others* 334; *Recognize Quality Sources* 416; *Using Latitude and Longitude, Research* 534; *Communication* 658 *Chapter Activities: 21st Century Skills: Analyzing Images* 392 **Teacher Edition:** **MMR: CEO Ch** 1, 16, 32, 46, 62, 86, 106, 130, 152, 172, 190, 210, 230, 246, 262, 280, 296, 318, 336, 360, 382, 398, 412 **HOCP: Ch** 1, 3, 19, 35, 49, 65, 89, 109, 133, 155, 175, 193, 213, 233, 249, 265, 283, 299, 321, 339, 363, 385, 401, 415 **ENGAGE: MD** 11 **TEACH & ASSESS: D** 13; **DS** 351; **E** 431; **S** 435 **IYHMT: ALL** 23; **R** 51, 331, 369, 435; **C** 59; **E** 75, 207; **CAC** 83; **I** 99; **AG** 115; **MC** 123, 307; **MI** 161; **AV** 165; **HS** 301; **COR** 329; **HACD** 347; **E** 405; **D** 405, 409, 429, 433; **S** 409
9. Draw evidence from literary or informational texts to support analysis, reflection, and research.	**Student Edition:** *Biography* 8, 35, 66, 87, 123, 142, 162, 188, 201, 222, 260, 295, 326, 343, 362, 374, 377, 401, 410, 435, 464, 476, 492, 526, 574, 594, 610, 626, 646, 675, 695, 702 *Focusing Research* 14 *Primary Source* 16, 17, 58, 85, 101, 111, 131, 146, 149, 150, 153, 156, 158, 167, 182, 185, 193, 195, 203, 216, 226, 228, 229, 231, 233, 240, 254, 258, 267, 287, 298, 308, 319, 324, 331, 356, 362, 374, 400, 401, 414, 427, 431, 434, 439, 479, 480, 486, 487, 488, 495, 497, 501, 521, 526, 531, 543, 549, 558, 574, 588, 593, 597, 601, 611, 653, 655, 666, 673, 680, 681, 683, 694, 700 *Researching History* 18–21 *Chapter Activities: 21st Century Skills: Analyze and Interpret Media* 22; *Collaborate With Others* 334; *Analyzing Images* 392; *Recognize Quality Sources* 416; *Using Latitude and Longitude, Research* 534; *Communication* 658 *Thinking Like A Historian: Internet Tips* 41; *Researching on the Internet* 102, 161, 231, 252, 342, 427, 555; *Predicting Consequences* 623 *The World's Literature* 84–85, 348–349, 496–497, 596–597 *What Do You Think? DBQ, Read to Write, Personal* 443 *Chapter Assessment: Extended Response, Expository Writing* 446 **Teacher Edition:** **MMR: CEO Ch** 1, 16, 32, 46, 62, 86, 106, 130, 152, 172, 190, 210, 230, 246, 262, 280, 296, 318, 336, 360, 382, 398, 412 **HOCP:** 3, 19, 35, 49, 65, 89, 109, 133, 155, 175, 193, 213, 233, 249, 265, 283, 299, 321, 339, 363, 385, 401, 415 **ENGAGE: MG** 77 **TEACH & ASSESS: APS** 103; **A** 139; **DC** 143; **I** 163; **DS** 351; **E** 431; **S** 435 **CLOSE & REFLECT: E** 127, 141; **HS** 143; **P** 267; **S** 379 **IYHMT: R** 51, 347, 369, 435; **C** 59; **E** 75, 207, 405; **CAC** 83; **D** 83; **I** 99; **AG** 115; **MI** 161; **AV** 165; **HS** 301; **MC** 307; **COR** 329; **HACD** 347; **D** 405, 409, 429; **S** 409

Codes used for the Teacher Edition pages are the initial caps of headings on that page.

Range of Writing	
10. Write routinely over extended time frames (time for research, reflection, and revision) and shorter time frames (a single sitting or a day or two) for a range of tasks, purposes, and audiences.	**Student Edition:** *Lesson Review: Expository Writing* 9, 15, 37, 43, 107, 119, 147, 159, 182, 205, 219, 241, 256, 264, 285, 299, 319, 333, 347, 379, 435, 458, 488, 495, 547, 555, 563, 569, 588, 595, 627, 679, 689, 695; *Descriptive Writing* 47, 189, 271, 391, 515, 533; *Persuasive Writing* 21, 69, 83, 93, 127, 133, 167, 197, 227, 291, 311, 357, 365, 481, 503, 519, 605, 649, 657, 671; *Personal Writing* 61, 153, 327, 379, 385, 441, 703; *Narrative Writing* 235, 401, 467, 527; *Creative Writing* 623, 635 *Chapter Activities: Exploring the Essential Question, Descriptive Writing* 48, 272, 612; *Expository Writing* 70, 98, 134, 168, 206, 242, 300, 366, 416, 444, 468, 504, 534, 576, 636, 658, 704; *Persuasive Writing* 334;*Creative Writing* 392 *Chapter Assessment: Extended Response, Personal Writing* 24, 72; *Persuasive Writing* 50, 274, 706; *Descriptive Writing* 136, 368, 394, 418, 614, 638; *Comparative Writing* 170; *Expository Writing* 208, 302, 446, 506, 536 *Descriptive Writing* 244, 368, 418, 470, 660; *Outlining a Reference Article* 578 *Thinking Like a Historian: Comparing and Contrasting* 242; *Researching on the Internet, Summarize* 427; *Researching Using Internet Resources* 555 *Chapter Activities: 21st Century Skills: Recognize Quality Sources* 416; *Creating a Blog* 636 *What Do You Think? DBQ, Read to Write, Personal* 443 *Thinking Like a Historian: Predicting Consequences* 623 **Teacher Edition:** **HOCP:** 3, 19, 35, 49, 65, 89, 109, 133, 155, 175, 193, 213, 233, 249, 265, 283, 299, 321, 339, 363, 385, 401, 415 **TEACH & ASSESS: D** 73; **A** 79; **DCAE** 127; **E** 135, 255; **MC** 139; **DC** 143; **S** 149, 435; **DS** 351 **CLOSE & REFLECT: IW** 55; **S** 97, 117; **C** 119; **E** 141, 235, 427; **MC** 181, 225, 227; **E** 197; **TAS** 243; **D** 357 **IYHMT: C** 59, 435; **D** 83, 405; **I** 99, 227; **AG** 115; **S** 123; **AV** 165; **S** 183; **S** 227; **MC** 307; **COR** 329; **R** 347; **R** 435

Reading Standards for Literacy in History/Social Studies, Grades 6–8

Key Ideas and Details	
1. Cite specific textual evidence to support analysis of primary and secondary sources.	**Student Edition:** *Biography* 8, 35, 66, 87, 123, 142, 162, 188, 201, 222, 260, 295, 326, 343, 362, 374, 377, 401, 410, 435, 464, 476, 492, 526, 574, 594, 610, 626, 646, 675, 695, 702 *What Is the Evidence?* 10–11 *Thinking Like A Historian: Analyzing Primary Sources* 41; *Analyzing Primary and Secondary Sources* 177, 308; *Analyzing Sources* 282; *Researching on the Internet* 342, 427; *Predicting Consequences* 623 *The World's Literature* 84–85, 348–349, 496–497, 596–597 **Teacher Edition:** **HOCP:** 3, 19, 35, 49, 65, 89, 109, 133, 155, 175, 193, 213, 233, 249, 265, 283, 299, 321, 339, 363, 385, 401, 415 **ENGAGE: P** 57 **TEACH & ASSESS: E** 5, 7, 143; **APS** 7, 93, 95, 97, 145, 199, 203; **MC** 91, 143; **IW** 121, 377; **PS** 127; **CAC** 139; **I** 159; **PSA** 167; **S** 199, 301, 313, 315, 357 **CLOSE & REFLECT: S** 97, 307, 373; **E** 99 **IYHMT: D** 83, 113; **I** 99, 311

Codes used for the Teacher Edition pages are the initial caps of headings on that page.

Key Ideas and Details	
2. Determine the central ideas or information of a primary or secondary source; provide an accurate summary of the source distinct from prior knowledge or opinions.	**Student Edition:** *Primary Source* 16, 17, 58, 85, 101, 111, 131, 146, 149, 150, 153, 156, 158, 167, 182, 185, 193, 195, 203, 216, 226, 228, 229, 231, 233, 240, 254, 258, 267, 287, 298, 308, 319, 324, 331, 356, 362, 374, 400, 401, 414, 427, 431, 434, 439, 479, 480, 486, 487, 488, 495, 497, 501, 521, 526, 531, 543, 549, 558, 574, 588, 593, 597, 601, 611, 653, 655, 666, 673, 680, 681, 683, 694, 700 *Chapter Assessment: Document-Based Questions* 24, 50, 72, 100, 136, 170, 208, 244, 274, 302, 336, 368, 394, 418, 446, 471, 507, 537, 579, 615, 661; *Short Response* 24, 50, 72, 100, 136, 170, 208, 244, 274, 302, 336, 368, 394, 418, 446, 471, 507, 537, 579, 615, 661 *Finding the Main Idea* 37, 43, 47, 50, 231, 660, 695 *Thinking Like A Historian: Analyzing Primary Sources* 41; *Analyzing Primary and Secondary Sources* 177, 308; *Analyzing Sources* 282; *Researching on the Internet, Summarize* 427; *Predicting Consequences* 623 *Summarizing* 43, 61, 127, 147, 170, 182, 235, 256, 311, 319, 327, 336, 342, 357, 415, 418, 435, 458, 495, 503, 515, 533, 547, 555, 578, 614, 631, 649, 657, 752, 753, 579 *Reading HELPDESK: Reading Strategy: Paraphrasing* 376 *Reading HELPDESK: Taking Notes: Summarizing* 624 *Identifying Central Issues* 681 **Teacher Edition:** **ENGAGE: P** 57 **TEACH & ASSESS: APS** 7, 93, 95, 97, 145, 199, 203; **E** 7, 143; **S** 11, 199, 285, 291, 305, 313, 419; **MC** 91, 143; **IW** 121, 377; **PS** 127; **S** 145, 271, 301, 315, 357; **PSA** 167; **ICI** 367, 417, 419; **FTMI** 375 **CLOSE & REFLECT: S** 23, 97, 307, 367, 373, 391; **P** 267; **FTMI** 375 **IYHMT: D** 83, 113; **S** 325; **ICI** 343; **FTMI** 423
3. Identify key steps in a text's description of a process related to history/social studies (e.g., how a bill becomes law, how interest rates are raised or lowered).	**Student Edition:** *Reading HELPDESK: Taking Notes, Sequencing* 10, 54, 128, 320 *Sequencing* 122 *Thinking Like a Historian: Using a Time Line, Sequence Events* 403, 416 *Lesson Review: Sequencing* 441 **Teacher Edition:** **TEACH & ASSESS: I** 195, 309; **S** 199, 203, 255; **E** 207; **MG** 393 **CLOSE & REFLECT: S** 103, 259 **IYHMT: S** 227, 259; **MC** 379

Codes used for the Teacher Edition pages are the initial caps of headings on that page.

Craft and Structure	
4. Determine the meaning of words and phrases as they are used in a text, including vocabulary specific to domains related to history/social studies.	**Student Edition:** *Reading HELPDESK: Content Vocabulary* 4, 10, 18, 28, 29, 38, 39, 44, 45, 54, 62, 76, 85, 86, 100, 108, 120, 128, 140, 148, 154, 160, 174, 183, 190, 198, 212, 220, 230, 236, 248, 257, 265, 278, 286, 292, 306, 312, 320, 328, 340, 350, 360, 372, 380, 386, 398, 404, 411, 422, 430, 436, 450, 459, 474, 482, 489, 498, 510, 516, 520, 528, 540, 548, 556, 564, 570, 582, 589, 598, 606, 618, 624, 628, 642, 643, 650, 665, 672, 682, 690, 696 *Reading HELPDESK: Academic Vocabulary* 5, 6, 11, 14, 20, 30, 32, 35, 41, 46, 56, 58, 64, 65, 77, 80, 82, 87, 90, 101, 102, 106, 109, 110, 111, 112, 115, 116, 118, 124, 125, 126, 129, 130, 145, 146, 150, 151, 152, 155, 156, 157, 161, 162, 163, 164, 166, 175, 176, 177, 179, 184, 185, 186, 187, 188, 191, 194, 196, 200, 202, 203, 214, 218, 221, 222, 224, 231, 232, 237, 238, 239, 252, 254, 258, 260, 261, 262, 266, 268, 269, 270, 279, 280, 281, 287, 289, 293, 295, 297, 298, 307, 308, 309, 310, 313, 315, 316, 322, 324, 326, 329, 330, 331, 332, 342, 344, 352, 362, 374, 375, 381, 382, 387, 399, 400, 407, 408, 413, 414, 423, 424, 431, 432, 434, 437, 438, 440, 452, 454, 456, 460, 462, 464, 476, 480, 484, 490, 494, 502, 512, 517, 518, 522, 530, 532, 541, 544, 549, 550, 558, 560, 562, 565, 566, 570, 572, 586, 590, 592, 598, 602, 604, 608, 619, 620, 622, 625, 626, 629, 630, 633, 634, 643, 644, 648, 653, 656, 666, 670, 673, 674, 678, 686, 688, 692, 698, 700 *Reading HELPDESK: Reading Strategy: Context Clues* 6 *Reading HELPDESK: Build Vocabulary: Word Parts* 8; *Multiple Meanings* 193, 325; *Word Forms* 116, 250; *Word Origins*, 178, 361, 390, 558; *Suffixes* 262, 683; *Prefixes* 457 *Lesson Review: Review Vocabulary* 9, 15, 21, 37, 43, 47, 61, 69, 83, 93, 107, 119, 127, 133, 147, 153, 159, 167, 182, 189, 197, 205, 219, 227, 235, 241, 256, 264, 271, 285, 291, 299, 311, 319, 327, 333, 347, 357, 365, 379, 385, 391, 403, 410, 415, 429, 435, 441, 458, 467, 481, 488, 495, 503, 515, 519, 527, 533, 547, 555, 563, 569, 575, 588, 595, 605, 611, 623, 627, 635, 649, 657, 671, 679, 689, 695, 703 *Reading HELPDESK: Visual Vocabulary* 57, 89, 142, 239, 249, 296, 332, 345, 465, 526 *Chapter Assessment: Extended Response, Expository Writing* 536 **Teacher Edition:** **SITP:** 19 **ENGAGE: D** 29, 135, 181, 341, 417, 425; **MC** 81, 169; **AS** 115; **LS** 115; **LS** 123; **CAC** 145, 161; **P** 147, 203; **A** 405; **C** 421; **S** 427 **TEACH & ASSESS: D** 5, 13, 41, 67, 93, 119, 163, 277, 345, 373, 393, 407, 421, 425; **MC** 5, 37, 127, 135, 139; **CAC** 5, 113, 141, 345, 433; **LS** 7, 51, 53, 55; **L** 21, 255; **E** 29, 195, 273, 277, 327, 369; **C** 29, 37, 117, 159, 223, 313, 345, 365, 375; **B** 53; **MG** 73; **I** 113, 117, 291; **A** 117, 369, 433; **I** 119, 207, 235; **DCAE** 127; **S** 137, 165, 197, 393; **APS** 145, 203; **MD** 203; **P** 367; **W** 373; **VIW** 391; **M** 191; **R** 425, 435 **CLOSE & REFLECT: E** 101, 427; **C** 137 **IYHMT: PTS** 25; **D** 59, 113, 427; **UCC** 103; **CAC** 149; **MC** 183; **A** 259; **S** 301; **TCAE** 395; **UGO** 395

Codes used for the Teacher Edition pages are the initial caps of headings on that page.

Craft and Structure	
5. Describe how a text presents information (e.g., sequentially, comparatively, causally).	**Student Edition:** *Reading HELPDESK: Taking Notes: Categorizing* 4, 312, 482, 642; *Analyzing* 278; *Finding Main Idea* 18, 154, 436; *Identifying* 28, 62, 76, 86, 100, 190, 198, 220, 265, 286, 328, 340, 372, 422, 474, 510, 516, 528, 540, 582, 618, 650; *Describing* 38, 236, 257, 398, 589; *Organizing* 108, 120, 350, 411, 430, 459, 564, 682; *Listing* 148, 360, 362, 380, 386, 628; *Summarizing* 404, 450, 548, 624; *Finding the Main Idea* 436; *Sequencing* 489, 556, 672, 690; *Determine Cause and Effect* 498, 598, 606, 664; *Sharing Relationships* 520; *Explaining* 696 *The World's Literature* 84–85, 348–349, 496–497, 596–597 *Reading HELPDESK: Reading Strategy: Listing* 440 **Teacher Edition:** **TEACH & ASSESS: S** 81; **CAC** 349
6. Identify aspects of a text that reveal an author's point of view or purpose (e.g., loaded language, inclusion or avoidance of particular facts).	**Student Edition:** *What Is Point of View?* 12 *What Do You Think?* 16–17, 228–229, 358–359, 442–443, 680–681 *Primary Source* 16, 17, 58, 85, 101, 111, 131, 146, 149, 150, 153, 156, 158, 167, 182, 185, 193, 195, 203, 216, 226, 228, 229, 231, 233, 240, 254, 258, 267, 287, 298, 308, 319, 324, 331, 356, 362, 374, 400, 401, 414, 427, 431, 434, 439, 479, 480, 486, 487, 488, 495, 497, 501, 521, 526, 531, 543, 549, 558, 574, 588, 593, 597, 601, 611, 653, 655, 666, 673, 680, 681, 683, 694, 700 *Chapter Assessment: Document-Based Questions: Identifying Point of View* 24 *Thinking Like A Historian: Analyzing Primary Sources* 41; *Analyzing Primary and Secondary Sources* 177, 308; *Analyzing Sources* 282; *Researching on the Internet* 427; *Identifying Points of View* 704 *What Do You Think? DBQ, Describing* 359 *Critical Thinking: Identifying Points of View* 479, 557, 689 *The World's Literature: Analyzing Literature, DBQ* 597 *Chapter Assessment: Extended Response, Descriptive Writing* 660 **Teacher Edition:** **HOCP:** 415 **ENGAGE: P** 57; **R** 143; **D** 389 **TEACH & ASSESS: S** 11; **MC** 91, 125, 139; **IPOV** 95, 143, 181, 183, 197, 277, 301, 309, 351, 375, 417; **C** 97; **MI** 99; **E** 101, 203; **APS** 103, 203; **I** 121, 159, 199; **A** 139; **PSA** 167; **E** 239, 303; **VIW** 391 **CLOSE & REFLECT: IPOV** 53, 221, 369 **IYHMT: E** 9; **PTS** 25; **D** 113, 303; **A** 121; **APOV** 199

Codes used for the Teacher Edition pages are the initial caps of headings on that page.

Integration of Knowledge and Ideas	
7. Integrate visual information (e.g., in charts, graphs, photographs, videos, or maps) with other information in print and digital texts.	**Student Edition:** *Step Into the Place* 2–3, 26–27, 52–53, 74–75, 98–99, 138–139, 172–173, 210–211, 246–247, 276–277, 304–305, 338–339, 370–371, 396–397, 420–421, 448–449, 472–473, 508–509, 538–539, 580–581, 616–617, 640–641, 662–663 *Map* 12, 29, 30, 31, 34, 37, 60, 63, 68, 78, 89, 90, 101, 106, 124, 131, 151, 161, 164, 175, 180, 184, 191, 194, 204, 232, 234, 249, 253, 266, 269, 279, 281, 284, 294, 298, 314, 317, 332, 346, 354, 364, 381, 388, 399, 405, 408, 423, 426, 433, 437, 440, 451, 453, 455, 466, 468, 475, 477, 490, 491, 499, 501, 504, 511, 513, 517, 529, 534, 541, 545, 559, 561, 562, 571, 573, 576, 583, 602, 608, 612, 620, 625, 632, 634, 656, 658, 665, 678, 685, 687, 691, 704 *Infographics* 7, 39, 41, 42, 45, 114, 116, 143, 145, 200, 201, 213, 218, 224, 251, 255, 288, 290, 331, 341, 355, 375, 384, 390, 424, 428, 477, 552, 621, 630, 647, 693 *Using Charts, Graphs, and Diagrams* 35–36 *Chapter Activities: Reading Maps* 48; *Geography Activity* 70, 134, 168, 206, 242, 272, 300, 334, 366, 392, 416, 444, 468, 504, 534, 576, 612, 636, 658, 704; *Using Latitude and Longitude* 534 *Chapter Assessment: Document-Based Questions* 72, 170 *Reading HELPDESK: Reading Strategy: Reading a Map* 131 *Reading HELPDESK: Reading in the Content Area: Content Area* 145; *Charts* 354; *Pie Chart or Pie Graph* 432 *Chart* 152, 178, 239, 406, 649 *Chapter Activities 21st Century Skills, Analyzing News Media* 300; *Analyzing Images* 392; *Communication* 658 *Chapter Activities Thinking Like a Historian, Comparing and Contrasting* 392; *Sequencing, Create a Time Line* 468, 612 *Thinking Like a Historian: Using a Time Line, Sequence Events* 403, 416 *Analyzing Visuals* 456, 554, 561, 566, 572, 595, 656, 677 *Photographs (with questions)* 512, 565, 667, 694 **Teacher Edition:** **MMR: CEO Ch** 1, 16, 32, 46, 62, 86, 106, 130, 152, 172, 190, 210, 230, 246, 262, 280, 296, 318, 336, 360, 382, 398, 412; **ATM** 32, 46, 62, 86, 106, 130, 152, 172, 190, 210, 230, 262, 318, 336, 382, 398, 412 **HOCP:** 19, 49, 109, 133, 155, 213, 233, 249, 265, 299, 385, 415 **SITT:** 3 **ENGAGE: AV** 37, 77, 111, 177, 185, 225, 271, 343, 365, 433; **M** 55, 253; **C** 67; **I** 91, 149, 157, 267, 309, 375, 435; **P** 91, 113, 135, 147, 161, 199, 241, 285, 289; **MC** 119, 169, 331, 429; **CAC** 161; **SS** 185, 351, 403; **E** 235, 325; **A** 277, 323; **D** 313, 345, 353; **MG** 355 **TEACH & ASSESS: E** 5, 99, 101, 117, 251, 257, 369, 387; **L** 21, 199, 349, 369; **CAC** 21, 167; **A** 21, 91, 93, 145, 149, 157, 163, 293; **MC** 23, 51, 113, 147, 159, 221; **G** 25; **C** 29, 291; **D** 51, 95, 147, 157, 163, 167, 207, 239, 251, 253, 317; **SS** 53, 111, 137, 301, 305; **MG** 77, 371; **I** 77, 121, 149, 159, 167, 195, 201, 243, 327, 329, 331, 387, 389, 427; **AV** 95, 101, 125, 145, 157, 181, 205, 221, 239, 267, 285, 291, 293, 331, 365, 377, 391, 427; **S** 119, 177, 199, 271, 341; **V** 121; **LS** 137; **CTT** 147; **DC** 157; **IWA** 157, 391; **AS** 223; **C** 253; **S** 269, 271, 323, 345; **AVI** 285; **O** 365 **CLOSE & REFLECT: MC** 21; **L** 77; **I** 269 **IYHMT: ALL** 23; **OLL** 23; **BLL** 23; **CAC** 41; **C** 59, 123; **A** 69; **MC** 93, 123; **AG** 115; **I** 121, 311, 419; **AV** 165; **UV** 183; **L** 253; **AVI** 287; **HS** 301; **D** 307; **E** 315; **R** 347, 369

Codes used for the Teacher Edition pages are the initial caps of headings on that page.

Integration of Knowledge and Ideas	
8. Distinguish among fact, opinion, and reasoned judgment in a text.	**Student Edition:** *Distinguishing Fact From Opinion* 19 *Thinking Like A Historian: Internet Tips* 41 *Chapter Activities: Analyzing and Making Judgments* 70, 206 *Chapter Activities: Thinking Like a Historian, Distinguishing Fact From Opinion* 366 **Teacher Edition:** **TEACH & ASSESS: DFAO** 11, 117; **IW** 11; **IS** 293 **CLOSE & REFLECT: HS** 427 **IYHMT: E** 9, 429; **PM** 141
9. Analyze the relationship between a primary and secondary source on the same topic.	**Student Edition:** *What Do You Think?* 16–17, 228–229, 358–359, 442–443, 680–681 *Document-Based Questions* 17, 229 *Thinking Like A Historian: Comparing Sources* 22; *Analyzing Primary Sources* 41; *Classifying and Categorizing Information* 83; *Analyzing Primary and Secondary Sources* 177, 308; *Analyzing Sources* 282 *Reading HELPDESK: Taking Notes: Contrasting* 110, 160; *Comparing* 174, 183, 292 *Infographic: Greek Philosophers* 224; *Chinese Philosophers* 288 **Teacher Edition:** **TEACH & ASSESS: E** 7, 9

Codes used for the Teacher Edition pages are the initial caps of headings on that page.

Range of Reading and Level of Text Complexity	
10. By the end of grade 8, read and comprehend history/social studies texts in the grades 6–8 text complexity band independently and proficiently.	**Student Edition:** *Biography* 8, 35, 66, 87, 123, 142, 162, 188, 201, 222, 260, 295, 326, 343, 362, 374, 377, 401, 410, 435, 464, 476, 492, 526, 574, 594, 610, 626, 646, 675, 695, 702 *Primary Source* 16, 17, 58, 85, 101, 111, 131, 146, 149, 150, 153, 156, 158, 167, 182, 185, 193, 195, 203, 216, 226, 228, 229, 231, 233, 240, 254, 258, 267, 287, 298, 308, 319, 324, 331, 356, 362, 374, 400, 401, 414, 427, 431, 434, 439, 479, 480, 486, 487, 488, 495, 497, 501, 521, 526, 531, 543, 549, 558, 574, 588, 593, 597, 601, 611, 653, 655, 666, 673, 680, 681, 683, 694, 700 *Thinking Like A Historian* 20, 41, 67, 83, 102, 161, 177, 231, 252, 282, 308, 342, 403, 427, 555, 467, 485, 555, 587, 623 *The World's Literature* 84–85, 348–349, 496–497, 596–597 *Reading HELPDESK: Reading in the Content Area* 426 **Teacher Edition:** **MMR: RL Ch** 1, 16, 32, 46, 62, 86, 106, 130, 152, 172, 190, 210, 230, 246, 262, 280, 296, 318, 336, 360, 382, 398, 412 **HOCP:** 3, 19, 35, 49, 65, 89, 109, 133, 155, 175, 193, 213, 233, 249, 265, 283, 299, 321, 339, 363, 385, 401, 415 **ENGAGE: C** 67 **TEACH & ASSESS: S** 11, 145, 177, 301; **D** 95; **CAC** 125, 271; **I** 141, 309; **C** 159; **E** 167; **L** 255; **MG** 371 **CLOSE & REFLECT: D** 67; **I** 71 **IYHMT: R** 51; **CAC** 51, 83; **D** 83, 303

Codes used for the Teacher Edition pages are the initial caps of headings on that page.

UNDERSTANDING BY DESIGN®

by Jay McTighe

Understanding by Design® (UbD™) offers a planning framework to guide curriculum, assessment, and instruction. Its two key ideas are contained in the title: 1) focus on teaching and assessing for understanding and transfer, and 2) design curriculum "backward" from those ends.

UbD is based on seven key tenets:

1. UbD is a way of thinking purposefully about curricular planning, not a rigid program or prescriptive recipe.
2. A primary goal of UbD is developing and deepening student understanding: the ability to make meaning of learning via "big ideas" and transfer learning.
3. Understanding is revealed when students autonomously make sense of and transfer their learning through authentic performance. Six facets of understanding—the capacity to explain, interpret, apply, shift perspective, empathize, and self assess—serve as indicators of understanding.
4. Effective curriculum is planned "backward" from long-term desired results though a three-stage design process (Desired Results, Evidence, Learning Plan). This process helps to avoid the twin problems of "textbook coverage" and "activity-oriented" teaching in which no clear priorities and purposes are apparent.
5. Teachers are coaches of understanding, not mere purveyors of content or activity. They focus on ensuring learning, not just teaching (and assuming that what was taught was learned); they always aim and check for successful meaning making and transfer by the learner.
6. Regular reviews of units and curriculum against design standards enhance curricular quality and effectiveness.
7. UbD reflects a continuous improvement approach to achievement. The results of our designs —student performance—inform needed adjustments in curriculum as well as instruction.

Three Stages of Backward Design

In UbD, we propose a 3-stage "backward design" process for curriculum planning. The concept of planning "backward" from desired results is not new. In 1949 Ralph Tyler described this approach as an effective process for focusing instruction. More recently, Stephen Covey, in the best selling book, *Seven Habits of Highly Effective People*, reports that effective people in various fields are goal-oriented and plan with the end in mind. Although not a new idea, we have found that the deliberate use of backward design for planning curriculum units and courses results in more clearly defined goals, more appropriate assessments, more tightly aligned lessons, and more purposeful teaching.

Backward planning asks educators to consider the following three stages:

Stage 1 – Identify Desired Results

What should students know, understand, and be able to do? What content is worthy of understanding? What "enduring" understandings are desired? What essential questions will be explored?

In the first stage of backward design we consider our goals, examine established Content Standards (national, state, province, district), and review curriculum expectations. Since there is typically more "content" than can reasonably be addressed within the available time, teachers must make choices. This first stage in the design process calls for setting priorities.

More specifically, Stage 1 of UbD asks teachers to identify the "big ideas" that we want students to come to understand, and then to identify or craft companion essential questions. Big ideas reflect transferable concepts, principles and processes that are key to understanding the topic or subject. Essential questions present open-ended, thought-provoking inquiries that are explored over time.

More specific knowledge and skill objectives, linked to the targeted Content Standards and Understandings, are also identified in Stage 1. An important point in UbD is to recognize that factual knowledge and skills are not taught for their own sake, but as a means to larger ends. Ultimately, teaching should equip learners to be able to use or transfer their learning; i.e., meaningful performance with content. This is the "end" we always want to keep in mind.

Stage 2 – Determine Acceptable Evidence

How will we know if students have achieved the desired results? What will we accept as evidence of student understanding and proficiency? How will we evaluate student performance?

Backward design encourages teachers and curriculum planners to first "think like an assessor" before designing specific units and lessons. The assessment evidence we need reflects the desired results identified in Stage 1. Thus, we consider in advance the assessment evidence needed to document and validate that the targeted learning has been achieved. Doing so invariably sharpens and focuses teaching.

In Stage 2, we distinguish between two broad types of assessment—Performance Tasks and Other Evidence. The performance tasks ask students to apply their learning to a new and authentic situation as means of assessing their understanding. In UbD, we have identified six facets of understanding for assessment purposes[1]. When someone truly understands, they:

- Can **explain** concepts, principles and processes; i.e., put it in their own words, teach it to others, justify their answers, show their reasoning.
- Can **interpret**; i.e., make sense of data, text, and experience through images, analogies, stories, and models.
- Can apply; i.e., effectively use and adapt what they know in new and complex contexts.
- Demonstrate **perspective**; i.e., can see the big picture and recognize different points of view.
- Display **empathy**; i.e., perceive sensitively and "walk in someone else's shoes."
- Have **self-knowledge**; i.e., show metacognition, use productive habits of mind, and reflect on the meaning of their learning and experience.

These six facets do not present a theory of how people come to understand something. Instead, the facets are intended to serve as indicators of how understanding is revealed, and thus provide guidance as to the kinds of assessments we need to determine the extent of student understanding. Here are two notes regarding assessing understanding through the facets:

1) All six facets of understanding need not be used all of the time in assessment. In social studies, Empathy and Perspective may be added when appropriate.
2) Performance Tasks based on one or more facets are not intended for use in daily lessons. Rather, these tasks should be seen as culminating performances for a unit of study.

In addition to Performance Tasks, Stage 2 includes Other Evidence, such as traditional quizzes, tests, observations, and work samples to round out the assessment picture to

Examples of Essential Questions in Social Studies

Understandings or Big Ideas	Essential Questions
History involves interpretation, and different people may interpret the same events differently.	*Whose "story" is this? How do we know what really happened in the past?*
The geography, climate, and natural resources of a region influence the culture, economy, and lifestyle of its inhabitants.	*How does where we live influence how we live?*
History often repeats itself. Recognizing the patterns of the past can help us better understand the present and prepare for the future.	*Why study the past? What does the past have to do with today?*
Governments can change based on the changing needs of their people, the society, and the world.	*What makes an effective government? Why do/should governments change?*

[1] Wiggins, G. and McTighe, J. and (1998, 2005). *Understanding by Design.* Alexandria, VA: The Association for Supervision and Curriculum Development.

UNDERSTANDING BY DESIGN®
(continued)

determine what students know and can do. A key idea in backward design has to do with alignment. In other words, are we assessing everything that we are trying to achieve (in Stage 1) or only those things that are easiest to test and grade? Is anything important slipping through the cracks because it is not being assessed? Checking the alignment between Stages 1 and 2 helps insure that *all* important goals are appropriately assessed.

Stage 3 – Plan Learning Experiences and Instruction

How will we support learners in coming to an understanding of important ideas and processes? How will we prepare them to autonomously transfer their learning? What enabling knowledge and skills will students need in order to perform effectively and achieve desired results? What activities, sequence, and resources are best suited to accomplish our goals?

In Stage 3 of backward design, teachers now plan the most appropriate learning activities to help students acquire important knowledge and skills, come to understand important ideas and processes, and transfer their learning in meaningful ways. When developing a plan for learning, we propose that teachers consider a set of instructional principles, embedded in the acronym W.H.E.R.E.T.O. These design elements provide the armature or blueprint for instructional planning in Stage 3 in support of our goals of understanding and transfer.

Each of the W.H.E.R.E.T.O. elements is presented in the form of questions to consider.

W = *How will I help learners know – What they will be learning? Why this is worth learning? What evidence will show their learning? How will their performance be evaluated?*

Learners of all ages are more likely to put forth effort and meet with success when they understand the learning goals and see them as meaningful and personally relevant. The "W" in W.H.E.R.E.T.O. reminds teachers to clearly communicate the goals and help students see their relevance. In addition, learners need to know the concomitant performance expectations and assessments through which they will demonstrate their learning so that they have clear learning targets and the basis for monitoring their progress toward them.

H = *How will I hook and engage the learners?*

There is wisdom in the old adage: "Before you try to teach them, you've got to get their attention." The best teachers have always recognized the value of "hooking" learners through introductory activities that "itch" the mind and engage the heart in the learning process, and we encourage teachers to deliberately plan ways of hooking their learners to the topics they teach. Examples of effective hooks include provocative essential questions, counter-intuitive phenomena, controversial issues, authentic problems and challenges, emotional encounters, and humor. One must be mindful, of course, of not just coming up with interesting introductory activities that have no carry-over value. The intent is to match the hook with the content and

PHOTO: Banana Stock/Picture Quest

the experiences of the learners—by design—as a means of drawing them into a productive learning experience.

E = *How will I equip students to master identified standards and succeed with the transfer performances? What learning experiences will help develop and deepen understanding of important ideas?*

Understanding cannot be simply transferred like a load of freight from one mind to another. Coming to understand requires active intellectual engagement on the part of the learner. Therefore, instead of merely covering the content, effective educators "uncover" the most enduring ideas and processes in ways that engage students in constructing meaning for themselves. To this end, teachers select an appropriate balance of constructivist learning experiences, structured activities, and direct instruction for helping students acquire the desired knowledge, skill, and understanding. While there is certainly a place for direct instruction and modeling, teaching for understanding asks teachers to engage learners in making meaning through active inquiry.

R = *How will I encourage the learners to rethink previous learning? How will I encourage on-going revision and refinement?*

Few learners develop a complete understanding of abstract ideas on the first encounter. Indeed, the phrase "coming to understand" is suggestive of a process. Over time, learners develop and deepen their understanding by thinking and re-thinking, by examining ideas from a different point of view, from examining underlying assumptions, by receiving feedback and revising. Just as the quality of writing benefits from the iterative process of drafting and revising, so to do understandings become more mature. The "R" in W.H.E.R.E.T.O. encourages teachers to explicitly include such opportunities.

E = *How will I promote students' self-evaluation and reflection?*

Capable and independent learners are distinguished by their capacity to set goals, self-assess their progress, and adjust as needed. Yet, one of the most frequently overlooked aspects of the instructional process involves helping students to develop the meta-cognitive skills of self-evaluation, self-regulation, and reflection. The second "E" of WHERETO reminds teachers to build in time and expectations for students to regularly self-assess, reflect on the meaning of their learning, and set goals for future performance.

T = *How will I tailor the learning experiences to the nature of the learners I serve? How might I differentiate instruction to respond to the varied needs of students?*

"One size fits all teaching" is rarely optimal. Learners differ significantly in terms of their prior knowledge and skill levels, their interests, talents, and preferred ways of learning. Accordingly, the most effective teachers get to know their students and tailor their teaching and learning experiences to connect to them. A variety of strategies may be employed to differentiate *content* (e.g., how subject matter is presented), *process* (e.g., how students work), and *product* (e.g., how learners demonstrate their learning). The logic of backward design offers a cautionary note here: the Content Standards and Understandings should *not* be differentiated (except for students with Individualized Education Plans—I.E.P.s). In other words, differentiate means keeping the end in mind for all.

O = *How will I organize the learning experiences for maximum engagement and effectiveness? What sequence will be optimal given the understanding and transfer goals?*

When the primary educational goals involve helping students acquire basic knowledge and skills, teachers may be comfortable "covering" the content by telling and modeling.

However, when we include understanding and transfer as desired results, educators are encouraged to give careful attention to how the content is organized and sequenced. Just as effective story tellers and filmmakers often don't begin in the "beginning," teachers can consider alternatives to sequential content coverage. For example, methods such as the Case Method, Problem or Project-Based Learning, and Socratic Seminars immerse students in challenging situations, even before they may have acquired all of the "basics." They actively engage students in trying to make meaning and apply their learning in demanding circumstances without single "correct" answers.

Conclusion

Many teachers who are introduced to the backward design process have observed that while the process makes sense in theory, it often feels awkward in use. This is to be expected since the principles and practices of UbD often challenge conventional planning and teaching habits. However, with some practice, educators find that backward design becomes not only more comfortable, but a way of thinking. The resources found in this program support teaching and assessing for understanding and transfer.

WHY TEACH WITH TECHNOLOGY?

by Tom Daccord and Justin Reich, EdTechTeacher

✔ **Technology is transforming the practice of historians and should transform history classrooms as well.** While printed documents, books, maps, and artwork constitute the bulk of the historical record before 1900, the history of the last century is also captured in sound and video recording and in Web sites and other Internet resources. Today's students need to learn how to analyze and build arguments using these multimedia records as well as traditional primary sources.

✔ **So many of the sources that helped historians and history teachers fall in love with the discipline are now available online.** In recent decades, universities, libraries, archives, and other institutions have scanned and uploaded many vast treasure troves of historical sources. The Internet-connected classroom increasingly has access to the world's historical record, giving students a chance to develop critical thinking skills as well as learning historical narratives.

✔ **Whoever is doing most of the talking or most of the typing is doing most of the learning, and the more people listening the better.** Technology allows us to transfer the responsibility for learning from teachers to students, and to put students in the driver's seat of their own learning. Students who are actively engaged in creating and presenting their understandings of history are learning more than students passively listening. Technology also allows students to publish their work to broader audiences of peers, parents, and even the entire Internet-connected world. Students find the opportunities challenging, exciting, and engaging.

Technology Extension

- Find an additional activity online that incorporates technology for this project.
- Visit the EdTechTeacher Web sites (included in the Technology Extension for this chapter) for more links, tutorials, and other resources.

Teaching With Technology

In addition to the many other online resources embedded in this program, EdTechTeacher Technology Extensions are provided for every Hands-On Chapter Project. These detailed instructions and inspiration help history teachers creatively and effectively integrate technology in their classrooms. Each Technology Extension describes a technology project, explains the rationale for the suggested technology, and provides guidelines for classroom teachers to help conduct and facilitate the activity. Each Technology Extension also provides links to pages on Teaching History with Technology (www.thwt.org) with up-to-date tutorials, guides, links to examples, and exemplary projects.

✔ **The more ways students have to engage with content, the more likely they are to remember and understand that content.** The Internet can provide students and teachers with access to text documents, images, sounds and songs, video, simulations, and games. The more different ways students engage with historical content, the more likely they are to make meaning of that material.

✔ **Students live in a technology-rich world, and classrooms should prepare students for that world.** When students spend most of their waking hours connected to a worldwide, online network of people, resources, and opportunities, they experience dissonance and disappointment in entering a "powered-down" school. Many students will leave school to go on to workplaces completely transformed by technology, and teachers have a responsibility to prepare students for these environments.

Integrating Technology Effectively

Ben Shneiderman, in his book *Leonardo's Laptop*, lays out a four-part framework for teaching with technology: Collect-Relate-Create-Donate. This framework is a helpful blueprint for designing projects and learning experiences with technology.

Collect Students should begin a project by collecting the resources necessary to produce a meaningful presentation of their understanding. In some cases, students might collect these resources through textbook reading and teacher lecture, but students should also collect resources from online collections, school library Web sites, and online searches.

Relate Technology greatly facilitates the process of students working together socially. The ability to collaborate is essential to the workplace and civic sphere of the future. In creating technology projects, students should have the chance to work together, or at least comment on each other's work, using blogs, wikis, podcasts, and other collaborative publishing tools.

Create Using multimedia publishing tools, students should have the opportunity to design presentations and performances of their historical understanding. They should make historical arguments in linear text, as well as through images, audio and video recordings, and multimedia presentations.

Donate Finally, students should create work not just for their teachers, but for broader audiences. Students who have a chance to share their work with their peers, their families, their community, and the Internet-connected world find that opportunity rewarding. Today's students experience very few barriers to expression in their networked lives, and they crave these opportunities in schools.

Guidelines for Successful Technology Projects

1) **Plan for problems.** Things can go wrong when working with technology, and learning how to deal with these challenges is essential for students, and for their teachers. As you start using technology in the classroom, try to have an extra teacher, aide, student-teacher, or IT staff member in the room with you to help troubleshoot problems. When things do go wrong, stay calm, and ask your students to help you resolve challenges and make the most of class time. Always have a back up, "pencil and paper" activity prepared in case there are problems with computers or networks. Over time, teachers who practice teaching with technology experience fewer and fewer of these problems, but they can be very challenging the first time you experience them!

2) **Practice from multiple perspectives.** Whenever you develop a technology project, try to do everything that students will do from a student's perspective. If you create a blog or wiki with a teacher account, create a student account to test the technology.

3) **Adapt to your local technology resources, but don't let those resources keep you from using technology.** Some schools have excellent and ample technology resources—labs and laptop carts—that make completing technology projects straightforward. Other schools have fewer resources, but virtually every student can get access to a networked computer in school, at the library or at home, especially if you give them a few nights to do so. Many technology activities are described as if you could complete them in a few class periods, but if resources are limited, you might consider spreading the activity out over a few days or weeks to give students the chance to get online.

4) **Plan with a partner.** Going it alone can be scary. If possible, have another teacher in your department or on your team, design and pilot technology projects with you to help solve the challenges that crop up whenever trying out new pedagogies.

5) **It's harder, then it gets easier.** Learning new teaching strategies is always hard. With technology, however, once you get past the initial learning curve there are all sorts of ways technology can make teaching more efficient and simultaneously make learning more meaningful for students.

Learn More about Teaching History with Technology

EdTechTeacher has several Web sites designed to help social studies and history teachers learn more about teaching with technology. The Best of History Web Sites (www.besthistorysites.net) is the Internet's authoritative directory of history-related resources, Web sites, games, simulations, lesson plans, and activities. Teaching History with Technology (www.thwt.org) has a series of white papers, tutorials, and guides for enriching history teaching strategies (lecturing, discussion, presentations, assessments, and so forth) with educational technology. EdTechTeacher (www.edtechteacher.org) has additional teaching resources and information about learning opportunities such as free webinars and other professional development workshops.

Tom Daccord and Justin Reich are co-Directors of EdTechTeacher. Together they authored Best Ideas for Teaching With Technology: A Practical Guide for Teachers by Teachers.

BACKGROUND KNOWLEDGE: THE KEY TO UNDERSTANDING

by Doug Fisher, Ph.D., and Nancy Frey, Ph.D.

Mention background knowledge and most middle school educators will tell you that it is an essential component of history and social studies learning. They will discuss the importance of activating it in their students and building it when there are gaps. Yet most will also confess to being unsure of how to accomplish this in a systematic way beyond asking some questions about prior experiences. As for the gaps, how can anyone find the time to build it when there is so much new information to be covered?

The answer is to integrate background knowledge activation, building, and assessment into the heart of the lesson, not just as bookends to new learning. The reasons for this are pretty striking. Background knowledge directly influences a learner's ability to understand new information and act upon it (RAND Reading Study Group, 2002). In addition, background knowledge is demonstrated through the use of academic vocabulary and academic language, an important measure of content learning (Cromley & Azevedo, 2007). Finally, students with strong background knowledge about a topic process text better, especially in their ability to monitor and correct comprehension difficulties (Cakir, 2008).

Cultivating Background Knowledge

The key to understanding new information is to link it to what is already known. A feature of initial learning is that we aren't very good at doing so. Our efforts to focus on what is unfamiliar temporarily blind us to what we already know. It is helpful to have well-placed reminders about what is already known, because it assists us in marshalling the familiar in order to understand the new.

When we ask questions of students about prior experiences, or invite them to engage in a quickwrite about a previously taught topic, we are activating their background knowledge. More importantly, we are providing the signposts they need to direct them to the most salient information they will need to learn the new material. For example, a study of Ancient Rome doesn't merely begin with the legendary founding of a great city by two boys raised by wolves. It also requires knowledge of the influence of ancient Greek civilization on Rome's governance, military, art, and culture. It is easy, however, for students to temporarily forget everything they have learned about Greece in their effort to assimilate new information. Well-placed questions, writing opportunities, and graphic organizers can remind them of what they have previously learned.

Another means for cultivating background knowledge is to assess what students know (or think they know) about a topic. This shouldn't be a quiz of isolated facts, but instead should focus on the anticipated misconceptions that a learner is likely to hold about a new topic. For instance, it is easy for students to confuse what they have learned about Greek mythology when learning about Roman gods and goddesses. Those terms (gods and goddesses) alone suggest that for Romans this was at the heart of their religious beliefs. But Roman mythology differs from Greek mythology. For Greeks, mythology formed the heart of religion. For Romans, the gods and goddesses made for good stories, but weren't necessarily worshipped. Posing questions that are designed to surface misconceptions such as this help to rectify incorrect perceptions before they are ingrained.

Assessing Background Knowledge

Despite the efforts of caring educators, families, and communities, students come to us with gaps in their background knowledge. This can be due to a variety of causes, including frequent moves, second language acquisition, lack of experience with a topic, or difficulty with the content itself. Students at the middle school level face the additional well-documented challenges of transitioning from elementary school, where one teacher made connections for them to background knowledge, to a middle school schedule with many teachers and content areas. These changes require them to make more of their own connections across subjects.

In addition, a middle school schedule leaves us with less time across the day to get to know our students and the background knowledge they possess. It is useful to have formative assessment embedded into lessons in order to gauge where gaps might exist.

Activities that draw on core background knowledge necessary for deep understanding of new information provide these opportunities. Lessons that invite students to construct graphic organizers using both new knowledge and background knowledge give us such a window. A well-placed question invites students to consider what they already know.

If and when students have difficulty with activities like this, the teacher can pause to supply missing background knowledge. This may be done through direct explanation, by drawing their attention to features in the text, and even to returning to a previous chapter to revisit information. These need not be seen as delays, but rather as time well spent to solidify foundational knowledge.

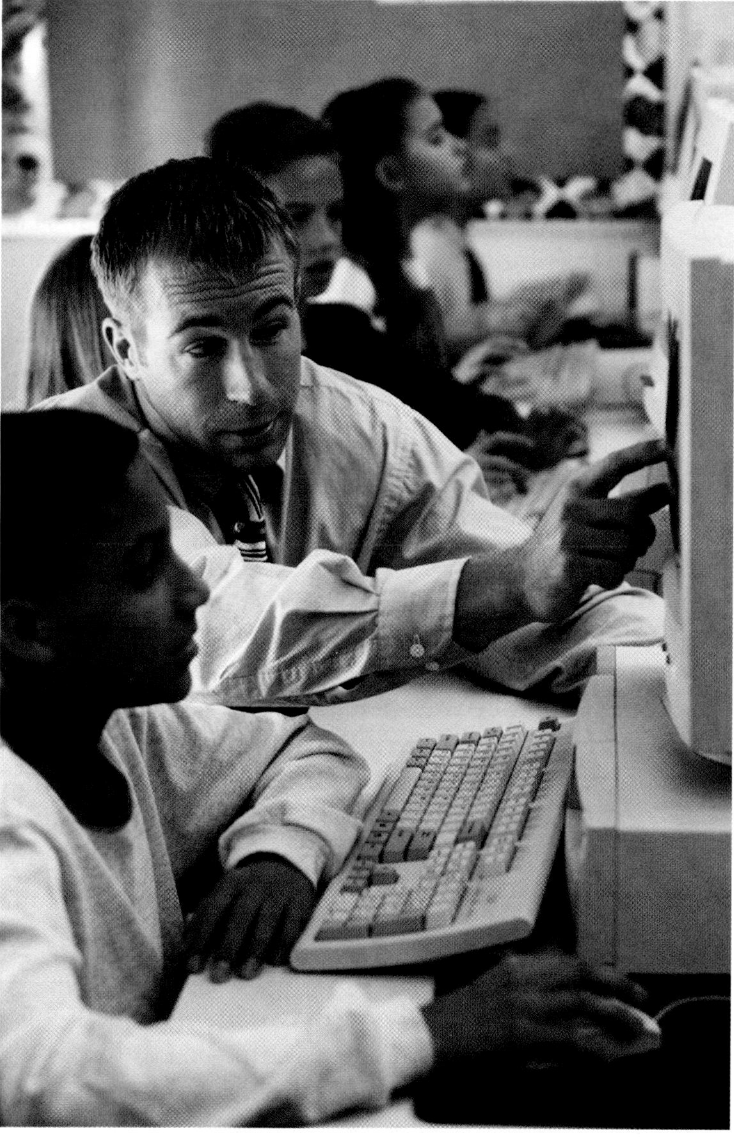

Building Background Knowledge

Effective middle school educators take a proactive stance to building background knowledge by creating opportunities to do so. They conduct read alouds and shared readings of text and provide visual information to build students' mental image banks. Texts and images related to necessary background knowledge are especially useful in history and social studies, where students are required to understand and use primary source documents. A challenge is that many of these are hard for students to make sense of on their own, as they often use archaic language and represent ideas that are not contemporary to adolescent lives. Texts and images carefully selected with middle school students in mind can build their background knowledge of the people and times being studied, and help them more fully appreciate the influences one culture has upon another. For example, illustrations of Greek and Roman architecture invite comparison. Maps of the ancient world highlight why empires fought over land.

Student background knowledge is also built through deeper understanding of the academic vocabulary and language that lies at the heart of history and social studies. By using a think aloud technique, teachers build their students' background knowledge about the derivation of the term, as well as the way they approach an unfamiliar word. This ensures that students will recall the term more precisely while also equipping them with a problem-solving strategy to apply to other new words.

Conclusion

McGraw-Hill **networks** learning system offers middle school educators the tools needed to activate, assess, and build student background knowledge by infusing approaches like this into the lesson design. The habit of mind of drawing on what one already knows and seeking information to fill in knowledge gaps begins with educators like you who show students how this is done.

Doug Fisher, Ph.D., and Nancy Frey, Ph.D., are professors in the School of Teacher Education at San Diego State University.

Cakir, O. (2008). The effect of textual differences on children's processing strategies. *Reading Improvement, 45*(2), 69-83.

Cromley, J. G., & Azevedo, R. (2007). Testing and refining the direct and inferential mediation model of reading comprehension. *Journal of Educational Psychology, 99*(2), 311-325.

RAND *Reading Study Group. (2002). Reading for understanding: Toward an R&D program in reading comprehension.* Office of Educational Research and Improvement. Santa Monica, CA: RAND.

professional development

USING FOLDABLES® IN THE CLASSROOM

by Rhonda Meyer Vivian, Ph.D., and Nancy F. Wisker, M.A.

Graphic Organizers

Current research shows that graphic organizers are powerful teaching and learning tools. Most of us are familiar with common graphic organizers such as diagrams, maps, outlines, and charts, all of which are two-dimensional. Foldables® are three-dimensional, interactive graphic organizers that were created more than 30 years ago by educator Dinah Zike.

Graphic organizers are visual representations combining line, shape, space, and symbols to convey facts and concepts or to organize information. Graphic organizers, when designed and used appropriately:

- Speed up communication
- Help organize information
- Are easy-to-understand
- Show complex relationships
- Clarify concepts with few words
- Convey ideas and understanding
- Assess comprehension

Graphic organizers help students organize information in a visual manner. This is a profound concept, especially as the number of non-native English-speaking students increases. A student is able to use graphic organizers to clarify concepts or to convey ideas and understandings with fewer words.

Graphic organizers also make complex relationships or concepts easier to understand, particularly for visual learners. Foldables take that process to the next level, most notably, for tactile/kinesthetic learners.

When to Use Graphic Organizers

Graphic organizers may be used at any point during instruction, but just as with any other instructional strategy, they are most successful when they are built into the instructional plan, rather than presented as an "extra" activity.

Graphic organizers may work better than outline notes in helping students discover or understand relationships between concepts. Foldables help teach students how to take notes by visually and kinesthetically chunking information into sections.

Foldables may be used as an alternative form of assessment in the classroom. Because the Foldable has readily identifiable sections, a teacher can quickly see gaps in student knowledge.

Reading, Writing, and Social Studies

Graphic organizers have been shown to be highly effective in literacy development. In numerous studies, graphic organizers help improve the development of literacy skills—including oral, written, and comprehension.

Graphic organizers have been found to help students organize information from expository social studies texts and comprehend content area reading. They also help students develop critical thinking skills and help transfer these skills to new situations and content areas.

Students With Special Needs

Graphic organizers may help English language learners improve higher-order thinking skills.

Because of their visual organization, graphic organizers seem to be quite beneficial for use with learning disabled students. They appear to help students understand content area material, to organize information, and to retain and recall content.

Conclusions

Graphic organizers may lead to improved student performance, whether measured by classroom-based observation, textbook assessments, or standardized assessments, when compared with more traditional forms of instruction.

When students construct their own graphic organizers, as they do with Foldables, they are active participants in their learning.

Our goal as educators is to help students glean important information and understand key concepts and to be able to relate these concepts or apply them to real-world situations. Graphic organizers help support and develop students' note-taking skills, summarizing skills, reading comprehension, and vocabulary development, which leads to better understanding and application of social studies content.

Dinah Zike is an award-winning author, educator, educational consultant, and inventor, known internationally for graphic organizers known as Foldables®. Based outside of San Antonio, Texas, Zike is a frequent keynote speaker and conducts seminars for over 50,000 teachers and parents annually.

Rhonda Myer Vivian, Ph.D., is CEO of Dinah-Might Adventures, LP, and Nancy F. Whisker, M.A., is Director of Math and Science for Dinah-Might Adventures, L.P.

Notebook Foldables®

Using Foldables® in the *Reading Essentials and Study Guide* will help your students develop note-taking and critical thinking skills while directly interacting with the text.

Templates allow students to make their own Notebook Foldables®.

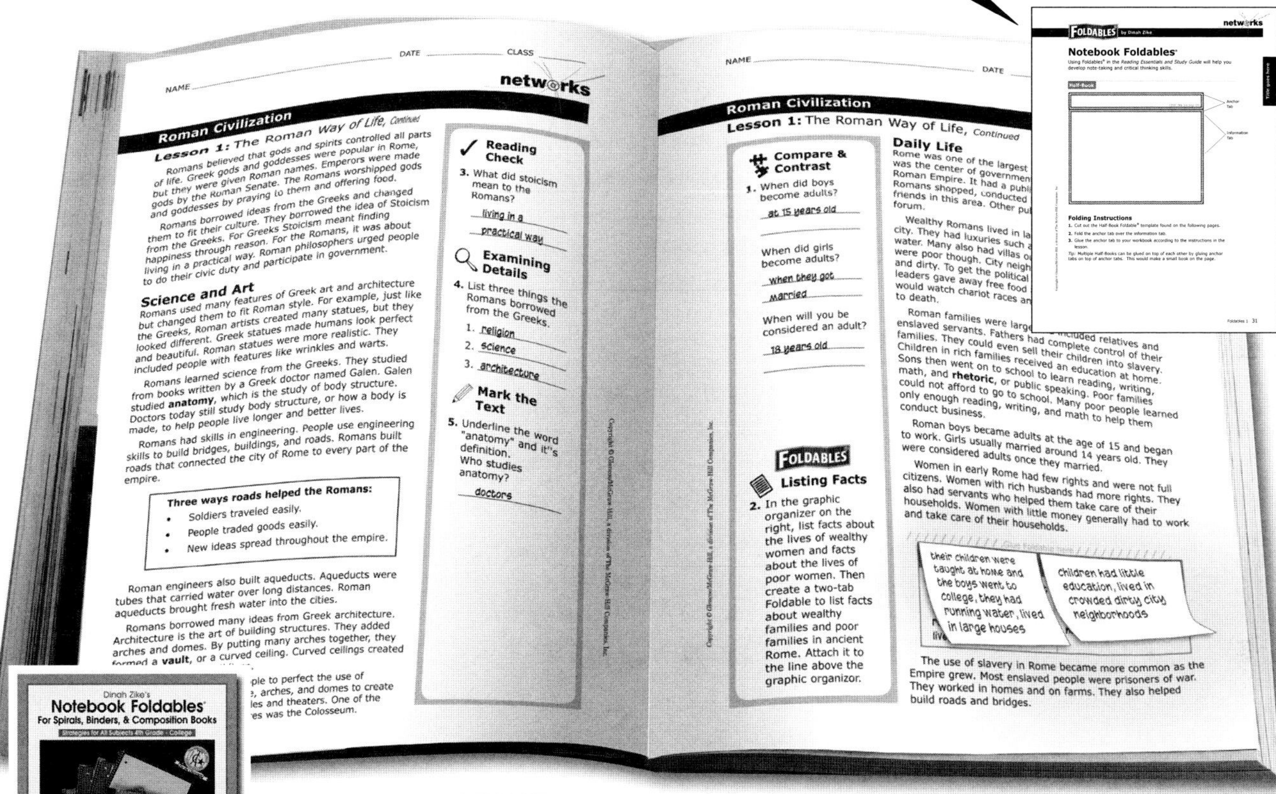

The *Reading Essentials and Study Guide* extends learning with Dinah Zike's award winning Notebook Foldables®. Notebook Foldables are specially designed to fit in workbooks and composition books. In partnership with Dinah, McGraw-Hill has developed the *Reading Essentials and Study Guide* with Notebook Foldables® to engage students more fully in social studies content.

It is easy to make Notebook Foldables®

1. **FOLD** an anchor tab and the desired number of information tabs.
2. **GLUE** the anchor tab.
3. **CUT** information tabs.

Students will master social studies concepts, ideas, and facts as they complete the side margin activities in this workbook, along with the many Notebook Foldables activities placed within the pages.

professional development

COLLEGE AND CAREER READINESS

Why Is College & Career Readiness Crucial?

- Only 70% of American students receive a high school diploma.
- Of that 70% of high school graduates, 53% of those who make it to college require remedial help.
- Over 90% of new jobs that will be available to students in the 21st century will require some postsecondary education.
- Most employers today cannot compete successfully without a workforce that has solid academic skills.
- The average difference in salary between someone with a high school degree and someone with postsecondary credentials can be $1 million over their lifetimes.

What Is College & Career Readiness?

Students are college and career ready when they have the level of preparation needed to academically, socially, and cognitively complete a postsecondary course of study without remediation. Students are prepared when they can enter the workforce at a level at which they are in line for promotion and career enhancement.

The ultimate goal of the college & career readiness initiative is to maintain America's competitive edge in the global economy of today. The workforce of the 21st century is an increasingly global, knowledge-based economy that demands the ability to:

- Think critically
- Solve problems
- Create and innovate
- Communicate
- Collaborate
- Learn new skills
- Use ICT (information and communications technology)

Explain College & Career Readiness to Students

One of the first steps you should take is to provide students with a framework that will help them see the relevancy of what they do in school. The three principal elements of College & Career Readiness (CCR) are:

- an understanding of core academic skills and the ability to apply them in educational and employment settings
- familiarity with skills valued by a broad range of employers such as communication, critical thinking, and responsibility
- mastery of the technologies and skill sets associated with a career pathway

Once students have been exposed to these elements, it is critical for them to see how they relate to their own plans for continuing education and career choice. Mention that CCR is more than just a personal issue, and it affects the country and our quality of life.

Most students—as well as many adults—consider work to be an obligation that they must perform in order to have money. Earning a salary is, of course, a central benefit of working, but so is the sense of satisfaction that comes from doing a job well. Moreover, every job contributes to the quality of life in our communities and our nation. Being prepared to pursue an education or get a job after high school is the hallmark of a good citizen.

Recognize That All Careers Are Important

Without question, the greatest challenge faced by educators, parents, and the public is recognizing that all jobs are important. When you discuss careers, be generous with your reflections and encourage your students to do the same. Be sure to mention the enormous variety of opportunities

PHOTO: Mark Scott/Photographer's Choice/Getty Images

available to them in diverse fields. The more that students can recognize the rich possibilities of whatever career they pursue, the more likely they will be to enjoy success and personal satisfaction.

Students typically have a relatively narrow perspective on the careers and jobs available to them. As part of the discussion of careers, broaden this perspective by reviewing some opportunities that your students might not be aware of. An interesting place to start is in the high profile industries of sports and entertainment.

Many students dream of being celebrities and have no idea about how unlikely this is. What they don't realize is that for every professional athlete, singer, or movie star, there are a hundred or more fascinating careers including sports trainers, writers, administrative assistants, drivers, and a seemingly endless list of other jobs. Not surprisingly, students usually respond positively when they learn that just in case they are not the next superstar in sports or entertainment, there are other opportunities that will allow them to achieve their dream in a slightly different way.

Students can explore careers in many ways; one way is by reviewing the 16 career clusters. Career clusters are groups of similar occupations and industries. They were developed by the U.S. Department of Education as a way to organize career planning. Students can visit the Career Center at http://ccr.mcgraw-hill.com/ to begin their explorations.

Make It Clear That There Are Various Paths To Success

A surprisingly small percentage of adults reach their careers through a direct and well-planned strategy. Familiarizing students with the various paths to success provides them with a realistic view of what life is like after high school and college. It may also give them an anchor in their own lives in the future when they find that they are wandering, which most of them will inevitably do.

Divergence from a direct path to a career is almost inevitable, and in many cases, is a desirable and enriching experience. Helping students to recognize this will make their future challenges seem less intimidating.

Have students investigate and discuss the career paths of people they know personally and by reputation, including celebrities. This discussion will promote engagement while showing the twists and turns that usually lead to success. Be sure to include some common but less-known paths, like the college benefits associated with military service or the arrangements nurses might make with a hospital to exchange tuition payments for a commitment of several years.

Make College & Career Readiness a regular part of interactive classroom discussions.

Unlike many other school subjects, a critical aspect of College & Career Readiness is its focus is on the future of each student, not the content of a course. Perhaps the best way to have students recognize this is to be sure that the time you spend discussing students' future pathways is truly interactive, with at least as much commentary from students as there is from you or other adult participants.

Because students are more willing to participate in discussions that have personal meaning to them, consider using these questions as starting points. These are "self-mentoring" questions that will help students clarify their thinking.

- What is something you really want to do in the next 10 years?
- How do you plan to get there?
- What is your back-up plan?
- What is something that you have done that made you proud?
- In which postsecondary courses do you think you would do best? Why do you think this?
- Imagine that you are going into the military. This choice involves activities that are hard physically and mentally. How would you handle these challenges?
- When you can't make up your mind about something important, what do you do?

Have students explore college & career readiness on their own at http://ccr.mcgraw-hill.com/ .

professional development

MEETING THE DIVERSE NEEDS OF OUR STUDENTS

by Douglas Fisher, Ph.D.

Today's classroom contains students from a variety of backgrounds with a variety of learning styles, strengths, and challenges. As teachers we are facing the challenge of helping students reach their educational potential. With careful planning, you can address the needs of all students in the social studies classroom. The basis for this planning is universal access. When classrooms are planned with universal access in mind, fewer students require specific accommodations.

What Is a Universal Access Design for Learning?

Universal design was first conceived in architectural studies when business people, engineers, and architects began making considerations for physical access to buildings. The idea was to plan the environment in advance to ensure that everyone had access. As a result, the environment would not have to be changed later for people with physical disabilities, people pushing strollers, workers who had injuries, or others for whom the environment would be difficult to negotiate. The Center for Universal Design at www.design.ncsu.edu/cud defines Universal Design as:

The design of products and environments to be usable by all people, to the greatest extent possible, without the need for adaptation or specialized design.

Universal Design and Access in Education

Researchers, teachers, and parents in education have expanded the development of built-in adaptations and inclusive accommodations from architectural space to the educational experience, especially in the area of curriculum.

In 1998, the National Center to Improve the Tools of Educators (NCITE), with the partnership of the Center for Applied Special Technology (CAST), proposed an expanded definition of universal design focused on education:

In terms of learning, universal design means the design of instructional materials and activities that allows the learning goals to be achievable by individuals with wide differences in their abilities to see, hear, speak, move, read, write, understand English, attend, organize, engage, and remember.

How Does Universal Design Work in Education?

Universal design and access, as they apply to education and schooling, suggest the following:

- **Inclusive Classroom Participation** Curriculum should be designed with all students and their needs in mind. The McGraw-Hill social studies print and online texts and materials were designed with a wide range of students in mind. For example, understanding that English learners and students who struggle with reading would be using this text, vocabulary is specifically taught and reinforced. Similarly, the teacher-support materials provide multiple instructional points to be used depending on the needs of the students in the class. Further, the text is written such that essential questions and guiding questions are identified for all learners.
- **Maximum Text Readability** In universally designed classrooms that provide access for all students, texts use direct language, clear noun-verb agreements, and clear construct-based wording. In addition to these factors, the McGraw-Hill social studies texts use embedded

PHOTO: BananaStock/PictureQuest

definitions for difficult terms, provide for specific instruction in reading skills, use a number of visual representations, and include note-taking guides.

- **Adaptable and Accommodating**
  The content in this textbook can be easily translated, read aloud, or otherwise changed to meet the needs of students in the classroom. The lesson and end-of-chapter activities and assessments provide students with multiple ways of demonstrating their content knowledge while also ensuring that they have practice with thinking in terms of multiple-choice questions. Critical thinking and analysis skills are also practiced.

How Is Differentiated Instruction the Key to Universal Access?

To differentiate instruction, teachers must acknowledge student differences in background knowledge and current reading, writing, and English language skills. They must also consider student learning styles and preferences, interests, and needs, and react accordingly. There are a number of general guidelines for differentiating instruction in the classroom to reach all students, including:

- **Link Assessment With Instruction**
  Assessments should occur before, during, and after instruction to ensure that the curriculum is aligned with what students do and do not know. Using assessments in this way allows you to plan instruction for whole groups, small groups, and individual students. Backward planning, where you establish the assessment before you begin instruction, is also important.
- **Clarify Key Concepts and Generalizations**
  Students need to know what is essential and how this information can be used in their future learning. In addition, students need to develop a sense of the big ideas—ideas that transcend time and place.
- **Emphasize Critical and Creative Thinking**
  The content, process, and products used or assigned in the classroom should require that students think about what they are learning. While some students may require support, additional motivation, varied tasks, materials, or equipment, the overall focus on critical and creative thinking allows for all students to participate in the lesson.
- **Include Teacher- and Student-Selected Tasks**
  A differentiated classroom includes both teacher- and student-selected activities and tasks. At some points in the lesson or day, the teacher must provide instruction and assign learning activities. In other parts of the lesson, students should be provided choices in how they engage with the content. This balance increases motivation, engagement, and learning.

How Do I Support Individual Students?

The vast majority of students will thrive in a classroom based on universal access and differentiated instruction. However, wise teachers recognize that no single option will work for all students and that there may be students who require unique systems of support to be successful.

Classroom Activity

Display a map of imperialism in Africa around 1914. Discuss with students the map's general information and have them list each country under the European power that controlled it.

To differentiate this activity:

- Have students imagine they are living in the early 1900s. Have them write a letter to a British newspaper about colonial rule in Africa.
- Have students record the number of African countries under European rule. Have them take the data and create a bar graph that shows which European powers were the most active colonizers at the time.
- Have students compose a song or poem about European rule in Africa, from an African's point of view.
- Have students choose a country of modern Africa to research. Have them write a three-page paper discussing how that country was affected by colonialism and how it has changed since the days of European rule.

professional development

MEETING THE DIVERSE NEEDS OF OUR STUDENTS
(continued)

Tips For Instruction

The following tips for instruction can support your efforts to help all students reach their maximum potential.

- ✔ Survey students to discover their individual differences. Use interest inventories of their unique talents so you can encourage contributions in the classroom.
- ✔ Be a model for respecting others. Adolescents crave social acceptance. The student with learning differences is especially sensitive to correction and criticism, particularly when it comes from a teacher. Your behavior will set the tone for how students treat one another.
- ✔ Expand opportunities for success. Provide a variety of instructional activities that reinforce skills and concepts.
- ✔ Establish measurable objectives and decide how you can best help students who meet them.
- ✔ Celebrate successes and make note of and praise "work in progress."
- ✔ Keep it simple. Point out problem areas if doing so can help a student effect change. Avoid overwhelming students with too many goals at one time.
- ✔ Assign cooperative group projects that challenge all students to contribute to solving a problem or creating a product.

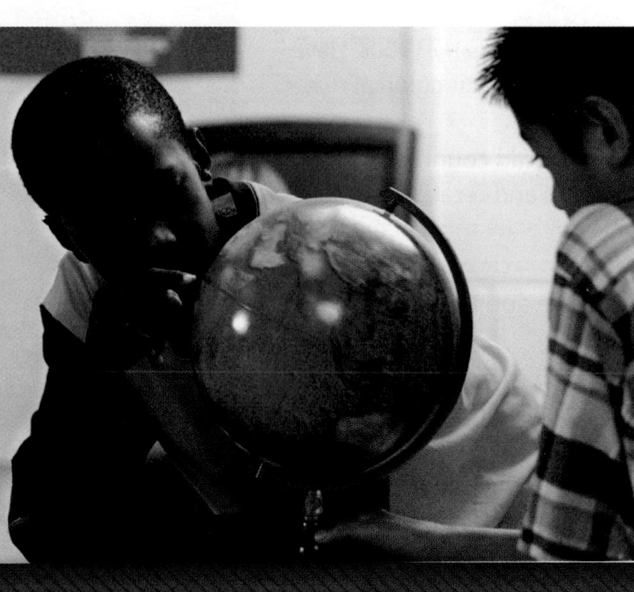

How Do I Reach Students With Learning Disabilities?

- ✔ Provide support and structure. Clearly specify rules, assignments, and responsibilities.
- ✔ Practice skills frequently. Use games and drills to help maintain student interest.
- ✔ Incorporate many modalities into the learning process. Provide opportunities to say, hear, write, read, and act out important concepts and information.
- ✔ Link new skills and concepts to those already mastered.
- ✔ If possible, allow students to record answers on audio.
- ✔ Allow extra time to complete assessments and assignments.
- ✔ Let students demonstrate proficiency with alternative presentations, including oral reports, role plays, art projects, and musical presentations.
- ✔ Provide outlines, notes, or recordings of lecture material.
- ✔ Pair students with peer helpers, and provide class time for pair interaction.

How Do I Reach Students With Behavioral Challenges?

- ✔ Provide a structured environment with clear-cut schedules, rules, seat assignments, and safety procedures.
- ✔ Reinforce appropriate behavior and model it for students.
- ✔ Cue distracted students back to the task through verbal signals and teacher proximity.
- ✔ Set goals that can be achieved in the short term. Work for long-term improvement in the big areas.

How Do I Reach Students With Physical Challenges?

- ✔ Openly discuss with the student any uncertainties you have about when to offer aid.
- ✔ Ask parents or therapists and students what special devices or procedures are needed and whether any special safety precautions need to be taken.
- ✔ Welcome students with physical challenges into all activities, including field trips, special events, and projects.
- ✔ Provide information to assist class members and adults in their understanding of support needed.

How Do I Reach Students with Visual Impairments?

- ✔ Facilitate independence. Modify assignments as needed.
- ✔ Teach classmates how and when to serve as visual guides.
- ✔ Limit unnecessary noise in the classroom if it distracts the student with visual impairments.
- ✔ Provide tactile models whenever possible.

- ✔ Foster a spirit of inclusion. Describe people and events as they occur in the classroom. Remind classmates that the student with visual impairments cannot interpret gestures and other forms of nonverbal communication.
- ✔ Provide recorded lectures and reading assignments for use outside the classroom.
- ✔ Team the student with a sighted peer for written work.

How Do I Reach Students With Hearing Impairments?

- ✔ Seat students where they can see your lip movements easily and where they can avoid any visual distractions.
- ✔ Avoid standing with your back to the window or light source.
- ✔ Use an overhead projector so you can maintain eye contact while writing information for students.
- ✔ Seat students where they can see speakers.
- ✔ Write all assignments on the board, or hand out written instructions.
- ✔ If the student has a manual interpreter, allow both student and interpreter to select the most favorable seating arrangements.
- ✔ Teach students to look directly at each other when they speak.

How Do I Reach English Learners?

- ✔ Remember, students' ability to speak English does not reflect their academic abilities.
- ✔ Try to incorporate the students' cultural experience into your instruction. The help of a bilingual aide may be effective.
- ✔ Avoid any references in your instruction that could be construed as cultural stereotypes.
- ✔ Preteach important vocabulary and concepts.
- ✔ Encourage students to preview text before they begin reading, noting headings.
- ✔ Remind students not to ignore graphic organizers, photographs, and maps since there is much information in these visuals.
- ✔ Use memorabilia and photographs whenever possible to build background knowledge and understanding. An example of this would be coins in a foreign currency or a raw cotton ball to reinforce its importance in history.

How Do I Reach Gifted Students?

- ✔ Make arrangements for students to take selected subjects early and to work on independent projects.
- ✔ Ask "what if" questions to develop high-level thinking skills. Establish an environment safe for risk taking in your classroom.
- ✔ Emphasize concepts, theories, ideas, relationships, and generalizations about the content.
- ✔ Promote interest in the past by inviting students to make connections to the present.
- ✔ Let students express themselves in alternate ways such as creative writing, acting, debates, simulations, drawing, or music.
- ✔ Provide students with a catalog of helpful resources, listing such things as agencies that provide free and inexpensive materials, appropriate community services and programs, and community experts who might be called upon to speak to your students.
- ✔ Assign extension projects that allow students to solve real-life problems related to their communities.

Classroom Activity

Students respond eagerly to a subject when they can relate it to their own experiences. With the growing number of students who come from other world regions, explaining geography through a global theme (such as volcanoes) can give them a worldwide as well as a regional perspective. To develop this awareness, display a large world map. Have students use the library or the Internet to research the latitude and longitude of 15 major volcanoes around the world. Ask them to mark these locations on the map and answer the following questions:

- What patterns do you see in volcanic activity?
- What causes volcanic activity?
- Where in the world are volcanoes most active?

As a follow-up, suggest students go to http://volcano.und.nodak.edu/vwdocs/kids/legends.html to find legends about the origins of some of the world's volcanoes. Encourage students to share what they find with the class.

professional development

ACADEMIC VOCABULARY

How Can I Help My Students Learn Academic Vocabulary?

What Is Academic English?

Academic English is the language used in academics, business, and courts of law. It is the type of English used in textbooks, and contains linguistic features associated with academic disciplines like social studies. Proficiency in reading and using academic English is especially related to long-term success in all parts of life.

By reinforcing academic English, teachers can help learners to access authentic, academic texts—not simplified texts that dummy down the content. In this way, they can provide information that will help build their students' background knowledge rapidly.

What Is Academic Vocabulary?

Academic vocabulary is based on academic English. By the time children have completed elementary school, they must have acquired the knowledge needed to understand academic vocabulary. How many words should they acquire to be able to access their texts? A basic 2,000-word vocabulary of high-frequency words makes up 87% of the vocabulary of academic texts. Eight hundred other academic words comprise an additional 8% of the words. Three percent of the remaining words are technical words. The remaining 2% are low-frequency words. There may be as many as 123,000 low-frequency words in academic texts.

Why Should Students Learn Academic Vocabulary?

English learners who have a basic 2,000-word vocabulary are ready to acquire most general words found in their texts.

Knowledge of academic words and general words can significantly boost a student's comprehension level of academic texts. Students who learn and practice these words before they graduate from high school are more likely to master

PHOTO: BananaStock/PictureQuest

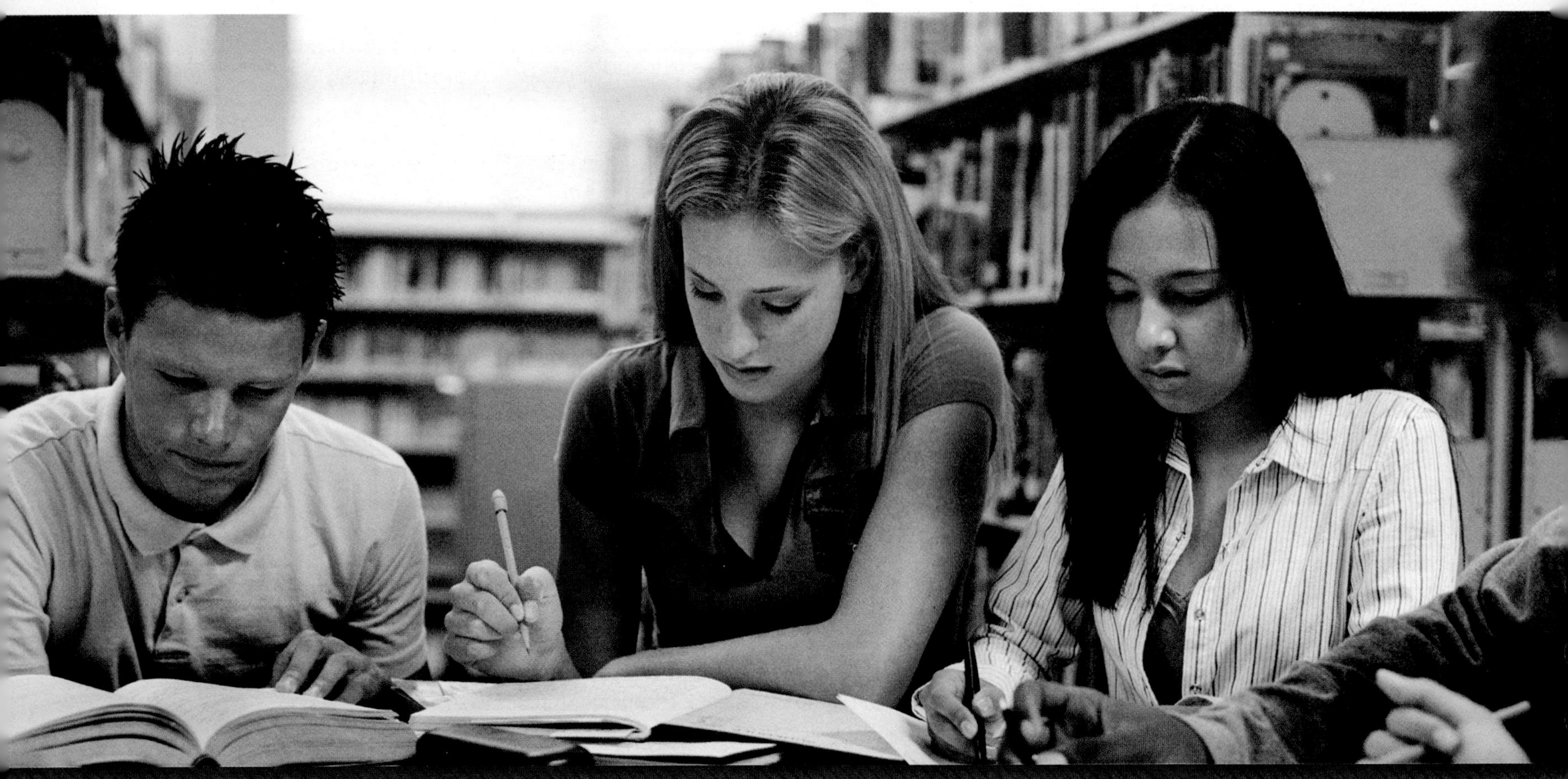

academic material with increased confidence and speed. They waste less time and effort in guessing words or consulting dictionaries than those who only know the basic 2,000 words that characterize general conversation.

How Do I Include Academic Vocabulary and Academic English in My Teaching?

Teachers can provide students with academic vocabulary and help students understand the academic English of their text.

To develop academic English, learners must have already acquired basic proficiency in everyday English.

Academic English should be taught within contexts that make sense. In terms of instruction, teaching academic English includes providing students with access to core curriculum—in this case social studies.

Academic English arises in part from social practices in which academic English is used. The acquisition of academic vocabulary and grammar is necessary to advance the development of academic English.

Tips for Teaching Academic Vocabulary

- ✔ **Expose Students to Academic Vocabulary** You do not need to call attention to words students are learning because they will acquire them subconsciously.
- ✔ **Do Not Correct Students' Mistakes When Using the Vocabulary Words** All vocabulary understanding and spelling errors will disappear once the student reads more.
- ✔ **Help Students Decode the Words Themselves** Once they learn the alphabet, they should be able to decode words. Decoding each word they don't recognize will help them more than trying to focus on sentence structure. Once they can recognize the words, they can read "authentic" texts.
- ✔ **Do Not Ignore the English Learner in This Process** They can learn academic vocabulary before they are completely fluent in oral English.
- ✔ **Helping Students Build Academic Vocabulary Leads to Broader Learning** Students who have mastered the basic academic vocabulary are ready to acquire words from the rest of the groups. To help determine which words are in the 2,000-word basic group, refer to *West's General Service List of English Words,* 1953. The list is designed to serve as a guide for teachers and as a checklist and goal list for students.

Guidelines for Teaching Academic Vocabulary

1. Direct and planned instruction
2. Models—that have increasingly difficult language
3. Attention to form—pointing out linguistic features of words

Classroom Activity

Writing About Modern America

Give students a brief writing assignment. Ask them to write a short essay about one of the topics listed below in the left column. Have students use as many of the academic vocabulary words in the right column as they can in their essay. When completed, ask student volunteers to share their writing. Note what academic vocabulary words they use.

Topic	Academic Vocabulary
The challenges of reducing poverty in America	sufficient minimum medical income
Recent technological advances	innovate technology media potential data transmit

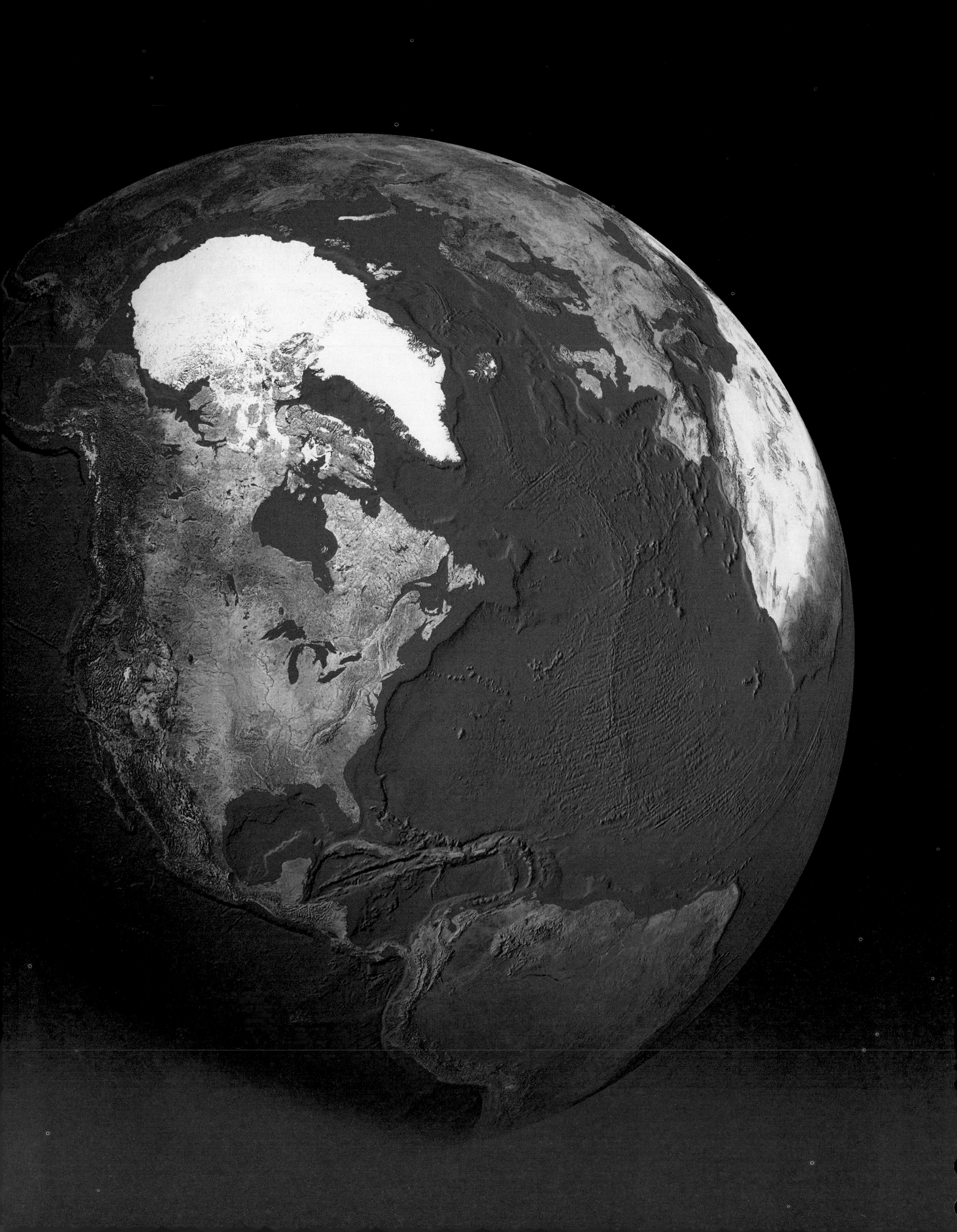

Reference Atlas

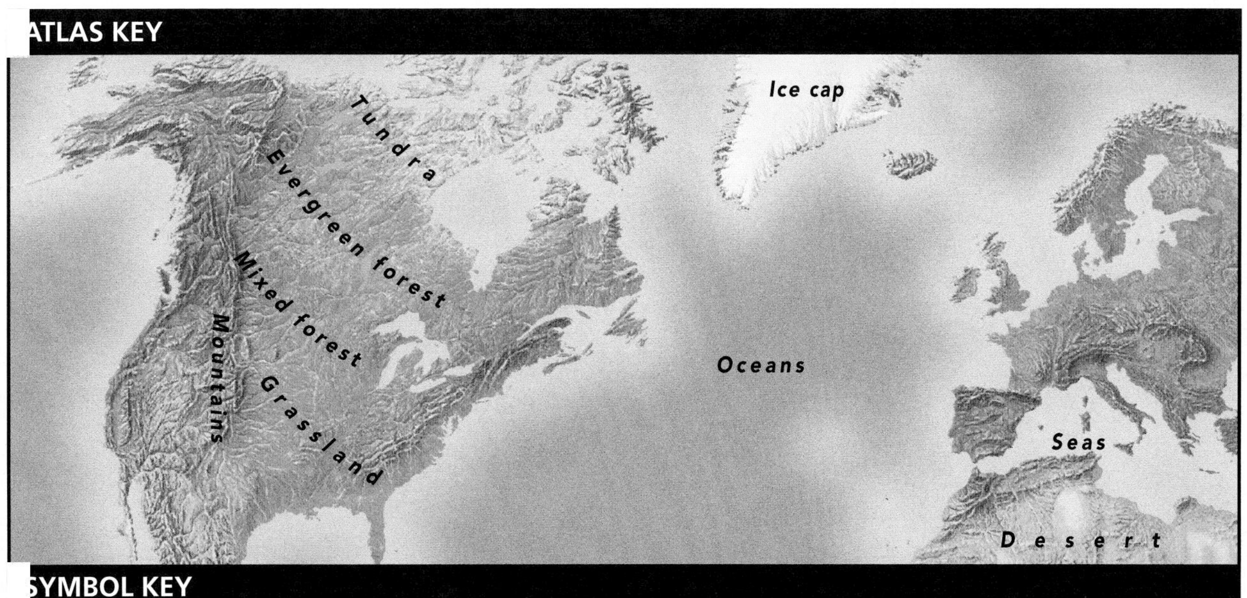

SYMBOL KEY

- Canal
- Claimed boundary
- International boundary
- Depression
- Elevation
- National capital
- Towns
- Below sea level
- Dry salt lake
- Lake
- Rivers
- Lava
- Sand
- Swamp

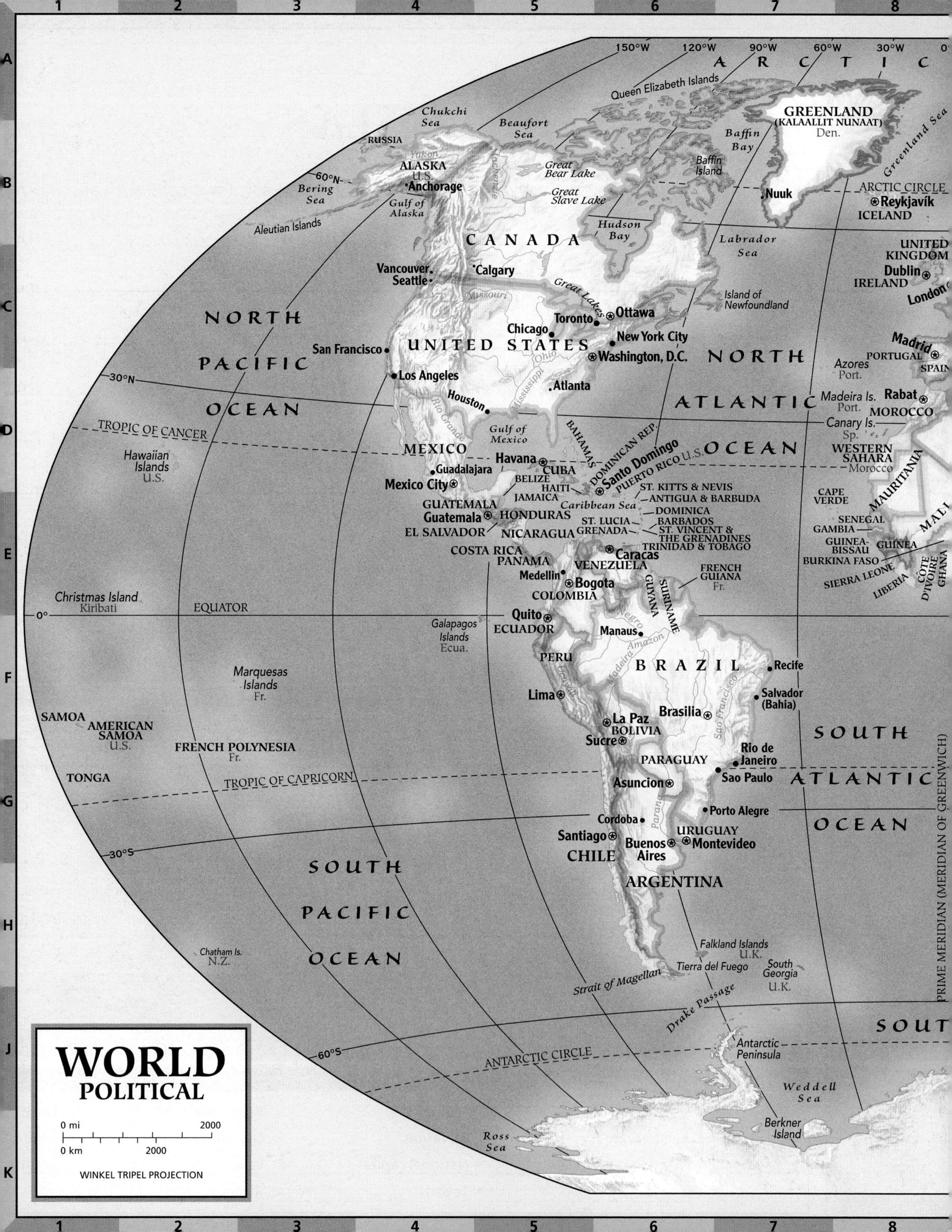

WORLD
POLITICAL
0 mi
2000
0 km
2000
WINKEL TRIPEL PROJECTION
NORTH PACIFIC OCEAN
NORTH ATLANTIC OCEAN
SOUTH PACIFIC OCEAN
SOUTH ATLANTIC OCEAN
ARCTIC
CANADA
UNITED STATES
MEXICO
BRAZIL
GREENLAND (KALAALLIT NUNAAT) Den.
ALASKA U.S.
Anchorage
Vancouver
Seattle
Calgary
San Francisco
Los Angeles
Houston
Chicago
Toronto
Ottawa
New York City
Washington, D.C.
Atlanta
Havana
CUBA
Mexico City
Guadalajara
Santo Domingo
Caracas
Bogota
Medellin
Quito
Lima
La Paz
Sucre
Brasilia
Rio de Janeiro
Sao Paulo
Asuncion
Santiago
Buenos Aires
Montevideo
Manaus
Recife
Salvador (Bahia)
Porto Alegre
Cordoba
Nuuk
Reykjavík
ICELAND
Dublin
IRELAND
UNITED KINGDOM
London
Madrid
PORTUGAL
SPAIN
Rabat
MOROCCO
TROPIC OF CANCER
EQUATOR
TROPIC OF CAPRICORN
ARCTIC CIRCLE
ANTARCTIC CIRCLE
PRIME MERIDIAN (MERIDIAN OF GREENWICH)

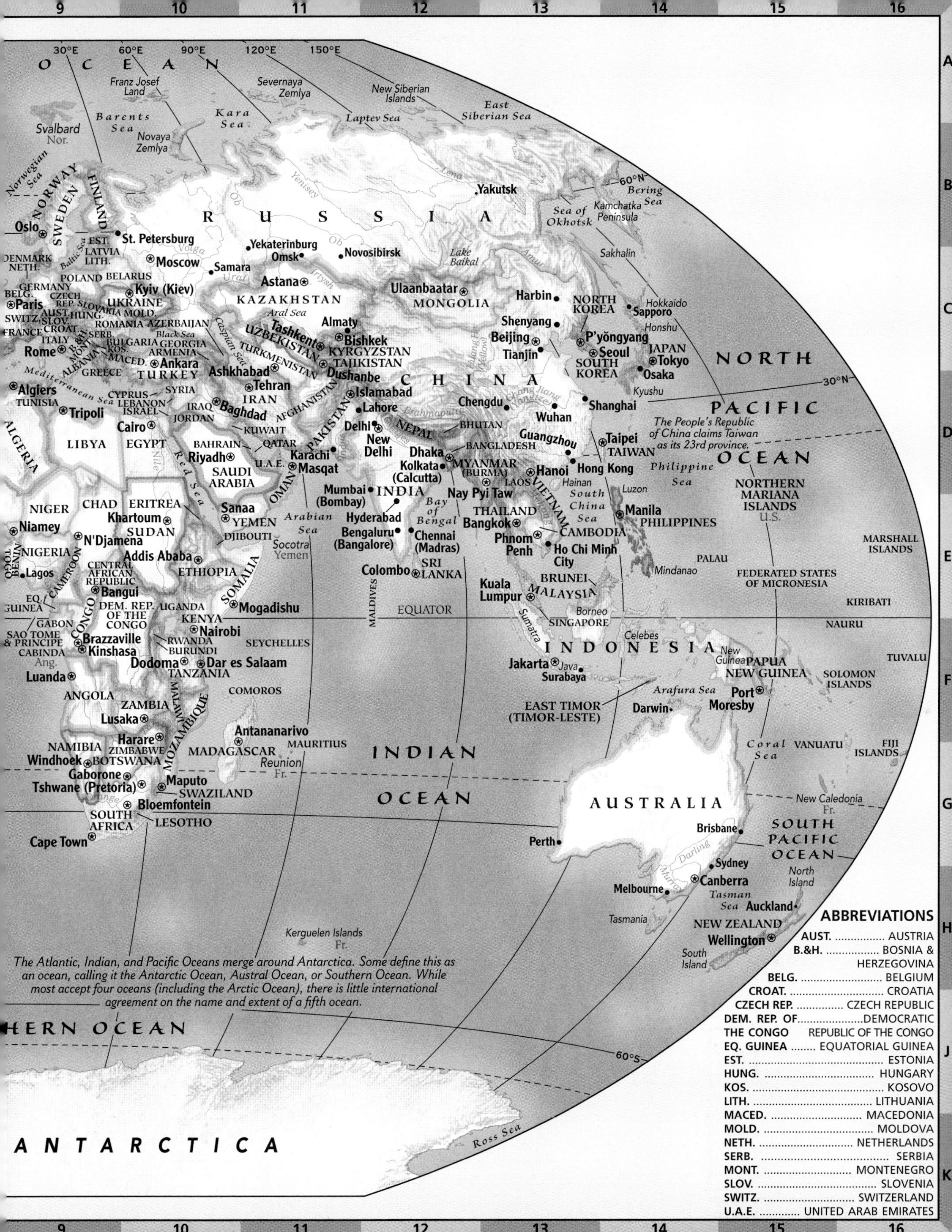
9
10
11
12
13
14
15
16
A
B
C
D
E
F
G
H
J
K
30°E
60°E
90°E
120°E
150°E
OCEAN
Franz Josef Land
Severnaya Zemlya
New Siberian Islands
East Siberian Sea
Barents Sea
Kara Sea
Laptev Sea
Svalbard Nor.
Novaya Zemlya
Norwegian Sea
NORWAY
SWEDEN
FINLAND
Lena
Yenisey
Ob
60°N
Bering Sea
Yakutsk
Sea of Okhotsk
Kamchatka Peninsula
RUSSIA
Oslo
St. Petersburg
EST.
LATVIA
LITH.
Baltic Sea
Volga
Yekaterinburg
Omsk
Novosibirsk
Lake Baikal
Amur
Sakhalin
DENMARK
NETH.
Moscow
Samara
Ural
Irtysh
BELG.
GERMANY
POLAND
BELARUS
Astana
Ulaanbaatar
Harbin
NORTH KOREA
Hokkaido
Sapporo
Paris
CZECH REP.
SLOVAKIA
Kyiv (Kiev)
UKRAINE
KAZAKHSTAN
MONGOLIA
SWITZ.
AUST.
HUNG.
MOLD.
Aral Sea
FRANCE
SLOV.
CROAT.
ROMANIA
AZERBAIJAN
Almaty
Shenyang
Honshu
ITALY
B.&H.
SERB.
BULGARIA
Black Sea
GEORGIA
Tashkent
Bishkek
Beijing
P'yŏngyang
Rome
MONT.
KOS.
ARMENIA
UZBEKISTAN
KYRGYZSTAN
Huang He (Yellow)
Tianjin
Seoul
JAPAN
Tokyo
ALBANIA
MACED.
Ankara
Caspian Sea
TURKMENISTAN
TAJIKISTAN
SOUTH KOREA
Osaka
NORTH
GREECE
TURKEY
Ashkhabad
Dushanbe
CHINA
Mediterranean Sea
Tehran
Kyushu
30°N
Algiers
CYPRUS
SYRIA
Islamabad
Chang Jiang (Yangtze)
TUNISIA
LEBANON
ISRAEL
IRAN
AFGHANISTAN
Lahore
Brahmaputra
Chengdu
Wuhan
Shanghai
PACIFIC
Tripoli
IRAQ
Baghdad
JORDAN
ALGERIA
Cairo
KUWAIT
PAKISTAN
Delhi
New Delhi
NEPAL
BHUTAN
The People's Republic of China claims Taiwan as its 23rd province.
LIBYA
EGYPT
BAHRAIN
QATAR
Indus
Ganges
BANGLADESH
Guangzhou
Taipei
TAIWAN
Riyadh
Karachi
Dhaka
Nile
Red Sea
U.A.E.
Masqat
Kolkata (Calcutta)
MYANMAR (BURMA)
Hanoi
Hong Kong
OCEAN
SAUDI ARABIA
OMAN
LAOS
Hainan
Philippine Sea
NORTHERN MARIANA ISLANDS U.S.
Mumbai (Bombay)
INDIA
Nay Pyi Taw
VIETNAM
South China Sea
Luzon
NIGER
CHAD
ERITREA
Bay of Bengal
THAILAND
Mekong
Manila
PHILIPPINES
Khartoum
Sanaa
YEMEN
Arabian Sea
Hyderabad
Bangkok
Niamey
SUDAN
DJIBOUTI
Bengaluru (Bangalore)
Chennai (Madras)
Phnom Penh
CAMBODIA
N'Djamena
Socotra Yemen
Ho Chi Minh City
MARSHALL ISLANDS
BENIN
TOGO
NIGERIA
Addis Ababa
PALAU
Lagos
CAMEROON
CENTRAL AFRICAN REPUBLIC
ETHIOPIA
SOMALIA
Colombo
SRI LANKA
Mindanao
FEDERATED STATES OF MICRONESIA
BRUNEI
Kuala Lumpur
MALAYSIA
Bangui
EQ. GUINEA
CONGO
DEM. REP. OF THE CONGO
UGANDA
Mogadishu
MALDIVES
KIRIBATI
KENYA
EQUATOR
Borneo
GABON
Nairobi
Sumatra
SINGAPORE
NAURU
SAO TOME & PRINCIPE
Brazzaville
RWANDA
BURUNDI
SEYCHELLES
Celebes
CABINDA Ang.
Kinshasa
INDONESIA
New Guinea
Dodoma
Dar es Salaam
Jakarta
Java
PAPUA NEW GUINEA
TUVALU
Luanda
TANZANIA
Surabaya
SOLOMON ISLANDS
MALAWI
COMOROS
Arafura Sea
Port Moresby
ANGOLA
EAST TIMOR (TIMOR-LESTE)
Darwin
ZAMBIA
MOZAMBIQUE
Lusaka
Antananarivo
NAMIBIA
Harare
ZIMBABWE
MAURITIUS
INDIAN
Coral Sea
VANUATU
FIJI ISLANDS
Windhoek
BOTSWANA
MADAGASCAR
Reunion Fr.
Gaborone
Maputo
Tshwane (Pretoria)
SWAZILAND
OCEAN
New Caledonia Fr.
Orange
Bloemfontein
AUSTRALIA
SOUTH AFRICA
LESOTHO
Brisbane
SOUTH PACIFIC OCEAN
Cape Town
Perth
Darling
Sydney
North Island
Murray
Canberra
Melbourne
Tasman Sea
Auckland
Tasmania
NEW ZEALAND
Kerguelen Islands Fr.
Wellington
South Island
The Atlantic, Indian, and Pacific Oceans merge around Antarctica. Some define this as an ocean, calling it the Antarctic Ocean, Austral Ocean, or Southern Ocean. While most accept four oceans (including the Arctic Ocean), there is little international agreement on the name and extent of a fifth ocean.
HERN OCEAN
60°S
Ross Sea
ANTARCTICA
ABBREVIATIONS
AUST. .... AUSTRIA
B.&H. .... BOSNIA & HERZEGOVINA
BELG. .... BELGIUM
CROAT. .... CROATIA
CZECH REP. .... CZECH REPUBLIC
DEM. REP. OF THE CONGO .... DEMOCRATIC REPUBLIC OF THE CONGO
EQ. GUINEA .... EQUATORIAL GUINEA
EST. .... ESTONIA
HUNG. .... HUNGARY
KOS. .... KOSOVO
LITH. .... LITHUANIA
MACED. .... MACEDONIA
MOLD. .... MOLDOVA
NETH. .... NETHERLANDS
SERB. .... SERBIA
MONT. .... MONTENEGRO
SLOV. .... SLOVENIA
SWITZ. .... SWITZERLAND
U.A.E. .... UNITED ARAB EMIRATES

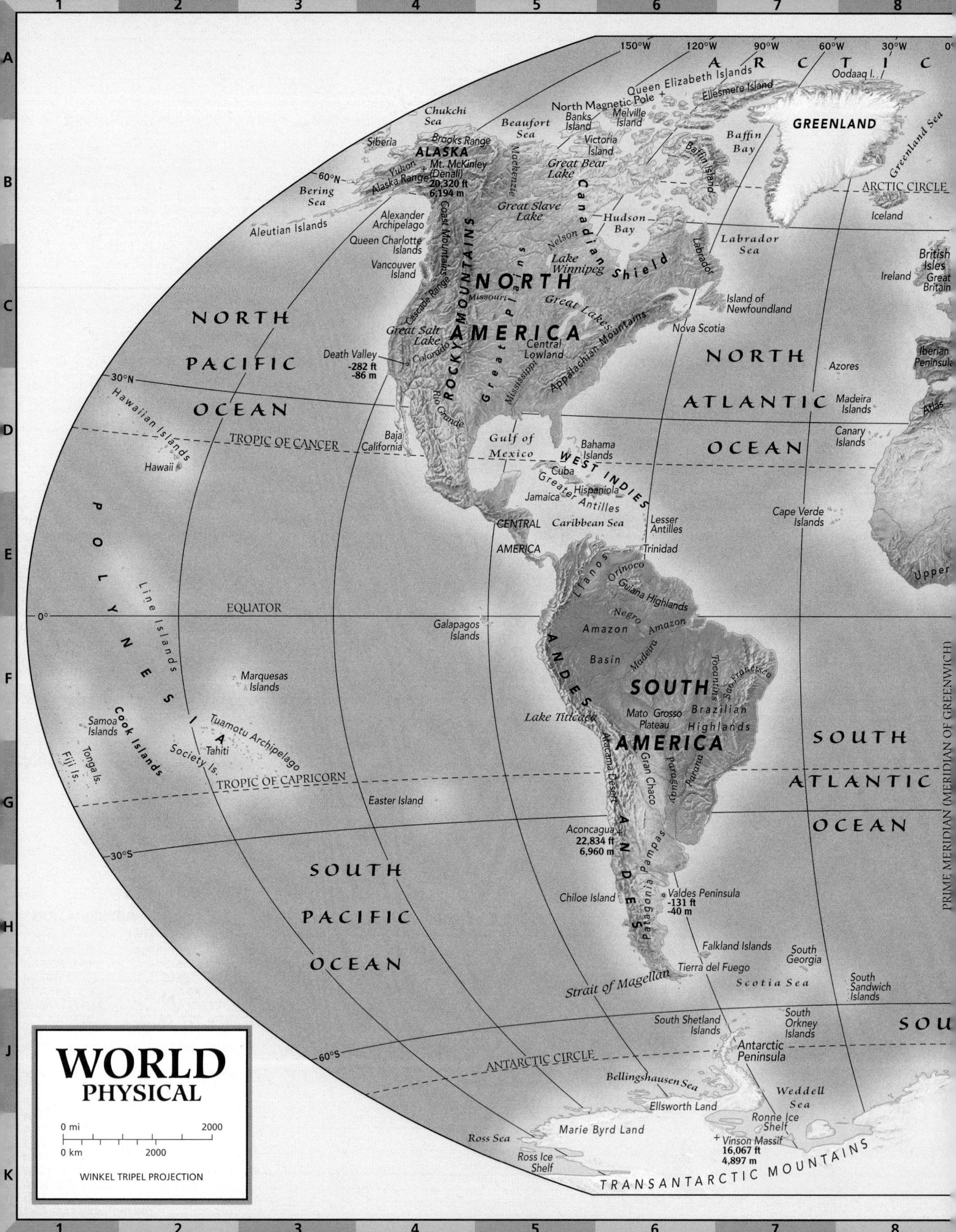

WORLD
PHYSICAL
0 mi
2000
0 km
2000
WINKEL TRIPEL PROJECTION
ARCTIC
150°W
120°W
90°W
60°W
30°W
Queen Elizabeth Islands
Oodaaq I.
Ellesmere Island
North Magnetic Pole
GREENLAND
Greenland Sea
Chukchi Sea
Beaufort Sea
Banks Island
Melville Island
Victoria Island
Baffin Bay
Baffin Island
Siberia
Brooks Range
ALASKA
Yukon
Mt. McKinley (Denali)
20,320 ft
6,194 m
Alaska Range
60°N
Bering Sea
Aleutian Islands
Mackenzie
Great Bear Lake
Great Slave Lake
Canadian Shield
Hudson Bay
ARCTIC CIRCLE
Iceland
Alexander Archipelago
Queen Charlotte Islands
Vancouver Island
Coast Mountains
Nelson
Lake Winnipeg
Labrador
Labrador Sea
British Isles
Ireland
Great Britain
Cascade Range
ROCKY MOUNTAINS
NORTH AMERICA
Missouri
Great Plains
Great Lakes
Island of Newfoundland
Nova Scotia
NORTH PACIFIC OCEAN
Great Salt Lake
Appalachian Mountains
Central Lowland
Death Valley
-282 ft
-86 m
Colorado
Mississippi
NORTH ATLANTIC OCEAN
Azores
Iberian Peninsula
30°N
Hawaiian Islands
Rio Grande
Madeira Islands
Atlas
Hawaii
TROPIC OF CANCER
Baja California
Gulf of Mexico
Bahama Islands
WEST INDIES
Canary Islands
Cuba
Greater Antilles
Hispaniola
Jamaica
Caribbean Sea
Lesser Antilles
Cape Verde Islands
CENTRAL AMERICA
Trinidad
POLYNESIA
Llanos
Orinoco
Guiana Highlands
Upper
Line Islands
0°
EQUATOR
Negro
Amazon
Amazon Basin
Galapagos Islands
Madeira
Tocantins
São Francisco
ANDES
SOUTH AMERICA
Marquesas Islands
Mato Grosso Plateau
Brazilian Highlands
Lake Titicaca
Samoa Islands
Cook Islands
Tuamotu Archipelago
Tahiti
Society Is.
Tonga Is.
Fiji Is.
Atacama Desert
Gran Chaco
Paraguay
Paraná
SOUTH ATLANTIC OCEAN
TROPIC OF CAPRICORN
Easter Island
PRIME MERIDIAN (MERIDIAN OF GREENWICH)
Aconcagua
22,834 ft
6,960 m
Pampas
30°S
SOUTH PACIFIC OCEAN
Chiloe Island
Patagonia
Valdes Peninsula
-131 ft
-40 m
Falkland Islands
South Georgia
Tierra del Fuego
Scotia Sea
South Sandwich Islands
Strait of Magellan
South Shetland Islands
South Orkney Islands
SOU
Antarctic Peninsula
60°S
ANTARCTIC CIRCLE
Bellingshausen Sea
Weddell Sea
Ellsworth Land
Ronne Ice Shelf
Marie Byrd Land
Ross Sea
Vinson Massif
16,067 ft
4,897 m
Ross Ice Shelf
TRANSANTARCTIC MOUNTAINS

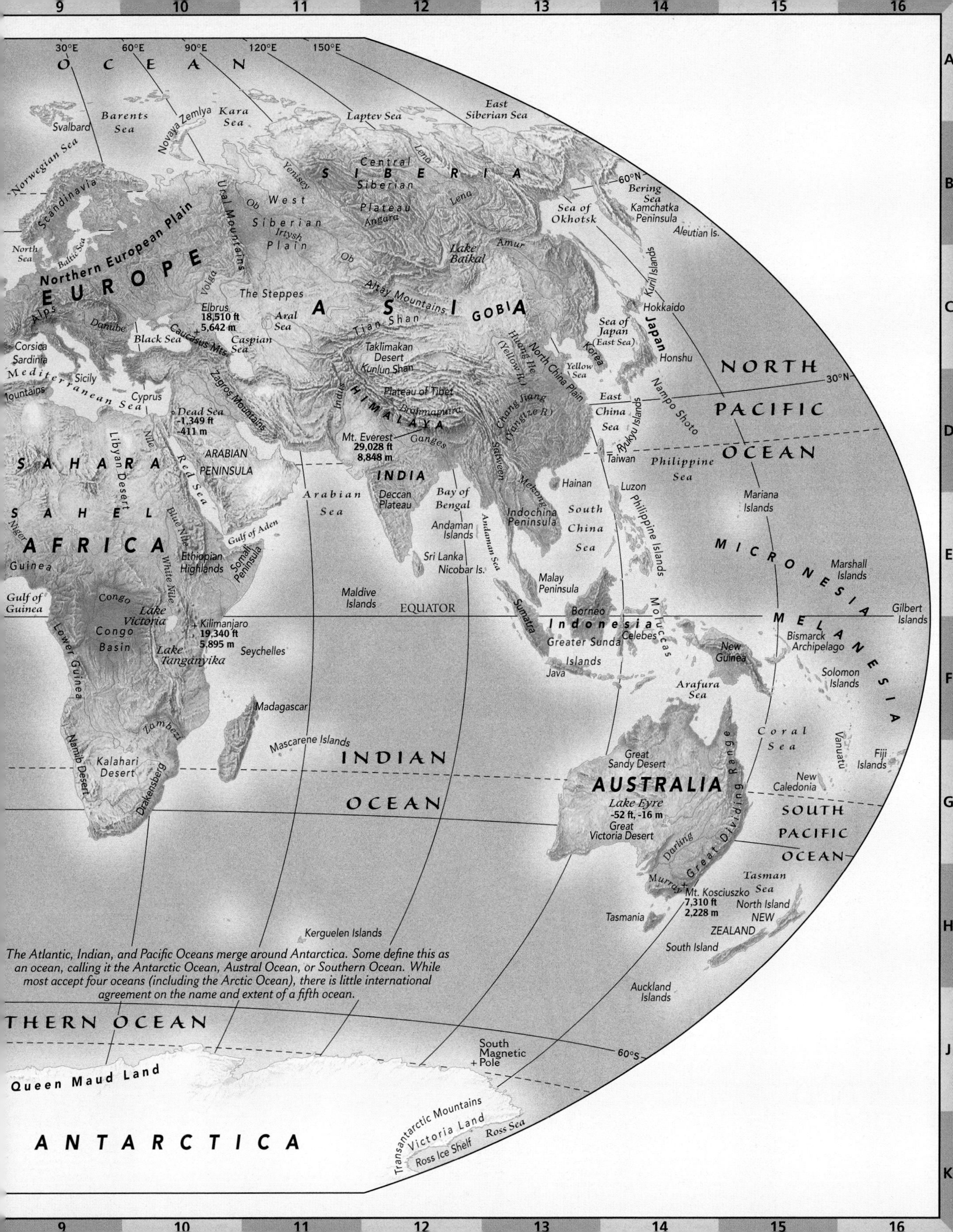

OCEAN
Barents Sea
Kara Sea
Laptev Sea
East Siberian Sea
Svalbard
Novaya Zemlya
Norwegian Sea
Scandinavia
North Sea
Baltic Sea
Northern European Plain
EUROPE
Ural Mountains
West Siberian Plain
Central Siberian Plateau
SIBERIA
Yenisey
Ob
Irtysh
Lena
Angara
Lake Baikal
Amur
Sea of Okhotsk
Bering Sea
Kamchatka Peninsula
Aleutian Is.
Kuril Islands
Hokkaido
Japan
Honshu
Sea of Japan (East Sea)
Korea
Yellow Sea
Volga
The Steppes
Alps
Danube
Elbrus 18,510 ft 5,642 m
Black Sea
Caucasus Mts.
Caspian Sea
Aral Sea
ASIA
Altay Mountains
GOBI
Tian Shan
Taklimakan Desert
Kunlun Shan
Huang He (Yellow R.)
North China Plain
Corsica
Sardinia
Mediterranean Sea
Sicily
Cyprus
Mountains
Dead Sea -1,349 ft -411 m
Zagros Mountains
Indus
HIMALAYA
Plateau of Tibet
Brahmaputra
Chang Jiang (Yangtze R.)
East China Sea
Ryukyu Islands
Nampo Shoto
NORTH PACIFIC OCEAN
Mt. Everest 29,028 ft 8,848 m
Ganges
SAHARA
Libyan Desert
Nile
Red Sea
ARABIAN PENINSULA
INDIA
Salween
Taiwan
Philippine Sea
Arabian Sea
Deccan Plateau
Bay of Bengal
Mekong
Hainan
Luzon
Mariana Islands
SAHEL
Niger
Blue Nile
Gulf of Aden
Andaman Islands
Andaman Sea
Indochina Peninsula
South China Sea
Philippine Islands
AFRICA
Guinea
White Nile
Ethiopian Highlands
Somali Peninsula
Sri Lanka
Nicobar Is.
MICRONESIA
Marshall Islands
Gulf of Guinea
Congo
Maldive Islands
Malay Peninsula
Moluccas
EQUATOR
Borneo
Sumatra
Lake Victoria
Kilimanjaro 19,340 ft 5,895 m
Indonesia
Celebes
Gilbert Islands
MELANESIA
Congo Basin
Lower Guinea
Lake Tanganyika
Seychelles
Greater Sunda Islands
Java
New Guinea
Bismarck Archipelago
Solomon Islands
Arafura Sea
Madagascar
Zambezi
Mascarene Islands
INDIAN OCEAN
Coral Sea
Vanuatu
Fiji Islands
Namib Desert
Kalahari Desert
Drakensberg
Great Sandy Desert
Great Dividing Range
AUSTRALIA
New Caledonia
Lake Eyre -52 ft, -16 m
Great Victoria Desert
SOUTH PACIFIC OCEAN
Darling
Murray
Mt. Kosciuszko 7,310 ft 2,228 m
Tasman Sea
Tasmania
North Island
NEW ZEALAND
South Island
Kerguelen Islands
Auckland Islands
The Atlantic, Indian, and Pacific Oceans merge around Antarctica. Some define this as an ocean, calling it the Antarctic Ocean, Austral Ocean, or Southern Ocean. While most accept four oceans (including the Arctic Ocean), there is little international agreement on the name and extent of a fifth ocean.
THERN OCEAN
South Magnetic Pole
Queen Maud Land
ANTARCTICA
Transantarctic Mountains
Victoria Land
Ross Sea
Ross Ice Shelf
30°E
60°E
90°E
120°E
150°E
60°N
30°N
60°S
9
10
11
12
13
14
15
16
A
B
C
D
E
F
G
H
J
K

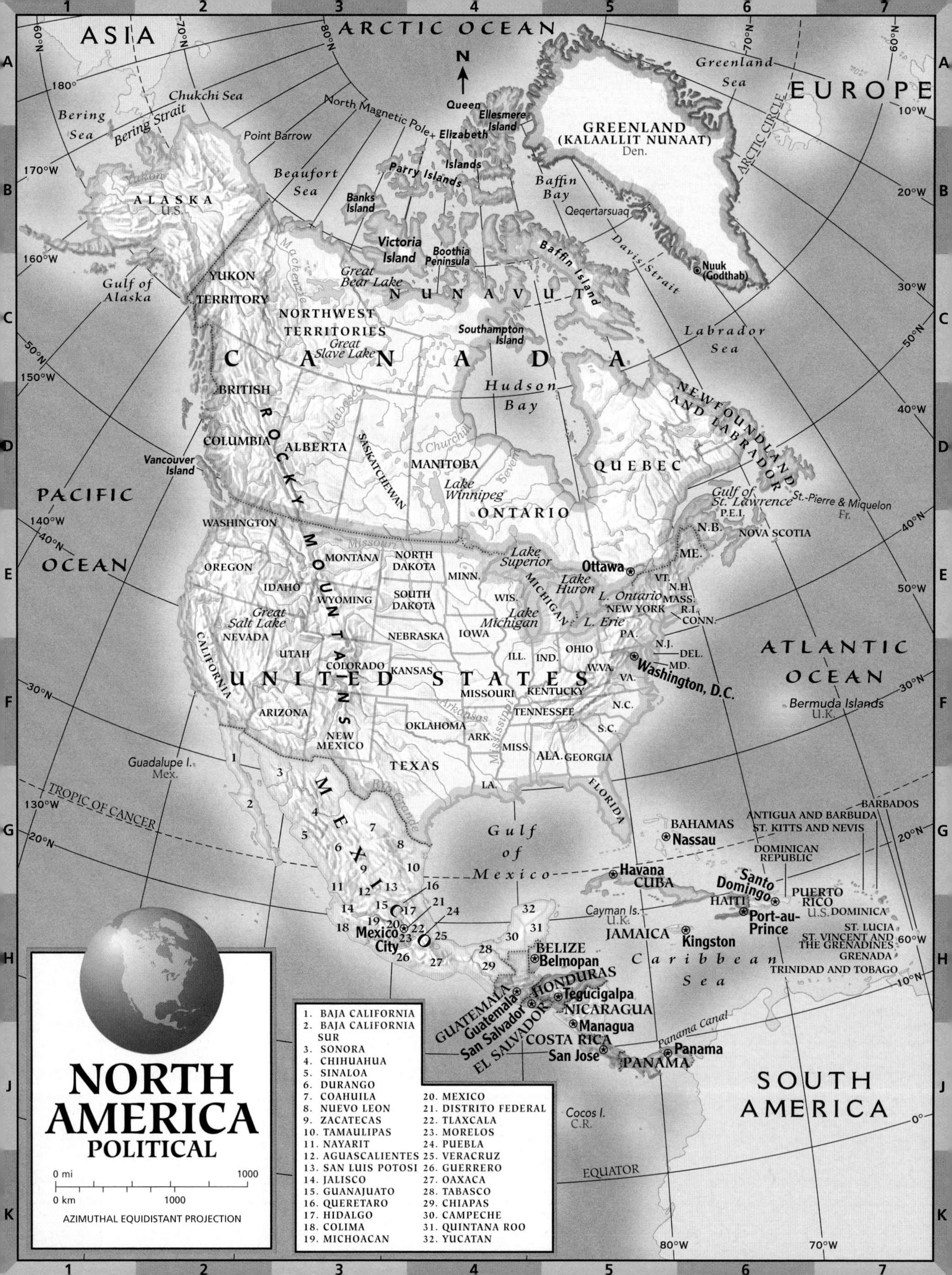

NORTH AMERICA
POLITICAL
AZIMUTHAL EQUIDISTANT PROJECTION
0 mi 1000
0 km 1000
ARCTIC OCEAN
ASIA
EUROPE
PACIFIC OCEAN
ATLANTIC OCEAN
SOUTH AMERICA
Chukchi Sea
Bering Sea
Bering Strait
Point Barrow
Beaufort Sea
North Magnetic Pole
Queen Elizabeth Islands
Ellesmere Island
Parry Islands
Banks Island
Victoria Island
Boothia Peninsula
Baffin Bay
Baffin Island
Davis Strait
Greenland Sea
GREENLAND (KALAALLIT NUNAAT)
Den.
Qeqertarsuaq
Nuuk (Godthab)
ARCTIC CIRCLE
ALASKA
U.S.
Yukon
Gulf of Alaska
YUKON TERRITORY
NORTHWEST TERRITORIES
NUNAVUT
Great Bear Lake
Great Slave Lake
Mackenzie
Southampton Island
Labrador Sea
CANADA
Hudson Bay
BRITISH COLUMBIA
ALBERTA
SASKATCHEWAN
MANITOBA
ONTARIO
QUEBEC
NEWFOUNDLAND AND LABRADOR
Athabasca
Churchill
Severn
Lake Winnipeg
Vancouver Island
ROCKY MOUNTAINS
Gulf of St. Lawrence
St.-Pierre & Miquelon
Fr.
P.E.I.
N.B.
NOVA SCOTIA
Ottawa
Lake Superior
Lake Huron
Lake Michigan
L. Ontario
L. Erie
WASHINGTON
OREGON
IDAHO
MONTANA
WYOMING
NORTH DAKOTA
SOUTH DAKOTA
MINN.
WIS.
MICHIGAN
ME.
VT.
N.H.
MASS.
R.I.
CONN.
NEW YORK
PA.
N.J.
DEL.
MD.
Missouri
Great Salt Lake
NEVADA
CALIFORNIA
UTAH
COLORADO
NEBRASKA
IOWA
KANSAS
ILL.
IND.
OHIO
W.VA.
VA.
Washington, D.C.
UNITED STATES
MISSOURI
KENTUCKY
N.C.
TENNESSEE
S.C.
ARIZONA
NEW MEXICO
OKLAHOMA
ARK.
Arkansas
Mississippi
MISS.
ALA.
GEORGIA
TEXAS
LA.
FLORIDA
Bermuda Islands
U.K.
Guadalupe I.
Mex.
TROPIC OF CANCER
Rio Grande
MEXICO
Gulf of Mexico
BAHAMAS
Nassau
Havana
CUBA
Cayman Is.
U.K.
JAMAICA
Kingston
HAITI
Port-au-Prince
Santo Domingo
DOMINICAN REPUBLIC
PUERTO RICO
U.S.
ANTIGUA AND BARBUDA
ST. KITTS AND NEVIS
BARBADOS
DOMINICA
ST. LUCIA
ST. VINCENT AND THE GRENADINES
GRENADA
TRINIDAD AND TOBAGO
Caribbean Sea
Mexico City
BELIZE
Belmopan
GUATEMALA
Guatemala
HONDURAS
Tegucigalpa
San Salvador
EL SALVADOR
NICARAGUA
Managua
COSTA RICA
San Jose
PANAMA
Panama
Panama Canal
Cocos I.
C.R.
EQUATOR
1. BAJA CALIFORNIA
2. BAJA CALIFORNIA SUR
3. SONORA
4. CHIHUAHUA
5. SINALOA
6. DURANGO
7. COAHUILA
8. NUEVO LEON
9. ZACATECAS
10. TAMAULIPAS
11. NAYARIT
12. AGUASCALIENTES
13. SAN LUIS POTOSI
14. JALISCO
15. GUANAJUATO
16. QUERETARO
17. HIDALGO
18. COLIMA
19. MICHOACAN
20. MEXICO
21. DISTRITO FEDERAL
22. TLAXCALA
23. MORELOS
24. PUEBLA
25. VERACRUZ
26. GUERRERO
27. OAXACA
28. TABASCO
29. CHIAPAS
30. CAMPECHE
31. QUINTANA ROO
32. YUCATAN

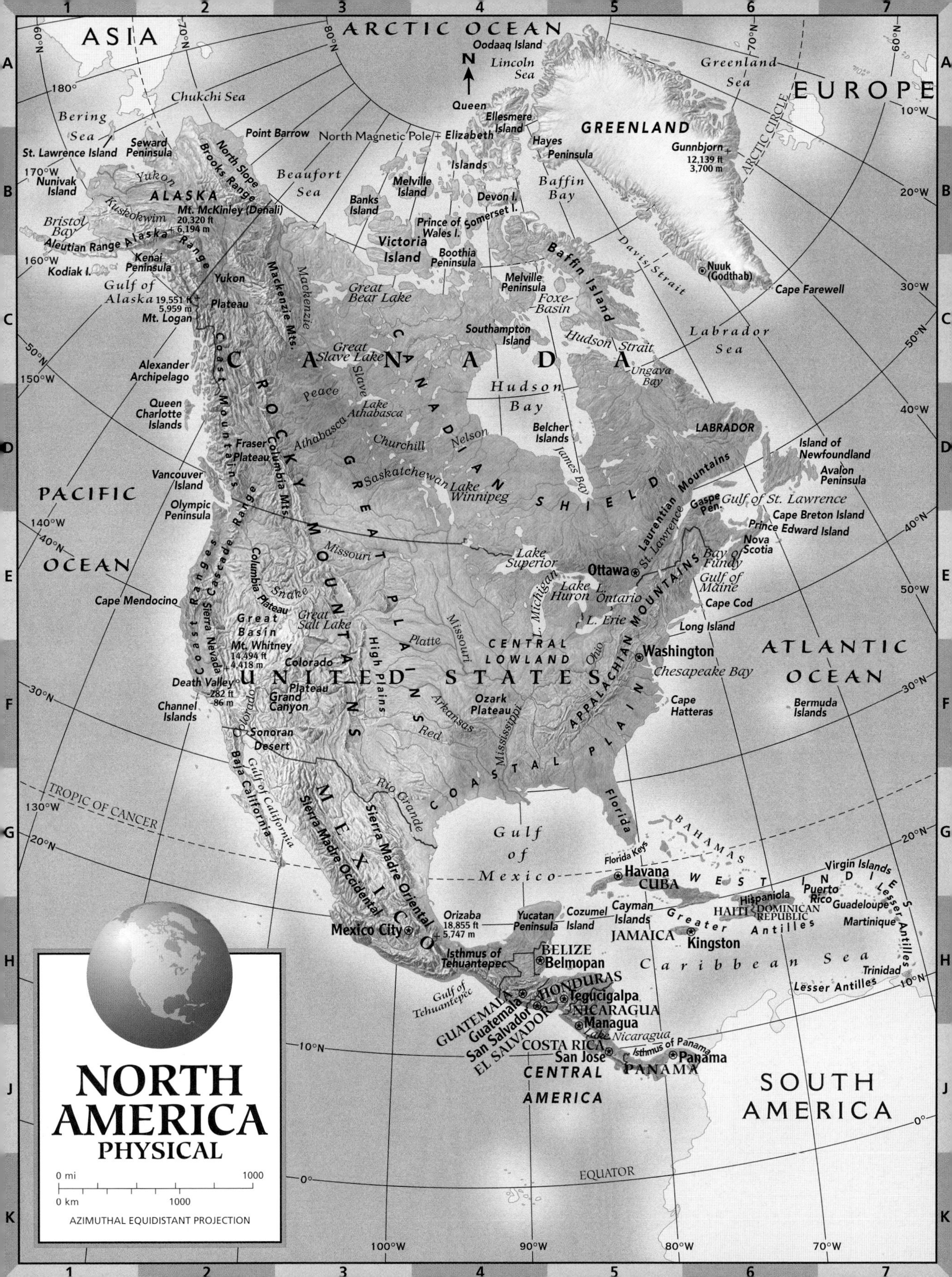

NORTH AMERICA
PHYSICAL
0 mi
1000
0 km
1000
AZIMUTHAL EQUIDISTANT PROJECTION
ARCTIC OCEAN
ASIA
EUROPE
GREENLAND
CANADA
UNITED STATES
MEXICO
CENTRAL AMERICA
SOUTH AMERICA
PACIFIC OCEAN
ATLANTIC OCEAN
Oodaaq Island
Lincoln Sea
Greenland Sea
Chukchi Sea
Bering Sea
St. Lawrence Island
Seward Peninsula
Point Barrow
North Magnetic Pole
Queen Elizabeth Islands
Ellesmere Island
Hayes Peninsula
Gunnbjorn
12,139 ft
3,700 m
ARCTIC CIRCLE
Nunivak Island
Yukon
ALASKA
North Slope
Brooks Range
Beaufort Sea
Melville Island
Banks Island
Devon I.
Baffin Bay
Mt. McKinley (Denali)
20,320 ft
6,194 m
Kuskokwim
Bristol Bay
Alaska Range
Aleutian Range
Kenai Peninsula
Kodiak I.
Prince of Wales I.
Somerset I.
Victoria Island
Boothia Peninsula
Baffin Island
Davis Strait
Nuuk (Godthab)
Cape Farewell
Mackenzie Mts.
Mackenzie
Great Bear Lake
Melville Peninsula
Foxe Basin
Gulf of Alaska
19,551 ft
5,959 m
Mt. Logan
Yukon Plateau
Southampton Island
Hudson Strait
Labrador Sea
Great Slave Lake
Alexander Archipelago
Coast Mountains
ROCKY MOUNTAINS
Peace
Slave
Lake Athabasca
Athabasca
Hudson Bay
Ungava Bay
Queen Charlotte Islands
CANADIAN SHIELD
Churchill
Nelson
Belcher Islands
James Bay
LABRADOR
Fraser Plateau
Columbia Mts.
Saskatchewan
Lake Winnipeg
Laurentian Mountains
Island of Newfoundland
Avalon Peninsula
Vancouver Island
GREAT PLAINS
Gaspe Pen.
Gulf of St. Lawrence
Cape Breton Island
Olympic Peninsula
Cascade Range
Prince Edward Island
Nova Scotia
Missouri
Lake Superior
St. Lawrence
Ottawa
Bay of Fundy
Columbia Plateau
Snake
L. Michigan
Lake Huron
L. Ontario
APPALACHIAN MOUNTAINS
Gulf of Maine
Cape Mendocino
Coast Ranges
Sierra Nevada
Great Basin
Great Salt Lake
Cape Cod
L. Erie
Long Island
Mt. Whitney
14,494 ft
4,418 m
High Plains
Platte
CENTRAL LOWLAND
Ohio
Washington
Colorado Plateau
Chesapeake Bay
Death Valley
-282 ft
-86 m
Grand Canyon
Arkansas
Ozark Plateau
Mississippi
Cape Hatteras
Bermuda Islands
Channel Islands
Colorado
Red
COASTAL PLAIN
Sonoran Desert
Baja California
Gulf of California
Rio Grande
Sierra Madre Oriental
Sierra Madre Occidental
Florida
TROPIC OF CANCER
BAHAMAS
Gulf of Mexico
Florida Keys
Havana
CUBA
WEST INDIES
Virgin Islands
Hispaniola
HAITI
DOMINICAN REPUBLIC
Puerto Rico
Guadeloupe
Martinique
Greater Antilles
Lesser Antilles
Orizaba
18,855 ft
5,747 m
Mexico City
Yucatan Peninsula
Cozumel Island
Cayman Islands
JAMAICA
Kingston
Isthmus of Tehuantepec
BELIZE
Belmopan
Caribbean Sea
Trinidad
Gulf of Tehuantepec
GUATEMALA
Guatemala
HONDURAS
Tegucigalpa
NICARAGUA
Managua
San Salvador
EL SALVADOR
Lake Nicaragua
COSTA RICA
San Jose
Isthmus of Panama
Panama
PANAMA
EQUATOR
180°
170°W
160°W
150°W
140°W
130°W
100°W
90°W
80°W
70°W
60°N
70°N
80°N
50°N
40°N
30°N
20°N
10°N
0°
10°W
20°W
30°W
40°W
50°W

MIDDLE AMERICA
PHYSICAL/POLITICAL
0 mi
400
0 km
400
AZIMUTHAL EQUIDISTANT PROJECTION
UNITED STATES
MEXICO
CENTRAL AMERICA
PACIFIC OCEAN
Gulf of Mexico
Gulf of California
Bay of Campeche
Gulf of Tehuantepec
Gulf of Honduras
Sonoran Desert
Baja California
Sierra Madre Occidental
Sierra Madre Oriental
Sierra Madre del Sur
Sierra Madre
Rio Grande
Yucatan Peninsula
Isthmus of Tehuantepec
False Cape
Revillagigedo Islands
Mex.
Cozumel Island
Cocos Island
C.R.
Orizaba
18,855 ft
5,747 m
Popocatepetl
17,802 ft
5,426 m
BAJA CALIFORNIA
BAJA CALIFORNIA SUR
SONORA
CHIHUAHUA
COAHUILA
SINALOA
DURANGO
NUEVO LEON
TAMAULIPAS
ZACATECAS
SAN LUIS POTOSI
NAYARIT
AGUASCALIENTES
JALISCO
GUANAJUATO
QUERETARO
VERACRUZ
HIDALGO
TLAXCALA
COLIMA
MICHOACAN
DISTRITO FEDERAL
MEXICO
MORELOS
PUEBLA
GUERRERO
OAXACA
TABASCO
CHIAPAS
CAMPECHE
YUCATAN
QUINTANA ROO
BELIZE
GUATEMALA
EL SALVADOR
HON
Tijuana
Mexicali
Ciudad Juarez
Chihuahua
Nuevo Laredo
Monterrey
Matamoros
La Paz
Mazatlan
Ciudad Madero
Tampico
San Luis Potosi
Guadalajara
Leon
Mexico City
Veracruz
Acapulco
Merida
Belize City
Belmopan
Guatemala
San Salvador
Tegucigalpa
Leon
N
110°W
100°W
90°W
30°N
20°N
10°N
0°
1
2
3
4
5
6
7
8
A
B
C
D
E
F
G
H
J
K

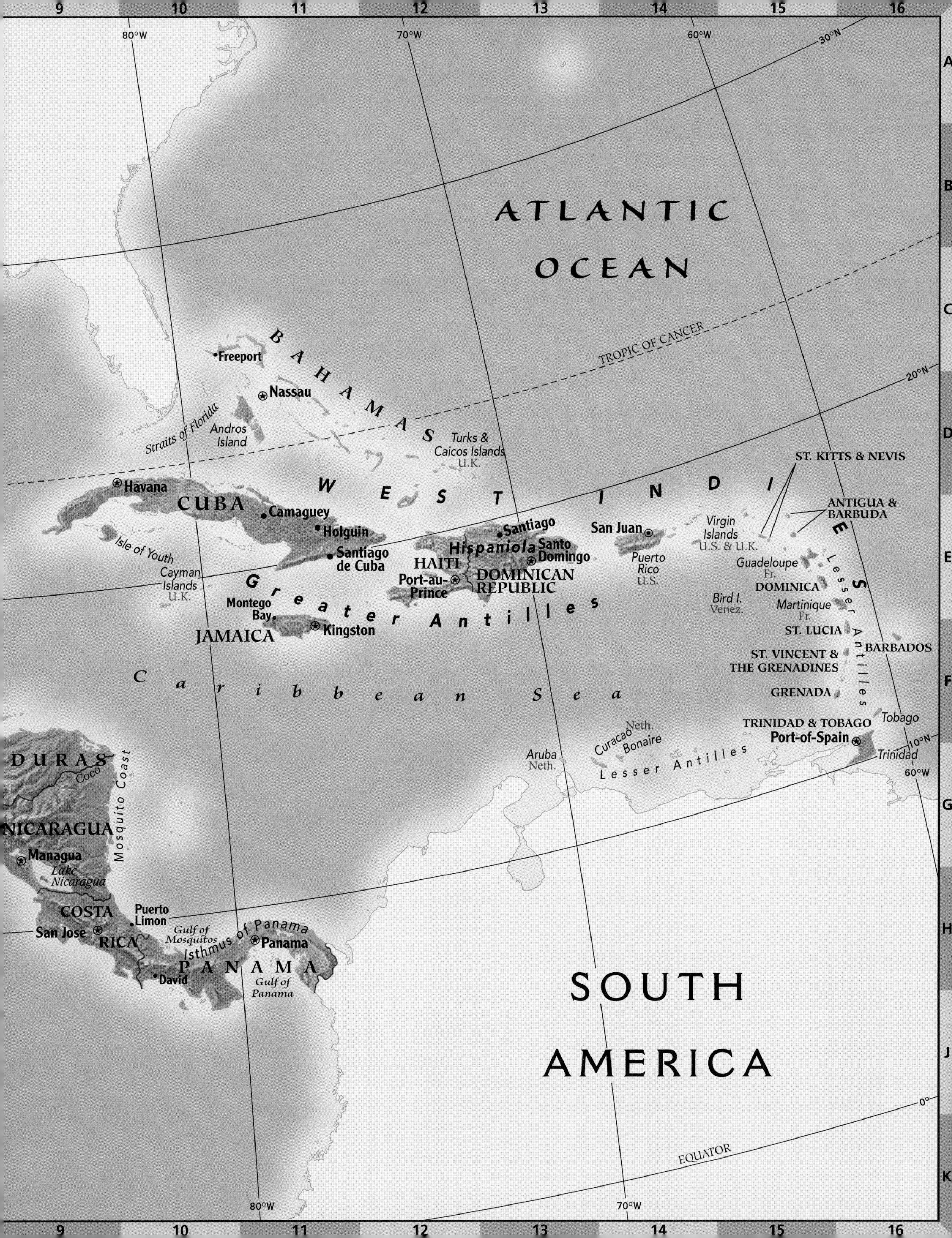

9
10
11
12
13
14
15
16
A
B
C
D
E
F
G
H
J
K
80°W
70°W
60°W
30°N
20°N
10°N
0°
ATLANTIC
OCEAN
TROPIC OF CANCER
EQUATOR
BAHAMAS
Freeport
Nassau
Andros Island
Straits of Florida
Turks & Caicos Islands
U.K.
WEST INDIES
Havana
CUBA
Camaguey
Holguin
Santiago de Cuba
Isle of Youth
Cayman Islands
U.K.
Santiago
Hispaniola
Santo Domingo
HAITI
Port-au-Prince
DOMINICAN REPUBLIC
San Juan
Puerto Rico
U.S.
Virgin Islands
U.S. & U.K.
ST. KITTS & NEVIS
ANTIGUA & BARBUDA
Guadeloupe
Fr.
DOMINICA
Martinique
Fr.
ST. LUCIA
BARBADOS
ST. VINCENT & THE GRENADINES
GRENADA
Tobago
TRINIDAD & TOBAGO
Port-of-Spain
Trinidad
Lesser Antilles
Bird I.
Venez.
Greater Antilles
Montego Bay
Kingston
JAMAICA
Caribbean Sea
Aruba
Neth.
Curacao
Neth.
Bonaire
Lesser Antilles
DURAS
Coco
Mosquito Coast
NICARAGUA
Managua
Lake Nicaragua
COSTA RICA
Puerto Limon
San Jose
Gulf of Mosquitos
Isthmus of Panama
Panama
PANAMA
David
Gulf of Panama
SOUTH
AMERICA

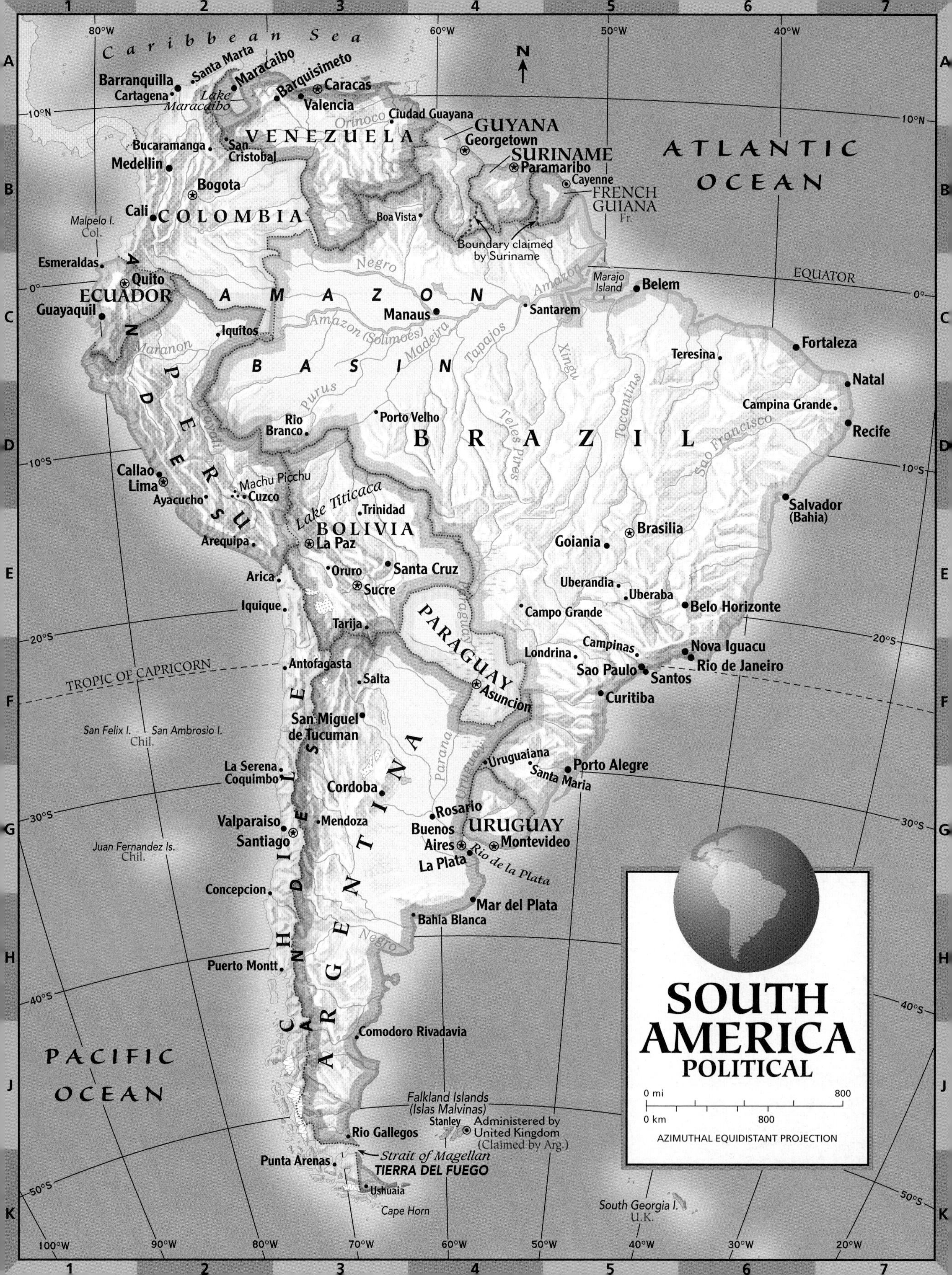

SOUTH AMERICA
POLITICAL
AZIMUTHAL EQUIDISTANT PROJECTION
0 mi 800
0 km 800
Caribbean Sea
ATLANTIC OCEAN
PACIFIC OCEAN
VENEZUELA
GUYANA
SURINAME
FRENCH GUIANA
Fr.
COLOMBIA
ECUADOR
PERU
BRAZIL
BOLIVIA
PARAGUAY
URUGUAY
ARGENTINA
CHILE
AMAZON BASIN
ANDES
Barranquilla
Santa Marta
Maracaibo
Barquisimeto
Caracas
Valencia
Cartagena
Lake Maracaibo
Orinoco
Ciudad Guayana
Georgetown
Paramaribo
Cayenne
Bucaramanga
San Cristobal
Medellin
Bogota
Cali
Malpelo I.
Col.
Boa Vista
Boundary claimed by Suriname
Negro
Amazon
Marajo Island
Belem
EQUATOR
Esmeraldas
Quito
Guayaquil
Manaus
Santarem
Iquitos
Amazon (Solimoes)
Madeira
Tapajos
Xingu
Maranon
Teresina
Fortaleza
Natal
Campina Grande
Recife
Purus
Ucayali
Porto Velho
Rio Branco
Teles Pires
Tocantins
Sao Francisco
Callao
Lima
Machu Picchu
Cuzco
Ayacucho
Lake Titicaca
Trinidad
Salvador (Bahia)
Brasilia
Goiania
Arequipa
La Paz
Oruro
Santa Cruz
Sucre
Arica
Iquique
Uberandia
Uberaba
Campo Grande
Belo Horizonte
Tarija
Paraguay
Campinas
Londrina
Nova Iguacu
Rio de Janeiro
Sao Paulo
Santos
Antofagasta
TROPIC OF CAPRICORN
Salta
Asuncion
Curitiba
San Felix I.
San Ambrosio I.
Chil.
San Miguel de Tucuman
Parana
Uruguay
Uruguaiana
Santa Maria
Porto Alegre
La Serena
Coquimbo
Cordoba
Rosario
Valparaiso
Mendoza
Santiago
Buenos Aires
Montevideo
Juan Fernandez Is.
Chil.
La Plata
Rio de la Plata
Concepcion
Mar del Plata
Bahia Blanca
Negro
Puerto Montt
Comodoro Rivadavia
Falkland Islands (Islas Malvinas)
Stanley
Administered by United Kingdom
(Claimed by Arg.)
Rio Gallegos
Punta Arenas
Strait of Magellan
TIERRA DEL FUEGO
Ushuaia
Cape Horn
South Georgia I.
U.K.
N
80°W
60°W
50°W
40°W
10°N
0°
10°S
20°S
30°S
40°S
50°S
100°W
90°W
80°W
70°W
60°W
50°W
40°W
30°W
20°W
1 2 3 4 5 6 7
A B C D E F G H J K

SOUTH AMERICA
PHYSICAL
Caribbean Sea
ATLANTIC OCEAN
PACIFIC OCEAN
Lake Maracaibo
Caracas
Orinoco
LLANOS
VENEZUELA
GUYANA
Georgetown
SURINAME
Paramaribo
Cayenne
FRENCH GUIANA
Angel Falls
Total drop
3,212 ft 979 m
Bogota
GUIANA HIGHLANDS
COLOMBIA
Boundary claimed by Suriname
Malpelo I.
Quito
ECUADOR
Negro
Amazon
Marajo Island
EQUATOR
AMAZON
Selvas
BASIN
Madeira
Tapajos
Xingu
Purus
Ucayali
ANDES
Teles Pires
Tocantins
Sao Francisco
BRAZIL
PERU
Lima
Machu Picchu
Lake Titicaca
MATO GROSSO PLATEAU
BRAZILIAN HIGHLANDS
Brasilia
BOLIVIA
La Paz
Altiplano
Sucre
Salar de Uyuni
Paraguay
PARAGUAY
GRAN CHACO
TROPIC OF CAPRICORN
Iguazu Falls
Asuncion
San Felix I.
San Ambrosio I.
Parana
Uruguay
ARGENTINA
CHILE
PAMPAS
Aconcagua 22,834 ft 6,960 m
Santiago
Buenos Aires
URUGUAY
Montevideo
Rio de la Plata
Juan Fernandez Is.
Negro
PATAGONIA
Chiloe Island
-131 ft -40 m
Valdes Peninsula
Gulf of San Jorge
Taitao Peninsula
Wellington I.
Falkland Islands (Islas Malvinas)
Stanley
Strait of Magellan
Tierra del Fuego
Cape Horn
South Georgia I.
N
10°N
0°
10°S
20°S
30°S
40°S
50°S
80°W
60°W
50°W
40°W
100°W
90°W
70°W
30°W
20°W
0 mi 800
0 km 800
AZIMUTHAL EQUIDISTANT PROJECTION
1 2 3 4 5 6 7
A B C D E F G H J K

EUROPE
POLITICAL
0 mi
400
0 km
400
AZIMUTHAL EQUIDISTANT PROJECTION
Akureyri
Reykjavík
ICELAND
ARCTIC CIRCLE
PRIME MERIDIAN (MERIDIAN OF GREENWICH)
Norwegian Sea
Tromso
Faeroe Islands
Den.
Torshavn
Trondheim
Are
Alesund
Sundsvall
Gulf of
Shetland Islands
Lerwick
Rockall
U.K.
Bergen
NORWAY
SWEDEN
Isle of Lewis
Orkney Islands
Oslo
Uppsala
Stavanger
Inverness
UNITED
Aberdeen
Stockholm
SCOTLAND
Glasgow
Edinburgh
Skagerrak
Goteborg
NORTHERN IRELAND
Belfast
Gotland
North Sea
Arhus
IRELAND
Irish Sea
Dublin
Liverpool
DENMARK
Copenhagen
Malmo
Manchester
Baltic
Cork
KINGDOM
Kiel
WALES
Birmingham
Gdansk
Celtic Sea
Cardiff
ENGLAND
Hamburg
NETH.
The Hague
Amsterdam
London
Bydgoszcz
Land's End
Southampton
Berlin
ATLANTIC OCEAN
English Channel
Brussels
GERMANY
POLAND
BELGIUM
Bonn
Lodz
Le Havre
Wroclaw
Brest
Frankfurt
LUX.
Rhine
Oder
Paris
Rennes
Prague
CZECH REP.
Nantes
Strasbourg
SLOVAKIA
Bratislava
FRANCE
Munich
Vienna
La Rochelle
Bay of Biscay
Zurich
LIECH.
Bern
AUSTRIA
Budapest
Limoges
SWITZERLAND
HUNGARY
Bordeaux
Geneva
La Coruña
Lyon
ALPS
SLOVENIA
Vigo
Donostia-San Sebastian
Milan
Ljubljana
Zagreb
Bilbao
Turin
CROATIA
Toulouse
Venice
Porto
Pyrenees
Genoa
BOSNIA & HERZEGOVINA
MONACO
Valladolid
SAN MARINO
Sarajevo
Coimbra
ANDORRA
Nice
Adriatic Sea
Marseille
Zaragoza
ITALY
MONTENEGRO
Madrid
Lisbon
Barcelona
Corsica
Fr.
Podgorica
PORTUGAL
SPAIN
VATICAN CITY
Rome
Valencia
Tiranë
ALBANIA
Cape St. Vincent
Cordoba
Palma
Balearic Islands
Sp.
Sardinia
It.
Naples
Seville
Murcia
Cadiz
Cartagena
Cagliari
Tyrrhenian Sea
Ionian Sea
GIBRALTAR
U.K.
Malaga
Strait of Gibraltar
Mediterranean
Palermo
Messina
Sicily
Catania
AFRICA
Valletta
MALTA
60°N
50°N
40°N
30°N
70°N
40°W
30°W
20°W
10°W
0°
10°E
N

A commonly accepted division between Asia and Europe—here marked by a gray line—is formed by the Ural Mountains, Ural River, Caspian Sea, Caucasus Mountains, and the Black Sea with its outlets, the Bosporus and the Dardanelles.
Europe-Asia boundary
RUSSIA
ASIA
KAZAKHSTAN
URAL MOUNTAINS
Barents Sea
White Sea
Kola Peninsula
LAPLAND
FINLAND
Bothnia
Lake Onega
Lake Ladoga
ESTONIA
LATVIA
LITHUANIA
RUSSIA
BELARUS
UKRAINE
MOLDOVA
ROMANIA
SERBIA
BULGARIA
KOSOVO
MACED.
TURKEY
GREECE
GEORGIA
AZERBAIJAN
CYPRUS
Carpathian Mts.
Balkan Mts.
Caucasus Mountains
Black Sea
Caspian Sea
Sea of Azov
Crimea
Bosporus
Dardanelles
Sea of Marmara
Aegean Sea
Peloponnesus
Crete
Rhodes
Sea
Volga
Ural
Dniester
Danube
Tobseda
Murmansk
Ivalo
Kirovsk
Umba
Kiruna
Kemi
Lulea
Oulu
Umea
Vaasa
Kuopio
Pori
Tampere
Turku
Helsinki
St. Petersburg
Kem
Arkhangel'sk
Severodvinsk
Pechora
Syktyvkar
Perm
Kirov
Ufa
Kazan
Tallinn
Velikiy Novgorod
Yaroslavl
Nizhniy Novgorod
Tver
Moscow
Riga
Samara
Orenburg
Daugavpils
Ryazan
Penza
Vitsyebsk
Smolensk
Oral
Kaunas
Vilnius
Minsk
Bryansk
Saratov
Warsaw
Homyel
Kursk
Chernihiv
Sumy
Kharkiv
Volgograd
Kyiv (Kiev)
Poltava
Krakow
Lviv
Donetsk
Astrakhan
Vinnytsya
Dnipropetrovsk
Rostov
Chişinău
Odesa
Stavropol
Kerch
Grozny
Simferopol
Yalta
Sevastopol
Belgrade
Bucharest
Constanta
Baku
Varna
Pristina
Sofia
Skopje
Istanbul
Thessaloniki
Athens
Nicosia
Iraklio
30°E
40°E
50°E
70°E
80°E
70°N
60°N
50°N
40°N
30°N

EUROPE
PHYSICAL
0 mi 400
0 km 400
AZIMUTHAL EQUIDISTANT PROJECTION
ICELAND
Reykjavík
ARCTIC CIRCLE
PRIME MERIDIAN (MERIDIAN OF GREENWICH)
Norwegian Sea
Faeroe Islands
Shetland Islands
Orkney Islands
Outer Hebrides
British Isles
Highlands
Edinburgh
Belfast
UNITED KINGDOM
IRELAND
Dublin
Irish Sea
Great Britain
Cardiff
London
North Sea
NORWAY
SWEDEN
SCANDINAVIA
Oslo
Stockholm
Gulf of
Jutland
DENMARK
Copenhagen
Zealand
Baltic
Amsterdam
NETH.
BELGIUM
Brussels
LUX.
Berlin
GERMANY
NORTH
POLAND
Oder
Elbe
Prague
CZECH REP.
Rhine
Danube
ATLANTIC OCEAN
English Channel
Brittany
Seine
Paris
Loire
FRANCE
Bay of Biscay
Mont Blanc
15,771 ft
4,807 m
Bern
SWITZ.
LIECH.
AUSTRIA
Vienna
Bratislava
SLOVAKIA
Budapest
HUNGARY
ALPS
Massif Central
Rhone
MONACO
SLOVENIA
Ljubljana
Zagreb
CROATIA
Drava
Sava
BOSNIA &
Sarajevo
HERZEGOVINA
Po
Adriatic Sea
Cantabrian Mountains
Pyrenees
Douro
PORTUGAL
IBERIAN PENINSULA
SPAIN
Madrid
Ebro
Tagus
Lisbon
ANDORRA
Riviera
SAN MARINO
Apennines
Corsica
ITALY
VATICAN CITY
Rome
MONTENEGRO
Tiranë
ALBANIA
Sardinia
Tyrrhenian Sea
Ionian Sea
Balearic Islands
Baetic Mountains
GIBRALTAR
Strait of Gibraltar
Mediterranean
Sicily
Etna
10,902 ft
3,323 m
Valletta
MALTA
AFRICA
60°N
50°N
40°N
30°N
70°N
40°W
30°W
20°W
10°W
0°
10°E
N

North Cape
Barents Sea
Kola Peninsula
White Sea
Pechora
URAL MOUNTAINS
FINLAND
Bothnia
Lake Region
Lake Onega
Lake Ladoga
Northern Dvina
EUROPEAN PLAIN
RUSSIA
Europe-Asia boundary
ASIA
Helsinki
Gulf of Finland
Tallinn
ESTONIA
Kama
Ural
Volga
Riga
LATVIA
Moscow
LITHUANIA
Oka
Vilnius
RUSSIA
CENTRAL RUSSIAN UPLAND
Minsk
BELARUS
Dnieper
Don
Warsaw
KAZAKHSTAN
Caspian Depression
Kyiv (Kiev)
Vistula
UKRAINE
Carpathian Mountains
Dniester
MOLDOVA
Chişinău
Sea of Azov
Caspian Sea
Crimea
Elbrus 18,510 ft 5,642 m
ROMANIA
Caucasus Mountains
AZERBAIJAN
Belgrade
Bucharest
Danube
GEORGIA
Baku
BALKAN PENINSULA
Black Sea
SERBIA
BULGARIA
Balkan Mountains
Sofia
KOSOVO
Skopje
MACED.
Bosporus
TURKEY
GREECE
Dardanelles
Sea of Marmara
Aegean Sea
Athens
Peloponnesus
Rhodes
Crete
Nicosia
CYPRUS
Sea
30°E
40°E
50°E
60°E
70°E
80°E
70°N
60°N
50°N
40°N
30°N

EUROPE
Black Sea
Sea of Marmara
Istanbul
ANATOLIA
Ankara
TURKEY
Tunis
TUNISIA
Tripoli
Mediterranean Sea
Taurus Mountains
Aleppo
CYPRUS
SYRIA
LEBANON
Damascus
Beirut
ISRAEL
Syrian Desert
Jerusalem
Amman
Alexandria
Cairo
JORDAN
El Giza
LIBYA
Sinai Pen.
See inset below
EGYPT
Nile R.
Hejaz
Aswan High Dam
Red Sea
SAHARA
Boundary claimed by Sudan
SUDAN
AFRICA
Khartoum
Eastern Mediterranean Area
TURKEY
Aleppo
N
CYPRUS
SYRIA
LEBANON
Mediterranean Sea
Beirut
Damascus
Sea of Galilee
Golan Heights
Jordan River
Tel Aviv–Jaffa
West Bank
Jerusalem
Amman
Suez Canal
Gaza Strip
Dead Sea
ISRAEL
JORDAN
El Giza
Cairo
EGYPT
SAUDI ARABIA
Nile River
Gulf of Suez
Gulf of Aqaba
0 mi 100
0 km 100
Red Sea
10°E
20°E
30°E
40°E
40°N
30°N

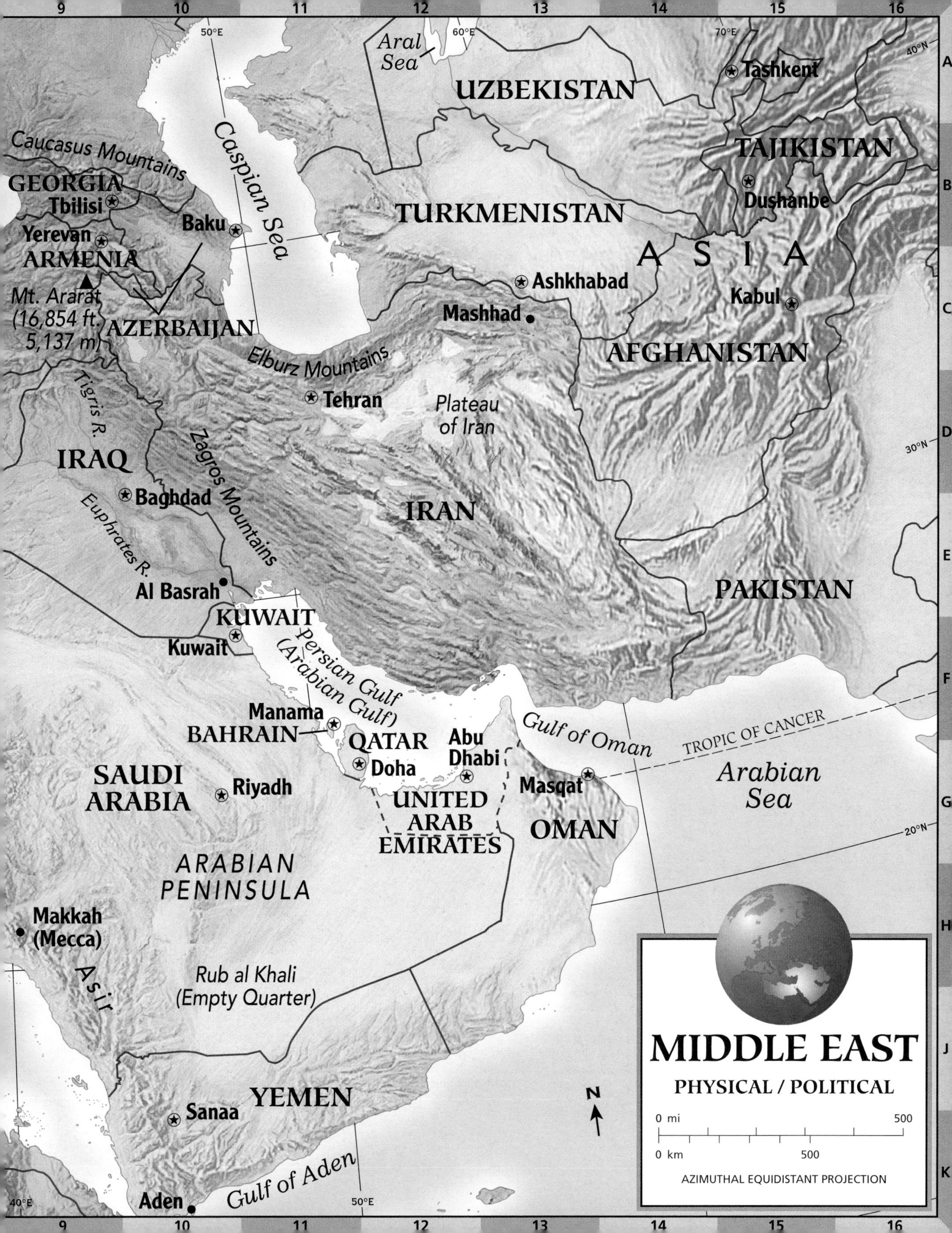

MIDDLE EAST
PHYSICAL / POLITICAL
0 mi
500
0 km
500
AZIMUTHAL EQUIDISTANT PROJECTION
N
Aral Sea
UZBEKISTAN
Tashkent
TAJIKISTAN
Dushanbe
TURKMENISTAN
Caspian Sea
Caucasus Mountains
GEORGIA
Tbilisi
Baku
Yerevan
ARMENIA
Mt. Ararat (16,854 ft. 5,137 m)
AZERBAIJAN
A S I A
Ashkhabad
Kabul
Mashhad
AFGHANISTAN
Elburz Mountains
Tehran
Plateau of Iran
Tigris R.
Zagros Mountains
IRAQ
Baghdad
Euphrates R.
IRAN
PAKISTAN
Al Basrah
KUWAIT
Kuwait
Persian Gulf (Arabian Gulf)
Manama
BAHRAIN
QATAR
Doha
Abu Dhabi
UNITED ARAB EMIRATES
Gulf of Oman
Masqat
TROPIC OF CANCER
Arabian Sea
OMAN
SAUDI ARABIA
Riyadh
ARABIAN PENINSULA
Makkah (Mecca)
Asir
Rub al Khali (Empty Quarter)
YEMEN
Sanaa
Gulf of Aden
Aden
40°N
30°N
20°N
40°E
50°E
60°E
70°E

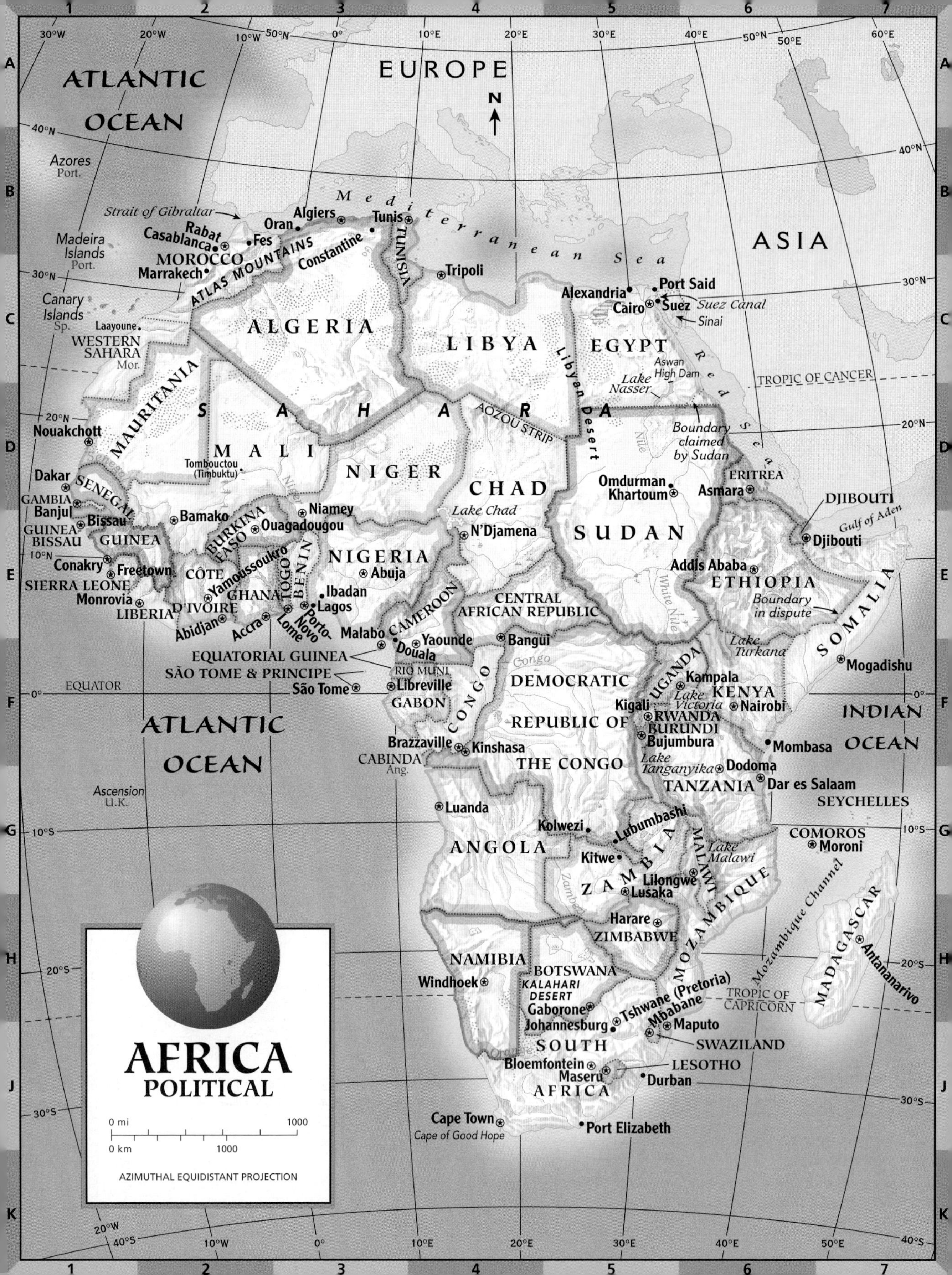

AFRICA
POLITICAL
AZIMUTHAL EQUIDISTANT PROJECTION
0 mi
1000
0 km
1000
ATLANTIC OCEAN
EUROPE
ASIA
INDIAN OCEAN
N
Azores
Port.
Madeira Islands
Port.
Canary Islands
Sp.
Strait of Gibraltar
Mediterranean Sea
Rabat
Casablanca
Fes
MOROCCO
Marrakech
ATLAS MOUNTAINS
Oran
Algiers
Constantine
Tunis
TUNISIA
Tripoli
Alexandria
Port Said
Cairo
Suez
Suez Canal
Sinai
Laayoune
WESTERN SAHARA
Mor.
ALGERIA
LIBYA
EGYPT
Libyan Desert
Aswan High Dam
Lake Nasser
Red Sea
TROPIC OF CANCER
MAURITANIA
SAHARA
AOZOU STRIP
Boundary claimed by Sudan
Nouakchott
MALI
Tombouctou (Timbuktu)
NIGER
CHAD
Nile
Omdurman
Khartoum
ERITREA
Asmara
Dakar
SENEGAL
GAMBIA
Banjul
Bamako
Niamey
Lake Chad
DJIBOUTI
Djibouti
Gulf of Aden
GUINEA-BISSAU
Bissau
GUINEA
BURKINA FASO
Ouagadougou
N'Djamena
SUDAN
Conakry
Freetown
SIERRA LEONE
CÔTE D'IVOIRE
Yamoussoukro
GHANA
TOGO
BENIN
NIGERIA
Abuja
Addis Ababa
ETHIOPIA
Monrovia
LIBERIA
Abidjan
Accra
Lome
Porto-Novo
Ibadan
Lagos
CENTRAL AFRICAN REPUBLIC
White Nile
Boundary in dispute
SOMALIA
Malabo
CAMEROON
Douala
Yaounde
Bangui
Lake Turkana
Mogadishu
EQUATORIAL GUINEA
SÃO TOME & PRINCIPE
RIO MUNI
Congo
EQUATOR
São Tome
Libreville
GABON
CONGO
DEMOCRATIC REPUBLIC OF THE CONGO
UGANDA
Kampala
Lake Victoria
KENYA
Nairobi
Kigali
RWANDA
BURUNDI
Bujumbura
Mombasa
Brazzaville
Kinshasa
CABINDA
Ang.
Lake Tanganyika
Dodoma
TANZANIA
Dar es Salaam
SEYCHELLES
Ascension
U.K.
Luanda
Kolwezi
Lubumbashi
COMOROS
Moroni
ANGOLA
Kitwe
ZAMBIA
MALAWI
Lake Malawi
Lilongwe
Lusaka
Zambezi
MOZAMBIQUE
Mozambique Channel
MADAGASCAR
Antananarivo
Harare
ZIMBABWE
NAMIBIA
Windhoek
BOTSWANA
KALAHARI DESERT
Gaborone
Tshwane (Pretoria)
Mbabane
Maputo
TROPIC OF CAPRICORN
Johannesburg
SWAZILAND
SOUTH AFRICA
Orange
Bloemfontein
Maseru
LESOTHO
Durban
Cape Town
Cape of Good Hope
Port Elizabeth

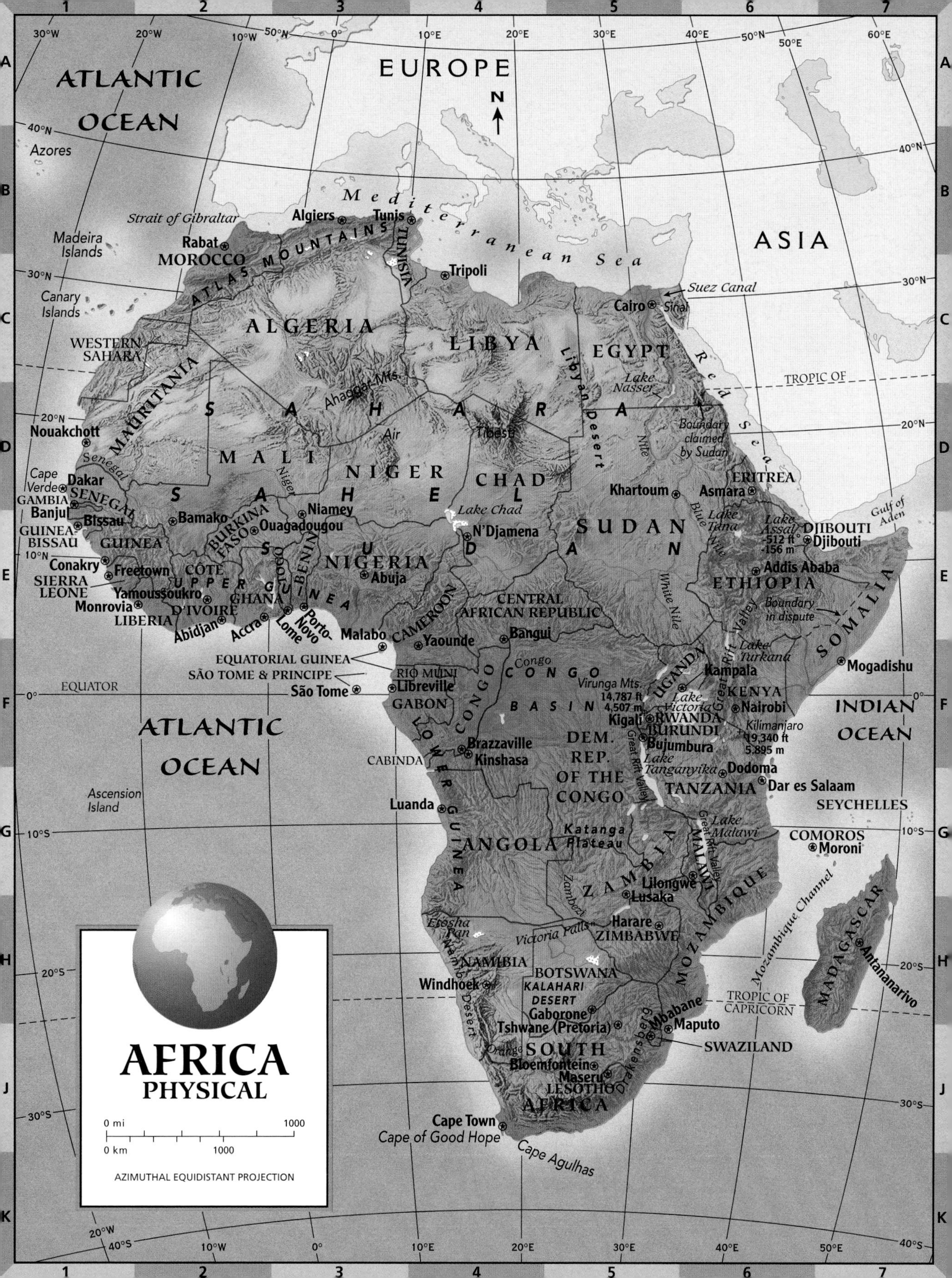

AFRICA
PHYSICAL
AZIMUTHAL EQUIDISTANT PROJECTION
0 mi
1000
0 km
1000
ATLANTIC OCEAN
EUROPE
ASIA
INDIAN OCEAN
Mediterranean Sea
Red Sea
Gulf of Aden
Mozambique Channel
Azores
Madeira Islands
Canary Islands
Strait of Gibraltar
Ascension Island
ATLAS MOUNTAINS
SAHARA
SAHEL
Ahaggar Mts.
Air
Tibesti
Libyan Desert
UPPER GUINEA
LOWER GUINEA
CONGO BASIN
KALAHARI DESERT
Namib Desert
Etosha Pan
Katanga Plateau
Drakensberg
Great Rift Valley
Virunga Mts. 14,787 ft 4,507 m
Kilimanjaro 19,340 ft 5,895 m
Lake Assal -512 ft -156 m
Lake Chad
Lake Nasser
Lake Tana
Lake Turkana
Lake Victoria
Lake Tanganyika
Lake Malawi
Victoria Falls
Nile
Blue Nile
White Nile
Niger
Senegal
Congo
Zambezi
Orange
Suez Canal
Sinai
Cape Verde
Cape of Good Hope
Cape Agulhas
Boundary claimed by Sudan
Boundary in dispute
TROPIC OF CANCER
EQUATOR
TROPIC OF CAPRICORN
MOROCCO
Rabat
ALGERIA
Algiers
TUNISIA
Tunis
LIBYA
Tripoli
EGYPT
Cairo
WESTERN SAHARA
MAURITANIA
Nouakchott
MALI
Bamako
NIGER
Niamey
CHAD
N'Djamena
SUDAN
Khartoum
ERITREA
Asmara
DJIBOUTI
Djibouti
ETHIOPIA
Addis Ababa
SOMALIA
Mogadishu
SENEGAL
Dakar
GAMBIA
Banjul
GUINEA-BISSAU
Bissau
GUINEA
Conakry
SIERRA LEONE
Freetown
LIBERIA
Monrovia
CÔTE D'IVOIRE
Yamoussoukro
Abidjan
BURKINA FASO
Ouagadougou
GHANA
Accra
TOGO
Lome
BENIN
Porto-Novo
NIGERIA
Abuja
CAMEROON
Yaounde
EQUATORIAL GUINEA
Malabo
RIO MUNI
SÃO TOME & PRINCIPE
São Tome
GABON
Libreville
CENTRAL AFRICAN REPUBLIC
Bangui
CONGO
Brazzaville
DEM. REP. OF THE CONGO
Kinshasa
CABINDA
UGANDA
Kampala
KENYA
Nairobi
RWANDA
Kigali
BURUNDI
Bujumbura
TANZANIA
Dodoma
Dar es Salaam
SEYCHELLES
COMOROS
Moroni
ANGOLA
Luanda
ZAMBIA
Lusaka
MALAWI
Lilongwe
MOZAMBIQUE
Maputo
ZIMBABWE
Harare
NAMIBIA
Windhoek
BOTSWANA
Gaborone
SOUTH AFRICA
Tshwane (Pretoria)
Bloemfontein
Cape Town
LESOTHO
Maseru
SWAZILAND
Mbabane
MADAGASCAR
Antananarivo

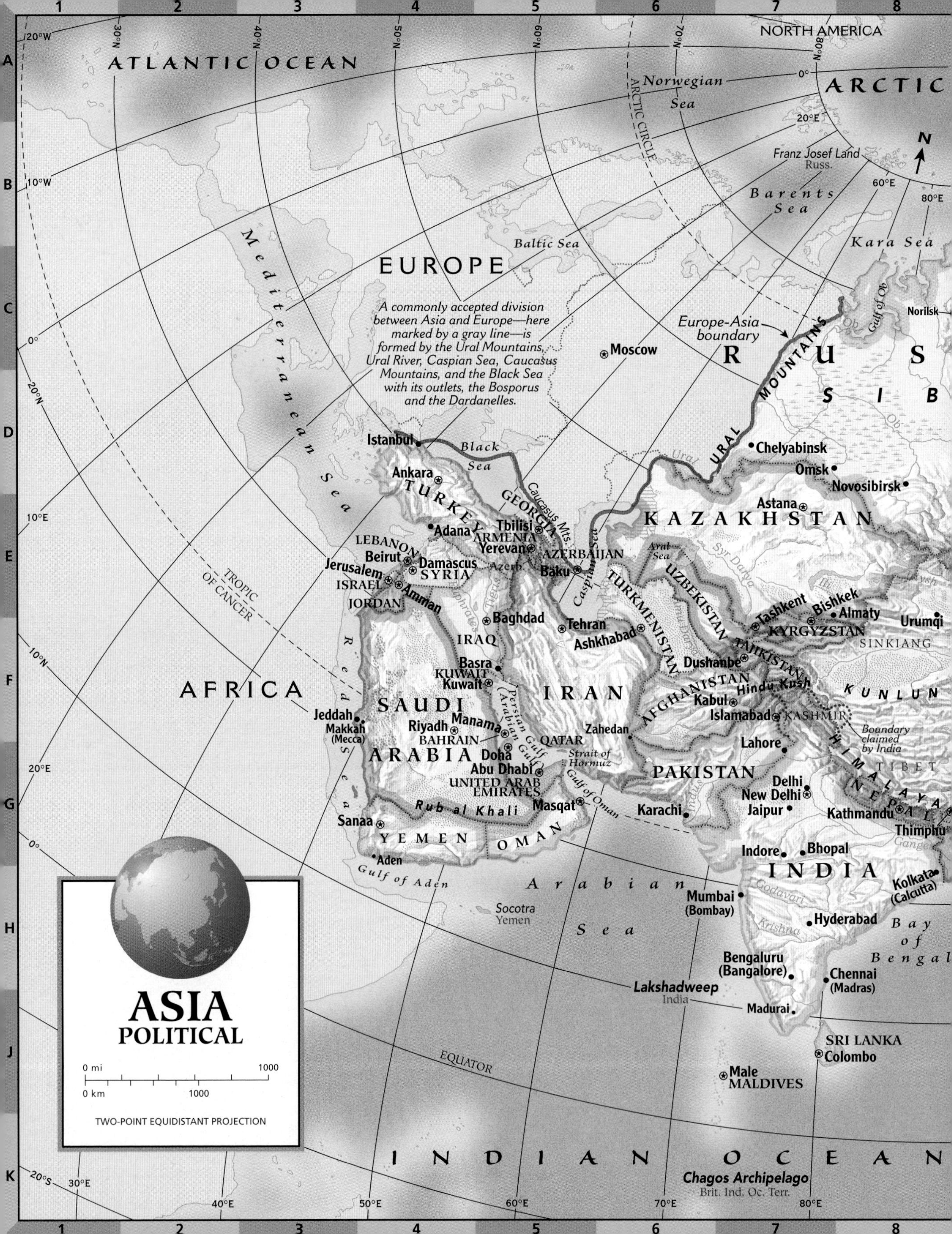

ASIA
POLITICAL
0 mi 1000
0 km 1000
TWO-POINT EQUIDISTANT PROJECTION
A commonly accepted division between Asia and Europe—here marked by a gray line—is formed by the Ural Mountains, Ural River, Caspian Sea, Caucasus Mountains, and the Black Sea with its outlets, the Bosporus and the Dardanelles.
Europe-Asia boundary
ATLANTIC OCEAN
NORTH AMERICA
ARCTIC
Norwegian Sea
ARCTIC CIRCLE
Franz Josef Land
Russ.
Barents Sea
Kara Sea
Baltic Sea
EUROPE
Mediterranean Sea
Moscow
URAL MOUNTAINS
Gulf of Ob
Norilsk
Istanbul
Black Sea
Ankara
TURKEY
GEORGIA
Caucasus Mts.
Tbilisi
Adana
ARMENIA
Yerevan
AZERBAIJAN
Azerb.
Baku
Caspian Sea
LEBANON
Beirut
Damascus
SYRIA
Jerusalem
ISRAEL
Amman
JORDAN
TROPIC OF CANCER
Chelyabinsk
Omsk
Novosibirsk
Astana
KAZAKHSTAN
Aral Sea
Syr Darya
UZBEKISTAN
TURKMENISTAN
Tashkent
Bishkek
Almaty
KYRGYZSTAN
Urumqi
SINKIANG
Baghdad
Tehran
Ashkhabad
IRAQ
Basra
KUWAIT
Kuwait
Dushanbe
TAJIKISTAN
AFGHANISTAN
Hindu Kush
Kabul
Islamabad
KASHMIR
KUNLUN
Boundary claimed by India
AFRICA
SAUDI ARABIA
IRAN
Jeddah
Makkah (Mecca)
Riyadh
Manama
BAHRAIN
Persian Gulf (Arabian Gulf)
QATAR
Doha
Zahedan
Strait of Hormuz
Abu Dhabi
UNITED ARAB EMIRATES
Gulf of Oman
Masqat
PAKISTAN
Lahore
TIBET
HIMALAYA
NEPAL
Delhi
New Delhi
Jaipur
Karachi
Kathmandu
Thimphu
Rub al Khali
Sanaa
YEMEN
OMAN
Aden
Gulf of Aden
Red Sea
Arabian Sea
Indore
Bhopal
INDIA
Kolkata (Calcutta)
Mumbai (Bombay)
Socotra
Yemen
Hyderabad
Bay of Bengal
Bengaluru (Bangalore)
Chennai (Madras)
Lakshadweep
India
Madurai
SRI LANKA
Colombo
EQUATOR
Male
MALDIVES
INDIAN OCEAN
Chagos Archipelago
Brit. Ind. Oc. Terr.

NORTH AMERICA
Bering Strait
North Pole
OCEAN
Chukchi Sea
Wrangel I.
Gulf of Anadyr
Anadyr
Bering Sea
East Siberian Sea
New Siberian Islands
North Land
Laptev Sea
Kolyma Range
Cherskiy Range
Verkhoyanski Mountains
Magadan
Commander Is.
Kamchatka Peninsula
Sea of Okhotsk
Yakutsk
SIA
ERIA
Sakhalin
Kuril Islands
Lake Baikal
Irkutsk
Hokkaido
Sapporo
MANCHURIA
Vladivostok
Sea of Japan (East Sea)
JAPAN
Tokyo
Ulaanbaatar
MONGOLIA
ALTAY MTS.
GOBI
Changchun
Shenyang
NORTH KOREA
P'yŏngyang
Seoul
SOUTH KOREA
Honshu
Kyoto
Osaka
Hiroshima
Kyushu
Marcus I. Jap.
TROPIC OF CANCER
Bonin Is. Jap.
Volcano Is. Jap.
Beijing
Qingdao
Shijiazhuang
Yellow Sea
Huang He (Yellow R.)
Xuzhou
Lanzhou
Xian
CHINA
Nanjing
Shanghai
East China Sea
Ryukyu Islands
Okinawa
Parece Vela Jap.
PACIFIC OCEAN
Chang Jiang (Yangtze R.)
Nanchang
Chengdu
Fuzhou
Taipei
Changsha
Boundary claimed by China
TAIWAN
The People's Republic of China claims Taiwan as its 23rd province.
BHUTAN
BANGLADESH
Guiyang
Guangzhou
Kunming
Hong Kong
Macau
Dhaka
MYANMAR (BURMA)
Hanoi
Haiphong
Luzon
Philippine Sea
South China Sea
Hainan
Nay Pyi Taw
Vientiane
LAOS
Quezon City
Manila
Samar
PHILIPPINES
Da Nang
Mindoro
Panay
Leyte
Negros
THAILAND
Bangkok
CAMBODIA
VIETNAM
Palawan
Mindanao
EQUATOR
Andaman Islands India
Phnom Penh
Ho Chi Minh City
Andaman Sea
Gulf of Thailand
Bandar Seri Begawan
BRUNEI
SABAH
Halmahera
Morotai
Biak
Jayapura
New Guinea
Nicobar Islands India
MALAYSIA
Kuala Lumpur
Medan
SARAWAK
Moluccas
Kepi
Merauke
Aru Is.
Dolak
SINGAPORE
Borneo
Celebes
Buru
Ceram
INDONESIA
Sumatra
Tanimbar Is.
Jambi
GREATER SUNDA ISLANDS
Mentawai Islands
Dili
EAST TIMOR (TIMOR-LESTE)
Timor Sea
Java Sea
AUSTRALIA
Jakarta
Java
Kupang

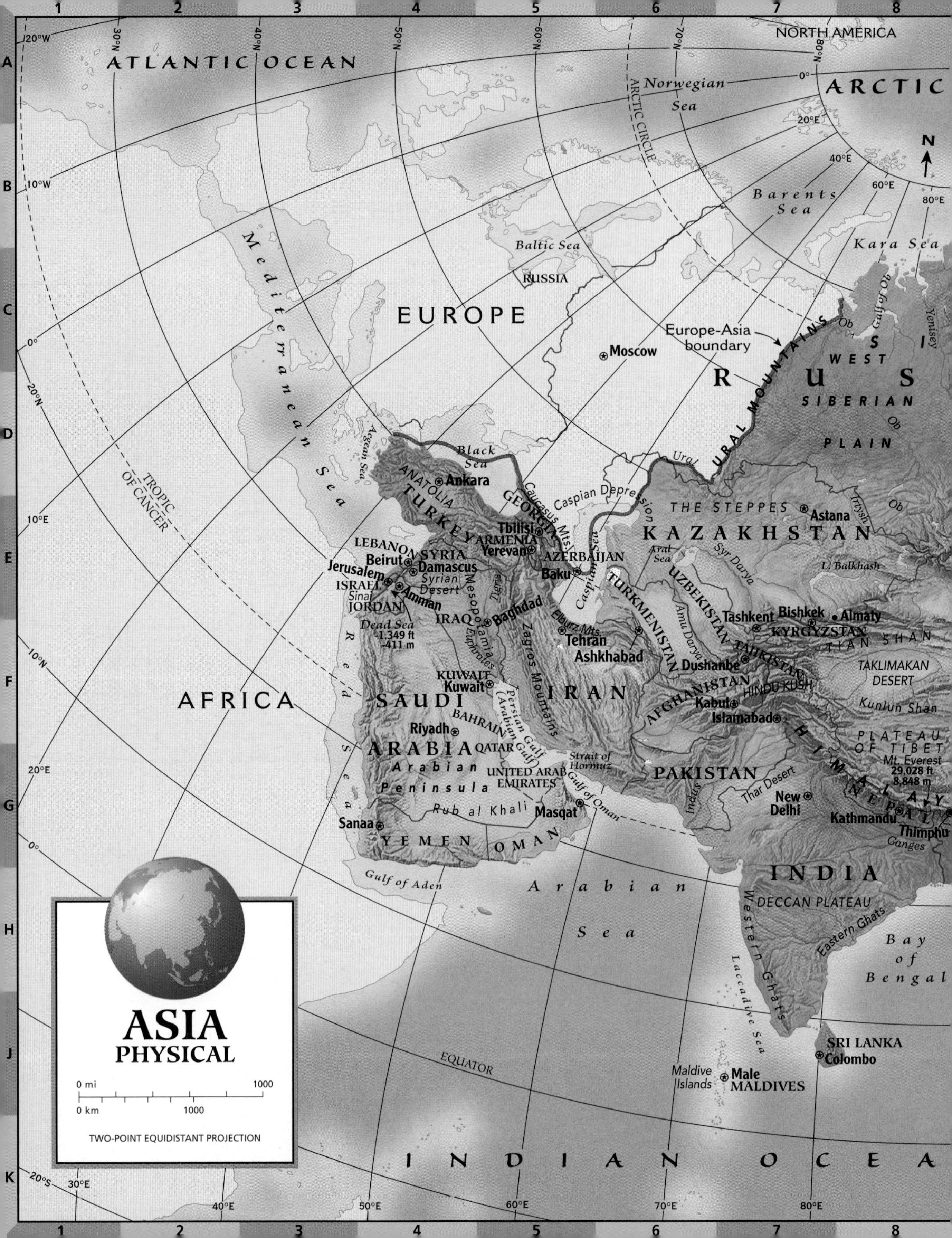
ASIA
PHYSICAL
TWO-POINT EQUIDISTANT PROJECTION
0 mi
1000
0 km
1000
ATLANTIC OCEAN
NORTH AMERICA
ARCTIC
Norwegian Sea
ARCTIC CIRCLE
Barents Sea
Kara Sea
Baltic Sea
RUSSIA
EUROPE
Mediterranean Sea
Moscow
Europe-Asia boundary
URAL MOUNTAINS
RUSSIA
WEST SIBERIAN PLAIN
Ob
Gulf of Ob
Yenisey
Irtysh
Ural
Black Sea
Aegean Sea
ANATOLIA
Ankara
TURKEY
GEORGIA
Caucasus Mts.
Tbilisi
ARMENIA
Yerevan
AZERBAIJAN
Baku
Caspian Depression
Caspian Sea
THE STEPPES
Astana
KAZAKHSTAN
Aral Sea
Syr Darya
L. Balkhash
UZBEKISTAN
TURKMENISTAN
Amu Darya
Tashkent
Bishkek
Almaty
KYRGYZSTAN
TIAN SHAN
TAJIKISTAN
Dushanbe
TAKLIMAKAN DESERT
LEBANON
SYRIA
Beirut
Damascus
Syrian Desert
Jerusalem
ISRAEL
Sinai
JORDAN
Amman
Dead Sea
-1,349 ft
-411 m
IRAQ
Mesopotamia
Tigris
Euphrates
Baghdad
Elburz Mts.
Tehran
Ashkhabad
Zagros Mountains
IRAN
KUWAIT
Kuwait
AFGHANISTAN
HINDU KUSH
Kabul
Islamabad
Kunlun Shan
PLATEAU OF TIBET
Mt. Everest
29,028 ft
8,848 m
HIMALAYA
AFRICA
TROPIC OF CANCER
Red Sea
SAUDI ARABIA
BAHRAIN
Riyadh
QATAR
Persian Gulf (Arabian Gulf)
Strait of Hormuz
UNITED ARAB EMIRATES
Gulf of Oman
Arabian Peninsula
Rub al Khali
Masqat
Sanaa
YEMEN
OMAN
PAKISTAN
Indus
Thar Desert
New Delhi
NEPAL
Kathmandu
Thimphu
Ganges
INDIA
DECCAN PLATEAU
Western Ghats
Eastern Ghats
Gulf of Aden
Arabian Sea
Bay of Bengal
Laccadive Sea
SRI LANKA
Colombo
Maldive Islands
Male
MALDIVES
EQUATOR
INDIAN OCEAN

NORTH AMERICA
Bering Strait
North Pole
OCEAN
Chukchi Sea
Chukchi Peninsula
Wrangel Island
Gulf of Anadyr
East Siberian Sea
Bering Sea
Aleutian Islands
North Land
New Siberian Islands
Laptev Sea
Taymyr Peninsula
Kolyma
Kolyma Range
Commander Islands
Cherskiy Range
Kamchatka Peninsula
Verkhoyanski Mountains
Lena
Aldan
CENTRAL SIBERIAN PLATEAU
SIBERIA
ASIA
Sea of Okhotsk
Sakhalin
Kuril Islands
PACIFIC OCEAN
Angara
Amur
Sikhote Alin Range
Hokkaido
Lake Baikal
Yablonovyy Range
Greater Khingan Range
Manchurian Plain
Yenisey
Sea of Japan (East Sea)
JAPAN
Tokyo
Ulaanbaatar
MONGOLIA
GOBI
ALTAY MOUNTAINS
NORTH KOREA
P'yongyang
Seoul
SOUTH KOREA
Honshu
Shikoku
Kyushu
Nampo Shoto
TROPIC OF CANCER
Beijing
North China Plain
Yellow Sea
Huang He (Yellow R.)
Qaidam Basin
East China Sea
Ryukyu Islands
CHINA
Mekong
Yangtze
Salween
Sichuan Basin
Chang Jiang (Yangtze R.)
Mariana Islands
Gongga Shan 24,790 ft 7,556 m
Taipei
TAIWAN
Philippine Sea
BHUTAN
Brahmaputra
BANGLADESH
Dhaka
Hanoi
MYANMAR (BURMA)
LAOS
Luzon
PHILIPPINE ISLANDS
Caroline Islands
Nay Pyi Taw
Vientiane
Hainan
South China Sea
Manila
PHILIPPINES
THAILAND
Bangkok
CAMBODIA
VIETNAM
EQUATOR
Andaman Islands
Phnom Penh
Sulu Sea
Mindanao
Andaman Sea
Gulf of Thailand
Malay Peninsula
Bandar Seri Begawan
BRUNEI
MALAYSIA
Celebes Sea
Moluccas
New Guinea
Nicobar Islands
Kuala Lumpur
SINGAPORE
Borneo
Celebes
INDONESIA
Sumatra
Arafura Sea
GREATER SUNDA ISLANDS
Mentawai Islands
Java Sea
Dili
EAST TIMOR (TIMOR-LESTE)
Timor Sea
AUSTRALIA
Jakarta
Java

1
2
3
4
5
6
7
8
A
B
C
D
E
F
G
H
J
K
RUSSIA
KAMCHATKA PENINSULA
Bering Sea
Sea of Okhotsk
ALEUTIAN ISLANDS
Lake Baikal
Yablonovyy Range
Sakhalin
Amur
Sikhote Alin Range
KURIL ISLANDS
Greater Khingan Range
Manchurian Plain
Ulaanbaatar
MONGOLIA
ALTAY MOUNTAINS
GOBI
Hokkaido
Beijing
P'yŏngyang
NORTH KOREA
Sea of Japan (East Sea)
Seoul
SOUTH KOREA
Honshu
JAPAN
Tokyo
Huang He (Yellow)
Yellow Sea
NORTH PACIF
CHINA
Kyushu
Shikoku
NAMPO SHOTO
Chiang Jiang (Yangtze)
Mekong
East China Sea
RYUKYU ISLANDS
Hawaiian
INDIA
Taipei
TAIWAN
MYANMAR (BURMA)
Hanoi
Nay Pyi Taw
Hainan
LAOS
VIETNAM
Vientiane
THAILAND
Bangkok
CAMBODIA
Phnom Penh
Luzon
South China Sea
Manila
PHILIPPINE ISLANDS
PHILIPPINES
Philippine Sea
NORTHERN MARIANA ISLANDS U.S.
MARIANA ISLANDS
MICRONESIA
GUAM U.S.
MARSHALL ISLANDS
Ratak Chain
Ralik Chain
Majuro
POLYNESIA
Andaman Sea
Sulu Sea
PALAU
Melekeok
CAROLINE ISLANDS
Palikir
Bandar Seri Begawan
BRUNEI
Mindanao
FEDERATED STATES OF MICRONESIA
Kuala Lumpur
MALAYSIA
SINGAPORE
Borneo
Celebes Sea
Tarawa (Bairiki)
Gilbert Islands
Yaren
NAURU
KIRIBATI
Phoenix Is.
Sumatra
INDONESIA
GREATER SUNDA ISLANDS
Celebes
MOLUCCAS
NEW GUINEA
MELANESIA
Jakarta
Java Sea
PAPUA NEW GUINEA
SOLOMON ISLANDS
TUVALU
Funafuti
Tokelau N.Z.
Java
LESSER SUNDA ISLANDS
Dili
EAST TIMOR (TIMOR-LESTE)
Arafura Sea
Port Moresby
Solomon Is.
Honiara
Santa Cruz Islands
WALLIS AND FUTUNA IS. Fr.
AMERICAN SAMOA U.S.
SAMOA
Apia
CORAL SEA ISLANDS TERRITORY Austral.
VANUATU
Port-Vila
Suva
FIJI ISLANDS
TONGA
Niue N.Z.
NEW CALEDONIA Fr.
Nuku'alofa
TROPIC OF CAPRICORN
Coral Sea
AUSTRALIA
Norfolk Island Austral.
Darling
Lord Howe Island Austral.
Kermadec Islands N.Z.
Great Australian Bight
Canberra
Tasman Sea
NEW ZEALAND
Wellington
INDIAN OCEAN
Tasmania
Chatham Island N.Z.
105°E
120°E
135°E
150°E
165°E
180°

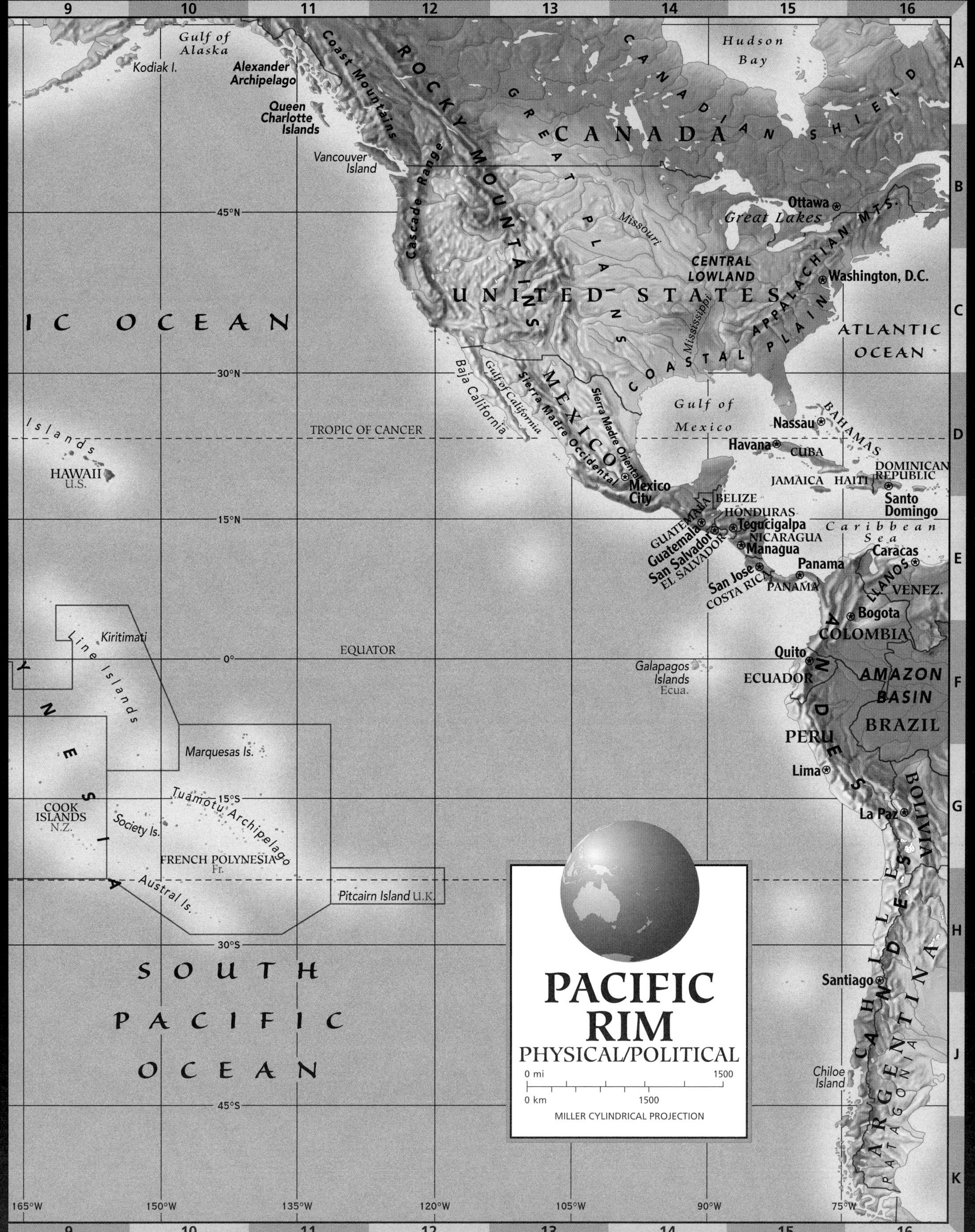
PACIFIC
RIM
PHYSICAL/POLITICAL
0 mi
1500
0 km
1500
MILLER CYLINDRICAL PROJECTION
Gulf of Alaska
Kodiak I.
Alexander Archipelago
Queen Charlotte Islands
Vancouver Island
Coast Mountains
ROCKY MOUNTAINS
GREAT PLAINS
CANADIAN SHIELD
CANADA
Hudson Bay
Cascade Range
Missouri
Great Lakes
Ottawa
APPALACHIAN MTS.
CENTRAL LOWLAND
Washington, D.C.
UNITED STATES
Mississippi
COASTAL PLAIN
ATLANTIC OCEAN
IC OCEAN
Baja California
Gulf of California
Sierra Madre Occidental
Sierra Madre Oriental
MEXICO
Gulf of Mexico
Nassau
BAHAMAS
TROPIC OF CANCER
Islands
HAWAII
U.S.
Havana
CUBA
JAMAICA
HAITI
DOMINICAN REPUBLIC
Santo Domingo
Mexico City
BELIZE
HONDURAS
GUATEMALA
Guatemala
Tegucigalpa
San Salvador
EL SALVADOR
NICARAGUA
Managua
Caribbean Sea
Caracas
Panama
San Jose
COSTA RICA
PANAMA
LLANOS
VENEZ.
Bogota
COLOMBIA
Kiritimati
Line Islands
EQUATOR
Quito
Galapagos Islands
Ecua.
ECUADOR
AMAZON BASIN
BRAZIL
PERU
Marquesas Is.
Lima
ANDES
Tuamotu Archipelago
COOK ISLANDS
N.Z.
Society Is.
FRENCH POLYNESIA
Fr.
La Paz
BOLIVIA
Austral Is.
Pitcairn Island U.K.
Santiago
CHILE
ARGENTINA
SOUTH PACIFIC OCEAN
Chiloe Island
PATAGONIA
45°N
30°N
15°N
0°
15°S
30°S
45°S
165°W
150°W
135°W
120°W
105°W
90°W
75°W

GEOGRAPHIC DICTIONARY

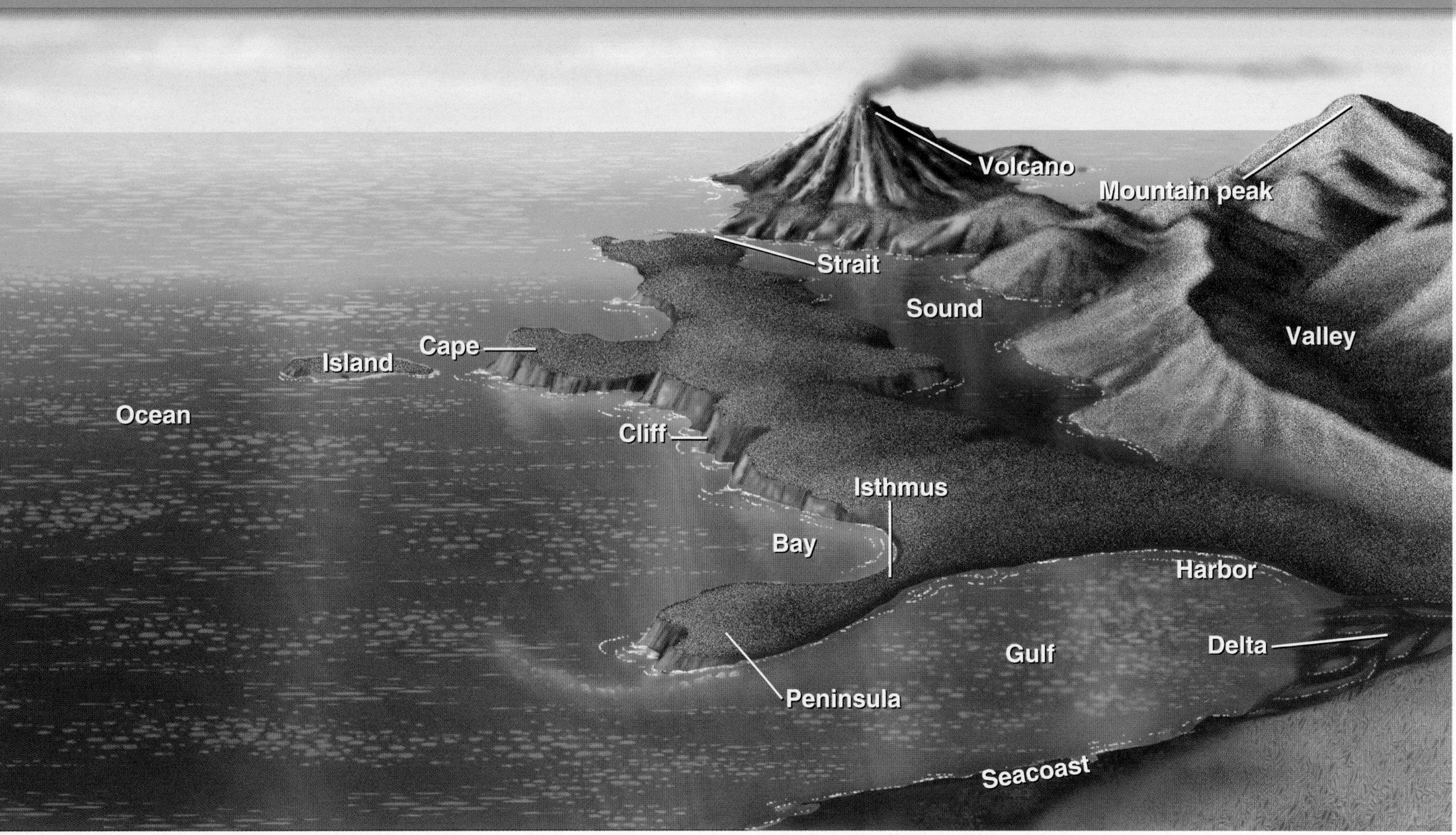

absolute location exact location of a place on the Earth described by global coordinates

basin area of land drained by a given river and its branches; area of land surrounded by lands of higher elevations

bay part of a large body of water that extends into a shoreline, generally smaller than a gulf

canyon deep and narrow valley with steep walls

cape point of land that extends into a river, lake, or ocean

channel wide strait or waterway between two landmasses that lie close to each other; deep part of a river or other waterway

cliff steep, high wall of rock, earth, or ice

continent one of the seven large landmasses on the Earth

cultural feature characteristic that humans have created in a place, such as language, religion, housing, and settlement pattern

delta flat, low-lying land built up from soil carried downstream by a river and deposited at its mouth

divide stretch of high land that separates river systems

downstream direction in which a river or stream flows from its source to its mouth

elevation height of land above sea level

Equator imaginary line that runs around the Earth halfway between the North and South Poles; used as the starting point to measure degrees of north and south latitude

glacier large, thick body of slowly moving ice

gulf part of a large body of water that extends into a shoreline, generally larger and more deeply indented than a bay

harbor a sheltered place along a shoreline where ships can anchor safely

highland elevated land area such as a hill, mountain, or plateau

hill elevated land with sloping sides and rounded summit; generally smaller than a mountain

island land area, smaller than a continent, completely surrounded by water

isthmus narrow stretch of land connecting two larger land areas

lake a large inland body of water

latitude distance north or south of the Equator, measured in degrees

longitude distance east or west of the Prime Meridian, measured in degrees

lowland land, usually level, at a low elevation

map drawing of the Earth shown on a flat surface

meridian one of many lines on the global grid running from the North Pole to the South Pole; used to measure degrees of longitude

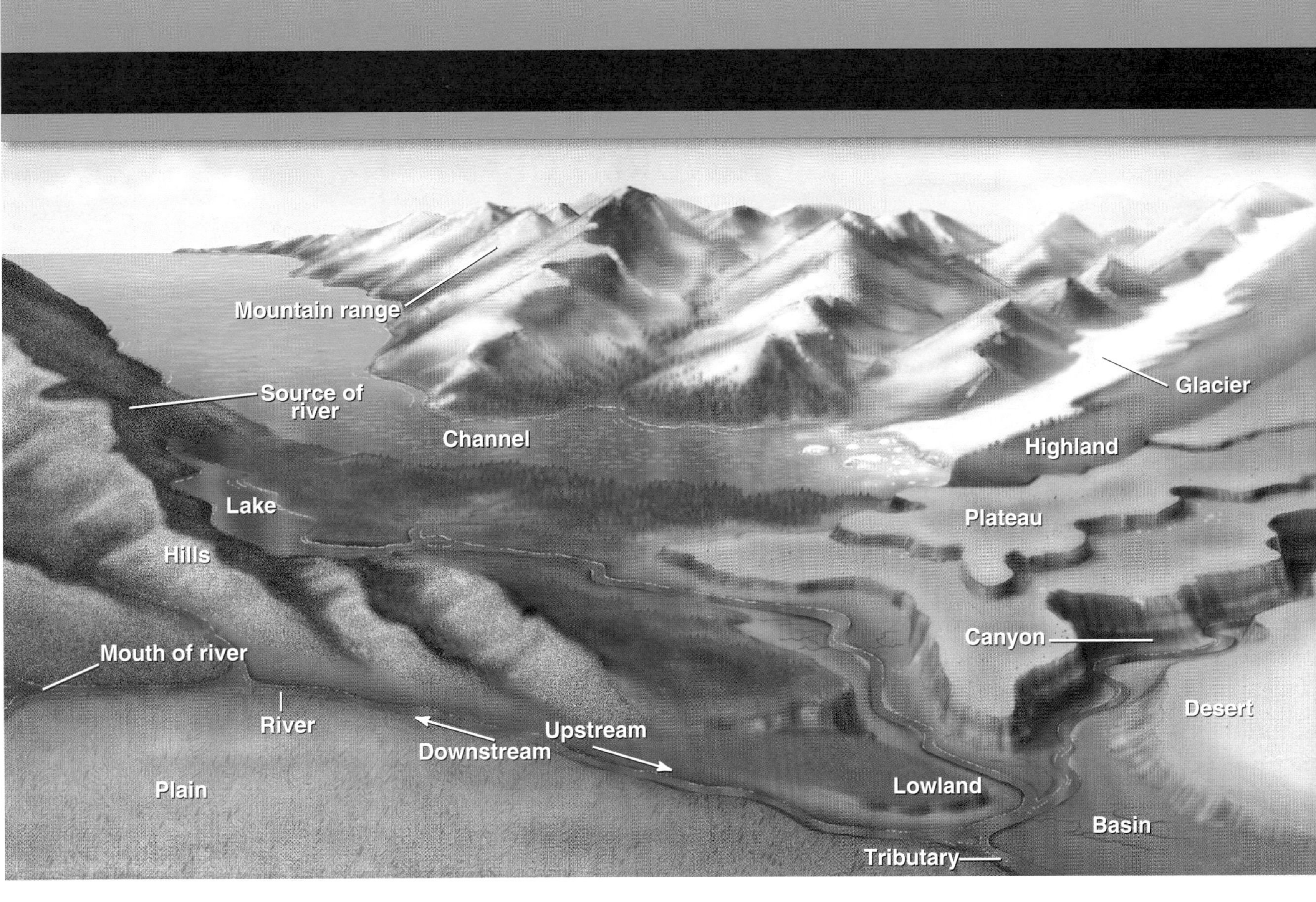

mesa broad, flat-topped landform with steep sides; smaller than a plateau

mountain land with steep sides that rises sharply (1,000 feet or more) from surrounding land; generally larger and more rugged than a hill

mountain peak pointed top of a mountain

mountain range a series of connected mountains

mouth (of a river) place where a stream or river flows into a larger body of water

ocean one of the four major bodies of salt water that surround the continents

ocean current stream of either cold or warm water that moves in a definite direction through an ocean

parallel one of many lines on the global grid that circle the Earth north and south of the Equator; used to measure degrees of latitude

peninsula body of land jutting into a lake or ocean, surrounded on three sides by water

physical feature characteristic of a place occurring naturally, such as a landform, body of water, climate pattern, or resource

plain area of level land, usually at a low elevation and often covered with grasses

plateau large area of flat or rolling land at a high elevation, about 300 to 3,000 feet (90 to 900 m) high

Prime Meridian line of the global grid running from the North Pole to the South Pole at Greenwich, England; starting point for measuring degrees of east and west longitude

relief changes in elevation over a given area of land

river large natural stream of water that runs through land

sea large body of water completely surrounded by land

seacoast land lying next to a sea or ocean

sea level position on land level with surface of nearby ocean or sea

sound body of water between a coastline and one or more islands off the coast

source (of a river) place where a river or stream begins, often in highlands

strait narrow stretch of water joining two larger bodies of water

tributary small river or stream that flows into a larger river or stream; a branch of the river

upstream direction opposite the flow of a river; toward the source of a river or stream

valley area of low land between hills or mountains

volcano mountain created as ash or liquid rock erupts from inside the Earth

A WORLD OF EXTREMES

1. **The largest continent** is Asia with an area of 12,262,691 sq. miles (31,758,898 sq. km).

2. **The smallest continent** is Australia with an area of 2,988,888 sq. miles (7,741,184 sq. km).

3. **The largest country** is Russia with an area of 6,592,819 sq. miles (17,075,322 sq. km).

4. **The smallest country** is Vatican City with an area of 1 sq. mile (2.6 sq. km).

5. **The longest river** is the Nile River with a length of 4,160 miles (6,695 km).

6. **The deepest lake** is Lake Baikal with a maximum depth of 5,715 feet (1,742 m).

7. **The highest waterfall** is Angel Falls with a height of 3,212 feet (979 m).

8. **The highest mountain** is Mount Everest with a height of 29,028 feet (8,848 m) above sea level.

9. **The largest desert** is the Sahara with an area of 3,500,000 sq. miles (9,065,000 sq. km).

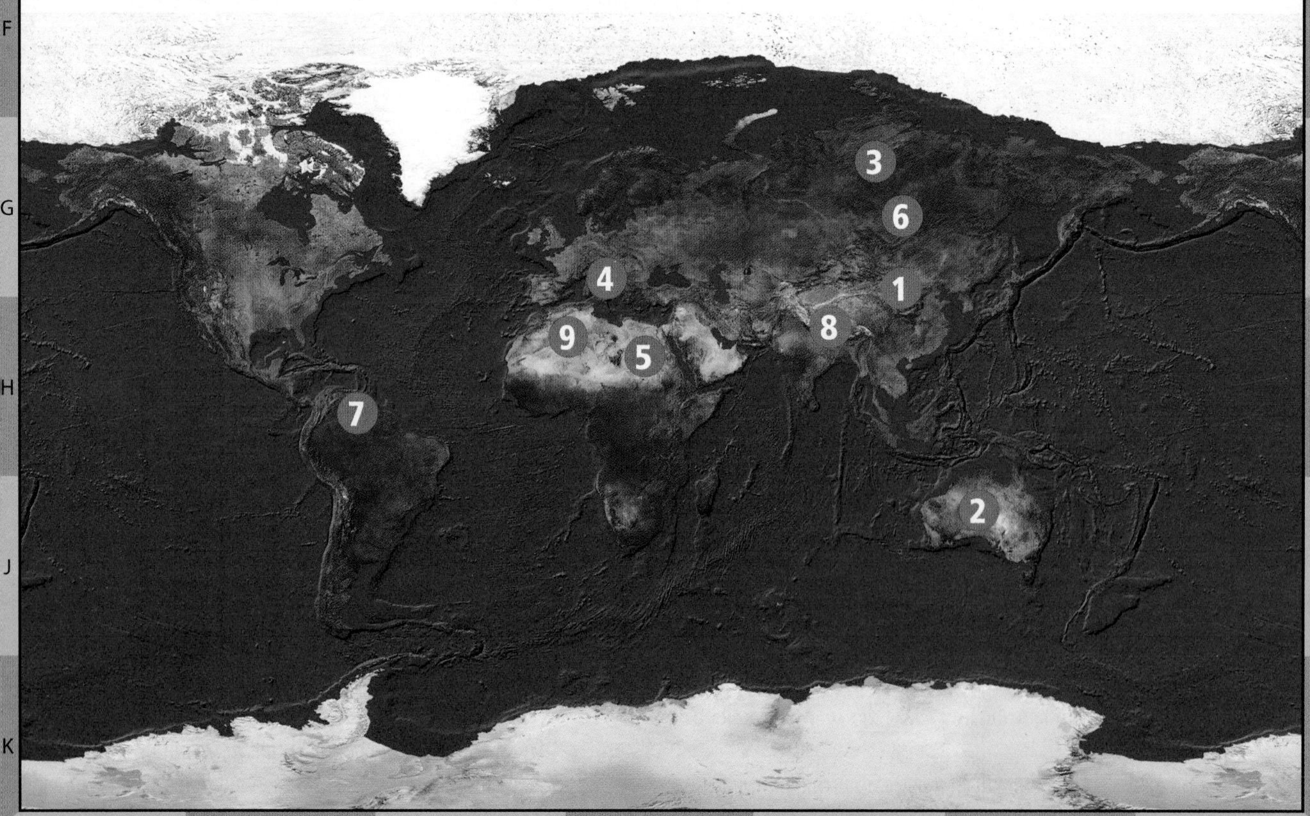

SCAVENGER HUNT

NETWORKS contains a wealth of information. The trick is to know where to look to access all the information in the book. If you complete this scavenger hunt exercise with your teachers or parents, you will see how the textbook is organized and how to get the most out of your reading and studying time. Let's get started!

1 **How many chapters are in this book?** 23

2 **Where in the front of the book can you find page numbers for each lesson?** Table of Contents

3 **What is the title of Chapter 2?** Studying Geography, Economics, and Citizenship

4 **What Essential Questions will you answer in Chapter 5?**
How does geography influence the way people live? What makes a culture unique? Why do civilizations rise and fall?

5 **Who is discussed in the biography feature of Chapter 6, Lesson 1?** Moses

6 **What is the *Thinking Like a Historian* activity for Chapter 8?**
Researching on the Internet. Students should use reliable sources to learn what Philip's goals were and why he wanted to conquer the Greeks as opposed to being their allies.

7 **What time period does Chapter 11 cover?**
500 B.C. to A.D. 180

8 **What is the title of Lesson 2 in Chapter 12?**
Rome's Decline

9 **Where in the back of the book can you find the meaning of vocabulary words such as *ephor*?**
Glossary

10 **Where in the back of the book can you find page numbers for information about citizenship?**
Index

ONLINE RESOURCES
networks

There's More Online!

- INTERACTIVE WORKSHEETS
- BIOGRAPHIES
- CHARTS/GRAPHS
- GAMES
- GRAPHIC ORGANIZERS
- IMAGES
- MAPS
- PRIMARY SOURCES
- SLIDE SHOWS
- TIME LINE
- LECTURE SLIDES
- INTERACTIVE WHITEBOARD ACTIVITIES
- ASSESSMENTS
- VIDEOS

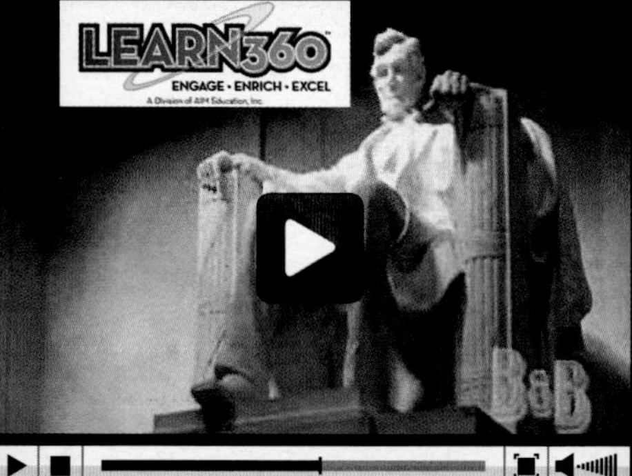

Great Reasons to Learn History

Uncovering the Past

Internet Research Techniques

Chapter 1

What Does a Historian Do?

Dear World History Teacher,

Before you plan your lessons for this chapter, think about the following information to help you focus on the concepts to cover during class.

People have said that history is everything that has happened since the beginning of time. This definition, however, is so broad that it is ineffective. History has a more common meaning as a record of the past. To create this record, historians use documents, artifacts such as pottery, tools, and weapons, and even artworks. History, according to this definition, really began over five thousand years ago when people first started to write and keep records.

History could also be defined as a special field of study. Herodotus, who lived in Greece during the fifth century B.C., is often regarded as the "father of history" in Western civilization. In his historical accounts of the Greek and Persian Wars, Herodotus used evidence, tried to tell a good story, and showed a concern for the causes and effects of events.

In the nineteenth and twentieth centuries, history became an academic discipline—a formal field of study that is taught in schools and universities. Leopold von Ranke, a nineteenth-century German historian, is often thought of as the father of this new approach to history. He created techniques for the critical analysis of documents and supported the creation of formal courses in universities to train new historians. As a result, historians today not only uncover factual evidence, but also use critical thinking to explain the cause-and-effect relationships that exist among the facts.

Jackson J. Spielvogel

More Media Resources

Current Events Online

Visit McGraw-Hill's current events Web site for high-interest news stories and activities for your students. Access the site through the Student or Teacher Center in **networks.**

Reading List

Grade 6 reading level:
Ancient Celts: Archaeology Unlocks the Secrets of the Celts' Past, by Jen Green

Grade 7 reading level:
Archaeology, by Trevor Barnes

Grade 8 reading level:
Take Me Back: A Trip through History from the Stone Age to the Digital Age, by DK Publishing

CHAPTER 1 Planner

UNDERSTANDING BY DESIGN®

Enduring Understanding

- ***Learning about the past helps us understand the present and make decisions about the future.***

Essential Questions

- ***Why is history important?*** • ***How do we learn about the past?***
- ***How do you research history?***

Students will know:

- *why people study history*
- *what artifacts historians use to understand the past*
- *guidelines for researching*
- *how to work safely using the Internet*

Students will be able to:

- **contribute** to a group activity about why people study history
- **understand and recall** concepts of time
- **synthesize** their understanding of how eras are named and apply this understanding to naming today
- **analyze** what makes a source reliable
- **categorize** by primary or secondary source
- **evaluate** reliable sources
- **distinguish** fact from opinion
- **recognize** bias

Predictable Misunderstandings

Students may think:

- It is unnecessary to learn about the past.
- It is acceptable to copy information from sources, especially those they find on the Internet.
- All sources are equally reliable.

Assessment Evidence

Performance Task

- Hands-On Chapter Project

Other Evidence

- Lesson Reviews
- Primary Source Activity
- 21st Century Skills Activities
- Answers to identifying names for the current time period
- Identification of classroom artifacts
- *What Do You Think?* questions
- Interactive Graphic Organizers
- Responses to place mat cooperative learning activity
- Participation in class discussion about primary and secondary sources
- Participation in a discussion about where to find answers
- Responses to Interactive Whiteboard Activities

Pacing Guide

Introducing the Chapter	1 day
Lesson 1 What Is History?	1 day
Lesson 2 How Does a Historian Work?	1 day
What Do You Think?	1 day
Lesson 3 Researching History	1 day
Chapter Activities and Assessment	1 day
TOTAL TIME	**6 Days**

Differentiated Instruction

These lesson plans are written to address the needs of your On Level students. Discussion and activities that are well-suited to your Approaching Grade Level learners, Beyond Grade Level learners, as well as your English Language Learners are coded as follows:

AL Approaching Grade Level

BL Beyond Grade Level

ELL English Language Learner

NCSS Standards in "What Does a Historian Do?"

Learners will understand:

2 TIME, CONTINUITY, AND CHANGE

1. The study of the past provides representation of the history of communities, nations, and the world.

2. Concepts such as: chronology, causality, change, conflict, complexity, multiple perspectives, primary and secondary sources, and cause and effect.

3. That learning about the past requires the interpretation of sources, and that using varied sources provides the potential for a more balanced interpretive record of the past.

4. That historical interpretations of the same event may differ on the basis of such factors as conflicting evidence from varied sources, national or cultural perspectives, and the point of view of the researcher.

4 INDIVIDUAL DEVELOPMENT AND IDENTITY

6. That perceptions are interpretations of information about individuals and events, and can be influenced by bias and stereotypes.

8 SCIENCE, TECHNOLOGY, AND SOCIETY

3. Our lives today are media and technology dependent.

CHAPTER 1

Introducing the Chapter

(Student Edition p. 1)

The Story Matters . . .

Read "The Story Matters . . ." aloud in class. Alternately, ask a volunteer to read it aloud. Then, challenge students to brainstorm a list of people who would have worked to make the museum exhibit possible.

Ask: **Who would have to work on this project to make it happen?** Remind students that someone had to find, clean, replicate, transport, reassemble, and advertise the museum exhibit.

Then ask: **Why do you think people would be interested in learning more about the terra-cotta warriors?**

Explain to students that the terra-cotta warriors were part of an elaborate burial ceremony for China's first emperor. Compare them to the pyramids in Egypt, which are also part of elaborate burial rituals. Explain that just as people all over the world are interested in learning about the Egyptian pyramids, so too are they interested in the warriors of China. People are interested in the customs of people throughout history.

What Does a Historian Do?

ESSENTIAL QUESTIONS • *Why is history important?* • *How do we learn about the past?* • *How do you research history?*

networks

There's More Online about historians and how they work.

CHAPTER 1

Lesson 1 *What Is History?*

Lesson 2 *How Does a Historian Work?*

Lesson 3 *Researching History*

The Story Matters . . .

Hundreds of terra-cotta warriors stood, silent and without expression, in the empty exhibit hall. They were replicas of the original statues found in China in 1974. Since their discovery, the warriors, dating from 210 B.C., had fascinated historians. Why were they created? How had they remained a buried secret for centuries?

The mystery of the warriors captured the imaginations of people all over the world. Museums asked for a chance to show the statues in their cities. Researchers carefully created exact replicas of the statues that would be strong enough to travel around the world. Museum workers like this one in Dresden, Germany, assembled heads, arms, and bodies in exactly the correct order. Thousands of visitors came to marvel at the beautiful and mysterious warriors.

◄ *A museum employee places the head on a statue in the Terra-cotta Warriors exhibit at the Dresden Energy Museum.*

AFP/Getty Images

1

Introducing Place and Time (Student Edition pp. 2–3)

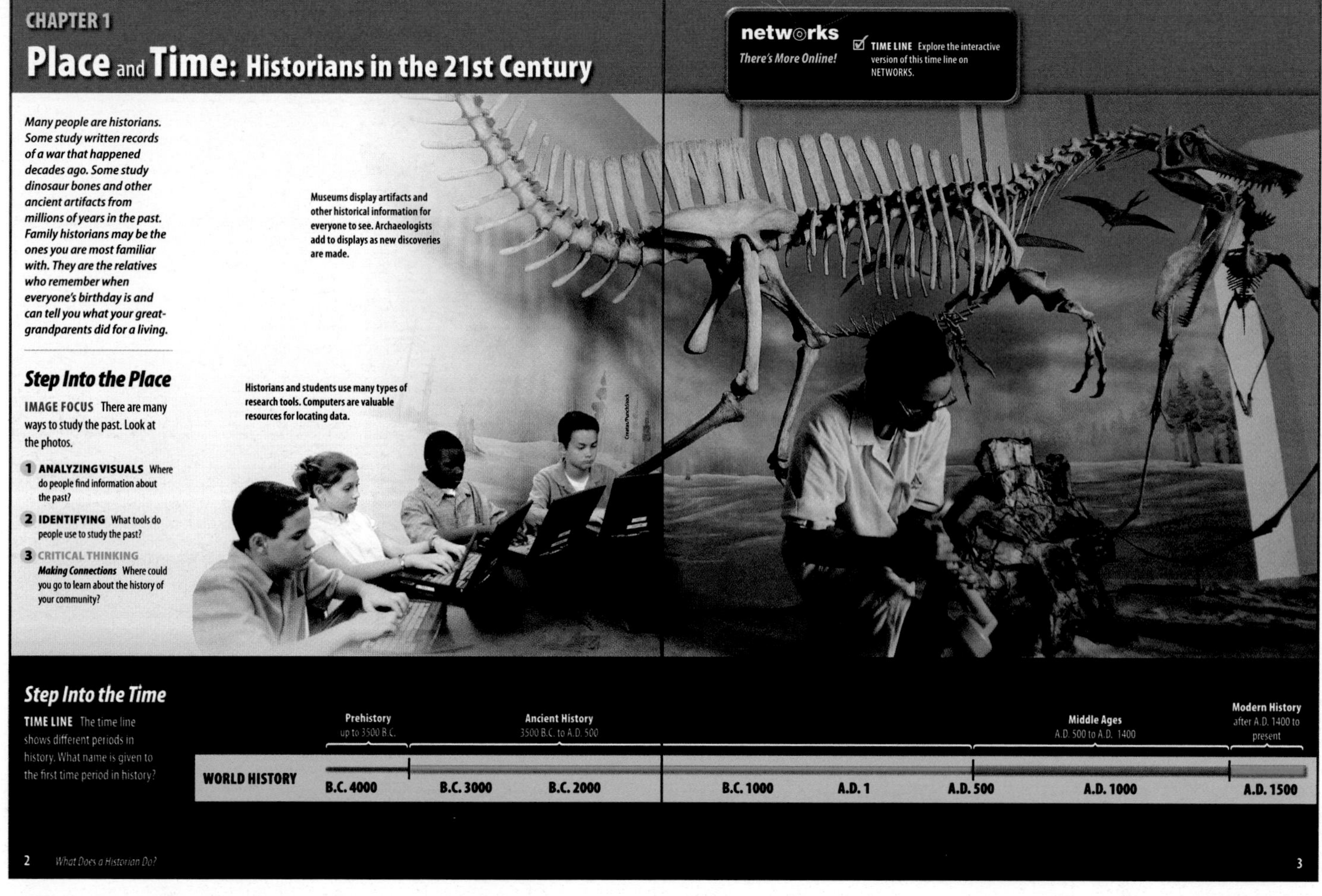

CHAPTER 1

Place and Time: Historians in the 21st Century

networks *There's More Online!* TIME LINE Explore the interactive version of this time line on NETWORKS.

Many people are historians. Some study written records of a war that happened decades ago. Some study dinosaur bones and other ancient artifacts from millions of years in the past. Family historians may be the ones you are most familiar with. They are the relatives who remember when everyone's birthday is and can tell you what your great-grandparents did for a living.

Museums display artifacts and other historical information for everyone to see. Archaeologists add to displays as new discoveries are made.

Historians and students use many types of research tools. Computers are valuable resources for locating data.

Step Into the Place

IMAGE FOCUS There are many ways to study the past. Look at the photos.

1 ANALYZING VISUALS Where do people find information about the past?

2 IDENTIFYING What tools do people use to study the past?

3 CRITICAL THINKING *Making Connections* Where could you go to learn about the history of your community?

Step Into the Time

TIME LINE The time line shows different periods in history. What name is given to the first time period in history?

2 *What Does a Historian Do?* 3

edtechteacher
21st Century Learning

Technology Extension

- Find an additional activity online that incorporates technology for this project.
- Visit the EdTechTeacher Web sites (included in the Technology Extension for this chapter) for more links, tutorials, and other resources.

Assessing Background Knowledge

What Do You Know? Activity

INTERACTIVE WORKSHEET

Have students complete the What Do You Know? Sentence Starter about what historians do, before they study the chapter. Have students think about the skills historians need to study the past. Then have them circle each task that historians must perform for their work.

After students complete the chapter, have them return to the list. Discuss how the historian's job might be different from what they expected.

INTERACTIVE WORKSHEET

Guided Reading Activities

There is a Guided Reading Activity for each lesson in this chapter. You might want to assign the Guided Reading Activity for Lesson 1 after introducing the chapter content.

Hands-On Chapter Project

Students will learn how to evaluate sources and determine their reliability and credibility.

- Through class discussion, students will review the definitions of primary and secondary sources, the concept of bias, and methods for determining whether a Web site is reliable.
- Guided by discussion and worksheets, students will choose a research topic of interest.
- Next, students will research their topic using at least one Web site and one print resource.
- Once they have completed their individual research, students will form small groups to discuss the quality and reliability of their sources.
- Finally, students will use an Assessment Rubric to evaluate their research, their understanding of reliable and unreliable sources, and their collaboration.

Visit **networks** online to see the full project and rubric.

Step Into the Place

Human-Environment Interaction Direct students' attention to the Chapter Opener images of historians at work. Ask volunteers to read the captions. Have students identify the activities in each picture and then explain how the images relate to history.

Find images of archaeologists at work and show them to students. Have students consider what it might be like to be part of a research team digging for artifacts. Have them explain what the job might involve. Encourage them to use details from the images to support their answers.

Ask: Is this what you would expect to be the job of a historian?

As a class, discuss the Image Focus questions.

Step Into the Time

Interpreting Have students review the time line for the chapter. Point out elements that are common to many time lines, including the letters B.C. and A.D., the numbers that indicate the year that something took place, and benchmark dates. Have students explain what each element of the time line means. Explain that they will learn about the parts of a time line in this chapter.

Ask students: On the time line, point out the time in which you live. *(Modern History)*

Answers for pages 2–3

Step Into the Place

1. People find information about the past in the ground, in books and documents, in museums, and online.
2. People use digging tools and computers.
3. Students should identify local libraries and museums as sources of local history.

Step Into the Time Prehistory

ONLINE RESOURCES

networks

Assign these interactive worksheets and quizzes from your Teacher Lesson Center. All resources are print-ready.

It's ALL Online!

CHAPTER 1 RESOURCES

- ☑ CHAPTER SUMMARY
- ☑ VOCABULARY BUILDER
- ☑ WHAT DO YOU KNOW?
- ☑ HANDS-ON CHAPTER PROJECT

Lesson 1 Resources

- ☑ INTERACTIVE GRAPHIC ORGANIZER
- ☑ PRIMARY SOURCE ACTIVITY
  The White House Renovation
- ☑ GUIDED READING ACTIVITY
- ☑ READING ESSENTIALS AND STUDY GUIDE
- ☑ ONLINE SELF-CHECK QUIZ

Lesson 2 Resources

- ☑ INTERACTIVE GRAPHIC ORGANIZER
- ☑ 21ST CENTURY SKILLS ACTIVITY
  Recognize Bias
- ☑ GUIDED READING ACTIVITY
- ☑ READING ESSENTIALS AND STUDY GUIDE
- ☑ ONLINE SELF-CHECK QUIZ

Lesson 3 Resources

- ☑ INTERACTIVE GRAPHIC ORGANIZER
- ☑ 21ST CENTURY SKILLS ACTIVITY
  Distinguish Facts and Opinions
- ☑ GUIDED READING ACTIVITY
- ☑ READING ESSENTIALS AND STUDY GUIDE
- ☑ ONLINE SELF-CHECK QUIZ

ASSESSMENT RESOURCES

- ☑ LESSON REVIEWS
- ☑ ONLINE SELF-CHECK QUIZZES
- ☑ CHAPTER ACTIVITIES AND ASSESSMENT
- ☑ STANDARDIZED TEST PRACTICE

REMEDIATION RESOURCES

- ☑ READING ESSENTIALS AND STUDY GUIDE
- ☑ GUIDED READING ACTIVITIES
- ☑ ONLINE SELF-CHECK QUIZZES
- ☑ CHAPTER SUMMARY

networks
There's More Online!
- **GAME** Time Periods
- **GRAPHIC ORGANIZERS**
  - Studying History
  - The Julian and Gregorian Calendars
- **SLIDE SHOW** Heinrich Schliemann

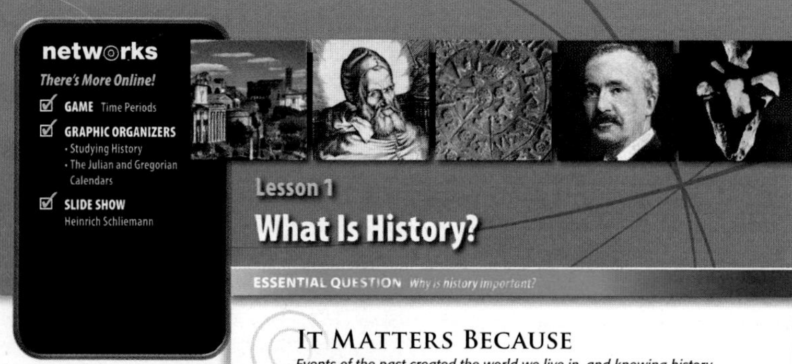

Lesson 1

What Is History?

ESSENTIAL QUESTION *Why is history important?*

IT MATTERS BECAUSE

Events of the past created the world we live in, and knowing history can help us make decisions about the future.

1 Why Study History?

GUIDING QUESTION *What types of things can history reveal about the past?*

History is the study of the people and events of the past. History explores both the way things change and the way things stay the same. History tells the story of the ways that cultures change over time.

People who study history are called historians. A historian's job is to examine the causes, or reasons, that something happened in the past. They also look for the effects, or results, of the event. They ask, "What happened?" and "Why did it happen?" They ask, "How did things change?" and "How has it influenced today?" Sometimes they ask, "What would have happened if . . . ?"

History explains why things are the way they are. The invention of the wheel in prehistoric times paved the way for the use of horse-drawn carts in later time periods. The carts were a step toward the invention of the automobile in modern times. Today, cars are an **integral** part of our culture.

Learning about the past helps us understand the present. It helps us make decisions about the future. Historical instances of conflict and cooperation are examples we can learn from. We can use that knowledge when we face similar choices.

Reading HELPDESK

Taking Notes: ***Categorizing***

Use a graphic organizer like the one shown here to list the important details about studying history.

Studying History		
Reasons to Study History	Measuring Historical Time	People Who Study Time

Content Vocabulary
- era
- archaeology
- artifact
- paleontology
- fossil
- anthropology
- species

Studying history helps us understand how we fit into the human story. Some of the clues are the languages we speak, the technologies we use, and the pastimes we enjoy. All these are results of events that happened in the past. History teaches us who we are.

PROGRESS CHECK

Explaining Why is it important to understand cause and effect when studying the past?

2 Measuring Time

GUIDING QUESTION *What are historical periods?*

To study the past, historians must have a way to identify and describe when things happened. They do that by measuring and labeling time in different ways.

Periods of History

One way to measure time is to label groups of years. For example, a group of 10 years is called a **decade**. A group of 100 years is known as a *century*. Centuries are grouped into even longer time periods. Ten centuries grouped together is called a *millennium*, which is a period of 1,000 years.

Historians also divide the past into larger blocks of time known as **eras.** *Prehistory* is the first of these long periods. Prehistory is the time before people developed writing.

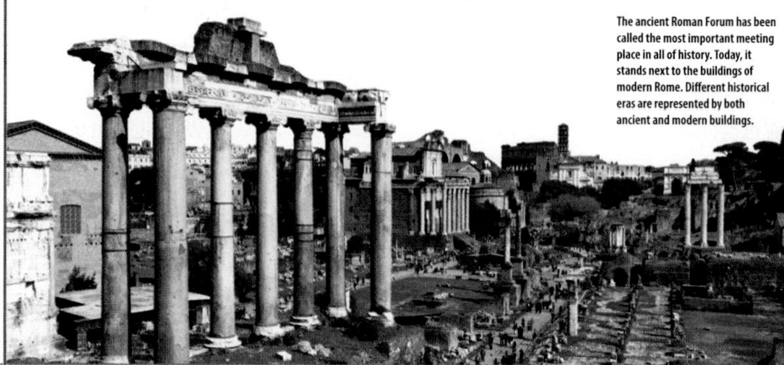

The ancient Roman Forum has been called the most important meeting place in all of history. Today, it stands next to the buildings of modern Rome. Different historical eras are represented by both ancient and modern buildings.

era a large division of time

Academic Vocabulary

integral essential; necessary

decade a group or set of 10 years

Writing was invented about 5,500 years ago. The period known as *Ancient History* comes next. It ends c. A.D. 500 (c., or circa, means "about"). Historians call the time period between about A.D. 500 and about A.D. 1400 the *Middle Ages*, or the medieval period. *Modern History* begins about A.D. 1400. It continues to the present day.

Calendars

A *calendar* is a system for arranging days in order. Different cultures in the world have developed about 40 different calendars.

Some cultures developed calendars based on nature, such as the cycle of the moon. The Chinese and Jewish calendars base their months on the appearance of the new moon. The ancient Egyptians also based one of their calendars on the moon.

The Gregorian calendar is named for its creator, Pope Gregory XIII. Why is it important that most of the world uses a form of the calendar he developed?

Julian Calendar

The calendar we use today is based in part on a calendar developed by Julius Caesar, a Roman leader. This calendar is called the Julian calendar, and it started counting years at the **founding** of Rome. A year on the Julian calendar was 365¼ days long. The calendar added an extra day every four years. The year with the extra day was called a leap year. However, the Julian calendar was still not **precisely,** or exactly, right. It lost several minutes each year, which added up to about one lost day every 128 years.

Gregorian Calendar

By A.D. 1582, the Julian calendar was losing time—about 10 days. Pope Gregory XIII decided to create a new calendar. First, he started counting from the birth of Jesus. Next, he ordered that the days between October 4th and October 15th of that year be dropped from the calendar. Like the Julian calendar, the Gregorian calendar includes leap years. However, in the Gregorian calendar, no century year will be a leap year unless it is divisible by 400, such as the years 1600 or 2000. That way, it will take thousands of years before there is another lost day.

Reading HELPDESK

Academic Vocabulary

found to create or set up something, such as a city

precise exact

Reading Strategy: ***Context Clues***

Context clues are words or phrases that give hints about the meaning of another word. Which phrase provides a clue about the meaning of the word *precisely*?

Not all countries accepted the Gregorian calendar right away. It took more than three centuries for the calendar to be recognized around the world. Today, most of the world uses this calendar. Like the Gregorian calendar, other calendars are also based on events of religious importance. The Jewish calendar begins about 3,760 years before the Gregorian calendar. According to Jewish tradition, that is when the world was created. Muslims date their calendar from the time that Muhammad, their first leader, left the city of Makkah (Mecca) to go to Madinah (Medina). This was the year A.D. 622 in the Gregorian calendar.

This stone calendar was made by the Minoans, people who lived on ancient Crete.

Dating Events

In the Gregorian calendar, the years before the birth of Jesus are known as "B.C.," or "before Christ." The years after are called "A.D.," or *anno domini*. This phrase comes from the Latin language and means "in the year of the Lord."

To date events before the birth of Jesus, or "B.C.," historians count backwards from A.D. 1. There is no year "0." The year before A.D. 1 is 1 B.C. (Notice that "A.D." is written before the date and "B.C." is written after the date.) For example, on the time line below, the founder of Buddhism was born about 563 B.C., or 563 years before the birth of Jesus. To date events after the birth of Jesus, or "A.D.," historians count forward, starting at A.D. 1. A date in the first 100 years after the birth of Jesus is between A.D. 1 and A.D. 100. Therefore, on the time line below, Buddhism spread to China in A.D. 100, or 100 years after the birth of Jesus.

To avoid a religious reference in dating, many historians prefer to use the initials B.C.E. ("before the common era") and C.E. ("common era"). These initials do not change the numbering of the years.

Using Time Lines

A time line is another way to track the passage of time. Time lines show the order of events within a period of time. They also show the amount of time between events. Most time lines are divided into even sections of time. Events are placed on a time line at the date when the event occurred.

INFOGRAPHIC

Time lines can trace the growth and decline of civilizations. This time line tracks the events of ancient India.

1. **IDENTIFYING** Around what year did the Mauryan Empire's Golden Age begin?
2. **CRITICAL THINKING** ***Analyzing*** Which dates and events on this time line give information about the Aryans?

ANCIENT INDIA

- c. 2600 B.C. Mohenjo-Daro flourishes
- c. 2500 B.C. Harappa flourishes
- c. 1500 B.C. Aryans bring Hindu ideas to India
- c. 1000 B.C. Aryans control northern India
- c. 563 B.C. Birth of the Buddha
- c. 265 B.C. Mauryan Empire's Golden Age begins

B.C. 2500 | B.C. 2000 | B.C. 1500 | B.C. 1000 | B.C. 500 | 0 | 500 A.D.

LESSON 1

ENGAGE

Describing Introduce the idea that historians keep track of time.

Ask: **How do we keep track of time during the day?** *(a watch or clock)* **How do we keep track of time during a month? A year?** *(a calendar, an organizer, the computer)* **More than a year?** *(a calendar or history textbook, an organizer, the computer)* AL ELL

Explain that many historians study long time periods and they use a variety of tools to organize their work.

TEACH & ASSESS

1 Why Study History?

GUIDING QUESTION *What types of things can history reveal about the past?*

Explaining Organize students into groups of four. Give each group a place mat made out of butcher paper.

Ask each group to draw an oval in the center of the paper.

Out of the center oval, have them draw four rules that extend to the corners of the paper. These divide the paper into four sections, one section for each student to write on.

Pose a question to the group.

Ask: **Why do people study history?**

Have one student write this question in the center oval. Then, each group member should write answers to that question in his or her section of the place mat.

The team should compare their answers and circle or highlight any answers that all four team members have in common.

Finally, have each group share its ideas with the class as a whole. AL ELL

INTERACTIVE WORKSHEET

Primary Source Activity

Evaluating Explain to students that one of the most important jobs for a historian is to determine the causes and effects of a historical event.

Remind students that a cause is the reason an event happens and an effect is the result, or consequence, of the event.

Provide examples from daily life, such as "The car stopped because it ran out of gas"; "The alarm did not go off, so Joey overslept"; and "Olivia scored high on the test because she studied."

Have students give more examples of cause and effect.

Assign the Primary Source Activity on the White House renovation for homework. Instruct students to evaluate the primary sources, looking for causes and effects of the event.

2 Measuring Time

GUIDING QUESTION *What are historical periods?*

Defining Review the terms related to accounting for time: *A.D., B.C., periods, decades, centuries, epoch, era, millennia, Prehistory, Ancient History, Middle Ages,* and *Modern History.*

Explain that the words we use to describe the passing of time are simply tools to organize the way we think about history.

GAME You may choose to have students play the concentration game for extra practice with these words. ELL

LECTURE SLIDE **Making Connections** Display on the board the lecture slide with the words *decade, century,* and *millennium.*

Ask:

Tell me something that happened in the past decade. *(Students should name a recent event.)*

Name a person who lived in the last century. *(Possible answers: Ronald Reagan, John F. Kennedy, Michael Jackson)*

Now name an event that happened about a millennium ago. *(Accept any reasonable answer. For example: Shakespeare wrote his plays, America was discovered by Europeans, and so on.)*

INTERACTIVE WHITEBOARD ACTIVITY

Applying Guide students through the Interactive Whiteboard Activity about time lines.

Before having students create their individual time lines, work as a class to create a time line of the school year.

Ask:

When did school start?

When does the term end?

What big events happen during each school term? AL

Have volunteers mark each event on the class time line.

Then, have students create time lines of their lives as described in the Interactive Whiteboard Activity.

Guide students by **asking:**

When were you born?

When did you start going to school?

Did you ever move to a new home or start something new? If so, when?

3 Digging Up the Past

GUIDING QUESTION *What do students of prehistory look for?*

LECTURE SLIDE **Comparing and Contrasting** Show the descriptions of a paleontologist, an archaeologist, and an anthropologist from the lecture slide.

Have students read the textbook to explain how each historian is similar to and different from the others.

Ask: **Which type of historian would students most like to be?** Have students explain why they made their choices. AL ELL

Have students complete the Lesson 1 Review.

Answers for pages 4–7

P. 4 Taking Notes Reasons to Study History: to find causes and effects; **Measuring Historical Time:** time lines, calendars, A.D. and B.C.; **People Who Study Time:** anthropologist, archaeologist, paleontologist

P. 5 ☑ PROGRESS CHECK Learning about the causes and effects of past events helps us understand the present and anticipate the future.

P. 6 It is important for people to use the same calendar so that there is a universal system for dating events that can be used and understood by people of all backgrounds. The Gregorian calendar is the one used in most of the world.

P. 6 Reading Strategy The phrase "lost several minutes each year" provides a clue about the meaning of the word *precisely.*

P. 7 INFOGRAPHIC

1. 265 B.C.
2. CRITICAL THINKING c. 1500 B.C. Aryans bring Hindu ideas to India; c. 1000 B.C. Aryans control northern India

BIOGRAPHY

Heinrich Schliemann (A.D. 1822–1890)

As a boy, Heinrich Schliemann (SHLEE • MAHN) loved stories about ancient Greece. He dreamed of finding Troy, an ancient city destroyed during the Trojan War.

In 1871, Schliemann began to dig through a human-made mound in Hissarlik (HIH • suhr • LIHK), Turkey. Two years later, he uncovered the remains of a mysterious ancient city in the area where Troy had stood. Some archaeologists believe that Schliemann actually found Troy. Others are unsure. Nevertheless, his work led to the discovery of many ancient Greek treasures. Because of his work, Schliemann is considered the founder of prehistoric Greek archaeology.

► CRITICAL THINKING

Making Inferences Archaeologists study and catalog evidence they find. What might be the historical value of uncovering evidence of an entire city?

Usually, the dates on a time line are evenly spaced. Sometimes, however, a time line covers events over too many years to show on one page. In this case, a slanted or jagged line might be placed on the time line. This shows that a certain period of time is omitted from the time line.

Time lines help historians make sense of the flow of events. A time line can be a single line, or it can be two or more lines stacked on top of each other. Stacked time lines are called multilevel time lines.

☑ PROGRESS CHECK

Applying When would a historian use a calendar? When would a historian use a time line?

3 Digging Up the Past

GUIDING QUESTION *What do students of prehistory look for?*

Since the invention of writing, people have recorded important events. These written records give historians a window to the past. Students of prehistory look into an even deeper past, one without writing. They must find a different kind of window.

History and Science

These historians use science to study history. As scientists, they study physical evidence to learn about our ancestors.

Archaeology (ahr • kee • AHL • luh • jee) is the study of the past by looking at what people left behind. Archaeologists dig in the earth for places where people once lived. They never know what they will find. They often discover **artifacts** (AHR • tih • FAKTS)—objects made by people. Common artifacts include tools, pottery, weapons, and jewelry. Archaeologists study artifacts to learn what life was like in the past.

Paleontology (PAY • lee • AHN • TAH • luh • jee) also looks at prehistoric times. Paleontologists study fossils to learn what the world was like long ago. **Fossils** are the remains of plant and animal life that have been preserved from an earlier time.

Anthropology (AN • thruh • PAH • luh • jee) is the study of human culture and how it develops over time. Anthropologists study artifacts and fossils, too. They look for clues about what people valued and believed.

Human Discoveries

In 1974, a team led by paleontologist Donald Johanson made an exciting find in Ethiopia in Africa. They discovered a partial skeleton of a human ancestor who lived more than 3.2 million years ago. Lucy, as she was called, was about three and a half feet tall (1.07 m) and weighed about 60 pounds (27.2 kg). She had long arms and short legs, and she walked upright.

Lucy belonged to the species *Australopithicus afarensis*. A **species** is a class of individuals with similar physical characteristics. Lucy lived long before the species called *Homo sapiens* evolved. All modern human beings belong to this species. The term *Homo sapiens* is Latin for "wise man." Scientists believe that Homo sapiens probably developed about 150,000 to 195,000 years ago.

☑ PROGRESS CHECK

Comparing How are archaeologists, paleontologists, and anthropologists like detectives?

Connections to TODAY

How Lucy Got Her Name

The night that Lucy was discovered, the team that found her was listening to the song "Lucy in the Sky with Diamonds" by the singing group the Beatles. They nicknamed the skeleton "Lucy," which was more attractive than her official name, AL 288-1.

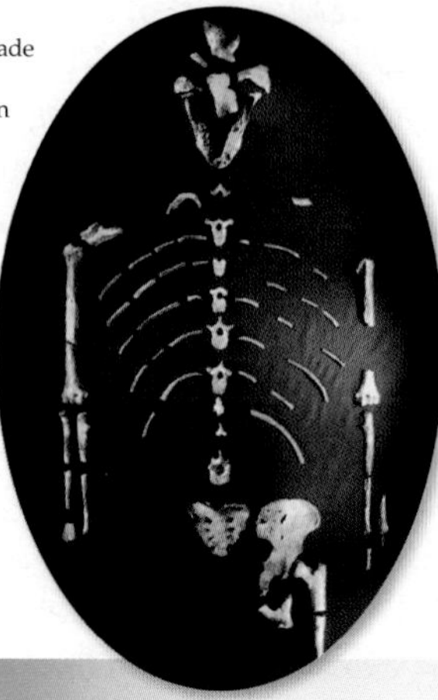

Scientists have found and pieced together about 40 percent of Lucy's skeleton.

Reading HELPDESK

archaeology the study of objects to learn about past human life
artifact an object made by people
paleontology the study of fossils
fossil plant or animal remains that have been preserved from an earlier time
anthropology the study of human culture and how it develops over time
species a class of individuals with similar physical characteristics

Build Vocabulary: *Word Parts*

The suffix *-ology* means "the study of." The suffix *-ist* means "a person who." For example, *biology* is the study of life. A *biologist* is a person who studies life. What are archaeologists, paleontologists, and anthropologists?

LESSON 1 REVIEW

Review Vocabulary

1. Explain what a historical *era* is.
2. Compare and contrast *artifacts* and *fossils*.

Answer the Guiding Questions

3. ***Making Connections*** Name one example of how the past influences daily life today.
4. ***Listing*** Identify different ways that historians measure time.
5. ***Describing*** How do historians learn about people who lived in the earliest historical eras?
6. **EXPOSITORY WRITING** How would a historian describe your life? Write a short essay that identifies the era in which you live and the artifacts that tell about your culture.

networks *There's More Online!*

☑ GRAPHIC ORGANIZER
- How a Historian Works
- Understanding Primary and Secondary Sources

☑ SLIDE SHOW
- Ancient Art
- Terra-cotta Army

Lesson 2 How Does a Historian Work?

ESSENTIAL QUESTION *How do we learn about the past?*

IT MATTERS BECAUSE

Knowing how historians work helps us understand historical information.

1 What Is the Evidence?

GUIDING QUESTION *What types of evidence do historians use to understand the past?*

Historians ask questions about the information they find from the past. Why did some nations go to war? How were the people affected by that war? How did events of the past change people's lives? These questions help us focus on historical problems.

To learn the answers to the historical questions, historians look for **evidence** (EH • vuh • duhnts). Evidence is something that shows proof or an indication that something is true. Evidence could be in the form of material objects, such as a soldier's uniform or scraps of pottery from an archaeological dig.

Other evidence may appear in documents or written materials that were created during a historical event. Historians use the evidence they read in historical **sources** to interpret what happened in the past.

Primary and Secondary Sources

Historians look for clues about the past in primary and secondary sources. **Primary sources** are firsthand pieces of evidence. They were written or created by the people who saw or experienced an event. Primary sources include letters, diaries, or government records. Literature or artwork from a particular time and place is a primary source. Spoken interviews and objects, such as tools or clothing, are also primary sources. Primary sources help historians learn what people were thinking while the events took place. They use the sources to find evidence that explains historical events.

Historians also use **secondary sources**. Secondary sources are created after an event. They are created by people who were not part of the historical event. The information in secondary sources is often based on primary sources. Examples of secondary sources are biographies, encyclopedias, history books, and textbooks.

A secondary source contains background information. Secondary sources also offer a broad view of an event. However, a historian must use primary sources to find new evidence about a subject.

Reliable Sources

Suppose you were studying the history of England and you wanted to know how ancient people lived. You might look in a book called the *Domesday Book*. This book was created in A.D. 1086 by administrators under William I. The book is a primary source from the period. It contains information about the people of England at the time it was written.

These sculptures of warriors are evidence of life in China during the Qin Dynasty. They give archaeologists and historians information about China's culture and its first emperor.

Reading HELPDESK

Taking Notes: *Sequencing*

As you read, think about the steps in finding and evaluating evidence. Use the sequence chart to note the steps in the process.

Step 1 → Step 2 → Step 3

Content Vocabulary
- evidence
- primary source
- secondary source
- point of view
- bias
- conclusion
- scholarly

evidence something that shows proof that something is true
primary source firsthand evidence of an event in history
secondary source a document or written work created after an event

Academic Vocabulary

source document or reference work

LESSON 1 (cont.)

CLOSE & REFLECT

Making Connections Explain to students that historians often name periods in history after events or achievements of the people who defined that period (for example, the Stone Age, the Industrial Age, the Victorian Age).

Have students speculate about appropriate names we might use to describe the period in which we live. Students may refer to current events or the president who is in office.

BACKGROUND KNOWLEDGE

Prehistoric findings are evident throughout the United States. For example, land near Koshkonong, Wisconsin, is hilly and wooded. The Wisconsin Department of Transportation planned to pave the area for a highway expansion project to be completed in 2013.

As the land was dug, a large, ancient dumping ground for artifacts that spans several eras was discovered. The land contains more than 100,000 prehistoric Native American artifacts. Artifacts include broken cookware, knife points, and even a 1,200-year-old deer bone with markings on it from an ancient tool.

In addition to Wisconsin, housing developers in Sandusky, Ohio, discovered prehistoric artifacts in 2003. Construction workers discovered skeletal remains and cooking pots from an ancient Native American group that occupied the region about 5,000 years ago.

Answers for pages 8–9

P. 8 CRITICAL THINKING Uncovering evidence of an entire city would give archaeologists a more complete picture of how people in earlier eras lived.

P. 8 ☑ PROGRESS CHECK A historian would use a calendar to find out when something happened and a time line to figure out the order in which things happened.

P. 8 Build Vocabulary Archaeologists are people who study artifacts to learn about the past. Paleontologists are people who study fossils. Anthropologists are people who study the history of human culture.

P. 9 ☑ PROGRESS CHECK Each uncovers and analyzes evidence of past events.

LESSON 1 REVIEW

1. A historical era is a large block of time.
2. Artifacts are human-made objects, such as tools and jewelry. Fossils are evidence of early plant or animal life that has been preserved from an earlier time. Both help historians understand life in the past.
3. Students might say that the writing of the U.S. Constitution gave them the freedoms they enjoy, or they may identify a more personal historical event, such as a relocation that required them to go to a new school and make new friends.
4. Historians measure time in small blocks, such as decades and centuries, and larger blocks, such as millennia and eras.
5. They look for physical evidence such as fossils and artifacts that tell how people lived.
6. Students should recognize that they live in the era of Modern History. They should identify that they've lived longer than a decade. They should also identify artifacts such as cell phones, computers, backpacks, electronic music players, and so forth as indicative of their culture.

Teaching *How Does a Historian Work?* (Student Edition pp. 10–15)

LESSON 2

ENGAGE

Making Connections Bring in a variety of present-day artifacts, including newspapers, magazines, photos, or objects, such as an electronic music player, a microwave popcorn bag, a cell phone, and so on.

Ask: What do these objects reflect about our culture?

Explain that these objects are artifacts that tell about our society. In the future, historians will study these objects to learn about our lives.

Ask: If a historian finds a saddle and horseshoes, what does that tell him or her about the culture? *(that the people rode horses)* AL

Point out that historians use documents and artifacts from the past to learn about cultures from long ago.

TEACH & ASSESS

1 What Is the Evidence?

GUIDING QUESTION *What types of evidence do historians use to understand the past?*

2 Writing About History

GUIDING QUESTION *How do we write about history?*

LECTURE SLIDE Use the lecture slide to review types of evidence.

SLIDE SHOW **Analyzing Primary Sources** Tell students that art is a type of primary source. We can learn about a culture through the art the people of the time produced.

Show students the slide show for this lesson. Point out that artistic works such as paintings or sculptures contain details about the culture of the past. Help students analyze each image for what it tells about the culture it depicts. ELL

INTERACTIVE WORKSHEET

21st Century Skills Activity

Explaining Explain that students will read two primary sources about Genghis Khan and evaluate whether the sources contain bias. Point out that the writers of the sources have different opinions about the historical figure.

Ask: How do primary sources lead historians to disagree about how to interpret historical events? *(The authors of primary sources take different positions on events. This sometimes leads historians to draw different conclusions.)*

Evaluating Remind students that some sources contain a bias—an unreasoned, emotional opinion about something.

Ask: Are primary or secondary sources more likely to contain bias? *(Primary sources are more likely to contain the bias of the eyewitness. Reliable secondary sources should not contain bias, but sometimes do.)*

Answers for pages 10–11

P. 10 Taking Notes Step 1: Collect sources.
Step 2: Compare sources to known facts.
Step 3: Make an inference or draw a conclusion.

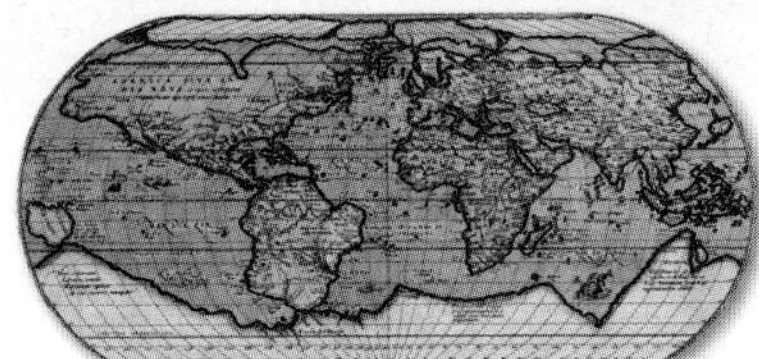

Maps can be primary sources. The map on the left was created around A.D. 1500. How does it compare with the modern world map on the right? What can historians learn by comparing these maps?

Connections to TODAY

The Census

In A.D. 1086, King William I of England decided to collect information about the land and people in his country. Today, our government collects similar data every ten years in the U.S. Census. Questions in the census do not include details about mills and animals as in the *Domesday Book*. They instead focus on age, race, and living arrangements. The census information is a primary source about the people who live in the United States.

The *Domesday Book* is a long list of manors and the names of their owners. It includes details about how many workers worked the land. It lists the number of fishponds, mills, and animals owned by each person. It also estimated the value of each property. The historian's job is to analyze and interpret the information from primary sources. They consider where and when a source was created. They also look for the reasons that the source was created. Was it a secret letter? Was it a document created for the king, such as the *Domesday Book*? Was it written so that all the people in a town or country would read it?

What is Point of View?

Historians interpret the document and the reasons it was created. Then they form an opinion about whether the source is trustworthy and reliable in its facts. This step is important since each source was written with a particular **point of view** or general attitude about people or life. The authors of primary sources use their points of view to decide what information is important and what to include in the document. Historians evaluate a primary source to find its point of view. They decide if it has a trustworthy viewpoint.

Sometimes a point of view is expressed as a **bias** or an unreasoned, emotional judgment about people and events. Sources with a bias cannot always be trusted.

PROGRESS CHECK

Explaining What is a historian's job when looking at primary sources?

Reading HELPDESK

point of view a personal attitude about people or life

bias an unreasoned, emotional judgment about people and events

2 Writing About History

GUIDING QUESTION *How do we write about history?*

When historians write about an event, they interpret the information from primary sources to draw conclusions and make inferences.

Making an inference means choosing the most likely explanation for the facts at hand. Sometimes the inference is simple. For example, if you see a person who is wearing a raincoat walk into a room with a dripping umbrella, you can infer that it is raining outside. The dripping umbrella and the raincoat are the evidence that combine with your prior knowledge about weather to infer that it is raining.

Making inferences about historical events is more complex. Historians check the evidence in primary sources and compare it to sources already known to be trustworthy. Then, they look at secondary sources that express different points of view about an event. In this way, historians try to get a clear, well-rounded view of what happened. The inference they make is how they explain what happened in the past. This explanation is based on the evidence in primary and secondary sources.

For example, you might read the *Domesday Book* to analyze the types of animals raised in 1086. You could add this knowledge to additional evidence from another source about grain that was planted. Then, you could think about what you know to be true about food. You might use all of this information to make an inference about the types of food people ate in eleventh-century England.

This cave painting was made during the Paleolithic era. It is a primary source.

▶ CRITICAL THINKING

Analyzing Primary Sources What information does the painting give historians?

Looking at History

Professional historians become experts on their historical subject. Historians gather artifacts and data about a subject and then write what they have learned from the study. Such writing may become an article in a **scholarly** (SKAH•luhr•lee) journal, or magazine. It may become a book on the specific subject.

In most cases, historical books and articles are reviewed by other scholars for accuracy. Experts in the field will review the sources and write their own articles. They evaluate how the historian has interpreted the facts. This study of historical interpretations is called historiography. Historians must keep accurate notes and be careful that their inferences are reasonable.

If you were researching World War I, this photo of American soldiers could help you. Using photos as evidence is a good way to expand information. What do you think these soldiers are waiting for?

Focusing Research

Some historians keep their areas of study very narrow. For example, someone could spend an entire career investigating the events that occurred on a single day, such as the day in the year A.D. 79 that Mount Vesuvius, a volcano in the region that is now Italy, erupted and destroyed the city of Pompeii. This subject is a **finite** place and time. Other historians focus on broader subjects. For example, some historians study the economic history of a period. Others study the political history of a country during a certain period of time. Still others might study military history, the history of medicine, or the history of technology in a certain place.

Drawing Conclusions

A **conclusion** (kuhn•KLOO•zhun) is a final decision that is reached by reasoning. You draw conclusions all the time. For example, you may notice that a friend often wears T-shirts from music concerts that he has attended. You might also remember he can never get together on Thursday nights because he has guitar lessons on Thursdays. Based on these two clues, you could draw the conclusion that your friend is really interested in music. Historians draw conclusions in the same way. They look for facts and evidence in their primary and secondary sources. Then, they use reasoning to make a judgment or draw a conclusion.

Reading HELPDESK

scholarly concerned with academic learning or research

conclusion a decision reached after examining evidence

Academic Vocabulary

finite limited; having boundaries

interpretation an explanation of the meaning of something

Historical Interpretations

Sometimes historians disagree about their **interpretations** of the facts. For example, historians disagree about how to evaluate the historical figure of Genghis Khan. There are historians who argue that Genghis Khan was a fierce and bloodthirsty warrior. Some have expressed horror at the tremendous destruction that Genghis Khan's fierce soldiers brought as they conquered new lands. Yet some historians see Genghis Khan differently. They look at the way Genghis Khan ruled his great Mongol empire. Sources show that this was a time of peace, prosperity, and stability in a huge portion of central and eastern Asia. The people living in the Mongol empire enjoyed a remarkable degree of religious tolerance, higher learning, and consistent laws.

Which conclusion is correct? Was Genghis Khan a ruthless warrior or a strong, intelligent leader of a great land? A historian may rely on evidence to support either position. However, it is the job of the historian to evaluate the primary sources and explain why both interpretations can be argued.

Genghis Khan and his Mongol warriors expanded the Mongol Empire. The violence of their invasions contrasted with the peace inside the empire.

PROGRESS CHECK

Analyzing Why do historians draw different conclusions about events of the past?

LESSON 2 REVIEW

Review Vocabulary

1. Name one way a *primary source* is different from a *secondary source.*
2. Why does a historian have to understand what *point of view* is?

Answer the Guiding Questions

3. ***Drawing Conclusions*** Why does drawing a conclusion come at the end of a research process?
4. ***Making Generalizations*** How does a primary source help a historian understand the past?
5. ***Assessing*** Explain why some historians differ in their interpretations of historical events.
6. **EXPOSITORY WRITING** Think of the reading you do every day. In a short paragraph, give an example of one primary source and one secondary source that you have read recently. Explain why each example fits into the category you have chosen.

LESSON 2 (cont.)

Historians should recognize the bias as they study each source. Ask students to identify written materials they have read recently that contain biased information. Then have students complete the 21st Century Skills worksheet for this lesson.

INTERACTIVE WHITEBOARD ACTIVITY **Evaluating** Review with students what they have read about reliable sources, as well as the difference between primary and secondary sources.

Then, guide students through the Interactive Whiteboard Activity as they sort sources for a research paper about Ancient Greece.

Ask: Are all of these sources reliable? How do you know? *(Student answers will vary. The primary sources include ancient artifacts, maps, literature, and an essay. Some students may note that these primary sources might include bias or inaccuracies. The secondary sources include standard reference materials that are generally assumed to be reliable, such as an atlas, an encyclopedia, and a history book.)*

Have students complete the Lesson 2 Review.

CLOSE & REFLECT

Identifying Have students identify objects in the classroom that would make appropriate artifacts for future historians. Have students speculate about what these artifacts would reveal about the class to people in the future.

IF YOU HAVE MORE TIME . . .

Teach Active Reading Strategies

Questioning Several types of questioning are important in reading strategically. Students need to ask general questions about the text before, during, and after they read. They also need to question their own understanding of the content as they read—that is, they need to conduct a running dialogue with themselves as part of the metacognitive process of thinking about their own thinking. This metacognitive process will naturally lead students to ask specific questions to clarify text. Finally, students need to ask themselves what information is most important in a selection and what concepts or information teachers will require them to know.

Reviewing As students read, teachers should pause at various points to review. Periodic review helps students negotiate their way through difficult text and keep struggling readers on task.

Evaluating As students have access to increasingly larger amounts of print materials, including a variety of electronic resources, they need to be able to evaluate what they read. Students evaluate expository texts—newspapers, editorials, advertisements, and essays—when they distinguish between fact and opinion. To evaluate whether information is reliable, students should pose questions such as: **Is the author qualified to write on this subject? Is the point of view biased? Is there another point of view not expressed here? Are opinions backed up with facts, statistics, and examples?**

BACKGROUND KNOWLEDGE

What Do Historians Do?

Anthropologist

Scientists work to uncover clues to learn about early human life. Anthropologists focus on human society. They study how humans developed and related to one another. Some anthropologists are interested in finding clues about ancient civilizations that no longer exist. Others prefer researching modern societies ranging from disappearing native cultures to urban teenagers.

Archivist

Libraries and museums have collections, or archives, of historical artifacts and manuscripts. Archivists are responsible for cataloging and preserving these materials so they can be used for research or public display.

Archaeologist

When digging begins for the construction of a new building, workers sometimes find artifacts or ruins of earlier societies. Officials will usually call an archaeologist to study the discoveries before building continues. Archaeologists work around the world, studying past societies by analyzing what people left behind.

Genealogist

Many people are curious about their own family's past. Are they descended from kings or queens? Why and when did their ancestors leave their native lands? Genealogists help people trace their roots in order to learn more about their families.

Historian

Historians are people who study and write about the human past to learn about important people and events. Historians work for many types of institutions—from the government to the football hall of fame—to study and record history.

Paleontologist

Man's earliest history has no written records and few artifacts for historians to study. Paleontologists find clues about prehistoric humans by studying bones and fossils.

Answers for pages 12–15

P. 12 The map from A.D. 1500 shows different land shapes than the modern map. By comparing these maps, historians can learn what people of the past knew about the world.

P. 12 ☑ **PROGRESS CHECK** When a historian looks at a primary source, he or she must identify point of view, detect bias, and determine the credibility of the source.

P. 13 **CRITICAL THINKING** Paintings like this one provide information about methods the artists used and about subjects that were important to them. This painting tells historians that the people who created it hunted animals using bows and arrows.

P. 14 They are waiting for orders to fire their guns at the enemy.

P. 15 ☑ **PROGRESS CHECK** Historians use different primary sources for their research. They decide which sources to use to support their conclusions. Sometimes historians make different choices about how to interpret a historical event.

LESSON 2 REVIEW

1. A primary source is a firsthand piece of evidence created by a person who experienced an event. A secondary source is created after the event took place by an individual who did not experience the event.
2. Historians should know what a point of view is because identifying a source's point of view will help them determine the reliability of the source and recognize bias.
3. Drawing conclusions comes at the end of the process because a historian first needs to find and evaluate sources.
4. A primary source contains details about a historical time period. Although it is written from a potentially biased point of view, a primary source contains concrete evidence from which to draw conclusions.
5. Historians use different historical sources to find evidence for their positions. Their interpretations may differ based on the facts in their sources.
6. Students should write a paragraph in which they identify at least two reading materials from their everyday lives, such as textbooks, social media, graphic novels, or young adult fiction. They should accurately identify the reading materials as primary or secondary sources and explain why each source fits in the designated category.

What Do You Think?

Should Artifacts Be Returned to Their Countries of Origin?

Imagine you were an archaeologist who found an important ancient artifact in another country. You would want to take that artifact home with you and display it in a museum. The country where you found the artifact might raise a protest. They may want the object to stay in their own country. Many such artifacts are displayed in museums far away from their country of origin. Who has the biggest claim to them? Should artifacts be returned to the countries in which they were found?

Yes

PRIMARY SOURCE

“The Oxford English Dictionary defines “repatriate” as “to restore (an artifact or other object) to its country of origin.” Many artifacts . . . have special cultural value for a particular community or nation. When these works are removed from their original cultural setting, they lose their context and the culture loses a part of its history. A request for repatriation of an artifact . . . usually has a strong legal basis. The antiquity was exported illegally, probably also excavated [dug up] illegally, and most importantly, it is now defined by U.S. courts as stolen property. Even in the United States, where private property rights are greatly respected, the government claims ownership of antiquities from federal lands—and would request their repatriation if they were to be privately excavated and exported.”

—Malcolm Bell III, professor emeritus, University of Virginia

The Cairo Museum holds countless artifacts from Egypt's long history. An example is this famous golden burial mask of Pharaoh Tutankhamen.

TEXT: "Who's Right? Repatriation of Cultural Property," Malcolm Bell III, america.gov, October 2010.
PHOTO: Michael Snell/Robert Harding World Imagery/Getty Images

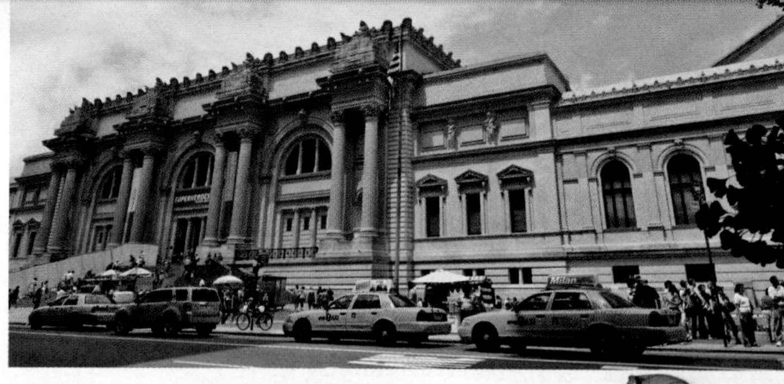

PHOTO: (t) Yoko Aziz/Age fotostock, (b) The Print Collector/Heritage/Age fotostock

The Metropolitan Museum of Art in New York is visited by millions of people every year. The museum's collection includes treasures from all over the world, including this sphinx of the Egyptian pharaoh Amenhotep II.

No

PRIMARY SOURCE

“History is long and untidy. Territory held today by a given nation-state in the past likely belonged to a different political entity [unit], one with other descendents. Does ancient Hellenistic [Greek] art made and found in Afghanistan, once on the edge of the Greek empire, belong to Greece or to Afghanistan? To which modern nation do they belong? The lines designating [assigning] claims to art and culture are not clear-cut.

I would argue that within the limits of the law, museums, wherever they are, should be encouraged to acquire works of art representative of the world's many and diverse cultures. This can be through purchase or long-term loan and working in collaboration [cooperation] with museums and nations around the world. These collections encourage a cosmopolitan [international] view of the world and promote a historically accurate understanding of the fluidity [constantly changing] of culture.”

—James Cuno, president and Eloise W. Martin Director of the Art Institute of Chicago

What Do You Think? DBQ

1. ***Identifying*** Why is repatriation a legal issue according to Bell?
2. ***Contrasting*** How do the arguments of Bell and Cuno differ?

CRITICAL THINKING

3. ***Problem Solving*** Describe a compromise that might solve a conflict over ownership of artifacts.

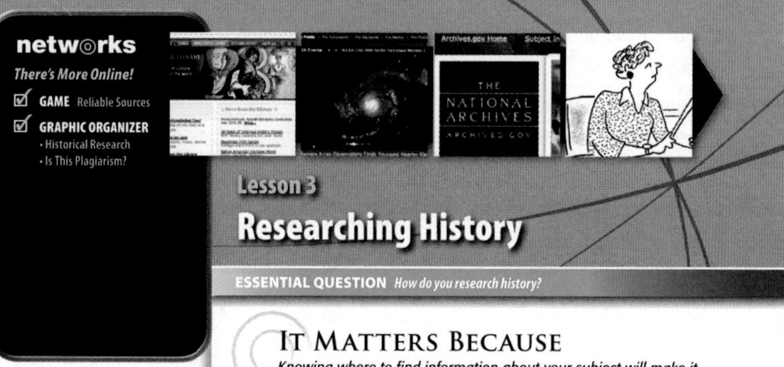

networks
There's More Online!
☑ **GAME** Reliable Sources
☑ **GRAPHIC ORGANIZER**
- Historical Research
- Is This Plagiarism?

Lesson 3

Researching History

ESSENTIAL QUESTION *How do you research history?*

It Matters Because

Knowing where to find information about your subject will make it easier to complete research projects and other schoolwork.

1 Planning Your Project

GUIDING QUESTION *How do you begin a research project?*

The first step in a history research project is to identify your topic. A topic should not be too broad (The Middle Ages) or too narrow (Middlebury, England, 1535). To test your topic, try looking it up in an encyclopedia. If there is no entry for your topic, it may be too small. If there are many entries, or a very long entry, the topic may be too large. Selecting a topic that is workable is the most important part of the project.

After you choose a topic, you need to decide what you want to learn about it. Create six questions to help you find out *who, what, when, where, why,* and *how.* Then write each question at the top of a note card. These cards will become your research tools. You may need to add additional cards as you research.

Choosing Research Materials

After selecting a topic and creating your question cards, the next step is to gather your research materials. Begin with general reference books, such as encyclopedias and textbooks, or your notes from class. Next, try looking for books about your subject at the library. Your research material must be nonfiction, rather than fiction or persuasive writing.

(l) Library of Congress, (cl) NASA
(cr) National Archives, (r) Aaron Bacall

Reading **HELPDESK**

Taking Notes: *Finding the Main Idea*

As you read, look for the main idea of each section. Use a graphic organizer like this one to write the details that support the main idea.

Main Ideas ↓ ☐ ↓ ☐ ↓ ☐ ↓ ☐

Content Vocabulary
- **credentials**
- **URL**
- **.gov**
- **.edu**
- **.org**
- **plagiarize**

Distinguishing Fact From Opinion

Scan each possible source to determine if the source is trustworthy. Look for opinion statements in the text. This will give you a clue that a resource could be biased or untrustworthy. Remember, a statement of fact expresses only what can be proven by evidence. A statement of opinion expresses an attitude. It is a conclusion or judgment about something that cannot be proven true or false. Historical research should rely on facts and primary sources rather than opinions.

Making Notes

As you find information, make a note about it on your cards. Your notes should be in your own words and in complete sentences. On the back of each card, make notes about the books in which you found the information.

☑ PROGRESS CHECK

Explaining Why is it important to distinguish fact from opinion in historical writing?

2 Researching on the Internet

GUIDING QUESTION *How do you safely research on the Internet?*

Looking for information on the Internet is quick and rewarding. However, it can be a challenge to find out if the information you located is true. Good historians follow a few important guidelines as they gather information.

Authorship

Many articles on the Internet are unsigned. A reader has no way of knowing who wrote the content and whether the author is an expert on the subject. However, reliable articles will be signed by well-known experts on the subject. The authors will include details about their **credentials** (kreh•DEN•shulz), or evidence that they are experts.

(t) Library of Congress
(c) NASA, (b) National Archives

Web sites such as these may be reliable for certain subjects. There are many clues on a Web site to let you know if it will have reliable information.

credentials something that gives confidence that a person is qualified for a task

Teaching *What Do You Think?* (Student Edition pp. 16–17)

ENGAGE

Assessing Ask students to consider the following list of artifacts from American history: the original Declaration of Independence, the original flag sewn by Betsy Ross, and the furniture owned by George Washington.

Ask:

- **Where should these historical items be kept?**
- **Should they remain in the United States?**
- **What if people from Europe or Asia purchased one of these objects?**
- **Should they display the item in their country?**
- **Would that object still be American?**

TEACH & ASSESS

Have students use the headings and images on the page to identify which passage will be written with a positive answer and which will be written with a negative answer. AL ELL

Summarizing Have students read the two primary source passages on their own. Review challenging words with students. ELL

Then have volunteers summarize the main argument in each passage.

Ask: Do you think the United States has the right to reclaim all the American artifacts in museums around the world?

Do you think American museums should return artifacts to other countries, where they originated? *(Students who support the "NO" argument in the feature should argue that American artifacts abroad belong to the museum where they are being kept. They should point out that such artifacts help others around the world appreciate and learn about American culture. Students who support the "YES" argument should argue that artifacts represent part of a unique cultural heritage that belongs to the people of those countries.)*

Have students support their answers with explanations and details from the text. BL

Finally, have students complete the *What Do You Think?* questions.

CLOSE & REFLECT

Discussing Point out that many ancient artifacts were smuggled out of the country by historians or researchers. They believed they could better care for them than those people in that country. Many also were seeking fame and fortune.

Ask: Should the way an artifact was originally obtained play a role in the decision to return the artifact? *(Responses will vary. Students may think that whether an artifact was stolen is an important criterion for returning it.)*

Answers to *What Do You Think?* DBQ

1. Bell argues that the U.S. court system considers antiquities stolen property when they are acquired from other countries illegally.
2. Bell argues that countries lose part of their culture when artifacts are taken from them, and it is considered illegal in U.S. courts. Cuno, however, argues that one country cannot own artifacts since numerous cultures in that country of origin have influenced the creation of them.
3. Students might suggest that museums work out loan programs or compensate countries for displaying their artifacts.

Teaching *Researching History* (Student Edition pp. 18–21)

LESSON 3

ENGAGE

Making Decisions Point out a few reference books in the classroom.

Ask:

- **Where do you go to find answers to questions?**
- **Do you look up the answers? If so, where?**
- **If you use a book, what type of book?**
- **Or do you use the Internet? If so, what type of site?**
- **Do you ask someone for help? If so, whom?**
- **How do you know if you have found the correct answer to your question?**

(Answers should show an understanding of the types of reliable places students should use to start a research project.)

TEACH & ASSESS

1 Planning Your Project

GUIDING QUESTION *How do you begin a research project?*

LECTURE SLIDE **Distinguishing Fact From Opinion**
Show the lecture slide that explains the difference between facts and opinions: Facts can be proven; opinions cannot.

Offer several examples of opinions, such as: *"The most interesting period of history is Ancient Egypt"* and *"The worst leader in history was Genghis Khan."* Remind students that these are opinions. They cannot be proven.

Then, have students write down two facts and one opinion about a topic of your choice.

Ask volunteers to read their examples aloud, and have classmates identify which statements are facts and which are opinions. AL

INTERACTIVE WORKSHEET
21st Century Skills Activity

Assign the 21st Century Skills Activity for homework. Explain to students that they will read two newspaper reports of a historical event. They will identify the facts and opinions in the articles that appear on the worksheet.

Answers for pages 18–19

P. 18 Taking Notes The main idea should contain a broad concept about interpreting research materials accurately. Detail boxes should contain facts that support the main idea.

P. 19 ☑ PROGRESS CHECK If a source contains opinions, it might be biased or untrustworthy.

Thinking Like a HISTORIAN

Internet Tips

Check it Out!

If you answer NO to any of the questions below, the Web page or Web site is probably not a reliable resource.

- Is the authorship of the article clear?
- Can you easily find out who is responsible for the Web site?
- Has the Web page been updated recently?
- Does the writing seem balanced or does it contain a bias toward one point of view?

There are other ways to decide if an article is worth using for research. You can look at the homepage for the article. If the article is on the site of a university, government office, or museum, it is probably reliable. For example, suppose you find a signed article about the foods eaten by American colonists. You find that the article is published by an academic journal at a university. You can assume that this page is a better source than an unsigned article about the same subject by a blogger on a cooking Web site.

Web URLs

A uniform resource locator, or **URL,** is the address of an online resource. The ending on a URL tells a great deal about the content. A URL that ends in **.gov** is most likely a government entity. This site probably contains accurate **data.** This data is usually as up to date as possible.

A URL that ends in **.edu** is usually a site for an educational institution, such as a college or university. Most .edu sites pride themselves on accuracy. However, it is possible that documents on these sites may contain opinions in addition to facts.

Nonprofit organizations usually use **.org** at the end of their URLs. These sites may be very accurate. However, these groups often gather information to support their cause. Their sites may contain biased information, and they often contain opinions.

You have gathered information and answered the questions on your note cards. Then organize your cards into categories. Once your cards are sorted, you can use them as an outline for writing your research paper.

PROGRESS CHECK

Speculating What are the consequences of using an Internet resource with biased information?

3 Writing Without Bias

GUIDING QUESTION *How do you interpret historical events accurately?*

You have chosen a good topic. You have created your question cards and used them while reading encyclopedia articles and library books. You have also used your cards while reviewing reliable Internet resources about your topic. You have turned the answers on your question cards into an outline. Now you are ready to write your research report. As you work, be aware of some important guidelines for writing about history.

Plagiarism

To **plagiarize** (PLAY•juh•RYZ) is to present the ideas or words of another person as your own without offering credit to the source. Plagiarism is similar to forgery, or copying something that is not yours. It also **violates** copyright laws. These laws prevent the unauthorized use of a writer's work. If you copy an idea or a written text exactly word-for-word, that is plagiarism. Some scholars have ruined their careers through plagiarism. They used content from books or the Internet without citing the source or giving credit.

To avoid plagiarism, follow these rules:

- Put information in your own words.
- When you restate an opinion from something you read, include a reference to the author: "According to Smith and Jones, . . ."
- Always include a footnote when you use a direct quotation from one of your sources.

"I didn't write the book report. I downloaded and printed it directly from the Internet, but I did collate and staple it myself."

Cartoons can make plagiarism seem humorous, but it is illegal and can lead to serious consequences.

Ancient History and Modern Values

Avoid using modern ideas to evaluate a historical event. For example, a scholar of women's history may want to apply modern ideas to women's rights in historical settings. Ideas have changed over time. Drawing conclusions about women's attitudes in the Middle Ages using modern ideas would be a mistake. Your evaluations of history should be based on the evidence, not on today's understanding of rights and society.

PROGRESS CHECK

Listing What is one way to avoid plagiarism when writing about history?

Reading HELPDESK

URL abbreviation for *uniform resource locator*; the address of an online resource

.gov the ending of a URL for a government Web site

.edu the ending of a URL for a Web site for an educational institution

.org the ending of a URL for an organization

plagiarize to present someone's work as your own without giving that person credit

Academic Vocabulary

data information, usually facts and figures

violate to disobey or break a rule or law

LESSON 3 REVIEW

Review Vocabulary

1. Why is it against the law to *plagiarize*?
2. Which URL ending would identify a Web site for a charity?
   a. .org b. .gov c. .edu

Answer the Guiding Questions

3. ***Assessing*** How do you know if a resource in a library book can be trusted?
4. ***Listing*** Identify the clues you would look for to decide if an online resource is trustworthy.
5. ***Determining Cause and Effect*** What is one negative effect that can come from applying modern values to a historical event?
6. **PERSUASIVE WRITING** Your teacher does not want students to use the Internet for research. Write two paragraphs in which you persuade the teacher that the Internet can be a reliable source of information.

NOTES

NOTES

LESSON 3 (cont.)

2 Researching on the Internet

GUIDING QUESTION *How do you safely conduct research on the Internet?*

VIDEO **Differentiating** Review the details about researching on the Internet. You may choose to show the short video "Internet Research Techniques."

Then, have students differentiate among the sites they may encounter while they research a topic. Create an idea web on the board using students' ideas about Internet research.

Ask: How is a government Web site different from a school Web site? *(A government site is developed by a government office and usually contains facts and statistics about a country or a government agency. A school site is developed by an academic institution and often contains research information.)* BL

GAME **Differentiating** Review with students how to determine which sources were reliable and which were unreliable. Launch the interactive game about reliable Web sites. Have students play the game as a class or in groups in which they sort the Web sites according to reliability.

3 Writing Without Bias

GUIDING QUESTION *How do you interpret historical events accurately?*

CHART **Defining** Ask students to define *plagiarism.* Have a student volunteer record the answers on the whiteboard.

Present students with scenarios, such as "Jane copied Johnny's homework" and "Lupe used her own words to describe the terra-cotta soldiers." Have students give a thumbs-down sign if the example is plagiarism and a thumbs-up sign if it is not. ELL

Then, have students work in pairs to complete the *Is It Plagiarism?* interactive chart.

Have students complete the Lesson 3 Review.

CLOSE & REFLECT

Making Generalizations Explain the class policy on plagiarism to students. Offer examples of how to avoid plagiarizing material they read in an encyclopedia or other research material.

Ask: Can you make any generalizations about historians or history students who plagiarize the work of others? *(Sample answer: Historians who plagiarize are careless or dishonest about their work.)*

IF YOU HAVE MORE TIME . . .

Review Additional Guidelines for Evaluating Internet Sites

Ask students to discuss ways that researching on the Internet is different from using books or other printed material.

Remind students that information on the Internet may be easier to find and more convenient, but it is more difficult to evaluate its reliability.

Then, explain to students that with so many Web sites available, it is important to determine which ones will be the most helpful. Also, with so many choices, it is easy to waste time using the Internet. By recognizing important details that distinguish reliable sites from unreliable sites, students will be able to find appropriate sites more easily and quickly.

The questions students should ask themselves when evaluating a Web site are:

- **Do the facts seem accurate, based on what I already know?**
- **Who is the author or sponsor of the site?**
- **What is the purpose of the site, and why is it maintained?** For example, consider whether the site is for entertainment, for information, to advertise a product or service, or to express a particular point of view.
- **Does the site have links to resources you already know to be reliable, such as government agencies, libraries, universities, or museums?**
- **Is the information easy to read and access?**

Answers for pages 20–21

P. 20 ☑ **PROGRESS CHECK** A biased resource would alter the interpretation of historical events. Conclusions will be inaccurate if historians do not use reliable sources for their research.

P. 21 ☑ **PROGRESS CHECK** Students may cite any of the following: put the ideas you read in your own words, give credit to the sources of ideas, and footnote direct quotations.

LESSON 3 REVIEW

1. Plagiarism is against the law because it is a form of stealing.
2. A is the correct answer. A charity would most likely have a URL that ends with .org.
3. A resource should not be trusted if it contains statements of opinion about a subject that are not backed up by verifiable facts.
4. Three clues are the authorship of the article, the ending of the URL, and the level of scholarship of the journal from which the article comes.
5. When modern values are used to evaluate an event in history, a writer may draw incorrect conclusions about the event.
6. Students' paragraphs should demonstrate an understanding of evaluating credible resources, especially as it applies to Internet sources.

CHAPTER 1 Activities

Write your answers on a separate piece of paper.

1. **Exploring the Essential Question**
   EXPOSITORY WRITING Using information you have read in this chapter, give three reasons why we study history.

2. **21st Century Skills**
   ANALYZE AND INTERPRET MEDIA Research a historical subject of your choice. Find three reliable sources and at least one source that would not be considered reliable. Write a paragraph that analyzes the online resources you discovered. Describe why each source is reliable or unreliable.

3. **Thinking Like a Historian**
   SEQUENCING Create a personal time line using the terms *before my birth* and *after my birth*. Fill in the time line with three key events that happened before and three key events that happened after you were born.

4. **GEOGRAPHY ACTIVITY**

Lewis and Clark expedition journal from the explorations of the Louisiana Territory

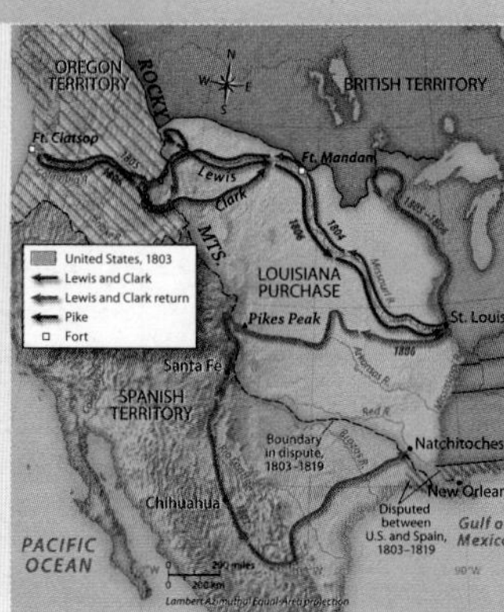

Modern map of Lewis and Clark journey, 1803

Comparing Sources
Which map is a primary source? Which is a secondary source? Include definitions of these terms in your answer. Then, explain why each source is useful to a historian.

CHAPTER 1 Assessment

REVIEW THE GUIDING QUESTIONS
Directions: Choose the best answer for each question.

1. How does the Gregorian calendar label events that happened after the birth of Jesus?
   A. B.C.E
   B. C.E.
   C. A.D.
   D. B.C.

2. An anthropologist is a historian who studies
   F. fossils found in sea beds.
   G. ancient plant life.
   H. animal behavior.
   I. the history of human culture.

3. A historian looks for firsthand evidence about an event in which type of resource?
   A. a secondary source
   B. a primary source
   C. the Internet
   D. an online scholarly journal

4. A work of scholarly history can be identified by
   F. its lively writing style.
   G. its biased point of view.
   H. its accuracy and lack of bias.
   I. its relevance to current events.

5. If you were researching data on the population of India, which online source would most likely contain reliable information?
   A. www.tourism-india.com
   B. www.cia.gov/india
   C. www.beautiful-people-of-india.org
   D. www.population.com

6. What is one way to avoid plagiarism?
   F. Always give credit to someone else for their ideas.
   G. Never use the Internet for research.
   H. Read a source three times.
   I. Always use the library for research.

CHAPTER 1 Assessment *(continued)*

DBQ DOCUMENT-BASED QUESTIONS

7. **Identifying** Historian William H. McNeill wrote an essay explaining why people should study history.

   "[We] can only know ourselves by knowing how we resemble and how we differ from others. Acquaintance [familiarity] with the human past is the only way to such self knowledge. …

   In [studying history], eternal and unchanging truth does not emerge. Only inspired, informed guesses about what mattered and how things changed through time. … Not very good, perhaps; simply the best we have in the unending effort to understand ourselves and others …"

   —Excerpt from "Why Study History?" by William H. McNeill

   According to McNeill, what do people gain from the study of history?
   A. They discover absolute truth.
   B. They discover that the past was not very good.
   C. They learn more about themselves.
   D. They learn to give their best effort in what they do.

8. **Identifying Point of View** With which statement would McNeill agree?
   F. Studying history is a waste of time.
   G. We have much to learn from history.
   H. History has no influence on the present time.
   I. We should look to history for the answers to all of our questions.

SHORT RESPONSE

"Historians do not perform heart transplants, improve highway design, or arrest criminals. … History is in fact very useful, actually indispensable [necessary], but the products of historical study are less tangible [physical], sometimes less immediate, than those that stem from some other disciplines."

—Excerpt from "Why Study History?" by Peter N. Stearns

9. Which part of this passage is fact? Which part is opinion?

10. According to Stearns, why is the usefulness of history difficult to identify?

EXTENDED RESPONSE

11. **Personal Writing** Write two paragraphs that identify primary sources and secondary sources about your life. Would these sources be biased? Explain.

Need Extra Help?

If You've Missed Question	1	2	3	4	5	6	7	8	9	10	11
Review Lesson	1	1	2	2	3	3	1	1	2	1	3

NOTES

REFLECT, REVIEW, & REMEDIATE

INTERACTIVE WORKSHEET

Chapter Summary

Provide students with the Chapter Summary worksheet to help review the chapter and prepare for assessment.

Reviewing the Enduring Understanding

Review this chapter's Enduring Understanding with students.

- Learning about the past helps us understand the present and make decisions about the future.

INTERACTIVE WHITEBOARD ACTIVITY

Draw a sample flowchart on the whiteboard. Explain that a flowchart shows a sequence of events. Organize students into small groups. Have each group work together to create a flowchart of how historians work. Each group should present its flowchart to the class. *(Flowcharts should include choosing a topic, finding evidence, evaluating sources, drawing conclusions/making inferences, and presenting findings.)*

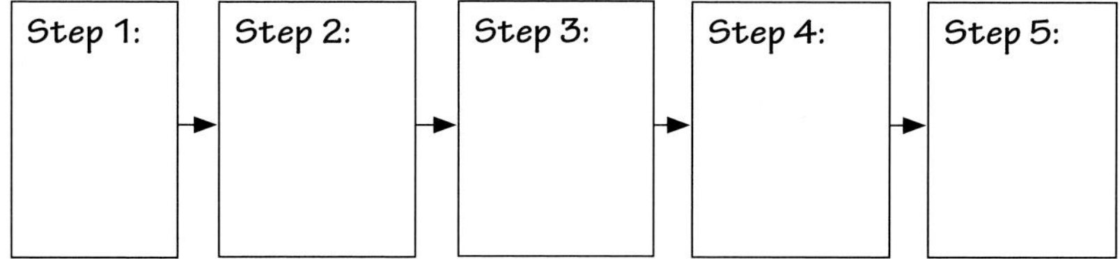

ACTIVITIES ANSWERS

Exploring the Essential Question

1. Possible answer: Reason 1: Historians who know about ancient peoples have been able to explain the meaning of the cave paintings discovered in Europe and to help preserve them for the future. Reason 2: Historians who study early religious documents are able to reveal the significance of early religious doctrines for modern worshipers. Reason 3: Historians who study wars can explain how events of the past led to wars in the present.

21st Century Skills

2. Students should be able to identify three reliable sources and explain why they should be trusted, using criteria such as credible authorship, scholarly journal, and appropriateness of the URL. Students should identify three unreliable resources and be able to point out why they are biased or lack credibility.

Thinking Like a Historian

3. Student time lines should reflect understanding of how time lines work, with events prior to students' birth and since their birth placed chronologically on the time line and clearly labeled.

Comparing Sources

4. The hand-drawn map created by Lewis and Clark when they explored the Louisiana Territory is a primary source. It shows details and evidence of their experience. The second map is a secondary source. It offers after-the-fact information about where the Lewis and Clark expedition traveled on their journey and how the land surrounding the Louisiana Territory was organized.

ASSESSMENT ANSWERS

Review the Guiding Questions

1. **C** Some historians use the designations C.E. and B.C.E., but the Gregorian calendar does not. The Gregorian calendar uses B.C. to identify events that occurred before the birth of Jesus and A.D. to identify events that occurred after Jesus's birth. Therefore, C is the correct answer.

2. **I** An anthropologist is interested in human beliefs and culture, not the history of sealife, plants, or animals. Thus, I is the correct answer.

3. **B** Firsthand evidence is found in primary sources, which were written by people who experienced an event. A scholarly journal is a secondary source, and the Internet is not always trustworthy. Thus, B is the correct answer.

4. **H** Historians who write scholarly history try to avoid bias, or a decided point of view. They focus instead on accuracy. Although the material may be relevant to current events, the focus of the writing does not have to be relevant to today. Therefore, H is the correct answer.

5. **B** Web sites such as "beautiful-people-of-india.org" and "population.com" do not have reliable URLs. Government (.gov) Web sites are usually considered reliable for population statistics. Thus, B is the correct answer.

6. **F** Plagiarism is not determined by which sources are used or how many times a source is read, but rather by how the sources are used. Sources from the library can be plagiarized as easily as sources from the Internet. Plagiarism is best avoided by giving credit where it is due. Therefore, F is the correct answer.

Document-Based Questions

7. **C** According to McNeill, learning about people of the past teaches us more about ourselves. He says that educated guesses, not truth, emerge from the study of history. It is this result, he says, that does not seem good. Thus, C is the correct answer.

8. **G** McNeill sees benefits in studying history so he would not see the effort as a waste of time, nor would he believe that history has no influence on the present. Because he believes there is no absolute truth in history, McNeill probably would not agree with statement I. Therefore, G is the correct answer.

Short Response

9. The first sentence in the passage ("Historians do not perform heart transplants . . .") is a fact. The second sentence ("History is in fact very useful . . .") is an opinion.

10. The usefulness of history is difficult to identify because studying history does not produce immediate, visible results the way work in other occupations does.

Extended Response

11. Students should mention primary sources, such as their letters, text messages, and diaries, and secondary sources, such as school yearbooks and descriptions of them written by others. They might indicate that diaries and letters could show a bias.

ONLINE RESOURCES

networks

There's More Online!

- ☑ INTERACTIVE WORKSHEETS
- ☑ BIOGRAPHIES
- ☑ CHARTS/GRAPHS
- ☑ GAMES
- ☑ GRAPHIC ORGANIZERS
- ☑ IMAGES
- ☑ MAPS
- ☑ PRIMARY SOURCES
- ☑ SLIDE SHOWS
- ☑ TIME LINE
- ☑ LECTURE SLIDES
- ☑ INTERACTIVE WHITEBOARD ACTIVITIES
- ☑ ASSESSMENTS
- ☑ VIDEOS

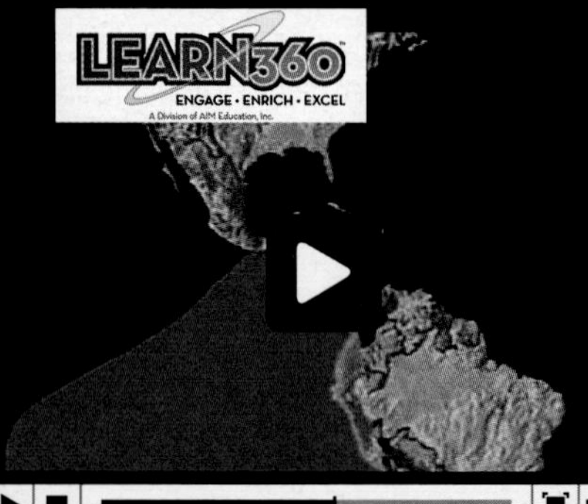

Geography Basics

Introduction to Economics, Part 1

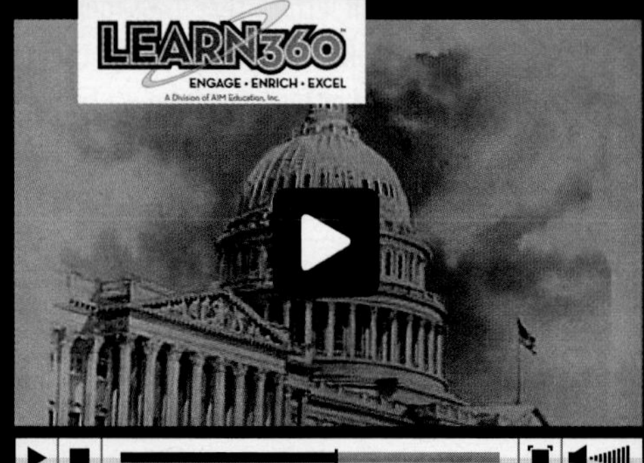

The Seven Dynamics of Citizenship

Chapter **2**

Studying Geography, Economics, and Citizenship

Dear World History Teacher,

As you begin to teach this chapter, it will help you to be aware of certain themes.

You are probably familiar with the reference by William Shakespeare that the world is a stage. Historians who study the events of the past must know something about the stage upon which the drama has been played out.

When people meet for the first time, they usually ask each other where they are from. People recognize that the environment in which we live greatly influences our development, opportunities, and even belief systems. Likewise, historians also must be aware of the physical geography of the Earth and how people interact with their environment. Thus, knowledge of human and physical geography is vital for anyone who studies history.

Also important to the study of history is an understanding of economics. All societies have resources. The way people accumulate, distribute, and use those resources, which are central to the study of economics, might be the most powerful gauge of people's beliefs, traditions, and actions. By studying a country's economic system, historians can begin to understand a country's priorities, values, and government policies.

The study of history is also crucial to being a good citizen. Americans continue to embrace a democratic political system and a mixed market economy. Learning about these features of American society provides students with the foundation for playing a productive and meaningful role in a democracy.

Jackson J. Spielvogel

More Media Resources

Current Events Online

Visit McGraw-Hill's current events Web site for high-interest news stories and activities for your students. Access the site through the Student or Teacher Center in **networks.**

Reading List

Grade 6 reading level:
Show Me the Money: How to Make Sense of Economics, by Alvin Hall

Grade 7 reading level:
A Tugging String: A Novel About Growing Up in the Civil Rights Era, by David T. Greenberg

Grade 8 reading level:
Earth Matters, by David de Rothschild

CHAPTER 2 Planner

UNDERSTANDING BY DESIGN®

Enduring Understandings

- *People, places, and ideas change over time.* • *Resources are limited, so people must make choices.* • *The value that a society places on individual rights is often reflected in that society's government.*

Essential Questions

- *How does geography influence the way people live?* • *Why do people trade?*
- *Why do people form governments?*

Students will know:

- *the Six Essential Elements of Geography and how geography relates to history*
- *the uses for longitude and latitude, map projections, and types of maps*
- *basic principles of economics and trade*
- *the meaning of representative government and the responsibilities of citizenship*

Students will be able to:

- **recall** information about the study of geography
- **apply** their understanding of geography to the interpretation of maps
- **synthesize** information about geography and its relationship with history
- **reflect** on their understanding of geography
- **identify** basic economic systems
- **explore** the role of trade in world history
- **compare and contrast** the advantages and disadvantages of trade
- **recall** key facts about the United States government
- **summarize** important facts about the rights, duties, and responsibilities of United States citizens
- **discuss** ways in which people can practice good citizenship in their communities
- **compare** their roles as American citizens with their roles as global citizens

Predictable Misunderstandings

Students may think:

- The study of geography and economics will not help them understand history.
- Maps and globes show the same information about Earth.
- Geographers study only the locations of places on Earth.
- Economics has little to do with their daily lives.
- Citizenship relates to rights but not duties or responsibilities.

Assessment Evidence

Performance Task

- Hands-On Chapter Project

Other Evidence

- Responses to Interactive Whiteboard Activities
- Comparing and contrasting different map projections
- Responses to Economics Simulation Activity
- Class discussion answers
- Interactive Graphic Organizers
- Economics of History Activity
- Geography and History Activities
- 21st Century Skills Activity
- Written Paragraphs
- Lesson Reviews

Pacing Guide

Introducing the Chapter	1 day
Lesson 1 Studying Geography	2 days
Lesson 2 Exploring Economics	1 day
Lesson 3 Practicing Citizenship	1 day
Chapter Activities and Assessment	1 day
TOTAL TIME	**6 Days**

Differentiated Instruction

These lesson plans are written to address the needs of your On Level students. Discussion and activities that are well-suited to your Approaching Grade Level learners, Beyond Grade Level learners, as well as your English Language Learners are coded as follows:

AL Approaching Grade Level

BL Beyond Grade Level

ELL English Language Learner

NCSS Standards covered in "Studying Geography, Economics, and Citizenship"

Learners will understand:

1 CULTURE

1. "Culture" refers to the socially transmitted behaviors, beliefs, values, traditions, institutions, and ways of living together for a group of people.

2. Concepts such as beliefs, values, institutions, cohesion, diversity, accommodation, adaptation, assimilation, and dissonance

4. That the beliefs, values, and behaviors of a culture form an integrated system that helps shape the activities and ways of life that define a culture

3 PEOPLE, PLACES, AND ENVIRONMENTS

1. The theme of people, places, and environments involves the study of the relationships between human populations in different locations and geographic phenomena such as climate, vegetation, and natural resources.

2. Concepts such as: location, region, place, migration, as well as human and physical systems

9. The use of a variety of maps, globes, graphic representations, and geospatial technologies to help investigate the relationships among people, places, and environments

5 INDIVIDUALS, GROUPS, AND INSTITUTIONS

6. That cultural diffusion occurs when groups migrate

7 PRODUCTION, DISTRIBUTION, AND CONSUMPTION

1. Individuals, government, and society experience scarcity because human wants and needs exceed what can be produced from available resources.

2. How choices involve trading off the expected value of one opportunity gained against the expected value of the best alternative

7. How markets bring buyers and sellers together to exchange goods and services

8. How goods and services are allocated in a market economy through the influence of prices on decisions about production and consumption

10 CIVIC IDEALS AND PRACTICES

2. Concepts and ideals such as: individual dignity, liberty, justice, equality, individual rights, responsibility, majority and minority rights, and civil dissent

6. The origins and function of major institutions and practices developed to support democratic ideals and practices

CHAPTER 2

Introducing the Chapter

(Student Edition p. 25)

The Story Matters . . .

Read "The Story Matters . . ." aloud in class or ask for a volunteer to read it aloud. Explain that the process of becoming a U.S. citizen is called naturalization. Discuss the reasons why a person might want to become a citizen of the United States.

Ask these questions: **What sorts of rights and responsibilities do U.S. citizens have? Do you know anyone who has become a naturalized U.S. citizen?**

Have a few students share their ideas about citizenship or their stories of naturalized citizens.

Then ask: **If you do not understand your duties and responsibilities as a citizen, what might happen? Who would protect your rights and freedoms?**

Tell the class that one of the responsibilities of citizenship is being informed about key issues. Explain that because the countries of the world are more connected now than ever before, it is important to understand geography. It is also important to learn about economics so that they can understand trade and manage their own money.

Studying Geography, Economics, and Citizenship

ESSENTIAL QUESTIONS • *How does geography influence the way people live?* • *Why do people trade?* • *Why do people form governments?*

networks *There's More Online* about the key ideas of geography, economics, and citizenship.

CHAPTER 2

Lesson 1 *Studying Geography*

Lesson 2 *Exploring Economics*

Lesson 3 *Practicing Citizenship*

The Story Matters . . .

Why is this woman smiling? She has just become a citizen of the United States. Though she was born in another country, she now enjoys all the rights and responsibilities of U.S. citizenship. Her last step toward gaining citizenship was taking the Oath of Allegiance. In this oath, people swear to "support and defend the Constitution against all enemies, foreign and domestic."

Whether you have taken this oath or not, as a U.S. citizen, you share this duty to defend the laws of your nation. Being a good citizen also means staying informed about the world around you. Understanding history, geography, and economics can help you fulfill this responsibility.

◀ *For many people, citizenship comes with being born in a certain country. For others, like this woman, citizenship is a matter of choice.*

Getty Images News/Getty Images

25

Introducing Place and Time (Student Edition pp. 26–27)

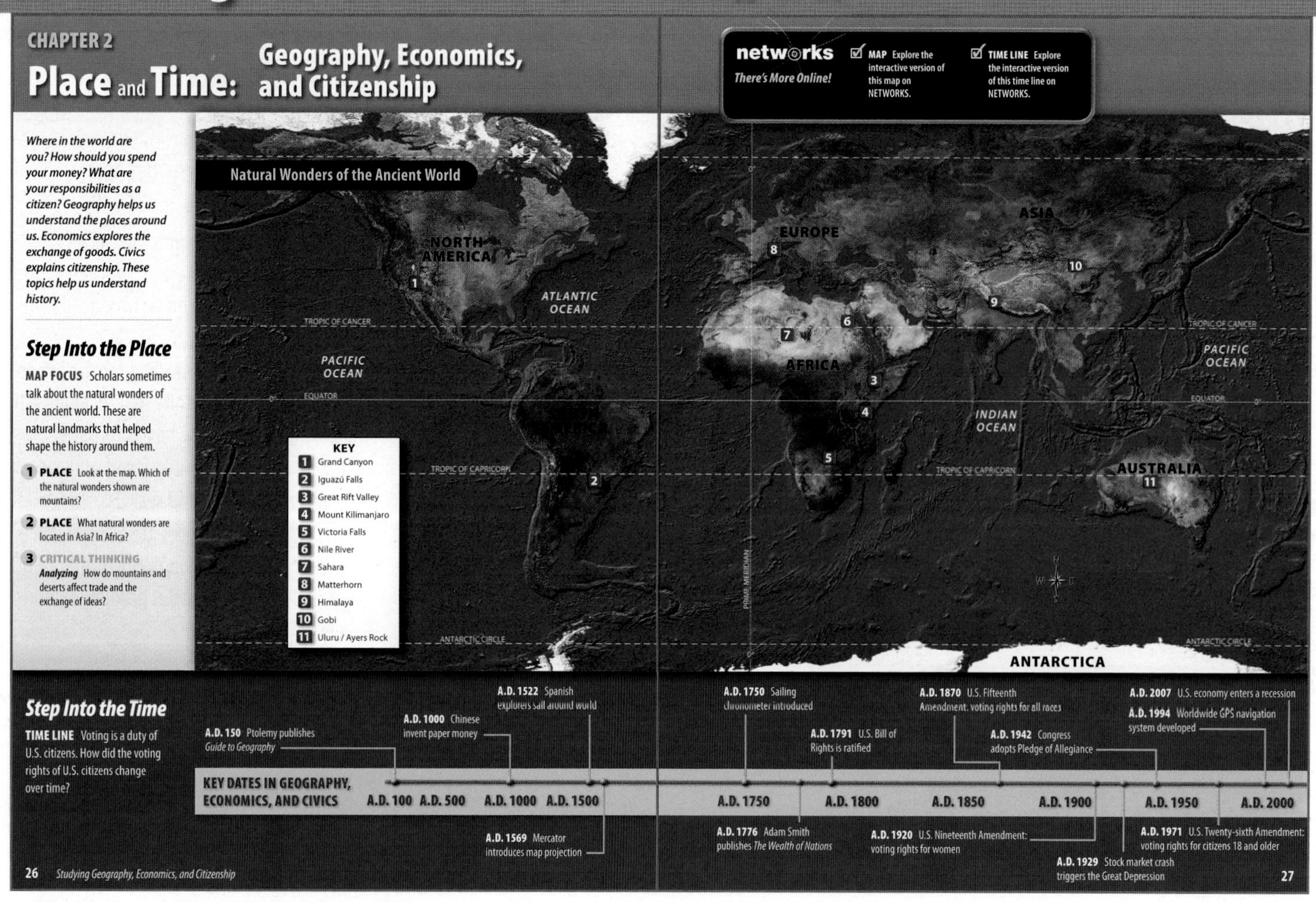

CHAPTER 2

Place and Time: Geography, Economics, and Citizenship

networks *There's More Online!* ☑ **MAP** Explore the interactive version of this map on NETWORKS. ☑ **TIME LINE** Explore the interactive version of this time line on NETWORKS.

Where in the world are you? How should you spend your money? What are your responsibilities as a citizen? Geography helps us understand the places around us. Economics explores the exchange of goods. Civics explains citizenship. These topics help us understand history.

Step Into the Place

MAP FOCUS Scholars sometimes talk about the natural wonders of the ancient world. These are natural landmarks that helped shape the history around them.

1. **PLACE** Look at the map. Which of the natural wonders shown are mountains?
2. **PLACE** What natural wonders are located in Asia? In Africa?
3. **CRITICAL THINKING** ***Analyzing*** How do mountains and deserts affect trade and the exchange of ideas?

Step Into the Time

TIME LINE Voting is a duty of U.S. citizens. How did the voting rights of U.S. citizens change over time?

26 *Studying Geography, Economics, and Citizenship*

27

Technology Extension

- Find an additional activity online that incorporates technology for this project.
- Visit the EdTechTeacher Web sites (included in the Technology Extension for this chapter) for more links, tutorials, and other resources.

Assessing Background Knowledge

INTERACTIVE WORKSHEET

What Do You Know? Activity

Have students complete the What Do You Know? Anticipation Guide about geography, economics, and citizenship before they study the chapter.

Direct students to read each statement on the chart. Then in the "Before" column, check whether they agree or disagree with the statement. Next, take a class poll so you can tailor your lessons to focus on students' misconceptions.

After students complete the chapter, have them reread the statements and note in the "After" column whether they now agree or disagree with the statement. Ask students who changed their responses to explain why they did so.

INTERACTIVE WORKSHEET

Guided Reading Activities

There is a Guided Reading Activity for each lesson in this chapter. You may wish to assign the Guided Reading Activity for Lesson 1 after introducing the chapter.

Hands-On Chapter Project

Students will participate in a simulation in order to learn how physical geography influences the way people live and trade.

- Students will work in small groups and use worksheets to invent a country and create a map of it.
- Through discussion and worksheets, students will name the country, identify its physical geographic features, specify its population and population distribution, identify its animals and vegetation, and specify its goods and services.
- Next, students will present their maps, describe their country, and watch other map presentations.
- Then, students will decide how their country will trade and with whom.
- Finally, the class will use an Assessment Rubric to evaluate their maps, presentations, and collaboration.

Visit **networks** online to see the full project and rubric.

ONLINE RESOURCES

networks

Assign these interactive worksheets and quizzes from your Teacher Lesson Center. All resources are print-ready.

It's ALL Online!

Chapter 2 Resources

- ☑ Chapter Summary
- ☑ Vocabulary Builder
- ☑ What Do You Know?
- ☑ Hands-On Chapter Project

Lesson 1 Resources

- ☑ Geography and History Activity: Latitude and Longitude
- ☑ Geography and History Activity: Physical Maps
- ☑ Guided Reading Activity
- ☑ Reading Essentials and Study Guide
- ☑ Online Self-Check Quiz

Lesson 2 Resources

- ☑ Economics of History Activity: Trade in the Ancient World
- ☑ Guided Reading Activity
- ☑ Reading Essentials and Study Guide
- ☑ Online Self-Check Quiz

Lesson 3 Resources

- ☑ 21st Century Skills Activity: Plan a Service Project
- ☑ Guided Reading Activity
- ☑ Reading Essentials and Study Guide
- ☑ Online Self-Check Quiz

Assessment Resources

- ☑ Lesson Reviews
- ☑ Online Self-Check Quizzes
- ☑ Chapter Activities and Assessment
- ☑ Standardized Test Practice

Remediation Resources

- ☑ Reading Essentials and Study Guide
- ☑ Guided Reading Activities
- ☑ Online Self-Check Quizzes
- ☑ Chapter Summary

Step Into the Place

Regions Project the chapter opener map on the whiteboard.

Tell students that major geographic features, such as large rivers and mountain ranges, can shape the development of civilizations. In some cases, such features provide valuable resources. In other situations, geography might be a barrier to travel and limit contact between different peoples.

Discuss as a class how some of the landmarks shown on the chapter opener map might provide benefits or disadvantages to the people living around them.

At your interactive whiteboard, have student volunteers categorize the different natural wonders of the ancient world shown on the map, identifying them as rivers, mountains, deserts, and so on. As a class, discuss the Map Focus questions.

Step Into the Time

Speculating Have students review the time line for the chapter. Ask them to pick out events related to geography. Advise them to look for key words like *map*, *globe*, and *world*.

Ask students: **Based on the information listed in the time line, how has our knowledge of geographic locations changed?** *(Our detailed knowledge of geographic locations has increased greatly. First, the world has been and is still being explored. Then, tools like the sailing chronometer and Mercator's map projection were made. Now, satellite imagery and GPS technology provide even more specific information about Earth's surface.)*

Answers for pages 26–27

Step Into the Place

1. Mount Kilimanjaro, Matterhorn, Himalaya
2. Asia: Gobi and Himalaya; Africa: Great Rift Valley, Mount Kilimanjaro, Victoria Falls, Sahara, Nile River
3. CRITICAL THINKING Mountains and deserts often form barriers to trade and the exchange of ideas.

Step Into the Time

The right to vote was expanded to include people of all races, women, and 18-year-old citizens.

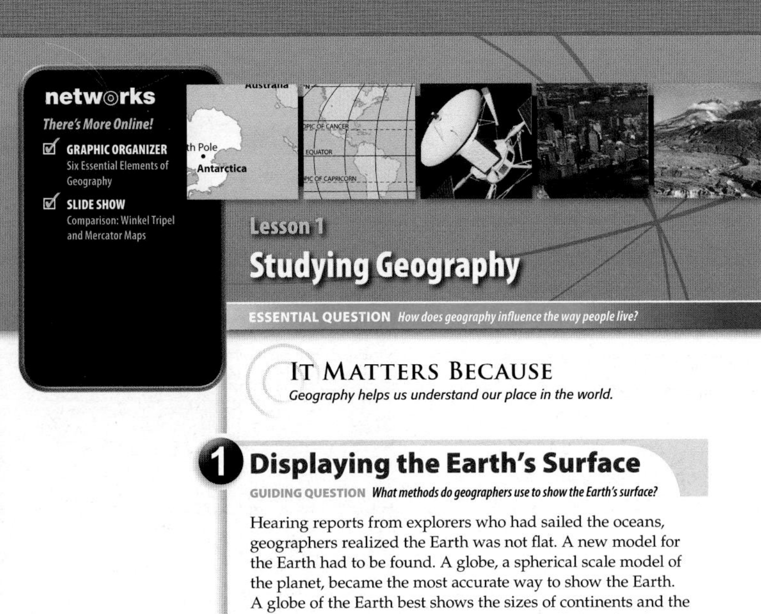

networks
There's More Online!
GRAPHIC ORGANIZER
Six Essential Elements of Geography
SLIDE SHOW
Comparison: Winkel Tripel and Mercator Maps
Antarctica
Lesson 1
Studying Geography

ESSENTIAL QUESTION *How does geography influence the way people live?*

IT MATTERS BECAUSE
Geography helps us understand our place in the world.

1 Displaying the Earth's Surface

GUIDING QUESTION *What methods do geographers use to show the Earth's surface?*

Hearing reports from explorers who had sailed the oceans, geographers realized the Earth was not flat. A new model for the Earth had to be found. A globe, a spherical scale model of the planet, became the most accurate way to show the Earth. A globe of the Earth best shows the sizes of continents and the shapes of landmasses and bodies of water. Globes also show true distance and direction.

Globes have their limitations. A globe is not as easy to carry as a map. Maps are flat drawings of all or part of the Earth's surface. Maps can show small areas in great detail. Maps can show many things—political borders, population densities, or even voting results. Plus, maps can be folded and carried in a pocket or placed in a car.

Maps, however, cannot show true size, shape, distance, and direction at the same time. The reason for this is they are flat drawings of a round object, the Earth.

Globes and maps have some features in common. Both are marked with imaginary lines that geographers use to locate places on Earth's surface. These lines divide the Earth into halves called hemispheres.

Reading **HELP**DESK

Taking Notes: ***Identifying***
Use a diagram like the one shown here to list the Six Essential Elements of Geography.

Six Essential Elements of Geography

Content Vocabulary
- **hemisphere**
- **latitude**
- **longitude**
- **projection**
- **physical map**
- **political map**

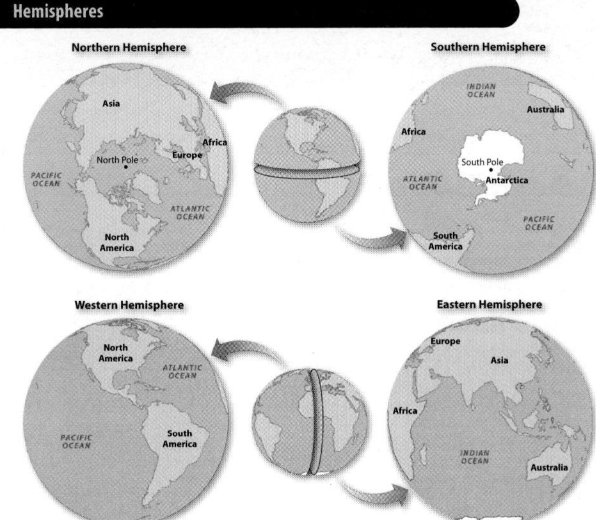

Dividing the Earth into hemispheres helps geographers locate places on the planet's surface. Which oceans are located in the Western Hemisphere? Which oceans are in the Eastern Hemisphere?

Hemispheres

To find a place on the Earth, geographers use a system of imaginary lines that crisscross the globe. The Equator (ih•KWAY•tuhr) is one of these lines. It circles the middle of the Earth like a belt. It divides the Earth into "half spheres," or **hemispheres** (HEH•muh•sfihrz). Everything north of the Equator is in the Northern Hemisphere. Everything south of the Equator is in the Southern Hemisphere. In which of these hemispheres do you live?

Another imaginary line divides the Earth into Eastern and Western Hemispheres. This line is called the Prime Meridian. Generally, the area east of the Prime Meridian is in the Eastern Hemisphere. Everything west of the Prime Meridian is in the Western Hemisphere.

Content Vocabulary
- **special-purpose map**
- **scale**
- **cardinal directions**
- **choropleth**
- **migration**
- **culture**

hemisphere a "half sphere," used to refer to one-half of the globe when divided into North and South or East and West

Finding Places on the Earth

The Equator and Prime Meridian are two of the lines on maps and globes that help you find places on the Earth. All the lines together are called latitude and longitude. Latitude and longitude lines cross one another, forming a pattern called a grid system.

Latitude and Longitude

Finding the intersection of latitude and longitude allows geographers to pinpoint absolute location. At what degree point is the Prime Meridian?

Lines of **latitude** (LA•tuh•tood) circle the Earth parallel to the Equator. They measure distance north or south of the Equator in degrees. The Equator is at 0° (zero degrees) latitude, while the North Pole is at latitude 90° N (90 degrees north).

Lines of **longitude** (LAHN•juh•tood) circle the Earth from Pole to Pole. These lines measure distances east or west of the Prime Meridian, which is at 0° longitude.

The grid system formed by lines of latitude and longitude makes it possible to find the absolute location of a place. This is the exact spot where a line of latitude crosses a line of longitude. An absolute location is written in special symbols called degrees (°) and minutes (′) (points between degrees). For example, the Empire State Building in New York City is located at a latitude of 40° 44′ North and a longitude of 73° 59′ West (40 degrees 44 minutes North and 73 degrees 59 minutes West).

Goode's Interrupted Equal-Area Projection

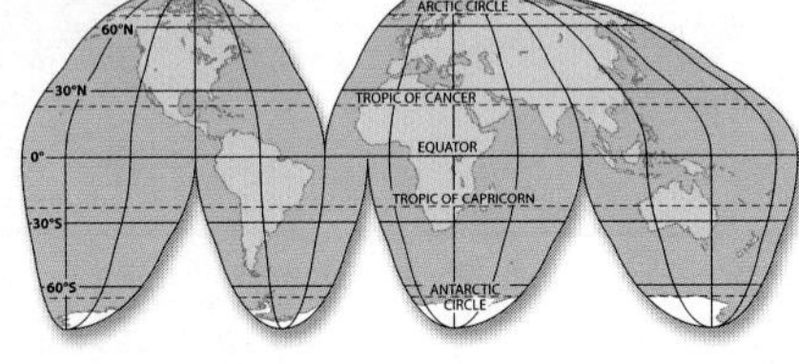

Goode's Interrupted Equal-Area projection shows a realistic representation of continents' sizes and shapes.

Reading **HELP**DESK

latitude imaginary lines that circle the Earth parallel to the Equator
longitude imaginary lines that circle the Earth from Pole to Pole, measuring distance east or west of the Prime Meridian
projection a way of showing the round Earth on a flat map

Academic Vocabulary
distort to twist out of shape or change the size of

From Globes to Maps

When the curves of a globe become straight lines on a map, the size, shape, distance, or area can change. Imagine taking an orange peel and trying to flatten it on a table. You would either have to cut it or **distort**, or stretch, parts of it. Mapmakers face a similar problem in showing the surface of the Earth on a map. Using mathematics, they have created different types of map **projections** (pruh•JEK•shuhnz), or ways of showing the Earth on a flat sheet of paper. Each kind of projection shows the Earth's surface in a slightly different way.

Flattening Out the Planet

When you take an image of the Earth and flatten it, big gaps open up. To fill in the gaps, mapmakers stretch parts of the Earth. They show either the correct shapes of places or their correct sizes. It is impossible to show both. As a result, mapmakers use different map projections depending on their goals.

Map Projections

Take another look at that flattened orange peel. You might see something that looks like a map based on Goode's Interrupted Equal-Area projection. A map made using this projection shows continents close to their true shapes and sizes. This projection is helpful for comparing land areas among continents.

The map on the top right was made using the Mercator projection. It shows true direction and land shapes fairly accurately. However, it does not show correct size or distance. Areas located far from the Equator are distorted on this projection. Alaska, for example, appears much larger on a Mercator map than it does on a globe.

A map using the Robinson projection is less distorted. Land on the western and eastern sides of the Robinson map appears much as it does on a globe. Areas near the North and South Poles are distorted the most on this projection.

The Winkel Tripel projection gives a good overall view of the continents' shapes and sizes. You can see that land areas in this projection are not as distorted near the Poles.

Mercator Projection

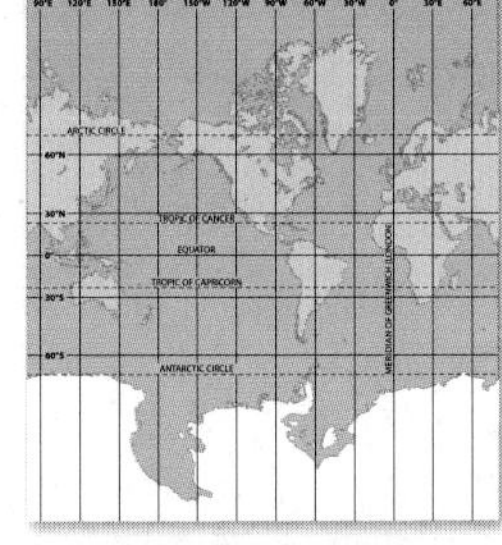

On a Mercator projection, land size and distance appear quite distorted.

Robinson Projection

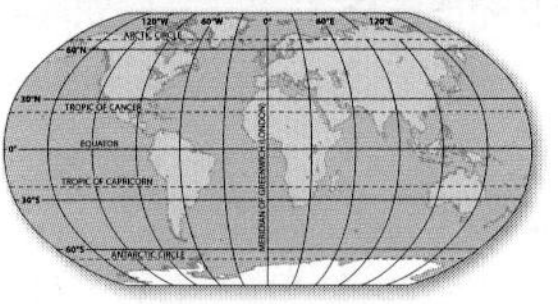

The Robinson projection shows a truer picture of land size and shape. However, the North and South Poles show a great deal of distortion.

Winkel Tripel Projection

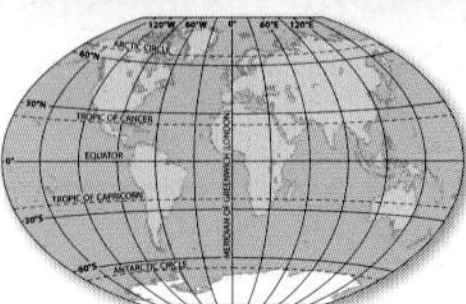

The representation of land areas on the Winkel Tripel projection most closely resembles the globe model.

PROGRESS CHECK

Analyzing What are an advantage and a disadvantage to using a map rather than a globe to study the Earth's geography?

LESSON 1 • Day 1

ENGAGE

Identifying Ask students to describe or identify what they think geographers study. Many students are likely to think that geography involves finding places on Earth and making maps. Note that geography deals with much more than just location.

Tell students that geographers use their tools to show us what the world looks like and describe how people, plants, animals, physical forces, and the environment interact with one another.

Point out that the study of geography can also help us understand the past. AL

TEACH & ASSESS

1 Displaying the Earth's Surface

GUIDING QUESTION ***What methods do geographers use to show the Earth's surface?***

Finding the Main Idea After reading "Hemispheres" and "Finding Places on the Earth," **ask:**

Why do geographers use imaginary lines when showing Earth's surface? *(so they can precisely identify regions and specific locations on Earth)*

What is the significance of the Equator and the Prime Meridian? *(They divide Earth into hemispheres, and they serve as starting points for measuring latitude and longitude.)*

INTERACTIVE WORKSHEET

Geography and History Activity

Locating Then have students begin the "Longitude and Latitude" Geography and History Activity. Review the meaning of the terms *hemisphere, longitude,* and *latitude.*

Students should complete the questions at the end of the worksheet, either individually or in groups. Tell students to look at the worksheet map.

Ask: Between which lines of latitude and longitude is our community located? *(Students should identify your community's lines of latitude and longitude.)*

Comparing and Contrasting If possible, compare the sizes and shapes of the continents shown on the map projections in this lesson with the sizes and shapes of continents on a globe.

Ask: Why do landmasses on maps look different from those on globes? *(Maps are flat representations of a round object. Each type of map distorts the view of Earth in some way.)*

Why do these map projections look different from each other? *(Each map projection distorts the view of Earth in a different way. A map can show correct shapes or correct sizes, but not both.)* BL

2 Five Themes and Six Essential Elements of Geography

GUIDING QUESTION ***How do geographers use the five themes and six essential elements of geography?***

GRAPHIC ORGANIZER

Categorizing Briefly review the Five Themes of Geography with students. Then show students the interactive graphic organizer on the Six Essential Elements of Geography.

Enter each of the elements into the organizer. Then prompt students to provide an example for each element.

INTERACTIVE WHITEBOARD ACTIVITY

For the theme "Physical Systems," show students the Lesson 1 Interactive Whiteboard Activity about food chains.

Guide them through making the connections among the different parts of the food chain.

CLOSE AND REFLECT

Making Connections Have students draw a simple map from their homes to the school from memory. Then ask them to consider and write down some tools of geography that would make their map easier to create and more accurate. Have students save this map for the Engage portion of Day 2. ELL

LESSON 1 • Day 2

ENGAGE

Visualizing Tell students to look at their "home to school" maps they drew on Day 1. Ask them to describe the types of features and landmarks they showed on their maps.

It is likely that students chose certain buildings or locations to use as reference points. Also ask students if they used any symbols or labels to make their maps easier to read. For example, students might have labeled street names, included a scale, or indicated cardinal directions. ELL

Explain to students that they will be learning about different types of maps and the types of information that they display.

TEACH & ASSESS

3 Types of Maps

GUIDING QUESTION ***What are some of the key ways that maps are used?***

4 Using Charts, Graphs, and Diagrams

GUIDING QUESTION ***What are the uses of charts, graphs, and diagrams?***

LECTURE SLIDE **Analyzing** Review the lecture slide that explains different types of maps. Discuss the differences among physical, political, and special-purpose maps.

Ask: What is the difference between a physical map and a political map? *(A physical map shows land and water features. A political map shows country names and borders.)* AL

When might you need to use a physical map? *(Student answers will vary, but they should suggest that a physical map would be needed in situations in which they need to look up information on physical features such as mountains, rivers, lakes, and so on.)*

Answers for pages 28–31

P. 28 Taking Notes The Six Essential Elements of Geography are the World in Spatial Terms, Places and Regions, Physical Systems, Human Systems, Environment and Society, and the Uses of Geography.

P. 29 The Pacific Ocean and the Atlantic Ocean are in the Western Hemisphere. The Indian Ocean is in the Eastern Hemisphere.

P. 30 The Prime Meridian is at 0° longitude.

P. 31 ☑ PROGRESS CHECK An advantage is that maps are portable. A disadvantage is that maps distort either the size or shape of Earth's landmasses and bodies of water.

Connections to — TODAY

GIS/GPS

Technology has changed the way we make maps. Most mapmakers use software programs called geographic information systems (GIS). This software combines information from satellite images, printed text, and statistics. A Global Positioning System (GPS) helps people locate places based on data broadcast by satellites.

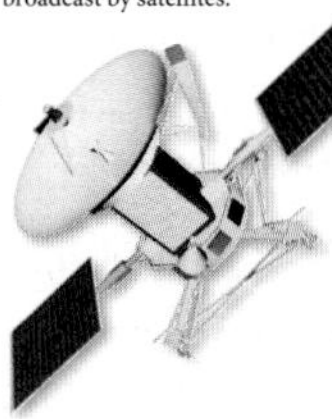

2 Five Themes and Six Essential Elements of Geography

GUIDING QUESTION *How do geographers use the five themes and six essential elements of geography?*

To understand how our world is connected, some geographers have broken the study of geography into five **themes** or six essential elements.

Five Themes of Geography

The Five Themes of Geography are (1) location, (2) place, (3) human-environment interaction, (4) movement, and (5) regions. You will see these themes highlighted in the geography skills questions throughout the book.

Six Essential Elements

Recently, geographers have begun to divide the study of geography into Six Essential Elements. Understanding these elements will help you build your knowledge of geography.

THE WORLD IN SPATIAL TERMS What do geographers do when studying a certain place? They first take a look at where the place is located. Location is a useful starting point. By asking "Where is it?" you begin to develop an **awareness** of the world around you.

PLACES AND REGIONS Place has a special meaning in geography. It refers to more than where a place is. It also describes what a place is like. It might describe physical characteristics such as landforms, climate, and plant or animal life. Or it might describe human characteristics, such as language and way of life.

To help organize their study, geographers often group places into regions. Regions are united by one or more common characteristics.

PHYSICAL SYSTEMS When geographers study places and regions, they analyze how physical systems—such as hurricanes, volcanoes, and glaciers—shape the Earth's surface. They also look at the communities of livings things. The populations of plants and animals depend upon one another and their surroundings for survival.

Reading **HELP**DESK

Academic Vocabulary

theme a topic that is studied or a special quality that connects ideas
awareness the state of having understanding or knowledge

HUMAN SYSTEMS Geographers are interested in human systems. Human systems refer to how people have shaped our world. Geographers look at how borders are decided and why people settle in certain places and not in others. A basic theme in geography is the movement of people, ideas, and goods.

ENVIRONMENT AND SOCIETY How does the relationship between people and their natural surroundings influence the way we live? The theme of human-environment interaction investigates this. It also shows how people use the environment and how their actions affect the environment.

Central Park in New York covers 843 acres of open land. People use the park for recreation. A yearlong study recorded about 35 million visits by people from the city and from around the world.

THE USES OF GEOGRAPHY Geography helps us understand the relationships among people, places, and environments. Mastering the tools and technology used for studying geography can also help us in our daily lives.

✓ PROGRESS CHECK

Identifying Which Essential Elements of Geography might be involved in the study of an area's landforms and how they affect people living there?

The 1980 eruption of Mount St. Helens in Washington state removed the top 1,314 feet (400 meters) of the volcano's peak and leveled nearly 230 square miles (595 square km) of surrounding forest. The destruction happened in a matter of minutes.

▶ CRITICAL THINKING

Analyzing What does this photo suggest about the wildlife living in the region?

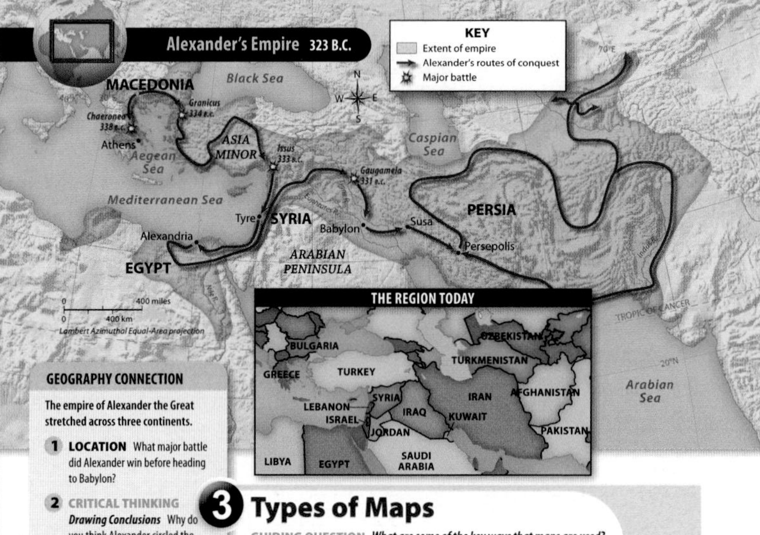

GEOGRAPHY CONNECTION

The empire of Alexander the Great stretched across three continents.

1. **LOCATION** What major battle did Alexander win before heading to Babylon?
2. CRITICAL THINKING ***Drawing Conclusions*** Why do you think Alexander circled the Mediterranean Sea but did not cross it?

3 Types of Maps

GUIDING QUESTION *What are some of the key ways that maps are used?*

Geographers use many different types of maps. Maps that show a wide range of information are called general-purpose maps. These maps are often collected into one book called an atlas. An atlas may be a collection of special area maps—such as North America maps—or general maps of the entire world. Two of the most common general-purpose maps found in an atlas are physical and political maps.

Physical maps show land and water features. The colors used on physical maps include brown or green for land and blue for water. Physical maps may also use colors to show elevation. Elevation is the height of an area above sea level. A key explains the meaning of each color. **Political maps** show the names and borders of countries. They also show the location of cities and other human-made features of a place. Often they identify major physical features of a land area.

Reading **HELP**DESK

physical map a map that shows land and water features
political map a map that shows the names and borders of countries
special-purpose map a map that shows themes or patterns such as climate, natural resources, or population

Reading Strategy: *Summarizing*

How do you read a map? Summarize how to read a map by identifying map parts and the information they provide.

Special-Purpose Maps

Some maps show specific kinds of information. These are called **special-purpose maps.** They usually show patterns such as climate, natural resources, or population. A road map is another example of a special-purpose map. Like this map of Alexander's empire, special-purpose maps may also display historical information, such as battles or territorial changes.

Reading Maps

An important step in reading a map is to study the map key. The key explains the lines and colors used on a map. It also explains any **symbols,** or signs and pictures, used on a map. For example, the map of Alexander's empire details the size of the empire, the route of Alexander's conquest, and some important battles. Cities are usually shown as a solid circle (•), like the one for Athens.

The map **scale** is a measuring line that tells you the distances represented on the map. Suppose you wanted to know the approximate distance from Tampa, Florida to New York City. Using the scale bar will help you calculate this distance.

A map has a symbol called a compass rose that tells you the position of the **cardinal directions**—north, south, east, and west. Cardinal directions help you explain the relative location of any place on Earth. Some maps also have a locator map, a small inset map. This shows where the region on the large map is located.

✓ PROGRESS CHECK

Drawing Conclusions Why is reading the map key important when looking at a special-purpose map?

4 Using Charts, Graphs, and Diagrams

GUIDING QUESTION *What are the uses of charts, graphs, and diagrams?*

Charts, graphs, and diagrams are tools for showing information. The first step to understanding these visual aids is to read the title. This tells you the subject.

Charts show facts in an organized way. They arrange information in rows and columns. To read a chart, look at the labels at the top of each column and on the left side of the chart. The labels explain what the chart is showing.

scale a measuring line that shows the distances on a map
cardinal directions north, south, east, and west

Academic Vocabulary

symbol a sign or image that stands for something else

LESSON 1 • Day 2 (cont.)

Point out to students that the map of Alexander's empire in their book shows one example of how geography can be used to help understand history.

By seeing the size of Alexander's empire, it is easier to understand the scale and importance of his conquests.

Ask students to consider other ways in which the tools of geography might be used to help understand historical events.

INTERACTIVE WORKSHEET

Geography and History Activity

Summarizing Then have students complete the "Physical Maps" Geography and History Activity. As students read the activity about the importance of water, **ask:**

What physical features does the activity discuss? *(water features such as oceans, seas, rivers, and lakes)*  AL

What water features are shown on the map? *(the Mediterranean Sea, Caspian Sea, Black Sea, Red Sea, Persian Gulf, Arabian Sea, and the Nile, Tigris, and Euphrates Rivers)*

Note to students that the worksheet describes one example of how geography affects history. The water features shown on the map shaped the development of nearby civilizations in significant ways.

Ask students to consider other ways in which physical geography might shape history.

5 Population and Culture

GUIDING QUESTION *How do geographers study population and culture?*

Making Connections Explain that studying population and culture is an important part of geography and history. Draw students' attention to the choropleth map.

Ask: What type of map is a choropleth? *(a special-purpose map)*

What does it show? *(population distribution)* BL

Ask students to think of examples of culture in their own lives. Note that music, fashion, language, and education vary from one culture to another.

Encourage students to think about how cultures influence each other and to consider what other cultures have influenced their taste in music, clothing, food, and so forth.  AL

Have students complete the Lesson 1 Review.

CLOSE & REFLECT

Summarizing Lead a discussion with students about the importance of geography in history. Draw the connection between the role of geography in their daily lives, which they have already discussed, and the role that geography played in the lives of people in the past. For example, people in the past interacted with their environment as do people in the present.

IF YOU HAVE MORE TIME . . .

Analyze Population Growth by Learner Level

Direct students to Datafinder on the Population Reference Bureau Web site to review the population growth of any country in the world: www.prb.org.

Approaching Level Learners Using the information provided on the Web site, have students gather data on the births per 1,000 and the deaths per 1,000 for one location on each continent. Then have students put this information in a bar graph. AL

On Level Learners Using the information provided on the Web site, have students gather data on the births per 1,000 and the deaths per 1,000 for each continent and for the entire world.

Then have students put this information in a bar graph where they will compare the world average to each continent's average and find which continents are below average.

Beyond Level Learners Using the information provided on the Web site, have students gather data on the births per 1,000 and the deaths per 1,000 for each continent. Have students create a bar graph of births and deaths for each region. BL

Then have them select one other variable, such as education, employment, environment, or health variables and create a second bar graph with this information. Have students write a short explanation about how this variable compares to the basic population rate.

Answers for pages 32–35

P. 33 CRITICAL THINKING The area around Mount St. Helens is not populated, perhaps because of the volcano, which has scarred the landscape. There would be little food for wildlife.

P. 33 ☑ PROGRESS CHECK Places and Regions would be involved in the description of the landforms. Environment and Society could be involved in studying how people have changed the landforms and adapted to them. The Uses of Geography could address the impact on the landforms over time.

P. 34 GEOGRAPHY CONNECTION

1. He won the Battle of Gauĝamela.
2. CRITICAL THINKING Students might say that the Mediterranean Sea provided too big a barrier or that Alexander did not have the ships to cross it.

P. 34 Reading Strategy To read a map, study the symbols that tell what the map shows, the scale that tells the distances on the map, and the compass rose that tells where the cardinal directions are.

P. 35 ☑ PROGRESS CHECK The map key contains information about the symbols, lines, and colors used on a special-purpose map. Without this information, such maps might be difficult to understand.

BIOGRAPHY

Gerardus Mercator (A.D. 1512 to A.D. 1594)

Gerardus Mercator was a European mapmaker. He is best known for creating the Mercator projection, the first map to show longitude and latitude as straight lines. His map helped sailors navigate at sea. Mercator was also the first person to call a collection of maps an *atlas*. Many people think Mercator was the greatest geographer of the 1500s.

▶ CRITICAL THINKING

Speculating Before sailors had a map such as Mercator's, how do you think they were able to find their way on the sea?

Graphs come in different types. Bar graphs use thick, wide lines to compare data. They are useful for comparing amounts. Line graphs show changes over a particular period of time. A climate graph, or climograph (KLY•muh•graf), combines a line graph and a bar graph. It shows the long-term weather patterns in a place.

To read a bar graph, line graph, or climograph, look at the labels along the side and bottom. The vertical line along the left side of the graph is the y-axis. The horizontal line along the bottom is the x-axis. One axis tells you what is being measured. The other axis tells what units of measurement are being used.

Pie graphs are circular graphs that show how the whole of something is divided into parts. Each "slice" shows a part or percentage of the whole "pie." The entire pie totals 100 percent.

Diagrams are special drawings. They show steps in a process, point out the parts of an object, or explain how something works. An elevation profile is a diagram that shows a piece of land as if it were sliced open. This shows changes in height.

☑ PROGRESS CHECK

Identifying What type of graph shows changes over time?

5 Population and Culture

GUIDING QUESTION *How do geographers study population and culture?*

Like geographers, historians study population, culture, and the movement of people, ideas, and goods. Historians are interested in how these things change over time.

Population Shifts

Population refers to how many people live in a specific area or place. Geographers study this in great detail. They look at what sorts of people make up a population. They examine how fast a population grows or shrinks over time. They also measure population density. This is the average number of people living in a square mile or square kilometer. A **choropleth** (KAWR•uh•plehth) uses colors to show population density.

Populations can also change location. The movement of people from one place to settle in another place is called **migration** (my•GRAY•shuhn). Throughout history there have been many migrations of human beings.

James Abercanto/SuperStock

Reading **HELP**DESK

choropleth a special-purpose map that uses color to show population density

migration the movement of people from one place to settle in another place

culture the set of beliefs, behaviors, and traits shared by a group of people

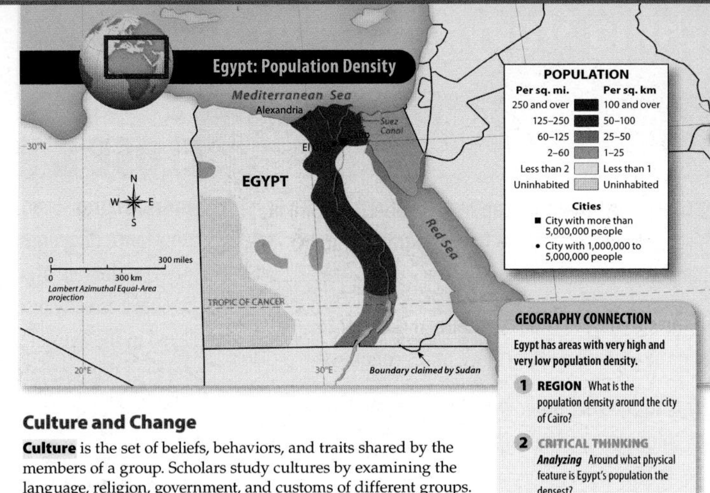

GEOGRAPHY CONNECTION

Egypt has areas with very high and very low population density.

1. **REGION** What is the population density around the city of Cairo?
2. CRITICAL THINKING ***Analyzing*** Around what physical feature is Egypt's population the densest?

Culture and Change

Culture is the set of beliefs, behaviors, and traits shared by the members of a group. Scholars study cultures by examining the language, religion, government, and customs of different groups.

Throughout history, different peoples have met through exploration, migration, and trade. These meetings often lead to cultural diffusion. In cultural diffusion, each group shares part of its culture with the other. Sometimes a completely new culture is formed. Many historians believe this happened in India as a result of the Aryan migrations.

☑ PROGRESS CHECK

Analyzing Why are geographers interested in contact between cultures?

LESSON 1 REVIEW

Review Vocabulary

1. How do *latitude* and *longitude* help identify your exact location on the Earth?
2. Why would a *scale* be helpful when trying to determine distances on a *physical map*?

Answer the Guiding Questions

3. ***Identifying*** What type of map would you choose to find the borders between countries? Why?
4. ***Finding the Main Idea*** Why do mapmakers have to choose between showing the correct land shapes or distances on the Earth?
5. ***Contrasting*** What is the difference between a chart and a diagram?
6. ***Making Inferences*** How might migration lead to the spread and mixing of cultures?
7. **EXPOSITORY WRITING** Write a paragraph explaining which Essential Elements of Geography you would use to study the weather in an area.

networks *There's More Online!*

☑ **GRAPHIC ORGANIZER** Characteristics of Economic Systems

☑ **GRAPH** Supply and Demand; Model of the Business Cycle

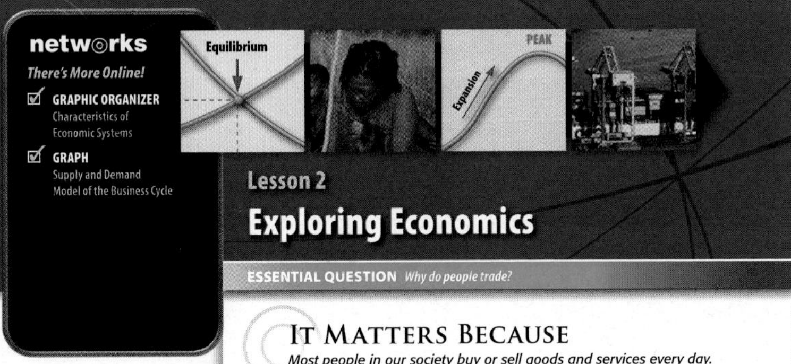

Lesson 2

Exploring Economics

ESSENTIAL QUESTION *Why do people trade?*

IT MATTERS BECAUSE

Most people in our society buy or sell goods and services every day. Trade has also shaped the course of history in major ways.

1 What Is Economics?

GUIDING QUESTION *What are the basic ideas of economics?*

There are three key questions to ask about any economy: *What* goods and services should we offer? *How* should we create and distribute these goods and services? *Who* will use these goods and services?

Resources and Production

In order to make goods and offer services, people need **resources.** There are four major kinds of resources: land, labor, capital, and entrepreneurship. Land includes the surface of the Earth and its natural resources, such as minerals and water. **Labor** is the ability of people to do work. You need labor to make goods and provide services. **Capital** is money and goods used to help people make or do things. You need capital to run a business. **Entrepreneurship** (ahn•truh•pruh•NUHR•shihp) is the act of running a business and taking on the risks of that business. Entrepreneurship usually describes individual or small businesses. Another kind of resource is **technology.** Technology is using knowledge in a practical way to accomplish a task. Technology can make it easier and cheaper to create goods.

(cl) Fabio Cheval/Workbook Stock/Getty Images; (r) Ian Murphy/Stone/Getty Images

Reading **HELP**DESK

Taking Notes: *Describing*

Use a chart like this one to list these two types of economic systems and their key elements.

Traditional	Command

Content Vocabulary

- capital
- entrepreneurship
- supply
- demand
- scarcity
- opportunity cost
- traditional economy
- command economy
- recession

All of these resources were important to early civilizations. Good land and freshwater were very important to farmers. Early rulers needed many workers for large projects. They gathered capital by collecting taxes. Merchants showed entrepreneurship. They traded goods to earn a profit, or an increase in the value of what they owned.

Supply and Demand

Getting the resources needed to offer a good or service is a first step to providing that good or service. Next, you need to know how much of that good or service to offer. You will also want to decide how much money to charge for the good or service. These choices are affected by the laws of supply and demand.

Supply is the amount of a good or service that a producer wants to sell. The law of supply says that the higher the price you can charge for a good or service, the more of it you will want to sell. **Demand** is the amount of something that a consumer wants to buy. The law of demand says that the lower the price of a good or service, the more of it people will want to buy.

You can see the supply and demand curves in the graph on this page. Look at the supply curve. It shows that people want to make more goods when the price is high. The demand curve shows that buyers want to buy less when the price is high. In a free market, these forces balance each other over time. The seller and buyer will agree on a price and amount that satisfies both.

Academic Vocabulary

resource something that is useful

labor the ability of people to do work

technology the use of advanced methods to solve problems

SUPPLY AND DEMAND CURVES INFOGRAPHIC

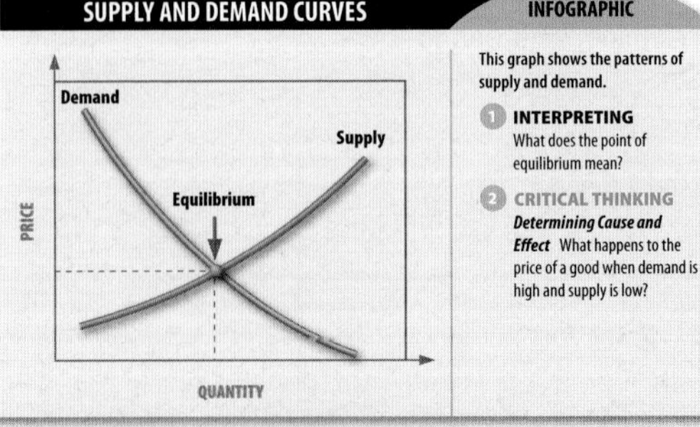

This graph shows the patterns of supply and demand.

1. **INTERPRETING** What does the point of equilibrium mean?
2. CRITICAL THINKING ***Determining Cause and Effect*** What happens to the price of a good when demand is high and supply is low?

Content Vocabulary

- inflation
- exports
- imports
- barter
- globalization

capital money and goods used to help people make or do things

entrepreneurship the act of running a business and taking on the risks of that business

supply the amount of a good or service that a producer wants to sell

demand the amount of something that a consumer wants to buy

LESSON 1 • Day 2 (cont.)

IF YOU HAVE MORE TIME . . .

Practice Recognizing Historical Perspective

As students study historical events or read primary sources of the past, they may be surprised by the actions taking place or the beliefs being expressed. To accurately evaluate the event or statement, students must carefully consider the time period and the experiences and viewpoints of the people involved.

Teach students how to recognize historical perspective by following these steps:

Look for context clues by asking when was the statement made. To what event or time does the statement refer? And what other related events had occurred before or were occurring at the time?

Ask who the author or speaker of the statement is. What past experiences or current considerations might influence that person's viewpoint?

Think about why it is important to think critically about historical perspectives.

Practice the skill by looking in a current newspaper, news Web site, or newsmagazine to find an example of a conflict between two or more groups of people. Write a short summary of how their perspectives of each other have determined their historical and current relationships.

Answers for pages 36–37

P. 36 CRITICAL THINKING Before Mercator's map, sailors used the stars to guide them. They probably also drew their own maps of their travels.

P. 36 ☑ PROGRESS CHECK A line graph best shows changes over time.

P. 37 GEOGRAPHY CONNECTION

1. Around the city of Cairo, there are more than 250 people per square mile or 100 per square kilometer.
2. CRITICAL THINKING Egypt's population is concentrated along the Nile River.

P. 37 ☑ PROGRESS CHECK Contact between cultures and the sharing of ideas often leads to changes in those cultures.

LESSON 1 REVIEW

1. A person must know where latitude and longitude intersect to know an absolute location on the surface of Earth.
2. The scale shows proportional distances displayed on the map, which helps a person measure the size of large physical features.
3. You would choose a political map because it displays country borders.
4. Because maps are a flat representation of a round object, they distort either size or shape.
5. A chart is a type of table that displays data in an organized way. A diagram is a drawing that shows how something works or how it looks on the inside.
6. Migration brings a new group of people to settle in an area. If other people are already living there, then one or both cultures might take on the characteristics of the other.
7. Student answers will vary. The study of weather might involve Physical Geography. Environment and Society could be involved in studying how the weather of the region affects people's activities.

Teaching *Exploring Economics* (Student Edition pp. 38–43)

LESSON 2

ENGAGE

Discussing Tell students that they will be learning about how economic ideas, such as limited resources and opportunity costs, affected early civilizations and the trade between them. Explain to the class that they are going to take part in a simulation in which they will make decisions about what to buy and sell.

TEACH & ASSESS

1 What Is Economics?

GUIDING QUESTION *What are the basic ideas of economics?*

Evaluating Tell students that they are living in an ancient civilization. They have 10 coins to spend on basic needs like clothing and food.

Note to students that their 10 coins represent a limited resource. It puts a limit on how much they can buy. As you work through the simulation, emphasize content vocabulary terms as you use them.

Ask: **How many rolls of cloth or bushels of grain would you buy if each item cost two coins?** *(Student answers will vary.)* Record student answers.

Then ask: **How many rolls of cloth or bushels of grain would you buy if each cost one coin?** *(Student answers will vary, but there is likely to be an increase in the number bought.)*

Discuss the differences in their answers with students. Explain that **demand** for goods usually increases as the price of those goods decreases. Also note that when an item is rare, the **demand** for it often grows. This is an example of how **scarcity** can increase the cost of goods. ELL

Now ask students: **If you could charge one coin per bushel of wheat and two coins for a roll of cloth, which would you rather sell?** *(Students will typically want to sell cloth for the higher amount.)* AL

GRAPH Discuss student responses. Note that the price at which they want to sell is different from the price at which they want to buy. Then explain that people who **supply** goods want to be able to charge the highest price that buyers are willing to pay. Illustrate these concepts using the interactive supply and demand graph.

Point out to students that when they spend coins on one item, they can no longer spend those coins on anything else. Their choices have become more limited. This limiting of choices is the **opportunity cost** of buying items. People in the past and the present have to be careful about their choices when they have limited resources.

Answers for pages 38–39

P. 38 Taking Notes In a traditional economy, people produce goods for their local group and typically use barter to trade. In a command economy, rulers decide what is made and how it is distributed.

P. 39 INFOGRAPHIC

1. The point of equilibrium means the amounts of items that consumers demand and producers sell are the same.
2. CRITICAL THINKING The price of the good will increase.

In a hunter-gatherer community, some members might provide food by hunting for meat or gathering vegetables. Others might turn furs into clothing.

There are other things that affect supply and demand. One is **scarcity** (SKEHR•suh•tee), or lack of a resource. When not much of a needed resource is available, then the demand for it will grow. The higher demand will raise the price. This may force people to seek replacements for that resource. Another factor is opportunity cost. The **opportunity cost** of something is what you give up to make it or buy it. Suppose you are a farmer. You choose to grow wheat on your land. You spend time and resources to grow the wheat. While you are growing wheat, you cannot use the land to grow beans. You are giving up the chance to grow something else when you grow wheat. The time, resources, and choices that you gave up are all part of the opportunity cost of growing wheat. People are always weighing the opportunity costs of their choices about what to make or buy.

✓ PROGRESS CHECK

Predicting How will the people who make goods and those who buy the goods react if the price goes down?

2 Managing and Measuring Economies

GUIDING QUESTION *What are the different types of economic systems?*

Dealing with resources, supply, and demand can be very hard. Each society organizes its economy using an economic system.

Economic Systems

A **traditional economy** is based on custom. In such an economy, children often do the same work as their parents. Members of a family or tribe make goods for the rest of their group. In this way, everyone's needs are met. Many hunter-gatherer groups had traditional economies.

In a **command economy,** a central government decides what goods will be made and who will receive them. The ancient civilizations of Egypt and Mesopotamia began as command economies. Rulers gathered the resources of their people. They used these resources to build large projects or raise powerful armies. Today, Cuba and North Korea have command economies.

In a market economy, each person, or **individual,** makes choices about what to make, sell, and buy. He or she buys and sells goods and services on an open market. The United States has a market economy.

Reading **HELP**DESK

scarcity the lack of a resource
opportunity cost what is given up, such as time or money, to make or buy something
traditional economy an economic system in which custom decides what people do, make, buy, and sell
command economy an economic system in which a central government decides what goods will be made and who will receive them

In a mixed economy, the government has some control over what and how much is made. Individuals make the rest of the economic choices. Some countries in Europe are mixed economies.

Measuring Economies

Economies grow and shrink over time. This pattern is called the business cycle. When the economy grows quickly, it is often called a boom. When the economy grows very slowly or shrinks, it is called a **recession** (rih•SEH•shuhn). In a recession, companies often close and people lose their jobs. The United States entered a recession in December 2007.

Governments try to keep their economies growing and avoid recessions. One way they do this is by watching prices. Rising prices are a sign of **inflation** (ihn•FLAY•shuhn). High inflation means that money buys less. This raises the cost of living. Say the yearly rate of inflation is 10 percent. This means that something that cost you $10 last year costs you $11 this year. Sometimes inflation can get very high. In Argentina in the 1980s, the yearly rate of inflation hit 1,000 percent. The same goods and services cost 10 times more than they did the year before.

Governments want to avoid having too much inflation. However, **experts** who study economics disagree about what causes inflation. So finding the right government policies is difficult.

✓ PROGRESS CHECK

Identifying In which type of economic system are all decisions made by a central government?

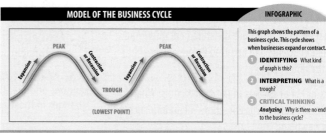

Thinking Like a **HISTORIAN**

Analyzing Primary Sources

In 1929, the United States and much of the world entered a long, painful depression. This period is called the Great Depression. Prices in the United States deflated by nearly one-third, and one in five Americans was unemployed. Historians still argue about the causes of this serious dip in the business cycle. Use your library to locate two primary sources dealing with the depression of the 1930s. Write a brief report analyzing the information and present your findings to the class. For more information about analyzing primary source material, read the chapter *What Does a Historian Do?*

MODEL OF THE BUSINESS CYCLE

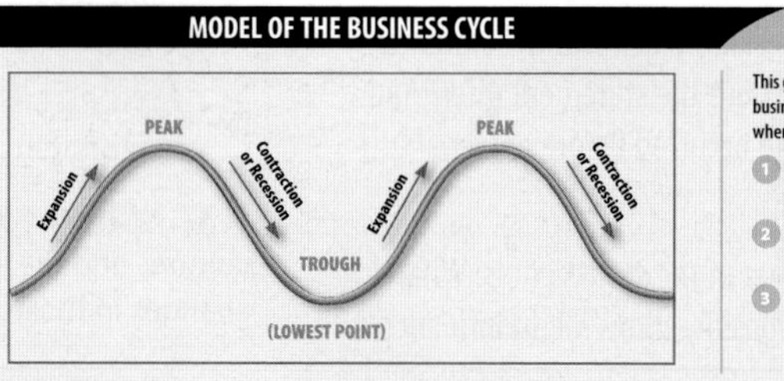

INFOGRAPHIC

This graph shows the pattern of a business cycle. This cycle shows when businesses expand or contract.

1. **IDENTIFYING** What kind of graph is this?
2. **INTERPRETING** What is a trough?
3. CRITICAL THINKING *Analyzing* Why is there no end to the business cycle?

recession a period of slow economic growth or decline
inflation a continued rise in prices or the supply of money

Academic Vocabulary

individual a single human being
expert a skilled person who has mastered a subject

3 Trade in World History

GUIDING QUESTION *What are the benefits and disadvantages of trade?*

Trade has been important to many different civilizations. What makes trade between different peoples so common?

Why Do People Trade?

Two countries trade with each other when both sides can gain something from the exchange. **Exports** are goods shipped out of a country and sold somewhere else. **Imports** are the goods and services that a country buys from other countries.

Countries want to export goods of which they have a large supply. They want to import goods that are hard to find in their own lands. For hundreds of years, Europeans traded wool, gold, and silver with Asians for rare goods such as silk and spices.

Early civilizations often traded by bartering. When people **barter,** goods and services are traded for other goods and services. For example, a merchant might trade fish for furs. Eventually, some ancient peoples invented money. Money had a set value, could be traded for anything, and was easier to carry.

Barriers to Trade

Barriers can make international trade difficult. Conflict can stop trade. Geography can make it hard to travel between two places. Sometimes a country chooses to cut off contact with other peoples. In the 1600s, Japan limited trade with European countries. The Japanese wanted to limit European influence on Japanese society.

INFOGRAPHIC

This graph shows the value of U.S. imports and exports over a ten year period.

1. **IDENTIFYING** In which year were U.S. exports at their lowest?
2. CRITICAL THINKING ***Determining Cause and Effect*** What is one effect of a country importing more than it exports?

U.S. IMPORTS AND EXPORTS, 2000–2009

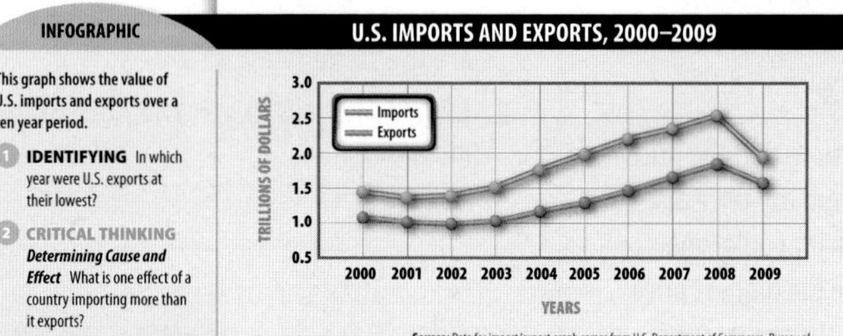

Source: Data for import/export graph comes from U.S. Department of Commerce, Bureau of Economic Analysis, International Economic Accounts, Trade in Goods and Services, 1992–present.

Reading **HELP**DESK

export a good sent from one country to another in trade
import a good brought into a country from another country
barter to trade by exchanging one good or service for another
globalization the growth in free trade between countries

Finally, nations may try to limit or ban trade that hurts producers in their own country. For example, in the Great Depression, U.S. farmers were worried about food imports from Europe. They feared that European farmers might drive them out of business. So they asked the U.S. government to raise taxes on imported European crops. The government did so to protect American farmers. This led other countries to tax U.S. goods to protect their own farmers and businesses.

Shipping through international ports is an important method of transporting goods. This global trade may help the economies of different countries grow.

▶ CRITICAL THINKING
Analyzing Where do you fit into the process of global trade?

Global Trade

Today, most of the world's countries take part in some form of international trade. The process is called **globalization** (gloh•buh•luh•ZAY•shuhn). Countries like the United States have numerous trade partners. Many large companies also have business branches in more than one country.

Much of this growth has come from efforts to increase free trade. The goal of free trade is a world market where people are free to choose what to buy and sell. People who favor free trade say that it boosts trade. It also cuts the prices of goods. These changes help economies grow. Those against free trade say that it makes imports and foreign labor costs too cheap. They fear that a country will lose companies and jobs to other countries.

Globalization has increased the ties among the world's economies. In 2009, the United States had the largest economy in the world. The U.S. economy was bigger than that of the next two leading countries, Japan and China, added together. Every day, Americans buy and use goods made in other countries. At the same time, American goods and services are sold around the world. When the U.S. economy struggles, it affects the entire world. The questions about what to make, how to make it, and who should buy it are no longer just national issues.

✓ PROGRESS CHECK

Finding the Main Idea Why do countries agree to trade with one another?

LESSON 2 REVIEW

Review Vocabulary

1. Why are *capital* and *labor* needed to make goods?
2. How does *demand* relate to buyers of a good?

Answer the Guiding Questions

3. ***Explaining*** What is opportunity cost?
4. ***Contrasting*** Describe the differences between a command economy and a traditional economy.
5. ***Summarizing*** What types of barriers might prevent trade between countries?
6. **EXPOSITORY WRITING** Write a paragraph describing how countries decide what goods to export and what goods to import.

LESSON 2 (cont.)

Managing and Measuring Economies

GUIDING QUESTION *What are the different types of economic systems?*

LECTURE SLIDE **Contrasting** Show students the lecture slide that explains the different economic systems.

Explain to students that in a traditional economy, they would have to barter one kind of good for another. Each family would make a few kinds of goods for itself. Anything extra could be traded for different types of goods.

Ask: **How does using money make it simpler to get the goods you want?** *(Money can be exchanged for a wide variety of goods. You don't have to find someone who is willing to trade for what you have.)*

Trade in World History

GUIDING QUESTION *What are the benefits and disadvantages of trade?*

INTERACTIVE WORKSHEET

Economics of History Activity

Analyzing Have students read the Economics of History Activity "Trade in the Ancient World." Point out that traders from ancient civilizations often traveled great distances to exchange goods and ideas. Note that this was voluntary trade, meaning people took these risks of their own free will.

Ask: **Why did these ancient civilizations trade with each other?** *(They traded to get basic goods they needed or to get luxury items that they wanted.)*

Ask students to give an example of a basic good and a luxury good that were traded. *(A basic good would be salt; a luxury good would be spices.)* AL

Ask: **What sorts of barriers did ancient traders have to overcome?** *(They had to travel long distances and across physical features such as mountains, deserts, and seas. They also had to travel through regions where warfare or robberies took place.)*

Have students complete the Lesson 2 Review.

CLOSE & REFLECT

Summarizing Lead a discussion with students about the importance of economics, especially trade, in history. Use the simulation and the discussions of trade to draw the connection between the role of economics in their daily lives and the role that economics played in the lives of people in the past.

IF YOU HAVE MORE TIME . . .

Explain What Balance of Trade Is

No country produces everything it needs to survive. Every country depends on trade with other countries. Exported goods are products that are sold to other countries. Because exports are sold to other countries, they provide additional profits at home. Imports are those goods that come from another country. The United States imports products from abroad that we need, like oil, or products that Americans would otherwise not be able to enjoy.

Balance of trade is the difference between the value of a nation's exports and its imports. A positive balance of trade creates a trade surplus. This is when the value of a nation's exports is greater than how much the nation imports from other countries. In this case, a nation is bringing in more money than it is paying out to other countries.

A trade deficit is a negative balance of trade. This occurs when a nation has to import needed goods more than it exports to other countries. A trade deficit can negatively affect other economic factors in a country, including income and employment. For example, with less demand for goods in affected import industries, less workers are needed causing rising unemployment.

Answers for pages 40–43

P. 40 ☑ PROGRESS CHECK According to the law of supply, producers will want to make less of the goods in order to maintain high prices. The law of demand states that consumers will want to buy more goods if prices are low.

P. 41 ☑ PROGRESS CHECK All decisions are made by a central government in a command economy.

P. 41 INFOGRAPHIC

1. a line graph
2. a low point in the business cycle
3. CRITICAL THINKING The business cycle continuously repeats.

P. 42 INFOGRAPHIC

1. 2002
2. CRITICAL THINKING The country will spend more money than it earns.

P. 43 CRITICAL THINKING Students may say that their role in global trade is that of a consumer, because they buy goods made in many different countries.

P. 43 PROGRESS CHECK Countries agree to trade because they benefit from the exchange of goods and services.

LESSON 2 REVIEW

1. Capital is the investment needed to start a business and pay its costs, while labor is needed to make things.
2. Demand is the amount of a good that consumers want to buy.
3. Opportunity cost is what a person gives up when he or she chooses to produce or buy a particular good or service.
4. Command economies rely on central government control; traditional economies rely on custom.
5. Geographical barriers or violent conflicts might discourage trade. Countries might also choose to limit trade.
6. Students should note that countries choose what to trade based on the scarcity of their own resources, their ability to make certain items, and which items offer them the greatest competitive advantage.

networks
There's More Online!
- GRAPHIC ORGANIZER Citizenship: Rights and Responsibilities
- SLIDE SHOW Citizens' Duties and Responsibilities
- VIDEO

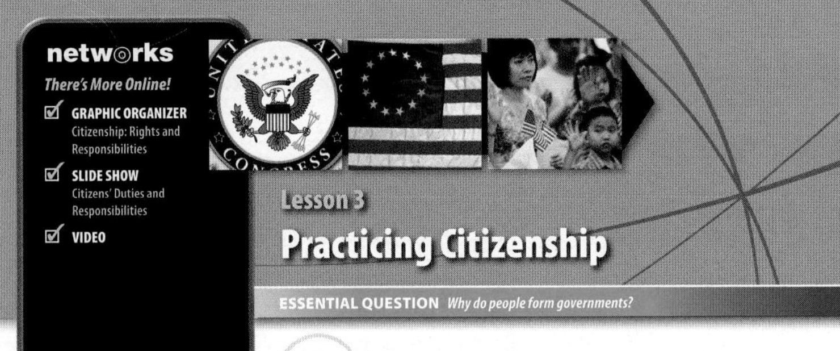

Lesson 3

Practicing Citizenship

ESSENTIAL QUESTION *Why do people form governments?*

It Matters Because

Our system of government needs active citizens who understand their rights and responsibilities.

1 Principles of Government

GUIDING QUESTION *What are the key principles of the U.S. government?*

The U.S. Constitution is the highest law in the United States. It contains the key ideas of America's government. Many of these ideas came from ancient Greece and Rome. The United States has a **representative government.** This means that citizens vote for officials who serve the will of the people. The government must act in the people's interests and protect their rights.

The Constitution created a **federal system** of government. The central, or federal, government is the highest authority. However, it also shares some powers with the state governments.

The federal government is split into three equal parts, or branches. Each branch has its own specific powers, an idea called **separation of powers.** This concept was adopted so that no one branch could become too powerful. An overly powerful government could harm its citizens. Each branch limits the power of the other branches. The diagram shows this system of **checks and balances.**

What do the three branches of government do? The **legislative** (LEH•juhs•lay•tihv) **branch** is known as the U.S. Congress. It passes laws for the whole country. The **executive branch** includes the office of the U.S. president. The president and other members of the executive branch ensure that the nation's laws are carried out.

(t) North Wind Picture Archives/North Wind Picture Archives, (c) Getty Images News/Getty Images

Reading HELPDESK

Taking Notes: ***Summarizing***

Use a graphic organizer like this one to show the rights and responsibilities of citizenship.

Citizenship
Rights
Responsibilities

Content Vocabulary
- representative government
- federal system
- separation of powers
- checks and balances

CHECKS AND BALANCES — INFOGRAPHIC

Can impeach, or remove, president; Can override veto; Can block appointments; Can refuse to approve treaties

Can impeach, or remove judges; Can block the appointment of judges

Can veto, or block, laws

LEGISLATIVE BRANCH

Can appoint, or choose, judges

Can declare acts of Congress to be unconstitutional, or illegal

Can declare presidential actions unconstitutional, or illegal

EXECUTIVE BRANCH

JUDICIAL BRANCH

The presidential veto is one example of checks and balances in action. However, if the president vetoes a bill, Congress can then vote to overturn the veto. This is another example of checks and balances.

1. **IDENTIFYING** How does the legislative branch act as a check on the judicial branch?
2. **CRITICAL THINKING** ***Drawing Conclusions*** Why did the authors of the Constitution create the system of checks and balances?

The **judicial** (joo•DIH•shuhl) **branch** includes the U.S. Supreme Court and various lesser courts. The judges in the judicial branch use the Constitution to interpret laws. They can strike down laws that violate the Constitution.

legislative branch part of government that passes laws
executive branch part of government that enforces laws
judicial branch part of government that interprets laws

PROGRESS CHECK

Identifying What type of government does the United States have?

2 What Is Citizenship?

GUIDING QUESTION *What are the civic rights, duties, and responsibilities of U.S. citizens?*

The system of government in the United States provides many freedoms. However, it also needs citizens to carry out certain duties and responsibilities. This idea, called civic participation, comes from ancient Greece and Rome. Good citizenship helps our government and communities work as well as possible.

Rights of Citizenship

All Americans have the right to **seek** life, liberty, and happiness. All Americans have the right to freedom of expression. This means that they can speak and write openly. They can attend peaceful gatherings. They can petition the government to address their needs. The Constitution also protects the right of people to worship as they choose. People who are accused of a crime have the right to receive a fair trial by a **jury** of their peers.

Content Vocabulary
- legislative branch
- executive branch
- judicial branch

representative government government in which citizens elect officials who govern
federal system government which divides power between central and state governments
separation of powers the division of power among the branches of government
checks and balances system in which each branch of government limits the power of another branch

THEN

The design of the American flag has changed over the years. However, its red and white stripes still honor the country's thirteen original states.

NOW

▶ CRITICAL THINKING
Analyzing Like the flags of other countries, the U.S. flag contains symbols. Each of the 50 stars represents a state. If the U.S. wanted a new flag to represent the country today, what symbols would you suggest, and why?

Citizens also have the right to vote for public officials and to serve in public office. The right to vote allows citizens to choose their leaders, while the right to serve lets them represent their fellow citizens in government.

Duties and Responsibilities of Citizenship

By law, citizens must carry out some duties. Obeying all federal, state, and local laws is one of the first duties of citizenship. Citizens also have a duty to pay their taxes to federal, state, and local governments. These taxes pay for the services provided by government to the American people.

Citizens must serve on a jury if the government asks them to. This service is needed in order to honor people's right to a fair trial by jury. Finally, citizens must be ready to defend the United States and the Constitution.

People born in other countries can also become U.S. citizens. First, they must go through naturalization. This is a process of applying for, and being granted, citizenship. To qualify, they have to have lived in the United States for a certain amount of time. They also need to show good moral character. They must be able to use basic English and must know about U.S. history and government. In addition, they must swear to uphold all duties of citizenship.

In addition to their duties, citizens also have responsibilities. Citizens should stay informed about important **issues,** or topics. An awareness of critical issues—such as concern for the global environment—will help them make wise choices when they vote in federal, state, and local elections. Voting is a powerful right and a key responsibility of citizenship. If people do not vote, they give away part of their voice in government.

Citizens should also respect the rights and views of other people. The United States welcomes people of many different backgrounds. They all share the same freedoms. Before you deny a right to someone else, put yourself in that person's place. Think how you would feel if someone tried to take away your rights.

Finally, citizens should take part in their local community. By working with one another, we help make our neighborhoods and towns better places to live. There are different ways to keep our communities strong. We can volunteer our time. We can join neighborhood groups, and we can serve in public office.

PROGRESS CHECK

Summarizing What duties do citizens have?

(t) North Wind Picture Archives/North Wind Picture Archives, (b) PhotoLink/Getty Images

Reading HELPDESK

Academic Vocabulary

seek to look for or try to achieve
jury a group of people sworn to make a decision in a legal case
issue a concern or problem that has not yet been solved

3 Being a Global Citizen

GUIDING QUESTION *What does it mean to be a global citizen?*

Today the world faces many problems that go beyond the borders of any one country. Threats to the health of the environment, such as pollution or the destruction of a tropical rain forest, affect people living in many different places. Many countries also have close economic ties to other nations. Because of these ties, economic problems in one country affect other countries. In addition, the idea is growing around the world that all people should have certain basic human rights. World leaders must often work together to deal with these issues.

Being a global citizen means learning about the different issues that affect the world as a whole. It means taking care of the environment. It also means understanding how people live in other countries. We are all affected by drought and hunger or economic troubles in other countries. Once we understand one another's ways of life, we can work together more easily to solve big problems.

Being a global citizen does not mean giving up your duties and responsibilities as a citizen of the United States. It means thinking about how you can make the world a better place by your actions. Making the effort to stay informed and to respect the views of others helps all Americans. Through that same effort, you can also help the rest of the world.

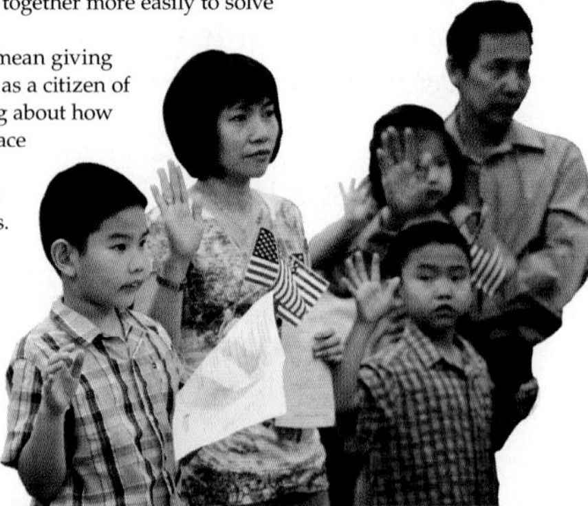

This family is taking the Oath of Allegiance. It is the final step in becoming a U.S. citizen through naturalization.

Getty Images News/Getty Images

PROGRESS CHECK

Finding the Main Idea What are some of the ways in which you could become a better global citizen?

LESSON 3 REVIEW

Review Vocabulary

1. What is a *federal system* of government?
2. How are *checks and balances* related to the idea of *separation of powers*?

Answer the Guiding Questions

3. ***Finding the Main Idea*** What is the main purpose of a representative government?
4. ***Drawing Conclusions*** Why do citizens have duties and responsibilities as well as rights?
5. ***Making Inferences*** What are some of the challenges of being a global citizen?
6. **DESCRIPTIVE WRITING** Write a paragraph describing how you can fulfill two of the responsibilities of citizenship in your daily life.

LESSON 3

ENGAGE

Discussing Introduce the term *citizen* to students. Ask them what they think it means to be a citizen of their local community, their state, and the United States. Following this discussion, have students write a short paragraph describing what citizenship means to them. AL

Ask student volunteers to share their paragraphs. Then tell students to save their paragraphs for the end of the lesson.

Explain to students that they will be learning about the structure of our government. They will also be learning about the rights and responsibilities of U.S. citizenship.

TEACH & ASSESS

1 Principles of Government

GUIDING QUESTION *What are the key principles of the U.S. government?*

LECTURE SLIDE **Explaining** Show the lecture slide that defines *federal system* and *separation of powers*. Have student volunteers explain each term in their own words.

INTERACTIVE WHITEBOARD ACTIVITY **Analyzing** Remind students that we have a federal republic, in which people elect their representatives and power is divided between the federal government and the state governments. **Ask:** What responsibility do citizens have in a representative government? *(Citizens have the responsibility to vote for their representatives.)*

Why is voting an important responsibility for citizens in a democracy? *(Democracies are representative governments. Citizens should use their right to vote so they can choose officials to protect their rights.)* AL

Point out the diagram on checks and balances in the student textbook. Review the main powers and tasks of each branch of government.

When finished, have students complete the Interactive Whiteboard Activity on the three branches of government. Guide them through the answers as necessary.

Ask: What is the purpose of having separation of powers and checks and balances? *(Each of these prevents any one branch of government from becoming powerful enough to dominate the other branches of the government.)*

2 What Is Citizenship?

GUIDING QUESTION *What are the civil rights, duties, and responsibilities of U.S. citizens?*

SLIDE SHOW **Categorizing** Have a student read the opening paragraph of "What Is Citizenship?" aloud. Then show students the slide show on the duties and responsibilities of citizenship.

Ask: What is the difference between a duty and a responsibility? *(A duty is an action required by law. A responsibility is an act that society does not require by law but expects people to carry out for their own good and for the good of others.)*

Give one example of a duty and one example of a responsibility. *(Serving on a jury when called is a duty that is required by law. Voting in an election is a responsibility that is not required by law but that benefits the individual voter and the system of government.)* BL

Why do citizens need to obey the law? *(Our government is based on rule of law. Everyone must follow the laws to keep order and to ensure that rights are protected.)* ELL

Making Connections Connect what students have learned about our system of government to what they have learned about citizenship. Ask students to describe the different ways in which citizens participate in government. *(Students should note that citizens vote, serve in public office, and petition members of government with their concerns.)* AL

INTERACTIVE WORKSHEET

21st Century Skills Activity

Applying Explain that citizens have duties and responsibilities in their local communities, as well as in their states and countries.

Ask: Why is it important for citizens to notice what is going on in their communities? *(Students should note that community issues might never be addressed or brought to the attention of government officials without the actions of citizens.)*

Assign students the 21st Century Skills Activity as homework. Students will identify specific ways in which they could carry out responsibilities of citizenship in their local community.

3 Being a Global Citizen

GUIDING QUESTION *What does it mean to be a global citizen?*

Ask students: What is one way in which you could be a good global citizen? *(Student answers will vary but will likely address global issues such as protecting the environment, acting on behalf of human rights, respecting other cultures, or staying informed on world issues.)* AL

Discuss our role as citizens of the United States compared to our roles as citizens of the world.

Ask: How is being a global citizen similar to being a United States citizen? *(Respecting the rights of others and staying informed are responsibilities for both types of citizenship.)*

How is it different from being a U.S. citizen? *(U.S. citizens have duties to the U.S., but they do not have duties to the rest of the world. They also cannot vote for world leaders and so cannot participate in government in the same way.)*

Have students complete the Lesson 3 Review.

CLOSE & REFLECT

Comparing Have students return to the paragraphs they wrote in the Engage activity. Invite students to compare their ideas about citizenship now to their views before the lesson.

Ask: How have your views about citizenship changed? *(Student answers will vary but should reflect an understanding of the rights and duties of citizenship.)*

Answers for pages 44–47

P. 44 Taking Notes ***Rights***: to seek life, liberty, happiness; freedom of expression; attend peaceful gatherings; petition the government; worship; fair trial by jury; to vote and serve ***Responsibilities***: stay informed; vote; respect the rights and views of others; take part in the community

P. 45 ☑ PROGRESS CHECK The United States has a federal, representative government.

P. 45 INFOGRAPHIC

1. A federal system is a strong central government that shares power with the states.
2. CRITICAL THINKING to prevent any one branch from becoming too powerful

P. 46 CRITICAL THINKING Students should identify relevant symbols that could be used to represent the United States.

P. 46 ☑ PROGRESS CHECK Citizens have a duty to obey laws, to pay taxes, to serve on juries, and to defend the country.

P. 47 ☑ PROGRESS CHECK People can become better global citizens by staying informed about world issues, learning about other cultures, and respecting the rights of others.

LESSON 3 REVIEW

1. A federal system of government is a government in which the central government has the highest authority but shares power with state governments.
2. Separation of powers gives each branch its own specific authority, but checks and balances limit the power of any one branch over another branch. Together they keep government from becoming too powerful.
3. It is to act in the people's interest and protect the people's rights.
4. Citizens have duties and responsibilities to ensure that rights are respected, that the voice of the people is heard in government, and that communities can be protected and strengthened.
5. Learning about global issues and other cultures takes effort, and some topics may be hard to understand. U.S. citizens must also remember that they have specific duties and responsibilities to the United States.
6. Students will not be able to vote, but they can stay informed on issues, respect the rights of others, and be active in their community.

CHAPTER 2 Activities

Write your answers on a separate piece of paper.

1. **Exploring the Essential Question**
DESCRIPTIVE WRITING Think about the role of the Six Essential Elements of Geography in your daily life. How do you affect the environment where you live? How does it affect you? Write a short essay answering these questions. Be sure to include descriptive details.

2. **21st Century Skills**
ANALYZING INFORMATION Imagine that the price of a gallon of gasoline has varied in the following way: January—$2.50, March—$2.45, May—$2.75, July—$3. Create a line graph that shows the rise and fall in gas prices over this period. According to the laws of supply and demand, when would gasoline producers want to sell the most gas?

3. **Thinking Like a Historian**
CITIZENSHIP AND SOCIETY Imagine that you are teaching a class of people seeking citizenship. What are the three topics you would be sure to include in your teaching?

4. **GEOGRAPHY ACTIVITY**

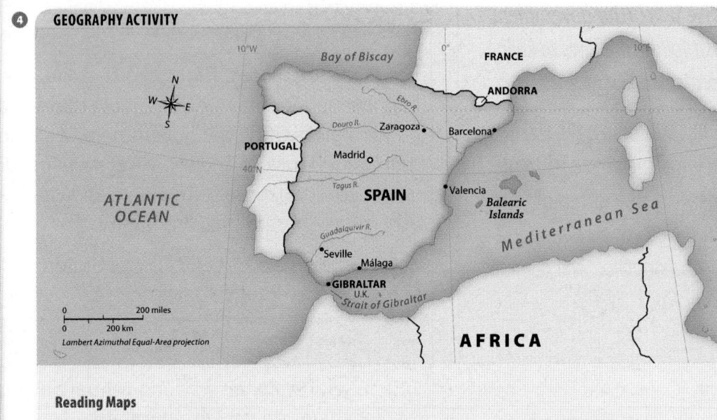

Reading Maps

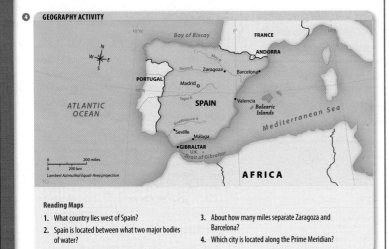

1. What country lies west of Spain?
2. Spain is located between what two major bodies of water?
3. About how many miles separate Zaragoza and Barcelona?
4. Which city is located along the Prime Meridian?

CHAPTER 2 Assessment

REVIEW THE GUIDING QUESTIONS
Directions: Choose the best answer for each question.

1. Which map projection shows correct direction and shape, but not size and distance?
   A. Goode's Interrupted Equal-Area
   B. Mercator
   C. Robinson
   D. Winkel Tripel

2. The line that divides the Earth into eastern and western halves is called the
   F. Equator.
   G. latitude.
   H. hemisphere.
   I. Prime Meridian.

3. A map showing population density would be considered a
   A. general-purpose map.
   B. political map.
   C. physical map.
   D. special-purpose map.

4. In a ______ economy, all decisions are made by a central government.
   F. command
   G. market
   H. mixed
   I. traditional

5. In economics, capital is
   A. how much of something someone wants to make.
   B. the price charged for goods or services.
   C. money or goods used to produce things.
   D. the willingness of people to take risks.

6. The ______ branch of the United States government interprets the laws.
   F. judicial
   G. federal
   H. executive
   I. legislative

CHAPTER 2 Assessment *(continued)*

DBQ DOCUMENT-BASED QUESTIONS

7. **Drawing Conclusions** Adam Smith wrote about reasons people trade in his 1776 economics book, *The Wealth of Nations*:

   "Whoever offers to another a bargain of any kind, proposes to do this [trade]. Give me that which I want, and you shall have this which you want, is the meaning of every such offer. . . . It is not from the benevolence [kindness] of the butcher, the brewer, or the baker that we expect our dinner, but from their regard [attention] to their own interest."

   —from *The Wealth of Nations*

   According to this passage, why do people trade with each other?
   A. to get something illegally
   B. to get something that they want
   C. to offer gifts
   D. to be benevolent

8. **Finding the Main Idea** According to the passage, what convinces the butcher, baker, or brewer to provide food for us?
   F. They do it because the government tells them to do it.
   G. They do it out of kindness.
   H. They do it because it serves their self-interest.
   I. They do it because we want the food.

SHORT RESPONSE

"Former Supreme Court Justice Louis Brandeis once said, 'The only title in our democracy superior to that of President [is] the title of citizen.' In the United States, the power of government comes directly from people like you. To protect freedom and liberty, U.S. citizens must participate in the democratic process and in their communities."

—from the *Citizen's Almanac*, U.S. Citizenship and Immigration Services

9. According to the passage, why do citizens need to take part in the democratic process?

10. Why does Brandeis say the title of citizen is greater than the title of President?

EXTENDED RESPONSE

11. **Persuasive Writing** You are a new American citizen. Write a letter to the editor explaining why citizens must fulfill their duties and responsibilities.

Need Extra Help?

If You've Missed Question	1	2	3	4	5	6	7	8	9	10	11
Review Lesson	1	1	1	2	2	3	2	2	3	3	3

NOTES

REFLECT, REVIEW, & REMEDIATE

INTERACTIVE WORKSHEET

Chapter Summary

Provide students with the Chapter Summary worksheet to help review the chapter and prepare for assessment.

Reviewing the Enduring Understandings

Review this chapter's Enduring Understandings with students:

- People, places, and ideas change over time.
- Resources are limited, so people must make choices.
- The value that a society places on individual rights is often reflected in that society's government.

INTERACTIVE WHITEBOARD ACTIVITY Organize the class into three groups. Have the first group brainstorm and write down examples of how geography affects their daily lives. Have the second and third groups do the same for economics and citizenship. Then have each group share its ideas with the class and discuss examples. Allow students from each group to offer suggestions for the other groups during the discussion. You might want to have one or more student volunteers record the best examples for each subject on the interactive whiteboard, using a chart like the one provided here.

	Matters In My Life Because . . .
Geography	
Economics	
Citizenship	

ACTIVITIES ANSWERS

Exploring the Essential Question

1 Student essays will vary. They should discuss some of the features of the environment in which they live, such as its weather patterns, physical features, or living things in the area. They may note how they and the people around them interact with this environment.

21st Century Skills

2 Student graphs should show the proper dates and prices, with a low in March and a peak in July. The law of supply states that gasoline producers would want to sell the most gas when the price is highest, which would be in July.

Thinking Like a Historian

3 Students might identify the duties, responsibilities, and rights of citizens. They may also want to teach about the structure of the government of the United States.

Reading Maps

4 **1.** Portugal; **2.** Atlantic Ocean and Mediterranean Sea; **3.** about 200 miles (322 km); **4.** Valencia

ASSESSMENT ANSWERS

Review the Guiding Questions

1 **B** The Mercator projection distorts size and distance but is still used because it shows directions and shapes with accuracy. The other map projections listed provide a more accurate representation of the size and distance of objects on Earth's surface. Therefore, the correct answer is B.

2 **I** A hemisphere is one-half of the globe, not a line. The Equator divides Earth into the Northern and Southern Hemispheres. The Prime Meridian divides the globe into the Eastern and Western Hemispheres. Greenwich is the name of the town that the Prime Meridian passes through. Thus, I is the correct answer.

3 **D** Physical maps show physical features rather than population. Political maps show borders and locations of cities. Population density is shown by choropleth maps, which are a type of special-purpose map. Therefore, D is the correct answer.

4 **F** Command economies are controlled by central governments. In mixed economies, only some economic decisions are controlled by the central government. In market economies, individuals make economic choices for themselves. Traditional economies are based on custom. Therefore, the correct answer is F.

5 **C** Capital is money or goods used to produce items. It is a type of investment. Answer A refers to the idea of supply, answer B deals with costs, and answer D deals with entrepreneurship. So C is the correct answer.

6 **F** The judicial branch interprets laws, the executive branch enforces laws, and the legislative branch makes laws. The term *federal* describes the division of power between the state and national governments. Thus, the correct answer is F.

Document-Based Questions

7 **B** Students should understand Smith's argument that people trade goods to get items they want in return for those goods. One of the traders might want money, while the other trader might want goods. The trading partners are not giving or receiving gifts. Trading is done for self-interest, not kindness. Therefore, B is the correct answer.

8 **H** The passage says that people provide these goods out of self-interest because they get something in return. The passage does not indicate that the government tells anyone to do anything and states that trade is not done out of kindness. The passage does not indicate that they provide food because we want it. Thus, H is the correct answer.

Short Response

9 The passage explains that citizens should participate in the democratic process to protect freedom and liberty.

10 The American democracy is based on the will of the people, shown by the votes and actions of its citizens. The justice is suggesting that this is a great responsibility and that honoring it deserves high praise.

Extended Response

11 Student answers will vary. Students should note that our representative form of government needs an informed, active set of voters so that the will of the people can be expressed. They should also note that our way of life includes many freedoms that are made possible when people carry out their duties and responsibilities.

ONLINE RESOURCES
networks

There's More Online!

- INTERACTIVE WORKSHEETS
- BIOGRAPHIES
- CHARTS/GRAPHS
- GAMES
- GRAPHIC ORGANIZERS
- IMAGES
- MAPS
- PRIMARY SOURCES
- SLIDE SHOWS
- TIME LINE
- LECTURE SLIDES
- INTERACTIVE WHITEBOARD ACTIVITIES
- ASSESSMENTS
- VIDEOS

How We Know About the Ice Ages

The Ice Man, Etruscans, the Roman Empire, and the Italian Renaissance.

Chapter 3

Early Humans and the Agricultural Revolution

Dear World History Teacher,

Over a long period of time, Paleolithic people created sophisticated tools, used fire for lighting and cooking, and adapted to and changed their physical environment. Paleolithic people were nomads who hunted animals and gathered wild plants. Although mostly concerned with survival, they also created a human culture that included sophisticated cave paintings.

The Agricultural Revolution of the Neolithic Age, which began around 10,000 B.C., dramatically changed human patterns of living. Growing food on a regular basis and taming animals made it possible for humans to end their nomadic ways and live in more permanent settlements. Gender patterns also changed from an equality-based relationship between men and women to a relationship in which men took on more dominant roles in the family and society. These organized permanent settlements gradually emerged into more complex human societies.

These complex human societies, which are defined as civilizations, appeared around 3000 B.C. in the river valleys of Mesopotamia, Egypt, India, and China. An increase in food production in these regions led to a significant growth in human population and the growth of cities.

Jackson J. Spielvogel

More Media Resources

Current Events Online

Visit McGraw-Hill's current events Web site for high-interest news stories and activities for your students. Access the site through the Student or Teacher Center in **networks.**

Reading List

Grade 6 reading level:
Exploring the Ice Age, by Margaret Cooper

Grade 7 reading level:
Bodies from the Ice: Melting Glaciers and the Recovery of the Past, by James M. Deem

Grade 8 reading level:
A Bone from a Dry Sea, by Peter Dickinson

At the MOVIES

Watch *Cave of Forgotten Dreams.* To make this film, director Werner Herzog was given unprecedented access to the Chauvet Cave in southern France, where some of the oldest artistic creations of humankind are found.

Discuss: Why would a 20th century film director be interested in cave paintings created more than 20,000 years ago?

NOTE: Be sure to preview any films to ensure that they are age-appropriate.

Search for more videos online in the **networks** Resource Library.

CHAPTER 3 Planner

UNDERSTANDING BY DESIGN®

Enduring Understanding

- ***People, places, and ideas change over time.***

Essential Question

- ***How do people adapt to their environment?***

Students will know:

- *how Paleolithic humans adapted to their environments to survive*
- *how advances during the Paleolithic Age made it possible for humans to survive the Ice Ages*
- *why some historians consider the Agricultural Revolution the most important event in human history*
- *why people created permanent settlements when they began to farm*
- *how tools and roles changed as a result of permanent communities*

Students will be able to:

- **analyze** photographs of shelters from the Paleolithic Age
- **use** trial-and-error methods to solve a problem
- **write** a descriptive paragraph on how trial and error helped humans survive
- **analyze** photographs of shelters from the Neolithic Age
- **connect** farming to their daily lives
- **draw conclusions** about why the Agricultural Revolution was a revolution

Predictable Misunderstandings

Students may think:

- The Paleolithic and Neolithic Ages were short spans of time.
- People during this time were not smart.
- People made few advances during this time.
- People did not live together as families.

Assessment Evidence

Performance Task

- Hands-On Chapter Project

Other Evidence

- Responses to Interactive Whiteboard Activities
- Answers to questions about Neolithic Age shelters
- Class discussion answers
- Writing activity to describe the relationship between trial and error and survival during the Paleolithic Age
- Brainstorming activity of phrases and adjectives that describe what life was like during the Paleolithic Age
- Concept Web creation
- Whiteboard Drag-and-Drop Activity
- 21st Century Skills Activity
- Lesson Reviews

Pacing Guide

Introducing the Chapter	1 day
Lesson 1 Hunter-Gatherers	1 day
Lesson 2 The Agricultural Revolution	1 day
Chapter Activities and Assessment	1 day
TOTAL TIME	**4 Days**

Differentiated Instruction

These lesson plans are written to address the needs of your On Level students. Discussion and activities that are well-suited to your Approaching Grade Level learners, Beyond Grade Level learners, as well as your English Language Learners, are coded as follows:

AL Approaching Grade Level

BL Beyond Grade Level

ELL English Language Learner

NCSS Standards covered in "Early Humans and the Agricultural Revolution"

Learners will understand:

1 CULTURE

3. How culture influences the ways in which human groups solve the problems of daily living;

4. That the beliefs, values, and behaviors of a culture form an integrated system that helps shape the activities and ways of life that define a culture

5. How individuals learn the elements of their culture through interactions with others, and how individuals learn of other cultures through communication and study

6. That culture may change in response to changing needs, concerns, social, political, and geographic conditions

2 TIME, CONTINUITY, AND CHANGE

5. Key historical periods and patterns of change within and across cultures (e.g., the rise and fall of ancient civilizations, the development of technology, the rise of modern nation-states, and the establishment and breakdown of colonial systems)

6. The origins and influences of social, cultural, political, and economic systems

7. Human modifications of the environment

4 INDIVIDUAL DEVELOPMENT AND IDENTITY

2. Concepts such as: development, change, personality, learning, individual, family, groups, motivation, and perception

5 INDIVIDUALS, GROUPS, AND INSTITUTIONS

3. Institutions are created to respond to changing individual and group needs

5. That groups and institutions change over time

6 POWER, AUTHORITY, AND GOVERNANCE

5. The ways in which governments meet the needs and wants of citizens, manage conflict, and establish order and society

7 PRODUCTION, DISTRIBUTION, AND CONSUMPTION

6. The economic gains that result from specialization and exchange as well as the trade-offs

8 SCIENCE, TECHNOLOGY, AND SOCIETY

1. Science is a result of empirical study of the natural world, and technology is the application of knowledge to accomplish tasks

CHAPTER 3

Introducing the Chapter

(Student Edition p. 51)

The Story Matters . . .

After students have read "The Story Matters . . .," begin a discussion with them about why archaeologists are excited about fossil finds such as the skull shown here.

Ask:

What do archaeologists hope to learn by studying the bones and artifacts of prehistoric people? Is the information that archaeologists learn from these artifacts important to contemporary life? What clues do you think we will leave behind for archaeologists to find 2 million years from now? Have students share their ideas.

Tell students that the movement of early people out of Africa is one of the earliest examples we have of the migration, or movement, of a large group of people. Begin a discussion with students about migration.

Ask:

Have you ever moved from one house to another? Why do individuals or families move? What causes a large number of people to leave one place and move to another? What might have caused early people to migrate out of Africa? How do you think these early migrations of people compare to the movement of people from one place to another that we see today? Tell students that as they continue their study of history, they will learn about other times when large groups of people moved from one place to another.

Early Humans and the Agricultural Revolution

8000 B.C. to 2000 B.C.

ESSENTIAL QUESTION • *How do people adapt to their environment?*

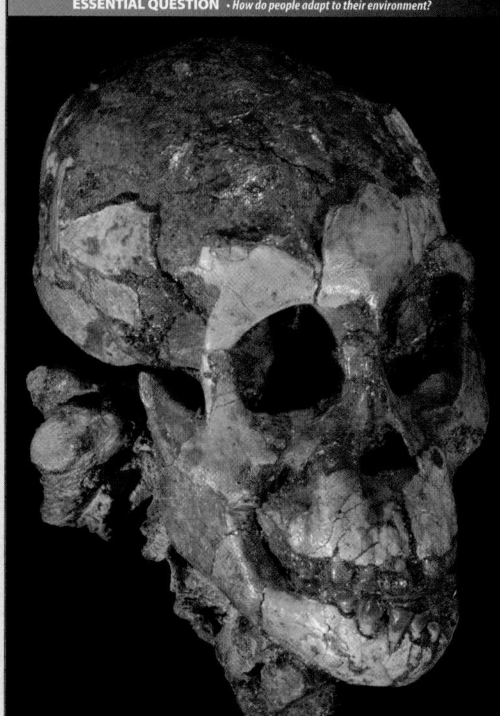

networks

There's More Online about the lives and customs of early humans.

CHAPTER 3

Lesson 1 *Hunter-Gatherers*

Lesson 2 *The Agricultural Revolution*

The Story Matters . . .

Was eastern Africa the home of the earliest humans? Many scientists believe that is where the first group of human-like beings lived. Some early human skeletons found in Africa are over six million years old. Scientists estimate that this skull may be more than 3.2 million years old. It may have belonged to a three-year-old child who lived in eastern Africa. Fossils like this one tell us a lot about early humans.

Some early people may have begun moving from Africa to other regions about 1.8 million years ago. Over a period of time humans were found in Europe and as far away as China. Everywhere early humans went, they left behind clues about their lives. By studying these clues, scientists can tell us about our past.

◄ *Ancient human-like fossils tell us about our early ancestors.*

AFP/Getty Images

51

Introducing Place and Time

(Student Edition pp. 52–53)

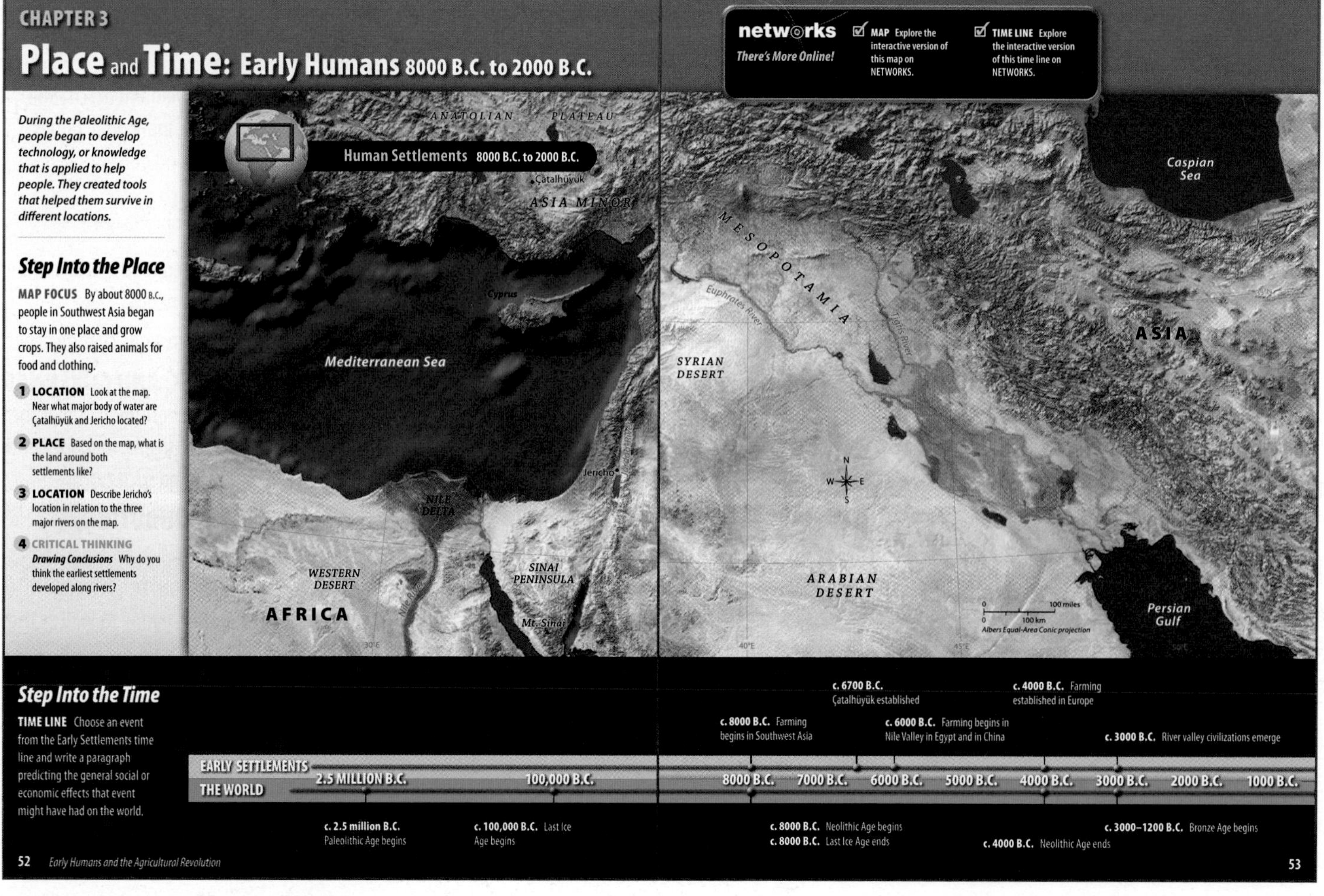

CHAPTER 3

Place and Time: Early Humans 8000 B.C. to 2000 B.C.

networks *There's More Online!* MAP Explore the interactive version of this map on NETWORKS. TIME LINE Explore the interactive version of this time line on NETWORKS.

During the Paleolithic Age, people began to develop technology, or knowledge that is applied to help people. They created tools that helped them survive in different locations.

Step Into the Place

MAP FOCUS By about 8000 B.C., people in Southwest Asia began to stay in one place and grow crops. They also raised animals for food and clothing.

1. **LOCATION** Look at the map. Near what major body of water are Çatalhüyük and Jericho located?
2. **PLACE** Based on the map, what is the land around both settlements like?
3. **LOCATION** Describe Jericho's location in relation to the three major rivers on the map.
4. **CRITICAL THINKING** ***Drawing Conclusions*** Why do you think the earliest settlements developed along rivers?

Step Into the Time

TIME LINE Choose an event from the Early Settlements time line and write a paragraph predicting the general social or economic effects that event might have had on the world.

52 *Early Humans and the Agricultural Revolution*

53

Technology Extension

- Find an additional activity online that incorporates technology for this project.
- Visit the EdTechTeacher Web sites (included in the Technology Extension for this chapter) for more links, tutorials, and other resources.

Assessing Background Knowledge

INTERACTIVE WORKSHEET

What Do You Know? Activity

Have students complete the Concept Circle for Early Humans and the Agricultural Revolution before they study the chapter.

Ask students if they think there is a term that does not belong with the others. *(Some students may say* technology *does not belong with other words about prehistoric times.)* Provide students with colored pencils to complete their drawings. After students complete the chapter, have them refer to their Concept Circles.

Discuss with students what they have learned about early humans and technology. Ask them how their illustrations of each of these terms would be different now that they have studied the chapter.

INTERACTIVE WORKSHEET

Guided Reading Activities

You might want to assign the Guided Reading Activity for Lesson 1 after introducing the chapter content.

Hands-On Chapter Project

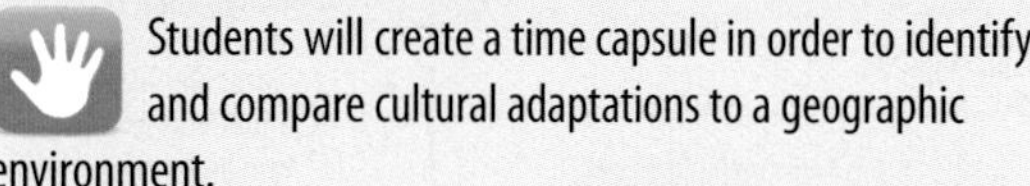

Students will create a time capsule in order to identify and compare cultural adaptations to a geographic environment.

- Students will work in small groups and use discussion and worksheets to create a time capsule.
- Students will begin by participating in a class discussion about the cultural regions of the United States and the types of cultural elements found in each region.
- Next, students will choose a region for their time capsule and assign tasks to group members.
- Then, students will discuss and research items to include in the time capsule.
- Students will present their completed time capsules to the class.
- Finally, the class will use an Assessment Rubric to evaluate their time capsules, presentations, and collaboration.

Visit **networks** online to see the full project and rubric.

ONLINE RESOURCES

networks

Assign these interactive worksheets and quizzes from your Teacher Lesson Center. All resources are print-ready.

It's ALL Online!

Chapter 3 Resources

- ☑ Chapter Summary
- ☑ Vocabulary Builder
- ☑ What Do You Know?
- ☑ Hands-On Chapter Project

Lesson 1 Resources

- ☑ Interactive Graphic Organizer
- ☑ 21st Century Skills Activity
  Critical Thinking and Problem Solving
- ☑ Interactive Guided Reading Activity
- ☑ Reading Essentials and Study Guide
- ☑ Online Self-Check Quiz

Lesson 2 Resources

- ☑ Interactive Graphic Organizer
- ☑ Interactive Guided Reading Activity
- ☑ Reading Essentials and Study Guide
- ☑ Online Self-Check Quiz

Assessment Resources

- ☑ Lesson Reviews
- ☑ Online Self-Check Quizzes
- ☑ Chapter Activities and Assessment
- ☑ Standardized Test Practice

Remediation Resources

- ☑ Reading Essentials and Study Guide
- ☑ Guided Reading Activities
- ☑ Online Self-Check Quizzes
- ☑ Chapter Summary

Step Into the Place

Movement Project the Chapter Opener map on the whiteboard. Direct students' attention to the locator map. Remind students of information in "The Story Matters . . ." about human migration out of Africa. Ask students how people might have traveled from Africa to the region shown on the map. *(They probably walked over the thin strip of land that connects Africa to Asia.)*

INTERACTIVE WHITEBOARD ACTIVITY At your interactive whiteboard, have student volunteers circle the names of major bodies of water. As a class, discuss the Map Focus questions.

Step Into the Time

Drawing Conclusions Have students review the time line for the chapter. Explain that they will be studying events from about 2,500,000 B.C. to 1000 B.C.

Ask students: **Based on the information in the time lines, what major development took place before the creation of settlements such as Jericho and Çatalhüyük?** *(farming)*

Answers for pages 52–53

Step Into the Place

1. They are near the Mediterranean Sea.
2. The land appears to be hilly.
3. Jericho is located between the major rivers and closest to Jordan.
4. CRITICAL THINKING Answers will vary but may include access to water for drinking, irrigation, and transportation.

Step Into the Time

Answers will vary but should demonstrate knowledge of early civilizations and the Agricultural Revolution.

networks
There's More Online!
☑ GRAPHIC ORGANIZER
Paleolithic Inventions
☑ SLIDE SHOW
Woolly Mammoth

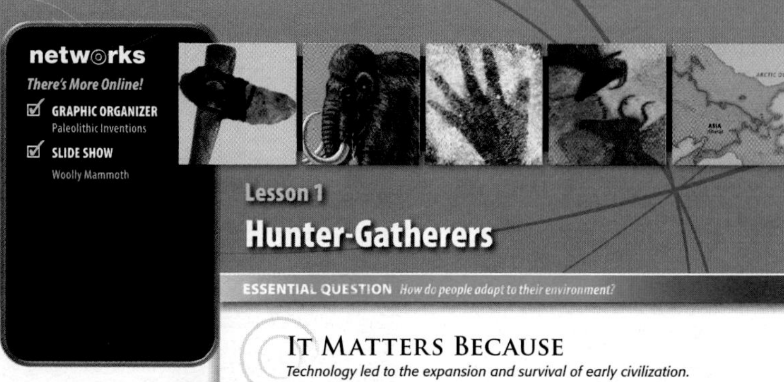

Lesson 1

Hunter-Gatherers

ESSENTIAL QUESTION *How do people adapt to their environment?*

It Matters Because

Technology led to the expansion and survival of early civilization.

1 The Paleolithic Age

GUIDING QUESTION *What was life like during the Paleolithic Age?*

Historians call the early period of human history the Stone Age. They do this because it was the time when people used stone to make tools and weapons. The earliest part of this period was the **Paleolithic** (pay•lee•uh•LIH•thick) Age. In Greek, *paleolithic* means "old stone." Therefore, the Paleolithic Age is also called the Old Stone Age. The Paleolithic Age began about 2.5 million years ago and lasted until around 8000 B.C. Remember, that is about 4,500 years earlier than recorded time, which starts about 5,500 years ago.

Surviving in the Paleolithic Age

Try to imagine what life was like during the Paleolithic Age. Think about living in a time long before any roads, farms, or villages existed. Paleolithic people often moved around in search of food. They were **nomads** (NOH•mads), or people who regularly move from place to place to survive. They traveled in groups, or bands, of about 20 or 30 members.

Paleolithic people survived by hunting and gathering. The search for food was their main activity, and it was often difficult. They had to learn which animals to hunt and which plants to eat. Paleolithic people hunted buffalo, bison, wild goats, reindeer,

Reading HELPDESK

Taking Notes: *Sequencing*

Use a diagram like the one on the right to list two important inventions of Paleolithic people. Then explain why these inventions were important.

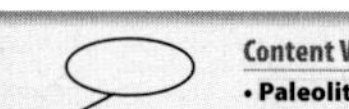

Content Vocabulary
- **Paleolithic**
- **nomads**
- **technology**
- **Ice Age**

and other animals, depending on where they lived. Along coastal areas, they fished. These early people also gathered wild nuts, berries, fruits, wild grains, and green plants.

Finding Food

Paleolithic men and women performed different tasks within the group. Men—not women—hunted large animals. They often had to search far from their camp. Men had to learn how animals behaved and how to hunt them. They had to develop tracking methods. At first, men used clubs or drove the animals off cliffs to kill them. Over time, however, Paleolithic people developed tools and weapons to help them hunt. The traps and spears they made increased their chances of killing their prey.

Women stayed close to the camp, which was often located near a stream or other body of water. They looked after the children and searched nearby woods and meadows for berries, nuts, and grains. Everyone worked to find food, because it was the key to the group's survival.

Paleolithic people traveled in bands to hunt and gather food. Bands lived together in the open, under overhangs such as the one pictured here, or in caves.

▶ CRITICAL THINKING
Analyzing Why did these people live together in groups?

Paleolithic relating to the earliest period of the Stone Age

nomads people who move from place to place as a group to find food for themselves

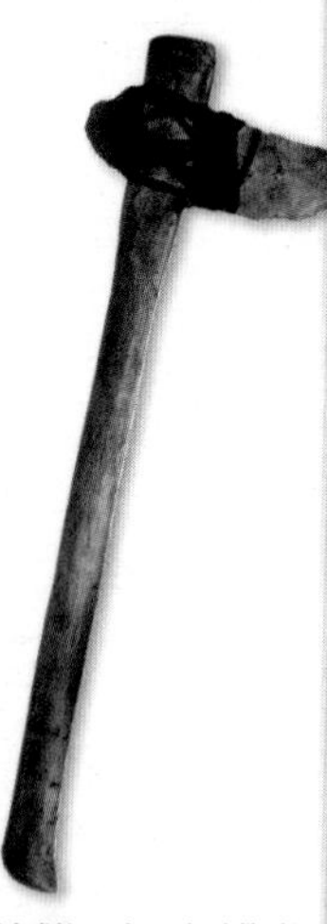

Paleolithic peoples used tools like this for many purposes. Look at this ax and decide what materials it was made of.

▶ CRITICAL THINKING
Predicting What do you think this tool was used for?

Some scientists believe that an equal relationship existed between Paleolithic men and women. It is likely that both made decisions that affected the band or group. Some evidence suggests that some men and women may have hunted in monogamous pairs. This means that a man and a woman worked together to find food for themselves and their children. Such groupings became the first families.

The Invention of Tools

Culture is the way of life for a group of people who share similar beliefs and customs. The **methods** Paleolithic people used to hunt and gather their food were part of their culture, as were the tools they used.

Technology (tehk•NAHL•uh•jee)—tools and methods to perform tasks—was first used by Paleolithic people. Before this time, sticks, stones, and tree branches served as tools. Later, people made devices from a hard stone called flint. Have you ever imagined how difficult it would be to prepare or eat food without a cutting tool? Paleolithic people learned that by hitting flint with another hard stone, the flint would flake into pieces. These pieces had very sharp edges that could be used for cutting. Hand axes, for example, were large pieces of flint tied to wooden poles. Flint technology was a major breakthrough for early peoples.

Over time, early people made better, more complex tools. Spears and bows and arrows made killing large animals easier. Harpoons, or spears with sharp points, and fishhooks increased the number of fish caught. Early humans used sharp-edged tools to cut up plants and dig roots. They used scraping tools to clean animal hides, which they used for clothing and shelter.

By the end of the Paleolithic Age, people were making smaller and sharper tools. They crafted needles from animal bones to make nets and baskets and to sew hides together for clothing. This technology had a far-reaching effect. It drove the development of more advanced farming tools and influenced where people settled.

Changing to Survive

Climate affected how Paleolithic people lived. Some early people lived in cold climates and made clothing from animal skins to stay warm. They sought protection in **available** natural shelters, such as caves and rock overhangs. Remember, there

Reading HELPDESK

technology an ability gained by the practical use of knowledge

Academic Vocabulary

method a way of doing something
available ready to be used
construct to build by putting parts together

were no houses or apartment buildings as we know them in the Paleolithic Age. Gradually, humans learned to make their own shelters. People **constructed** tents and huts of animal skins, brush, and wood. In very cold climates, some people made shelters from ice and snow. In regions where wood was scarce, Paleolithic people used the large bones from dead woolly mammoths, or hairy elephant-like animals, to build frames for shelters. They then covered the bones with animal hides.

People living in warmer climates, on the other hand, needed little clothing or shelter. For the purposes of safety and comfort, however, many lived in caves and huts. These shelters provided protection against attacks by large animals.

Fire Sparks Changes

Life became less difficult for Paleolithic people once they discovered how to make fire. People learned that fire provided warmth in cold caves. It provided light when it was dark and could be used to scare away wild animals. Armed with spears, hunters could also use fire to chase animals from bushes to be killed. Eventually, people gathered around fires to share stories and to cook. Cooked food, they discovered, tasted better and was easier to chew and digest. In addition, meat that was smoked by fire did not have to be eaten right away and could be stored.

How did people learn to use fire? Archaeologists believe early humans produced fire by friction. They learned that by rubbing two pieces of wood together, the wood became heated and charred. When the wood became hot enough, it caught fire. Paleolithic people continued rubbing wood together, eventually developing drill-like wooden tools to start fires. They also discovered that a certain stone, iron pyrite, gave off sparks when struck against another rock. The sparks could then ignite dry grass or leaves—another way to start a fire.

Visual Vocabulary

woolly mammoth a large, hairy, extinct animal related to modern-day elephants

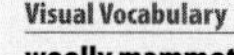

LESSON 1

ENGAGE

SLIDE SHOW **Analyzing Visuals** Present the slide show about Paleolithic animals. Begin a discussion with students about how the animals adapted to their environment.

Ask:
- **In what kind of climate would this animal live?**
- **What kind of food do you think it ate?**
- **How do you think this animal protected itself?**
- **How do you think speed would be important to an animal?**
- **Why do you think some animals were able to survive even though they were slow?**

(Students' responses will vary depending on the animal shown. Accept all answers that can be supported.)

Ask students to predict what kinds of adaptations early humans made to survive in harsh environments. AL

TEACH & ASSESS

1 The Paleolithic Age

GUIDING QUESTION *What was life like during the Paleolithic Age?*

LECTURE SLIDE **Previewing** Begin a discussion with students about what they would do if they were lost on a deserted island.

Ask:

What would you eat? How would you know if something is safe to eat? *(Students may say they would try just a little bit of a potential food and see if they got sick, or they might wait to see if an animal ate it and survived.)*

Tell students that these methods are examples of trial-and-error learning. Point out that in trial-and-error learning, you try different solutions to a problem until you find an answer. ELL

Making Connections Ask students if another subject they study in school sometimes requires them to use trial and error. *(Students might mention math or science.)*

LECTURE SLIDE Discuss the definition of trial-and-error learning from the Lecture Slide. Tell students to watch for ways in which humans used trial-and-error learning to help them adapt and survive.

INTERACTIVE WHITEBOARD ACTIVITY **Categorizing** Have students work in small groups or with a partner to brainstorm a list of words and phrases they would use to describe life in the Paleolithic Age.

Then have a member of each group come to the whiteboard to write down the words. When all the groups have written their words, compare the lists as a class.

Ask:

What words were on most groups' lists?

Then have students categorize the words into groups; for example, words about food, words about shelter, positive words, negative words, and so on. AL

2 The Ice Ages

GUIDING QUESTION *How did people adapt to survive during the Ice Ages?*

INTERACTIVE WHITEBOARD ACTIVITY **Comparing and Contrasting** Have students compare and contrast the Paleolithic Age with the Ice Ages.

Ask:
- **How were the Ice Ages different from the Paleolithic Age?**
- **How were they the same?**

Then show the Paleolithic and Ice Age Venn diagram on the whiteboard. Have students drag and drop images into the correct location on the diagram.

Have students complete the Lesson 1 Review.

CLOSE & REFLECT

Discussing Discuss with students how people were able to adapt to survive after the Ice Ages. Ask students how they think humans today might adjust if there were another drastic change in Earth's climate.

INTERACTIVE WORKSHEET

21st Century Skills Activity

Have students complete the 21st Century Skills Activity for this lesson about trial and error and problem solving.

BACKGROUND KNOWLEDGE

The Dig at Mezhirich

In 1965 a farmer dug to expand his cellar in Mezhirich, Ukraine, and struck a bone—a huge, lower-jaw bone of a mammoth.

After excavation, nearly 149 bones were discovered. The bones indicated the site dated back to the Ice Age of 15,000 years ago. These huge, heavy bones were formed into four oval-shaped dwellings.

The jaw bones were interlocked, forming a solid, circular base. Also, there were roof supports made of giant tusks.

Scientists guess that animal hides covered the buildings. The site at Mezhirich is the oldest example of architecture in the world.

Answers for pages 54–57

P. 54 Taking Notes Answers should include the use of fire, scraping tools, harpoons, spears, and the bow and arrow; all were important because they allowed the tools' users to live and hunt more efficiently.

P. 55 CRITICAL THINKING A group of people can gather more food and provide safety for one another.

P. 56 CRITICAL THINKING Answers will vary but should reflect an understanding of Paleolithic needs.

Paleolithic art has been found in caves in Argentina. Early people left a message that remains today.

▶ CRITICAL THINKING

Identifying What subjects were most common in cave paintings?

Language and Art

Other advancements took place during the Paleolithic Age. One important advancement was the development of spoken language. Up until this time, early people **communicated** through sounds and physical gestures. Then they began to develop language.

Ancient peoples started to express themselves in words for the same reasons we do. We use language to communicate information and emotions. Language makes it easier for us to work together and to pass on knowledge. We also use words to express our thoughts and feelings. The spoken language of early people was **constantly** growing and changing. New technology and more complicated experiences, for example, required new words.

Early people also expressed themselves through art. Some of this art can still be seen today, even though it is thousands of years old. For example, in 1879 a young girl named Maria de Sautuola wandered into a cave on her grandfather's farm near Altamira, Spain. She was startled by what she discovered on the walls of that cave:

PRIMARY SOURCE

> ❝ Maria entered the cave . . . and suddenly reappeared all excited, shouting 'Papa, mira, toros pintados! [Papa, look, painted bulls!]' Maria had discovered one of the most famous animal-art galleries in the world. ❞
>
> —from *Hands: Prehistoric Visiting Cards?* by August Gansser

Reading **HELP**DESK

Academic Vocabulary

communicate to share information with someone

constant always happening

About ten thousand years before Maria's visit, Paleolithic artists had painted mysterious signs, including what looked like a herd of animals—horses, boars, bison, and deer—on the cave's ceiling. In 1940, a cave with similar paintings to those in Spain was discovered near Lascaux (lah•SKOH) in southern France.

Paleolithic cave paintings have been found all around the world. Early artists crushed yellow, black, and red rocks and combined them with animal fat to make their paints. They used twigs and their fingertips to apply these paints to the rock walls. They later used brushes made from animal hair. Early people created scenes of lions, oxen, panthers, and other animals. Few humans, however, appear in these paintings.

Historians are not sure why early artists chose to make cave paintings. Early people may have thought that painting an animal would bring hunters good luck. Some scholars believe, however, that the paintings may have been created to record the group's history. They may have been created simply to be enjoyed.

☑ PROGRESS CHECK

Explaining Why was fire important for Paleolithic people?

The paintings in the Lascaux caves are the most famous examples of Paleolithic art. Scientists now believe that such paintings took thousands of years, and hundreds of generations, to produce.

▶ CRITICAL THINKING

Speculating Why do you think these paintings lasted so long?

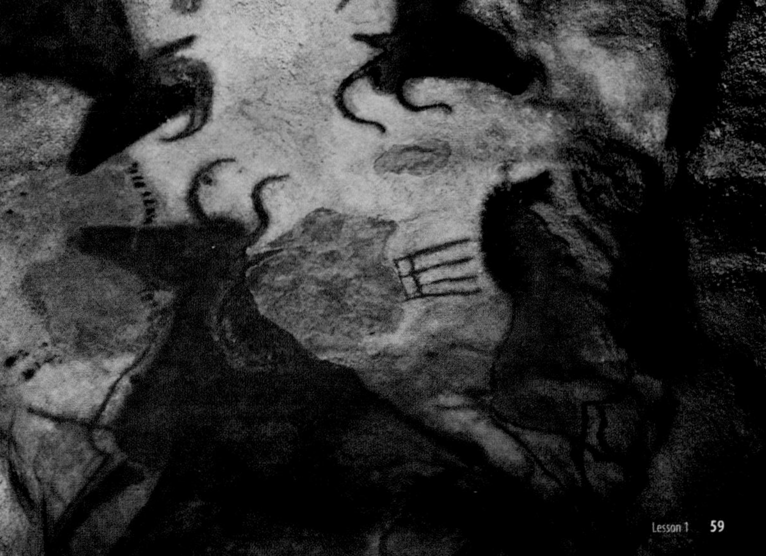

2 The Ice Ages

GUIDING QUESTION *How did people adapt to survive during the ice ages?*

Tools and fire were two important technological developments of Paleolithic people. Throughout history, people have used new technology to help them survive when the environment changes. The ice ages were major environmental disturbances. The changes they brought about threatened the very survival of humans.

What Changes Came With the Ice Ages?

The **ice ages** were long periods of extreme cold that affected all of Earth. The most recent Ice Age began about 100,000 years ago. Thick sheets of ice moved across large parts of Europe, Asia, and North America. As the ice sheets, or glaciers, grew larger, the water level of the oceans was lowered. The low sea levels exposed a strip of dry land connecting the continents of Asia and North America. This strip of land was known as a land bridge. The land bridge acted as a natural highway that allowed people to travel from Asia into North America. From there, Paleolithic peoples moved southward to settle in different regions.

GEOGRAPHY CONNECTION

During the most recent Ice Age, a strip of land connected the continents of Asia and North America.

1. **REGIONS** How did the geography of this region change when the most recent Ice Age ended?
2. CRITICAL THINKING ***Analyzing*** After people arrived in North America, what is a likely reason they moved south rather than staying near the land bridge?

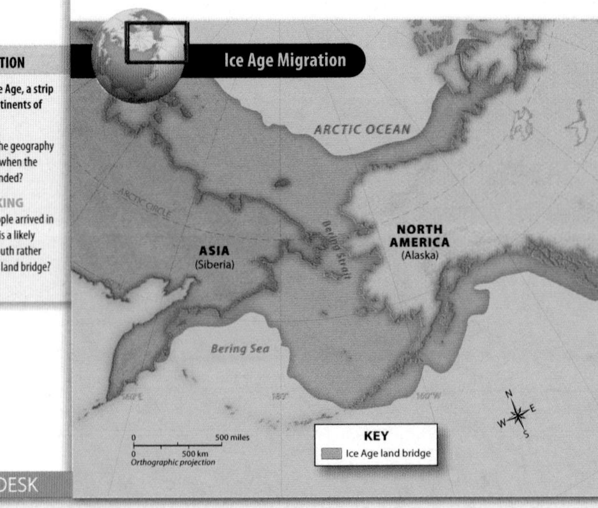

Reading **HELP**DESK

ice age a time when glaciers covered much of the land

How Did the Ice Ages Affect Humans?

Ice age conditions posed a grave threat to human life. To survive in the cold temperatures, humans had to adapt, or change, many areas of their lives. One way they adapted their diets was by enriching meals with fat. To protect themselves from the harsh environment, they learned to build sturdier shelters. They also learned to make warm clothing using animal furs. Paleolithic people used fire to help them stay warm in this icy environment. The last Ice Age lasted about 90,000 years, ending between about 9000 and 8000 B.C.

☑ PROGRESS CHECK

Explaining How were land bridges formed?

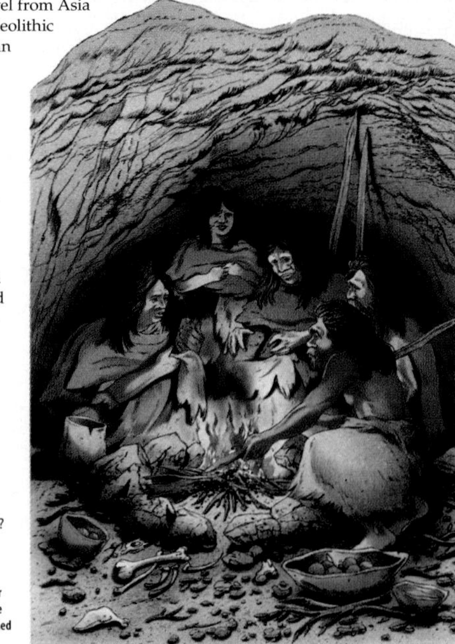

After early people controlled fire, they brought it into their shelters. At the site of some Stone Age huts, scientists have discovered an early form of a fireplace—a shallow hole lined with blackened stones.

LESSON 1 REVIEW

Review Vocabulary

1. What is another name for the *Paleolithic* Age?

Answer the Guiding Questions

2. ***Describing*** By what methods did Paleolithic people get food?
3. ***Summarizing*** How did fire help Paleolithic people survive?
4. ***Determining Cause and Effect*** How did the ice ages affect where people settled in the Americas?
5. ***Making Connections*** How does climate affect the type of house you live in or the clothes you wear?
6. **PERSONAL WRITING** You are a mother or father who lives in the early Paleolithic Age. In a few paragraphs, describe your daily life.

LESSON 1 (cont.)

IF YOU HAVE MORE TIME . . .

Read for a Reason

When students have a reason or purpose for reading, the task becomes relevant and meaningful, both of which are necessary for comprehension.

Good readers inherently set purposes for themselves, but less-proficient readers might need help finding a reason for reading.

Before Reading

Skimming
Help students establish a reason for reading by skimming the text. Point out section headings, illustrations, and boldfaced words. Tell students that these text features can help establish a purpose for reading. ELL

During Reading

Identifying a Reason for Reading
Give students a specific task to perform while they read, such as looking for a specific piece of information, summarizing content, finding details to support a position, or writing a response to what they have read. AL

After Reading

Paraphrasing
When students finish reading, have them work with a partner to paraphrase what they have read. Encourage them to reread sections of text or share notes and answers to questions in order to clarify reading. ELL

IF YOU HAVE MORE TIME . . .

Reinforce Map Skills

Use the following suggestions to reinforce map skills with students, if time allows.

These activities can be used in this lesson or any time you need to reinforce map skills.

- Have students identify the physical systems of their state or region.
- Have students look through their textbook to find different examples of map projections. Identify and discuss the advantages and disadvantages of the different projections they find.
- Write on a slip of paper the page number for a map in the book. Include a question on the paper that students would need to use the map and key to answer. Have volunteers randomly select a slip of paper, look for the map and key, and answer your question.
- Bring to class or ask volunteers to bring to class different special-purpose maps. Examples include trail maps from a park, road maps, building emergency exit maps, or even maps from a work of fiction. Allow time to compare the different maps and explain how each fulfills a special purpose.

Answers for pages 58–61

P. 58 CRITICAL THINKING Human handprints and the animals that people hunted were common subjects.

P. 59 CRITICAL THINKING They lasted so long because they were located and protected in caves.

P. 59 ☑ PROGRESS CHECK It offered protection, warmth, cooking, and a social element.

P. 60 GEOGRAPHY CONNECTION

1. When the Ice Age ended, sea levels rose and the land bridge disappeared underwater.
2. CRITICAL THINKING Answers will vary but should include the idea that regions to the south would be warmer and more hospitable to humans than the area near the land bridge.

P. 61 ☑ PROGRESS CHECK The ice lowered water levels in the oceans so the land that had been under water became visible.

LESSON 1 REVIEW

1. The Paleolithic Age is also called the Old Stone Age. People used stones to make tools and weapons.
2. They got food by hunting, gathering, and fishing.
3. Fire provided warmth, helped scare away animals, and lit the darkness. It was also used for cooking.
4. The ice ages created a land bridge from Asia to the Americas. When the ice ages ended, people were able to migrate to different regions.
5. Answers will vary. Accept all reasonable answers.
6. Students' writings should be consistent with the lesson content.

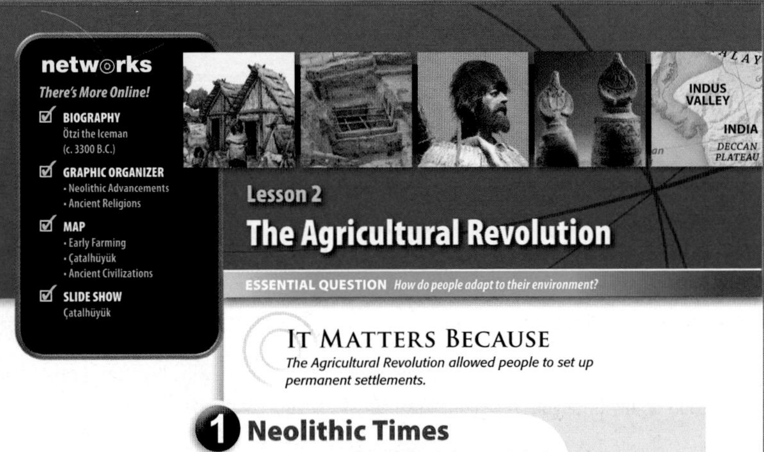

Lesson 2
The Agricultural Revolution

ESSENTIAL QUESTION *How do people adapt to their environment?*

It Matters Because
The Agricultural Revolution allowed people to set up permanent settlements.

1 Neolithic Times

GUIDING QUESTION *How did farming change people's lives?*

The earliest people were nomads who moved from place to place to hunt animals and gather plants. After the last Ice Age ended, Earth's temperatures rose. As the climate warmed, many nomads moved into areas with a mild climate and fertile land.

Another historical revolution then occurred. For the first time, people began staying in one place to grow grains and vegetables. Gradually, farming replaced hunting and gathering as the main source of food. At the same time, people began to **domesticate** (duh•MEHS•tih•kayt), or tame, animals for human use. Animals transported goods and provided meat, milk, and wool.

The Neolithic Age

This change in the way people lived marked the beginning of the **Neolithic Age** (nee•uh•LIH•thick). It began about 8000 B.C. and lasted until around 4000 B.C.—about 4,000 years. The word *neolithic* is Greek for "new stone." Calling this time period the New Stone Age, however, is somewhat misleading. Although new stone tools were made, the real change in the Neolithic Age was the shift from hunting and gathering to **systematic agriculture**. This is growing food on a regular basis.

Reading HELPDESK

Taking Notes: *Identifying*
Use a diagram like this to identify three advancements made during the Neolithic Age.

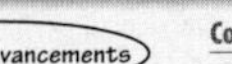

Content Vocabulary
- domesticate
- Neolithic Age
- systematic agriculture
- shrine
- specialization
- Bronze Age
- monarchy

This shift from hunting and gathering to food production, however, did not happen quickly. Even during the Mesolithic Age, or Middle Stone Age, some people continued to hunt and gather, while others began to grow their own food.

Big Changes for Humankind

Historians call this settled farming during the Neolithic Age the Agricultural Revolution. The word *revolution* refers to any change that has an enormous effect on people's ways of life. While hunter-gatherers ate wild grains that they collected, early farmers saved some of the grains to plant. Humans lived differently once they learned how to grow crops and tame animals that produced food. They now could produce a constant food supply. This allowed the population to grow at a faster rate. Nomads gave up their way of life and began living in settled communities. Some historians consider the Agricultural Revolution the most important event in human history.

GEOGRAPHY CONNECTION

Between about 7000 and 2000 B.C., farming developed on different continents.

1. **REGIONS** What crops were grown south of the Equator?
2. **CRITICAL THINKING** ***Speculating*** Why do you think so many different crops were grown in Central America?

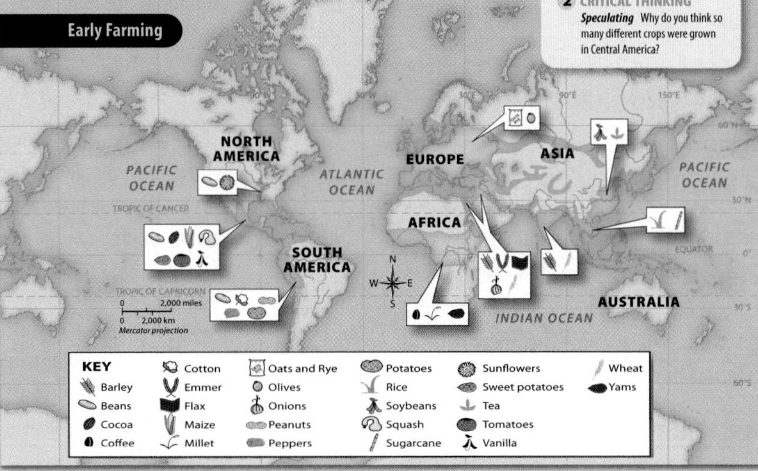

domesticate to adapt an animal to living with humans for the advantage of humans

Neolithic Age relating to the latest period of the Stone Age

systematic agriculture the organized growing of food on a regular schedule

Widespread Farming

By 8000 B.C., people in Southwest Asia began growing wheat and barley. They also domesticated pigs, cows, goats, and sheep. From there, farming spread into southeastern Europe. By 4000 B.C., farming was an established **economic** activity in Europe.

At about the same time, around 6000 B.C., people had begun growing wheat and barley in the Nile Valley in Egypt. Farming soon spread along the Nile River and into other regions in Africa. In Central Africa, different types of crops emerged. There, people grew root crops called tubers, which included yams. They also grew fruit crops, such as bananas. Wheat and barley farming moved eastward into India between 8000 and 5000 B.C.

By 6000 B.C., people in northern China were growing a food grain called millet and were domesticating dogs and pigs. By 5000 B.C., farmers in Southeast Asia were growing rice. From there, rice farming spread into southern China.

In the Western Hemisphere, between 7000 and 5000 B.C., people in Mexico and Central America were growing corn, squash, and potatoes. They also domesticated chickens and dogs.

PROGRESS CHECK

Explaining How did the spread of farming change the lives of nomads?

Originally, Neolithic people built large dwelling places that housed a small clan, or family group, along with their cattle and grain stores. Eventually, these were replaced by one- or two-room houses, which were usually clustered in groups.

CRITICAL THINKING
Analyzing Why would construction methods vary depending on geographical location?

Reading HELPDESK

Academic Vocabulary

economy the system of economic life in an area or country; an economy deals with the making, buying, and selling of goods or services

CRITICAL THINKING
Analyzing The village of Çatalhüyük grew into a large community. These ruins reveal well thought out construction. ***Why do you think some people were happy to settle in villages?***

2 Life in the Neolithic Age

GUIDING QUESTION *What was life like during the Neolithic Age?*

During the Neolithic Age, people settled in villages where they built permanent homes. They **located** villages near fields so people could plant, grow, and harvest their crops more easily. People also settled near water sources, especially rivers.

Neolithic Communities

Neolithic farming villages developed throughout Europe, India, Egypt, China, and Mexico. The biggest and earliest known communities have been found in Southwest Asia. One of the oldest communities was Jericho (JAIR•ih•koh). This farming village grew in an area between present-day Israel and Jordan called the West Bank. The village of Jericho was well established by about 8000 B.C. It extended across several acres. The area of sun-dried-brick houses was surrounded by walls that were several feet thick.

Academic Vocabulary

locate to set up in a particular place

LESSON 2

ENGAGE

Previewing Have students write down their favorite lunch. Begin a discussion about where the foods that make up their lunch came from. Prompt with questions such as the following.

Ask:

- **Where does the bread come from for your sandwich?**
- **Where is the wheat from?**
- **How do we get wheat?**

Continue with other questions of this sort. Lead students to understand that their food is the result of agriculture. AL ELL

Then ask:

How did people obtain food before agriculture? *(They hunted, fished, and gathered wild food.)*

Ask students to speculate on how agriculture might change people's lives. Write students' ideas on the board. Discuss which ideas were correct, which ideas might need to be changed, and which ideas they would like to add to the list. BL

TEACH & ASSESS

1 Neolithic Times

GUIDING QUESTION *How did farming change people's lives?*

Making Connections Tell students about the different types of crops that early farmers grew, such as beans, corn, potatoes, squash, wheat, rice, cocoa, tomatoes, onions, peppers, soybeans, and peanuts. Have students create menus using these types of foods.

Ask:

Which of these foods do you eat? In what form do you eat each one? *(Accept all reasonable responses.)* When students have completed their menus, have them share their menus with the class. Then begin a discussion with students about the source of the food they eat. AL

Ask:

Do you have a garden? Do you grow your own food? Do you know any people who grow most of the food they eat? Why would people choose to grow their own food? Tell students that in this lesson, they will find out that early peoples had to learn how to farm and that doing so changed human history. AL

2 Life in the Neolithic Age

GUIDING QUESTION *What was life like during the Neolithic Age?*

3 Civilizations Emerge

GUIDING QUESTION *What characteristics did early civilizations share?*

Defining Have students come up with a definition for *civilization.*

Ask:

What makes a civilization? *(Students should mention characteristics such as government, laws, art, and religion.)* Write students' ideas on the whiteboard.

Making Inferences Have pairs of students create concept webs showing the effects of agriculture on civilization.

Ask:

How is the agricultural revolution really a revolution? *(A revolution is any change that has an enormous effect on how people live. The move from hunting and gathering to systematic agriculture brought changes to all aspects of life. People lived in different kinds of houses; they ate different kinds of food. They no longer had to move from place to place, so they could build sturdier buildings. They were safer, and better food made them healthier.)* AL

Have students complete the Lesson 2 Review.

CLOSE & REFLECT

LECTURE SLIDE **Drawing Conclusions** Use the lecture slide on settled communities to discuss the benefits and drawbacks of a settled way of life with students.

Ask:

- **What were the benefits of living in settled communities?** *(People could be safer and healthier. They could form governments and build cities.)* Show the Lecture Slide answers.
- **What were the drawbacks of living in settled communities?** *(Answers will vary. Some students might not see any drawbacks. Others might point out that staying in one place is not as exciting or as interesting as moving from place to place. It might be harder for some people to live in a community and follow the rules than to be free to do as they want.)* AL

IF YOU HAVE MORE TIME . . .

Create a Graphic Organizer

Comparing and Contrasting Have students compare and contrast Paleolithic and Neolithic times. Students should complete this sentence to help them understand how to compare and contrast: "Paleolithic people ______, while people of Neolithic times ______."

Then ask students to create a two-column graphic organizer and fill in the details of each era under the appropriate headings. Remind students what it means to compare and contrast. Read through the facts on the graphic organizer and discuss the similarities and differences of the eras.

For Approaching Level and English Language Learners, read aloud passages in the text that include facts to complete the organizer and prompt students to discover these facts. Model how to compare and contrast the different facts in the graphic organizer. AL ELL

Encourage Beyond Level students to do additional research. They can create a slide presentation to share with the class based on what they find. BL

Answers for pages 62–65

P. 62 Taking Notes Answers include: systematic agriculture, domesticated animals, settled communities.

P. 63 GEOGRAPHY CONNECTION

1. Crops grown south of the Equator included beans, cotton, peanuts, peppers, potatoes, coffee, millet, and yams.
2. CRITICAL THINKING Answers will vary but should include the idea that the region's warm and rainy climate would allow a wide variety of crops to be grown.

P. 64 ☑ PROGRESS CHECK It allowed people to settle and form communities.

P. 64 CRITICAL THINKING Different materials, such as wood, stone, or clay (for bricks) would be available in different geographical locations. These different materials require different construction methods.

P. 65 CRITICAL THINKING Living in a community meant security and an easier life.

BIOGRAPHY

Ötzi the Iceman (c. 3300 B.C.)

Mystery Man Ötzi was a Neolithic man whose remains were discovered in 1991 in the Austrian Alps. Also called the "Iceman," Ötzi presented a mystery. Did he live where he died? Did he spend his life in another location? What did he do for a living? Scientists found the same form of oxygen in Ötzi's teeth as in the water of the southern Alpine valleys. They have concluded that, even though Ötzi was found in the mountains, he lived most of his life in the valleys south of the Alps. Scientists believe Ötzi was either a shepherd or a hunter who traveled from the valleys to the mountains.

▶ CRITICAL THINKING
Analyzing What types of clothing or tools do you think Ötzi used?

Another well-known Neolithic community was Çatalhüyük (chah•tahl•hoo•YOOK) in present-day Turkey. Although little evidence of the community remains, historians know that between 6700 and 5700 B.C., it covered 32 acres and was home to about 6,000 people. The people lived in simple mud-brick houses that were built close together. What if, instead of a front door, your house had a roof door? In Çatalhüyük, the houses did not have front doors. Instead of going through a door in the wall, people entered their homes through holes in the rooftops. They could also walk from house to house across the roofs. People decorated the inside of their homes with wall paintings.

In addition to homes, Çatalhüyük had special buildings that were **shrines** (SHREYENZ), or holy places. These shrines were decorated with images of gods and goddesses. Statues of women giving birth have also been found in the shrines. Both the shrines and the statues show that the role of religion was growing in the lives of Neolithic people.

Farmers grew fruits, nuts, and different grains on land outside Çatalhüyük. People grew their own food and kept it in storerooms within their homes. They raised sheep, goats, and cattle that provided milk and meat. They ate fish and bird eggs from nearby low-lying wetlands called marshes. Scenes drawn on the walls of the city's ruins show that the people of Çatalhüyük also hunted.

What Were the Benefits of a Settled Life?

Neolithic people needed protection from the weather and wild animals. A settled life provided greater security. Steady food supplies created healthier, growing populations. As the population increased, more workers became available. Those individuals could grow more crops. Villagers produced more than they could eat, so they began to trade their food for supplies they could not produce themselves.

Because an abundant amount of food was produced, fewer people were needed in the fields. Neolithic people began to take part in economic activities other than farming. **Specialization** (speh•shuh•leh•ZAY•shun) occurred for the first time. People took up specific jobs as their talents allowed. Some people became artisans, or skilled workers. They made weapons and jewelry that they traded with neighboring communities. People made pottery from clay to store grain and food. They made

Reading HELPDESK

shrine a place where people worship

specialization the act of training for a particular job

baskets from plant fibers. They also used plant fibers to weave cloth. Ötzi, the Neolithic Iceman, wore a cape made from woven grass fibers. These craftspeople, like farmers, also exchanged the goods they produced for other things they did not have.

The roles of men and women changed when people moved into settlements. Men worked in the fields to farm and herd animals. They gradually became more responsible for growing food and protecting the village. Men emerged as family and community leaders. Women bore the children and stayed in the villages. They wove cloth, using the wool from their sheep. They also used bone needles to make clothing from cloth and animal skins. In addition, women managed food supplies and performed other tasks.

The growth of communities did not always bring benefits. In some places, such as settlements in present-day Jordan, rapid population growth caused resources such as wood supplies to be used up quickly. On occasion, this loss of forestation caused desert-like conditions to spread. Where this type of ecological damage occurred, many settlements were abandoned.

The End of the Neolithic Age

During the late Neolithic Age, people made more technological advances. Toolmakers created better farming tools as the need for them arose. These included hoes for digging soil, sickles for cutting grain, and millstones for grinding flour. In some regions, people began to work with metals, including copper. Workers heated rocks and discovered melted copper inside them. They then experimented with making the copper into tools and weapons. These proved to be easier to make and use than those made of stone.

Craftspeople in western Asia discovered that mixing copper and tin formed bronze. This was a technological breakthrough because bronze was stronger than copper. Bronze became widely used between 3000 and 1200 B.C. This period is known as the **Bronze Age**. Few people, however, could afford bronze and continued to use tools and weapons made of stone.

PROGRESS CHECK

Explaining How did the spread of agriculture affect trade?

Thinking Like a **HISTORIAN**

Making Inferences

In Çatalhüyük the homes were built very close together. Each house had a door in its roof. People climbed into their homes using ladders. Use the Internet to research why the people of Çatalhüyük used this style of building. Then make an inference about the reason for the roof doors and present it to the class. For more information about making inferences, read the chapter *What Does a Historian Do?*

Bronze Age pottery shows fine details. The use of bronze for tools and weapons was another step forward for ancient peoples.

▶ CRITICAL THINKING
Analyzing Why do you think bronze tools and weapons would have been an important achievement?

Bronze Age the period in ancient human culture when people began to make and use bronze

Early Civilizations 3000 B.C.

KEY
Egypt
Indus Valley
Mesopotamia
China

Black Sea, ANATOLIAN PLATEAU, Mediterranean Sea, MESOPOTAMIA, WESTERN DESERT, EGYPT, ARABIAN DESERT, Persian Gulf, Red Sea, ARABIAN PENINSULA, Arabian Sea, INDUS VALLEY, INDIA, DECCAN PLATEAU, Bay of Bengal, HIMALAYA, PLATEAU OF TIBET, CHINA, Yellow Sea, South China Sea, INDOCHINA PENINSULA

0 1,000 miles
0 1,000 km
Lambert Azimuthal Equal-Area projection

GEOGRAPHY CONNECTION

Civilizations developed in the river valleys of Mesopotamia, Egypt, India, and China.

1. **PLACE** Along which rivers did the early civilizations of Mesopotamia and Egypt develop?
2. **CRITICAL THINKING** ***Analyzing*** As these cultures became more complex, what characteristics set some of them apart as civilizations?

3 Civilizations Emerge

GUIDING QUESTION ***What characteristics did early civilizations share?***

Humans continued to develop more complex cultures, or ways of life. By the beginning of the Bronze Age, communities were widespread. More complex cultures called civilizations began to develop in these communities. Four of the great river valley civilizations—Mesopotamia, Egypt, India, and China—emerged around 3000 B.C. All civilizations share similar characteristics.

Cities and Government

One characteristic of these early civilizations was that they developed cities and formed governments. The first civilizations developed in river valleys, where fertile land made it easy to grow crops and feed large numbers of people. The rivers provided fish and water. They also encouraged trade, which allowed the exchange of both goods and ideas. The cities that developed in these valleys became the centers of civilizations.

People formed governments to protect themselves and their food supplies. In these early civilizations, the first governments were monarchies. A **monarchy** is a type of government led by a king or queen. Monarchs created armies to defend against enemies and made laws to keep order. They also appointed government officials who managed food supplies and building projects.

Reading HELPDESK

monarchy a government whose ruler, a king or queen, inherits the position from a parent

Religions

Religions emerged in the new civilizations to help people explain their lives. For example, religions helped explain the forces of nature and the role of humans in the world.

Early people believed that gods were responsible for a community's survival. Priests performed religious ceremonies to try to win the support of the gods. Rulers claimed that their own power was based on the approval of the gods.

Social Structure

Early civilizations had social class structures. That is, people in society were organized into groups. These groups were defined by the type of work people did and the amount of wealth or power they had. Generally, rulers and priests, government officials, and warriors made up the highest social class. They set the rules and made the important decisions. Below this class was a large group of free people, including farmers, artisans, and craftspeople. At the bottom of the class structure were enslaved people, most of whom were captured from enemies during war.

Writing and Art

To pass on information, people invented ways of writing. These early systems used symbols in place of letters and words. Writing became an important feature of these new civilizations. People used writing to keep accurate records and to preserve stories.

Civilizations also created art for enjoyment and practical purposes. Artists created paintings and sculptures portraying gods and forces of nature. People designed massive buildings that served as places of worship or burial tombs for kings.

PROGRESS CHECK

Speculating Why did early peoples form governments?

LESSON 2 REVIEW

Review Vocabulary

1. What was *systematic agriculture*?
2. How did *specialization* affect the lives of Neolithic peoples?

Answer the Guiding Questions

3. ***Stating*** What was the Agricultural Revolution?
4. ***Identifying Cause and Effect*** How did farming lead to new types of economic activities?
5. ***Inferring*** What are the advantages and disadvantages when a community grows?
6. ***Identifying*** Which groups made up the largest social class in early civilizations?
7. **PERSUASIVE WRITING** You are the leader of a band of hunter-gatherers. You have seen other bands settle in river valleys and begin to farm. Write a speech to persuade your own band to settle and begin farming.

LESSON 2 (cont.)

IF YOU HAVE MORE TIME . . .

Use Art to Communicate Learning Proficiency

Students—especially those with limited verbal skills—can use art to show a great deal of information in a different way. Using art, students can demonstrate their knowledge and understanding of the material.

For this activity, students will create a "photograph" as another way of expressing the concepts in the lesson.

Background for Activity

Direct students' attention to a photograph or other image in their textbook. It does not have to be in this lesson or chapter.

Have students spend about five minutes identifying information imparted by the photograph to help them think about what they should include in their art.

Discuss what characteristics are specific to photographs to illustrate information.

For example, students should recognize that good photographs have a main subject. The photograph also captures specific details about the subject.

Help students identify that their art should incorporate specific details too, as a photograph does. Point out that visual communication can put a lot of information into a small space.

Activity

Provide each student with a sheet of blank $8\frac{1}{2}" \times 11"$ paper, a ruler, and drawing materials.

Have students use the rulers to draw an $8" \times 10"$ rectangle on the piece of paper. This will serve as the space for them to create a "photograph" to illustrate what they understand about the Neolithic Revolution or the emergence of civilizations.

Explain that the border is the "picture frame," and students can decorate that too.

After students have created their "photograph," ask volunteers to share their work with the class.

BACKGROUND KNOWLEDGE

Emergence of Early Civilizations

Why early civilizations developed remains difficult to explain. Since civilizations developed independently in different parts of the world, can general causes be identified that would explain why all of these civilizations emerged?

A number of possible explanations have been suggested. One theory maintains that challenges forced human beings to make efforts that resulted in the rise of civilization.

Some scholars have adhered to a material explanation. Material forces, such as the growth of food surpluses, made possible the specialization of labor and development of large communities with bureaucratic organization.

But the area of the Fertile Crescent, in which civilization emerged in Southwest Asia, was not naturally conducive to agriculture. Abundant food could be produced only with a massive human effort to carefully manage the water, an effort that created the need for organization and bureaucratic control and led to civilized cities.

Some historians have argued that nonmaterial forces, primarily religious, provided the sense of unity and purpose that made such organized activities possible. Finally, some scholars doubt that we are capable of ever discovering the actual causes of early civilization.

Answers for pages 66–69

P. 66 CRITICAL THINKING He probably used clothing made of hides, tools made of flint and wood, and a bow and arrows.

P. 67 CRITICAL THINKING Stronger tools would have made farming more efficient. Stronger weapons would give one people an advantage over nearby peoples if a battle were to be fought.

P. 67 ☑ PROGRESS CHECK People had an abundance of food and could trade for what they needed.

P. 68 GEOGRAPHY CONNECTION

1. In Mesopotamia, civilization developed along the Tigris and Euphrates Rivers. Civilization developed along the Nile River in Egypt.
2. CRITICAL THINKING As cultures became more complex, the need for organization—in the form of government—led to the development of civilizations.

P. 69 ☑ PROGRESS CHECK They wanted to protect themselves and bring order to their lives.

LESSON 2 REVIEW

1. At first, humans relied on hunting and gathering for their daily food. With the shift to systematic agriculture, humans grew their own food on a regular basis.
2. People took up specific jobs as their talents allowed. Some farmed, and others became artisans.
3. The Agricultural Revolution was a major change in the way people lived. They turned from hunting and gathering their food in nomadic communities to farming and herding in established, settled communities.
4. A steady food supply and food surplus meant not all people had to farm. Some people became skilled workers who produced goods.
5. When a community grows, one advantage is that more people are available to do work. Also, there may be more security and a steadier food supply for people. A disadvantage is that a larger population means the resources and goods must be shared among more people.
6. The largest social group in early civilizations was made up of free people, including farmers, artisans, and craftspeople.
7. Answers will vary. Speeches should provide persuasive reasoning for settling in communities and farming.

CHAPTER 3 Activities

Write your answers on a separate piece of paper.

1. **Exploring the Essential Question**
   EXPOSITORY WRITING How would you describe the ways people adapted to a colder environment during the Ice Age? Write an essay telling how some changes people made may have led to the development of agriculture when the last Ice Age was over.

2. **21st Century Skills**
   ANALYZING AND MAKING JUDGMENTS Early humans made several technical advancements during the Paleolithic Age. These included the use of fire, flint tools and weapons, spoken language, and tents and wooden structures. Write a paragraph telling which of these helped them most to become more efficient hunters and why.

3. **Thinking Like a Historian**
   COMPARING AND CONTRASTING Create a diagram like the one shown to compare and contrast the technological advancements of the Paleolithic Age with those of the Neolithic Age.

Paleolithic Age Advancements	Neolithic Age Advancements

4. **GEOGRAPHY ACTIVITY**

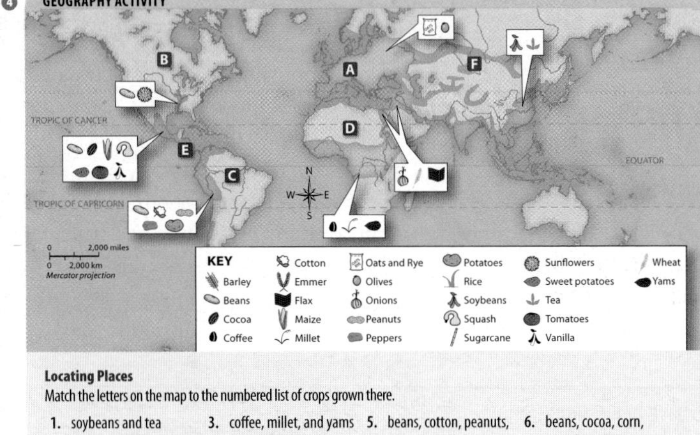

Locating Places
Match the letters on the map to the numbered list of crops grown there.

1. soybeans and tea
2. beans and sunflowers
3. coffee, millet, and yams
4. oats and olives
5. beans, cotton, peanuts, peppers, and potatoes
6. beans, cocoa, corn, squash, tomatoes, sweet potatoes and vanilla

CHAPTER 3 Assessment

REVIEW THE GUIDING QUESTIONS
Directions: Choose the best answer for each question.

1. Paleolithic people first used tools made of
   A. bronze.
   B. copper.
   C. sticks, stones, and tree branches.
   D. flint.

2. Which of the following developed after the Paleolithic Age?
   F. language
   G. farming
   H. art
   I. tools

3. What major change took place during the Neolithic Age?
   A. People built sturdier shelters.
   B. People began farming in a systematic way.
   C. People began to use spoken language to communicate.
   D. People learned to use fire to survive in cold environments.

4. Where did farming first develop?
   F. Southwest Asia
   G. southeastern Europe
   H. India
   I. China

5. Çatalhüyük had special buildings that were holy places, or
   A. fortresses.
   B. lofts.
   C. shrines.
   D. cathedrals.

6. Which of the following groups was at the bottom of early social class structures?
   F. farmers
   G. enslaved people
   H. craftspeople
   I. artisans

CHAPTER 3 Assessment *(continued)*

DBQ DOCUMENT-BASED QUESTIONS

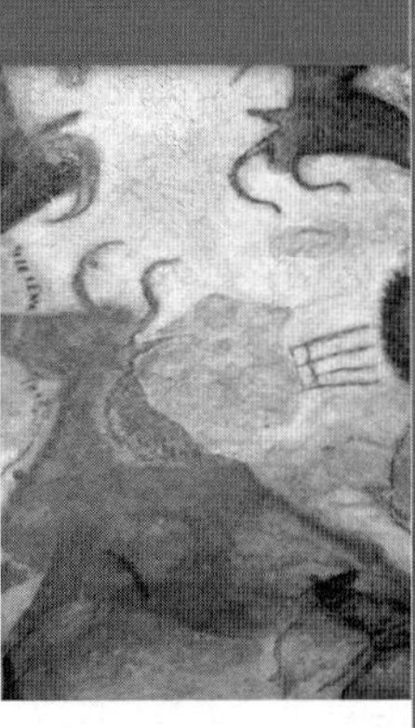

7. **Making Connections** Study this example of one of the oldest Paleolithic cave paintings.
   What kind of animals does this painting appear to represent?
   A. woolly mammoths
   B. cattle
   C. horses
   D. reindeer

8. **Identifying** What type of tools did Paleolithic people use for painting on the cave walls?
   F. wood blocks
   G. paint rollers
   H. pencils
   I. twigs

SHORT RESPONSE

Write your answers on a separate piece of paper.

"Agriculture developed at different times and in different places. . . . Over the years, people have domesticated many different plants and animals. Domestication of some species has been abandoned. Following the last Ice Age, people began to cultivate rice, wheat, potatoes, and corn. However, herding of reindeer declined because of the climate changes."

—from "History of Agriculture," *Encyclopaedia Britannica*

9. Was the change from hunting and gathering to agriculture sudden? Explain.

10. What are some possible reasons that people stopped raising some domesticated species?

EXTENDED RESPONSE

Write your answer on a separate piece of paper.

11. **Personal Writing** You are a member of a Paleolithic group of hunter-gatherers. Write a letter to a friend describing the hunting stories you are recording in cave paintings. Explain how you think your stories might help other hunters improve their skills.

Need Extra Help?

If You've Missed Question	1	2	3	4	5	6	7	8	9	10	11
Review Lesson	1	1, 2	2	2	2	2	1	1	2	2	1

NOTES

REFLECT, REVIEW, & REMEDIATE

INTERACTIVE WORKSHEET

Chapter Summary

Provide students with the Chapter Summary worksheet to help review the chapter and prepare for assessment.

Reviewing the Enduring Understanding

Review this chapter's Enduring Understanding with students:

- People, places, and ideas change over time.

INTERACTIVE WHITEBOARD ACTIVITY On the interactive whiteboard, have a student create a Venn diagram and write "Paleolithic Age" in one oval, "Neolithic Age" in the other, and "Both" in the area where the two ovals intersect. Then lead a discussion that allows students to recall characteristics of the two periods. Have a student write these characteristics in the correct area on the diagram.

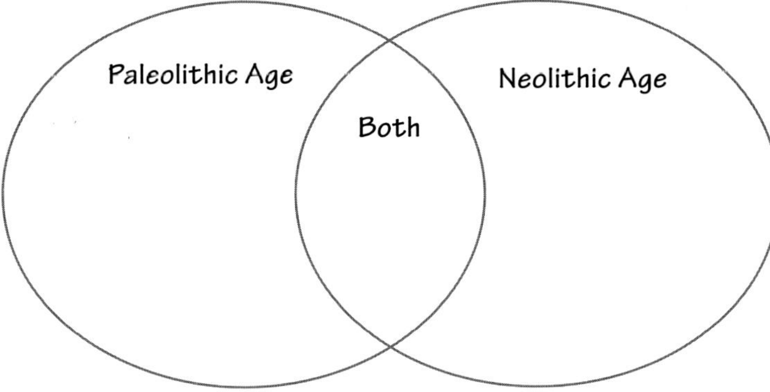

ACTIVITIES ANSWERS

Exploring the Essential Question

1. Students should note that people had to adapt their lives to survive the Ice Age. They changed their diets. They built sturdier shelters and made warm clothing. They used fire to help them survive. Sturdier shelters made moving from place to place harder, so permanent settlements began to develop. With permanent settlements, domesticating animals and plants became more practical.

21st Century Skills

2. Learning to shape flint into sharp-edged tools and weapons helped Paleolithic people become more efficient hunters. Flint arrowheads and spears were more efficient for bringing down prey.

Thinking Like a Historian

3. Paleolithic Age Advancements: nomadic life; hunters and gatherers; women gathered food and men hunted; primitive tools made of stone; developed spoken language; cave paintings

   Neolithic Age Advancements: settled life; farmers; men herded, farmed, and served as leaders, while women bore children, stayed in the villages, and wove cloth; more advanced tools made of copper and bronze; developed written language; art was for enjoyment and practical purposes

Locating Places

4. **1.** F, **2.** B, **3.** D, **4.** A, **5.** C, **6.** E

ASSESSMENT ANSWERS

Review the Guiding Questions

1. **C** The first tools were sticks, stones, and tree branches. Copper and bronze tools did not come into use until the Neolithic Era. Flint tools were used during the Paleolithic Era.

2. **G** Farming did not develop during the Paleolithic Age, but during the Agricultural Revolution of the Neolithic Age. The use of tools and the development of spoken language and art took place during the Paleolithic Age.

3. **B** The shift to systematic farming occurred during the Agricultural Revolution of the Neolithic Age. During the Ice Age of the Paleolithic Age, people built sturdier shelters, developed spoken language, and discovered how to use fire.

4. **F** Farming first developed in Southwest Asia around 8000 B.C. It developed later in India around 7000 B.C., in China around 6000 B.C., and in southeastern Europe around 4000 B.C.

5. **C** Cathedrals and shrines are holy places, but of these two, only shrines existed in Çatalhüyük. A fortress is not a holy place. A loft is part of a barn and is not a holy place.

6. **G** Enslaved people were at the bottom of the class structure. Farmers, craftspeople, and artisans were all members of a large group of free people.

Document-Based Questions

7. **B** The animals in the painting have horns and resemble modern cattle. Woolly mammoths and horses do not have horns. Reindeer have antlers rather than horns.

8. **I** Twigs were one of the first tools used in cave painting. F, G, and H are incorrect because they are more modern tools and would not have been used in the cave paintings.

Short Response

9. The change was probably gradual, with a period of intensive food gathering before farming actually began.

10. Answers will vary but may mention that more suitable species were discovered, that changes in the environment made raising a particular species more difficult, or that people's tastes changed and made certain species less desirable.

Extended Response

11. Answers will vary but should reflect what the student has learned from the chapter. Some historians believe that the Paleolithic hunters were seeking good luck by painting a particular animal. Others believe the paintings might have had religious significance or that they were done for enjoyment.

ONLINE RESOURCES

networks

There's More Online!

- INTERACTIVE WORKSHEETS
- BIOGRAPHIES
- CHARTS/GRAPHS
- GAMES
- GRAPHIC ORGANIZERS
- IMAGES
- MAPS
- PRIMARY SOURCES
- SLIDE SHOWS
- TIME LINE
- LECTURE SLIDES
- INTERACTIVE WHITEBOARD ACTIVITIES
- ASSESSMENTS
- VIDEOS

Mesopotamia: An Overview

Persepolis

Chapter **4**

Mesopotamia

Dear World History Teacher,

The peoples of Mesopotamia built one of the first civilizations. They developed cities and struggled with the problems of organization as they moved from individual communities to larger territorial units and eventually to empires. They invented writing to keep records and created literature. They constructed monumental buildings to please their gods, to give witness to their power, and to preserve their culture. They developed new political, military, social, and religious structures to deal with the basic problems of human existence and order. The Mesopotamians left detailed records that allow us to view how they wrestled with three of the fundamental problems that humans have pondered: the nature of human relationships, the nature of the universe, and the role of divine forces in that universe. Although later people provided different answers, the Mesopotamians were one of the first to pose the questions, give answers, and write them down.

By 1200 B.C., the cohesive civilization of Mesopotamia had given way to a number of small states that emerged and flourished for a short while. These states eventually were overshadowed by the rise of great empires. The Assyrian Empire, built upon the effective use of military force, was the first to unite almost all of the ancient Middle East.

Jackson J. Spielvogel

More Media Resources

Current Events Online

Visit McGraw-Hill's current events Web site for high-interest news stories and activities for your students. Access the site through the Student or Teacher Center in **networks.**

Reading List

Grade 6 reading level:
Seven Wonders of the Ancient World, by Lynn Curlee

Grade 7 reading level:
Ten Kings and the Worlds They Ruled, by Milton Meltzer

Grade 8 reading level:
Archaeology, by Trevor Barnes

At the MOVIES

Watch clips of documentaries about ancient Mesopotamia, such as Time Life's *Lost Civilizations* or *Ancient Mysteries: Seven Wonders of the Ancient World.*

Discuss: **Do documentaries convey different information about a topic than books convey?**

NOTE: Be sure to preview any clips to ensure they are age-appropriate.

Search for more videos online in the **networks** Resource Library.

CHAPTER 4 Planner

UNDERSTANDING BY DESIGN®

Enduring Understandings

- ***People, places, and ideas change over time.***
- ***Cultures are held together by shared beliefs and common practices and values.***

Essential Questions

- ***How does geography influence the way people live?*** • ***Why does conflict develop?***

Students will know:

- *why people settled in Mesopotamia*
- *how* Gilgamesh *relates to modern-day literature pieces*
- *what it was like to live in Sumer*
- *the Sumerian ideas and inventions that have been passed on to other civilizations*
- *the themes found in the epic poem genre*
- *how civilizations developed in Mesopotamia*
- *what contributions the Assyrians made to Southwest Asia*
- *why Babylon was an important city in the ancient world*

Students will be able to:

- **explain** how floods sometimes helped the farmers of Mesopotamia
- **draw conclusions** about why the Sumerians built cities with walls around them
- **analyze** why the Sumerians invented a writing system
- **describe** where the Fertile Crescent is located
- **compare** the social classes of Sumer
- **describe** why scribes were important in Sumerian society
- **find** the main reason why Hammurabi's Code was important
- **summarize** why Assyria's army was so strong
- **identify** the wonder of the ancient world that was located in Babylon
- **describe** how the Assyrians ruled their empire
- **explain** why the Chaldeans overthrew the Assyrians

Predictable Misunderstandings

Students may think:

- The wheel was invented before Sumer existed.
- The Mesopotamians had no laws before the Code of Hammurabi.
- Only one Babylonian Empire existed.

Assessment Evidence

Performance Task

- Hands-On Chapter Project

Other Evidence

- Interactive Graphic Organizers
- The World's Literature questions
- 21st Century Skills Activity
- Economics of History Activity
- Primary Source Activity
- Interactive Guided Reading Activities
- Written paragraphs
- Lesson Reviews

Pacing Guide

Introducing the Chapter		1 day
Lesson 1	The Sumerians	2 days
	The World's Literature	1 day
Lesson 2	Mesopotamian Empires	1 day
Chapter Activities and Assessment		1 day
TOTAL TIME		**6 Days**

Differentiated Instruction

These lesson plans are written to address the needs of your On Level students. Discussion and activities that are well-suited to your Approaching Grade Level learners, Beyond Grade Level learners, as well as your English Language Learners, are coded as follows:

AL **Approaching Grade Level**

BL **Beyond Grade Level**

ELL **English Language Learner**

NCSS Standards covered in "Mesopotamia"

Learners will understand:

2 TIME, CONTINUITY, AND CHANGE

6. The origins and influences of social, cultural, political, and economic systems

3 PEOPLE, PLACES, AND ENVIRONMENTS

1. The theme of people, places, and environments involves the study of the relationships between human populations in different locations and geographic phenomena such as climate, vegetation, and natural resources

2. Concepts such as: location, region, place, migration, as well as human and physical systems

7. Human modifications of the environment

5 INDIVIDUALS, GROUPS, AND INSTITUTIONS

2. Concepts such as: mores, norms, status, role, socialization, ethnocentrism, cultural diffusion, competition, cooperation, conflict, race, ethnicity, and gender

8. That when two or more groups with differing norms and beliefs interact, accommodation or conflict may result

6 POWER, AUTHORITY, AND GOVERNANCE

5. The ways in which governments meet the needs and wants of citizens, manage conflict, and establish order and society

7 PRODUCTION, DISTRIBUTION, AND CONSUMPTION

6. The economic gains that result from specialization and exchange as well as the trade-offs

8 SCIENCE, TECHNOLOGY, AND SOCIETY

2. Society often turns to science and technology to solve problems

CHAPTER 4 Introducing the Chapter

(Student Edition p. 73)

The Story Matters . . .

Guide the class in a discussion of what it might have been like to live in the palace in Nimrud during the time of the Assyrian Empire.

Ask: **Have you ever been inside a palace or a mansion? Have you seen a movie or a program on television that takes place in a palace or a mansion? What were they like?** Have a few students share their thoughts.

Then ask: **Do you think historical buildings, like palaces or mansions, should be preserved? Do these buildings have any benefit for the community? Does our community have any examples of historical buildings?**

Tell the class that the history of Mesopotamia at this time period is well documented because of the many Assyrian artifacts that have been found. Explain to interested students that they can find out more about the artifacts of Assyria online.

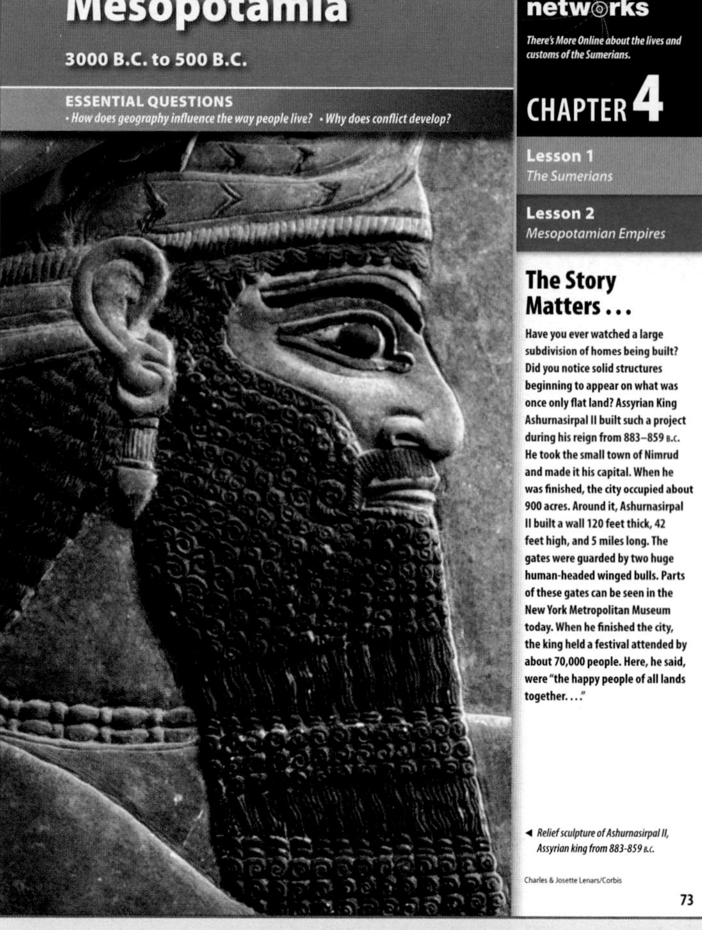

Mesopotamia

3000 B.C. to 500 B.C.

ESSENTIAL QUESTIONS
• *How does geography influence the way people live?* • *Why does conflict develop?*

networks

There's More Online about the lives and customs of the Sumerians.

CHAPTER 4

Lesson 1 *The Sumerians*

Lesson 2 *Mesopotamian Empires*

The Story Matters . . .

Have you ever watched a large subdivision of homes being built? Did you notice solid structures beginning to appear on what was once only flat land? Assyrian King Ashurnasirpal II built such a project during his reign from 883–859 B.C. He took the small town of Nimrud and made it his capital. When he was finished, the city occupied about 900 acres. Around it, Ashurnasirpal II built a wall 120 feet thick, 42 feet high, and 5 miles long. The gates were guarded by two huge human-headed winged bulls. Parts of these gates can be seen in the New York Metropolitan Museum today. When he finished the city, the king held a festival attended by about 70,000 people. Here, he said, were "the happy people of all lands together. . . ."

◄ *Relief sculpture of Ashurnasirpal II, Assyrian king from 883-859 B.C.*

Charles & Josette Lenars/Corbis

73

Introducing Place and Time (Student Edition pp. 74–75)

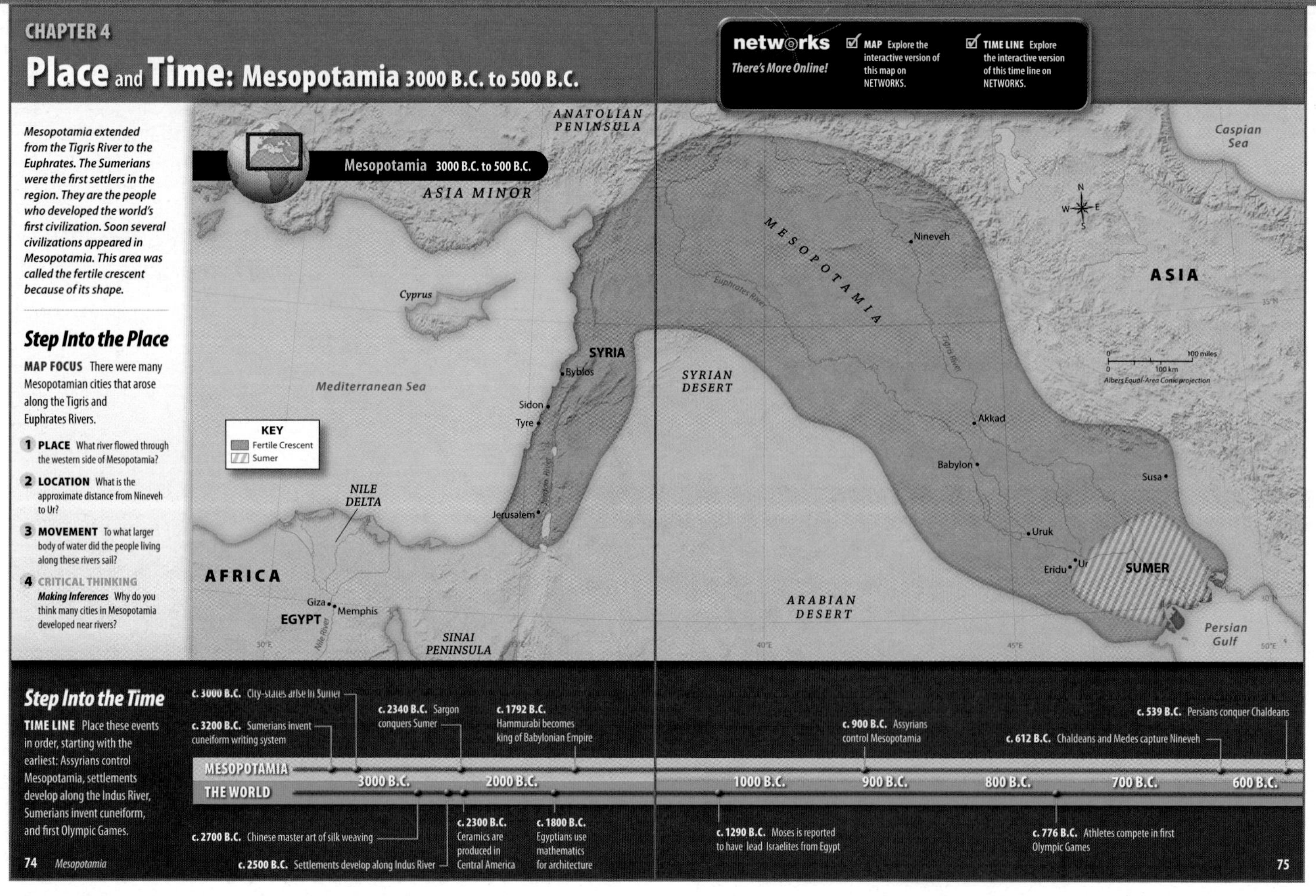

CHAPTER 4

Place and Time: Mesopotamia 3000 B.C. to 500 B.C.

Mesopotamia extended from the Tigris River to the Euphrates. The Sumerians were the first settlers in the region. They are the people who developed the world's first civilization. Soon several civilizations appeared in Mesopotamia. This area was called the fertile crescent because of its shape.

Step Into the Place

MAP FOCUS There were many Mesopotamian cities that arose along the Tigris and Euphrates Rivers.

1. **PLACE** What river flowed through the western side of Mesopotamia?
2. **LOCATION** What is the approximate distance from Nineveh to Ur?
3. **MOVEMENT** To what larger body of water did the people living along these rivers sail?
4. **CRITICAL THINKING** *Making Inferences* Why do you think many cities in Mesopotamia developed near rivers?

networks *There's More Online!*

☑ **MAP** Explore the interactive version of this map on NETWORKS.

☑ **TIME LINE** Explore the interactive version of this time line on NETWORKS.

Step Into the Time

TIME LINE Place these events in order, starting with the earliest: Assyrians control Mesopotamia, settlements develop along the Indus River, Sumerians invent cuneiform, and first Olympic Games.

74 *Mesopotamia*

75

Technology Extension

- Find an additional activity online that incorporates technology for this project.
- Visit the EdTechTeacher Web sites (included in the Technology Extension for this chapter) for more links, tutorials, and other resources.

Assessing Background Knowledge

INTERACTIVE WORKSHEET

What Do You Know? Activity

Have students complete the Anticipation Guide about Mesopotamia before they study the chapter. Then, in the "Before" column, have students check whether they agree or disagree with each statement. Next, take a class poll so you can tailor your lessons to focus on students' misconceptions.

After students complete the chapter, have them reread the statements and note in the "After" column whether they agree or disagree with each statement. Ask students who changed their responses to explain why they did so.

INTERACTIVE WORKSHEET

Guided Reading Activities

There is a Guided Reading Activity for each lesson in this chapter. You might want to assign the Guided Reading Activity for Lesson 1 after introducing the chapter content.

Hands-On Chapter Project

Students will create a poster of a person performing one of the occupations of Sumerian society.

- Students will work in pairs or small groups and use worksheets to create a poster. The poster should include visual details, written annotations, reasons the occupation is important, and a bibliography.
- Students will choose an occupation, conduct personal research, take notes, and document their sources.
- Then students will meet with their teams to share information, create the poster, and compile the bibliography. Visit **networks** online to see the full project and rubric.
- Students will present their posters to the class and discuss the importance of the occupation to a Sumerian village.
- Finally, the teacher and students will complete the Rubric Assessment for each poster.

ONLINE RESOURCES

networks

Assign these interactive worksheets and quizzes from your Teacher Lesson Center. All resources are print-ready.

It's ALL Online!

Chapter 4 Resources

- ☑ Chapter Summary
- ☑ Vocabulary Builder
- ☑ What Do You Know?
- ☑ Hands-On Chapter Project

Lesson 1 Resources

- ☑ Interactive Graphic Organizer
- ☑ 21st Century Skills Activity Collaboration
- ☑ Economics of History Activity Bartering
- ☑ Interactive Guided Reading Activity
- ☑ Reading Essentials and Study Guide
- ☑ Online Self-Check Quiz

Lesson 2 Resources

- ☑ Primary Source Activity The Code of Hammurabi
- ☑ Interactive Guided Reading Activity
- ☑ Reading Essentials and Study Guide
- ☑ Online Self-Check Quiz

Assessment Resources

- ☑ Lesson Reviews
- ☑ Online Self-Check Quizzes
- ☑ Chapter Activities and Assessment
- ☑ Standardized Test Practice

Remediation Resources

- ☑ Reading Essentials and Study Guide
- ☑ Guided Reading Activities
- ☑ Online Self-Check Quizzes
- ☑ Chapter Summary

Step Into the Place

Location Project the Interactive World Atlas on the whiteboard and project Asia and North Africa. Remind students about where early people first settled. Discuss with the class why these people settled in these locations. Tell students that civilizations developed where people settled.

INTERACTIVE WHITEBOARD ACTIVITY Using the Interactive World Atlas, have student volunteers analyze the map of Asia and mark where they think civilizations might start, based on students' understanding of desirable geographic features to settle by.

Next, project the Chapter Opener map on the whiteboard. As a class, discuss the Map Focus questions.

Step Into the Time

Making Inferences Have students review the time line for the chapter. Explain that they will be studying events from about 3000 B.C. to 500 B.C.

Ask students: **Based on the information in the time line, what can you infer about what was happening in Mesopotamia beginning around 3000 B.C.?** *(Sumerians developed an advanced civilization and formed city-states. Sargon conquered Sumer and all of Mesopotamia. Then a series of peoples took control of Mesopotamia: the Babylonians, the Assyrians, the Chaldeans and Medes, and finally the Persians.)*

Answers for pages 74–75

Step Into the Place

1. the Euphrates River
2. about 500 miles
3. the Persian Gulf
4. CRITICAL THINKING The rivers would provide water for farming and transportation for goods and people.

Step Into the Time

CRITICAL THINKING Sumerians invent cuneiform, settlements develop along the Indus River, Assyrians control Mesopotamia, first Olympic Games

Lesson 1

The Sumerians

ESSENTIAL QUESTION *How does geography influence the way people live?*

It Matters Because

The Sumerians made important advances in areas such as farming and writing that laid the foundation for future civilizations.

1 The First Civilizations in Mesopotamia

GUIDING QUESTION *Why did people settle in Mesopotamia?*

Civilizations first developed about 3000 B.C. in the river valleys of Mesopotamia (MEH•suh•puh•TAY•mee•uh), Egypt, India, and China. Throughout history, the need to have water for drinking and growing crops influenced where people settled. Although there were differences among the early civilizations, they were alike in many ways. As these early civilizations developed, people formed social classes. The social class people belonged to partly depended on their occupations. They did specialized types of work. Using improved technology, they made more and better goods. They set up governments to pass laws, defend their land, and carry out large building projects. The people of these civilizations also developed systems of values and beliefs that gave meaning to their lives.

The Two Rivers

Mesopotamia, the earliest known civilization, developed in what is now southern Iraq (ih•RAHK). Mesopotamia means "the land between the rivers" in Greek. The civilization began on the plain between the Tigris (TY•gruhs) and the Euphrates (yu•FRAY•teez) rivers.

Reading **HELP**DESK

Taking Notes: ***Identifying***

On a diagram like this one, identify two major inventions of the Sumerians.

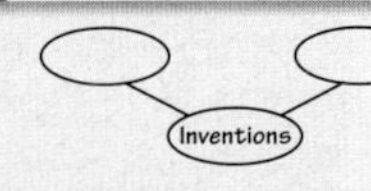

Content Vocabulary

- silt
- irrigation
- surplus
- city-state
- polytheism
- ziggurat
- cuneiform
- scribe
- epic

These rivers run about **parallel** to each other and flow more than 1,000 miles (1,600 km). They run southeast from the mountains of southeastern Asia to the Persian (PUR•zhuhn) Gulf.

Mesopotamia itself was located in the eastern part of the larger Fertile Crescent. This curving strip of good farmland extends from the Mediterranean (mehd•uh•tuh•RAY•nee•uhn) Sea to the Persian Gulf. The Fertile Crescent includes parts of the modern countries of Turkey, Syria, Iraq, Lebanon, Israel, and Jordan.

Early Valley Dwellers

For thousands of years, clues to Mesopotamia's history lay buried among its ruins and piles of rubble. In the 1800s, archaeologists began to dig up many buildings and artifacts. These finds revealed much about early Mesopotamia.

Historians believe that people first settled Mesopotamia about 7000 B.C. The first settlers were hunters and herders. By about 4000 B.C., some of these groups had moved to the plain of the Tigris-Euphrates valley. They built farming villages along the two rivers.

Irrigation canals help farmers grow crops in areas that would otherwise be dry and not suitable for farming.

Taming the Rivers

Early Mesopotamian farmers used water from the Tigris and Euphrates Rivers to water their fields. However, the farmers could not always rely on the rivers for their needs. Little or no rain fell in the summer. As a result, the rivers were often low. The farmers did not have enough water to plant crops in the fall.

During the spring harvest, rains and melting snow from the northern mountains caused rivers to overflow their banks. This flooded the plains. Sometimes, unexpected and violent floods swept away crops, homes, and livestock.

Yet farmers in Mesopotamia knew that the floods were also helpful. Flooded rivers were filled with **silt**, or small particles of soil. When the floods ended, silt was left on the banks and plains. The silt proved to be a very good soil for farming.

Over time, people in Mesopotamia learned to build dams to control the seasonal floods. They dug canals that let water flow from a water source to their fields. This method of watering crops is called **irrigation** (IHR • uh • GAY • shuhn).

silt fine particles of fertile soil

irrigation a system that supplies dry land with water through ditches, pipes, or streams

Academic Vocabulary

parallel moving or lying in the same direction and the same distance apart

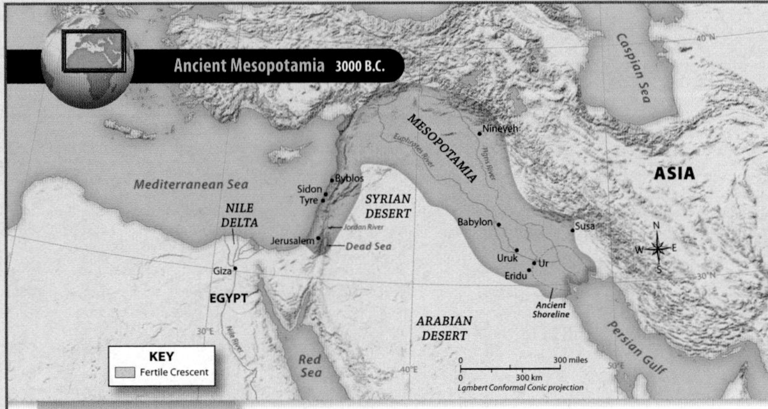

GEOGRAPHY CONNECTION

A number of great civilizations developed in Mesopotamia.

1. **LOCATION** What city was located in northern Mesopotamia?
2. **CRITICAL THINKING** ***Making Inferences*** Why do you think Mesopotamia was a good location for the growth of civilization?

Irrigation let these early farmers grow **surpluses** (SUHR•plus•ehz)—or extra amounts—of food. Farmers stored the surpluses for later use.

When food was plentiful, not all people needed to farm. Some became artisans, or skilled workers. They specialized in weaving cloth and making pottery, tools, and weapons.

As artisans made more goods, people's lives changed. People began to live together in places that favored trade. Small farming villages grew into cities. By 3000 B.C., several cities developed in Sumer (SOO•mer), a region in southern Mesopotamia.

PROGRESS CHECK

Explaining How did floods sometimes help farmers?

2 Sumer's Civilization

GUIDING QUESTION *What was life like in Sumer?*

Sumer's people were known as Sumerians. They built the first cities in Southwest Asia, including Ur (uhr), Uruk (OO•rook), and Eridu (ER•i•doo). These cities became centers of civilization that controlled the lower part of the Tigris and Euphrates valleys.

Reading **HELP**DESK

surplus an amount that is left over after a need has been met

city-state a city that governs itself and its surrounding territory

polytheism a belief in more than one god

City-States Arise

Sumer's cities were surrounded by mudflats and patches of scorching desert. The harsh landscape made it hard to travel by land and communicate with other groups. This meant that each city was largely cut off from its neighbors.

As a result, Sumerian cities became independent. The people of each city raised their own crops and made their own goods. As the cities grew, they gained political and economic control over the lands around them. By doing this, they formed **city-states**. Each city-state had its own government and was not part of any larger governing state. The population of the city-states ranged from about 5,000 to 20,000 people.

Historians think that each Sumerian city-state was protected by a large city wall. Ruins and artifacts have been found by archaeologists that support this theory. Because stone and wood were in short supply, the Sumerians used mud from the rivers as their main building material. They mixed mud with crushed reeds, formed bricks, and left them in the sun to dry. The gates of the wall stayed open during the day but were closed at night for protection. The ruler's palace, a large temple, and other public buildings were located in the center of the city.

Often, these city-states went to war with one another over resources and political borders. Sometimes, they fought to win glory or to gain more territory. During times of peace, city-states traded with each other. They also agreed to help each other by forming alliances (uh•LY•uhns•uhs) to protect their common interests.

In areas where there was little rainfall, farmers watered their fields using irrigation channels.

▶ **CRITICAL THINKING**

Analyzing What other water sources were available in addition to the river?

Gods, Priests, and Kings

The Sumerian people worshipped many gods, a type of belief known as **polytheism** (PAH•lee•thee•ih•zuhm). These multiple gods played different roles in Sumerian life. The Sumerians thought that some gods had power over parts of nature, such as the rain or the wind. They also believed that some gods guided the things that people did, such as plowing or brick-making. They honored whatever god would help their activity.

Although Sumerians honored all the gods, each city-state claimed one as its own.

LESSON 1 • Day 1

ENGAGE

Predicting

Have students skim "The First Civilizations in Mesopotamia," noting the headings, key terms, and images. Explain that archaeologists have found many things that provided information about early Mesopotamian civilizations.

Ask:

What do you think some of these artifacts might have been? *(Answers will vary, but students might mention remains of buildings and other structures, pottery, tools, and weapons.)* AL

TEACH & ASSESS

1 The First Civilizations in Mesopotamia

GUIDING QUESTION *Why did people settle in Mesopotamia?*

SLIDE SHOW

Describing Review with students how irrigation works. Then, have students watch the interactive slide show about irrigation. Have students describe in their own words how irrigation works. AL ELL

LECTURE SLIDE

Show the definition of *periodic flooding* from the lecture slide. Remind students that the Tigris-Euphrates valley was subject to periodic flooding.

Ask:

How were people affected when the Tigris or Euphrates River flooded the land? *(Answers will vary, but students might say that crops and homes were sometimes destroyed. They might also mention that the floodwaters deposited rich soil that was good for farming.)* AL ELL

2 Sumer's Civilization

GUIDING QUESTION *What was life like in Sumer?*

SLIDE SHOW

Making Connections Review the information about ziggurats. Then have students watch the interactive slide show to help them make connections between ziggurats and modern structures.

Ask:

- **Do you think ziggurats were important to the Sumerians? Explain.** *(Yes, Sumerians worshiped their gods at the ziggurats. Their gods were important to them and so were their ziggurats.)*
- **Are any buildings in the United States as important to American culture as the ziggurat was to Sumerian culture? Explain.** *(Answers will vary. For example, a student might say that the White House is important because the president lives there.)* AL

LECTURE SLIDE

Show the definition of *city-state* from the lecture slide. Review the formation of city-states.

Ask:

What caused city-states to develop? *(Answers will vary, but students might say people gathered in settlements along rivers. These settlements became isolated because of the desert. As farming improved, the settlements grew and people specialized in various types of work. As a result, the settlements developed into city-states.)*

Be sure students think about location, terrain, farming, and work specialization when analyzing the development of city-states.

Ask:

What were relations between city-states like? *(In times of peace, city-states traded with each other. Often, they went to war with one another over resources and political boundaries. However, they also formed alliances to help each other protect their common interests.)*

Ask:

What do you know about the present-day nations that are in the area that was once called Mesopotamia? *(Answers will vary, but students may mention that the area is important for oil production and that it was the site of the Iraq War.)*

CLOSE & REFLECT

Diagramming Have students review the material about city-states, including their layout and important buildings, such as the ziggurat.

Based on this information, have a student volunteer draw a basic diagram of a city-state on the board. Ask the class to suggest changes or additions to the diagram and explain them.

IF YOU HAVE MORE TIME . . .

Explore Natural Resources in Ancient Mesopotamia

Analyzing Discuss with students the importance of natural resources to the civilizations of ancient Mesopotamia. Mention that conflicts often arose over who controlled and used these resources.

Consider Natural Resources in the Region Today

Researching Ask students to research the present-day nations that are part of the Mesopotamian region. Use this information to facilitate a class discussion about recent or ongoing conflicts over natural resources in the region.

Comparing and Contrasting Students can create a graphic organizer to help them compare and contrast the conflicts over natural resources that occurred in the past with those conflicts of today. Students should first determine what type of organizer to use. Then, they should use their research and textbooks to complete the organizer. BL

Describe the Role of the United States in the Region Today

Explaining Have students discuss the United States's involvement in the region. Students might find current news articles that provide information to help the discussion. BL

Answers for pages 76–79

P. 76 Taking Notes Answers might include writing, the wheel, a number system based on 60, and the wooden plow.

P. 78 GEOGRAPHY CONNECTION

1. Nineveh
2. CRITICAL THINKING The Tigris and Euphrates Rivers provided water for drinking and for crops. Also, the flooding of these two rivers made the soil fertile. As a result, agriculture flourished.

P. 78 ☑ PROGRESS CHECK Rich silt, which helped crops grow, was left behind by floodwaters.

P. 79 CRITICAL THINKING rain and canals

The ziggurat was built to be visible throughout the city-state. The walls of the ziggurat enclosed the royal warehouses and the city's treasury.

▶ CRITICAL THINKING

Speculating Why do you think the Sumerians would want the ziggurat to be highly visible?

To honor its god, a city-state often included a large temple called a **ziggurat** (ZIG•oo•rat). The word *ziggurat* means "to rise high" in the ancient Akkadian (uh•KAY•dee•uhn) language. The very top of the ziggurat was a holy place. It was the god's home, and only special priests were allowed to go there. In the early days, priests of the ziggurat ruled the city-states. Groups of important men helped them govern. Later, Sumerian city-states became monarchies.

Sumerian kings claimed they received their power to rule from the city's god. The first kings were most likely war heroes. Over time, their rule became hereditary. This meant that after a king died, his son took over. In most cases, the wives of kings did not have political power. However, some controlled their own lands.

Social Groups

People in Sumer were divided into social classes. Generally, people remained in the social class into which they were born. Kings, priests, warriors, and government officials belonged to the upper class. The middle class **consisted** of merchants, farmers, fishers, and artisans. The middle class was Sumer's largest social group. Enslaved people made up Sumer's lowest class. Most of these workers had been captured in war. Also, criminals and people who could not pay their debts often were enslaved. Enslaved men and women worked for the upper class.

Women and men had different roles in Sumerian society. The basic unit of society was the family. Men were the head of the home. Boys went to school and were trained for a specific job. Sumerian women ran the home, taught their daughters to do the same, and cared for the children. Women had a few civil rights. Some owned businesses. Sumerian law required parents to care for their children. The law also required adult children to care for their parents if their parents needed help.

Reading HELPDESK

ziggurat a pyramid-shaped structure with a temple at the top

Academic Vocabulary

consist to be made up of

Reading Strategy: *Summarizing*

When you summarize, you find the main idea of a passage and restate it in your own words. Read the paragraph under the heading "Social Groups." On a separate sheet of paper, summarize the paragraph in one or two sentences.

Farmers and Traders

If you lived in Sumer, you were most likely a farmer. Each farmer had a plot of land located in the area around a city-state. Dams and waterways ran through this farmland. Wheat, barley, and dates were the major crops. Farmers also raised sheep, goats, and pigs.

Trade was another key part of Sumer's economy. The Sumerians did not have some of the goods that they needed. For example, even though many Sumerians were skilled metalworkers, they had to trade with other peoples to obtain most of their metals. Trade routes linked Sumer to places as far away as India and Egypt.

Sumerian merchants went to other lands. They traded wheat, barley, and tools for timber, minerals, and metals. The minerals and metals were then used to make jewelry or tools. For jewelry making, Sumerians valued a red stone called carnelian from India's Indus Valley. They also searched for a blue stone known as lapis lazuli from what is now Afghanistan. Traders returned with iron and silver from present-day Turkey.

Sumerian artisans produced a variety of goods, including jewelry. This piece is made of gold and lapis lazuli.

▶ CRITICAL THINKING

Speculating If you were an artisan in ancient times, what would you produce?

☑ PROGRESS CHECK

Analyzing Why do you think the Sumerians built cities with walls around them?

3 Sumerian Contributions

GUIDING QUESTION *What ideas and inventions did Sumerians pass on to other civilizations?*

The Sumerians created the first civilization that had a great influence on history. Later civilizations copied and improved many of the ideas and inventions that began in Sumer. As a result, Mesopotamia has been called the "cradle of civilization." It was the beginning of organized human society.

Writing

Of all the contributions made by Sumerians to the world, writing is perhaps the most important. The writing system they developed was the earliest known system in the world.

This Royal Standard of Ur—the royal design—shows scenes of everyday life in Sumer. *Which methods of travel are shown on this standard?*

Sumerians needed materials for building and making tools. They sailed to other lands to trade for wood logs to take home.

Writing was a way for Sumerians to keep records of their lives and their history. Writing was also a way to share information. They could pass on their ideas to later generations.

Sumerians created a way of writing called **cuneiform** (kyoo•NEE•uh•FAWRM). The cuneiform writing system was made up of about 1,200 different characters. Characters represented such things as names, physical objects, and numbers. Cuneiform was written by cutting wedge-shaped marks into damp clay with a sharp reed. The name *cuneiform* comes from a Latin word meaning "wedge." Sumerians wrote on clay because they did not have paper. Archaeologists have found cuneiform tablets that have provided important information about Mesopotamian history.

Only a few people—mostly boys from wealthy families—learned how to read and write cuneiform. After years of training, some students became **scribes** (SKRYBS), or official record keepers. Scribes wrote documents that recorded much of the everyday life in Mesopotamia, including court records, marriage contracts, business dealings, and important events. Some scribes were judges and government officials.

Sumerians told stories orally for centuries. After developing writing, they were able to record these stories. Their tales praised the gods and warriors for doing great deeds. The world's oldest known story is from Sumer. Written more than 4,000 years ago and still studied today, this story is called the *Epic of Gilgamesh* (GIHL•guh•MEHSH). An **epic** is a long poem that tells the story of a hero.

Reading HELPDESK

cuneiform a system of writing developed by the Sumerians that used wedge-shaped marks made in soft clay

scribe a person who copies or writes out documents; often a record keeper

epic a long poem that records the deeds of a legendary or real hero

Technology and Mathematics

The people of Mesopotamia also made many useful inventions. For example, the Sumerians were the first people to use the wheel. The earliest wheels were solid wood circles made from carved boards that were clamped together. A Sumerian illustration from about 3500 B.C. shows a wheeled vehicle. They built the first carts, which were pulled by donkeys. They also introduced vehicles into military use with the development of the chariot.

For river travel, Sumerians developed the sailboat. They invented a wooden plow to help them in the fields. Artisans made the potter's wheel, which helped to shape clay into bowls and jars. Sumerians were also the first to make bronze out of copper and tin. They used bronze to craft stronger tools, weapons, and jewelry.

The Sumerians also studied mathematics and astronomy. They used geometry to measure the size of fields and to plan buildings. They created a place-value system of numbers based on 60. They also devised tables for calculating division and multiplication. The 60-minute hour, 60-second minute, and 360-degree circle we use today are ideas that came from the Sumerians. Sumerians watched the positions of the stars. It showed them the best times to plant crops and to hold religious ceremonies. They also made a 12-month calendar based on the cycles of the moon.

Thinking Like a HISTORIAN

Classifying and Categorizing Information

The Sumerians invented or improved many items and methods. To classify these, look for topics with broad characteristics, such as *farming* or *communication*. Under each broad classification, you can divide the topic into narrower categories. Under farming, for example, include the category *irrigation*. Create a chart to organize broad topics and categories for the Sumerians' inventions and present your information to the class. For more about classifying and categorizing, read the chapter *What Does a Historian Do?*

☑ PROGRESS CHECK

Explaining Why did the Sumerians invent a writing system?

Sumerian writing etched on stone has been found by archaeologists.

LESSON 1 REVIEW

Review Vocabulary

1. How were *polytheism* and *ziggurats* related in Sumerian civilization?

Answer the Guiding Questions

2. ***Describing*** Where is the Fertile Crescent located? Where is Mesopotamia located?
3. ***Comparing*** How were the social classes of Sumer organized?
4. ***Identifying*** What was the most common role for women in Sumerian society?
5. ***Describing*** Why were scribes important in Sumerian society?
6. **PERSUASIVE WRITING** Sumerians developed many inventions. Choose the invention that you think is the most significant and explain why you made this choice.

LESSON 1 • Day 2

ENGAGE

Making Inferences Remind students about the terrain of Mesopotamia, mentioning the two rivers and the desert.

Ask:

What route do you think people would use if they were migrating into Mesopotamia? *(Answers will vary. Students might say people would use rivers because deserts are difficult to cross.)*

Ask:

What do you think were the results of this migration? *(Answers will vary. Students might mention that the population of the region increased and settlements were formed.)*

TEACH & ASSESS

2 Sumer's Civilization

GUIDING QUESTION *What was life like in Sumer?*

LECTURE SLIDE **Making Connections** Show the definition of *social class* from the lecture slide. After students have read "Sumer's Civilization," discuss with them the idea of social class in Sumer. Then have them define in their own words *upper class, middle class,* and *lower class.* Record their answers on the board. *(Sample answers—Upper Class: have most wealth in society; have power. Middle Class: have some money but not a lot; have limited power. Lower Class: have limited money; have very little power.)*

Ask:

Do you think today's society has social classes? *(Yes, today's society has people with high incomes, people with average incomes, and people with low incomes. These people can be grouped into upper, middle, and lower classes.)*

Making Inferences Review with students the roles of a monarch, a scribe, an artisan, and a slave.

Ask:

- **What do you think the daily life of a monarch was like?** *(Answers will vary, but students might say that monarchs had servants, good food, and a lot of leisure time.)* AL
- **What type of education did a monarch's children likely receive?** *(The children of monarchs probably went to excellent schools and received advanced educations.)* AL
- **What was the home of a monarch like?** *(Monarchs probably lived in a palace or a mansion.)* AL
- Then ask the same questions for a scribe, an artisan, and a slave. BL

Predict Ask: Which social class do you think most of the leaders of Mesopotamian society came from? *(The key leaders came from the upper class.)* Then have students skim the next lesson to see if their answers were correct.

INTERACTIVE WORKSHEET

Economics of History Activity

Bartering Have students work in groups to complete the Economics of History worksheet activity on bartering to help them understand the bartering system used in Sumer. Be sure students understand the information presented at the beginning of the activity so they can do the bartering exercise. After the activity,

Ask:

- **Was your bartering successful? Explain.** *(Answers will vary, but students might respond "no" because they did not get all the goods they needed.)*
- **Do you prefer an economic system that uses bartering or a system that uses money? Explain.** *(Answers will vary. Students might say they prefer using money because bartering seems too confusing. Also, with bartering, a person has to rely too much on what other people are willing to trade. Some students might say they like bartering because they can trade something they don't want for something they do want. They might like a direct exchange in which money is not needed.)*

INTERACTIVE WHITEBOARD ACTIVITY **Synthesizing** Have students use the Interactive Whiteboard Activity about bartering to practice their bartering skills. In this activity, a list of goods is provided. Students should choose goods they are willing to trade. They should also decide what goods they want to get in exchange. Students should then drag and drop these goods into the blanks provided. BL

SLIDE SHOW Have students watch the interactive slide show about precious stones traded in Sumer to help them understand more about these minerals. Make sure students read the captions for each image. BL ELL

3 Sumerian Contributions

GUIDING QUESTION *What ideas and inventions did Sumerians pass on to other civilizations?*

Remind students that the Sumerians made many important contributions that still affect us today, including the invention of writing, the wheel, the sailboat, bronze, and the 12-month calendar.

Ask:

Which of the Sumerian contributions do you think was the most important, and why? *(Answers will vary. Students might mention writing because it was a way to keep records and pass ideas to later generations.)*

Have students complete the Lesson 1 Review.

CLOSE & REFLECT

Identifying Points of View Have students volunteer to take the role of a monarch, a scribe, an artisan, and a slave. Ask them what their character's opinion might be about the economic system of bartering. AL

Answers for pages 80–83

P. 80 CRITICAL THINKING Answers will vary but may include the idea that they wanted to emphasize the religious importance of the temple.

P. 80 Reading Strategy Answers will vary but should include the ideas that most Sumerians were farmers and belonged to the middle class. Of the upper, middle, and lower classes, the middle class was the largest.

P. 81 CRITICAL THINKING Answers will vary, but students should try to identify various goods produced during ancient times.

P. 81 The standard shows people riding in chariots and walking.

P. 81 ☑ PROGRESS CHECK They built walled cities for protection.

P. 83 ☑ PROGRESS CHECK They invented a writing system to record business dealings and other important events.

LESSON 1 REVIEW

1. The Sumerian people practiced polytheism, or the worship of many gods and goddesses. The ziggurat was the temple in a Sumerian city that was dedicated to the chief god or goddess of the city.
2. The Fertile Crescent is a strip of land extending from the Mediterranean Sea to the Persian Gulf. Mesopotamia is the name for the region between the Tigris and Euphrates Rivers. Mesopotamia lies within the Fertile Crescent.
3. The upper class consisted of kings, priests, warriors, and government officials. The middle class included merchants, farmers, fishers, and artisans. Enslaved people made up the lower class.
4. Most women ran their households and took care of their children.
5. There were few scribes. Their important work included recording business transactions and documenting Sumerian history and literature.
6. Answers will vary, but students should demonstrate knowledge of the invention they chose and defend its importance.

Epic of Gilgamesh

Gilgamesh (c. 2000 B.C.)

Gilgamesh ruled Uruk in southern Mesopotamia sometime around 2000 B.C. According to mythology, he was a god and a human. It is believed that Gilgamesh was a harsh ruler until his friendship with Enkidu (EN • kee • doo) taught him to be fair and kind. In this epic poem, Gilgamesh faces many challenges. He suffers many losses and must confront his biggest fear: death. Eventually, Gilgamesh learns he cannot avoid death.

This excerpt tells the story of when Gilgamesh and his friend, Enkidu, decide to become heroes. They set out to kill Humbaba (hum•BAH•bah), a monstrous giant who ruled the cedar forest where gods lived. Humbaba has the face of a lion and his breath ignites fire, while his roar unleashes floods.

"Don't be afraid, said Gilgamesh. We are together. There is nothing We should fear"

—from Gilgamesh: A Verse Narrative
tr. Herbert Mason

PRIMARY SOURCE

"Enkidu was afraid of the forest of Humbaba
And urged him [Gilgamesh] not to go, but he
Was not as strong as Gilgamesh in argument,
And they were friends:

They had **embraced** and made their vow
To stay together always,
No matter what the **obstacle**.
Enkidu tried to hold his fear . . .

Don't be afraid, said Gilgamesh.
We are together. There is nothing
We should fear.

I learned, Enkidu said, when I lived
With the animals never to go down
Into that forest. I learned that there is death
In Humbaba. Why do you want
To raise his [Humbaba's] anger? . . .

After three days they reached the edge
Of the forest where Humbaba's watchman stood.
Suddenly it was Gilgamesh who was afraid,
Enkidu . . . reminded him to be fearless.
The watchman sounded his warning to Humbaba.
The two friends moved slowly toward the forest gate.

When Enkidu touched the gate his hand felt numb,
He could not move his fingers or his wrist,
His face turned pale like someone's witnessing a death[.]
He tried to ask his friend for help
Whom he had just encouraged to move on,
But he could only **stutter** and hold out
His paralyzed hand."

—from *Gilgamesh: A Verse Narrative*, tr. Herbert Mason

The Gilgamesh epic was written on 12 tablets and discovered in Nineveh, in present-day Iraq. The tablets were found in the library of the Assyrian king Ashurbanipal (ah • shur • BAH • nuh • puhl), who reigned 668–627 B.C.

Vocabulary

embrace to hug with arms around
obstacle something that stands in the way
stutter an uneven repetition of sounds and words

Analyzing Literature DBQ

1. ***Identifying*** How many times is death mentioned in this excerpt?
2. ***Describing*** How do you know that Gilgamesh and Enkidu are friends?
3. ***Speculating*** Enkidu is left in a risky situation. What do you think happens to him?

NOTES

NOTES

ENGAGE

Remind the class that understanding historical context can help them understand historical literature.

MAP Project the interactive version of the Chapter Opener map of ancient Mesopotamia. Remind students that a king named Gilgamesh ruled the city of Uruk. Have a student volunteer show the location of Uruk on the map.

Then ask:

What other cities or major features are located near Uruk? *(Students should identify the cities of Eridu, Ur, and Babylon, as well as the Euphrates River.)* ELL

Have students look at the Chapter Opener time line. Remind them that Gilgamesh is believed to have ruled around 2000 B.C.

TEACH & ASSESS

Explaining Explain to students that a historical king named Gilgamesh existed, and that the *Epic of Gilgamesh* is based on this king. Much of the story is exaggerated, though, it is not historically accurate. After students read the introduction to the epic:

Ask:

What clues tell you that at least part of the epic is a fictional story rather than a factual record? *(Students should note that Gilgamesh is described as both a god and a human in Mesopotamian mythology. The excerpt also describes him setting out to slay a monstrous giant.)* BL

Ask:

What evidence do we have that the *Epic of Gilgamesh* was popular in ancient times? *(The story of Gilgamesh was famous, and the tablets containing the story were kept in a royal library.)*

Have student volunteers read aloud the first two verses from the excerpt.

Ask:

- **How does Enkidu feel about entering the forest?** *(He is afraid.)* ELL
- **Why does he feel this way?** *(He is afraid that Humbaba will be angered and that he and Gilgamesh might die in the forest.)* AL
- **Why does Enkidu go into the forest?** *(His friend Gilgamesh insists on going, and Enkidu is persuaded because they have sworn to stay together.)*

Have students read the final three verses of the excerpt.

Ask:

- **What changes when the two heroes reach the forest?** *(Gilgamesh grows afraid, and Enkidu reassures him.)* AL
- **Is Humbaba powerful? How do you know?** *(Humbaba is clearly quite powerful, for Gilgamesh and Enkidu are afraid of him. Enkidu is paralyzed with fear when he reaches the forest gate.)*

Ask students to consider whether having to overcome fear makes Enkidu and Gilgamesh more realistic than they would seem if they were not afraid of anything.

Remind students that the *Epic of Gilgamesh* is a story of the heroic deeds of Gilgamesh and Enkidu.

Ask:

Do Gilgamesh and Enkidu seem heroic in this excerpt? Why or why not? *(Student answers will vary. Some might note that Gilgamesh and Enkidu seem afraid, which might not strike students as heroic. Others might note that Gilgamesh and Enkidu work to overcome their fear, which is a sign of bravery.)* BL

Hold a discussion with students about the meaning of *heroism* and what makes a person a hero. Encourage them to use examples from their own lives of people facing their fears and overcoming them.

Have students complete the Analyzing Literature questions.

CLOSE & REFLECT

INTERACTIVE WORKSHEET **Summarizing** Divide the class into groups of four. Tell each group that they will be doing publicity for the story of Gilgamesh as a novel or as a film. Assign the 21st Century Skills Activity on collaboration. Students can use the worksheet as a guide for their activities. They may complete the assignment as homework. Each group can present its film or book publicity to the class.

BACKGROUND KNOWLEDGE

The *Epic of Gilgamesh*

The Epic of Gilgamesh is about an actual king, the king of Uruk in Babylonia. The stories of his life—both truth and myth—were written in cuneiform onto 12 clay tablets. Unbelievably, these 12 tablets were found, damaged but readable, in the ruins of a library that had been destroyed by Persians. Have students research information about the *Epic of Gilgamesh*, either on the Internet or at the library. Then have them write a short paragraph describing its importance.

Answers for *Analyzing Literature* DBQ

1. twice
2. They have vowed to stay together, no matter what; they assure one another when they are each afraid; they ask each other for help.
3. Because tragedy often occurs in epic poems and because death is foreshadowed twice in this excerpt, students should speculate that Enkidu dies, which eventually he does.

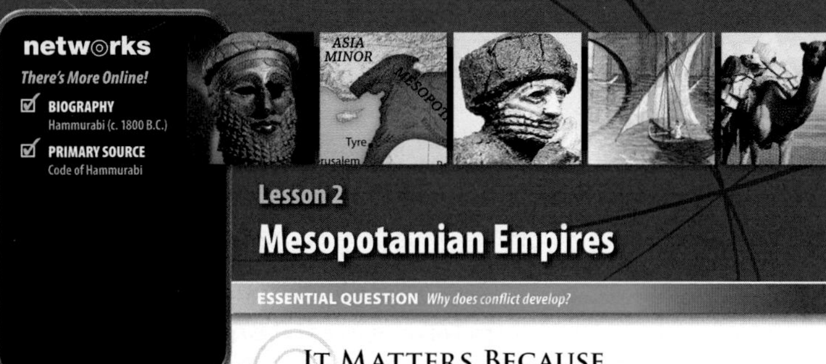

networks
There's More Online!
☑ **BIOGRAPHY** Hammurabi (c. 1800 B.C.)
☑ **PRIMARY SOURCE** Code of Hammurabi

Lesson 2

Mesopotamian Empires

ESSENTIAL QUESTION *Why does conflict develop?*

It Matters Because

Mesopotamia's empires greatly influenced other civilizations. Hammurabi's Code even influenced the legal codes of Greece and Rome.

1 The First Empires

GUIDING QUESTION *How did Mesopotamia's first empires develop?*

By 2400 B.C., Sumer's city-states were weakened by conflict. As the strength of Sumer faded, powerful kingdoms arose in northern Mesopotamia and in neighboring Syria. Seeking new lands, rulers of these kingdoms built empires. An **empire** (EHM•PYR) is a group of many different lands under one ruler. Through conquest and trade, these empires spread their cultures over a wide region.

Who Was Sargon?

The kingdom of Akkad (AK•ad) developed in northern Mesopotamia. Sargon (SAHR•GAHN) was an ambitious leader who ruled the people of Akkad, known as Akkadians (uh•KAY•dee•uhnz). About 2340 B.C., Sargon moved his well-trained armies south. He conquered the remaining Sumerian city-states one by one. Sargon united the conquered territory with Akkad and became known as the king of Sumer and Akkad. In doing so, he formed the world's first empire. Eventually, Sargon extended this empire to include all of the peoples of Mesopotamia. His Mesopotamian empire lasted for more than 200 years before invaders conquered it.

Reading **HELP**DESK

Taking Notes: ***Identifying***
On a diagram like this one, identify the major Mesopotamian empires from this lesson.

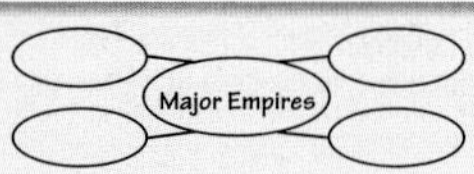

Content Vocabulary
- **empire**
- **tribute**
- **province**
- **caravan**
- **astronomer**

Who Was Hammurabi?

A people called the Amorites lived in the region west of Mesopotamia. In the 1800s B.C., they conquered Mesopotamia and built their own cities. Babylon (BA•buh•luhn) was the grandest of these cities. It was located on the eastern bank of the Euphrates River in what is now Iraq. Around 1792 B.C., the Babylonian king, Hammurabi (HA•muh•RAH•bee), began conquering cities controlled by the Amorites to the north and south. By adding these lands he created the Babylonian Empire. This new empire stretched north from the Persian Gulf through the Tigris-Euphrates valley and west to the Mediterranean Sea.

Hammurabi's Code

Hammurabi was thought to be a just ruler. He is best known for creating a set of laws for his empire. He posted this law **code** for all to read. The code dealt with crimes, farming, business, marriage, and the family—almost every area of life. The code listed a punishment for each crime.

The Code of Hammurabi was stricter than the old Sumerian laws. The code demanded what became known as "an eye for an eye, and a tooth for a tooth." This means that the punishment for a crime should match the seriousness of the crime. It was meant to limit punishment and do away with blood feuds.

The code also protected the less powerful. For example, it protected wives from abuse by their husbands. Hammurabi's Code influenced later law codes, such as those of Greece and Rome.

☑ **PROGRESS CHECK**
Finding the Main Idea Why was Hammurabi's Code important?

2 The Assyrian Empire

GUIDING QUESTION *How did the Assyrians influence Southwest Asia?*

The Assyrian Empire arose about 1,000 years after the empire of Hammurabi. Assyria (uh•SIHR•ee•uh) was a large empire, extending into four present-day countries: Turkey, Syria, Iran, and Iraq.

The Assyrians built a large and powerful **military** to defend their hills and fertile valleys. Around 900 B.C., their army began taking over the rest of Mesopotamia.

BIOGRAPHY

Sargon (c. 2300 B.C.)
What king created the world's first empire? Sargon united Akkad with Sumer in the region between the Tigris and Euphrates Rivers. Sargon's Akkadian name, Sharrum-kin, means "the true king."

Under Sargon's rule, the cultures of Akkad and Sumer mixed. The people of Mesopotamia spoke the Akkadian language, but they wrote in Sumerian cuneiform. They also worshipped Sumerian gods. Sargon's empire grew wealthy through its many trade routes.

▶ **CRITICAL THINKING**
Speculating What made Sargon a "true king"?

empire a large territory or group of many territories governed by one ruler

Academic Vocabulary
code a set of official laws
military having to do with soldiers, weapons, or war

The Assyrian Army

The army of Assyria was well trained and disciplined. In battle, the troops numbered around 50,000 soldiers. This army was made up of infantry, or foot soldiers; cavalry, or horse soldiers; and charioteers. The Assyrians fought with slingshots, bows and arrows, swords, and spears.

The Assyrians robbed people, set crops on fire, and destroyed towns and dams. They took **tribute**, or forced payments, from conquered people. The Assyrian army also drove people from their homes. Stories of Assyrian brutality spread. Sometimes people were so afraid of the Assyrians that they would surrender to them without a fight.

One of the key factors in the Assyrian successes was iron weapons. The Hittites (HIH•tyts), a people to the north, had mastered iron production, making iron stronger than tin or copper. The Assyrians learned from Hittite technology.

Kings and Government

Assyria extended from the Persian Gulf in the east to the Nile River in the west. The capital was located at Nineveh (NIH•nuh•vuh), along the Tigris River.

Assyrian kings had to be powerful leaders to rule such a large area. They divided their empire into **provinces** (PRAH•vuhn•suhs), or political districts. The government built roads that connected these provinces. The kings chose officials to govern, collect taxes, and carry out the laws in each province. Soldiers stood guard at stations along the roads to protect traders from bandits. Messengers on government business used the stations to rest and change chariot horses.

Life in Assyria

The lives of the Assyrians were built on what they learned from other Mesopotamian peoples. The Assyrians had law codes, but their punishments were harsher. Assyrians based their writing on Babylonian writing. They worshipped many of the same gods.

Assyrians built large temples and palaces filled with wall carvings and statues. They also wrote and collected stories. An ancient Assyrian king named Ashurbanipal (ah•shur•BAH•nuh•puhl) built one of the world's first libraries in Nineveh. It held 25,000 tablets of stories and songs to the gods. Historians have learned much about ancient civilizations from this library.

Hammurabi's Code was carved on stone slabs that were placed where the most people would see them. Sometimes a statue of the king was placed with it.

▶ **CRITICAL THINKING**
Drawing Conclusions Why was displaying the code important for Babylonians?

Reading **HELP**DESK

tribute a payment made to a ruler or state as a sign of surrender

province a territory governed as a political district of a country or empire

Assyrian Empire 900 B.C.

ASIA MINOR, MESOPOTAMIA, Caspian Sea, Nineveh, Mediterranean Sea, Tyre, Jerusalem, Babylon, EGYPT, Thebes, ARABIAN DESERT, Persian Gulf, Red Sea, 40°N, 30°E, 50°E
0 – 400 miles; 0 – 400 km; Lambert Conformal Conic projection
KEY: Assyrian Empire

GEOGRAPHY CONNECTION
The Assyrians conquered lands from Mesopotamia to Egypt.

1. **LOCATION** What geographic feature lay to the south of the Assyrian Empire?
2. **CRITICAL THINKING** ***Making Inferences*** Several major rivers flowed through the Assyrian Empire. Why were these rivers important?

Farming and trade were both important to the Assyrians. They brought in wood and metal from far away to supply their empire with material for building and for making tools and weapons.

☑ **PROGRESS CHECK**
Summarizing Why was Assyria's army so strong?

3 The Chaldean Empire

GUIDING QUESTION *Why was Babylon an important city in the ancient world?*

For 300 years, Assyria ruled the area from the Persian Gulf to Egypt. Because they were harsh rulers, people often rebelled. In about 650 B.C., fighting broke out over who would be the next Assyrian ruler. With the Assyrians in turmoil, a group of people called the Chaldeans (kal•DEE•uhns) took power.

A New Empire

Centuries before, about 1000 B.C., the Chaldean people had moved into southern Mesopotamia. At that time, the Assyrians had quickly conquered the Chaldeans' small kingdom. The Chaldeans hated their harsh new rulers and were never completely under Assyrian control.

Connections to **TODAY**
Libraries
The United States Library of Congress in Washington, D.C., ranks as the largest library in the world. It holds millions of books, photographs, and other documents.

Visual Vocabulary
slingshot a weapon that is used to throw stones or other objects

LESSON 2

ENGAGE

PRIMARY SOURCE **Previewing** Show students the primary source slide showing translations of the introduction and several excerpts from Hammurabi's Code.

Ask:

Why do you think Hammurabi created a code of laws? *(Answers will vary. Students might say that Hammurabi wanted to create a just system of laws that was fair for all people. Also, he probably wanted to maintain order in his empire.)*

TEACH & ASSESS

1 The First Empires

GUIDING QUESTION ***How did Mesopotamia's first empires develop?***

LECTURE SLIDE **Drawing Conclusions** To help students draw conclusions, show the lecture slide about Hammurabi's most significant accomplishment. Hold a class discussion about Hammurabi's Code and its influence on the Babylonian Empire.

Ask:

- **Did the code make clear what actions were crimes?** *(Hammurabi's Code was the first set of laws that made clear exactly what actions were crimes. It also let people know that any person committing a crime would be punished. The code was posted throughout the empire so that all the subjects would know the crimes and their punishments.)*
- **What was the guiding principle for the laws in Hammurabi's Code?** *(The guiding principle behind Hammurabi's Code was "an eye for an eye and a tooth for a tooth," which means that for every wrong done there should be a similar measure of justice. Also, the code helped the less powerful, such as women.)*
- **How do you think Hammurabi's Code helped the development of the Babylonian Empire?** *(Answers will vary. Students might mention that the code probably established more order throughout the empire, so less conflict and fewer uprisings occurred.)*

INTERACTIVE WORKSHEET Next, complete the Primary Source Activity as a class to help students understand the nature of Hammurabi's Code and its influence on the Babylonian Empire.

2 The Assyrian Empire

GUIDING QUESTION ***How did the Assyrians influence Southwest Asia?***

3 The Chaldean Empire

GUIDING QUESTION ***Why was Babylon an important city in the ancient world?***

INTERACTIVE WHITEBOARD ACTIVITY

Identifying Review with students "The Assyrian Empire" and "The Chaldean Empire," and then show them the Interactive Whiteboard Activity. Have students match the characteristics shown in the activity to the correct empire. AL

Comparing and Contrasting Ask students to consider the distinct characteristics of the empires of Akkad, Assyria, and Babylon. Have them think about the time periods, the rulers, the religions, and the locations of these empires.

Ask:

- **What did the Assyrian and Chaldean Empires have in common?** *(Each empire was based in Mesopotamia and expanded through conquest. Trade was important to both empires, and they each built mighty palaces and temples.)*
- **How were the two empires different?** *(The Assyrians had a reputation as harsh rulers, and their army was feared. The Chaldeans overthrew the Assyrians. The Assyrians developed iron weapons and tools, and the Chaldeans developed advanced astronomy.)*

Have students complete the Lesson 2 Review.

CLOSE & REFLECT

Making Connections Ask students to think about the significance of Hammurabi's Code. Then lead a class discussion about the importance of laws today. Ask students to think about which laws they approve of and which they do not, and about why laws are necessary.

IF YOU HAVE MORE TIME . . .

Debate Hammurabi's Code

Organize a class debate on this question: Which word—*fair* or *cruel*—better describes Hammurabi's Code of Laws?

Assign small groups one of the points of view, making sure to have an equal number of groups supporting each side. Tell them to prepare for the debate by reviewing the laws mentioned in the text.

Also, students should research more of Hammurabi's laws in library resources or on the Internet. The more laws they are able to find, the better able they will be to support their arguments. Remind them to use their graphic organizers to organize their thoughts.

When students are ready, conduct the debate. At the end, ask students to vote on who had the stronger argument.

When the debate is finished, point out that in the code, crimes against slaves are treated differently—and more lightly—than crimes against free people. Ask whether this changes their opinions. BL

Answers for pages 86–89

P. 86 Taking Notes Akkad, Babylonia, Assyria, Chaldea

P. 87 ☑ PROGRESS CHECK Hammurabi's Code created a new set of stricter, standard punishments for crimes in his empire. It thus affected all of his people. It also influenced the law codes of later societies.

P. 88 CRITICAL THINKING Displaying the code helped Babylonians understand which actions broke the law and what the punishments were for various criminal acts.

P. 89 GEOGRAPHY CONNECTION

1. the Arabian Desert
2. CRITICAL THINKING They provided water for drinking, farming, and trading.

P. 89 ☑ PROGRESS CHECK Its soldiers were well-trained and had advanced weapons.

GEOGRAPHY CONNECTION

1. **LOCATION** In which direction would someone travel from Sidon to reach the Persian Gulf?
2. **CRITICAL THINKING** ***Evaluating*** Why do you think the Chaldeans naturally became traders?

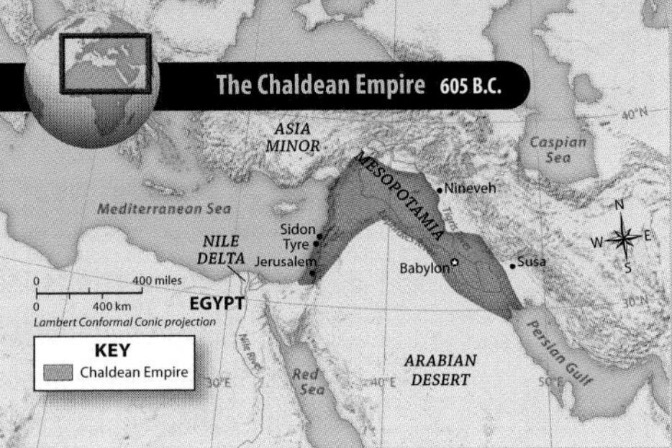

Years later, when the Assyrians were fighting each other, the Chaldean king Nabopolassar (NAH•buh•puh•LAH•suhr) decided to reclaim his kingdom.

In 627 B.C., Nabopolassar led a revolt against the Assyrians. Within a year, he had forced the Assyrians out of Uruk and was crowned king of Babylonia. The Medes, another people in the **region** who wanted to break free from Assyrian rule, joined the Chaldeans. Together, they defeated the Assyrian army. In 612 B.C., they captured the Assyrian capital of Nineveh and burned it to the ground. The hated Assyrian Empire quickly crumbled.

Nabopolassar and his son, Nebuchadnezzar (NEH•byuh•kuhd•NEH•zuhr), created a new empire. Most of the Chaldeans were descendants of the Babylonians who made up Hammurabi's empire about 1,200 years earlier. Through conquest, the Chaldeans gained control of almost all of the lands the Assyrians had once ruled. The city of Babylon served as their capital. Because of this, the Chaldean Empire is sometimes called the New Babylonian Empire.

The Greatness of Babylon

King Nebuchadnezzar rebuilt Babylon, making it the largest and richest city in the world. Huge brick walls surrounded the city. Soldiers kept watch in towers that were built into the walls.

Grand palaces and temples were located in the center of Babylon. A huge ziggurat stood more than 300 feet (92 m) tall. When the sun shone, its gold roof could be seen for miles.

Reading HELPDESK

Academic Vocabulary
region a geographic area

Academic Vocabulary
complex having many parts, details, or ideas

The richness of the ziggurat was equaled by that of the king's palace. The palace had a giant staircase of greenery known as the Hanging Gardens.

Babylon's Hanging Gardens were considered one of the Seven Wonders of the Ancient World. These terraced gardens—built like huge steps—included large trees, masses of flowering vines, and other beautiful plants. A **complex** irrigation system brought water from the Euphrates River to water the gardens. It is believed that Nebuchadnezzar built the gardens to please his wife. She missed the mountains and plants of her homeland in the northwest.

For his people, Nebuchadnezzar built a beautiful street near the palace that they could visit. It was paved with limestone and marble, and lined with walls of blue glaze tile.

These ruins of the original gardens stand today as a reminder of Babylon's glory.

The grand Hanging Gardens of Babylon were watered from the top down using irrigation. Water flowed from one level to the next.

▶ **CRITICAL THINKING**
Speculating Why do you think ancient cities had at least one magnificent building?

King Nebuchadnezzar in the Hanging Gardens.

Each spring, thousands of people crowded into Babylon to watch a gold statue of the god Marduk (MAHR•dook) as it was wheeled along the street. Chaldeans believed that the ceremony would bring peace and bigger crops to their empire.

The Babylonians built many new canals, making the land even more fertile. To pay for his building projects and to maintain his army, Nebuchadnezzar had to collect very high taxes and tributes. Because his empire stretched as far as Egypt, it had to have an efficient system of government.

One Greek historian in the 400s B.C. described the beauty of Babylon. He wrote, "In magnificence, there is no other city that approaches it." Outside the center of Babylon stood houses and marketplaces. There artisans made pottery, cloth, and baskets. The major trade route between the Persian Gulf and the Mediterranean Sea passed through Babylon. Merchants came to the city in traveling groups called **caravans** (KAR•uh•VANZ). They bought Babylonian goods —pottery, cloth, baskets, and jewelry. Babylon grew wealthy from this trade; under the Assyrians, the area had been fairly poor.

The people of Babylon also made many scientific advancements. The Chaldeans, like other people in Mesopotamia, believed that the gods showed their plans in the changes in the sky. Chaldean **astronomers** (uh•STRAH•nuh•muhrs)—people who study the heavenly bodies—mapped the stars, the planets, and the phases of the moon as it changed. The Chaldeans invented one of the first sundials to measure time. They also were the first to follow a seven-day week.

The Fall of the Empire

After Nebuchadnezzar died, a series of weak kings ruled the Chaldean empire. Poor harvests and slow trade further weakened the empire. In 539 B.C., the Persians recognized

caravan a group of merchants traveling together for safety, usually with a large number of camels

astronomer a person who studies planets and stars

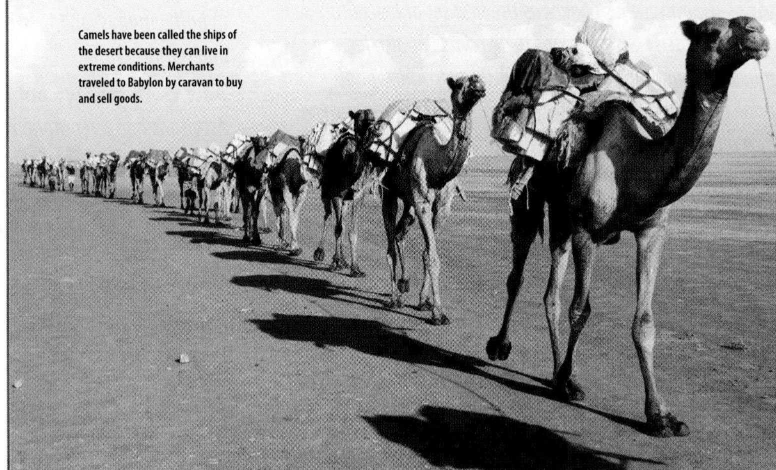

Camels have been called the ships of the desert because they can live in extreme conditions. Merchants traveled to Babylon by caravan to buy and sell goods.

that the Chaldeans had lost their strength and leadership. The Persians took advantage and captured Babylon and made Mesopotamia part of their empire. However, they allowed their newly captured land to keep its distinct culture. The Persians wisely did not want to destroy all the Chaldeans had accomplished.

PROGRESS CHECK

Identifying Which wonder of the ancient world was located in Babylon?

LESSON 2 REVIEW

Review Vocabulary

1. How could *caravans* passing through Babylon be helped by *astronomers*?
2. How might conquered people feel about paying *tribute* to the Assyrians?

Answer the Guiding Questions

3. ***Comparing*** How did Hammurabi's Code differ from earlier Sumerian laws?
4. ***Describing*** How did the Assyrians rule their empire?
5. ***Explaining*** Why did the Chaldeans overthrow the Assyrians?
6. **PERSUASIVE WRITING** You live in an area that the Assyrian army is attempting to conquer. Write a speech that you might give to your neighbors to persuade them either to defend themselves or to surrender without a fight.

LESSON 2

IF YOU HAVE MORE TIME . . .

Reexamine the Influence of Rivers on Mesopotamian Cultures

Making Inferences Have students make inferences about the influence of the Tigris and Euphrates Rivers on the empires of Mesopotamia.

Ask:

- **How do you think the Tigris and Euphrates Rivers helped the formation of the empires of Mesopotamia?** *(Answers will vary. Students might answer that the rivers helped with the movement of troops.)*
- **How did these rivers help unify these empires?** *(Answers will vary. Students might mention that the rivers could have been used to send messages and goods, which would help communication and trade.)*

Discuss Assyrian Innovations

Summarizing Remind students that the Assyrians built on what they learned from other Mesopotamian peoples. They were also innovators. An innovator is someone who comes up with a new idea.

Ask:

- **What are some of the ideas the Assyrians learned or adapted from other Mesopotamian peoples?** *(They learned about iron production from the Hittites. They had law codes and worshiped many of the same gods as other Mesopotamian peoples. They based their writing on Babylonian writing.)*
- **What are some Assyrian innovations, and how did they have a lasting effect?** *(Iron weapons were a factor in Assyrian success. The Assyrians divided their empire into provinces to make it easier to govern. They built one of the world's first libraries at Nineveh, which has helped historians learn about ancient civilizations.)*

Discuss the Wonders of the Ancient World

Classifying Remind students that the Hanging Gardens of Babylon were considered one of the Seven Wonders of the Ancient World.

Ask:

Can you name any of the six other wonders of the ancient world? *(Students may correctly guess that the pyramids of Egypt were another of the Seven Wonders.)*

Have students research the Seven Wonders of the Ancient World. Have each student write a paragraph about one of the Seven Wonders, describing it and explaining why it was considered so important. Suggest that students illustrate their reports if possible.

Ask:

If you were making a list of the Seven Wonders of the Modern World, what would you put on it? *(Answers will vary.)*

List students' suggestions on the whiteboard. Then have the class vote on a list of Seven Wonders of the Modern World.

Simulate Babylonian Trade Using an Economics of History Activity

INTERACTIVE WORKSHEET

Trading Using Money Tell students that the Babylonians began to use money when they traded. Have students complete the Economics of History Activity to help them understand how the Babylonians traded using coins.

Be sure students understand the information presented about haggling as a bargaining technique. This will assist them in doing the trading exercise. Have students work in groups to complete the activity.

Then, ask:

- **Was your trading successful? Explain.** *(Answers will vary, but students might respond "no" because they did not get all the goods they needed.)*
- **Do you like using haggling in the buying and selling process? Explain.** *(Answers will vary. Students might say they do not like haggling because some people could buy a good for less money than other people, depending on how well they haggled. Other students might say they liked the haggling process because they got bargains by using it or because they enjoyed the competitive aspect.)*

Compare and Contrast the Mesopotamian Empires

Discussing Conduct a brief class discussion to compare and contrast the empires of Sumer, Akkad, Assyria, and Babylon. Ask volunteers to describe each empire and its characteristics.

As students compare and contrast the empires, remind them to use words that reflect similarities and differences. Students should use words such as *similarly, like,* or *in the same way* to describe similar characteristics. They might use words such as *on the other hand, in a different way,* or *although.* AL

Answers for pages 90–93

P. 90 GEOGRAPHY CONNECTION

1. To reach the Persian Gulf, people would travel south and east from Sidon.
2. CRITICAL THINKING The Chaldeans became traders because they had easy access to other regions by way of the Mediterranean Sea and the Persian Gulf, which their empire bordered.

P. 91 CRITICAL THINKING People built large structures to honor their rulers or their gods.

P. 93 ☑ PROGRESS CHECK the Hanging Gardens

LESSON 2 REVIEW

1. Babylon was a trading center, and astronomers could help merchants traveling in caravans with scheduling and weather predictions.
2. People might feel upset. Paying tribute to the Assyrians meant the Assyrians had conquered them.
3. Hammurabi's Code provided the first written rule of law, forcing all people to follow the law in how they treated others.
4. The Assyrians divided their empire into provinces and chose officials to collect taxes and enforce laws.
5. The Assyrians were merciless to those they defeated. When the Assyrians fought among themselves, the Chaldeans rebelled and destroyed the Assyrian Empire.
6. The speeches should be informative and persuasive and reflect accurate details based on the description of Assyrian warfare in the text.

CHAPTER 4 Activities

Write your answers on a separate piece of paper.

1. **Exploring the Essential Question**
EXPOSITORY WRITING How would you describe the influence of Mesopotamia's physical geography on the region? Write an expository essay about how geography influenced the way people lived in Mesopotamia. Think about the Tigris River and the Euphrates River and the effect of flooding on the region. Include information about how geography influenced the formation of city-states in your essay.

2. **21st Century Skills**
CREATING A COMMUNICATIONS PRODUCT Write a script for a documentary about the technological and mathematical contributions made by the Sumerians. Divide your script into two columns. The left column should include the narration for your documentary. The right column should describe the images that will be shown. These images should match with the narration in the left column. Read your script to the class, or, if you have access to a video camera, shoot a short film based on your script.

3. **Thinking Like a Historian**
IDENTIFYING Create a diagram like the one here to identify types of archeological evidence that researchers might search for to learn about ancient Mesopotamia.

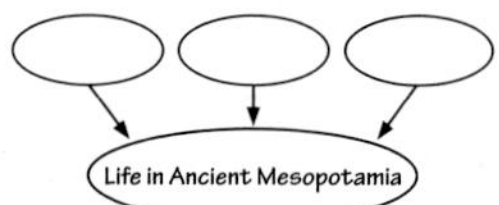

4. **GEOGRAPHY ACTIVITY**

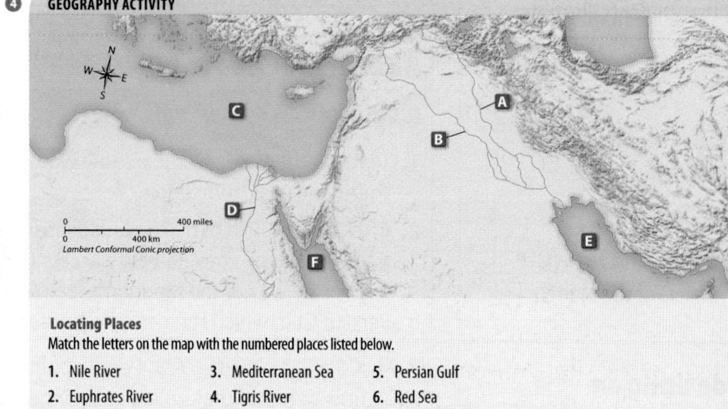

Locating Places
Match the letters on the map with the numbered places listed below.

1. Nile River
2. Euphrates River
3. Mediterranean Sea
4. Tigris River
5. Persian Gulf
6. Red Sea

CHAPTER 4 Assessment

REVIEW THE GUIDING QUESTIONS
Directions: Choose the best answer for each question.

1. In Mesopotamia, floods deposited silt, which made the soil
A. rocky.
B. fertile.
C. dry.
D. barren.

2. Which of the following groups belonged to the Sumerian middle class?
F. government officials
G. warriors
H. merchants
I. enslaved people

3. Sumerians developed a 12-month calendar by recording the
A. position of planets and stars.
B. length of the seasons.
C. amount of flooding.
D number of days with rainfall.

4. Who developed the first empire in Mesopotamia?
F. Hammurabi
G. Sargon
H. Ashurbanipal
I. Nabopolassar

5. What did Assyrians often demand from the people they conquered?
A. leaving their homes
B. participation in elections
C. volunteers for the army
D. the worship of gods

6. The astronomers of Babylon mapped
F. the irrigation canals.
G. the ocean currents.
H. the nearby mountains.
I. the stars and the planets.

DBQ DOCUMENT-BASED QUESTIONS

This excerpt comes from a poem called "The Mesopotamian View of Death" that was written by an unknown Mesopotamian mother.

Hark the piping!

My heart is piping in the wilderness
where the young man once went free.

He is a prisoner now in death's kingdom
lies bound where once he lived.

The ewe gives up her lamb
and the nanny goat her kid

My heart is piping in the wilderness,
an instrument of grief.

—"The Mesopotamian View of Death," *Poems of Heaven and Hell from Ancient Mesopotamia*, N. K. Sanders, trans

CHAPTER 4 Assessment *(continued)*

7. **Drawing Conclusions** What has happened to the young man in the poem?
A. He has died.
B. He is in prison for life.
C. He is a successful warrior.
D. He tends a flock of sheep.

8. **Explaining** How does the mother react to what has happened?
F. She wants a chance to hug her son again.
G. She blames the king for what has happened.
H. She says she should have been tending her sheep.
I. She believes that her body is acting out her feelings.

SHORT RESPONSE

"The vast majority of the inhabitants of Babylonia, Assyria, and other Mesopotamian empires were poor and had no political power. . . .

"Under some circumstances a person could change his or her social status. . . . a trader or merchant who was uncommonly diligent or lucky in business might . . . be able to afford his own plots of land."

—from *Empires of Mesopotamia* by Don Nardo

9. How might a trader improve his social status?

10. How did a person show their wealth at this time? Do you think people often improved their social status in ancient Mesopotamia? Explain your answer.

EXTENDED RESPONSE

11. **Descriptive Writing** You are a diplomat from Egypt who is visiting Babylon around 565 B.C. The leader of your country wants information about the city, including the Hanging Gardens. How is the city organized? What do the Hanging Gardens look like? Write a report that describes Babylon, and give your opinion about the city.

Need Extra Help?

If You've Missed Question	1	2	3	4	5	6	7	8	9	10	11
Review Lesson	1	1	1	2	2	2	2	1, 2	1	1	2

NOTES

REFLECT, REVIEW, & REMEDIATE

INTERACTIVE WORKSHEET

Chapter Summary

Provide students with the Chapter Summary worksheet to help review the chapter and prepare for assessment.

Reviewing the Enduring Understandings

Review this chapter's Enduring Understandings with students:
- People, places, and ideas change over time.
- Cultures are held together by shared beliefs and common practices and values.

INTERACTIVE WHITEBOARD ACTIVITY On the interactive whiteboard, have a student volunteer create a two-column chart and write "Sumer" in one column and "Assyria" in the other. Then lead a discussion that allows students to recall features of daily life, the economy, and key events for each civilization. The student volunteer should record these features in the chart.

	Sumer	Assyria
Daily Life		
Economy		
Key Events		

ACTIVITIES ANSWERS

Exploring the Essential Question

1. Students' essays should note the effect of the Tigris and Euphrates Rivers on Mesopotamians. They should discuss how these rivers affected transportation and farming. They might also include how Mesopotamians dealt with flooding and why city-states became independent units.

21st Century Skills

2. Students' scripts or videos should have narration that describes the major technological and mathematical contributions of the Sumerians in an engaging manner. Key contributions include the wheel, the calendar, bronze, the cuneiform system of writing, and the invention of a system of numbers. The visuals should be compelling and match the narration.

Thinking Like a Historian

3. Graphic organizers might contain responses such as archaeological evidence from ancient cities, uncovered artifacts such as pottery or tools, or writings on clay tablets.

Locating Places

4. Letters should match the correct geographic locations.
1. D, **2.** B, **3.** C, **4.** A, **5.** E, **6.** F

ASSESSMENT ANSWERS

Review the Guiding Questions

1. **B** Silt has small particles of soil. It does not contain rocks. Silt would not make the soil drier or wetter. It does not damage the soil and would not make the soil barren. When silt is deposited on the land, it makes the soil more fertile. Thus, choice B is the correct answer.

2. **H** Merchants belonged to the middle class. Government officials and warriors belonged to the upper class, and enslaved people belonged to the lower class. So choice H is the correct answer.

3. **A** The amount of flooding and the number of days with rainfall are not relevant. The length of seasons can vary and is not precise enough to use for a calendar. By recording the positions of the planets and the stars, Sumerians developed a 12-month calendar based on the phases of the moon. The correct answer is choice A.

4. **G** Hammurabi, Ashurbanipal, and Nabopolassar lived centuries after Sargon. As leader of Akkad, Sargon developed the first Mesopotamian Empire when he conquered the Sumerian cities. So G is the correct answer.

5. **A** The Assyrians often forced the people they conquered to leave their homes. They did not hold elections and did not force captives to join their army. They worshiped many of the same gods as people they conquered and did not force conquered people to worship. Thus, choice A is the correct answer.

6. **I** Astronomers do not map Earth's geographic features. Babylonian astronomers mapped the stars and the planets. Choice I is the correct answer.

Document-Based Questions

7. **A** Although the young man is imprisoned, it is in "death's kingdom," not a physical jail. The excerpt does not address his skills as a warrior and does not say whether he has been a shepherd. It does say that he is dead, so choice A is the correct answer.

8. **I** The excerpt does not address the mother's desire to hug her son and does not suggest that she assigns blame for his death. She speaks of sheep and goats giving up their young, not of tending sheep. She feels that her heart cries out her grief in the keening tones of a musical instrument. Choice I is the correct answer.

Short Response

9. Student responses should mention that the trader might make a lucky deal, prosper through hard work, or benefit from a combination of the two.

10. No, wealth is shown by owning land. The author states that most people in the Mesopotamian empires were poor and had no political power, which suggests that few people had high social status and that improving it was not a common occurrence.

Extended Response

11. Students' reports should contain phrases that describe the design of the city, the ziggurat, and the Hanging Gardens. Students should give their opinion as a visitor from Egypt.

ONLINE RESOURCES
networks

There's More Online!

- INTERACTIVE WORKSHEETS
- BIOGRAPHIES
- CHARTS/GRAPHS
- GAMES
- GRAPHIC ORGANIZERS
- IMAGES
- MAPS
- PRIMARY SOURCES
- SLIDE SHOWS
- TIME LINE
- LECTURE SLIDES
- INTERACTIVE WHITEBOARD ACTIVITIES
- ASSESSMENTS
- VIDEOS

The Nile River

Life in Ancient Egypt

Chapter 5
Ancient Egypt and Kush

Dear World History Teacher,

Egypt, like Mesopotamia, was a river valley civilization. Of central importance to the development of Egyptian civilization was the Nile River, whose significance was even celebrated by the people in song.

Of equal importance in Egyptian history was the pharaoh, who was, in theory, a god who maintained fundamental order and harmony within the kingdom. While obeying the pharaoh, subjects helped maintain the cosmic order. The pharaoh was also celebrated in song.

Egypt produced a culture that dazzled and awed its later conquerors. The Egyptians' technical achievements alone, especially visible in the construction of the pyramids, demonstrated a measure of skill that was unique to the world at that time. These achievements were part of a universal organization filled with the presence of the divine. The Egyptians had no word for religion because it was an inseparable element of the world order to which Egyptian society belonged.

The Egyptians made an impact in the south in Nubia, which became the independent state of Kush. Kushite culture borrowed elements from Egypt, including hieroglyphs, religious beliefs, and the practice of interring kings in pyramids.

Jackson J. Spielvogel

More Media Resources

Current Events Online

Visit McGraw-Hill's current events Web site for high-interest news stories and activities for your students. Access the site through the Student or Teacher Center in **networks.**

Reading List

Grade 6 reading level:
Voices of Ancient Egypt, by Kay Winters

Grade 7 reading level:
Ancient Egypt, by Andrew Haslam and Alexandra Parsons

Grade 8 reading level:
Curse of the Pharaohs: My Adventures with Mummies, by Zahi Hawass

At the MOVIES

Watch clips of popular culture films about Ancient Egypt, such as Cecil B. DeMille's *The Ten Commandments* (1956) or Warner Brothers' *The Prince of Egypt* (1998). Alternatively, view documentaries about Egyptian civilization, such as National Geographic's *The Mysteries of Egypt* (1998).

Discuss: **Can fictional movies capture historical events accurately?**

NOTE: Be sure to preview any clips to ensure they are age-appropriate.

Search for videos online in the **networks** Resource Library.

CHAPTER 5 Planner

UNDERSTANDING BY DESIGN®

Enduring Understandings

- *People, places, and ideas change over time.* • *Cultures are held together by shared beliefs and common practices and values.*

Essential Questions

- *How does geography influence the way people live?* • *What makes a culture unique?*
- *Why do civilizations rise and fall?*

Students will know:

- *why the Nile River was important to the ancient Egyptians*
- *characteristics of ancient Egyptian religion and society*
- *factors that led to the rise and fall of the ancient Egyptian empire*
- *how Kush and Egypt influenced each other*

Students will be able to:

- **compare** information on populations of the Fertile Crescent and Nile River valley
- **describe** a main agricultural product and its economic effect on ancient Egypt
- **predict** how the Nile River affected Egyptian life
- **analyze** the predictions about how the Nile River affected Egyptian life
- **analyze** how belief in the afterlife influenced ancient Egyptian life
- **describe** ancient Egyptian social classes
- **analyze** life from the perspective of one of ancient Egypt's social classes
- **organize** information on a pharaoh's responsibilities
- **analyze** visuals from Egypt's golden age
- **describe** an empire and how it is built
- **identify** reasons Egypt reached the height of its power
- **write** a description of characteristics of a pharaoh
- **explain** how the pharaoh contributed to the rise and fall of the Egyptian empire
- **analyze** the exchange of goods and ideas among Kush, Egypt, and Assyria
- **illustrate** the trade relationship between Kush and its trading partners

Predictable Misunderstandings

Students may think:

- Egypt is not part of Africa.
- All of Egypt is desert.
- The Nile River flows south from the Mediterranean Sea.

Assessment Evidence

Performance Task

- Hands-On Chapter Project

Other Evidence

- Class discussion answers
- Class simulation participation
- Interactive Whiteboard Activity responses
- Brainstorming activity
- Geography and History Activity
- Economics of History Activities
- 21st Century Skills Activities
- Lesson Reviews
- Evaluation of class simulation
- Writing activities

Pacing Guide

Introducing the Chapter	1 day
Lesson 1 The Nile River	2 days
Lesson 2 Life in Ancient Egypt	2 days
Lesson 3 Egypt's Empire	2 days
Lesson 4 The Kingdom of Kush	1 day
Chapter Activities and Assessment	1 day
TOTAL TIME	**9 Days**

Differentiated Instruction

These lesson plans are written to address the needs of your On Level students. Discussion and activities that are well-suited to your Approaching Grade Level learners, Beyond Grade Level learners, as well as your English Language Learners are coded as follows:

AL Approaching Grade Level

BL Beyond Grade Level

ELL English Language Learner

NCSS Standards covered in "Ancient Egypt and Kush"

Learners will understand:

1 CULTURE

4. That the beliefs, values, and behaviors of a culture form an integrated system that helps shape the activities and ways of life that define a culture

3 PEOPLE, PLACES, AND ENVIRONMENTS

1. The theme of people, places, and environments involves the study of the relationships between human populations in different locations and geographic phenomena such as climate, vegetation, and natural resources

7. Human modifications of the environment

4 INDIVIDUAL DEVELOPMENT AND IDENTITY

3. How factors such as physical endowment, interests, capabilities, learning, motivation, personality, perception, and beliefs influence individual development and identity

5 INDIVIDUALS, GROUPS, AND INSTITUTIONS

7. That institutions may promote or undermine social conformity

9. That groups and institutions influence culture in a variety of ways

8 SCIENCE, TECHNOLOGY, AND SOCIETY

2. Society often turns to science and technology to solve problems

4. Science and technology have had both positive and negative impacts upon individuals, societies, and the environment in the past and present

5. Science and technology have changed peoples' perceptions of the social and natural world, as well as their relationship to the land, economy and trade, their concept of security, and their major daily activities

CHAPTER 5

Introducing the Chapter

(Student Edition p. 97)

The Story Matters . . .

Read "The Story Matters . . ." aloud in class. Then discuss what it might have been like to have been a young person living in ancient Egypt, where death was the focus of daily life.

Ask:

How do you honor your ancestors or the people who came before you? Have a few students share their stories.

Then ask:

How would you like to be remembered by the generations that follow you? What stories or memories of your life would you like people to share?

Tell the class that Egypt's dry, sandy climate helped preserve ancient artifacts and monuments for thousands of years. Well-preserved carvings and other artifacts from the ancient pyramids tell us most of what we know about this ancient culture and its history.

Tell students that they can view the rediscovered treasures of ancient Egypt online.

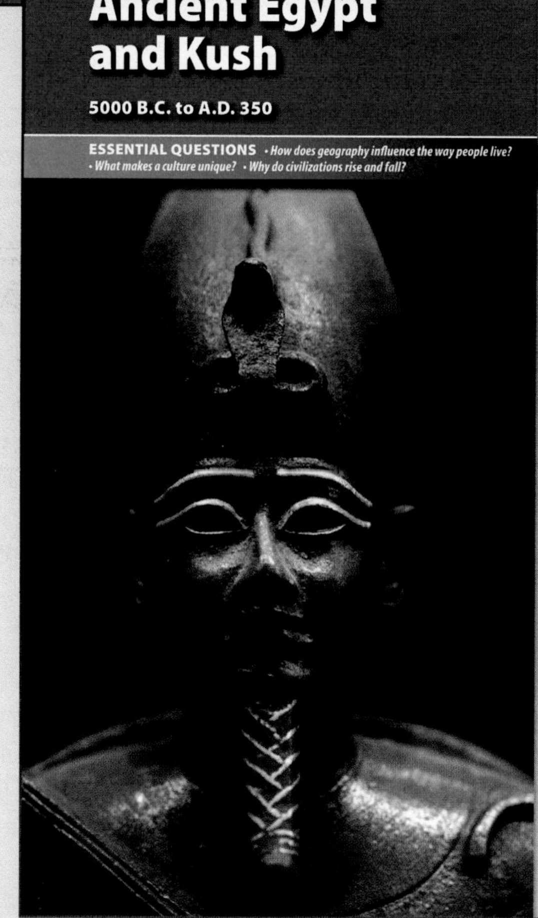

Ancient Egypt and Kush

5000 B.C. to A.D. 350

ESSENTIAL QUESTIONS *• How does geography influence the way people live? • What makes a culture unique? • Why do civilizations rise and fall?*

networks

There's More Online about the cultures of ancient Egypt and Kush

CHAPTER 5

Lesson 1 *The Nile River*

Lesson 2 *Life in Ancient Egypt*

Lesson 3 *Egypt's Empire*

Lesson 4 *The Kingdom of Kush*

The Story Matters . . .

When you think of the most powerful person in your country, who is it? Is it the president? For ancient Egyptians, one of the most important beings was the god Osiris. Osiris controlled the power of life and death. As the god of agriculture, he controlled the very food Egyptians ate. He allowed the Nile River to flood its banks and bring fertile soil and water to the Egyptian desert. Osiris also knew death. In the underworld, the souls of the dead met the god Osiris. He did not have the power to return the dead to life, but he was a symbol of ongoing life. As you read this chapter, you will learn how the forces of life and death shaped the daily life of the ancient Egyptians and Kushites.

◄ *The god Osiris was respected because he represented new life and new crops.*

Corbis

97

Introducing Place and Time

(Student Edition pp. 98–99)

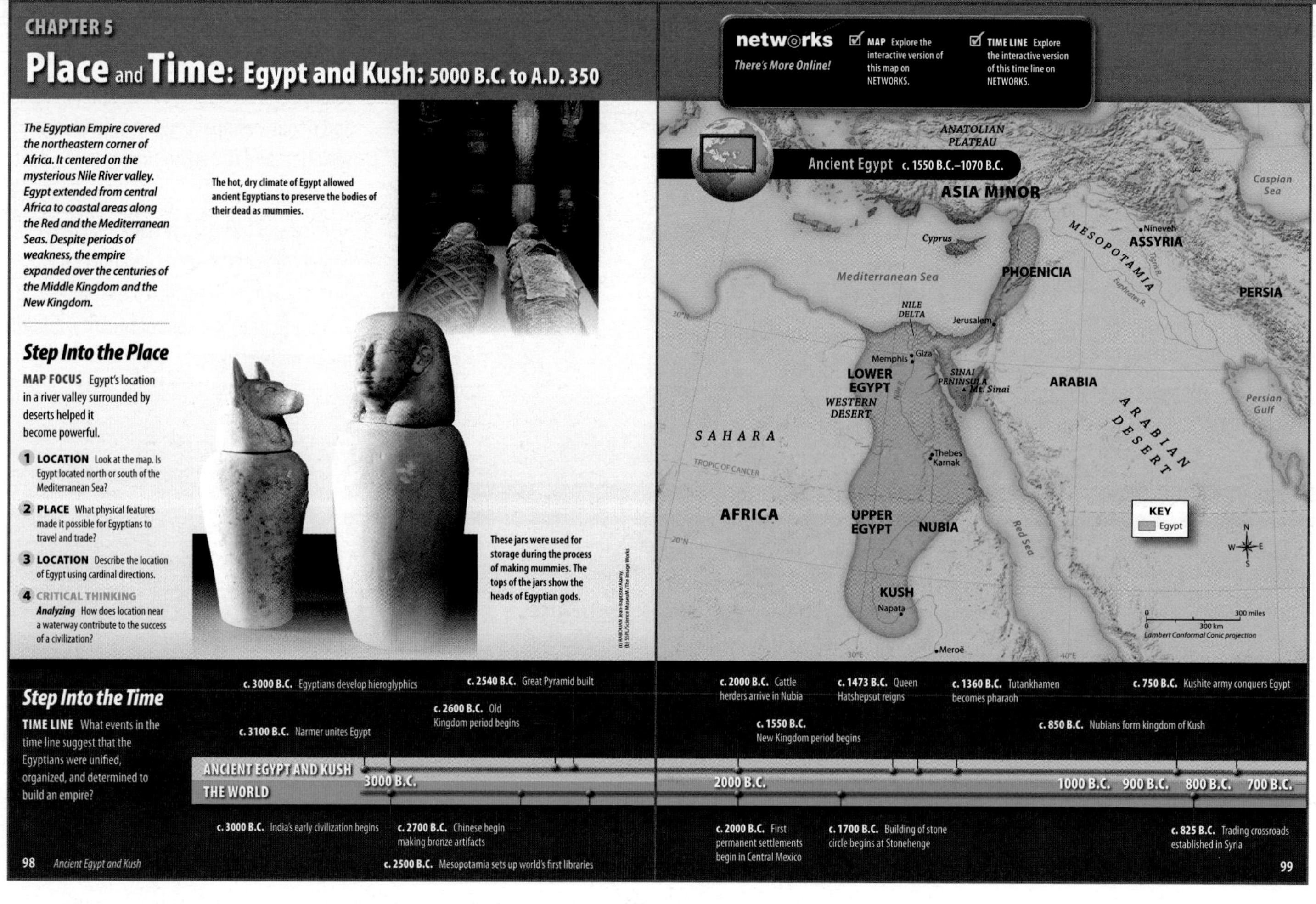

CHAPTER 5

Place and Time: Egypt and Kush: 5000 B.C. to A.D. 350

The Egyptian Empire covered the northeastern corner of Africa. It centered on the mysterious Nile River valley. Egypt extended from central Africa to coastal areas along the Red and the Mediterranean Seas. Despite periods of weakness, the empire expanded over the centuries of the Middle Kingdom and the New Kingdom.

The hot, dry climate of Egypt allowed ancient Egyptians to preserve the bodies of their dead as mummies.

Step Into the Place

MAP FOCUS Egypt's location in a river valley surrounded by deserts helped it become powerful.

1. **LOCATION** Look at the map. Is Egypt located north or south of the Mediterranean Sea?
2. **PLACE** What physical features made it possible for Egyptians to travel and trade?
3. **LOCATION** Describe the location of Egypt using cardinal directions.
4. **CRITICAL THINKING** *Analyzing* How does location near a waterway contribute to the success of a civilization?

These jars were used for storage during the process of making mummies. The tops of the jars show the heads of Egyptian gods.

(t) RABOUAN Jean-Baptiste/Alamy, (b) SSPL/Science Museum/The Image Works

networks *There's More Online!*

☑ MAP Explore the interactive version of this map on NETWORKS.

☑ TIME LINE Explore the interactive version of this time line on NETWORKS.

Step Into the Time

TIME LINE What events in the time line suggest that the Egyptians were unified, organized, and determined to build an empire?

ANCIENT EGYPT AND KUSH

- **c. 3100 B.C.** Narmer unites Egypt
- **c. 3000 B.C.** Egyptians develop hieroglyphics
- **c. 2600 B.C.** Old Kingdom period begins
- **c. 2540 B.C.** Great Pyramid built
- **c. 2000 B.C.** Cattle herders arrive in Nubia
- **c. 1550 B.C.** New Kingdom period begins
- **c. 1473 B.C.** Queen Hatshepsut reigns
- **c. 1360 B.C.** Tutankhamen becomes pharaoh
- **c. 850 B.C.** Nubians form kingdom of Kush
- **c. 750 B.C.** Kushite army conquers Egypt

3000 B.C. 2000 B.C. 1000 B.C. 900 B.C. 800 B.C. 700 B.C.

THE WORLD

- **c. 3000 B.C.** India's early civilization begins
- **c. 2700 B.C.** Chinese begin making bronze artifacts
- **c. 2500 B.C.** Mesopotamia sets up world's first libraries
- **c. 2000 B.C.** First permanent settlements begin in Central Mexico
- **c. 1700 B.C.** Building of stone circle begins at Stonehenge
- **c. 825 B.C.** Trading crossroads established in Syria

98 *Ancient Egypt and Kush*

99

Technology Extension

- Find an additional activity online that incorporates technology for this project.
- Visit the EdTechTeacher Web sites (included in the Technology Extension for this chapter) for more links, tutorials, and other resources.

Assessing Background Knowledge

INTERACTIVE WORKSHEET

What Do You Know? Activity

Have students complete the What Do You Know? Activity by looking at the photographs of ancient Egyptian pyramids and answering the questions.

Remind students that they are not expected to know the answers before reading the chapter. They should draw on prior knowledge and make their own inferences and conclusions based on the photographs.

After students complete the chapter, have them review the photographs and revise their answers to the questions, if necessary. Ask students to cite facts from the chapter to support their revised answers.

INTERACTIVE WORKSHEET

Guided Reading Activities

There is a Guided Reading Activity for each lesson in this chapter. You may wish to assign the Guided Reading Activity for Lesson 1 after introducing the chapter content.

Hands-On Chapter Project

Each student will create a sarcophagus that represents his or her identity and personal interests.

- Students will take part in a class discussion to activate their background knowledge about Egyptian sarcophagi.
- Then, each student will plan and construct a "shoe-box" sarcophagus, using worksheets as a guide.
- Next, students will write an explanation of their sarcophagi and its contents. They will present their work to the class.
- Finally, students will evaluate their sarcophagi, explanations, and presentations using an Assessment Rubric.

Visit **networks** online to see the full project and rubric.

ONLINE RESOURCES

networks

Assign these interactive worksheets and quizzes from your Teacher Lesson Center. All resources are print-ready.

It's ALL Online!

CHAPTER 5 RESOURCES

- ☑ CHAPTER SUMMARY
- ☑ VOCABULARY BUILDER
- ☑ WHAT DO YOU KNOW?
- ☑ HANDS-ON CHAPTER PROJECT

Lesson 1 Resources

- ☑ GEOGRAPHY AND HISTORY Understanding Location: Ancient Egypt
- ☑ ECONOMICS OF HISTORY ACTIVITY Scarcity and Ancient Egyptian Farmers
- ☑ GUIDED READING ACTIVITY
- ☑ READING ESSENTIALS AND STUDY GUIDE
- ☑ ONLINE SELF-CHECK QUIZ

Lesson 2 Resources

- ☑ INTERACTIVE GRAPHIC ORGANIZER
- ☑ 21ST CENTURY SKILLS Making Connections
- ☑ GUIDED READING ACTIVITY
- ☑ READING ESSENTIALS AND STUDY GUIDE
- ☑ ONLINE SELF-CHECK QUIZ

Lesson 3 Resources

- ☑ INTERACTIVE GRAPHIC ORGANIZER
- ☑ 21ST CENTURY SKILLS
- ☑ GUIDED READING ACTIVITY
- ☑ READING ESSENTIALS AND STUDY GUIDE
- ☑ ONLINE SELF-CHECK QUIZ

Lesson 4 Resources

- ☑ INTERACTIVE GRAPHIC ORGANIZER
- ☑ ECONOMICS OF HISTORY The Exchange of Goods and Ideas
- ☑ GUIDED READING ACTIVITY
- ☑ READING ESSENTIALS AND STUDY GUIDE
- ☑ ONLINE SELF-CHECK QUIZ

ASSESSMENT RESOURCES

- ☑ LESSON REVIEWS
- ☑ ONLINE SELF-CHECK QUIZZES
- ☑ CHAPTER ACTIVITIES AND ASSESSMENT
- ☑ STANDARDIZED TEST PRACTICE

REMEDIATION RESOURCES

- ☑ READING ESSENTIALS AND STUDY GUIDE
- ☑ GUIDED READING ACTIVITIES
- ☑ ONLINE SELF-CHECK QUIZZES
- ☑ CHAPTER SUMMARY

Step Into the Place

INTERACTIVE WHITEBOARD

Location Project the Interactive Atlas on the whiteboard. Focus on the region of North Africa and Southwest Asia. Remind students about the rise and fall of the Mesopotamians. Discuss as a class how geographical features of a place or region provided protection from enemies as well as opportunities for farming and trade.

At your whiteboard, have student volunteers analyze the map and draw circles around the deserts in the region. Then ask students what impact the deserts might have had on the development of ancient Egypt.

Next, as a class, discuss the Map Focus questions.

Step Into the Time

Sequencing Have students review the time line for the chapter. Explain that they will be studying events from about 5000 B.C. to 700 B.C. Use the time line in the chapter to remind students how B.C. dates are arranged from higher to lower numerals. Help students by suggesting that they think of B.C. dates as a countdown, beginning around 5000 and counting down to zero.

Ask students: **Was the year 1250 B.C. before or after 1400 B.C.?** *(after)* **Was the year 825 B.C. before or after 750 B.C.?** *(before)*

Continue to quiz students, using random dates until they demonstrate command of the concept.

Answers for pages 98–99

Step Into the Place

1. south
2. the Nile River, the Red Sea, and the Mediterranean Sea
3. Egypt is south of the Mediterranean Sea and west of the Red Sea.
4. CRITICAL THINKING A waterway provides water for drinking and growing crops as well as a trade route.

Step Into the Time

Students may cite: Narmer unites Egypt, the Egyptians develop hieroglyphics, and the Great Pyramid is built.

networks
There's More Online!
- ☑ **DIAGRAM** How Egyptians Made Papyrus
- ☑ **GRAPHIC ORGANIZER** Benefits of the Nile
- ☑ **MAP**
  - Ancient Egypt
  - Early Trade Routes

Lesson 1

The Nile River

ESSENTIAL QUESTION *How does geography influence the way people live?*

It Matters Because

The Nile River was the most important factor in the development of ancient Egypt.

1 The Nile River Valley

GUIDING QUESTION *Why was the Nile River important to the ancient Egyptians?*

While empires flourished and fell in Mesopotamia, two other civilizations developed along the Nile River in northeastern Africa. One of these civilizations was Egypt (EE•jihpt). It developed in the northern part of the Nile River valley. The other civilization, Kush (CUSH), emerged in the far southern part of the Nile River valley. Although Egypt and Kush were **unique** civilizations, they influenced one another throughout their long histories.

Valley Civilization

The Nile River valley was ideal for human settlement because of its fertile land. As early as 5000 B.C., hunters and gatherers from the drier areas of Africa and Southwest Asia began to move into the Nile River valley. Permanent settlements were created by early groups who farmed the land and built villages along the Nile's banks. These people were the earliest Egyptians and Kushites.

The early Egyptians lived in the northern region of the Nile River valley. They called their land *Kemet* (KEH•meht), which means "black land," after the dark, rich soil. Later, this northern Nile area would be called *Egypt*. Of the world's early river valley civilizations, you probably are most familiar with ancient Egypt. People still marvel at its ruins located in present-day Egypt. These ruins include the enormous stone Sphinx that has the body of a lion and a human head. Archaeologists also study the wondrous pyramids and the mummies found buried in tombs once full of riches.

The Gift of the River

Many of ancient Egypt's structures survived because Egypt has a hot, dry climate. Since the region receives little rainfall, ancient Egyptians depended on the Nile for drinking and bathing. The river also supplied water to grow crops. To the Egyptians, the Nile was the "creator of all good." They praised it in a hymn:

PRIMARY SOURCE

> "You create the grain, you bring forth the barley,
> Assuring perpetuity [survival] to the temples.
> If you cease your toil and your work,
> Then all that exists is in anguish [suffering]."
>
> —from "Hymn to the Nile"

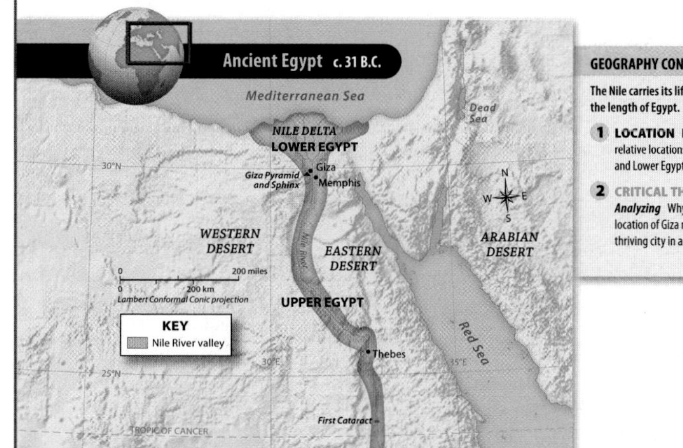

GEOGRAPHY CONNECTION

The Nile carries its life-giving water the length of Egypt.

1. **LOCATION** Describe the relative locations of Upper Egypt and Lower Egypt.
2. **CRITICAL THINKING** *Analyzing* Why do you think the location of Giza made it an early thriving city in ancient Egypt?

Reading HELPDESK

Taking Notes: *Identifying*
Use a web diagram like this one to identify three reasons why most ancient Egyptians lived near the Nile River.

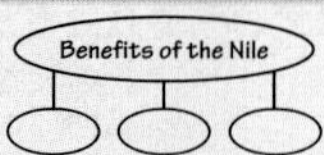

Content Vocabulary
- **cataract**
- **delta**
- **shadoof**
- **papyrus**
- **hieroglyphics**
- **dynasty**

Academic Vocabulary
unique one of a kind; different from all others

Thinking Like a HISTORIAN

Researching on the Internet

As the "lifeblood" of Egypt, the Nile River was and continues to be essential to daily life in Egypt. It is also important to the other places through which it flows. Use the Internet to find reliable sources about the lands through which the Nile River and its tributaries run. Identify three facts that you discover about the Nile River from your research and present them to the class. For more information about using the Internet for research, read the chapter *What Does a Historian Do?*

Narrow cataracts on the Nile limit river travel, especially for larger ships.

Do you know which is the world's longest river? It is the Nile that flows north about 4,000 miles (6,437 km) from central Africa to the Mediterranean Sea. It has been called the "lifeblood" of Egypt.

At its source, the Nile is two separate rivers: the Blue Nile and the White Nile. The Blue Nile begins in the snowy mountains of eastern Africa. The White Nile starts in the tropics of central Africa. The two rivers join just south of Egypt to form the Nile River. There, steep cliffs and large boulders form dangerous, fast-moving waters called **cataracts** (KA•tuh•RAKTS). Cataracts make traveling by ship along the Nile difficult.

A Protected Land

As with many rivers, the Nile's flow throughout the centuries has created a valley. You can see on the map on the previous page that the Nile looks like the long winding root of a plant. Shortly before the Nile reaches the Mediterranean Sea, it splits into many branches that resemble a plant's bloom. These waterways form a fan-shaped area of fertile marshland called a **delta** (DEHL•tuh).

In the Nile River valley, we see the effect that water has on the landscape. The lush, green Nile valley and delta contrast sharply with the barren deserts that stretch out on either side of the river. The change in landscape can be so sudden that a person can stand with one foot in fertile soil and one foot in barren sand.

The Nile borders the largest deserts in the world. To the west of the Nile River is the Libyan Desert, which forms part of the Sahara (suh•HAR•uh). To the river's east lies the Eastern Desert that extends to the Red Sea. The ancient Egyptians called these deserts the "Red Land" because of their scorching heat. These large desert areas were not favorable to humans or animals. They kept Egypt **isolated,** however, from outside invaders.

In addition to the deserts, other physical features protected Egypt. To the far south, the Nile's dangerous cataracts prevented enemy ships from attacking Egypt. In the north, delta marshes stopped invaders who sailed from the Mediterranean Sea. These physical features gave the Egyptians advantages that Mesopotamians lacked. The Egyptians rarely faced the danger of invasion. As a result, Egyptian civilization developed peacefully.

The Egyptians, though isolated, were not completely cut off from other peoples. The Mediterranean Sea to the north and the Red Sea to the east provided routes for trade.

The stark contrast between watered and not watered land can be seen along the banks of the Nile.

Egyptians took advantage of the region's wind patterns so that they could travel and trade. Although the natural flow of the Nile's currents carried boats north, winds from the north pushed sailboats south.

☑ **PROGRESS CHECK**

Explaining How were the Egyptians protected by their physical environment?

2 People of the River

GUIDING QUESTION *How did the ancient Egyptians depend on the Nile River to grow their crops?*

We know that the Mesopotamians controlled the floods of the Tigris and Euphrates Rivers to grow crops. They developed the technology to do so, but the unpredictable rivers constantly challenged them. In Egypt, however, the flooding of the Nile River was seasonal and consistent from year to year. So the Egyptians did not face the same challenge.

Predictable Floods

As in Mesopotamia, flooding along the Nile in Egypt was common. The Nile floods, however, were more predictable and less destructive than those of the Tigris and the Euphrates. As a result, the Egyptians were not afraid that heavy floods would destroy their homes and crops. Each year, during late spring, heavy tropical rains in central Africa and melting mountain snow in eastern Africa added water to the Nile. Around the middle of summer, the Nile overflowed its banks and flooded the land. Egyptian farmers were ready to take advantage of this cycle. When the waters returned to their normal level in late fall, thick deposits of fertile soil remained.

Reading HELPDESK

cataract a waterfall or rapids in a river

delta a fan-shaped area of silt near where a river flows into the sea

Academic Vocabulary
isolate to separate from others

LESSON 1 • Day 1

ENGAGE

Comparing As a class, compare the populations of the Fertile Crescent and the Nile River valley. Tell students to locate in their textbooks the map of the Fertile Crescent from the previous chapter and the map of the Nile River valley in this chapter.

Ask:
- **What do the maps tell you about the populations of the Fertile Crescent and the Nile River valley?** *(People lived near the rivers.)*
- **What geographic features do both areas have in common?** *(Both areas have rivers surrounded by deserts.)*
- **Why did people in both places live near water?** *(Water is an important resource for drinking and growing crops.)* AL

Tell students that in this lesson, they will learn why the Nile River was important to the development of the Egyptian civilization.

TEACH & ASSESS

1 The Nile River Valley

GUIDING QUESTION ***Why was the Nile River important to ancient Egyptians?***

GRAPHIC ORGANIZER **Describing** Discuss as a class why people originally settled near the Nile River. Have students describe the Nile River and the land around it. Then have students complete the Taking Notes interactive graphic organizer.

Ask volunteers to share their organizers with the class. If necessary, review the meanings of key terms, such as *crops*, *drinking*, *soil*, and *transportation*. ELL

INTERACTIVE WORKSHEET

Geography and History Activity

Describing As a class, have students complete the Geography and History Activity for this chapter. Remind students to refer to their textbook for details as they complete the map and answer questions about the location of ancient Egypt.

Ask students the following questions about the features of the Nile River valley:
- **Where does the Nile River flow?** *(It flows north from Central Africa to the Mediterranean Sea.)*
- **What is the land like around the Nile River?** *(Most of the land on either side of the Nile is hot, sandy desert.)*
- **How has the Nile River affected the land in which it flows?** *(It has created a valley of fertile land in the desert.)*
- **What important resources did the Nile provide for settlers?** *(water for drinking, bathing, cooking, and farming; fertile soil for growing crops)*
- **How did the Nile River protect the people who lived near it?** *(The cataracts in the south prevented enemies from reaching Egyptian settlements. The delta in the north was too marshy so there was no port that invaders could reach.)*
- **How did the desert protect the Egyptians?** *(It was so hot and difficult to travel over that it kept enemies from reaching Egypt by land.)*
- **How did the Nile River help relations among Egyptian villages?** *(The river allowed for trade and travel among the villages.)*
- **How did the Nile affect Egyptian trade with other cities in the region?** *(It provided a route to other places for trading.)*

Comparing and Contrasting Have students return to the maps they studied in the Engage activity. Then ask students to work with partners to create a T-chart graphic organizer that compares how the geographic features of Egypt and Mesopotamia helped or hindered their respective civilizations. *(Because of the Nile River, Egyptians had friendly trade and relations among Nile villages and natural defenses, such as cataracts and marshy deltas, that protected them from invaders. Mesopotamians, on the other hand, lived in open spaces with no protection and had to face the danger of invasion.)*

CLOSE & REFLECT

Predicting As a class, brainstorm a list of predictions that answer this question: How did the Nile River affect Egyptian life?

Write student responses on the board. If students need help, remind them to look at the web diagram they completed in the Describing Activity, which identifies reasons why people lived near the Nile River.

Guide students by asking:
- **If you were an ancient Egyptian farmer, how would the Nile River have helped you?**
- **If you lived in an Egyptian village, how would the Nile River have protected you and your village?**

LESSON 1 • Day 2

ENGAGE

Predicting As a class, review students' predictions from the Day 1 Close & Reflect activity. Lead students in a discussion of the reasoning behind their predictions.

If necessary, review the process for making and confirming predictions as students continue to read and gather more information.

Ask:
- **What groups of people depended most on the Nile River?** *(farmers, traders, and workers)*
- **How did the Nile help Egypt grow and develop?** *(The Nile provided water for farming and drinking so the settlements could grow and develop and farmers could grow more food. It also provided protection so villages were safe and could grow. It allowed people to trade and travel.)*

Tell students that in this lesson, they will learn how the ancient Egyptians farmed, developed tools, created a system of writing, and united under one ruler.

TEACH & ASSESS

2 People of the River

GUIDING QUESTION ***How did ancient Egyptians depend on the Nile River to grow their crops?***

Determining Cause and Effect Help students understand how the flooding of the Nile River helped farmers. Have students work in pairs or small groups to create a cause-and-effect chart that identifies two effects of the Nile's regular flooding. *(Regular and predictable flooding meant that Egyptians did not have to fear that floods would destroy their homes and villages. The floods left fertile soil behind, which was good for growing crops.)* AL

Answers for pages 100–103

P. 100 Taking Notes The Nile provided water for crops, drinking, and bathing; rich soil for farming; a means of transportation; and security against attack.

P. 101 GEOGRAPHY CONNECTION

1. Lower Egypt is located north of Upper Egypt.
2. CRITICAL THINKING Giza's location near the Nile Delta made trade easier. Its location along the Nile River would have made agriculture easier too.

P. 103 ☑ PROGRESS CHECK The Nile River's cataracts and its marshy delta kept invaders out of Egypt. The hot, sandy deserts also prevented outsiders from reaching Egypt.

How Did Egyptians Farm?

Special techniques and tools—such as this shadoof—helped farmers grow crops in the dry season.

Farmers planted wheat, barley, and flax seeds while the soil was still wet. Over time, they grew enough food to feed themselves and the animals they raised.

During the dry season, Egyptian farmers irrigated their crops. They scooped out basins, or bowl-shaped holes, in the earth to store river water. They then dug canals that extended from the basins to the fields, allowing water to flow to their crops. Raised areas of soil provided support for the basin walls.

In time, Egyptian farmers developed new tools to make their work easier. For example, farmers created a **shadoof** (shuh•DOOF), which is a bucket attached to a long pole that lifts water from the Nile and empties it into basins. Many Egyptian farmers still use this method today.

Egyptian farmers also needed a way to measure the area of their lands. When floods washed away boundary markers that divided one field from another, farmers used geometry to help them recalculate where one field began and the other ended.

Egyptians gathered **papyrus** (puh•PY•ruhs), a reed plant that grew wild along the Nile. They used the long, thin reeds to weave rope, sandals, baskets, and river rafts. Later, they used

We learn about ancient farming methods from Egyptian art murals such as this.

▶ CRITICAL THINKING

Describing What details about ancient farming methods can you find in this painting of farmers?

Reading HELPDESK

shadoof a bucket attached to a long pole used to transfer river water to storage basins

papyrus to make paper. To do this, the Egyptians cut strips from the stalks of the papyrus plant and soaked them in water. Next, the strips were laid side by side and pounded together. They were then set out to dry, forming a large sheet of papyrus on which the Egyptians could write.

Papyrus reeds grow wild along rivers. From harvesting the reeds to final product, the process of making paper from papyrus took many days.

▶ CRITICAL THINKING

Predicting If Egyptians had not developed papyrus, what other material could they have used to write on?

How Did the Egyptians Write?

Like the Mesopotamians, the Egyptians developed their own writing system. At first, Egyptian writing was made up of thousands of picture symbols that represented objects and ideas. A house, for example, would be represented by a drawing of a house. Later, Egyptians created symbols that represented sounds, just as the letters of our alphabet do. The combination of pictures and sound symbols created a complex writing system called **hieroglyphics** (hy•ruh•GLIH•fihks).

Few ancient Egyptians could read and write hieroglyphics. Some Egyptian men, however, attended special schools to prepare for careers as scribes in government or business. The Egyptians did not write on clay tablets like the Mesopotamians. For their daily tasks, Egyptian scribes developed a simpler script that they wrote or painted on papyrus. These same scribes carved hieroglyphics onto stone walls and monuments.

☑ PROGRESS CHECK

Identifying What kind of writing system did the Egyptians develop?

papyrus a reed plant that grew wild along the Nile

hieroglyphics a writing system made up of a combination of pictures and sound symbols

GEOGRAPHY CONNECTION

Trade routes brought new ideas to Egypt as well as money and goods.

1. **LOCATION** What two islands were the farthest north on Egyptian trade routes?
2. **MOVEMENT** A trader traveling from Memphis to Babylon might stop in which cities?
3. CRITICAL THINKING ***Analyzing*** Why do so many trade routes run along waterways?

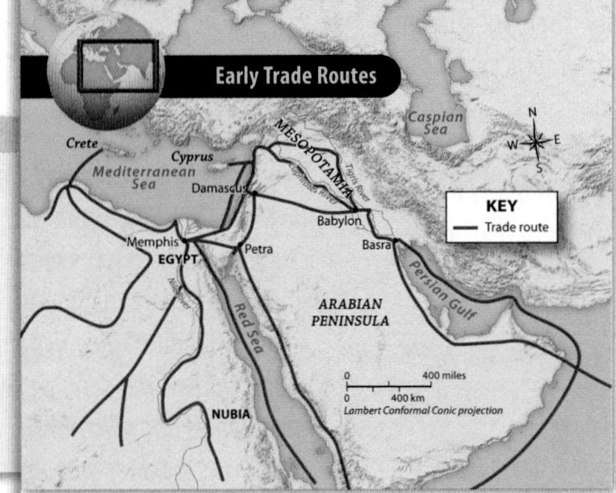

3 Uniting Egypt

GUIDING QUESTION *How did Egypt become united?*

Protected from outside attacks by desert barriers, Egyptian farmers were able to grow surpluses—extra amounts—of food. In Egypt, as in Mesopotamia, extra food meant that some people could leave farming to work in other occupations. Artisans, merchants, and traders began to play an important role in Egypt's economy. As more goods became available, villages along the Nile traded with one another. Before long, Egyptian caravans were carrying goods to Nubia (NOO•bee•uh) to the south, Mesopotamia to the northeast, and other places outside Egypt's borders. Along with the exchange of goods, Egyptian traders learned about the ways of life and governments of other societies.

Forming Kingdoms

The need for organized government became increasingly important as farming and trade increased. A government was necessary to oversee the construction and repair of irrigation ditches and dams. A government was needed to develop a process for storing and distributing grain during famines. In addition, conflicts over land ownership had to be settled.

dynasty a line of rulers from one family

Academic Vocabulary

unify to unite; to bring together into one unit

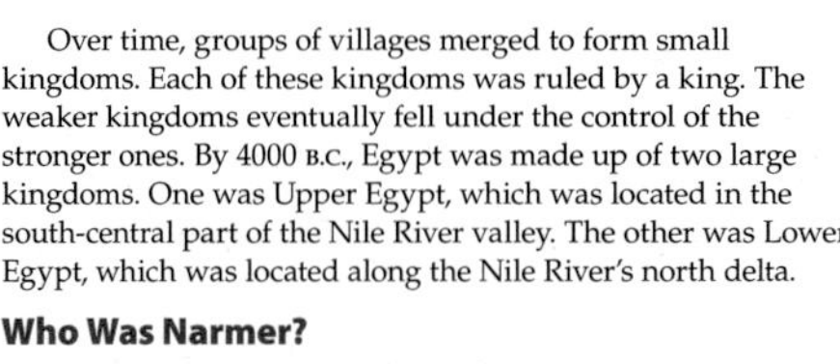

Over time, groups of villages merged to form small kingdoms. Each of these kingdoms was ruled by a king. The weaker kingdoms eventually fell under the control of the stronger ones. By 4000 B.C., Egypt was made up of two large kingdoms. One was Upper Egypt, which was located in the south-central part of the Nile River valley. The other was Lower Egypt, which was located along the Nile River's north delta.

Who Was Narmer?

Narmer (NAHR•mer) was a king of Upper Egypt. About 3100 B.C., he led his armies from the valley north into the delta. Narmer conquered Lower Egypt and married one of Lower Egypt's princesses, which **unified** the kingdoms. For the first time, all of Egypt was ruled by one king.

Narmer established a new capital at Memphis, a city on the border between Upper Egypt and Lower Egypt. He governed both parts of Egypt from this city. Memphis began to flourish as a center of government and culture along the Nile.

Narmer's kingdom lasted long after his death. The right to rule was passed from father to son to grandson. Such a line of rulers from one family is called a **dynasty** (DY•nuh•stee). When one dynasty died out, another took its place.

From about 3100 B.C. to 332 B.C., a series of 30 dynasties ruled Egypt. These dynasties are organized into three time periods: the Old Kingdom, the Middle Kingdom, and the New Kingdom. Throughout these three time periods, Egypt was usually united under a single ruler and enjoyed stable government.

Egyptian art often glorified rulers. The man in the center of this carving is Narmer.

▶ CRITICAL THINKING

Analyzing How does the carving show that Narmer was a powerful leader?

☑ PROGRESS CHECK

Explaining How did the separate kingdoms of Egypt unite?

LESSON 1 REVIEW

Review Vocabulary

1. Why did the Egyptians need *hieroglyphics*?
2. How does a *dynasty* work?

Answer the Guiding Questions

3. ***Identifying*** What physical feature is to the east and west of the Nile River? How did this feature help Egyptians?
4. ***Contrasting*** How did the flooding of major rivers affect both the Mesopotamians and the Egyptians?
5. ***Explaining*** What was significant about the joining of the two kingdoms under Narmer?
6. ***Analyzing*** How did the Nile River help the ancient Egyptians develop as a well-governed civilization?
7. **EXPOSITORY WRITING** Why has the Nile River been described as the "lifeblood" of Egypt? Why was the river essential to the Egyptians? Explain your answer in the form of a short essay.

LESSON 1 (cont.)

LECTURE SLIDE Show students the lecture slide that lists technological developments of ancient Egypt. Explain to students that some of these developments, such as irrigation, the shadoof, and geometry, were results of living near the Nile.

Ask: **How did the Nile make these developments possible?** *(Because of regular flooding, Egyptians needed geometry to mark their fields. They also needed the shadoof to move water from the Nile to their irrigation systems.)*

Have students add these cultural and technological developments to their cause-and-effect graphic organizers.

CHART Explain that papyrus was used for writing. Show students the sequence chart about papyrus.

Then ask: **Why did Egyptians need to develop a system of writing?** *(They needed a way to document their ideas and record information about their crops.)*

INTERACTIVE WORKSHEET

Economics of History Activity

Determining Cause and Effect Lead students in a discussion of how Egypt's natural resources helped Egyptians grow surpluses of food and goods and develop a system of trade. Then, have students complete the Economics of History Activity for this chapter.

As students think about the concept of scarcity, **ask:**

What kinds of foods did the ancient Egyptians grow? *(grains)*

What role did the Nile River play in the production, trade, and transportation of these goods? *(The Nile provided the water and the fertile soil to grow the product. The Nile was also the means for transporting the product to places outside Egypt.)* AL

3 Uniting Egypt

GUIDING QUESTION *How did Egypt become united?*

Explaining **Ask:** **Why was a united government necessary as ancient Egypt grew?** *(A government was needed to oversee the farming, trading, and land ownership in a growing Egypt.)*

Remind students that in this section, they read about the ruler who united Egypt and established a system of family rule called a *dynasty.*

Ask: **Why was the dynasty system important?** *(It created a stable and united system of government.)*

Predicting Have students predict the effect of the dynasty system on Egypt. Ask students to consider the benefits of such a system *(long-term political stability)* and the potential problems. *(A pharaoh might not have children to inherit the throne. A family that is corrupt or weak could damage Egypt.)* BL

Have students complete the Lesson 1 Review questions.

CLOSE & REFLECT

Have students discuss the predictions they made at the end of Day 1. Tell them to circle the predictions that came true. As a class, review the predictions that were not confirmed and discuss how they could be amended based on new information students have learned from the lesson.

IF YOU HAVE MORE TIME . . .

Explore Writing with Hieroglyphics

Applying Find examples of hieroglyphics online or in reference books. Display these examples to the class and explain the meaning of each hieroglyph. Explain that Egyptians used hieroglyphics to record their stories and histories.

Work with the class to create an alphabet of hieroglyphics. As an alternative, you may choose to find an existing, student-friendly, hieroglyphic alphabet on the Internet.

Have each student write two or three simple sentences using the class's hieroglyphic alphabet. In these sentences, students should introduce themselves ("My name is . . .") and share one or two interesting facts about themselves.

Ask student volunteers to share their hieroglyphic sentences with the class.

BACKGROUND KNOWLEDGE

The Rosetta Stone

Egyptian hieroglyphics were a mystery to historians for centuries. The Rosetta Stone was the key that unlocked the mystery. The stone is a slab with text on it in two languages (Egyptian and Greek) written in three scripts (Egyptian hieroglyphics, demotic Egyptian, and Greek). Demotic is the "everyday" writing that Egyptians used. Scholars were able to use their knowledge of Greek to decipher the meaning of the hieroglyphics. The text on the stone is the same in each language: a decree about the pharaoh Ptolemy V from the second century B.C.

The Rosetta Stone was discovered in 1799 by French soldiers in Napoleon's army. When Napoleon was defeated, the British took possession of the stone. The Rosetta Stone was put on display in the British Museum in 1802 and remains on display there today.

Answers for pages 104–107

P. 104 CRITICAL THINKING The painting shows that ancient Egyptians used plows and animals to help them farm.

P. 105 CRITICAL THINKING If the ancient Egyptians had not developed papyrus, they could have written on cloth, wood, or stone.

P. 105 ☑ PROGRESS CHECK The Egyptians developed hieroglyphics, a system of symbols that represent sounds.

P. 106 GEOGRAPHY CONNECTION

1. Cyprus and Crete
2. Petra and Damascus
3. CRITICAL THINKING Travel is faster on water than on land. Also, it was probably easier to carry large loads on a boat.

P. 107 CRITICAL THINKING Narmer is bigger than the other figures, and he is holding up a weapon.

P. 107 ☑ PROGRESS CHECK The weaker villages fell to the stronger ones until two powerful kingdoms remained—Upper Egypt and Lower Egypt. Both were united under Narmer, who, as king of Upper Egypt, conquered Lower Egypt and married one of its princesses.

LESSON 1 REVIEW

1. They needed hieroglyphics in order to communicate and record ideas and facts.
2. A dynasty is a system of rule in which power is handed down from grandfather to father to son.
3. The deserts that lie east and west of the river provided Egypt with a natural defense against intruders. The heat and sand kept outsiders from crossing lands that separated Egypt from other places.
4. The Mesopotamians could not predict or control the flooding of their rivers; as a result, property and lives were often lost. The floods in Egypt were regular and predictable, so people could plan their lives around them.
5. The unification of the two kingdoms was the first time that Egypt was united under one ruler. Unification represented an important step in the development of Egypt as a powerful civilization.
6. Students should explain that the Nile River provided resources and natural defenses to the ancient Egyptians. This allowed them to grow and develop a civilization.
7. Answers will vary but should include the idea that the Nile was an essential life-giving resource that provided water for crops, drinking, and bathing; rich soil for farming; a means of transportation; and security against attack.

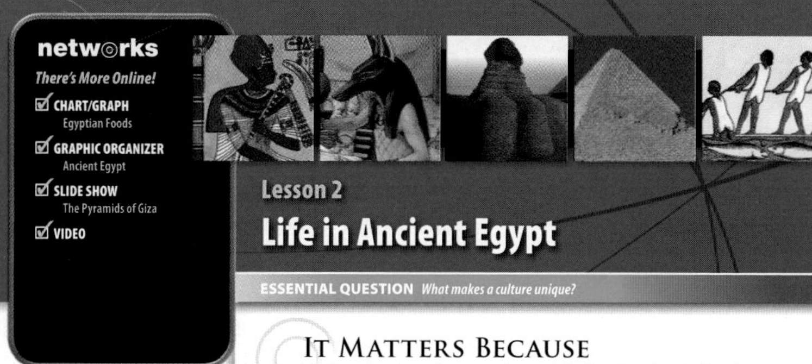

networks
There's More Online!
- ☑ CHART/GRAPH Egyptian Foods
- ☑ GRAPHIC ORGANIZER Ancient Egypt
- ☑ SLIDE SHOW The Pyramids of Giza
- ☑ VIDEO

Lesson 2

Life in Ancient Egypt

ESSENTIAL QUESTION *What makes a culture unique?*

It Matters Because

The Egyptian pharaohs were all-powerful rulers. Egyptians built such gigantic and sturdy pyramids in their honor that the pyramids still stand today.

1 Egypt's Early Rulers

GUIDING QUESTION *How was ancient Egypt governed?*

Around 2600 B.C., Egyptian civilization entered the period known as the Old Kingdom. The Old Kingdom lasted until about 2200 B.C. During these years, the Egyptians built magnificent cities and increased trade. They also formed a unified government. The Egyptians prized unity. They understood the importance of everyone working and living according to similar principles and beliefs. Therefore, they developed a government under an all-powerful ruler who controlled both religious and political affairs. A government in which the same person is both the political leader and the religious leader is called a **theocracy** (thee•AH•kruh•see).

A Political Leader

At first, the Egyptian ruler was called a king. Later, he was known as **pharaoh** (FEHR•oh). The word *pharaoh* originally meant "great house." It referred to the grand palace in which the king and his family lived.

The Egyptians were fiercely loyal to the pharaoh because they believed that a strong ruler unified their kingdom. The pharaoh held total power. He issued commands that had to be obeyed. Egyptians believed that a pharaoh's wise and far-reaching leadership would help their kingdom survive such disasters as war and famine.

The pharaoh appointed **bureaucrats** (BYUR•uh•kratz), or government officials, to carry out his orders. Bureaucrats supervised the construction and repair of dams, irrigation canals, and brick granaries. Granaries (GRAY•nuh•reez) were used to store grain from bountiful harvests so people would not starve during times of poor harvests.

The pharaoh owned all the land in Egypt and could use it as he pleased. The pharaoh's officials collected tax payments of grain from farmers. The pharaoh also **distributed** land to officials, priests, and wealthy Egyptians whom he favored.

A Religious Leader

Egyptians were also loyal to the pharaoh because they thought he was the son of Re (RAY), the Egyptian sun god. They believed their pharaoh was a god on earth who protected Egypt. Whenever the pharaoh appeared in public, people played music on flutes and cymbals and bowed their heads.

The pharaoh (left) had many servants to wait on him and provide him with all his needs.

▶ CRITICAL THINKING

Explaining What role did the pharaoh play as a political leader?

Reading **HELP**DESK

Taking Notes: *Organizing*

Use a diagram like this one to list information about ancient Egypt by adding one or more facts to each of the boxes.

Ancient Egypt → Ruler | Religion | Social Groups

Content Vocabulary
- **theocracy**
- **pharaoh**
- **bureaucrat**
- **embalming**
- **pyramid**

theocracy government by religious leaders
pharaoh ruler of ancient Egypt
bureaucrat a government official

Academic Vocabulary

distribute to divide into shares and deliver the shares to different people

As Egypt's religious leader, the pharaoh participated in ceremonies to help the kingdom thrive. For example, the pharaoh rode a bull around Memphis because the Egyptians believed that this would help keep the soil fertile. The pharaoh was also the first person to cut the ripened grain at harvest time. Egyptians believed this action would produce abundant crops.

☑ PROGRESS CHECK

Analyzing How was the pharaoh a political leader and a religious leader?

2 Religion in Egypt

GUIDING QUESTION *What kind of religion did the ancient Egyptians practice?*

Religion influenced every aspect of Egyptian life. Like the people of Mesopotamia, ancient Egyptians worshipped many gods and goddesses. The people of Egypt, however, thought their gods were more powerful. The Egyptians believed these deities (DEE•uh•teez) controlled natural forces as well as human activities.

The Egyptians depended on the sun to grow their crops and on the Nile River to make the soil fertile. Thus, two of the most **crucial** gods were the sun god Re and the river god Hapi (HAH•pee). Another important god was Osiris (oh•SY•ruhs). According to legend, Osiris was an early pharaoh who gave the Egyptian people laws and taught them farming. His wife Isis (EYE•suhs) represented the faithful wife and mother. Osiris and Isis together ruled over the world of the dead. Thoth (THOHTH) was the god of learning. He could take human or animal form—or both—as did most gods and goddesses.

The Egyptians gave offerings to their gods, whom they believed controll[ed] their lives.

▶ CRITICAL THINKING

Speculating Why do you think the god being offered a gift has the head of a bird?

The Afterlife

The Egyptians had a positive view of the afterlife. They believed that life after death would be even better than the present life. After a long journey, the dead arrived at a place of peace.

One of the most important writings of ancient Egypt was *The Book of the Dead*. Egyptians studied its prayers and magic spells to prepare for the afterlife. They believed that Osiris greeted those who had just died at the gate to the next world. If people had led good lives and knew the spells, Osiris would give them eternal life. This passage from *The Book of the Dead* explains what a person who enters the happy afterlife can expect:

PRIMARY SOURCE

> "Wheat and barley . . . shall be given unto him therein, and he shall flourish there just as he did upon earth."
>
> —from *Papyrus of Ani—The Egyptian Book of the Dead*

The earliest Egyptians believed that only the pharaohs could enjoy the afterlife. They thought that the pharaoh's soul **resided** in his body, and that the body had to be protected in order for the soul to complete the journey to the afterlife. There, the pharaoh would continue to protect Egypt. If the pharaoh's body decayed after death, his soul would not have a place to live. The pharaoh would not survive in the afterlife. As the centuries passed, however, Egyptians came to believe that the afterlife was not only for pharaohs. All people—rich and poor—could hope for eternal life with the help of the god Osiris. As a result, the process of **embalming** (ihm•BAHLM•ihng) emerged so that Egyptians could protect bodies for the afterlife.

Before a body was embalmed, priests removed the body's organs. The organs were stored in special jars that were buried with the body. Then the priests covered the body with a salt called natron and stored it for several days. The natron dried up the water in the body, causing it to shrink. The shrunken, dried body was then filled with burial spices and tightly wrapped with long strips of linen. The wrapped body was then known as a mummy (MUH•mee). The mummy was sealed in a coffin and placed in a decorated tomb.

The goddess Isis was the wife of the god Osiris. She was a powerful god respected on her own.

▶ CRITICAL THINKING

Inferring Why do you think the Egyptians worshipped some powerful gods that were men and others that were women?

Reading **HELP**DESK

Reading Strategy: *Contrasting*

Look for clue words such as *however, but,* and *although*. These words tell you that the author is contrasting two ideas. Which sentence on this page uses a contrasting clue word? What ideas are being contrasted?

Academic Vocabulary

crucial important or significant

embalming the process of treating a body to keep it from decaying

Academic Vocabulary

reside to be present continuously or have a home in a particular place

LESSON 2 • Day 1

ENGAGE

Making Connections In a Think-Pair-Share activity, have students brainstorm a list of objects, ideas, or images they associate with Egypt.

Ask:

What do you think of when you think of Egypt? *(Answers may include pyramids, deserts, mummies, hieroglyphics, and the Sphinx.)* ELL

Write student answers on the board.

Tell students that in this lesson they will learn how ancient Egypt was governed, what kind of religion the ancient Egyptians practiced, why and how the ancient Egyptians built the pyramids, and how Egyptian society was organized.

TEACH & ASSESS

1 Egypt's Early Rulers

GUIDING QUESTION ***How was ancient Egypt governed?***

GRAPHIC ORGANIZER

Identifying Work as a class to generate a list of the responsibilities of early Egyptian rulers.

Ask:

What was the role of the early ruler or pharaoh in Egypt? *(to unify the people of Egypt and to provide political and religious leadership)*

In addition, have students begin to complete the Taking Notes graphic organizer that appears on the first lesson page. Remind students to add to it as they read the lesson.

2 Religion in Egypt

GUIDING QUESTION ***What kind of religion did the ancient Egyptians practice?***

Discussing Return to the list of associations that students generated in the Engage activity. Explain that many of the images or objects that most people associate with ancient Egyptians, such as mummies and pyramids, are related to the topic of religion.

Ask:

How are mummies and pyramids related to the religion of the ancient Egyptians? *(Egyptians mummified bodies so the bodies could travel to the afterlife. Pyramids were meant to guide the pharaohs to the afterlife.)*

Lead a discussion of how the lives of ancient Egyptians were focused on the afterlife.

Ask:

What did the ancient Egyptians think the afterlife would be like? *(They thought it was better than the present life.)*

Who was allowed to reach the afterlife? *(At first, Egyptians believed that only the pharaohs could reach the afterlife, but later, Egyptians believed everyone could.)*

Making Connections Explain that ancient Egyptians' belief in the afterlife influenced all aspects of their lives. Then divide the class into small groups.

Assign each group an area of Egyptian life—science, religion, daily activities, and medicine.

Ask each group to make connections between Egyptians' belief in the afterlife and the area they were assigned.

Groups should present their findings to the class.

To help students, **ask:**

If you were a scientist or a doctor, how would your belief in the afterlife affect your work? *(A scientist might think the afterlife would provide answers to all questions. A doctor might hope the next life would have less suffering than this one.)*

If you were an Egyptian priest, how would your belief in the afterlife affect your work? *(You knew that your work was important in helping people reach the afterlife.)*

If you were an ordinary worker, how would your belief in the afterlife affect you? *(You would try to make good decisions so you could achieve eternal life.)* AL

CLOSE & REFLECT

INTERACTIVE WORKSHEET

21st Century Skills Activity

Identifying Place students into small groups. Tell them they will complete a graphic organizer that identifies pharaohs' political and religious responsibilities. Have them complete the 21st Century Skills Activity for this lesson. Remind them to return to their textbooks for details to fill in the graphic organizer.

If students need help, **ask:**

How did Egypt's rulers unify and lead the country? *(Possible summary: The early rulers and pharaohs were responsible for uniting Egypt politically and through religion.)*

How did the rulers serve as religious leaders? *(The pharaohs participated in religious ceremonies and were considered to gods.)* AL

Answers for pages 108–111

P. 108 Taking Notes Ruler: The pharaoh had total power in Egypt. **Religion:** Religion guided every part of life. **Social Groups:** Most Egyptians were farmers.

P. 109 CRITICAL THINKING The pharaoh issued commands that had to be obeyed and appointed bureaucrats to carry out his orders.

P. 110 ☑ PROGRESS CHECK Pharaohs had total control over all aspects of life. As political leaders, they issued commands about how land would be used and appointed bureaucrats to carry out their orders. They protected and led the people during times of trouble. As religious leaders, pharaohs represented the gods and participated in ceremonies that affected crops and farming.

P. 110 CRITICAL THINKING Students might speculate that the god is the god of the sky and, thus, takes the shape of a bird.

P. 110 Reading Strategy The contrasting clue word *however* is used in the sentence "The Egyptians, however, believed their gods were more powerful." The sentence is contrasting the religious beliefs of the Egyptians with the religious beliefs of the Mesopotamians.

P. 111 CRITICAL THINKING Students might say that some things were seen as "male" and others as "female." They might also note that the gods were seen as part of Egyptian history so they would have taken male and female forms like the Egyptians themselves.

Preparing the pharaoh's body for burial involved a mix of science and religion. Special priests performed the process.

▶ CRITICAL THINKING
Explaining What do you think Egyptians learned about the human body by embalming?

Wealthy people had their mummies placed in coffins and buried in tombs. Poorer people had their mummies buried in caves or in the sand. Even animals were embalmed. Egyptians viewed animals not only as pets, but also as sacred creatures. As a result, they buried the mummies of cats, birds, and other animals at temples honoring their gods and goddesses.

Medical Skills

The Egyptians learned much about the human body from embalming. This knowledge helped them to develop basic medical skills. Egyptian doctors sewed up cuts and set broken bones. They were the first to use splints, bandages, and compresses. Egyptians also wrote down medical information on papyrus scrolls. These records were the world's first medical books.

☑ PROGRESS CHECK
Analyzing Why did Egyptians protect a person's body after death?

Reading **HELP**DESK

pyramid great stone tomb built for an Egyptian pharaoh

Academic Vocabulary
labor work

Pyramid Tombs

GUIDING QUESTION *Why and how were pyramids built?*

The Egyptians honored their pharaohs in a special way. They built great tombs called **pyramids** (PIHR•uh•mihds) for the pharaohs. These enormous structures were made of stone and covered the area of several city blocks. Centuries after they were built, these monuments still tower over the desert sands. The pyramids protected the bodies of dead pharaohs from floods, wild animals, and robbers. The Egyptians believed the pharaohs would be happy after death if they had their personal belongings. For that reason, they placed the pharaoh's clothing, weapons, furniture, and jewelry in the pyramids.

The pyramids preserved, or saved, these objects in relatively good condition for centuries. Today, archaeologists are able to study the pyramids and the treasures they hold to learn about life in ancient Egypt.

How Were Pyramids Built?

Thousands of workers spent years of hard **labor** to build the pyramids. Farmers did much of the work during the summer months when the Nile River flooded and they could not farm.

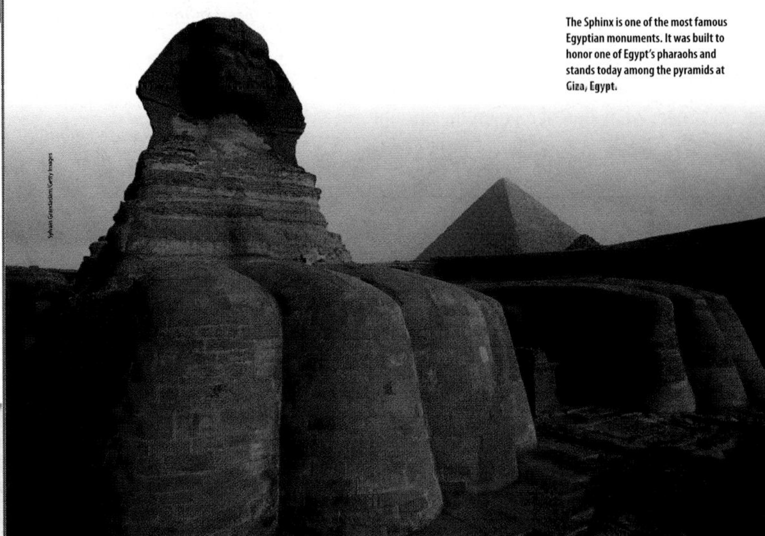

The Sphinx is one of the most famous Egyptian monuments. It was built to honor one of Egypt's pharaohs and stands today among the pyramids at Giza, Egypt.

INSIDE A PYRAMID

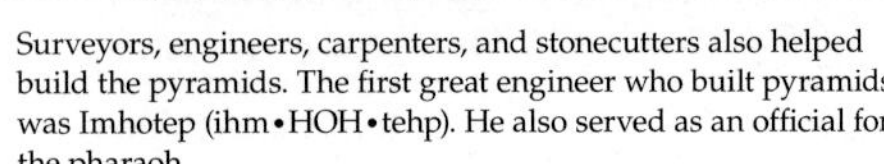

1. **Air Shaft**
2. **King's Burial Chamber** The king's mummified body was placed in a room at the pyramid's center.
3. **Grand Gallery** This tall, sloping hall held large granite blocks that sealed the tomb.
4. **Queen's Burial Chamber** This chamber held a statue of the king, not the queen's body.
5. **Entrance**
6. **Underground Burial Chamber** Sometimes kings were buried here instead.
7. **Queen's Pyramids** These smaller pyramids are believed to be tombs for the kings' wives.
8. **Mastaba** These tombs surrounding the pyramids held royal family members and other nobles.
9. **Valley Temple** This temple may have been used for rituals before the king was buried.

INFOGRAPHIC

The pyramids contained many rooms, each used for a different purpose.

▶ CRITICAL THINKING
Speculating Why was the king's burial chamber constructed in the middle of the pyramid and not at the top?

Surveyors, engineers, carpenters, and stonecutters also helped build the pyramids. The first great engineer who built pyramids was Imhotep (ihm•HOH•tehp). He also served as an official for the pharaoh.

Workers searched for stone in places throughout the Nile River valley or in Upper Egypt. After locating the stone, skilled artisans used copper tools to cut the stone into huge blocks. Next, workers used rope to fasten the blocks onto wooden sleds. The sleds were pulled along a path made of logs to the Nile River. There, the stones were moved onto barges that carried them to the building site. Workers unloaded the blocks and dragged or pushed them up ramps to be set in place at each new level of the pyramid.

The Egyptians faced many challenges as they built the pyramids. These challenges, however, led to important discoveries. For example, each pyramid rested on a square-shaped foundation, with an entrance facing north. To find north, the Egyptians studied the skies and developed an understanding of astronomy. With this knowledge, they invented a 365-day calendar with 12 months divided into three seasons. This calendar became the basis for our modern calendar.

Reading **HELP**DESK

Egyptians also made advancements in mathematics. Egypt's pyramid builders had to calculate how much stone was needed to build a pyramid. They had to measure angles in order to **construct** a pyramid's walls. To do this, they invented a system of written numbers based on 10. They also created fractions, using them with whole numbers to add, subtract, and divide.

An Egyptian Wonder

About the mid-2000s B.C., the Egyptians built the biggest and grandest of the pyramids—the Great Pyramid. It lies about 10 miles (16.1 km) from the modern city of Cairo. Built for King Khufu (KOO•foo), the Great Pyramid is one of three pyramids still standing at Giza on the Nile's west bank. It is about the height of a 48-story building, towering nearly 500 feet (153 m) above the desert. It extends over an area equal in size to nine football fields. More than 2 million stone blocks were used in the pyramid's construction, each weighing an average of 2.5 tons (2.3 metric tons). For more than 4,000 years, the Great Pyramid stood as the tallest structure in the world.

☑ PROGRESS CHECK
Explaining Why did the Egyptians build the pyramids?

In this photo of the Great Pyramid, the pyramid in the center belongs to King Khafre, son of Khufu. Khafre's pyramid has a width (at its base) to height ratio of about 708:471 ft (216:143 m). Khufu's pyramid has a ratio of about 756:481 ft (230:147 m).

▶ CRITICAL THINKING
Comparing Which pyramid is larger?

Academic Vocabulary
construct to build

LESSON 2 • Day 2

ENGAGE

LECTURE SLIDE **Making Generalizations** Show the definition of *social class* from the lecture slide. Explain to students that most societies have different social classes. A person's social class or status is mostly defined by the work he or she does.

Introduce the term *division of labor* and explain that the jobs people do may affect their place in society. To illustrate this point, ask students to name different kinds of work or professions.

Write their answers on the board.

Then have students consider whether these jobs can be sorted by social status.

Ask:

Why do you think some jobs have a higher status than others? *(They require more training or education. They are difficult or admired.)*

Which jobs do you think had the highest status in ancient Egypt? *(pharaoh, bureaucrat, priest, scribe, pyramid architect)*

Tell students they will learn about the way people lived and worked in ancient Egypt. They will apply their knowledge about social class to the ancient Egyptians.

TEACH & ASSESS

3 Pyramid Tombs

GUIDING QUESTION *Why and how were pyramids built?*

SLIDE SHOW

Making Connections Help students make a connection to the Engage activity and the previous day's lesson by pointing out that the pyramids were tombs built by Egyptian workers so the pharaohs would be happy after death. Show them the slide show about the pyramids at Giza.

Then lead students in a discussion of workers' efforts.

Ask:

Why did ancient Egyptian farmers, engineers, and stonecutters build tombs for their leaders? *(to protect the bodies of the pharaohs)*

Why was it important to protect the bodies of the pharaohs? *(They believed the pharaohs needed their bodies so the pharaohs could move on to and live in the afterlife.)* AL

Where did workers find the stone that made up the pyramids? *(throughout the Nile River valley and Upper Egypt)*

The tools used to cut the stone were made from what type of metal? *(copper)*

Then, help students recognize the types of scientific and mathematical knowledge Egyptians needed to build the pyramids.

Ask:

Why did the Egyptians need to better understand astronomy and study the skies in order to build a pyramid? *(They needed astronomy to find north so the pyramid entrance could face north.)*

Remind students that in order to construct pyramids, Egyptians needed to make calculations and measure angles.

Ask:

What did the Egyptians develop in mathematics to help them make calculations, such as how much stone was needed to make a pyramid? *(They invented a number system based on 10; they created fractions; and they used whole numbers and fractions to add, subtract, and divide.)* BL

Point out that Egyptian workers believed it was their duty to help the pharaohs achieve a happy afterlife by constructing the tomb.

4 Daily Life

GUIDING QUESTION *How was Egyptian society organized?*

Identifying Review with students the section "Daily Life." Work together to identify each social class, its members, and their jobs. Help students by drawing a three-column table on the whiteboard with the following headings: "Class," "Members," and "Their Jobs."

Then, ask students to identify each social class, starting with the most powerful. Write students' answers in the first column. *(Ruling, Upper, Middle, Working)*

Next, under "Members," have students identify which people belonged to each class. *(Ruling: pharaoh; Upper: priests, army commanders, and nobles; Middle: merchants and artisans; Working: farmers, unskilled workers, and slaves)*

Finally, ask students to tell what jobs each group did. Write their answers under "Their Jobs." *(Ruling: rule Egypt; Upper: run the army and the government; Middle: run shops; Working: grow food and build things)*

After students complete the organizer, **ask: What does each social class contribute to Egyptian society as a whole?** *(Each class performs a different role that helps society run smoothly.)* BL

Describing Assign or have students choose a member of ancient Egyptian society, such as a pharaoh, farmer, priest, merchant, or doctor. Then have each student write a paragraph or two that describes a day in that person's life. Remind students to write using "I" and to include details from the chapter about the person's social class. AL If necessary, have students meet with you or a partner to share a few phrases or sentences orally. ELL

Have students complete the Lesson 2 Review questions.

CLOSE & REFLECT

Analyzing Have students answer the following "debriefing" questions about what they learned about ancient Egyptian class structure. Students can answer the questions orally in small groups, or they can jot down and submit their answers on paper.

- Why did Egypt have different social classes?
- What roles did Egyptian social classes play in society?
- Based on what you learned, how are the social classes of ancient Egypt similar to or different from social classes in the modern world? AL

Answers for pages 112–115

P. 112 CRITICAL THINKING Embalming taught the Egyptians about anatomy, internal organs, and blood circulation.

P. 112 ☑ PROGRESS CHECK The Egyptians protected the body in order to preserve the person's soul so that it would have a successful journey through the afterlife.

P. 114 INFOGRAPHIC

CRITICAL THINKING The king's burial chamber was in the middle of the pyramid so the pharaoh's body and his treasures would be safe.

P. 115 ☑ PROGRESS CHECK They built the pyramids to provide tombs that would honor deceased pharaohs and protect them and all their belongings from floods, dust and heat, and robberies.

P. 115 CRITICAL THINKING Khufu's pyramid is larger.

4 Daily Life

GUIDING QUESTION *How was Egyptian society organized?*

At its peak, ancient Egypt was home to about 5 million people. This would be about equal to the number of people living today in the state of Colorado. Most ancient Egyptians lived in the fertile Nile valley and delta. The delta is found at the mouth of the river. These two areas, which make up only 3 percent of Egypt's land, are densely populated even today.

Egypt's Social Groups

The **roles** of the people in ancient Egypt reflected their social status, or position in society. Look at the diagram of the different social groups, or classes, in ancient Egypt. The king or pharaoh and his family held the highest social position in Egypt, followed by a small upper class of army commanders, nobles, and priests. The priests served as government officials and supervised people who worked as clerks and scribes. A larger group of traders, artisans, and scribes made up the middle class. The lowest but largest groups in Egyptian society

INFOGRAPHIC

SOCIAL STATUS IN ANCIENT EGYPT

People lived according to their social status and occupation. People who were ambitious could improve their status.

▶ CRITICAL THINKING
Identifying What level of society do you think a teacher would occupy?

Reading HELPDESK

Academic Vocabulary
role the function or part an individual fills in society

Build Vocabulary: *Word Forms*
As a noun, *official* means "someone who holds an office or who manages the rules of a game." As an adjective, it means "authorized." The verb *officiate* means "to act in an official role."

These ancient Egyptian women are chemists. Women were educated and valued for their special skills.

▶ CRITICAL THINKING
Analyzing What social class would these women belong to?

was made up of farmers and unskilled workers. Even though there were divisions in Egyptian class structures, ambitious people in the lower classes were able to improve their social position.

How People Lived

Egypt's upper class lived in elegant homes and on estates along the Nile River. Their homes were constructed of wood and sun-dried mud bricks, and some were two or three stories tall. Surrounding their homes were lush gardens and pools filled with fish and water lilies. Men and women from the upper class dressed in fashionable white linen clothes and wore dark eye makeup and jewelry. Servants waited on them and performed household tasks.

The middle class of ancient Egyptian society was made up of people who owned businesses and held skilled jobs. These jobs included trading and working as a scribe. Artisans were also important members of the middle class. These craft-makers produced linen cloth, jewelry, pottery, and metal goods. The middle class lived in smaller homes and dressed more simply than the upper class.

Reading Strategy: *Finding the Main Idea*
Remember that each paragraph contains ideas that are related. Usually one sentence summarizes the main idea of a paragraph. Find the main idea in the last paragraph on this page.

The felucca, an ancient Egyptian river craft, sailed the Nile. Sailors today still use the same ship and sail design.

▶ CRITICAL THINKING
Identifying Into what Egyptian social class would fishers fit?

The largest Egyptian social classes included farmers, unskilled workers, and enslaved people. Most farmers worked on land that was owned by wealthy nobles. They paid rent to the landowners, usually with a portion of their crops. Farmers lived in houses that were made of mud brick. The houses generally had only one room and a roof made of palm leaves. Farmers ate a simple diet of bread, vegetables, and fruit.

Unskilled workers performed **manual** labor, such as unloading cargo from boats and transporting it to markets. Some were fishers. Most unskilled workers settled in crowded city neighborhoods. They lived in small mud-brick houses with hard-packed dirt floors. Their houses sometimes included a courtyard. Families often gathered on the flat rooftops to socialize, play games, and sleep. Because of the hot Egyptian climate, they also did their cooking on the rooftop. This helped their homes stay cooler.

Some of these unskilled workers were enslaved people. Many of them had been captured in war, and they could earn their freedom over time. Some of these enslaved people helped build the pyramids.

Egyptian Families

The family was the most important group in ancient Egyptian society. Even the gods and goddesses were arranged in family groupings. The father was the head of the family in ancient Egypt, but women had more rights than women in other early civilizations had. Egyptian women held a legal status similar to that of men. They could own property, buy and sell goods, and **obtain** divorces.

Wealthy women even served as priests, managing temples and performing religious ceremonies. Wives of farmers often worked in the fields with their husbands. Women of the higher social classes were more likely to stay at home while their husbands worked at their jobs.

Reading HELPDESK

Academic Vocabulary
manual involving physical effort
obtain to gain something through a planned effort

Few Egyptian children attended school. Egyptian children had time for fun, playing with board games, dolls, spinning tops, and stuffed leather balls. As in many other cultures, Egyptian children were expected to respect their parents. Mothers taught their daughters to sew, cook, and run a household. Boys learned farming or other trades from their fathers. Learning their father's trade was important, because very often the oldest son would inherit his father's business.

When boys and girls became teenagers, they were expected to get married and start families of their own. In Egyptian cities and among the upper class, people usually lived in nuclear families. A nuclear family is made up of two parents and their children. Some farm families and others in the lower class lived as extended families. In an extended family, older adults, along with their married children and their families, live together. For farm families, this provided more people to work the fields.

The oldest son, and sometimes the oldest daughter, were also responsible for taking care of their parents when the parents became too old or sick to take care of themselves. This responsibility included making sure the parents were given a proper burial after they died.

Egyptian sons learned their fathers' trades, such as fishing or farming. This ancient art piece shows fishers hauling nets.

☑ PROGRESS CHECK
Identifying What types of people made up Egypt's upper class?

LESSON 2 REVIEW

Review Vocabulary

1. Explain the role a *pharaoh* played in a *theocracy.*
2. What was the social status of a *bureaucrat* in ancient Egypt?

Answer the Guiding Questions

3. ***Describing*** What kind of religion did the ancient Egyptians practice? Describe at least one way that their religion was tied to agriculture.
4. ***Analyzing*** What was the most important purpose of the pyramids? Explain your reasoning.
5. ***Comparing and Contrasting*** How was life for Egyptian children similar to or different from that of children today?
6. ***Defending*** Why did the Egyptians spend years and many resources to build enormous tombs for their dead pharaohs?
7. **EXPOSITORY WRITING** If you could be anyone in ancient Egypt except the pharaoh, who would you choose to be? Explain the reasons for your choice. Make sure to include the advantages and disadvantages of your social position.

LESSON 2 • Day 2 (cont.)

BACKGROUND KNOWLEDGE

The Sphinx

The Sphinx is one of the most recognizable landmarks in the world. Carved from limestone found in Giza, the monument shows a creature with the body of a lion and the head of a pharaoh. The sculpture is 240 feet (73 m) long and 66 feet (20 m) high. It is believed to be more than 4,600 years old. The face of the Sphinx once had a nose and a beard. The nose was shot off by soldiers conducting target practice. The beard was worn away by wind and erosion.

Historians are not certain which pharaoh is depicted by the Sphinx. However, because the monument faces Khafre's pyramid, some historians believe the Sphinx has some connection to Khafre.

IF YOU HAVE MORE TIME . . .

Show The Video "Ancient Egypt"

VIDEO Lead a class discussion about the video content. What new facts did students learn about Egyptian civilization?

Explore Egyptian Artifacts Online

You may also choose to have students explore more about Egyptian artifacts online. Many museums throughout the world have Egyptian art and artifact exhibits. Challenge students to conduct research and share their findings with the class. Remind students of the appropriate safety guidelines as well as guidelines for quality research sources. BL

Create Postcards That Describe Egyptian Monuments

Direct students to the photos of the Sphinx and the Great Pyramid in their textbooks. Ask them to imagine what it would be like to see these monuments in person. Encourage students to use a variety of descriptive words and phrases.

Organize students into pairs or trios. Have each pair or trio choose an Egyptian monument. Then, direct each pair or trio to find a color image of their chosen monument.

Have them use this image as the front of a postcard. Instruct students to write a brief description of the monument, as if they had seen it in person. Encourage students to sign and address their postcard too. AL

Use Drama to Depict Egyptian Social Classes

Simulating Have students use what they learned in the lesson to plan skits in which they portray members of ancient Egypt's social classes.

Have students form groups of four. Each group should choose a social class to portray. Tell students to refer to their textbooks and to outside sources to find information about their social class.

Students should then work together to think of a way to present information about the classes in a skit. For example, students might work with other groups to act out a scene on an ancient Egyptian street to show how the classes interacted.

Students can use costumes in their skits, if available, or indicate their social class with colored tags on clothing.

Debrief with students by discussing the importance of people performing different roles in society.

Point out examples from students' skits of social classes having contact with each other, such as a scribe recording a grain harvest or a doctor treating a farmer's injury.

Then, **ask:**

Would Egyptian society function effectively if everyone belonged to the ruling class? *(No; if everyone had been a ruler, no one would have been available to do manual labor or trading.)*

What if all ancient Egyptians were merchants? *(That would not work well, either. Someone had to make the goods for the merchants to sell. Someone also had to provide food and shelter for the Egyptians.)*

How did the social classes work together to help Egyptian society? *(Each class performed a different role that helped society run smoothly.)*

Answers for pages 116–119

P. 116 INFOGRAPHIC

CRITICAL THINKING A teacher would be in the middle level of society.

P. 117 CRITICAL THINKING The women chemists would belong to the middle social class.

P. 117 Reading Strategy The middle class of ancient Egyptian society was made up of business owners and skilled workers.

P. 118 CRITICAL THINKING Fishers would fall into the same social class as farmers.

P. 119 ☑ PROGRESS CHECK The nobles, army commanders, and priests made up the upper class.

LESSON 2 REVIEW

1. The pharaoh served as the religious leader. The pharaoh represented the gods and participated in religious ceremonies.
2. A bureaucrat was a member of the upper class. It was the bureaucrat's job to carry out the orders of the pharaoh.
3. The ancient Egyptians believed the gods controlled nature and human activities. Students should point out that an agricultural society would consider gods who were connected to the elements, such as sun and rain, to be most important.
4. The pyramid was important because it served as a tomb for the pharaoh and provided a place where the body would pass safely into the afterlife. Although the pyramid also protected the body from floods, dust, and heat, the journey of the pharaoh's soul was important to the beliefs of the Egyptians, and therefore was a priority.
5. Like children of today, Egyptian children played games. Unlike children of today, Egyptian youngsters did not attend school. Also, Egyptian girls learned housekeeping skills from their mothers. Today, both boys and girls learn how to take care of their homes.
6. Students may suggest that building tombs provided an opportunity for Egyptians to work together to preserve their culture and to follow their religious beliefs.
7. Students will probably suggest that life in the upper class was easier and more interesting than life in the other classes. Students who prefer the upper class should mention the benefits of wealth and power but also the drawbacks of having big responsibilities, such as winning battles or participating in religious ceremonies. Those who prefer the middle class may point to the ability of those people to make and sell things and to have a comfortable life without the responsibilities of power.

networks
There's More Online!

GRAPHIC ORGANIZER
- Middle and New Kingdoms
- Achievements of the Pharaohs

MAP Ancient Egyptian Kingdoms

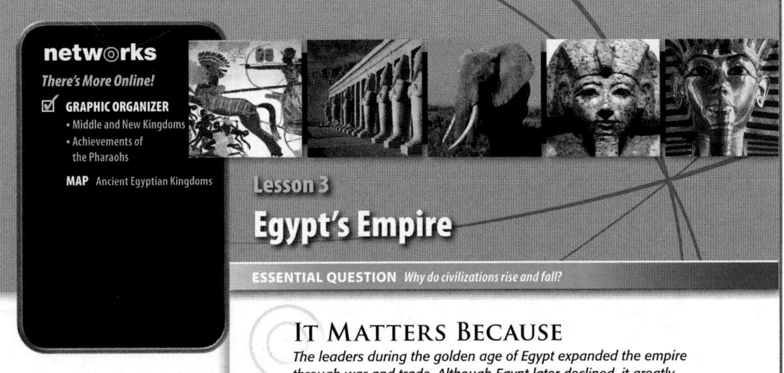

Lesson 3

Egypt's Empire

ESSENTIAL QUESTION *Why do civilizations rise and fall?*

It Matters Because

The leaders during the golden age of Egypt expanded the empire through war and trade. Although Egypt later declined, it greatly influenced other civilizations.

1 A Golden Age

GUIDING QUESTION *Why was the Middle Kingdom a "golden age" for Egypt?*

Around 2200 B.C., the ruling pharaohs in Memphis began to weaken. Ambitious nobles fought for control of Egypt. For more than 200 years, disorder and violence swept through the region. Finally, a new dynasty of pharaohs came to power. They moved the capital south to a city called Thebes (THEEBZ). These new pharaohs began a period of peace and order called the Middle Kingdom that lasted from about c. 2055 B.C. to c. 1650 B.C.

Conquests

During the Middle Kingdom, Egypt conquered new territories. Egyptian armies gained control of Nubia to the south and expanded northeast into present-day Syria. The Egyptian pharaohs added to their kingdom's wealth. They required tribute, or forced payments, from the peoples their armies had conquered.

Within Egypt, the pharaohs made many improvements. They added thousands of acres to the land already being farmed to increase crop production. They had more irrigation dams and channels built to supply more water to the population. The pharaohs also ordered the construction of a canal between the

Reading HELPDESK

Taking Notes: *Organizing*

As you read this lesson, complete a chart like this one about the Middle Kingdom and the New Kingdom.

	Middle Kingdom	New Kingdom
Date		
Government		
Economy		

Content Vocabulary
- incense
- envoy

Nile River and the Red Sea. As a result, Egyptian traders were able to send goods south by ship through the Red Sea. From there, the ships sailed to ports along the coasts of Arabia and East Africa.

The Arts Flourish

Egyptian arts and architecture thrived during the Middle Kingdom. Painters decorated the walls of tombs and temples with colorful scenes. These tomb paintings illustrated stories about the deities, as well as scenes from everyday life. Sculptors carved hunting, fishing, and battle scenes on large stone walls. They created statues of the pharaohs, showing them as ordinary humans rather than gods.

During the Middle Kingdom, the Egyptians developed a new kind of architecture. Pharaohs no longer had pyramids built. Instead, they had their tombs cut into limestone cliffs west of the Nile River. This area became known as the Valley of the Kings.

Artisans produced jewels for pharaohs and decorative objects from gold, such as this chair.

▶ CRITICAL THINKING
Differentiating What about this chair makes you think it was made for royalty?

The Hyksos

During the 1600s B.C., some Egyptian nobles challenged the power of the pharaohs. Civil war divided Egypt, ending an era of peace and prosperity. As the Middle Kingdom weakened, outsiders invaded Egypt. A people from western Asia known as the Hyksos (HIHK•sahs) swept across the desert into Egypt.

The Hyksos were powerful warriors who used methods of warfare unknown to the Egyptians. The Hyksos rode in horse-drawn chariots and fought with sturdy weapons made of bronze and iron. As a result, they overwhelmed the Egyptian soldiers and took control of the land.

For more than 100 years, Hyksos kings ruled Egypt. The Hyksos borrowed some Egyptian customs but remained separate from the Egyptian people. Meanwhile, most Egyptians hated the Hyksos and planned to overthrow them. The Egyptians learned how to steer horse-drawn chariots and use Hyksos weapons. Around 1550 B.C., an Egyptian prince named Ahmose (AH•mohs) formed an army and drove the Hyksos out of Egypt.

PROGRESS CHECK
Analyzing How were the Egyptians able to defeat the Hyksos?

The Hyksos introduced chariots to Egypt. Battle scenes show the advantage a soldier on a chariot has over those on foot.

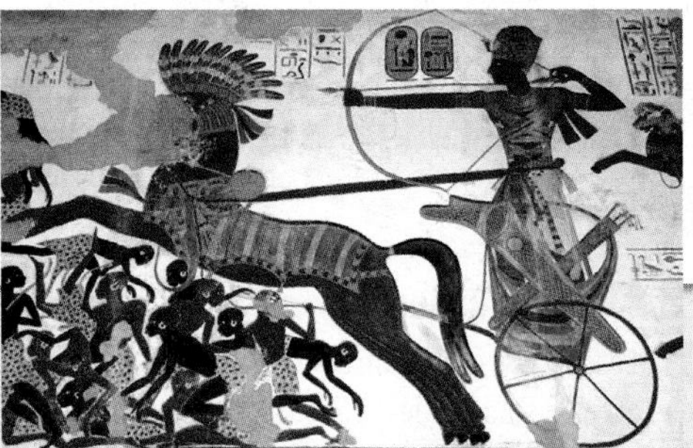

Connections to TODAY

Ivory

Ivory comes from mammals with tusks, such as elephants and walruses.

2 Building an Empire

GUIDING QUESTION *Why was the New Kingdom a unique period in ancient Egypt's history?*

Ahmose founded a new dynasty. It began a period known as the New Kingdom, which lasted from about 1550 B.C. to 1070 B.C. During this time, Egypt prospered through trade, gained more lands through conquest, and reached the height of its power. No longer isolated, Egyptians benefited from the spread of goods, ideas, and cultures within their empire.

A Woman Pharaoh

A queen named Hatshepsut (hat•SHEHP•soot) was one of the few women to rule Egypt. She came to power in about 1473 B.C. and governed with her husband. Then, after his death, she made herself pharaoh and ruled on behalf of her young nephew.

Because the title of pharaoh was usually passed from father to son, Hatshepsut had to prove that she was a good leader. In order for the people to accept her, Hatshepsut dressed in the clothes of a male pharaoh. She even wore the false beard to copy the one worn by male Egyptian kings. She built magnificent temples and restored old monuments. Her tomb in the Valley of the Kings contains large wall carvings that illustrate some of the major events of her reign.

One of the few women to govern Egypt, Hatshepsut ruled with the support of her subjects. This enormous tomb stands today in honor of her reign.

Reading HELPDESK

Reading Strategy: *Sequencing*

Key words such as *then*, *later*, and *after* are clues to the order in which events happened. Which of these key words is used on this page?

Growth of Trade

Hatshepsut was more interested in promoting trade than starting wars. She made great efforts to restore trade relations that had been interrupted by the Hyksos invasion.

During the rule of Hatshepsut, Egyptian seafarers sailed to ports in Arabia and East Africa. There, Egyptian traders exchanged beads, metal tools, and weapons for gold, ivory, ebony wood, and **incense** (IN•sens), a material burned for its pleasant smell.

The Egyptians valued wood products because the Nile River valley had few trees. They needed wood to build boats, furniture, and other items. To find wood, Egyptian traders traveled to the east coast of the Mediterranean Sea where the present-day country of Lebanon is located. The people in this region were called the Phoenicians (fih•NEE•shuns). The Phoenicians had a great impact on other cultures in the region. Their invention of an alphabet and a system of writing influenced others. Phoenician trade routes and settlements also encouraged the spread of goods and ideas across a large part of the ancient world.

Trade and Politics

The Egyptians traded wheat, paper, gold, copper, tin and tools to the Phoenicians for purple dye, wood and furniture. The traders exchanged goods they had for supplies they needed, rather than selling goods for money. The Phoenicians in turn traded Egyptian goods to other people. By trading with the Phoenicians, Egyptians spread their food and goods across Southwest Asia. Trade in the eastern Mediterranean helped make the Egyptian kingdom wealthier. Hatshepsut used some of this wealth to build monuments.

In addition to trade, New Kingdom pharaohs developed political ties between Egypt and nearby kingdoms. For example, the Egyptian dynasty became joined by treaty or marriage with ruling families in the Babylonian Empire in Mesopotamia, the Mittani (mih•TAH•nee) in Syria, and the Hittite Empire in Anatolia (ah•nuh•TOH•lee•uh).

To maintain close ties, pharaohs and the other rulers also exchanged **envoys** (EHN•voyz), or representatives. These actions marked the first time in history that a group of nations tried working together to reach common goals.

BIOGRAPHY

Hatshepsut (reigned 1473–1458 B.C.)

Hatshepsut was one of the most successful rulers of Egypt. Hatshepsut chose people who were loyal to her to serve in government positions. She valued the opinions of common Egyptians and sought their support for decisions she made. After her death, Thutmose III, Hatshepsut's nephew, had her name removed from royal texts and monuments. Historians believe that he did this to show that no female ruler interrupted the royal line of males.

▶ CRITICAL THINKING
Drawing Conclusions What actions of hers helped make Hatshepsut a successful ruler?

incense a material that produces a pleasant smell when burned

envoy a government representative to another country

LESSON 3 • Day 1

ENGAGE

Analyzing Visuals Explain that a golden age is the period in which a civilization is at its greatest political, cultural, and economic power. Have students skim Lesson 3 for images of artifacts from Egypt's golden age. Guide students toward understanding that the objects represent ancient Egypt at its height.

To make a connection to the modern world, **ask:**

What objects today suggest that we are living in a golden age? *(Students may suggest that handheld computers and other technology represent a culture at its height.)*

Tell students that in this lesson they will be learning about ancient Egypt at its most powerful. They will also learn about several leaders who caused the growth and decline of the Egyptian empire.

TEACH & ASSESS

1 A Golden Age

GUIDING QUESTION ***Why was the Middle Kingdom a "golden age" for Egypt?***

Determining Cause and Effect Lead students in a discussion of the steps ancient Egyptians took to expand or improve their territory and gain wealth during the Middle Kingdom. *(conquering new territories, collecting tribute, building more farms and canals, increasing trade with other places, and building new temples and tombs)*

Help students see a connection between Egypt acquiring more land and having more political power, wealth, and cultural influence.

INTERACTIVE WHITEBOARD ACTIVITY Use your interactive whiteboard to help students identify the characteristics of the Hyksos and the Egyptians at the end of the Middle Kingdom.

Ask: How did the Hyksos help the Egyptians? *(They provided knowledge that ultimately made the Egyptians more powerful.)*

2 Building an Empire

GUIDING QUESTION ***Why was the New Kingdom a unique period in ancient Egypt's history?***

Identifying Point out that two of Egypt's leaders—Hatshepsut and Thutmose III—took different steps to increase the size and influence of the Egyptian empire during the New Kingdom. Ask students to identify those steps. *(Hatshepsut developed strong trade relations rather than wage war to gain new territory. Thutmose III conquered territories to expand Egypt's empire.)*

Making Generalizations Tell students to locate the map "Ancient Egyptian Kingdoms" in their textbooks. Have students identify the shaded areas on the map that indicate the borders of the Old Kingdom, the Middle Kingdom, and the New Kingdom. Challenge students to make a generalization about how Egypt changed over time, based on the details on the map. *(Egypt grew in size over time, covering more territory.)* **AL**

Ask: How did the ancient Egyptians increase the size and power of their empire? *(They conquered and developed lands, took resources and goods, enslaved their enemies, and increased their trade with other people.)*

GRAPHIC ORGANIZER **Determining Cause and Effect** Make sure students understand that an empire is a large area of land that is ruled by one government or leader.

Ask: How did the ancient Egyptians increase the power and wealth of their empire during the Middle and New Kingdoms? *(They conquered and developed lands, took resources and goods, enslaved their enemies, built more farms and canals, developed new artistic and architectural methods, and increased their trade with other places.)*

Allow students time to record their answers in the Taking Notes interactive graphic organizer.

CLOSE & REFLECT

Listing Lead students in a discussion that focuses on Egypt at the height of its empire. Have students meet in small groups to list reasons why ancient Egypt was at the height of its powers during the New Kingdom. Ask students to share their lists with the class. **AL**

LESSON 3 • Day 2

ENGAGE

INTERACTIVE WORKSHEET

21st Century Skills Activity

Making Generalizations As a class, create a list of qualities that a good leader should have. Write students' answers on the board. *(Possible answers include integrity, intelligence, honesty, strength, willingness to take risks, and ability to lead during difficult times.)*

Then have students discuss the leadership qualities exhibited by the ancient Egyptian rulers they have read about so far.

Next, have students work alone or in pairs to write an employment advertisement for a pharaoh, using the 21st Century Skills Activity for this lesson. The ad should identify the responsibilities of a pharaoh as well as the qualities that are necessary to rule an empire.

Ask volunteers to share their advertisements with the class.

Tell students they will be learning more about rulers of the Egyptian empire as they continue with the lesson. They will also discover the reasons for the decline of Egyptian power.

TEACH & ASSESS

3 Two Unusual Pharaohs

GUIDING QUESTION ***How did two unusual pharaohs change Egypt?***

4 Recovery and Decline

GUIDING QUESTION ***Why did the Egyptian empire decline in the late 1200s B.C.?***

LECTURE SLIDE **Identifying** Show students the lecture slide with the list of pharaohs of the New Kingdom.

Ask:

- **What changes did Amenhotep IV make?** *(He started a new religion. He took away power from the priests. He moved the capital city from Thebes to Akhetaton.)*
- **What effect did these changes have on ancient Egypt?** *(They unsettled the people and caused Egypt to lose power and influence.)*

Answers for pages 120–123

P. 120 Taking Notes **Middle Kingdom**—Dates: c. 2055 B.C.–c. 1650 B.C. Government: Pharaohs increased farm acreage and improved irrigation. Economy: Trade expanded. **New Kingdom**—Dates: 1550 B.C.–1070 B.C. Government: Ahmose established a new dynasty; Hatshepsut expanded Egypt through trade; Thutmose III expanded the kingdom; and Ramses II expanded the kingdom and formed political ties with neighboring kingdoms. Economy: Trade increased; the building of temples under Ramses II helped the economy grow.

P. 121 CRITICAL THINKING The chair is decorated with great detail and with lion heads.

P. 121 ☑ PROGRESS CHECK During Hyksos rule, the Egyptians improved their fighting skills by learning to drive chariots and to use new weapons. Later, these skills helped the Egyptians, under the leadership of Ahmose, drive out the Hyksos.

P. 122 Reading Strategy The key words *then* and *after* are used in the first paragraph under the head "A Woman Pharaoh."

P. 123 CRITICAL THINKING Hatshepsut was successful because she chose loyal government officials and paid attention to common Egyptians.

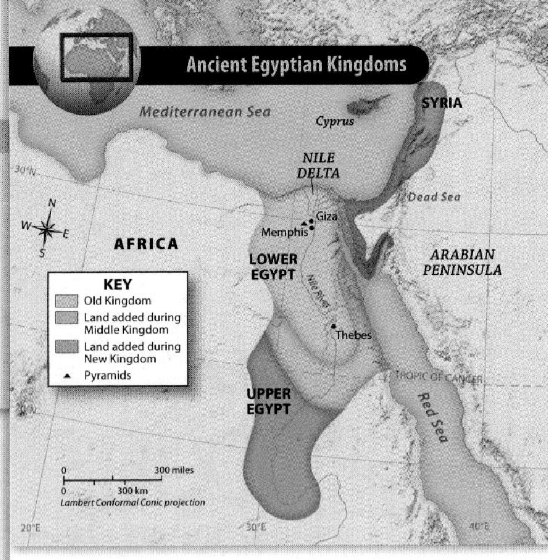

GEOGRAPHY CONNECTION

During the Middle Kingdom, the capital of Egypt was moved from Memphis to Thebes.

1. **LOCATION** Identify the relative location of Thebes.
2. **PLACE** Describe the borders of the New Kingdom.
3. **CRITICAL THINKING** ***Comparing*** Which kingdom added the most territory?

Expanding the Empire

When Hatshepsut died, her nephew, Thutmose III (thoot•MOH•suh), became pharaoh. Thutmose was a strong leader and general who expanded Egypt's control north to the Euphrates River in Mesopotamia. His troops also moved south far up the Nile and conquered Nubia, which had once thrown off Egyptian rule. Egyptian armies captured nearly 350 cities during Thutmose's reign.

As Thutmose and his armies conquered more areas, the Egyptian empire grew wealthy, and slavery became more common. Egypt **acquired** gold, copper, ivory and other valuable goods from conquered peoples. Egyptians captured and enslaved many prisoners of war. Enslaved people had some rights, however, including the right to own land, marry, and eventually gain their freedom.

PROGRESS CHECK

Explaining Why did the Egyptians want to trade with the Phoenicians?

Reading HELPDESK

Academic Vocabulary

acquire to get possession of something

3 Two Unusual Pharaohs

GUIDING QUESTION *How did two unusual pharaohs change ancient Egypt?*

During the New Kingdom, two remarkable pharaohs came to power. One pharaoh, Amenhotep IV, tried to make dramatic changes, and one, Tutankhamen, was very young. Their actions set them apart from other rulers in Egypt's long history.

A Religious Founder

A new pharaoh named Amenhotep IV (ah•muhn•HOH•tehp) came to power in about 1370 B.C. Supported by his wife, Nefertiti (nehf•uhr•TEE•tee), Amenhotep tried to change Egypt's religion, which was based on the worship of many deities.

Amenhotep believed that Egypt's priests had grown too powerful and wealthy. He felt threatened by their power. To lessen the priests' **authority,** Amenhotep started a new religion. He introduced the worship of Aton (AHT•n), the sun god, as Egypt's only god. When Egypt's priests opposed this change, Amenhotep removed many of them from their posts, took their lands, and closed temples. He then changed his name to Akhenaton (ahk•NAH•tuhn), meaning "Spirit of Aton." The capital was moved to a new city north of Thebes called Akhetaton (ahk•heh•TAH•tuhn).

These changes unsettled Egypt. Most Egyptians rejected Aton and continued to worship many deities. In addition, the priests of the old religion resisted their loss of power. The discontent with Akhenaton's rule spread to the army leaders. They believed Akhenaton, devoted to his new religion, neglected his duties as pharaoh. Under Akhenaton's weak rule, Egypt lost most of its lands in western Asia to outside invaders.

Who Was "King Tut"?

When Akhenaton died about 1360 B.C., his son-in-law, 10-year-old Tutankhamen (too•tang•KAH•muhn), became pharaoh. The young pharaoh relied on advice from priests and officials to rule Egypt. Tutankhamen quickly restored the worship of many deities. Tutankhamen's short rule ended after only nine years when he died unexpectedly. The cause of his death is still a mystery to historians.

King Tut is shown wearing the false beard worn by all pharaohs. Tut was a child when he became pharaoh. He died at the age of 19.

Academic Vocabulary

authority the right or power to give orders, make decisions, or control people

Even though "King Tut," played a small role in the history of Egypt, he is the most famous of the pharaohs. British archaeologist Howard Carter attracted public attention when he discovered Tut's tomb in 1922. Carter's find was amazing because most tombs of the pharaohs had been robbed by thieves. Tut's tomb, however, contained the pharaoh's mummy and many treasures, including a brilliant gold mask of the young ruler's face.

PROGRESS CHECK

Evaluating Why are Akhenaton and Tutankhamen considered unusual pharaohs?

4 Recovery and Decline

GUIDING QUESTION *Why did the Egyptian empire decline in the late 1200s B.C.?*

During the 1200s B.C., the pharaohs worked to restore Egypt's greatness. They fought battles for more territory, increased Egypt's wealth through trade, and built large temples and monuments.

Ramses II

The most successful of these pharaohs was Ramses II (RAM•seez), who ruled from 1279 B.C. to 1213 B.C. Ramses conquered the region of Canaan and moved north into Syria. To get this territory, he fought the Hittites, who lived in present-day Turkey. After many battles, Ramses and the Hittite king signed a peace treaty.

Age of Temples

During his 66-year reign, Ramses also devoted himself to peaceful activities. Ramses II and other New Kingdom rulers had many temples built throughout Egypt. One of the most magnificent was Karnak (KAHR•nack) at Thebes. Its huge columned hall still impresses visitors today. A poem celebrating a victory by Ramses is carved in the temple. In part of the poem, Ramses says this to his chariot driver:

> "Halt! take courage, charioteer, As a sparrow-hawk swoops down upon his prey,
> So I swoop upon the foe, and I will slay, I will hew [cut] them into pieces,
> I will dash them into dust."
>
> —from *Pen-ta-tur: The Victory of Ramses II Over the Khita*

Most Egyptians prayed in their homes, so temples were used only for special occasions. Egyptians saw the temples as the

Few rulers reigned as long as Ramses. He reigned three years longer than England's Queen Victoria, who ruled for 63 years. What mathematical expression would tell you the length of Ramses' reign?

Academic Vocabulary

decline to become weaker

Reading Strategy: *Understanding Cause and Effect*

The word *so* indicates the effect of an event. Read the first sentence in the last paragraph above. The *effect* is that temples were used only for special occasions. What is the cause?

Still in use after more than 3,000 years, Karnak remains to honor Ramses' many achievements.

homes of their deities. Priests and priestesses performed daily rituals, washed the statues of the deities, and brought them food.

Temples were important to Egypt's economy. Priests hired people to work in temple workshops and granaries. Temples also served as banks. Egyptians used them to store valuable items, such as gold jewelry, fragrant oils, and finely woven textiles.

Why Did Egypt Decline?

After Ramses II died, Egypt **declined.** Pharaohs fought costly wars. Armies from the eastern Mediterranean attacked Egypt. By 1150 B.C., the Egyptian empire controlled only the Nile delta.

In the 900s B.C., the Libyans conquered Egypt. Then, the people of Kush seized power. Finally, in 670 B.C., Egypt was taken over by the Assyrians from Mesopotamia.

PROGRESS CHECK

Summarizing What were the accomplishments of Ramses II?

LESSON 3 REVIEW

Review Vocabulary

1. Why would someone want to buy *incense*?
2. What might have been the duties of an ancient Egyptian *envoy*?

Answer the Guiding Questions

3. ***Describing*** Discuss two reasons why the Middle Kingdom period was a "golden age" for Egypt.
4. ***Explaining*** Why was the New Kingdom a unique period in ancient Egypt's history?
5. ***Summarizing*** Describe the religious changes brought about by Akhenaton and Tutankhamen.
6. ***Analyzing*** In what ways were temples important to Egypt's economy?
7. **PERSUASIVE WRITING** You are a scribe who works for Queen Hatshepsut. Write a brief report that explains why she is a good pharaoh and deserves the support of the people.

LESSON 3 (cont.)

Comparing and Contrasting Remind students of what they learned about Hatshepsut and Thutmose III. Lead students in a discussion of how those rulers compare to Ramses II and Amenhotep IV. Make sure students understand that, like Hatshepsut and Thutmose III, Ramses II knew the importance of increasing ancient Egypt's territory and maintaining peace. Amenhotep IV, however, did not make the empire stronger or wealthier; instead, he caused it to decline.

LECTURE SLIDE **Discussing** Show students again the lecture slide that lists the pharaohs of the New Kingdom. Make sure students understand that the pharaohs were all-powerful and influenced all aspects of Egyptians' daily life.

Ask: What are two specific examples of how the pharaohs of the New Kingdom used their power over Egyptian daily life? *(Amenhotep IV, also called Akhenaton, was able to change the religion; Hatshepsut was able to increase the empire's wealth through trade, which meant Egypt's merchants and artisans made more money from the sale of goods.)* BL

Identifying Read aloud the following list of actions taken by Egyptian pharaohs. As you read each item, ask students to give a thumbs-up sign if the activity helped strengthen Egypt. Students should give a thumbs-down sign for all activities that led to the empire's decline. Make sure students are in agreement in their answers. AL ELL

Challenge students to identify specific rulers who took these actions. You may choose to display the lecture slide of New Kingdom pharaohs for students to reference. BL

- Building new temples and restoring old tombs *(thumbs-up) (Hatshepsut, Ramses II)*
- Seeking the opinions of common Egyptians *(thumbs-up) (Hatshepsut)*
- Promoting trade *(thumbs-up) (Hatshepsut)*
- Removing a pharaoh's name from public records *(thumbs-down) (Thutmose III)*
- Conquering new territories *(thumbs-up) (Thutmose III, Ramses II)*
- Acquiring resources and valuables *(thumbs-up) (Thutmose III)*
- Founding a new religion and removing priests from power *(thumbs-down) (Amenhotep/Akhenaton)*
- Neglecting duties as a pharaoh *(thumbs-down) (Amenhotep/Akhenaton)*
- Signing a peace agreement with neighbors *(thumbs-up) (Ramses II)*

INTERACTIVE GRAPHIC ORGANIZER Use your interactive whiteboard to help students complete the graphic organizer that matches Egyptian pharaohs to their achievements.

Analyzing Ask students to write a paragraph in which they answer the following questions: **What is an empire? How did a pharaoh help an empire rise or fall?**

Invite one or two volunteers to share their answers with the class. Discuss volunteers' answers with the class.

Have students complete the Lesson 3 Review questions.

CLOSE & REFLECT

Applying Lead students in a discussion of the following question about empire building.

Ask: If you were a new pharaoh, knowing what you do about empire building, what is the first step you would take to build up the Egyptian empire? *(Students may mention conquering new territory, developing new trade routes, building new temples, and restoring tombs as ways to build and strengthen the empire.)*

BACKGROUND KNOWLEDGE

Amenhotep and Changes to Art and Architecture

Along with changing the religion of Egypt and moving the capital, Amenhotep, renamed Akhenaton, changed Egyptian art and architecture as well. For the millennium before his rule, traditional royal Egyptian art was formal and reserved. Akhenaton showed how different his reign would be by breaking from this tradition. This new style had highly exaggerated forms that were almost grotesque and shocking. For example, the royal family was shown with small torsos but large hips and thighs. The skulls were exaggerated and long. Their arms, however, were thin.

Not only was the visual style different, the subject matter of royal art changed. Although art of the period continued to show the king worshiping, ordinary life began to be depicted as well. For example, artists showed Akhenaton and his wife Nefertiti playing with their daughters. Animals and birds also were shown in nature.

The traditional focus on the eternal was replaced by depictions of the here and now. This new art included scenes of everyday life—life that occurs out in the light of the sun, or Aton, the new focus of Akhenaton's religion.

Akhenaton also made changes in temple architecture and how buildings were made. Smaller stone blocks with strong mortar were used. Even official inscriptions changed. The language inscribed on these new buildings began to reflect the spoken language and moved away from the formal, traditional language on monuments in the past. These changes had a profound effect on Egyptian life.

Answers for pages 124–127

P. 124 GEOGRAPHY CONNECTION

1. Thebes is south of Memphis but north of the Tropic of Cancer.
2. The New Kingdom was bordered by the Mediterranean Sea, the Dead Sea, and the Red Sea.
3. CRITICAL THINKING The New Kingdom added the most territory.

P. 124 ☑ PROGRESS CHECK They traded with the Phoenicians to obtain goods they could not make or grow for themselves, especially furniture and wood for building ships.

P. 126 ☑ PROGRESS CHECK Akhenaton took the unusual step of changing the Egyptian religion to the worship of one deity. Tutankhamen is well-known today for the riches found in his tomb, but he was an unusually young pharaoh who died after ruling for only nine years.

P. 126 The length of Ramses' reign can be calculated using the mathematical expression 63 + 3.

P. 126 Reading Strategy The cause is that most Egyptians prayed in their homes.

P. 127 ☑ PROGRESS CHECK Ramses II regained lost territory in western Asia and signed a peace treaty with the Hittite king. He also had temples built, which helped the Egyptian economy.

LESSON 3 REVIEW

1. Someone would want to buy incense to make his or her home smell better or to use in a religious ceremony.
2. An envoy's duties may have included representing the Egyptian empire by meeting with important political leaders in other places and sending reports back to the pharaoh.
3. Egypt acquired new territory and reached the height of its power. With the building of great tombs and statues, the arts and architecture flourished.
4. During the New Kingdom, two remarkable pharaohs came to power. Amenhotep IV tried to change Egypt's religion. Tutankhamen was only a boy.
5. Akhenaton tried to change Egypt's religion. The changes were not popular. They unsettled the people and the Egyptian social structure. The pharaoh's interest in religion made him an ineffective ruler, and Egypt lost territory. Tutankhamen restored the religion but was too young and died too soon to become a ruler who made much impact.
6. Priests hired people to work in the temples' storage buildings and workshops. People also used temples as banks.
7. Students' answers should take the form of a letter and point out that Hatshepsut was a peaceful leader who valued loyalty and believed that trading relations could help maintain the empire better than war could. She also solicited the opinions of ordinary Egyptians before making decisions that affected the empire.

networks
There's More Online!
- ☑ **GRAPHIC ORGANIZER** Kush Conquers Egypt
- ☑ **MAP** Kush Kingdom, c. 250 B.C.

Lesson 4

The Kingdom of Kush

ESSENTIAL QUESTION *Why do civilizations rise and fall?*

It Matters Because

The kingdoms of Nubia and Kush were influenced by Egyptian culture, and they continued many Egyptian traditions.

1 The Nubians

GUIDING QUESTION *How did Nubia and Egypt influence each other?*

In addition to Egypt, other civilizations flourished in Africa. One of these African civilizations was Nubia, later known as Kush. Nubia was located south of Egypt along the Nile River in present-day Sudan.

Cattle herders were the first people to settle in this region, arriving about 2000 B.C. They herded long-horned cattle on the **savannas** (suh•VA•nuhs), or grassy plains, that stretch across Africa south of the Sahara. Later, people settled in farming villages along the Nile River.

Unlike the Egyptians, the Nubians did not **rely** on the Nile floods to create fertile soil. Their land had fertile soil and received rainfall all year long. Nubian villagers grew crops such as beans, yams, rice, and grains. The Nubians also hunted for food. Their hunters and warriors excelled at using the bow and arrow.

The Rise of Kerma

Gradually, the stronger Nubian villages took over the weaker ones and formed the kingdom of Kerma (KAR•muh). The Nubians of Kerma grew wealthy from agriculture and the mining of gold. Their kingdom developed a close relationship with Egypt in the north. Kerma's central location in the Nile valley benefited the Nubians. It made Kerma an important trade link between Egypt and the tropical areas of southern Africa. From Kerma, the Egyptians acquired cattle, gold, incense, ivory, giraffes, leopards, and enslaved people. They also hired Nubians to serve in their armies because of their skills in warfare. Kerma's artisans produced fine pottery, jewelry, and metal goods.

Workers built tombs for Kerma's kings, usually on a smaller scale than Egyptian tombs. Like the Egyptian pharaohs, the kings of Kerma were buried with their personal belongings, including valuable gems, gold, jewelry, and pottery. These artifacts were as magnificent as those found in Egypt's royal tombs that were built during the same time period.

Egyptian Invasion

Egyptian armies invaded Nubia in the 1400s B.C. After a 50-year war, the Egyptians conquered the kingdom of Kerma and ruled it for the next 700 years.

As a result of Egyptian rule, the Nubians adopted many of the beliefs and customs of Egyptian culture. For example, the Nubians worshipped Egyptian gods and goddesses along with their own Nubian deities. They learned to use copper and bronze to make tools. The Nubians adapted Egyptian hieroglyphs to fit their own language and created an alphabet.

☑ **PROGRESS CHECK**

Analyzing Why did Kerma become an important center for trade?

The savannas of Africa are grassy and dotted with trees and herds of wildlife. The grasses can withstand long, hot periods without rain. These broad plains covered much of Nubia.

Reading HELPDESK

Taking Notes: *Sequencing*

Use a diagram like this one to list events that led up to the Kush conquest of Egypt.

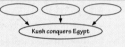

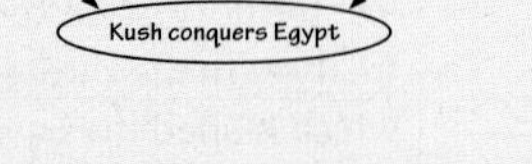

Content Vocabulary
- savanna
- textile

savanna a flat grassland, sometimes with scattered trees, in a tropical or subtropical region

Academic Vocabulary

rely to depend on someone or something

2 The Kushite Kingdom

GUIDING QUESTION *Why did the kingdom of Kush prosper?*

By the end of the Middle Kingdom, Egypt was weak. It could no longer govern its conquered peoples effectively, and the Nubians were able to break away from Egyptian rule.

The Rise of Kush

By 850 B.C., the Nubians had formed an independent kingdom known as Kush. Powerful kings ruled the country from its capital at Napata (NA•puh•tuh).

The city of Napata was located where trade caravans crossed the upper part of the Nile River. Caravans came from central Africa, bringing ivory and other goods. They stopped at Napata for Kushite products and then continued on to Egypt. The Egyptians traded with Kush for goods the Egyptians could not make. Such trade brought wealth to the traders and kings of Kush.

Kush Conquers Egypt

In time, Kush became powerful enough to **challenge** Egypt. About 750 B.C., a Kushite king named Kashta (KAHSH•tuh) invaded Egypt. His soldiers reached the city of Thebes. After Kashta died, his son Piye (PY) became king and completed the conquest of Egypt in 728 B.C. Piye founded the Twenty-fifth Dynasty that governed Egypt and Kush from Napata.

The kings and wealthy people of Kush continued to admire Egyptian culture. Kushites built white sandstone temples and monuments similar to those in Egypt. The Kushites also believed in a close relationship between their rulers and their deities, many of whom were Egyptian. For example, when a king died, Kushite officials met at the temple to ask the Egyptian god Amon-Re to appoint a new leader:

In this scene, Nubian royalty offer gifts to an Egyptian pharaoh. The procession shows respect for the pharaoh.

Kush Kingdom c. 250 B.C.

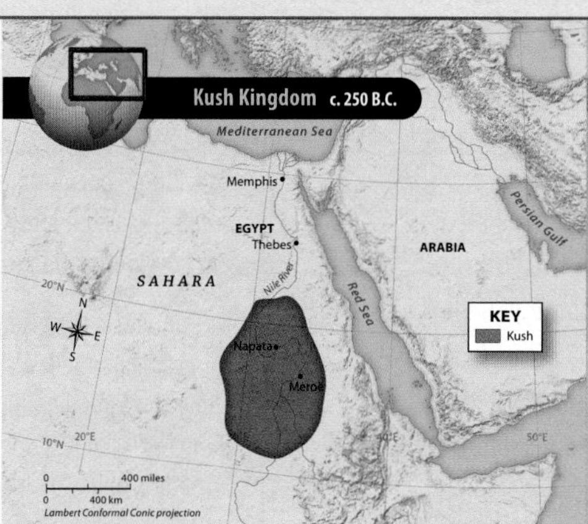

GEOGRAPHY CONNECTION

Trade caravans crossed the Nile near Napata, which made the city a busy trading center.

1. **LOCATION** In what direction would traders travel to get from Napata to Meroë?
2. **CRITICAL THINKING** ***Analyzing*** How is the Nile different south of Meroë?

PRIMARY SOURCE

> "So the commanders of His Majesty and the officials of the palace . . . [found] the major priests waiting outside the temple. They said to them, "Pray, may this god, Amon-Re . . . give us our lord. . . . We cannot do a thing without this god. It is he who guides us. . . ." Then the commanders . . . and the officials . . . entered into the temple and put themselves upon their bellies before this god. They said, "We have come to you, O Amon-Re, . . . that you might give to us a lord, to revive us, to build the temples of the gods, . . ."
>
> —from *The Selection of Aspalta as King of Kush*

The Kushites also built small, steeply-sloped pyramids as tombs for their kings. Some people in Kush, however, adopted customs and styles similar to those worn by southern Africans. This included wearing ankle and ear jewelry. By this time, the people of Kush also had developed their own style of painted pottery. The elephant, a sacred animal in Kush, was used as a theme in sculpture and other arts.

Kushite artisans worked in gold, creating objects such as this statue of Amon-Re. They also made fine pottery.

Reading HELPDESK

Academic Vocabulary

challenge to invite the start of a competition

Reading Strategy: *Reading a Map*

When reading a map, first locate the key. It will help you identify what is being shown on the map. What is the key identifying on the map above?

LESSON 4

ENGAGE

LECTURE SLIDE

Making Connections Begin by showing students the lecture slide that defines *cultural diffusion.* Lead students in a discussion of how cultures interact and shape one another.

Ask students for examples of how their lives are affected or influenced by other cultures.

Ask:

Do you enjoy music, food, clothing, or games that are from other cultures?

How or why do certain cultures "rub off" on each other? AL ELL

Students should understand that cultures that are close geographically often influence each other.

Explain that the ancient Egyptians influenced many civilizations in the region. Tell students that in this lesson they will learn how Nubia and Egypt influenced each other and why the kingdom of Kush rose to power.

TEACH & ASSESS

1 The Nubians

GUIDING QUESTION *How did Nubia and Egypt influence each other?*

GRAPHIC ORGANIZER

Sequencing After students have finished reading the lesson, have them complete the Taking Notes sequencing activity in the lesson opener.

Make sure students understand that a weakened Egypt allowed the formerly conquered Nubians to regain territories and become powerful.

Have students reinforce the sequence by turning the information in the diagram into a time line. Students should refer to their textbooks for dates to insert in their time lines.

Making Generalizations After students read about the rise of the Nubian kingdom of Kerma and its time under Egyptian rule, ask them to make a generalization about how the two cultures interacted.

Ask:

Why was Egypt an influence on the Nubians? *(Nubia traded with Egypt and later was under Egyptian rule.)*

In what ways did Egypt shape Nubian culture? *(Nubians adopted Egyptian religious practices as well as hieroglyphics and tool-making skills.)* BL

2 The Kushite Kingdom

GUIDING QUESTION *Why did the kingdom of Kush prosper?*

INTERACTIVE WORKSHEET

Economics of History Activity

Making Connections Explain that Kush, Assyria, and Egypt had strong economic and cultural ties. Have students turn to the Economics of History Activity for this lesson to help them identify the exchanges among the three cultures.

As students complete the activity,

ask:

What ideas or goods were exchanged among the Egyptians, Kushites, and Assyrians? *(Egypt gave Kush its religion and the idea to build pyramids and monuments; the Assyrians gave the Kushites the technology to make iron tools and weapons; Kush traded goods with Egypt.)*

Then lead students in a class discussion.

Ask:

- **Why would the Kushites continue to admire the ancient Egyptians even after conquering them?** *(The Kushites lived with the Egyptians for many years and had adopted their customs and culture.)*
- **How did southern Africans influence the Kushites?** *(The Kushites adopted ankle and ear jewelry worn by southern Africans.)*
- **Why did the Kushites want to learn how to make iron from the Assyrians?** *(Kushite bronze weapons and tools were not as strong as iron ones. Iron tools allowed them to grow more food, and iron weapons boosted the Kushites' military strength.)*
- **How was the city of Meroë like and unlike an Egyptian city?** *(Its layout was like an Egyptian city, and it contained tombs and monuments. Unlike Egypt's cities, Meroë had many iron furnaces.)*

Have students complete the Lesson 4 Review questions.

CLOSE & REFLECT

Identifying Discuss as a class the best graphic organizer for identifying the trade relationships between the Kushites and other peoples.

Suggest that students draw a web diagram with the center circle labeled "Kush." Have students work in small groups to draw satellite circles and label them with the names of Kushite trading partners. *(Egypt, southern Africa, India, Arabia, China, and Rome)*

Students should then draw arrows to and from the center circle to each smaller one. On the arrows, students should write the goods that were traded or exchanged.

For example, the Kushites sent leopard skins, wood, slaves, and iron products to Rome. They received woven cloth and other goods in return. AL ELL

Answers for pages 128–131

P. 128 Taking Notes New Kingdom declines; Nubians rebel and found Kush; Kush grows rich from trade; Kush conquers Egypt.

P. 129 ☑ PROGRESS CHECK Kerma was centrally located in Nubia and had close relations with Egypt.

P. 131 Reading Strategy The key identifies the color used to show Kush.

P. 131 GEOGRAPHY CONNECTION

1. Traders would travel southeast to get from Napata to Meroë.
2. CRITICAL THINKING South of Meroë, the Nile is two rivers instead of one.

Using Iron

Kush ruled Egypt for about 60 years. In 671 B.C., the Assyrians invaded Egypt. Armed with iron weapons, the Assyrians defeated the Kushites, who only had bronze weapons, which were not as strong. The Kushites fled Egypt and returned to their homeland in the south.

Despite their defeat in Egypt, the Kushites learned how to make iron from the Assyrians. Farmers in Kush used iron to make their hoes and plows instead of copper or stone. With better tools, they were able to grow more grain and other crops. Kushite warriors also created iron weapons, which boosted their military strength.

The Capital of Meroë

About 540 B.C., Kush's rulers moved their capital to the city of Meroë (MEHR•oh•ee), near one of the Nile's cataracts. This move made them safer from Assyrian attacks. The Nile River continued to provide a means for trade and transportation for the Kushites. Large deposits of iron ore and trees were nearby and were used to fuel furnaces for making iron. As a result, Meroë became a major center for iron production as well as a busy trading city.

Kushite kings modeled the layout and design of Meroë after Egypt's great cities. A temple dedicated to the god Amon-Re stood at the end of a long avenue lined with sculptures of rams. The walls of palaces and houses were decorated with paintings. Small pyramids stood in the royal graveyard, modeled on the larger pyramids of Egypt. Meroë, however, was different from a typical Egyptian city because it contained iron furnaces. Huge columns of smoke poured out of iron furnaces. Heaps of shiny black slag, or waste from iron making, lay around the furnaces.

The Kushites adopted pyramids as tombs. They usually built tombs that were smaller than those of the Egyptians, however.

Reading **HELP**DESK

textile woven cloth

Modeled on Egyptian cities, Meroë had a special purpose. It was an iron-making city with smokestacks and soot.

A Trading Center

Meroë was at the heart of a large web of trade that ran north to Egypt's border and south into central Africa. Kush's merchants received leopard skins and valuable woods from the tropical interior of Africa. They traded these items, along with enslaved workers and their own iron products, to places as far away as Arabia, India, China, and Rome. In return, they brought back cotton, **textiles** (TEHK•styls), or woven cloth, and other goods. Kush's merchants used their wealth to build fine houses and public baths like ones they had seen in Rome.

Kush remained a great trading kingdom for nearly 600 years. Then, another kingdom called Axum (AHK•soom) emerged near the Red Sea in eastern Africa. Axum is located in the present-day country of Ethiopia. Axum gained its strength from its location on the Red Sea. Goods from Africa flowed into Axum. Over time, it served as a trading center for the ancient Mediterranean and East African worlds. Around A.D. 350, the armies of Axum invaded Kush and destroyed Meroë.

✓ PROGRESS CHECK

Explaining How did the use of iron affect Kush?

LESSON 4 REVIEW

Review Vocabulary

1. What are the characteristics of a *savanna*?
2. What are *textiles* used to make?

Answer the Guiding Questions

3. ***Explaining*** How did Nubia and Egypt influence one other?
4. ***Comparing and Contrasting*** How were the cities of Kush similar to and different from those of Egypt?
5. ***Drawing Conclusions*** How did natural resources help make Meroë a great trading city?
6. **PERSUASIVE WRITING** Create an advertisement that could have been used in ancient Egypt and Kush to encourage people to use iron.

NOTES

NOTES

IF YOU HAVE MORE TIME . . .

Examine Power Exchange Between Nubia and Egypt

Explaining Explain that Nubia was an important trading partner with Egypt. Nubia spent many centuries under Egyptian control, but when Egypt weakened, the Nubians conquered their former ruler.

Have students think of examples of countries today that are located near each other but have troubled relationships. *(Students may draw on their own experiences or on their understanding of current events. For example, they might point to the relationship between India and Pakistan or North Korea and South Korea.)*

Ask:

What often happens when one group suddenly becomes more powerful than another? *(The relationships between the groups can change. One group might become more influential or important than the other.)*

Work in Groups to Compare and Contrast Egyptian and Nubian Culture

Comparing and Contrasting Have students work in small groups to examine Egyptian and Nubian culture, institutions, and ways of life.

Tell students first to brainstorm categories, such as religion, agriculture, and art.

Have them consult their textbooks or do research in the library or on the Internet.

Remind students of safety guidelines for Internet research. Also, students should be aware of what quality source material consists of.

After they have finished their research, ask students to create a Venn diagram that identifies similarities and differences between Egyptian and Nubian civilizations.

Have students share their findings with the class.

Make the Connection Between Nubian Skills

Analyzing Point out to students that the Nubians were excellent warriors and served in Egyptian armies because of these skills.

Ask students to speculate why the Nubians were excellent at warfare. Help students make the connection between their hunting skills and their skills in warfare. BL

Summarize Nubian Civilization

Describing For reinforcement, have students write a description of the Nubian civilization. Students should explain who the Nubians were, where they lived, how their civilization developed, and what their relationship was like with the Egyptians. AL ELL Students should practice using descriptive vocabulary in their summaries.

Encourage students to use create a chart, if needed, to help organize the information in their summaries. Students can browse through the textbook and refer to heads in the Lesson to help guide them. AL ELL

Ask volunteers to share their descriptions with the class.

BACKGROUND KNOWLEDGE

Reading Strategy: Reviewing

As students read, teachers should pause at various points to review. Periodic review is especially important when students read informational text that is dense with new concepts. Reading guides help students negotiate their way through difficult text and keep struggling readers on task. These guides are also helpful models to use when reviewing a selection. Outlines, charts, graphic organizers, and other visual aids help students organize information as they read and are valuable aids for reviewing information after reading. Students can also use these aids when they are summarizing.

Answers for pages 132–133

P. 133 ☑ PROGRESS CHECK Tools and weapons made from iron were stronger than those made from copper. As a result, the Kushites had stronger weapons for fighting and stronger tools for growing more crops. With these tools, Kush grew militarily and economically.

LESSON 4 REVIEW

1. Savannas are grassy plains that stretch across Africa south of the Sahara Desert.
2. Textiles are used to make clothes and other items, such as sheets and towels.
3. Egypt admired Nubia's skills in warfare and traded for goods they needed. Nubian leaders were buried in tombs, much like the pharaohs of Egypt. Nubians also worshiped Egyptian gods and adopted hieroglyphics.
4. Kush cities had a design and layout similar to the design of cities in Egypt. Kush cities, like Egyptian cities, contained temples and pyramid tombs. Unlike Egyptian cities, the Kush capital of Meroë contained wood-fueled iron furnaces.
5. The land contained rich deposits of iron ore. The city had access to the Nile River for trade and transportation.
6. Students' advertisements should point out that iron has many uses; for example, it can be used in the manufacturing of weapons and tools. Iron tools and weapons would help people become more productive farmers and more effective soldiers.

CHAPTER 5 Activities

Write your answers on a separate piece of paper.

1. **Exploring the Essential Question**
   EXPOSITORY WRITING Why did ancient Egyptian civilization fail? Write an essay that explains the events and decisions that led to the end of Egypt's role as a political, economic, and cultural power.

2. **21st Century Skills**
   GIVING A PRESENTATION Prepare a presentation that identifies the key events and achievements of Egypt's Old Kingdom, Middle Kingdom, and New Kingdom. Compare and contrast the developments in each time period. End your presentation with a brief statement about the importance of the Egyptian civilization.

3. **Thinking Like a Historian**
   UNDERSTANDING PROS AND CONS Create a chart like the one here to identify the pros and cons of living along the Nile River. Then write a sentence that tells why early Egyptians settled there.

Characteristics of the Nile River	Pros	Cons
Regular flooding		
Cataracts		
Downhill flow		

4. **GEOGRAPHY ACTIVITY**

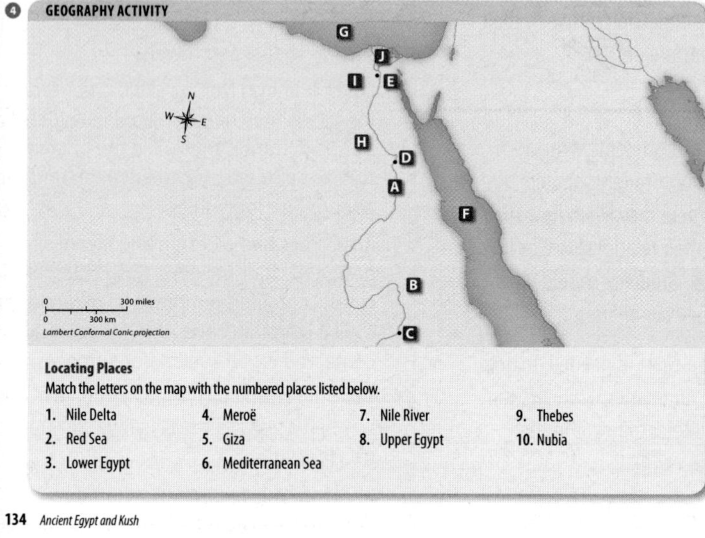

Locating Places
Match the letters on the map with the numbered places listed below.

1. Nile Delta	4. Meroë	7. Nile River	9. Thebes
2. Red Sea	5. Giza	8. Upper Egypt	10. Nubia
3. Lower Egypt	6. Mediterranean Sea		

CHAPTER 5 Assessment

REVIEW THE GUIDING QUESTIONS
Directions: Choose the best answer for each question.

1. What did the delta of the Nile River provide Egyptians?
   A. trade route to the Mediterranean Sea
   B. protection from invaders
   C. fertile soil for growing crops
   D. regular rainfall

2. Who was responsible for uniting and governing Egypt?
   F. bureaucrats
   G. priests
   H. workers
   I. pharaohs

3. Egyptians built pyramids because they
   A. wished to honor the achievements of their leaders.
   B. desired to please the gods.
   C. hoped to impress later civilizations with their buildings.
   D. wanted to protect the dead pharaohs' bodies.

4. The largest group in Egyptian society was made up of
   F. farmers and workers.
   G. scribes and traders.
   H. artisans and merchants.
   I. army commanders and nobles.

5. What was the main focus of Queen Hatshepsut's rule?
   A. building pyramids
   B. developing trade
   C. preparing for the afterlife
   D. conquering new territory

6. How were Kushites different from the Egyptians?
   F. They produced large amounts of iron.
   G. They built temples and tombs for their kings.
   H. They used a system of writing with hieroglyphics.
   I. They sailed the Nile to reach faraway trading partners.

CHAPTER 5 Assessment *(continued)*

DBQ DOCUMENT-BASED QUESTIONS

7. **Drawing Conclusions** An epic poem describes the victory of King Ramses II over the Hittites.

Then the King spake [spoke] to his squire,
"Halt! take courage, charioteer,
As a sparrow-hawk swoops down on his prey
So I swoop upon the foe [enemy], and I will slay."

—from *Pen-ta-tur: The Victory of Ramses II Over the Khita*

Which word best describes Ramses as he is depicted in the poem?
A. bird-like
B. innocent
C. uncertain
D. courageous

8. **Inferring** How might the Egyptians have reacted to this poem?
   F. It made them afraid of their king.
   G. It made them regret going to war.
   H. It made them feel proud to be Egyptian.
   I. It made them worry about losing to the enemy.

SHORT RESPONSE

"To build such monumental structures, the Egyptians needed a highly organized workforce. From tomb inscriptions and from laborers' instructions on walls, [...] researchers can now draw something close to a modern personnel chart for the ancient workers. 'Every project like a pyramid had a crew of workers,' explains Ann Roth, an Egyptologist who has studied the groups of workers in detail. 'And each group was responsible for one part of the pyramid complex.'"

— from "The Pyramid Builders" by Virginia Morell

9. How did Egyptian workers cooperate to build the pyramids?

10. Why did workers need to be organized to build the pyramids?

EXTENDED RESPONSE

11. **Descriptive Writing** You are an Egyptian trader visiting the Kush city of Meroë. Write a journal entry in which you describe the city and compare it to your Egyptian home.

Need Extra Help?

If You've Missed Question	1	2	3	4	5	6	7	8	9	10	11
Review Lesson	1	2	2	2	3	4	3	3	2	2	4

NOTES

REFLECT, REVIEW, & REMEDIATE

INTERACTIVE WORKSHEET

Chapter Summary

Provide students with the Chapter Summary worksheet to help review the chapter and prepare for assessment.

Reviewing the Enduring Understandings

Review this chapter's Enduring Understandings with students:

- People, places, and ideas change over time.
- Cultures are held together by shared beliefs and common practices and values.

INTERACTIVE WHITEBOARD On the whiteboard, have student volunteers create a three-column chart and write "Ancient Egypt" in one column and "Ancient Kush" in the other. Then lead a discussion that allows students to recall features of daily life, the economy, and key events for each empire. A student volunteer should record answers in the chart.

	Ancient Egypt	Ancient Kush
Daily Life		
Economy		
Key Events		

ACTIVITIES ANSWERS

Exploring the Essential Question

1. Students should note that Egyptian civilization lasted many centuries and experienced several declines or downturns, but it usually recovered and entered a new period of prosperity and influence. They should identify factors that caused ancient Egypt to decline, such as weak leadership, costly wars, and loss of land, as well as the arrival of other powerful groups, such as the Kushites and Assyrians, who had superior weapons.

21st Century Skills

2. Students should highlight the historical and cultural events of each time period and be able to compare them. For example, students should mention the establishment of the dynastic system of rule, the development during the Old Kingdom of a religion based on belief in an afterlife, and the empire building of Hatshepsut, Thutmose III, and Ramses II. Students' presentations should include a statement that summarizes the contributions of Egyptian civilization to world history.

Thinking Like a Historian

3. Graphic organizers should identify advantages and disadvantages. For example, regular flooding meant being displaced, but it also enriched the soil for growing crops. Cataracts provided a natural defense but made travel on the Nile difficult. A northward, downhill flow meant that using the Nile to travel to the Nile Delta and the Mediterranean Sea was easy but traveling to southern Africa on the Nile was difficult.

Locating Places

4. **1.** J, **2.** F, **3.** I, **4.** C, **5.** E, **6.** G, **7.** A, **8.** H, **9.** D, **10.** B

ASSESSMENT ANSWERS

Review the Guiding Questions

1. **B** The marshy delta of the Nile prevented invaders from entering Egypt. It did not provide a trade route, fertile soil for growing crops, or regular rainfall. Thus, B is the correct answer.

2. **I** Workers were members of Egypt's lowest social class. They could not be responsible for the government. Priests and bureaucrats performed vital tasks in the Egyptian empire, but ultimately it was the pharaoh's job to unite and govern Egypt. Therefore, I is the correct answer.

3. **D** Egyptians believed in the afterlife; therefore, it was important to preserve a pharaoh's body so that his soul, which resided in his body, could complete the journey through the afterlife. As a result, they built pyramids to protect the pharaohs' bodies from floods, dust and heat, and robbers. Thus, the correct answer is D.

4. **F** Farmers and workers made up the lowest and largest group in Egyptian society. Scribes, traders, artisans, merchants, army commanders, and nobles belonged to groups that made up a smaller percentage of the population. Thus, F is the correct answer.

5. **B** Unlike leaders before and after, Hatshepsut was more interested in improving trading ties with neighboring lands than with starting wars to gain more territory. Trade increased during her reign. Thus, B is correct.

6. **F** Students should understand that the Kushites were greatly influenced by the Egyptians even after Kush had conquered Egypt. The Kushites built cities and burial grounds like those of the Egyptians and adapted the Egyptian writing system. Unlike the Egyptians, however, the Kushites had access to wood and iron ore and built furnaces to produce iron. Therefore, F is correct.

Document-Based Questions

7. **D** In addition to references to sparrows and swooping, the king's speech contains strong words about fighting and courage. He speaks as a person who is confident in his leadership abilities and unafraid of battle. D is the best answer.

8. **H** The poem speaks of strength and victory, so Egyptians probably felt pride when they read or heard it. Thus, H is the correct answer.

Short Response

9. Students should understand that building the pyramids required the labor of many people working together to cut and move large objects and to fit them together. As the excerpt suggests, they would have had to cooperate and coordinate their efforts to get the work done.

10. Students should understand that the pyramids were massive projects that involved many different structures and required many people to build them. In order to get the pyramids built properly, workers would have needed to organize themselves and plan how and when to work.

Extended Response

11. Students' journal entries should contain descriptive phrases indicating that Meroë was a busy trading city that was influenced by Egyptian culture. Their entries should include specific details about the layout and design of the city, including the presence of wood-burning iron furnaces.

ONLINE RESOURCES

networks

There's More Online!

- INTERACTIVE WORKSHEETS
- BIOGRAPHIES
- CHARTS/GRAPHS
- GAMES
- GRAPHIC ORGANIZERS
- IMAGES
- MAPS
- PRIMARY SOURCES
- SLIDE SHOWS
- TIME LINE
- LECTURE SLIDES
- INTERACTIVE WHITEBOARD ACTIVITIES
- ASSESSMENTS
- VIDEOS

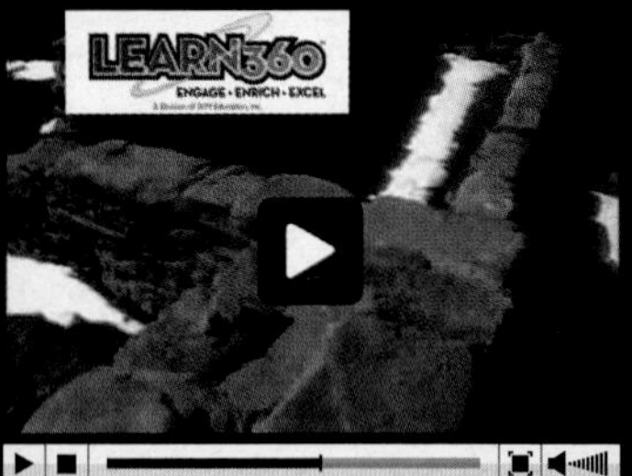

Assignment: Galilee–Israeli Culture

The Middle East: A Region of Contrasts

Temple Mount

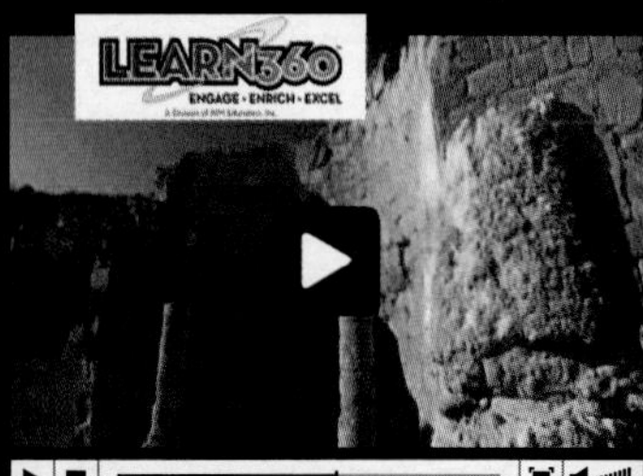

Temple of Herod

Chapter 6

The Israelites

Dear World History Teacher,

Despite some differences, scholars today agree that between 1200 and 1000 B.C., the Israelites emerged as a distinct group of people. They organized into tribes or a league of tribes, who eventually established a kingdom.

Three leaders—Saul, David, and Solomon—were influential in establishing Israelite control over Canaan in the 900s B.C. After Solomon's death, tensions between the northern and southern tribes in Israel led to the formation of two separate kingdoms—the kingdom of Israel in the north and the southern kingdom of Judah. The Assyrians conquered the kingdom of Israel in 722 B.C., and Judah fell to the Chaldeans in 586 B.C. Judeans, as the people of Judah were called, were exiled in Babylon, the Chaldean capital. Later, under the Persians, the Judeans, now known as the Jews, were allowed to return to Jerusalem and rebuild their city. The Jews gave their name to Judaism, a world religion that influenced Christianity and Islam.

The major tenet of Judaism is the belief in one God. The Jews collected sacred writings in the Hebrew Bible. From the Hebrew Bible came concepts that ultimately enriched Western civilization, including social justice and the belief in an ultimate age of universal peace.

Jackson J. Spielvogel

More Media Resources

Current Events Online

Visit McGraw-Hill's current events Web site for high-interest news stories and activities for your students. Access the site through the Student or Teacher Center in **networks.**

Reading List

Grade 6 reading level:
Exodus, by Brian Wildsmith

Grade 7 reading level:
Words and Miracles: A Passover Companion, by Eric A. Kimmel

Grade 8 reading level:
It's a Miracle! A Hanukkah Storybook, by Stephanie Spinner

At the MOVIES

Watch clips of popular culture films about the Israelites, such as *The Ten Commandments* (1956, Paramount).

Discuss: **Can fictional movies accurately capture historical events?**

NOTE: Be sure to preview any clips to ensure they are age-appropriate.

Search for more videos online in the **networks** Resource Library.

CHAPTER 6 Planner

UNDERSTANDING BY DESIGN®

Enduring Understandings

- *People, places, and ideas change over time.* • *The value that a society places on individual rights is often reflected in that society's government.* • *Countries have relationships with each other.*

Essential Questions

- *How do religions develop?* • *What are the characteristics of a leader?*
- *How does religion shape society?* • *Why does conflict develop?*

Students will know:

- *the differences between monotheism and polytheism*
- *the beliefs of the ancient Israelites*
- *the key leaders of the ancient Israelites*
- *about the Jewish exile in Babylon and the Jews' return to Judah*
- *what life was like for Jews during Greek and Roman rule*

Students will be able to:

- **contrast** religious concepts
- **identify** leaders and key historical figures
- **read** a historical map of Southwest Asia/Canaan
- **analyze** how geography contributes to settlement
- **draw** a map of Canaan or of a dwelling in Canaan
- **analyze** the role of kings in ancient Israel
- **summarize** information about the ancient Israelites
- **read** a map depicting the Jewish exile to Babylon
- **identify** the role of scribes in spreading ideas
- **demonstrate** understanding of Jewish culture and interpret what they learned
- **analyze** how conflicts develop
- **read and interpret** primary sources
- **make** the connection between historical events and religious holidays
- **use** a graphic organizer to differentiate four different Jewish groups under Roman rule

Predictable Misunderstandings

Students may think:

- Judaism did not influence other world religions.
- The Phoenicians made no lasting contributions to world culture.
- All the Jewish people supported Roman rule over their homeland.

Assessment Evidence

Performance Task

- Hands-On Chapter Project

Other Evidence

- Interactive Graphic Organizer activities
- Geography and History Activity
- 21st Century Skills Activities
- Primary Source Activities
- Lesson Reviews
- Interactive Whiteboard Activities
- Classroom discussions
- Summary paragraph

Pacing Guide

Introducing the Chapter	1 day
Lesson 1 Beginnings	2 days
Lesson 2 The Israelite Kingdom	2 days
Lesson 3 The Development of Judaism	2 days
Lesson 4 The Jews in the Mediterranean World	2 days
Chapter Activities and Assessment	1 day
TOTAL TIME	**10 Days**

Differentiated Instruction

These lesson plans are written to address the needs of your On Level students. Discussion and activities that are well-suited to your Approaching Grade Level learners, Beyond Grade Level learners, as well as your English Language Learners, are coded as follows:

AL **Approaching Grade Level**

BL **Beyond Grade Level**

ELL **English Language Learner**

NCSS Standards in "The Israelites"

Learners will understand:

1 CULTURE

4. That the beliefs, values, and behaviors of a culture form an integrated system that helps shape the activities and ways of life that define a culture

5. How individuals learn the elements of their culture through interactions with others, and how individuals learn of other cultures through communication and study

2 TIME, CONTINUITY, AND CHANGE

7. The contributions of key persons, groups, and events from the past and their influence on the present

3 PEOPLE, PLACES, AND ENVIRONMENTS

8. Factors that contribute to cooperation and conflict among peoples of the nation and world, including language, religion, and political beliefs

5 INDIVIDUALS, GROUPS, AND INSTITUTIONS

8. That when two or more groups with differing norms and beliefs interact, accommodation or conflict may result

CHAPTER 6

Introducing the Chapter

(Student Edition p. 137)

The Story Matters . . .

Read "The Story Matters . . ." aloud in class or ask for a volunteer to read it aloud. Discuss with students David's rise to greatness.

Ask:

Who are some other important historical leaders who rose to power from humble beginnings?

Have students share examples with which they are familiar, such as Abraham Lincoln or Andrew Jackson.

Then ask:

How do the life stories of historical figures affect the way we think about them?

Guide the class in a discussion of this question. Point out that knowing about a historical figure's life can make learning about the events involving that person more interesting or easier to understand. Tell students they can learn more online about the story of David's life.

The Israelites

1800 B.C. to A.D. 70

ESSENTIAL QUESTIONS • *How do religions develop?* • *What are the characteristics of a leader?* • *How does religion shape society?* • *Why does conflict develop?*

networks *There's More Online* about the lives and customs of the Israelites.

CHAPTER 6

Lesson 1 *Beginnings*

Lesson 2 *The Israelite Kingdom*

Lesson 3 *The Development of Judaism*

Lesson 4 *The Jews in the Mediterranean World*

The Story Matters . . .

David is regarded as the greatest Israelite king, yet he was not born into royalty. David, a shepherd, became a leader of the Israelite people. As their king, he united the Israelites and expanded their lands. He was also the author of the Psalms, or poems often used in prayer and song. David stands as the greatest among many important leaders who guided the Israelites throughout their history.

◄ *As a young man, David was known for his bravery and his skill in playing the lyre, a type of harp.*

Lebrecht Music and Arts Photo Library/Alamy

137

Introducing Place and Time

(Student Edition pp. 138–139)

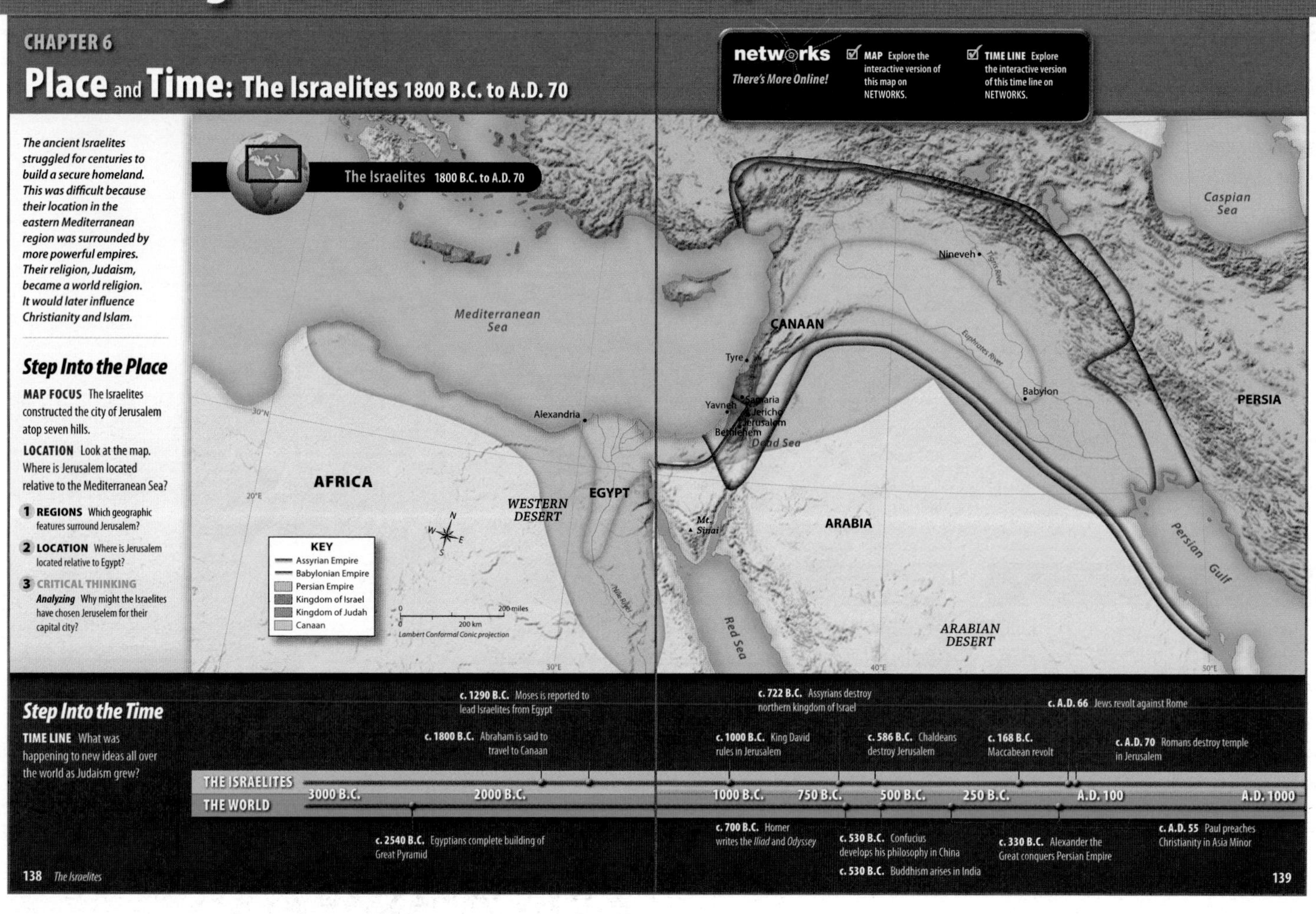

CHAPTER 6
Place and Time: The Israelites 1800 B.C. to A.D. 70
networks There's More Online!
MAP Explore the interactive version of this map on NETWORKS.
TIME LINE Explore the interactive version of this time line on NETWORKS.
The ancient Israelites struggled for centuries to build a secure homeland. This was difficult because their location in the eastern Mediterranean region was surrounded by more powerful empires. Their religion, Judaism, became a world religion. It would later influence Christianity and Islam.
Step Into the Place
MAP FOCUS The Israelites constructed the city of Jerusalem atop seven hills.
LOCATION Look at the map. Where is Jerusalem located relative to the Mediterranean Sea?
1 REGIONS Which geographic features surround Jerusalem?
2 LOCATION Where is Jerusalem located relative to Egypt?
3 CRITICAL THINKING Analyzing Why might the Israelites have chosen Jeruselem for their capital city?
The Israelites 1800 B.C. to A.D. 70
Mediterranean Sea
AFRICA
Alexandria
EGYPT
WESTERN DESERT
KEY
Assyrian Empire
Babylonian Empire
Persian Empire
Kingdom of Israel
Kingdom of Judah
Canaan
200 miles
200 km
Lambert Conformal Conic projection
CANAAN
Tyre
Yavneh
Samaria
Jericho
Jerusalem
Bethlehem
Dead Sea
Mt. Sinai
Red Sea
ARABIA
ARABIAN DESERT
Nineveh
Babylon
Euphrates River
Tigris River
PERSIA
Caspian Sea
Persian Gulf
Step Into the Time
TIME LINE What was happening to new ideas all over the world as Judaism grew?
c. 1800 B.C. Abraham is said to travel to Canaan
c. 1290 B.C. Moses is reported to lead Israelites from Egypt
c. 1000 B.C. King David rules in Jerusalem
c. 722 B.C. Assyrians destroy northern kingdom of Israel
c. 586 B.C. Chaldeans destroy Jerusalem
c. 168 B.C. Maccabean revolt
c. A.D. 66 Jews revolt against Rome
c. A.D. 70 Romans destroy temple in Jerusalem
THE ISRAELITES
THE WORLD
3000 B.C.
2000 B.C.
1000 B.C.
750 B.C.
500 B.C.
250 B.C.
A.D. 100
A.D. 1000
c. 2540 B.C. Egyptians complete building of Great Pyramid
c. 700 B.C. Homer writes the Iliad and Odyssey
c. 530 B.C. Confucius develops his philosophy in China
c. 530 B.C. Buddhism arises in India
c. 330 B.C. Alexander the Great conquers Persian Empire
c. A.D. 55 Paul preaches Christianity in Asia Minor
138 The Israelites
139

Technology Extension
- Find an additional activity online that incorporates technology for this project.
- Visit the EdTechTeacher Web sites (included in the Technology Extension for this chapter) for more links, tutorials, and other resources.

Assessing Background Knowledge

INTERACTIVE WORKSHEET

What Do You Know? Activity

Have students complete the What Do You Know? Activity, a concept ladder about the Israelites, before they study the chapter. Direct students to read each question.

Explain that they will use their prior knowledge to write an answer or a prediction for each question. Encourage students to use these questions as a guide to important themes found in this chapter.

After students complete the chapter, have them reread their answers and make any changes or corrections they believe are needed. Ask students who changed their responses to explain why they did so. *(Students should cite facts from the chapter.)*

INTERACTIVE GUIDED READING

Guided Reading Activities

There is a Guided Reading Activity for each lesson in this chapter. You may wish to assign the Guided Reading Activity for Lesson 1 after introducing the chapter content.

Hands-On Chapter Project

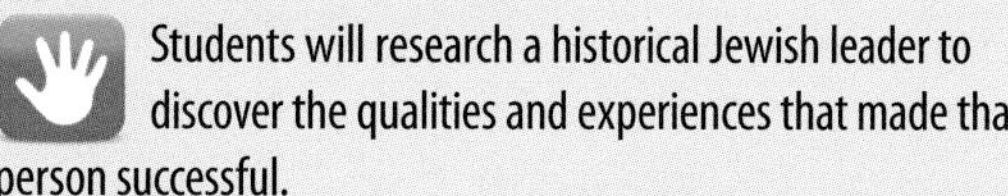

Students will research a historical Jewish leader to discover the qualities and experiences that made that person successful.

- Students will participate in a class discussion to identify key qualities possessed by successful leaders.
- Then, students will choose a leader to research. They will use worksheets to help them plan and prepare a presentation on their chosen leader.
- Next, students will deliver their completed presentations to the class.
- Finally, students will evaluate their research and presentations using an Assessment Rubric.

Visit **networks** online to see the full project and rubric.

Step Into the Place

INTERACTIVE WHITEBOARD ACTIVITY

Location Project the chapter opener map on the whiteboard and then point to the homelands of the ancient Israelites.

Remind students of some geographic features that people might look for when choosing the location of a capital city. Students might suggest features such as a central location or access to water and transportation routes.

At your interactive whiteboard, have student volunteers analyze the map and identify alternate locations for a capital of the ancient Israelites. Ask each volunteer to explain why Jerusalem might have been chosen over these alternate locations.

Next, discuss the Map Focus questions.

Step Into the Time

Making Inferences Have students review the time line for the chapter. Explain that they will be studying events from about 1800 B.C. to A.D. 70.

Ask students: **Based on the information listed in the time line, what can you infer about the history of the Israelites after the reign of David?** *(After the reign of David, the history of the Israelites was marked by conflict with various other groups.)*

Answers for pages 138–139

Step Into the Place

1. Jerusalem is surrounded by hills and desert. The Dead Sea lies to the east. The Mediterranean Sea lies to the west.
2. Jerusalem is northeast of Egypt.
3. CRITICAL THINKING The hilltops of Jerusalem allowed residents to see approaching attackers.

Step Into the Time

Civilizations in the rest of the world also experienced political changes and the development of religious beliefs.

ONLINE RESOURCES

networks

Assign these interactive worksheets and quizzes from your Teacher Lesson Center. All resources are print-ready.

It's ALL Online!

Chapter 6 Resources
- ☑ Chapter Summary
- ☑ Vocabulary Builder
- ☑ What Do You Know?
- ☑ Hands-On Chapter Project

Lesson 1 Resources
- ☑ Interactive Graphic Organizer
- ☑ Geography and History Activity Human-Environment Interaction; The Israelites and Canaan
- ☑ Guided Reading Activity
- ☑ Reading Essentials and Study Guide
- ☑ Online Self-Check Quiz

Lesson 2 Resources
- ☑ Interactive Graphic Organizer
- ☑ 21st Century Skills Activity Creativity and Innovation Problem Solving
- ☑ Primary Source Activity The Prophets
- ☑ Guided Reading Activity
- ☑ Reading Essentials and Study Guide
- ☑ Online Self-Check Quiz

Lesson 3 Resources
- ☑ Interactive Graphic Organizer
- ☑ Primary Source Activity The Hebrew Bible
- ☑ Guided Reading Activity
- ☑ Reading Essentials and Study Guide
- ☑ Online Self-Check Quiz

Lesson 4 Resources
- ☑ Interactive Graphic Organizer
- ☑ 21st Century Skills Activity Information Literacy
- ☑ Guided Reading Activity
- ☑ Reading Essentials and Study Guide
- ☑ Online Self-Check Quiz

Assessment Resources
- ☑ Lesson Reviews
- ☑ Online Self-Check Quizzes
- ☑ Chapter Activities and Assessment
- ☑ Standardized Test Practice

Remediation Resources
- ☑ Reading Essentials and Study Guide
- ☑ Guided Reading Activities
- ☑ Online Self-Check Quizzes
- ☑ Chapter Summary

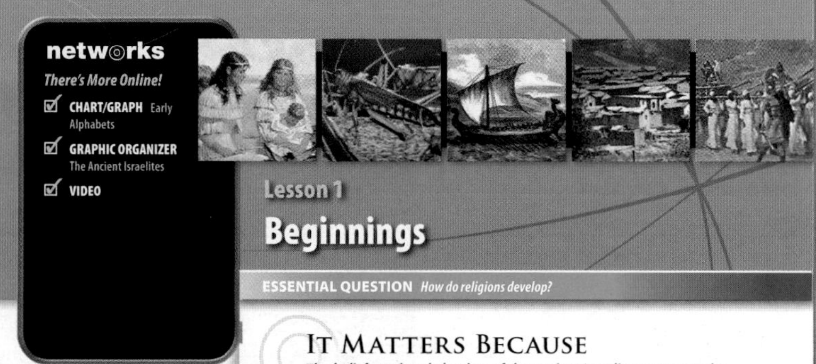

networks
There's More Online!
- CHART/GRAPH Early Alphabets
- GRAPHIC ORGANIZER The Ancient Israelites
- VIDEO

Lesson 1
Beginnings

ESSENTIAL QUESTION *How do religions develop?*

It Matters Because
The beliefs and early leaders of the ancient Israelites represent the foundations of Judaism.

1 Beginnings
GUIDING QUESTION *What did the ancient Israelites believe?*

You probably have heard of the religion of Judaism (JOO•dee•ih•zuhm). You may not know, however, that it is both an ancient and modern religion. Many ancient societies worshipped many deities, or gods. The worship of more than one god is called polytheism. A group of people in Southwest Asia known as the Israelites (IHZ•ree•ah•lites) were different. Unlike other **cultures** of the day, they worshipped only one God.

The Israelites believed that God sent **prophets** (PRAH•fehts), or messengers, to share God's word with the people. The prophets communicated to the Israelites that their God created and ruled the world. They argued that God is very powerful but also just and good. The prophets wanted the Israelites to understand that God expects goodness from his people.

The prophets also believed that every individual could connect personally to God through prayer, religious study, and good and just acts. The belief in one all-powerful, just, and personal God is called **monotheism** (MAH•nuh•thee•ih•zuhm). The practice of monotheism made Judaism unique among ancient religions.

Reading **HELP**DESK

Taking Notes: ***Summarizing***
Use a diagram like this one to list at least two facts about each category.

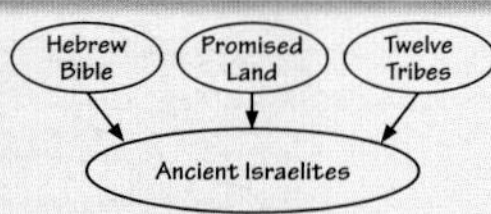

Content Vocabulary
- **prophet**
- **monotheism**
- **tribe**
- **Exodus**
- **covenant**
- **Torah**
- **commandment**
- **alphabet**

The Hebrew Bible
The Israelites recorded their beliefs and history. These writings became known as the Hebrew Bible or Tanakh (TAH•nahk). Through the Hebrew Bible, the beliefs and faith of the ancient Israelites lived on to become the religion of Judaism. The followers of Judaism are today known as Jews.

Although the original Israelite population was small, their influence was great. Judaism played an important part in the development of two other major monotheistic religions—Christianity and Islam. Christians call the Hebrew Bible the Old Testament. Christianity grew directly out of Judaism. Islam also accepted many of Judaism's beliefs and practices. Through the Hebrew Bible, Judaism influenced the values, ethics, and principles of many other societies.

Abraham
Around 1200 B.C. great changes took place in the Mediterranean region. Egypt's empire ended, and new peoples, including the Israelites, created kingdoms in the region. The early Israelites depended on herding and trading to survive. According to the Hebrew Bible, Abraham and his family migrated from Mesopotamia and settled in Canaan (KAY•nuhn) along the Mediterranean Sea. Today, the countries of Lebanon, Israel, and Jordan occupy the land that was once Canaan.

According to Jewish belief, the ancestors of the ancient Israelites were a man named Abraham and his family. The Hebrew Bible gives this account of Abraham's family and the early history of the Israelites. The Hebrew Bible states that God told Abraham to journey to Canaan, which would belong to Abraham and his descendants forever. According to the Hebrew Bible, Abraham, his wife Sarah, and their entire household accepted God's promise and settled in Canaan. The land is often called the Promised Land because of God's promise to Abraham.

The Hebrew Bible says that Abraham led his family to Canaan. In addition to his role in Judaism, Abraham is regarded as an important figure in Christianity and Islam.

prophet a messenger sent by God to share God's word with people
monotheism a belief in one God

Academic Vocabulary
culture the beliefs and behaviors of a group of people

BIOGRAPHY

Moses (c. 14th–13th century B.C.)
According to the Hebrew Bible, Moses, as a baby, was floated down the Nile River. He was born in Egypt to an Israelite woman enslaved by the pharaoh. After the pharaoh demanded all newborn Israelite boys be killed, Moses's mother hid him in a basket to float on the Nile. The pharaoh's daughter rescued him and adopted him.

▶ CRITICAL THINKING
Explaining What important leadership traits did Moses show?

Isaac and Jacob
After Abraham died, his son Isaac and later his grandson Jacob headed the family. An angel gave Jacob the new name of Israel, which means "one who struggles with God." Later Jacob's descendants were called "Israelites." As stated in the Hebrew Bible, Jacob's 12 sons became the leaders of **tribes** (TRYBS), or separate family groups. Jacob's sons were the ancestors of the Twelve Tribes of Israel.

After living in Canaan for many years, Jacob's family left because of a famine. They migrated to Egypt and lived there in peace for several generations. As the Israelite population increased, however, the Egyptian pharaoh grew uneasy. He feared that one day the Israelites would rebel. To prevent this, the Egyptians reduced the Israelites to slavery.

Moses and the Exodus
The Israelites were forced to work at hard labor, so they prayed to God to be set free. According to the Hebrew Bible, an Israelite prophet named Moses turned out to be their deliverer. While tending sheep in the wilderness outside Egypt, Moses saw a bush in flames. God called to Moses from the burning bush. He told Moses to tell the pharaoh to let the Israelites go.

Moses went before the pharaoh to demand the release of the Israelites. When the pharaoh refused, the Hebrew Bible says that God sent 10 plagues upon Egypt. These plagues were events that caused problems for the Egyptians, such as **locusts** devouring the fields or outbreaks of disease. The plagues convinced the pharaoh to free the Israelites. After the Israelites left Egypt for Canaan, the pharaoh decided to send his army to pursue them.

When the Israelites reached the Red Sea, there was no way to cross the waters. According to the Hebrew Bible, God parted the Red Sea to let his people cross to the other side. When the pharaoh's army tried to follow, the waters flooded back and drowned them. The departure of the Israelites out of slavery in Egypt is known as the **Exodus** (EHK•suh•duhs). Jews celebrate a holy festival called Passover to remember their freedom from slavery.

The Covenant
On their way from Egypt, according to the Hebrew Bible, the Israelites received a **covenant** (KUHV • uh • nuhnt), or agreement with God. In the agreement, God promised to return the Israelites

Reading **HELP**DESK

tribe a social group made up of families or clans
Exodus the departure of the Israelites out of slavery in Egypt
covenant an agreement with God

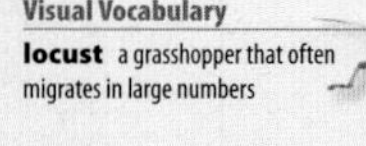
Visual Vocabulary
locust a grasshopper that often migrates in large numbers

THE TEN COMMANDMENTS
1. Do not worship any god except me.
2. Do not . . . bow down and worship idols.
3. Do not misuse my name.
4. Remember the Sabbath Day and keep it holy.
5. Honor your father and your mother.
6. Do not murder.
7. Be faithful in marriage.
8. Do not steal.
9. Do not testify falsely [tell lies] about others.
10. Do not want anything that belongs to someone else.

—**Paraphrased** from Exodus 20:3-17

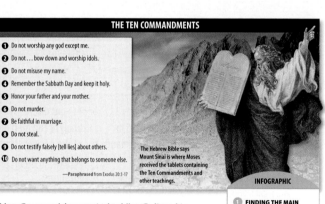

The Hebrew Bible says Mount Sinai is where Moses received the tablets containing the Ten Commandments and other teachings.

INFOGRAPHIC
1. **FINDING THE MAIN IDEA** What is the main idea of the fourth commandment?
2. CRITICAL THINKING ***Identifying*** Which commandments address family relationships?

safely to Canaan and they promised to follow God's teachings. Moses climbed to the top of Mount Sinai (SY • ny). There, as God's chosen leader, he received teachings from God. Known as the **Torah** (TAWR • uh), these teachings later became part of the Hebrew Bible.

The Torah made clear what God considered to be right and wrong. One important part of the Torah is the Ten **Commandments** (kuh•MAND•muhnts).

Loyalty to God is the central idea of the Ten Commandments. The name of God was never to be misused. The Israelites were not to worship any other gods or images. This belief that there is only one God became the basis for both Christianity and Islam.

In addition, the Ten Commandments later helped shape the moral principles of many nations. Think about the laws and rules we have today and how they might relate to these commandments. For example, the principles on which many laws are based, such as rules against stealing or killing, come from the Ten Commandments. The Ten Commandments also promoted social justice and a feeling of community. They contribute to the democratic belief that laws should apply equally to all.

☑ PROGRESS CHECK
Comparing and Contrasting How did the Israelites' beliefs differ from the beliefs of most other ancient peoples?

The Ark of the Covenant was a wooden chest, overlaid in gold, that held the tablets on which the Ten Commandments—part of God's covenant with the Israelites—appeared.

Torah teachings that Moses received from God; later became the first part of the Hebrew Bible
commandment a rule that God wanted the Israelites to follow

LESSON 1 • Day 1

ENGAGE

IMAGE

Identifying Present the interactive feature on Moses as a baby. Have volunteers read the text aloud. **Ask:** **How do you think Moses was able to preserve his Israelite heritage while living in an Egyptian palace as a prince?** *(Possible answer: He may have heard stories about the Israelites while growing up and may have felt a bond with the people.)*

Tell students they will be learning about the religious beliefs of the ancient Israelites as well as the Israelites' settlement in Canaan.

Explain that they will also examine how the Israelites' religious beliefs differed from those of earlier groups.

TEACH & ASSESS

1 Beginnings

GUIDING QUESTION *What did the ancient Israelites believe?*

Comparing Refer students to the section titled "Beginnings."

Ask: **How were Abraham and Moses similar?** *(Possible answer: They were prophets who led people to settle in new lands.)* BL

Identifying Help students locate the information about the Israelites' belief in prophets.

Ask: **What did the Israelites believe about the role of prophets?** *(The Israelites believed the role of the prophets was to share God's words with the people. They believed these prophets were messengers from God.)*

IMAGE

Discussing Present the interactive feature on locusts. Ask volunteers to share their responses to the discussion question.

Point out that a plague of locusts can completely destroy crops. Loss of crops would have been extremely disruptive in a society such as ancient Egypt in which agriculture was an important economic activity. ELL

INTERACTIVE WHITEBOARD ACTIVITY

Making Connections Present the Interactive Whiteboard Activity on the Ten Commandments. Review with students that the central idea of the Ten Commandments is loyalty to God.

Ask: **What should be the central idea of the 10 rules you write for your school?** *(Answers may vary but could include that the central idea of these rules should be school safety and/or success.)* Encourage students to refer to the central idea they have chosen as they write their rules for the school. AL

Drawing Conclusions

Ask: **Why are the Ten Commandments considered an influential list of rules?** *(Possible answer: The ideas in the Ten Commandments shaped the principles on which many laws, rules, and morals are based even today. For example, many places have laws against stealing and killing. Laws such as these originate in the Ten Commandments. Other important principles such as justice, community, and equality also have roots in the Ten Commandments.)* BL

CLOSE & REFLECT

Making Connections Ask students to think about other early civilizations with which they are already familiar. Direct them to brainstorm a list of key leaders from these civilizations and record their responses on the board. Then, ask students to evaluate their responses and identify similar leaders in the development of Judaism. As a class, discuss the significance of the leaders they identified.

LESSON 1 • Day 2

ENGAGE

Previewing Have students look again at the Chapter Opener map. Point them to the area on the map that comprises Canaan. Remind students that Canaan was located along the Mediterranean Sea where the present-day countries of Lebanon, Israel, and Jordan are found. Inform students that nomadic groups first inhabited Canaan around 3000 B.C.

Ask: **How might the location and geography of Canaan have affected its development?** *(Students might suggest that Canaan's location along the Mediterranean Sea might have drawn groups seeking a strategic location for trade or defense.)*

TEACH & ASSESS

2 The Land of Canaan

GUIDING QUESTION *How did the Israelites settle Canaan?*

INTERACTIVE WORKSHEET

Geography and History Activity

Determining Cause and Effect Remind students why the Israelites moved to Canaan from Egypt. Point out that over time, the Egyptian pharaoh began to fear the growing Israelite population and forced them into slavery.

Ask:

What was the Exodus? *(the departure of the Jews from slavery in Egypt)* AL

Have students complete the Geography and History worksheet on the Israelites and Canaan. Explain that this worksheet explores different ways the Canaanites adapted to their environment.

Ask: **How did the environment of Canaan shape the lifestyle of the Israelites?** *(Possible answers include: The rocky, dry environment affected the building design and materials used in Canaanite homes. The lack of water also required the Canaanites to store rainwater for agricultural purposes.)*

LECTURE SLIDE

Analyzing Explain to students that the Phoenicians were another group living in Canaan when the Israelites arrived. The Phoenicians were known for sailing and trading. They also developed an alphabet so they could communicate. Show students the lecture slide about the Phoenicians and their trading partners.

INTERACTIVE GRAPHIC ORGANIZER

Analyzing Show students the flowchart about the Phoenicians and their shipbuilding.

Ask: **What characteristics of the Phoenicians indicate that they were skilled sailors?** *(The Phoenicians used the sun and stars to plot long voyages. They also built ships with oars and sails that were able to travel great distances.)* BL

Answers for pages 140–143

P. 140 Taking Notes Answers may vary. Sample answer: Hebrew Bible: The Torah is the first part of the Hebrew Bible. The Ten Commandments are part of the Torah. Promised Land: Canaan was the Promised Land. According to Jewish tradition, God ordered Abraham to settle in Canaan. Twelve Tribes: Jacob's sons became the leaders of tribes or family groups. Jacob's sons were the ancestors of the Twelve Tribes of Israel.

P. 142 CRITICAL THINKING Moses showed independence by demanding the Israelite's release from the pharaoh and leading the Israelites from Egypt.

P. 143 INFOGRAPHIC

1. The main idea is to honor God by dedicating one day to worship.
2. CRITICAL THINKING The fifth and seventh commandments address family life.

P. 143 ☑ PROGRESS CHECK The Israelites believed in a single, just, all-powerful God. Many other ancient peoples believed in worshiping multiple deities.

The Phoenicians' small, yet durable, ships influenced shipbuilding for centuries. Phoenician sailors also helped advance the use of astronomy in navigation.

▶ CRITICAL THINKING

Differentiating How do the Phoenician ships appear to be similar to and different from contemporary ships?

2 The Land of Canaan

GUIDING QUESTION *How did the Israelites settle Canaan?*

The Hebrew Bible states that Moses died before the Israelites reached the land God had promised them. A new leader named Joshua guided the Israelites into Canaan, but they found other people living there. These peoples included the Canaanites (KAY•nuh•NYTS) and—somewhat later—the Philistines (FIH•luh•STEENS). Unlike the Israelites, these people of Canaan worshipped many gods and goddesses. They also had different ways of life.

Who Were the Canaanites?

Nomadic tribes probably settled in Canaan as early as 3000 B.C. At first, most of the people were herders. They journeyed with their flocks of sheep and other animals from pasture to pasture. Later, they settled in villages, farmed the land, and learned to trade.

Many different groups lived in Canaan. One Canaanite group was the Phoenicians (fih•NEE•shuhns). The Phoenicians lived in cities along the Mediterranean Sea in northern Canaan. Located near a major waterway, the Phoenicians were skilled sailors and talented traders. They used the sun and the stars to plot long sea voyages. Well-built Phoenician ships with oars and sails carried trade goods across the Mediterranean Sea to Greece, Spain, and even western Africa. Phoenician sailors may even have traveled as far as the British Isles in northwestern Europe.

Reading **HELP**DESK

alphabet a set of letters or other characters used to write a language

The Phoenicians soon controlled Mediterranean shipping and trade. At various ports, they exchanged cedar logs, glass, and jewelry for tin and other precious metals. One of the most valued Phoenician products was cloth colored with a beautiful purple dye. This dye was **extracted** from shellfish along the Phoenician coast.

As they traded, the Phoenicians founded settlements throughout the Mediterranean world. Carthage, a settlement on the coast of North Africa, in time became the most powerful city in the western Mediterranean.

As a result of these settlements, Phoenician ideas and goods spread to other peoples. Think what your life might be like without written language. One of the Phoenicians' important contributions was an **alphabet** (AL•fuh•beht), or a group of letters that stand for sounds. The letters could be used to spell out the words in their language. The alphabet made writing simpler and helped people keep better records.

Connections to TODAY

Alphabets

The Phoenicians began using the alphabet as a way to keep track of trade. Later, the Greeks adapted the Phoenician alphabet. From the Greek alphabet, the Romans created their alphabet. The Roman alphabet is the most widely used writing system in the world today.

Philistines

Another group in Canaan, the Philistines, migrated from near present-day Greece. They were one of the groups known as the "Sea People" who invaded the Mediterranean area about 1200 B.C. The Philistines set up five walled towns in southern Canaan along the Mediterranean coast. They were skilled in making iron tools and weapons, which helped them create the strongest army in Canaan. The Philistines kept their own language and religion. Still, they accepted many ideas and practices from their neighbors in Canaan.

EARLY ALPHABETS

INFOGRAPHIC

Modern Characters	Ancient Phoenician	Ancient Hebrew	Ancient Greek	Early Roman
A	≮ ≠	≮	ᐊ ᐱ A	⋒ ⋏ A
B	9 9	4 9	ᙖ B	B B
G	7 3	1 1	‹ Γ 7 1	C C
D	◁ ɑ	9 ◁	Δ ◁ A	Δ D
E	∃	∃	∃ F E	E
F	1	Y	T F F	F
Z	Z		I	Z
TH	⊗		⊙	
I	? ?	Z	Z Z	I

The Phoenician alphabet contained 22 letters. Unlike our alphabet today, it was written from right to left.

▶ CRITICAL THINKING

Making Inferences How would the lack of written language have made trade more difficult for ancient people?

Academic Vocabulary

extract to remove by a physical or chemical process

Reading in the Content Area

Tables organize information in a way that helps you remember it. To read a table, look first at the title and headings. Ask yourself questions such as "How is the information organized? What is the table trying to show me?"

Military Conquest

Because other groups lived in the region, the Israelites faced a challenge establishing Canaan as their new homeland. They believed, however, that it was God's will that they claim the land. Joshua led them in a series of battles to conquer Canaan.

The Hebrew Bible tells about the battle at the city of Jericho. There, Joshua told the Israelites to march around the city walls. For six days, they marched while priests blew their trumpets. On the seventh day, according to the account:

PRIMARY SOURCE

> ❝ Joshua commanded the people, "Shout, for the LORD has given you the city. . . . At the sound of the trumpet, when the people gave a loud shout, the wall collapsed. ❞
>
> —from the Hebrew Bible, the book of Joshua, 6: 16–20

The Israelites took control of the city after the walls of Jericho crumbled.

According to the Hebrew Bible, Joshua led the Israelites in other battles. Any land they seized was divided among the 12 tribes. After Joshua died, political and military leaders called judges ruled the tribes. The judges settled disputes. They also led troops into battle. The Hebrew Bible tells of a woman judge named Deborah, who was admired for her wisdom and bravery. She told the commander Barak (Buh•RAHK) to attack the army of the Canaanite king Jabin. Deborah went to the battlefield as an adviser. With her help, Barak and 10,000 Israelites destroyed the Canaanite forces.

Jericho is one of the oldest continuously inhabited sites in the world. Here we see an illustration of the Hebrew Bible story of Joshua bringing down the walls of the city.

Academic Vocabulary

ensure to make certain or make sure of

Life in Canaan

After many battles, the Israelite tribes won control of the hilly region of central Canaan and settled there. Most Israelites farmed and herded animals. The land was rocky and dry, with little water. So during the rainy season, farmers collected the rainwater. They stored it in small caves or under the ground. They used the stored water to irrigate crops such as olives, flax, barley, and grapes.

Imagine a rocky countryside dotted by square white houses. Most Israelites lived in houses with two levels. The walls of the houses were made of mud-brick or stone plastered with mud and white-washed. Floors were made of clay. Wooden beams supported a flat, thatched roof, covered with clay. During the day, people cooked and did household chores in the home's lower level. At night, donkeys and goats bedded down there. The family slept on the upper level.

The ancient tabernacle was a tent constructed from beautiful tapestries, or woven fabric, that were decorated with angels. It was an elaborate structure, containing a courtyard and two rooms. The measurements of the structure were said to have come directly from God, according to the Hebrew Bible.

The Tabernacle

According to the Hebrew Bible, the Israelite tribes worshipped God in a large tent-like structure called the tabernacle (TA•buhr•na•kuhl). The Israelites believed that the tabernacle housed God's presence. This structure was taken down and put away as the Israelites moved from place to place. In Canaan, they erected the tabernacle at a religious center called Shiloh.

The Hebrew Bible says that the tabernacle housed a sacred object called the Ark of the Covenant. The ark, a gold-covered wooden chest, held tablets, or stone slabs. The Israelites believed that the Ten Commandments were written on these tablets. The Israelites believed the ark was a sign of God's presence and that having it with them in battle would **ensure** victory.

☑ PROGRESS CHECK

Identifying Who were the Phoenicians, and what was their major contribution to world civilization?

LESSON 1 REVIEW

Review Vocabulary

1. Describe the difference between *monotheism* and *polytheism*.

Answer the Guiding Questions

2. ***Describing*** What subjects are covered in the Hebrew Bible?
3. ***Explaining*** How did the Israelites settle Canaan?
4. ***Summarizing*** What is the central theme of the Ten Commandments?
5. ***Identifying*** Which group living in Canaan included skilled sailors and traders?
6. **EXPOSITORY WRITING** Moses was chosen to lead the Israelites out of Egypt. Write a paragraph to explain the qualities you think Moses possessed to undertake this difficult task.

LESSON 1 • Day 2 (cont.)

CHART

Discussing Show students the interactive chart on the Phoenician alphabet. Click on the visual to learn more about the meaning of the term *alphabet*. Encourage students to share and discuss their responses to the discussion question.

Ask: **Which of the alphabets shown do you think most closely resembles the modern alphabet? What might this resemblance suggest about the alphabet you chose?** *(Possible answers: The early Roman alphabet most closely resembles the modern alphabet. This likely suggests that the early Roman alphabet is the most recent of the other alphabets shown. It might also suggest that the modern alphabet evolved most directly from this alphabet.)* AL ELL

IMAGE

Analyzing Primary Sources Have students focus on the section about the Israelites' military struggle against the Philistines. Then present the interactive image about the battle of Jericho. Direct students to the discussion question for this activity. Then, guide them as they locate the passage from the Hebrew Bible in their text that will help them answer this question.

Analyzing Direct students' attention to the section titled "Military Conquest." Help students recognize that Joshua's death brought a change in leadership to the Israelites.

Ask: **How did the leadership of the Israelites change after Joshua's death?** *(After Joshua's death, political and military leaders known as judges ruled the Twelve Tribes.)*

PRIMARY SOURCE

Describing Explain to students that after many conflicts, the Israelites regained control of central Canaan, where they lived and worshiped.

Discuss the tabernacle's importance to the Israelites. Then show students the quotation from the Hebrew Bible about the building of a tabernacle. Ask students to describe a tabernacle and explain its purpose. *(The tabernacle was a large, tentlike structure that served as the place of worship for the Israelites and where they believed God's presence was found. The Hebrew Bible states that the tabernacle housed the Ark of the Covenant.)*

IMAGE

Analyzing Direct students' attention to the image of the Ark of the Covenant. Invite volunteers to read the information aloud.

Ask: **Why did the Israelites treasure the ark?** *(They believed it was a sign of God's presence and that it would ensure their victory in battles.)*

INTERACTIVE GRAPHIC ORGANIZER

Explaining Remind students to complete the lesson's Taking Notes graphic organizer. Then have students complete the Lesson 1 Review questions.

CLOSE & REFLECT

Summarizing Lead students in a brief discussion in which they summarize the important role that the geography of Canaan played in the development of Judaism.

BACKGROUND KNOWLEDGE

The Red Sea

Scholars disagree about where the Israelites might have crossed the Red Sea. Some believe the name for the Red Sea was incorrectly translated long ago and that the correct reference is to the "Sea of Reeds," a marshy, inland lake north of the Red Sea.

IF YOU HAVE MORE TIME . . .

Use a Flowchart to Learn Early the History of the Israelites

Sequencing Have students work alone or in pairs to create a flowchart of important events that occurred during the early history of the Israelites.

Then have students or pairs compare charts with others in the class. Students should discuss any differences or discrepancies in their flowcharts.

Conclude the activity by having all students contribute to a final flowchart that you draw on the whiteboard.

Research the Phoenician Alphabet

Making Connections Invite students to research the alphabets that were influenced by the Phoenician alphabet, including the ancient Hebrew, ancient Greek, early Roman, and modern alphabets.

Students should create a chart that shows similar characters in the different alphabets and draw conclusions from their work.

Ask students to share their findings with the class. 

Answers for pages 144–147

P. 144 CRITICAL THINKING Answers will vary, but students should correctly identify features of the ships in the illustration and compare them to modern ships.

P. 145 CRITICAL THINKING The lack of written language would have made it difficult to identify or label items that were being traded. It would have made communication about things like shipping and prices challenging.

P. 147 ☑ PROGRESS CHECK The Phoenicians were skilled shipbuilders and traders who lived in northern Canaan; their major contribution to the world was their alphabet.

LESSON 1 REVIEW

1. Monotheism is the worship of one god. Polytheism is the worship of two or more gods.
2. The history and religious beliefs of the Israelites are covered in the Hebrew Bible.
3. They fought the Canaanites to return to their promised land.
4. Loyalty to God is the central theme of the Ten Commandments.
5. The Phoenicians were the group living in Canaan; the group included skilled sailors and traders.
6. Answers will vary, but students might note that Moses was a strong leader, brave, and fair; his faith in God was unique.

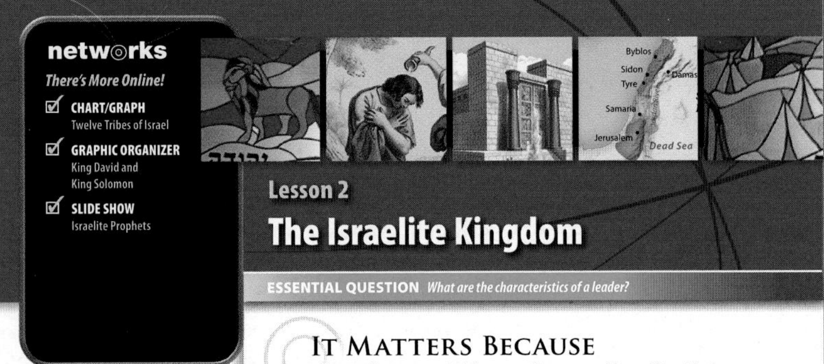

networks
There's More Online!
- CHART/GRAPH Twelve Tribes of Israel
- GRAPHIC ORGANIZER King David and King Solomon
- SLIDE SHOW Israelite Prophets

Lesson 2
The Israelite Kingdom

ESSENTIAL QUESTION *What are the characteristics of a leader?*

It Matters Because

The Israelites were ruled by several important kings. After this time, they were divided into two kingdoms and faced threats from neighboring empires.

1 Early Kings

GUIDING QUESTION *What was the role of kings in Israelite history?*

By 1100 B.C., the Israelites had settled much of the land of Canaan. They developed a prosperous culture, creating an alphabet and a calendar based on Canaanite ideas. Yet one powerful enemy—the Philistines—remained. When the Philistines moved inland from the Mediterranean Sea, they came into conflict with the Israelites. Many Israelites called for a king to unite the Twelve Tribes and lead them in battle against the Philistines.

Saul: The First King

According to the Hebrew Bible, the Israelites asked the judge Samuel to choose a king. Samuel, though, warned that a king would tax them and enslave them. The Israelites, however, still demanded a king so Samuel chose a young man named Saul (SAWL). Samuel anointed Saul as king, pouring holy oil on him to show that God had blessed him.

Under Saul's leadership, the Israelites won many battles against the Philistines. With each victory, Saul gained greater fame. Later, however, Saul lost the support of the people. According to the Hebrew Bible, Saul disobeyed some of God's commands.

Reading HELPDESK

Taking Notes: *Listing*
Use a chart like this one to list the achievements of King David and King Solomon.

King David	King Solomon

Content Vocabulary
- **psalm**
- **exile**
- **proverb**

God then instructed Samuel to choose and anoint another king. Samuel chose a young shepherd named David.

King David

Even before he became Israel's king, David had won praise for his bravery. The Hebrew Bible provides an account of David and his victory over Goliath, a giant Philistine warrior. In a bragging fashion, Goliath dared any Israelite to fight him one-on-one. Young David stepped forward with his shepherd's staff, a slingshot, and five smooth stones. With a heavy spear in hand, Goliath rushed forward. David hurled one stone straight at the giant's forehead. Goliath dropped dead.

Impressed by David's skill, King Saul placed his army under David's command. As David won more and more victories, the women of Israel sang his praises: "Saul has slain his thousands, and David his tens of thousands." Then, seized by jealousy, Saul tried to kill David, but David escaped. When Saul died in battle against the Philistines, David returned and became king.

According to the Hebrew Bible, once David was in power, he united the Israelite tribes. David and his army defeated the Philistines. He then established a capital city for Israel at Jerusalem (juh•ROO•suh•lehm). The Israelites built their capital in the hill country away from the coast. A fine musician and poet, David is believed to have written many of the sacred songs found in the Hebrew Bible's Book of **Psalms** (SALMZ)—also found in the Christian Bible. One of the most famous is Psalm 23, which begins:

The Twelve Tribes of Israel were family groups. According to the Hebrew Bible, each family descended from a son of Jacob. Scholars note that family connections and a common religion bound the tribes together long before they united under David.

PRIMARY SOURCE

> “The LORD is my shepherd, I shall not be in want.
> He makes me lie down in green pastures,
> he leads me beside quiet waters,
> he restores my soul.
> He guides me in the paths of righteousness [fairness]
> for his name's sake.”
>
> —Psalm: 23:1–3

According to the Hebrew Bible, David was tending sheep when Samuel arrived to anoint him.

psalm a sacred song or poem used in worship

Solomon built the First Temple on a site David had selected, the Temple Mount. The spot had religious significance. It was the place, according to the Hebrew Bible, where Abraham had tried to sacrifice Isaac.

Under David's rule, the Israelites enjoyed prosperous times. Farmers cultivated the tough, dry land by building terraces on the steep hillsides. Terraced fields are strips of land cut out of a hillside like stair steps. Terraces prevented soil from washing down the hillside when it rained. After David's death, the Israelites honored him as their greatest king, as do Jews today. King David's son Solomon (SAH•luh•muhn) became the next Israelite king around 970 B.C. Through trade and treaties with other peoples, Solomon brought a long **period** of peace to the region. He constructed many cities and, according to the Hebrew Bible, built the first temple in Jerusalem. Built of fragrant cedar wood and costly stone, Solomon's temple—also called the First Temple—held the Ark of the Covenant and other sacred objects.

King Solomon was also known for his wisdom. He is believed to be the author of **proverbs** (PRAHV•uhrbz), or wise sayings, that are recorded in the Hebrew Bible. Solomon shared his proverbs in hopes of helping his people:

PRIMARY SOURCE

> “Whoever walks in integrity walks securely,
> but whoever takes crooked paths will be found out.”
>
> —Proverbs: 10:9

Despite Solomon's accomplishments, many Israelites turned against him. They did not like working on his building projects or paying the high taxes he demanded. After Solomon's death around 922 B.C., the Israelites entered a troubled period in their history. Deep disagreements split their kingdom. In addition, powerful neighbors threatened their survival.

PROGRESS CHECK

Evaluating Why did the Israelites believe David was their greatest king?

Reading HELPDESK

proverb a wise saying

Academic Vocabulary
period a division of time that is shorter than an era

2 Two Kingdoms

GUIDING QUESTION *How did neighboring empires respond to the Israelites?*

After Solomon's death, the ten northern tribes rebelled against the government in Jerusalem. These tribes **founded** a separate kingdom, Israel. Its capital was Samaria. The two tribes in the south founded the smaller kingdom of Judah (JOO•duh). Judah's capital was Jerusalem. Although split politically, the people of Israel and Judah preserved the Israelite religion.

During this time, large empires formed around Israel and Judah. As you read previously, the Assyrians and the Chaldeans built powerful empires. Their rulers wanted to control the trade routes that ran through the Israelite kingdoms. Small and weak, the kingdoms of Israel and Judah felt threatened by their powerful neighbors.

The Fall of Israel

The Assyrians spread fear throughout the region. They forced conquered peoples to pay tribute. If they did not receive tribute, the Assyrians destroyed towns, burned estates, and carried away all valuable goods. Then they forced the conquered people to move to different areas to start new settlements.

When the kingdom of Israel refused to pay tribute, the Assyrians invaded Israel in 722 B.C. The Assyrians captured major cities, including the capital at Samaria. They wanted absolute control.

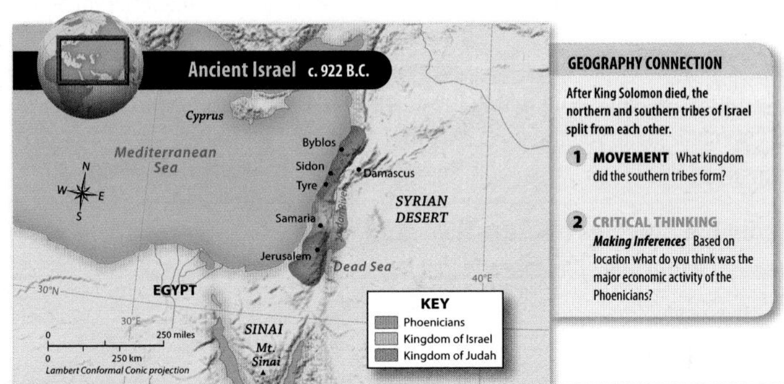

GEOGRAPHY CONNECTION

After King Solomon died, the northern and southern tribes of Israel split from each other.

1. **MOVEMENT** What kingdom did the southern tribes form?
2. **CRITICAL THINKING** ***Making Inferences*** Based on location what do you think was the major economic activity of the Phoenicians?

Academic Vocabulary
found to set up or establish

Teaching *The Israelite Kingdom*

(Student Edition pp. 148–153)

LESSON 2 • Day 1

ENGAGE

INTERACTIVE GRAPHIC ORGANIZER

Identifying Direct students' attention to the Taking Notes graphic organizer on the first page of Lesson 2. Point out the names of the Israelite leaders David and Solomon. Explain to students that this lesson contains information about important early leaders of the Israelites. Ask students why good leaders are important. *(Leaders can help groups through difficult challenges and periods of change.)* As students prepare to read this lesson, encourage them to look for information about the leaders for later recall. AL

TEACH & ASSESS

1 Early Kings

GUIDING QUESTION *What was the role of kings in Israelite history?*

INTERACTIVE WORKSHEET

21st Century Skills Activity

Problem Solving Point out to students that by 1100 B.C., many Israelites called for a king to unite the Twelve Tribes. David eventually became the second king of the Israelites.

Present the 21st Century Skills Activity about King David and his approach to problem solving. Have students complete the questions on the worksheet. Assign the final written paragraph as homework.

Ask: **Why would the ability to solve large problems be important for a successful leader?** *(Answers may vary but should include that leadership is about helping others reach a common goal. Large obstacles are usually encountered along the way to any significant goal. Therefore, the ability to solve problems and thus remove obstacles would be essential for any successful leader.)* BL

IMAGE

Making Inferences Present the interactive feature on King David. Click the image to read the information provided. Direct students to review the information about David's background and achievements, as well as life in Israel under his rule.

Ask: **How would you describe David before he was king?** *(Possible answer: David was courageous for fighting Goliath, and he came from humble beginnings.)* BL

IMAGE

Drawing Conclusions Present the interactive feature on King Solomon. Click the image to read the information provided.

Ask: **Why was Solomon considered wise?** *(Solomon used unusual methods to find the truth.)*

CLOSE & REFLECT

Summarizing Ask students to think about what they have learned about the early Israelite kings in this lesson. Lead students in a brief discussion that summarizes the impact that each king had on early Israelite society. AL

LESSON 2 • Day 2

ENGAGE

Discussing Ask students to think about examples of conflict with which they are familiar. Explain that these can be conflicts that have affected countries, groups, or people.

Ask: **How did these conflicts affect the parties involved in the dispute?** *(Answers will vary, but students might suggest that conflict weakens or proves harmful to the parties involved.)* Ask volunteers to share their examples and discuss how the conflicts affected the parties involved. Explain that they will learn how conflict among the Twelve Tribes divided the Israelites and affected their interactions with neighboring empires.

TEACH & ASSESS

2 Two Kingdoms

GUIDING QUESTION *How did neighboring empires respond to the Israelites?*

MAP

Analyzing Visuals Remind students that the Israelites split into two kingdoms following the death of their third king, Solomon. Click on the map key to view the locations of the different kingdoms in ancient Israel.

Ask: **To which Israelite kingdom would the Phoenicians have posed a greater threat?** *(Israel)* **What body of water lay east of Judah?** *(the Dead Sea)*

IMAGE

Describing Direct students' attention to the text about the split between the Israelite tribes.

Ask: **How did this split occur?** *(After Solomon's death, the 10 northern tribes rebelled against the government in Jerusalem. The northern tribes founded a separate kingdom called Israel. The two southern tribes established a smaller kingdom called Judah.)*

Then show the image of the Twelve Tribes, and have volunteers read aloud the information about their leaders.

LECTURE SLIDE

Discussing Show students the lecture slide about the Israelite tribes and their neighbors, the Assyrians and the Chaldeans.

Ask students to use the information they have learned to draw simple outline maps of the split between Israel and Judah. Tell students to add labels for Israel, Judah, Jerusalem, and Samaria to their maps. AL ELL

Comparing and Contrasting Direct students to review the final paragraph in the section on the fall of Israel.

Ask: **How were the Israelites and the Samaritans alike and different?** *(Like the Israelites, the Samaritans worshiped the God of Israel, read the Torah, and followed religious teachings. However, the Samaritans also adopted religious practices that the Israelites did not accept. Over time, the two groups grew more and more different.)* AL ELL

INTERACTIVE WORKSHEET

Primary Source Activity

Analyzing Primary Sources Guide students to recognize that today's Judaism developed from the religious practices preserved mainly in the kingdom of Judah.

Explain that the prophets played an important role in Judean life. Present the Primary Source Activity worksheet on the prophets.

Have student volunteers read out loud the two selections from the worksheet. Then allow the students to answer the worksheet questions in small groups. AL ELL

Determining Cause and Effect

Ask: **How did Judah's failed revolt against Chaldean rule affect the people of Judah?** *(After the revolt failed, Nebuchadnezzar destroyed Jerusalem and took many of Judah's people to live in the Chaldean capital of Babylon.)*

SLIDE SHOW **Identifying Points of View** Refer students to the section titled "What Was the Prophets' Message?" Help them locate the information about the teachings and beliefs of the prophets. Then, show the slide show.

Answers for pages 148–151

P. 148 Taking Notes King David—drove the Philistines out; created an empire; built Jerusalem; wrote many psalms. King Solomon—built temple in Jerusalem; brought peace to the region

P. 150 ☑ PROGRESS CHECK David united the Twelve Tribes of Israel, defeated the Philistines, and established the capital city of his kingdom, Jerusalem.

P. 151 GEOGRAPHY CONNECTION

1. They formed Judah.
2. CRITICAL THINKING The Mediterranean was important for trade and transportation.

CHART

ISRAELITE PROPHETS

Jeremiah was one of several prophets. The Israelites believed the prophets brought them the word of God.

▶ CRITICAL THINKING

Comparing What do the teachings of Hosea and Jeremiah have in common?

Name	Time Periods	Teachings
Elijah	874–840 B.C.	Only God should be worshipped—not idols or false gods.
Amos	780–740 B.C.	The kingdom of King David will be restored and will prosper.
Hosea	750–722 B.C.	God is loving and forgiving.
Isaiah	738–700 B.C.	God wants us to help others and promote justice.
Micah	735–700 B.C.	Both rich and poor have to do what is right and follow God.
Jeremiah	626–586 B.C.	God is just and kind—he rewards as well as punishes.
Ezekiel	597–571 B.C.	Someone who has done wrong can choose to change.

So they forced some of the Israelites to resettle in the Assyrian Empire. Assyrians then brought in people from other parts of their empire to live in Israel. These settlers mixed with the Israelites still living there. A new mingled culture developed. These people became known as Samaritans.

The Samaritans adopted many of the Israelites' religious beliefs. They worshipped the God of Israel, read the Torah, and followed the Israelites' religious laws. The Samaritans, however, adopted religious practices that the Israelites did not accept. In time, the Samaritans and the people of Israel had little in common. Today's Judaism developed from the religious practices preserved mainly in the kingdom of Judah.

The Fall of Judah

The people of Judah **survived** the Assyrian conquests, but their freedom did not last. In 597 B.C., the Chaldeans under King Nebuchadnezzar (NEHB•uh•kuhd•NEHZ•zuhr), forced thousands of people to leave Jerusalem and live in Babylon (BAB•uh•lahn), the Chaldean capital. Nebuchadnezzar chose a new king, a Judean, to rule Judah.

At first, Judah's king did as he was told. Soon, however, he plotted to set Judah free. A prophet named Jeremiah warned that God did not want Judah to rebel, but the king refused to listen. The king led the people of Judah to revolt. The Chaldeans retook Jerusalem in 586 B.C. Nebuchadnezzar then leveled Jerusalem to the ground. He destroyed the temple, captured the king, and took him and thousands of Judah's people to Babylon.

Reading HELPDESK

exile a forced absence from one's home or country

Academic Vocabulary

survive to continue to live; to live through a dangerous event

In Jewish history, this time became known as the Babylonian **Exile** (EHG•zyl). When people are exiled, they are forced to leave their home or country. Psalm 137 in the Hebrew Bible describes the sadness many of Judah's people felt in living far away from their homeland:

PRIMARY SOURCE

> ❝By the rivers of Babylon we sat and wept. . . .
> How can we sing the songs of the LORD while in a foreign land?
> If I forget you, O Jerusalem, may my right hand forget its skill.
> May my tongue cling to the roof of my mouth if I do not remember you,
> if I do not consider Jerusalem my highest joy . . .❞
>
> —Psalm 137:1–6

What Was the Prophets' Message?

The prophets had an important role in Judean life. They offered words of hope in times of despair. At other times, the prophets explained that the people were not obeying God. They urged people to change their ways and make the world a better place.

The prophet Amos said, "But let justice roll on like a river, righteousness like a never-failing stream!" This means that all people should work for a just society in which everyone is treated fairly. Dr. Martin Luther King, Jr. quoted the prophet's words in the 20th century in his "I Have a Dream" speech. The goal of a just society later became a primary part of the teachings of Christianity and Islam. Jewish prophets also stressed the importance of leading a moral life and helping others in order to connect with God.

☑ PROGRESS CHECK

Identifying What empires conquered Israel and Judah?

LESSON 2 REVIEW

Review Vocabulary

1. How might reading a series of *proverbs* affect people?

Answer the Guiding Questions

2. ***Explaining*** Why was it important that King David united the tribes of Israel?
3. ***Explaining*** How did Solomon's death affect the Israelites?
4. ***Identifying*** Which group mixed with the Israelites to form the Samaritan culture?
5. ***Identifying*** What was the Babylonian Exile?
6. **PERSONAL WRITING** The Jews were exiled and forced to spend 70 years in Babylon. If you were forced to live far away from your homeland, how would you react to your situation? Write a journal entry describing your thoughts about being forced to live away from your homeland.

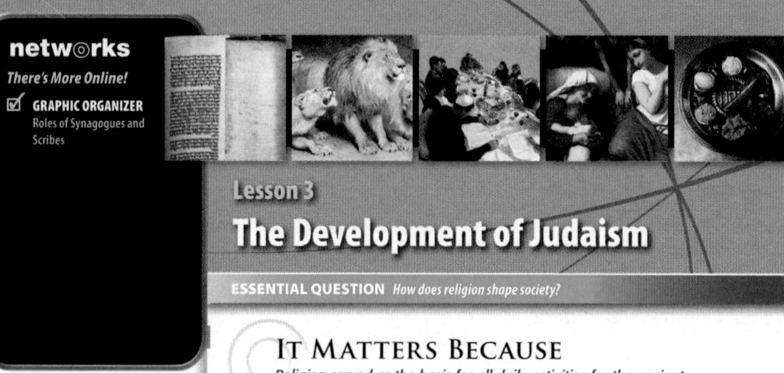

networks

There's More Online!

☑ GRAPHIC ORGANIZER Roles of Synagogues and Scribes

Lesson 3

The Development of Judaism

ESSENTIAL QUESTION *How does religion shape society?*

IT MATTERS BECAUSE

Religion served as the basis for all daily activities for the ancient Israelites. Many of their religious beliefs and practices continue today.

1 Return to Judah

GUIDING QUESTION ***How did the people of Judah practice their religion while in exile and in their homeland?***

The families of Judeans who were exiled to Babylon spent 70 years away from Judah. During their exile, they became known as the Jews. We call their religion Judaism.

While in Babylon, the Jews no longer had a temple in which to worship God. It is believed that small groups of Jews began to meet at **synagogues** (SIHN•uh•GAHGS), or Jewish houses of worship. They worshipped on the **Sabbath** (SA•buhth). According to **tradition**, the Sabbath lasts from sundown Friday to nightfall Saturday. During this weekly day of worship and rest, Jews prayed and talked about their religion and history. Jews still observe the Sabbath today.

Rebuilding Judah

While some Jews accepted Babylon as their permanent home, others hoped to return to Judah some day. This hope was achieved when a group of people called the Persians swept across Southwest Asia. The Persians defeated the Chaldeans and took over Babylon. In 538 B.C., the Persian king Cyrus II let Jews return to Judah.

Reading HELPDESK

Taking Notes: Identifying the Main Idea

As you read, complete a graphic organizer like this one to describe the roles of both synagogues and scribes in the survival of Judaism.

Synagogues → Roles ← Scribes

Content Vocabulary

- **synagogue**
- **scroll**
- **Sabbath**
- **kosher**

Some Jews stayed in Babylon, but many returned to Judah. They rebuilt Jerusalem and constructed a new temple to replace the one destroyed by the Chaldeans. This new place of worship became known as the Second Temple.

Meanwhile, the Persians chose officials to rule the country and collect taxes from the people. They did not allow the Jews to have their own government or king. The Jews depended on religious leaders—the temple priests and scribes—to guide their society.

Many priests were religious scholars. These priests had a deep understanding of the Jewish faith. Scribes often lectured in the synagogues and taught in the schools. Led by a scribe named Ezra, the Jews wrote the five books of the Torah on pieces of parchment. They sewed the pieces together to make long **scrolls** (SKROHLZ). The Torah and writings that were added later make up the Hebrew Bible.

What Is In the Hebrew Bible?

Isn't it easier to follow rules when they are clearly explained? That is what the Hebrew Bible provided for the ancient Jews. Three parts—the Torah, the Prophets, and the Writings—make up the Hebrew Bible. It contains a series of 24 books written and collected over many centuries. The Hebrew Bible presents the laws and rules of the Israelites. It also reflects the culture of the people. Jewish history, art, literature, poetry, and proverbs are also part of the Hebrew Bible.

Genesis, the first book of the Torah, presents the Israelite view of human beginnings. It tells how God created the Earth in six days and rested on the seventh day. Genesis also describes how God punished the world for wicked behavior. In this book, God warns a man named Noah that a flood is coming and commands him to build an ark, or large boat. As the rains poured and flood waters rose, Noah, his family, and two of every animal on Earth boarded the ark. The Earth flooded and many perished. Only those on the ark escaped drowning. After the rain stopped, God placed a rainbow in the sky as a sign that the world would never again be destroyed by a flood.

Genesis also explains why the people of the world speak many different languages. It tells how the citizens of the city of Babel tried to build a tower to reach heaven.

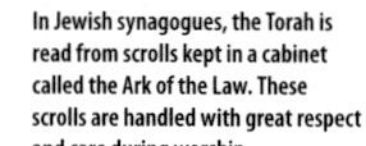

In Jewish synagogues, the Torah is read from scrolls kept in a cabinet called the Ark of the Law. These scrolls are handled with great respect and care during worship.

synagogue a Jewish house of worship

Sabbath a weekly day of worship and rest

scroll a long document made from pieces of parchment sewn together

Academic Vocabulary

tradition a custom, or way of life, passed down from generation to generation

Teaching *The Israelite Kingdom* (cont.)

(Student Edition pp. 148–153)

LESSON 2 • Day 2 (cont.)

Discuss with the class why the prophets' teachings might remain relevant today. Guide students to understand that the prophets' belief in a just society remains an important topic of discussion and debate.

Ask: **What was the prophets' point of view on being faithful to God?** *(The prophets argued that being faithful to God meant more than going to a temple to worship. They also believed it was important to live a moral life and help others connect with God.)*

Have students complete the Lesson 2 Review questions.

CLOSE & REFLECT

Summarizing Have students write a paragraph summarizing what they have learned from this lesson about important people and events of the early Israelites.

Ask volunteers to read their summary paragraphs aloud to the class. Invite the class to discuss whether these summaries differ, and if so, students should consider which facts are essential to include in a summary. Summaries should focus on facts that are essential to understanding the lesson content. BL

IF YOU HAVE MORE TIME . . .

Make Personal Connections to Text

Discussing Students who connect what they read to personal experiences and beliefs, as well as to other selections they have read, often find it easier to construct meaning in text materials.

Making connections between what they read and their ideas, feelings, and experiences also helps increase students' enjoyment of reading for information. As students read for class, have them ask themselves these questions:

- **How would I feel if I were forced to leave my home, family, and friends?**
- **What difference can a good leader make to a team or group?**
- **What kinds of things do I feel proud about?**

Suggest that students write their answers to these questions in journals or notebooks. Encourage students to use this strategy over the course of the entire chapter. Then ask volunteers to share their thoughts about whether this process helped them comprehend more as they read. AL

Answers for pages 152–153

P. 152 CHART

CRITICAL THINKING Both believed that God is loving and kind.

P. 153 ☑ PROGRESS CHECK First the Assyrians and then the Chaldeans conquered the Jewish people.

LESSON 2 REVIEW

1. Proverbs are short, wise sayings meant to reinforce good behavior. Reading a series of proverbs might cause people to examine and possibly change their behavior.
2. By uniting the tribes, David helped give the Israelites an identity as a group.
3. After Solomon's death, the Israelite tribes split into two separate kingdoms—Israel and Judah.
4. Assyrians mingled with the Israelites to form the Samaritan culture.
5. The Babylonian Exile was the deportation, or forced move, of many Jews to Babylon.
6. Answers will vary, but students should demonstrate thoughtful consideration of the experience of living in exile. They might refer to living in an unfamiliar place, facing difficult conditions, or confronting intolerance.

Teaching *The Development of Judaism*

(Student Edition pp. 154–159)

LESSON 3 • Day 1

ENGAGE

Discussing Remind students that in Lesson 2 they learned that the people of Judah were exiled to Babylon after being captured by the Chaldeans. Discuss with students some of the reasons why groups of people might be forced into exile. Guide students to understand that exiles are usually caused by political factors.

Explain that in this lesson they will learn about the important figures and events surrounding the movements of the Jews into and out of exile in Babylon.

TEACH & ASSESS

1 Return to Judah

GUIDING QUESTION *How did the people of Judah practice their religion while in exile and in their homeland?*

INTERACTIVE GRAPHIC ORGANIZER

Previewing Remind students to complete the lesson's Taking Notes graphic organizer. Then, direct their attention to the title of this section and ask them what they might learn about in this section. *(Students should infer that they will likely learn about the Judeans' return to their homeland from exile in Babylon.)*

Explaining Ask: **How did the name of the Judeans and their religion change during their exile in Babylon?** *(During this time, the Judeans became known as "the Jews." Their religion became known as "Judaism.")*

Analyzing Focus students' attention on the section titled "Rebuilding Judah." Discuss with students that during the period of Babylonian exile, Judaism spread in the ancient world. Guide students to recognize that although many Jews eventually returned to Judah, others stayed in Babylon, thereby spreading their belief system in this area.

IMAGE

Classifying Present the interactive image on Torah scrolls. Click on the image to reveal information about the books of the Torah. **Ask:** **Which book of the Torah includes the story of Moses?** *(Exodus)* **Which book provides directions for people preparing to live in the Promised Land?** *(Deuteronomy)*

INTERACTIVE WORKSHEET

Primary Source Activity

Analyzing Primary Sources Make sure students understand that the Torah scrolls, along with other writings, make up the Hebrew Bible.

Assign students the Primary Source Activity worksheet on the Hebrew Bible. Have them complete the worksheet questions individually or in small groups.

SLIDE SHOW **Evaluating** Discuss with students some of the qualities they associate with heroes. Students may suggest characteristics such as courage, strength, and determination. Explain that the book of Daniel in the Hebrew Bible uses the story of a heroic figure to express hope for a better world.

Ask: **What heroic qualities did Daniel demonstrate?** *(Possible answer: Daniel demonstrated heroic qualities such as courage, faith, and goodness.)* Then, present the interactive slide show about Daniel. BL

Comparing Tell students to choose one of the other Jewish heroes featured in this activity. **Ask:** **What is one heroic characteristic that this figure shares with Daniel?** *(Possible answer: Like Daniel, Akiva had to overcome difficult circumstances to become a Jewish hero.)*

Answers for pages 154–155

P. 154 Taking Notes Possible answers: Synagogues were places where Jews could meet and worship while in exile. Scribes were religious scholars who studied and taught about the Jewish faith. They also wrote the books of the Torah.

Daniel's faith in God protected him from the lions. As a result, Daniel became a model of faith and strength to Jews facing difficult challenges.

▶ CRITICAL THINKING

Analyzing What lesson does the story of Daniel provide for Jewish people, especially during hard times?

God disapproved and made the people speak in different languages. The people could not **communicate** with one another. As a result, they could not work together to complete the tower. God then scattered the people across the Earth.

Later parts of the Hebrew Bible describe Jewish hopes for the future. The book of Isaiah describes what the Jews believed to be God's plan for a peaceful world. It says that the nations:

PRIMARY SOURCE

> "[W]ill beat their swords into plowshares and their spears into pruning hooks. Nation will not take up sword against nation, nor will they train for war anymore."
>
> — Isaiah 2:4 (New International Version)

The book of Daniel explains that the Jews also believed that evil and suffering would eventually be replaced by goodness. Daniel was a trusted adviser to a Babylonian king. As a Jew, however, he refused to worship Babylonian gods. For punishment, the Chaldeans threw Daniel into a lions' den. God, however, protected Daniel from the wild beasts. The story of Daniel reminds Jews that God will rescue them. Christians and Muslims share with the Jews the hope of a better world in which good triumphs over evil.

☑ PROGRESS CHECK

Explaining Why did religious leaders guide Jewish society after the Jews returned from exile?

Academic Vocabulary

communicate to exchange knowledge or information

2 Jewish Daily Life

GUIDING QUESTION *How did religion shape the Jewish way of life?*

The Torah provides teachings for daily living. These teachings shaped the family life of the early Jews. The teachings gave instructions about what foods to eat and what clothes to wear. They also required Jews to help the poor, deal honestly with their neighbors, and apply laws fairly. Jewish teachings emphasized individual worth and responsibility, as well as self-discipline. It also reminded Jews of their loyalty to God.

Connections to TODAY

Heroes

Stories of brave leaders like Daniel have inspired Jews to maintain their faith during times of trial and trouble. Brainstorm a list of present-day individuals or groups who inspire others with their bravery in the face of great difficulty or danger.

The Jewish Family

The ancient Israelites stressed the importance of family life. The Torah identifies specific roles for the father and the mother of the house. If a father died, his sons would take his place to lead the family.

The Jewish family also stressed education—especially for young men. When sons grew old enough, fathers taught them to worship God and to learn a trade. Later, under the guidance of religious teachers, boys learned to read the Torah. Everything the students learned—from the alphabet to Jewish history—they learned from the Torah. Because reading the Torah was central to Jewish life, religious teachers became important **community** leaders.

Daughters, who were educated at home by their mothers, learned to be wives, mothers, and housekeepers. This included learning Jewish teachings about food, the Sabbath, and holidays. They also learned about the women of ancient Israel. Two of these women were Ruth and her mother-in-law, Naomi.

According to the Hebrew Bible, Naomi's husband and her two sons died. One of the sons was married to Ruth. Ruth, who was not a Jew herself, made a difficult decision. To help Naomi, Ruth chose to leave her Moabite homeland. She moved to Bethlehem to be with Naomi. Naomi had urged Ruth to stay with her own people, but Ruth responded:

Sabbath comes from the Hebrew word *Shabbat*, which means "cease or desist." The Sabbath is the day of the week when, according to Jewish tradition, people stop working in order to worship. In traditional Jewish homes, the Sabbath begins with a prayer and a family meal.

Academic Vocabulary

community a group of people with common interests living in an area

Because Ruth was Naomi's daughter-in-law, she was accepted with kindness in Bethlehem.

PRIMARY SOURCE

> "Where you go I will go, and where you stay I will stay. Your people will be my people and your God my God. Where you die I will die, and there I will be buried."
>
> —The Book of Ruth 1:16-17 (New International Version)

Ruth's courage and devotion to her family provided an example for Jewish girls to follow.

Dietary Laws

Jewish law tells Jews what they can eat. Ancient Jews could eat the meat of only certain animals. For example, they could eat beef and lamb but not pork. Laws about food are known as *kashrut*, which means "that which is proper." By following laws related to food, Jews believed they were showing obedience to God.

Today, food that is prepared according to Jewish dietary laws is called **kosher** (KOH•shuhr). Many items you see in a grocery store have the symbol for kosher on the label. Animals used for kosher meat must be killed in a certain way. The meat must be inspected, salted, and soaked in water. Foods that are not kosher are considered to be unclean. Dietary law prohibits Jews from eating meat and dairy products together. Jews also cannot eat shellfish such as crab or shrimp.

This symbol can be found on some food packages. It indicates that foods have been prepared according to Jewish dietary laws.

kosher prepared according to Jewish dietary law

Specific foods with religious significance are eaten during some meals. For example, the seder (SAY•duhr) is a special meal eaten during the festival of Passover. It is a holiday that celebrates the Exodus of the Jewish people from Egypt. Foods such as lamb, hardboiled eggs, vinegar, salt water, herbs, and flat bread called matzoh, are served at the seder. During the meal, the youngest child at the table asks a series of questions about the food and the meaning of Passover. The adults and older children at the table recite the answer to the question together. For example, they tell how the bitter herbs reflect the bitter experience of the Jews living in exile. The tradition of eating special foods at Passover and reflecting on history is sacred to the Jewish people.

The foods of the seder are symbolic. For example, the egg is a symbol of God's kindness. Bitter herbs are dipped in fruit juice or honey to symbolize the sweetness and bitterness of life.

▶ CRITICAL THINKING

Comparing What is a particular food your friends or family include when you have a special dinner?

☑ PROGRESS CHECK

Evaluating Why did religious teachers become important leaders in Jewish communities?

LESSON 3 REVIEW

Review Vocabulary

1. Use the terms *synagogue*, *Sabbath*, and *kosher* to describe traditional Jewish practices.

Answer the Guiding Questions

2. ***Identifying*** What are the three parts of the Hebrew Bible?
3. ***Explaining*** How did the people of Judah practice their religion while in exile?
4. ***Comparing*** How were Jewish sons and daughters educated differently?
5. ***Identifying*** What is one type of food that is considered unclean according to Jewish dietary laws?
6. **EXPOSITORY WRITING** What do you think is the main lesson to be learned from the story of Daniel in the lions' den? Write a paragraph describing your thoughts.

LESSON 3 • Day 1 (cont.)

CLOSE & REFLECT

Determining Cause and Effect Write the word *exile* on the whiteboard. As a class, identify effects of the exile from and return to Judah on the Jewish people. Make sure students understand that the exile caused the Jews to unify—they became known as Jews and began the tradition of meeting in synagogues and worshiping on the Sabbath. After their return to Judah, they worked together to build a new temple and to create the Hebrew Bible.

LESSON 3 • Day 2

ENGAGE

Making Connections Invite students to skim the lesson content and to think about the ways that religion likely influenced the daily lives of the ancient Israelites. Then, ask volunteers to suggest ways in which religious beliefs influence daily life today.

TEACH & ASSESS

2 Jewish Daily Life

GUIDING QUESTION *How did religion shape the Jewish way of life?*

LECTURE SLIDE

Making Inferences Direct students to read the introductory text under the heading "Jewish Daily Life." Then show the lecture slide about the history and content of the Torah. Point out to them the ways in which the teachings of the Torah shaped the behaviors of early Jews.

Ask: How did the teachings of the Torah encourage Jews to behave responsibly? *(Possible answer: The teachings of the Torah encouraged Jews to help the poor, to deal honestly with other people, and to apply laws fairly. The Torah also encouraged them to show self-discipline in their daily lives.)*

IMAGE

Hypothesizing Explain to students that because of the Torah's importance to Jewish life, Israelite families stressed the value of education. Present the interactive feature on education and the scrolls.

IMAGE

Identifying Lead students in a discussion about why the story of Ruth and Naomi is important.

Ask: What traits did Ruth demonstrate that made her a role model for Jewish girls? *(Ruth showed courage and devotion to her family in her decision to remain with Naomi. These traits made her a leader on which Jewish girls could model their actions.)* Then show students the image of the story of Esther. Have them answer the discussion question.

IMAGE

Explaining Show students the image of the head coverings and clothing traditionally worn by ancient Jews.

Ask: Why did ancient Jews wear special clothing? *(Students should understand that the head coverings and other clothing helped distinguish the Jews from the Greeks. They wore special items to remind themselves to think of God.)*

Ask students to hypothesize why religious education would be important to the survival of any religion. *(It would help ensure that the teachings, beliefs, and practices of the religion were passed down to younger generations.)* BL

INTERACTIVE WHITEBOARD ACTIVITY

Categorizing Clarify for students that Jewish families emphasized following Jewish dietary laws. Then, review with students the types of foods that are considered kosher and not kosher. Next, present the Interactive Whiteboard Activity on kosher foods. Assist students as they categorize each type of food as kosher or not kosher. When students have completed the activity, discuss as a class any other types of laws that might affect what people eat. ELL

Have students complete the Lesson 3 Review questions.

CLOSE & REFLECT

Explaining Remind students of the primary sources they have learned about in this lesson, including the Hebrew Bible and the Torah scrolls. Discuss with students why sources such as these documents can prove valuable when learning about the ancient Israelites. Note the information that such sources provide about the rules that governed daily life. AL

BACKGROUND KNOWLEDGE

The Dead Sea

The Dead Sea is the lowest-lying body of water in the world. It lies an average of 1,312 feet (400 m) below sea level. Its name, which dates from the 300s B.C., comes from its extreme saltiness. Nothing lives in its water except certain kinds of bacteria. Fish carried into the sea by the Jordan River die almost instantly.

IF YOU HAVE MORE TIME . . .

Research and Make Connections Among Cultures

Identifying The Jewish religion is not the only one that includes dietary guidelines. For example, Muslims do not eat pork or drink alcohol; Hindus do not eat beef; Mormons do not drink alcohol, coffee, or tea; and many Buddhists and Quakers are vegetarians. Then invite students to research the dietary practices of a religious group and prepare a brief report for the class. Students should explain the reasons for the practices and guidelines. After students give their presentations, lead the class in a discussion that compares and contrasts the practices. BL

Answers for pages 156–159

P. 156 CRITICAL THINKING The story of Daniel reminds them to maintain their faith in God, because God will protect them during hard times.

P. 156 ☑ PROGRESS CHECK Because the Persians who ruled Judah did not allow Jews to form their own government, the Jewish people depended on religious leaders—the temple priests and scribes—to guide them.

P. 159 CRITICAL THINKING Answers will vary.

P. 159 ☑ PROGRESS CHECK Religious teachers became important leaders because of the Torah's great influence on daily life in Jewish communities.

LESSON 3 REVIEW

1. Jews worship in synagogues, or houses of worship, on the weekly religious holiday, the Sabbath. Many Jews eat foods that are kosher, meaning they are prepared according to Jewish dietary laws.
2. The Torah, the Prophets, and the Writings are three parts of the Hebrew Bible.
3. Small groups of Jews met at synagogues to worship.
4. Sons learned how to read the Torah and worship. They also learned a trade. Daughters learned how to be wives, mothers, and housekeepers.
5. Students may respond that pork and shellfish are considered unclean under Jewish dietary law.
6. Answers will vary but might include the following: God will rescue good people from evil; good eventually will triumph.

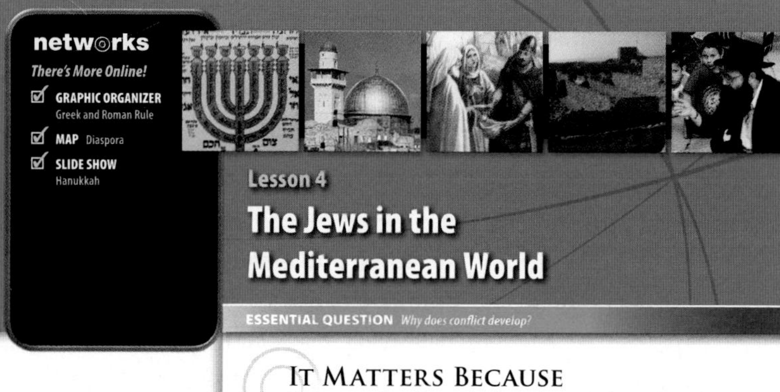

networks
There's More Online!
- GRAPHIC ORGANIZER Greek and Roman Rule
- MAP Diaspora
- SLIDE SHOW Hanukkah

Lesson 4

The Jews in the Mediterranean World

ESSENTIAL QUESTION *Why does conflict develop?*

It Matters Because

The Jews experienced many significant changes under Greek and Roman rule.

1 The Arrival of Greek Rule

GUIDING QUESTION *What was life like for the Jews in Greek-ruled lands?*

The Jews of Judah remained under Persian rule for nearly 200 years. That is about the same amount of time as the entire history of the United States. Then, in 331 B.C., a king from Macedonia, who had conquered Greece, defeated the Persians. This king was Alexander the Great. Alexander admired Greek ways and wanted to spread them. He introduced the Greek language and culture to Judah. Alexander allowed the Jews to stay in Judah.

How Did Jewish Ideas Spread?

Under Alexander, Judah remained the center of Judaism. Many Jews at that time, however, had long lived outside Judah. Thousands had been exiled to Babylon in 586 B.C. When in 538 B.C. the conquering Persians gave them permission to return to Judah, many chose to stay in Babylon or go to other Mediterranean lands instead. These groups of Jews living outside of the Jewish homeland became known as the **Diaspora** (deye•AS•puh•ruh). *Diaspora* is a Greek word that means "scattered." Where these Jews settled, they practiced their customs, and Jewish ideas spread.

The Jews of the Diaspora remained loyal to Judaism. At the same time, many learned the Greek language and adopted features of Greek culture. A group of Jewish scholars in Egypt copied the Hebrew Bible into Greek. This Greek **version**, called the Septuagint (sehp•TOO•uh•juhnt), helped people who were not Jews to read and understand the Hebrew Bible. As a result, Jewish ideas spread throughout the Mediterranean world.

The Revolt of Maccabeus

After Alexander's death, four of his generals divided his empire into separate kingdoms. One kingdom covered much of Southwest Asia. A family known as the Seleucids (suh•LOO•suhds) ruled this kingdom. By 200 B.C., Judah was under the control of Seleucid kings.

In 176 B.C., Antiochus IV (an•TEE•uh•kuhs) came to power as the Seleucid king. As ruler of Judah, Antiochus required the Jews to worship the many Greek gods and goddesses.

Taking Notes: *Comparing and Contrasting*

As you read, complete a diagram like this one by identifying similarities and differences between Greek rule and Roman rule.

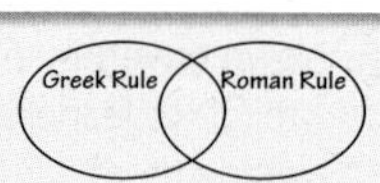

Content Vocabulary
- Diaspora
- rabbi

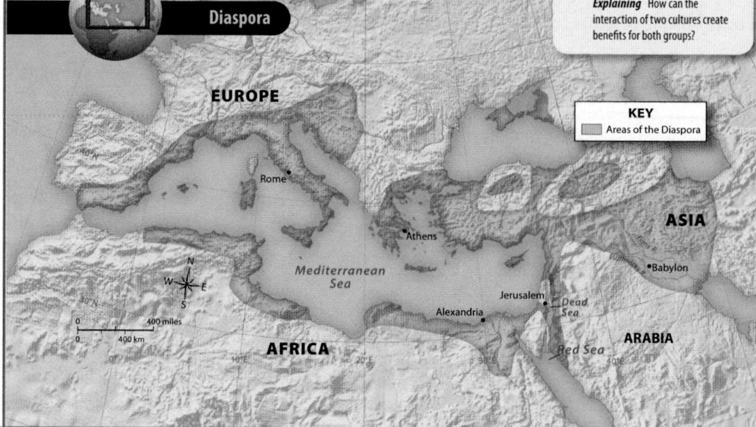

GEOGRAPHY CONNECTION

The Diaspora continued throughout Alexander's Greek empire. During the first century A.D., Jews represented about 40 percent of the empire's population.

1 **MOVEMENT** How did the Diaspora help spread Jewish ideas?

2 **CRITICAL THINKING** *Explaining* How can the interaction of two cultures create benefits for both groups?

Diaspora the groups of Jews living outside of the Jewish homeland

Academic Vocabulary

version a different form or edition; a translation of the Bible

BIOGRAPHY

Judas Maccabeus (c. 190 B.C.–160 B.C.)

Judas Maccabeus and his followers engaged in guerrilla warfare against the Greek armies. Guerrilla warfare is irregular combat carried out by small groups of independent soldiers. This strategy helped the Maccabees succeed in battle against the Seleucids. The family of Judas Maccabeus ruled Judah and expanded its lands. With more territory protecting it, Judah remained free until the Roman conquest.

▶ CRITICAL THINKING
Explaining Why is Judas Maccabeus considered a hero?

A large number of Jews, however, refused to abandon their religion. In 167 B.C., Judas Maccabeus (JOO•duhs MAK•uh•BEE•uhs), a Jewish priest, led the fight against Seleucid rule. He and his followers fled to the hills. They formed a rebel army known as the Maccabees.

After many battles, the Maccabees succeeded in capturing the Temple. They cleared it of all statues of Greek gods and goddesses. They then rededicated the temple to the worship of God. Each year, Jews recall the cleansing of the Temple when they celebrate the festival of Hanukkah (HAH•nuh•kuh).

PROGRESS CHECK

Analyzing How did Alexander and later the Seleucids affect the people of Judah?

2 Roman Rule in Judaea

GUIDING QUESTION *How did the Jews react to Roman rule of their homeland?*

By 100 B.C., the Romans controlled much of the eastern Mediterranean lands. The name *Roman* came from Rome, their capital. Rome was located far to the west in what is known today as Italy. Led by powerful generals, the Romans **expanded** their empire. In 63 B.C., Roman forces conquered Judah and renamed it Judaea (joo•DEE•uh).

At first, the Romans chose a follower of the Jewish religion, Herod (HEHR•uhd), to rule as king of Judaea. Herod built many forts and cities in Judaea. The Second Temple in Jerusalem, rebuilt during Herod's reign, served as the center of Jewish worship.

Jewish Groups

After Herod's death, Roman officials ruled Judaea. At that time, disagreement grew about how Judaism should be practiced. Jews also had different views on how to deal with the Romans.

One group of Jews was known as the Pharisees (FEH•ruh•seez). The Pharisees gained the support of the common people. They taught in the synagogues and applied the teachings of the Torah to daily life. Through their teachings, the Pharisees helped to make Judaism a religion of the home and family. The Pharisees wanted to help people obey the commandments. To do this, they stressed both written and oral law. Oral law is the unwritten interpretations passed down over time by word of mouth.

Reading HELPDESK

Academic Vocabulary

expand to enlarge

Herod was primarily responsible for developing the fortress at Masada. It was the scene of a major Roman and Jewish battle. Visitors may tour its mountainous ruins today.

The Pharisees wanted Judaea free of Roman rule. However, they did not urge Jews to fight the Romans. Instead, they told people to resist Roman control. They urged the people to practice the Torah's teachings with greater **devotion**.

Another Jewish group made up of wealthy noble families was the Sadducees (SA•juh•SEEZ). Many of them served as priests and scribes in the Temple. The Sadducees accepted the laws of the Torah. They were more concerned, however, with applying the laws to temple ceremonies. They also did not agree with many of the Pharisees' teachings. For example, the Sadducees emphasized the written law but rejected oral law. The Sadducees favored **cooperation** with the Romans. They wanted to keep peace and order in Judaea.

A third group was called the Essenes (ih•SEENZ). They were priests who broke away from the Temple in Jerusalem. Many Essenes lived at Qumrān, an area in the desert near the Dead Sea. They spent their lives praying and waiting for God to deliver the Jews from Roman rule. The Essenes followed only the written law of the Torah.

Centuries later, in A.D. 1947, ancient scrolls were found in caves at Qumrān. Because the caves were near the Dead Sea, the scrolls became known as the Dead Sea Scrolls. Many of the scrolls were most likely written by Essenes. The scrolls are important to historians because they provide a window into a particular place and time.

Academic Vocabulary

devotion dedication, a strong commitment
cooperation working together

Teaching *The Jews in the Mediterranean World*

(Student Edition pp. 160–167)

LESSON 4 • Day 1

ENGAGE

SLIDE SHOW

Making Connections Present the interactive slide show about Hanukkah and discuss the information provided. Invite students to describe what they know about Hanukkah and its traditions.

Also, ask volunteers to describe similar traditions from their backgrounds that commemorate important historical events.

Inform students that in this lesson they will learn about this holiday's origins as well as other key events in Jewish history. AL ELL

TEACH & ASSESS

1 The Arrival of Greek Rule

GUIDING QUESTION ***What was life like for the Jews in Greek-ruled lands?***

MAP

Analyzing Visuals Discuss with students the meaning of the word *empire*. Guide them to understand that empires often controlled huge areas of land and included people of many different cultures.

Then present the interactive maps of the Diaspora. Click on the maps, and read the information provided.

Help students answer the discussion question by pointing out the concentration of dense Jewish settlements along the Mediterranean coast.

Ask: How do you think the settlement patterns of the Diaspora might have changed over time? *(Possible answer: The Diaspora likely moved gradually outward from Judah. Those areas located farther away from Judah might have become more populated by Jews over time.)* BL

LECTURE SLIDE

Explaining Show students the lecture slide about the Diaspora. Discuss how Jews settled and thrived in major cities outside Judah, such as Alexandria, and influenced other cultures.

Ask: What was the Septuagint? Why was it important to the spread of Jewish ideas in the Mediterranean world? *(The Septuagint was a version of the Hebrew Bible that had been copied into Greek. It helped people who were not Jewish read and understand the ideas in the Hebrew Bible.)* ELL

Hypothesizing Review with students the text about the groups of Jews that became known as the Diaspora.

Ask: How do you think living outside the Jewish homeland affected the ways in which families of the Diaspora practiced Judaism? *(Possible answer: Living outside the Jewish homeland likely had little effect on these families. Jewish ideas spread throughout the Diaspora, so this suggests that these families likely continued to practice Judaism as they had previously.)* BL

IMAGE Present the image about Judas Maccabeus and the Maccabees. **Ask: How do you think guerilla warfare helped the Maccabees beat the Seleucids?** *(The Seleucids may not have been prepared for the surprise attacks and the constant strain of being on guard may have taken its toll.)* Review with students the connection between the victory of the Maccabees and the annual festival of Hanukkah.

Ask: Who wrote the First Book of Maccabees? *(a Jewish historian who lived in Judah during the second century B.C.)*

CLOSE & REFLECT

Explaining Have students explain why the Diaspora was important to the survival of the Jewish religion. Write students' answers on the board. Use the answers to summarize what the Diaspora was.

LESSON 4 • Day 2

ENGAGE

Discussing Ask students what they know about the Romans and the Roman Empire. Write their responses on the board. Challenge students to draw on what they have learned about Jewish experience under the rule of other cultures, such as the Chaldeans, the Babylonians, and the Greeks.

Ask: How are the Jewish people likely to respond to life under Roman rule? *(Accept reasonable answers. Students may suggest that if the Romans allow the Jewish people to worship and carry out their traditions, everything will be fine, but if the Romans impose rules on them, they might revolt.)*

TEACH & ASSESS

2 Roman Rule in Judaea

GUIDING QUESTION ***How did the Jews react to Roman rule of their homeland?***

IMAGE

Analyzing Visuals Refer students to the section titled "Jewish Groups." Present the interactive image on the fortress at Masada.

Ask: Why is Masada considered an important historic site? *(It is the site of an ancient fortress that was developed primarily by Herod. It was also the location of an important battle between Jewish and Roman forces in the struggle for independence.)*

Making Inferences Direct students' attention to the text about Jewish groups under Roman rule, and guide them to determine the types of people who made up each group.

Ask: Which group probably had the support of common families? *(the Pharisees)* **Which group was made up of wealthy noble families?** *(the Sadducees)*

IMAGE **Explaining** Present the interactive image of the Dead Sea Scrolls. Click on the image, and read the information provided. **Ask: Why might the Dead Sea Scrolls have been placed in caves?** *(The documents might have been placed in caves to hide them from Roman armies.)*

Identifying Point students to the section titled "Jewish-Roman Wars." **Ask: Which Jewish group led a revolt against Roman rule?** *(the Zealots)*

Discuss with students the outcome of Jewish revolts against Roman rule. Help them understand that the Romans eventually put down these revolts, leading to stricter controls and harsh penalties on the Jews.

IMAGE **Finding the Main Idea** Tell students to focus on the text about the Romans' destruction of the Second Temple in Jerusalem. Then present the interactive image feature on the Western Wall of the Temple.

Ask: Why is the Western Wall still important to modern Jews? *(It is the only part of the Temple complex available to Jews for prayer. It is a monument to their faith. It is a symbol of how their faith has outlasted their enemies.)*

Answers for pages 160–163

P. 160 Taking Notes Similarities—Both conquered Judah; introduced their culture to Judah. Differences—Greeks allowed Jews to stay in Judah; many Jews (the Diaspora) settled in other parts of Greek empire.

P. 161 GEOGRAPHY CONNECTION

1. As Jews moved and settled around the world, they practiced their beliefs. Other cultures learned from them.
2. CRITICAL THINKING Each culture can learn from the knowledge, customs, and beliefs of the other group.

P. 162 CRITICAL THINKING Maccabeus led Jewish rebels against the Seleucid army and recaptured the Temple. By rededicating the Temple, Maccabeus reclaimed the central Jewish site for worship.

P. 162 ☑ PROGRESS CHECK Under Alexander, Judah remained the center of Judaism; the Diaspora took place; and a Greek version of the Hebrew Bible was written, which helped spread Jewish ideas in the Mediterranean world. Under the Seleucid kings, Jews had to worship other gods, which led to a revolt by the Maccabees.

GEOGRAPHY CONNECTION

There are rocky cliffs along the shores of the Dead Sea. Caves in these cliffs contained the Dead Sea scrolls.

1. **LOCATION** Describe the location of the Dead Sea in relation to the Mediterranean Sea.
2. **CRITICAL THINKING** *Explaining* Why would the discovery of the Dead Sea Scrolls be considered so significant?

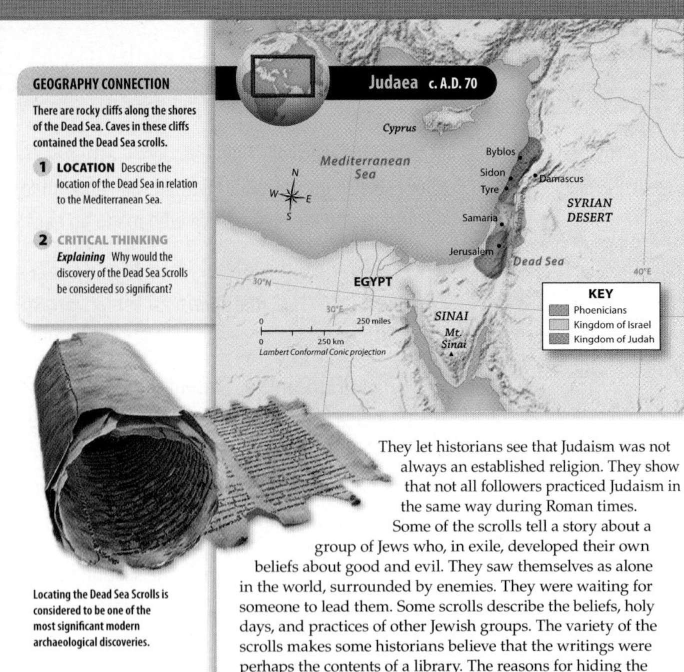

Locating the Dead Sea Scrolls is considered to be one of the most significant modern archaeological discoveries.

They let historians see that Judaism was not always an established religion. They show that not all followers practiced Judaism in the same way during Roman times.

Some of the scrolls tell a story about a group of Jews who, in exile, developed their own beliefs about good and evil. They saw themselves as alone in the world, surrounded by enemies. They were waiting for someone to lead them. Some scrolls describe the beliefs, holy days, and practices of other Jewish groups. The variety of the scrolls makes some historians believe that the writings were perhaps the contents of a library. The reasons for hiding the scrolls are unclear. Someone may have wanted to protect them from destruction during times of conflict with the Romans. Since their discovery, however, the scrolls have helped historians understand more about Judaism during Roman times.

A fourth Jewish group, the Zealots, lived in Judaea. They wanted to fight for their freedom against the Romans. During the A.D. 60s, Jewish hatred of Roman rule reached its peak. Hope remained in the Jewish faith, however. Many Jews were waiting for God to send a deliverer to free them from Roman rule. As **tensions** between Romans and Jews in Judaea increased, the Zealots prepared to act.

Reading HELPDESK

Academic Vocabulary

tensions opposition between individuals or groups; stress

Jewish-Roman Wars

In A.D. 66, the Zealots revolted. They overpowered the small Roman army in Jerusalem. Four years later, Roman forces retook the city. They killed thousands of Jews and forced many others to leave. The Romans also destroyed the Second Temple in Jerusalem. Today the Western Wall still stands in Jerusalem. This structure is all that remains of the Temple complex. It is a long-standing Jewish custom to come to this spot to pray.

After a number of years passed, some Jews rebelled once again. In A.D. 132, a military leader named Simon ben Kosiba, known as Bar Kochba, led the Jews in the battle for freedom. However, three years later, Roman forces crushed the revolt. They killed Bar Kochba and many other Jewish leaders during the fighting.

With the revolt put down, the Romans imposed stricter controls and did not allow Jews to live in or even visit Jerusalem. The Romans renamed Judaea and called it Palestine. This name refers to the Philistines, whom the Israelites had conquered centuries before.

The ancient Western Wall is the only remaining structure of the Temple of Jerusalem. Coming here to pray has been a Jewish custom for hundreds of years. Those who visit the wall often leave prayers on paper stuffed into its cracks.

▶ **CRITICAL THINKING**

Explaining Why might people still come to this site to pray?

Connections to TODAY

Dead Sea Scrolls

In A.D. 1947, a shepherd in the Judaean desert entered a cave along the shore of the Dead Sea. There he discovered several large clay jars. Some jars were empty, but in others he found ancient scrolls of leather, papyrus, and copper. These **documents**, written between 200 B.C. and A.D. 68, are called the Dead Sea scrolls. The scrolls found in several caves in the area include the oldest complete copy of the Book of Isaiah and pieces of many other books of the Hebrew Bible. Among the documents are works in ancient Hebrew, Greek, and Aramaic. Most scholars believe that the scrolls were part of a library that belonged to an early Jewish community.

The Rabbis

Despite losing their struggle for independence, the Jews regrouped with the help of their **rabbis** (RA•byz), or religious leaders. The Jewish people no longer had a temple or priests. Instead, the synagogues and rabbis gained importance. The rabbis taught and explained the Torah. They provided moral guidance—accepted notions of right and wrong—to the people.

One of the most famous rabbis was Yohanan ben Zaccai (YOH•kah•nahn behn zah•KY). Ben Zaccai lived in Judaea when Jerusalem fell to the Romans in A.D. 70. He persuaded the Romans to spare the Jewish city of Yavneh. There, he founded a school to continue teaching the Torah.

Ben Zaccai helped the Judaic spirit survive the destruction of the temple and the loss of Jerusalem. He placed great importance on the study of the Torah. He also stressed acts of loving kindness and community service. Because of ben Zaccai's efforts, the school at Yavneh became a center of Torah studies and a model for other schools. Other rabbis founded Torah schools in places as far away as Babylon and Egypt.

Through the efforts of ben Zaccai and other rabbis, the basic beliefs of Judaism were preserved. Eventually, the rabbis gathered their oral discussions about Jewish law and recorded them in a work known as the Mishnah. Later, the Mishnah was combined with other Jewish legal traditions into an authoritative collection of Jewish tradition known as the Talmud. The word *Talmud* is a Hebrew term that means "instruction." The Talmud became the basis for Jewish teachings throughout the ages.

A part of the Talmud called the Mishnah began as an oral history of Jewish law passed from one generation of rabbis to another.

Reading HELPDESK

rabbi the official leader of a Jewish congregation

Academic Vocabulary

document an official paper used as proof or support of something

Rabbis continue to educate students today. They might also perform charity or social functions for their congregations.

To this day, the Talmud remains central to Jewish teaching and is the ultimate authority on Jewish law. A prayer at the end of part of the Talmud reveals the Jewish reverence for the Torah:

PRIMARY SOURCE

> "Make sweet, O Lord, our God, the words of Thy Law in our mouths, and in the mouth of Thy people the house of Israel; and may we, our children, and the children of Thy people the house of Israel, all know Thy Name and learn Thy Law."
>
> —from *The Babylon Talmud, Book 1: Tract Sabbath*

✓ PROGRESS CHECK

Explaining How did the rabbis help Judaism survive after the Roman conquest?

LESSON 4 REVIEW

Review Vocabulary

1. In what way did *rabbis* help the Jews during the period of Roman rule?

Answer the Guiding Questions

2. *Explaining* What was life like for the Jews in Greek-ruled lands?
3. *Identifying* Which group gained control of Judah following Alexander's death?
4. *Explaining* How did the Jews react to Roman rule of their homeland?
5. *Identifying* Who established a school for teaching the Torah at Yavneh?
6. **PERSUASIVE WRITING** Imagine you are living in Judaea during the Roman conquest. Write a letter to a friend describing what action you would like to see taken to make Judaea free again.

LESSON 4 • Day 2 (cont.)

Explaining Help students locate the text on rabbis, and discuss with them how the rabbis helped the Jewish people regroup after their unsuccessful struggle for independence. Guide this discussion to focus on the rabbis' roles as religious leaders and teachers.

Ask: How did Yohanan ben Zaccai help the Jewish religion survive? *(Zaccai persuaded the Romans to spare the city of Yavneh. He also founded a school that continued to teach the Torah and preserve the basic beliefs of Judaism.)*

Drawing Conclusions Review with students the changes that took place after the Jews lost their struggle for independence from the Romans.

Ask: Why do you think the rabbis became important during this time? *(Possible answer: During this time, the Jewish people no longer had the Temple or priests. This helped the rabbis become important. The Jewish people also might have been looking for guidance during this difficult period. The rabbis provided this guidance. The work of the rabbis to preserve Judaism also likely helped give them a leadership role among the Jewish people.)*

IMAGE

Analyzing Primary Sources Direct students' attention to the slide describing the Mishnah and the Talmud.

Make sure students understand that rabbis developed these works to preserve important ideas about Jewish law. Then, present the interactive image with information about and text from the Talmud.

Click on the image to read the information provided, and then click again to hear quotes from the Talmud. Ask students to reflect on the quotations from the Talmud.

Ask: How do these quotations reflect what you know about the purpose of the Talmud? *(Possible answer: The Talmud discusses issues faced in daily life. These quotations offer practical advice that could be applied to everyday situations.)* BL

INTERACTIVE GRAPHIC ORGANIZER

Comparing and Contrasting Ask volunteers to describe important characteristics of life for Jews under Roman rule.

Then, discuss with the class how these characteristics were similar or different under Greek rule. Record students' responses in a Venn diagram. *(Possible answers include the following. Greek rule: Jews were forced to worship Greek gods. Hebrew texts were translated into Greek. Jewish rebellion overthrew Greek rule. Both: Jews opposed foreign rule. Some Jews fought against Greek and Roman rulers. Roman rule: Romans defeated Jewish rebellions and cast Jews out of Jerusalem.)*

Have students complete the Lesson 4 Review questions.

CLOSE & REFLECT

INTERACTIVE WORKSHEET

21st Century Skills Activity

Sequencing Present the 21st Century Skills Activity on making a time line. If necessary, have a student read aloud the instruction about making a time line.

Make sure students understand the concept of a time line before asking them to complete the activity and answer the questions.

If time allows, ask students to share their time lines with the class. Finally, close by asking students why time lines help students of history remember events. *(Students should suggest that the linear organization of events helps them remember the order of events. The time line helps them visualize history as it unfolded.)*

IF YOU HAVE MORE TIME . . .

Use Graphic Organizers to Visualize Cause and Effect

Determining Cause and Effect Have students work in pairs to create cause-and-effect charts for the sections "The Arrival of Greek Rule" and "Roman Rule in Judaea." Tell students to identify as many causes and effects as they can. If students need guidance, ask them to identify the causes and effects of the Diaspora or the causes and effects of Jewish rebellion against the Romans. Ask students to share their charts with the class.

Discuss any differences or discrepancies in the charts. Close by having students make generalizations about life for the Jews under the Greeks and under the Romans.

Use Context Clues to Determine Meaning

Analyzing Students can use context clues to determine the meaning of a word they do not know. Context refers to the words and sentences that surround the unknown word. Here is a list of context clues that students can look for.

- **Synonyms** Students should look for a synonym to the unknown word. Synonyms are often found in context when two things are compared.
- **Antonyms** Students might also look for antonyms for the unknown word. Antonyms often appear in context when two things are contrasted.
- **Definitions** Students might find a phrase that defines or describes an unknown word. Commas, dashes, or parentheses often surround a phrase that gives this type of clue.
- **Examples** Sometimes a reading contains examples that reveal the meaning of a word.

There are also other techniques for using context to determine the meaning of a word that students can use.

- Ask students to look before, at, and after the unknown word for a context clue.
- Have students connect what they already know with what the author has written.
- Have students predict a possible meaning.
- Have students apply the meaning in a sentence.
- Ask students if their meaning makes sense. If not, have them try again. AL ELL

Answers for pages 164–167

P. 164 GEOGRAPHY CONNECTION

1. The Dead Sea is east of the Mediterranean Sea.
2. CRITICAL THINKING The discovery of the Dead Sea Scrolls provided firsthand information about Judaism during the period of Roman rule.

P. 165 CRITICAL THINKING They come to the Western Wall in order to honor what remains of the Second Temple. By doing so, they show that their faith has outlasted the Romans who tried to destroy them.

P. 167 ☑ PROGRESS CHECK Rabbis taught and explained the Torah, and they provided moral guidance to others. Some rabbis founded schools that preserved the basic beliefs of Judaism.

LESSON 4 REVIEW

1. The rabbis helped by explaining and teaching the Torah and providing moral guidance.
2. The Jews were allowed to stay in Judah. The Greek language and Greek ways were introduced to Judah.
3. The Seleucids gained control of Judah following Alexander's death.
4. They rebelled against Roman rule.
5. The rabbi Yohanan ben Zaccai established this school at Yavneh.
6. Letters will vary but should show thoughtful consideration of the difficulties of Jewish life under Roman rule.

CHAPTER 6 Activities

Write your answers on a separate piece of paper.

❶ **Exploring the Essential Question**
EXPOSITORY WRITING Write an expository essay about how key leaders influenced the Israelites during the time periods discussed in this chapter. Identify specific leaders who had the most significant effect. Explain how they led during times of conflict.

❷ **21st Century Skills**
CREATING A SLIDE SHOW Create a slide show about an aspect of Jewish culture that you have studied in this chapter. When presenting, briefly introduce each image, and offer a clear interpretation of why it is significant.

❸ **Thinking Like a Historian**
COMPARING AND CONTRASTING Create a diagram like the one shown to compare and contrast the Jewish groups that existed under Roman rule.

❹ **GEOGRAPHY ACTIVITY**

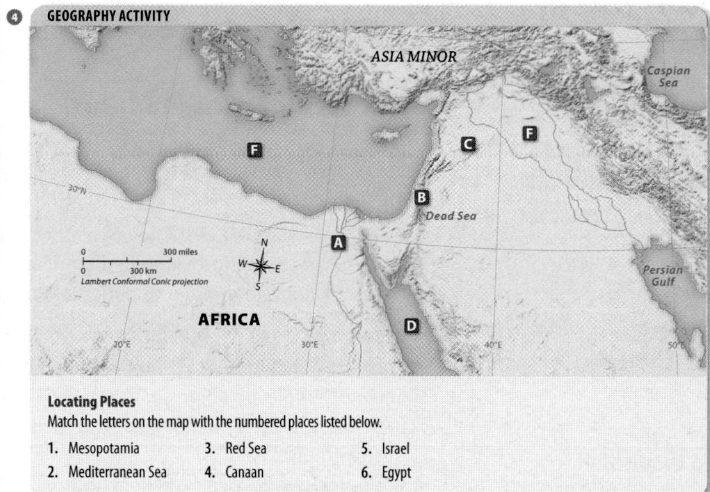

Locating Places
Match the letters on the map with the numbered places listed below.

1. Mesopotamia
2. Mediterranean Sea
3. Red Sea
4. Canaan
5. Israel
6. Egypt

CHAPTER 6 Assessment

REVIEW THE GUIDING QUESTIONS
Directions: Choose the best answer for each question.

❶ The Israelites differed from many other ancient civilizations by
A. battling neighboring civilizations.
B. settling in Canaan.
C. worshiping only one God.
D. creating written documents.

❷ According to the Hebrew Bible, from which location did the Israelites migrate to Canaan?
F. Mesopotamia
G. Egypt
H. Lebanon
I. Jordan

❸ Which of the following is considered the greatest king in Israelite history?
A. David
B. Alexander
C. Solomon
D. Samuel

❹ Though it had survived earlier conquests, in 586 B.C., Jerusalem was destroyed by the
F. Chaldeans.
G. Assyrians.
H. Samaritans.
I. Israelites.

❺ While in exile in Babylon, Jews began to
A. believe in one God.
B. construct new temples.
C. join the Maccabees.
D. worship in synagogues.

❻ Which group overpowered the Romans and captured Jerusalem in 66 B.C.?
F. Sadducees
G. Essenes
H. Pharisees
I. Zealots

CHAPTER 6 Assessment *(continued)*

DBQ DOCUMENT-BASED QUESTIONS

❼ **Summarizing** Which of the following best states the main purpose of the Ten Commandments?
A. to suggest ways to observe the Sabbath
B. to describe the qualifications for kings
C. to reveal warnings to Israelites
D. to provide rules for living

❽ **Drawing Conclusions** The message found in the Ten Commandments can best be seen today in
F. modern biology.
G. modern geography.
H. modern politics.
I. modern law.

The Ten Commandments
❶ Do not worship any god except me.
❷ Do not . . . bow down and worship idols.
❸ Do not misuse my name.
❹ Remember the Sabbath Day and keep it holy.
❺ Honor your father and your mother.
❻ Do not murder.
❼ Be faithful in marriage.
❽ Do not steal.
❾ Do not testify falsely [tell lies] about others.
❿ Do not want anything that belongs to someone else.
—**Paraphrased** from Exodus 20:3-17

SHORT RESPONSE

"The biblical King Solomon was known for his wisdom, his wealth and his writings. . . . Solomon's downfall came in his old age. . . . Within Solomon's kingdom, he placed heavy taxation on the people, who became bitter. He also had the people work as soldiers, chief officers and commanders of his chariots and cavalry. He granted special privileges to the tribes of Judah and this alienated [angered] the northern tribes."

—from "Solomon" by Shira Schoenberg

❾ What is believed to have weakened Solomon as a king?

❿ Why might Solomon granting special privileges to the tribes of Judah have displeased the other tribes?

EXTENDED RESPONSE

⓫ **Comparative Writing** Write a short essay in which you compare and contrast the daily life of Jews under Greek and Roman rule. Consider how Greek and Roman rule affected the Jewish peoples' ability to practice their religion. Describe how conflicts eventually developed between the Jews and the ruling groups.

Need Extra Help?

If You've Missed Question	❶	❷	❸	❹	❺	❻	❼	❽	❾	❿	⓫
Review Lesson	1	1	2, 4	2, 3	2	4	1	1	2	2	4

NOTES

REFLECT, REVIEW, & REMEDIATE

INTERACTIVE WORKSHEET

Chapter Summary

Provide students with the Chapter Summary worksheet to help review the chapter and prepare for assessment.

Reviewing the Enduring Understandings

Review this chapter's Enduring Understandings with students:

- People, places, and ideas change over time.
- The value that a society places on individual rights is often reflected in that society's government.
- Countries have relationships with each other.

Guide students in small-group discussions about the ways in which the individual rights of the Israelites changed during the time period of this chapter. Ask them to consider what these changes might suggest about the various groups that governed the Israelites. Guide students to recognize that governments that sought to limit the Israelites' freedom to practice their beliefs did not place great value on individual rights.

INTERACTIVE WHITEBOARD ACTIVITY On the interactive whiteboard, draw a web diagram and write the phrase "Individual Rights of the Israelites" in the center. Then have volunteers from each group add to the diagram the key ideas they discussed about individual rights and freedoms related to the Israelites.

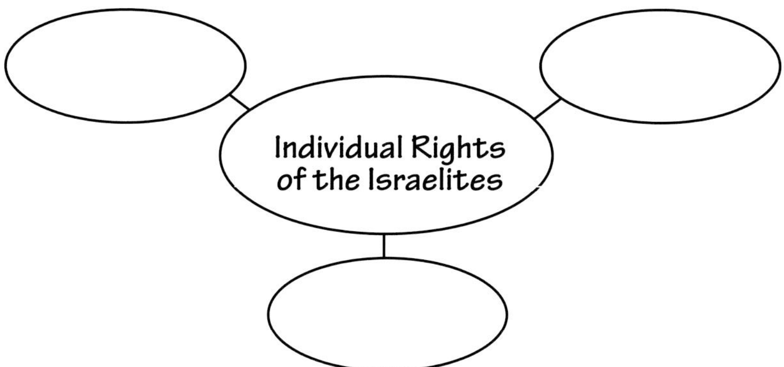

ACTIVITIES ANSWERS

Exploring the Essential Question

1. Students' essays should correctly identify key leaders discussed in the chapter. Their writing should clearly explain the roles of these leaders in the development of Judaism and the conflicts that arose during this time period. Students may highlight leaders such as Abraham, Moses, Joshua, David, Daniel, Judas Maccabeus, and Yohanan ben Zaccai in their essays.

21st Century Skills

2. Students should select relevant, informative images and clearly explain how each image relates to their selected topics.

Thinking Like a Historian

3. Graphic organizers might include the following information: Pharisees—resisted by practicing the Torah's teachings with greater devotion; Sadducees—disagreed with Pharisees, favored cooperation with Romans; Essenes—rebellious priests broke away from Temple and followed only the Torah; Zealots—wanted to fight Romans for freedom.

Locating Places

4. **1.** Mesopotamia F; **2.** Mediterranean Sea E; **3.** Red Sea D; **4.** Canaan C; **5.** Israel B; **6.** Egypt A

ASSESSMENT ANSWERS

Review the Guiding Questions

1. **C** Unlike many other ancient civilizations that practiced polytheism, the Israelites practiced monotheism, or the worship of only one god.

2. **F** The Hebrew Bible indicates that the Israelites migrated to Canaan from Mesopotamia.

3. **A** Because of factors such as his successes in battle, his construction of a capital city, and the prosperous economic conditions during his reign, David is considered the greatest king in Israelite history.

4. **F** Despite having withstood earlier Assyrian conquests, in 597 B.C., Jerusalem was captured by the Chaldeans and then destroyed by them in 586 B.C.

5. **D** During the Babylonian Exile, Jews did not have a temple in which to worship. As a result, they began meeting at synagogues to worship on the Sabbath.

6. **I** The Zealots wanted to be free from Roman rule and rebelled in 66 B.C., capturing Jerusalem.

Document-Based Questions

7. **D** The main purpose of the Ten Commandments is to provide rules for living, not to suggest ways to observe the Sabbath, describe qualifications for kings, or reveal warnings.

8. **I** Modern laws incorporate the moral principles of the Ten Commandments by punishing bad behavior (murder and theft, for example) and promoting a fair society. Modern biology and geography are based on scientific fact, not moral principles. Modern politics do not consistently uphold moral principles.

Short Response

9. Students should explain that Solomon's power was weakened by his decisions to tax the people heavily and to expect them to serve as soldiers, officers, and commanders of his army. Also, he favored the tribe of Judah over the other tribes.

10. Students' responses should indicate that Solomon's granting of favors to only one tribe likely made the other tribes feel they were being treated unfairly.

Extended Response

11. Students' essays should detail the conditions of Jewish life under Greek and Roman rule. For instance, they might suggest that under the Greek rule of Alexander, Judah remained the center of Judaism. Greek culture spread into Judah, and many Jews also moved to other parts of the Greek empire. This helped spread Jewish ideas throughout the Mediterranean region. Later, Greek rulers ordered Jews to give up their beliefs, which led to a conflict. Disagreements also grew during the period of Roman rule. Several Jewish groups suggested different responses to Roman policies, including a revolt. The Romans eventually defeated several Jewish rebellions.

ONLINE RESOURCES
networks

There's More Online!

- ☑ INTERACTIVE WORKSHEETS
- ☑ BIOGRAPHIES
- ☑ CHARTS/GRAPHS
- ☑ GAMES
- ☑ GRAPHIC ORGANIZERS
- ☑ IMAGES
- ☑ MAPS
- ☑ PRIMARY SOURCES
- ☑ SLIDE SHOWS
- ☑ TIME LINE
- ☑ LECTURE SLIDES
- ☑ INTERACTIVE WHITEBOARD ACTIVITIES
- ☑ ASSESSMENTS
- ☑ VIDEOS

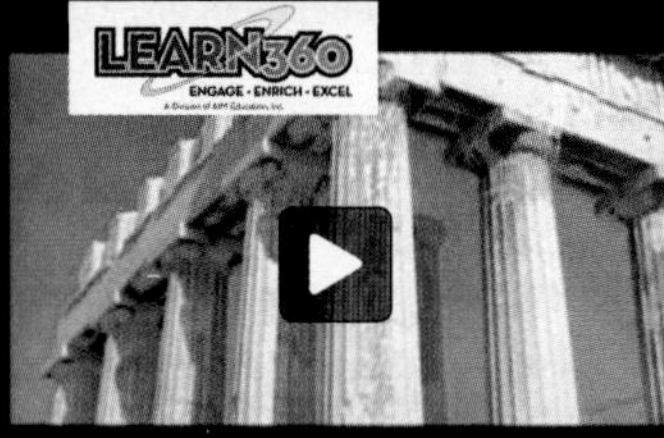

Ancient Greece: Geography and Government

Athens

Chapter 7

The Ancient Greeks

Dear World History Teacher,

The earliest Greek-speaking people migrated from Asia into Greece about 2000 B.C. By 1600 B.C., they had established the Mycenaean civilization, named for the ancient Greek city of Mycenae. After the civilization's collapse in the 1100s B.C., Greece entered its Dark Age. With the end of the Dark Age around 800 B.C., the era of the polis, or city-state, began.

The polis was a community of people that was ruled by its male citizens. The two most famous city-states were Sparta, a militaristic polis ruled by an oligarchy, and Athens, which became known for its democratic institutions despite the fact that many slaves and women had no political rights. Many of our political terms are Greek in origin. Our concepts of the rights and duties of citizenship were also conceived in Athens, which introduced the idea of democracy to the Western world.

The Greek city-states flourished and reached their height in the Classical Period of the 400s B.C. At the beginning of the century, the Persian Wars temporarily unified the Greeks, who were victorious against the powerful Persian Empire. However, the growth of an Athenian empire led to a mighty conflict with Sparta—the Great Peloponnesian War. The conflict weakened the Greek city-states and opened the door to an invasion by Philip II of Macedonia that ended their freedom in 338 B.C.

Jackson J. Spielvogel

More Media Resources

Current Events Online

Visit McGraw-Hill's current events Web site for high-interest news stories and activities for your students. Access the site through the Student or Teacher Center in **networks.**

Reading List

Grade 6 reading level:
Mythological Creatures: A Classical Bestiary, written and illustrated by Lynn Curlee

Grade 7 reading level:
Eyewitness Books: Olympics, by Chris Oxlade and David Ballheimer

Grade 8 reading level:
Troy, by Adele Geras

At the MOVIES

Watch clips of popular culture films and shows such as *The Odyssey*, a television miniseries based on Homer's epic poem about the Greek hero Ulysses's 10-year voyage home following the Trojan War. This retelling of one of the greatest adventures of all time was produced by the Hallmark Channel.

Ask: Why do you think stories written by the Greeks so many years ago are still popular today?

NOTE: Be sure to preview any film to ensure that it is age-appropriate.

Search for more videos online in the **networks** Resource Library.

CHAPTER 7 Planner

UNDERSTANDING BY DESIGN®

Enduring Understandings

- *People, places, and ideas change over time.* • *The value that a society places on individual rights is often reflected in that society's government.* • *Countries have relationships with each other.*

Essential Questions

- *How does geography influence the way people live?* • *Why do people form governments?*
- *Why does conflict develop?* • *How do governments change?*

Students will know:

- *how geography affected the early Greeks*
- *what contributed to the development of the Minoan civilization*
- *how the Mycenaeans became a powerful military force*
- *how Greek culture spread to other parts of the world*
- *the different types of government that developed among the Greek city-states*
- *why Sparta became a military society*
- *what characteristics made Athens unique*
- *how the Persians successfully ruled their large empire*
- *what the Greeks did to defeat the Persians*
- *what it was like to live in Athens during the rule of Pericles*

Students will be able to:

- **explain** how geography affected the settlement of Greece
- **identify** similarities and differences between the rights and responsibilities of ancient Greek citizens and U.S. citizens today
- **describe** the characteristics of tyranny, oligarchy, and democracy
- **explain** differences between Sparta and Athens
- **identify** the location of the Persian Empire
- **explain** how the Greeks won the Persian Wars
- **explain** differences between Athenian democracy and American democracy
- **identify** characteristics of life in Athens
- **explain** why Pericles was able to convince Athenians to continue fighting the Peloponnesian War
- **identify** what happened to the Greek city-states after the Peloponnesian War
- **analyze** what could have changed the outcome of the war

Predictable Misunderstandings

Students may think:

- Democracy was the same in Athens as in the United States.
- The Greek city-states were friendly to one another because they were all located in Greece.

Assessment Evidence

Performance Task

- Hands-On Chapter Project

Other Evidence

- Responses to Interactive Whiteboard Activities
- Comparing and contrasting photos of Greek culture
- Class discussions of the Peloponnesian War
- Economics of History Activity
- 21st Century Skills Activity
- Geography and History Activity
- Primary Source Activities
- Written essay
- Lesson Reviews

Pacing Guide

Introducing the Chapter	1 day
Lesson 1 Rise of Greek Civilization	2 days
Lesson 2 Sparta and Athens: City-State Rivals	2 days
Lesson 3 Greece and Persia	1 day
Lesson 4 Glory, War, and Decline	2 days
Chapter Activities and Assessment	1 day
TOTAL TIME	**9 Days**

Differentiated Instruction

These lesson plans are written to address the needs of your On Level students. Discussion and activities that are well-suited to your Approaching Grade Level learners, Beyond Grade Level learners, as well as your English Language Learners, are coded as follows:

AL **Approaching Grade Level**

BL **Beyond Grade Level**

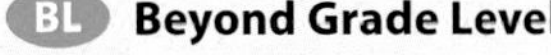

ELL **English Language Learner**

NCSS Standards covered in "Ancient Greece"

Learners will understand:

1 CULTURE

4. That the beliefs, values, and behaviors of a culture form an integrated system that helps shape the activities and ways of life that define a culture

8. That language, behaviors, and beliefs of different cultures can both contribute to and pose barriers to cross-cultural understanding

2 TIME, CONTINUITY, AND CHANGE

7. The contributions of key persons, groups, and events from the past and their influence on the present

3 PEOPLE, PLACES, AND ENVIRONMENTS

8. Factors that contribute to cooperation and conflict among peoples of the nation and world, including language, religion, and political beliefs

4 INDIVIDUAL DEVELOPMENT AND IDENTITY

3. How factors such as physical endowment, interests, capabilities, learning, motivation, personality, perception, and beliefs influence individual development and identity

4. How personal, social, cultural, and environmental factors contribute to the development and the growth of personal identity

5 INDIVIDUALS, GROUPS, AND INSTITUTIONS

2. Concepts such as: mores, norms, status, role, socialization, ethnocentrism, cultural diffusion, competition, cooperation, conflict, race, ethnicity, and gender

6. That cultural diffusion occurs when groups migrate

9. That groups and institutions influence culture in a variety of ways

8 SCIENCE, TECHNOLOGY, AND SOCIETY

6. Values, beliefs, and attitudes that have been influenced by new scientific and technological knowledge (for example, invention of the printing press, conceptions of the universe, applications of atomic energy, and genetic discoveries)

CHAPTER 7

Introducing the Chapter

(Student Edition p. 171)

The Story Matters . . .

Read "The Story Matters . . ." aloud in class or ask a volunteer to read it aloud. Then discuss what it might have been like living in Greece as a young person when Greek culture was a strong influence in the Mediterranean area.

Ask:

What are the effects of American cultural influence in the world? Ask a few students to share their views.

Then ask:

Does living in a dominant culture affect the way people in that culture live and view the rest of the world?

Tell the class that Greek civilization developed from the Minoans and Mycenaeans. By the 700s B.C., Greek city-states and colonies flourished in the Mediterranean region. The Persian Empire attempted unsuccessfully to invade Greece. However, by the end of the 400s B.C., Greek culture declined after a bitter war between the two most powerful city-states, Athens and Sparta.

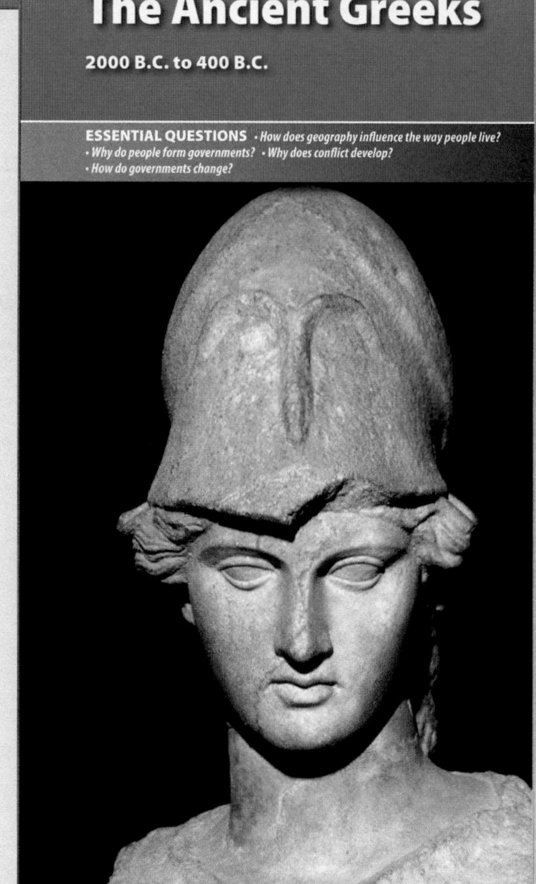

The Ancient Greeks

2000 B.C. to 400 B.C.

ESSENTIAL QUESTIONS • *How does geography influence the way people live?* • *Why do people form governments?* • *Why does conflict develop?* • *How do governments change?*

networks

There's More Online about the lives and the culture of the ancient Greeks.

CHAPTER 7

Lesson 1 *Rise of Greek Civilization*

Lesson 2 *Sparta and Athens: City-State Rivals*

Lesson 3 *Greece and Persia*

Lesson 4 *Glory, War, and Decline*

The Story Matters . . .

In ancient times, Greek language, culture, and mythology spread throughout the Mediterranean region. Traditional figures, such as the goddess Athena, were featured in art and on pottery and other household objects.

In time, ancient Greek civilization was absorbed by the more powerful Romans. Because the Romans imitated Greek culture in many ways, the achievements of the Greeks in politics, philosophy, and literature were passed on through the centuries. In this way, the ancient Greeks continue to influence Western civilization.

◀ *The gods and goddesses of Greek mythology are part of our most enduring literature. As shown here, the goddess Athena is usually depicted with a helmet ready for battle.*

Danita Delimont/Gallo Images/Getty Images

171

Introducing Place and Time

(Student Edition pp. 172–173)

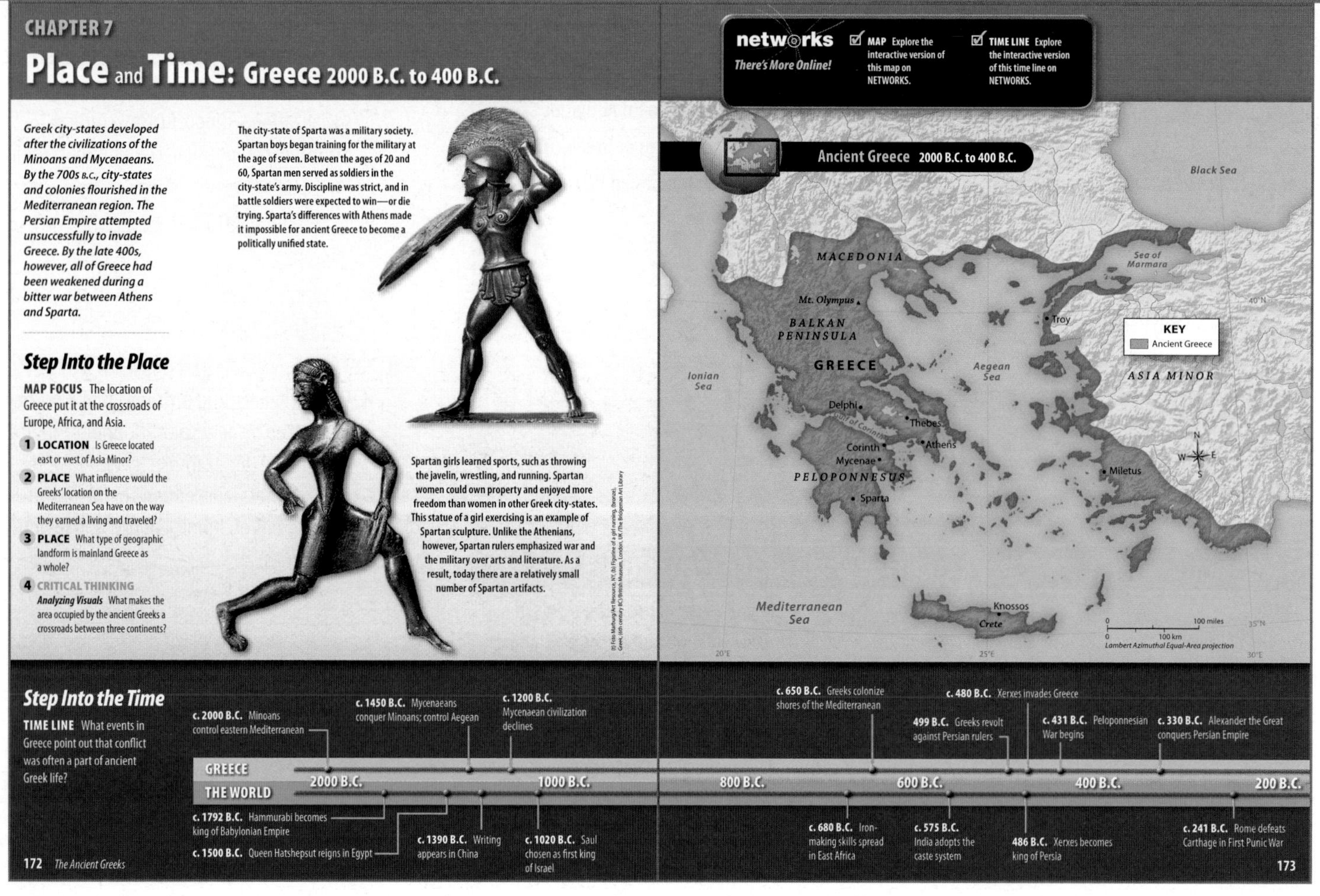

CHAPTER 7

Place and Time: Greece 2000 B.C. to 400 B.C.

Greek city-states developed after the civilizations of the Minoans and Mycenaeans. By the 700s B.C., city-states and colonies flourished in the Mediterranean region. The Persian Empire attempted unsuccessfully to invade Greece. By the late 400s, however, all of Greece had been weakened during a bitter war between Athens and Sparta.

The city-state of Sparta was a military society. Spartan boys began training for the military at the age of seven. Between the ages of 20 and 60, Spartan men served as soldiers in the city-state's army. Discipline was strict, and in battle soldiers were expected to win—or die trying. Sparta's differences with Athens made it impossible for ancient Greece to become a politically unified state.

Spartan girls learned sports, such as throwing the javelin, wrestling, and running. Spartan women could own property and enjoyed more freedom than women in other Greek city-states. This statue of a girl exercising is an example of Spartan sculpture. Unlike the Athenians, however, Spartan rulers emphasized war and the military over arts and literature. As a result, today there are a relatively small number of Spartan artifacts.

(t) Foto Marburg/Art Resource, NY, (b) Figurine of a girl running, (bronze), Greek, (6th century BC)/British Museum, London, UK/The Bridgeman Art Library

Step Into the Place

MAP FOCUS The location of Greece put it at the crossroads of Europe, Africa, and Asia.

1. **LOCATION** Is Greece located east or west of Asia Minor?
2. **PLACE** What influence would the Greeks' location on the Mediterranean Sea have on the way they earned a living and traveled?
3. **PLACE** What type of geographic landform is mainland Greece as a whole?
4. **CRITICAL THINKING** ***Analyzing Visuals*** What makes the area occupied by the ancient Greeks a crossroads between three continents?

networks *There's More Online!* MAP Explore the interactive version of this map on NETWORKS. TIME LINE Explore the interactive version of this time line on NETWORKS.

Step Into the Time

TIME LINE What events in Greece point out that conflict was often a part of ancient Greek life?

GREECE

- **c. 2000 B.C.** Minoans control eastern Mediterranean
- **c. 1450 B.C.** Mycenaeans conquer Minoans; control Aegean
- **c. 1200 B.C.** Mycenaean civilization declines
- **c. 650 B.C.** Greeks colonize shores of the Mediterranean
- **499 B.C.** Greeks revolt against Persian rulers
- **c. 480 B.C.** Xerxes invades Greece
- **c. 431 B.C.** Peloponnesian War begins
- **c. 330 B.C.** Alexander the Great conquers Persian Empire

2000 B.C. 1000 B.C. 800 B.C. 600 B.C. 400 B.C. 200 B.C.

THE WORLD

- **c. 1792 B.C.** Hammurabi becomes king of Babylonian Empire
- **c. 1500 B.C.** Queen Hatshepsut reigns in Egypt
- **c. 1390 B.C.** Writing appears in China
- **c. 1020 B.C.** Saul chosen as first king of Israel
- **c. 680 B.C.** Iron-making skills spread in East Africa
- **c. 575 B.C.** India adopts the caste system
- **486 B.C.** Xerxes becomes king of Persia
- **c. 241 B.C.** Rome defeats Carthage in First Punic War

172 *The Ancient Greeks*

173

Technology Extension

- Find an additional activity online that incorporates technology for this project.
- Visit the EdTechTeacher Web sites (included in the Technology Extension for this chapter) for more links, tutorials, and other resources.

Assessing Background Knowledge

INTERACTIVE WORKSHEET

What Do You Know? Activity

Have students complete the Anticipation Guide about the ancient Greeks before they study the chapter. Tell students to read each statement and in the "Your Opinion" column, circle *A* or *D* to indicate whether they agree or disagree with the statement. Students' responses will give you a good idea of the kinds of misconceptions you should address.

After students have completed the chapter, have them revisit the Anticipation Guide and note answers they would change now that they have learned more about the topic. Ask students to share some of their previous misconceptions with the class.

INTERACTIVE WORKSHEET

Guided Reading Activities

There is a Guided Reading Activity for each lesson in this chapter. You may wish to assign the Guided Reading Activity for Lesson 1 after introducing the chapter content.

Hands-On Chapter Project

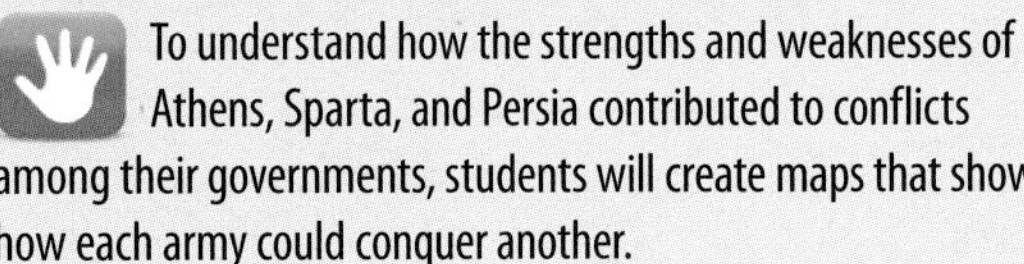

To understand how the strengths and weaknesses of Athens, Sparta, and Persia contributed to conflicts among their governments, students will create maps that show how each army could conquer another.

- Students will participate in a class discussion about conflicts between governments or cultures.
- Students will divide into small groups. Each group will be assigned to study Athens, Sparta, or Persia.
- Next, students will plan, research, and create their maps, using worksheets to guide their preparation.
- Then, student groups will present their completed maps to the class and discuss what they have learned.
- Finally, students will evaluate their research, maps, presentations, and collaboration using an Assessment Rubric.

Visit **networks** online to see the full project and rubric.

ONLINE RESOURCES

networks

Assign these interactive worksheets and quizzes from your Teacher Lesson Center. All resources are print-ready.

It's ALL Online!

Chapter 7 Resources

- ☑ Chapter Summary
- ☑ Vocabulary Builder
- ☑ What Do You Know?
- ☑ Hands-On Chapter Project

Lesson 1 Resources

- ☑ Geography and History Activity
  Understanding Location: The Greek Peninsula
- ☑ 21st Century Skills Activity
  Communication: Outlining
- ☑ Interactive Guided Reading Activity
- ☑ Reading Essentials and Study Guide
- ☑ Online Self-Check Quiz

Lesson 2 Resources

- ☑ Economics of History Activity
  Economics and Greek Governments
- ☑ Interactive Guided Reading Activity
- ☑ Reading Essentials and Study Guide
- ☑ Online Self-Check Quiz

Lesson 3 Resources

- ☑ Primary Source Activity
  Herodotus's Account of the Battle of Salamis
- ☑ Interactive Guided Reading Activity
- ☑ Reading Essentials and Study Guide
- ☑ Online Self-Check Quiz

Lesson 4 Resources

- ☑ Primary Source Activity
  Pericles' s Funeral Oration
- ☑ Interactive Guided Reading Activity
- ☑ Reading Essentials and Study Guide
- ☑ Online Self-Check Quiz

Assessment Resources

- ☑ Lesson Reviews
- ☑ Online Self-Check Quizzes
- ☑ Chapter Activities and Assessment
- ☑ Standardized Test Practice

Remediation Resources

- ☑ Reading Essentials and Study Guide
- ☑ Interactive Guided Reading Activities
- ☑ Online Self-Check Quizzes
- ☑ Chapter Summary

Step Into the Place

INTERACTIVE WHITEBOARD ACTIVITY

Location Project a world map (from the Interactive World Atlas) on the interactive whiteboard. Ask students how many of them know where Greece is. Ask them what present-day countries are close to Greece.

Have students find ancient Greece on the chapter opener map.

Ask students: What can you tell about the geography of ancient Greece by looking at this map? What would you say are the two most important geographic features of this area? As a class, discuss the Map Focus questions.

Step Into the Time

Sequencing Have students review the time line for the chapter. Explain that they will be studying events from about 2000 B.C. up to about 400 B.C.

Ask: What are some events you already know about that happened during those years? *(Students might answer that Hammurabi became the king of the Babylonian Empire and that Saul was chosen as the first king of Israel.)*

Remind students to use the time lines in their books to identify other events that occurred during this time period.

Answers for pages 172–173

Step Into the Place

1. Greece is west of Asia Minor.
2. The location of Greece in the Mediterranean Sea would encourage its people to fish for a living. A major form of transportation would be by boat.
3. The mainland is a peninsula. Greece also has several nearby islands.
4. CRITICAL THINKING Greece lies at the crossroads of Europe, Africa, and Asia. Its location increased the likelihood of contact between Greeks and people from other continents.

Step Into the Time

Students will note the uprising and wars listed on the time line. Their answers would include: Greek revolt of 499 B.C., invasion by Xerxes in 480 B.C., Peloponnesian War beginning in 431 B.C.

networks
There's More Online!
- ☑ CHART/GRAPH Greek Alphabet
- ☑ GRAPHIC ORGANIZER Compare Minoans and Mycenaeans
- ☑ SLIDE SHOW Mycenaean Artifacts

Lesson 1

Rise of Greek Civilization

ESSENTIAL QUESTION *How does geography influence the way people live?*

It Matters Because

The early Greeks developed important settlements, trade routes, and political ideas in the Mediterranean region.

1 Mountains and Seas

GUIDING QUESTION *How did physical geography influence the lives of the early Greeks?*

Greece was the first civilization to develop in Europe and the westernmost part of Asia. In other early civilizations, people first settled in river valleys that had rich soil. Greek civilization began in an area **dominated** by mountains and seas.

If you flew over this region today, you would see rugged landscapes and beautiful seas. The Greek mainland is on the southern part of Europe's Balkan Peninsula. A **peninsula** (puh•NIHN•suh•luh) is a body of land with water on three sides. Far to the east of the Greek mainland is another peninsula called Anatolia. It is part of present-day Turkey.

Between these two land areas are the dazzling blue waters of the Aegean Sea. The Aegean Sea is part of the larger Mediterranean Sea. There are hundreds of islands in the Aegean Sea. They look like stepping stones between the Greek mainland and Anatolia.

The Greeks traded goods and ideas between islands and along the area's coastlines. Today many Greeks fish and trade for a living, much as the ancient Greeks did before them. Other ancient Greeks settled in farming **communities**. These settlements began on narrow, fertile plains that ran along the coast and between the mountains. In the area's mild climate, farmers grew crops, such as wheat, barley, olives, and grapes. They also raised sheep and goats.

Even though some Greek communities were near the sea, others were far from the coast. Inland communities were separated from each other by rugged mountains and deep valleys. As a result, communities in many parts of ancient Greece became fiercely independent. They came to think of their communities almost as small separate countries.

☑ **PROGRESS CHECK**

Understanding Cause and Effect How did seas influence the way many ancient Greeks lived?

Reading HELPDESK

Taking Notes: ***Comparing***

Use a Venn diagram like the one here to compare the Minoans and Mycenaeans.

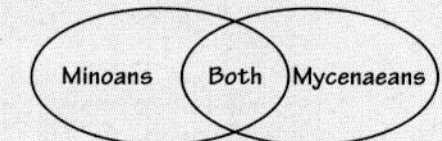

Content Vocabulary
- peninsula
- bard
- colony
- polis
- agora
- phalanx

GEOGRAPHY CONNECTION

All parts of ancient Greece were near water.

1. **LOCATION** Which body of water lies east of the Balkan Peninsula?
2. **CRITICAL THINKING** ***Making Inferences*** What type of transportation was probably most useful to the early Greeks?

peninsula a piece of land nearly surrounded by water

Academic Vocabulary

dominate to control or influence something or someone

community people with common interests living in a particular area; the area itself

2 An Island Civilization

GUIDING QUESTION *How did the civilization of the Minoans develop?*

Greek myths describe an early civilization that developed on Crete (KREET), an island southeast of the Greek mainland. About A.D. 1900, a British archaeologist named Arthur Evans discovered a site on Crete called Knossos (NAH•suhs). He unearthed the amazing palace of a legendary king named Minos (MY•nuhs).

Evans **concluded** that Minos and his family lived in the palace. The palace had numerous rooms that were connected by twisting passageways. Some of these rooms were used to store oil, wine, and grain. Other rooms were workshops where people made jewelry, vases, and statues. There were even bathrooms in the palace.

An ancient people called the Minoans (muh•NOH•uhnz) built the palace at Knossos. The Minoan civilization was the first to develop in the Aegean region, but they were not Greeks. Their civilization lasted from about 2500 B.C. to 1450 B.C.

Trade was an important **economic** activity for the Minoans. They built ships using the wood from Crete's forests of oak and cedar trees. The Minoans sailed to Egypt and Syria. There they traded pottery and stone vases for ivory and metals. Minoan ships also patrolled the eastern Mediterranean Sea to protect Minoan trade from pirates.

Sometime around 1450 B.C., however, the Minoan civilization collapsed. Historians do not know why this happened. One theory for the collapse is that undersea earthquakes caused huge waves that destroyed Minoan cities. Other historians think that people from the Greek mainland, known as Mycenaeans (my•suh•NEE•uhns), invaded Crete.

The palace at Knossos included a large outdoor theater. Colorful wall paintings decorated the palace, both inside and outside.

▶ **CRITICAL THINKING** ***Analyzing*** What kind of activities do the ruins of the palace suggest?

☑ **PROGRESS CHECK**

Explaining What did the discovery at Knossos reveal about the Minoans?

3 A Mainland Civilization

GUIDING QUESTION *How did the Mycenaeans gain power in the Mediterranean?*

About 2000 B.C., the Mycenaeans left their homeland in central Asia. They moved into mainland Greece. There, they gradually mixed with the local people and set up several kingdoms.

Reading HELPDESK

Academic Vocabulary

conclude to reach an understanding; to make a decision

economic the system in a country that involves making, buying, and selling goods

Mycenaean Kingdom

Little was known about the Mycenaeans until the late 1800s. That was when a German archaeologist named Heinrich Schliemann (HYN•rihk SHLEE•mahn) discovered the ruins of a palace in Mycenae (my•SEE•nee). He named the people of this civilization the Mycenaeans.

Each Mycenaean king lived in a palace built on a hill. Thick stone walls circled the palace and protected the kingdom's people. Nobles lived outside the walls on large farms, called estates. The workers and enslaved people who farmed the land lived in villages on these estates.

Mycenaean palaces were centers of government. Artisans there made leather goods, clothes, and jars for wine and olive oil. Other workers made swords and ox-hide shields. Government officials recorded the wealth of the kingdom's residents. They also collected wheat, livestock, and honey as taxes.

Traders and Warriors

Minoan traders from Crete visited the Greek mainland. Gradually, the Mycenaeans adopted features of Minoan culture. They built ships and worked with bronze. They used the sun and stars to navigate the seas. The Mycenaeans also worshipped the Earth Mother, the Minoans' chief god.

By the mid-1400s B.C., the Mycenaeans had conquered the Minoans and controlled the Aegean area. This brought new wealth to the Mycenaeans, which they used to expand their military strength. The Mycenaeans were proud of their military successes in the Trojan War.

A Dark Age

However, the Mycenaean civilization **declined** over time. Mycenaean kingdoms fought one another, and earthquakes destroyed their palace fortresses. By 1100 B.C., the Mycenaean civilization had crumbled.

About this time, groups of warring peoples moved from place to place throughout the eastern Mediterranean region.

Thinking Like a **HISTORIAN**

Analyzing Primary and Secondary Sources

German historian Heinrich Schliemann is considered the modern discoverer of the Mycenaean world. Schliemann (1822–1890) discovered several palaces and the ancient city of Troy. Research a biography or articles about Schliemann to create a short report about the archaeologist. Present your report to the class. For more information about using primary and secondary sources, read the chapter *What Does a Historian Do?*

Mycenaean artisans made golden masks to cover the faces of their dead kings. This is known as the Mask of Agamemnon.

Academic Vocabulary

decline to move toward a weaker condition

LESSON 1 • Day 1

ENGAGE

Analyzing Visuals

Project the interactive map of Greece, Crete, and the Mediterranean Sea from the chapter opener. Tell students that the Greek peninsula and the surrounding islands were the location of two early civilizations: the Minoans on the island of Crete and the Mycenaeans on the Greek peninsula.

LECTURE SLIDE **Identifying**

Show students the chart of trade between the Minoans and the Mycenaeans from the lecture slide. Tell them that trade was important to both civilizations.

Ask:

What happens when people from different places meet and trade? *(They trade ideas and culture as well as goods.)* AL ELL

TEACH & ASSESS

1 Mountains and Seas

GUIDING QUESTION *How did physical geography influence the lives of the early Greeks?*

SLIDE SHOW **Describing**

After watching the interactive slide show, discuss as a class how geography affected the lives of the early Greeks.

Ask:

- **What three major bodies of water surround the Greek peninsula?** *(the Ionian Sea, the Mediterranean Sea, and the Aegean Sea)*
- **What is most of the land like on the Greek peninsula?** *(Most of the land is rugged and mountainous.)*
- **How did the many islands in the Aegean Sea affect life in Greece?** *(The Greeks traded goods and ideas among islands.)*
- **What made inland communities in ancient Greece so fiercely independent?** *(Inland communities were fiercely independent because they were separated by rugged mountains and deep valleys.)* AL
- **How do you think these geographic features might have affected life in ancient Greece?** *(Geography influenced how people earned a living, what they ate, and how they traveled and communicated.)* BL

2 An Island Civilization

GUIDING QUESTION *How did the civilization of the Minoans develop?*

Explaining

Tell students that the Minoan civilization was the first to develop in the Aegean region. Artifacts of the civilization were only discovered in the early 1900s.

Remind students that the Minoans were not Greeks. They lived near Greece on the island of Crete, and their civilization lasted from about 2500 B.C. to 1450 B.C.

Ask:

- **What was an important economic activity for the Minoans?** *(They traded goods with Egypt and Syria by sea.)*
- **Why did Minoan ships patrol the Mediterranean Sea?** *(They sought to protect Minoan trade from pirates.)*
- **Why did the Minoan civilization collapse around 1450 B.C.?** *(Historians don't know for certain, but some suggest that the Mycenaean people from the Greek mainland invaded Crete.)*

3 A Mainland Civilization

GUIDING QUESTION *How did the Mycenaeans gain power in the Mediterranean?*

SLIDE SHOW While viewing the slide show, ask for volunteers to read the captions.

Ask:

- **What do these artifacts tell about the Mycenaean civilization?** *(Artisans knew how to work in bronze.)*
- **How did the Mycenaean civilization interact with the Minoan civilization?** *(The Mycenaeans learned to work in bronze. They gradually adopted other features of the Minoan culture like using the sun and stars to navigate the seas and worshiping the Minoan goddess.)*

INTERACTIVE WORKSHEET

21st Century Skills Activity

Assign for homework the 21st Century Skills Activity.

CLOSE & REFLECT

INTERACTIVE WORKSHEET

Geography and History Activity

Have students complete the Geography and History Activity that summarizes how geography influenced the development of civilizations on the Greek peninsula and the islands surrounding it. Review the worksheet in class, moderating a class discussion of the worksheet answers.

Ask:

- **How was the peninsula's location connected to its importance?** *(Greece was a crossroads of trade between the eastern and western areas of the Mediterranean Sea.)*
- **As the Greeks traveled the Mediterranean to trade, what effect did that have on countries in the Mediterranean region?** *(It spread Greek ideas and traditions throughout the Mediterranean region.)*
- **What conclusion can you make about the geography of a particular area and the development of civilization there?** *(Answers would include that geography contributes greatly to how and where a civilization develops.)*

Answers for pages 174–177

P. 174 Taking Notes Answers for Minoans include island civilization and mysterious collapse. Answers for Mycenaeans include mainland civilization, warfare, and detailed records. Answers for both include large palaces, kings, and trade.

P. 175 ☑ PROGRESS CHECK Seas provided a living for many Greek fishers and traders.

P. 175 GEOGRAPHY CONNECTION

1. The Aegean Sea lies east of the Balkan Peninsula.
2. CRITICAL THINKING Ships were probably most useful.

P. 176 CRITICAL THINKING The ruins suggest that the inhabitants enjoyed activities that related to the arts.

P. 176 ☑ PROGRESS CHECK It revealed that the Minoans were economically prosperous and artistically talented.

THE GREEK ALPHABET

Greek Letter	Written Name	English Sound
Α	alpha	a
Β	beta	b
Γ	gamma	g
Δ	delta	d
Ε	epsilon	e
Ζ	zeta	z
Η	eta	e
Θ	theta	th
Ι	iota	i
Κ	kappa	c,k
Λ	lambda	l
Μ	mu	m
Ν	nu	n
Ξ	xi	x
Ο	omicron	o
Π	pi	p
Ρ	rho	r
Σ	sigma	s
Τ	tau	t
Υ	upsilon	y,u
Φ	phi	ph
Χ	chi	ch
Ψ	psi	ps
Ω	omega	o

One of these groups was a Greek-speaking people known as the Dorians (DOHR•ee•uhns). They invaded the Greek mainland from the north and took control of most of the region.

Historians call the next 300 years of Greek history a Dark Age. During this difficult time, trade slowed down, people made fewer things to sell, and most were very poor. Farmers grew only enough food to feed their families. Many people also stopped writing and keeping records.

In Greece, several positive developments also happened during this time. Dorian warriors introduced iron weapons and the skill of iron making. Iron weapons and farm tools were stronger and cheaper than the bronze ones used by the Mycenaeans. As the Dorians pushed into Greece, thousands of people fled the Greek mainland. They settled on the Aegean islands and the western shore of Anatolia.

The Hellenes

By 750 B.C., many descendants of the people who ran away returned to the Greek mainland. They brought back new ideas, crafts, and skills. Small independent communities developed under local leaders who became kings. These people called themselves Hellenes, or Greeks. Farmers in these communities grew more food than their families could use. The Greeks traded their surplus food with each other and with neighboring peoples, such as the Egyptians and Phoenicians. As trade increased, a new need for writing developed. The Greeks adopted an alphabet from Phoenician traders who sailed from the Mediterranean coast.

The Greek alphabet had 24 letters that represented different sounds. It greatly simplified reading and writing in the Greek language. Record keeping became easier. Soon, people wrote down the tales that had been told by **bards**, or storytellers. Previously, these tales had been passed down from generation to generation orally. Now they could finally be kept in written form.

✓ PROGRESS CHECK

Determining Cause and Effect How did the Dorian invasion help spread Greek culture?

Reading **HELP**DESK

bard someone who writes or performs epic poems or stories about heroes and their deeds

Build Vocabulary: *Word Origins*

Geographers call the place where a large river divides into smaller rivers near the ocean a *delta*. Deltas often form in the shape of a triangle, like the Greek letter delta. Try writing a word using the Greek alphabet.

4 Colonies and Trade

GUIDING QUESTION *How did early Greeks spread their culture?*

As Greece recovered from the Dark Age, its population increased rapidly. By 700 B.C., local farmers could not produce enough grain to feed the growing population. To solve this problem, Greek communities began to send people outside the Aegean area to establish **colonies** (KAH•luh•nees). A colony is a settlement in a new territory that has close ties to its homeland.

The Greeks founded many colonies along the coasts of the Mediterranean Sea and the Black Sea between 750 B.C. and 550 B.C. Greek culture spread into new areas, such as southern Italy, Sicily, France, Spain, North Africa, and western Asia.

The colonies traded with their "parent" cities on the Greek mainland. They shipped grains, metals, fish, timber, and enslaved people to Greece. In return, the Greek mainland sent wine, olive oil, and pottery to the colonies. As the Greeks began to make coins from metal, this **affected** their trade. Trade expanded as merchants traded money for goods rather than bartered for goods. This system increased a colony's wealth. As the demand for goods grew, artisans made more goods to meet the demand. People in different colonies specialized in making certain products. For example, in colonies where farmers raised sheep, people began to make cloth from the sheep's wool.

Connections to TODAY

Coins

The Greeks began making coins from silver in the 600s B.C. Current American quarters and dimes are made of layers of copper and nickel and covered with a copper-nickel alloy or blend. Many American coins have symbols similar to ones used on ancient Greek coins. If you could create a new American coin, whose image would you place on it?

✓ PROGRESS CHECK

Determining Cause and Effect How did the colonies affect trade and industry in the Greek world?

5 The Greek City-State

GUIDING QUESTION *How did Greek city-states create the idea of citizenship?*

Mountains and seas separated Greek communities from each other. As a result, people developed a loyalty to the community in which they lived. Communities became fiercely independent. By the end of the Dark Age, nobles who owned large estates had overthrown the Greek kings. Across Greece, nobles ruled numerous city-states.

colony a group of people living in a new territory who have ties to their homeland; the new territory itself

Academic Vocabulary

affect to influence; to cause a change

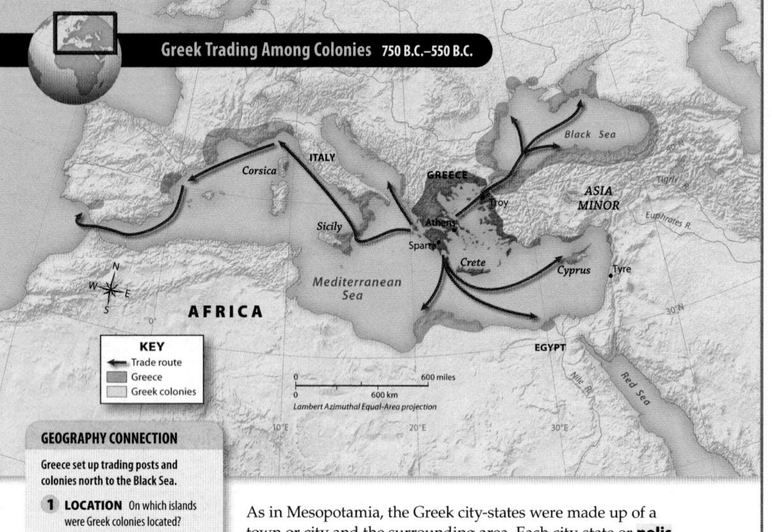

GEOGRAPHY CONNECTION

Greece set up trading posts and colonies north to the Black Sea.

1. **LOCATION** On which islands were Greek colonies located?
2. **CRITICAL THINKING** ***Drawing Conclusions*** In addition to the buying and selling of goods, what effect would Greece have on the people of its colonies and surrounding lands?

As in Mesopotamia, the Greek city-states were made up of a town or city and the surrounding area. Each city-state or **polis** (PAH•luhs), was like an independent country. Today, English words such as *police* and *politics* come from the Greek word *polis.*

What Did a Polis Look Like?

The polis was the basic political unit of Greek civilization. At the center of each polis was a fort built on a hilltop. The hilltop that a fort stood on was called an acropolis (uh•KRAH•puh•luhs). Local people could take refuge in the acropolis when invaders attacked. The Greeks built temples on the acropolis to honor local gods.

Outside the acropolis was an open area called an **agora** (A•guh•ruh). This space was used as a marketplace. It was also an area where people could gather and debate issues, choose officials, pass laws, and carry out business. City neighborhoods surrounded the agora. Just beyond the city were the villages and farmland that also were part of the polis.

Reading **HELP**DESK

polis a Greek city-state

agora a gathering place; marketplace in ancient Greece

Because most city-states were surrounded by mountains and seas, they were usually small. Some were only a few square miles in area, while others covered hundreds of square miles. By 500 B.C., nearly 300,000 people lived in the city-state of Athens. Most city-states, however, were much smaller.

What Did Citizenship Mean to the Greeks?

Today, in the United States, a person who is born here is considered a citizen. We owe many of our ideas about citizenship to the ancient Greeks.

Who was a Greek citizen? Citizens were members of a political community with rights and responsibilities. In Greece, male citizens had the right to vote, hold public office, own property, and defend themselves in court. In return, citizens had the responsibility to serve in government and to fight for their polis as citizen soldiers. Ancient Greek citizenship was very different from that of ancient Mesopotamia or Egypt, where most people were subjects. They had no rights, no voice in government, and no choice but to obey their rulers.

In most Greek city-states, only free, land-owning men born in the polis could be citizens. They believed the responsibility to run the city-state was theirs because the polis was made up of their property. Some city-states later ended the requirement of owning land for a person to be a citizen. Women and children might qualify for citizenship, but they had none of the rights that went with it.

When people today take the American oath of citizenship, a new life of rights and responsibilities begins.

In the agora at Athens, people of different professions met in different parts of the space. Theatrical performances were also held here.

LESSON 1 • Day 2

ENGAGE

Project on the interactive whiteboard the map of Greece showing how the Greeks traded among colonies. Remind students that the landscape was rugged in Greece, so towns and cities were isolated.

Ask students what they do when they are feeling alone. Responses should suggest that they reach out to friends, family, or neighbors.

Tell students that when the population of city-states grew, the city-states could not produce enough food to feed everyone.

Lead students in a discussion about why the city-states established colonies away from the mainland. Explain that they will learn how geography influenced colonial trade and the creation of citizenship in Greece.

TEACH & ASSESS

4 Colonies and Trade

GUIDING QUESTION *How did early Greeks spread their culture?*

LECTURE SLIDE

Drawing Conclusions

Show the types of goods traded between Greece and her colonies from the lecture slide. Point out to students that Greece had trading colonies in Europe, Asia, and Africa.

Ask:

What else besides goods got exchanged as Greek influence grew in the Mediterranean? *(Greek ideas and culture)*

Making Connections

Have students compare the map of Greece and her trading colonies with a map of the modern Mediterranean world.

Ask:

- **In which modern nations did Greece have colonies?** *(Spain, France, Italy, Ukraine, Romania, Bulgaria, Syria, Libya, Egypt, Cyprus, Georgia, Turkey)*
- **Did trade increase or decrease the spread of Greek culture and ideas?** *(Trade increased the spread of Greek culture and ideas.)*
- **How might the difficulty of growing enough food be a disadvantage and an advantage for the Greeks?** *(While not being able to grow enough food made it necessary for the Greeks to begin colonies, that led the Greeks to develop better ships and become a greater power in the region around the Mediterranean.)*

5 The Greek City-State

GUIDING QUESTION *How did Greek city-states create the idea of citizenship?*

Identifying

Tell students that our concept of modern citizenship evolved from citizenship in Greek city-states.

Ask:

- **What role did mountains and the sea play in developing the Greek city-states?** *(The mountains on the peninsula and the sea separated Greek city-states from each other, which caused city-states to develop different ideas of citizenship.)*
- **Who ruled the Greek city-states?** *(Nobles who owned large properties ruled the Greek city-states.)*
- **What did the city-states consist of?** *(a town or a city and the surrounding countryside)*
- **What is another name for a Greek city-state, and how important were they?** *(A polis; city-states were the basic political unit of Greek civilization.)* AL

Comparing and Contrasting

Tell students that similarities and differences can be found in citizenship in ancient Greece and citizenship in the United States today.

On the interactive whiteboard, create a two-column chart. Label one column "Ancient Greek Citizenship" and the other column "U.S. Citizenship Today." Work as a class to answer the following questions about ancient Greece and the United States today.

- **Who can be a citizen?** *(Everyone born in the United States is a citizen. If a person is born elsewhere, he or she can become a citizen of the United States by a process called "naturalization." Citizenship in Greek city-states varied, but usually only free, landowning men who were born in the polis could be citizens.)*
- **Who has the rights of citizenship?** *(In the United States, all citizens have the rights of citizenship. In Greek city-states, only landowning males who were born in the polis had the rights of citizenship.)*
- **What are the rights of citizenship?** *(In the United States, citizens have the right to vote, hold political office, and defend themselves in court. They also have numerous personal rights such as the freedom of religion and the right to free speech. In the Greek city-states, the rights of citizenship included the right to vote, hold public office, own property, and defend oneself in court.)*
- **What are the responsibilities of citizenship?** *(In the United States, the responsibilities of citizenship include obeying the law, voting, and paying taxes. The responsibilities of citizenship in ancient Greek city-states included serving in government and fighting for the polis as citizen soldiers.)*

Write the answers in the appropriate column in the graphic organizer on the interactive whiteboard. BL

Have students complete the Lesson 1 Review.

CLOSE & REFLECT

Drawing Conclusions Ask students if the strong loyalty of Greek citizens to their polis led to Greece's downfall. Moderate a class discussion of this question.

IF YOU HAVE MORE TIME . . .

Examine What It Means to Be a Citizen

Defining As written in 1787, the U.S. Constitution did not offer citizenship to all Americans. In the 1860s, however, the Fourteenth Amendment provided guidelines to protect citizenship status. Distribute Sections 1 and 2 of this amendment, and have a student read them aloud. ELL

Ask:

- **How does Section 1 of the Constitution define *citizenship*?** *(People born or naturalized in the United States are U.S. citizens.)*
- **What rights are guaranteed to citizens?** *(rights to life, liberty, property, due process, equal protection under the law, and the right to vote)*

Ask students to compare the rights associated with citizenship in ancient Greece with those in the United States and decide which are more inclusive.

If time permits, ask students what type of graphic organizer is best for making comparisons. *(Venn diagrams)*

Then, use the interactive whiteboard to create a class graphic organizer. Ask volunteers to record class responses on the board.

Students should refer to their textbooks, as needed, to participate in the discussion and review what rights were associated with ancient Greek citizenship. AL

Answers for pages 178–181

P. 178 ☑ PROGRESS CHECK The Dorians introduced iron weapons and farm tools. As a result of the invasions, Greek communities spread throughout the Aegean and into Anatolia.

P. 179 ☑ PROGRESS CHECK Trade expanded between the colonies and their "parent" cities.

P. 180 GEOGRAPHY CONNECTION

1. Cyprus, Sicily, and Corsica were home to Greek colonies.
2. CRITICAL THINKING Greek ideas and customs would spread to people in its colonies and the surrounding lands.

Citizen Soldiers

In Greece, wars were fought by wealthy nobles riding horses and driving chariots. By 700 B.C., citizens called hoplites (HAHP•lyts) made up the city-state armies. The hoplites fought on foot. Each heavily armed soldier carried a round shield, a short sword, and a spear. During battles, rows of hoplites marched forward together, shoulder to shoulder. They raised their shields above them to protect them from the enemy's arrows. This unified formation is called a **phalanx** (FAY•langks).

The success of the hoplites came from their pride in fighting as brave warriors. In Athens, for example, soldiers took this oath:

PRIMARY SOURCE

> "I will not disgrace my sacred arms nor desert my comrade, [fellow soldier] wherever I am stationed [located]. . . And I will observe the established laws and whatever laws in the future may be reasonably established. If any person seek to overturn the laws . . . I will oppose him. I will honor the religion of my fathers."
>
> —from *Athenian Ephebic Oath*, tr. Clarence A. Forbes

phalanx a group of armed foot soldiers in ancient Greece arranged close together in rows

North Wind/North Wind Picture Archives

The polis gave Greek citizens a sense of belonging. This is similar to how people feel about their home states today. The citizens put the needs of the polis above their own. Such strong loyalty to their own city-state divided the Greeks. They were not as unified as a whole country. This lack of unity weakened Greece, making it easier to conquer.

PROGRESS CHECK

Explaining What were the rights and responsibilities of Greek citizens?

LESSON 1 REVIEW

Review Vocabulary

1. Explain the difference between a *colony* and a *polis*.

Answer the Guiding Questions

2. ***Analyzing*** What were the ancient Greeks' most important economic activities?
3. ***Explaining*** How did the Minoans develop wealth?
4. ***Summarizing*** What happened to Mycenaean civilization during the Dark Age?
5. ***Explaining*** Why did the Greeks establish colonies?
6. **EXPOSITORY WRITING** How did Greek city-states apply democracy? How did they limit democracy? Write a short essay explaining your answers.

NOTES

NOTES

networks
There's More Online!
GRAPHIC ORGANIZER Compare Sparta and Athens

Lesson 2

Sparta and Athens: City-State Rivals

ESSENTIAL QUESTION *Why do people form governments?*

IT MATTERS BECAUSE

The city-states of Athens and Sparta had two quite different governments. Athenian democracy strongly influenced later forms of democracy.

1 Political Changes

GUIDING QUESTION *Which types of government did the Greek city-states have?*

As Greek city-states grew, wealthy nobles seized power from kings. They did not rule very long, however. Owners of small farms resented the nobles' power. Many of the farm owners had borrowed money from the nobles to buy land. When the farmers could not repay the loans, the nobles often took their land. The farmers then had to work for the nobles or move to the city to find jobs. In some cases, they even had to sell themselves into slavery.

By 650 B.C., small farmers wanted political change and a greater voice in government. Merchants and artisans also called for reforms. Merchants and artisans had earned a good living in the growing city-states. However, because they did not own land, they were not **considered** citizens. That meant they had no role in ruling the polis.

The growing unrest led to the rise of tyrants. A **tyrant** (TY•ruhnt) is someone who seizes power and rules with total authority. Most tyrants who commanded city-states ruled fairly.

Reading HELPDESK

Taking Notes: *Comparing*

Use a Venn diagram like this one to compare life in Sparta and Athens.

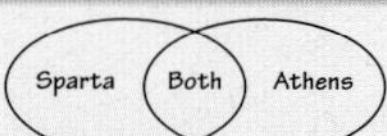

Content Vocabulary
- **tyrant**
- **oligarchy**
- **democracy**
- **helot**
- **ephor**

LESSON 1 • Day 2 (cont.)

BACKGROUND KNOWLEDGE

Discover Facts About Ancient Greek Politics and Citizenship

- The English word *idiot* is derived from the Greek *idiotes*, which means "private person or individual"—in other words, someone who does not get involved in politics.
- Citizens were obligated to take an intelligent and active role in governing Athens. They voted for legislation, made decisions on war or peace, elected officials, and spoke in the Assembly.
- Losing citizenship was a punishment for crimes such as bribery, cowardice in battle, violence against your parents, and anti-democratic activity.
- After 451 B.C., only males with a father who had Athenian citizenship and a mother whose father had citizenship could be citizens.
- Occasionally, but rarely, it was possible for voters to allow a foreigner, a free Greek, a woman, or an enslaved person to receive citizenship as a reward for extraordinary service to the democracy.

IF YOU HAVE MORE TIME . . .

Analyze Geography Using Creativity

Have pairs of students create a postcard that illustrates the geographic characteristics of early Greece and explains the role these characteristics played in the development of the Greek city-states. Students may use maps and diagrams in this chapter, the Reference Atlas, and outside resources as needed to identify the distinctive geography of the region.

Students should begin by locating the region and identifying its geographic characteristics. On the front of the postcard, they may illustrate these characteristics with photos, their own drawings, maps, or diagrams. On the back of the postcard, they should explain how the characteristics influenced the development of city-states.

Answers for page 182

P. 182 ☑ PROGRESS CHECK Citizens had the right to vote, hold public office, own property, and defend themselves in court. Their responsibilities included serving in government and fighting for their polis.

LESSON 1 REVIEW

1. A colony is a settlement in a new territory that keeps close ties to its homeland. A polis is an ancient Greek city-state.
2. Their most important economic activities were farming and trading.
3. The Minoans prospered because of their overseas trade.
4. The Mycenaean civilization collapsed. People became poor, Greece was invaded by the Dorians, and the art of writing was lost during the Dark Age.
5. The Greeks established colonies because farmers could not grow enough grain to feed the increasing population.
6. Answers will vary. Students should point out that city-states extended democracy by including more diverse social classes in government. However, they limited democracy by excluding noncitizens, women, and enslaved people from government.

Teaching *Sparta and Athens: City-State Rivals* (Student Edition pp. 183–189)

LESSON 2 • Day 1

ENGAGE

Ask students what kind of government they think the United States has. *(Most students will say the United States is a democracy.)* Then have students define what they think is meant by *democracy*. Tell students that the word *democracy* comes from the ancient Greek words *demos,* meaning "people," and *cracy,* meaning "rule." Have students come up with a definition of *democracy* based on these Greek roots. Tell students that as they read they will learn more about the Greek roots of democracy and other forms of government.

Ask:

What other forms of government can you name? *(Answers might include dictatorship and monarchy.)*

LECTURE SLIDE

Show the forms of government from the lecture slide. Tell students that after the Dark Age in Greece, three forms of government developed. Those three forms are *tyranny*, *oligarchy*, and *democracy*.

TEACH & ASSESS

1 Political Changes

GUIDING QUESTION *What types of government did the Greek city-states have?*

Explaining

Tell students that changes to government in ancient Greece started with common people being dissatisfied with the nobles running the city-states.

Ask:

- **Why were farmers unhappy with nobles ruling?** *(Many farmers borrowed money from nobles to buy land. When they could not repay their debts, the nobles took back the land. The farmers had to work for the nobles, move to another city-state to find other work, or sell themselves into slavery.)*
- **Why were merchants unhappy with nobles ruling city-states?** *(Although merchants and artisans made a good living, they did not own land. Only landowners were citizens and could participate in government and politics.)*
- **What did merchants, artisans, and small farmers want?** *(They wanted political change and a greater voice in government.)*
- **What was the first political change to happen because of this unrest?** *(The common people of Greece supported the overthrow of the nobles by the tyrants.)*

Answers for page 183

P. 183 Taking Notes Answers for Sparta include warlike society, strict military training, comparative freedom for women, oligarchic government. Answers for Athens include diverse culture, seclusion of women, democratic government. Answers for both include successful city-state.

GEOGRAPHY CONNECTION

Sparta and Athens were the dominant city-states in ancient Greece.

1 **LOCATION** About how many miles apart were Sparta and Athens?

2 **CRITICAL THINKING**
Analyzing Which city-state's geography might make it more open to attack in a military battle? Explain.

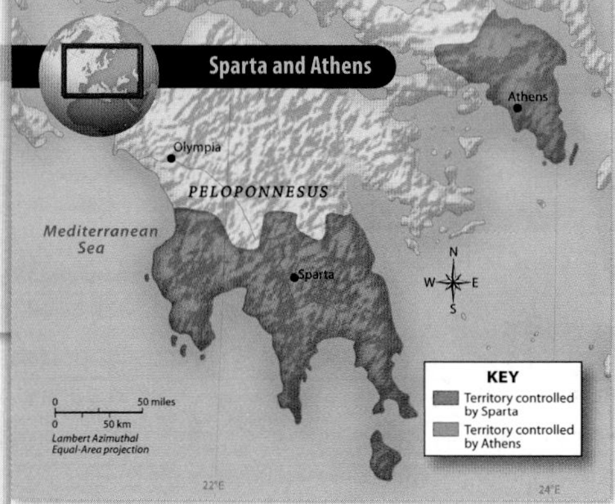

However, the harsh rule of a few tyrants gave the word *tyranny* its current meaning; that is, rule by a cruel and unjust person.

The common people of Greece supported the tyrants when they overthrew the nobles during the 600s B.C. Tyrants also gained support from the hoplites, or citizen soldiers, in the army. Tyrants strengthened their popularity by building new temples, fortresses, and marketplaces. Nevertheless, most Greeks objected to rule by a single person. They wanted a government in which all citizens could participate.

Tyrants ruled many of the Greek city-states until about 500 B.C. From then until 336 B.C., most city-states developed into either oligarchies or democracies. In an **oligarchy** (AH•luh•gahr•kee), a few wealthy people hold power over the larger group of citizens. In a **democracy** (dih•MAH•kruh•see), all citizens share in running the government. Two of the major city-states, Sparta and Athens, were governed differently and created very different societies.

PROGRESS CHECK

Evaluating Why were tyrants able to hold power in various Greek city-states?

Reading HELPDESK

tyrant an absolute ruler unrestrained by law

oligarchy a government in which a small group has control

democracy a government by the people

Academic Vocabulary

consider to give careful thought

2 Sparta: A Military Society

GUIDING QUESTION *Why did the Spartans focus on military skills?*

The city-state of Sparta was located on the Peloponnesus (peh•luh•puh•NEE•suhs) Peninsula in southern Greece. The Spartans were descended from the Dorians who invaded Greece in the Dark Age. Like other city-states, Sparta's economy was based on agriculture.

Sparta did not set up overseas colonies. Instead, Sparta invaded neighboring city-states and enslaved the local people. The Spartans called their enslaved laborers **helots** (HEH•luhts), a word that comes from the Greek word for "capture."

A Strong Military

About 650 B.C., the helots revolted against their Spartan masters. The Spartans crushed that uprising. Sparta's leaders wanted to prevent future revolts. They decided to make Sparta a **military** society that stressed discipline. They also believed in simplicity, and strength through self-denial. The leaders thought that a military society created more obedient and loyal citizens.

Sparta's government prepared all boys and men for a life of war. Boys left their homes at age seven to join the military. In military camps, they learned to read, write, and use weapons. They also were treated harshly. The military leaders believed that harsh treatment would turn the young boys into adults who would survive the pain of battle. The Greek historian Plutarch (PLOO•tahrk) described life for Spartan boys:

PRIMARY SOURCE

> ❝They were enrolled in certain companies . . ., where they all lived under the same order and discipline, doing their exercises and taking play together. Of these he who showed the most conduct and courage was made captain; they . . . obeyed his orders and underwent patiently whatsoever punishment he inflicted [delivered]; so that the whole course of their education was one continued exercise of a ready and perfect obedience.❞
>
> —from *Plutarch: The Lives of the Noble Grecians and Romans*

Spartan warriors depended on their training to help them survive.

▶ CRITICAL THINKING
Synthesizing What types of weapons were used in hand-to-hand combat?

helots enslaved people in ancient Sparta

Academic Vocabulary

military relating to soldiers, arms, or war

Spartan men entered the regular army at age 20. Men could marry during their twenties, but they were not allowed to live at home. Instead, they stayed in military camps, sharing barracks and eating meals with other soldiers. A typical army meal was a dish called black broth—pork boiled in animal blood, salt, and vinegar. Spartan men could live at home again when they reached the age of 30, but they continued to train for combat. They finally retired from the army at age 60.

Since many Spartan men lived away from home, Spartan women enjoyed more freedom than the women of other Greek city-states. They could own property and travel. Girls were trained in sports, such as wrestling and throwing the javelin. They remained physically fit to fulfill their roles as mothers. Their main goal was to raise sons who were brave, strong Spartan soldiers.

Spartan women expected their men to either win or die in battle. Spartan soldiers must never surrender. One Spartan mother ordered her son to "Come home carrying your shield or being carried on it."

Physical fitness was important for Spartan women. Girls trained in sports to increase their athletic abilities.

How Was Sparta Governed?

Sparta's government was an oligarchy. Two kings ruled jointly, but they had little power. Their only duties were to lead the army and carry out religious ceremonies. In addition to the kings, Sparta had two other governing bodies, the assembly and the council of elders.

The assembly included all male citizens over the age of 30. The assembly made decisions about war and peace. However, the council of elders was the most powerful body in the government. Council members served as judges. They were the only officials who could order executions or exile. Each year, the council elected five people to be **ephors** (EH•fuhrs). The ephors enforced the laws and managed the collection of taxes.

Sparta's strict government brought **stability**. But that stability cost the people of Sparta. Because the government feared losing the helots, it discouraged free thinking and new ideas. Officials believed learning could lead to unrest. As a result, Sparta did not welcome foreign visitors and prevented citizens from traveling outside the city-state except for military reasons. It even discouraged people from studying literature and the arts.

Reading HELPDESK

ephor a high-ranked government official in Sparta who was elected by the council of elders

Academic Vocabulary

stability the condition of being steady and unchanging

In addition, Sparta resisted other types of change. For example, Spartans continued to use heavy iron bars for money when other Greeks used coins. This discouraged trade and isolated Sparta from the rest of Greece. While other city-states built up business and trade and improved their standard of living, Sparta remained a poor farming society.

For Sparta's strong, well-trained army, the only important goals were military power and victory. The Spartans **achieved** Greece's greatest military strength and power. Sparta would play a key role in defending Greece against invaders.

PROGRESS CHECK

Determining Cause and Effect Why did Sparta fall behind other Greek city-states in many areas?

3 Athens: A Young Democracy

GUIDING QUESTION *How did the culture in Athens differ from other Greek city-states?*

The Italian artist Raphael painted this picture, *School of Athens*, in 1510–11. This shows younger students mixing with teachers and older students.

Another great Greek city-state was Athens. It was located northeast of Sparta, about a two-day trip away. Athens was founded by the descendants of the Mycenaeans and differed from Sparta in its ideas about society and government.

An Athenian Education

Athenians received an education far different from that of the Spartans. Athens educated its males, as Sparta did. In Athenian schools, boys studied subjects such as arithmetic, geometry, drawing, music, and public speaking. They also participated in sports. The Athenians believed that this type of education produced young people with strong minds and bodies. At age 18, when boys finished school, they were expected to take an active role in public affairs.

Academic Vocabulary

achieve to succeed; to gain something as the result of work

LESSON 2 • Day 1 (cont.)

LECTURE SLIDE

Identifying

Most of the tyrants of Greek city-states ruled fairly, but a few were cruel.

Ask:

What does the word *tyranny* as it is used today mean? *(rule by a cruel and unjust person)*

Show students the list of words belonging to the *tyranny* word family from the lecture slide. Tell students that a tyrant rules with total authority and often harshly. Ask students if they can name any other historical or modern-day tyrants. *(Responses will vary but should be reasonable. Students may name Hitler, Mussolini, Stalin, Saddam Hussein, Kim Jung Il, or other tyrants.)*

INTERACTIVE WHITEBOARD ACTIVITY

Analyzing

On the interactive whiteboard, create a three-column, four-row graphic organizer. Label the columns *Tyranny, Oligarchy,* and *Democracy.* Label the four rows *Ruled by, Citizenship, Advantages,* and *Disadvantages.*

During the class discussion, fill in the horizontal columns for each of the three types of government. Keep the graphic organizer to use again as you teach the rest of the chapter.

Contrasting

Ask: How is an oligarchy different from a monarchy? *(In an oligarchy, a few people rule; in a monarchy, one person rules.)*

Distinguishing Fact and Opinion

Read the following statements about political changes in ancient Greece and have students say whether the statements are fact or opinion.

- Many of the tyrants of ancient Greece ruled fairly. *(opinion)*
- Oligarchy, in which a few wealthy people hold power, is the most dangerous form of government. *(opinion)*
- In a democracy, citizens hold political power. *(fact)*
- Democracy is the best form of government. *(opinion)*

CLOSE & REFLECT

Synthesizing

Have students write a paragraph explaining whether they would want to live in a country governed by one of these three forms of government: tyranny, oligarchy, or democracy.

LESSON 2 • Day 2

ENGAGE

Analyzing Visuals Direct students' attention to the images that represent Sparta and the images that represent Athens from the chapter on society and government.

Lead a class discussion about why Sparta and Athens became so different. Tell students that these differences helped lead to a war between the two city-states—the Peloponnesian War.

TEACH & ASSESS

2 Sparta: A Military Society

GUIDING QUESTION ***Why did the Spartans focus on military skills?***

Determining Cause and Effect

Ask:

What effect did the revolt of the helots have on Sparta? *(Sparta become more militaristic.)*

Analyzing Visuals Have students use the map of Sparta and Athens to answer these questions.

Ask:

- **What is one major difference between the locations of Sparta and Athens?** *(Lead students to understand that Sparta was located inland, and Athens was located by the sea.)*
- **How might their locations have influenced the development of Sparta and Athens?** *(Sparta's inland location might have caused it to become more isolated. It also may have prompted the development of a strong army instead of a navy. Athens, with its location on the coast, had more interaction with other cultures and developed a strong navy.)*

Explaining

Tell students that the city-state of Sparta developed into a military society.

Ask:

- **At what age did boys in Sparta join the military?** *(seven)*
- **What was their education like?** *(They went to military camps where they learned to read, write, and use weapons.)*
- **How were the students treated?** *(They were treated harshly because military leaders believed harsh treatment turned young boys into strong, tough adults who could take the pain of battle.)*
- **What freedoms did Spartan women have?** *(They could own property and travel. Young girls were trained in sports.)* AL

LECTURE SLIDE

Identifying

Show the definitions of *oligarchy* and *democracy* from the lecture slide. Tell students that Sparta was ruled by an oligarchy. The most powerful body in the government was the council of elders. It passed laws; however, the assembly had the power to make decisions about war and peace. Sparta's oligarchy was known for its military strength and played a key role in defending Greece against invaders.

Ask:

- **Who was in the Spartan assembly?** *(all male citizens over the age of 30)*
- **What did the Spartan government discourage?** *(It discouraged change and new ideas, and it outlawed travel outside the city-state.)*
- **How was trade discouraged?** *(Sparta continued to use heavy iron bars for money while other Greek city-states developed coins. This discouraged trade, and the standard of living did not improve.)*

3 Athens: A Young Democracy

GUIDING QUESTION ***How did the culture in Athens differ from other Greek city-states?***

LECTURE SLIDE

Evaluating

Show the lecture slide with the chart comparing the education of males in Athens and Sparta. Tell students that life in Athens was different from life in Sparta. Males in Athens were educated in arithmetic, geometry, drawing, music, and public speaking. They participated in sports. The people in Athens believed this type of education produced young people with strong minds and bodies. At age 18, when males finished school, they took an active role in public issues and affairs.

Answers for pages 184–187

P. 184 GEOGRAPHY CONNECTION

1. They were about 100 miles apart.
2. CRITICAL THINKING Answers will vary, but students should refer to physical barriers, such as mountains and water, in their answers.

P. 184 ☑ PROGRESS CHECK Tyrants could hold power because they had the support of the hoplites, or citizen soldiers, in the army.

P. 185 CRITICAL THINKING Spears and knives were used in hand-to-hand combat.

P. 187 ☑ PROGRESS CHECK Spartans were basically conservative. They thought free thinking and learning might lead to unrest and weaken their control over the helots, so they resisted change.

BIOGRAPHY

Solon (c. 630 B.C.–560 B.C.)

The great reformer Solon was the son of a well-to-do family, but he did not live the life of a rich Greek. Solon was a poet and a lawmaker. His goal was to find agreement between nobles and farmers who needed to be able to work together. He improved the economy by requiring all sons to continue in the same job their fathers had. He promoted trade by farmers and rewrote the Athenian constitution.

▶ CRITICAL THINKING

Predicting How do you think people today would accept Solon's ruling that sons follow fathers in their life's work?

Athenian mothers educated their daughters at home. Girls were taught spinning, weaving, and other household duties. In some wealthy families, they learned to read, write, and play music. Women were expected to marry and care for their children. For the most part, women were not active in business or government in Athens.

Early Reforms

The history of Athens was much like that of the other Greek city-states. By about 600 B.C., most Athenian farmers owed money to the nobles. Some farmers were forced to sell themselves into slavery to repay their debts. Athenians began to rebel. Farmers called for an end to all debts. They also asked that land be distributed to the poor.

To avoid an uprising, the nobles agreed to make some changes. They turned to a respected merchant named Solon (SOH•luhn) for leadership. In 594 B.C., Solon ended the farmers' debts and freed those who were enslaved. He also opened the assembly and the law courts to all male citizens. The assembly was responsible for passing laws written by a council of 400 wealthy citizens.

The common people praised Solon's reforms. Still, many Athenians were unhappy. Wealthy people felt Solon had gone too far, while poor people thought he had not gone far enough. By the time Solon left office, he had lost much of his support.

In 560 B.C., a tyrant named Peisistratus (py•SIHS•truht•uhs) took over the government. A relative of Solon, Peisistratus made reforms that went even further than those that Solon had made. Peisistratus divided large estates among farmers who had no land. He provided loans to help farmers buy equipment to work their farms. He gave citizenship to Athenians who did not own land. He also hired the poor to **construct** temples and other public works. Since religion was important in Athens, Peisistratus built additional shrines to different gods. He also encouraged the worship of the goddess Athena. Under Peisistratus, festivals held to honor Athena were expanded by the addition of athletic contests.

This clay ballot was used to select jurors for Athenian courts. How different is the ballot voters use today?

Reading **HELP**DESK

Academic Vocabulary

construct to build

Toward Democracy

After the death of Peisistratus, a noble named Cleisthenes (KLYS•thuh•neez) became the next leader of Athens. Prizing democracy, Cleisthenes made the assembly the city-state's major governing body. As before, all male citizens could participate in the assembly and vote on laws. Assembly members could now discuss issues freely, hear legal cases, and appoint army officials.

Cleisthenes also created a new council of 500 citizens. They were to help the assembly manage daily government affairs. The council introduced laws and controlled the treasury. They also managed relations with other city-states. Each year Athenian citizens held a lottery to choose the council members. Athenians preferred the lottery system over an election. In their view, an election might unfairly favor the rich, who were well-known. Terms on the council were limited to one year, and no one could serve on the council for more than two terms. Thus, every citizen had a chance to be a council member.

While Cleisthenes's reforms made the government of Athens more democratic, many residents were still excluded from the political process. People who were not citizens still could not participate in the government. This group included all Athenian women, foreign-born men, and enslaved people.

☑ PROGRESS CHECK

Explaining Why was Solon chosen to be leader of Athens?

Connections to **TODAY**

The Olympics

The ancient Olympic Games were held every four years at Olympia, in the western part of Greece, in honor of the god Zeus. The first Olympics were organized in 776 B.C. According to one legend, the founder of the games was the hero Hercules. The modern Olympics began in 1896 in Athens.

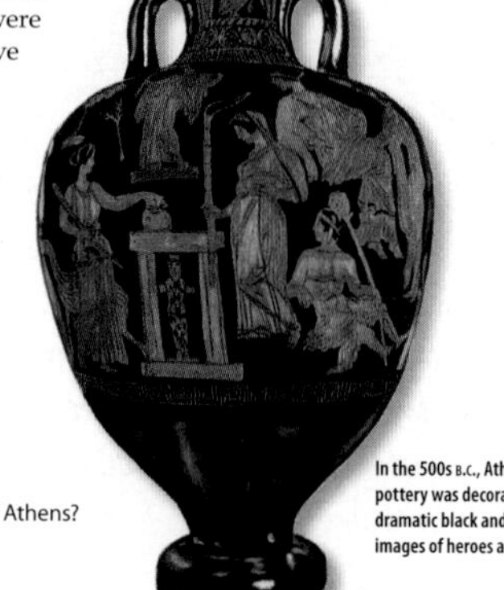

In the 500s B.C., Athenian pottery was decorated with dramatic black and red images of heroes and gods.

LESSON 2 REVIEW

Review Vocabulary

1. What might a *tyrant* say to citizens who are asking for democracy?

Answer the Guiding Questions

2. ***Explaining*** Why were the tyrants able to seize control in Athens?
3. ***Determining Cause and Effect*** Why did the Spartans emphasize military training?
4. ***Describing*** How did Athenians feel about the changes Solon put in place?
5. ***Identifying*** What was a major accomplishment of Cleisthenes?
6. **DESCRIPTIVE WRITING** You are a student living in ancient Sparta or Athens. Write a journal entry that describes a day in your life.

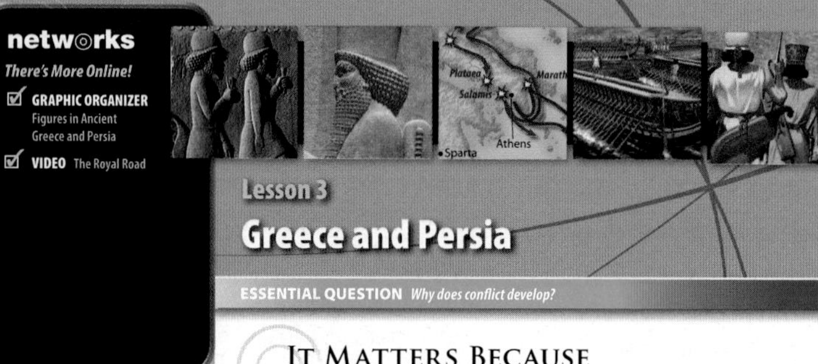

Lesson 3
Greece and Persia

ESSENTIAL QUESTION *Why does conflict develop?*

IT MATTERS BECAUSE

Although it was large and powerful, the Persian Empire could not defeat the Greeks.

1 Persia's Empire

GUIDING QUESTION ***How did the Persians rule a vast empire?***

About the time that the government in Athens was undergoing political changes, the Persians were building a powerful empire in Southwest Asia. Persia (PUHR•zhuh), the homeland of the Persians, was located in what is today southwestern Iran.

Early Persians were warriors and cattle herders from the grasslands of central Asia. After settling in the highlands of Persia, they came under the control of other peoples. Then a dynasty of kings brought the Persians together into a powerful kingdom. In the 500s B.C., a talented king named Cyrus (SY•ruhs) the Great built a strong Persian army. With that army, he began creating an empire that became the largest in the ancient world.

Creating an Empire

During the 540s B.C., Persian troops swept into neighboring lands. They brought Mesopotamia, Syria, Judah, and the Greek city-states of the area of Anatolia under Persian rule. King Cyrus held his growing empire together by treating conquered peoples fairly. He allowed them to keep their own languages, religions, and laws. In addition, Cyrus decided that the Jews exiled in Babylon would be allowed to return to their homeland.

Reading **HELP**DESK

Taking Notes: *Identifying*

As you read the lesson, fill in a chart like this one with the names of participants.

Persian Kings Attacking Greece	Greek Defenders

Content Vocabulary
- **satrapy**
- **satrap**
- **Zoroastrianism**

After Cyrus, other Persian rulers continued to expand the empire. Their armies took over Egypt, western India, and lands to the northeast of Greece. From west to east, the Persian Empire stretched a distance of some 3,000 miles (4,800 km). This is about the size of the continental United States today.

To link this large territory, the Persians improved the network of roads begun by the Assyrians. The most important route, the Royal Road, ran more than 1,500 miles (2,400 km) from Persia to Anatolia. Travelers could **obtain** food, water, and fresh horses at roadside stations along the route. Using the Royal Road, messengers could travel from Persia to Anatolia in just seven days. That same journey had taken three months before the road was built.

Persian Government

As the Persian Empire expanded, its increasing size made it more difficult to manage. Darius I (duh•RY•uhs), who ruled Persia from 522 to 486 B.C., reorganized the government to make it more efficient. He divided the empire into provinces called **satrapies** (SAY•truh•peez). Each satrapy was ruled by a governor called a **satrap** (SAY•trap), which means "defender of the kingdom." The satrap collected taxes, judged legal cases, managed the police, and recruited soldiers for the Persian army.

GEOGRAPHY CONNECTION

Persian kings built the Royal Road to connect the areas of their large empire.

1. **MOVEMENT** About how far was the shortest distance from Greece to the western end of the Royal Road?
2. **CRITICAL THINKING** ***Making Inferences*** Based on the map, why might the Persian Empire have posed a danger to Greece?

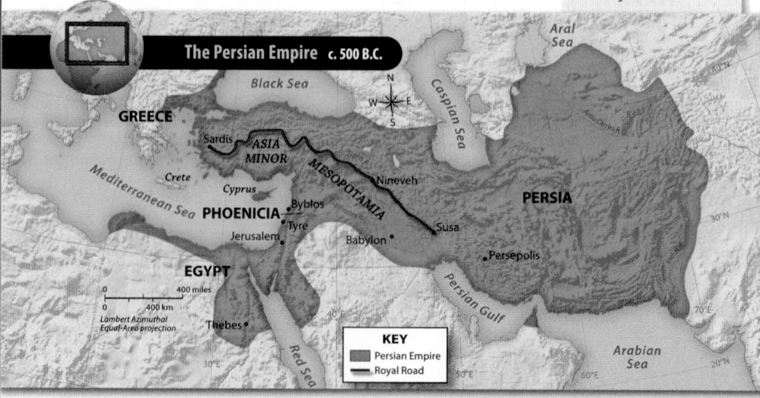

satrapy the territory governed by an official known as a satrap

satrap the governor of a province in ancient Persia

Academic Vocabulary

obtain to acquire or receive something

Teaching *Sparta and Athens: City-State Rivals* (cont.)

(Student Edition pp. 183–189)

LESSON 2 • Day 2 (cont.)

Ask:

Which system—Spartan or Athenian—do you think provided young men with a better education? *(Responses will vary, but insist that students support their opinions with reasons.)*

If time allows, hold a debate on the issue.

INTERACTIVE WHITEBOARD ACTIVITY

Identifying Project the drag-and-drop whiteboard activity. Explain that this activity enables students to select words that describe Sparta or Athens from a word bank. Students then move those words into one of two appropriate columns or groups. These columns have the headings "Sparta" and "Athens." Moderate a class discussion using the activity as a starting point. AL ELL

CLOSE & REFLECT

Comparing

Organize the class into two groups: Spartans and Athenians. Have students write a letter describing life in their assigned city-state. Their goal is to persuade the reader that theirs is the greatest city-state in Greece.

Tell students to use details from the chapter in their letters.

INTERACTIVE WORKSHEET

Economics of History

Assign the Economics of History worksheet for homework. Have students complete the Lesson 2 Review.

Answers for pages 188–189

P. 188 CRITICAL THINKING Answers will vary. Most people would disagree with such a ruling.

P. 188 Most students will say ballots today are paper or electric.

P. 189 ☑ PROGRESS CHECK Solon was chosen because he was a wealthy merchant who was respected by all classes of Athenians.

LESSON 2 REVIEW

1. A tyrant probably would reply that public order demanded the rule of a single person.
2. They were able to seize power because of civic unrest, which led to demands for political change.
3. They emphasized military training because they feared an uprising by the helots, whom they had enslaved.
4. Some wealthy Athenians believed Solon had gone too far, but poor Athenians thought he had not gone far enough.
5. One of Cleisthenes's major accomplishments was to make the city-state's assembly in Athens the city's major governing body. He also created a new council of citizens.
6. Answers will vary. Students should point out that daily life in Athens involved diverse activities, but life in Sparta had an almost exclusively military focus.

Teaching *Greece and Persia*

(Student Edition pp. 190–197)

LESSON 3

ENGAGE

MAP **Making Inferences**

On the interactive whiteboard, project the map from the lesson showing the Persian Empire. Tell students that while political changes were going on in Greek city-states, Persia was building an empire that grew as large as the continental United States.

Ask:

Why might the ancient Greeks and the Persians come into conflict? Where might such conflict have first taken place? Moderate a class discussion, reminding students that the Greeks were expanding and founding overseas colonies. Note that Asia Minor was a region that lay between both civilizations.

Tell students that in this lesson they will be learning about the rise of the Persian Empire and its conflict with the Greek city-states.

Making Connections

Have students compare the map of the Persian Empire to a modern map of the same area.

Ask:

What modern-day nations were once part of the Persian Empire? *(All or part of the these countries were once part of the Persian Empire: Iran, Afghanistan, Pakistan, Kuwait, Iraq, Armenia, Georgia, Russia, Bahrain, Yemen, Oman, Turkey, Macedonia, Bulgaria, Syria, Lebanon, Israel, Palestine, Jordan, Libya, Sudan, Egypt, Turkmenistan, Uzbekistan, Kazakhstan, and Tajikistan.)*

TEACH & ASSESS

1 Persia's Empire

GUIDING QUESTION *How did the Persians rule a vast empire?*

Summarizing

Keep the map of the Persian Empire projected on the interactive whiteboard. Discuss as a class what happened in Persia that led to the establishment of a large empire.

Ask:

- **Which king first expanded the Persian Empire?** *(Cyrus)* AL
- **How did Cyrus rule?** *(He ruled fairly. He let the conquered peoples keep their languages, religions, and laws.)*
- **How did Darius I reorganize the Persian Empire?** *(He divided the empire into provinces. Each province was ruled by a governor, or satrap, who collected taxes, judged legal cases, managed the police, and recruited soldiers for the Persian army.)*

Defining

Review the meaning of the terms *satrapies* and *satraps* with students. ELL

Answers for pages 190–191

P. 190 Taking Notes Persian Kings Attacking Greece: Darius I and Xerxes; Greek Defenders: King Leonidas of Sparta, Themistocles of Athens

P. 191 GEOGRAPHY CONNECTION

1. Greece was about 311 miles (500 km) away.
2. CRITICAL THINKING The Persian Empire was within easy striking distance of Greece on two fronts. It bordered the Greek mainland in the northeast and was less than 100 miles (161 km) from Greece across the Mediterranean.

King Darius I of Persia established Persepolis as the center of his government. This sculpture from one of the main buildings in Persepolis shows a line of nobles and dignitaries waiting to speak with the king.

▶ CRITICAL THINKING

Speculating The artist shows all of the nobles, except one, facing forward. Why do you think the artist chose to show one person looking back?

Persia maintained a full-time, paid, professional army. In comparison, the Greek army consisted of citizens called to serve only during times of war. The best fighters in the Persian army were the 10,000 soldiers who were trained to guard the king. They were known as the Immortals because when a member died, another soldier immediately took his place.

This Zoroastrian holy site is in present-day Iran.

Who Was Zoroaster?

The Persians at first worshipped many gods. Then, sometime in the 600s B.C., a religious teacher named Zoroaster (ZOHR•uh•WAS•tuhr) preached a new monotheistic religion. Most Persians accepted his religion, which was called **Zoroastrianism** (zohr•uh•WAS•tree•uh•nih•zuhm).

Zoroaster taught that there was one supreme god. This deity was called Ahura Mazda, or "Wise Lord." Ahura Mazda was the creator of all things and the leader of the forces of good. Zoroaster believed that evil existed in the world. People were free to choose between good and evil, but at the end of time, goodness would be victorious. Zoroastrian teachings, prayers, and hymns (sacred songs) were written down in a holy book. Because of Zoroastrianism, the Persians began to view their monarchy as a sacred institution or role.

Reading HELPDESK

Zoroastrianism a Persian religion based on the belief of one god

Persian kings believed that they ruled by the power of Ahura Mazda and were responsible to him alone. Darius I had the following statement carved on a cliff:

PRIMARY SOURCE

> "For this reason Ahura Mazda [the Zoroastrian god] bore me aid . . . because I was not an enemy, I was not a deceiver, I was not a wrong-doer, neither I nor my family; according to rectitude [righteousness] I ruled."
>
> —from Darius I, *Behistun Inscription*, column 4, line 4.13

After Darius's rule ended, the Persians continued to practice Zoroastrianism for centuries. The religion has about 200,000 followers today. Most of them live in South Asia.

✔ PROGRESS CHECK

Explaining How did Persian rulers unite their vast empire?

King Darius I, shown in this carving, believed that the Zoroastrian god approved of his rule.

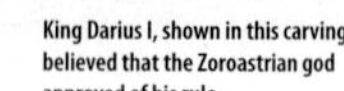

2 The Persian Wars

GUIDING QUESTION *How did the Greeks defeat the Persians?*

As the 400s B.C. began, the Persians were ready to expand into Europe. However, they soon clashed with the Greeks, who had colonies in the Mediterranean area. Persia and Greece were very different civilizations. While the Persians obeyed an all-powerful king, many of the Greeks believed that citizens should choose their own rulers and government.

As a result of the conquests made by Cyrus, the Persians already controlled the Greek cities in Anatolia. In 499 B.C., these Greeks revolted against their Persian rulers. The Athenians sent warships to help the rebels, but the Persians crushed the uprising. The Persian king Darius was angry that the Athenians interfered. He decided to punish the mainland Greeks for meddling in his empire.

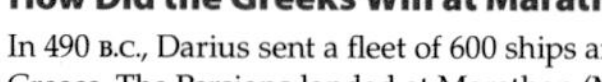

How Did the Greeks Win at Marathon?

In 490 B.C., Darius sent a fleet of 600 ships and an army to invade Greece. The Persians landed at Marathon (MAR•uh•thahn), which was a plain about 25 miles (40 km) northeast of Athens. The Persians waited there for several days. They expected the Greeks to come there and fight them. However, the Athenians did not come forward. They had only 10,000 troops compared to the Persians' 20,000 soldiers.

Build Vocabulary: *Words With Multiple Meanings*

One word can have many meanings, depending on how the word is used in a sentence. The noun *fleet*, for example, means "a group of vehicles operated under one control." As an adjective, *fleet* means "fast" or "temporary."

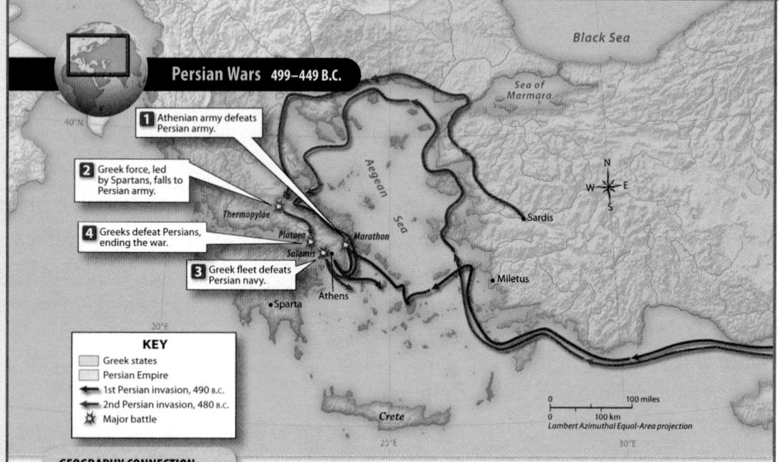

GEOGRAPHY CONNECTION

The Greek city-states successfully defended their territory against two invasions by the Persian Empire.

1. **LOCATION** Which Greek city-state defeated the Persian army in a major battle?
2. CRITICAL THINKING ***Speculating*** Why might the Greek city-states have had an advantage over the Persians?

When their enemy refused to fight, the Persians decided to sail directly to Athens and attack it by sea. The Persians began loading their ships with their strongest units—the cavalry. As soon as the Persian horsemen were on the ships, the Athenians charged down the hills and onto the plain of Marathon. The Athenians caught the Persian foot soldiers standing in the water, out of formation. They were without any help from their cavalry.

The Persians suffered a terrible defeat. According to Greek legend, a young messenger raced 25 miles from Marathon to Athens with news of the victory. When the runner reached Athens, he cried out "Victory" and then **collapsed** and died from exhaustion. Today's marathon races are named for that famous run and are just over 26 miles (41.8 km) long.

Land and Sea Battles

After the defeat at Marathon, the Persians vowed revenge against the Athenians. In 480 B.C., a new Persian king named Xerxes (ZUHRK•seez) invaded Greece with about 200,000 troops and thousands of warships and supply vessels. The Greek city-states banded together to fight the Persians.

Reading HELPDESK

Academic Vocabulary

collapse to break down; to lose effectiveness

Reading Strategies: *Ask Questions*

Asking questions as you read helps you understand what you read. Ask questions with the words *who, what, why, where, when,* and *how.*

King Leonidas (lee•AH•nuh•duhs) of Sparta supplied the most soldiers. Themistocles (thuh•MIHS•tuh•kleez) of Athens directed the Greek naval forces and devised a battle plan.

Persian ships supplied the invaders with food. Themistocles wanted to attack the Persians' ships and cut off the army's supplies. To do this, the Greeks had to stop the Persian army from reaching Athens. Sparta's King Leonidas led 7,000 soldiers into a battle that lasted for three days. The Spartans' bravery at Thermopylae (thur•MAH•puh•lee) was much celebrated.

The Greeks, however, could not stop the Persians at Thermopylae. A traitor showed the Persians a trail leading around the Greek line, allowing them to attack from behind. Realizing that his Greek army would soon be surrounded, Leonidas dismissed most of the troops. He and 300 Spartans remained and fought to the death. The Greek historian Herodotus (hair•RAH•deh•tuhs) gave this description of the battle:

PRIMARY SOURCE

> "They [the Spartans] defended themselves to the last, those who still had swords using them, and the others resisting with their hands and teeth; till the barbarians [Persians], who in part . . . had gone round and now encircled them upon every side, overwhelmed and buried the remnant [remainder] which was left beneath showers of missile weapons."
>
> —from *The Histories* by Herodotus

Connections to TODAY

Marathons

The first marathon runner is said to have been a Greek soldier. He is thought to have run from Athens to Sparta.

The first Olympic marathon—which took its name from that battle—was held when the modern games began in 1896. In 1924, the Olympic marathon distance was set at 26 miles and 385 yards (42.195 km).

At the Battle of Salamis, smaller, faster Greek ships defeated the Persian fleet.

▶ CRITICAL THINKING

Analyzing Why were the Persians at a disadvantage in the battle?

LESSON 3 (cont.)

LECTURE SLIDE **Identifying**

Show the beliefs of Zoroastrians from the lecture slide. Tell students that in the 600s B.C., a religious teacher named Zoroaster taught the Persians to follow a single god, named Ahura Mazda. Most Persians accepted this religion, called Zoroastrianism.

Ask:

How was Zoroastrianism related to the rule of Persian kings? *(Persian kings believed they ruled by the power of Ahura Mazda and were responsible only to him.)*

LECTURE SLIDE **Comparing and Contrasting**

Show the blank Venn diagram about the Persian Wars from the lecture slide. Have students work in small groups to complete Venn diagrams comparing and contrasting ancient Greece and ancient Persia during the Persian Wars.

Tell students to focus on the following points of comparison: geography, government, religion, and daily life. After students have finished their diagrams, ask them to speculate about why conflict might have developed between the Greeks and the Persians.

2 The Persian Wars

GUIDING QUESTION *How did the Greeks defeat the Persians?*

IMAGE **Identifying**

Show students the image of the naval battle between the Greek and Persian fleets at Salamis.

Ask:

- **Who won the Battle of Salamis?** *(The Greek navy destroyed almost the entire Persian fleet.)*
- **How did the Greeks, with a smaller navy, win?** *(The Greek ships were smaller in size and faster, so they could be maneuvered more easily.)*

INTERACTIVE WORKSHEET

Primary Source Activity Tell students that before the Persian King Xerxes fought with the Greek navy at Salamis, he asked the advice of his allies. Then have the class read the Primary Source worksheet and answer the questions. Moderate a discussion of the answers.

Have students complete the Lesson 3 Review.

CLOSE & REFLECT

Making Predictions Hold a class discussion on the war between the Greeks and Persians. Ask students what happened to Persia as a result of the war. Then ask them to predict what happened to Greece after the war. Did Greece become more united or less united, or did it remain the same?

IF YOU HAVE MORE TIME . . .

Take a Closer Look at the Persian Empire

Identifying

Project the map of the Persian Empire on the interactive whiteboard.

Ask:

What is Persia called today? *(Iran)*

Identifying and Analyzing

Persian rulers built a vast and important system of roads. One such road was the Royal Road.

Ask:

- **Where did the Royal Road begin and end?** *(It extended from Persia to Anatolia. Travelers could get food, water, and fresh horses at roadside stations along the way.)*
- **How did the new roads change Persian life?** *(The roads connected Persia with different areas and different peoples of the empire. They promoted trade and the exchange of ideas.)*

Comparing and Contrasting

Tell students that as the Persian Empire grew, it became more difficult to manage. Darius I reorganized the government to make it easier to rule the empire. He divided the empire into provinces called *satrapies*. Each province was ruled by a governor called a *satrap*.

Ask:

How was this system of provinces similar to and different from the system of states in the United States today? *(Answers will vary. Among other points of comparison, students might note that Persian provinces and American states have governors. However, the Persian satraps were appointed, but U.S. governors are elected.)* BL

Analyzing

Show the beliefs of Zoroastrians from the lecture slide. Tell students that like many people in ancient times, the Persians worshiped many gods. In the 600s B.C., however, a religious teacher preached a religion that worshiped one god. The preacher's name was Zoroaster, and the religion he preached was called Zoroastrianism.

Point out to students that Zoroaster believed in one god who was the creator of all things and the leader of the forces of good. The one god was called Ahura Mazda.

Ask:

- **Did Zoroaster believe evil existed in the world?** *(yes)*
- **Did Zoroaster believe evil would win out over good? Why or why not?** *(No; he believed that people had a choice between good or evil and that good would prevail over evil.)*
- **What did Persian kings believe about themselves and their rule?** *(Persian kings believed they ruled by the power of Ahura Mazda and were responsible only to him.)*
- **What did Darius I have carved on a cliff about his relationship with Ahura Mazda?** *(that Ahura Mazda gave him aid in ruling and that he ruled righteously)*

Create a Graphic Organizer

Analyzing

Project on the interactive whiteboard the map showing the Persian Wars. Tell students that three major land battles and one major sea battle were fought.

Create a graphic organizer on the interactive whiteboard entitled "Land Battles." The organizer should have three columns with the headings "Battle Location," "Details," and "Outcome." Under "Location," label the rows "Marathon," "Thermopylae," and "Plataea."

As a class, fill in the graphic organizer. *(Answers will vary but should include: **Marathon:** Greeks waited until Persians were loading their ships; Greeks won. **Thermopylae:** Spartans in united Greek force made heroic effort to protect Athens; Persians won, marched into Athens. **Plataea:** United Greek city-states had large, well-trained army; Greeks defeated Persians.)*

Answers for pages 192–195

P. 192 CRITICAL THINKING Answers will vary. Perhaps he has turned to discuss something with the person behind him.

P. 193 ☑ PROGRESS CHECK They divided the empire into satrapies and assigned important government responsibilities to each satrap. They also treated their conquered peoples fairly.

P. 194 GEOGRAPHY CONNECTION

1. Athens defeated the Persian army at Marathon.
2. CRITICAL THINKING The armies of the city-states were fighting in their home territories, while the Persians were in unfamiliar territory and far from supply bases.

P. 195 CRITICAL THINKING The narrow strait gave them less room to maneuver because the Persians' ships were larger and more difficult to maneuver.

The Persian king Xerxes watches his fleet battle the Greeks at the Battle of Salamis.

▶ CRITICAL THINKING

Contrasting Xerxes led his armies into battle. How is his role in wartime different from that played by most modern political leaders?

The Spartans' heroic stand gave Themistocles time to carry out his plan to attack Persia's ships. The Athenian fleet of ships lured the Persian fleet into the strait of Salamis (SA•luh•muhs), near Athens. A strait is a narrow **channel** of water between two pieces of land. The Greeks hoped this move would give them an advantage in battle. Themistocles believed that the heavy Persian ships would crowd together in the strait, making them difficult to move. His assumption proved to be correct. Vigorous fighting took place between the two navies. The Greeks had fewer ships, but their boats were smaller and faster, and could outmaneuver the Persian ships. The plan worked. The Greeks sank about 300 Persian ships and lost only about 40 ships of their own. The Persian fleet was almost entirely destroyed. Still, the Persian foot soldiers marched on to Athens. Finding the city almost deserted, the Persians set it on fire.

The combined forces of the Greek city-states in 479 B.C. formed their largest army yet. They had improved their fighting forces with better armor and weapons. At Plataea (pluh•TEE•uh), northwest of Athens, the Greek army again faced the Persians. In numbers, the two sides were evenly matched. Each fielded a force of about 100,000 men. This time, however, the Greeks defeated the Persian army. Fighting continued as the Greeks went on the defensive to free the city-states in Anatolia from Persian rule. Peace between the Greek allies and the Persians did not come until 449 B.C.

Academic Vocabulary

channel a strait or narrow sea between two landmasses

Decline of Persia

After its losses in Greece, Persia faced many challenges. The Persian army was no longer strong enough to defend the entire empire. Also, the Persian people grew unhappy with their government. The kings taxed the people heavily to pay for magnificent palaces and other luxuries. Members of the royal family disagreed about who should rule.

As Persia weakened, it became open to outside attacks. In the 300s B.C., Persia could not resist the invasion of an army led by a young and powerful ruler named Alexander. The Persian Empire ended, and a new Greek empire emerged that extended beyond even Persia's boundaries.

☑ PROGRESS CHECK

Explaining After the losses in Greece, why did the Persians grow unhappy with their government?

LESSON 3 REVIEW

Review Vocabulary

1. What were the responsibilities of the *satrap?*

Answer the Guiding Questions

2. ***Explaining*** Why did Darius I create satrapies?
3. ***Determining Cause and Effect*** What brought Sparta and Athens together as allies?
4. ***Analyzing*** Why did Persia invade Greece?
5. ***Differentiating*** Which Persian leader do you think made the biggest contribution? Why?
6. **PERSUASIVE WRITING** You are an officer in the Athenian army. The Persians have just landed at Marathon to invade Greece. Write a letter to a friend explaining why the Athenian army did not go out to fight the Persians when they arrived at Marathon.

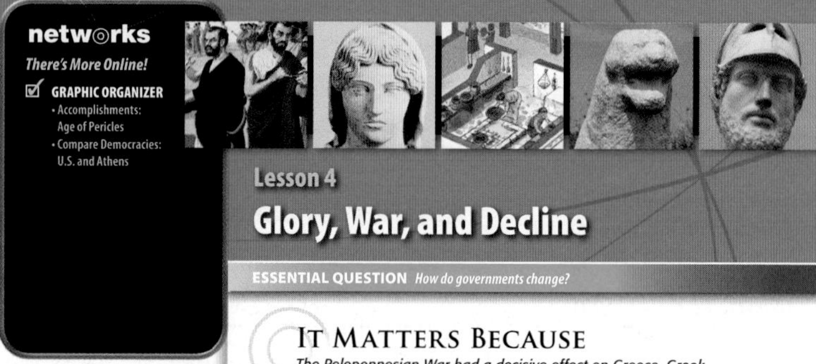

networks

There's More Online!

☑ **GRAPHIC ORGANIZER**
- Accomplishments: Age of Pericles
- Compare Democracies: U.S. and Athens

Lesson 4

Glory, War, and Decline

ESSENTIAL QUESTION *How do governments change?*

It Matters Because

The Peloponnesian War had a decisive effect on Greece. Greek culture declined after the Athenian loss to Sparta.

1 The Rule of Pericles

GUIDING QUESTION ***How did Pericles influence government and culture in Athens?***

As the Persian Wars ended, Athens became a powerful and self-confident city-state. From 461 B.C. to 429 B.C., the Athenians, under their new leader Pericles (PEHR•uh•kleez), enjoyed a golden age of prosperity and achievement. Their city-state became the economic and cultural center of Greece. Athens also practiced democratic government.

Democracy in Athens

Athenians took great pride in their democratic system. The form of government practiced by the Athenians is called **direct democracy** (dih•MAH•kruh•see). In a direct democracy, all citizens meet to debate and vote on government matters. In a **representative democracy**, such as the one we have in the United States today, citizens elect a smaller group of people. This group represents them, makes laws, and governs on their behalf.

In ancient Athens, direct democracy worked because of its relatively small number of citizens. The assembly consisted of some 43,000 male citizens over the age of 18. Often, however, fewer than 6,000 participated in the meetings, which were held every 10 days. At those meetings, participating citizens passed laws, elected officials, and made policy on war and foreign affairs. The ten top officials, elected each year, were known as generals.

Reading **HELP**DESK

Taking Notes: *Identifying*

Use a chart like this one to list the accomplishments during the age of Pericles.

Age of Pericles

Content Vocabulary
- **direct democracy**
- **representative democracy**
- **philosopher**

Pericles in Charge

After the Persian Wars, the most important general in Athenian government was Pericles. His wise rule guided the city-state for more than 30 years.

Pericles made Athens a more democratic city-state. He appointed people to positions because of their abilities, not because they were members of a certain social class. Pericles brought more ordinary Athenians into government. As a result, even shopkeepers and laborers could, for the first time, share in the government along with nobles and farmers.

Under Pericles's rule, Athens became a center of learning and the arts. The Persians had burned much of the city during the Persian Wars. Under Pericles, Athens was rebuilt. He erected new temples, monuments, and statues throughout the city.

Pericles also supported writers, artists, teachers, sculptors, and architects. **Philosophers** (fuh•LAH•suh•fuhrs) also flourished during the rule of Pericles. Philosophers are thinkers who reflect on the meaning of life. Athens became a great center for knowledge. Pericles called the city "the school of Greece."

☑ PROGRESS CHECK

Explaining How was Athens able to become a direct democracy?

Political discussion was highly popular in Athens.

▶ CRITICAL THINKING

Speculating Citizens in Athens would meet on a hill in the city set aside for political discussion. What issues do you think Athenian citizens might have debated there?

direct democracy a form of democracy in which all citizens can participate firsthand in the decision-making process

representative democracy a form of democracy in which citizens elect officials to govern on their behalf

philosopher a person who searches for wisdom or enlightenment

LESSON 3 (cont.)

IF YOU HAVE MORE TIME . . .

Make Postcards to Illustrate the Persian Wars

Creating Have pairs of students create a postcard that illustrates the conflict between Greece and Persia.

Students might focus on the causes of the conflict, important people involved in the conflict, specific battles, or the outcome.

Students should begin by selecting a topic for their postcards. They can use the information in their textbooks to help them choose a topic to illustrate, or they might conduct outside research.

Summarizing On the front of the postcard, students might use photos, their own drawings, maps, or diagrams. On the back of the postcard, they should provide analysis of their topic and summarize their illustration.

Learn More About the First Marathon

Making Connections Have students perform research online to learn more about the ancient roots of modern marathon races.

Ask:

- **Who was Pheidippides?** *(Pheidippides was the messenger who, according to the Greek story, ran 25 miles from Marathon to Athens to announce the Athenian victory.)*
- **What happend when Pheidippides reached Athens?** *(He is said to have yelled, "Nike!", or victory, and then fallen dead, exhausted by his run.)*
- **Do you think Pheidippides would be an inspiration to modern marathon runners?** *(Some students may say "yes" because he endured a grueling run. Others may say his death following his run would be discouraging rather than inspirational.)*

Then have students make a map of the route Pheidippides took from Marathon to Athens to announce the victory.

Answers for pages 196–197

P. 196 CRITICAL THINKING Most modern political leaders do not take an active part in battles.

P. 197 ☑ PROGRESS CHECK Persians were unhappy because the kings taxed the people heavily.

LESSON 3 REVIEW

1. The satrap collected taxes, judged legal cases, managed the police, and recruited soldiers for the army.
2. He created satrapies to make the government more efficient.
3. Sparta and Athens formed an alliance to fight off Persian invasions.
4. Persia invaded in order to punish Greece for aiding the rebellious cities of Anatolia.
5. Answers will vary but should be supported by valid reasons.
6. Letters will vary. Students may mention that the Athenians had far fewer troops than the Persians. They may also mention the Athenians' decision to wait and catch the Persians off-guard without the protection of their cavalry.

Teaching *Glory, War, and Decline* (Student Edition pp. 198–205)

LESSON 4 • Day 1

ENGAGE

LECTURE SLIDE Show the definition of *golden age* from the lecture slide. Tell students that the golden age in Athens was a significant time in Western world history. Many major Western ideas about philosophy, government, and the arts developed during this period.

TEACH & ASSESS

1 The Rule of Pericles

GUIDING QUESTION *How did Pericles influence government and culture in Athens?*

Making Connections

Lead the class in a discussion about life in Athens during the time of Pericles. Remind students that during the Persian War, Athens was burned. It was rebuilt after the war ended, and under the leadership of Pericles, it experienced a golden age of prosperity, cultural achievement, and democracy.

Ask:

- **What form of government was practiced in Athens during its golden age?** *(direct democracy)*
- **How does direct democracy work?** *(All citizens meet to debate and vote on government matters.)*
- **What kind of democracy do we have in the United States?** *(We have a representative democracy.)*
- **How does democracy work in the United States?** *(Citizens elect a small group of people, the Congress, to represent them.)*
- **What does this small group of representatives do?** *(They make laws and govern on behalf of the people.)*

Tell students that in Greece, direct democracy worked because of the small number of citizens. Remind students that only free males over 18 years old were citizens and could participate in the government. On average, about 6,000 people participated in the government meetings. BL

Answers for pages 198–199

P. 198 Taking Notes Answers should include rebuilding of Athens; political leadership during the period of the Delian League; support of writers, artists, and philosophers; expansion of democratic government.

P. 199 CRITICAL THINKING Answers will vary but may include politics or philosophy.

P. 199 ☑ PROGRESS CHECK The population of Athenian citizens attending the assembly meetings was relatively small, making direct democracy possible. In addition, Pericles, the most important leader in Athens, encouraged direct democracy and participation in government by all classes of citizens.

INFOGRAPHIC

Athens was able to have a direct democracy because it had a low number of citizens.

1. **IDENTIFYING** In Athens, what involvement could citizens have in the passage of laws?
2. CRITICAL THINKING
Analyzing Under which government does a broader segment of the population have the right to vote?

COMPARING GOVERNMENTS

	Athenian Democracy	American Democracy
Type of Democracy	Direct	Representative
Right to Vote	Only adult males born in Athens	All citizens, male and female age 18 or over
Laws	Proposed by the council and approved by a majority in the assembly	Approved by both houses of Congress and signed by the president
Citizen Involvement	Citizens with voting rights can vote for or against any law	Citizens with voting rights can vote for or against the officials who make the laws

2 Athenian Life

GUIDING QUESTION *What was life like for Athenians under the rule of Pericles?*

At its height in the 400s B.C., Athens was the largest Greek city-state. Its population numbered about 285,000. Of this number, about 150,000 were citizens. Only 43,000 of these citizens, however, were males who had political rights. Athens was home to about 35,000 foreigners and 100,000 enslaved people.

Athenian Men and Women

Athenian men worked as farmers, artisans, and merchants. They often finished their daily work in the morning. They spent afternoons exercising at the gymnasium. In the evening, upper-class men enjoyed all-male gatherings where they ate, drank, and discussed philosophy or politics.

Athenian women focused on their homes and families. Girls married at a young age, often in their mid-teens. Their duties centered on having children and taking care of their households. Women of poor families helped with the farm work or sold goods in the local marketplace. Most upper-class women rarely left their houses except to attend funerals and festivals. Even then, they had to be **accompanied** by a male relative. Upper-class women generally supervised the servants and spun, dyed, or wove cloth.

Athenian women could not attend school, but many learned to read and to play music. However, Athenian society did not consider educated women as equal to men. Women could not participate in political activities or own property. Greek women were always under the care of a male family member. Husbands were responsible for their wives and unmarried daughters. Sons looked after their widowed mothers.

A few women had more freedom, especially foreigners, who were regarded differently than Athenian-born women. One well-regarded woman was Aspasia (as•PAY•zhuh). She was known for her intelligence and charm. Aspasia taught public speaking, and her ideas were popular among Athenians. Both Plato (PLAY•toh), the famous Greek philosopher, and Pericles were influenced by her.

Reading **HELP**DESK

Academic Vocabulary

accompany to go with someone as a companion

BIOGRAPHY

Aspasia (c. 470–400 B.C.)

Aspasia originally came from the Greek-speaking city of Miletus in Asia Minor. Her beauty and intellect made her a democratic symbol to many Greeks who treated her like a modern rock star.

She aggressively entered into the male-dominated society and government of Greece. She was one of the first women to encourage other females to participate in government and demand their rights.

What Was the Role of Slavery in Athens?

Slavery was common in ancient civilizations. It was often considered to be a normal part of life, even by enslaved people themselves. Even in a democracy like Athens, slavery was common. Most Athenian households had at least one enslaved person. Wealthy Athenian families often had several.

Many enslaved people were prisoners who had been captured in battle. These included both Greeks and non-Greeks. Enslaved men worked on farms, in the shops of artisans, or at hard labor. Enslaved women were cooks and servants in wealthy homes and sometimes taught upper-class children. The treatment of enslaved people varied. Those who labored in mines often died very young. Slaves who worked as craftspeople had easier lives. Sometimes, enslaved people could earn money and, in rare cases, buy their freedom. Slavery might have helped Athens develop its prosperous economy.

ATHENIAN ARCHITECTURE

Wool Room Yarn was spun and cloth was woven here.

Family Room

Altar and Courtyard Greek courtyards usually had an altar to the favorite family god.

Bedroom

Dining Room Men ate their meals alone while served by women.

Kitchen Cooking was often done over an open fire.

INFOGRAPHIC

Wealthy Athenians often had large homes. Houses were built with mud bricks and had tiled roofs.

CRITICAL THINKING
Inferring How does the architecture of a Greek home reflect the role of women in ancient Greece?

The Athenian Economy

Farming was a common occupation among Athenians. Local farmers grew grains, vegetables, and fruits, including grapes and olives to make wine and olive oil for shipment to foreign markets.

Athenian farms lacked **sufficient** land to grow enough food to support the city-state. Although Athenians grew some grain, they had to import more from other places. Athens built a large fleet of ships to trade with colonies and other city-states in the Mediterranean world. During the 400s B.C., Athens led the Greek world in trade. Important goods made and traded in Athens included pottery and leather products.

PROGRESS CHECK

Comparing and Contrasting How did the roles of Athenian men and women differ?

Marble lions like this one guarded the way from the harbor to the temples in Delos.

3 War Between Athens and Sparta

GUIDING QUESTION *How did the Peloponnesian War affect the Greek city-states?*

As time passed, the Greek city-states learned that their survival depended on cooperation. Even after the Persian Wars ended, the Persian threat against Greece remained. In 478 B.C., Athens joined with other city-states to form a defensive league, or protective group, to defend its members against the Persians. Because the league at first had its headquarters on the island of Delos (DEE•LAHS), it became known as the Delian League.

Athens provided the Delian League with most of its sailors and soldiers, while the other city-states supplied money and ships. During the next several **decades**, the league drove Persia out of the remaining Greek territories in Anatolia. Free of Persian domination, Greece grew richer through increased overseas trade.

The Athenian Empire

In spite of its successes, the Delian League failed. Athens was the strongest city-state, and the league's officials and commanders and most of the troops were Athenian. Over time, Athens began to use its influence to control the other member city-states. The league was no longer an alliance of equal city-states fighting Persia. It had become a group of city-states controlled by Athens.

Reading **HELP**DESK

Academic Vocabulary

sufficient enough
decade a period of ten years

Pericles's leadership helped Athens dominate the Delian League. He treated the other city-states like subjects, demanding strict loyalty and regular payments from them. He even insisted that they use Athenian coins and measures. In 454 B.C., the Athenians moved the Delian League's treasury from Delos to Athens. They also sent troops to other Greek city-states to help the common people rebel against the nobles in power.

War Breaks Out

As the economic and political power of Athens grew, other city-states, especially Sparta, became alarmed. Politically and socially, Sparta and Athens were quite different. Neither trusted the other. Both wanted to be the major power in the Greek world.

Sparta became the leader of an alliance of city-states opposed to Athens. In 433 B.C., Athens began interfering with some of Sparta's allies. These allies pressured Sparta to attack Athens. War broke out in 431 B.C. and continued until 404 B.C. The possibility of future cooperation among the Greek city-states disappeared as a result of this war. Historians call this **conflict** the Peloponnesian War because Sparta was located in the Peloponnesus.

Pericles's Funeral Oration

During the war's first winter, Athens held a public funeral to honor soldiers who had died in battle. Afterward, the Athenian families gathered to mourn their losses. In a famous speech, called the *Funeral Oration*, Pericles talked about the greatness of Athens and reminded the people that they made their government strong. He reminded them that citizens had to obey the rules in their constitution—their framework of government. They accepted certain duties, such as paying taxes and defending the city. They were also awarded certain rights, such as the ability to vote and run for office.

PRIMARY SOURCE

> "Our constitution is called a democracy because power is in the hands not of a minority but of the whole people. When it is a question of settling private disputes, everyone is equal before the law. . . ."
>
> —Pericles, *Funeral Oration*, quoted in *History of the Peloponnesian War*

In his speech, Pericles **emphasized** that the democratic way of life is worth protecting. He urged his listeners to have the courage to continue fighting. The ideas Pericles expressed are still valued by citizens of democratic countries today.

The historian Thucydides described Pericles as "the first citizen" of Athens.

CRITICAL THINKING
Evaluating Pericles was not an emperor, a king, or even a president, yet he was able to lead Athens to the greatest glories the city would ever know. How do you think he was able to accomplish what he did?

Academic Vocabulary

conflict a battle or war
emphasize to attach a sense of importance to something; to express the importance of something

LESSON 4 • Day 1 (cont.)

LECTURE SLIDE

Making Inferences

Show students the list of Pericles's achievements from the lecture slide. Tell students that under Pericles, Athens became a center of learning and the arts. He supported writers, artists, teachers, sculptors, and architects. People who reflected on the meaning of life, called philosophers, also flourished.

Ask:

- **What did Pericles call Athens?** *(the school of Greece)*
- **What did he mean by that?** *(Answers will vary, but students should recognize that Athens was the center of learning in Greece.)*

Analyzing Visuals

Have students answer these questions based on the illustration of Athenians engaged in political discussion.

Ask:

- **What does this illustration tell you about life in Athens during the time of Pericles?** *(Accept all reasonable responses. Students may mention that only men are shown in the illustration.)*
- **What is the name of the building on top of the hill that you can see in the background ?** *(the Parthenon)*
- **What conclusions can you draw from this illustration about architecture during the time of Pericles?** *(It was advanced. The Greeks built in a variety of styles.)*
- **Have you ever seen buildings similar to the buildings shown here?** *(Students may mention more modern buildings such as the White House or the Capitol in Washington that incorporate elements, such as columns or domes, from Greek architecture. They may also mention buildings in their community that have these elements.)*

2 Athenian Life

GUIDING QUESTION *What was life like for Athenians under the rule of Pericles?*

Comparing and Contrasting

Create a three-column chart on the interactive whiteboard entitled "Life in Athens." The three vertical columns should be labeled "Men over 18", "Women," and "Enslaved People."

Organize the class into pairs. Have each pair copy the blank chart onto a piece of paper. Tell students to fill out the chart with details describing the lives of men over 18, women, and enslaved people in Athens.

Tell students to consult their textbooks and to include as many details as possible in their charts.

In a class discussion, have each pair tell one detail of life in Athens for one of the groups.

(Answers will vary but might include: Men: worked as farmers, artisans, merchants; spent afternoons exercising; upper-class men met in the evenings, ate, drank, and discussed politics and philosophy.

Women: married young and focused on having children and caring for the household; upper-class women rarely left home but if they did, they were accompanied by a male; poor women did farmwork or worked in shops; no women had political rights or participated in government.

Enslaved People: enslaved men were often captured in battles; worked on farms, in shops, or in mines; enslaved women worked as cooks and servants in wealthy homes.)

Fill in the chart on the interactive whiteboard as students provide the details. AL

Remind students that although Pericles was influential in Athens, the city-state remained a democracy.

Have students complete the Lesson 4 Review.

CLOSE & REFLECT

Speculating

Ask:

Do you think most people enjoyed life in Athens when Pericles was in charge? Why?

Guide the class in a discussion.

Making Connections

Ask:

- **Would you like to have lived in Athens during the time of Pericles?**
- **How would that life be different from your life now?**
- **Would life be the same in any ways?**

Encourage students to consider life in Athens from different points of view; for example, as a free adult man, an adult woman, a slave, a young man, and a young woman.

Assessing

Quickly assess students' comprehension of this section by reading these statements and having students indicate by a thumbs up or a thumbs down if the statement is true or false.

- Athenian men would often go to a gymnasium to exercise. *(true)*
- Education was equally available to boys and girls. *(false)*
- Upper-class Athenian women spent their mornings shopping in the marketplace. *(false)*
- Many of Athens's slaves were prisoners who had been captured in battle. *(true)*

LESSON 4 • Day 2

ENGAGE

Speculating Ask students if they ever were members of a group in which one person tried to take charge of the group and tell everyone else what to do.

Ask:

How did you feel when one person tried to take charge and tell everyone else what to do? Then **ask: What happened?** *(Students will probably say that conflict developed within the group.)* Tell students they are about to learn how a similar conflict developed in Greece.

TEACH & ASSESS

3 War Between Athens and Sparta

GUIDING QUESTION *How did the Peloponnesian War affect the Greek city-states?*

LECTURE SLIDE

Explaining

Show information about the Delian League from the lecture slide. Tell students that even after the Persian Wars, the Persians were still a threat to the Greek city-states. The city-states joined together in a league in which each city-state had equal power. They cooperated with each other on defense matters. This league was named the Delian League because at first its headquarters were on the island of Delos. Sparta did not join this league.

Answers for pages 200–203

P. 200 INFOGRAPHIC

1. Citizens who had voting rights could vote directly for or against all laws.
2. CRITICAL THINKING A broader segment of the population has the right to vote in the United States than it did under Athenian democracy.

P. 201 INFOGRAPHIC

CRITICAL THINKING Rooms were set aside for tasks such as spinning and cooking, which were women's work. Only men ate in the dining room, where they were served by women.

P. 202 ☑ PROGRESS CHECK Men did farmwork, exercised at the gymnasium, and attended gatherings in the evening to talk about politics and philosophy. Women did housework and raised families.

P. 203 CRITICAL THINKING Answers will vary. Pericles expanded Athenian democracy, which helped broaden his base of support. He was able to maintain power for more than 30 years, which allowed him to carry out his plans to rebuild Athens and make it a great center for knowledge.

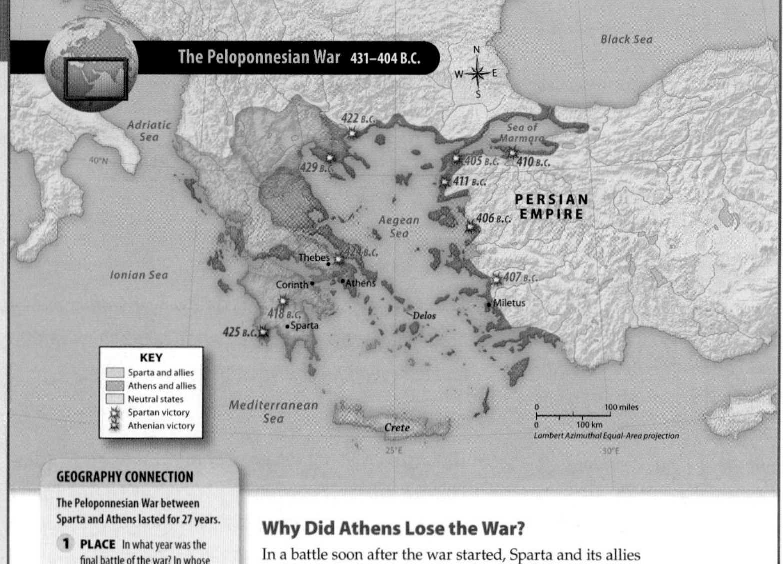

GEOGRAPHY CONNECTION

The Peloponnesian War between Sparta and Athens lasted for 27 years.

1. **PLACE** In what year was the final battle of the war? In whose territory was it fought?
2. **CRITICAL THINKING** ***Speculating*** Which cities were on the side of Athens? Why do you think having those allies was not enough help for Athens to win the war?

Why Did Athens Lose the War?

In a battle soon after the war started, Sparta and its allies surrounded Athens. They knew that, in an open battle, they could easily defeat the Athenian army. Pericles understood the weakness of the Athenian troops. He chose to keep his army and the people within the walls of the surrounded city. The powerful Athenian navy would bring supplies to the city from its colonies and allies. Sparta lacked a navy and could not stop the Athenian ships.

For almost two years, Athens remained safe. Then a deadly disease broke out within the overcrowded city's population. More than a third of the people died, including Pericles. During the next 25 years, each side won some victories but was unable to defeat its opponent.

Finally, Sparta made a deal with the Persian Empire. The Spartans agreed to give the Persians some Greek territory in Anatolia. In return, Sparta received enough Persian gold to build its own navy.

Reading HELPDESK

Reading Strategy: *Rereading*

When a paragraph is difficult to understand, try reading it again. Read it once to understand the main idea. Read it again to understand the details.

As the war dragged on, Athens fell into a state of unrest. The democracy had been overthrown. The government that replaced it was then overthrown. By the end of 411 B.C., democracy had been restored. The war, however, continued. In 405 B.C., Sparta's newly built navy destroyed the Athenian fleet. Sparta then placed a blockade around Athens, preventing food and other supplies from entering the city. Starving, the Athenians finally surrendered a year later. The Spartans and their allies then knocked down the city walls. The Athenian empire collapsed.

The Effects of the War

The Peloponnesian War brought disaster to the Greek city-states. The governments were left divided and weak. Many people had died in battle or from disease. Fighting had destroyed farms and left many people with no way to earn a living. As a result, thousands of young Greeks left Greece to join the Persian army.

After the conflict, Sparta ruled its newly acquired empire, much as Athens had ruled its empire before. This harsh treatment angered Sparta's former allies. An uneasy political situation developed. During the next 30 years, Sparta tried to put down rebellions and fought Persia again. Finally, in 371 B.C., the city-state of Thebes seized Sparta and ended the Spartan empire. About 10 years later, Thebes also collapsed.

As the city-states fought, they failed to notice the growing threat from the kingdom of Macedonia to the north. Macedonia's strength and desire for expansion would eventually cost the Greek city-states their independence.

✓ PROGRESS CHECK

Explaining Why was Sparta's deal with Persia so important in the war against Athens?

LESSON 4 REVIEW

Review Vocabulary

1. Explain why a group taking a vote on something is an example of a *direct democracy*.

Answer the Guiding Questions

2. ***Describing*** How did Pericles choose people for positions in the government in Athens?
3. ***Explaining*** What jobs did Athenian slaves do?
4. ***Determining Cause and Effect*** Why did the Delian League break apart?
5. ***Identifying*** What was the most important accomplishment of Pericles?
6. **EXPOSITORY WRITING** Ancient Athens was a direct democracy. The United States Constitution provides for a representative democracy. Do you think the United States should change to a direct democracy? Why or why not?

NOTES

NOTES

LESSON 4 • Day 2 (cont.)

Ask:

- **In its early years, what did the Delian League accomplish?** *(The Delian League drove the Persians from the Greek territories in Anatolia.)*
- **What role did Athens play in this league?** *(Athens provided the league with most of its soldiers and sailors.)*
- **What did the other city-states in the league provide?** *(They provided ships and money.)*
- **Did the Delian League succeed?** *(No, it failed.)*
- **Why did it fail?** *(Athens, the strongest city-state, began to control the other member city-states.)*
- **What role did Pericles have in this?** *(He treated the other city-states like subjects and demanded strict loyalty and regular payment of money. He even insisted that the other city-states use Athenian coinage and measures.)* AL

Determining Cause and Effect

Have students work in small groups to create cause-and-effect chains that illustrate the fall of Athenian power. Remind students that some effects have more than one cause and some causes have more than one effect.

Challenge groups to make their chains as detailed as possible. Then, ask groups to explain their cause-and-effect chains to the class. BL

English Language Learners might benefit from writing paragraphs to describe these cause-and-effect relationships listed in their chains. Paragraphs should include words such as *as a result of, because,* or *then* that identify cause-and-effect relationships.

Once students have written their paragraphs, they should underline any of these clue words to see if their paragraphs accurately describe the relationships found in their chains. ELL

Making Connections

Point out to students that placing a blockade around a town, a city, or a country has been used as a military strategy throughout history.

Ask:

- **What is the goal of a blockade?** *(The goal of a blockade is to force one side to surrender by cutting off supplies, such as food.)*
- **How might the people living in a blockaded city or town get around the blockade?** *(Accept reasonable answers. Students may mention that people could build tunnels. In modern times, they might be able to have supplies airlifted in.)*
- **What are the advantages and disadvantages of a blockade for those who enforce it?** *(One advantage of a blockade is that the enforcing side will not suffer many losses. The disadvantege is that it could take a long time to be effective.)*

PRIMARY SOURCE

Tell students that a year after Sparta surrounded Athens, Pericles held a funeral for fallen soldiers and sailors in Athens. The Funeral Oration, or speech, he gave to the Athenians is still read today.

Have students complete the Primary Source Activity. Review their answers in a class discussion.

Ask:

- **What did Pericles say the rights of democracy came with?** *(With democracy comes responsibilities.)*
- **What were some of those responsibilities?** *(to obey the laws and to defend the city-state)*
- **In today's U.S. democracy, do citizens have those same responsibilities?** *(yes)*

Encourage student volunteers to read the speech aloud.

CLOSE & REFLECT

Explaining

Tell students that a famous Greek historian, Thucydides, who lived during the Peloponnesian War, said that war "is a violent teacher."

Ask:

What do you think he meant by that? *(Students will probably mention that the lessons learned from a war come about only as a result of great suffering on both sides.)*

Drawing Conclusions

Ask students:

How could the results of the Peloponnesian War have been avoided?

Guide the class in a discussion of this question.

Have students complete the Lesson 4 Review.

BACKGROUND KNOWLEDGE

Biography of Pericles

Pericles was born in about 495 B.C. to a wealthy and powerful family just outside of Athens. He received his education from philosophers. As a young man, he was known for his skill with words. Later, when he became a political leader, he strongly supported democracy.

Although he was from a wealthy family, he believed that citizenship should not be limited to the wealthy and powerful. He made changes to take power from the few and give it to the many. The "Age of Pericles" was Athens's Golden Age, and the city blossomed under his leadership.

Pericles wanted Athens to be a model for the world. He hired hundreds of workers to construct public buildings in Athens. The best known is the Parthenon. Workers hauled 20,000 tons of marble from a nearby mountain and spent almost 15 years completing it.

Pericles was a private person. He avoided being in public as much as possible. He spent most of his time alone, with family, or with close friends. He married and had three sons. In 429 B.C. Pericles died from the plague.

Answers for pages 204–205

P. 204 GEOGRAPHY CONNECTION

1. The final battle was fought in 405 B.C. in the territory of Athens.
2. **CRITICAL THINKING** Miletus and the Island of Delos were allied with Athens. These cities were much farther away than Sparta and Sparta's allies. It would be more difficult for them to provide aid than it was for Sparta's allies.

P. 205 ☑ **PROGRESS CHECK** The alliance gave Sparta enough money to build its own navy.

LESSON 4 REVIEW

1. The group is an example of direct democracy because everyone in the group has a vote.
2. Pericles appointed people to government positions because of their abilities rather than their social class.
3. Enslaved Athenians worked on farms or in the shops of artisans. They also performed hard labor. Enslaved women worked as cooks, servants, and tutors.
4. It broke apart because Athens assumed an ever-more-oppressive role, demanding tribute from league members.
5. Pericles's most important accomplishments were leading the city of Athens, expanding democratic government there, and helping Athens dominate the Delian League.
6. Answers will vary. Many students will say that the population of the United States is too large for the country to function effectively as a direct democracy.

CHAPTER 7 Activities

Write your answers on a separate piece of paper.

1. **Exploring the Essential Question**
   EXPOSITORY WRITING Why does conflict develop? Write an essay describing the ways that conflict played an important role in the lives of the ancient Greeks. In your writing, discuss such examples as Mycenaeans versus Minoans, Persia versus Greece, and Athens versus Sparta.

2. **21st Century Skills**
   ANALYZING AND MAKING JUDGMENTS Which of these experiences would help you to better understand the meaning of *democracy?*
   A. running for class president
   B. trading CDs with your friend
   C. picking up litter in your neighborhood
   D. checking out a book at a library

3. **Thinking Like a Historian**
   COMPARING AND CONTRASTING Create a diagram like the one below to compare and contrast the causes and effects of the Persian War with those of the Peloponnesian War.

Persian War	Peloponnesian War

4. **GEOGRAPHY ACTIVITY**

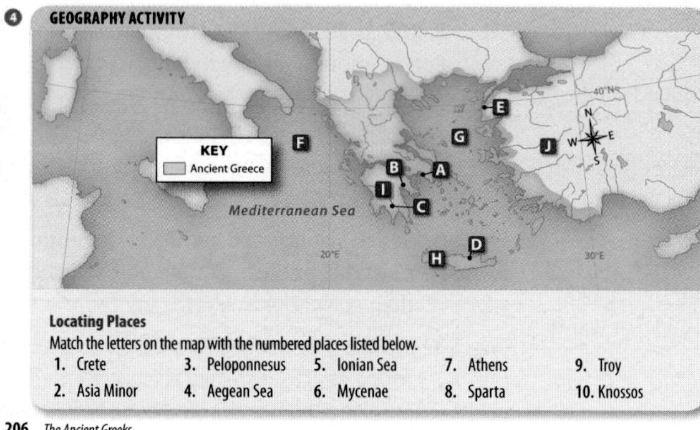

Locating Places
Match the letters on the map with the numbered places listed below.

1. Crete
2. Asia Minor
3. Peloponnesus
4. Aegean Sea
5. Ionian Sea
6. Mycenae
7. Athens
8. Sparta
9. Troy
10. Knossos

CHAPTER 7 Assessment

REVIEW THE GUIDING QUESTIONS
Directions: Choose the best answer for each question.

1. Where was Knossos located?
   A. Sparta
   B. Persia
   C. Athens
   D. Crete

2. Why did Greek colonies spread throughout the Mediterranean region?
   F. Tyrants created many of them.
   G. Population pressures caused them to develop.
   H. Persia attacked mainland Greece.
   I. Pericles founded them.

3. What is the rule of a few wealthy people called?
   A. tyranny
   B. direct democracy
   C. oligarchy
   D. representative democracy

4. The officials who enforced the law and collected taxes in ancient Sparta were called
   F. kings.
   G. generals.
   H. ephors.
   I. helots.

5. Which of the following was a Persian king?
   A. Xerxes
   B. Alexander the Great
   C. Pericles
   D. Leonidas

6. About how long did the Peloponnesian War last?
   F. 10 years
   G. 17 years
   H. 27 years
   I. 50 years

CHAPTER 7 Assessment *(continued)*

DBQ DOCUMENT-BASED QUESTIONS

Greek historian Plutarch describes the state-run education of boys in Sparta:

"Reading and writing they gave them, just enough to serve their turn; their chief care was to make them good subjects, and to teach them to endure pain and conquer in battle."

—from Plutarch, *The Lives of the Noble Grecians and Romans*

7. **Identifying** Spartans were educated and trained to be
   A. lawyers.
   B. politicians.
   C. soldiers.
   D. doctors.

8. **Drawing Conclusions** According to Plutarch, what Spartan educators most wanted from students was for them to
   F. write epics.
   G. win wars.
   H. reject discipline.
   I. serve in the assembly.

SHORT RESPONSE

"Further, we [Athenians] provide plenty of means [ways] for the mind to refresh itself from business. We celebrate games and sacrifices all the year round, and the elegance of our private establishments forms a daily source of pleasure . . . while the magnitude [large size] of our city draws the produce of the world into our harbor."

—from Pericles' Funeral Oration, quoted in *The Complete Writings of Thucydides*

9. How did Athenians live a more varied lifestyle than Spartans?

10. In what ways might a modern city want to imitate ancient Athens?

EXTENDED RESPONSE

11. **Expository Writing** The lives of Athenian girls were very different from the lives of girls today. Write a brief essay that explains the differences, giving real-life examples.

Need Extra Help?

If You've Missed Question	1	2	3	4	5	6	7	8	9	10	11
Review Lesson	1	1	2	2	3	4	1	1	2	2	2

NOTES

REFLECT, REVIEW, & REMEDIATE

INTERACTIVE WORKSHEET

Chapter Summary

Provide students with the Chapter Summary worksheet to help review the chapter and prepare for assessment.

Reviewing the Enduring Understandings

Review this chapter's Enduring Understandings with students:
- People, places, and ideas change over time.
- The value that a society places on individual rights is often reflected in that society's government.
- Countries have relationships with each other.

Lead the class in a discussion of how Greece has provided examples of change and unity.

Ask questions such as: **How does geography influence the way people live? Why do people form governments? Why does conflict develop? How do governments change?**

INTERACTIVE WHITEBOARD You might want to have one or more student volunteers record the best examples for each subject on the interactive whiteboard, using a chart like the one provided here.

Major Changes in Greek History	Times When the Greeks United

ACTIVITIES ANSWERS

Exploring the Essential Question

1. Students should note that the Mycenaeans took aggressive action to gain supremacy in the Mediterranean world, first by subduing the Minoans and then through their military successes in the Trojan War. Students may also mention economic conflicts such as the debts of farmers to the nobles in Greek city-states; political friction resulting from the concentrated power of tyrants; international tensions resulting from Greek aid to the Anatolian cities that revolted against the Persians; and Spartan resentment of the Athenian buildup of power as a result of Athens's leadership of the Delian League.

21st Century Skills

2. **A** Democracy is a political system, and running for class president would provide political experience. Answers B, C, and D are not good choices because these activities are not necessary to a democracy.

Thinking Like a Historian

3. **Persian War:** vast extent of Persian Empire, Persian resentment when Greek city-states aided Greek revolts in western Anatolia; Persian defeats at Marathon and Salamis; Greek recovery under the leadership of Athens; Athenian buildup of power in the Delian League
Peloponnesian War: resentment of Athens by other Greek city-states, especially Sparta; leadership of Pericles; Pericles's death from the plague; Spartan alliance with Persia; Spartan defeat of Athenian navy; decline of Athens and Sparta after the war

Locating Places

4. **1.** H, **2.** J, **3.** I, **4.** G, **5.** F, **6.** B, **7.** A, **8.** C, **9.** E, **10.** D

ASSESSMENT ANSWERS

Review the Guiding Questions

1. **D** Knossos was located on the island of Crete. Sparta is located on the Peloponnesus, and Athens lies about 100 miles east of Sparta on the Greek mainland. Persia is on the Asian continent. Therefore, D is the correct answer.

2. **G** The population grew, and city-states needed colonies to grow food for the increased population. Tyrants did not create colonies, although they sometimes governed them. Pericles lived after the great age of Greek colonization. The Persian attack had no influence on the formation of Greek colonies. Thus, the correct answer is G.

3. **C** The rule of a few wealthy people is called an oligarchy. Tyranny is the rule of a single, all-powerful individual. Direct democracy and representative democracy are systems in which the majority of the citizens play a role in government. Thus, C is the correct answer.

4. **H** Men called ephors were the officials who enforced the law. Kings ruled Mycenaean states, and generals were the highest public officials in Athens. Helots were enslaved people in Sparta. Therefore, H is the correct answer.

5. **A** Xerxes was king of Persia and fought the Persian war against Greek city-states. Alexander was from Macedon, north of Greece, and later built an empire. Pericles was an Athenian statesman during its golden age. Leonidas was a Spartan king. Thus, A is the correct answer.

6. **H** The Peloponnesian War broke out in 431 B.C. and ended in 404 B.C., for a total span of 27 years. The war continued longer than 10 and 17 years but did not last as long as 50 years.

Document-Based Questions

7. **C** Although Spartan boys might go on to become teachers, lawyers, or doctors, the purpose of their education was to train them for the military, so the correct choice is C.

8. **G** Spartan boys were expected to later be victorious in battle. Although they were taught to read and write, these skills were not emphasized. Students were disciplined strictly, and rejecting discipline was not allowed. Serving in the assembly was not the prime expectation. Therefore, G is the correct answer.

Short Response

9. Whereas the Spartans' lifestyle was centered almost exclusively on physical fitness and military training, the Athenian lifestyle included a diverse education, physical activity, discussions of politics and philosophy, and the exploration of new ideas.

10. Answers will vary but may mention the concepts of pluralism, diversity, prosperity, and innovation.

Extended Response

11. Essays should discuss topics such as education and mention activities that girls do today that they were not permitted to do in ancient Athens, such as go to school and go out unaccompanied by a male family member.

ONLINE RESOURCES

networks

There's More Online!

- INTERACTIVE WORKSHEETS
- BIOGRAPHIES
- CHARTS/GRAPHS
- GAMES
- GRAPHIC ORGANIZERS
- IMAGES
- MAPS
- PRIMARY SOURCES
- SLIDE SHOWS
- TIME LINE
- LECTURE SLIDES
- INTERACTIVE WHITEBOARD ACTIVITIES
- ASSESSMENTS
- VIDEOS

Ancient Greece: Farmers and Daily Life

Famous People, Incredible Lives: Alexander the Great

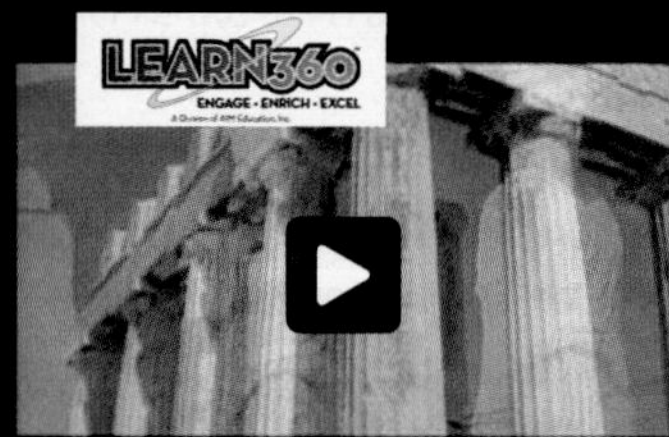

Alexander the Great's Empire

Chapter 8

Greek Civilization

Dear World History Teacher,

Ancient Greek civilization was the fountainhead of Western culture. Socrates, Plato, and Aristotle established the foundations of Western philosophy. Herodotus and Thucydides created the discipline of history. Our Western literary forms are derived from Greek poetry and drama. Greek notions of harmony and proportion have remained the standards for Western art and architecture. A rational method of inquiry was conceived in ancient Greece. During the Classical period, the Greeks debated fundamental questions, such as the purpose of human existence, that have concerned Western thinkers since.

Despite these achievements, an element of tragedy remains. The Greeks were unable to rise above rivalries that caused them to fight and undermine their own civilization.

Although the independent Greek city-states were conquered by the Macedonians, Greek culture did not die. Under Alexander the Great, Macedonians and Greeks invaded and conquered the Persian Empire. Greeks and non-Greeks came together during the time known as the Hellenistic Era. Greek culture survived, but in a new form, mixed with the local cultures conquered by Alexander.

Jackson J. Spielvogel

More Media Resources

Current Events Online

Visit McGraw-Hill's current events Web site for high-interest news stories and activities for your students. Access the site through the Student or Teacher Center in **networks.**

Reading List

Grade 6 reading level:
Everyday Life in the Ancient World, by Sally Tagholm, Julie Ferris, Jonathan Stroud, and Sue Nicholson

Grade 7 reading level:
Alexander the Great: The Legend of a Warrior King, by Peter Chrisp

Grade 8 reading level:
The Library of Alexandria, by Kelly Trumble

At the MOVIES

Watch clips of popular culture films about Ancient Greece, such as *Jason and the Argonauts* or *Barefoot in Athens*. Or view documentaries about the civilization, such as *The Greeks: Crucible of Civilization.*

Discuss: **Can fictional movies capture historical events accurately?**

NOTE: Be sure to preview any clips to ensure they are age-appropriate.

Search for more videos online in the **networks** Resource Library.

CHAPTER 8 Planner

UNDERSTANDING BY DESIGN®

Enduring Understandings

- *Cultures are held together by shared beliefs and common practices and values.*
- *People, places, and ideas change over time.* • *Leaders can bring about change in society.*

Essential Questions

- *What makes a culture unique?* • *How do new ideas change the way people live?*
- *What are the characteristics of a leader?*

Students will know:

- *how the ancient Greeks honored gods and goddesses*
- *the ideas that the ancient Greeks expressed in their literature, drama, art, and architecture*
- *ancient Greek beliefs about history and science*
- *how successful Alexander was in achieving his goals*
- *how Hellenistic kingdoms spread Greek culture*
- *ideas developed during the Hellenistic Era*

Students will be able to:

- **analyze** images of Greek gods and goddesses
- **organize** information about Greek gods and goddesses
- **write** a paragraph about a god or goddess
- **compare** ancient and modern Greek beliefs
- **describe** ancient Greek philosophy
- **explain** the philosophy of Socrates
- **discuss** the life of Socrates
- **compare and contrast** Socrates, Plato, and Aristotle
- **interpret** ancient Greek philosophical ideas
- **compare and contrast** the qualities of a great military leader and an effective ruler
- **categorize** Alexander's leadership qualities and military achievements
- **analyze** images of culture from the Hellenistic Era
- **explain** the meaning of *Hellenistic*
- **identify** contributions from the Hellenistic Era
- **write** a newspaper article describing an idea or a discovery from the Hellenistic Era
- **illustrate** an idea from the Hellenistic Era

Predictable Misunderstandings

Students may think:

- The Greeks and Greek culture remained in a remote area.
- There is little or no connection between the Greeks and life in the United States today.
- The Greeks excelled mostly in the arts and not in math and science.

Assessment Evidence

Performance Task

- Hands-On Chapter Project

Other Evidence

- Answers to class discussion comparing beliefs
- Discussion answers about ancient Greek thinkers
- Participation in small-group activity
- Newspaper article on idea of Hellenistic Era
- Economics of History Activity
- 21st Century Skills Activity
- Booklet on philosophical ideas
- Primary Source Activity
- Geography and History Activities
- Lesson Reviews
- Graphic organizer activities
- Interactive Whiteboard Activity responses

Pacing Guide

Introducing the Chapter		1 day
Lesson 1	Greek Culture	1 day
Lesson 2	The Greek Mind	1 day
	What Do You Think?	1 day
Lesson 3	Alexander's Empire	1 day
Lesson 4	Hellenistic Culture	1 day
Chapter Activities and Assessment		1 day
TOTAL TIME		**7 Days**

Differentiated Instruction

These lesson plans are written to address the needs of your On Level students. Discussion and activities that are well-suited to your Approaching Grade Level learners, Beyond Grade Level learners, as well as your English Language Learners, are coded as follows:

AL **Approaching Grade Level**

BL **Beyond Grade Level**

ELL **English Language Learner**

NCSS Standards covered in "Greek Civilization"

Learners will understand

1 CULTURE

1. "Culture" refers to the socially transmitted behaviors, beliefs, values, traditions, institutions, and ways of living together for a group of people

2. Concepts such as beliefs, values, institutions, cohesion, diversity, accommodation, adaptation, assimilation, and dissonance

3. How culture influences the ways in which human groups solve the problems of daily living

4. That the beliefs, values, and behaviors of a culture form an integrated system that helps shape the activities and ways of life that define a culture

8. That language, behaviors, and beliefs of different cultures can both contribute to and pose barriers to cross-cultural understanding

2 TIME, CONTINUITY, AND CHANGE

2. Concepts such as: chronology, causality, change, conflict, complexity, multiple perspectives, primary and secondary sources, and cause and effect

3. That learning about the past requires the interpretation of sources, and that using varied sources provides the potential for a more balanced interpretive record of the past

4. That historical interpretations of the same event may differ on the basis of such factors as conflicting evidence from varied sources, national or cultural perspectives, and the point of view of the researcher

5. Key historical periods and patterns of change within and across cultures (e.g., the rise and fall of ancient civilizations, the development of technology, the rise of modern nation-states, and the establishment and breakdown of colonial systems)

7. The contributions of key persons, groups, and events from the past and their influence on the present

CHAPTER 8

Introducing the Chapter

(Student Edition p. 209)

The Story Matters . . .

Read "The Story Matters . . ." aloud in class. Tell students that Alexander was tutored by the famous philosopher Aristotle.

Ask: How do you think Aristotle's influence affected Alexander? *(Answers will vary, but students may mention that Aristotle taught Alexander to be interested in many different fields of study. This teaching probably influenced Alexander to want to spread many different Greek ideas and aspects of Greek culture to the lands he conquered.)*

Tell students that Alexander was a commander in his father's armies by the time he was 16 years old.

Ask: How do you think childhood and the teenage years were different in the time of Alexander than they are now? *(Answers will vary, but students may mention that children had to grow up and take responsibility at a much younger age than they do now.)*

Tell the class that Alexander became king at a young age, after his father, Philip II, was killed. Alexander went on to fulfill his father's dream of conquering the Persian Empire and creating a new Hellenistic, or Greek-influenced, empire. Then, Alexander also died at a young age, but the impact of Greek culture lived on for a long time.

Even after the end of the Hellenistic Era, the Romans, who conquered Alexander's former empire, were strongly influenced by Greek culture. There are countless ways in which the influence of Alexander and Greek culture are still important today. An online search will show many connections between ancient Greece and our culture.

networks

There's More Online about the lives and customs of the ancient Greeks.

CHAPTER 8

Lesson 1 *Greek Culture*

Lesson 2 *The Greek Mind*

Lesson 3 *Alexander's Empire*

Lesson 4 *Hellenistic Culture*

The Story Matters . . .

Alexander became king of Macedonia when he was only 20 years old. Before his death at age 32, he built the largest empire the world had known. His strong will and personality enabled him to lead armies to victory. He is considered one of the greatest generals who ever lived.

Alexander's childhood tutor was the Greek philosopher Aristotle, who encouraged Alexander's interest in philosophy, medicine, and science. As an adult, Alexander spread Greek art, ideas, language, and architecture into all the lands he conquered. The impact of his rule lasted for centuries.

◄ *This marble bust of Alexander the Great, carved in 330 B.C., is in the Louvre, a famous museum located in Paris, France.*

Danita Delimont/Gallo Images/Getty Images

209

Introducing Place and Time

(Student Edition pp. 210–211)

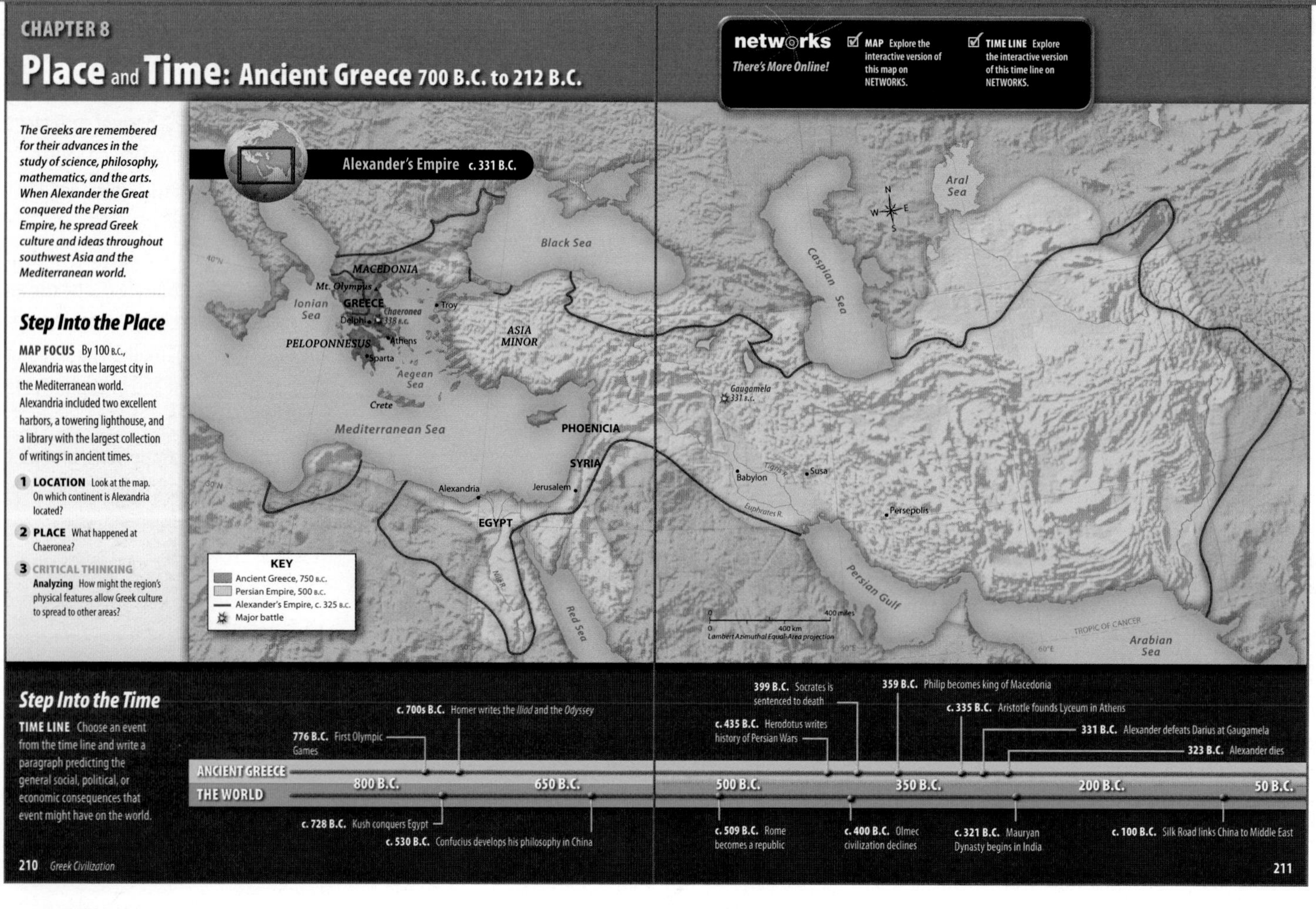

CHAPTER 8

Place and Time: Ancient Greece 700 B.C. to 212 B.C.

networks *There's More Online!*

☑ **MAP** Explore the interactive version of this map on NETWORKS.

☑ **TIME LINE** Explore the interactive version of this time line on NETWORKS.

The Greeks are remembered for their advances in the study of science, philosophy, mathematics, and the arts. When Alexander the Great conquered the Persian Empire, he spread Greek culture and ideas throughout southwest Asia and the Mediterranean world.

Step Into the Place

MAP FOCUS By 100 B.C., Alexandria was the largest city in the Mediterranean world. Alexandria included two excellent harbors, a towering lighthouse, and a library with the largest collection of writings in ancient times.

1. **LOCATION** Look at the map. On which continent is Alexandria located?
2. **PLACE** What happened at Chaeronea?
3. **CRITICAL THINKING** **Analyzing** How might the region's physical features allow Greek culture to spread to other areas?

Step Into the Time

TIME LINE Choose an event from the time line and write a paragraph predicting the general social, political, or economic consequences that event might have on the world.

ANCIENT GREECE

- **776 B.C.** First Olympic Games
- **c. 700s B.C.** Homer writes the *Iliad* and the *Odyssey*
- **c. 435 B.C.** Herodotus writes history of Persian Wars
- **399 B.C.** Socrates is sentenced to death
- **359 B.C.** Philip becomes king of Macedonia
- **c. 335 B.C.** Aristotle founds Lyceum in Athens
- **331 B.C.** Alexander defeats Darius at Gaugamela
- **323 B.C.** Alexander dies

800 B.C. — 650 B.C. — 500 B.C. — 350 B.C. — 200 B.C. — 50 B.C.

THE WORLD

- **c. 728 B.C.** Kush conquers Egypt
- **c. 530 B.C.** Confucius develops his philosophy in China
- **c. 509 B.C.** Rome becomes a republic
- **c. 400 B.C.** Olmec civilization declines
- **c. 321 B.C.** Mauryan Dynasty begins in India
- **c. 100 B.C.** Silk Road links China to Middle East

210 *Greek Civilization*

211

Technology Extension

- Find an additional activity online that incorporates technology for this project.
- Visit the EdTechTeacher Web sites (included in the Technology Extension for this chapter) for more links, tutorials, and other resources.

Assessing Background Knowledge

INTERACTIVE WORKSHEET

What Do You Know? Activity

Have students complete the What Do You Know? activity before they study the chapter. Tell students to read each statement and circle *T* or *F* to indicate whether they think the statement is true or false. Students' responses will give you a good idea of the kinds of misconceptions you can address when teaching the lessons.

After students have completed the chapter, have them revisit the activity and note answers they would change after having learned more about the topic. Ask students to share some of their previous misconceptions with the class.

INTERACTIVE WORKSHEET

Guided Reading Activities

There is a Guided Reading Activity for each lesson in this chapter. You may wish to assign the Guided Reading Activity for Lesson 1 after introducing the chapter content.

Hands-On Chapter Project

Students will create a model of a Greek-styled building to learn about Greek architecture.

- Students will participate in a classroom discussion about the ideas that the Greeks expressed in their architecture.
- Students will form small groups, with each group working on a certain type of building. Groups will use worksheets and discussion to guide their project plan and research.
- Next, each group will create a model of its chosen building.
- Then, students will present their models to the class.
- Finally, students will evaluate their research, presentation, and collaboration using an Assessment Rubric.

Visit **networks** online to see the full project and rubric.

ONLINE RESOURCES

networks

Assign these interactive worksheets and quizzes from your Teacher Lesson Center. All resources are print-ready.

It's ALL Online!

Chapter 8 Resources

- ☑ Chapter Summary
- ☑ Vocabulary Builder
- ☑ What Do You Know?
- ☑ Hands-On Chapter Project

Lesson 1 Resources

- ☑ Interactive Graphic Organizer
- ☑ Economics of History Activity
  Support for the Arts in Ancient Greece
- ☑ Guided Reading Activity
- ☑ Reading Essentials and Study Guide
- ☑ Online Self-Check Quiz

Lesson 2 Resources

- ☑ Interactive Graphic Organizer
- ☑ 21st Century Skills Activity
  Writing in Expository Style
- ☑ Guided Reading Activity
- ☑ Reading Essentials and Study Guide
- ☑ Online Self-Check Quiz

Lesson 3 Resources

- ☑ Interactive Graphic Organizer
- ☑ Geography and History Activity
  Understanding Movement: Greek Migration
- ☑ Primary Source Activity Alexander the Great: Hero or Villain?
- ☑ Guided Reading Activity
- ☑ Reading Essentials and Study Guide
- ☑ Online Self-Check Quiz

Lesson 4 Resources

- ☑ Interactive Graphic Organizer
- ☑ Geography and History Activity
  Understanding Movement: Hellenistic Cities
- ☑ Guided Reading Activity
- ☑ Reading Essentials and Study Guide
- ☑ Online Self-Check Quiz

Assessment Resources

- ☑ Lesson Reviews
- ☑ Online Self-Check Quizzes
- ☑ Chapter Activities and Assessment
- ☑ Standardized Test Practice

Remediation Resources

- ☑ Reading Essentials and Study Guide
- ☑ Guided Reading Activities
- ☑ Online Self-Check Quizzes
- ☑ Chapter Summary

Step Into the Place

INTERACTIVE WHITEBOARD ACTIVITY

Location Project the Chapter Opener map on the whiteboard. Invite volunteers to point out the locations of civilizations they have already studied. *(Mesopotamia, Egypt, Kush, and the area that is now modern-day Israel)* Point out that their locations helped these civilizations thrive.

Discuss how the locations of these civilizations gave them opportunities for trade and access to the spread of ideas but also made them vulnerable to attack.

Next, point out the mainland and islands of Greece. Explain that Greece's location helped it become a powerful civilization. As a class, discuss the Map Focus questions.

Step Into the Time

Making Inferences Call students' attention to the time line for this chapter. Explain that between about 800 B.C. and 200 B.C., Greece became a thriving kingdom.

Draw students' attention to the entries on the Ancient Greece time line that refer to Alexander the Great. Note that Alexander was born in 356 B.C. **Ask: How might Alexander's age have made his accomplishments seem more impressive?** *(Answers will vary, but students should note that Alexander was only 25 when he defeated Darius, and he conquered all the lands shown on the map by the time of his death at age 33.)*

Answers for pages 210–211

Step Into the Place

1. Africa
2. A major battle took place.
3. CRITICAL THINKING Bodies of water, such as the Mediterranean Sea, connected the seagoing Greeks with lands throughout the region.

Step Into the Time

Students should pick an event and make specific predictions regarding its consequences. They might tell how the event will affect the government or the relations between empires, or they might tell how the event will affect trade, commerce, or business.

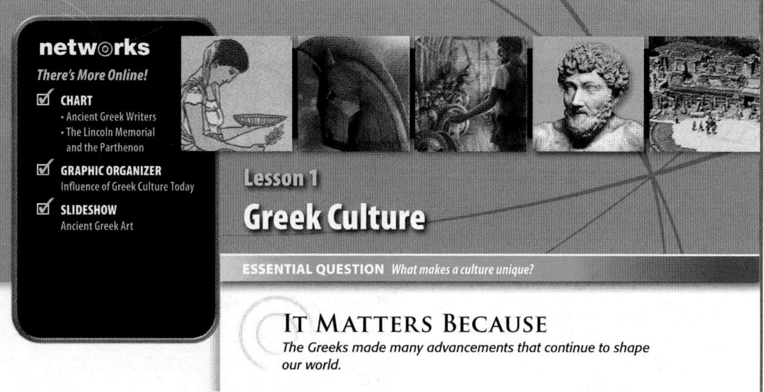

networks
There's More Online!
- **CHART**
  - Ancient Greek Writers
  - The Lincoln Memorial and the Parthenon
- **GRAPHIC ORGANIZER** Influence of Greek Culture Today
- **SLIDESHOW** Ancient Greek Art

Lesson 1

Greek Culture

ESSENTIAL QUESTION *What makes a culture unique?*

It Matters Because

The Greeks made many advancements that continue to shape our world.

1 Greek Beliefs

GUIDING QUESTION *How did the ancient Greeks honor their gods?*

You have learned that the ancient Greeks formed city-states. These are independent states made up of a city and the land that surrounds it. Although city-states separated Greece politically, the Greek people were united by a common culture. They spoke the Greek language. They shared many beliefs and customs. The Greek people also believed many of the same **myths**, or traditional stories about gods and heroes. Greek myths expressed the religious beliefs of the ancient Greeks.

Who Were the Greek Gods?

Like other people of the ancient world, the Greeks believed in gods and goddesses. The Greeks, however, did not think of their gods as all-powerful beings. In Greek myths, the gods have great powers, but they look and act like human beings. In Greek mythology, they marry and have children. At times, they act like children, playing tricks on each other. Because the gods showed human qualities, the Greek people did not fear them. Greeks believed that the 12 most important gods and goddesses lived on Mount Olympus (uh•LIHM•puhs), Greece's highest mountain.

Reading **HELP**DESK

Taking Notes: *Summarizing*
Use a diagram like this one to identify three ways Greek culture influences our world today.

Content Vocabulary
- **myth**
- **ritual**
- **oracle**
- **fable**
- **oral tradition**
- **drama**
- **tragedy**
- **comedy**

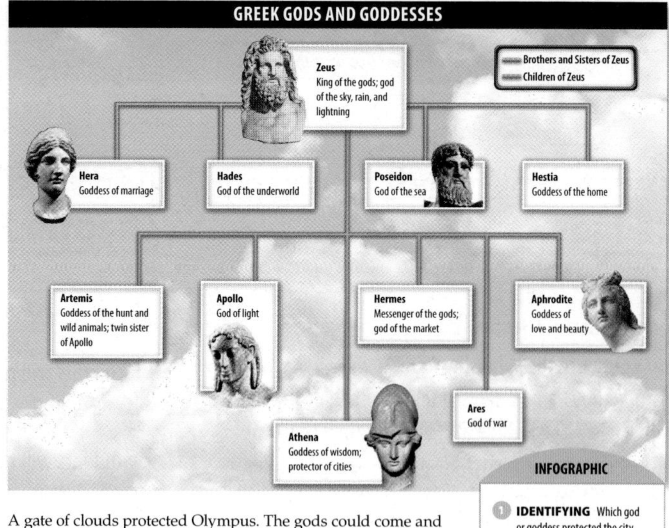

INFOGRAPHIC

1. **IDENTIFYING** Which god or goddess protected the city of Athens?
2. **CRITICAL THINKING** ***Analyzing*** How were Athena and Hera related?

A gate of clouds protected Olympus. The gods could come and go as they pleased, but humans were stopped from entering through the gate of clouds.

Zeus was the king of the Olympian gods, while Athena was the goddess of wisdom and crafts. Apollo was worshipped as the god of the sun and poetry. People looked up to Aphrodite, the goddess of love. Two fierce gods were Ares, the god of war, and Poseidon, the god of the seas and earthquakes.

All Greeks worshipped Zeus as their chief god. Each city-state also chose one god or goddess as its protector. To win the favor of their god, the people of the city-state performed rituals. A **ritual** (RIH•chuh•wuhl) is an action that is part of a religious ceremony. The people worshipped the god in temples and at home. They prayed and offered gifts to the god. Through these rituals, the Greeks hoped the god would reward them.

myth a traditional story that explains the practices or beliefs of a people, or something in the natural world

ritual words or actions that are part of a religious ceremony

Greeks visited oracles for predictions and advice about their futures.
CRITICAL THINKING
Analyzing Why do you think people sometimes misunderstood the oracles' predictions?

Festivals honoring the gods and goddesses were an important part of Greek life. Each city-state scheduled public feasts and sacrifices. Every four years, Greek athletes took part in athletic competitions. These games were "for the greater glory of Zeus." They were held at the city of Olympia and were called the Olympic Games. Beginning in 776 B.C., the ancient Olympic Games took place for more than 1,000 years. The first modern Olympics were held in 1896 in Athens.

The Greeks believed their gods would be pleased if people showed skill in the arts, in athletic games, or in thinking.

Greek Oracles

The Greeks believed that each person had a fate or destiny. Certain events were going to happen no matter what they did. They also believed in prophecy, or a prediction about the future. The Greeks believed that the gods gave prophecies to warn people about the future in time to change it.

To find out about the future, many Greeks visited an **oracle** (AWR•uh•kuhl). This was a sacred shrine where a priest or priestess spoke for a god. The most famous was the oracle at the Temple of Apollo at Delphi (DEHL•fy). The oracle chamber was deep inside the temple. The room had an opening in the floor where volcanic smoke hissed from a crack in the earth.

There a priestess sat on a stool and listened to questions. The priests translated her answers. State leaders or their messengers traveled to Delphi to ask advice from the Oracle of Apollo.

PROGRESS CHECK

Explaining Why did the ancient Greeks seek advice from oracles?

2 Epics and Fables

GUIDING QUESTION *Why were epics and fables important to the ancient Greeks?*

Greek poems and stories are some of the oldest literature in Western civilization. For hundreds of years, Europeans and Americans used ancient Greek works as models for writing their own literature. England's William Shakespeare is an example.

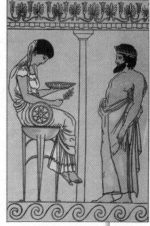

Reading **HELP**DESK

oracle a sacred shrine where a priest or priestess spoke for a god or goddess

Academic Vocabulary

construct to build

He borrowed Greek plots and settings for his many dramas. He also organized his plays similarly to the way Greek dramas were organized.

The first Greek stories were epics. Two great epics of ancient Greece were the *Iliad* and the *Odyssey*. The poet Homer (HOH•muhr) composed them during the 700s B.C. Homer based these epics on stories about a war between Greece and the city of Troy. Troy once existed in the area that is today northwestern Turkey.

The Trojan Horse

In the *Iliad*, a prince of Troy falls in love with Helen, the wife of a Greek king, and kidnaps her. The kidnapping angers the Greeks, who attack Troy in revenge. The Greeks, however, cannot break through the thick walls surrounding the city. In order to get into the city, the Greeks trick the Trojans and **construct** a huge, hollow wooden horse. The finest Greek soldiers hide inside the horse. All the other Greek soldiers board ships and sail away.

The Trojans think they have won the war and that the horse is a victory prize from the Greeks. The Trojans roll the giant horse into the city. That night, the Greeks creep out of the horse and open the city gates. They allow the rest of the Greek army, who have sailed back to Troy after dark, to enter the city. The Greeks then capture the city, rescue Helen, and take her home.

The *Odyssey* tells the story of Odysseus (oh•DYS•ee•uhs), a Greek hero of the Trojan War. It describes his long trip home after the fall of Troy. He faces storms, monsters, and witches along the way. Odysseus finally returns to his wife. According to the poem, it takes Odysseus 10 years to accomplish his arrival in Greece. Today, people use the word *odyssey*—a word taken from his name—to describe a long, exciting journey.

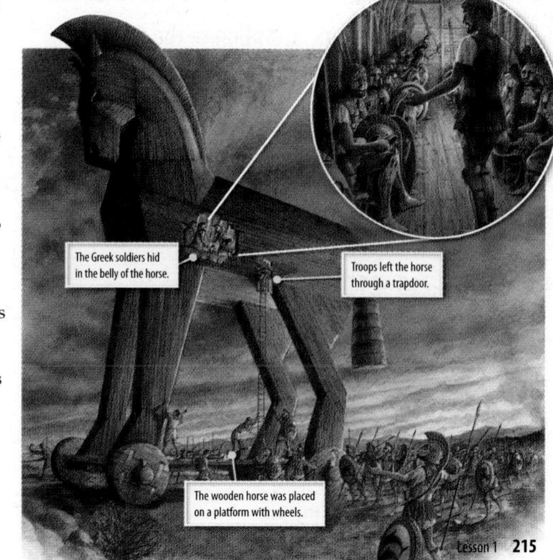

The epic the *Iliad* tells how the Greeks built the Trojan Horse as a way to get a small group of soldiers into Troy. The term "Trojan Horse" is still used today to mean a trick played on someone.

LESSON 1

ENGAGE

GAME **Defining** Have students work in pairs or small groups to play the game in which they match words from the lesson to their definitions. Give them time to complete the activity, and then supply the correct answers. Have students check their own work. AL ELL

INTERACTIVE WHITEBOARD ACTIVITY **Previewing** Ask students to preview the text by looking at the images of gods and goddesses in their textbook.

In a class discussion, have students share what they know about Greek gods and goddesses and briefly describe any myths they know about Greek deities.

Then have students match the gods and goddesses with their functions in the sorting Interactive Whiteboard Activity.

Ask: **Why do you think the Greeks had so many gods and goddesses?** *(Answers will vary but may include that the different gods and goddesses represented different parts of nature or aspects of human life.)* Then have them play the game in which they match gods' and goddesses' functions to their names and images. AL BL ELL

Tell students that they will be learning about the religious beliefs of the ancient Greeks and about their accomplishments in literature, drama, the arts, and architecture.

TEACH & ASSESS

1 Greek Beliefs

GUIDING QUESTION *How did the ancient Greeks honor their gods?*

GRAPHIC ORGANIZER **Making Connections** As a class, brainstorm a list of answers to this question: How are our lives today influenced by people or ideas from ancient Greece? Encourage students to think about many different aspects of life, including literature, the arts, science, and architecture.

To prompt students, **ask:** **How are public buildings, especially in our nation's capital, influenced by Greek architecture? What mathematical ideas discovered by the ancient Greeks are still important today? How are our stories influenced by tales of Greek heroes?**

Then have students work alone or in pairs to complete the Taking Notes interactive graphic organizer. Tell them that after they have finished studying the entire chapter, they will revisit the graphic organizer and see how much more they can add to it. AL

GAME **Hypothesizing** Have students complete the game of matching the gods' and goddesses' functions to their names and images. Point out that the ancient Greeks believed the gods and goddesses controlled nature.

Ask: **How do modern people explain nature?** *(Modern people explain nature by using science.)* **Why do you think the ancient Greeks believed gods and goddesses controlled nature?** *(Students should understand that modern scientific techniques for understanding the world had not yet been developed, so the Greeks based their beliefs on religion instead.)*

IMAGE **Making Connections** Show students the image about the Oracle of Delphi. Ask students to explain what a ritual is in their own words. Then have volunteers describe religious rituals in the United States, such as those in churches, mosques, synagogues, temples, or out in nature, such as sun dances.

Ask: **Why do people perform rituals?** *(Answers will vary but may include that people perform rituals to honor religious beliefs or to create a feeling of community among the members of a religion.)* ELL

Explaining Have students write a paragraph for homework about their favorite Greek god or goddess. Have them explain why that one is their favorite and include information they learned in the lesson.

At some point, have pairs of students exchange papers and read each other's paragraphs. Students can ask their partners questions about anything in the paragraph that is not clear. Ask volunteers to share their paragraphs with the class. BL

2 Epics and Fables

GUIDING QUESTION *Why were epics and fables important to the ancient Greeks?*

Making Connections Remind students that an epic is a long narrative poem that tells of a hero's great adventures. After discussing the epics of the *Iliad* and the *Odyssey*, ask students to think of movies, stories, or even video games that draw on the themes or elements of the Greek epics. *(Students' responses will vary, but students should understand that almost any story that involves a long journey toward home in part is derived from Homer's* Odyssey.*)*

PRIMARY SOURCE **Discussing** Ask students how many of them know the story of the boy who cried wolf. Explain that this story is one of Aesop's fables.

Assign the Primary Source activity for this lesson, "The Boy Who Cried Wolf." Have students take turns reading the fable out loud, paragraph by paragraph.

Ask: **What clues within the text tell you that this story is a fable?** *(None of the characters have names; the story has a moral.)*

Ask: **How are the characters in this fable different from those in many other fables?** *(The main characters in this fable are people, not animals.)* BL

Discussing After students have discussed epics and fables, ask them to consider the impact of both forms on the stories we tell today. Point out that many of our stories have morals, like fables, and many of our stories feature heroes doing great deeds, as in Greek epics.

3 The Impact of Greek Drama

GUIDING QUESTION *How did Greek dramas develop?*

CHART **Identifying** Give students the interactive chart on ancient Greek playwrights. Have them work alone or in pairs to complete the activity, matching the names of the four most important playwrights in ancient Greece with their themes and stories.

Remind students to skim their textbooks for information about the playwrights to help them complete the chart.

Answers for pages 212–215

P. 212 Taking Notes Answers will vary but may include the following: Aristotle's ideas influenced European and American governmental systems; *pi*, Pythagorean theorem; Hippocratic Oath; Socratic method; Greek classical architecture—columns; Olympic Games; Greek plays and writings served as models for more modern writers; term *Trojan horse* describes computer viruses; Aesop's fables used to teach morals

P. 213 INFOGRAPHIC

1. Athena was the protector of cities.
2. CRITICAL THINKING As the sister of Athena's father, Hera was Athena's aunt. Athena was Hera's niece.

P. 214 CRITICAL THINKING The oracles often gave their answers in the form of riddles, which were open to different interpretations.

P. 214 ☑ PROGRESS CHECK They believed oracles could speak for the gods, see into the future, and give wise advice.

Greeks believed the *Iliad* and the *Odyssey* were more than stories. They looked on the epics as real history. These poems gave the Greeks an ideal past with a cast of heroes. One Athenian wrote, "My father, in his pains to make me a good man, compelled me to learn the whole of Homer's poems."

Homer's stories taught courage and honor. They also taught that it was important to be loyal to your friends and to value the relationship between husband and wife. The stories showed heroes striving to be the best they could be. Heroes fought to protect their own honor and their family's honor. Homer's heroes became role models for Greek boys.

PRIMARY SOURCE

"O friends, be men; so act that none may feel
Ashamed to meet the eyes of other men.
Think each one of his children and his wife,
His home, his parents, living yet or dead."

— from *The Iliad* by Homer,

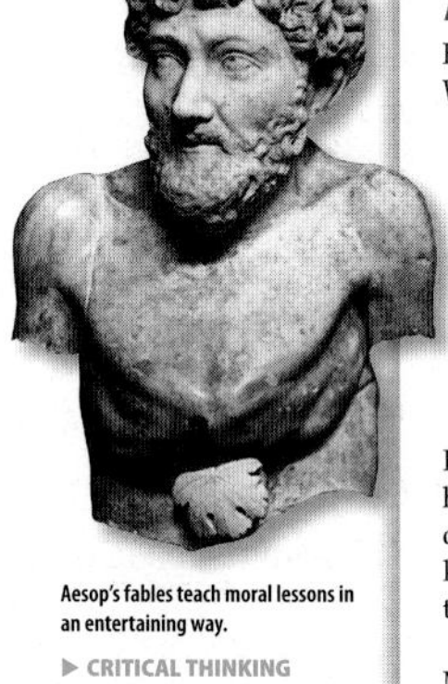

Aesop's fables teach moral lessons in an entertaining way.

▶ CRITICAL THINKING

Theorizing Why might Aesop have used animal characters to tell his fables?

Aesop's Fables

Have you heard the stories "The Fox and the Grapes" or "The Boy Who Cried Wolf"? These stories have traditionally been credited to a man named Aesop (EE•sahp). He is supposed to have lived and told his stories around 550 B.C. Historians now know that Aesop probably never existed. However, the stories he is supposed to have told certainly do exist. They are known as Aesop's fables. A **fable** (FAY•buhl) is a short tale that teaches a lesson. In most of Aesop's fables, animals speak and act like people. These stories are often funny and show human weaknesses and strengths. Each fable ends with a moral, or useful truth.

One of Aesop's popular fables is "The Hare and the Tortoise." In this fable, a slow-moving tortoise, or turtle, and a speedy hare, or rabbit, race each other. Soon, the hare is far ahead. Sure of victory, the hare stops to take a nap. Meanwhile, the tortoise keeps slowly moving. He passes the sleeping rabbit and wins the race.

The moral of the story is "slow and steady wins the race." Many phrases from Aesop's fables are still in use, including: "It is easy to dislike something you cannot have," and "Appearances can be deceiving."

Reading HELPDESK

fable a story meant to teach a lesson

oral tradition the custom of passing along stories by speech

Aesop's fables were told during the time that is known as the Golden Age of Greece. During this period, art, philosophy, architecture, and literature flourished.

For 200 years, Aesop's fables were a part of Greek **oral tradition**. This means that the stories were passed from generation to generation by word of mouth. It took many years before these tales were written down. Since then, Aesop's fables have been translated into many languages. They are still read by people around the world today.

☑ PROGRESS CHECK

Describing How do fables usually end?

Theaters in ancient Greece were often located outside. Plays took place in a level semicircle partially surrounded by stepped seating.

Today, most plays are performed in enclosed theaters like the one below. However, you can still attend plays at outdoor theaters in Greece and in other parts of the world.

▶ CRITICAL THINKING

Speculating Why do you think Greek plays were performed outside?

3 The Impact of Greek Drama

GUIDING QUESTION *How did Greek dramas develop?*

The ancient Greeks created and performed the first dramas (DRAH•muhs). A **drama** is a story told mainly through the words and actions of a cast of characters. A drama is performed by actors. In ancient Greece, they were performed on stage. Many of today's movies, plays, and television shows are dramas.

Think about your favorite movie. How would you describe it? Is it humorous? Is it a serious story? Greek drama can be divided into two categories: tragedy and comedy. In a **tragedy** (TRA•juh•dee), the main character struggles to overcome hardships but does not succeed. As a result, the story has a tragic, or unhappy, ending. The earliest Greek plays were tragedies. Later, the Greeks also wrote comedies. In a **comedy** (KAH•muh•dee), the story ends happily. Today, the word *comedy* means a story filled with humor.

During the fifth century B.C., four writers emerged as the greatest Greek dramatists, or writers: Aeschylus, Sophocles, Euripides, and Aristophanes. These four dramatists wrote their plays during the Golden Age of Greece, which was from about 500 to 350 B.C.

Aeschylus (EHS•kuh•luhs) was the earliest Greek dramatist. One of his dramas is a set of three plays called the *Oresteia* (ohr•eh•STY•uh). This drama tells about a Greek king's return from the Trojan War and the troubles that strike his family. The Oresteia is a story about revenge and murder. It shows how one evil action can lead to another. Although the play ends tragically, good triumphs over evil in the end.

drama a story written in the form of a play

tragedy a play or film in which characters fail to overcome serious problems

comedy a play or film that tells a humorous story

THE PARTHENON

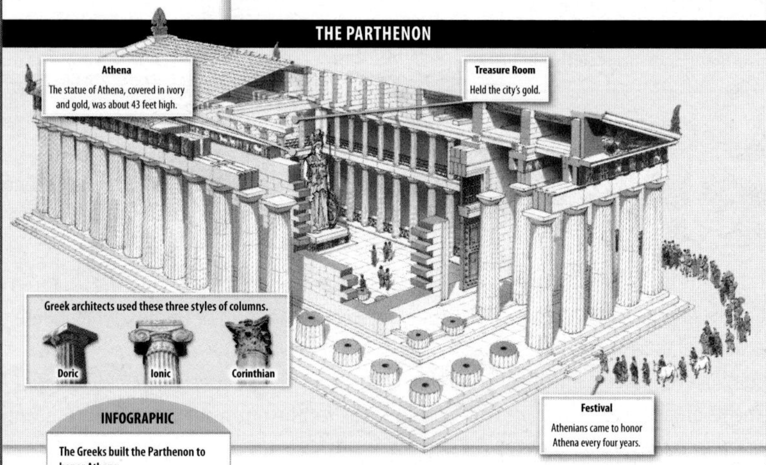

INFOGRAPHIC

The Greeks built the Parthenon to honor Athena.

1. **DESCRIBING** What features of the temple tell you that it was built by the Greeks?
2. CRITICAL THINKING ***Drawing Conclusions*** Why were temples the most important buildings in Greek city-states?

Sophocles (SAH•fuh•kleez) was a great Athenian writer. In his plays, Sophocles accepted suffering as a real part of life. He also stressed courage and understanding. In his play *Antigone* (an•TIH•guh•nee), Sophocles questions whether it is better to obey orders or to do what one believes to be right.

Another leading Greek dramatist was Euripides (yuh•RIH•puh•deez). Unlike Aeschylus and Sophocles, Euripides wrote about ordinary human beings in realistic situations. His plays often show the suffering caused by war.

In theaters today, the actors include men, women, and children. In ancient Greece, however, only men could be actors. Even female characters were played by male actors. The most famous writer of Greek comedies was Aristophanes (ar•uh•STAH•fuh•neez). His works poked fun at the leaders and issues of his day. He encouraged people to think and laugh. Many of Aristophanes' comedies included jokes, just as television comedy shows do today.

Reading HELPDESK

Academic Vocabulary

conflict a fight or disagreement

style a distinctive form or type of something

How Greek Drama Developed

Drama was more than entertainment for the people of ancient Greece. It was part of religious festivals and a way to show loyalty to their city-state.

In early Greek dramas, a group of performers, called the chorus, presented the story through singing and dancing. Later, dramas used several actors on stage. Then, stories were created using action and **conflicts** among the characters.

☑ PROGRESS CHECK

Determining Cause and Effect How did Greek drama influence how people are entertained today?

4 Greek Art and Architecture

GUIDING QUESTION *What ideas did the Greeks express in their art and architecture?*

The ancient Greeks excelled in the arts and architecture. They created works that expressed the ideals of reason, balance, and harmony. The characteristics of Greek art became the artistic **style** that we now call classical. Classical Greek art set standards of beauty that people still admire today.

The Greeks constructed beautiful buildings. Every Greek city-state had a temple dedicated to a god or goddess. Temples such as the Parthenon included a central room that housed statues of the gods. Large, graceful columns supported many Greek buildings. Some famous buildings in Washington, D.C., such as the White House and the Capitol, have Greek columns.

Sculpture decorated many Greek temples. The human body was the favorite subject of Greek artists. Greek sculptors tried to show ideal beauty in perfect human forms.

The design of the Lincoln Memorial in Washington, D.C., is similar to the Parthenon. Its 36 columns represent the number of states in the union at the time President Lincoln died.

☑ PROGRESS CHECK

Explaining How did the Greeks design their buildings?

LESSON 1 REVIEW

Review Vocabulary

1. How is a *fable* part of an *oral tradition*?

Answer the Guiding Questions

2. ***Explaining*** Why was Mount Olympus important to the Greeks?
3. ***Identifying*** What epic included the story of the Trojan horse?
4. ***Comparing*** What two types of drama did the Greeks create? How do they differ?
5. ***Inferring*** Why are some computer viruses called Trojan horses?
6. **EXPOSITORY WRITING** Compare Greek theater actors to modern theater actors. How are they alike and different? Write a paragraph or two that compares these types of actors.

LESSON 1 (cont.)

INTERACTIVE WORKSHEET

Economics of History Activity

Simulating Hand out the Economics of History Activity for this lesson. If time allows, ask student volunteers to read aloud paragraphs of the Background Information. Pause and ask students to summarize or paraphrase the information. Make sure students understand the concepts and specialized vocabulary introduced in the text. After reading, students should be able to identify the main idea of the passage—that the government and wealthy patrons supported the arts in order to glorify ancient Greek culture. AL ELL

Ask: **Who supported the arts in ancient Greece by providing funds?** *(The government and wealthy citizens were the main financial supporters of the arts.)*

Why might a Hellenistic king or a famous athlete want to have a large marble statue carved in his or her likeness? *(Answers may include the following: to show his or her greatness and importance, so his or her fame will live on even after death.)*

Have students complete the activity for homework.

Greek Art and Architecture

GUIDING QUESTION *What ideas did the Greeks express in their art and architecture?*

LECTURE SLIDE **Making Connections** Show students the lecture slide that discusses the characteristics of Greek art and architecture.

Ask: **What elements of Greek architecture do you see in modern buildings today?** *(Answers may include the following: columns, white marble fronts, geometric designs.)*

IMAGE Show students the image of the Lincoln Memorial and the Parthenon.

Ask: **How are public buildings, especially in our nation's capital, influenced by Greek architecture?** *(Students should note that many public buildings use elements of Greek architecture such as columns.)*

SLIDE SHOW Have students look at the illustrations of Greek art in the text, and then show them the images of ancient Greek art in the interactive slide show for this lesson.

Ask: **What values and ideals did ancient Greek art express?** *(The art of ancient Greece expressed their ideas and values of beauty, harmony, and moderation.)*

Have students complete the Lesson 1 Review questions.

BACKGROUND KNOWLEDGE

The Parthenon

The Parthenon was built on the Acropolis, the fortified center of Athens. It was a holy site. Many other temples were built there, including the Erechtheum—a small temple dedicated to Athena and Poseidon; the Temple of Athena Nike—dedicated to the goddess of victory; and the Sanctuary of Zeus—where burnt offerings were made to the chief god. The Parthenon stood as the grandest of all temples on the hill. It was built to honor the goddess Athena with money collected from Athens's empire. High walls surrounding the rocky hill protected the temples there. The Athenians would flee to the Acropolis for shelter during times of war.

The Temple of Delphi

The ancient Greeks considered the site of the Temple of Delphi to be the center of the world. Legend said that Zeus, the king of the gods, released two eagles. One flew from the east, and the other flew from the west. They met at Delphi, on the slopes of Mount Parnassus, indicating the location's importance. A stone marking the spot where the eagles met was called the *omphalos*, or navel. The influential oracle of Apollo was known all over the Greek world. People around the ancient world consulted the oracle, a woman over the age of 50, about matters of political, military, and even personal importance.

CLOSE & REFLECT

Comparing To close, have a class discussion comparing our beliefs today to the beliefs of ancient Greeks. Base the discussion on the Essential Question: What makes a culture unique?

Guide students to see the ways in which the religious beliefs in ancient Greece affected people's lives.

For example, the ancient Greeks believed they had personal relationships with gods that possessed supernatural powers yet were very human-like; they had no fear of their gods and goddesses; they believed in prophecy and consulted oracles; they were inspired by and modeled their lives on stories of gods and heroes. BL ELL

Answers for pages 216–219

P. 216 CRITICAL THINKING Using animals was a nonthreatening way to get the message across without forcing listeners to see themselves in the story.

P. 217 CRITICAL THINKING Outside areas could hold the most people.

P. 217 ☑ PROGRESS CHECK Many fables end with a moral, or useful truth.

P. 218 INFOGRAPHIC

1. The large, graceful columns indicate that the structure was built by ancient Greeks.
2. CRITICAL THINKING They were important because they were the places where ancient Greeks worshiped.

P. 219 ☑ PROGRESS CHECK The two types of Greek drama—comedy and tragedy—are still the basis for most modern entertainment. Modern plays, movies, and television shows almost always have elements of comedy or tragedy, or both.

P. 219 ☑ PROGRESS CHECK They used a mathematical formula that helped them design buildings with attractive proportions.

LESSON 1 REVIEW

1. A fable is a short story that teaches a lesson. A fable is an example of the oral tradition because it can be passed down from generation to generation by word of mouth, as was the case for Aesop's fables.
2. The ancient Greeks considered Mount Olympus the home of their 12 most important gods and goddesses.
3. The *Iliad* includes the story of the Trojan Horse.
4. The ancient Greeks created tragedy and comedy. In a tragedy, a person tries but fails to overcome hardships; the story has a tragic, or sad, ending. In contrast, a comedy is a story with funny parts, and it ends happily.
5. Trojan horse viruses are put into a computer in a sneaky way in order to cause harm. This process is similar to the way the original Trojan horse was put in Troy in a deceitful way in order to destroy the city.
6. Students should suggest that modern and ancient Greek actors are similar in that they act out stories on the stage. They are different in that ancient Greek actors usually told stories through speeches or singing and dancing. Modern actors usually tell stories through realistic actions and exchanging words with other actors. Another difference is that ancient Greek actors were always men. Modern actors can be men, women, or children.

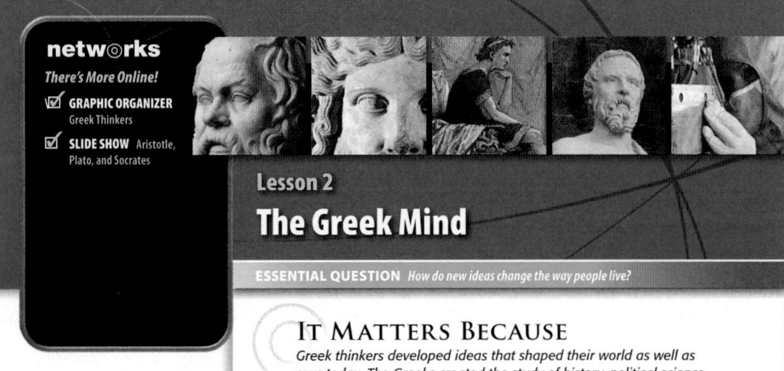

networks
There's More Online!
GRAPHIC ORGANIZER Greek Thinkers
SLIDE SHOW Aristotle, Plato, and Socrates

Lesson 2

The Greek Mind

ESSENTIAL QUESTION *How do new ideas change the way people live?*

It Matters Because

Greek thinkers developed ideas that shaped their world as well as ours today. The Greeks created the study of history, political science, biology, and logic.

1 Greek Thinkers

GUIDING QUESTION *What ideas did the Greeks develop to explain the world around them?*

The Greeks believed the human mind was capable of great understanding. During the Golden Age of Greece, from approximately 500 B.C. to 350 B.C., art, architecture, and literature all flourished. This was also a very fertile time for the life of the mind. Most of the thinkers discussed in this chapter were part of that exciting time. They were pondering deep questions about truth and also developing the study of science and mathematics. Greek thinkers produced some of the most remarkable ideas the world has ever known.

One type of thinker was involved in creating a new body of knowledge. These thinkers were known as philosophers. The body of knowledge they created is called philosophy (fih•LAH•suh•fee). Philosophy is a Greek word that means "love of wisdom." Through philosophy, Greek philosophers helped develop the study of many subjects, including history, political science, biology, and logic, or the study of reasoning.

Reading **HELP**DESK

Taking Notes: ***Identifying***

Use a diagram like the one here to list the Greek thinkers you read about in this lesson. With each name you list, write down one thing the person is known for.

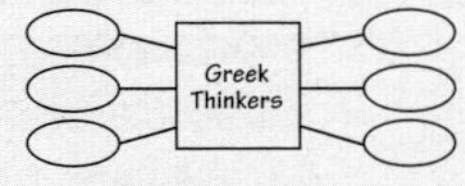

Content Vocabulary
- **Sophists**
- **rhetoric**
- **Socratic method**
- **Hippocratic Oath**

The Sophists

Many Greek philosophers were teachers. A group of philosophers known as the **Sophists** (SAH•fihsts) traveled from polis to polis. They made a living by teaching. The Sophists taught many subjects, including mathematics, science, and history. However, they were best known for teaching **rhetoric**, or the art of public speaking and debate.

Sophists did not believe that the gods influenced human actions. They also **rejected** the idea of absolute right or wrong. For the Sophists, a way of life that was right for one person might be wrong for another.

The Sophists not only challenged Greek traditions, but they also accepted money for their teaching. Other Greek philosophers did not approve of this practice. Many Greeks also thought that the Sophists lacked ideals and values. Critics claimed the Sophists taught students to win arguments rather than seek truths.

Who Was Socrates?

Although a sculptor by training, Socrates (SAH•kruh•teez) loved philosophy. He lived in Athens and spent most of his time teaching. Socrates did not leave a written record of his beliefs. Information about him is found in his students' writings. These writings **reveal** that Socrates was a harsh critic of the Sophists.

Unlike the Sophists, Socrates believed in absolute truth and that all real knowledge was within each person. In his search for truth, Socrates created a new way of questioning called the **Socratic** (suh•KRA•tihk) **method**. Today, many university professors use the Socratic Method when they teach. Socrates did not lecture. Instead, he asked pointed questions and waited for his students to respond. He wanted students to find the answers for themselves and form their own opinions.

Some Athenian leaders believed that the Socratic method was dangerous. At one time, Athens had allowed its people to speak freely. They could publicly question their leaders. However, when Athens lost the Peloponnesian War, its new rulers limited this freedom. The Athenians no longer trusted open debate. This method of discussion, however, was exactly what Socrates thought was necessary. He continued to teach his students.

Socrates believed that obeying the law was more important than his own life. Rather than leave Athens, he accepted a sentence of death.

rhetoric the art of public speaking and debate
Sophists Greek teachers of philosophy, reasoning, and public speaking
Socratic method philosophical method of questioning to gain truth

Academic Vocabulary
reject to refuse to accept or consider
reveal to make information public; to tell a secret

BIOGRAPHY

Plato (c. 428–347 B.C.)

Plato had planned a career in government. However, he was horrified by the death of his teacher, Socrates. As a result, Plato left politics and spent many years traveling and writing. When Plato returned to Athens in 387 B.C., he started the Academy, which was a school where students learned using Socrates' method of questioning. His academy attracted young people from Athens and other Greek city-states. He believed that by training the mind, people could discover truth. Plato's teachings and writings would influence the Western world for centuries.

▶ **CRITICAL THINKING**
Speculating Why do you think Plato felt he could not have a career in government?

In 399 B.C., city leaders—fearing his influence— arrested Socrates. They charged that he had urged young people to rebel against the government. A jury found Socrates guilty and sentenced him to death.

Following the verdict of the court, Socrates was given the opportunity to leave Athens and live. Instead, he stayed. Surrounded by his students and friends, Socrates gave his last speech.

He said that he was living under the city's laws. As a result, he stated, he was committed to obeying them. Socrates then drank poison to carry out the jury's sentence, and died.

Plato's Ideas

The two Greek philosophers you may have heard of are Plato and Aristotle. The philosopher Plato (PLAY•toh) was one of Socrates' students. Plato became a teacher and founded a school in Athens called the Academy. Unlike Socrates, Plato recorded his ideas in writing. One work Plato wrote was *The Republic*. It presented his plan for an ideal society and government.

In *The Republic*, Plato organized society into three groups. At the top were philosopher kings. They ruled through logic and wisdom. Warriors, the second group, defended society from attack, using force. The third group included the rest of the people. Their role was to produce society's food, clothing, and shelter. They lacked the wisdom of the kings and the courage of the warriors.

Plato believed that an ideal society must have a just and reasonable government. In *The Republic*, Plato noted his dislike of Athenian democracy. He wrote that the common people did not think for themselves and that they could be easily influenced into making foolish decisions. Plato believed that "philosopher kings" were intelligent and well-educated. He felt these kings would place the needs of the community ahead of their own needs. Plato wanted only these philosopher kings to govern the citizens of Greece.

Despite his distrust of the common people, Plato was willing to grant more rights to women. He believed that women should have the same opportunities for education and jobs that men have.

Reading **HELP**DESK

Academic Vocabulary
despite in spite of, regardless of

Before starting his own school, the Lyceum, Aristotle taught at Plato's Academy. Here he tutors a young man who soon would be called Alexander the Great.

Who Was Aristotle?

Another great thinker of ancient Greece was Aristotle (AR•uh•stah•tuhl). He wrote more than 200 works on topics such as government, astronomy, and political science. In 335 B.C., Aristotle started a school called the Lyceum. At this school, he taught his students the "golden mean." The mean is the middle position between two extremes. The idea of the golden mean is that people should live moderately. For example, **individuals** should not eat too little or too much. Instead, they should eat just enough to stay well.

Aristotle had many interests, including science. He studied the stars, plants, and animals and carefully recorded what he observed. Aristotle classified living things according to their similarities and differences. Aristotle's methods were an important step in the development of modern science.

Like Plato, Aristotle also wrote about government. He studied and compared the governments of different city-states and hoped to find the best political system. In his book *Politics*, Aristotle divided governments into three types.

Academic Vocabulary
individuals human beings, persons

LESSON 2

ENGAGE

Previewing Have students read "It Matters Because" in their textbooks and look at the illustrations, captions, and headings in the lesson.

Explain that ancient Greece was remarkable for how many new fields of study were explored then. Challenge students to make a list of the fields of study, based on their preview of the lesson.

Write their answers on the whiteboard. *(Answers should include philosophy, history, and science.)*

Make sure students understand that many of the subjects taught in schools today, except for technological ones, were first developed and studied in ancient Greece.

Ask students what they know about Greek thinkers, or philosophers. Remind them that they might have learned about these philosophers in other classes, such as science or math class.

Have students share their information with the class. *(Some students might know something about the Socratic method, Plato, Aristotle, the Pythagorean theorem, or the Hippocratic Oath.)* AL ELL

Tell students that in this lesson they will study the first philosophers and scientists in the world.

TEACH & ASSESS

1 Greek Thinkers

GUIDING QUESTION ***What ideas did the Greeks develop to explain the world around them?***

GRAPHIC ORGANIZER **Identifying** Tell students to write in the Taking Notes graphic organizer the names of any Greek thinkers they know and the accomplishment(s) that made the person famous. Students may draw on the discussion from the Engage section of the lesson. Have students continue to fill in the graphic organizer as they read the lesson.

Ask:

If you could spend a day with one of the thinkers you learned about here, which one would you choose? Explain why. *(Students' responses should state a definite choice, and the reasons for their choices should include details from the text about the thinker they chose.)*

SLIDE SHOW **Sequencing** Have students review the section "Greek Thinkers," and then show them the slide show of Socrates, Plato, and Aristotle. Have students identify the order in which these three philosophers lived and who taught whom. *(Socrates was the oldest, and he taught Plato. Plato was the next one, and he taught Aristotle. Aristotle was the last of the three.)* BL

Point out that the relationship among the three thinkers is important. Because Socrates taught Plato, and Plato taught Aristotle, each thinker used the previous one as a foundation for his ideas.

Students should also understand that without Plato and his writings, we would have no firsthand account of Socrates's life and ideas. AL ELL

PRIMARY SOURCE **Analyzing** Show students the excerpt from Plato's *Republic*. Ask volunteers to read the parts of the dialogue aloud for the class. Make sure students understand the ideas expressed in the dialogue. If necessary, ask students to work with partners to paraphrase the dialogue. AL ELL

INTERACTIVE WORKSHEET

21st Century Skills Activity

Making Connections Read aloud the passage in the Student Edition that explains Aristotle's beliefs about the three types of government. ELL

Make sure students have a clear understanding of the terms *monarchy*, *oligarchy*, and *democracy* and can explain the terms in their own words. Then as a class, complete the 21st Century Activity on how Aristotle's ideas influenced the founders of the United States.

Have students write their short essays for the worksheet. Remind students that a strong expository essay has a clearly stated main idea that is supported by several key pieces of evidence. Students should draw directly from Aristotle's ideas in their papers. During revision, allow students to work in pairs or small groups and give each other feedback on the clarity of their ideas, evidence, and expression. BL

LECTURE SLIDE **Discussing** Explain to students that today philosophers do not generally become so famous that their names are known to the average person. The great thinkers who are likely to be famous are usually people who have made advances in technology or science.

Show students the lecture slide about the great Greek thinkers. Then have students make connections with modern thinkers.

Ask:

Who are some of the great thinkers of the past 75 years? What are they known for? *(Answers may include Albert Einstein, theory of relativity; Rachel Carson, key figure in creating global environmental movement; Francis Crick and James Watson, discovered structure of DNA molecule; Jane Goodall, discovered tool-making abilities in chimpanzees; Stephen Hawking, physics and astronomy, new information about black holes in space; Stephanie Kwolek, invented Kevlar, used in bullet-proof vests; Hannah Arendt, German-born American philosopher; Steve Jobs and Bill Gates, advances in computer technology)*

Finally, ask students to summarize the importance of ancient Greece's thinkers. Students should be able to identify Socrates, Plato, and Aristotle and explain their key contributions to philosophy.

2 New History and Science Ideas

GUIDING QUESTION ***What did the Greeks believe about history and science?***

PRIMARY SOURCE **Comparing and Contrasting** Show students the image of papyrus with writing by Herodotus. Ask a volunteer to read aloud the excerpt. If necessary, have the volunteer pause after each sentence or two to allow listening students to absorb and understand Herodotus's ideas. ELL

As a class, paraphrase Herodotus's words. Allow students time to answer the discussion question about Herodotus's purpose for writing history. Students should understand from reading and listening to the excerpt that Herodotus was interested in recording specific details of events that had an impact on history.

Answers for pages 220–223

P. 220 Taking Notes Students may suggest any six of the following thinkers and facts about them: Socrates, Socratic method; Plato, ideal government; Aristotle, golden mean, classified living things; Herodotus, historian, father of history, wrote history of Persian wars; Thucydides, historian, did careful research, wrote History of the Peloponnesian Wars; Thales, first scientist, studied astronomy and math; Pythagoras, Pythagorean theorem; Hippocrates, Hippocratic Oath, developed cures for diseases.

P. 222 CRITICAL THINKING Plato did not want to participate in a government that put his teacher, Socrates, to death.

GREEK PHILOSOPHERS

Thinker Or Group	Sophists	Socrates	Plato	Aristotle
Main Idea	Sophists like Libanius (above) thought that people should use knowledge to improve themselves. They believed that there is no absolute right or wrong.	Socrates was a critic of the Sophists. He believed that there was an absolute truth.	Plato rejected the idea of democracy as a form of government. He believed that philosopher-kings should rule society.	Aristotle taught the idea of the "golden mean." He believed observation and comparison were necessary to gain knowledge.
Important Contribution	They developed the art of public speaking and debate.	He created the Socratic method of teaching.	He described his vision of the ideal government in his work the *Republic*.	He wrote over 200 books on philosophy and science. He divided all governments into three basic types.
Influence on Today	The importance of public speaking can be seen in political debates between candidates.	His methods influenced the way teachers interact with their students.	He introduced the idea that government should be fair and just.	His political ideas still shape political ideas today.

INFOGRAPHIC

The influence of Greek thinkers is felt today in education and politics.

1. **IDENTIFYING** What did the Sophists believe?
2. **CRITICAL THINKING** ***Analyzing*** Would Plato approve or disapprove of the American system of government? Why?

The first was monarchy, or rule by one person. The second was oligarchy (OHL•uh•gahr•kee), which is rule by a few people. The third type was democracy, or rule by many.

Aristotle believed the best government had features of all three. A chief executive would serve as head of state. A council or legislature would assist this leader and be supported by the people.

Aristotle's ideas influenced the way Europeans and Americans thought about government. The authors of the United States Constitution, like Aristotle, believed that no one person or group should have too much power.

PROGRESS CHECK

Explaining Why did Plato dislike Athenian democracy?

Reading HELPDESK

Academic Vocabulary

investigate to observe or study by examining closely and questioning systematically

2 New History and Science Ideas

GUIDING QUESTION *What did the Greeks believe about history and science?*

The Greeks used their thinking skills to write history. They also **investigated** the natural world. They developed new ways of studying science and history.

The Greeks and History

In many ways, the ancient Greeks were like most people living at that time. They believed that legends and myths were true. People did not analyze events in order to explain the past. Then, in 435 B.C., the Greek thinker Herodotus (hih•RAH•duh•tuhs) wrote a history of the Persian Wars. Herodotus wrote that the gods played a role in historical events. However, he made a great effort to separate fact from fiction. Like a news reporter, he questioned many people to get information, but then he investigated the truthfulness of these sources. Because of Herodotus's careful research, many European and American historians consider him "the father of history."

Another famous historian of ancient Greece was Thucydides (thoo•SIH•duh•deez). He was a general in the Peloponnesian War. The two great Greek city-states of Athens and Sparta fought in this conflict, which lasted nearly 30 years. Thucydides considered this war to be a major event in world history. After the war, he wrote *The History of the Peloponnesian War.*

Unlike Herodotus, Thucydides rejected the idea that the gods affected human history. Thucydides believed that only people made history. In his writing, Thucydides tried hard to be accurate and impartial. Thucydides acted like a modern roving reporter. He visited battle sites, and he also carefully examined documents. In addition, he accepted only actual eyewitness reports of events.

Herodotus was careful about any information he recorded. He wanted to be sure of the accuracy of what he wrote.

Thales was one of the first scientists to explain the physical world using examples from nature. He is pictured here with some of the tools he used to develop his theories.

Thucydides did not just state the facts. He also explored the causes and effects of events. He believed that future generations could learn from the past. Moreover, as a historian, he wanted to leave behind ideas and commentary so that others could learn.

For example, in *The History of the Peloponnesian War,* Thucydides wrote of a warning to Sparta:

PRIMARY SOURCE

> ❝ And yet, [Sparta], you still delay. You fail to see that peace stays longest with those who . . . show their determination not to submit to injustice. . . . Your habits are old-fashioned as compared with [those of Athens]. It is the law as in art, so in politics, that improvements [will win out]. . . . Athens has [made greater progress] than you on the path of innovation. ❞
>
> —from *The History of the Peloponnesian War,* by Thucydides, c. 431 B.C.

The First Scientists

The ancient Greeks developed many scientific ideas. These ideas have influenced scientific thinking for centuries. In ancient times, most people thought that their gods controlled nature. Early Greek scientists had a different idea. They thought that natural events could be explained logically and that people could discover the causes of these events by using reason.

The first important Greek scientist was Thales (THAY•leez) of Miletus. Born in the mid-600s B.C., Thales studied astronomy and mathematics. He did not have telescopes and other instruments that scientists use today. Thales made discoveries and developed theories by observing and thinking.

Another Greek scientist, Pythagoras (puh•THA•guh•ruhs), taught his pupils that the universe followed the same laws that governed music and numbers. He believed that all relationships could be expressed in numbers. As a result, he developed many new ideas about mathematics. Most people know his name because of the Pythagorean Theorem that is still used in geometry today. It is a way to determine the length of the sides of a triangle.

Reading HELPDESK

Hippocratic Oath a set of promises about patient care that new doctors make when they start practicing medicine

Today's scientist have the use of many tools that were not available to Thales and other ancient Greeks.

CRITICAL THINKING

Analyzing What might Thales have discovered about water if he had been able to use a modern microscope?

Ancient Greek Medicine

Greek scientists also studied medicine, or the science of treating diseases. Hippocrates (hih•PAH•kruh•TEEZ) was a physician in ancient Greece who is regarded as the "father of medicine." He believed diseases came from natural causes. Most people at that time thought evil spirits caused diseases. Hippocrates traveled all over Greece to help the sick. He used his new ideas to diagnose different illnesses. He also discovered his own treatments to help cure sick people.

Hippocrates created a list of rules about how doctors should use their skills to help patients. His rules are listed in the **Hippocratic Oath** (HIH•puh•KRAT•ihk). The oath says that doctors should do their best to help the patient. It also says that they should protect the patient's privacy. Today, doctors around the world still promise to honor the Hippocratic Oath.

PROGRESS CHECK

Explaining Why is Herodotus called "the father of history"?

LESSON 2 REVIEW

Review Vocabulary

1. How would someone use *rhetoric* in everyday life?

Answer the Guiding Questions

2. ***Comparing and Contrasting*** What was one important similarity between Plato and Aristotle? What was one major difference?
3. ***Describing*** What is the Hippocratic Oath?
4. ***Explaining*** Who are the three most important and famous philosophers from ancient Greece? Explain the teacher-student relationships among the three of them. What do all three have in common?
5. **PERSUASIVE WRITING** Think about the people you read about in this lesson. Whose ideas are still important to us today? Why? Express your opinion in a one-page paper.

LESSON 2 (cont.)

IMAGE **Comparing and Contrasting** Then show students the image of the statue of Thucydides. Ask a volunteer to read aloud the text. If necessary, explain what an eyewitness account is and how it is different from other types of recorded history. ELL

Ask:

How were the approaches to the history of Herodotus and Thucydides similar, and how were they different? *(They both questioned many people to find out the truth of what happened; they both investigated the truthfulness of their sources; they both believed people could learn about the present by studying the past. Herodotus believed the gods affected human history, but Thucydides rejected that idea. Thucydides believed that people made their own history. Thucydides also visited places where events had occurred, examined documents, and accepted only eyewitness accounts.)* BL

IMAGE **Identifying** Show students the image that contains information about Thales. If time allows, ask a volunteer to read aloud the information. Invite a student who is knowledgeable about mathematics or geometry to explain Thales's diagram of a triangle inside a circle.

Ask:

What is a hypothesis? *(an educated guess)*

What is the scientific method? *(It is a way of using logic and educated guesses to explain things in the natural world.)*

What was new about the way Greek scientists thought? *(They did not believe that everything in nature was caused by the gods. They thought natural events could be explained logically.)* BL

INTERACTIVE WHITEBOARD ACTIVITY **Identifying** Have students complete the Interactive Whiteboard Activity, matching facts about ancient Greek scientists to their names. If necessary, remind students to scan their textbooks for information that will help them complete the Interactive Whiteboard Activity.

Ask:

Why is Hippocrates known as the father of medicine? *(He was the first doctor to believe that diseases came from natural causes rather than from evil spirits.)*

Have students complete the Lesson 2 Review as homework.

CLOSE & REFLECT

Explaining Have each student make a booklet about the three ideas he or she likes best from Socrates, Plato, and Aristotle. In their booklets, students should explain the ideas and discuss how the ideas apply to their own lives. AL BL ELL

IF YOU HAVE MORE TIME . . .

Practice Making Generalizations About Greek Democracy

Remind students that a generalization is a statement that links together or summarizes certain facts. To form a generalization about democracy during the time of the ancient Greeks, first have students brainstorm a list of facts about it.

Write students' facts on the board, and ask students to identify and eliminate any opinions. Then have them form a valid generalization about the topic. Write it and leave it on the whiteboard for the duration of the lesson.

Examine Greek Thinkers and Historians

Evaluating Have students consider the advancements made by Greek thinkers and identify which one they consider to be the most important.

Once they have identified the most significant advancement, they should defend their evaluation by writing down at least two or three reasons it is most important.

Have volunteers share their responses with the class.

Debate The Greek historian Thucydides considered an understanding of one's place in history important to one's life. Have students arrange an informal debate about the idea. Students should form sides and present arguments about the role of history in modern life.

GAME **Identifying** Have students read each statement in the game about ancient Greek philosophers and historians. As they read each statement, they should decide whether it is true or false.

Ask students what was similar about all the philosophers, historians, and scientists in this lesson. *(They were changing the world by thinking in a new way and believing it was possible to use logic to understand the world around them.)*

Answers for pages 224–227

P. 224 ☑ PROGRESS CHECK Plato believed that the common people were too easily persuaded to make poor decisions. He believed that only the "philosopher-kings," the best-educated citizens, would place the people's best interests above personal goals.

P. 224 INFOGRAPHIC

1. Sophists believed people should use knowledge to improve themselves and that there is no absolute right or wrong.
2. CRITICAL THINKING He would disapprove because he rejected democracy in favor of rule by philosopher-kings.

P. 227 CRITICAL THINKING Answers will vary but should include the idea that he probably would have discovered that water contains living organisms.

P. 227 ☑ PROGRESS CHECK Herodotus is considered the "father of history" because he was the first historian to distinguish fact from fiction. He questioned many people to get his information, and he investigated the truthfulness of his sources.

LESSON 2 REVIEW

1. A person could use rhetoric when giving presentations in class, in debates, or when participating in various club or volunteer activities.
2. Similarity: Plato and Aristotle were interested in government. Difference: Plato didn't believe in democracy; he believed in rule by philosopher-kings; Aristotle believed the best government has elements of monarchy, oligarchy, and democracy.
3. The oath gives a code of ethics and behavior that physicians agree to uphold in their professional lives.
4. The three most important and famous philosophers in ancient Greece were Socrates, Plato, and Aristotle. Socrates was the teacher of Plato. Plato was the teacher of Aristotle. Answers may vary regarding what those three have in common, but students may say they all used the Socratic method, they all sought to find the truth about life and the world, and they all enjoyed teaching their ideas.
5. Answers will vary but may include Socrates, Plato, Aristotle, Herodotus, Thucydides, Thales, Pythagoras, and Hippocrates. Students should note at least one key idea the thinker is known for and explain why they think that contribution is important or valuable.

What Do You Think?

Did Socrates Commit Treason?

After Athens lost the Peloponnesian War, there was a period of political disorder in the city-state. Athenian leaders restricted free speech to help keep peace and order in Athens.

Socrates was critical of the decision to limit free speech. He taught his students to question everything and to think for themselves. The Athenian leaders felt his criticisms were a threat. They thought that his influence with the young people was dangerous. They accused Socrates of misleading students by teaching them to question authority. Following a trial, Socrates was found guilty of treason and sentenced to death.

Defending himself before a jury, Socrates used his method of questioning, urging jury members to think critically. At his death, he was still committed to reason.

Yes

PRIMARY SOURCE

“Socrates is guilty of . . . corrupting [misguiding] the young. Did not Socrates cause his associates to despise the established laws. . . . [His] [w]ords . . . tended to incite the young to contemn [to treat with scorn] the established constitution, rendering them violent and headstrong. . . . Socrates taught sons to pour contumely [harshly] upon their fathers by persuading his young friends that he could make them wiser than their sires [fathers], or by pointing out that the law allowed a son to sue his father for aberration [lapse] of mind, and to imprison him.”

—Socrates' accusers, Meletus, Anytus, and Lycon, quoted in *The Memorabilia: Recollections of Socrates* by Xenophon (translated by Henry Graham Dakyns)

Freedom of speech was not guaranteed in ancient Greece. Citizens gathered daily to discuss current issues.

No

PRIMARY SOURCE

“Men of Athens, I honor and love you; but I shall obey God rather than you, and while I have life and strength I shall never cease from the practice and teaching of philosophy, exhorting [urging] anyone . . . I meet . . . saying: my friend—a citizen of the great and mighty and wise city of Athens,—are you not ashamed of heaping up [so much] money and honor and reputation, and caring so little about wisdom and truth and the greatest improvement of the soul, which you never regard or heed [pay attention to] at all? . . . For I do nothing but go about persuading you all, old and young alike, not to take thought for your persons and your properties, but . . . to care about the greatest improvement of the soul. . . . This is my teaching, and if this is the doctrine which corrupts the youth, I am a mischievous person. But if any one says that this is not my teaching, he is speaking an untruth. Wherefore, O men of Athens, I say to you . . . whichever you do, understand that I shall never alter my ways, not even if I have to die many times.”

—Socrates, as quoted in *Apology*, by Plato (translated by Benjamin Jowett)

What Do You Think? DBQ

1. ***Explaining*** Socrates' accusers claim that he is teaching young people to question their constitution. Why do the accusers say this is an example of Socrates being a bad influence on the young?
2. ***Describing*** What does Socrates say is the main idea he teaches?
3. ***Evaluating*** Who do you think makes the stronger argument, Socrates or his accusers?

NOTES

NOTES

ENGAGE

GAME **Reviewing** To review Socrates's ideas and beliefs and how they were different from those of other philosophers of the time, have students complete the game sorting the philosophies and characteristics of Socrates and the Sophists. Ask the following question, and write students' responses on the whiteboard.

Ask:

Other than the ones listed in the game, what ideas did Socrates have, and what did he believe in? *(Answers will vary but could include: created Socratic method of questioning, wanted students to think for themselves and form their own opinions; believed that all real knowledge was within each person.)*

Explaining Tell students that in this lesson they will read two arguments about whether Socrates was guilty of misleading the youth of Athens. The argument that he was guilty is based on official accusations of three people. The opinion that he was not guilty is offered in a quotation from Socrates, recorded later by Plato.

Remind students that Socrates did not write down any of his own ideas. We only know what he said and thought about this and other issues from what Plato and other philosophers wrote later.

Tell students they will read primary source material arguing for and against the charge that Socrates was guilty of misleading the youth of Athens.

Before studying the first argument, ask students to jot down whether or not they think Socrates was guilty. Make sure students understand that the stakes for Socrates were high. If found guilty, he would be put to death.

TEACH & ASSESS

Identifying Points of View Ask a volunteer to read the introductory paragraphs that give the background for the arguments. Make sure students understand the events leading up to the trial.

Then ask another volunteer to read aloud the "Yes" argument. As a class, paraphrase the primary source material. Make sure all students understand the source material. AL ELL

Ask:

What did Socrates's accusers say Socrates had done? *(He persuaded sons that he could make them wiser than their fathers, and he pointed out that the sons could sue their fathers and have them imprisoned.)*

Ask:

Why was teaching the young men of Athens to question their parents a serious offense? *(Students should understand that encouraging young people to question their parents was seen as a way to undermine authority and as a threat to civic order. Many considered Socrates's actions to be dangerous to the well-being of Athens.)*

Making Connections Discuss ways that an adult can influence young people.

Ask:

Which adults in your life influence what you think and how you behave?

Are those people close family members, people you know in the community, or famous people you admire?

How do they influence you? *(Students' answers will vary but should include a reasoned analysis of which adults in their lives influence them and how they are influenced.)*

Close this part of the lesson by asking student volunteers to summarize the "Yes" argument. Take a poll to see which students were influenced by the argument. Write the results on the whiteboard. Leave the results on the whiteboard during the discussion of the opposing argument.

Identifying Points of View Tell students that next they will read primary source material arguing that Socrates was not guilty of misleading the youth of Athens.

Repeat the same process with the "No" argument. First read the argument aloud. Then, have a new volunteer paraphrase the "No" argument. Make sure all students understand the quotation. ELL

Ask:

What did Socrates say he was trying to persuade people to do? *(to care about the improvement of their souls)*

Ask:

Do you think that Socrates's defense is a good one? *(Students' answers will vary. They should provide reasons for why they do or do not think the defense is a good one.)*

Take another poll. This time ask if students are convinced by the "No" argument, and write the number who are on the board. Compare the No votes to the Yes votes from earlier. Discuss which side "won" based on the arguments in the text. If time allows, discuss the outcome of the voting.

Discussing Review with students how Socrates was tried and convicted. As a class, discuss why he chose to accept his sentence. Remind the class that Socrates was given the choice to accept the sentence of death or to leave Athens.

Ask:

Do you think Socrates was right to accept his sentence of death rather than to leave Athens? *(Students might say they agree with Socrates's idea that as a citizen of Athens, his duty was to accept the sentence even though he did not agree with it.*

Others may say that he might have accepted the sentence because he was getting old and did not want to have to leave Athens and go somewhere else to live.

Still others may suggest that he was foolish to accept the sentence, and he could have gone somewhere else and continued teaching.) AL ELL

Have students work alone or with a partner to complete the What Do You Think? questions.

Drawing Conclusions Have students write an open letter to the people of Athens explaining either why Socrates was guilty or why Socrates was innocent. Remind students to support their arguments with reasons and evidence and to make them as persuasive as possible.

If necessary, review that persuasive writing involves stating an opinion and supporting it with reasons and evidence. Students should draw on the "Yes" and "No" primary sources for evidence.

In addition, students should include emotional appeals as well as logical appeals. *(Students' letters will vary but should present their arguments logically. Students' letters should include reasons, evidence, and persuasive techniques.)*

CLOSE & REFLECT

Have students share their letters to the citizens of Athens by reading them aloud in small groups. Ask a few volunteers to share their letters with the whole class.

Then have the class as a whole discuss whether they think Socrates was guilty. Ask students whether their original opinions changed after they studied the two arguments.

Answers for *What Do You Think?* 

1. Socrates's accusers are saying that Socrates is setting a bad example for the youth by disagreeing with the current laws and that this influence also causes the young to question the law and become "violent and headstrong."
2. Socrates says the main idea he teaches is to care about wisdom, truth, and the improvement of the soul and to pay less attention to money, honor, and reputation.
3. Answers will vary, but students should point out that while Socrates's accusers make more specific claims, Socrates himself makes a more general argument, reaffirming his teaching doctrines of leading students to truth and wisdom through philosophy.

networks
There's More Online!

- ☑ **CHART** Seven Wonders of the World
- ☑ **GRAPHIC ORGANIZER**
  - Accomplishments of Philip II and Alexander the Great
  - Rise of Alexander the Great
- ☑ **VIDEO**

Lesson 3

Alexander's Empire

ESSENTIAL QUESTION *What are the characteristics of a leader?*

It Matters Because

Strong leaders can bring change to society. Philip II and Alexander the Great, as strong leaders, spread many Greek ideas to conquered lands.

1 Philip II of Macedonia

GUIDING QUESTION *Why did Macedonia become powerful?*

As you learned earlier, the Persians set out to conquer the Greek city-states but failed. The Macedonians (ma•suh•DOH•nee•uhnz) were people who lived north of Greece. In the 300s B.C., they conquered Greece.

Conquering Greece

The Macedonians were farmers. They raised sheep and horses and grew crops in their river valleys. For much of its history, Macedonia was not a very strong kingdom. Under King Philip II, however, Macedonia became a superpower in the ancient world.

As a young man, Philip had lived in Greece. He came to admire Greek culture and military skill. Philip became king of Macedonia in 359 B.C. He **created** a strong army. Philip planned to unite the Greek city-states under his rule and destroy the mighty Persian Empire. Philip trained a vast army of foot soldiers to fight like the Greeks. At this time, the Greek city-states were weak. They had been divided by the Peloponnesian War. As a result, they could not defend themselves against Philip's powerful army.

Reading **HELP**DESK

Taking Notes: *Summarizing*

Use a diagram like this one to describe how Philip II and Alexander changed Greece.

Content Vocabulary
- **cavalry**
- **Hellenistic Era**

Philip took control of the city-states one by one. He defeated some city-states in battle, and he bribed the leaders of others to surrender. A few city-states **voluntarily** agreed to join with Macedonia.

Many Greeks worried about Philip's plans. Demosthenes (dih•MAHS•thuh•neez) was an Athenian who opposed Philip. He was a lawyer and one of Athens's great public speakers. Demosthenes warned the Athenians that Philip was a threat to Greek freedom. He urged all the city-states to join together to fight the Macedonians:

PRIMARY SOURCE

> "Remember only that Philip is our enemy, that he has long been robbing and insulting us . . . that the future depends on ourselves, and that unless we are willing to fight him there we shall perhaps be forced to fight here. . . . You need not speculate [guess] about the future except to assure yourselves that it will be disastrous unless you face the facts and are willing to do your duty."
>
> —Demosthenes, "The First Philippic" in *Orations of Demosthenes*

By the time the Greeks tried to unite, it was too late. The Athenians joined with Thebes and a few other free city-states. They battled Philip's army, but they could not stop his invasion. In 338 B.C., the Greeks and the Macedonians fought one last major battle. At the Battle of Chaeronea (kehr•uh•NEE•uh), Philip's army crushed the Greeks. Philip now ruled most of Greece.

☑ **PROGRESS CHECK**

Summarizing How was Philip II able to gain control over most of Greece?

2 Alexander Takes Over

GUIDING QUESTION *What were Alexander's goals as a ruler?*

After conquering Greece, Philip hoped to lead the Greeks and Macedonians to war against the Persian Empire. Before Philip could carry out his plans, however, he was killed. His son Alexander became king.

Alexander was only 20 when he became ruler of Macedonia and Greece, but Philip had carefully prepared his son for the job. By age 16, Alexander was serving as a commander in the Macedonian army. He quickly won the respect of his soldiers.

Thinking Like a **HISTORIAN**

Researching on the Internet

Philip II of Macedonia admired the art and ideas of the Greeks—and their armies. Philip set out to take over the Greek city-states. Why do you think Philip wanted to conquer the Greeks rather than be allies with them? Use the Internet to find reliable sources about Philip's goals. Then present them to your class. For more information about using the Internet for research, read *What Does a Historian Do?*

▶ **CRITICAL THINKING**

Finding the Main Idea Demosthenes spoke out against Philip. Why was Demosthenes opposed to Philip's plans?

Academic Vocabulary

create to make or produce something; to bring something into existence

voluntarily by choice or free will; willingly

Alexander's Empire 323 B.C.

MACEDONIA, Black Sea, Chaeronea 338 B.C., Granicus 334 B.C., Aegean Sea, Athens, ASIA MINOR, Issus 333 B.C., Gaugamela 331 B.C., Caspian Sea, Mediterranean Sea, Tyre, SYRIA, Babylon, Susa, PERSIA, Persepolis, Alexandria, EGYPT, WESTERN DESERT, ARABIAN DESERT, Persian Gulf, Red Sea, TROPIC OF CANCER

0 — 400 miles; 0 — 400 km; Lambert Azimuthal Equal-Area projection

KEY
- Extent of empire
- Alexander's routes of conquest
- Major battle

The Region Today

BULGARIA, GREECE, TURKEY, UZBEKISTAN, TURKMENISTAN, SYRIA, LEBANON, ISRAEL, IRAQ, IRAN, AFGHANISTAN, JORDAN, KUWAIT, PAKISTAN, LIBYA, EGYPT, SAUDI ARABIA

GEOGRAPHY CONNECTION

Alexander the Great's empire covered parts of three different continents.

1. **PLACE** In what place today are the people known as Persians living?
2. **CRITICAL THINKING** ***Analyzing Visuals*** Why did Alexander go primarily east and south from Macedonia and Greece in his conquests?

They admired him for his bravery and military skill. After Philip's death, Alexander was ready to fulfill his father's dream. He prepared to invade the Persian Empire.

War with Persia

In the spring of 334 B.C., Alexander led about 40,000 Macedonian and Greek soldiers into Asia Minor. Their goal was to defeat one of the strongest armies in the world—the Persians. Alexander's **cavalry** (KAV•uhl•ree), or soldiers on horseback, proved to be a stronger force. They fought a battle at Granicus, in what is today northwestern Turkey. In that battle, Alexander's cavalry crushed the Persian forces. Alexander's forces continued to march across Asia Minor. They freed Greek city-states that had been under Persian rule.

Reading **HELP**DESK

cavalry part of an army in which the soldiers ride horses

Academic Vocabulary

pursue to follow in order to capture or defeat

A year and a half later, in November 333 B.C., Alexander fought the next major battle against the Persians at Issus (IH•suhs), in Syria. Once again, Alexander's military skills resulted in a victory. The Persian king Darius III was forced to flee from Issus.

Alexander and his troops did not **pursue** Darius, though. Instead, they moved south along the Mediterranean coast. In early 331 B.C., they conquered Egypt. Alexander built a new city in Egypt and named it Alexandria (a•lihg•ZAN•dree•uh) after himself. As a center of business and trade, Alexandria became one of the most important cities of the ancient world. It remains a vital city in the Mediterranean region today.

In late 331 B.C., Alexander's army headed back north. He turned eastward and invaded Mesopotamia, now ruled by the Persians. Alexander's army smashed Darius's forces at Gaugamela (gaw•guh•MEE•luh), near the Tigris River. After this victory, Alexander's army took over the rest of the Persian Empire.

After he conquered Persia, Alexander did not stop. In 327 B.C., he marched his army into northwestern India. There he fought a number of bloody battles. His soldiers were tired of constant fighting and refused to go farther. Alexander agreed to lead them home.

On the return march, the troops crossed a desert in what is now southern Iran. Heat and thirst killed thousands of soldiers. At one point, a group of soldiers found a little water and scooped it up in a helmet. They offered the water to Alexander. According to a Greek historian:

PRIMARY SOURCE

> "Alexander, with a word of thanks for the gift, took the helmet, and, in full view of his troops, poured the water on the ground. So extraordinary was the effect of this action that the water wasted by Alexander was as good as a drink for every man in the army."
>
> —*The Campaigns of Alexander* by Arrian, tr. by Aubrey De Sélincourt

At the far left of this battle scene is Alexander the Great, who fought alongside his soldiers.

▶ **CRITICAL THINKING**

Hypothesizing What was Alexander trying to show when he threw water on the ground in front of his thirsty soldiers?

Teaching *Alexander's Empire*

(Student Edition pp. 230–235)

LESSON 3

ENGAGE

Comparing and Contrasting Divide the class into four groups.

For two of the groups, **ask:** **What does it mean to be a great military leader?** Have them write their answers on a piece of paper. *(Answers will vary but may include the following: must be brave, intelligent, able to inspire people to follow you, good at military strategy, and good at choosing generals.)*

For the other two groups, **ask:** **What does it mean to be an effective ruler?** *(Answers will vary but may include the following: must be able to inspire people to follow you, be good at choosing advisers, be able to get people to trust you, and be fair and just.)*

Have groups share their responses and discuss the similarities and differences between the responses to each question.

Tell students that in this lesson they will study the life of Alexander the Great and learn about his achievements as a ruler and military leader. Review with students the characteristics of a great military leader compared with a great ruler. AL ELL

TEACH & ASSESS

1 Phillip II of Macedonia

GUIDING QUESTION *Why did Macedonia become powerful?*

GRAPHIC ORGANIZER **Summarizing** Have students fill in the Taking Notes graphic organizer on how Philip II and Alexander changed Greece. Remind students that they may consult their textbooks for details and information for their organizers.

IMAGE **Making Connections** Show students the image of Demosthenes. Explain to the class that when Demosthenes was a boy, he spoke with a stammer and bad pronunciation. He practiced speaking with pebbles in his mouth so he could speak more clearly. He also practiced speaking in front of a large mirror. He is considered to be one of the most famous orators of all time.

Ask: **What characteristics helped make Demosthenes a great orator and leader?** *(Answers may include that he displayed perseverance, willingness to work hard, and ingenuity [cleverness].)*

2 Alexander Takes Over

GUIDING QUESTION *What were Alexander's goals as a ruler?*

MAP **Analyzing Visuals** Have students find the map "Alexander's Empire" in their textbooks.

Ask:

- **What do the arrows and red lines represent?** *(the path Alexander and his armies took)*
- **What modern countries make up the eastern borders of the empire?** *(Afghanistan, Pakistan, Uzbekistan, Turkmenistan)*
- **What geographic feature marks the eastern reach of Alexander's empire?** *(the Indus River)*
- **Near what river was the battle of Gaugamela fought?** *(the Tigris River)* ELL

Hypothesizing Point out that Alexander was strongly influenced by his father.

Ask: **Do you think that following in the footsteps of one's parents was more common in Alexander's day than it is now? Why?** *(Answers will vary. Possible answer: Yes, it was probably more common in Alexander's day. In those days, most people did the same kind of work their parents did. Young people now have many more choices than people did in Alexander's time.)* BL

Listing Draw a two-column chart on the board. Label Column A "Leadership Qualities" and Column B "Military Achievements."

GRAPHIC ORGANIZER **Identifying** Have student volunteers fill in the chart based on what they know about Alexander the Great. Allow students to refer to their textbooks. *(Answers may include the following: Leadership Qualities: inspired men to follow him; founded city of Alexandria; spread Greek culture throughout Southwest Asia and Egypt; learned new ideas from people in conquered lands; tried to bring unity by appointing Persians to top government positions. Military Achievements: was commander in father's army by the time he was 16; inspired his armies to march into unknown lands; was fearless in battle; risked his life; defeated the Persian Empire; conquered lands all the way to India; created empire that covered most of the known world.)* Then have students use their answers to complete the graphic organizer, "Rise of Alexander." AL

3 Alexander's Legacy

GUIDING QUESTION *How successful was Alexander in achieving his goals?*

INTERACTIVE WHITEBOARD ACTIVITY **Analyzing** Have students complete the activity "Conquests of Alexander the Great" to match Alexander's achievements with the places on the map where the achievements were accomplished.

INTERACTIVE WORKSHEET

Primary Sources Activity

Analyzing Primary Sources Have students complete the Primary Source Activity "Alexander The Great: Hero or Villain?" Have students work in pairs to read aloud the material from primary sources. Provide resources that help English language learners with difficult vocabulary. ELL

INTERACTIVE WORKSHEET

Geography and History Activity

Understanding Movement As a class, review how Alexander's conquests helped spread Greek culture. Then, have students complete the Geography and History Activity "Greek Migration" for homework.

Displaying Have students work alone, in pairs, or in small groups to design a Web site home page for Alexander the Great. The page should explain why Alexander is considered "great" and should include images, drawings, and text that represent his achievements.

LECTURE SLIDE **Summarizing** Show the lecture slide and then discuss with students Alexander's goals and what happened to Alexander's empire after he died.

Have students refer to the last section of this lesson in their textbooks and to the Geography and History worksheet to refresh their memories about the details.

Answers for pages 230–233

P. 230 Taking Notes ended freedom of Greek city-states, defeated Persian Empire, expanded the economy, spread Greek culture, exposed Greece to Eastern culture

P. 231 Thinking Like a Historian Answers will vary, but most students should mention that the Greek city-states were not unified and their army was weak, so they were an easy target; Philip was an empire builder; Philip's ambitions to be a ruler made him more interested in conquering Greece than in being a friendly ally and neighbor; and Philip needed to conquer Greece so he could topple the Persian Empire.

P. 231 CRITICAL THINKING Demosthenes was worried about the Greeks' loss of freedom.

P. 231 ☑ PROGRESS CHECK The Greek city-states were not unified, and they were weakened by the Peloponnesian War. Philip conquered some city-states and bribed others. Some willingly joined him.

P. 232 GEOGRAPHY CONNECTION

1. People in Iran are known as Persians because Iran is the modern name for the area that was known as Persia.
2. CRITICAL THINKING Alexander wanted to invade and conquer the Persian Empire, which was located to the east and to the south of Greece and Macedonia.

P. 233 CRITICAL THINKING He was showing that he was no better than his soldiers; if they did not have water to drink, then he would not drink either. He inspired them to continue, despite the hardships.

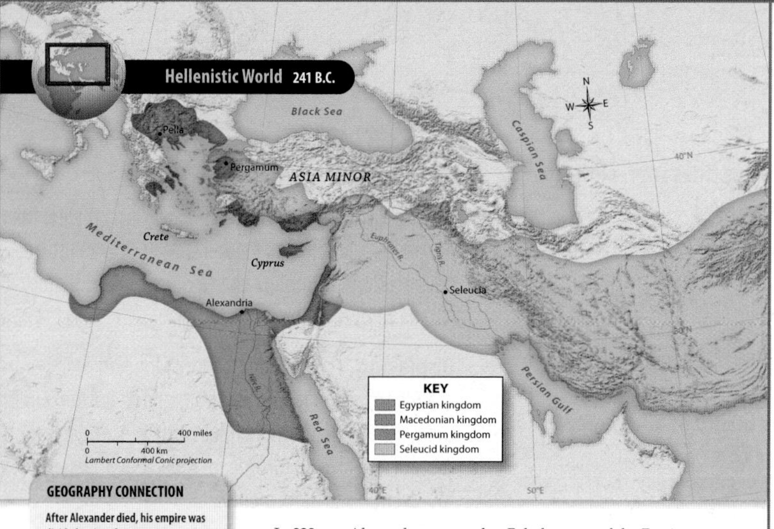

GEOGRAPHY CONNECTION

After Alexander died, his empire was divided up into four separate kingdoms, which were all part of the Hellenistic World.

1. **LOCATION** In which kingdom was Greece mostly located?
2. **CRITICAL THINKING** ***Analyzing Visuals*** How many different continents was Alexander's empire on, and which continents were they?

In 323 B.C., Alexander returned to Babylon, one of the Persian cities now under his control. The hardships of the journey had wrecked his health. Suffering from wounds and worn out by fever, Alexander died. He was only 32 years old.

PROGRESS CHECK

Explaining Why was the Battle of Gaugamela so important to Alexander?

3 Alexander's Legacy

GUIDING QUESTION *How successful was Alexander in achieving his goals?*

Alexander was a great general who feared nothing. He rode into battle ahead of his soldiers and marched into unknown lands. The key to Alexander's courage may have been his early education. As a boy, Alexander read the Greek epics. His role model was Homer's warrior-hero Achilles. Today, Alexander is called Alexander the Great.

Alexander's armies extended Greek rule over a vast region. They spread Greek language, ideas, art, and architecture throughout Southwest Asia and Egypt. Alexander's successes marked the beginning of the **Hellenistic Era** (heh•luh•NIHS•tihk EHR•uh). *Hellenistic* means "like the Greeks." The Hellenistic Era refers to when Greek culture spread to the non-Greek peoples that Alexander had conquered.

Reading HELPDESK

Hellenistic Era the time period following the death of Alexander during which Greek culture spread through the known world

Reading Strategy: *Summarizing*

When you finish reading a section of text about an important person or event in history, write a paragraph that tells what the person did or what happened. Use your own words. Then compare your summary to the text and check any facts.

A Divided Empire

Alexander planned to unite Macedonians, Greeks, Egyptians, and Asians in his new empire. His dream of creating one great empire, however, didn't last. After Alexander died, his generals divided the empire into four separate kingdoms. These kingdoms were Macedonia, Pergamum (PUHR•guh•muhm), Egypt, and the Seleucid (suh•LOO•suhd) Empire.

The Hellenistic Kings

People who served in the governments of the Hellenistic kings had to speak Greek. The Hellenistic kings preferred to give jobs to Greeks and Macedonians. In this way, they were able to keep control of the governments.

By 100 B.C., Alexandria, in Egypt, was the largest city in the Mediterranean world. It included two excellent harbors and a towering lighthouse. It stood on a harbor island with a burning flame at its top. The library at Alexandria had the largest collection of writings in ancient times.

The Hellenistic kings also created new cities and military posts. These new Greek communities needed architects, artists, engineers, and philosophers. Hellenistic rulers encouraged Greeks and Macedonians to settle in the conquered lands. These colonies spread Greek culture widely—into Egypt and India.

PROGRESS CHECK

Explaining What happened to Alexander's empire after he died?

The lighthouse at Alexandria was one of the Seven Wonders of the Ancient World. It was completed about 280 B.C. and stood on an island in the harbor.

CRITICAL THINKING

Analyzing Why was a fire kept burning on top of the lighthouse at night?

LESSON 3 REVIEW

Review Vocabulary

1. Why was the *cavalry* an important part of Alexander's army?

Answer the Guiding Questions

2. ***Summarizing*** What did Demosthenes want the Greek city-states to do about the Macedonians? Did they follow his advice?
3. ***Describing*** What is the Hellenistic Era?
4. ***Identifying*** What were some of the policies of Alexander and the Hellenistic kings that helped to spread Greek culture throughout the empire?
5. **NARRATIVE WRITING** Alexander admired the heroes of the Trojan War so much that he traveled with a copy of Homer's *Iliad*. What book would you carry if you traveled as Alexander did? Write a description of your choice and explain your reasons for it.

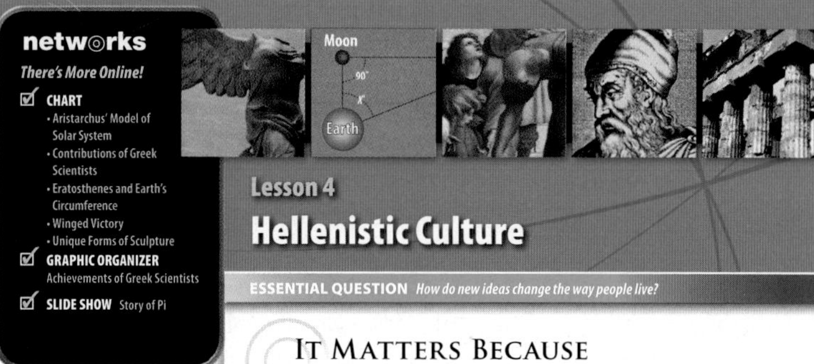

networks
There's More Online!
CHART
• Aristarchus' Model of Solar System
• Contributions of Greek Scientists
• Eratosthenes and Earth's Circumference
• Winged Victory
• Unique Forms of Sculpture
GRAPHIC ORGANIZER
Achievements of Greek Scientists
SLIDE SHOW Story of Pi
Moon
90°
Earth

Lesson 4

Hellenistic Culture

ESSENTIAL QUESTION *How do new ideas change the way people live?*

IT MATTERS BECAUSE

Hellenistic cities became centers of learning and culture. Philosophy and the arts flourished, and new discoveries that were made are still important to us today.

1 Hellenistic Arts

GUIDING QUESTION *How did Greek culture spread during the Hellenistic Era?*

During the Hellenistic Era, philosophers, scientists, poets, and writers moved to the new Greek cities of Southwest Asia and Egypt. Alexandria, for example, served as the Greek capital of Egypt and was a major center of learning. Many scholars were attracted to Alexandria's library. It contained more than 500,000 scrolls. Alexandria also had a museum that attracted scholars to do research. The city's reputation as a place of learning and its location on the Mediterranean Sea contributed to Alexandria's economic growth. Today, Alexandria remains a vital city in Egypt where nearly 4 million people live and work.

Buildings and Statues

Greek architects served an important role in expanding Alexander's empire. They planned public building projects for new cities that were being founded and for old cities that were being rebuilt. Hellenistic kings wanted to make these cities like Athens and other cultural centers in Greece. They were willing to spend huge amounts of money to do so. These kings wanted to line the streets with Greek temples, theaters, and baths.

Hellenistic kings and other wealthy citizens hired Greek sculptors, who created thousands of statues for towns and cities. Hellenistic sculptors proved as talented as the sculptors of Greece's Golden Age. These sculptors, however, developed new styles. They did not carve ideal figures to reflect beauty and harmony. Instead, they showed people in a more realistic style. They even created statues that looked angry or sad.

Reading HELPDESK

Taking Notes: *Describing*

Use a chart like this one to describe the achievements of the Greek scientists.

Greek Scientist	Achievements
Eratosthenes	
Euclid	
Archimedes	

Content Vocabulary

- **Epicureanism**
- **Stoicism**
- **circumference**
- **plane geometry**
- **solid geometry**

Hellenistic Writers

Hellenistic rulers also supported talented writers. As a result, poets and writers produced a large amount of literature during the Hellenistic Era. Very little of this writing has survived today.

One work that we do know about is an epic poem called *Argonautica*. Written by Appolonius (a•puh•LOH•nee•uhs) of Rhodes (ROHDZ), the poem tells the story of Jason and his band of heroes. You may have read or seen a modern version of this poem, often called *Jason and the Argonauts*. Jason and his band sail the seas **seeking** a ram with a golden fleece. Along the way, they have many adventures. Another poet, Theocritus (thee•AH•kruh•tuhs), wrote short poems about the beauty of nature.

Athens remained the center for Greek theater. There, writers of plays produced comedies, not tragedies. These comedies are known as Greek New Comedy. However, the comedies of the Hellenistic Era were not like the comedies of Greece's Golden Age. Those of the Hellenistic Era did not poke fun at political leaders. Instead, the plays told stories about love and relationships of ordinary people. One of the best known of the new playwrights was Menander (muh•NAN•duhr). He lived from 343 B.C. to 291 B.C. and is considered the most important poet of Greek New Comedy. The temple of Apollo at Delphi had an inscription that read "Know thyself." Making a humorous comment on that inscription, Menander said "This 'Know Yourself' is a silly proverb in some ways; To know the man next door is a much more useful rule." His works were later adapted by Roman writers. Through his works, Menander influenced the development of European comedy during the Renaissance (reh•nuh•ZAHNTS) and even comedy today.

PROGRESS CHECK

Explaining How did Greek sculpture and drama change during the Hellenistic Era?

Hellenistic artists were masters at capturing movement and emotion. This statue, *Winged Victory*, seems to be walking forcefully forward.

CRITICAL THINKING

Drawing Conclusions Washington D.C.'s buildings showcase many statues in the Greek style. Why do you think so many of them are in this style?

Academic Vocabulary

seek to search for

LESSON 3 (cont.)

IMAGE **Making Connections** Show the image of modern Alexandria and lead the class in a discussion of how the modern city has or has not changed since Alexander the Great's day. AL

Have students complete the Lesson 3 Review as homework.

CLOSE & REFLECT

Summarizing Ask volunteers to summarize the impact of Alexander the Great on the ancient world.

Suggest that students first summarize Alexander's military exploits and then his impact as a ruler of a great empire.

IF YOU HAVE MORE TIME . . .

Explore Macedonia

Geography Alexander's homeland of Macedonia had a long, complicated history. Its strategic location on the Balkans made it a prize many empires wanted to control. In the twentieth century, parts of it were controlled by Yugoslavia, Greece, and Bulgaria.

Have students consult a world almanac, the Internet, or another resource to put together a time line of major events in Macedonia.

Answers for pages 234–235

P. 234 ☑ PROGRESS CHECK It was the battle in which his forces defeated the Persians and that gave Alexander control of the Persian Empire.

P. 234 GEOGRAPHY CONNECTION

1. Greece was mostly located in the Macedonian kingdom.
2. CRITICAL THINKING Alexander's empire was on three continents: Europe, Asia, and Africa.

P. 234 READING STRATEGY Student paragraphs should have a topic sentence and contain facts to support it.

P. 235 CRITICAL THINKING to guide ships into the harbor

P. 235 ☑ PROGRESS CHECK It was divided into four kingdoms: Egypt, Macedonia, Pergamum, and Seleucid.

LESSON 3 REVIEW

1. Alexander's soldiers on horseback—his cavalry—were a strong force. At Granicus, they crushed the local Persian forces, leading to the final downfall of the Persian Empire.
2. Demosthenes wanted the Greek city-states to unite to fight Philip and the Macedonians. The Athenians finally did try to unite, but it was too late.
3. The Hellenistic Era refers to a time when Greek language and ideas spread to the non-Greek peoples that Alexander had conquered.
4. Alexander and the Hellenistic rulers had ambitious building programs, creating new cities and military posts. They recruited Greeks and Macedonians to come settle in the conquered lands and work as artists, architects, engineers, writers, philosophers, government officials, and soldiers.
5. Answers will vary, but students should name a book they value or admire and clearly state the reasons they would find it valuable to have it with them all the time and in different life situations they encounter.

Teaching *Hellenistic Culture* (Student Edition pp. 236–241)

LESSON 4

ENGAGE

LECTURE SLIDE **Previewing** Have students look at the images in their textbook in the sections on the arts and writers in the Hellenistic Era.

Ask: How are the sculptures of human figures different from those in the Golden Age of Greece? *(The figures are more realistic. They show more emotion and movement.)* Tell students there was a similar change in the writing of the Hellenistic Era. For example, dramas told stories about ordinary people, not gods and heroes. AL ELL

Then show the lecture slide that defines the Hellenistic Era.

Ask: What does the word *Hellenistic* mean? *("like the Greeks")* Discuss with the class how the arts were supported in the Hellenistic Era by the rulers of the kingdoms and wealthy citizens who were eager to import Greek culture to their lands and especially to the new cities they were building.

Explain to students that in this lesson they will learn about artists, writers, playwrights, philosophers, scientists, and mathematicians in the Hellenistic world.

TEACH & ASSESS

1 Hellenistic Arts

GUIDING QUESTION *How did Greek culture spread during the Hellenistic Era?*

GRAPHIC ORGANIZER **Identifying** Tell students they will complete the Taking Notes graphic organizer by writing the achievements of the three scientists listed. Students may draw on what they already know to begin filling in the chart. Later, they may also draw on details from their textbooks and the information they learn from the chart "Contributions of Greek Scientists." AL

INTERACTIVE WORKSHEET

Geography and History Activity

Discussing As a class, work through the Geography and History Activity about Hellenistic Cities. Pay particular attention to the map. Have students compare the map in the digital worksheet to the map of the Hellenistic World in their textbooks. Point out that the map in the worksheet has more detail as it shows more cities and some of the geographic features around those cities.

IMAGE **Connecting to Today** Show students the images of the two sculptures Winged Victory at Samothrace and Unique Forms of Continuity in Space. Have volunteers read aloud the text that accompanies the images.

Ask: How does *Winged Victory at Samothrace* reflect the Hellenistic culture of its time? *(Answers will vary but may include that it has a heroic feel and it portrays strength and powerful, dynamic movement.)*

Making Connections Discuss with students how Greek dramas served as a basis for theater plays today. Have students list where else today––in addition to the theater––we can see the impact of the Greek drama.

Answers for pages 236–237

P. 236 Taking Notes Eratosthenes: determined that Earth is round; measured Earth's circumference, distance to sun, distance to moon; concluded sun is larger than moon. **Euclid:** described plane geometry. **Archimedes:** worked on solid geometry, established science of physics, calculated value of pi, invented machinery and weapons.

P. 237 The classical style is associated with formality and realism.

P. 237 ☑ PROGRESS CHECK Sculpture became more realistic, showing people as they really are. Some dramas were written about ordinary people rather than about the gods.

2 Thinkers and Scientists

GUIDING QUESTION *What ideas and discoveries emerged during the Hellenistic Era?*

During the Hellenistic Era, Athens continued to support Greek philosophers. These philosophers tried to answer questions such as, "What is a good life?" and "How can people find peace of mind in a troubled world?" The two most important Hellenistic philosophers were Epicurus and Zeno.

Who Was Epicurus?

Epicurus founded a philosophy known as **Epicureanism** (eh•pih•kyu•REE•uh•nih•zuhm). He taught his students that finding happiness was the goal of life. He believed that the way to be happy was to avoid pain.

Today the word *epicurean* means the love of physical pleasure, such as good food or comfortable surroundings. For Epicurus, however, pleasure meant spending time with friends. It meant learning not to be upset about problems in life. Epicureans avoided worry. They limited their wants and lived simply.

The Stoics

A Phoenician thinker named Zeno developed a philosophy called **Stoicism** (STOH•uh•sih•zuhm). Zeno did not have the money to rent a lecture hall in which to teach. Instead, he taught at a building called the "painted porch". The Greek word for *porch* was *stoa*. The term "Stoicism" thus comes from the Greek word *stoa*.

The Stoics claimed that people who were guided by their emotions lived unhappy lives. They believed that happiness resulted from using reason. Sound thinking, they thought, should guide decisions. Today, the word *stoic* is used to describe someone who seems not affected by joy or sadness. Unlike Epicureans, Stoics thought people had a duty to serve their **community**. The ideas of the Stoics would later influence Roman thinkers.

Other astronomers would not believe Aristarchus when he stated that the solar system moved around the sun. This diagram shows his idea.

MODEL OF SOLAR SYSTEM BY ARISTARCHUS

Moon
Sun
Earth
90°
X°

Science and Mathematics

Science also flourished during the Hellenistic Era. Even though Hellenistic scientists used simple instruments, they performed many experiments and developed new theories.

Reading HELPDESK

Epicureanism the philosophy of Epicurus, stating that the purpose of life is to look for happiness and peace

Stoicism the philosophy of the Stoics who believed that people should not try to feel joy or sadness

Academic Vocabulary

community a group of various kinds of people living in a particular area or a common location

Aristarchus (ar•uh•STAHR•kuhs) claimed that the sun was at the center of the universe. He said that Earth circled the sun. At the time, other astronomers rejected his ideas. They thought that Earth was the center of the universe. Euclid taught others his theories about geometry. If you study geometry today, you will be learning about the same topics studied by ancient Greeks.

Another scientist, Eratosthenes (ehr•uh•TAHS•thuh•neez), was the chief librarian at the library at Alexandria. After study and research, Eratosthenes concluded that Earth was round. He then used his knowledge to measure Earth's **circumference** (suhr•KUHM•fuhr•ens)—the distance around Earth.

In order to measure the Earth's circumference, Eratosthenes put two sticks in the ground far apart from each other. When the sun was directly over one stick, he measured its shadow. By measuring the shadows, he was able to calculate the curve of Earth's surface.

Using his measurements, Eratosthenes tried to figure the distance around Earth. Remarkably, his estimate was within 185 miles (298 km) of the actual distance. Using similar **methods**, he tried to determine how far it was to the sun and to the moon. Although his measurements were not **accurate**, he concluded that the sun was much larger than Earth and the moon.

The modern age owes a great debt to the Hellenistic thinkers. Here the mathematician Euclid is immortalized in "The School of Athens," a painting by sixteenth-century artist Raphael. The work can be viewed today at the Vatican in Rome.

GREEK SCIENTISTS AND THEIR CONTRIBUTIONS — CHART

Scientist	Scientific "Firsts"
Archimedes	Established the science of physics Explained the lever and compound pulley
Aristarchus	Established that Earth revolves around the sun
Eratosthenes	Figured out that Earth is round
Euclid	Wrote a book that organized information about geometry
Hipparchus	Created a system to explain how planets and stars move
Hippocrates	Known as the "Father of Medicine" First to write a medical code of good behavior
Hypatia	Expanded knowledge of mathematics and astronomy
Pythagoras	First to establish the principles of geometry

The ancient Greeks made advances in science.

1 **IDENTIFYING** How was Euclid's achievement important for the study of geometry?

2 **CRITICAL THINKING** ***Analyzing*** Why did Aristarchus' ideas upset some people?

circumference the outer border of a circle; the measurement of that border

Academic Vocabulary

method a procedure or process; a way of doing something

accurate free from error; in agreement with truth

Connections to TODAY

Constant *pi*

Astronomers in the Hellenistic Era made amazing discoveries. Many of the measurements they made were very accurate. Even though scientists today can measure more accurately, no one has ever been able to improve on Archimedes' calculation of *pi*. The number *pi* (π) is a ratio. When the circumference of a circle is divided by its diameter, you get *pi*. *Pi* is always the same for every circle—about 3.1416.

Archimedes' calculation of *pi* is used daily in mathematics, more than 2,000 years after he worked it out.

Euclid (YOO•kluhd) of Alexandria advanced the field of mathematics. His best-known book *Elements* describes plane geometry. **Plane geometry** is one branch of mathematics. It shows how points, lines, angles, and surfaces relate to one another. Around 300 B.C., Egypt's King Ptolemy I (TAH• luh• mee) asked Euclid if he knew a faster way to learn geometry. Euclid answered that "there is no royal way" to learn geometry. In other words, if the king wanted to understand Euclid's ideas, he would have to study. Euclid's theories still influence mathematicians today.

The most famous scientist of the Hellenistic Era was Archimedes (ahr • kuh• MEE• deez). Archimedes worked on **solid geometry**. He studied ball-like shapes, called spheres, and tube-like shapes, called cylinders. He also figured out the value of *pi*. This number is used to measure the area of circles. It is represented by the Greek symbol π.

Archimedes was also an inventor. He developed machinery and weapons of war. Archimedes was known as a modest man. According to one story, however, he boasted, "Give me a lever and a place to stand on . . . and I will move the earth."

The king of Syracuse heard of Archimedes' boast. He asked Archimedes to build a machine to defend the city, so Archimedes designed catapults. These machines could throw rocks, arrows, and spears over long distances.

When the Romans attacked Syracuse in 212 B.C., the catapults drove them back. It took the Romans three years to capture the city. During the massacre that followed, Archimedes was killed.

Hellenistic thought and culture had long-lasting effects. The mathematician Hypatia (hy• PAY• shuh) lived in Alexandria in Egypt around A.D. 400, more than 700 years after the Hellenistic Era. She kept up the Greek tradition of studying philosophy and mathematics. Like the great Greek thinkers of the past, Hypatia also championed the use of reason over superstition:

PRIMARY SOURCE

> "To teach superstitions as truth is a most terrible thing."
> "Reserve your right to think, for even to think wrongly is better than not to think at all."
>
> —from Hypatia, *Encyclopaedia Britannica Profiles, 300 Women Who Changed the World*

PROGRESS CHECK

Comparing and Contrasting How were Epicureanism and Stoicism similar? How were they different?

Reading HELPDESK

plane geometry a branch of mathematics centered around measurement and relationships of points, lines, angles, and surfaces of figures on a plane

solid geometry a branch of mathematics about measurement and relationships of points, lines, angles, surfaces, and solids in three-dimensional space

3 Greece and Rome

GUIDING QUESTION *How did Greece fall under Roman rule?*

The four kingdoms that formed from Alexander's empire shared Hellenistic culture. Despite their common culture, the kingdoms were unable to work together. They often fought wars with one another.

Macedonia held power over Greece for a time. It could not keep the Greek city-states permanently under control, though. Sparta and some other city-states regained their independence. These city-states had Hellenistic cultures, but they did not have strong armies. They remained free for only a short time.

Rome was a city-state in central Italy. In the late 200s B.C., Rome conquered the entire Italian Peninsula. Greece lost its lands in southern Italy. The Greeks now feared that Rome would take control of Greece.

The Greeks tried to stop Rome's growing power, but failed. They began supporting Rome's enemies in various wars. The Romans won these conflicts, however. Gradually, Rome gained control of the Greek mainland.

PROGRESS CHECK

Explaining How did the Greek city-states react to Rome's growing power?

Sicily is a beautiful island in the Mediterranean. Ruled by ancient Greeks and then the Romans, it is the home today of many historic ruins of both cultures.

LESSON 4 REVIEW

Review Vocabulary

1. Why did Greek scientists study the *circumference* of Earth?

Answer the Guiding Questions

2. ***Explaining*** Why did Alexandria become a major center of learning?
3. ***Describing*** What contributions did Archimedes make to science?
4. ***Explaining*** How did the Greeks attempt to stop Rome's invasion of Greece?
5. ***Drawing Conclusions*** What beliefs about Earth and the heavens were proved by the discoveries of Aristarchus and Eratosthenes?
6. **EXPOSITORY WRITING** Compare the Stoic and Epicurean views about life. Which of these views appeals to you? Write a paragraph that explains the reasons for your choice.

LESSON 4 (cont.)

2 Thinkers and Scientists

GUIDING QUESTION *What ideas and discoveries emerged during the Hellenistic Era?*

CHART Show students the chart, Greek Scientists and Their Contributions, that summarizes the discoveries of Eratosthenes, Euclid, and Aristarchus. Challenge students to explain how the discoveries of these thinkers affect modern life.

SLIDE SHOW **Applying** Show students the slide show on *pi*. Read the text on the slides aloud.

Tell students that Archimedes figured out the value of *pi* (3.14). That contribution helped mathematicians to make great advances in geometry.

Lead the class in finding the circumference of a circle drawn on a piece of paper by measuring the circle's diameter and multiplying that by *pi*.

They could check their work by carefully putting a piece of string around the circumference of the circle and then measuring the string.

IMAGE **Specifying** Show students the slide of Hypatia. Ask a volunteer or volunteers to read the text aloud to the class.

Ask:

Where did Hypatia work? *(She taught philosophy and advanced mathematics in Alexandria.)*

Ask:

How does Hypatia's work as a scholar stand out from others you have learned about? *(She is the only female scholar. She is considered the first female scholar of her time.)*

Synthesizing Have students choose one idea or discovery that emerged during the Hellenistic Era and write a newspaper article about it. Students should describe the idea or discovery as if it were new as well as "predict" what might happen in the future because of the idea.

Have students create an illustration and a caption to go with the article. BL

3 Greece and Rome

GUIDING QUESTION *How did Greece fall under Roman rule?*

Comparing and Contrasting Direct students to the section "Greece and Rome." Have students return to the predictions they made earlier about the reasons for the end of the Hellenistic Era.

Discuss the reasons that students learned during class discussion. On the board, write the reasons the Hellenistic Era came to an end, as students identify them.

Ask:

Which reason seems the most important or the most likely to have caused the end of the Hellenistic Era? *(Answers will vary, but students should point out that the Greeks were divided and had weak armies. They could not hold off the Romans.)*

Have students complete the Lesson 4 Review as a homework assignment.

CLOSE & REFLECT

Discussing Have students share their newspaper articles and illustrations about an idea or a discovery during the Hellenistic Era.

If time allows, ask students to discuss their choice of event or discovery. If students' selections show a trend, take a moment to discuss why so many students thought it was important.

IF YOU HAVE MORE TIME . . .

Examine the Cultural Diversity of Ancient Greece

Compare and Contrast The Hellenistic world included many different cultural and ethnic groups. Have students explain how this diversity could have been a strength and a weakness. *(Diversity could have led to many different good ideas, although it also could have led to conflict among the groups.)*

Then have them compare the diversity of the Greek world after Alexander's death to the diversity in the United States today. Write students' responses on the whiteboard.

Answers for pages 238–241

P. 239 CHART

1. His book, *Elements*, organized information on geometry in a way that made it easier to teach.
2. CRITICAL THINKING His ideas required people to consider the idea that Earth was not the center of the universe.

P. 240 ☑ PROGRESS CHECK Epicureans and Stoics wanted to have simple and happy lives, but their ideas about how to achieve that goal were different. Epicureans saw happiness as a goal of life. They thought the way to happiness was to avoid pain and worry and spend time with friends. Stoics believed they had a duty to serve their community, that their lives should be ruled by reason and sound thinking, and that emotions could cause unhappiness. Therefore, they believed they should be indifferent to joy or sadness.

P. 241 ☑ PROGRESS CHECK They were afraid; they tried to stop Rome by supporting Rome's enemies in wars, but they were not successful and were defeated by the Romans.

LESSON 4 REVIEW

1. Studying the circumference of Earth was part of the studies of astronomy and geography. The Greek scientists used that measurement to calculate the size of the sun and moon and the distance from Earth to the sun and to the moon.
2. Alexandria was in a good location on the Mediterranean coast. It had the largest library in the world and a museum that many researchers used for their work.
3. Archimedes established the science of physics, explained the lever and compound pulley, worked on solid geometry, calculated the value of *pi*, and invented weapons of war.
4. The Greeks supported Rome's enemies in various wars.
5. Aristarchus disproved the belief that Earth is the center of the universe by discovering that Earth circles the sun. Eratosthenes disproved the idea that Earth is flat by discovering that it is round.
6. In their comparisons, students should mention several characteristics of both groups. The Epicureans believed that happiness was the goal of life and that the way to happiness was to seek pleasure, spend time with friends, not worry, and live simply. The Stoics believed happiness came from following reason, not emotions, and that everyone had a duty to serve their community. Responses to which view appeals to them will vary, but students should state their preferences clearly and support them with specific reasons related to Epicureanism and Stoicism.

CHAPTER 8 Activities

Write your answers on a separate piece of paper.

1. **Exploring the Essential Question**
EXPOSITORY WRITING Write an expository essay about what made the Greek people and their culture unique. Think of the new ideas they developed in philosophy and the sciences. Think of the new forms of art and architecture that they created. Include in your essay a discussion of the lasting influences that Greece has had on the world.

2. **21st Century Skills**
APPLY TECHNOLOGY EFFECTIVELY Create a blog entry to compare and contrast the sculpture and architecture of the Hellenistic Era with that of the modern world. Choose photos that show the general differences and details. Write copy that analyzes the styles and points out the differences. Include your personal opinions of the two styles.

3. **Thinking Like a Historian**
COMPARING AND CONTRASTING Select one of the historical maps from the chapter. Then search the Internet for maps of the same area today. Write one or two paragraphs explaining how the area has changed or remained the same between the time of ancient Greece and now.

4. **GEOGRAPHY ACTIVITY**

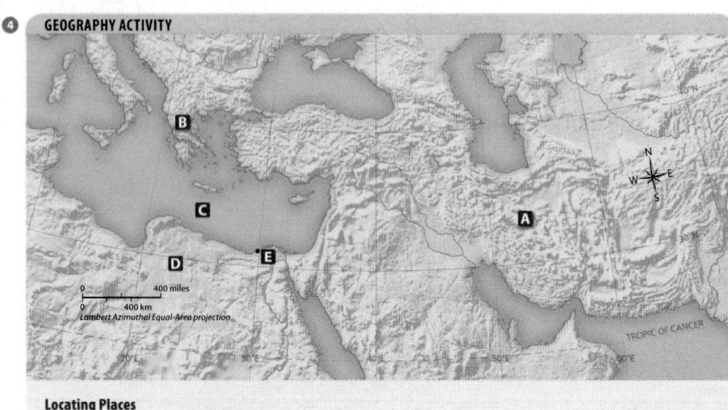

Locating Places
On a separate sheet of paper, match the letters on the map with the numbered places listed here.

1. Greece
2. Africa
3. Alexandria
4. Persia
5. Mediterranean Sea

CHAPTER 8 Assessment

Directions: Choose the best answer for each question.

1. The original Olympic games were held
A. to honor the goddess Aphrodite.
B. to appease the god Poseidon, king of the sea.
C. for the greater glory of the god Zeus.
D. for the god Ares to make the people strong in war.

2. Socrates was sentenced to death because
F. some people thought his teaching was dangerous.
G. he did not believe in absolute right and wrong.
H. he accepted money for his teaching.
I. some people did not like his ideas about philosopher kings.

3. Who taught the idea of the golden mean?
A. Socrates
B. Aristotle
C. the Sophists
D. Plato

4. Alexander's plan to unite a great empire didn't last because
F. the Persians reconquered their lost lands.
G. his generals divided the kingdom after his death.
H. his armies grew frustrated and wished to return home.
I. the Romans rose to power and conquered his weakened empire.

5. Sculptors in the Hellenistic Era carved figures that
A. appeared abstract, only partly looking like real people.
B. showed the beauty and harmony of the ideal human.
C. represented people realistically, with emotions.
D. emphasized the humorous side of life.

6. Who was the first scientist to calculate the value of *pi*?
F. Aristarchus
G. Eratosthenes
H. Hypatia
I. Archimedes

CHAPTER 8 Assessment *(continued)*

DBQ DOCUMENT-BASED QUESTIONS

7. **Inferring** This excerpt is from a speech by Demosthenes. He spoke to the people of Athens about Philip II of Macedonia.

"Remember only that Philip is our enemy, that he has long been robbing and insulting us, ... that the future depends on ourselves, and that unless we are willing to fight him there we shall perhaps be forced to fight here [our homeland]. ... You need not speculate [guess] about the future except to assure yourselves that it will be disastrous unless you face the facts and are willing to do your duty."

—from "The First Philippic," *Orations of Demosthenes*

Demosthenes says the Athenians must "do their duty." What is their duty?
A. to fight Philip when he comes to Athens
B. to speculate about what will happen in the future
C. to go fight Philip now
D. to seek aid from other city-states

8. **Predicting** What does Demosthenes predict?
F. If the Athenians are not good to Philip, he will rob them.
G. It is still possible to make peace with Philip.
H. There are others who will help the Athenians fight Philip.
I. If the Athenians ignore Philip, there will be disaster.

SHORT RESPONSE

"The choice of the site ... was determined by the abundance of water from [the lake] ... and by the good anchorage [harbor]. ... Alexandria became, within a century of its founding, one of the Mediterranean's largest cities and a centre of Greek scholarship and science."

—from *Encyclopaedia Britannica Online,* "Alexandria."

9. How did Alexandria's physical features help make it a great city?

10. Why do you think the city flourished, even after the death of Alexander?

EXTENDED RESPONSE

11. **Descriptive Writing** You are a citizen in a new city of the Hellenistic Era. Write a description of the ideal Hellenistic city.

Need Extra Help?

If You've Missed Question	1	2	3	4	5	6	7	8	9	10	11
Review Lesson	1	2	2	3	4	4	3	3	3, 4	4	4

NOTES

REFLECT, REVIEW, & REMEDIATE

INTERACTIVE WORKSHEET

Chapter Summary

Provide students with the Chapter Summary worksheet to help review the chapter and prepare for assessment.

Reviewing the Enduring Understandings

Review this chapter's Enduring Understandings with students:

- Cultures are held together by shared beliefs and common practices and values.
- People, places, and ideas change over time.
- Leaders can bring about change in society.

INTERACTIVE WHITEBOARD ACTIVITY Have a student volunteer create a three-column chart on the interactive whiteboard and write "Golden Age" in one column and "Hellenistic Era" in the other. Then lead a discussion that allows students to recall philosophers, writers and playwrights, and scientists from each period and what their main accomplishments were. The student volunteer should record names of the Greek thinkers in the chart.

	Golden Age	Hellenistic Era
Philosophers		
Writers and playwrights		
Scientists		

ACTIVITIES ANSWERS

Exploring the Essential Question

1. Students should note the ideas of some of the Greek philosophers and the discoveries of some of the Greek astronomers and mathematicians. There should be mention of Greek theater, writing, art, and sculpture. Their answer should discuss the importance that gods and goddesses played in the lives of Greek citizens. Lasting influences could include art, architecture, and political ideas.

21st Century Skills

2. The blog entry should include photos and written descriptions that illustrate the way statues of the human form were idealized in the Golden Age and became more realistic and emotional in the Hellenistic Era. The illustration and description of architecture could show the evolution of styles of columns and the same changes in human figures as part of friezes and bas-reliefs that occurred in statues. The blog entry should also include the writer's opinions and preferences. The visuals should be compelling and match the print copy.

Thinking Like a Historian

3. Students should identify places and explain why the historical and modern maps do not exactly correspond (for example, where an area that used to be one country is now two countries). They also should give some general commentary on the changes that have taken place, noting whether there have been many changes or just a few, for instance.

Locating Places

4. Letters should match the correct geographic locations.
   1. D; **2.** C; **3.** F; **4.** G **5.** A

ASSESSMENT ANSWERS

Review the Guiding Questions

1. **C** Zeus was the head of all the gods and goddesses and the most powerful. The Olympic Games were held to honor him, so C is the correct answer. Other gods and goddesses were honored in ceremonies, but the Olympics were always held in honor of Zeus.

2. **F** Socrates was sentenced to death because many Athenians thought he was encouraging the youth to rebel. As a result, they thought his teachings were dangerous. Thus, the answer is F. The Sophists did not believe in absolute right and wrong. The Sophists also accepted money for their teaching, but Socrates did not. Socrates did not teach about philosopher-kings; Plato did.

3. **B** Aristotle taught his students the principle of the golden mean—that a person should live moderately and avoid extremes in behavior. Choice B is the correct answer.

4. **G** After Alexander the Great's death, his generals divided the empire among themselves. Thus, choice G is the correct answer. Much of Alexander's empire was eventually conquered by Romans and others, but those takeovers took place many years after the empire was established. Alexander's troops threatened to rebel during the general's lifetime; their threats, however, did not cause the breakup of the empire.

5. **C** By the time of the Hellenistic Era, sculptors were carving the human figure more realistically and even depicting strong emotions. Thus, the answer is C. Sculptures showing the beauty and harmony of the ideal human were from the Golden Age of Greece.

6. **I** Archimedes first calculated the value of *pi*. Aristarchus claimed the sun was the center of the solar system, Eratosthenes discovered that Earth was round, and Hypatia lived after the Hellenistic Era.

Document-Based Questions

7. **C** Choice C is the correct answer. Demosthenes told the Athenians they need not speculate about the future, that the future was certain "unless they were willing to fight him there," and that they should not wait until he comes to Athens.

8. **I** Choice I is the correct answer. Demosthenes says "the future . . . will be disastrous" if the Athenians don't "do [their] duty" and conquer Philip.

Short Response

9. Students' responses should mention that the lake provided freshwater for drinking and watering crops, and the harbor made the city a major port for ships sailing on the Mediterranean Sea.

10. Students should note that Alexandria was able to thrive and grow because the Hellenistic Era (following Alexander's death) was a flourishing time for commerce and trade, the arts, building, science, and scholarship. Alexandria's location and the library, museum, and lighthouse made it a main center in that region of the world.

Extended Response

11. Students' reports should contain a description of an ideal city that reflects the values of Hellenistic culture. They should include some specific details about how they would plan the city's layout and buildings. Students may say they would encourage people to live there by paying them to come work on building the city (for example, architects and sculptors) and by providing good library facilities, support for the arts, and beautiful, open public spaces.

ONLINE RESOURCES

networks

There's More Online!

- INTERACTIVE WORKSHEETS
- BIOGRAPHIES
- CHARTS/GRAPHS
- GAMES
- GRAPHIC ORGANIZERS
- IMAGES
- MAPS
- PRIMARY SOURCES
- SLIDE SHOWS
- TIME LINE
- LECTURE SLIDES
- INTERACTIVE WHITEBOARD ACTIVITIES
- ASSESSMENTS
- VIDEOS

Timelines of Ancient Civilizations: India–Indus River Civilizations to Buddhism, Part 1

India's History From the Hindus to the Buddhists

India's History from the Golden Age to Today

Chapter **9**

Ancient India

Dear World History Teacher,

The first civilization in India arose in the Indus River valley during the fourth millennium B.C. It grew into two major cities, Harappa and Mohenjo-Daro. Harappan civilization achieved significant political and social gains for some 2,000 years, but internal decline weakened it. The migration of the Aryans finally brought its end around 1500 B.C.

The Aryans were an Indo-European-speaking people who established political control throughout all of India and created a new Indian civilization. A caste system, in which people were divided into distinct social classes, became a chief feature of the new Indian civilization.

Two of the world's great religions, Hinduism and Buddhism, began in India. Hinduism was an outgrowth of the religious beliefs of the Aryan peoples. Buddhism was the product of one man, Siddhartha Gautama, whose simple message created a new spiritual philosophy.

Between 325 B.C. and A.D. 500, India was a land of many different states, but two major empires emerged. The Mauryan Empire in northern India lasted from 321 B.C. until 183 B.C. The Gupta Empire lasted from A.D. 320 until the invasion of the Huns in the late fifth century. Both empires experienced strong government and a thriving of the arts. Indian civilization was extensive and eventually, in the form of Hinduism and Buddhism, spread to China and Southeast Asia.

Jackson J. Spielvogel

More Media Resources

Current Events Online

Visit McGraw-Hill's current events Web site for high-interest news stories and activities for your students. Access the site through the Student or Teacher Center in **networks.**

Reading List

Grade 6 reading level:
I Remember India, by Anita Ganeri

Grade 7 reading level:
Archeaology, by Trevor Barnes

Grade 8 reading level:
India: People, Place, Culture, History, DK Publishing

At the MOVIES

Watch clips of popular culture films about ancient India, such as *Little Buddha* (1993)

Discuss: From the information given in the film, what do you think Buddhists believe?

NOTE: Be sure to preview any clips to ensure they are age-appropriate.

Search for more videos online in the **networks** Resource Library.

CHAPTER 9 Planner

UNDERSTANDING BY DESIGN®

Enduring Understandings

- *People, places, and ideas change over time.* • *Religion can influence a society's beliefs and values.*

Essential Questions

- *How does geography influence the way people live?* • *How do religions develop?*
- *What makes a culture unique?*

Students will know:

- *how the Indus Valley civilization developed*
- *the origins of the caste system in India*
- *fundamental concepts of Hinduism and Buddhism*
- *what Ashoka accomplished during his rule*
- *the achievements of the Golden Age of the Gupta Empire*
- *the contributions of Indian culture to literature, art, math, and science*

Students will be able to:

- **recognize** why people settle by rivers
- **analyze** how human culture evolves
- **describe** early civilizations in India
- **recall** the names of the castes in India
- **distinguish** among the terms *varna*, *jati*, and *caste*
- **identify** key terms in Hindu beliefs
- **analyze** religious concepts
- **present** their own ideas in class
- **participate** in classroom discussion
- **compare and contrast** Ashoka's rule before and after he embraced Buddhism
- **compare and contrast** ancient Indian rule during Ashoka with modern day
- **synthesize** information to form opinions and make observations about ancient Indian culture

Predictable Misunderstandings

Students may think:

- Early civilizations were primitive and completely unlike ours.
- It only took a few hundred years for the early Indian societies to form, develop, and disappear.
- Indian culture had no influence on western people.

Assessment Evidence

Performance Task

- Hands-On Chapter Project

Other Evidence

- Interactive Graphic Organizers
- Primary Source Activity
- 21st Century Skills Activities
- Geography and History Activity
- Answers to Guided Reading Activity sheets
- Classroom discussion and group activity answers
- Answers from Analyzing Visuals
- Interactive Whiteboard Activity responses
- What Do You Think? questions
- Written paragraphs
- Lesson Reviews

Pacing Guide

Introducing the Chapter	1 day
Lesson 1 Early Civilizations	1 day
Lesson 2 Religions of Ancient India	1 day
Lesson 3 The Mauryan Empire	2 days
Chapter Activities and Assessment	1 day
TOTAL TIME	**6 Days**

Differentiated Instruction

These lesson plans are written to address the needs of your On Level students. Discussion and activities that are well-suited to your Approaching Grade Level learners, Beyond Grade Level learners, as well as your English Language Learners, are coded as follows:

Approaching Grade Level

Beyond Grade Level

ELL **English Language Learner**

NCSS Standards covered in "Ancient India"

Learners will understand:

1 CULTURE

1. "Culture" refers to the socially transmitted behaviors, beliefs, values, traditions, institutions, and ways of living together for a group of people;

5. How individuals learn the elements of their culture through interactions with others, and how individuals learn of other cultures through communication and study;

2 TIME, CONTINUITY, AND CHANGE

3. That learning about the past requires the interpretation of sources, and that using varied sources provides the potential for a more balanced interpretive record of the past;

5. Key historical periods and patterns of change within and across cultures (e.g., the rise and fall of ancient civilizations, the development of technology, the rise of modern nation-states, and the establishment and breakdown of colonial systems);

6. The origins and influences of social, cultural, political, and economic systems;

3 PEOPLE, PLACES, AND ENVIRONMENTS

1. The theme of people, places, and environments involves the study of the relationships between human populations in different locations and geographic phenomena such as climate, vegetation, and natural resources;

2. Concepts such as: location, region, place, migration, as well as human and physical systems;

6. Patterns of demographic and political change, and cultural diffusion in the past and present (e.g., changing national boundaries, migration, and settlement, and the diffusion of and changes in customs and ideas);

4 INDIVIDUAL DEVELOPMENT AND IDENTITY

4. How personal, social, cultural, and environmental factors contribute to the development and the growth of personal identity;

6. That perceptions are interpretations of information about individuals and events, and can be influenced by bias and stereotypes.

5 INDIVIDUALS, GROUPS, AND INSTITUTIONS

1. This theme helps us know how individuals are members of groups and institutions, and influence and shape those groups and institutions;

2. Concepts such as: mores, norms, status, role, socialization, ethnocentrism, cultural diffusion, competition, cooperation, conflict, race, ethnicity, and gender;

6. That cultural diffusion occurs when groups migrate;

7. That institutions may promote or undermine social conformity;

CHAPTER 9

Introducing the Chapter

(Student Edition p. 245)

The Story Matters . . .

Read "The Story Matters . . ." aloud in class. Then, lead a discussion about Radha and Krishna.

Ask: **Why do you think people wanted to hold up Radha and Krishna as examples of true love and loyalty?** *(Responses will vary. Students might point out that early Hindus valued the emotion of love and honored their deities.)*

Then ask: **Why is it important to know about deities such as Radha and Krishna?** *(Responses will vary. Students may suggest that knowing about deities such as Radha and Krishna will provide insight into ancient Indian culture and help them see connections between modern and ancient cultures and beliefs.)*

To help students answer these questions, encourage them to think about what they know of the deities and gods honored by other cultures. Encourage students to apply this knowledge to help them think about Hindu culture. Explain how knowledge of another culture's beliefs helps lead toward cultural understanding. Then, tell them they can learn more about Radha and Krishna online.

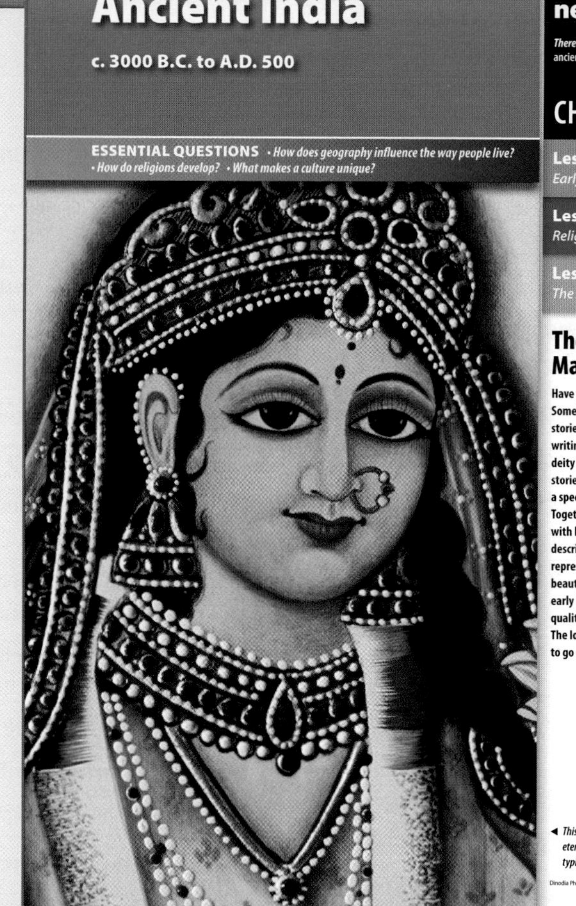
Ancient India

c. 3000 B.C. to A.D. 500

ESSENTIAL QUESTIONS • How does geography influence the way people live? • How do religions develop? • What makes a culture unique?

networks

There's More Online about the culture of ancient India.

CHAPTER 9

Lesson 1 Early Civilizations

Lesson 2 Religions of Ancient India

Lesson 3 The Mauryan Empire

The Story Matters . . .

Have you ever read a love story? Some of the earliest immortal love stories are found in ancient Indian writing. Radha is the supreme deity featured in many of these stories. She is the Hindu deity with a special companion—Krishna. Together they appear in many tales with happy events and beautiful descriptions. Radha and Krishna represent examples of true love, beauty, loyalty, and devotion. The early Hindu culture honored these qualities as necessary for a good life. The love of Radha and Krishna is said to go on for eternity.

This picture of Radha emphasizes her eternal beauty. The ornate jewelry is typical of ancient Indian art.

Dinodia Photo Library/Age fotostock

245

Introducing Place and Time

(Student Edition pp. 246–247)

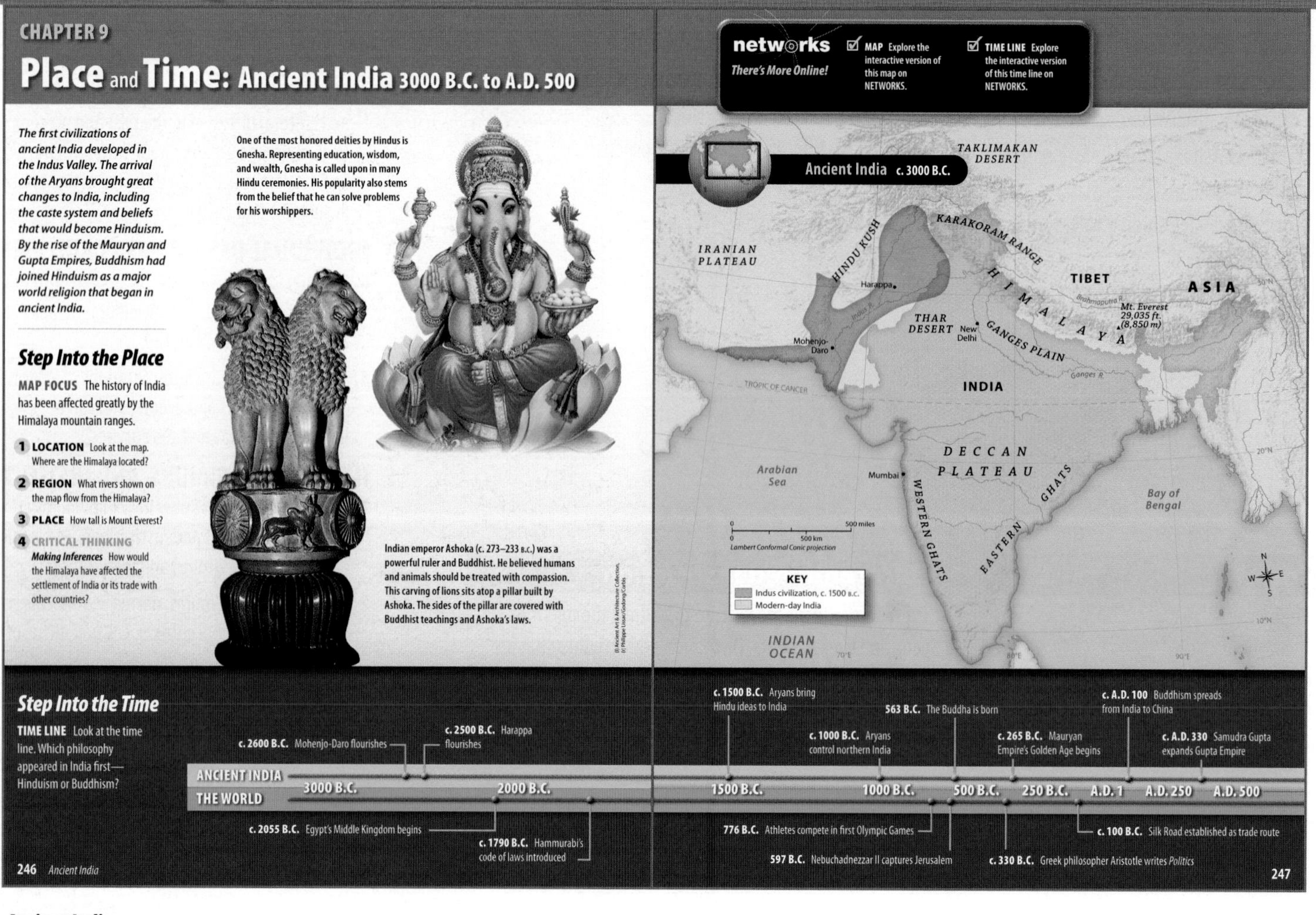
CHAPTER 9

Place and Time: Ancient India 3000 B.C. to A.D. 500

The first civilizations of ancient India developed in the Indus Valley. The arrival of the Aryans brought great changes to India, including the caste system and beliefs that would become Hinduism. By the rise of the Mauryan and Gupta Empires, Buddhism had joined Hinduism as a major world religion that began in ancient India.

Step Into the Place

MAP FOCUS The history of India has been affected greatly by the Himalaya mountain ranges.

1 LOCATION Look at the map. Where are the Himalaya located?

2 REGION What rivers shown on the map flow from the Himalaya?

3 PLACE How tall is Mount Everest?

4 CRITICAL THINKING *Making Inferences* How would the Himalaya have affected the settlement of India or its trade with other countries?

One of the most honored deities by Hindus is Gnesha. Representing education, wisdom, and wealth, Gnesha is called upon in many Hindu ceremonies. His popularity also stems from the belief that he can solve problems for his worshippers.

Indian emperor Ashoka (c. 273–233 B.C.) was a powerful ruler and Buddhist. He believed humans and animals should be treated with compassion. This carving of lions sits atop a pillar built by Ashoka. The sides of the pillar are covered with Buddhist teachings and Ashoka's laws.

(l) Ancient Art & Architecture Collection, (r) Philippe Lissac/Godong/Corbis

networks There's More Online! MAP Explore the interactive version of this map on NETWORKS. TIME LINE Explore the interactive version of this time line on NETWORKS.

Step Into the Time

TIME LINE Look at the time line. Which philosophy appeared in India first—Hinduism or Buddhism?

ANCIENT INDIA

c. 2600 B.C. Mohenjo-Daro flourishes

c. 2500 B.C. Harappa flourishes

c. 1500 B.C. Aryans bring Hindu ideas to India

c. 1000 B.C. Aryans control northern India

563 B.C. The Buddha is born

c. 265 B.C. Mauryan Empire's Golden Age begins

c. A.D. 100 Buddhism spreads from India to China

c. A.D. 330 Samudra Gupta expands Gupta Empire

3000 B.C. 2000 B.C. 1500 B.C. 1000 B.C. 500 B.C. 250 B.C. A.D. 1 A.D. 250 A.D. 500

THE WORLD

c. 2055 B.C. Egypt's Middle Kingdom begins

c. 1790 B.C. Hammurabi's code of laws introduced

776 B.C. Athletes compete in first Olympic Games

597 B.C. Nebuchadnezzar II captures Jerusalem

c. 330 B.C. Greek philosopher Aristotle writes *Politics*

c. 100 B.C. Silk Road established as trade route

246 Ancient India

247

Technology Extension

- Find an additional activity online that incorporates technology for this project.
- Visit the EdTechTeacher Web sites (included in the Technology Extension for this chapter) for more links, tutorials, and other resources.

Assessing Background Knowledge

INTERACTIVE WORKSHEET

What Do You Know? Activity

Have students complete the What Do You Know? Activity. Review students' answers to spot any misconceptions they may have. Address these misconceptions with students as they complete the chapter. Students who continue to have misconceptions may need additional help.

After students complete the chapter, have them reread the statements and review and change their answers as needed. Ask students to explain why they changed any answers they did. *(Students should cite facts from the chapter.)*

INTERACTIVE WORKSHEET

Guided Reading Activities

There is a Guided Reading Activity for each lesson in this chapter. You may wish to assign the Guided Reading Activity for Lesson 1 after introducing the chapter content.

Hands-On Chapter Project

Students will create a slide show presentation about life in ancient India.

- Students will participate in a class discussion about ways in which physical geography has influenced the development of ancient civilizations.
- Students will divide into small groups, with each group researching a different topic about ancient Indian life.
- Then, using worksheets and class discussions to guide the process, each group will plan, research, and create a slide show presentation on its chosen topic.
- Next, students will present their slide shows to the class.
- Students will then work as a team to combine each group's slide show into a single class presentation.
- Finally, students will evaluate their research, presentations, and collaboration using an assessment rubric.

Visit **networks** online to see the full project and rubric.

ONLINE RESOURCES

networks

Assign these interactive worksheets and quizzes from your Teacher Lesson Center. All resources are print-ready.

It's ALL Online!

Chapter 9 Resources

- ☑ Chapter Summary
- ☑ Vocabulary Builder
- ☑ What Do You Know?
- ☑ Hands-On Chapter Project

Lesson 1 Resources

- ☑ Interactive Graphic Organizer
- ☑ Geography and History Activity
  Understanding Human-Environment Interaction
- ☑ Guided Reading Activity
- ☑ Reading Essentials and Study Guide
- ☑ Online Self-Check Quiz

Lesson 2 Resources

- ☑ Interactive Graphic Organizer
- ☑ 21st Century Skills Activity
  Communication: Summarizing
- ☑ Guided Reading Activity
- ☑ Reading Essentials and Study Guide
- ☑ Online Self-Check Quiz

Lesson 3 Resources

- ☑ Interactive Graphic Organizer
- ☑ Primary Source Activity
  Buddhism and Hinduism
- ☑ 21st Century Skills Activity
  Communication: Create and Give a Presentation
- ☑ Guided Reading Activity
- ☑ Reading Essentials and Study Guide
- ☑ Online Self-Check Quiz

Assessment Resources

- ☑ Lesson Reviews
- ☑ Online Self-Check Quizzes
- ☑ Chapter Activities and Assessment
- ☑ Standardized Test Practice

Remediation Resources

- ☑ Reading Essentials and Study Guide
- ☑ Guided Reading Activities
- ☑ Online Self-Check Quizzes
- ☑ Chapter Summary

Step Into the Place

INTERACTIVE WHITEBOARD ACTIVITY

Location Project the Chapter Opener map on the whiteboard. Remind students of other civilizations they have studied.

Ask: **What are some of the geographic features that people might look for when choosing a place to settle?**

Have student volunteers first identify places where civilizations have formed and places where civilizations might have formed. Ask each volunteer to explain his or her choice. As a class, discuss the Map Focus questions.

Step Into the Time

Making Inferences Have students review the time line for the chapter. Explain that they will be studying events from about 300 B.C. to A.D. 500.

Ask: **Notice that several civilizations are listed. How long did each one last? What are possible reasons why some civilizations last longer than others?** *(Answers may include for longer-lasting civilizations: good leadership, successful farming, no invasions or natural disasters; for shorter-lasting civilizations: natural disasters, war and conquest, and the gradual weakening of society and leadership)*

Answers for pages 246–247

Step Into the Place

1. The Himalaya run along India's northern border.
2. The Indus and Ganges Rivers flow from the Himalaya.
3. Mount Everest is more than 29,000 feet (8,839 m) tall.
4. **CRITICAL THINKING** The Himalaya made travel into India difficult. The mountains also presented a barrier to trade with other countries.

Step Into the Time

The Aryans introduced Hindu beliefs around 1500 B.C., which was before the Buddha's birth.

networks
There's More Online!
☑ GRAPHIC ORGANIZER
• Indian Social Classes
• Ways Aryans Changed India
☑ SLIDE SHOW
Crafts in India

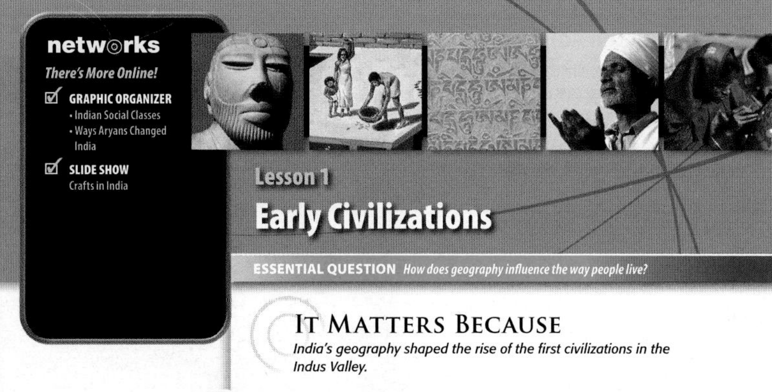

Lesson 1
Early Civilizations

ESSENTIAL QUESTION *How does geography influence the way people live?*

It Matters Because

India's geography shaped the rise of the first civilizations in the Indus Valley.

1 The Geography of India

GUIDING QUESTION *How did physical geography and climate influence the development of civilization in India?*

India and several other modern-day countries make up the **subcontinent** of India. A subcontinent is a large landmass that is smaller than a continent. The Indian subcontinent is part of the continent of Asia.

Mountains, Plains, and Rivers

On its northern border, India is separated from the rest of Asia by rugged mountain systems. The Himalaya are one of these mountain systems. You have probably heard of Mount Everest, the highest peak in the Himalaya. Mount Everest is more than 29,000 feet tall. That is nearly 5.5 miles (8.8 km), which makes Mount Everest the tallest mountain in the world.

Wide fertile plains lie at the foot of India's extensive mountain ranges. The plains owe their rich soil to the three great rivers that flow through the region. These rivers are the Indus (IHN•duhs), the Ganges (GAN•jeez), and the Brahmaputra (BRAHM•uh•POO•truh). India's people rely on these rivers for farming, transportation, and trade.

Reading **HELP**DESK

Taking Notes: ***Summarizing***
Using a diagram like this one, describe three ways the Aryans changed India.

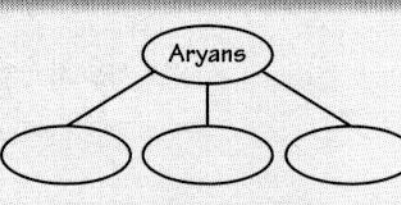

Content Vocabulary
• **subcontinent** • **raja** • **caste**
• **monsoon** • **Sanskrit** • **guru**
• **language family** • **Vedas**

The Geography of India

KARAKORAM RANGE
HINDU KUSH
Harappa
Indus R.
Mohenjo-Daro
HIMALAYA
Mt. Everest 29,035 ft. (8,850 m)
GANGES PLAIN
Ganges R.
INDIA
TROPIC OF CANCER
DECCAN PLATEAU
WESTERN GHATS
EASTERN GHATS
Arabian Sea
Bay of Bengal
INDIAN OCEAN
0 800 miles
0 800 km
Albers Equal-Area projection
30°N 20°N 10°N 70°E 80°E 90°E
KEY
Winter monsoon (dry winds)
Summer monsoon (wet winds)
▲ Mountain peak

GEOGRAPHY CONNECTION

The mighty Himalaya and major bodies of water border the Indian subcontinent.

1 **PLACE** Which two rivers are found in northern India?

2 **CRITICAL THINKING**
Predicting What might happen to India's farmers if the summer monsoons did not occur?

The landforms in central and southern India are much different from the landforms in the north. Along the west and east coasts of the subcontinent are lush fertile lands. Farther inland, there are two chains of mountains that have worn down over time. As the mountains eroded, they left areas of rugged hills. Between the mountains is a dry highland known as the Deccan Plateau (DEH•kuhn pla•TOH). The southern two-thirds of India is part of this huge **plateau**.

India's civilization has been shaped by its climate as well as by its physical landscape. Seasonal winds called **monsoons** (mahn•SOONZ) have a large influence on India's climate.

During winter, monsoon winds blow cold, dry air from the Himalaya east to west across India. During summer, warmer land temperatures cause the winds to change direction. Summer monsoon winds blow west to east from the Arabian Sea. They bring warm, wet air and pouring rains.

subcontinent a large landmass that is smaller than a continent
monsoon seasonal wind, especially in the Indian Ocean and southern Asia

Visual Vocabulary
plateau a broad flat area of high land

The summer rains bring farmers water that they need for their crops. With good rainfall, farmers can grow large amounts of food. Because of this, people celebrate the arrival of the monsoon rains. However, monsoon rains can also cause damage. Very heavy rains sometimes cause floods that destroy crops. Floods can even kill people and animals.

Too little rain can also be a problem. If the rains come late, there may be a long dry period called a drought. A serious drought can bring disaster to farmers. If lots of farm crops are ruined, many people may go hungry or starve.

☑ **PROGRESS CHECK**

Explaining How do monsoon winds affect life in India?

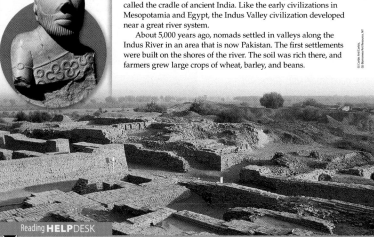

Archaeologists have studied the ruins of Mohenjo-Daro (below) and found many artifacts. These include statues of priest-kings, jewelry, and pottery.

2 The Indus Valley Civilization

GUIDING QUESTION *How did the people of the Indus River Valley build cities?*

Thousands of years ago, India's first civilization began in the valley around the Indus River. The Indus Valley civilization is called the cradle of ancient India. Like the early civilizations in Mesopotamia and Egypt, the Indus Valley civilization developed near a great river system.

About 5,000 years ago, nomads settled in valleys along the Indus River in an area that is now Pakistan. The first settlements were built on the shores of the river. The soil was rich there, and farmers grew large crops of wheat, barley, and beans.

Reading **HELP**DESK

Build Vocabulary: ***Word Forms***
The word *celebrate* exists in several forms. The verb form means "to honor a person or a holiday with festivities." The noun *celebration* means "an event held to honor a holiday or person." The adjective used to describe a celebration is *celebratory*.

HOUSES IN MOHENJO-DARO

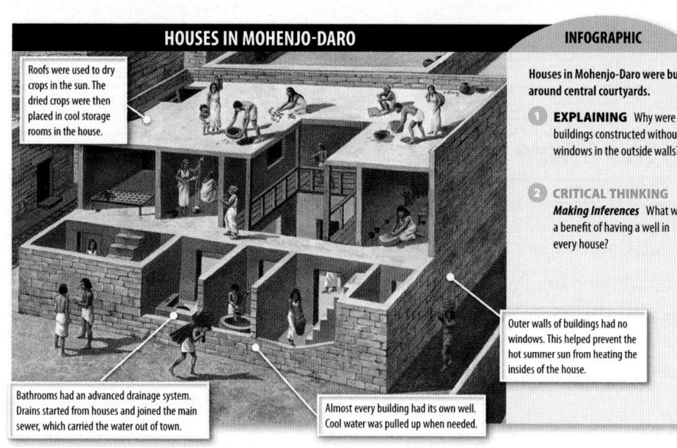

Roofs were used to dry crops in the sun. The dried crops were then placed in cool storage rooms in the house.
Bathrooms had an advanced drainage system. Drains started from houses and joined the main sewer, which carried the water out of town.
Almost every building had its own well. Cool water was pulled up when needed.
Outer walls of buildings had no windows. This helped prevent the hot summer sun from heating the insides of the house.

INFOGRAPHIC

Houses in Mohenjo-Daro were built around central courtyards.

1 **EXPLAINING** Why were buildings constructed without windows in the outside walls?

2 **CRITICAL THINKING**
Making Inferences What was a benefit of having a well in every house?

With abundant crops, not all the people needed to farm. Many people made tools and constructed houses. Some supported themselves by trading extra food and goods. The Indus people prospered and built cities. The Indus civilization spread over much of western India and Pakistan.

Mohenjo-Daro and Harappa

The Indus culture flourished between 2600 B.C. and 1900 B.C. We know about the Indus culture from studying the ruins of two major cities, Mohenjo-Daro (moh•HEHN•joh DAHR•oh) and Harappa (huh•RA•puh).

At their peak, both Mohenjo-Daro and Harappa had more than 35,000 residents. The cities were designed almost exactly alike. Each city had dozens of streets. Larger streets were paved with tan-colored bricks. The smaller streets that crossed them were often left unpaved. At the west end of each city stood a fortress built on a brick platform and surrounded by strong, thick walls.

The Indus Valley people used oven-baked bricks to build their homes. Most houses had flat wooden roofs. The houses had enclosed courtyards, and some were several stories tall.

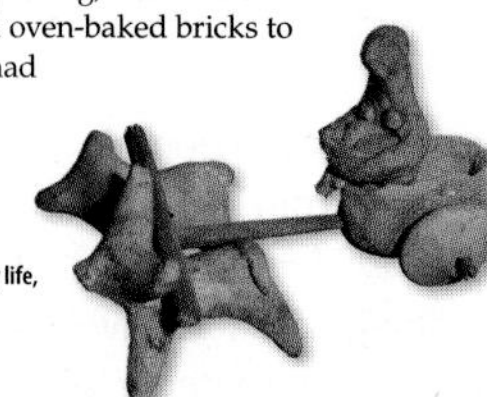
Ancient Indian art portrays daily life, such as driving this ox cart.

LESSON 1

ENGAGE

IMAGE Show students the interactive images of the Deccan Plateau.

Ask:

What do these pictures suggest about the environment of the plateau? *(It is higher than the area around it. The environment is diverse. It has rivers, so people might settle there.)*

Why do civilizations tend to settle near rivers? *(Rivers provide water and rich soil for good crops. Ample food in turn allows the population to grow, and it allows people to take up jobs other than farming, such as trading and craft making. Rivers also provide transportation as well as access to trade and other cultures and beliefs.)*

Explain to students that river valleys like these were the location of the earliest civilizations to develop in India. These civilizations adapted to the diverse environments of the region. AL

TEACH & ASSESS

1 The Geography of India

GUIDING QUESTION ***How did physical geography and climate influence the development of civilization in India?***

LECTURE SLIDE

Discussing Direct students to the map "Geography of India" in their textbooks and then show the lecture slide on the geography of India.

Ask:

How many rivers supported the Indian civilizations, and what were they called? *(three; the Indus, the Ganges, and the Brahmaputra)* AL ELL

MAP

Analyzing Have students return their focus to the map "The Geography of India." Help students find the patterns of the monsoons on the map.

Ask:

How might these winds have affected human life in the river valley? *(They would bring rain for crops, but this extra rain might also bring floods. If the monsoons didn't come, drought could result.)*

2 The Indus Valley Civilization

GUIDING QUESTION ***How did the people of the Indus River Valley build cities?***

IMAGE

Drawing Conclusions Direct students to the diagram of the Mohenjo-Daro buildings in their textbooks. Then show them the images of early Indian civilization and daily life in Mohenjo-Daro. Discuss the features of the cities including construction with bricks, grid patterns, and evidence of city life. Guide students to an understanding of how well planned these buildings were.

Ask:

What did the river supply for building the cities? *(mud for bricks; water for plumbing)*

How do we know that Mohenjo-Daro was a city rather than a rural village? *(It was large. There is evidence of trade and different kinds of work people did, including crafting, buying and selling, building, and engineering.)*

IMAGE

Analyzing Visuals Show students the image of the Harappan unicorn seal. Ask a volunteer to read aloud the text that explains how ancient Indians used seals like the one shown. As a class, answer the discussion questions.

Then ask:

Why do you think scholars believe these seals may show a form of written language? *(Answers may include: The pictographs on the seal resemble a form of writing.)* BL

INTERACTIVE WHITEBOARD ACTIVITY

Then have students complete the sorting exercise from the Interactive Whiteboard Activity. Students should draw on what they learned about symbols and seals in the previous activity. Allow students to work alone or in pairs to match the type of community with the images in the image bank. AL ELL

INTERACTIVE WORKSHEET

Geography and History Activity

Comparing and Contrasting Assign students the Geography and History Activity to work on individually or in groups. Have students read the text about the how the Harappan and Aryan civilizations, discussed in the next part of the lesson, were affected by geography. Students may use what they learn about the Aryans in this activity to guide the discussion in the next part of the lesson.

Answers for pages 248–251

P. 248 Taking Notes Possible answers include: introducing the Vedas, introducing the caste system, developing a written language, introducing new agricultural techniques

P. 249 GEOGRAPHY CONNECTION

1. The Indus and the Ganges Rivers are found in northern India.
2. CRITICAL THINKING The farmers would be lacking the water needed for crops.

P. 250 ☑ PROGRESS CHECK The summer monsoon winds bring rains that can help farmers produce more crops but can also cause destructive floods.

P. 251 INFOGRAPHIC

1. Buildings without windows were cooler because windows let in the intense summer heat.
2. CRITICAL THINKING Households with their own wells had a steady source of water. Wells made a household more efficient because people did not have to take time to find and collect water.

Thinking Like a HISTORIAN

Researching on the Internet

Historians have found many clay seals and stamps in Harappa. These objects are covered in writing and pictures. Historians have not determined the meaning of these writings. Use the Internet to find images of some of these seals. Create a list of what you think each might mean. Then discuss your theories with your class. For more information about using the Internet for research, read the chapter *What Does a Historian Do?*

The civilization's engineers and builders were highly skilled. Large buildings stored grain for the entire population. Wells supplied water, and every house had at least one indoor bathroom. Wastewater flowed through pipes to pits outside the city walls. Houses also had garbage chutes connected to bins in the streets.

What was life like?

Archaeologists have learned much about Indus Valley culture by studying its city ruins. For example, the ruins show that cities' royal palaces and temples may have been enclosed in a fortress. This shows the importance of both religion and government in the settlements of the Indus Valley.

Most Indus Valley people **resided** in farming villages surrounding the cities. They grew rice, barley, wheat, peas, and cotton. City residents were merchants, shopkeepers, and artisans. They made and sold copper and bronze tools, clay pottery, and cotton cloth. Artisans also made jewelry from shells, ivory, and gold. Archaeologists have even found toys among the ruins.

Indus Valley merchants traveled as far as Mesopotamia to trade. Some traders made the difficult trip through the mountains to Mesopotamia. Others probably sailed to Mesopotamia along the southern coast of Asia.

✔ PROGRESS CHECK

Describing How did most Indus Valley people earn a living?

3 Aryan Migrations and Settlements

GUIDING QUESTION *How did the Aryans influence early India?*

Sometime around 1900 B.C., the people of the Indus Valley began to **abandon** their cities and villages. Why did the people leave? Archaeologists have found several possible causes. There was a severe drought that lasted for hundreds of years. It destroyed crops and caused people to starve. Earthquakes and floods killed many more people and changed the course of the Indus River. Meanwhile, groups of people called the Aryans (AR•ee•uhnz) **migrated** to India. Soon a new civilization **emerged**.

Reading HELPDESK

Academic Vocabulary

reside to live
abandon to leave and not return
migrate to move from one place to another
emerge to come into being or become known

The Indo-Europeans

The Aryans were not a race or ethnic group. Many historians believe that the Aryan people's language was part of a large language family known as Indo-European. A **language family** is a group of similar languages. Many modern Indian languages, like Hindi, are part of the Indo-European family. So are many European languages, including English. The Aryans were speakers of Indo-European languages.

Indo-European people lived in central Asia but began migrating to other places. Some moved west to Europe or south to Iran. The Aryans went to India. Like most Indo-Europeans, the Aryans raised cattle for meat, milk, and butter. They moved from place to place to find pastures and water for their cattle. The Aryans were expert horse riders and hunters, as well as fierce warriors. As they moved about, the Aryans sometimes raided nearby villages for food.

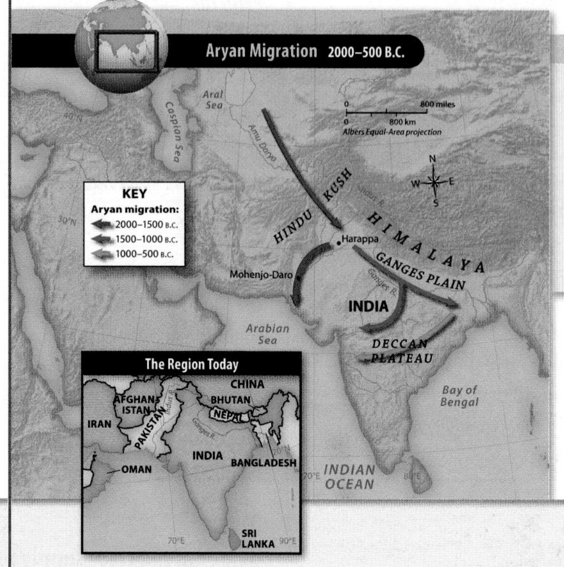

GEOGRAPHY CONNECTION

The Aryans migrated into India and spread throughout the subcontinent.

1. **MOVEMENT** From what general direction did the Aryan migration flow?
2. **CRITICAL THINKING** ***Identifying*** What physical features did the Aryans settle along during their first migrations? Why did they settle there?

language family a group of similar languages

Hindi, India's national language, developed over time from ancient Sanskrit. The Aryans used Sanskrit to record many things.

CRITICAL THINKING

Drawing Conclusions Why did early people develop a system of writing once they settled in groups?

From about 1500 to 1000 B.C., bands of Aryans moved throughout India. These groups mixed with the descendants of the Indus Valley people. Together, they created a new culture. Over time, the Aryans in India adopted a new way of life. They settled down in one place and became farmers, though they still raised cattle. Eventually, the Aryans saw their herds as sacred and banned the use of cattle as food.

The Aryans began to make iron tools to clear forests so they could farm the land. They also built irrigation systems. Gradually, they turned the Ganges River valley into productive farmland. In the north, farmers grew grains such as wheat, millet, and barley. Millet is a grain that is still an important food in many parts of the world. Farmers planted rice in the fertile river valleys. In the south, farmers grew crops such as cotton, vegetables, pepper, ginger, and cinnamon.

The Aryans lived in tribes. Each tribe was led by a **raja** (RAH•jah), or prince. The rajas created their own small kingdoms, which often fought each other over cattle, treasure, and land.

Like most nomadic people, the early Aryans had no written language. After they settled in villages, they developed a written language called **Sanskrit** (SAN•skriht). Sanskrit gave people a way to record sales, trade, and land ownership. Eventually, Aryan hymns, stories, poems, and prayers were also written in Sanskrit. Later, they were recorded and collected into sacred **texts** known as the **Vedas** (VAY•duhs). Examples of the Vedas remain today. This prayer in the Vedas asks for divine help in offering sacrifices:

PRIMARY SOURCE

> "Let us invoke [call upon] today, to aid our labour, the Lord of Speech, . . . May he hear kindly all our invocations [prayers] who gives all bliss for aid, whose works are righteous."
>
> —from Visvakarman," *Rig-Veda*, Book 10, Hymn LXXXI

✔ PROGRESS CHECK

Identifying How did the Aryans change their way of life after they settled in India?

Reading HELPDESK

raja an Indian prince
Sanskrit the first written language of India
Vedas ancient sacred writings of India
caste an Indian social class whose members are restricted in the jobs they may take and in their association with members of other castes
guru a teacher

Academic Vocabulary

text words written down in a particular form, such as a book
manual work done by hand

4 Ancient Indian Society

GUIDING QUESTION *How was society in ancient India organized?*

As the Aryans settled into India, people set up towns along India's Ganges River. Most people still farmed for a living. Some workers specialized in crafts such as carpentry or weaving. Others took part in trade. As India's economy grew, a system of social classes gradually developed.

What were the *Varnas*?

The four social classes of ancient India are called *varnas* (VUR•nehs). People were considered members of the *varna* into which they were born. The most powerful *varnas* were the Brahmins (BRAH•mihns) and Kshatriyas (KSHA•tree•uhs). The Brahmins were the priests—the people who performed religious ceremonies. The Kshatriyas were warriors who ran the government and army.

INFOGRAPHIC

Indian society was divided into four major castes.

1. **IDENTIFYING** Which caste was the largest? Which was the smallest?
2. **CRITICAL THINKING** ***Analyzing*** Why do you think unskilled workers and servants were grouped in the Sudra caste?

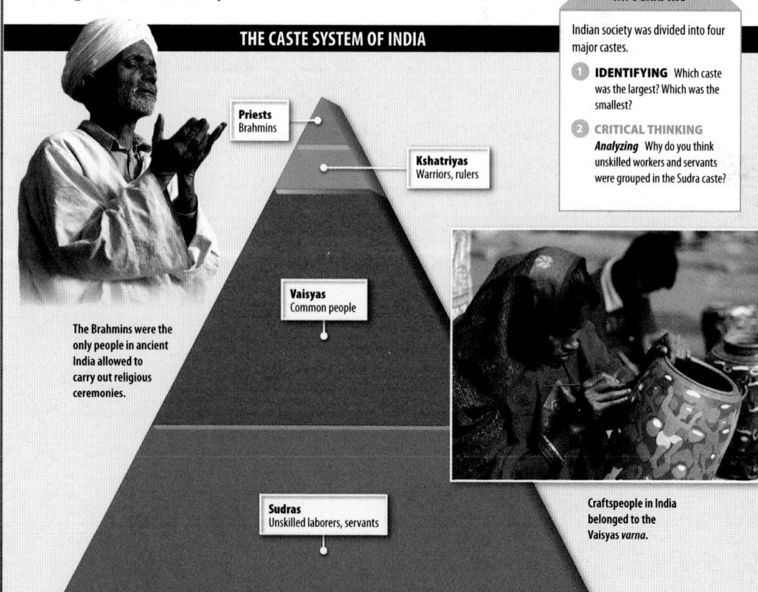

The Brahmins were the only people in ancient India allowed to carry out religious ceremonies.

Craftspeople in India belonged to the Vaisyas *varna*.

LESSON 1 (cont.)

CLOSE & REFLECT

Explaining Discuss the achievements of the Indus Valley and Aryan civilizations with students. Ask them if they were surprised by the relative sophistication of cities such as Mohenjo-Daro. Encourage them to consider the lasting impact that the Aryan migration has had on the culture and society of India.

IF YOU HAVE MORE TIME . . .

Research Languages in Modern India

Making Inferences Make sure students understand that the Aryans introduced a new language, Sanskrit, to ancient India. Explain that today many languages are spoken in India. Invite interested students to work alone or in pairs or small groups to research and identify modern India's languages, which include the two official languages of English and Hindi, along with Bengali, Gujarati, Kashmiri, Malayalam, Marathi, Oriya, Punjabi, Tamil, Telugu, Urdu, Kannada, Assamese, Sanskirit, and Sindhi. Suggest that students make a map or other visual that shows where these languages are mostly spoken in India. Students should present their findings to the class and be able to discuss how having a population that speaks many different languages might make it difficult to unify the country politically or culturally. BL

Answers for page 256

P. 256 ☑ PROGRESS CHECK Families were the center of daily life. Many generations lived together in a household controlled by the oldest male.

LESSON 1 REVIEW

1. The development of the written language Sanskrit allowed the Vedas to be preserved in written form.
2. The summer monsoons bring much-needed rain to the Indus Valley region, making farming more productive.
3. Cities such as Harappa and Mohenjo-Daro were well planned and organized, with paved streets, sewer systems, and garbage collection in addition to their fortified walls.
4. The Aryans began as migrants but eventually mixed with the descendants of the Indus Valley peoples to form a new culture.
5. The four main groups are Brahmin, or priests; Kshatriyas, or warriors and rulers; Vaisyas, or commoners who were farmers, craftspeople, and merchants; and the Sudras, or manual laborers and servants.
6. Student answers will vary, but they should note that the Aryans established new kingdoms, introduced the *varna* system to India, and created a new culture that introduced the Vedas.

Teaching *Religions of Ancient India* (Student Edition pp. 257–264)

LESSON 2

ENGAGE

LECTURE SLIDE

Comparing and Contrasting Explain to students that people in most cultures of the world practice some form of religion. Show the lecture slide that explains the difference between monotheism and polytheism. Have a student volunteer read the slide aloud. Make sure students understand how to pronounce the words *monotheism* and *polytheism* and know their meanings. ELL

Then ask: **Based on your prior knowledge of ancient cultures, which believed in many gods?** *(Sumerians, most of the Egyptians, Greeks, Romans)* **Which ancient cultures believed in one God?** *(Israel and, briefly, Egypt)*

Explain to students that in this lesson they are going to learn about some Eastern religions. Tell them that as they read, they should look for ways in which Eastern religions differ from—and are similar to—those they have studied previously.

TEACH & ASSESS

1 Origins of Hinduism

GUIDING QUESTION *What are the basic beliefs of Hinduism? How did Hinduism develop?*

IMAGE

Previewing Explain to students that some Hindu beliefs are common to all three religions they will study in this lesson. List the following core Hindu beliefs on the board:

- All souls are connected to one great soul, known as Brahman.
- People are reincarnated, or reborn, again and again in a cycle.
- The cycle ends when the soul is united with Brahman.

Then show students the image with information about the Upanishads. Ask a volunteer to read the text aloud. Ask for students' reactions to the images.

Ask: **What do you think the images represent, or stand for?** *(Possible answers: a god, the power of or the spread of Hinduism)* Explain to students that some Hindu beliefs are common to all three of the religions they will study in this lesson.

INTERACTIVE GRAPHIC ORGANIZER

Describing Allow students time in class to begin completing the Taking Notes graphic organizer with facts about the religions of ancient India. Students may continue to fill in the organizer as they work their way through the lesson. AL

Answers for page 257

P. 257 Taking Notes Answers may include: Hinduism: Belief in one universal spirit, belief in reincarnation and karma, support for caste system; Buddhism: Belief in reincarnation, importance of karma, opposition to caste system, search for nirvana; Jainism: Belief in *ahimsa*

The Upanishads (upper right) present basic Hindu views about the universe. Many Hindus regard the deity Vishwakarma as the universe's divine builder. They honor him as the protector of all artisans and architects. Images of Vishwakarma show him with four arms and hands, holding building plans and tools.

The Upanishads say that a soul that becomes one with Brahman is like a lump of salt thrown into water. The lump of salt is gone, but the water tastes salty. The salt has become part of the water.

Most ancient Indians, however, could not easily understand the idea of Brahman. They believed in many different deities that were more like people. Hindus built temples and statues and held ceremonies for these deities. Eventually, three deities became the most important: *Brahma* the Creator, *Vishnu* the Preserver, and *Shiva* the Destroyer. Over time, many Hindus came to think of all the deities as different parts of Brahman, the one universal spirit.

Another part of Hinduism is the belief in **reincarnation** (REE•ihn•kahr•NAY•shuhn), or the rebirth of the soul. Hindus strive for *moksha*, the ultimate peace. Hindus believe that most souls do not reunite with Brahman immediately after death. Instead, each soul must first pass through many lives. The Upanishads describe reincarnation as a process in this way:

PRIMARY SOURCE

> “As a caterpillar, having reached the end of a blade of grass, takes hold of another blade, then draws its body from the first, so the Self having reached the end of his body, takes hold of another body, then draws itself from the first.”
>
> —from *Brihadaranyaka Upanishad, Fourth Brahmana*, line 3

Reading HELPDESK

Hinduism a major religion that developed in ancient India

Brahman the universal spirit worshipped by Hindus

reincarnation the rebirth of the soul

karma a force that decides the form that people will be reborn into in their next lives

dharma a person's personal duty, based on the individual's place in society

Academic Vocabulary

status a person's rank compared to others

In Hinduism, the idea of reincarnation is closely related to another idea known as **karma** (KAHR•muh). According to karma, people's **status** in life is not an accident. It is based on what they did in past lives. In addition, the things people do in this life decide how they will be reborn. If someone leads a bad life, that person is reborn into a lower form of life. When good people die, their souls are reborn into a higher form of life.

Hindus believe they have to earn a better existence in the next life. To do that, they must follow **dharma** (DAHR•muh), or their personal duty. People's duties are different, depending on their place in society. A farmer has different duties than a priest. Men have different duties than women.

How did Hindu beliefs shape the way of life in ancient India? For one thing, Indians accepted the Hindu idea that all life is sacred. Animals as well as people were treated with kindness and respect.

Beliefs such as reincarnation also made many Indians more accepting of the *varna* system. A devout Hindu believed that the people in a higher *jati* were superior and deserved their status. At the same time, the belief in reincarnation gave hope to people from every walk of life. A person who leads a good life is reborn into a higher *jati*.

Connections to TODAY

Hindu Beliefs

Many Hindus today believe that a man should go through four stages in his life: a student (preparing to live in the world), a married man (accepting worldly responsibilities), a forest dweller (retirement from the world), and finally, a wandering monk (completely renouncing the world).

✓ **PROGRESS CHECK**

Understanding Cause and Effect How did Hinduism affect the way ancient Indians lived day to day?

Indian Hindus believe the Ganges River is sacred. They believe that the river is the physical form of a female deity, and they bathe in the river to purify themselves. What tells you this photo shows Hindus in modern times?

BIOGRAPHY

The Buddha (c. 563 B.C.–c. 483 B.C.)

In his search for wisdom, Siddhartha Gautama lived a very simple life. He lived apart from people and slept on the ground. To clear his mind, he stopped eating for a time.

Still, after years, he felt he was no closer to the truth. One day he sat down in the shade of a tree to meditate. At last, Buddhist texts say, he learned the truth he had been seeking. Once he began teaching, he became known to his followers as the Buddha, or "Enlightened One."

▶ **CRITICAL THINKING**

Speculating Why do you think Siddhartha Gautama sought wisdom by living in such a simple way?

2 Rise of Buddhism

GUIDING QUESTION ***Why did Buddhism appeal to many people in various parts of Asia?***

During the 500s B.C., some Indians felt unhappy with the many ceremonies of the Hindu religion. They wanted a simpler, more spiritual faith. They left their homes and looked for peace in the hills and forests. Many trained their minds to **focus** and think in positive ways. This training was called meditation. Some seekers developed new ideas and became religious teachers.

One of these teachers was Siddhartha Gautama (sih•DAHR•tuh GOW•tah•muh). He became known as the Buddha (BOO•dah). He founded a new religion called **Buddhism** (BOO•dih•zuhm).

The Buddha

Today, Buddhism is one of the major world religions. Most Buddhists live in Southeast Asia and East Asia. Only a few live in India, Buddhism's birthplace.

Siddhartha Gautama was born around the year 563 B.C. The exact date of his birth is not known. He grew up as a prince in a small kingdom near the Himalaya. Today, this area is in southern Nepal (nuh • PAWL).

As a young man, Siddhartha seemed to have everything. He was rich, handsome, and happily married with a newborn son. Then one day he left his palace to explore the life of ordinary people in the kingdom. As he traveled, Siddhartha was shocked at the misery and poverty around him. He saw beggars, people who were sick, and aged people with nowhere to live. For the first time, he understood that the world was filled with suffering.

Siddhartha gave up all he had and became a monk. Saying goodbye to his wife and son, he began his journey to find the meaning of life. Dressed in a yellow robe, he traveled the country, stopping to **meditate**, or think deeply. As he preached his message to people, he gathered followers. His teachings became known as Buddhism.

What did the Buddha teach?

Some of the Buddha's ideas were not new to India. He followed some Hindu ideas and changed others. Like Hindus, the Buddha believed that the world of the spirit was more important than the everyday world. He felt that one reason people suffered in life was that they cared too much about the wrong things. These included fame, money, and personal possessions. Wanting such

Reading HELPDESK

Buddhism a religion founded in ancient India by the religious teacher Buddha

Academic Vocabulary

focus to place all of one's attention on something

meditate to focus one's thoughts to gain a higher level of spiritual awareness

things could fill people with bad emotions like greed or anger. But seeking spiritual truth, he believed, led to inner peace.

The Buddha taught his followers the Four Noble Truths. He believed these would help people seek spiritual truth.

The Four Noble Truths:

1. Life is full of suffering.
2. People suffer because they desire worldly things and want to satisfy themselves.
3. The way to end suffering is to stop desiring things.
4. The only way to stop desiring things is to follow the Eightfold Path.

The Buddha's fourth truth says that people can end suffering by following eight steps.

The Eightfold Path:

1. Know and understand the Four Noble Truths.
2. Give up worldly things and do not harm others.
3. Tell the truth, do not gossip, and do not speak badly of others.
4. Do not **commit** evil acts, such as killing, stealing, or living an unclean life.
5. Do rewarding work.
6. Work for good and oppose evil.
7. Make sure your mind keeps your senses under control.
8. Practice meditation to see the world in a new way.

When people were finally free from all earthly concerns, they would reach **nirvana** (nihr•VAH•nuh). According to Buddhist teaching, nirvana is not a physical place. It is an emotional or spiritual state, a feeling of perfect peace and happiness.

Buddhism spread because it welcomed people from all walks of life. The Buddha placed little importance on the *varna* system. He believed people's place in life did not depend on the *varna* into which they were born. The Buddha explained that the success of life depended on peoples' behavior now.

Like Hindus, the Buddha believed in reincarnation, but in a different way. He taught that people could end the cycle of rebirth by following the Eightfold Path rather than their dharma.

Buddhist monks devote their lives to honoring the Buddha through prayer and gifts. Monks are considered to be on a higher spiritual level than other people, and they serve as spiritual teachers.

nirvana a state of perfect happiness and peace

Academic Vocabulary

commit to carry out or do

LESSON 2 (cont.)

IMAGE

Describing Present again the image of the Upanishads. As a class, discuss what the images and text reveal about the Upanishads and Hindu beliefs. Then have students work individually, in pairs, or in small groups to answer the following questions. Students should use a graphic organizer for their answers:

- **What was Aryan culture like when the Vedas were written?** *(The Aryans were gradually becoming settled farmers instead of wandering nomads.)*
- **Which Hindu practices developed with a more settled life?** *(Rituals, music, temple-building, and reading developed with a settled life. The caste system arose around varieties of work that developed in settled areas.)*
- **How did life under Hinduism change Aryan culture?** *(The caste system became more rigid; rituals were complicated.)*

Examples of graphic organizers include a three-column chart or a cause-and-effect diagram, such as a box (cause) with arrows to several circles (effects). You may choose to provide students with a premade graphic organizer, such as a sequence or flowchart.

VIDEO

Analyzing Present the video to reinforce the importance of Hinduism in the development of the culture and society of ancient India. The video can also serve as a transition from exploring Hinduism to exploring Buddhism. After students watch the video, **ask: How did Hindu beliefs shape the way of life in ancient India?** *(Hindu beliefs taught acceptance of the caste system and dharma, the necessity of rituals for every part of life, and the importance of living a good life.)* AL ELL

How did the Hindu beliefs of karma and dharma support the caste system? *(Karma, the good or evil a person creates by doing good or evil deeds, is what determines the caste a person is in. The only way to rise to a different caste is to follow dharma [duty] and create better karma for the next life.)* BL

2 Rise of Buddhism

GUIDING QUESTION ***Why did Buddhism appeal to many people in various parts of Asia?***

Interpreting Ask student volunteers to read aloud the section in their textbooks about the Four Noble Truths. Model for students how to paraphrase, or restate, each of the truths in their own words. For example, say: "This is one way to restate the first Truth: 'There is a lot of pain in the world.'" Then ask volunteers to restate the other three truths. Write their paraphrases on the whiteboard.

Then present the Eightfold Path one step at a time. Ask students to paraphrase each step in their own words. ELL

IMAGE

Discussing Present the image of the Buddhist monk. Explain that more than 2 million people in the United States are practicing Buddhists.

Ask: Do you think following the Eightfold Path would be difficult for people in today's modern world? Why or why not? *(Possible answers: Yes; it would be hard because our society is so fast-paced. No; if people truly believe, then they will dedicate themselves to following the path's steps.)* Then show students the image of the Buddhist monk. Have students answer the discussion question.

SLIDE SHOW

Discussing Show students the slide show of the Buddhist temples. Ask students for their reactions to the images on the slides. Challenge them to think of words that describe the temples. (*Students may suggest* pensive, thoughtful, *or* calm.) As a class, discuss how the temples reflect the principles of Buddhism that students have learned about in class.

INTERACTIVE GRAPHIC ORGANIZER

Describing Have students return to the Taking Notes graphic organizers they began earlier. Ask the following questions, and have them add the information to their charts:

Ask:

- **What are the basic beliefs of Buddhism?** *(The only way to end earthly suffering is to eliminate desire. A person eliminates desire by meditating, avoiding wrong-doing, and concentrating on right thoughts and actions.)*
- **How did Buddhism change life for its followers in contrast to Hinduism?** *(Everyone was equal. Anyone could reach enlightenment. Meditation, not ritual, was the key to spiritual growth.)*

Speculating Ask: Why do you think Buddhism died out in Indian culture but grew in other parts of Asia? *(Students' speculations will vary but should be reasonable. Possible answers: Hinduism and the caste system were already in place and difficult to change. The more powerful castes might not have wanted to lose status by converting to a belief system in which everyone is equal. The more powerful castes might have suppressed Buddhism. Buddhism does not stress winning converts.)* BL

3 Jainism

GUIDING QUESTION ***What are the teachings of Jainism?***

PRIMARY SOURCE

Defining Show the image of Mahavira, and have students read the primary source text. Then have students answer the discussion question. Next, discuss Jainism as a class.

Ask:

- **What is *ahimsa*?** *(the main belief of Jainism—practicing nonviolence toward all living things)*
- **How do Jains practice this belief?** *(They are careful not to kill even insects or worms.)*
- **How is Jainism similar to Buddhism?** *(Both share beliefs in giving up worldly things and not harming others.)* AL ELL

SLIDE SHOW

Making Connections Show the slide show of Gandhi's acts of protest. If necessary, provide context about Gandhi's life and his impact on the politics of the twentieth century. Explain that he was greatly influenced by the idea of *ahimsa*.

Ask: How might acts of nonviolence help people who are seeking freedom? *(Possible answer: It gets the attention of those in power who are used to people using only force, and it continues to remind them of what the freedom-fighters want.)* BL

Answers for pages 258–261

P. 259 ☑ PROGRESS CHECK Hinduism guided most aspects of people's lives through such regulations as the *varna* system and the belief in reincarnation and karma.

P. 259 the style of building construction, the photo is in color, that there are women and men in the river

P. 260 CRITICAL THINKING Students should note that he sought a simple way of life because he did not want his worldly possessions to distract him from his meditations.

Many people accepted the Buddha's message, especially Untouchables and Indians in the lower *jati*. For the first time, these groups heard that they, too, could reach enlightenment.

For more than 40 years, the Buddha taught his ideas. After his death, Buddha's followers disagreed over the meaning of the Buddha's ideas. Eventually, the Buddhists divided into two groups: Theravada (ther•uh•VAH•duh) Buddhists and Mahayana (mah•huh•YAH•nuh) Buddhists.

Theravada Buddhism

Theravada means "teachings of the elders." Followers of Theravada view the Buddha as a great teacher, but not a god. Theravada Buddhism is the major religion of the modern-day country of Sri Lanka (sree LAHN•kuh). Buddhist teachers spread the ideas of Theravada to Myanmar (MEEAHN•mahr), Thailand (TEYE•land), Cambodia (kam•BOH•dee•uh), and Laos (LAH•ohs).

Mahayana Buddhism

Mahayana Buddhism teaches that the Buddha is a god. Followers of Mahayana Buddhism believe that the Eightfold Path is too difficult for most people. By worshipping the Buddha, people will go to a heaven after they die. There, they can follow the Eightfold Path and reach nirvana.

Bodhisattvas (BOH•dih•SUHT•vuhz) hold a special place in Mahayana Buddhism. Bodhisattvas are enlightened people who do not enter heaven. Instead, they stay on Earth to do good deeds and help others on the path to nirvana.

Mahayana Buddhism spread northward into China and from there to Korea and Japan. A special kind of Mahayana Buddhism arose in the central Asian country of Tibet (tih•BEHT).

Buddhist leaders called lamas led the government of Tibet. The Dalai Lama (DAH•ly LAH•muh) led Tibet's government, and the Panchen Lama led the religion. Tibetans considered both leaders to be reincarnations of the Buddha.

Today, few Buddhists live in India where the Buddha first preached. Buddhism, however, is widely practiced in Southeast Asia and East Asia. There are an **estimated** 376 million Buddhists in the world today.

✓ PROGRESS CHECK

Identifying Where is Buddhism practiced today and in what forms?

Reading **HELP**DESK

Build Vocabulary: *Suffixes*

The suffix *-ward* means "in the direction of" or "toward." It is used in many words that indicate direction, such as *northward, upward, forward,* or *outward*. Create a list of six directional words using the suffix *-ward*.

Academic Vocabulary

estimate to determine an approximate value, size, or nature of something

It is a tradition for Buddhist monks in Tibet to create geometric patterns using brightly colored powders, stones, or pieces of metal. The shapes in the patterns represent the cosmos, or universe, and are believed to have special powers.

3 Jainism

GUIDING QUESTION *What are the teachings of Jainism?*

Along with Hinduism and Buddhism, another Indian faith known as **Jainism** (JEYE•nih•zihm) arose about 500 B.C. Today, there are 6 million followers of Jainism. Most of them live in India.

Who is Mahavira?

The exact origins of Jainism are unknown. Its current form was developed by a religious leader named Mahavira. Mahavira lived in India at about the same time as Siddhartha Gautama.

Like Siddhartha, Mahavira came from a wealthy royal family in northern India. After his parents died, Mahavira gave up his wealth and property. He owned nothing and begged for his food.

Mahavira became known as the Jina, or the conqueror. His followers came to be known as Jains. Many of Mahavira's teachings were like those of the Buddha. Both taught that people needed to stop wanting worldly things. Only by doing so could they escape the cycle of rebirth and reach nirvana. The Jains practiced strict poverty.

Jainism a religion of ancient India that does not believe in a supreme being. It emphasizes nonviolence and respect for all living things.

Gandhi (center) used nonviolence as an effective protest tool. He often protested by fasting, or not eating, to show support for a cause.

What is *Ahimsa*?

The key value of Jainism is *ahimsa* (ah•HIM•sah). This means practicing nonviolence toward all living things. Believing that all life is sacred, Mahavira's followers tried to avoid harming any living creature. For example, they used brooms to sweep away insects so that they would not step on them. Jains did not farm because they were afraid of plowing under worms and other living things in the soil.

The idea of *ahimsa* has long influenced India's culture and politics. In the 1900s, the Indian leader Mohandas Gandhi (MOE•han•dahs GANH•dee) wanted to free India from Great Britain. He led a nonviolent struggle against British rule. Thousands would come to hear Gandhi speak or to simply sit with him while he prayed. At the time, Indians refused to pay taxes or buy British goods as a show of protest. Many protesters were jailed, but India eventually gained its independence. Gandhi himself was jailed many times.

Gandhi's method of nonviolent resistance influenced many others. In the United States, Dr. Martin Luther King, Jr., led nonviolent protests to gain rights for African Americans. Like Gandhi, Dr. King was able to use nonviolence to bring about great change in his country.

✓ PROGRESS CHECK

Identifying What is the belief of *ahimsa*?

LESSON 2 REVIEW

Review Vocabulary

1. What do the ideas of *reincarnation* and *karma* have in common?
2. How would practicing *Buddhism* affect people's daily lives?

Answer the Guiding Questions

3. ***Explaining*** What do Hindus believe about Brahman?
4. ***Drawing Conclusions*** How did the Buddha say people should live?
5. ***Comparing*** What beliefs do Buddhism and Jainism share?
6. **EXPOSITORY WRITING** Write a paragraph comparing Hindu and Buddhist beliefs about reincarnation and how one should live.

NOTES

LESSON 2 (cont.)

INTERACTIVE WORKSHEET

21st Century Skills Activity

Summarizing For additional practice summarizing, have students complete the 21st Century Skills Activity sheet. Students may work alone or in pairs to read the instruction and complete the activity. Make sure students understand all the specialized vocabulary that appears in the text students must summarize. ELL

INTERACTIVE GRAPHIC ORGANIZER

Identifying Allow students time to complete the Taking Notes graphic organizer that appears on the first lesson page or have them complete it for homework.

Have students complete the Lesson 2 Review questions.

CLOSE AND REFLECT

Making Connections

Lead a discussion in which the class compares the eastern religions—Hinduism, Buddhism, and Jainism—to other religions they have studied or know about, such as Christianity, Judaism, and Islam. How are these religions similar, and how are they different? *(Responses will vary but should be reasonable and based on details from the text.)*

Guide students to have a respectful attitude toward all religions.

IF YOU HAVE MORE TIME . . .

Learn About Ancient Cultures Through Art

Analyzing Visuals Have students research in reference books and online for images of Hindu and Buddhist art. Ask them to research the images that are associated with depictions of the Hindu deities and the Buddha. Students may work in groups to gather art and write brief descriptions of the art they find. Ask groups to share their findings with the class, including illustrations, if possible.

BACKGROUND KNOWLEDGE

Instruction Techniques for English Learners

The techniques below will be most helpful to English learners in your classroom.

Clarify what the students should know. Teachers clearly explain the social studies standards for the students in student-friendly language. They "unpack" these standards—that is, they take them apart for the students and explain exactly what information and concepts the students should learn in the lesson to help them reach the standards.

Set high expectations. Teachers set high standards for their English learners and remember that the students are capable of acquiring the English they need to access their social studies lessons and to participate in classroom activities.

Provide a strong conceptual foundation. Teachers help English learners develop a strong conceptual foundation in social studies. Concepts are explained clearly and accurately.

Expose students to a broad range of reading materials. Teachers build their students' English language proficiencies by providing them with extensive exposure to increasingly challenging social studies/history readings that serve as appropriate models of English.

Answers for pages 262–264

P. 262 ☑ PROGRESS CHECK Buddhism is widely practiced in Eastern and Southeastern Asian countries such as Myanmar, Thailand, Cambodia, Laos, and Tibet. It is divided into the Theravada and Mahayana forms.

P. 262 Students should list six words with a *ward* suffix: *northward, southward*

P. 264 ☑ PROGRESS CHECK It is the practice of nonviolence toward all living things.

LESSON 2 REVIEW

1. The karma one earns in life determines the type of life he or she will be reborn into as part of the cycle of reincarnation.
2. Buddhism teaches people to give up worldly desires and possessions, so it would make people live simpler, more spiritual lives.
3. Hindus believe that Brahman is a universal spirit. Many Hindus believe that the major deities of the Hindu faith are incarnations of Brahman in different forms.
4. Buddha said that people should follow the Eightfold Path, which involves steps such as giving up worldly things and avoiding doing harm to others in order to gain enlightenment and inner peace.
5. Both believe in reincarnation, meditation, and that the attainment of enlightenment will lead to nirvana.
6. Students should note that Buddhists and Hindus believe in reincarnation, the concept that souls are reborn after the body dies. Hindus support the caste system, but Buddhists believe it is not of great importance. Hindus believe that people must follow their dharma, or duty, to earn good karma in life. This dharma is different for each person. Buddhists believe that, instead of living by the dharma of a caste, all people can earn good karma by following the Eightfold Path.

NOTES

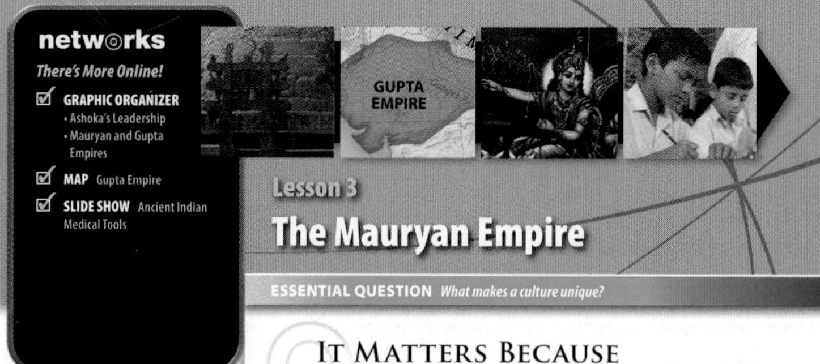

networks
There's More Online!
- GRAPHIC ORGANIZER
  - Ashoka's Leadership
  - Mauryan and Gupta Empires
- MAP Gupta Empire
- SLIDE SHOW Ancient Indian Medical Tools

Lesson 3

The Mauryan Empire

ESSENTIAL QUESTION *What makes a culture unique?*

IT MATTERS BECAUSE

The Mauryan and Gupta dynasties formed the first great Indian empires. Their cultures were the basis for civilizations that followed.

1 Origin of an Empire

GUIDING QUESTION *How did religion affect the development of the Mauryan Empire?*

By the 500s B.C., India was divided into many small kingdoms. Conflict over land and trade weakened the kingdoms, leaving them open to foreign invasion. Persian armies conquered the Indus Valley in the 500s B.C. and made it part of the Persian Empire. The Greeks, under Alexander the Great, then defeated the Persians. Alexander entered India but turned back in 325 B.C., when his homesick troops threatened to rebel.

India's First Empire

After Alexander left India, an Indian military officer named Chandra Gupta Maurya (CHUHN•druh GUP•tuh MAH•oor•yuh) built a strong army. He knew that only a large and powerful empire could defend India against invasion. In 321 B.C., Chandra Gupta set out to conquer northern India and unify the region under his rule.

Chandra Gupta was the first ruler of the Mauryan dynasty. He was a skilled administrator. He set up a well-run government in his capital city of Pataliputra (PAH•tah•lih•POO•truh). One of his major achievements was an efficient postal system. The system improved communications throughout his empire.

Reading **HELP**DESK

Taking Notes: ***Identifying***

Use a chart like this one to identify important information about the Mauryan and Gupta Empires.

Mauryan	Gupta

Content Vocabulary
- **stupa**
- ***Bhagavad Gita***
- **pilgrim**

GEOGRAPHY CONNECTION

The Mauryan dynasty built the first great Indian empire.

1. **REGION** Which part of India was not in the Mauryan Empire?
2. **CRITICAL THINKING** ***Analyzing*** What does the map key tell you about the religion of the Mauryan Empire?

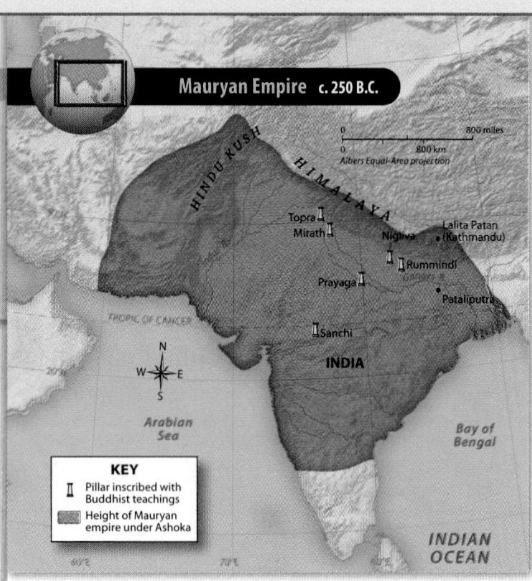

Chandra Gupta's powerful army crushed any resistance to his rule. He also used spies to report any disloyalty among his subjects. While he was a strong ruler, Chandra Gupta was very cautious. He was afraid of being poisoned, so he had servants taste his food before he ate it. He was so concerned about being attacked that he never slept two nights in a row in the same bed.

What did Ashoka Accomplish?

The Mauryan Empire reached the height of its glory under Chandra Gupta's grandson Ashoka (uh•SOH•kuh). Ashoka governed most of northern and central India from about 273 B.C. to 232 B.C.

Ashoka was an unusual king. Like many rulers, Ashoka began his rule with fierce wars of conquest. **Eventually**, he came to hate killing. After one battle, he looked at the fields covered with dead and wounded soldiers. He was horrified by what he saw. He decided that he would follow Buddhist teachings and become a man of peace.

Reading **HELP**DESK

stupa a Buddhist shrine, usually dome-shaped

Academic Vocabulary

eventual taking place at an unnamed later time
promote to encourage the doing of something

Ashoka kept his promise. During the rest of his life, he tried to improve the lives of his people. Ashoka made laws that encouraged people to do good deeds, practice nonviolence, and respect others. He created hospitals for people and for animals. He built fine roads, with rest houses and shade trees for the travelers' comfort.

Ashoka was the first ruler to **promote** Buddhism. He sent teachers to spread the religion throughout India and other parts of Asia. Buddhist teachings and the laws of Ashoka were carved on rocks and tall stone pillars for all the people to read. Carved on one rock is the idea that:

PRIMARY SOURCE

> "Father and mother must be hearkened [listened to]; similarly, respect for living creatures must be firmly established; truth must be spoken. These are the virtues of the Law of Piety [devotion] which must be practiced."
>
> —from "Summary of the Law of Piety," The Edicts of Ashoka

Ashoka also had thousands of **stupas** (stoo•puhs) built throughout India. Stupas are Buddhist shrines shaped like a dome or burial mound. The stupas contained religious objects and served as a place of worship. Although he was a devout Buddhist, Ashoka was tolerant of all beliefs and allowed his Hindu subjects to practice their religion.

Ashoka's able leadership helped the Mauryan Empire prosper. India's good roads helped it become the center of a large trade network that stretched to the Mediterranean Sea.

Ashoka—shown here—made regular visits to rural people of his empire to spread Buddhist ideas and learn about their needs. He also had this "Great Stupa" built in honor of Buddha.

CRITICAL THINKING
Speculating Why do you think Ashoka had so many stupas built?

LESSON 3 • Day 1

ENGAGE

Discussing As a class, discuss the qualities that make an effective leader. Have students list the names of some of the leaders from the past that they know about or have studied, such as King David, the ancient Egyptian pharaohs, Pericles, and Alexander the Great. Talk about the accomplishments of each one and whether he or she was a good leader, a bad leader, or both.

Ask: **What qualities does a good leader need?** *(Positive qualities might include wisdom and concern for people as well as the ability or desire to treat everyone fairly, solve problems, and listen.)*

What qualities does a bad leader have? *(Negative qualities might include greed, dishonesty, giving certain people special favors, and not solving problems.)*

Tell students that they will learn about several different leaders in ancient India and how these leaders influenced their people. Encourage students to look for examples in the text of positive effects and negative effects of each leader's actions.

TEACH & ASSESS

1 Origin of an Empire

GUIDING QUESTION *How did religion affect the development of the Mauryan Empire?*

MAP

Identifying Have students locate the map of the Mauryan Empire in their textbooks and notice the cities that are marked.

Ask: **What do the locations of the cities have in common?** *(They are next to rivers.)*

What does the symbol next to each one mean? *(Ashoka placed a pillar there.)* AL ELL

PRIMARY SOURCE

Differentiating Show students the slide with the quotation from the *Bhagavad Gita*. Explain that the words express a Hindu belief about leadership. Ask students to paraphrase the quotation in their own words. *(Possible answer: Leaders who are wise and know themselves are calm and focused. A good leader treats everyone the same.)* Have students consider the quotation as they answer the following questions about Chandra Gupta Maurya's leadership qualities.

Ask: **In what way was Chandra Gupta Maurya a good leader? What things did he do for his people?** *(He united the people, ran an efficient government, and started a postal service.)*

In what way was he a bad leader? *(He was cruel and cared mostly about his personal safety.)*

In general, do you think Chandra Gupta Maurya followed his beliefs? Why or why not? *(Responses will vary. Sample responses: He did because he followed his dharma, or duty. He did not because he did not look on everyone equally and with compassion.)* BL

INTERACTIVE GRAPHIC ORGANIZER

Analyzing Use the graphic organizer about Ashoka to generate a discussion. Discuss the accomplishments of Ashoka and his attitude toward his people. Then **ask:**

What kind of leader was he at first? *(violent)*

What happened to him that changed his life? *(He converted to Buddhism.)*

Did he follow his beliefs? How do you know? *(He followed his beliefs because he gave up violence for peace and tried to make life better for his people.)*

Give specific examples of improvements that Ashoka sponsored. *(Improvements included creating good roads, hospitals, shade trees and comfortable rest stops for travelers, and establishing pillars and stupas to spread Buddhist teachings.)*

Summarizing Segue to the Gupta Empire with a review of "The End of the Mauryan Empire."

Ask: **What happened to the Mauryan Empire after Ashoka's death? Why?** *(The empire declined and split into warring kingdoms because the rulers that followed Ashoka were not as wise or as unselfish as he had been. They raised taxes and seized land.)* AL

2 The Gupta Empire

GUIDING QUESTION *Why did the Gupta Empire become powerful?*

MAP

Comparing and Contrasting Have students focus on the maps "Mauryan Empire" and "Gupta Empire."

Ask: **How are the two empires similar?** *(Both empires controlled the land around the Indus River.)*

How are the two empires different? *(The Mauryan Empire was much larger than the Gupta Empire. Buddhism was promoted during the Mauryan Empire, as seen by the stupa icons on the map.)* AL

Evaluating **Ask:** **Do you think Samudra Gupta was a good leader or a bad leader?** *(Most will say he was a good leader because under his leadership, Indian entered a golden age. Have students provide evidence from the text to support their opinions.)*

IMAGE

Discussing Show students the image of the sculpture and murals created in the Ajanta Caves during the Gupta Empire.

Ask: **Why is it important that these caves be preserved?** *(They should be preserved so people in the future can see the great art created during the Gupta Empire.)*

INTERACTIVE GRAPHIC ORGANIZER

Summarizing Have students complete the Taking Notes graphic organizer that appears on the first lesson page, summarizing the achievements of the Mauryan and Gupta Empires.

INTERACTIVE WORKSHEET

Primary Sources Activity

Assign the Primary Source Activity, which compares the words of the Buddhist ruler Ashoka with a passage from the Hindu Upanishads.

Ask students to reflect upon how the ideas about leadership expressed in these excerpts compare with their own views about leadership that they shared earlier in Lesson 3.

Students may complete the worksheet questions as homework if needed.

CLOSE AND REFLECT

To close, have students summarize the achievements of the Mauryan and Gupta Empires.

Ask: **Do you think the leadership qualities these men possessed inspired their people to produce great art and science? Why or why not?** *(Possible answer: yes; because the leader of the country sets an example for the people)*

Answers for pages 265–267

P. 265 Taking Notes Possible answers: Mauryan: India's first empire, founded by Chandra Gupta Maurya, reached its height during reign of Ashoka—a soldier who became a Buddhist. Gupta: a power in the Ganges River valley, led by rulers who practiced Hinduism and built temples

P. 266 GEOGRAPHY CONNECTION

1. The southern tip of the Indian subcontinent was not part of the Mauryan Empire.
2. CRITICAL THINKING The symbols for pillars inscribed with Buddhist teachings show that Buddhism was important in the empire.

P. 267 CRITICAL THINKING Ashoka wanted to spread Buddhist teachings, and the stupas provided places for Buddhists to worship and learn.

The End of the Mauryan Empire

After Ashoka died in 232 B.C., the Mauryan Empire **declined**. The kings who came after Ashoka lacked his kindness and skills. The new rulers made merchants pay heavy taxes and took lands from the peasants. The Indian people rebelled against the harsh treatment. In 183 B.C., the last Mauryan king was murdered by one of his own generals. The land of the Mauryan Empire split into many small warring kingdoms.

PROGRESS CHECK

Explaining What caused Ashoka to denounce violence? What was the result?

2 The Gupta Empire

GUIDING QUESTION *Why did the Gupta Empire become powerful?*

For 500 years, the small warring kingdoms fought one another for control of India. Then, in A.D. 320, the Gupta dynasty came to power in the Ganges River valley. The city of Pataliputra had been the capital of the old Mauryan Empire. It now became the capital of the Gupta Empire. Chandra Gupta I, the first Gupta ruler, had the same name as the first ruler of the Mauryan dynasty.

Chandra Gupta I ruled for 10 years. He chose his son, Samudra Gupta (suh•MOO•druh GUP•tuh), to rule after him. Samudra Gupta expanded the Gupta Empire in northern India. He was a great military leader and a patron of arts and literature. Under Samudra Gupta, India entered a golden age.

Gupta rulers practiced the Hindu religion like many of their subjects did. They donated money to support Hindu scholars and build Hindu temples. Many temples had brightly painted sculptures of deities and images from Hindu sacred writings.

Trade helped the Gupta Empire thrive. Salt, cloth, and iron were common goods traded in India. Indian merchants also traded with China and with lands in Southeast Asia and the Mediterranean area. The Gupta rulers benefited from their control of much of the trade. They owned silver and gold mines and large estates.

Cities arose along trade routes. People called **pilgrims** (PIHL•gruhms) used the trade routes to journey to holy sites. Cities with famous temples grew wealthy from visiting pilgrims.

PROGRESS CHECK

Explaining How did the Gupta Empire profit from trade routes?

Reading HELPDESK

pilgrim a person who travels to holy sites

Academic Vocabulary

decline to become smaller or weaker

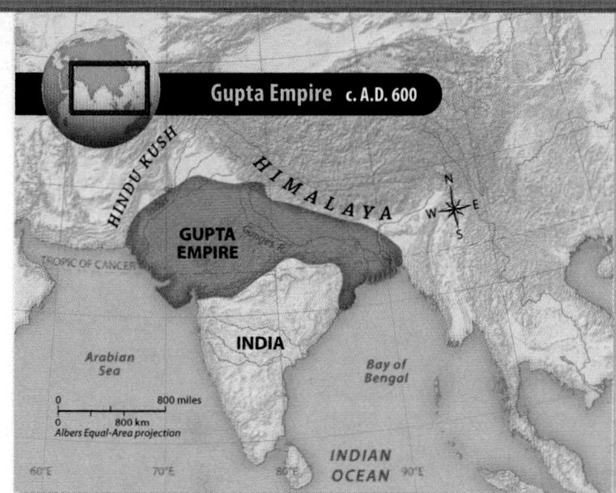

GEOGRAPHY CONNECTION

The Gupta dynasty founded the second great Indian empire.

1 LOCATION Where was the Gupta Empire located? Around what river valleys was it formed?

2 CRITICAL THINKING *Analyzing* What does this map suggest about the power of the Gupta Empire?

3 Culture in Ancient India

GUIDING QUESTION *What were the cultural contributions of the Mauryan and Gupta Empires?*

Ancient India produced a brilliant culture. Artists, builders, writers, and scientists made many **contributions** while the Mauryan and Gupta kings ruled.

The Literature of India

The Vedas were among the first works written in the Sanskrit language. The literature of ancient India also includes epics. Hindu epics are sacred texts that teach important moral lessons. The people could learn the correct and acceptable behavior through interesting stories.

The *Mahabharata* (muh•HAH•BAH•ruh•tuh) is an ancient religious epic. It is also the longest poem in any written language, with about 90,000 verses. The *Mahabharata* describes a struggle for control of an Indian kingdom that took place about 1100 B.C. Its exciting stories about great heroes influenced Hindus then and now.

The best-known section of the *Mahabharata* is the ***Bhagavad Gita*** (BAH•guh•VAHD GEE•tuh), or "Song of the Lord." In it, the deity Krishna goes with a prince into battle. The prince does not want to fight because members of his family are on the other side.

Bhagavad Gita a section of the Indian epic the *Mahabharata*

Academic Vocabulary

contribute to give or donate something

Hindu artists tried to depict the dieties. This picture shows Krishna and Prince Arjuna.

Krishna reminds the prince to obey his duty as a warrior. The prince makes the painful choice to fight his family.

A second epic, the *Ramayana* (rah•mah•YAH•nah), is a poem that grew to about 25,000 verses before it was written down. It tells the story of Rama, the perfect king, and Sita, his faithful wife. When Sita is kidnapped by an evil king, Rama rushes to her rescue with the help of friends.

The Arts and Architecture

The ancient Hindus believed that music was a gift from the gods. Many sacred texts, such as the Bhagavad Gita, were probably sung. At yearly festivals, people danced, sang, and played music. Musical instruments included tambourines, flutes, drums, and lutes.

Much of early India's art was created on fragile materials, such as paper, and has not survived. What is left today is mostly religious art—elaborate sculptures carved in stone. Sculptors carved images of the Buddha as early as the A.D. 100s.

The most important **structures** in early India were the rulers' palaces and the temples used for religious worship. During Ashoka's reign, many stone pillars carved with Buddhist messages were placed alongside roads.

Mathematics

Indian mathematicians of the Gupta period made important contributions. Aryabhata (AHR•yuh•BUHT•uh) was one of the first scientists known to have used algebra. Indian mathematicians explained the idea of infinity—something without an end. They also invented the symbol "0" and connected it with the idea of nothing. The Indians' invention of zero affected the study of mathematics and science. Modern technology, such as computers, would not be possible without the concept of zero.

Reading HELPDESK

Academic Vocabulary

structure a building or other built object

Gupta mathematicians developed symbols for the numbers 1 to 9 that we use today. In the A.D. 700s, Arab traders adopted these number symbols, or numerals. European traders later borrowed them from the Arabs. In the A.D. 1200s, use of these numbers spread though Europe and replaced Roman numerals. Today, this system of number symbols is known as the Indian-Arabic numerical system.

Advances in Science

Scientists and scholars in ancient India also made important advances in astronomy and technology. Indian astronomers mapped the movements of planets and stars. They proposed the theory that the Earth was round and revolved around the sun. During the Gupta period, scientists advanced metalworking. Among their most impressive constructions is the pillar of iron of Delhi, dating from around A.D. 400. It is still standing, and, in spite of its age, it has hardly rusted.

Advances in Medicine

Can you imagine doctors performing dental surgery 1600 years ago? Indian doctors treated dental problems using tools such as the bow drill. The doctors used this tool, which was usually used to make fire, to drill teeth.

Doctors during the Gupta era were advanced for their time. They could set broken bones, sew wounds, and perform complicated surgeries. They also were skilled in making medical instruments, such as scalpels and needles.

A doctor named Shushruta (shoosh•ROO•tah) repaired damaged noses in an early type of plastic surgery. Indian doctors used herbs to cure illnesses. They also believed in healing the causes of a disease, not just treating the disease itself.

PROGRESS CHECK

Analyzing What lasting achievement did Indian mathematicians make?

Connections to TODAY

Math Poems

Some writings about mathematics from the Gupta dynasty have survived. The math formulas are written as poems. Scholars had to find ways to fit numbers into the poems so that they would sound correct. Imagine having to turn in your math homework in the form of a poem.

Ancient Indian contributions to mathematics made much of today's math-based technology possible.

LESSON 3 REVIEW

Review Vocabulary

1. How would a *pilgrim* in ancient India use a *stupa*?
2. What is the *Bhagavad Gita*?

Answer the Guiding Questions

3. ***Determining Cause and Effect*** How did religion influence the Mauryan Empire?
4. ***Describing*** How did the Gupta Empire grow powerful?
5. ***Identifying*** What were the written epics of the Mauryan and Gupta period?
6. **DESCRIPTIVE WRITING** You are living in India during the rule of Ashoka. Write a letter to a friend describing the things Ashoka is doing as a leader. In your letter, explain whether you think Ashoka is a great ruler.

LESSON 3 • Day 2

ENGAGE

LECTURE SLIDE

Making Connections Remind students that India experienced a golden age under the first Gupta rulers. Show students the lecture slide on the golden age of ancient Indian civilization.

Ask: **What is a "golden age"?** *(Possible answer: a time of prosperity and creativity)*

How is trade connected to India's golden age? *(The success of trade made India's rulers wealthy. They used this money from trade to pay for projects in the arts and literature.)*

TEACH & ASSESS

3 Culture in Ancient India

GUIDING QUESTION *What were the cultural contributions of the Mauryan and Gupta Empires?*

CHART

Calculating Show students the interactive chart of ancient Indian number symbols. Demonstrate the importance of the concept of zero by asking students to identify written numbers with and without zero.

For example, write the numeral one and then add a numeral zero to make the numeral ten, and ask what has changed. *(The number is now a ten.)*

You may show another one or two of these examples if time permits. Indian mathematicians were the first to invent a symbol for the concept of nothing, or zero.

Ask: **What would happen to our understanding of numbers if there were no zero?** *(We might not be able to read or write numbers in an understandable way.)*

In what way is the zero important to computers? *(Possible answer: Computer codes are written in ones and zeros, which represent on/off or yes/no. Some students might know the word* binary.*)* BL

IMAGE

Comparing and Contrasting Discuss what kinds of tools surgeons use today. List some on the board. *(Examples include various kinds of scalpels; separator and clamps; machines such as X-ray machines and CAT scans; and other devices.)*

Then show images of ancient and modern surgical tools and discuss their similarities and differences. *(Similar—some are used for cutting or sewing; Different—today's tools can give surgeons more information, can do more complicated tasks, and are more precise.)*

INTERACTIVE WORKSHEET

21st Century Skills Activity

Analyzing Assign students to work on the 21st Century Skills Activity for Lesson 3 in small groups or as individuals.

Explain that they will be choosing a topic for a presentation about India's culture. Suitable topics would include religion, art, literature, and science. Allow class time for students to discuss ideas.

Have students complete the Lesson 3 Review.

CLOSE & REFLECT

Provide students with an opportunity to discuss their ideas for presentation topics.

Ask students to identify their topics and explain why they believe those topics are interesting and significant. As homework, students may work on actual presentations or prepare an outline of a presentation to turn in, as class time permits.

BACKGROUND KNOWLEDGE

The *Ramayana*

The *Ramayana* is perhaps the most popular Sanskrit text. More than 2,000 years old, it was most likely written by a poet named Valmiki around 300 B.C. It is an epic poem that is nearly 50,000 lines long (24,000 couplets) that tells the story of Rama, the Hindu deity and royal prince. It describes his birth, his childhood and education, and his marriage. The poem also describes the kidnapping of Rama's wife by Ravana, a demon-king, and Rama's heroic efforts to rescue her.

In the centuries since it was written, the *Ramayana* has been translated into many languages. The events of the poem are even today acted out in festivals around India. Many Indians still make an effort to memorize and recite the poem aloud for entertainment and to much acclaim.

Answers for pages 268–271

P. 268 ☑ PROGRESS CHECK Ashoka witnessed bloodshed on a battlefield and became a devout Buddhist. This led him to achieve many good works and to promote religious tolerance among his people.

P. 268 ☑ PROGRESS CHECK Trade routes allowed trade within India to flourish and brought goods from other countries to India. In addition, cities grew along trade routes and benefited from pilgrimages to shrines.

P. 269 GEOGRAPHY CONNECTION

1. in northern India, in the Indus and Ganges River valleys
2. CRITICAL THINKING The Gupta Empire was significantly smaller than the Mauryan Empire, which suggests that it was less powerful.

P. 271 ☑ PROGRESS CHECK Indian mathematicians made many breakthroughs, including the creation of algebra and the use of what we call Arabic numerals, including the idea of nothing, or zero.

LESSON 3 REVIEW

1. A Buddhist pilgrim might visit a stupa because of its religious significance as a shrine.
2. It is a well-known segment of the *Mahabharata*, an ancient religious epic.
3. Ashoka, the leader of the Mauryan Empire, became a devoted Buddhist and put many Buddhist principles into practice, including the humane treatment of people and animals and tolerance for other religions. This helped the empire prosper during his reign.
4. The Gupta were skilled in battle and prospered from wide-ranging trade networks, becoming powerful through a mixture of military strength and trade.
5. The *Mahabharata*, its subsection the *Bhagavad Gita*, and the *Ramayana* were the major literary epics of the period.
6. Student answers will vary. They should note the tolerance of Ashoka's reign as well as the many public works he undertook and the religious stupa that he erected around the empire. Students should also express an opinion about Ashoka as a leader.

CHAPTER 9 Activities

Write your answers on a separate piece of paper.

❶ **Exploring the Essential Question**
DESCRIPTIVE WRITING You are a scholar living in India among the descendants of the Aryans. One day you stumble across a great mural that shows what life was like in the city of Mohenjo-Daro at its height. Write a description to your friends of what the art shows about people and daily life in the city. How does it compare to your life?

❷ **21st Century Skills**
MANAGE INFORMATION Create a poster that displays what you have learned about the Hindu religion. Include the concepts of karma and dharma, with pictures and captions that help show the meaning of each.

❸ **Thinking Like a Historian**
GEOGRAPHY AND CIVILIZATION Use a graphic organizer like the one shown here to show why river valleys were the best locations for early civilizations. Write "River" in the center circle and the advantages of living by a river in the surrounding circles. Refer back to the way the citizens of Harappa and Mohenjo-Daro --and later the Aryans-- used the river in their daily lives.

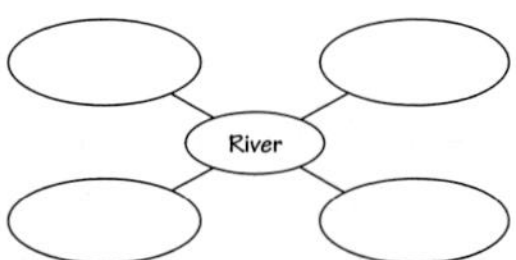

❹ **GEOGRAPHY ACTIVITY**

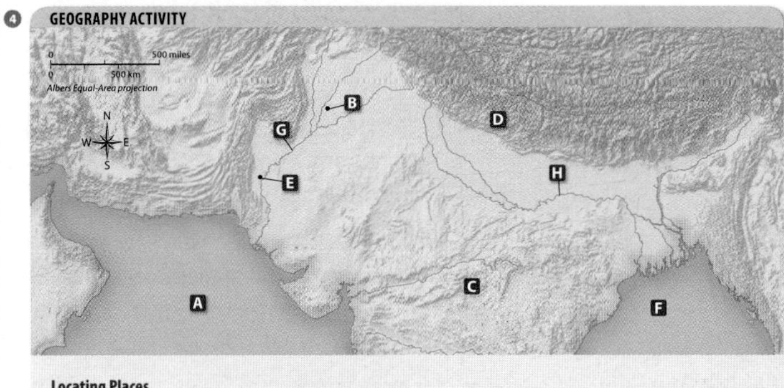

Locating Places
Match the letters on the map with the numbered places listed below.

1. Himalaya
2. Arabian Sea
3. Ganges River
4. Harappa
5. Bay of Bengal
6. Deccan Plateau
7. Mohenjo-Daro
8. Indus River

CHAPTER 9 Assessment

REVIEW THE GUIDING QUESTIONS
Directions: Choose the best answer for each question.

❶ Farming, transportation, and trade in the Indus Valley were all dependent on
A. mountains.
B. rivers.
C. monsoons.
D. lakes.

❷ The Aryans were the first Indians to develop
F. foreign trade.
G. indoor plumbing.
H. major cities.
I. written language.

❸ In the Indian caste system, your karma was largely decided by
A. whether you were reincarnated.
B. whether you followed your dharma.
C. whether you learned the Four Noble Truths.
D. whether you belonged to a *jati*.

❹ Buddhism appealed to a wider range of people than Hinduism because
F. Buddhists believed in many gods.
G. The Buddha traveled to many places.
H. Buddhism treated all people equally.
I. Buddhist poetry was so beautiful.

❺ If a mosquito lands on my hand and I refuse to kill it, I am practicing
A. ahimsa.
B. the Eightfold Path.
C. Theravada.
D. dharma.

❻ The *Ramayana* is
F. a beautiful temple.
G. an epic poem.
H. a sacred city.
I. a metalworking technique.

CHAPTER 9 Assessment *(continued)*

DBQ DOCUMENT-BASED QUESTIONS

❼ **Drawing Conclusions** This passage is from the text *The Word of the Buddha*:

"He avoids the killing of living beings. . . . He avoids stealing and abstains from [avoids] taking what is not given to him. Only what is given to him he takes, waiting till it is given; and he lives with a heart honest and pure."

According to the passage, what is the correct way to obtain something?
A. by taking whatever one needs
B. by giving something in return
C. by demanding what one wants
D. by waiting for it to be given

❽ **Comparing and Contrasting** The first line of the passage expresses a view similar to what belief?
F. ahimsa
G. karma
H. varna
I. jati

SHORT RESPONSE

"There were a number of similarities [between Buddhism and Jainism]. Religious rituals were essentially congregational [performed in groups]. [M]onasteries [groups of men—monks—who center their lives entirely on religion] [were] organized on democratic lines, and initially accepting persons from all strata [walks] of life. Such monasteries were dependent on their neighborhoods for material support. Some of the monasteries developed into centres of education. The functioning of monks in society was greater, however, among the Buddhist orders. Wandering monks, preaching and seeking alms, gave the religions a missionary flavour. The recruitment of nuns signified a special concern for the status of women."

— Encyclopaedia Britannica Online

❾ Buddhism and Jainism both established monasteries. Why were these groups called monasteries and how did they choose their members?

❿ What purpose did a monk serve in the Buddhist religion and in the Jain religion?

EXTENDED RESPONSE

⓫ **Persuasive Writing** You are the ruler Ashoka. You have converted to Buddhism and want to tell your people why. You also want to persuade people to practice acceptance of others. Write a speech that tells why you believe converting to Buddhism would be a positive step in their lives.

Need Extra Help?

If You've Missed Question	❶	❷	❸	❹	❺	❻	❼	❽	❾	❿	⓫
Review Lesson	1	1	2	2	2	3	2	2	2	2	2, 3

NOTES

REFLECT, REVIEW, & REMEDIATE

INTERACTIVE WORKSHEET

Chapter Summary

Provide students with the Chapter Summary worksheet to help review the chapter and prepare for assessment.

Reviewing the Enduring Understandings

Review this chapter's Enduring Understandings with students:

- People, places, and ideas change over time.
- Religion can influence a society's beliefs and values.

INTERACTIVE WHITEBOARD ACTIVITY Organize the class into four groups. Make a chart on the interactive whiteboard with rows for the Indus Valley civilization, Aryan civilization, Mauryan Empire, and Gupta Empire. Assign one group to review the accomplishments of each culture. Have each group identify on the chart the two greatest accomplishments of their assigned culture and explain their reasons for choosing those accomplishments.

Culture	Major Accomplishments
Indus Valley civilization	
Aryan civilization	
Mauryan Empire	
Gupta Empire	

Discuss the basic beliefs of Hinduism and Buddhism. **Ask:** **In what ways are Hinduism and Buddhism the same?** *(They believe in one great spirit and in reincarnation and union with the great spirit after death.)* **In what ways are they different?** *(Buddhists consider all people equally able to reach enlightenment and believe that they should give up worldly goods for a spiritual life. Hinduism supports the caste system, which Buddhism rejects.)*

ACTIVITIES ANSWERS

Exploring the Essential Question

1. Student answers will vary, but they should note factors such as the sophisticated planning seen in the city of Mohenjo-Daro and evidence of religion and trade. They should comment on the architecture, dress, and visible art and compare these to modern-day life.

21st Century Skills

2. Student displays will vary but should indicate all levels of the caste system and demonstrate an understanding that one's karma in this life helps determine the form that one will be reincarnated into in the next life. They should also demonstrate an understanding that it is important to follow one's dharma in order to behave in a proper fashion.

Thinking Like a Historian

3. Students should note that the rivers provided water for drinking and for irrigating crops during the dry season. In addition, the presence of the rivers helped make the soil in the area fertile and productive for crops. People also used the rivers for trade and transportation.

Locating Places

4. **1.** Himalaya, D; **2.** Arabian Sea, A; **3.** Ganges River, H; **4.** Harappa, B; **5.** Bay of Bengal, F; **6.** Deccan Plateau, C; **7.** Mohenjo-Daro, E; **8.** Indus River, G

ASSESSMENT ANSWERS

Review the Guiding Questions

1. **B** The correct choice is B. The Indus and Ganges Rivers were the lifeblood of the region and supported farming, transportation, and trade. The monsoons benefited farming but would not benefit trade or transportation. The mountains could present barriers to trade and transportation and would not affect farming. India's lakes were of less use for farming, transportation, or trade than its rivers, as they do not span the country as the rivers do.

2. **I** The correct choice is I. Aryans developed the written language Sanskrit. Before the Aryans arrived, Indus Valley people were trading as far away as Mesopotamia. Indoor plumbing and grid-based city layouts were developed in the earlier Indus Valley civilization.

3. **B** The correct choice is B. In the caste system, people must follow the dharma, or duty, associated with their caste in order to gain good karma. People's karma would influence how they were reincarnated. People's *jati* would not have an effect on their karma. The Four Noble Truths are a part of Buddhism.

4. **H** The correct choice is H. Buddha treated people equally and offered an end to the cycle of reincarnation, which appealed to those of lower castes. The Buddha's travels would not greatly influence followers, nor would Buddhist poetry. Buddhists did not believe in many gods.

5. **A** The correct choice is A. *Ahimsa* is the principle of nonviolence toward all living things. The Eightfold Path is a Buddhist concept. Theravada is a sect of Buddhism. *Dharma* is the duty associated with a person's caste.

6. **G** The correct choice is G. The *Ramayana* is an epic poem about Prince Rama.

Document-Based Questions

7. **D** The passage says that a Buddhist should wait until something is given, rather than asking for it or taking it.

8. **F** The line "He avoids the killing of living beings" is the definition of *ahimsa*.

Short Response

9. Monasteries served as religious centers and sometimes as centers of education. They accepted people who were willing to center their lives around religion.

10. Monks, particularly in Buddhism, helped spread the beliefs of the religion by wandering the land.

Extended Response

11. Student answers will vary, but they should emphasize the idea that following Buddhist principles will promote the greater good of the people by encouraging good behavior and nonviolence.

ONLINE RESOURCES
networks

There's More Online!

- INTERACTIVE WORKSHEETS
- BIOGRAPHIES
- CHARTS/GRAPHS
- GAMES
- GRAPHIC ORGANIZERS
- IMAGES
- MAPS
- PRIMARY SOURCES
- SLIDE SHOWS
- TIME LINE
- LECTURE SLIDES
- INTERACTIVE WHITEBOARD ACTIVITIES
- ASSESSMENTS
- VIDEOS

The Chinese Landscape

Chinese History from Peking Man to Confucius

Chinese History From the First Emperor to the Romance of the Three Kingdoms

Chapter **10**

Early China

Dear World History Teacher,

China was the last of the river valley civilizations to fully develop. By the time the Shang dynasty emerged as an organized state, the societies in Mesopotamia, Egypt, and India had already reached an advanced level of civilization.

The Shang dynasty formed an organized government, created a system of writing, and developed advanced skills for making bronze vessels. During the Zhou dynasty, China adopted many of the features that characterized China's civilization for centuries. Especially important politically was the "Mandate of Heaven," which gave kings a supposedly divine right to rule. The family, with its ideal of filial piety, also emerged as a powerful economic and social unit during the Zhou dynasty.

Between 500 B.C. and 200 B.C., three major schools of thought emerged in China—Confucianism, Daoism, and legalism. All three sought to define the principles that would create a stable order in society.

After 200 years of civil war, the Qin dynasty created a new era of Chinese unity. The first Qin emperor, Qin Shihuangdi, however, was also the last. The Han established an empire that lasted over 400 years. During the Han dynasty, China extended its boundaries into Central Asia and southward into what is modern-day Vietnam. Chinese culture appeared unrivaled, and its scientific achievements were unsurpassed.

Jackson J. Spielvogel

More Media Resources

Current Events Online

Visit McGraw-Hill's current events Web site for high-interest news stories and activities for your students. Access the site through the Student or Teacher Center in **networks.**

Reading List

Grade 6 reading level:
Chee-Lin: A Giraffe's Journey, by James Rumford

Grade 7 reading level:
Through Time: Beijing, by Richard Platt

Grade 8 reading level:
Exploring the Life, Myth, and Art of Ancient China, by Edward L. Shaughnessy

At the MOVIES

In *Hero*, a minor official defeats three warlords who are plotting to assassinate Qin Shihuangdi, China's powerful emperor. **Discuss:** **What does the movie tell us about the need for a strong ruler? Can you make a connection between the events shown in the movie and events in contemporary China?**

The documentary *Confucius: Words of Wisdom* explores the life and legacy of Confucius. **Which of Confucius's "five virtues" do you think are most useful for today's world? Why?**

NOTE: Be sure to preview any film to ensure that it is age-appropriate.

Search for more videos online in the **networks** Resource Library.

CHAPTER 10 Planner

UNDERSTANDING BY DESIGN®

Enduring Understandings

- *People, places, and ideas change over time.* • *The movement of people, goods, and ideas causes societies to change over time.*

Essential Questions

- *What makes a culture unique?* • *How do new ideas change the way people live?*
- *How do governments change?*

Students will know:

- *how geography shaped the development of China's civilization*
- *why Shang rulers were able to remain powerful*
- *the ways society and government were influenced by Chinese thinkers*
- *what changes the Qin emperor made to unite China*
- *how life improved under Han rulers*
- *how China and the rest of the world benefited from the Silk Road*
- *why Buddhism became popular in China*

Students will be able to:

- **explain** the role of geography in the development of Chinese civilization and in its isolation
- **compare and contrast** the Shang dynasty with the Zhou dynasty
- **compare and contrast** Huang He Valley civilizations with other river valley civilizations, including those along the Tigris-Euphrates, Nile, and Indus Rivers
- **identify** Confucius, Laozi, and Hanfeizi and how their philosophies affected society and government
- **describe** Confucianism, Daoism, and legalism
- **apply** a Chinese philosophy to a real-world situation and predict its effects
- **predict** what life was like in the Qin dynasty and the Han dynasty based on images from each
- **identify** geographical features along the Silk Road
- **apply** the concepts of monopoly and competition to the economics of trade along the Silk Road
- **discuss** how increased trade benefits civilization

Predictable Misunderstandings

Students may think:

- The Chinese people are all the same.
- Confucianism is a religion.
- All Chinese rulers were strict dictators.

Assessment Evidence

Performance Task

- Hands-On Chapter Project

Other Evidence

- Participation in Interactive Whiteboard Map Activity
- Graphic organizer on Shang and Zhou dynasties
- Answers to discussion of definition of *philosophy*
- Answers to discussion of three philosophies
- Contribution to small-group activity
- Identification of sayings and philosophers
- Interpretations of slide show images
- Predictions of what life was like in the Qin and Han dynasties
- Discussion answers about the Silk Road
- Discussion answers on trade benefits
- Time line of Shang and Zhou dynasties
- Answers comparing and contrasting river valley civilizations
- Letter-writing assignment
- Geography and History Activity
- 21st Century Skills Activity
- Economics of History Activity
- Lesson Reviews

Pacing Guide

Introducing the Chapter	1 day
Lesson 1 The Birth of Chinese Civilization	1 day
Lesson 2 Society and Culture in Ancient China	1 day
Lesson 3 The Qin and the Han Dynasties	2 days
Chapter Activities and Assessment	1 day
TOTAL TIME	**6 Days**

Differentiated Instruction

These lesson plans are written to address the needs of your On Level students. Discussion and activities that are well-suited to your Approaching Grade Level learners, Beyond Grade Level learners, as well as your English Language Learners, are coded as follows:

AL **Approaching Grade Level**

BL **Beyond Grade Level**

ELL **English Language Learner**

NCSS Standards covered in "Early China"

Learners will understand:

1 CULTURE

4. That the beliefs, values, and behaviors of a culture form an integrated system that helps shape the activities and ways of life that define a culture

5. How individuals learn the elements of their culture through interactions with others, and how individuals learn of other cultures through communication and study

8. That language, behaviors, and beliefs of different cultures can both contribute to and pose barriers to cross-cultural understanding

2 TIME, CONTINUITY, AND CHANGE

6. The origins and influences of social, cultural, political, and economic systems

9. The influences of social, geographic, economic, and cultural factors on the history of local areas, states, nations, and the world

3 PEOPLE, PLACES, AND ENVIRONMENTS

1. The theme of people, places, and environments involves the study of the relationships between human populations in different locations and geographic phenomena such as climate, vegetation, and natural resources

6. Patterns of demographic and political change, and cultural diffusion in the past and present (e.g., changing national boundaries, migration, and settlement, and the diffusion of and changes in customs and ideas)

8. Factors that contribute to cooperation and conflict among peoples of the nation and world, including language, religion, and political beliefs

5 INDIVIDUALS, GROUPS, AND INSTITUTIONS

7. That institutions may promote or undermine social conformity

6 POWER, AUTHORITY, AND GOVERNANCE

5. The ways in which governments meet the needs and wants of citizens, manage conflict, and establish order and society

7 PRODUCTION, DISTRIBUTION, AND CONSUMPTION

1. Individuals, government, and society experience scarcity because human wants and needs exceed what can be produced from available resources

10 CIVIC IDEALS AND PRACTICES

4. The common good, and the rule of law

CHAPTER 10 Introducing the Chapter

(Student Edition p. 275)

The Story Matters . . .

After students have read "The Story Matters . . .," begin a discussion with them about Confucius.

Ask:

Have you heard of Confucius before?

What did you know about Confucius before you read this?

Have students share their responses.

Then ask:

Why do you think the early Chinese were receptive to the ideas of Confucius?

Which of Confucius's ideas do you think are still relevant in the modern world?

Why do you think Confucius emphasized respect for education?

What do you think Confucius meant by saying that people should fulfill their duties toward their parents?

What duties do you think you have toward your parents?

Tell students that as they read this chapter, they will learn more about Confucius and other ancient Chinese thinkers.

Early China

1750 B.C. to A.D. 220

ESSENTIAL QUESTIONS • *What makes a culture unique?* • *How do new ideas change the way people live?* • *How do governments change?*

networks *There's More Online* about the lives and customs of the people of early China.

CHAPTER 10

Lesson 1 *The Birth of Chinese Civilization*

Lesson 2 *Society and Culture in Ancient China*

Lesson 3 *The Qin and the Han Dynasties*

The Story Matters . . .

Confucius is considered to be one of early China's great teachers. Thousands of years after his death, his teachings are still followed. During his lifetime, Confucius taught people there was a way to build a better life for themselves and for society. To do that, he said, people must put the needs of their families and community above their own wants. He urged people to honor traditions and seek knowledge.

The teachings of Confucius spread throughout China. His legacy includes a respect for education and the importance of fulfilling all duties toward one's parents and community. That philosophy influences many Asian countries today.

◄ *More than 2,000 years ago, Confucius founded a system of beliefs. He unknowingly had an impact on the whole world.*

Hulton Archives/Getty Images

275

Introducing Place and Time (Student Edition pp. 276–277)

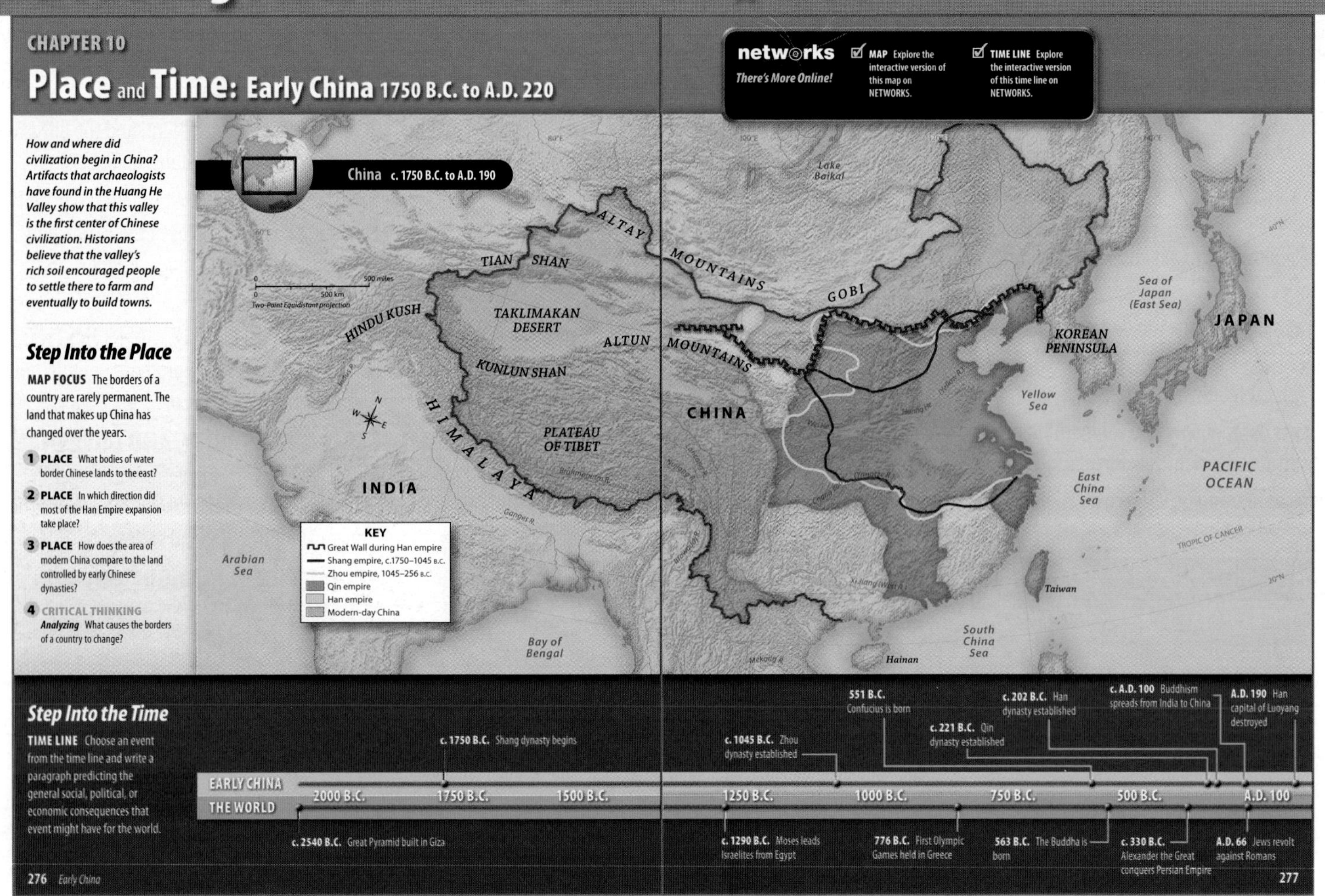
CHAPTER 10
Place and Time: Early China 1750 B.C. to A.D. 220
How and where did civilization begin in China? Artifacts that archaeologists have found in the Huang He Valley show that this valley is the first center of Chinese civilization. Historians believe that the valley's rich soil encouraged people to settle there to farm and eventually to build towns.
Step Into the Place
MAP FOCUS The borders of a country are rarely permanent. The land that makes up China has changed over the years.
1 PLACE What bodies of water border Chinese lands to the east?
2 PLACE In which direction did most of the Han Empire expansion take place?
3 PLACE How does the area of modern China compare to the land controlled by early Chinese dynasties?
4 CRITICAL THINKING Analyzing What causes the borders of a country to change?
China c. 1750 B.C. to A.D. 190
networks There's More Online!
MAP Explore the interactive version of this map on NETWORKS.
TIME LINE Explore the interactive version of this time line on NETWORKS.
Lake Baikal
ALTAY MOUNTAINS
TIAN SHAN
GOBI
HINDU KUSH
TAKLIMAKAN DESERT
ALTUN MOUNTAINS
KUNLUN SHAN
PLATEAU OF TIBET
HIMALAYA
CHINA
INDIA
KOREAN PENINSULA
Sea of Japan (East Sea)
JAPAN
Yellow Sea
East China Sea
PACIFIC OCEAN
TROPIC OF CANCER
Taiwan
South China Sea
Hainan
Arabian Sea
Bay of Bengal
KEY
Great Wall during Han empire
Shang empire, c.1750–1045 B.C.
Zhou empire, 1045–256 B.C.
Qin empire
Han empire
Modern-day China
Step Into the Time
TIME LINE Choose an event from the time line and write a paragraph predicting the general social, political, or economic consequences that event might have for the world.
EARLY CHINA
THE WORLD
2000 B.C.
1750 B.C.
1500 B.C.
1250 B.C.
1000 B.C.
750 B.C.
500 B.C.
A.D. 100
c. 1750 B.C. Shang dynasty begins
c. 1045 B.C. Zhou dynasty established
551 B.C. Confucius is born
c. 221 B.C. Qin dynasty established
c. 202 B.C. Han dynasty established
c. A.D. 100 Buddhism spreads from India to China
A.D. 190 Han capital of Luoyang destroyed
c. 2540 B.C. Great Pyramid built in Giza
c. 1290 B.C. Moses leads Israelites from Egypt
776 B.C. First Olympic Games held in Greece
563 B.C. The Buddha is born
c. 330 B.C. Alexander the Great conquers Persian Empire
A.D. 66 Jews revolt against Romans
276 Early China
277

Technology Extension

- Find an additional activity online that incorporates technology for this project.
- Visit the EdTechTeacher Web sites (included in the Technology Extension for this chapter) for more links, tutorials, and other resources.

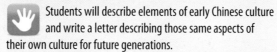

Assessing Background Knowledge

INTERACTIVE WORKSHEET

What Do You Know? Activity

Have students complete the Anticipation Guide about early China before they study the chapter. Direct students to read each statement and then, in the "Before" column, check off whether they think the statement is true or false. Next, check students' answers so you can tailor your lesson to focus on the content that students need the most help understanding.

After students complete the chapter, have them refer back to the Anticipation Guide. Have them find the page in the chapter where each idea was discussed and note the page number in the guide. Students should also note whether or not they were right and, if not, what they learned.

INTERACTIVE WORKSHEET

Guided Reading Activities

You may wish to assign the Guided Reading Activity for Lesson 1 after introducing the chapter content.

Hands-On Chapter Project

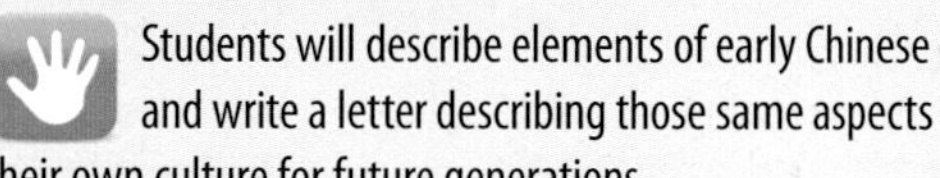

Students will describe elements of early Chinese culture and write a letter describing those same aspects of their own culture for future generations.

- Students will take part in a class discussion about early Chinese culture and draw connections to present-day life in the United States.
- Next, students will use worksheets to guide them through the process of taking notes and gathering ideas for their letters.
- Then, students will write their letters and present them to the class.
- Finally, students will evaluate their research, letters, and presentations using an Assessment Rubric.

Visit **networks** online to see the full project and rubric.

ONLINE RESOURCES

networks

Assign these interactive worksheets and quizzes from your Teacher Lesson Center. All resources are print-ready.

It's ALL Online!

CHAPTER 10 RESOURCES

- ☑ Chapter Summary
- ☑ Vocabulary Builder
- ☑ What Do You Know?
- ☑ Hands-On Chapter Project

Lesson 1 Resources

- ☑ Geography and History Activity
  Understanding Place: China
- ☑ Interactive Guided Reading Activity
- ☑ Reading Essentials and Study Guide
- ☑ Online Self-Check Quiz

Lesson 2 Resources

- ☑ 21st Century Skills Activity
  Create and Give a Presentation
- ☑ Interactive Guided Reading Activity
- ☑ Reading Essentials and Study Guide
- ☑ Online Self-Check Quiz

Lesson 3 Resources

- ☑ Economics of History Activity
  Trade Along the Silk Road
- ☑ Interactive Guided Reading Activity
- ☑ Reading Essentials and Study Guide
- ☑ Online Self-Check Quiz

Assessment Resources

- ☑ Lesson Reviews
- ☑ Online Self-Check Quizzes
- ☑ Chapter Activities and Assessment
- ☑ Standardized Test Practice

Remediation Resources

- ☑ Reading Essentials and Study Guide
- ☑ Guided Reading Activities
- ☑ Online Self-Check Quizzes
- ☑ Chapter Summary

Step Into the Place

Place Project the Chapter Opener map of China on the whiteboard. Tell students that the map shows the borders of modern China. Discuss with students how they think the borders of China might have changed over the years. *(China might have lost or gained territory over the years.)*

Ask: **What could cause a country to gain or lose territory?** Write students' ideas on the board and return to them as they complete the chapter. Then display the subsequent maps showing the land area of different Chinese dynasties. As a class, discuss the Map Focus questions.

Step Into the Time

Drawing Conclusions Have students review the time line for the chapter. Explain that they will be studying events from about 2000 B.C. to A.D. 200.

Ask: **What conclusion can you draw from comparing the time line entries for the Buddha and for Buddhism?**

(The World Time Line states that the Buddha was born in c. 563 B.C. in Nepal. The China time line states that Buddhism reached China in c. A.D. 100. Students should draw the conclusion that it took more than 600 years for Buddhism to reach China.)

Answers for pages 276–277

Step Into the Place

1. Yellow Sea, East China Sea, South China Sea, Pacific Ocean
2. south
3. Modern China is much larger.
4. CRITICAL THINKING War often results in a change of borders when a country loses or gains land. Natural disasters can also result in the loss of land.

Step Into the Time

Student answers will vary. Students should pick an event and make some specific predictions regarding the consequences of the event in one of the areas mentioned in the question. They might describe how the event will affect families, the government, or the relations between countries; or they might discuss how the event will affect trade, commerce, or business.

netw◎rks
There's More Online!
- CHART/GRAPH Art and Culture: Dragons
- GRAPHIC ORGANIZER Changes Under Shang and Zhou Rule
- VIDEO

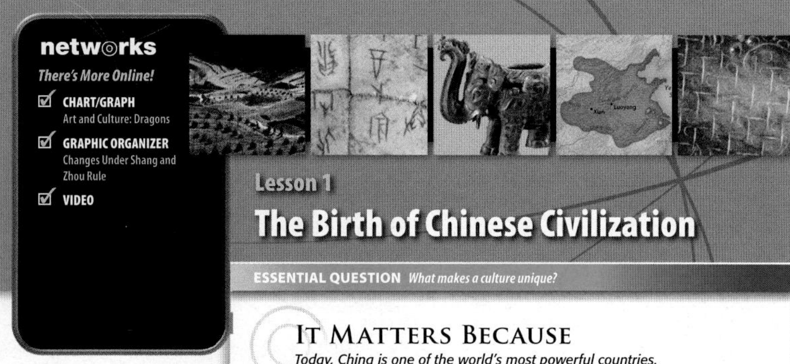

Lesson 1
The Birth of Chinese Civilization

ESSENTIAL QUESTION *What makes a culture unique?*

IT MATTERS BECAUSE
Today, China is one of the world's most powerful countries.

1 The Land of China

GUIDING QUESTION *How have rivers, mountains, and deserts shaped the development of China's civilization?*

The ancient civilizations of Egypt, Mesopotamia, and India developed along large rivers. Hundreds of years later in East Asia, another civilization began along the Huang He (HWANG HUH). In Chinese, Huang He means "yellow river." This civilization was China. China has gone through many changes over the centuries, but it is still a strong and growing civilization today.

Powerful Rivers

The Huang He stretches east across China for more than 2,900 miles (4,666 km). It begins in China's western mountains and flows to the Pacific Ocean. On its way, the Huang He cuts through thick layers of rich, yellow soil. This soil is called loess (LEHS). The river carries away large amounts of loess and spreads it farther downstream. The yellow color of the soil in the Huang He gives the river its name.

The rich soil helps farmers grow large amounts of food on small plots of land. As a result, the Huang He valley **emerged** as one of the great wheat-producing areas of the ancient world.

The Huang He has benefited the people of the Huang He valley. The river has also brought great misfortune. The Huang He often overflows its banks, causing enormous floods. Since

Reading HELPDESK

Taking Notes: *Analyzing*
Use a web diagram like this one to identify three ways the lives of the Chinese people changed under Shang rule.

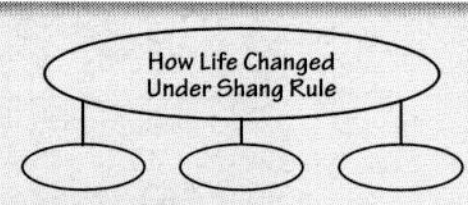

Content Vocabulary
- warlord
- aristocrat
- ancestor
- pictograph
- ideograph
- bureaucracy

600 B.C., the Chinese have recorded more than 1,500 floods of the Huang He. These floods have taken millions of lives. The Chinese call the Huang He "China's Sorrow" in honor of the people killed by the floods.

Over time, the people of China moved south and settled near another great river, the Chang Jiang (CHAHNG JYAHNG), or the Yangtze River. The Chang Jiang flows from west to east across central China. It flows through spectacular canyons and broad plains on its way to the East China Sea. The Chang Jiang is about 3,915 miles (6,300 km) long. Only the Amazon in South America and the Nile in Africa are longer.

Like the Huang He, the Chang Jiang provides rich soil for farming. Early farmers grew rice along the river's shores. The Chang Jiang was also an important waterway for trade and transportation.

Mountains and Desert

China has fertile river valleys, but only about one-tenth of its land can be farmed. Mountains and desert cover much of the country's land. To the southwest, the towering Himalaya separate China from South Asia. The Kunlun Shan and Tian Shan mountain ranges slice through western China. East of the Tian Shan is a vast, rocky desert known as the Gobi.

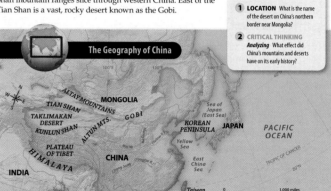

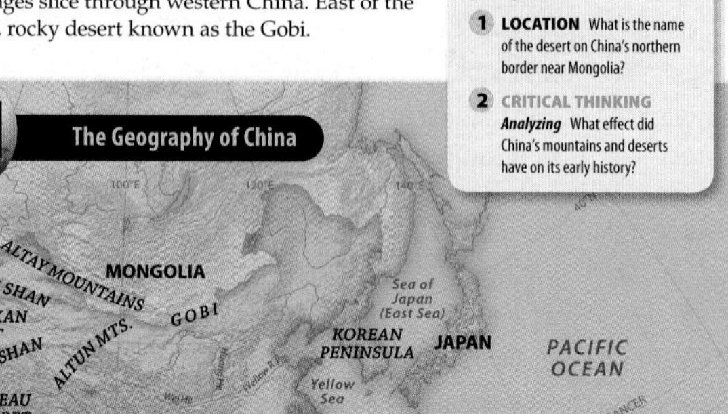

GEOGRAPHY CONNECTION

While the country of China has one of the world's largest populations, it has little land that it can use for growing food.

1. **LOCATION** What is the name of the desert on China's northern border near Mongolia?
2. **CRITICAL THINKING** *Analyzing* What effect did China's mountains and deserts have on its early history?

- hereditary
- Mandate of Heaven
- Dao

Academic Vocabulary
emerge to become known

Terraced farming, shown here, helps overcome the difficult landscape in China. Farmers plant every strip of land they can, even in the mountains.

For centuries, these rugged mountains and the barren desert acted like walls around the country. These barriers limited contacts between China and other civilizations. The Chinese developed a unique culture and a strong sense of independence. They called their land "the Middle Kingdom." To them, it was the center of the world.

PROGRESS CHECK
Identifying How did rivers help civilization develop in China?

2 The First Chinese Dynasty

GUIDING QUESTION *Why did China's Shang rulers become powerful?*

What we know about the early people of China comes from the things they left behind. Archaeologists have unearthed clay pots and cups in the Huang He valley that date back thousands of years. These artifacts show that the Huang He valley was the birthplace of Chinese civilization.

Archaeologists think that people settled in the valley because of its rich soil. Early settlers farmed the land. As in other early civilizations, people here also used the river for travel and trade. As the population grew, the Chinese began building towns.

Myths and Legends

Like other early peoples, the ancient Chinese created myths to explain the creation of their world. Many Chinese myths celebrate the deeds of great heroes. Yü the Great was one of these heroes. According to myths, Yü dug the first **channels** to control the floodwaters of the Huang He. Yü chased away the dragon that caused the floods. Then, he started digging the channels. According to the myth, Yü was aided in his task by other dragons. One dragon used its tail to help dig the channels. Still, it took 13 long years to complete the work. After the channels were finished, the flood waters could flow safely away to the sea.

Legend has it that Yü founded China's first dynasty. That dynasty, named the Xia (SHYAH), began about 2000 B.C.

Reading HELPDESK

Academic Vocabulary
channel a canal; a narrow body of water between two landmasses

Archaeologists, however, have not found any historical evidence of the Xia. Based on written records, China's first dynasty is the Shang. Shang kings ruled China from about 1750 B.C. to 1045 B.C.

Who Were the Shang?

Archaeologists have unearthed long-buried walls and buildings. These ruins show that the Shang built the first cities in China. Among these cities was the royal capital of Anyang (AHN • YAHNG). A palace and temple stood at the center of the city. Public buildings and the homes of government officials circled this central area. Beyond the city's center stood workshops and other homes.

The king was the most powerful person, serving as the political, religious, and military leader of Shang China. At first, Shang kings controlled only a small area of northern China. In time, the Shang conquered neighboring areas. They ruled over most of the people of the Huang He valley.

As the Shang kingdom grew, kings sent out large armies to defend the kingdom's borders. They appointed people called warlords to govern local territories. **Warlords** are **military** leaders who lead their own armies. Shang kings **relied** on the warlords to stay in power.

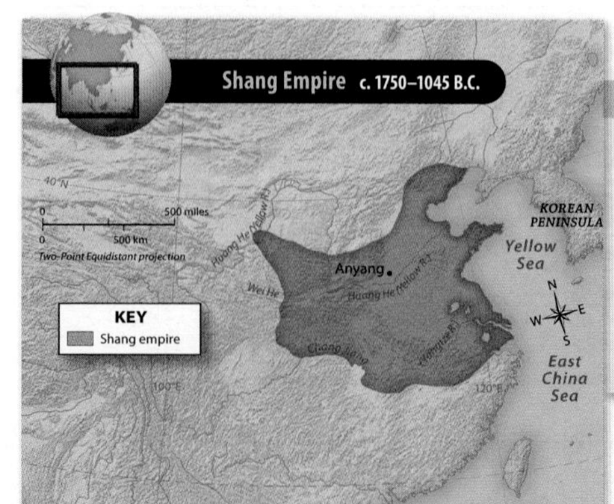

GEOGRAPHY CONNECTION

The Shang are thought to have built the first Chinese cities.

1. **LOCATION** What rivers were found within the borders of the Shang dynasty?
2. **CRITICAL THINKING** *Analyzing* Anyang is the only Chinese city shown on the map. Where would you expect other Chinese cities to be located?

warlord a military commander exercising civil power by force, usually in a limited area

Academic Vocabulary
military related to soldiers, arms, or war
rely to be dependent

LESSON 1

ENGAGE

MAP **Analyzing Visuals** Show the map of ancient China and the surrounding area on the interactive whiteboard. Have students locate geographic features marked on the map.

Ask students to locate the Gobi, the Taklimakan Desert, the Himalaya, the Huang He, the Chang Jiang River, and the Altay and Altun Mountains.

LECTURE SLIDE

Ask:

Where do you think early Chinese people were most likely to have settled?

Have volunteers come to the board and circle these places. *(Based on their study of other early civilizations, students will most likely circle river valleys as places where the ancient Chinese settled.)* As students circle the places, have them read the names aloud. ELL

Ask:

What geographic features helped isolate the Chinese civilization?

Have volunteers circle these features. Have students explain their choices. *(Places that helped isolate the Chinese include the Himalaya, the Altay and the Altun Mountains, and the Gobi and Taklimakan deserts. Students may also circle the bodies of water that form China's eastern coast.)*

Show the blank pro-and-con chart from the lecture slide. Have students complete a pro-and-con chart for China's different geographic features.

TEACH & ASSESS

1 The Land of China

GUIDING QUESTION ***How have rivers, mountains, and deserts shaped the development of China's civilization?***

INTERACTIVE WORKSHEET Complete the Geography and History Activity as a class to help students understand the effect China's geography has had on its history.

2 The First Chinese Dynasty

GUIDING QUESTION ***Why did China's Shang rulers become powerful?***

3 The Zhou: China's Longest Dynasty

GUIDING QUESTION ***How did the Zhou claim the right to rule China?***

GRAPHIC ORGANIZER **Summarizing** Discuss as a class the changes that the Shang and Zhou dynasties brought to China.

Then show the Interactive Graphic Organizer for this lesson and have students complete it. *(Changes noted can include: writing introduced, bronze arts developed, idea of Mandate of Heaven introduced, irrigation developed, first cities built, trade expanded, kings become leaders of religion and government, strong army created, and borders of China expanded.)* AL

INTERACTIVE WHITEBOARD ACTIVITY **Analyzing** Point out to students that one of the achievements of the early Chinese was the development of a writing system.

Ask:

- **How is the writing system developed by the early Chinese different from the writing system used in English?** *(Chinese writing uses pictographs and ideographs. English has 26 characters representing sounds that are put together to form words.)*
- **What is the difference between a pictograph and an ideograph?** *(A pictograph is a character that represents an object. An ideograph combines two or more pictographs to represent an idea.)*

Present the Interactive Whiteboard Activity on Chinese writing. BL

Sequencing Have students create a time line showing the dates of the Shang and Zhou dynasties. Students should list rulers and the dates they ruled as well as major events, characteristics, discoveries, and accomplishments of each dynasty.

Students may use their textbook and Interactive Graphic Organizer as references. *(Events to list include, in order: 1750 B.C. Shang dynasty begins, first cities built, kings rule China, capital at Anyang established, kingdom expands, ancestors honored, bronze arts flourish; 1045 B.C. Wu Wang starts the Zhou dynasty, kings rule China, Mandate of Heaven; 400s B.C.–200s B.C. Period of the Warring States)* AL

Have students complete the Lesson 1 Review.

CLOSE & REFLECT

Comparing and Contrasting

Ask students to name similarities and differences between the Shang and Zhou civilizations that developed in the Huang He Valley.

They can use the graphic organizers they created earlier for assistance.

Answers for pages 278–281

P. 278 Taking Notes Changes noted can include: writing introduced, bronze arts developed, idea of Mandate of Heaven introduced, irrigation developed, first cities built, trade expanded, kings become leaders of religion and government, strong army created, and borders of China expanded.

P. 279 GEOGRAPHY CONNECTION

1. It is the Gobi.
2. CRITICAL THINKING They limited farmland and separated China from the outside world.

P. 280 ☑ PROGRESS CHECK Rivers provided fertile soil and irrigation that made it easier to grow food. They provided waterways for trade and transportation.

P. 281 GEOGRAPHY CONNECTION

1. Huang He and Chang Jiang
2. CRITICAL THINKING Students will most likely expect other cities to have been built along China's rivers or along its coastline.

Thinking Like a HISTORIAN

Analyzing Sources

Archaeologists study what ancient societies have left behind. Some of what we know about early China and Chinese writing comes from the study of oracle bones. They are a primary source. Suppose you were an archaeologist who dug up a collection of oracle bones. You would want to analyze them. Use the library to find secondary sources about oracle bones. Write a brief report summarizing your findings and present it to the class. For more information about analyzing sources, read the chapter *What Does a Historian Do?*

Under the king, warlords and other royal officials formed the upper class. They were **aristocrats** (uh•RIHS•tuh•krats), people of noble birth whose wealth came from the land they owned. Aristocrats passed their land and power to their children or to younger family members.

Most people of Shang China were farmers. There were much smaller groups of merchants, artisans, and slaves. The farmers lived in rural villages and worked the land that belonged to the aristocrats. They raised cattle, sheep, and chickens and grew grains, such as millet, wheat, and rice.

People in Shang China worshipped many gods. The god Shang Ti ruled as supreme god over the lesser gods. According to legend, the gods lived in the mountains, rivers, and seas.

The early Chinese both admired and feared the gods. They believed the gods could bring good or bad fortune. They attempted to please the gods by offering gifts of food and other goods.

The Chinese also honored their **ancestors**, or long-dead family members. They made offerings to their ancestors. They hoped that their ancestors would bring good luck and help in difficult times. Today, many Chinese still pay respect to their ancestors by going to temples and burning small paper copies of food, clothing, and other items. These copies represent things that departed relatives need in the afterlife.

Seeking Guidance from Ancestors

Shang kings believed that they received their power to rule from the gods and their wisdom from their ancestors. For this reason, religion and government were closely linked. For the kings, an important duty was to contact the gods and the ancestors before making important decisions.

The kings asked for help by using oracle (AWR•uh•kuhl) bones. They instructed priests to scratch questions on the bones, such as "Will I win the battle?" or "Will there be an abundant harvest?" Priests heated the oracle bones over a fire until they cracked. The pattern of cracks provided answers from the gods and ancestors to the king's questions.

The ancient Chinese wrote in pictographs and ideographs. **Pictographs** (PIKH•tuh•grafs) are characters that represent objects. For example, the Chinese characters for the sun and the moon are pictographs. **Ideographs** (IH•dee•uh•grafs) are another kind of character used in Chinese writing. They link

Messages written on animal bones show that the Chinese language originated with pictures representing words.

Panorama Media/Panorama Stock RF/Age fotostock

Reading HELPDESK

aristocrat a member of an upper class of society, usually made up of hereditary nobility

ancestor a person that someone is descended from

pictograph a symbol in a writing system based on pictures

ideograph a symbol in a writing system that represents a thing or an idea

two or more pictographs to express an idea. For example, the ideograph that stands for "forest" combines three pictographs of the word "tree."

Unlike the Chinese language, English and many other languages have writing systems based on an alphabet. An alphabet uses characters that represent sounds. Most characters in the Chinese language represent entire words.

Chinese ideographs combine the pictographs of single items to form a more complex word.

▶ CRITICAL THINKING

Speculating Why do you think many Chinese today practice the ancient craft of pictographs?

Shang Arts

During the Shang dynasty, the Chinese created objects made of bronze. These works of art are some of the finest bronzes ever made. To make bronze objects, artisans made clay molds in several parts. Then they carved designs into the clay. Finally, they joined the parts of the mold together and poured in melted bronze. When the bronze cooled, the artisans removed the mold. The finished object was a beautifully decorated work of art.

Shang bronze objects included sculptures, daggers, vases, cups, and urns—or large ceremonial containers. The Shang used bronze urns to prepare and serve food for ceremonies to honor their ancestors.

Chinese artists and artisans made many other important advances. Farmers raised silk worms that produced silk. Weavers then made the silk into colorful clothing for wealthy people. Artisans crafted vases and dishes from kaolin (KAY•eh•lehn), a fine, white clay. They also carved statues from ivory and a green stone called jade.

☑ PROGRESS CHECK

Explaining Why did Shang kings have questions scratched on oracle bones?

3 The Zhou: China's Longest Dynasty

GUIDING QUESTION *How did the Zhou claim the right to rule China?*

According to legend, the last of the Shang rulers was a wicked tyrant. Many Chinese turned against him. In 1045 B.C., rebels led by an aristocrat named Wu Wang (WOO WAHNG) overthrew the Shang government. When his victory was complete, Wu declared a new dynasty called the Zhou (JOH). The Zhou ruled China for more than 800 years—longer than any other dynasty in Chinese history.

The Chinese made bronze objects for many uses. What do you think this elephant might have been used for?

(b) Asian Art & Archaeology, Inc./CORBIS

GEOGRAPHY CONNECTION

Zhou rulers maintained the longest lasting dynasty in Chinese history.

5 **LOCATION** What body of water made up the eastern border of Zhou territory?

6 CRITICAL THINKING ***Analyzing*** Why did the Zhou divide their kingdom into smaller territories?

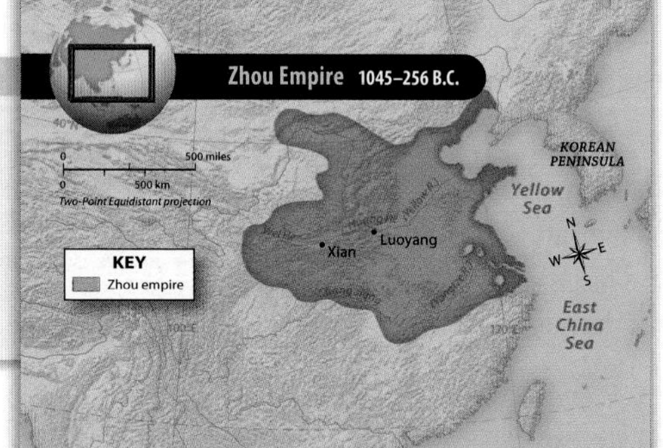

How did the Zhou Rule China?

Zhou kings governed China much as Shang rulers had. The king led the government, ruling with the help of a bureaucracy (byu•RAH•kruh•see). A **bureaucracy** is made up of officials who carry out the tasks of government. The king also put together a strong army to bring weaker kingdoms under Zhou rule.

Soon the Zhou kingdom was larger than that of the Shang. To govern effectively, the king divided the kingdom into territories. He assigned loyal aristocrats to govern each of the territories. The positions the aristocrats held were **hereditary**. This meant that when an aristocrat died, a son or another member of his family governed the territory.

The Chinese believed their king represented them before the gods. The king's chief duty was to carry out religious ceremonies to please the gods. Zhou kings claimed that kings ruled China because they had the Mandate of Heaven.

The Right to Rule

The **Mandate of Heaven** is the belief that the Chinese king's right to rule came from the gods. The Mandate stated the idea that the gods chose a wise and good person to rule. The person chosen by the gods would govern honestly and well.

The Mandate of Heaven changed what the Zhou people expected from their king. The king must rule by the proper

Reading HELPDESK

bureaucracy a group of non-elected government officials

hereditary having title or possession by reason of birth

Mandate of Heaven the belief that the Chinese king's right to rule came from the gods

Dao Chinese system of beliefs which describes the way a king must rule

"Way," known as the **Dao** (DOW). His duty was to honor and please the gods. If there was a natural disaster or a bad harvest, that meant the king had failed and he could be replaced.

Technology and Trade

For many centuries, Chinese farmers had to depend on rain to water their crops. Under Zhou kings, the Chinese developed new systems to irrigate the land. With a better water supply, farmers were able to grow more crops than ever before.

China's trade also expanded. Archaeologists have found pieces of Chinese silk in central Asia and as far away as Greece.

War Between the States

Over time, the aristocrats who ruled the territories of the Zhou kingdom grew more powerful. They ignored the king's commands and took control of their own territory. The aristocrats began to fight one another for power. These wars began in the 400s B.C. and went on for nearly 200 years. Because each aristocrat formed his own state, this time in China's history is called the "Period of the Warring States."

To fill the ranks of their armies, the aristocrats forced farmers to serve as soldiers. Chinese soldiers were armed with swords, spears, and crossbows. As the fighting continued through the years, warriors began using horses. The Chinese developed the saddle and stirrup. Now soldiers could ride around the battlefield while throwing spears or shooting crossbows. The wars fought at this time would result in a new dynasty.

This dragon is an example of bronze work from the Zhou dynasty.

Burstein Collection/CORBIS

☑ PROGRESS CHECK

Identifying What technology was developed in China during the Zhou dynasty?

LESSON 1 REVIEW

Review Vocabulary

1. How did a *pictograph* differ from an *ideograph*?

Answer the Guiding Questions

2. ***Describing*** What geographic features isolated ancient China from other civilizations?
3. ***Explaining*** How did Shang rulers gain power?
4. ***Identifying*** What was the chief duty of Zhou kings?
5. ***Describing*** Describe the biggest change for the Chinese people during the Zhou dynasty.
6. **EXPOSITORY WRITING** China's geographic features separated it from other civilizations. Write a paragraph explaining the advantages and disadvantages of isolation.
7. **EXPOSITORY WRITING** Write a paragraph that explains why "China's Sorrow" is an appropriate description of the Huang He.

IF YOU HAVE MORE TIME . . .

Discuss the Qualities of a Leader

Identifying Begin a discussion with students about what makes a good leader. Include in the discussion what characteristics are required to successfully lead an especially large empire, such as China.

Ask:

What qualities do people look for in a leader? What makes a leader strong?

Write students' responses on the board. If students have trouble coming up with the qualities of a good leader, prompt them with the following questions.

Ask:

- **Does a good leader need to be persuasive?**
- **Does a good leader need to be ethical and responsible?**
- **Should a leader be able to inspire others?**
- **Do good leaders lead by example?**
- **Does the size of an empire affect what skills a leader needs to be successful?**

As students read about different dynasties that ruled China, remind them to think about the qualities they think a good leader needs when they evaluate each leader's success. Students should base their opinions on the class responses to these questions.

Make a Graphic Organizer to Compare and Contrast the Shang and Zhou Dynasties

Ask:

What type of graphic organizer would be most useful for comparing and contrasting the Shang and Zhou dynasties? *(a Venn diagram)*

Work with students to complete a Venn diagram to compare and contrast the Shang and Zhou dynasties. Draw a sample Venn diagram on the whiteboard. Label one circle "Shang Dynasty" and the other circle "Zhou Dynasty." Label the overlapping sections of the circles "Both."

Ask:

- **Who founded each dynasty?**
- **Who led the government?**
- **What were the greatest accomplishments of each dynasty?**
- **How did each dynasty end?**

Have volunteers come to the whiteboard and write the answers to the questions in the correct area of the diagram. As needed, have a volunteer read aloud each of the answers.

Have students add other information about the two dynasties to the diagram and read the answers aloud. 

Discuss River Valley Civilizations

Comparing and Contrasting Ask students to name similarities and differences between the civilizations that developed in the Huang He Valley and civilizations in other river valleys such as along the Tigris-Euphrates, Nile, and Indus Rivers.

Create a four-column chart on the whiteboard. Label the columns *Tigris-Euphrates, Nile, Indus,* and *Huang He*. Have students come to the board and complete the chart with information about each of the river valley civilizations.

Using the chart on the board for reference, discuss the ways in which the civilization that arose along the Huang He was the same as or different from other river valley civilizations. *(Answers will vary but may include similarities such as farming and differences such as isolation.)* BL

Answers for pages 282–285

P. 282 Thinking Like a Historian Answers will vary but should reflect an understanding of the importance of this archaeological find and how oracle bones were used in the Shang dynasty.

P. 283 Answers will vary but should give a reasonable use for the bronze elephant.

P. 283 CRITICAL THINKING Pictographs are still part of the Chinese culture.

P. 283 ☑ PROGRESS CHECK They had priests scratch questions on oracle bones as a way of asking questions of the gods and ancestors.

P. 284 GEOGRAPHY CONNECTION

1. the Yellow Sea
2. CRITICAL THINKING to make ruling easier

P. 285 ☑ PROGRESS CHECK New irrigation systems, saddles, and stirrups were developed during the Zhou dynasty.

LESSON 1 REVIEW

1. Each pictograph represents an object; ideographs join two or more pictographs to represent another thing or to express an idea.
2. Deserts and mountains isolated China from other civilizations.
3. Shang rulers used military force to gain power.
4. The chief duty of a Zhou king was to carry out religious ceremonies to please the gods.
5. The biggest change for the Chinese during the Zhou dynasty was the development of the Mandate of Heaven. According to the Mandate of Heaven, the gods chose a wise and good person to rule China. The Mandate of Heaven changed what Chinese people expected from a king. The king's duty was to honor and please the gods. If the king failed in his duty, the people had the right to replace him.
6. A civilization that is cut off from other civilizations might have the advantage of being able to develop peacefully. The people of the civilization might develop a stronger national identity. However, isolation also keeps people from being exposed to new ideas and new ways of doing things. A civilization could grow weak without the exposure to new ideas.
7. Although the Huang He provides China with rich soil that makes it possible to grow large amounts of food on small plots of land, the river has also brought misery to China. The river often floods, which causes immense damage and many deaths. Millions of people have died as a result of the flooding of the Huang He.

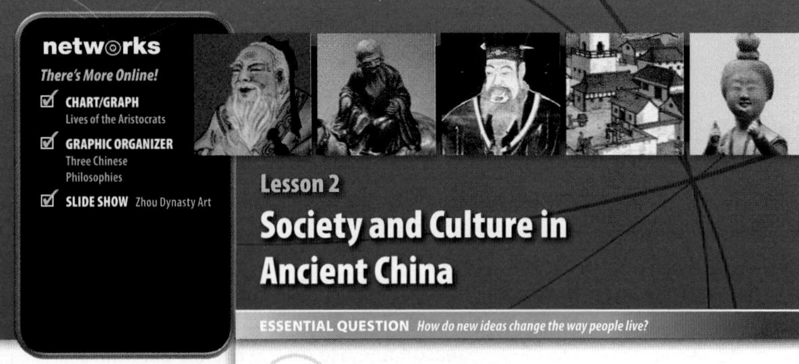

networks
There's More Online!
- CHART/GRAPH Lives of the Aristocrats
- GRAPHIC ORGANIZER Three Chinese Philosophies
- SLIDE SHOW Zhou Dynasty Art

Lesson 2

Society and Culture in Ancient China

ESSENTIAL QUESTION *How do new ideas change the way people live?*

It Matters Because

Ideas that started in early China continue to influence today's world.

1 Chinese Philosophies

GUIDING QUESTION *How did Chinese thinkers influence society and government?*

During the Period of the Warring States, rulers of rival states fought each other. Armies wiped out entire villages of men, women, and children. Many Chinese looked for ways to stop the killing. They wanted to bring order to society.

Between 500 B.C. and 200 B.C., Chinese thinkers developed three major **philosophies**. They were Confucianism, Daoism, and legalism. These philosophies were different from one another. However, the philosophies had the same goal. Each philosophy aimed to create a well-run and peaceful society. After decades of war, Chinese people welcomed these new ideas.

What Ideas Did Confucius Teach?

Confucianism (kuhn•FYOO•shuh•nih•zuhm) was based on the teachings of a man named Confucius (kuhn•FYOO•shuhs). Born about 550 B.C. to a farming family, Confucius lived when rival kings fought each other for power. Confucius criticized the misrule of these kings. He urged the people to follow the beliefs of their ancestors. If people would do that, Confucius believed, it would bring peace and harmony to China.

Reading **HELP**DESK

Taking Notes: *Identifying*

Use a graphic organizer like the one shown here to identify the three Chinese philosophies that emerged after the fall of the Zhou dynasty.

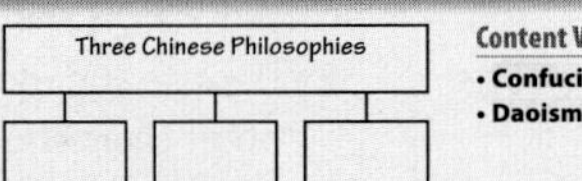

Content Vocabulary
- **Confucianism**
- **legalism**
- **Daoism**
- **filial piety**

Duty is a central idea of Confucianism. Duty means that a person places the needs of family and community above his or her own needs. Each **individual** has certain duties to fulfill. It is the duty of parents to love their children, and it is the children's duty to respect their parents. Husbands should support their wives, and wives should obey their husbands. Above all, a ruler had a duty to rule justly and to set an example of right living. In return, subjects should be loyal and obey the law.

Confucius believed that if each individual carried out his or her duties, society would do well. He urged the people to be good. This meant behaving moderately, keeping one's promises, honoring traditions, and respecting the elderly. Confucius also advised people to seek knowledge:

Connections to TODAY

Confucianism in Asia

Confucianism still has millions of followers today. Most of these followers are in China. Over the centuries, however, the basic teachings of Confucius spread across Asia. The concepts he handed down—a belief in duty and correct behavior and respect for education—are a part of the culture in many Asian countries today.

PRIMARY SOURCE

> "By extensively . . . studying all learning, and keeping himself under the restraint [control] of the rules of propriety [correct behavior], one may thus likewise not err . . . from what is right."
>
> —Confucius, *Analects*, XII, 15

To Confucius, the right way to live was **similar** to the idea known as the Golden Rule: "Do unto others as you would have others do unto you."

The Influence of Confucius

Confucius believed that government service should be open to all men of ability and merit and not limited to those of noble birth. The aristocrats did not want to open government to more people. They did not want to lose their power. However, over time Chinese emperors developed the practice of choosing government officials through civil service tests.

Many people honored Confucius as a great teacher. His followers wrote down his sayings and collected them in a work called the *Analects*. After Confucius died in 479 B.C., his teachings spread throughout China. Confucianism continued to shape Chinese society and government until the early A.D. 1900s.

The Chinese philosopher Confucius taught that people should do their duty and keep promises.

Confucianism a system of beliefs based on the teachings of Confucius

Academic Vocabulary

philosophy the study of the basic ideas about society, education, and right and wrong

individual a single human being as contrasted with a group

similar having things in common

INFOGRAPHIC

Three philosophies developed in early China. Each had a strong leader.

1. **IDENTIFYING** Which philosophy encourages followers to concentrate on duty and humanity?
2. **CRITICAL THINKING** *Analyzing* Which of these philosophies do you think would be most popular in the world today? Explain.

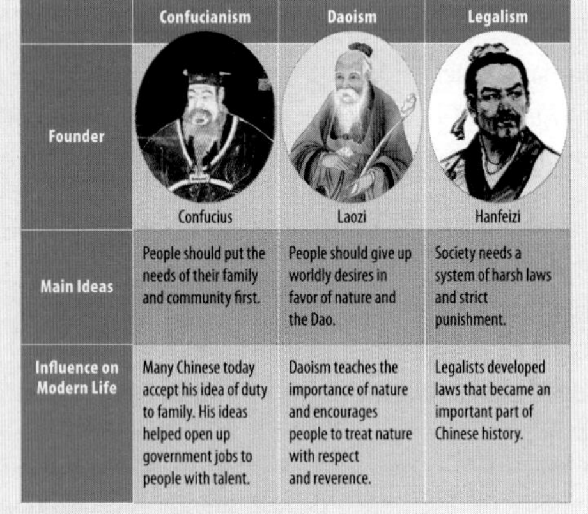

CHINESE PHILOSOPHERS

	Confucianism	Daoism	Legalism
Founder	Confucius	Laozi	Hanfeizi
Main Ideas	People should put the needs of their family and community first.	People should give up worldly desires in favor of nature and the Dao.	Society needs a system of harsh laws and strict punishment.
Influence on Modern Life	Many Chinese today accept his idea of duty to family. His ideas helped open up government jobs to people with talent.	Daoism teaches the importance of nature and encourages people to treat nature with respect and reverence.	Legalists developed laws that became an important part of Chinese history.

The Philosophy of Daoism

Another Chinese philosophy, known as **Daoism** (DOW•ih•zuhm) also promoted a peaceful society. The word *Dao* means "path" and is often translated as "the Way." Daoism began with the ideas of Laozi (LOW•DZUH). Laozi is believed to have lived during the same time as Confucius.

Like Confucianism, Daoism teaches people how to live a good life. Daoists believed that people should free themselves from worldly desires and live simply. They should turn to nature and the Dao—the spiritual force that guides all things. In this way, they would enjoy a happy life.

Daoism is different from Confucianism in some ways. Followers of Confucius taught that people should work hard to make the world better. Daoism taught people to turn away from worldly affairs and live in harmony with nature. Many Chinese followed both Confucianism and Daoism. They believed that the two philosophies supported each other.

Reading **HELP**DESK

Daoism a Chinese philosophy concerned with obtaining long life and living in harmony with nature

Legalism

A third philosophy stressed the importance of a system of laws. This philosophy became known as **legalism** (lee•guh•lih•zuhm), or the "School of Law."

A thinker named Hanfeizi (HAN•fay•DZOO) introduced the ideas of legalism during the 200s B.C. Unlike Confucius or Laozi, Hanfeizi believed that humans are naturally evil. Strict laws and harsh punishments were necessary to force people to do their duty.

Many aristocrats supported legalism because it emphasized force. Legalism did not require rulers to consider the needs or wishes of their people. Its ideas led to cruel punishments for even the smallest crimes.

PROGRESS CHECK

Comparing and Contrasting How are the ideas of Confucius and Laozi similar? How are they different?

2 Chinese Life

GUIDING QUESTION *How was early Chinese society organized?*

Early Chinese society was made up of four social classes. A **social class** includes people who have the same economic and social position. In ancient China, these social classes were land-owning aristocrats, farmers, artisans, and merchants.

Lives of the Aristocrats

China's aristocratic families were wealthy. They owned large estates and lived in tile-roofed houses with courtyards and gardens. Walls surrounded their homes as protection against bandits. Inside, fine furniture and carpets filled the rooms.

Aristocratic families owned large plots of land. After the father died, a family's land was divided equally among all of the male heirs. As a result, sons and grandsons owned much less land than their fathers and grandfathers owned.

Lives of the Farmers

About nine out of ten Chinese farmed for a living. The farmers lived in rural villages surrounded by mud walls. Beyond the village walls were fields owned by the aristocrats. The farmers rented the fields by turning over part of their crops to the owners.

The ideas of Laozi became popular in China between around 500 B.C. and 300 B.C. Here he is shown riding a water buffalo into the desert.

legalism a Chinese philosophy that stressed the importance of laws

Academic Vocabulary

social class a group of people who are at a similar cultural, economic, or educational level

LESSON 2

ENGAGE

Making Connections Ask students to think about how their actions affect or influence others. Lead students into a discussion of why laws are created.

Then discuss how a society's values might be reflected in its laws. Ask volunteers to cite a law and then discuss whether it reflects a value of our society. If it does, identify what that value is.

LECTURE SLIDE

Defining

Ask:

What is meant by the term *philosophy*? Lead students to understand that philosophy is the study of the beliefs and laws that rule life and nature. Show students the definition of *philosophy* from the lecture slide.

Ask:

How does philosophy shape the way we live? *(Students might say that what people consider true and important will determine how they act.)* Ask students if they think philosophies differ from culture to culture.

Encourage students to use what they have learned so far about early China to speculate about what the early Chinese might have believed about life and nature. AL

TEACH & ASSESS

1 Chinese Philosophies

GUIDING QUESTION *How did Chinese thinkers influence society and government?*

INTERACTIVE WHITEBOARD ACTIVITY **Identifying Points of View** Have students complete the Interactive Whiteboard Activity matching sayings of Chinese philosophers to the correct school of philosophy.

Then divide students into three groups to create a matching game. One group will be Confucians, another will be Daoists, and the third will be legalists.

Thinking about what they have learned, students in each group should write sayings that represent something the followers of their group's philosophy might have said.

For example, students in the Daoist group might write, "Put aside your desire for money."

Each group should prepare a list of four or five sayings. After collecting the lists, read the sayings aloud to the class.

INTERACTIVE WORKSHEET **Evaluating** Have students complete the 21st Century Skills Activity in which they create a slide show presentation about one of the three philosophies they have studied.

Provide time in class for students to work on and then make their presentations. Students may need additional time outside of class to complete and practice their presentations.

2 Chinese Life

GUIDING QUESTION *How was early Chinese society organized?*

SLIDE SHOW **Analyzing Visuals** Present the slide show on art produced by Chinese artisans.

Ask: What do these images tell you about the wealth of ancient China? *(The quality of the art and the expensive materials suggest that ancient China had great wealth.)*

Ask: How did art styles change during the Zhou dynasty? *(Zhou artists experimented with new styles in forms such as jade carving and bronze work.)* AL

Have students complete the Lesson 2 Review.

CLOSE & REFLECT

Making Connections Have students choose one of the three philosophies (Confucianism, Daoism, legalism) that they believe would make school better if everyone followed it. Have students write a short letter to the principal describing one or more key changes their chosen philosophy could result in at the school. AL

IF YOU HAVE MORE TIME . . .

Discuss the Effect of Confucius on Family Life in China

Determining Cause and Effect Guide students in a discussion of the effect the teachings of Confucius had on Chinese family life.

Ask:

How were the teachings of Confucius reflected in the lives of Chinese families? *(Confucius stressed the importance of respect for parents and the elderly. In Chinese families, children put the wants of their parents, especially their fathers, above their own wants.)*

Answers for pages 286–289

P. 286 Taking Notes Confucianism, Daoism, legalism

P. 288 INFOGRAPHIC

1. Confucianism
2. CRITICAL THINKING Answers will vary but should be logical.

P. 289 PROGRESS CHECK Confucius and Laozi offered people a guide on how to live a good life. Confucius believed that to live a good life, people should work hard to make the world better. Laozi, on the other hand, believed that to have a good life, people should turn away from the material world and focus on nature.

CHINESE VILLAGE

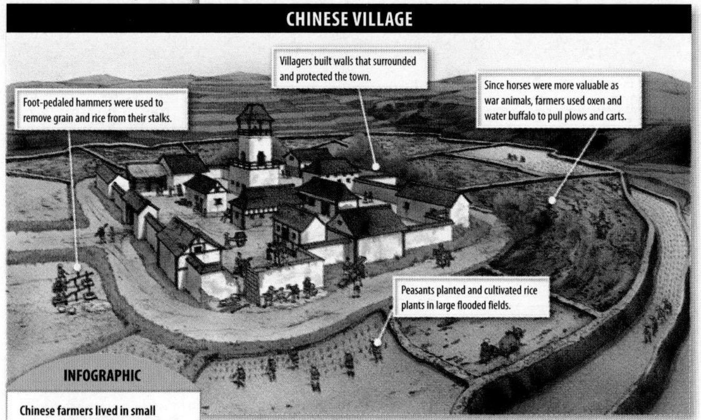

Villagers built walls that surrounded and protected the town.
Foot-pedaled hammers were used to remove grain and rice from their stalks.
Since horses were more valuable as war animals, farmers used oxen and water buffalo to pull plows and carts.
Peasants planted and cultivated rice plants in large flooded fields.

INFOGRAPHIC

Chinese farmers lived in small villages made up of several families. They farmed fields outside the village walls.

▶ CRITICAL THINKING

Analyzing What are some possible disadvantages for farmers of working on land they do not own?

In northern China, farmers grew wheat and a grain called millet. In the south, where the climate was warmer and wetter, they grew rice. Most farmers also owned a small plot of land where they grew food for their own use.

The government required farmers to pay taxes and to work one month each year on projects such as building roads. In wartime, farmers were forced to serve as soldiers. In addition, farmers had to face constant threats from famine and floods.

Lives of the Artisans and Merchants

Artisans are skilled workers who make useful objects. The artisans of Zhou China crafted iron tools and weapons, silk cloth, and vessels made of bronze or jade. Many were architects, artists, and woodworkers. Most artisans learned their skills from their fathers and, in turn, passed them along to their sons.

Shopkeepers, traders, and bankers made up the merchant class. Merchants lived in towns and provided goods and services to the aristocrats.

Some merchants became wealthy, but they were not respected members of society. People believed that merchants worked only for their own gain, not for the good of society.

Reading **HELP**DESK

filial piety the responsibility children have to respect, obey, and care for their parents

While artisans made useful goods and farmers grew food for all, merchants made money for themselves. Merchants were also barred from government jobs.

What Were Chinese Families Like?

The family was at the center of early Chinese society. Farming in ancient China required many workers, so parents had many children to help them with the work. Even young children worked in the fields. Chinese families took care of those members in need—the aged, the young, and the sick.

Chinese families practiced **filial piety** (FIH•lee•uhl PY•uh•tee). Filial refers to a son or daughter. Piety refers to duty or devotion. Therefore, *filial piety* refers to people's responsibility to respect and obey their parents.

It also requires people to take care of their parents as they grow older. Family members placed the needs of the head of the family before their own. The head of the family was the oldest male, usually the father. Respect for parents and the elderly were central to the teachings of Confucius. Even today, filial piety is an important part of Chinese culture.

Roles of Men and Women

Men and women had very different roles in early China. Men were respected because of the jobs they did—growing crops, attending school, running the government, and fighting wars. The Chinese considered these jobs more important than the work carried out by women. Most women raised children and saw to their education. They also managed the household and family finances.

The Man and woman here are shown in brightly colored dress. The colors on these ancient Chinese figures have lasted thousands of years. Why do you think there is such attention to detail?

☑ PROGRESS CHECK

Explaining Why were merchants not respected in ancient China?

LESSON 2 REVIEW

Review Vocabulary

1. Describe a situation in which you might show *filial piety*.

Answer the Guiding Questions

2. ***Explaining*** Why did many aristocrats support legalism?
3. ***Identifying*** What were the main social classes of early China?
4. ***Assessing*** Which philosophy do you most strongly agree with—Confucianism, Daoism, or legalism? Why?
5. ***Paraphrasing*** Read the following quotation by Confucius. Then restate the quotation in your own words: "A journey of a thousand miles begins with a single step."
6. **PERSUASIVE WRITING** Which system of belief—Confucianism, Daoism, or legalism—would lead to the best government? Write a paragraph expressing your opinion in order to convince others.

NOTES

NOTES

LESSON 2 (cont.)

IF YOU HAVE MORE TIME . . .

Explore Chinese Philosophies

Making Connections Review with students what the term *philosophy* means. Have students provide examples of values that guide their lives, such as the golden rule.

Ask:

Have you ever heard of the golden rule? What is it? *(The golden rule states that you should treat others the way you would want to be treated.)*

Ask:

Do you agree with the golden rule? What would society be like if everyone followed this rule? *(Accept all reasonable responses.)* AL ELL

Identifying Points of View Have students work in small groups to create a matching game. One third of the group represents the ideas of Confucius, one third represents the ideas of Laozi, and one third represents the ideas of Hanfeizi.

Thinking about what they have learned in the lesson and using the interactive whiteboard chart, students should write sayings that represent something their philosopher might have said. For example, students in the group representing Laozi might write, "Put aside your desire for money."

Each group should prepare a list of four or five sayings. After collecting the lists of example sayings, read them aloud to the class. Have students match the saying with the correct philosopher.

Think About Class in Chinese Society

Comparing and Contrasting Guide students in a discussion comparing and contrasting the different classes that existed in ancient China: aristocrats, farmers, artisans, and merchants.

Ask:

- **What class did most of the people of China belong to?** *(farmers)*
- **Which classes of people lived in rural areas?** *(farmers and aristocrats)*
- **Who lived in towns?** *(merchants)*
- **Which people were wealthy?** *(aristocrats and some merchants)*

LECTURE SLIDE **Comparing and Contrasting** Then, have students write sentences on sheets of paper, comparing and contrasting the different classes. Provide ELL students with this contrast sentence stem: ______ were ______, but ______ were ______.

Show the sample contrast sentence from the lecture slide: *Aristocrats were wealthy, but farmers were poor.*

Provide this sentence stem for comparing: Both ______ and ______. Create a sample sentence with students.

For example: *Both farmers and aristocrats lived in rural areas.*

After students write their examples, have volunteers write their sentences on the whiteboard and review the sentences as a class. ELL

SLIDE SHOW **Using Visuals** Present the "Lives of the Artisans and Merchants" slide show and discuss the information it includes.

Answers for pages 290–291

P. 290 INFOGRAPHIC

CRITICAL THINKING One disadvantage is that farmers who do not own the land they farm cannot enjoy all the profits because they must pay rent. Another disadvantage is that farmers might not take good care of the land because they do not own it.

P. 291 Possible answer: because the Chinese valued art and made their art as realistic as possible

P. 291 ☑ PROGRESS CHECK Merchants were not respected because most people believed merchants were only interested in making money for themselves, not in improving society.

LESSON 2 REVIEW

1. Students' answers will vary but should reflect an understanding that filial piety involves the obligation of children to respect, obey, and take care of their parents.
2. Many aristocrats supported legalism because it did not require rulers to consider the needs or wishes of their people; rather, it allowed them to rule by force.
3. The main social classes of early China were aristocrats, farmers, artisans, and merchants.
4. Answers may vary but should demonstrate an understanding of the philosophy students chose to write about.
5. Answers may vary but should state something such as, "The hardest part of doing something difficult can be getting started. Start off with something small and keep going."
6. Answers may vary but should reflect an understanding of the role of government and the belief system students chose to write about.

networks
There's More Online!
- GAME Chinese Inventions
- GRAPHIC ORGANIZER Comparing and Contrasting: Qin and Han Dynasties
- SLIDE SHOW Qin Tomb Soldiers

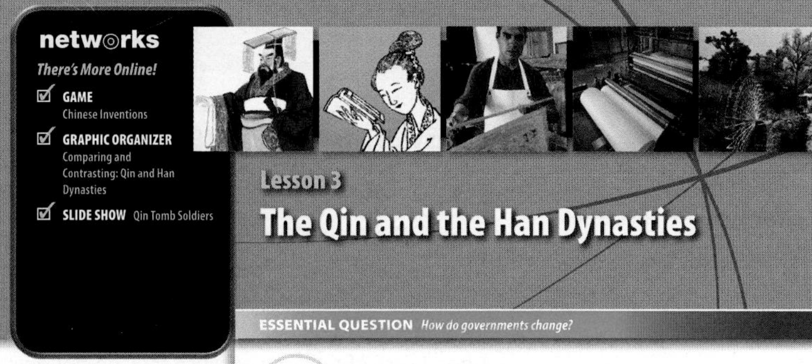

Lesson 3

The Qin and the Han Dynasties

ESSENTIAL QUESTION *How do governments change?*

IT MATTERS BECAUSE

Stable government builds solid growth and strength in a civilization.

1 The Qin Emperor

GUIDING QUESTION *How did the Qin Emperor unite China?*

You have read about the fighting in China from about 400 B.C. to 200 B.C. During the Period of the Warring States, the strong rulers of local states fought one another and ignored the weak Zhou kings. One of these states was called Qin (CHIHN). In 221 B.C., the ruler of Qin sent a large cavalry force to defeat the other states and end the Zhou dynasty. The Qin then controlled China from the Huang He to the Chang Jiang.

To mark a new beginning for China, the Qin ruler declared himself Qin Shihuangdi (CHIHN SHEE•hwahng•dee), which means "the First Qin Emperor." Qin brought changes to Chinese government that would last for many centuries.

How Did Qin Change China?

Qin wanted to strengthen and **unify** China. To do that, he took direct control of China's provinces. Under the Zhou rulers, the governors of the provinces had passed on their positions to sons or relatives. Now, only Qin had the power to appoint the governors.

Qin ruled China with absolute control and swift, harsh punishment. Anyone who disagreed with him was punished or killed. Writings that displeased Qin were burned.

Reading HELPDESK

Taking Notes: *Comparing*
Use a Venn diagram like the one shown here to compare and contrast the Qin and Han dynasties.

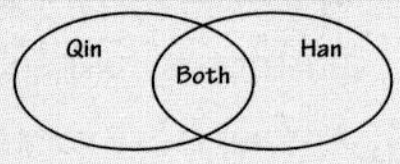

Content Vocabulary
- **censor**
- **currency**
- **civil service**
- **tenant farmer**
- **acupuncture**

Qin also increased the power of his government by appointing officers known as **censors**. The censors' job was to make sure government workers did their work.

Qin developed other policies and projects to unify the empire. He created a **currency**, or type of money, that everyone had to use. He hired scholars to simplify and set rules for the Chinese writing system. Qin also undertook building projects, including the construction of his own tomb. Qin's tomb was so large that it housed an army of life-sized clay soldiers and horses. Qin also ordered tens of thousands of farmers to build palaces, roads, dams, and a huge canal. The canal connected the Chang Jiang in central China to what is today the city of Guangzhou (GWAHNG•JOH) in southern China. The government transported supplies on the canal to soldiers in distant territories.

Why Was the Great Wall Built?

Qin united the different parts of China into one empire. He wanted to keep the empire safe from invasion. A vast desert known as the Gobi was on the edge of China's northern border. Nomads, people who move from place to place with herds of animals, lived in the Gobi. The Chinese knew them as the Xiongnu (SYEHN•NOO). The Xiongnu were skilled warriors who fought on horseback and often attacked Chinese settlements. Earlier Chinese rulers had constructed separate walls in the north to keep out the Xiongnu. Qin planned to have the walls joined and strengthened.

The End of Qin Rule

In 221 B.C., Qin boasted that his dynasty would rule China forever. The Qin dynasty actually ended soon after Qin's death in 210 B.C. Both aristocrats and farmers revolted against the harsh Qin rule. Fighting erupted throughout China. By 206 B.C. the Qin dynasty was over and a new dynasty arose.

PROGRESS CHECK

Explaining How would you describe Qin as a ruler?

Connections to **TODAY**

The Great Wall

Many things get built and rebuilt over time. Building the Great Wall in China took several years. Qin forced hundreds of thousands of farmers to leave their fields to work on the wall. Thousands of laborers died before the project was completed. The finished wall, the Great Wall of China, was built mainly on the northern slopes of mountains, using stone, sand, and rubble. However, Qin did not build the wall that stands today. The Great Wall today consists of a series of walls and towers built during the Ming dynasty beginning in the late 1400s.

Qin Shihuangdi had a large goal: to organize and strengthen the country.

censor an official who watches others for correct behavior
currency something, such as coins or paper money, that is used as a medium of exchange

Academic Vocabulary
unify to make into a single unit

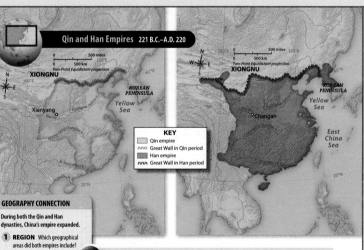

Qin and Han Empires 221 B.C.–A.D. 220

XIONGNU · KOREAN PENINSULA · Yellow Sea · Xianyang · Changan · East China Sea · Two-Point Equidistant projection · 0–500 miles · 0–500 km

KEY
- Qin empire
- Great Wall in Qin period
- Han empire
- Great Wall in Han period

GEOGRAPHY CONNECTION

During both the Qin and Han dynasties, China's empire expanded.

1. **REGION** Which geographical areas did both empires include?
2. CRITICAL THINKING ***Drawing Conclusions*** Why do you think the Han empire was able to expand farther west than the Qin?

2 Han Rulers

GUIDING QUESTION *What improvements did the Chinese make under Han rulers?*

In 202 B.C., a new dynasty known as the Han dynasty came to power in China. Its founder was Liu Bang (LYOO BAHNG), a farmer turned soldier. His family began the powerful Han dynasty that would rule China for more than 400 years.

Han Wudi

The first strong emperor of the Han dynasty was Han Wudi (HAHN WOO•DEE), who ruled from 141 B.C. to 87 B.C. Han Wudi took important steps to improve China's government. Earlier emperors chose family members and loyal aristocrats to help them run the government. Han Wudi wanted to end this practice. He recruited dedicated and talented people for **civil service**, government workers who were chosen on the basis of competitive tests.

First, scholars and officials recommended qualified candidates. Then, the candidates took long, difficult written examinations. Finally, officials graded the tests, and the emperor reviewed the results. The candidates with the highest scores got the jobs.

Reading HELPDESK

civil service the administrative service of a government

Although this system of selecting government officials raised the quality of government, the system also had its faults. Supposedly, government work was open to anyone with talent and ability. Realistically, the system actually favored the rich. Only wealthy families could afford to educate their sons for the difficult civil service tests.

Education

The Han government created schools to prepare students for civil service. Students prepared for the exams by studying law, history, and the ideas of Confucius. After many years of schooling, the students took the civil service examinations. If they passed, they earned jobs as government workers or teachers. They also won great respect in society because they were well educated.

The Empire Expands

During the years of Han rule, China's population rose to about 60 million. To meet the needs of China's growing population, farmers needed to produce more food. However, China's farmers faced special challenges in doing so.

When farmers died, their land was divided among their sons. Gradually, over several **generations**, the amount of land farmed by a family became smaller and smaller. By the middle of the Han dynasty, the average farmer owned only about one acre of land.

Farmers could not raise enough food to feed their families on such small plots of land. They had no choice but to sell their land and work as tenant farmers. **Tenant farmers** work land owned by someone else. Eventually, wealthy landlords owned thousands of acres. The tenant farmers remained very poor.

As China's population grew, the Han Empire took in new territory. Han armies conquered lands to the north, including Korea. They moved south into Southeast Asia and west as far as northern India. After Han Wudi's armies pushed back the Xiongnu—the nomads to the north—the Chinese lived in peace for almost 150 years.

Han Culture

During this era of peace, literature and the arts blossomed. Writers wrote about current events. They made copies of old historical works. In the arts, painters and sculptors reached out to new audiences.

BIOGRAPHY

Ban Zhao (c. A.D. 45–A.D. 116)

Ban Zhao was the first female Chinese historian. She served as the imperial historian during the Han dynasty. Along with her historical pieces, she wrote poems and essays. One well-known work is a guide for women titled *Nu Jie (Lessons for Women)*. It details how women should behave and encourages education for females. The Chinese followed her teachings for hundreds of years, though her emphasis on education was largely ignored.

CRITICAL THINKING
ANALYZING Why do you think Ban Zhao emphasized education for women?

tenant farmer a farmer who works land owned by someone else and pays rent in cash or as a share of the crop

Academic Vocabulary
generation a group of individuals born and living at the same time

LESSON 3 • Day 1

ENGAGE

Making Predictions Tell students they will be viewing a slide show about a building project that took place during the Qin dynasty, which ruled China from 221 B.C. to 206 B.C. Tell students that as they watch the slides, they should write down predictions about what life was like under this dynasty based on what they see.

SLIDE SHOW Present the slide show about the Qin tomb and discuss it.

Have student volunteers write their predictions about what life was like during the Qin dynasty on the interactive whiteboard. Ask students what they based their predictions on. Discuss the predictions, asking students if they agree with the predictions others have made.

TEACH & ASSESS

1 The Qin Emperor

GUIDING QUESTION *How did the Qin emperor unite China?*

2 Han Rulers

GUIDING QUESTION *What improvements did the Chinese make under Han rulers?*

Differentiating Have students work with a partner to complete the following activity. Have each pair of students write a list of four or five facts about the Qin or the Han dynasty without using the dynasty name *Qin* or *Han*. For example, students might write "Han Wudi was the first strong emperor of this dynasty." While students are writing, create a two-column chart on the interactive whiteboard. Label the columns "Qin" and "Han." Ask students to read their facts aloud to the class. Have students decide where each fact belongs. Then, have a student write the fact in the correct column.

Sequencing To help students think about the influence of Confucius's ideas on the Han dynasty, review with students the dates of Confucius's life.

Ask: When was Confucius born? *(about 550 B.C.)*

Ask: Was this before or after the beginning of the Han dynasty? *(about 300 years before)*

Remind students that Confucius's ideas were not immediately popular in China. It was not until long after Confucius's death that his ideas took hold in China.

Simulating Then, have students imagine that they are the new emperor of China, Han Wudi.

Ask: As the new emperor, what teachings of Confucius will help you govern? How will they help? *(Answers will vary. Students might say they would choose to follow Confucius's rules for good conduct. As the new emperor, they might also want to spread the ideal of filial piety, encouraging their subjects to look upon the emperor as the father of the entire nation, who should be respected and obeyed.)*

Determining Cause and Effect Guide the class in a discussion of the ways in which the creation of a new civil service affected the quality of government workers.

Ask: What might have resulted from having all the best students in China study for the same exam? *(All students were studying to take the same test, so everyone would read and study the same texts. All students who studied would know basically the same material. Because all students studied Confucian teachings, they would learn the same values. All successful applicants would come to the government with the same body of knowledge. This could help unify the country. On the other hand, it could deprive the country of new ideas.)* BL

Drawing Conclusions Have students refer back to the map of the Shang Empire and the map of the Zhou Empire.

Ask: What region of China did all the dynasties control? *(All the dynasties controlled the region between the Huang He and the Chang Jiang.)*

Ask: What conclusion can you draw from this? *(Border regions might fall in and out of Chinese control, but the area between the Huang He and the Chang Jiang forms the heart of China.)*

LECTURE SLIDE **Identifying** Remind students that during the peaceful Han dynasty, the Chinese developed many new inventions. Show Han dynasty inventions from the lecture slide. Have students identify the inventions. *(Inventions include the cast-iron plow, the waterwheel, the wheelbarrow, and paper.)* AL

Ask: Which of these inventions do you think had the greatest impact? Why? *(Accept all reasonable responses.)*

Ask: What connection can you find between the strides made in technology during the Han dynasty and the teachings of Confucius? *(Confucius's emphasis on education increased knowledge, which led to new inventions. Confucius's emphasis on putting the good of the community over that of the individual also might have led people to find ways to improve life for all.)*

CLOSE & REFLECT

Connecting Return to the predictions that students made about life under the Qin based on the slide show. Discuss with students which predictions were correct and which were not and why.

Ask: Based on what you have read, would you rather have lived during the Qin dynasty or the Han dynasty? Have students support their choices with facts from the lesson.

LESSON 3 • Day 2

ENGAGE

MAP **Analyzing Visuals** Show the interactive map "Trading in the Ancient World" on the whiteboard.

Then **ask:**

- **What does this map show?** *(trading routes across Asia)*
- **What does the solid purple line represent?** *(the Silk Road)*
- **What do the solid yellow lines represent?** *(other trading routes)*
- **What geographic features did traders on the Silk Road have to cross?** *(mountains, deserts, rivers)*
- **What were some of the goods traded?** *(Students may name any of the items listed in the map key.)*
- **How might you group the items that were traded? In what categories do the different items belong?** *(Students might mention that one category is spices, which include pepper, cardamom, cloves, cinnamon, nutmeg, and ginger. Other groups that students may mention are metals including gold and copper, and woods including teakwood and sandalwood.)* ELL AL

Answers for pages 292–295

P. 292 Taking Notes Possible answers for Qin: appointed censors, ruled harshly, created a uniform currency, simplified writing system, began large building projects, lasted 15 years; Possible answers for Han: civil service system, growth of Confucianism, artists created works for more people, lasted 400 years; Possible answers for both: wanted to strengthen and unify China, expanded China's borders, most people were poor farmers, had social classes

P. 293 ☑ PROGRESS CHECK Qin was a harsh ruler. He was ambitious and had a vision of China that he was intent on achieving.

P. 294 GEOGRAPHY CONNECTION

1. Huang He and Chang Jiang valleys, much of the eastern coast and western mountains
2. CRITICAL THINKING Students may answer that the Han Empire had a stronger army and could therefore conquer more land. Accept other reasonable answers that students can support.

P. 295 CRITICAL THINKING Answers may vary. Students may say that she emphasized the need for education for women because she was a woman and probably had experienced firsthand the difficulty women had in getting an education.

In early China, people made paper one sheet at a time from hemp or rag pulp. This modern artist (above) makes paper the ancient way. Today's paper mills (below) manufacture huge rolls of paper on machines like this one.

▶ CRITICAL THINKING

Analyzing What would be the effect on today's publishing industry if all paper were once again made by hand?

In earlier times, artists had created religious works for rulers and aristocrats. Now, under Han rule, artists created beautiful works of art for less prominent families.

Under the Han, the ideas of Confucius gained influence. The idea of filial piety became very strong. The stability of the government also helped strengthen family ties. The new class of scholarly civil servants greatly influenced government, but other social classes in China remained the same. Daily life also was very similar to what it had been before.

Chinese Inventions

During the Han dynasty, new technology helped Chinese farmers and workers produce more than ever before. One major development was the cast-iron plow, which could break up the soil more easily than wooden plows could. New iron tools and techniques were used to drain swamps and direct water to parched fields. As a result, land that was once unfit for farming now produced food and other crops.

Improvements took place in areas besides farming. Millers invented **waterwheels** to grind more grain, and miners fashioned iron drill bits to mine more salt. Another Chinese invention, the wheelbarrow, was first used to carry heavy material on building sites. Artisans developed silk manufacturing and invented paper. Used first for wrapping, paper became an ideal writing material. Like Egyptian papyrus, paper provided a way to keep written records.

Two remarkable achievements of Han inventors were the rudder and a new way to move the sails of ships. With these inventions, ships could sail against the wind for the first time. They could also travel farther than ever before. As a result, China's merchants shipped their goods to areas as far away as India and the Red Sea.

Medical Advances

Chinese medicine advanced under the Han. Doctors discovered that certain foods prevented disease. They used a variety of herbs to treat illnesses. Doctors also relieved pain by piercing patients' skin at vital points with thin needles. This treatment is known as **acupuncture** (A•kyuh•puhngk•chuhr). Acupuncture renews the body by increasing the flow of energy.

☑ PROGRESS CHECK

Explaining Why did Han rulers create civil service examinations?

Reading **HELP**DESK

Visual Vocabulary

waterwheel a wheel made to turn by the water flowing against it

3 On the Silk Road

GUIDING QUESTION *How did the Silk Road benefit China and the rest of the world?*

During the Han period, Chinese traders grew rich by sending expensive goods to other parts of the world. Over time, both sea and land trade routes led to an exchange of many different goods and ideas between China and other areas.

New Contacts With the West

China's trade increased in part as a result of Chinese exploration. In 139 B.C., the emperor Han Wudi sent out a general named Zhang Qian (JAHNG CHYEHN) to explore areas west of China. Zhang's mission was to recruit allies to help China fight against its enemies, especially the Xiongnu to the north.

Thirteen years later, Zhang returned to China. He had failed to find allies. He had learned, however, about the people, geography, and culture of the areas west of China. He also visited a kingdom far to the west, probably in the area of present-day Kazakhstan. There, he saw horses of great strength and size.

Emperor Han Wudi was delighted to hear this report. He wanted horses for his soldiers, so he encouraged trade between China and western regions.

In exchange for the horses, Chinese merchants traded silk, spices, and other luxury goods. The trade route to the west was later called the Silk Road in honor of China's most famous export.

Trade Expands

The Silk Road was not just one road. It was a **network** of trade routes. When the road was completed in the A.D. 100s, it was 4,000 miles (6,436 km) long and stretched from western China to the Mediterranean. The distance, rough terrain, and bandits along the road made travel difficult and dangerous.

Over the years, merchants traded many items in addition to luxury goods. These included fruits, vegetables, flowers, and grains. For example, China sent peaches and pears to India, while India sent cotton and spinach to China. In time, Chinese inventions, such as paper, would also travel to other regions along the Silk Road.

Acupuncture is based on finding pressure spots in the human body to help ease pain. Chinese doctors detected certain places on the body that correspond to spots on the foot. Needles can be applied to these spots to help the pain.

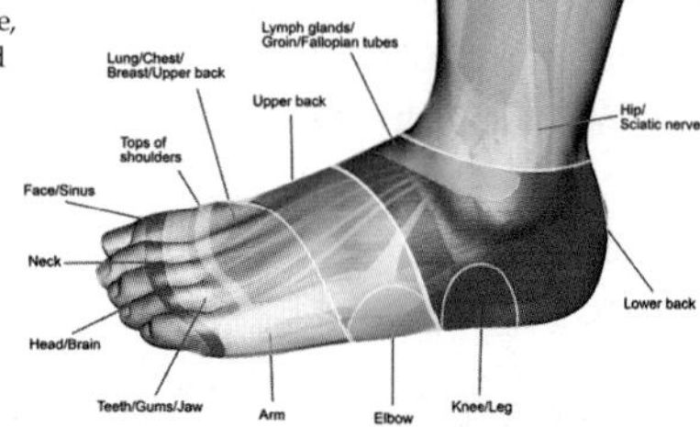

acupuncture an originally Chinese practice of inserting fine needles through the skin at specific points to treat disease or relieve pain

Academic Vocabulary

network a connected group or system

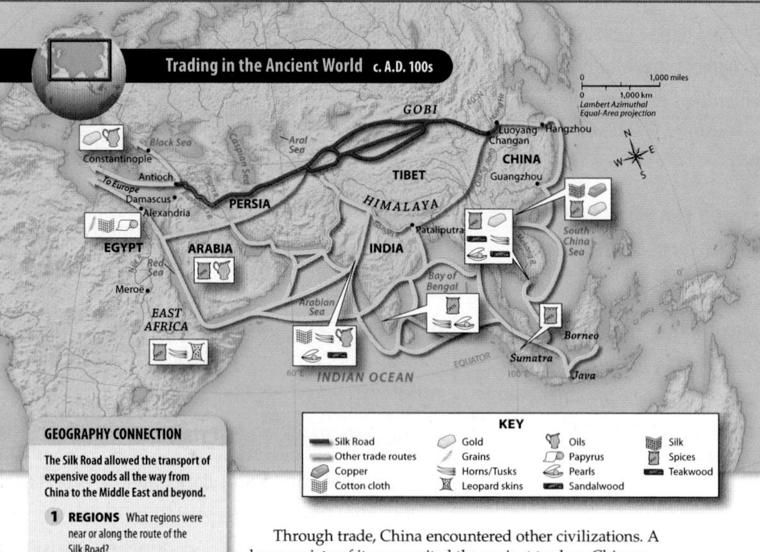

GEOGRAPHY CONNECTION

The Silk Road allowed the transport of expensive goods all the way from China to the Middle East and beyond.

1. **REGIONS** What regions were near or along the route of the Silk Road?
2. **CRITICAL THINKING** ***Analyzing Visuals*** Chinese merchants sold many products along the Silk Road. What products do you think Chinese merchants bought as they traveled and traded?

Through trade, China encountered other civilizations. A huge variety of items awaited the ancient traders. Chinese writers described a mighty empire to the far west:

PRIMARY SOURCE

> ❝It has more than four hundred walled towns. . . . The walls of the towns are made of stone. . . . The common people are farmers. . . . The country produces plenty of gold, silver, and precious jewels. . . . They make gold and silver coins. . . .❞
>
> —from *Hou Hanshu* 88, Second Edition

The Chinese writers were describing the Roman Empire. For more than 1,000 years, the Silk Road was the main trade **link** between Asia and Europe.

☑ PROGRESS CHECK

Identifying Cause and Effect What developments led to the creation of the Silk Road?

Reading **HELP**DESK

Academic Vocabulary

link a connecting element or factor

4 Buddhism Reaches China

GUIDING QUESTION *Why did Buddhism become a popular religion in China?*

The Silk Road served as a way to spread knowledge, culture, and religions. Buddhism, in particular, spread across the Silk Road from India to China. Buddhism won few followers in China at first. The fall of the Han dynasty and the long period of unrest that followed, however, spurred the spread of Buddhism.

Why Did the Han Dynasty Collapse?

Many of the emperors who succeeded Han Wudi were weak and dishonest. Corrupt officials and greedy aristocrats took over more of the land, forcing many farmers to give up their property. People began to rise up and rebel against the Han rulers.

Rebel armies destroyed the Han capital, Luoyang (LWAW•YAHNG) in A.D. 190. By A.D. 220, civil war divided China. For the next 400 years, China remained divided into many small kingdoms.

Buddhism Wins Followers

The fall of the Han dynasty and the long years of civil war frightened many Chinese. Feeling anxious, fearful, and unsafe, many people turned to Buddhist ideas. Followers of Confucius and Daoists also admired Buddhist ideas, which influenced their own religious rituals and moral ideas. By the A.D. 400s, Buddhism had become one of China's major religions.

☑ PROGRESS CHECK

Determining Cause and Effect Why did the fall of the Han dynasty help Buddhism spread in China?

LESSON 3 REVIEW

Review Vocabulary

1. What are the advantages of having a *civil service* system to select government workers?

Answer the Guiding Questions

2. ***Describing*** How did Qin rulers unite China?
3. ***Explaining*** How did the civil service system change China's government?
4. ***Determining Cause and Effect*** What was one result of the building of the Great Wall?
5. ***Explaining*** What caused the downfall of the Han dynasty?
6. ***Analyzing Visuals*** What was one fact that you put in the "Both" part of the Venn diagram comparing the Qin and Han?
7. **EXPOSITORY WRITING** How do you think early China's history would be different if the Silk Road had never developed? Write a paragraph expressing your view.

LESSON 3 • Day 2 (cont.)

TEACH & ASSESS

3 On the Silk Road

GUIDING QUESTION *How did the Silk Road benefit China and the rest of the world?*

Making Connections Have students brainstorm a list of explorers and write their suggestions on the whiteboard. Ask students what these explorers have in common. *(Students will likely name European explorers who came to the Americas or looked for sea routes to Asia to increase trade.)*

Ask: **Do you know of any explorers from Asia?** *(If students don't mention his name, remind them of Zhang Qian, whom they read about in this chapter.)* **What area did Zhang explore?** *(areas west of China)* **Who sent Zhang on his exploration?** *(Han Wudi)* **How long was Zhang gone?** *(13 years)* **What did Zhang learn on his travels?** *(He learned about the people, geography, and culture of the areas west of China.)*

Have students compare and contrast Zhang's explorations with those of European explorers such as Christopher Columbus or Ferdinand Magellan. *(Students should suggest that Europeans were also looking for new trade routes. For example, Columbus was looking for a new trade route to Asia when he first came to the Americas.)*

INTERACTIVE WORKSHEET

Economics of History Activity

Have students complete the Economics of History Activity for this chapter, "Trade Along the Silk Road." As students complete the activity, remind them to think about how the Silk Road benefited China and the rest of the world.

Making Connections Begin a discussion with students comparing how ideas spread from one place to another during the Han dynasty to how ideas spread today.

Ask:

- **In addition to goods, what else was exchanged along the Silk Road?** *(ideas)* Discuss with students how the exchange of ideas has changed since the time of early China.
- **How are ideas exchanged today?** *(via the Internet and other media)*
- **How does today's easier exchange of ideas affect the way we live?** *(Students might say that because ideas travel much faster, it is now harder to keep ideas from spreading.)*

4 Buddhism Reaches China

GUIDING QUESTION *Why did Buddhism become a popular religion in China?*

Determining Cause and Effect Be sure to point out to students that Buddhism is one of the ideas that was exchanged along the Silk Road. Then, discuss with students the reasons for the fall of the Han dynasty and the rise in popularity of Buddhism in China.

Ask: **What caused the Han dynasty to fall?** *(Many of the emperors who succeeded Han Wudi were weak. Corrupt and greedy officials stole land; people began to rebel against the Han leaders.)*

Ask: **What caused the Chinese people to embrace Buddhism?** *(The years of civil war and instability resulting from the decline of the Han dynasty frightened the Chinese people. Buddhism provided comfort to people facing fear and anxiety.)*

LECTURE SLIDE **Diagramming** Show the blank cause-and-effect chart from the lecture slide. Have students complete a cause-and-effect chart to represent the chain of events involved in the fall of the Han dynasty and the rise of Buddhism in China.

Cause	Effect
Emperors after Han Wudi were weak and dishonest.	*People began to rebel against Han rulers.*
Civil war divided China.	*People felt unsafe and frightened.*
Many Chinese felt frightened and unsafe after years of civil war.	*People turned to Buddhism, which helped them overcome their fear.*

LECTURE SLIDE **Making Connections** Remind students that Buddhism first developed in India. Show the basic beliefs of Buddhism from the lecture slide and discuss them with students. *(Suffering exists and it has a cause, but it also has an end. Nothing is permanent; change is always possible.)* Then, discuss with students which specific Buddhist ideas might have appealed to Chinese people during the long civil war that followed the fall of the Han dynasty.

CLOSE & REFLECT

Summarizing Discuss with students the movement of ideas as well as goods along the Silk Road. Ask volunteers to summarize for the class the fall of the Han dynasty and the growth of Buddhism in China.

Have students complete the Lesson 3 Review as an in-class or homework activity.

Answers for pages 296–299

P. 296 CRITICAL THINKING If all paper were still made by hand, it would be extremely scarce and expensive. The publishing industry would be able to produce very few books. Those books they did produce would be so expensive that not many people could afford them. Most publishing companies would probably go out of business.

P. 296 ☑ PROGRESS CHECK Han rulers created civil service examinations to stop the practice of having royal family members and other aristocrats run the government. Up to this point, government jobs were used as a reward for loyalty to the government. The civil service exam system opened government service to other people with talent and ability.

P. 298 GEOGRAPHY CONNECTION

1. China, Tibet, India, Persia, Arabia, Egypt
2. CRITICAL THINKING Students' answers can include any product that the map indicates China did not produce, such as pearls, leopard skins, and horns and tusks.

P. 298 ☑ PROGRESS CHECK Chinese exploration and Emperor Han Wudi's desire for horses for his army helped lead to the creation of the Silk Road.

P. 299 ☑ PROGRESS CHECK The fall of the Han dynasty led to many years of civil war in China. The disorder made people feel unsafe. Buddhist ideas helped people overcome their anxiety and fear.

LESSON 3 REVIEW

1. The civil service helped ensure that government officials were qualified for their jobs.
2. Qin rulers united China by taking direct control of the provinces. Qin created a currency that everyone in the empire had to use. He also built roads as well as a canal that joined central and southern China.
3. The civil service made it possible for bright and talented people to serve in the government. Before the civil service system, those in power appointed government employees.
4. One result of the building of the Great Wall under the Qin was that the forced labor of hundreds of thousands of farmers turned the farming class against their rulers.
5. Many of the emperors who ruled after Han Wudi were dishonest and weak, which led people to rebel against them.
6. Answers may vary. One possible answer is that they both wanted to strengthen and unify China.
7. Without the Silk Road, China might not have come into contact with other countries and civilizations when it did. Without this contact, new ideas and philosophies might not have come to the country. China might never have embraced Buddhism. Without trade, China would have had less wealth.

CHAPTER 10 Activities

Write your answers on a separate sheet of paper.

1 Exploring the Essential Question
EXPOSITORY WRITING How would you compare the culture of China to other ancient cultures you have read about? Write an essay explaining how the culture of ancient China is different from these other civilizations. What factors led to the development of a unique culture in China?

2 21st Century Skills
ANALYZING NEWS MEDIA Work with a partner. Find an article from the business section of a newspaper or magazine about China and trade. What does the article tell you about trade and China today? What goods does China trade today? With whom does China trade? Present your article and your findings to the class. In your presentation, discuss how trade today between China and her trading partners is different from trade in the time of the Han dynasty.

3 Thinking Like a Historian
UNDERSTANDING RELATIONSHIPS A pyramid diagram can be used to show relationships. In a pyramid diagram, the group with the most members goes on the bottom. Create a pyramid diagram like the one on the right showing the social classes in ancient China from most powerful (top) to least powerful (bottom).

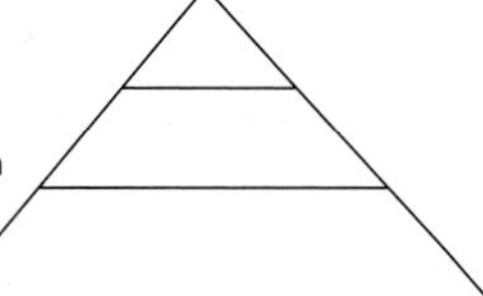

4 GEOGRAPHY ACTIVITY

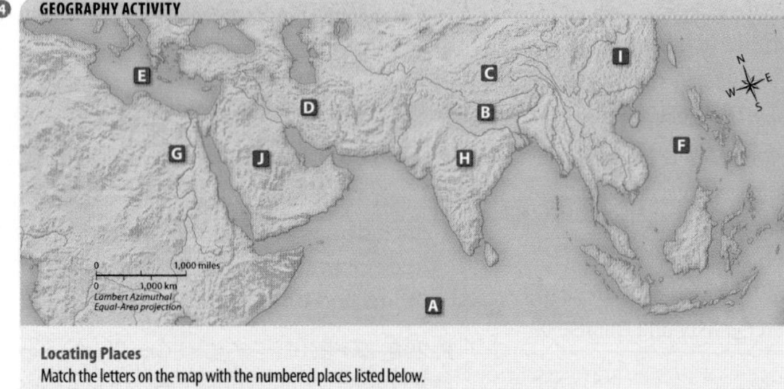

Locating Places
Match the letters on the map with the numbered places listed below.

1. Egypt
2. Arabia
3. Persia
4. India
5. Tibet
6. China
7. Indian Ocean
8. South China Sea
9. Himalaya
10. Mediterranean Sea

CHAPTER 10 Assessment

REVIEW THE GUIDING QUESTIONS
Directions: Choose the best answer for each question.

1. How did mountains and deserts help Chinese civilization develop?
   A. They provided fertile farmland.
   B. They made transportation easier.
   C. They gave China safe borders.
   D. They made it difficult for the Chinese to grow crops.

2. Shang rulers expanded their kingdom by
   F. military conquest.
   G. marriage with neighboring rulers.
   H. land purchases.
   I. forming colonies.

3. What is the Mandate of Heaven?
   A. a group of officials in China who worked for the government
   B. the rule of China by a wicked tyrant
   C. the belief that a son had the right to inherit his father's land
   D. the belief that the Chinese king's right to rule came from the gods

4. Confucius's belief that government service should be open to all able men led to
   F. the rule of China by a strong leader.
   G. wars by rival kings.
   H. the creation of a system of civil service tests.
   I. the rule of China by farmers and workers.

5. Most people in ancient China were
   A. aristocrats.
   B. farmers.
   C. soldiers.
   D. merchants.

6. Trade increased during the Han dynasty because of
   F. the expansion of the Roman Empire into China.
   G. lower taxes and better roads.
   H. food surpluses in China.
   I. Chinese exploration and improved technology.

CHAPTER 10 Assessment *(continued)*

DBQ DOCUMENT-BASED QUESTIONS

7. **Assessing** The main ideas of Daoism are explained in a book titled *Dao De Jing* (*The Way of the Dao*).

   "When leading by the way of the Tao [Dao], abominate [hate] the use of force, for it causes resistance, and loss of strength. . . .

   The wise leader achieves results, but does not glory in them . . . and does not boast of them.

   —"A Caveat Against Violence," The *Tao Te Ching*, Stan Rosenthal, trans.

   According to Daoist thought, what is the result of using force or violence?
   A. It causes resistance and loss of strength.
   B. It builds strength and breaks down resistance.
   C. It causes resistance without an effect on strength.
   D. It builds strength and resistance.

8. **Analyzing** What do you think this statement means? "The wise leader achieves results, but does not glory in them."
   F. The wise leader finishes projects but is not pleased with them.
   G. The wise leader reaches goals but does not notice them.
   H. The wise leader is effective but not proud.
   I. The wise leader is efficient and is boastful.

SHORT RESPONSE

"A hundred years ago the Shang (SHAHNG) dynasty was . . . lost . . . existing only in historical texts. . . . But over the course of the 20th century, the Shang steadily reappeared, the myths replaced by tangible [easily seen] artifacts: massive bronzes, eloquent oracle bones, burial complexes."

—Peter Hessler, "The New Story of China's Past," *National Geographic*, (July 2003)

9. How would your study of early China have been different if you were studying 100 years ago?

10. What might "tangible artifacts" tell us about the Shang?

EXTENDED RESPONSE

11. **Expository Writing** Write a brief report that compares and contrasts the characteristics of the four ancient Chinese dynasties you have read about.

Need Extra Help?

If You've Missed Question	1	2	3	4	5	6	7	8	9	10	11
Review Lesson	1	2	2	3	3	3	2	2	1	1	1, 3

NOTES

REFLECT, REVIEW, & REMEDIATE

IINTERACTIVE WORKSHEET

Chapter Summary

Provide students with the Chapter Summary worksheet to help review the chapter and prepare for assessment.

Reviewing the Enduring Understandings

Review this chapter's Enduring Understandings with students:

- People, places, and ideas change over time.
- The movement of people, goods, and ideas causes societies to change over time.

INTERACTIVE WHITEBOARD ACTIVITY On the interactive whiteboard, create a graphic organizer that will help students see the effects that the Silk Road had on life in China. Have student volunteers come to the board to complete the organizer.

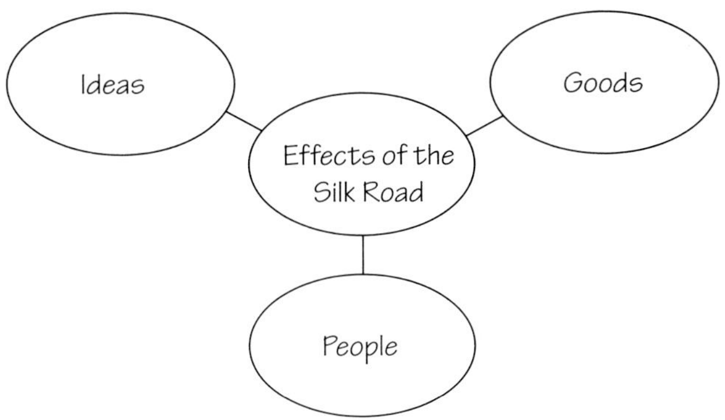

ACTIVITIES ANSWERS

Exploring the Essential Question

1 Answers will vary, but students should mention how the geography of China, which isolated it from other civilizations, helped China form a unique culture. Some unique features of Chinese culture include its writing system—which uses symbols to represent objects that are then combined to represent ideas—and its belief systems, including Confucianism, Daoism, and legalism.

21st Century Skills

2 Answers may vary depending on the article students select. Answers may include that the goods China trades and the way the goods are traded today are different. Also, China has different trading partners today from those of early China.

Thinking Like a Historian

3 Students' pyramids should show farmers at the bottom of the pyramid, artisans and merchants in the center, and the aristocracy at the top.

Locating Places

4 **1.** G, **2.** J, **3.** D, **4.** H, **5.** C, **6.** I, **7.** A, **8.** F, **9.** B, **10.** E

ASSESSMENT ANSWERS

Review the Guiding Questions

1 **C** Mountains and deserts cut off China from other civilizations. Isolated from others, the Chinese were able to develop a unique culture and a strong sense of independence. Fertile farmland was found in river valleys, not mountains and deserts. Mountains and deserts made transportation more difficult, not easier. They did not provide fertile farmland.

2 **F** Shang rulers had large armies that they used to conquer neighboring areas. G, H, and I are not correct answers because Shang rulers did not purchase land, form colonies, or make political marriages to increase their empire.

3 **D** The Mandate of Heaven is the belief that the Chinese king's right to rule came from the gods. A group of officials who work for the government is called a bureaucracy. Although Chinese aristocrats passed on the territory they ruled to a son or another family member, this practice is not what is known as the Mandate of Heaven.

4 **H** The civil service examination system was an attempt to open government service to all qualified men. Prior to the creation of the exam system, only hereditary aristocrats served in the government.

5 **B** About 9 out of 10 Chinese farmed for a living. The aristocracy made up only a small percentage of Chinese society. Merchants were also a very small percentage. Although many soldiers served in the Chinese armies, most of the soldiers were from the farming class.

6 **I** Inventions such as the rudder and a new way to move the sails of ships made it possible for Chinese ships to travel farther than before. Chinese ships could now reach India and the Red Sea. The combination of new technology and expanded exploration led to an increase in trade.

Document-Based Questions

7 **A** According to this quote from *The Way of the Dao,* the "use of force . . . causes resistance and loss of strength." Force does not build strength or break down resistance.

8 **H** The wise leader is effective but does not brag about results. The wise leader is effective and notices results. It is likely the leader would be pleased. Not being overly proud, the leader might be humble.

Short Response

9 Students studying early China 100 years ago might not have learned about the Shang dynasty.

10 Historians use oracle bones, bronze sculptures, and burial sites to learn more about the Shang. Oracle bones tell historians what concerns the Shang had and what was important to them. Bronzes can tell historians about Shang art and technology. Burial sites can tell historians about Shang religion.

Extended Response

11 Answers may vary but should include information about each of the dynasties. Students may mention that each dynasty relied on military force to expand its borders and to hold on to power. During each dynasty, the country's borders varied, but each dynasty sought to expand the country. The country was larger under the Zhou than it was under the Shang, and it was larger under the Han than it was under the Qin. Chinese social classes were fundamentally the same under all the dynasties, with a large class of farmers ruled by a small aristocracy headed by a king. The civil service system of the Han dynasty was an effort to bring people other than the aristocracy into government service. In fact, however, most people who passed the civil service exams were the sons of the wealthiest families.

ONLINE RESOURCES
networks

There's More Online!

- INTERACTIVE WORKSHEETS
- BIOGRAPHIES
- CHARTS/GRAPHS
- GAMES
- GRAPHIC ORGANIZERS
- IMAGES
- MAPS
- PRIMARY SOURCES
- SLIDE SHOWS
- TIME LINE
- LECTURE SLIDES
- INTERACTIVE WHITEBOARD ACTIVITIES
- ASSESSMENTS
- VIDEOS

Roman Empire Cultural Contributions

Chapter 11

Rome: Republic to Empire

Dear World History Teacher,

Sometime in the eighth century B.C., a group of Latin-speaking people built Rome, a small community along the Tiber River in Italy. Between 509 and 264 B.C., this city expanded to include almost everyone who lived on the Italian Peninsula. Roman diplomacy was as important as its armies. Roman rule was tolerated by people throughout the Mediterranean region because Rome allowed for local autonomy and granted Roman citizenship to non-Romans.

During this time of expansion, Rome also developed the political institutions of a republic ruled by an aristocratic oligarchy. Although Rome had no master plan for expansion, its relationship with its neighbors outside of Italy soon led to conflict. Between 264 and 133 B.C., Rome expanded to the west and east and became master of the Mediterranean Sea.

The Roman Republic was one of the largest empires in antiquity, but the traditional values of Rome declined as affluence and individualism increased. All too soon, Rome's republican institutions proved inadequate for ruling such a vast empire. After a series of bloody civil wars, Augustus created a new order that began the Roman Empire, now led by a series of autocratic rulers who used the title of imperator, or emperor. Augustus created a new era of prosperity referred to as the *Pax Romana*, or "Roman peace."

Jackson J. Spielvogel

More Media Resources

Current Events Online

Visit McGraw-Hill's current events Web site for high-interest news stories and activities for your students. Access the site through the Student or Teacher Center in **networks.**

Reading List

Grade 6 reading level:
The Romans and Their Empire, by Trevor Cairns

Grade 7 reading level:
Bodies from the Ash: Life and Death in Ancient Pompeii, by James M. Deem

Grade 8 reading level:
Galen: My Life in Imperial Rome, by Marissa Moss

At the MOVIES

Watch clips from popular culture films about the Roman Empire, such as the 2002 television miniseries *Caesar.*

Discuss: **What can we learn about historical events from fictional movies?**

NOTE: Be sure to preview any clips to ensure they are age-appropriate.

Search for more videos online in the **networks** Resource Library

CHAPTER 11 Planner

UNDERSTANDING BY DESIGN®

Enduring Understandings

- *People, places, and ideas change over time.* • *Conflict can lead to change.*
- *Leaders can bring about change in society.*

Essential Questions

- *How does geography influence the way people live?* • *How do governments change?*
- *Why does conflict develop?* • *What are the characteristics of a leader?*

Students will know:

- *the effect that geography had on the rise of Rome*
- *how Rome gained control of the Mediterranean region*
- *how conflict between Rome's social classes led to change in its government*
- *what caused the decline of the Roman Republic*
- *the events that enabled Rome to become an empire*
- *what caused the Roman Empire to prosper*

Students will be able to:

- **explain** how geographic features contributed to the settlement and growth of Rome
- **analyze** the perspective of a member of a Roman-conquered community
- **identify** reasons why inequality exists
- **discuss** the perspective of the Roman social classes
- **explain** how conflict was resolved between patricians and plebeians
- **discuss** how conflict between Rome and Carthage led to the Punic Wars
- **describe** the events of the Punic Wars
- **analyze** problems that can cause a nation's decline
- **identify** the causes of the Roman Republic's decline
- **determine** the impact of Julius Caesar
- **identify** the events and people that led to the establishment of the Roman Empire
- **identify** qualities of a good leader
- **determine** the impact of Augustus
- **compare** actions of Roman leaders with today's U.S. leaders.

Predictable Misunderstandings

Students may think:

- The Romans enslaved everyone they conquered.
- All Roman emperors were cruel dictators.
- The Roman Republic was a strong democracy that gave equal power to all citizens.

Assessment Evidence

Performance Task

- Hands-On Chapter Project

Other Evidence

- Responses to Think-Pair-Share activity
- Journal entries
- Brainstorming situations of unequal treatment
- Discussion responses
- Flowchart on Punic Wars
- Family tree activity
- Explanations of Julius Caesar quote
- Completion of time line activity
- Debate on emperors during *Pax Romana*
- Writing assignments and activities
- Interactive Graphic Organizers
- Geography and History Activities
- 21st Century Skills Activity
- Primary Source Activity
- Lesson Reviews
- Class discussion answers

Pacing Guide

Introducing the Chapter	1 day
Lesson 1 The Founding of Rome	1 day
Lesson 2 Rome as a Republic	2 days
Lesson 3 The End of the Republic	2 days
Lesson 4 Rome Builds an Empire	1 day
Chapter Activities and Assessment	1 day
TOTAL TIME	**8 Days**

Differentiated Instruction

These lesson plans are written to address the needs of your On Level students. Discussion and activities that are well-suited to your Approaching Grade Level learners, Beyond Grade Level learners, as well as your English Language Learners, are coded as follows:

AL **Approaching Grade Level**

BL **Beyond Grade Level**

ELL **English Language Learner**

NCSS Standards covered in "Rome: Republic to Empire"

Learners will understand:

1 CULTURE

2. Concepts such as beliefs, values, institutions, cohesion, diversity, accommodation, adaption, assimilation, and dissonance

4. That the beliefs, values, and behaviors of a culture form an integrated system that helps shape the activities and ways of life that define a culture

6. That culture may change in response to changing needs, concerns, social, political, and geographic conditions

2 TIME, CONTINUITY, AND CHANGE

2. Concepts such as: chronology, causality, change, conflict, complexity, multiple perspectives, primary and secondary sources, and cause and effect

5. Key historical periods and patterns of change within and across cultures (e.g., the rise and fall of ancient civilizations, the development of technology, the rise of modern nation-states, and the establishment and breakdown of colonial systems)

7. The contributions of key persons, groups, and events from the past and their influence on the present

3 PEOPLE, PLACES, AND ENVIRONMENTS

1. The theme of people, places, and environments involves the study of the relationships between human populations in different locations and geographic phenomena such as climate, vegetation, and natural resources

5 INDIVIDUALS, GROUPS, AND INSTITUTIONS

8. That when two or more groups with differing norms and beliefs interact, accommodation or conflict may result

6 POWER, AUTHORITY, AND GOVERNANCE

2. Fundamental ideas that are the foundation of American constitutional democracy (including those of the U.S. Constitution, popular sovereignty, the rule of law, separation of powers, checks and balances, minority rights, the separation of church and state, and Federalism)

5. The ways in which governments meet the needs and wants of citizens, manage conflict, and establish order in society

7 PRODUCTION, DISTRIBUTION, AND CONSUMPTION

1. Individuals, government, and society experience scarcity because human wants and needs exceed what can be produced from available resources

3. The economic choices that people make have both present and future consequences

10 CIVIC IDEALS AND PRACTICES

1. The theme of civic ideals and practices helps us to learn about and know how to work for the betterment of society

2. Concepts and ideals such as: individual dignity, liberty, justice, equality, individual rights, responsibility, majority and minority rights, and civil dissent

3. Key practices involving the rights and responsibilities of citizenship and the exercise of citizenship (e.g., respecting the rule of law and due process, voting, serving on a jury, researching issues, making informed judgments, expressing views on issues, and collaborating with others to take civic action)

4. The common good, and the rule of law

7. Key past and present issues involving democratic ideals and practices, as well as the perspectives of various stakeholders in proposing possible solutions to these issues

Introducing the Chapter

(Student Edition p. 303)

The Story Matters . . .

Read "The Story Matters . . ." aloud in class. Discuss with students the importance of understanding lost civilizations.

Ask: **Why do you think people like archaeologists were interested in unearthing Pompeii?**

What did they want or expect to learn? Have students suggest reasons why scientists and others want to know about past times and people. Students should point out that scientists can learn about how people lived long ago from studying the remains of past cities and homes.

Tell the class that the history of Pompeii and its destruction has been pieced together since the discovery of the city's ruins. Remind interested students that they can explore the ruins of Pompeii online.

Rome: Republic to Empire

500 B.C. to A.D. 180

ESSENTIAL QUESTIONS • *How does geography influence the way people live?* • *How do governments change?* • *Why does conflict develop?* • *What are the characteristics of a leader?*

networks

There's More Online about the cultures of the Roman Republic and Roman Empire

CHAPTER 11

Lesson 1 *The Founding of Rome*

Lesson 2 *Rome as a Republic*

Lesson 3 *The End of the Republic*

Lesson 4 *Rome Builds an Empire*

The Story Matters . . .

When the volcano Vesuvius erupted in A.D. 79, it covered the Roman city of Pompeii with a thick layer of burning ash. As many as 20,000 people were killed, and the buried city was lost for centuries. When explorers dug into its remains in the early 1700s, they discovered a time capsule of Roman times, with buildings, art, and everyday objects all perfectly preserved.

This mosaic, which is an image of a woman created out of small stones and glass, was discovered in one of the homes of Pompeii. Historians have learned much about the daily life of Romans from artifacts unearthed at Pompeii and other archaeological sites.

◄ *Goddesses were depicted in Roman mosaics, but this woman was most likely a wealthy woman of Pompeii.*

Araldo de Luca/CORBIS

303

Introducing Place and Time

(Student Edition pp. 304–305)

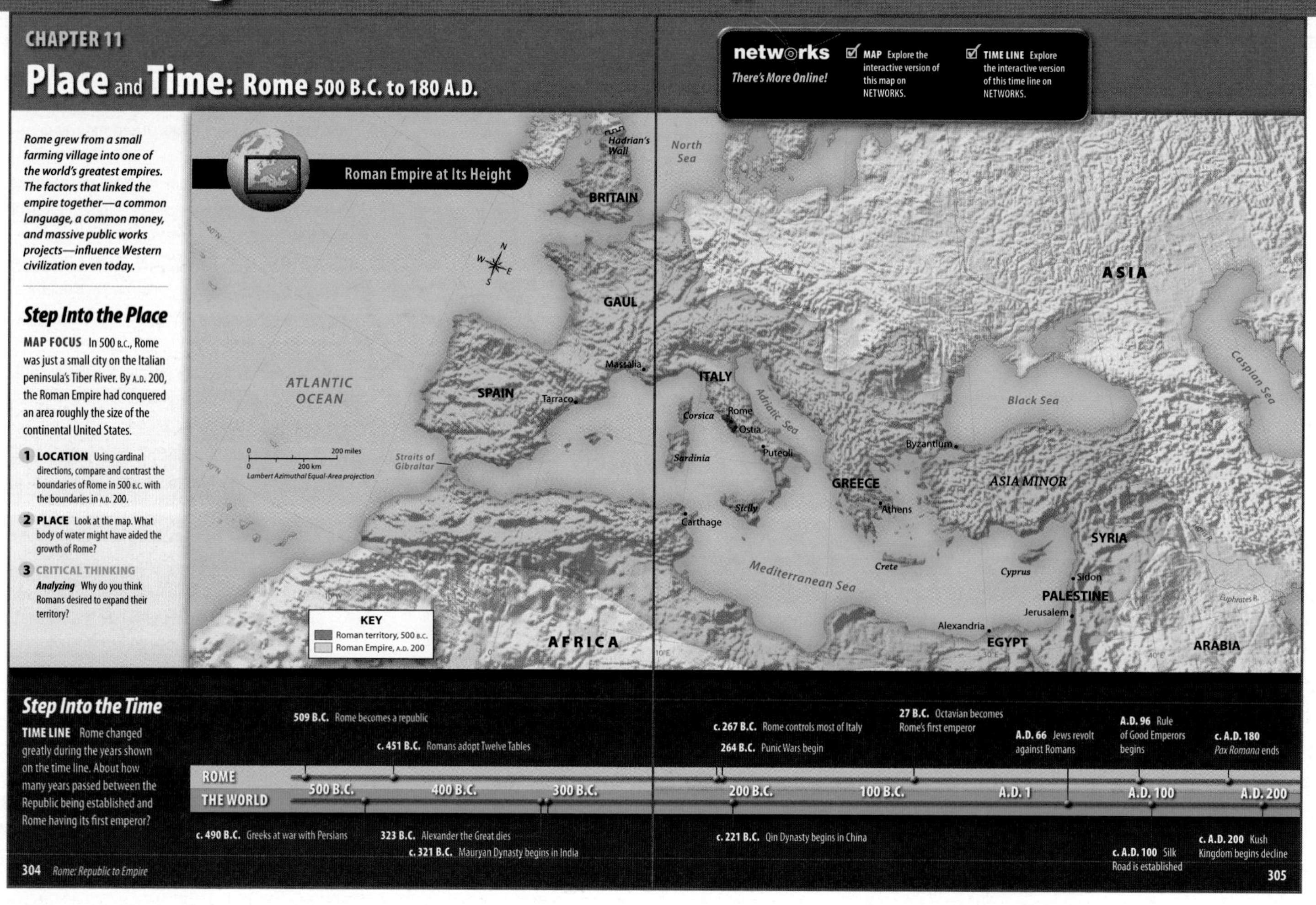

CHAPTER 11

Place and Time: Rome 500 B.C. to 180 A.D.

Rome grew from a small farming village into one of the world's greatest empires. The factors that linked the empire together—a common language, a common money, and massive public works projects—influence Western civilization even today.

Step Into the Place

MAP FOCUS In 500 B.C., Rome was just a small city on the Italian peninsula's Tiber River. By A.D. 200, the Roman Empire had conquered an area roughly the size of the continental United States.

1. **LOCATION** Using cardinal directions, compare and contrast the boundaries of Rome in 500 B.C. with the boundaries in A.D. 200.
2. **PLACE** Look at the map. What body of water might have aided the growth of Rome?
3. **CRITICAL THINKING** *Analyzing* Why do you think Romans desired to expand their territory?

networks *There's More Online!* ☑ MAP Explore the interactive version of this map on NETWORKS. ☑ TIME LINE Explore the interactive version of this time line on NETWORKS.

Step Into the Time

TIME LINE Rome changed greatly during the years shown on the time line. About how many years passed between the Republic being established and Rome having its first emperor?

304 *Rome: Republic to Empire* 305

Technology Extension

- Find an additional activity online that incorporates technology for this project.
- Visit the EdTechTeacher Web sites (included in the Technology Extension for this chapter) for more links, tutorials, and other resources.

Assessing Background Knowledge

INTERACTIVE WORKSHEET

What Do You Know? Activity

Have students complete the Concept Ladder on the What Do You Know? Activity. Students should answer the questions about the Roman Republic and the Roman Empire before they study the chapter. Then take a class poll of student answers so you can tailor your lessons to focus on any student misconceptions.

After students complete the chapter, have them reread the questions in the Concept Ladder and note any corrections to their original answers. Ask students who changed their responses to explain why they did so. *(Students should cite facts from the chapter.)*

INTERACTIVE WORKSHEET

Guided Reading Activities

You may wish to assign the Guided Reading Activity for Lesson 1 after introducing the chapter content.

Hands-On Chapter Project

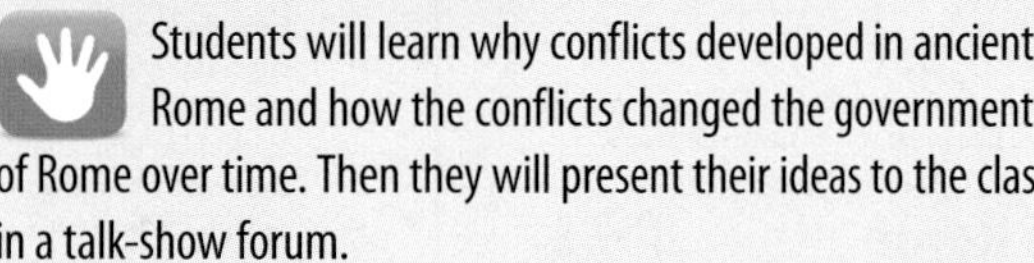

Students will learn why conflicts developed in ancient Rome and how the conflicts changed the government of Rome over time. Then they will present their ideas to the class in a talk-show forum.

- Students will meet in groups to discuss the project plan.
- Students will distribute and read worksheets, select conflicts, conduct research, and formulate interview questions.
- Then, groups will plan and gather props for a talk-show forum.
- Finally, students in their groups will act out the talk show, filming it with an audience.

Visit **networks** online to see the full project and rubric.

Step Into the Place

Location Project on the whiteboard the Chapter Opener map of the wider Mediterranean region. Point out the Italian Peninsula. Discuss, in a general way, how Italy's geographic features (climate, location, natural resources, physical features, and so on) can provide advantages and disadvantages for settlement and expansion.

Ask students to brainstorm advantages and disadvantages of Rome's location. Invite them to write their responses on the whiteboard. *(Advantages: mild climate; proximity to the sea provides access to trading; protected by water. Disadvantages: isolated; vulnerable to invasion by sea)* Then, as a class, discuss the Map Focus questions.

Step Into the Time

Drawing Conclusions Have students review the time line for the chapter. Explain that they will be studying events from about 500 B.C. to A.D. 180.

Ask: **Based on the information in the time line, which event do you think represents the transition from republic to empire?** *(27 B.C.—Octavian becomes Rome's first emperor. The word* emperor *is similar to the word* empire*. This event likely represents the transition from republic to empire.)*

Answers for pages 304–305

Step Into the Place

1. Rome's boundaries expanded north, east, west, and south.
2. Rome's location along the Tiber River made Rome accessible from the Mediterranean Sea.
3. **CRITICAL THINKING** Answers may include that Romans wanted to spread their ideas and culture or that they desired power over the region.

Step Into the Time

Student answers should be at or close to 482 years.

ONLINE RESOURCES

networks

Assign these interactive worksheets and quizzes from your Teacher Lesson Center. All resources are print-ready.

It's ALL Online!

CHAPTER 11 RESOURCES

- ☑ Chapter Summary
- ☑ Vocabulary Builder
- ☑ What Do You Know?
- ☑ Hands-On Chapter Project

Lesson 1 Resources

- ☑ Interactive Graphic Organizer
- ☑ Geography and History Activity Early Rome
- ☑ Guided Reading Activity
- ☑ Reading Essentials and Study Guide
- ☑ Online Self-Check Quiz

Lesson 2 Resources

- ☑ Interactive Graphic Organizer
- ☑ 21st Century Skills Critical Thinking
- ☑ Guided Reading Activity
- ☑ Reading Essentials and Study Guide
- ☑ Online Self-Check Quiz

Lesson 3 Resources

- ☑ Interactive Graphic Organizer
- ☑ Primary Source Activity Julius Caesar
- ☑ Guided Reading Activity
- ☑ Reading Essentials and Study Guide
- ☑ Online Self-Check Quiz

Lesson 4 Resources

- ☑ Interactive Graphic Organizer
- ☑ Geography and History Activity Roman Roads
- ☑ Guided Reading Activity
- ☑ Reading Essentials and Study Guide
- ☑ Online Self-Check Quiz

Assessment Resources

- ☑ Lesson Reviews
- ☑ Online Self-Check Quizzes
- ☑ Chapter Activities and Assessment
- ☑ Standardized Test Practice

Remediation Resources

- ☑ Reading Essentials and Study Guide
- ☑ Guided Reading Activities
- ☑ Online Self-Check Quizzes
- ☑ Chapter Summary

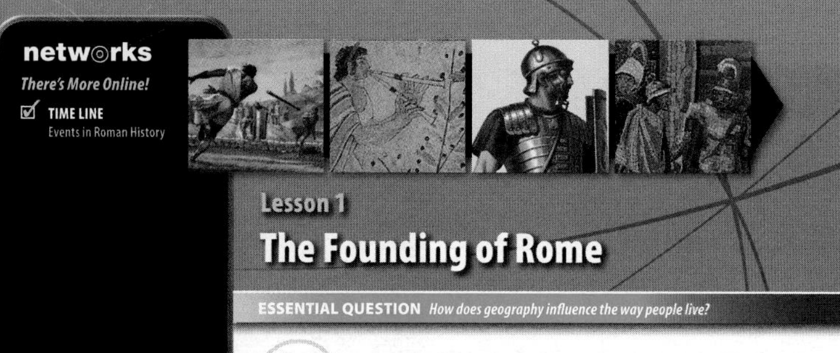

networks *There's More Online!*
TIME LINE Events in Roman History

Lesson 1
The Founding of Rome

ESSENTIAL QUESTION *How does geography influence the way people live?*

It Matters Because
Rome's location, especially its nearby farmlands and easy access to the Mediterranean Sea, enabled it to grow and influence the world.

1 The Beginning of Rome
GUIDING QUESTION *What effect did geography have on the rise of Roman civilization?*

Greek culture did not die when Greece's power declined. Parts of it were adapted and used by the Romans. The Romans had been mostly isolated from the great civilizations of the eastern Mediterranean region. Over time, however, they learned from these civilizations and used their new knowledge to build a vast and powerful empire. Roman rule extended throughout much of present-day Europe, Africa, and Asia.

The Settling of Italy
Italy's location has attracted people for thousands of years. Italy is centrally located in the Mediterranean region. People can easily travel to it from Africa, Asia, and Europe. In addition, people and goods moved with little difficulty through passes in Italy's rugged mountains. These mountain passes also linked settlements together.

There is another key reason why Italy has attracted settlers. Italy has a sunny, mild climate and fertile farmland. Its mountain slopes level off to large flat plains that are ideal for growing crops. With the ability to grow plenty of food, Italy could support a large population.

Reading HELPDESK

Taking Notes: *Creating a Time Line*
Use a time line like this one to order events from the founding of Rome through the Roman Republic's conquest of most of Italy.

800 B.C. — 200 B.C.

Content Vocabulary
- republic
- legion

Rome's Location
The Romans made their home on the Italian Peninsula. This long, thin peninsula juts out from central Europe into the Mediterranean Sea. On a map, Italy looks like a high-heeled boot. The boot's heel points to Greece. The toe points to the island of Sicily (SIH•suh•lee). The Alps are like shoelaces that are strung across the top of the boot. These rugged mountains separate Italy from northern Europe. Another mountain range in Italy is the Apennines (A•puh•NYNZ). These mountains extend from north to south. Volcanoes dot southern Italy's landscape. Italy has long been affected by volcanic eruptions and earthquakes.

Physical features influenced Rome's development. Rome was **founded** about 15 miles (24 km) up the Tiber (TY•buhr) River from the Mediterranean Sea. People used the river to move goods easily between northern and southern Italy. Merchants could also ship their goods out to the Mediterranean Sea using the river. In addition, Rome was far enough up the Tiber River to escape raids by sea-going pirates. Rome's location across seven steep hills made it easy to defend against enemy attacks.

Roman Origins
Several different legends describe how Rome began. One legend about the founding of Rome is contained in *The Aeneid* (ih•NEE•ihd), written by the Roman poet Virgil. He described what took place after the Greeks captured the city of Troy. First, the Trojan Aeneas (ih•NEE•uhs) and his soldiers escaped from Troy to find a new homeland. The Trojans settled in Italy and waged war. Then Aeneas married a local king's daughter. Their marriage united the Trojans with a group of Latin-speaking people who lived in this region. Because of this, Aeneas is known as the "father" of the Romans.

Another legend describes the founding of Rome much differently. This tale **involves** twin brothers, Romulus (RAHM•yuh•luhs) and Remus (REE•muhs). After they were born, they were left beside the Tiber River. A female wolf discovered the boys and cared for them. A shepherd and his wife found and raised the twins.

According to legend, Romulus and Remus were the sons of the Roman war god, Mars. The historian Livy tells of the brothers' argument about how to build Rome's first walls. As depicted here, Romulus killed Remus in the conflict.

Academic Vocabulary
found to establish or create
involve to include

Thinking Like a HISTORIAN
Analyzing Primary and Secondary Sources
The Roman historian Livy wrote about the history of Rome. What were his sources? What other sources about these events do we have that are as reliable as Livy's? For example, is a fresco an historical source? If so, is it a primary or secondary source? Which type of source is more trustworthy? Write a brief explanation of how you would compare sources if sources were reliable, such as Livy's writing and images painted on a wall. For more information about analyzing primary and secondary sources, read the chapter *What Does a Historian Do?*

When the brothers grew up, they planned to build a city along the Tiber River. However, the two boys argued about the construction of the city. Remus made fun of the walls that Romulus built. The Roman historian Livy (LIH•vee) tells what happened next:

PRIMARY SOURCE

> "Then followed an angry altercation [argument]; heated passions [emotions] led to bloodshed; in the tumult [uproar] Remus was killed. The more common report is that Remus contemptuously [spitefully] jumped over the newly raised walls and was forthwith killed by the enraged Romulus, . . . Romulus thus became sole ruler, and the city [Rome] was called after him, its founder."
>
> —from *History of Rome*, by Livy

Historically, little is known about the first people to settle in Italy. Archaeological artifacts (AHR•tih•fakts) suggest that Neolithic people might have settled in Italy as early as 5000 B.C. These early groups built farming villages but moved after they had used up the nutrients in the soil. Between 2000 B.C. and 1000 B.C., other groups of people settled permanently in the hills and on the plains. Latin-speaking people, called Latins, settled on the plain of Latium (LAY•shee•uhm) in central Italy.

One group of Latins built straw-roofed huts on Rome's hills. They tended animals and grew crops. This settlement, which **occurred** (uh•KUHRD) between 800 B.C. and 700 B.C., marks the birth of Rome. The people living there became known as Romans.

Influences of Greeks and Etruscans
After 800 B.C., other groups moved into the region where the Romans lived. Two of these groups, the Greeks and the Etruscans (ih•TRUHS•kuhnz), would greatly influence Roman civilization.

From about 750 B.C. to 500 B.C., Greeks settled in farming villages in southern Italy. The Greeks introduced grape and olive farming to the region. The Greeks also passed on the Greek alphabet to the Romans. Later, the Romans would model their buildings, sculpture, and literature after those of the Greeks.

The Etruscans had an even greater influence on Roman civilization. The Etruscans settled north of Rome in Etruria (ih•TROOR•ee•uh). After 650 B.C., they moved south. The Etruscans **eventually** (ee•VEN•choo•uh•lee) took control of Rome and its surrounding area.

Reading HELPDESK

Academic Vocabulary
occur to happen
eventual final or ultimate

Etruscan wall paintings were frescoes, meaning they were painted on wet plaster. Many Etruscan frescoes show people enjoying music or dance.

▶ CRITICAL THINKING:
Analyzing What does the image suggest about how the Etruscans lived?

The Etruscans were ruled by nobles, who grew wealthy from trade and mining. Other Etruscans **devoted** themselves to the study of the arts. Skilled Etruscan artisans worked with copper, iron, lead, and tin. They turned these metals into weapons, tools, and jewelry. Etruscan artists covered the walls of tombs with colorful paintings. They painted men and women feasting, dancing, and playing music. Some wall paintings also displayed violent battle scenes. These images showed that the Etruscans were proud of their powerful army.

The Etruscans taught the Romans to build with brick and to roof their homes with tiles. They drained the water from marshes that lay between Rome's hills. They laid out city streets. The Etruscans built temples, passing on their religious rituals to the Romans. They even influenced the style of clothing that the Romans wore. Roman men adopted the Etruscan fashion of wearing short cloaks and togas. Finally, the Etruscan army served as the model for the mighty army that the Romans would later create.

PROGRESS CHECK
Explaining How did the Etruscans influence early Rome?

Academic Vocabulary
devote to give one's time, effort, or attention earnestly

LESSON 1

ENGAGE

MAP **Think-Pair-Share** Show students the Chapter Opener map. Have them examine the map with the time line from the Chapter Opener in mind.

Ask:

What geographic features do you think influenced Rome's development? Have students break into pairs to discuss the question for a few moments. Then, ask each pair to share their conclusions with the class. *(Rome's location along a river, its proximity to the Mediterranean Sea, and its proximity to Greeks and Etruscans influenced its development.)* Make sure students understand that the Tiber River is the river that flows through Rome.

Tell students they will be learning about the development of the Roman Republic. They will use their responses to examine how geographic factors influenced Rome's development.

TEACH & ASSESS

1 The Beginning of Rome

GUIDING QUESTION ***What effect did geography have on the rise of Roman civilization?***

IMAGE **Listing** Have students list the physical and geographic features that made Italy an appealing place to settle. Have them compare their answers with their responses from the Think-Pair-Share activity above. Then show students the images of Rome today and in ancient times. Discuss how the physical and geographic features that made it a good place to settle likely still affect life in that city today. AL

Evaluating Discuss the two legends of Rome's founding.

Ask:

Which legend of Rome's origins is more likely to be based on fact? Why? *(Answers may vary, but students might identify the legend told in the Aeneid as more likely to have a factual basis because it is more realistic and based on actual history. The Remus and Romulus story is less likely to be factual because the idea of two boys being raised by wolves seems unlikely.)* BL

INTERACTIVE WORKSHEET

Geography and History Activity

Making Connections Have students complete the Geography and History Activity for Lesson 1. After students have filled in the graphic organizer at the end of the worksheet, ask them to share their responses with the class.

Write their responses on the board in a cause-and-effect format similar to the worksheet. Be sure to point out any geographic features of the area that students did not note.

LECTURE SLIDE **Discussing** Present the lecture slide on how the Greeks incluenced the Romans..

Ask:

How did the Greeks influence the Romans? *(Greek settlers introduced grape and olive farming and passed on the Greek alphabet. The Romans would be influenced also by Greek architecture, sculpture, and literature.)*

IMAGE **Drawing Conclusions** Show students the image of the Etruscan mural. Then discuss with the class the different ways cultures can influence one another—as a result of living in close proximity and exchanging ideas or as a result of the power one culture holds over another.

Ask:

Why did the Etruscans have a greater influence over Roman civilization than the Greeks? *(The Greeks' influence resulted mainly from living near the Romans in southern Italy, whereas the Etruscans took control of Rome and its surrounding area.)*

INTERACTIVE GRAPHIC ORGANIZER **Identifying** Allow students time throughout the lesson to add entries to the time line. Students should identify key historical events that indicate Rome's growth from its founding to its conquest of most of Italy.

2 Becoming a Republic

GUIDING QUESTION ***How did Rome become a great power?***

IMAGE **Organizing Ideas** Discuss as a class what type of graphic organizer would be best to use to identify the general categories of things that helped Rome become powerful. For instance, categories could include "geographic advantages," "military strength," and "leadership." Then, focus on the Roman soldier. Show students the slide with information about Roman soldiers. Ask volunteers to read the text aloud.

INTERACTIVE WHITEBOARD ACTIVITY **Identifying** Display the image of the Roman soldier in the Interactive Whiteboard Activity. Have students identify the components of the soldier's uniform and arms, and drag and drop the terms to the correct spot on the image.

Ask:

How did legionnaires identify different groups on the battlefield? *(by looking at the standards, or battle flags)*

Ask:

Why would this have been important? *(to find each other on the battlefield)* AL ELL

Evaluating Discuss with students the differences between giving conquered peoples citizenship and making them allies of Rome.

Ask:

What were the advantages and disadvantages of being a citizen of Rome compared to being an ally? *(Answers will vary. Students may say that citizenship was preferable, because as citizens they were given the rights and responsibilities of other Roman citizens. Others might argue that it was better for groups to be allies and continue to govern their own affairs.)*

Have students complete the Lesson 1 Review.

Answers for pages 306–309

P. 306 Taking Notes Answers may vary.
c. 753 B.C. Latins establish the community of Rome;
c. 750 B.C. Greeks settle in southern Italy;
650 B.C. Etruscans take control of Rome;
509 B.C. Roman Republic is established;
267 B.C. Rome rules most of Italy.

P. 309 CRITICAL THINKING The Etruscans enjoyed the arts, especially music and dance. They had leisure time for appreciating the arts.

P. 309 ☑ PROGRESS CHECK The Etruscans influenced Roman architecture, religious rituals, clothing styles, and the Roman military.

ROMAN LEGIONARY

A soldier's armor was made of iron strips joined by leather ties.
The long iron point on the spear was made to bend after the spear was thrown, preventing an enemy from using it.
Shields were made from sheets of wood glued together and covered with leather or cloth.

INFOGRAPHIC

Originally the soldiers in the Roman army were untrained citizens. Through harsh training, the Roman army became known as one of the world's best.

▶ CRITICAL THINKING

Analyzing *Why was it an advantage to Rome to have a professional army?*

2 Becoming a Republic

GUIDING QUESTION *How did Rome become a great power?*

The Romans greatly **benefited** from the contributions of the Etruscans. However, they grew weary of Etruscan rulers. According to Roman tradition, in 509 B.C., the Romans overthrew Tarquin the Proud, the Etruscan king, and established a **republic** (rih•PUH•blihk). A republic is a form of government in which citizens elect their leaders. The creation of a republic began a new era in Rome's history. When Rome became a republic, it was still a small city. It was also still surrounded by different groups of people. These groups included Etruscans, Greeks, and other Latins. Over the next 200 years, the Romans fought many wars against these neighbors. By 267 B.C., Rome controlled almost all of Italy. The Roman Republic was able to **acquire** land because of its strong army. During the early years of the republic, every male citizen who owned land had to serve in the army. Roman soldiers were well trained, and deserters were punished by death. This strict discipline ensured soldiers stayed loyal to Rome.

The Romans also developed new battle strategies. In the early days of the republic, the Romans fought like the Greeks. Rows of soldiers moved in a single large group. They attacked from only one direction. Roman generals realized that this way of fighting was slow and hard to control. They reorganized their soldiers into smaller groups, called **legions** (LEE•juhnz). Each legion had about 6,000 men. A legion was further divided into groups of 60 to 120 soldiers. These smaller groups could move quickly around the battlefield to wherever they were most needed.

Roman soldiers were also well armed. Most soldiers carried a short, double-edged iron sword called a *gladius* (GLAY•dee•uhs) and an iron spear called a *pilum* (PY•luhm). Each of the small groups in a legion carried its own standard into battle. The standard was a tall pole topped with a symbol, such as an eagle.

Reading **HELP**DESK

republic a form of government in which citizens elect their leaders
legions large groups of Roman soldiers

Academic Vocabulary

benefit to receive help; to gain
acquire to get as one's own

Because the standard could be seen above the action, it showed soldiers where they were supposed to be on the battlefield.

Who Ruled Rome?

In addition to having a strong army, the Romans ruled effectively. After they conquered a region, they built permanent military outposts to protect it. These settlements were built at strategic locations, such as on a high hill or at a river crossing. They also built roads between settlements. As a result, troops and supplies could move quickly within the conquered lands.

The Romans stressed the need to treat conquered people fairly. If conquered people were treated well, the Romans believed, the people would become loyal subjects. To encourage fair treatment, the Romans created the Roman Confederation. This system gave some conquered peoples, especially other Latins, full Roman citizenship. They could vote and serve in the government of Rome. They were treated the same as other citizens under the law.

Other conquered peoples became allies, or friends, of Rome. As allies, they paid Roman taxes. In addition, they were required to supply soldiers to fight for Rome. Allies, however, were free to manage their own local affairs.

With these policies, the Romans hoped to maintain the peace in their conquered lands. If conquered peoples turned against Rome, its rulers were ready to crush any revolts. Rome's generosity paid off. The republic grew stronger and more unified.

The Roman soldiers, called legionaries, were disciplined and well trained. In groups called legions, they developed new battle strategies.

☑ PROGRESS CHECK

Analyzing Why were the Romans able to expand their control of Italy?

LESSON 1 REVIEW

Review Vocabulary

1. How was the growth of the *republic* aided by the Roman army's use of *legions* in warfare?

Answer the Guiding Questions

2. ***Explaining*** How did Rome's location affect its development?
3. ***Summarizing*** How did the Roman government maintain control over conquered territories?
4. ***Differentiating*** How did the attitude of Romans toward the Etruscans change over time?
5. **PERSUASIVE WRITING** You are a Roman living about 650 B.C. The Etruscans have taken over, and your friends are worried about the new rulers. Write a persuasive speech in which you encourage them to adopt Etruscan ways. Tell what Romans may learn from the Etruscans and why they should not turn against the new rulers.

netw⊙rks

There's More Online!

☑ GRAPHIC ORGANIZER Roman Society
☑ SLIDE SHOW Symbols of Authority
☑ VIDEO

Lesson 2

Rome As a Republic

ESSENTIAL QUESTION *How do governments change?*

IT MATTERS BECAUSE

Rome's ideas about democracy would greatly influence the people who founded the United States many centuries later.

1 Governing Rome

GUIDING QUESTION *How did conflict between classes change Rome's government?*

Not everyone was treated fairly in the Roman Republic. Rome's government reflected divisions within its society.

Early Romans were divided into two classes: patricians and plebeians. The **patricians** (puh•TRIH•shuhnz) were Rome's ruling class. Patricians were wealthy landowners. They came from Rome's oldest and most prominent families. Most Romans, however, were **plebeians** (plih•BEE•uhnz). Plebeians were not as wealthy as the patricians. In some cases, they were very poor. Plebeians included artisans, shopkeepers, and owners of small farms.

Patrician and plebeian men were Roman citizens and had the right to vote. Both groups were required to pay taxes and serve in the army. Plebeians, however, had a lower social position than the patricians. For example, it was illegal for a patrician and a plebeian to marry each other. Plebeians also lacked important basic rights. They could not hold public office or lead the public ceremonies that honored the gods of Rome. Rome's republic would be shaped by a struggle between the patricians and the plebeians over the right to govern.

Reading **HELP**DESK

Taking Notes: *Categorizing Information*

Use a web diagram like the one here to list facts about patricians and plebeians and their roles in the government of Rome.

Content Vocabulary

- patrician
- veto
- dictator
- plebeian
- praetor
- civic duty
- consul
- tribune

Government of the Republic

The government of the Roman Republic was organized into three branches. One branch made laws; another ran the daily affairs of government; a third branch acted as judges. The republic had a system of checks and balances. This system was designed to prevent one branch from becoming too strong. It did not separate powers like the United States government does today, however. Judges helped run the government and could lead armies. Some leaders who ran the government also helped make laws.

Two patrician **consuls** (CAHN•suhlz) headed the government. The consuls were administrators and army leaders. Each consul served one year in office. Their terms of office were short so that they would not become too powerful. Each consul could **veto** (VEE•toh), or reject, the other's decision. The word veto is Latin for "I forbid." Rome also had other major government officials called **praetors** (PREE•tuhrz). They interpreted the law and served as judges in court. They could also lead armies.

The Senate was Rome's **legislature.** The Senate was a group of 300 patrician men. These senators served the republic for life. During the early republic, the Senate only advised the consuls. By the 200s B.C., however, senators debated foreign policy, proposed laws, and approved the construction of roads and temples.

The Assembly of Centuries was another legislative body in Rome. It elected consuls and praetors and passed laws. The Assembly of Centuries was, like the Senate, controlled by patricians.

This plebeian strike to gain a voice in government turned violent. The Roman plebeians went on at least five strikes in order to establish their rights.

Conflict Between Classes

As time passed, the plebeians grew frustrated. They had to serve in the army and pay taxes, yet they had no power in the government.

In 494 B.C., many plebeians went on strike, refusing to fight in the army. They even left Rome to create a government of their own. The patricians feared that the republic was in danger of collapsing, so they agreed to share power with the plebeians.

The patricians allowed the plebeians to have their own body of representatives, called the Council of the Plebs. The Council of the Plebs elected officials called **tribunes** (TRIH•byoonz). Tribunes voiced plebeian concerns to the government.

patricians the ruling class
plebeians ordinary citizens
consul head of government, usually with a limited term in office
veto to reject
praetors government officials who interpret the law and serve as judges
tribune an elected official who protects the rights of ordinary citizens

Academic Vocabulary

legislature a group of people who make the laws

LESSON 1 (cont.)

CLOSE & REFLECT

Explaining Have students write a journal entry from the perspective of a person whose community was recently conquered by Rome. Have students explain whether this is a positive event and why. Ask volunteers to read aloud from their journal entries. Use these as a starting point to discuss why being conquered can be tolerable in some situations.

IF YOU HAVE MORE TIME . . .

Use Mathematics to Analyze the Number of Soldiers in a Roman Legion

Calculating Point out to students that Roman legions usually had 6,000 men. In turn, each legion was divided into groups of 60 to 120 soldiers.

Ask: **Into how many 60-soldier groups could a Roman legion be divided?** *(100)* **Into how many 120-soldier groups could one legion be divided?** *(50)*

Answers for pages 310–311

P. 310 INFOGRAPHIC

P. 310 CRITICAL THINKING A professional army would be well trained, disciplined, and focused only on defending Rome, whereas a volunteer army would be trained only when volunteers could take time away from their work.

P. 311 ☑ PROGRESS CHECK The Romans were disciplined and fair. They built a strong army, used effective military strategies, and ruled the people they conquered fairly. As a result, they were able to expand control of Italy.

LESSON 1 REVIEW

1. The use of legions helped the Roman army fight battles more effectively, which allowed the Romans to conquer more areas and expand the Roman republic, a form of government in which citizens elect their leaders.
2. Rome's location along the Tiber River allowed for movement of goods in and out of the area. Its distance from the Mediterranean Sea provided protection from seagoing pirates, and the steep hills across which Rome extended provided protection from other enemies.
3. The Roman government controlled conquered territories by governing fairly and allowing conquered peoples to become full citizens or allies of the republic. They also crushed any revolts.
4. Although Etruscans had a lot of influence over Roman life, over time Romans tired of being ruled by the Etruscans.
5. Answers will vary. Speeches should mention that the Etruscans are educated, cultured, and wealthy. They know and can teach the Romans many skills, such as how to build better houses and cities and how to farm more effectively. They can teach the Romans about the arts and how to make better weapons. The Romans can learn skills from the Etruscans that will make Rome stronger and better.

Teaching *Rome as a Republic* (Student Edition pp. 312–319)

LESSON 2 • Day 1

ENGAGE

INTERACTIVE WORKSHEET

21st Century Skills Activity

Making Connections Show students the 21st Century Skills Activity worksheet on making connections. Guide students through the Practicing the Skills questions. Ask students to brainstorm examples from history of situations in which people have not been treated equally, such as slavery, women not being allowed to vote, and segregated schools. Write their responses on the interactive whiteboard. Discuss with students why they think inequality exists.

Ask: **What methods have groups in the United States used to try to gain equal treatment under the law?** *(Examples include organizing marches and rallies, taking their cases to court, using strikes and boycotts, and pressuring lawmakers.)*

Assign the rest of the worksheet as homework.

Tell students that in this lesson, they will be learning about the rights of people living in the Roman Republic.

TEACH & ASSESS

1 Governing Rome

GUIDING QUESTION *How did conflict between classes change Rome's government?*

INTERACTIVE GRAPHIC ORGANIZER **Summarizing** Review the lesson's Taking Notes graphic organizer with students.

Ask: **Who were the plebeians and patricians?** *(Possible answer: The plebeians and patricians were the two social classes that had a conflict.)* Remind students that they may consult their textbooks for details that will help them complete the graphic organizer.

INTERACTIVE GRAPHIC ORGANIZER

Making Connections Have students look at the graphic organizer that makes connections between the Roman and U.S. legal systems.

Ask: **How were the two systems similar and different?** *(The Roman system did not separate powers, as the U.S. government does. Roman judges helped run the government and the armies. U.S. judges are not permitted to do such things.)*

LECTURE SLIDE **Identifying Points of View** Present the lecture slide about the plebeians and patricians. Then have students consider the points of view of both sides.

Ask: **What did the plebeians want?** *(to participate in the government equally with patricians)* **Did the patricians want the plebeians to have the same rights as they did? Why or why not?** *(Possible answer: No, because the patricians wanted to hold onto their power in the government; if plebeians had equal rights, they might take control of the republic.)*

Answers for pages 312–313

P. 312 Taking Notes **Patricians:** ruling class, landowners, prominent families, men were citizens; Role in Roman Government: men were citizens, paid taxes, served in army, could hold public office and lead public ceremonies. **Plebeians:** majority of Romans, poor artisans, shopkeepers, farmers, illegal to marry patricians; Role in Roman Government: men were citizens, paid taxes, served in army, Council of Plebs represented plebeians in government

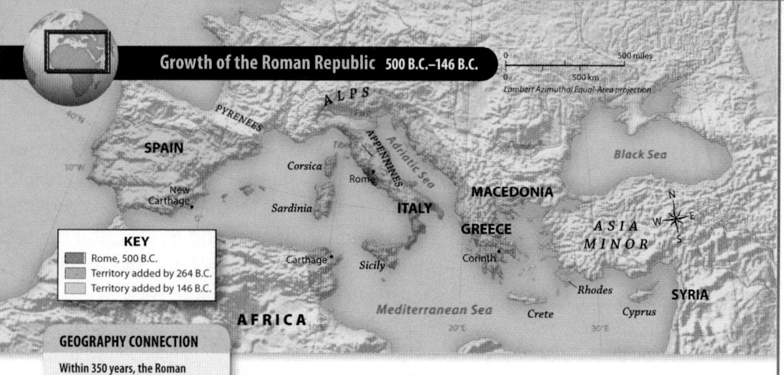

GEOGRAPHY CONNECTION

Within 350 years, the Roman Republic conquered territory along much of the Mediterranean Sea's northern coast.

1 **PLACE** What major islands did Rome conquer?

2 **CRITICAL THINKING** *Making Inferences* Why do you think Rome did not expand farther north?

Tribunes could also veto government decisions. Later, plebeians were even allowed to become consuls, and marriages between plebeians and patricians were made legal.

In 287 B.C., the plebeians won another important political victory. The Council of the Plebs was given the right to pass laws for all Romans. Politically, all male citizens were now considered equal. In practice, however, a few wealthy patrician families still held most of the power. Women did not have any political rights. The Roman Republic had become more representative, but it was still not democratic.

Cincinnatus and Civic Duty

The Romans believed that there were times when the republic needed a strong leader. To lead Rome, the Romans created the office of **dictator** (DIHK•tay•tuhr). Today, this word is used to describe an oppressive ruler who has total control over a country. In the Roman Republic, however, the consuls resigned during difficult or dangerous times, and the senate appointed a dictator to lead the republic. During a crisis, the dictator had complete control over Rome. After the crisis was over, the dictator was expected to give up his power, and the regular government's power would then be restored.

One of the most famous Roman dictators was Cincinnatus (SIHN•suh•NA•tuhs). Cincinnatus had been a respected Roman consul who was known for his loyalty to Rome. In 458 B.C., a powerful enemy of Rome threatened to destroy the Roman army. The Senate appointed Cincinnatus as dictator to handle this emergency. Messengers were sent to his farm to tell him about his appointment. They found him plowing his fields. Cincinnatus accepted the role of dictator, and he immediately created an army. Then, he led it into battle, easily defeating the enemy. Next, Cincinnatus marched his army back to Rome and resigned as dictator. Just 16 days after taking control of the republic, Cincinnatus returned to his farm.

Reading **HELP**DESK

dictator a person granted absolute power

When called to serve, Cincinnatus willingly left his farm to fulfill his civic duty.

▶ **CRITICAL THINKING**
Analyzing What role did Cincinnatus play in government to fulfill his civic duty?

Cincinnatus was widely admired because he fulfilled his **civic duty**. Civic duty is the idea that citizens have a responsibility to help their country. This idea was important to the Romans and has been valued by other people as well. George Washington, for example, was inspired by Cincinnatus. Like Cincinnatus, Washington was a farmer who was asked to lead an army: the Continental Army in the American War for Independence. After leading the Americans to victory, Washington returned to his farm in Virginia. Later, he **reluctantly** agreed to become the first president of the United States.

Rome's System of Law

One of Rome's greatest contributions to later civilizations was its system of law. Roman law has influenced the legal systems of the United States and other countries.

At first, Roman laws were not written down. This sparked criticism from the plebeians. They believed that patrician judges would always rule in favor of the upper classes if there were no written laws. The plebeians demanded that laws be put into writing. Thus, the judges would have to refer to the laws when they made a legal decision. The patricians eventually agreed.

In 451 B.C., Rome adopted its first written code of laws known as the Twelve Tables. The laws were carved on twelve bronze tablets and placed in Rome's marketplace, called the Forum (FOHR•uhm). These laws served as the foundation for all future Roman laws. The Twelve Tables supported the ideal that all free citizens—patrician and plebeian alike—had the right to be treated equally in the Roman legal system.

These bundles of rods and axes, called fasces, were carried by Roman officials as a symbol of legal authority.

civic duty the idea that citizens have a responsibility to help their country

Academic Vocabulary

reluctantly hesitantly or unwillingly

The Roman court system shared many similarities with the legal system in the United States today. Judges heard cases before an audience of citizens.

As the Romans conquered more people, they expanded their system of laws. They created laws that would apply to people who were not Roman citizens. These new laws were known as the Law of Nations. The Law of Nations identified the laws and rights that applied to all people everywhere in the Roman lands.

Roman Justice

The ideas found in Roman laws are woven throughout the American legal system today. For example, the American legal system, like the Roman legal system, **assumes** that a person is innocent until proven guilty. People accused of crimes have the right to defend themselves before a judge. Judges must carefully consider all the evidence in a case before making a decision.

The *rule of law* is one of the key ideas that the Romans passed on to the world. The rule of law means that laws apply to everyone equally. It also means that the legal system should treat everyone the same way. Before the Romans, the rule of law was unfamiliar to people.

In many regions, people of the upper classes enjoyed special privileges. They often had different laws and courts from the lower classes. People in the lower classes, however, had few legal rights or none at all. The Romans extended the idea of the rule of law to all their lands. Today, the rule of law is the guiding principle of the American legal system.

✓ **PROGRESS CHECK**

Explaining What was the emergency that caused Cincinnatus to be appointed dictator?

2 The Punic Wars

GUIDING QUESTION *How did Rome conquer the Mediterranean region?*

Rome continued to grow as a republic. Its power, however, was threatened by another civilization in the Mediterranean region. Carthage (KAHR•thihj) was a powerful trading empire based along the north African coast. Carthage traced its beginnings to the Phoenicians, who created a trading colony there about 800 B.C. Carthage became the largest and wealthiest city in the western Mediterranean area because of trade. Its territory included parts of northern Africa and southern Europe.

Reading **HELP**DESK

Academic Vocabulary

assume to take for granted to be true

intensify to become stronger

innovation the introduction of something new

Carthage became Rome's main rival. Each wanted to control the entire Mediterranean world. In 264 B.C., their rivalry **intensified**. It grew into a series of wars that took place over a period of nearly 120 years.

The Punic Wars Begin

War between the Romans and the Carthaginians, or the people of Carthage, erupted in 264 B.C. The original conflict is known as the First Punic War. The First Punic War began when Rome sought control of the fertile island of Sicily. The Carthaginians had already established colonies on the island. So they were determined to stop the Roman invasion.

Carthage used its strong navy to protect its trading empire. Although Rome had a powerful army, it did not have a navy. It was forced to build a fleet quickly in order to fight Carthage. The Romans modeled their new warships after those of Carthage. They made one key **innovation**. They built a small moveable bridge on the front of each ship. This bridge allowed Roman soldiers to board a Carthaginian ship and fight hand-to-hand on its decks. In a way, it changed a sea war into a land war.

For more than 20 years, the Romans and Carthaginians fought each other at sea. Finally, in 241 B.C., a Roman fleet badly defeated Carthage's navy off the coast of Sicily. Carthage was forced to give up Sicily and pay a huge fine to the Romans. Rome then took control of the island.

GEOGRAPHY CONNECTION

After defeating Carthage in the Second Punic War, Rome was the strongest power in the Mediterranean region.

1 **LOCATION** From what direction did Hannibal of Carthage attack Rome?

2 **CRITICAL THINKING** *Analyzing* Why did Hannibal take the route he did instead of sailing directly to Rome?

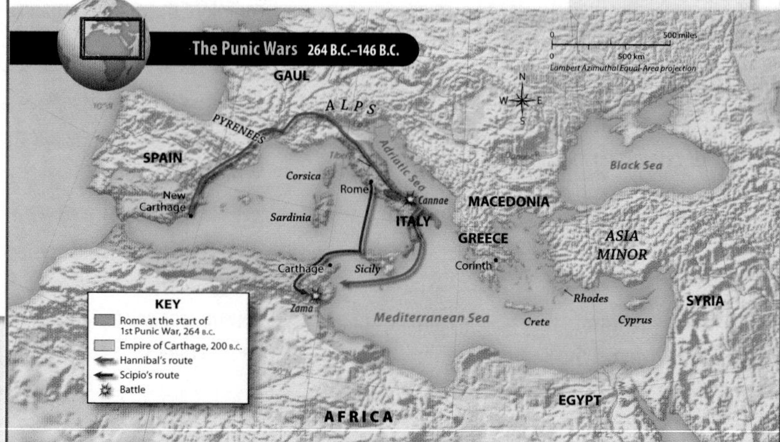

LESSON 2 • Day 1 (cont)

PRIMARY SOURCE **Summarizing** Present the quotation about Cincinnatus. Ask volunteers to read aloud the informative text and the quotation. Take time to have students paraphrase the quotation. Make sure students understand what qualities Livy is emphasizing in his description of Cincinnatus.

Ask: **Why was Cincinnatus an important figure?** *(He fulfilled his civic duty by leaving his farm to become dictator, but then he returned to his farm when the crisis was over rather than staying in power.)*

LECTURE SLIDE **Making Connections** Show students the lecture slide"Governing Rome." Discuss the concept of civic duty with students.

Ask: **What are some ways people can perform their civic duty in the United States today?** Write their responses on the whiteboard. *(Possible answers: voting, doing volunteer work, serving in government office, serving in the military)*

PRIMARY SOURCE **Identifying** Share with students text from the Twelve Tables. Ask volunteers to read the text of the laws. As a class, discuss the meaning of each law.

INTERACTIVE WHITEBOARD ACTIVITY **Categorizing** Show students the Interactive Whiteboard Activity on the Twelve Tables. Read each law with students. Then, help students paraphrase each law. Next, discuss each law's likely meaning, and have students match each law with a category in the item bank.

SLIDE SHOW **Making Connections** Project the slide show about symbols of authority and then discuss Rome's influence on modern symbols of power.

CLOSE & REFLECT

Synthesizing Ask students to think about what the conflict between plebeians and patricians achieved. Lead students in a discussion of how the conflict was resolved and what changes it brought about in the Roman Republic.

LESSON 2 • Day 2

ENGAGE

Summarizing Have students recall the conflict between the classes of Roman citizens.

Ask: **What was the conflict about?** *(The conflict was about plebeians having equal rights with patricians.)*

Previewing Have students preview the map "The Punic Wars 264–126 B.C." in their textbooks. Tell students that in this section, they will learn about Rome's conflict with its great rival, Carthage. This struggle for power between Rome and Carthage in the Mediterranean region lasted more than 100 years. Ask students to locate the following places on the map: Italy, Sicily, and Carthage. Explain that the Punic Wars first started over control of Sicily.

TEACH & ASSESS

2 The Punic Wars

GUIDING QUESTION *How did Rome conquer the Mediterranean region?*

Describing Ask: **What made Carthage a rich and powerful force in the Mediterranean region?** *(trade)*

Identifying Ask: **What did Rome need to do to prepare to fight Carthage for control of Sicily?** *(Rome needed to build a naval fleet because Carthage was protecting Sicily with its navy.)* Ask students to consider why Carthage might have had a strong navy in the first place. *(because of its location on the sea)*

MAP **Locating** Direct students again to the map of the Punic Wars. Have students locate the main battle sites of the Punic Wars on the map. *(Cannae in southern Italy, Zama in north Africa)*

Ask: **What territory did Rome gain as a result of the Punic Wars?** *(Sicily, Spain, and Carthage)* AL

Analyzing Primary Sources Have students read the excerpt in their textbook from *The Histories of Polybius.*

Ask: **What did the Senate instruct the Roman commanders to do?** *(The Senate ordered the Roman commanders to battle Hannibal's forces.)* BL

Sequencing Have students work in pairs or small groups to create a flowchart that illustrates the sequence of events in the Punic Wars. AL

Have students complete the Lesson 2 Review.

CLOSE & REFLECT

MAP **Speculating** Direct students to write a short response to the following question: **Why do you think the Romans were so determined to beat the Carthaginians?** *(Possible response: The Romans were determined to beat the Carthaginians because the Romans wanted control over Carthage's territory.)* AL

Ask students to share their responses with the class. Then present the interactive map "Growth of the Roman Republic." Invite students to revise their responses after studying the map. *(Possible response: By defeating the Carthaginians, the Romans would greatly increase their control over most of the Mediterranean region.)*

IF YOU HAVE MORE TIME . . .

Use Role-Playing to Explore Conflict Between Plebeians and Patricians

Analyzing Point of View Have students do a role-playing activity in which one group plays the role of plebeians and another group plays the patricians. Tell students that it is 494 B.C. and the plebeians are on strike from the army. A group of plebeians have gathered at the Forum, ancient Rome's central market area, and has encountered a group of patricians.

Ask: **How would each side explain its point of view?** Allow a few minutes for the groups to prepare a response before guiding them to role-play a debate or a discussion. BL

Answers for pages 314–317

P. 314 GEOGRAPHY CONNECTION

1. **Place** Corsica, Sardinia, Sicily, and Corinth
2. CRITICAL THINKING Rome did not want to conquer lands too far from the coast. Roman forces probably could not support efforts to conquer more areas.

P. 315 CRITICAL THINKING He served as Rome's leader during a time of crisis.

P. 316 ☑ PROGRESS CHECK The Roman Senate appointed Cincinnatus as dictator because Rome was under threat from a powerful enemy.

P. 317 GEOGRAPHY CONNECTION

1. Hannibal attacked Rome from the northwest.
2. CRITICAL THINKING Hannibal wanted to surprise the Romans, who would have expected him to make a direct attack from the southwest—from Carthage, across the Mediterranean Sea. Instead, he took a longer, indirect route.

Hannibal Attacks: The Second Punic War

After losing Sicily, Carthage tried to expand its empire into Spain. They wanted to make up for the losses caused by Rome taking over Sicily. Spain had valuable resources of silver, copper, gold, lead, and iron.

The Romans bitterly opposed Carthage's attempt to establish territory so near to Rome. So the Romans encouraged the Spanish to rebel against Carthage. In response, Carthage sent its greatest general, Hannibal (HA•nuh•buhl), to attack Rome. This event, in 218 B.C., started the Second Punic War.

Hannibal planned to fight the Romans in Italy. To do this he gathered an army of about 46,000 men and 37 elephants. He sailed from Carthage to Spain. Then, his soldiers marched through southern Gaul, or present-day France.

Next, they crossed the Alps into Italy. The Carthaginians crossed the Alps with their elephants, hoping to overpower the Roman army. Instead, the bitter cold and attacks by mountain tribes killed almost half of the Carthaginian soldiers and most of the elephants. The remaining army, however, was still a powerful fighting force when it reached Italy.

In December 218 B.C., the Carthaginian forces defeated the Romans in northern Italy. Hannibal made good use of his elephants in the attack. Unfortunately, most of the animals died after the conflict.

▶ CRITICAL THINKING
Analyzing Why was this battle important?

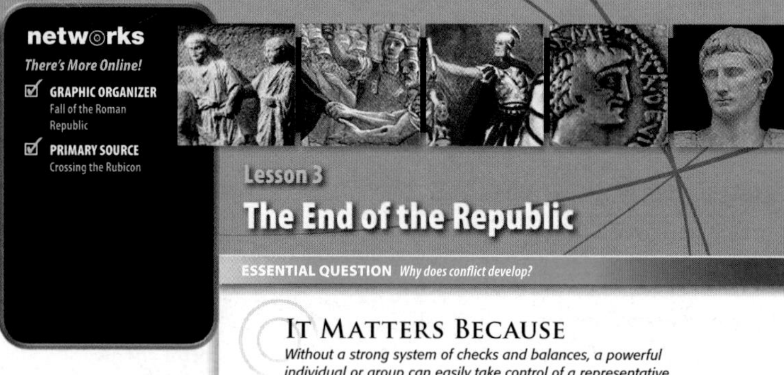

Reading **HELP**DESK

As Hannibal and his army grew closer and closer to Italy and the Roman forces, Roman military leaders looked to the Senate for advice.

PRIMARY SOURCE

> "They [the Roman commanders] therefore sent frequent messages to Rome asking for instructions, . . . in view of the fact that the country was being plundered, . . . The Senate passed a resolution . . . give the enemy battle."
>
> —from *The Histories of Polybius*, by Polybius

In 216 B.C., Hannibal defeated the Romans at the Battle of Cannae (KA•nee) in southern Italy. Following the battle, Hannibal's army raided the country. In response, the Romans assembled another army to stop the Carthaginians. In 206 B.C. Roman forces, led by Scipio (SIH•pee•oh), captured Spain and then attacked the city of Carthage. Hannibal returned home to North Africa to defend his people. Scipio's troops defeated the Carthaginians in 202 B.C. at the Battle of Zama (ZAY•muh). Carthage was forced to give up its navy and pay Rome a large sum of money. It also had to give its Spanish territory to Rome. As a result, Rome became the supreme power in the western Mediterranean.

The Third Punic War

Rome still considered Carthage a military threat. In 146 B.C., Rome finally destroyed it in the Third Punic War. At the same time, Rome also waged war against other states in the eastern Mediterranean region. In the 140s B.C., all of Greece fell under Roman rule. About twenty years later, Rome acquired its first province in Asia.

✓ PROGRESS CHECK

Describing How did Hannibal lose the Second Punic War?

Connections to TODAY

Hannibal's Elephants

Historians have wondered how Hannibal obtained elephants for his march. Were they Indian or African elephants? Indian elephants are easier to train. In fact, most circus elephants today are Indian elephants. However, it would have been very difficult for Hannibal to obtain elephants from India. Even African elephants are not native to North Africa, where Hannibal started his march. Historians continue to question which type of elephant Hannibal used—or how he obtained them.

LESSON 2 REVIEW

Review Vocabulary

1. Why were Roman *consuls* awarded the power of the *veto*?

Answer the Guiding Questions

2. *Explaining* How did plebeians gain power in the republic? For what changes were they responsible?
3. *Summarizing* Describe how Rome defeated Carthage to become the ruler of the Mediterranean region.
4. *Distinguishing Fact from Opinion* Identify whether the following statement is a fact or an opinion: "At first, patricians had more rights than plebeians."
5. **EXPOSITORY WRITING** In an essay, describe what the idea of "rule of law" meant to the average Roman.

networks
There's More Online!
☑ GRAPHIC ORGANIZER Fall of the Roman Republic
☑ PRIMARY SOURCE Crossing the Rubicon

Lesson 3

The End of the Republic

ESSENTIAL QUESTION *Why does conflict develop?*

IT MATTERS BECAUSE

Without a strong system of checks and balances, a powerful individual or group can easily take control of a representative government.

1 Problems in the Republic

GUIDING QUESTION *What factors led to the decline of the Roman Republic?*

The Roman army won victories abroad, but the republic faced mounting economic troubles at home. The gap between the rich and the poor grew wider. Many farmers faced financial ruin. The cities of the republic were becoming overcrowded and dangerous.

Romans—Rich and Poor

Most Romans were plebeians who farmed small plots of land. The plebeians had made some political gains in the Roman Republic, but they lacked real power. Power was still held by the patricians. The upper class still made up most of the Senate and served in key government positions. They also managed Rome's finances and directed its wars.

In the 100s B.C., farmers began to fall into poverty and debt. Why? Many small farmers had neglected their fields while fighting in Roman wars. Others had their farms destroyed by the Carthaginians. Now, the farmers did not have crops to harvest. As a result, they could not pay back loans they owed.

Reading **HELP**DESK

Taking Notes: *Sequencing*

Complete a diagram like this one to identify the events that led to the fall of the Roman Republic. You may add more boxes if necessary.

[ ] → [ ] → [Republic Falls]

Content Vocabulary
- **latifundia**
- **triumvirate**

In addition, small farmers could not compete with wealthy Romans, who owned **latifundia** (la•tuh•FUHN•dee•uh), or large farming estates. Farmers could not even find jobs on these huge farms. Those jobs went to a new source of labor—the thousands of prisoners captured in the Roman wars. Wealthy landowners did not have to pay wages to enslaved workers. Instead, they bought more land for their latifundia. Small farms were pushed out of business.

As small farms shut down, thousands of poor unemployed people left the countryside. They poured into Rome's cities looking for jobs. Even in the cities, however, enslaved people did most of the work. Paying jobs were hard to find. If free people could find a paying job, it was generally for a low wage.

Desperate economic conditions created mounting anger among the poor. Roman leaders worried about a rebellion. To prevent a revolt, Roman leaders began offering cheap food and free entertainment to the poor. Numerous Roman rulers used this policy of "bread and circuses" to acquire or stay in power.

Roman Reformers

Not all wealthy Romans ignored the problems of the poor. Two government officials, who were also brothers, worked for reforms. Tiberius and Gaius Gracchus (GRA•kuhs) thought that Rome's problems were caused by the actions of wealthy landowners. The brothers wanted to stop the wealthy from taking over small farms to create their latifundia. They urged the Senate to take some land from the latifundia and return it to the poor.

Stone carvings such as this show that artists felt farming was an important topic to include. Oxen did the heavy work for farmers.

▶ CRITICAL THINKING
Analyzing How did the reforms of the Gracchus brothers affect Roman farmers?

latifundia large farming estates

LESSON 2 • Day 2 (cont.)

Discussion After the role-playing, have students share and discuss the feelings they might have experienced as patricians or plebeians. Create a two-column chart on the whiteboard. Label one column "Patricians" and the other "Plebeians." Write students' responses in the appropriate columns on the chart. *(Possible answers: Patricians—They feel threatened, concerned about losing control of the government, and worried that plebeians will try to take their land and wealth. They feel determined to maintain their higher status and power in society. Plebeians—They feel frustrated with their lack of rights, hopeful that a strike will work, and determined to seek an equal role in government to improve the lot of all plebeians.)*

BACKGROUND KNOWLEDGE

The Second Punic War

During the Second Punic War, Hannibal's army, traveling in the Alps, was far from Carthage and, thus, far from needed supplies and fresh troops. Hannibal wasn't worried, though. He was confident that he would find allies in Italy to join him in his fight against Rome.

The allies, however, remained loyal to Rome. Hannibal would need to acquire more supplies and troops from Carthage's territory in Spain. The Romans set about conquering Spain to cut off Hannibal. After conquering Spain, the Romans traveled to Carthage. Hannibal was forced to retreat from the Italian Peninsula to defend Carthage.

Answers for pages 318–319

P. 318 CRITICAL THINKING It was the first encounter between Carthaginian forces and the Roman army during the Second Punic War, and Hannibal's army won.

P. 319 ☑ PROGRESS CHECK Hannibal's forces tried to overpower the Roman army by marching through southern Gaul into Italy while riding on elephants.

LESSON 2 REVIEW

1. The veto prevented any one consul from becoming too powerful. Answers should demonstrate an understanding that the consuls were the heads of the government and that a veto means to reject the other's decision.
2. The plebeians went on strike from serving in the army and left Rome to create their own government. The patricians then allowed them to form the Council of Plebs and gave them the right to elect their own officials, become consuls, and pass laws.
3. Rome used its military power to fight the Punic Wars and eventually defeat Carthage and take control of the Mediterranean region.
4. The statement is a fact.
5. Answers will vary, but students should explain that Roman law emphasized the right of all free citizens to be treated equally under the law.

Teaching *The End of the Republic*

(Student Edition pp. 320–327)

LESSON 3 • Day 1

ENGAGE

Discussing Tell students that in this lesson they will be learning about an unstable period in Rome's history. During this time, Rome was in transition from a republic to an empire.

Ask:

What problems can cause the decline or instability of a government or a nation? Have students think about this question on their own for a few moments.

Then have them partner with a classmate to discuss it and write down their responses. Each pair can share their responses with the class. *(Possible responses: poverty, unemployment, corruption, crime, violence)*

Have students discuss examples of these problems that they are familiar with from world history and U.S. history and how these problems are affecting the country's stability today.

TEACH & ASSESS

1 Problems in the Republic

GUIDING QUESTION ***What factors led to the decline of the Roman Republic?***

Previewing Tell students that in this section, they will learn about the factors that led to the decline of the Roman Republic and its transition to an empire. Have students scan the headings and captions in this section.

Ask: Based on the headings and captions, what factors do you think led to the decline of the republic? *(poverty, class conflict, problems with the army, reform efforts)*

INTERACTIVE GRAPHIC ORGANIZER

Analyzing Discuss with students the factors that made life difficult for the plebeians. Show students the graphic organizer on poverty in Rome. Guide them in a discussion about why life became so hard for this particular group.

Speculating Tell students that martyrs are people who are so committed to a certain cause or belief that they are willing to suffer or die defending it.

Ask: In what ways do you think the Gracchus brothers suffered for trying to help the poor? *(Possible answers: They might have been hated and shunned by other senators and patricians.)*

LECTURE SLIDE **Identifying** Show students the lecture slide, which provides an overview of the challenges Marius faced as consul and how he solved them. Ask students to list on the interactive whiteboard the changes that Marius made to the Roman army. *(The army became a paid force; many jobless Romans joined the army; military generals grew powerful.)*

Evaluating Ask: Is it dangerous for military leaders to have political power? Why or why not? *(Possible response: It is dangerous because military leaders can use their troops to take power by force, which weakens the democracy.)*

Answers for pages 320–321

P. 320 Taking Notes Answer to graphic organizer: Marius elected consul → Creates professional army → Sulla becomes dictator → First Triumvirate rules Rome → Caesar takes power → Caesar is killed → Second Triumvirate fails → Octavian becomes emperor

P. 321 CRITICAL THINKING Some farmers neglected their land to fight in the wars; other farms were destroyed.

The Gracchus brothers tried to help the poor farmers who had lost their land to latifundia.

▶ CRITICAL THINKING

Analyzing What does the murder of these brothers tell us about the Roman government at this time?

The Senate was made up of wealthy Romans, some of whom owned the latifundia. They fought the Gracchus brothers' proposals. A group of senators even killed Tiberius in 133 B.C. Gaius was also murdered 12 years later. Dark days had fallen on the Roman Republic. The people charged with making and upholding the laws repeatedly broke them.

Roman Politics and the Army

The republic soon faced more challenges. Rome's military leaders began to seek political power. In 107 B.C., a general named Marius (MARE•ee•uhs) became consul. Marius, the son of a worker, was not a patrician. Marius believed that he could solve Rome's economic problems. He **transformed** the army in order to provide opportunities for the poor. Until then, only property owners served in the military. Marius, however, recruited soldiers from the landless poor. In return for their service, he paid them wages—and promised them land. The Roman army was no longer a force of citizen volunteers. It was now a force of **professional** soldiers.

The plan that Marius put into action provided work for many jobless, landless Romans. However, it also weakened the republican form of government. Soldiers felt more loyalty to the general who hired and paid them than to the republic. As a result, military generals grew enormously powerful. Some generals sought political office. This allowed them to pass laws that gave land to their soldiers—and increased their power.

The creation of a professional army led to new power struggles. Marius was soon opposed by another general, named Sulla (SUH•luh), who commanded his own army. In 82 B.C., Sulla drove his enemies out of Rome and named himself dictator. It marked the first time a Roman general had led his army into the capital.

Over the next three years, Sulla made changes to the government. He reduced the power of the tribunes and gave the senators more responsibilities. Sulla then stepped down as dictator. Sulla hoped that his reforms would restore the Roman Republic to its earlier days of glory. Instead, Rome plunged into conflict that lasted for the next 50 years. Some Romans took notice of how Sulla had used an army to achieve his goals. Those who were eager for power decided that they would do the same thing.

☑ PROGRESS CHECK

Analyzing What was the purpose of "bread and circuses"?

Reading HELPDESK

Academic Vocabulary

transform to change the structure of

professional relating to a type of job that usually requires training and practice

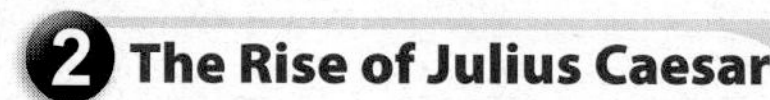

2 The Rise of Julius Caesar

GUIDING QUESTION *How did Julius Caesar rise to power in Rome?*

After Sulla left office, different Roman leaders fought among themselves for power. Many of them were military officials who relied on their loyal armies to support them. In 60 B.C., three men ruled the Roman Republic: Crassus, Pompey (PAHM•pee), and Julius Caesar (JOOL•yuhs SEE•zuhr). Crassus was a general and one of Rome's wealthiest men. Pompey and Caesar were also rich and known for their military accomplishments. These three men formed the First Triumvirate to rule Rome. A **triumvirate** (try•UHM•vuh•ruht) is a political group of three people who share equal power.

Julius Caesar made himself Rome's first dictator for life in 44 B.C. As dictator, Caesar was greatly admired by the poor for his reforms. But he was hated by his enemies for his ambition.

Caesar's Conquests

Each Triumvirate member commanded a military post in an outlying area of the Roman Republic. Pompey led in Spain, Crassus in Syria, and Caesar in Gaul. Gaul was made up mostly of what are now France and Belgium. While serving in Gaul, Caesar fought the Celts and invaded Britain. He won the admiration and support of the poorer classes. Roman senators grew uneasy with Caesar, however. They feared that he was becoming too popular and would seek power as Sulla had.

By 50 B.C., the First Triumvirate no longer existed. Crassus had died in battle, and Pompey emerged as Caesar's main rival. In 49 B.C., the Senate gave its support to Pompey. It ordered Caesar to give up his army and return to Rome. Caesar, however, refused. He knew that if he returned to Rome, he might be imprisoned or killed by his rivals. Caesar gathered his loyal troops and crossed the Rubicon (ROO•bih•KAHN) River.

triumvirate three rulers who share equal political power

Connections to **TODAY**

Crossing the Rubicon

Caesar crossed the Rubicon at great risk. Even today, the phrase "crossing the Rubicon" is used when a person makes a decision that cannot be undone.

Caesar crossed the Rubicon even though he knew it would lead to civil war.

▶ CRITICAL THINKING

Predicting What might have happened if Caesar had not decided to cross the Rubicon?

This small river separated Caesar's military command area from Roman Italy. According to legend, Caesar saw a vision that inspired him to cross the Rubicon. He exclaimed to his troops:

PRIMARY SOURCE

> "Even yet we may draw back; but once cross yon little bridge, and the whole issue is with the sword. . . . Take we the course which the signs of the gods and false dealing of our foes point out. The die is cast."
>
> —from *Life of Julius Caesar* by Suetonius

Caesar had refused to obey the Senate and was now marching on Rome. He realized that he was starting a **civil** war. His decision, however, could not be reversed.

Caesar and his soldiers swiftly captured all of Italy. They drove Pompey's forces out of the country. The fighting then spread eastward, with Caesar finally crushing Pompey's army in Greece in 48 B.C.

Reading HELPDESK

Academic Vocabulary

civil of or relating to citizens

Caesar Takes Power

In 44 B.C., Caesar took over the Roman government. He ended the practice of dictators serving in office for short terms by declaring himself dictator for life. To strengthen his power, Caesar appointed people to the Senate who supported him.

Meanwhile, Caesar introduced reforms that made him popular with Romans, especially the poor. He gave citizenship to many people living in Roman territories. He created jobs for the unemployed. In the countryside, he organized new settlements for landless laborers. He ordered landowners using slave labor to hire more free workers.

One of the most famous reforms that Caesar introduced was the creation of a new calendar. It had 12 months, 365 days, and a leap year. Known as the Julian calendar, it was used throughout Europe until A.D. 1582. Then it was changed slightly to become the Gregorian calendar. The Gregorian calendar is based on the date of the birth of Jesus. This calendar is still used by most countries in the world today.

Caesar developed the new calendar with the help of the astronomer Sosigenes (soh•SIHJ•ee•neez). It has movable pegs to allow for changing days.

Many Romans praised Caesar as a wise ruler because he brought peace and good government to Rome. Others, however, hated him. They believed that he wanted to be a king. Caesar's enemies, led by the senators Brutus and Cassius, plotted to kill him. In 44 B.C., Caesar's opponents gathered around him as he entered the Senate and stabbed him to death. Caesar was killed on March 15, also known as the "Ides of March" in the Julian calendar. His murder was made famous in the play *Julius Caesar*, by William Shakespeare. In the play, Caesar was warned to "Beware the Ides of March."

☑ PROGRESS CHECK

Explaining Why did some Romans oppose Caesar?

Build Vocabulary: *Words With Multiple Meanings*

plot: a secret plan

plot: (verb) to plan; to locate; to invent a story line

LESSON 3 • Day 1 (cont.)

GRAPHIC ORGANIZER **Determining Cause and Effect** Display the interactive graphic organizer about the cycle of Roman society. Ask a volunteer to read aloud the text. Students should draw on that text as they complete the cause-and-effect diagram. After students complete the diagram, ask a volunteer to summarize it.

CLOSE & REFLECT

Evaluating Remind students of the discussion you had at the opening of this lesson about problems that can cause instability in a government or a nation.

Have students identify ways a nation could reverse the problems they identified during that discussion. Write their suggestions on the interactive whiteboard. *(Possible answers: changing leadership, modifying laws, working to improve the economy)*

LESSON 3 • Day 2

ENGAGE

Previewing Write "Veni, vidi, vici" on the board. Tell students that it is a Latin phrase. Then write the English translation on the board: "I came, I saw, I conquered."

Ask students if they can guess who might have said this. If students have not already guessed, reveal that Julius Caesar was the speaker of the quotation.

TEACH & ASSESS

2 The Rise of Julius Caesar

GUIDING QUESTION *How did Julius Caesar rise to power in Rome?*

IMAGE **Analyzing** Show students the image of Caesar's life before he ruled Rome. Ask a volunteer to read the information aloud. Then challenge the class to think of adjectives that describe Caesar and his life. *(Students may suggest words such as* noble intellectual, physically fit, *and* ambitious.) Write students' responses on the whiteboard.

Ask:

What leadership qualities did Caesar possess? *(He was physically strong and intellectual. He had a strong drive to survive and succeed.)*

PRIMARY SOURCE **Making Decisions** Present Plutarch's description of Caesar crossing the Rubicon. Discuss the idiom "crossing the Rubicon," which refers to that event.

Ask:

What does this phrase mean? *(making a decision that cannot be undone)*

Discuss how people make important decisions—by weighing the risks and benefits of each choice. Explain that all decisions carry some risk because the outcome is unknown.

Challenge students to think of their own personal "Rubicon moments" and to share their thoughts with the class, if they want to. Alternately, have students think of other "Rubicon moments" in history, such as Alexander's decision to turn back from India or Moses's decision to lead the ancient Israelites from Egypt. Ask students to recall the risks and benefits of each decision. AL ELL

IMAGE **Analyzing** Present the interactive image of Julius Caesar and his assassination. Ask students for their reactions to the image. They should observe that Caesar is wearing red robes that match his spilled blood, while his attackers are dressed in white.

Challenge students to draw conclusions about the guilt and innocence of the figures based on the use of color. Then ask a volunteer to read aloud the text accompanying the image. Finally, direct students to the Primary Source Activity for the lesson.

INTERACTIVE WORKSHEET

Primary Source Activity

Analyzing Primary Sources Ask volunteers to read aloud the monologues from Shakespeare's play. Help them with the more challenging vocabulary, including archaic terms, such as *thrice*.

Then lead the class in a discussion of whose argument is more convincing, that of Antony or that of Brutus. Have students complete the discussion questions as part of their homework.

Sequencing Work as a class to create a time line that spans from 60 B.C. to 27 B.C. Complete the time line with events that led Rome from a republic to an empire, beginning with the rise of Julius Caesar. Students may add to the time line after discussing the next section in their textbooks.

3 From Republic to Empire

GUIDING QUESTION *How did Rome become an empire?*

IMAGE **Making Inferences** Present the interactive images of Antony and Cleopatra. Ask volunteers to read aloud the captions and informative text on the slides. Invite students to share their observations and thoughts about the lives of two figures.

Ask:

Why do you think the Romans wanted to stop Antony and Cleopatra from ruling Rome? *(Possible response: Cleopatra was not a Roman, so they might have feared Egypt would take control of Rome.)*

PRIMARY SOURCE **Evaluating** Present Virgil's description of Octavian. Discuss with students the way Octavian voiced his support for the republic while taking steps to become emperor.

Ask:

Why didn't Octavian just declare himself emperor? *(By voicing support for the republic, Octavian was able to gain support of the Romans and the senators, who then agreed to name him emperor anyway.)*

Have students complete the Lesson 3 Review questions.

CLOSE & REFLECT

Analyzing Have students discuss the pros and cons of Caesar's decision to cross the Rubicon. Create a two-column chart on the interactive whiteboard to record students' responses. *(Possible responses: Pros to crossing Rubicon: chance to rule Rome, chance to achieve goals for Rome. Cons to crossing: risk being killed or imprisoned. Pros to turning back: chance to maintain position he had and remain safe. Cons to turning back: his enemies already knew his goals, so they might kill him anyway; he would be giving up his chance to rule Rome.)*

After students share their responses, challenge them to draw a conclusion about whether Caesar was right to cross the Rubicon and take Rome. AL

Answers for pages 322–325

P. 322 CRITICAL THINKING Senators broke the law in order to silence someone they disagreed with.

P. 322 ☑ PROGRESS CHECK They provided bread (food) and circuses (entertainment) to the urban poor to win their support and prevent a rebellion.

P. 324 CRITICAL THINKING If Caesar had not crossed the Rubicon, he might not have become Rome's leader.

P. 325 ☑ PROGRESS CHECK They thought he had become too powerful and that he wanted to be king.

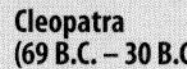

Mark Antony
(83 B.C. – 30 B.C.)

Mark Antony, a Roman, supported Caesar during the civil war between Caesar and Pompey. Antony was known as a wise politician. He was also a talented orator, meaning he was an effective public speaker. Antony was married twice before he fell in love with the Egyptian queen Cleopatra. He first met her around 40 B.C., when he accused her of assisting his enemies. Soon after, they formed a romantic and military partnership that lasted until their famous deaths.

Cleopatra
(69 B.C. – 30 B.C.)

Cleopatra was the daughter of an Egyptian king. When her father died in 51 B.C., Cleopatra took the throne with her brother. They soon became rivals. To hold onto the throne, Cleopatra formed an alliance with Julius Caesar. After Caesar died, Cleopatra allied herself with Mark Antony. When they fled to Egypt, Antony, it is said, heard a false report that Cleopatra had died. Deeply saddened, he killed himself. After Cleopatra buried him, she then took her own life.

▶ CRITICAL THINKING
Explaining Why did Mark Antony and Octavian first join forces? Why did Mark Antony and Octavian become divided?

3 From Republic to Empire

GUIDING QUESTION *How did Rome become an empire?*

After Caesar's death, civil war broke out. Caesar's 18-year-old grandnephew Octavian (ahk•TAY•vee•uhn) joined two of Caesar's top generals, Mark Antony (AN•tuh•nee) and Marcus Lepidus (LEH•puh•duhs). The three leaders' forces defeated those who killed Caesar. In 43 B.C., they formed the Second Triumvirate. Next, they divided the Roman Empire among themselves. Octavian took command of Italy and the west. Antony ruled in Greece and the east. Lepidus took charge in North Africa.

Antony and Cleopatra

The Second Triumvirate, however, did not last long. Lepidus retired from politics. Soon Octavian and Antony became rivals. Antony fell in love with the Egyptian queen Cleopatra. Together, they formed an alliance. Octavian accused Antony and Cleopatra of plotting against Rome. According to Octavian, Antony planned to make himself the sole ruler of the republic with Cleopatra's help. Many Romans grew alarmed at this news. Their support **enabled** Octavian to declare war on Antony.

In 31 B.C., Octavian and Antony's navies clashed off the coast of Greece. At the Battle of Actium (AK•shee•uhm), Octavian's forces defeated those of Antony and Cleopatra. Within a year, Octavian captured Alexandria and made Egypt Roman territory. Antony and Cleopatra killed themselves to avoid being captured by Octavian. Octavian became the supreme ruler of Rome. The civil wars had ended and so, too, did the Roman Republic.

Reading HELPDESK

Academic Vocabulary
enable to make possible

Octavian—a New Direction

Octavian could have made himself a life-long dictator. However, he knew that many Romans favored a republic. These Romans were influenced by Cicero (SIH•suh•ROH) who was a well-known political leader and writer in Rome. Cicero strongly supported the representative, republican government. Cicero also did not trust dictators.

Throughout Rome's civil wars, Cicero had argued that a representative government should be restored to Rome. He died before Octavian rose to power. Cicero's ideas, however, would influence the writers of the United States Constitution centuries later.

Publicly, Octavian voiced his support for a republic. Privately, however, Octavian felt differently. He believed that a republican government was too weak to solve Rome's problems. Octavian felt that Rome needed a strong leader. With a strong and loyal army supporting Octavian, the Senate consented to his wishes. It declared Octavian consul, tribune, and commander-in-chief for life in 27 B.C. Octavian, however, took the title *Augustus* (aw•GUHS•tuhs), or "the majestic one." Caesar Augustus, as Octavian was now called, became Rome's first emperor, or all-powerful ruler.

Octavian overcame many obstacles to become emperor of Rome.

▶ CRITICAL THINKING
Analyzing How did Octavian's leadership differ from Caesar's?

☑ PROGRESS CHECK

Predicting How do you think Cicero might have reacted when the Senate named Octavian the first emperor of Rome?

LESSON 3 REVIEW

Review Vocabulary

1. Why did the creation of *latifundia* cause poor people to move to cities?

Answer the Guiding Questions

2. ***Understanding Cause and Effect*** How did the election of Marius as consul reflect a change in Rome's government?
3. ***Summarizing*** What changes did Julius Caesar bring about as ruler of Rome?
4. ***Explaining*** How did Octavian's rule serve as a transition from Roman republic to empire?
5. ***Identifying*** Who was Caesar Augustus?
6. **PERSONAL WRITING** You own a small Roman farm in the 100s B.C. Write a letter to a friend describing the changes you have witnessed in agriculture and the Roman government. Describe how those changes have affected you personally.

networks
There's More Online!
☑ **GRAPHIC ORGANIZER** Achievements of Emperor Augustus
☑ **SLIDE SHOW**
• Mt. Vesuvius and Pompeii
• Roman Architecture

Lesson 4

Rome Builds an Empire

ESSENTIAL QUESTION *What are the characteristics of a leader?*

IT MATTERS BECAUSE
The achievements of the Roman Empire influenced the Western world for centuries and continued to affect the modern world today.

1 The Rule of Augustus

GUIDING QUESTION *How did Augustus create a new age of prosperity for Rome?*

The rule of Caesar Augustus (formerly called Octavian) marked the beginning of a new era. For nearly two hundred years, the Roman world enjoyed peace and prosperity. This time period lasted until about A.D. 180. It is known as the ***Pax Romana*** (PAHKS roh•MAH•nah), or "Roman Peace." During this time, Rome reached the height of its power.

What Reforms Did Augustus Make?

As emperor, Augustus was determined to protect the empire. To do this, he created a permanent professional army. About 150,000 soldiers—all Roman citizens—made up this powerful military force. In addition, Augustus created a special unit known as the Praetorian Guard. The 9,000 men in this select unit guarded the emperor.

Augustus thought that Rome's borders should be easier to defend. He established the empire's boundaries along natural physical features. These included the Rhine (RYN) River and Danube (DAN•yoob) River to the north, the Atlantic Ocean to the west, the Sahara to the south, and near the Euphrates River to the east. Troops were stationed along these frontier areas to protect the empire from invaders.

In addition to protecting the empire, Augustus wanted to display the power of Rome. Augustus had many public buildings, fountains, and palaces rebuilt to reflect the greatness of Rome. "I found Rome a city of brick," he boasted, "and left it a city of marble."

Augustus rebuilt many of Rome's buildings in marble to reflect the city's grandeur.

Augustus also worked to improve Rome's government. During his reign, more than 50 million people lived within the empire's borders. This is slightly fewer than the number of people living in Italy today. To maintain control over his empire, Augustus named an official called a **proconsul** (PROH•KAHN•suhl), or governor, to oversee each of Rome's provinces. These new local officials replaced the politicians who had been appointed by the Senate. Augustus himself often visited the provinces to **inspect** the work of the proconsuls.

With new leaders in place, Augustus changed the empire's tax system. Before Augustus, tax collectors paid the government for the right to collect taxes. Tax collectors could keep some of what they collected from the people. Many tax collectors, however, were dishonest and took too much from the people. To solve this problem, Augustus made tax collectors permanent government officials and paid them regular wages.

Augustus also changed Rome's legal system. He created a code of laws for people living in the provinces who were not Roman citizens. As time passed, most of these people became citizens, so eventually, the laws were applied to everyone. However, the legal system often favored the authority of the empire over individual citizens' rights.

Reading HELPDESK

Taking Notes: *Identifying*
Use a web diagram like this one to identify the important achievements of Emperor Augustus.

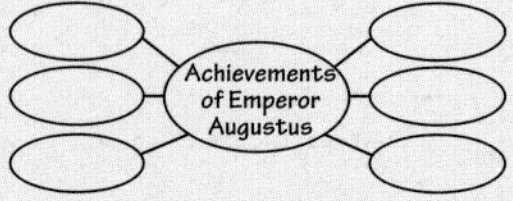

Content Vocabulary
• ***Pax Romana***
• **proconsul**

Pax Romana Roman peace
proconsul governor

Academic Vocabulary
inspect to look over carefully

LESSON 3 • Day 2 (cont.)

IF YOU HAVE MORE TIME . . .

Create a Family Tree and Discuss Memorials

Making Connections Point out to students that many of the leaders of Rome, starting with Caesar, were related in some way. Have students work in groups to create a graphic organizer that shows the relationships among the people who helped change Rome from a republic to an empire. Direct students to include short explanations of what each person did. BL

Discussing Explain that Quintilis, the month in which Julius Caesar was born, was renamed July in his honor while Caesar was still alive. Discuss with students what problems might occur when such a great honor is bestowed on a living figure. *(Students may suggest that it is different to judge a person's real importance while he or she is still alive and that passing years provide some perspective.)* Challenge students to think of contemporary examples of this problem. If students need guidance, ask them for their thoughts about erecting memorials for troops killed in recent wars.

BACKGROUND KNOWLEDGE

Bread and Circuses

The Roman circus referred to in the policy of "bread and circuses" was not like the circus of today. A Roman circus was a great arena that held spectators who came to see chariot races, footraces, and gladiator fights. In fact, the circuses were more like sports events.

Answers for pages 326–327

P. 326 CRITICAL THINKING They were supporters of Caesar and wanted to avenge his death. Octavian accused Antony of plotting to take over Rome with Cleopatra's help.

P. 327 CRITICAL THINKING Octavian did not support the Republic. He favorted one all-powerful ruler.

P. 327 ☑ PROGRESS CHECK He might have spoken out against the decision to make Octavian an emperor because he favored a republic, with elected leaders, rather than a dictatorship.

LESSON 3 REVIEW

1. *Latifundia* were large estates whose owners used slaves and would not hire farmers. As a result, farmers lost their land and moved to the city for work.
2. Marius was the first military general to become consul, which led to more military leaders seeking control of the government.
3. Caesar expanded citizenship and introduced reforms that helped the poor, but he also ended the republic by becoming Rome's first dictator for life.
4. Octavian's rule served as a transition because he came to power at the end of the republic, but then the Senate declared him commander-in-chief for life. In addition, Octavian took the title of emperor.
5. Caesar Augustus was the name Octavian took when he became Rome's first emperor.
6. Responses will vary. Letters should reflect the changes in farming and government described in the lesson.

LESSON 4

ENGAGE

Think-Pair-Share Ask students to choose the most important accomplishment they have learned about so far in this chapter and identify two reasons why the accomplishment is the most important one. Have students share their ideas in a Think-Pair-Share activity. Then, invite students to share their conclusions with the class.

Explain that in this lesson, students will learn about the events and accomplishments that marked the rule of Augustus.

TEACH & ASSESS

1 The Rule of Augustus

GUIDING QUESTION *How did Augustus create a new age of prosperity for Rome?*

Previewing Allow students time to preview the lesson, looking at the images, captions, and subheads. As they preview, they should formulate thoughts about the lesson.

Ask: Based on your preview, was Augustus's rule characterized by peace or more wars? *(peace)*

INTERACTIVE GRAPHIC ORGANIZER
Explaining Introduce the Taking Notes graphic organizer for the lesson. Lead a discussion of the accomplishments of Augustus. Have students begin completing the organizer.

Ask: Why was Augustus considered a great leader? *(Students may suggest that he was a great leader because he took many steps to make Rome stronger and safer, and he did not abuse his power.)* AL ELL

Making Inferences Ask students to discuss the changes Augustus made to local government. *(He replaced the local politicians appointed by the Senate with proconsuls that he appointed.)*

Ask: How did the changes made by Augustus affect Rome's representative government? *(It weakened it because local officials were now appointed by a dictator instead of elected by the people.)* BL

SLIDE SHOW **Analyzing Visuals** Present the interactive slide show on the Roman Colosseum, the Roman Forum, and the Theater of Marcellus. Explain that these structures were public projects that were also architectural wonders of their time.

Ask students to brainstorm examples of other large structures that are considered wonders today. Then **ask:** How did these buildings serve the people of Rome? *(The theater held performances and displayed art and sculptures. The Forum was a center of Roman government. The Colosseum was a massive stadium that hosted contests for the public's entertainment.)* Make sure students understand that the buildings were not only prized for their functionality but also for their grandeur. They made Rome look like a sophisticated and wealthy place.

Contrasting Have students discuss the section "Emperors After Augustus."

Ask: How did Caligula and Nero differ from Tiberius and Claudius? *(Caligula and Nero were cruel rulers; Tiberius and Claudius ruled effectively.)*

Answers for pages 328–329

P. 328 Taking Notes created permanent professional army; established defendable boundaries; built many public buildings and palaces; established proconsuls; reformed tax system; reformed legal system

THEN

Natural disasters can shape people's interactions with their environment. In August A.D. 79 the volcano Mt. Vesuvius erupted and destroyed the city of Pompeii, in what is now Italy. Several thousand people escaped, while thousands more died. Today, about 600,000 people live near the volcano, although scientists warn it may be due to erupt again soon.

NOW

▶ CRITICAL THINKING
Analyzing Why might people live in an area where a natural disaster has happened?

Despite all of his reforms, Augustus feared that people might still be unhappy with his leadership. To preserve his rule and the empire, Augustus imported grain from Africa and **distributed** it to the poor. Augustus believed that a well-fed population would be less likely to revolt against him.

Emperors After Augustus

Augustus ruled Rome for almost 40 years. After Augustus died in A.D. 14, his adopted son, Tiberius, became emperor. After Tiberius, three other emperors from Augustus's family ruled Rome—Caligula (kuh•LIH•gyuh•luh), Claudius, and Nero (NEE•roh). They are known as the Julio-Claudian emperors. Tiberius and Claudius governed the empire effectively. In **contrast**, Caligula and Nero proved to be cruel rulers.

Caligula murdered many people and spent money recklessly. He even appointed his favorite horse as consul. The Praetorian Guard murdered him and made Claudius emperor.

Nero was also a brutal emperor who killed many people. Among his victims were his mother and two wives. Nero committed suicide after the Senate had sentenced him to death for treason.

PROGRESS CHECK
Explaining How did Augustus protect Rome's borders?

2 The Roman Peace

GUIDING QUESTION *How did the Roman Empire become rich and prosperous?*

After Nero died, violence erupted throughout the Roman Empire. Then, in A.D. 69, a general named Vespasian (veh•SPAY•zhee•uhn), became emperor. Vespasian restored order, but he treated harshly anyone who opposed Roman rule. Vespasian crushed several uprisings throughout the empire. One such uprising was the Jewish revolt in the eastern province of Judaea. Vespasian's son, Titus, commanded troops that defeated the Jewish rebels. Roman soldiers also destroyed the Jewish temple in Jerusalem in A.D. 70.

Vespasian began the construction of the Colosseum, the huge amphitheater located in central Rome. After Vespasian died, his sons Titus and Domitian each governed Rome. While Titus was emperor, two disasters struck the empire. In A.D. 79, the volcano Mount Vesuvius erupted, destroying the city of Pompeii. A year later, a great fire badly damaged Rome. Both sons, however, ruled during an era of relative growth and prosperity.

Reading HELPDESK

Academic Vocabulary
distribute to give or deliver to members of a group
contrast the act of comparing by looking at differences

THE "GOOD EMPERORS" OF THE *PAX ROMANA*

Nerva
A.D. 96–A.D. 98
Revised taxes; land reforms helped the poor

Trajan
A.D. 98–A.D. 117
Greatly expanded the empire; gave money for education

Hadrian
A.D. 117–A.D. 138
Made Roman law easier to understand and apply

Antoninus Pius
A.D. 138–A.D. 161
Enacted laws that assisted orphans

Marcus Aurelius
A.D. 161–A.D. 180
Reformed Roman law; assisted in uniting empire's economy

INFOGRAPHIC

These emperors, who earned the title the Five Good Emperors, together ruled for almost 75 years.

1 IDENTIFYING Under which emperor did the empire grow significantly?

2 CRITICAL THINKING
Analyzing How would the contributions of Hadrian and Marcus Aurelius affect the empire's legal system?

Five Good Emperors

During the early A.D. 100s, several emperors who were not related to Augustus or Vespasian ruled the empire. Nerva, Trajan, Hadrian, Antoninus Pius, and Marcus Aurelius are known as the "good emperors." The five "good emperors" did not abuse their power. They were among the most **capable** rulers in Rome's history.

The five emperors governed during a time of economic growth. Agriculture and trade flourished during this period, which lasted from A.D. 96 to A.D. 180. Tertullian, a Roman writer, described this time:

PRIMARY SOURCE

> "All places are now accessible [easy to reach], all are well known, all open to commerce . . . cultivated fields have subdued [tamed] forests . . . marshes are drained; and where once were . . . solitary cottages, there are now large cities . . . everywhere are houses, and inhabitants, and settled government, and civilized life."
>
> —from *Treatise on the Soul* by Tertullian

The five emperors introduced programs to help the empire's people. For example, Trajan made money available so that poor children could receive an education. Hadrian made Roman laws easier for ordinary citizens to understand.

Academic Vocabulary
capable able, competent

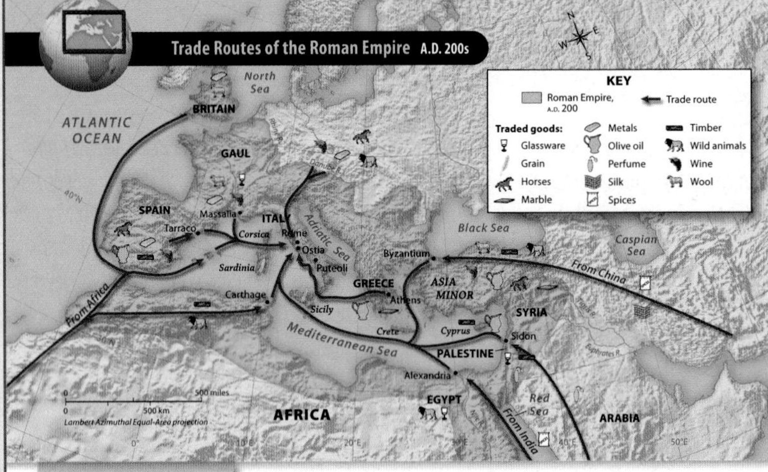

GEOGRAPHY CONNECTION

Trade goods flowed to Rome and kept the city well supplied.

1 PLACE Which areas of the empire shipped timber to Rome?

2 CRITICAL THINKING
Drawing Conclusions Why do you think Romans traded for horses and wild animals?

The five emperors also improved Roman cities. They spent tax money to build arches and monuments, bridges, roads, and harbors. They also built extensive **aqueducts** (A•kwuh•duhkts) to bring water from the country to the city.

A United Empire

The Emperor Trajan expanded the Roman Empire to its maximum size. The empire's borders extended to Britain in the northwest and Mesopotamia in the east.

Trajan's **successors** believed that the empire had become too large to rule effectively. They withdrew Roman forces from regions they could not defend and reinforced areas that were easier to protect. Hadrian pulled troops from Mesopotamia but strengthened defenses at the Rhine and Danube rivers.

By the A.D. 100s, the Roman Empire was one of the largest empires in history. Its land area was about 3.5 million square miles (9.1 million square km), almost the size of the United States.

Reading HELPDESK

Academic Vocabulary
successor one that comes after

Visual Vocabulary
aqueduct a human-made channel that carries water long distances

Many groups of people lived in the Roman Empire. Roman law, Roman rule, and a shared Roman identity united them all. By A.D. 212, every free person within the empire was considered a Roman citizen. All citizens were treated equally under Roman laws.

The Empire's Economy

Agriculture remained the most important economic activity in the Roman Empire. Most people were farmers. Farmers in northern Italy and in the provinces of Gaul and Spain grew grapes and olives to make wine and olive oil. Grain from Britain, Sicily, and Egypt supplied Rome's people with food.

Industry thrived in the cities. Potters, weavers, and jewelers produced pottery, cloth, and jewelry. Other artisans made glass, bronze, and brass. These goods were exported throughout the Mediterranean region.

Trade flourished. By A.D. 100, a common Roman system of money was used within the empire. Merchants used the same money in Gaul, Greece, or Egypt as they did in Rome. People also used a standard system of weights and measurements.

A network of paved roads extended throughout the empire. The roads allowed the Romans to communicate and move armies and goods easily. The Roman navy eliminated piracy on the Mediterranean Sea and other waterways. As a result, goods could be shipped safely to and from the empire's ports.

Traders from all over the empire arrived in Rome's port cities. Traders sold luxury goods to wealthy Romans. The Romans also imported raw materials, such as British tin and Spanish silver and lead. Roman workshops turned them into different goods.

Trade made many people wealthy. The wealth, however, did not extend to all Romans. Most city dwellers and farmers remained poor, and many other people remained enslaved.

PROGRESS CHECK
Analyzing Why were five of Rome's rulers known as the "good emperors"?

LESSON 4 REVIEW

Review Vocabulary

1. What was the role of a *proconsul* under Augustus?

Answer the Guiding Questions

2. *Explaining* How did the changes that Augustus made to the Roman tax system reduce government corruption?
3. *Analyzing* How did roads contribute to the empire's success?
4. *Drawing Conclusions* What do you think was the greatest achievement of Augustus?
5. **EXPOSITORY WRITING** You are a Roman living around A.D. 215. Write an essay about how the Roman Empire has changed since the reign of Trajan. As an ordinary citizen, which change affects you most?

LESSON 4 (cont.)

The Roman Peace

GUIDING QUESTION *How did the Roman Empire become rich and prosperous?*

SLIDE SHOW **Discussing** Present the images of Pompeii and Mount Vesuvius. After a volunteer reads aloud the informational text to the class, ask students for their reactions to the images. Allow students time to answer the discussion question on the last slide.

SLIDE SHOW **Listing** Show the interactive slide show about the Five Good Emperors. Have students identify the accomplishments of each emperor. Then, have students discuss this question:

Which of these five emperors do you think did the most for Rome? Provide examples to support your opinion. *(Sample response: I think Hadrian did the most for Rome. He strengthened Rome's borders and kept the empire safe from invaders.)*

Next, ask for volunteers to read their responses to the class. Allow students to discuss any differences in their opinions. Then ask students if they have changed their opinions as a result of listening to others present their responses. AL

IMAGE **Discussing** Present the interactive image of an aqueduct. After a volunteer reads aloud the text, discuss the technical achievement of building the massive aqueduct. Students should understand that building the structure required excellent engineering skills as well as the efforts of many people.

Ask:

Why was the aqueduct system important to Rome? *(It provided the city with water.)*

Ask:

How would Rome have been different without the aqueduct system? *(Rome would not have been such an efficient city because people would have had to spend a lot of time finding and carrying water instead of focusing on business, politics, or the arts.)*

INTERACTIVE WORKSHEET

Geography and History Activity

Identifying Introduce the Geography and History Activity about the Roman road system. Discuss with students how having a good road system, like the aqueducts, helped Rome prosper and thrive. If time allows, ask a volunteer to read aloud the text about Roman roads. Make sure students understand the language and can articulate the main idea—that Roman roads helped the empire expand and prosper. Assign the worksheet questions for homework.

LECTURE SLIDE **Evaluating** Show students the lecture slide for the lesson, which identifies the Roman emperors from Augustus through Marcus Aurelius.

Have students work in pairs to create a time line or other graphic organizer that illustrates what different Roman leaders did that affected Rome's prosperity and wealth—for better or for worse—from the decline of the republic through the *Pax Romana*.

Students should note significant changes and events related to Rome's economy. When they are finished, have each pair share its graphic organizer with the class. *(Student responses should include: Augustus—helped; funded building projects, improved tax system, fed poor. Caligula—hurt; spent money recklessly. Vespasian—helped; restored order, constructed Colosseum; Titus and Domitian—helped; maintained prosperity despite disasters in Pompeii and Rome; Five Good Emperors—helped; funded building projects and aqueducts, created common currency, improved road system)*

Have students complete the Lesson 4 Review.

CLOSE & REFLECT

Making Connections Have students identify similarities between the actions of the Roman emperors covered in this lesson and modern governments. *(Possible answers include the concept that both governments used or use tax money for building projects, for education, to improve roads, and so on.)*

Discuss how effective these actions were in creating or maintaining wealth, prosperity, and stability in the Roman Empire. Then, discuss how effective students think these actions are in modern times. BL

IF YOU HAVE MORE TIME . . .

Create Slogans for Augustus

Discussing Have students work in small groups to come up with slogans that Augustus could have used to promote his accomplishments throughout the land. Have students present their slogans to the rest of the class. Discuss how, even though he was dictator, Augustus still made efforts to keep the public's opinion of him favorable.

Research the "Good Emperors" of Rome

Explaining Organize students into five groups, and assign each group one of Rome's "Good Emperors"—Nerva, Trajan, Hadrian, Antoninus, or Marcus Aurelius. Tell the groups to research their assigned emperor and then prepare a short presentation that explains why the emperor was a good one. Students should divide tasks among members in their groups. Their presentations should include text and visuals, if possible. After all groups give their presentations, lead the class in a brief debate about which emperor was the greatest of the good ones.

BACKGROUND KNOWLEDGE

Romance Languages

Many European languages are called Romance languages, including Portuguese, Spanish, French, Italian, and Romanian. These languages are not called Romance languages because they sound romantic when spoken. They are considered Romance languages because they derive from Latin, the language of the Romans. Today more than 900 million people speak Romance languages.

Answers for pages 330–333

P. 330 ☑ PROGRESS CHECK He established them along natural boundaries and stationed troops along the borders to fight off invaders.

P. 330 CRITICAL THINKING Answers will vary but may include: jobs and family are nearby; the area is "home"; people might think the natural disaster will not happen again.

P. 331 INFOGRAPHIC

1. Trajan
2. CRITICAL THINKING Under Hadrian, more people would understand the law. Marcus Aurelius reformed the law.

P. 332 GEOGRAPHY CONNECTION

1. Spain, Africa, Cyprus, and Asia Minor shipped timber to Rome.
2. CRITICAL THINKING Horses and wild animals were probably not native to Rome. They had to be imported.

P. 333 ☑ PROGRESS CHECK They were known as the "good emperors" because they ruled competently and did not abuse their power.

LESSON 4 REVIEW

1. The proconsul acted as a governor over the provinces.
2. Augustus converted tax collectors into paid government employees.
3. Roads made trading, communication, and military movement easier.
4. Answers will vary. Sample answer: Augustus's greatest achievement was stabilizing the Roman government, which led to the formation of the Roman Empire.
5. Essays should mention that the empire began to shrink since the reign of Trajan, when it was at its maximum size. Roman forces withdrew from places they could not easily defend. Also, all free people were treated equally under Roman law. Students may suggest that legal reforms would have had the most impact on their lives as ordinary citizens. Because of these changes, a judge would have to treat ordinary citizens fairly, even though they were not wealthy or powerful.

CHAPTER 11 Activities

Write your answers on a separate piece of paper.

1 Exploring the Essential Question
PERSUASIVE WRITING Suppose you support the efforts of Tiberius and Gaius Gracchus to reform Rome. Write a letter or speech to other Romans that explains why reform is needed and what types of reforms should occur.

2 21st Century Skills
COLLABORATE WITH OTHERS Use the Internet and your local library to research the Twelve Tables of Rome. Work with your classmates to design a similar series of laws that are needed in society today. Record them, using modern language. How is your law code similar to and different from the Twelve Tables?

3 Thinking Like a Historian
PROBLEM SOLVING Roman leaders faced many problems and obstacles in expanding the empire and creating a peaceful society. Using a chart like this one, list some of the major problems they faced and how they solved these problems.

Problem	Solution

4 GEOGRAPHY ACTIVITY

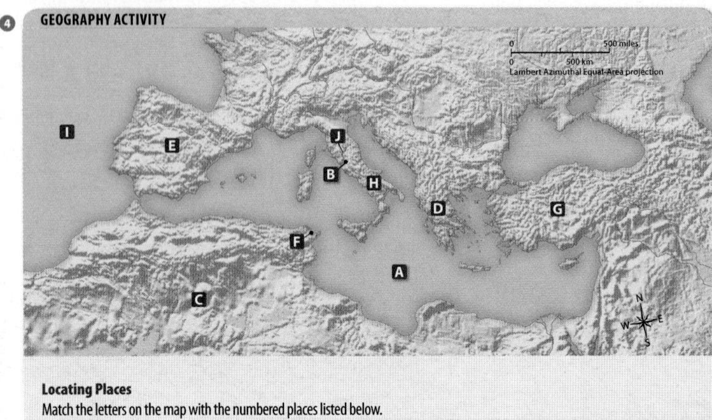

Locating Places
Match the letters on the map with the numbered places listed below.

1. Rome
2. Spain
3. Tiber River
4. Africa
5. Mediterranean Sea
6. Carthage
7. Asia Minor
8. Italy
9. Atlantic Ocean
10. Greece

CHAPTER 11 Assessment

REVIEW THE GUIDING QUESTIONS
Directions: Choose the best answer for each question.

1. Rome conquered Italy by
   A. modeling their army after the Greeks.
   B. treating everyone fairly.
   C. creating an alliance with the Etruscans.
   D. developing a flexible, strong army.

2. Early Rome was protected from pirate raids because
   F. it had a strong army.
   G. pirates were afraid of Romulus, the founder of Rome.
   H. it was located far enough from the Mediterranean Sea.
   I. there was no treasure in Rome.

3. Plebeians forced the patricians to treat them more equally by
   A. vetoing the law that did not allow plebeians and patricians to marry.
   B. refusing to serve in the army.
   C. electing more plebeians to the Senate.
   D. demanding that women be allowed to vote.

4. What was the body of laws that served as the foundation for all future Roman laws called?
   F. Twelve Tables
   G. Roman Constitution
   H. Law of Nations
   I. Rule of Law

5. Caesar took control of the republic by
   A. making peace with his rivals.
   B. starting a civil war with Pompey.
   C. winning support of the poor Romans.
   D. taking control of the Rubicon River.

6. During the *Pax Romana*
   F. textiles became the empire's most important industry.
   G. agriculture, industry, and trade flourished.
   H. the Empire decreased in power.
   I. Emperor Hadrian built the Colosseum.

CHAPTER 11 Assessment *(continued)*

DBQ DOCUMENT-BASED QUESTIONS

7. **Drawing Conclusions** Augustus wrote a historical document describing his accomplishments. This passage is about his military leadership:

   "About 500,000 Roman citizens were under military oath to me. Of these, when their terms of service were ended, I settled in colonies . . . and to all these I allotted lands or granted money as rewards for military service.

   " —Augustus, *Res Gestae*, from *Aspects of Western Civilization, Vol. I*

   Why would Roman citizens have wanted to serve in Augustus's army?
   A. for the opportunity to travel and see new places
   B. for the chance to show off Rome's military strength
   C. for the honor of serving under a great military leader
   D. for the benefits of land and money after serving

8. **Summarizing** How did rewarding retired soldiers benefit Augustus?
   F. It made the soldiers want to hurry through their time in service.
   G. It caused the soldiers to become ambitious and daring.
   H. It ensured the soldiers would always remain loyal to Augustus.
   I. It improved Augustus's reputation as a kind-hearted leader.

SHORT RESPONSE

The historian Plutarch wrote of Julius Caesar's leadership:

"He was so much master of the good-will and hearty service of his soldiers that those who in other expeditions [special trips] were but ordinary men displayed a courage past defeating ... when they went upon any danger where Caesar's glory was concerned. ... there was no danger to which he [a soldier] did not willingly expose himself, no labour from which he pleaded an exemption [asked to be excused]."

—from *Caesar* by Plutarch

9. How did Caesar's soldiers perform under his leadership?

10. What aspect of Caesar's leadership inspired his soldiers' actions?

EXTENDED RESPONSE

11. **Persuasive Writing** Who do you think was the greatest leader of Rome? Write a persuasive essay in support of your candidate.

Need Extra Help?

If You've Missed Question	1	2	3	4	5	6	7	8	9	10	11
Review Lesson	1	1	2	2	3	4	4	4	3	3	3, 4

NOTES

REFLECT, REVIEW, & REMEDIATE

INTERACTIVE WORKSHEET

Chapter Summary

Provide students with the Chapter Summary worksheet to help review the chapter and prepare for assessment.

Reviewing the Enduring Understandings

Review this chapter's Enduring Understandings with students:

- People, places, and ideas change over time.
- Conflict can lead to change.
- Leaders can bring about change in society.

INTERACTIVE WHITEBOARD On the interactive whiteboard, have students create a chain of events (sequence) graphic organizer. Ask for volunteers to write one key event in the organizer. Then, ask another volunteer to write the event that followed the previous event. Continue until you have reached the *Pax Romana*. *(Answers should be factually and chronologically correct based on the text.)*

ACTIVITIES ANSWERS

Exploring the Essential Question

1. Suggestions for reform will vary, but students should mention the plan of Tiberius and Gaius Gracchus to provide more land for farmers.

21st Century Skills

2. Students' laws should reflect modern times and situations. Students should compare and contrast their laws to the Twelve Tables, explaining similarities and differences.

Thinking Like a Historian

3. Answers may vary, but some examples might include:

Problem	Solution
Greek battle strategies too slow	Develop legions
Plebeians go on strike	Give them the right to pass laws
Carthage threatens Rome	Fight Punic Wars and defeat Carthage
Urban poor become desperate and angry	Use "bread and circuses" to maintain peace

Locating Places

4. **1.** B Rome, **2.** E Spain, **3.** J Tiber River, **4.** C Africa, **5.** A Mediterranean Sea, **6.** F Carthage, **7.** G Asia Minor, **8.** H Italy, **9.** I Atlantic Ocean, **10.** D Greece

ASSESSMENT ANSWERS

Review the Guiding Questions

1. **D** Rome developed a disciplined and loyal army. Romans also created more flexible battle strategies, which allowed them to fight more effectively and conquer more territory. Although the Romans treated conquered peoples fairly, they did not find success in modeling their army after the Greeks, and they did not form an alliance with the Etruscans.

2. **H** Rome's location along the Tiber River, about 15 miles from the Mediterranean Sea, helped protect it from pirate raids. Early Rome did not have a strong army, a scary founder, or a lack of treasure.

3. **B** It was the plebeians' strike against serving in the military that prompted the patricians to give them more equal rights under the law.

4. **F** The Twelve Tables were the original foundation of Roman Law. None of the other statements apply to the question.

5. **B** Caesar started and won a civil war with Pompey, which led to him becoming dictator for life. He crossed but did not control the Rubicon. He won the support of poor Romans after becoming dictator. He did not make peace with his rivals.

6. **G** It is true that during the *Pax Romana,* agriculture, industry, and trade flourished. None of the other statements are true about the *Pax Romana.*

Document-Based Questions

7. **D** It is clear from the quote that Augustus rewarded his soldiers well—with money and land—and that is why citizens wanted to serve in the Roman army.

8. **H** The most likely benefit to Augustus was troop loyalty.

Short Response

9. They were more courageous under Caesar's leadership than under the leadership of others.

10. Students' answers may vary but might include that Caesar's soldiers were inspired by their leader's bravery and the fact that he would not use his rank to get out of doing any type of work.

Extended Response

11. Responses will vary. Students should cite their chosen leader's accomplishments. They should use evidence from the text to explain why that leader was better than the other Roman leaders.

ONLINE RESOURCES

networks

There's More Online!

- INTERACTIVE WORKSHEETS
- BIOGRAPHIES
- CHARTS/GRAPHS
- GAMES
- GRAPHIC ORGANIZERS
- IMAGES
- MAPS
- PRIMARY SOURCES
- SLIDE SHOWS
- TIME LINE
- LECTURE SLIDES
- INTERACTIVE WHITEBOARD ACTIVITIES
- ASSESSMENTS
- VIDEOS

The Geography of Italy

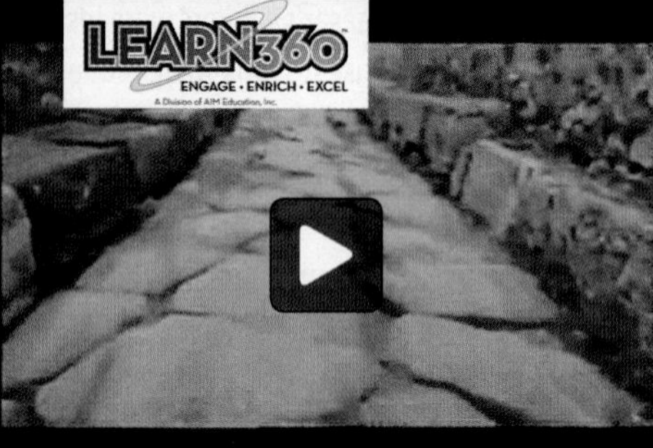

The Coliseum

Chapter 12

Roman Civilization

Dear World History Teacher,

The Roman Empire accomplished a remarkable series of achievements that were fundamental to modern Western civilization. The Romance languages of today are based on Latin. Roman legal ideas influenced Western practices of impartial justice and trial by jury. Roman monuments provided architectural models for public buildings in the West for hundreds of years. Roman aqueducts and roads are still used today.

Crises in the third century and the rise of Christianity gradually brought a transformation of the Roman Empire in the fourth and fifth centuries. Diocletian and Constantine had restored an aura of stability in the late empire. Both rulers tried to bring about reforms. Constantine even moved the capital from Rome to the Greek city of Byzantium in the east in an attempt to save the empire.

The efforts of these emperors, however, proved to be in vain as the empire continued to decline. With fewer resources and little desire to resolve problems, the government was unable to defend itself against the Germanic groups that moved into the western region of the empire. In A.D. 476, the last Western emperor was deposed.

As the western part of the Roman Empire disintegrated, the Eastern Roman Empire, also known as the Byzantine Empire, flourished.

Jackson J. Spielvogel

More Media Resources

Current Events Online

Visit McGraw-Hill's current events Web site for high-interest news stories and activities for your students. Access the site through the Student or Teacher Center in **networks.**

Reading List

Grade 6 reading level:
Pompeii: Lost and Found, by Mary Pope Osborne

Grade 7 reading level:
What Do We Know About the Romans? by Mike Corbishley

Grade 8 reading level:
Bodies From the Ash: Life and Death in Ancient Pompeii, by James M. Deem

At the MOVIES

Watch clips of popular culture films about Ancient Rome, such as *Ben-Hur*.

Discuss: **Can fictional movies capture historically accurate events?**

NOTE: Be sure to preview any clips to ensure they are age-appropriate.

Search for more videos online in the **networks** Resource Library.

CHAPTER 12 Planner

UNDERSTANDING BY DESIGN®

Enduring Understandings

- *People, places, and ideas change over time.*

Essential Questions

- *What makes a culture unique?* • *Why do civilizations rise and fall?*
- *How does geography influence the way people live?*

Students will know:

- *how the Greeks influenced Roman religion, science, art, architecture, and literature*
- *the reasons for the decline of the Roman Empire*
- *why the Byzantine Empire became powerful*

Students will be able to:

- **compare and contrast** information about Roman women and women today
- **identify and organize** information about what it was like in Rome
- **analyze** a primary source document about the Oppian Law
- **analyze and compare** photographs about the ways the Greeks influenced the Romans
- **identify and evaluate** Rome's contributions to our society today
- **make predictions** about why an empire might collapse
- **analyze** photos in the textbook to predict factors for the fall of the Roman Empire
- **draw conclusions** about the success of Diocletian's reforms
- **analyze** how the economy influenced the fall of the Roman Empire
- **identify** points of view in Roman society
- **make connections** with trading cities in the United States today and Rome
- **analyze** a map of the Byzantine Empire's trade routes
- **explain** why Justinian was a successful ruler
- **compare and contrast** information about Justinian and today's rulers

Predictable Misunderstandings

Students may think:

- All Romans were gladiators.
- The Roman Empire collapsed because it was invaded.
- Only one empire had its capital in Rome.

Assessment Evidence

Performance Task

- Hands-On Chapter Project

Other Evidence

- Economics of History Activity
- Geography and History Activity
- Primary Source Activity
- Responses to Interactive Whiteboard Activities
- Interactive Graphic Organizers
- Interactive Self-Check Quizzes
- The World's Literature questions
- Graphic Organizer Activities
- What Do You Think? questions
- Written paragraphs
- Lesson Reviews
- Participation in class discussions

Pacing Guide

Introducing the Chapter		1 day
Lesson 1	The Roman Way of Life	2 days
	The World's Literature	1 day
Lesson 2	Rome's Decline	2 days
	What Do You Think?	1 day
Lesson 3	The Byzantine Empire	2 days
Chapter Activities and Assessment		1 day
TOTAL TIME		**10 Days**

Differentiated Instruction

These lesson plans are written to address the needs of your On Level students. Discussion and activities that are well-suited to your Approaching Grade Level learners, Beyond Grade Level learners, as well as your English Language Learners are coded as follows:

AL **Approaching Grade Level**

BL **Beyond Grade Level**

ELL **English Language Learner**

NCSS Standards covered in "Roman Civilization"

Learners will understand:

1 CULTURE

3. How culture influences the ways in which human groups solve the problems of daily living

4. That the beliefs, values, and behaviors of a culture form an integrated system that helps shape the activities and ways of life that define a culture

5. How individuals learn the elements of their culture through interactions with others, and how individuals learn of other cultures through communication and study

6. That culture may change in response to changing needs, concerns, social, political, and geographic conditions

2 TIME, CONTINUITY, AND CHANGE

6. The origins and influences of social, cultural, political, and economic systems

7. The contributions of key persons, groups, and events from the past and their influence on the present

6 POWER, AUTHORITY, AND GOVERNANCE

2. Fundamental ideas that are the foundation of American constitutional democracy (including those of the U.S. Constitution, popular sovereignty, the rule of law, separation of powers, checks and balances, minority rights, the separation of church and state, and Federalism)

5. The ways in which governments meet the needs and wants of citizens, manage conflict, and establish order and society

CHAPTER 12

Introducing the Chapter

(Student Edition p. 337)

The Story Matters . . .

Read "The Story Matters . . ." aloud in class or ask a volunteer to read it aloud.

Ask:

Why was "thanking 'the God of the Christians' for his victory" a significant thing for Constantine to do? *(As emperor, he showed support for the Christians. Also, Christians were still persecuted in Rome, so he risked persecution himself.)*

Remind the class that the mosaic depiction of Constantine honors him and is symbolic of some of his accomplishments.

Tell the class that Constantine did many things to help the Roman Empire survive during a time of great trouble. In fact, he is also called "Constantine the Great."

The things Constantine accomplished were important to the survival of the Roman Empire, and they still influence our lives today. If students look online, they will find that a great deal has been written about him.

Roman Civilization

50 B.C. to A.D. 600

ESSENTIAL QUESTIONS • *What makes a culture unique?* • *Why do civilizations rise and fall?* • *How does geography influence the way people live?*

networks *There's More Online* about the lives and customs of the ancient Romans.

CHAPTER 12

Lesson 1 *The Roman Way of Life*

Lesson 2 *Rome's Decline*

Lesson 3 *The Byzantine Empire*

The Story Matters . . .

When Constantine defeated his brother-in-law in battle, he became emperor of the Western Roman Empire. At that time, Christians were persecuted in Rome, but Constantine thanked "the God of the Christians" for his victory.

This mosaic shows more than just how Constantine looked. The crown on his head represents his power. This reminds us that Constantine granted religious freedom to Christians and made it possible for Christianity to become widespread in the Roman Empire.

Constantine's influence was so great that 10 other Roman emperors were named after him.

◄ *This mosaic depicts Emperor Constantine I. Mosaics like this one can be seen covering the inside walls of Hagia Sophia, a mosque in the present-day city of Istanbul.*

337

Introducing Place and Time

(Student Edition pp. 338–339)

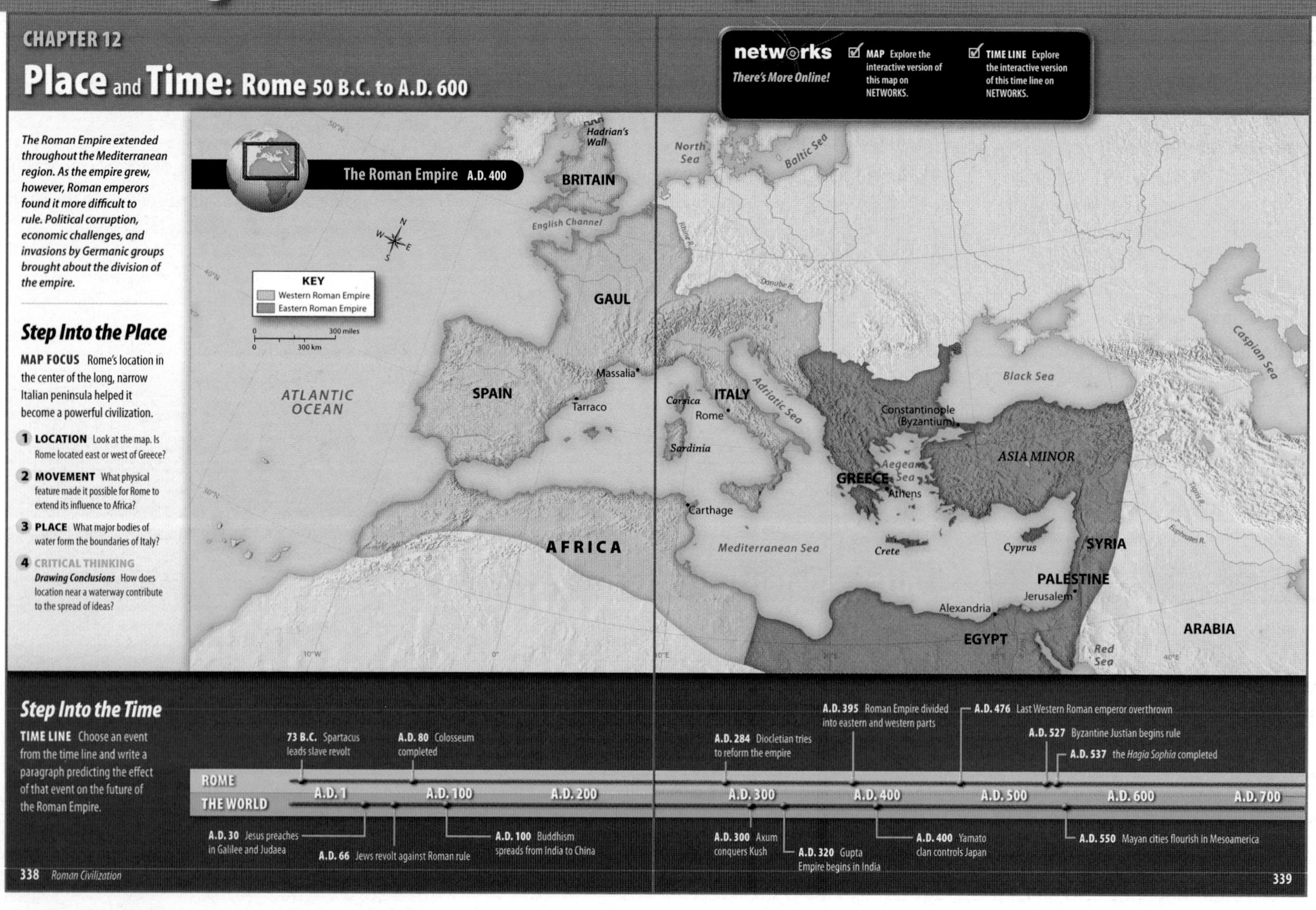

CHAPTER 12

Place and Time: Rome 50 B.C. to A.D. 600

The Roman Empire extended throughout the Mediterranean region. As the empire grew, however, Roman emperors found it more difficult to rule. Political corruption, economic challenges, and invasions by Germanic groups brought about the division of the empire.

Step Into the Place

MAP FOCUS Rome's location in the center of the long, narrow Italian peninsula helped it become a powerful civilization.

1. **LOCATION** Look at the map. Is Rome located east or west of Greece?
2. **MOVEMENT** What physical feature made it possible for Rome to extend its influence to Africa?
3. **PLACE** What major bodies of water form the boundaries of Italy?
4. **CRITICAL THINKING** *Drawing Conclusions* How does location near a waterway contribute to the spread of ideas?

networks *There's More Online!* ☑ **MAP** Explore the interactive version of this map on NETWORKS. ☑ **TIME LINE** Explore the interactive version of this time line on NETWORKS.

Step Into the Time

TIME LINE Choose an event from the time line and write a paragraph predicting the effect of that event on the future of the Roman Empire.

338 *Roman Civilization*

339

Technology Extension

- Find an additional activity online that incorporates technology for this project.
- Visit the EdTechTeacher Web sites (included in the Technology Extension for this chapter) for more links, tutorials, and other resources.

Assessing Background Knowledge

INTERACTIVE WORKSHEET

What Do You Know? Activity

Have students complete the What Do You Know? matching game about Roman civilization before they study the chapter. Direct students to cut out the cards and match each term to its definition. Tell students the cards review terms and ideas from the previous chapter about Rome. You may choose to have students work in pairs.

Once students have matched the cards, review with them the correct answers. Then have students mix up and match the cards again.

INTERACTIVE WORKSHEET

Guided Reading Activities

There is a Guided Reading Activity for each lesson in this chapter. You may wish to assign the Guided Reading Activity for Lesson 1 after introducing the chapter content.

Hands-On Chapter Project

Students will create a museum exhibit displaying information about an aspect of Roman culture.

- Students will begin by participating in a class discussion about the different features that help define a culture.
- Next, students will divide into small groups. Using worksheets and discussions as guides, each group will create a plan for their exhibit.
- Then, each group will research and create an exhibit on its chosen cultural subject.
- Students will share their exhibits with the rest of the class.
- Finally, students will evaluate their research, exhibit presentation, and collaboration using an Assessment Rubric.

Visit **networks** online to see the full project and rubric.

ONLINE RESOURCES

networks

Assign these interactive worksheets and quizzes from your Teacher Lesson Center. All resources are print-ready.

It's ALL Online!

Chapter 12 Resources

- ☑ Chapter Summary
- ☑ Vocabulary Builder
- ☑ What Do You Know?
- ☑ Hands-On Chapter Project

Lesson 1 Resources

- ☑ Interactive Graphic Organizer
- ☑ Primary Source Activity
  Women in Protest
- ☑ Guided Reading Activity
- ☑ Reading Essentials and Study Guide
- ☑ Online Self-Check Quiz

Lesson 2 Resources

- ☑ Interactive Graphic Organizer
- ☑ Economics of History Activity
  Inflation and the Fall of the Roman Empire
- ☑ Guided Reading Activity
- ☑ Reading Essentials and Study Guide
- ☑ Online Self-Check Quiz

Lesson 3 Resources

- ☑ Interactive Graphic Organizer
- ☑ Geography and History Activity
  Understanding Location: Constantinople
- ☑ Guided Reading Activity
- ☑ Reading Essentials and Study Guide
- ☑ Online Self-Check Quiz

Assessment Resources

- ☑ Lesson Reviews
- ☑ Online Self-Check Quizzes
- ☑ Chapter Activities and Assessment
- ☑ Standardized Test Practice

Remediation Resources

- ☑ Reading Essentials and Study Guide
- ☑ Guided Reading Activities
- ☑ Online Self-Check Quizzes
- ☑ Chapter Summary

Step Into the Place

Location Project the Interactive World Atlas map of Europe, Asia, and North Africa on the whiteboard. Invite volunteers to point out the locations of civilizations they have already studied this year. *(Mesopotamia, Egypt, Israel, and Greece)* Discuss how the locations of these civilizations gave them opportunities for trade and access to the spread of ideas but also made them vulnerable to attack. Next, project the Chapter Opener map and point out the Italian peninsula and Rome. Explain that like some of the civilizations they studied earlier, Rome's location helped it become a powerful civilization. As a class, discuss the Map Focus questions.

Step Into the Time

Making Inferences Call students' attention to the time line for this chapter. Explain that between 73 B.C. and A.D. 550, Rome flourished but also faced difficult times.

Draw students' attention to the event "A.D. 476 Last Western Roman emperor overthrown" on the Rome time line.

Ask: How might other events on the Rome time line have helped cause this event? *(Sample answer: A slave revolt and the splitting of the empire might have helped weaken the empire, making it easier to take over.)*

Answers for pages 338–339

Step Into the Place

1. west
2. the Mediterranean Sea
3. the Mediterranean Sea and the Adriatic Sea
4. CRITICAL THINKING Sample answer: When people travel on a waterway to trade, they come into contact with other people and learn new ideas from one another.

Step Into the Time

Sample answer: The division of the Roman Empire in A.D. 395 will lead to the end of the Roman Empire because countries are stronger when they are united.

networks
There's More Online!
- GRAPHIC ORGANIZER The Greeks and the Romans
- SLIDE SHOW Roman Homes
- VIDEO

Lesson 1

The Roman Way of Life

ESSENTIAL QUESTION *What makes a culture unique?*

It Matters Because

The Romans have influenced our science, art, architecture, and literature.

1 Daily Life

GUIDING QUESTION *What was daily life like for the Romans?*

Many Romans lived in cities throughout the Roman Empire. Like cities and towns of today, Roman cities were centers for culture, business, and government. We know quite a lot about life in places like Rome and Pompeii from studying the archaeological ruins. Even though the Roman Empire was widespread, the heart of the empire was on the Italian Peninsula in the city of Rome.

The Empire's Chief City

Rome was one of the largest cities in the ancient world. By about A.D. 1, more than a million people lived there. People traveled to Rome from every part of the empire. Like many other Roman cities, Rome was carefully planned. It was laid out in a square with the main streets crossing at right angles.

The emperor lived in Rome in a splendid palace on the top of a hill. At the foot of the hill was the Forum (FOHR•uhm). This was a large open space that served as a marketplace and public square, much like the malls we visit today. In the Forum marketplace, Romans shopped for food and luxury items, played games, and chatted with their friends. Temples and other public buildings surrounded the Forum.

Reading HELPDESK

Taking Notes: *Identifying*

Use a table like the one here to list the ideas the Romans borrowed from the Greeks to create their own culture.

Greeks Ideas Borrowed by Romans

Greeks	Romans

Content Vocabulary
- **gladiator**
- **satire**
- **anatomy**
- **ode**
- **vault**

Like the emperor, wealthy Romans lived in large, comfortable houses on the city's hills. Their homes had marble walls, tiled floors, and running water. Houses were built around a courtyard called an atrium, which was open to the sky. The atrium often had a garden. Wealthy Romans also had homes called villas on large farms outside the city.

Romans who were less wealthy worked as shopkeepers or artisans. Most Romans, however, were poor. Many did not have jobs, while others performed unskilled labor, such as delivering goods. Poor Romans lived in crowded, noisy, dirty neighborhoods in wooden apartment buildings six or seven stories tall. These buildings often collapsed or caught fire. People tossed garbage into the streets, and thieves prowled the areas at night.

To gain the support of Rome's poor, political leaders offered "bread and circuses." On some days, teams of chariot racers competed in the Circus Maximus, an arena seating more than 150,000 people. On other days, crowds watched **gladiators** (GLA•dee•ay•tuhrz) fight each other to the death or battle wild animals in stadiums such as the Colosseum. Most gladiators were enslaved people, criminals, prisoners of war, or poor people. Romans admired the gladiators' skills and bravery.

INFOGRAPHIC

Many wealthy Romans lived in homes built around courtyards.

1. **IDENTIFYING** In which part of the home did Romans entertain guests?
2. **CRITICAL THINKING** ***Comparing and Contrasting*** How is a Roman home similar to homes in your neighborhood? How is it different?

ROMAN HOME

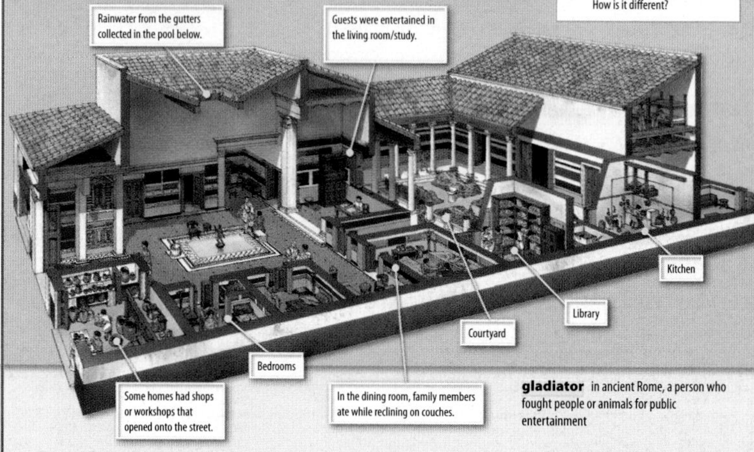
Rainwater from the gutters collected in the pool below.
Guests were entertained in the living room/study.
Kitchen
Library
Courtyard
Bedrooms
Some homes had shops or workshops that opened onto the street.
In the dining room, family members ate while reclining on couches.

gladiator in ancient Rome, a person who fought people or animals for public entertainment

Thinking Like a HISTORIAN

Researching on the Internet

Spartacus--a gladiator— has been portrayed as a hero in literature and in the movies. Use the Internet to find reliable sources about what his life was like and what he tried to accomplish. Identify three facts that you discover from your research and present them to the class. For more about using the Internet for research, read *What Does a Historian Do?*

The Roman Family

At the heart of Roman society was the family. When Rome was a republic, large families were common. Married children often lived in the same house with their parents and other relatives. The father closely watched over his wife and her activities. The law even allowed fathers to sell children into slavery or have them put to death. In later times, fathers lost some of this power, and wives gained some legal rights. Families had fewer children, and Romans were more likely to divorce and remarry.

Fathers in upper-class families were responsible for the education of their children. When they were young, wealthy boys and girls learned from private lessons at home. As they grew older, boys from wealthy families went to schools where they studied reading, writing, arithmetic, and rhetoric, or public speaking. Older girls continued to study at home. Poorer Romans could not afford to go to school, but some of them learned enough reading, writing, and arithmetic to help them conduct business.

At about the age of 15, a Roman boy celebrated becoming an adult. He would burn his toys as offerings to the household gods. Then he would put on a white toga, a loose-fitting robe that Roman men wore. Once he became an adult, a man might work at his family's business, join the army, or get a job in the government. Men tended to marry later, but women usually married around the age of 14. Once they married, Roman women were considered adults.

Upper-class Roman women were often educated and expected to teach their children about Roman culture.

▶ **CRITICAL THINKING**
Analyzing How were the roles of Roman men and women different?

What Was Life Like for Roman Women?

Women in early Rome were not full citizens and had few rights. They had a strong influence on their families, however, and often advised their husbands in private. When Rome was an empire, the wives of emperors began to exercise more power. For example, while the emperor Septimius fought rebels in distant parts of the empire, the empress Julia Domna **administered,** or was in charge of, political affairs in Rome.

The freedoms a Roman woman enjoyed depended on her husband's wealth and position. By the A.D. 100s, wealthy women had more independence.

Reading HELPDESK

Reading Strategy: *Summarizing*

When you summarize, you find the main idea of a passage and restate it in your own words. Read how the Romans treated enslaved people. On a separate sheet of paper, summarize the passage in one or two sentences.

Academic Vocabulary

administer to be lawfully in charge of
protect to defend from trouble or harm

They could own land, run businesses, and sell property. They managed the household while enslaved people did the housework. This left women free to study literature, art, and fashion. Outside the home, they could go to the theater or attend races and fights, but they had to sit in areas separate from men.

Women with less money had less freedom. They spent their time doing housework or helping their husbands in family-run shops. They were allowed to leave home to shop, visit friends, worship at temples, or go to the baths. A few women worked independently outside the home. Some served as priestesses, carrying out religious rituals in temples, while others worked as hairdressers and even doctors.

Rome and Slavery

Slavery was a part of Roman life from early times. The use of slave labor grew, however, as Rome acquired more territory. Roman soldiers took conquered peoples as prisoners. These captives were brought to Rome and sold into slavery. By 100 B.C., about 40 percent of the people in Italy were enslaved.

Enslaved people performed many different jobs. They worked in homes and harvested crops. They mined ore and helped build roads, bridges, and aqueducts throughout the empire. Many enslaved Greeks, though, were well educated. They served as teachers, doctors, and artisans.

For most enslaved people, life was miserable. They were often forced to work long hours and could be sold at any time. They were punished severely for poor work or for running away. To escape their hardships, enslaved people often rebelled.

In 73 B.C., a gladiator named Spartacus (SPAHR•tuh•kuhs) led a slave rebellion. As Spartacus and his forces moved through Italy, their numbers swelled to 70,000. Spartacus planned to reach the Alps. From there, the enslaved people could return to their homelands. The Roman army, however, crushed the revolt. Spartacus was killed in battle and 6,000 of his followers were crucified, or put to death by being nailed to a cross.

Religion and Philosophy

Romans believed that gods controlled all parts of life. Household spirits protected the home and family. Gods **protected** the entire empire. Greek gods and goddesses were given Roman names. For example, Zeus became Jupiter, the sky god, and Aphrodite became Venus, the goddess of love and beauty. Beginning with Augustus, emperors were officially made gods by the Roman Senate.

Romans worshipped their gods and goddesses by praying and offering food to them. Every Roman home included an altar for its household gods. At altars, the head of the family made offerings of incense, wine, honey, and the family meal.

BIOGRAPHY

Livia (58 B.C.–A.D. 29)

Livia Augustus, as she was later called, stood out among Roman women. As the wife of Caesar Augustus for 52 years, she was a symbol of Roman marriage and family. She was also seen as a model of Roman morality. When her grandson, Claudius, became emperor, she took the title of Augustus and held a position of high honor.

▶ **CRITICAL THINKING**
Making Inferences What does the honoring of Livia tell us about the beliefs of the Roman people?

LESSON 1 • Day 1

ENGAGE

Identifying As a class, brainstorm a list of responses that answer this question: What types of rights and freedoms do women in the United States have today?

Ask:

- **Are women allowed to vote?**
- **Can they serve in the military?**
- **Can they own property?**
- **Can they go to college?**
- **Can they pursue any career?**

(Sample answers: Yes; women can vote, serve in the military, own property, attend college, and pursue a wide variety of careers.) AL ELL

Tell students that they will be learning about what life was like in the Roman Empire, including what life was like for women. They will return to this list and compare and contrast the rights and freedoms of women in the United States today with those of Roman women.

TEACH & ASSESS

1 Daily Life

GUIDING QUESTION *What was daily life like for the Romans?*

INTERACTIVE WHITEBOARD ACTIVITY

Organizing Discuss as a class what type of graphic organizer would be best to summarize information about what it was like to live in Rome. You might suggest a multi-column chart or a web diagram. Draw an example of the diagram on the whiteboard.

Then, as a class, write categories in the graphic organizer so that students can list details about what life was like in Rome.

For example, categories might include Housing, Work, Neighborhoods, and Entertainment. Supporting details for Housing might describe how housing differed between the wealthy and the poor.

Guide students to help them identify the graphic organizer categories. Have them think about how they might categorize what their life is like to identify these categories.

Ask:

Think about your daily life. What do you have in common with the Romans? How could you organize this information into categories?

Then use the information in "Daily Life" to help students complete the graphic organizer. AL

INTERACTIVE WORKSHEET

Primary Source Activity

Evaluating Have students complete the Primary Source Activity "Women in Protest." As students read the primary sources that describe why some people supported and others rejected the need for the Oppian law, **ask:**

What were the women protesting? *(the continuation of the Oppian law)*

Was Cato for or against the law? *(for)*

Was Valerius for or against the law? *(against)*

As students read the opinions, have them look up in a dictionary any words they do not understand. Students should complete the questions at the end of the worksheet. Ask students to evaluate whether the information in the excerpts reflects the information in their textbooks about the status of women.

Explaining

Ask: How do you think the education of young people affects a civilization? *(Possible answer: Education might make a civilization more prosperous because young people would learn basic skills such as mathematics.)*

Tell students that in this section, they read about people who received an education in Rome.

Ask: How was the Roman family important to the education of young people during the time of the republic and Empire? *(Sample answer: The Roman family served as the means by which young people became educated.)*

Explain that not all Romans had the right to an education.

Ask: In Rome, who was most likely to get an education? *(Romans who came from wealthy families)*

INTERACTIVE WHITEBOARD ACTIVITY

Comparing and Contrasting Return to the rights and freedoms list that students created in the Engage activity. Point out that in early Rome, wealthy women had more freedoms than women with less money. Project the Interactive Whiteboard Activity for this lesson.

As students review "What Was Life Like for Roman Women?", have volunteers drag items from the Item Bank to the correct box on the interactive chart.

Next, have students circle the freedoms that women have today. *(Students may circle all items.)* AL ELL

Ask: What are some other rights and freedoms enjoyed by women in the United States today that Roman women did not have? *(Sample answers: voting, higher education, traveling where they choose)*

Explaining Have students consider the role of slavery in Roman culture.

Ask: How much of the Roman population was made up of enslaved people? *(By 100 B.C., it included about 40 percent of the population.)*

Where did enslaved people work? *(Enslaved people worked in homes, on farms, and in mines.)*

How do you think the dependence on slavery might have affected Rome's economy? *(Students might say that slavery had a negative effect on the birth of new businesses or industries because so many people were enslaved.)* BL

CLOSE & REFLECT

Summarizing To summarize, ask students to brainstorm a list of adjectives that describe life in the Roman Empire. Write their responses on the board. AL BL ELL

Answers for pages 340–343

P. 340 Taking Notes
Greeks: Statues were made to look perfect; bodies were young and healthy. Homer's *Odyssey* served as the basis for Roman literature ideas; Greeks identified themes to be used in plays.
Romans: Statues were more realistic; showed wrinkles, warts, and other less attractive features. Virgil took ideas from Greece's *Odyssey* to create the *Aeneid*; Horace used Greek ideas to create satires and odes.

P. 341 INFOGRAPHIC

1. Romans entertained guests in the living room/study.
2. CRITICAL THINKING Students should note similarities and differences between their homes and Roman homes. These similarities may include the use of a living room to entertain guests. The differences may include the absence of an attached shop and courtyard in modern homes.

P. 342 CRITICAL THINKING Men were the heads of the household, were responsible for their children's education, and ran the family's business. They could work outside the home and own property. Women had a strong influence on their families and often advised their husbands in private. They did housework or worked in the family business. Few women worked outside their homes.

P. 342 Reading Strategy Summaries should include the idea that enslaved people had hard lives but that they played an important role in Roman society.

P. 343 CRITICAL THINKING The honoring of Livia tells us that the Roman people respected women who were loyal to their families.

Government officials made offerings in temples where important gods and goddesses of Rome were honored. Temples were open to all people.

The Romans also adapted ideas from Greek **philosophy,** such as the philosophy of Stoicism. For the Greeks, Stoicism was about finding happiness through reason. Romans, however, believed Stoicism was about learning to live in a practical way. Stoic philosophers urged people to participate in public affairs, to do their civic duty, and to treat conquered peoples well.

As the empire grew, Romans came into **contact** with people who practiced different religions. Rome allowed these people to practice their religions if they did not threaten the government.

✓ PROGRESS CHECK

Explaining Why was the family important in Roman society?

2 Science and Art

GUIDING QUESTION *How did the Greeks influence Roman culture?*

As a republic and later as an empire, Rome was influenced by Greek civilization. The Romans admired and studied Greek art, architecture, and philosophy. They copied the Greeks in many ways but changed, or adapted, what they borrowed to match their own needs.

This urn is an example of the glass objects that were made and traded throughout the Roman Empire. Just as people recycle glass today, so did ancient Roman glass workers.

Science

The Romans learned from Greek science. A Greek doctor named Galen introduced many **medical** ideas to Rome. He emphasized the importance of **anatomy** (uh•NA•tuh•mee), the study of body structure. To learn about inner organs, Galen cut open dead animals and recorded his findings. Doctors in the Western world studied Galen's work for more than 1,500 years.

An important scientist of the Roman Empire was Ptolemy (TAH•luh•mee). Ptolemy lived in the city of Alexandria, in Egypt. He studied the sky and carefully mapped over 1,000 different stars. He studied the motion of planets and stars and created rules to explain their movements. Educated people in Europe accepted his ideas for centuries.

The Romans developed practical engineering skills. They built roads that connected Rome to every part of the empire. The first major Roman road, the Appian Way, linked Rome to southeastern Italy. The roads allowed Roman soldiers to travel quickly to different regions. Merchants used the roads, to trade their goods in different regions throughout the empire.

DEA/A.DAGLI ORTI/De Agostini Picture Library/Getty Images

Reading HELPDESK

anatomy the study of the body's structure

Academic Vocabulary

philosophy basic beliefs, concepts, and attitudes
contact communication or connection
medical relating to the practice of medicine

Roman engineers supplied cities with fresh water using aqueducts. They built aqueducts to bring water from the hills into the cities. Aqueducts were long troughs supported by rows of high **arches.** Aqueducts carried water over long distances. One Roman-built aqueduct in Segovia, Spain, is still used today—nearly 1,900 years after it was completed.

The Roman system of numbers, also called numerals, helped business people with their accounting. The system used letter-like symbols borrowed from the Greeks and the Etruscans. We still use Roman numerals to show dates on buildings, to create outlines, and to count items in a series, like Super Bowl games.

THEN

The Greeks and Romans used medical tools they designed themselves. Greek physicians passed medical knowledge to the Romans, who advanced it further. The Romans then passed medical techniques to the Western world that are still used today.

NOW

▶ CRITICAL THINKING

Making Connections What are some of the medical ideas the Romans learned from the Greeks? How are these ideas in use today?

Art and Architecture

The Romans also adopted many features of Greek art and architecture. Roman artists, however, developed their own styles. The Greeks made statues that showed perfect-looking people with beautiful bodies. Roman statues were more realistic and included wrinkles, warts, and other less attractive features.

Roman builders also introduced their own features to Greek ideas. They used arches in bridges, aqueducts, and buildings. Rows of arches were often built against one another to form a **vault,** or curved ceiling. Using this method, the Romans were able to create domes from many rings of shaped stone.

The Romans were the first people to master the use of concrete, a mixture of volcanic ash, lime, and water. When it dried, this mix was as hard as rock. The Romans used concrete, domes, and arches to build many different structures. One of the most famous Roman structures is the Colosseum, a huge arena completed about A.D. 80. Another example is the Pantheon (PAN•thee•AHN), a temple built to honor Rome's gods. The Pantheon's domed roof was the largest of its time. Today, it is one of the oldest undamaged buildings in the world.

Literature

Like the Greeks, Romans respected writers and philosophers. The Romans were also idealists searching for the meaning of life. Roman writers, however, went beyond the Greek myths and plays to create their own style. They honored their gods but also wrote comedies about them. The Romans praised military successes but also wrote about failures in battle.

vault a curved ceiling made of arches

Visual Vocabulary

arch a curved part of a structure that serves as a support

Roads of the Roman Empire A.D. 117

GEOGRAPHY CONNECTION

Before the Romans built a system of roads, much long-distance travel and trade was done by water. Roads reached areas that ships could not, so trade and travel improved.

1. **LOCATION** In relation to the rest of the empire, where is Rome located?
2. **CRITICAL THINKING** ***Drawing Conclusions*** Why were so many Roman roads built along waterways?

The Greeks presented inspirational plays ending with a moral. The Romans did the same but also added a touch of reality. Sometimes situations did not work out well for their characters. The Romans added a twist to their writing, revealing a more human side to people. They were not afraid to poke fun at the gods, political leaders, and heroes.

The Roman poet Virgil (VUHR•juhl) drew ideas from the *Odyssey*, an epic poem by a Greek writer named Homer. Virgil's epic poem, the *Aeneid* (uh•NEE•uhd), tells the story of the founding of Rome. In the *Aeneid*, Virgil expresses the values that he believed should guide Rome:

PRIMARY SOURCE

> ❝But you, remember, are to be a Roman. . . . Your task is to impose peace by law and order: to protect the downtrodden, and to crush the arrogant [very proud] in war.❞
>
> —from the *Aeneid*, Book VI. 1151–1154, by Virgil

Reading HELPDESK

satire verse or prose that pokes fun at human weaknesses

ode a lyric poem that expresses strong emotions about life

Using Greek models, the Roman poet Horace (HAWR•uhs) dow wrote **satires** (SA•tyrs). These works poked fun at human weaknesses, much like comedians do today. Horace also wrote **odes,** or poems that express strong emotions about life.

Inspired by the Greek historian Herodotus (hih•RAH•duh•tuhs), Livy and Tacitus (TA•suh•tuhs) wrote about Roman history. In his *History of Rome*, Livy described Rome's rise to power. He said that history had moral lessons to teach people.

While Livy celebrated Rome's greatness, Tacitus took a more critical view. He believed that Rome's emperors had taken away people's freedom. Tacitus also thought Romans were losing the values that made them strong. He accused them of wasting time on sports and other pleasures.

Theater and Language

One of the most popular pastimes in Rome was attending plays. Roman plays were staged as part of religious celebrations or national festivals. The actors wore masks to represent the characters. Masks allowed actors to play different roles. For most of Rome's history, men and boys played all the roles in a play. Women were allowed to act only in comedy plays called mimes.

Romans attending the theater sat in stadiums much like those in sports arenas today.

Latin, the language of the Romans, had an even bigger impact than Roman writings. Latin became Europe's language for government, trade, and learning until about A.D. 1500. Latin is the basis of many modern European languages, such as Italian, French, and Spanish. It shaped several others as well. Some of the English words we use today come from Latin.

Richard Hamilton Smith/CORBIS

✓ PROGRESS CHECK

Explaining Describe Roman improvements to Greek architecture.

LESSON 1 REVIEW

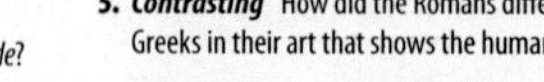

Review Vocabulary

1. What is the difference between a *satire* and an *ode*?
2. Why would a doctor today need to study *anatomy*?

Answer the Guiding Questions

3. ***Identifying*** What were the different roles a father played in the Roman family?
4. ***Describing*** What was daily life like for Roman women? Describe two differences that existed between women who were wealthy and those who were poor.
5. ***Contrasting*** How did the Romans differ from the Greeks in their art that shows the human body?
6. ***Differentiating*** How did the Greeks influence Roman writers?
7. **EXPOSITORY WRITING** Why do civilizations borrow elements from earlier civilizations? Think of two elements of American culture that have been borrowed from ancient Roman cultures. Explain what they are in a short essay.

LESSON 1 • Day 2

ENGAGE

Making Connections In a Think-Pair-Share activity, have students brainstorm a list of the elements or features that cultures share. Write the correct answers on the board. *(Answers may include government, religion, and the economy.)* AL ELL

Tell students that in this lesson, they will learn how the Romans adapted ideas from the Greeks and created a unique culture.

TEACH & ASSESS

Science and Art

GUIDING QUESTION *How did the Greeks influence Roman culture?*

GRAPHIC ORGANIZER

Comparing and Contrasting
Show the Taking Notes graphic organizer "The Greeks and the Romans" for this lesson. After students have learned about how the Romans adapted Greek ideas, have them list these developments in the graphic organizer.

SLIDE SHOW Share the slide show featuring Roman architecture for Lesson 1, and discuss the developments illustrated in each photo. Help students notice the Greek influence in each Roman structure. AL ELL

Have students use the Internet to find photos and information to create their own mini slide show presentations that illustrate one example of how the Greeks influenced Roman science, art, architecture, literature, or theater.

For example, students might find photos of the Greek Parthenon and compare this to the Roman Pantheon. Students should first describe the Greek example and then explain how the Romans adapted it to meet their needs.

LECTURE SLIDE **Justifying** Show students the lecture slide that lists Roman achievements. Have students explain the significance of each achievement.

Ask students to consider the development of Roman roads.

Ask: How could a reliable road system help extend and maintain an empire? *(Students might explain that a reliable road system makes trade easier and allows troops to move quickly throughout an empire.)* BL

Have students complete the Lesson 1 Review as homework.

CLOSE & REFLECT

Summarizing Have students work as a class to summarize the lesson. Ask each student to retell one important fact or idea from the lesson. Remind students that they should not repeat other students' facts and ideas. AL ELL

BACKGROUND KNOWLEDGE

Roman Roads

The roads in the Roman Empire connected to Rome. At the center of the capital city was a "golden milestone" *(milliareum aureum)* from which the Roman road system extended.

The first of the Roman roads was the Appian Way, built in 312 B.C. to connect Rome and the city of Brundisium (modern Brindisi) on the Adriatic coast. By A.D. 200, the Roman Empire featured 50,000 miles (80,000 km) of roadways stretching from Britain to Mesopotamia and from the Danube River to Spain and northern Africa.

The Roman roads were noted for being straight, having solid foundations and sufficient drainage, and being built using concrete. Though they adapted to local terrain and resources, Roman engineers followed basically the same principles in building abroad as they did in Italy.

The Roman road system made it easier to conquer and administer far-flung territories and later provided a means for great migrations into the empire. The roads also served as a means for the spread of Christianity.

Despite deterioration from neglect, Roman roads continued to serve Europe throughout the Middle Ages, and many fragments of the roads—including the Appian Way—survive today.

Answers for pages 344–347

P. 344 ☑ PROGRESS CHECK The family was the center of Roman life. A family's wealth determined the level of education available to the children and the amount of freedom available to the women in the family.

P. 345 CRITICAL THINKING The Romans learned the study of the body's anatomy from Galen, a Greek, who learned about the body's structure by dissecting dead animals and documenting his findings. We still use the same knowledge of anatomy to examine and treat people.

P. 346 GEOGRAPHY CONNECTION

1. Rome is located in the center of the empire.
2. CRITICAL THINKING Roads were built near waterways to connect towns that were already established along the waterways.

P. 347 ☑ PROGRESS CHECK The Romans created domes and arches so they could build structures that were more useful for their own purposes. They also used new materials such as concrete.

LESSON 1 REVIEW

1. Students should indicate that satire is a free-form piece of writing meant to poke fun at someone or something, and an ode is a poem that expresses strong emotions about life.
2. By studying anatomy, a doctor learns about the structure of the human body.
3. A father was the head of his household and was responsible for his children's education and his family's business.
4. Women advised their husbands in private, did the housework, shopped, and helped in the family business. Unlike poor women, wealthy women had enslaved people do their housework and were free to study and engage in leisure activities.
5. Greek statues showed perfect-looking people with beautiful bodies. Roman sculpture was more realistic, often showing less attractive details.
6. Greek myths honored their gods and praised military successes. Romans honored their gods but also wrote comedies about their mishaps, and they praised the success of their military generals but also wrote about their failures in battle.
7. Student essays should reflect an awareness that people learn from past generations and from the cultures with which they have interacted. They should mention two or more specific cultural elements—such as language and architectural styles—that Americans have borrowed from Roman civilization.

THE WORLD'S LITERATURE

The Aeneid

by Virgil (70 B.C. –19 B.C.)

Virgil (70 B.C.–19 B.C.), the author of the epic *The Aeneid*

Virgil is one of ancient Rome's greatest poets. He grew up on a farm and spent much of his life away from Rome. Virgil also served as a member in the court of Emperor Augustus.

After Emperor Augustus defeated his rivals and took power, he asked the poet Virgil to write a poem to honor Rome. Virgil wrote the *Aeneid*. It is an epic that retells the Greek legend of the battle of Troy from a Roman point of view.

In writing the *Aeneid*, Virgil did what many Roman artists did—he modeled his work on the earlier works of the Greeks. In the *Aeneid*, Virgil echoed the words of the Greek poet Homer.

In this excerpt, Aeneas (ih • NEE • uhs) is visiting the Underworld, the mythical world of the Dead, where he finds his father, Anchises (an • KEE • seez). There, Anchises explains some of the mysteries of the Underworld and predicts that future members of Aeneas's family will found Rome.

"But you, remember, are to be a Roman. … Your task is to impose peace by law and order: to protect the downtrodden, and to crush the arrogant in war."

—from *Aeneid*, Book VI, by Virgil

Aeneas carries Anchises—his father—from burning Troy.

PRIMARY SOURCE

"Now: I will describe to you the glory that will come upon the future generations of Trojans. I will tell you who our Italian **descendants** (dih • SEHN • duhnts) will be, and what distinction they will bring to our name. Do you see that young man leaning on a simple spear? He . . . will be the first to have in his veins a mixture of Trojan and Italian blood. He will be your son, Silvius. His mother will be called Lavinia. . . . She will bring him up in the woods to be a king and the father of kings. . . . And there are his glorious successors, next to him. Look especially at Silvius Aeneas, who will share your name: if ever he comes to the throne, he will be remembered equally for his devotion to the gods and for his courage in war. What excellent young men they are—don't you think?

"Next comes Romulus: he will be the son of Mars and Rhea Silvia, herself descended from my grandfather. Do you see the double **plume** (PLOOM) on the crest of his helmet? And how he is marked out by his father to be a god himself? He will be the founder of Rome—a wall will enclose her seven hills, but her empire will reach to the farthest edges of the world, her fame to the heights of Olympus. She will be fortunate in the race that she will nurture [care for]. . . .

"To sum up: there are some places where **smiths** and sculptors will shape bronze more subtly, or carve more lifelike portraits out of marble; in others, **orators** (AWR • uh • tuhrs) will argue more persuasively, and astronomers will observe more accurately the motion of the heavenly bodies and predict the rising stars. But you, remember, are to be a Roman, and the Romans' art is to be art of a different kind: the art of government, of ruling nations. Your task is to impose peace by law and order: to protect the **downtrodden**, and to crush the arrogant in war."

—from Vergil's* *Aeneid: Hero, War, Humanity*. tr. G.B. Cobbold.

*Vergil is an alternate spelling of Virgil

Vocabulary

descendant
future member of a family

smith
craftsperson who works with metal

orator
public speaker

downtrodden
people who are poor or suffering

Visual Vocabulary

A **plume** is a group of feathers or horse hair often worn on the top of a headpiece.

Analyzing Literature DBQ

1. ***Analyzing*** What is the purpose of Anchises's speech to Aeneas? What parts of the passage show that purpose?
2. ***Interpreting*** What does Anchises describe as the "Romans' art"?

networks
There's More Online!
- ☑ CHART/GRAPH Infographic: The Fall of Rome
- ☑ GRAPHIC ORGANIZER The Empire Collapses
- ☑ MAP Germanic Migrations A.D. 200–500
- ☑ SLIDE SHOW The U.S. Capitol

Lesson 2

Rome's Decline

ESSENTIAL QUESTION *Why do civilizations rise and fall?*

IT MATTERS BECAUSE

The fall of Rome resulted from political uproar, distant wars, and economic crises.

1 A Troubled Empire

GUIDING QUESTION *What problems led to Rome's decline?*

Marcus Aurelius was the last of five emperors who reigned during the *Pax Romana*, a time of peace and progress. Nearly a century of confusion and violence followed.

Political Confusion

During this time, Rome's government grew weak, while the army became very powerful. To stay in office, an emperor had to pay increasingly higher wages to the soldiers who supported him. When these payments could not be made, soldiers would turn against the emperor. Then civil wars broke out, as legion fought legion to put a new emperor on the throne. In a span of about 50 years, ending in A.D. 284, Rome had 22 different emperors. Most were murdered by the army or by their bodyguards.

Roman society also suffered during this period. Many Romans no longer honored the traditional values of duty, courage, and honesty. Dishonest government officials took bribes, and few talented citizens wanted to hold government office. Interest and support for education declined, and many wealthy Romans simply stopped paying taxes. Enslaved laborers now made up a large part of the empire's population.

Reading **HELP**DESK

Taking Notes: *Organizing*

Use a graphic organizer like the one shown here to identify reasons the Roman Empire collapsed.

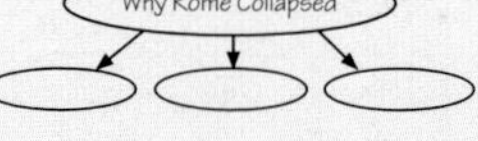

Content Vocabulary
- **reforms**

Economic Weaknesses

Rome's weakened government led to a weakened economy during the A.D. 200s. Roman soldiers and foreign invaders attacked farms and disrupted trade. These attacks led to food shortages, and food prices soared. People had less money to spend, so they bought fewer goods. The price of wheat from Egypt rose from seven or eight drachmae (DRAYK • muh) per unit to 120,000. Merchants saw their profits decline, forcing many out of business. Many workers lost their jobs.

To stop this economic decline, the government produced more coins. The government, however, did not have a large supply of gold and silver. As a result, the new coins had less of these precious metals in them, which reduced their value. In order to get the same profit for their goods, farmers and merchants continued to raise their prices. These actions led to inflation, or a steep rise in prices with a matching decline in the value of money. As the value of Roman coins decreased, people began to barter, or to exchange goods instead of money.

When Roman coins were made, they were imprinted with the image of the ruling emperor.

Invasions

While Rome continued to struggle, Germanic tribes raided the western empire, and Persian armies invaded in the east. People living in cities built protective walls around them. With less money to use, the government started to hire Germanic soldiers. Germanic soldiers, however, had no loyalty to the empire.

These well-preserved walls were built by the Romans in the late A.D. 200s to protect the town of Lugo, Spain.

▶ CRITICAL THINKING
Drawing Conclusions Why did Roman towns require protection in the A.D. 200s?

Teaching *The World's Literature*

(Student Edition pp. 348–349)

ENGAGE

Identifying Remind the class that understanding historical context can help them understand historical literature. List the following names on the board: the *Aeneid,* Virgil, and Augustus. Read the introduction.

Ask: What is the *Aeneid*? *(an epic poem)* Who was Virgil? *(a Roman poet)* Who was Augustus? *(a Roman emperor)* AL

Ask: Why is it important to know that Virgil served in the court of Augustus? *(Virgil's writings might have been influenced by Augustus. Virgil might be writing to impress or to please Augustus.)*

TEACH & ASSESS

Have the class read the quotation chorally (aloud, in unison) as you lead them using a slightly louder voice.

Tell students they have just read the words of a father, Anchises, to his son, Aeneas.

Ask: How do you think Anchises feels about Rome? *(Sample responses: Anchises is proud because Rome will be his son's city. Anchises sees Rome as a benevolent guardian of its people.)* BL

Ask students if they have ever seen a genealogy chart. Explain that it is like a flowchart with the eldest known relatives at the top. Tell them they will create a simple genealogy chart for this excerpt of the *Aeneid*. Read only the first paragraph of the primary source aloud.

Next, write the name *Anchises* in the upper-left corner of the whiteboard. As you ask the following questions, add each name in the proper position, below and slightly to the right, with a line connecting it to the relative(s).

Ask: Who is Anchises's son? *(Aeneas)* Who is Aeneas's son? *(Silvius)* Silvius's son? *(Silvius Aeneas)* AL Who is Aeneas's wife, and where does she belong on the diagram? *(Lavinia; she belongs next to Aeneas, with a line connecting down to her son, Silvius.)* BL

Review the third paragraph with students.

Ask: Does Anchises think that people in Rome will do everything better than people in other places? *(No; he says that some places will do a variety of things better.)* What will Rome do best? *(rule nations)*

Have students review the final paragraph for the main idea behind Anchises's conversation with his son.

Ask: How do you think Emperor Augustus might have felt about Virgil's poem? Why? *(Sample answer: He might have been pleased because the poem gives a positive view of Rome and how it will treat its people.)* BL

At the end of the discussion, have students complete the Analyzing Literature questions.

CLOSE & REFLECT

Identifying Tell students that many great pieces of literature feature a hero who does brave deeds. To summarize, ask students to tell who the hero might be and explain why. *(Sample answers: Anchises—because he is guiding his son to make Rome great; Aeneas—because he will return from the Underworld to lead Rome to greatness)*

Answers to *Analyzing Literature* DBQ

1. He wants to show Aeneas that his descendants will have an important future in Italy. "I have long wished to show you, to let you see for yourself, the generations of our family that are yet to come, so that when you have made your mark in Italy, you may share my pride in them; Now: I will describe to you the glory that will come upon the future generations of Trojans. I will tell you who our Italian descendants will be, and what distinction they will bring to our name."
2. Roman art is to be the art of government, of ruling nations. The Romans are to impose peace by law and order, to protect the downtrodden, and to crush the arrogant in war.

Teaching *Rome's Decline*

(Student Edition pp. 350–357)

LESSON 2 • Day 1

ENGAGE

Predicting On the board, have students brainstorm a list of Rome's contributions to the modern world. Then ask students to consider each contribution and its value in the world today. Take a poll, and rank the contributions in order of their value. Write this information on the list.

Remind students that although Rome made all these contributions, the empire collapsed.

Ask:

What factors might cause an empire like Rome to disintegrate? *(Students might identify economic problems, political scandals, or military invasions.)*

Write this list on the board under "Reasons an Empire Might Collapse."

Tell students that in this lesson they are learning why the Roman Empire collapsed. They will later compare their predictions with the reasons described in their textbooks.

TEACH & ASSESS

1 A Troubled Empire

GUIDING QUESTION *What problems led to Rome's decline?*

Previewing Have students review the photos in this lesson. **Ask:** Which photo hints that Rome was threatened by forces outside its empire? *(the photo showing the walls around Lugo, Spain)* AL ELL

GRAPHIC ORGANIZER **Drawing Conclusions** Remind students that as they review this section, they will fill in "Why Rome Collapsed," the graphic organizer for this lesson.

Ask: In "A Troubled Empire," what are some of the factors that led to the Roman Empire's decline? *(political confusion, economic problems, dependence on slave labor)*

Refer to the factors students listed on the board at the beginning of the lesson. Have them add to their graphic organizers the factors they listed that are similar to those presented in the text. *(Sample answers: economic problems, political scandals, military invasions)* AL ELL

Summarizing Ask students to summarize the reforms Diocletian made and their results. Guide student responses by **asking:**

What was one of the reforms Diocletian made? *(the political change of dividing the empire into parts)*

What problem was Diocletian trying to solve by enacting this reform? *(Diocletian tried to bring about political and economic reforms to help the empire survive. He had forts built along the empire's border to help protect it from invading Germanic groups. He divided the empire into four parts, each with its own ruler, but he held ultimate authority over all of them. To stop prices from rising, he set maximum prices on wages and goods. In order for certain industries to remain productive, he ordered workers to stay at their jobs until they died. Diocletian also made local leaders responsible for collecting taxes.)* BL

Answers for pages 350–351

P. 350 Taking Notes political confusion, economic weakness, invasions

P. 351 CRITICAL THINKING Roman towns required protection because more groups were invading the empire.

Who Was Diocletian?

A general named Diocletian (DY•uh•KLEE•shuhn) became emperor in A.D. 284. He introduced **reforms,** or political changes to make things better. To defend the empire against invasions, Diocletian built forts along its frontiers. To rule the large empire more efficiently, he divided it into four parts, each with its own ruler. He held ultimate authority over all of them.

Diocletian also tried to strengthen the economy. He set maximum prices for wages and goods in order to prevent prices from rising further. To improve productivity, he ordered workers to remain at the same jobs until they died. Diocletian also made local officials personally responsible for the taxes their communities had to pay. Despite these efforts, Diocletian's reforms did not succeed. People ignored his rules, and Diocletian was not a strong enough emperor to enforce them.

PROGRESS CHECK

Explaining How did Diocletian try to improve Rome's economy?

A giant's foot? No, it is actually a replica of a foot from a statue of the Roman Emperor Constantine. This 30-foot (9.1 m) statue once stood in a public building in the Roman Forum.

CRITICAL THINKING

Hypothesizing Why do you think Constantine's reforms did not end Rome's decline?

2 The Fall of Rome

GUIDING QUESTION *What effect did Germanic invaders have on the Roman Empire?*

When Diocletian left office in A.D. 305, conflict again broke out in the empire. Fighting continued until another general named Constantine (KAHN•stuhn•TEEN) became emperor in A.D. 312.

Constantine's Rule

To improve the economy, Constantine issued several orders to **reinforce** the rules of Diocletian. Constantine also wanted a stable workforce and military. For example, the sons of workers had to follow their fathers' trades. The sons of farmers had to work their fathers' lands. The sons of soldiers served in the army.

In spite of Constantine's reforms, the empire continued to decline. In A.D. 330, Constantine moved the capital from a failing Rome to a new city in the east—the Greek city of Byzantium (buh•ZAN•tee•uhm) in present-day Turkey. This city became known as Constantinople (kahn•stan•tuh•NOH•puhl). After Constantine died a few years later, Theodosius (THEE•uh•DOH•shuhs) took power in Constantinople.

Reading **HELP**DESK

reforms changes to bring about improvement

Academic Vocabulary

reinforce to strengthen

expand to spread out

Following their rebellion and victory at Adrianople, the Visigoths invaded Rome.

After taking power, Theodosius found the empire difficult to govern. The empire covered a vast area and faced threats from both inside and outside its borders. Theodosius realized the empire had become too large to control from one seat of government. Theodosius decided that—when he died—the eastern and western parts should become separate empires. This division took place in A.D. 395. One empire was the Western Roman Empire, with its capital remaining at Rome. The other was the Eastern Roman Empire, with its capital city at Constantinople.

Germanic Invaders

During the late A.D. 300s and 400s, many Germanic tribes migrated from northern Europe and fought to **expand** their hold over Roman territory. Some were looking for better land for raising livestock and farming. Many, however, were fleeing the Huns, a fierce group of warriors from Mongolia in Asia.

In the late A.D. 300s, the Huns entered Eastern Europe. Fearing a Hun attack, one Germanic tribe, the Visigoths (VIH•zuh•gahths), asked the Roman government for protection. The Romans let them settle just inside the empire's border. Here they were under the protection of the Roman army. In return, the Visigoths promised to be loyal to the empire. They promised not to attack the empire from the inside.

The Romans, however, treated the Visigoths badly. They charged them high prices for food and enslaved some of their people. Tired of Roman demands, the Visigoths finally rebelled. In A.D. 378, they fought and defeated the Roman legions at Adrianople (AY•dree•uh•NOH•puhl).

The modern city of Istanbul was known as Byzantium during the last days of the Western Roman Empire. When Emperor Constantine moved the capital of the empire there from Rome, Byzantium became Constantinople.

CRITICAL THINKING

Analyzing Why did Constantine move the capital to Byzantium?

Germanic Migrations c. A.D. 200–500

KEY: Western Roman Empire; Eastern Roman Empire; Battle; Angles/Saxons; Franks; Huns; Ostrogoths; Vandals; Visigoths

GEOGRAPHY CONNECTION

Numerous invasions led to the fall of the Roman Empire.

1. **MOVEMENT** Who attacked both Britain and northern Gaul?
2. CRITICAL THINKING ***Drawing Conclusions*** Why do you think the Eastern Roman Empire experienced very few invasions?

The Visigoths' victory brought more attacks on Roman territory. Soon, Germanic tribes invaded Gaul, which is today France. Then, in A.D. 410, the Visigoth leader Alaric (A•luh•rihk) led his people into Italy and captured Rome itself. The Visigoths looted the city's government buildings and private homes. Rome's conquest by Alaric made it clear that the empire would not, as many Romans believed, last forever.

The Vandals, another Germanic group, attacked Roman lands in Spain and northern Africa. Then they sailed to Italy, and in A.D. 455, entered Rome. They were able to overcome the Romans living there. The Vandals spent almost two weeks seizing valuables and burning buildings. The English word *vandalism,* meaning "the willful destruction of property," comes from the actions of the Vandals.

The Germanic people had entered every part of Rome's organization. By the mid-A.D. 400s, Germanic soldiers had been working for the Roman government for centuries.

Reading **HELP**DESK

Reading in the Content Area: *Charts*

Flowcharts can show a chain of events. To read a flowchart, follow the arrows. Ask yourself questions such as, "What are the steps in this event? How does one event lead to another?"

Roman Emperor Forced Out

As a result, several Germanic leaders held high posts in Rome's government and army. In A.D. 476, the Germanic general named Odoacer (OH•duh•WAY•suhr) had enough support from soldiers that he was able to take control. Odoacer overthrew the western emperor, a 14-year-old boy named Romulus Augustulus (RAHM•yuh•luhs aw•GUHS•chah•luhs).

After Odoacer seized control, no Roman emperor ever again ruled from Rome. From then on, foreign powers ruled what had been the Roman Empire. Historians often use this event to mark the end of the Western Roman Empire. It was a major turning point in history.

Odoacer controlled Rome for almost 15 years. The Germanic peoples, however, continued to fight amongst themselves. During Odoacer's rule, a group of Visigoths attacked the city of Rome. After much fighting, they seized the city and killed Odoacer. They set up their new kingdom in Italy under their leader, Theodoric (thee•AH•duh•rihk). Elsewhere in Europe, other Germanic kingdoms arose and came to power.

The Western Roman Empire ceased to exist. Pope Gregory I wrote about the fall of Rome and how it affected people who had lived within its borders.

Connections to TODAY

Vandalism

Vandalism is a word with Roman origins. It means "the intentional destruction or damage to property." Graffiti is a type of vandalism. It involves writing, drawing, or carving words or symbols on any surface without the permission of the owner. A person who destroys or damages property on purpose is called a *vandal.*

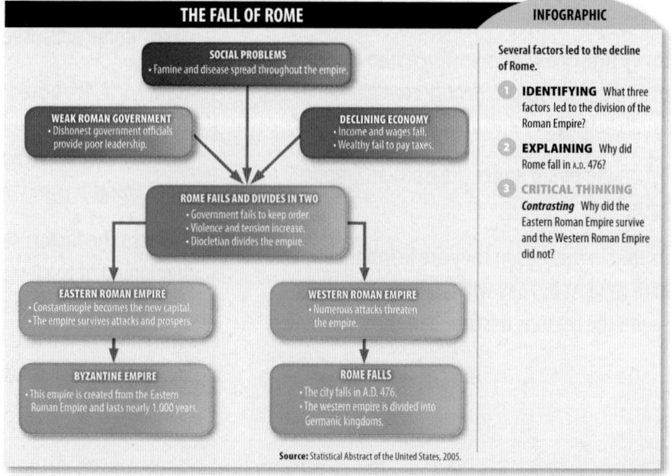
THE FALL OF ROME
INFOGRAPHIC
SOCIAL PROBLEMS
• Famine and disease spread throughout the empire.
WEAK ROMAN GOVERNMENT
• Dishonest government officials provide poor leadership.
DECLINING ECONOMY
• Income and wages fall.
• Wealthy fail to pay taxes.
ROME FAILS AND DIVIDES IN TWO
• Government fails to keep order.
• Violence and tension increase.
• Diocletian divides the empire.
EASTERN ROMAN EMPIRE
• Constantinople becomes the new capital.
• The empire survives attacks and prospers.
WESTERN ROMAN EMPIRE
• Numerous attacks threaten the empire.
BYZANTINE EMPIRE
• This empire is created from the Eastern Roman Empire and lasts nearly 1,000 years.
ROME FALLS
• The city falls in A.D. 476.
• The western empire is divided into Germanic kingdoms.
Source: Statistical Abstract of the United States, 2005.

Several factors led to the decline of Rome.

1. **IDENTIFYING** What three factors led to the division of the Roman Empire?
2. **EXPLAINING** Why did Rome fall in A.D. 476?
3. CRITICAL THINKING ***Contrasting*** Why did the Eastern Roman Empire survive and the Western Roman Empire did not?

LESSON 2 • Day 1 (cont.)

Drawing Conclusions

Ask: Did the reforms solve the empire's problems? Why or why not? *(No; the reforms were ineffective because people ignored them, and Diocletian's power was weak.)* BL

LECTURE SLIDE Show students the lecture slide that defines *scarcity* and *inflation*.

Ask students to give an example of each that relates to the Roman Empire. AL ELL

INTERACTIVE WORKSHEET

Economics of History Activity

Assign the Economics of History Activity for homework. Be sure students understand the information presented at the beginning of the activity so they can answer the questions.

CLOSE & REFLECT

Identifying Points of View Ask students to take on the perspective of a Roman citizen who owns a small business. Have students explain how Rome's political and economic issues might affect that citizen. AL BL

LESSON 2 • Day 2

ENGAGE

Predicting Have students discuss previous empires they have studied.

Ask:

What caused those empires to end? *(Students might name military invasions, weak economies, extended geography, or lack of strong leaders.)* AL

Write the reasons on the whiteboard. Have students use the list to generate predictions about the fate of Rome.

Tell students they will be learning about the events that weakened and eventually ended the Roman Empire.

TEACH & ASSESS

2 The Fall of Rome

GUIDING QUESTION ***What effect did Germanic invaders have on the Roman Empire?***

MAP **Analyzing Visuals** Show students the interactive map "Germanic Migrations."

Ask:

- What do the arrows represent? *(the paths that the Germanic tribes took)*
- Which invader traveled the farthest south? *(Vandals)*
- Who attacked both Britain and northern Gaul? *(Angles, Saxons)*
- Which groups captured Rome? *(Vandals, Visigoths)*
- Why do you think the Eastern Roman Empire experienced few invasions? *(Many invading Germanic tribes traveled westward to escape the Huns in the east. Also, mountains and rivers made traveling eastward more difficult.)* AL ELL

Making Inferences After students have read "The Fall of Rome," discuss how invasions affected Rome's collapse.

Ask:

Why might a vast, divided empire be more likely to be invaded? *(Students might say that a large, divided empire would be more difficult to defend because it would need many more soldiers to protect it.)*

Have students describe how other factors, such as the enslavement of Germanic groups, might have affected the stability of the empire. *(After the Romans allowed some Visigoths to settle within the empire's borders, Rome treated them poorly by charging them high prices for food and enslaving some of them. Hostilities between the two groups increased, leading to the rebellion of the Visigoths.)* BL

3 Rome's Legacies

GUIDING QUESTION ***What are the key achievements and contributions of Roman civilization?***

SLIDE SHOW **Making Connections** Show students the slide show about Roman influences on the architecture of the U.S. Capitol. Then discuss how Rome has influenced American culture today.

For example, **ask:**

Based on what you have learned about Rome, how has Rome influenced:

- the type of government we have in the United States? *(a republic, though a democratic one)*
- the ideas Americans have about laws? *(innocent until proven guilty; everyone is equal under the law; judges decide legal cases)* BL
- the language we speak and write? *(the use of the Latin alphabet; Latin basis of many words we use)*
- the architecture of buildings? *(the use of concrete, arches, vaults, and domes)* AL

Encourage students to identify some examples not found in the textbook.

Determining Cause and Effect

Ask: What are some reasons for the fall of Rome? Have students complete the lesson's graphic organizer and review the answers with them. *(political problems, military invasions, economic problems)*

Answers for pages 352–355

P. 352 ☑ PROGRESS CHECK Diocletian set maximum prices for wages and goods to prevent prices from rising. He ordered workers to remain in the same job until they died. Also, he made local officials personally responsible for the taxes their communities had to pay.

P. 352 CRITICAL THINKING Students might say the damage was too great to be fixed by Constantine's reforms or that Constantine's reforms did not address the right problems facing the empire.

P. 353 CRITICAL THINKING Constantine moved the capital to Byzantium to escape the political unrest, economic problems, and invasions in the western part of the empire.

P. 354 GEOGRAPHY CONNECTION

1. The Angles/Saxons attacked Britain and northern Gaul.
2. CRITICAL THINKING Possible answer: Physical barriers made the eastern part of the empire harder to reach.

P. 355 INFOGRAPHIC

1. Weak Roman government, social problems, and a declining economy led to the division of the Roman Empire.
2. Numerous attacks threatened the empire.
3. CRITICAL THINKING The Eastern empire survived the attacks against it. The Western empire did not.

PRIMARY SOURCE

“We see on all sides sorrows; We hear on all sides groans. Cities are destroyed, fortifications razed [forts destroyed] to the ground, fields devastated [left in ruin], land reduced to solitude. No husbandman [farmer] is left in the fields, few inhabitants remain in the cities. . . . What Rome herself, once deemed [regarded as] the Mistress of the World, has now become, we see—wasted away with . . . the loss of citizens, the assaults of enemies, the frequent fall of ruined buildings.”

—from *Homiliarum in Ezechielem*, by Pope Gregory I

By A.D. 550, a group of Germanic-ruled territories had replaced the Western Roman Empire, yet Roman culture did not completely disappear. Western Europe's new Germanic rulers adopted the Latin language, Roman laws, and Christianity. In the eastern Mediterranean, the Eastern Roman Empire thrived. It became known as the Byzantine Empire and lasted nearly 1,000 more years.

✓ PROGRESS CHECK

Identifying Why do historians consider A.D. 476 an important date?

3 Rome's Legacies

GUIDING QUESTION *What are the key achievements and contributions of Roman civilization?*

The influence of the ancient Romans still surrounds us. Roman achievements live on in our system of laws and government today. The peace and order created by Roman rule helped with the rapid growth and spread of the Christian religion.

Rome's Influence on Law and Government

Many beliefs about law and justice in the American legal system come from Roman ideas. Like the Romans, we believe that everyone is equal under the law. We also believe that a person is considered innocent until proven guilty. We, like the Romans, require our judges to decide cases fairly.

The republican form of government was developed in ancient Rome. Certain citizens in a republic elected their leaders. The United States and a number of other countries today are democratic republics. We also believe that a republic works best if all adult citizens vote, **participate** in government, and help to improve their communities.

Reading HELPDESK

Academic Vocabulary

participate to take part

Rome's Cultural Impact

Many Western countries use the Latin alphabet, which has expanded from 22 to 26 letters. The Italian, French, Spanish, Portuguese, and Romanian languages are derived from Latin—the language of the Romans. Many English words have Latin roots. Latin phrases are part of the vocabulary of scientists, doctors, and lawyers. The Romans continue to influence the literature we read and enjoy. The great Roman writers such as Virgil, Horace, Livy, and Tacitus are still admired and studied. Architecture and construction also owe much to the ancient Romans. Government buildings in Washington, D.C. and the capital cities of many states often use domes and arches inspired by Roman architecture. Concrete, a Roman development, remains a major building material today.

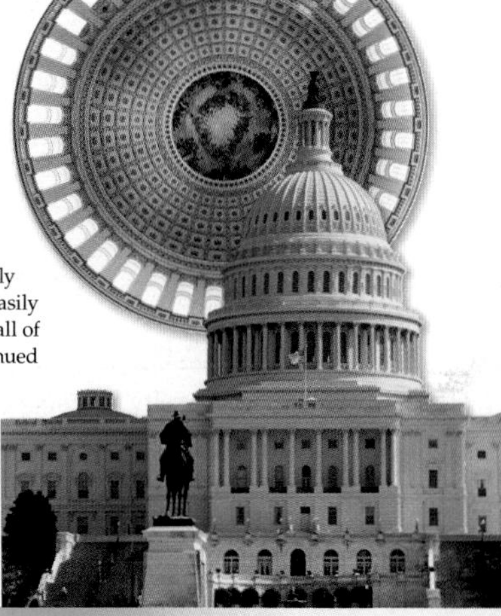

The Roman arch can support large domes. The design of our U.S. Capitol Building was influenced by the Romans. The image above shows what the U.S. Capitol dome looks like on the interior.

Ancient Rome and Christianity

Christianity is a major world religion. It began in the eastern part of the Roman Empire and was adopted by Rome's emperors in the A.D. 300s. Those emperors helped the new religion grow and spread.

The Roman road system allowed the early Christians to travel throughout the empire safely and quickly. As a result, Christian ideas were easily shared with other groups of people. After the fall of the Western Roman Empire, Christianity continued to attract new believers.

✓ PROGRESS CHECK

Comparing What Roman contributions still influence our lives today?

LESSON 2 REVIEW

Review Vocabulary

1. Why were Diocletian's *reforms* unsuccessful?

Answer the Guiding Questions

2. ***Describing*** Discuss two problems that led to Rome's decline.
3. ***Explaining*** How did the division of the Roman Empire make it easy for people to invade it?
4. ***Summarizing*** Describe how Rome contributed to the development of world languages.
5. **PERSUASIVE WRITING** What do you think was the greatest accomplishment of Roman civilization? Write a one-page essay that describes the accomplishment and why you feel it was the civilization's greatest.

What Do You Think?

Did People Benefit from Roman Rule?

Throughout their vast empire, the Romans built roads, bridges, and irrigation systems. These improvements allowed trade and agriculture to flourish. To accomplish these changes, however, the Romans had to sail to other lands to obtain materials. With the traders came Roman soldiers.

Some people, however, did not want to be ruled by the Romans. Many died fighting against the Roman invaders.

Mosaic of Romans unloading a boat

Yes

PRIMARY SOURCE

“From neighboring continents far and wide a ceaseless [endless] flow of goods pours into Rome. From every land and every sea come each season's crops, the produce of countryside, rivers, and lakes, and articles skillfully made by Greeks and foreigners.

. . . So many merchants arrive from all points of the compass with their cargoes throughout the year, and with each return of harvest, that the city is like the common warehouse of the world . . . clothing from Babylonia, luxuries from barbarian lands beyond. . . . Egypt, Sicily and Africa are your farms. . . . Everything converges [comes together] here—trade, shipping, agriculture, metallurgy [making products from metals], all the skills that exist and have existed, everything that is bred or grown. Anything that cannot be seen in Rome does not exist.”

—Aelius Aristides, *To Rome*

The Destruction of the Temple in Jerusalem by the Emperor Titus, a painting by Nicolas Poussin

No

PRIMARY SOURCE

“As the legions [soldiers] charged in, neither persuasion nor threat could check [stop] their impetuosity [impulsive behavior]: passion [frenzy] alone was in command. . . . Most of the victims were peaceful citizens, weak and unarmed, butchered [killed] wherever they were caught. While the Sanctuary [Temple] was burning, looting went on right and left and all who were caught were put to the sword. There was no pity for age, no regard for rank; little children and old men, laymen and priests alike were butchered; every class was held in the iron embrace of war, whether they defended themselves or cried for mercy . . . They also burnt the treasuries which housed huge sums of money, huge quantities of clothing, and other precious things.”

—(Flavius) Josephus describing the destruction of the Jewish temple by the Romans in A.D. 70, *The Jewish War*

What Do You Think? DBQ

1. ***Identifying*** Which person has a favorable view of Rome?
2. ***Describing*** Does (Flavius) Josephus believe the Romans were merciful when they conquered people? How does he try to persuade the reader to support his belief?
3. ***Making Inferences*** What do you think Aristides meant when he said, “Anything that cannot be seen in Rome does not exist”?

LESSON 2 • Day 2 (cont.)

Categorizing List the following words on the board:

A. Barter

B. Constantine

C. Diocletian

D. Inflation

E. Constantinople

F. Rome

Then write the following phrases. As you read each of these phrases aloud, ask volunteers to respond with the matching word.

1. Established maximum prices for wages and goods to stop prices from rising *(C)*
2. Rise in prices and a decline in the value of money *(D)*
3. To exchange using goods instead of money *(A)*
4. Capital of the Western Roman Empire *(F)*
5. Moved capital of empire to Byzantium *(B)*
6. Present-day Istanbul *(E)* AL

Have students complete the Lesson 2 Review.

CLOSE & REFLECT

Predicting Have students make predictions about how the fall of Rome will affect Europe and the Eastern Roman Empire. AL BL

Answers for pages 356–357

P. 356 ☑ PROGRESS CHECK In A.D. 476, the Germanic general Odoacer invaded Rome and overthrew the emperor. Afterward, no emperor ever ruled the empire from Rome again.

P. 357 ☑ PROGRESS CHECK Students might say that the Romans have influenced our beliefs about law, justice, government, and citizenship; our use of the Latin alphabet and language; our modern languages; literature, architecture, and the use of concrete in construction; the languages we speak; and our religious beliefs.

LESSON 2 REVIEW

1. Diocletian's reforms were unsuccessful because people ignored his new rules. He was also too weak as an emperor to enforce them.
2. Students could discuss two of the following three: the weak Roman government, social problems, and the declining economy.
3. The invasions focused on the Western Roman Empire, which was far too extended, and with fewer soldiers, it was too weak to defend itself.
4. The language of the Romans, Latin, shaped other languages, including Italian, French, Spanish, Portuguese, and Romanian. These languages, like English, use the Latin alphabet. Many English words have Latin roots.
5. Essay topics might focus on Roman contributions to law, justice, government, language, architecture, or religion.

Teaching *What Do You Think?* (Student Edition pp. 358–359)

ENGAGE

Categorizing Prepare two columns on the board headed "Benefit" and "Did Not Benefit."

Ask:

Now that you have read about the Roman Empire, in what ways do you think people benefited from or did not benefit from Roman rule? List responses on the chart. *(Answers may include: Benefit: culture, law, engineering, arts; Did Not Benefit: slavery, poverty)*

Students will return to this list to compare their responses with those of the writers from the quotations.

TEACH & ASSESS

Ask students to review the introductory paragraphs. Have the class focus on the background illustration featuring Roman architectural ruins.

Ask:

What do these ruins tell us about Roman skills? *(The Romans were skilled in architecture.)*

Which writer do you think would have most appreciated the beauty of this architecture? Why? *(Aelius Aristides, because it shows off the Romans' skill)* BL

What kind of benefits does Aelius Aristides mention? *(the availability of agricultural and manufactured products from far away; all known skills)*

Call students' attention to the mosaic illustration.

Ask:

Why was this mosaic a good choice to illustrate Aristides's opinion? *(It shows men unloading products, which represents the main benefit Aristides mentions: the availability of many trade goods that enter Roman ports.)*

Call students' attention to the "No" primary source.

Ask:

Which three words describe the citizens? *(peaceful, weak, unarmed)*

Which words and phrases describe the actions of the soldiers? *(passion alone was in command, butchered, burning, looting, put to the sword, burnt the treasuries)*

Call students' attention to the painting *The Destruction of the Temple in Jerusalem by the Emperor Titus.*

Ask:

What seems to be happening here? *(Roman soldiers are killing people.)* **How does this image support Flavius Josephus's argument?** *(It shows that Romans could be violent and destructive.)* AL ELL

Ask:

Based on what each author writes, what can you guess about their lives within the Roman Empire? *(Aelius Aristides: may have been a merchant or a wealthy buyer; Josephus: may have witnessed the destruction of the Jewish temple and escaped)* BL

Return to the "Benefit" and "Did Not Benefit" lists that students created in the Engage activity. Invite volunteers to circle the items on their lists that were mentioned by the writers. Have volunteers add more items, if needed, to the lists.

CLOSE & REFLECT

Have students complete the "What Do You Think?" questions in class or as a homework assignment.

Answers to *What Do You Think?* 

1. Aelius Aristides
2. Flavius Josephus believes the Romans had no mercy. He wrote that they destroyed or stole items from those they conquered and killed children and old people.
3. This statement reflects Aristides's belief that Rome was the center of civilization. Any new trend could be seen in Rome.

networks
There's More Online!
- GRAPHIC ORGANIZER Why the Byzantine Empire Thrived
- MAP Justinian's Conquests
- SLIDE SHOW
  - Hagia Sophia
  - The Hippodrome of Constantinople

Lesson 3

The Byzantine Empire

ESSENTIAL QUESTION *How does geography influence the way people live?*

It Matters Because

At the height of its power, the Byzantine Empire united people on three continents. Its system of laws and its strong leadership helped the empire flourish.

1 The New Rome

GUIDING QUESTION *How did the Byzantine Empire become rich and powerful?*

After the Roman Empire was divided in A.D. 395, the eastern half eventually became known as the Byzantine Empire. At the height of its power in the A.D. 500s, the Byzantine territory extended west to Italy, south to Egypt, and east to the Arabian border. A variety of peoples lived within the empire's borders. Greeks made up the largest population. Egyptians, Syrians, Arabs, Armenians, Jews, Persians, Slavs, and Turks also lived in the empire. Under Emperor Justinian, the laws improved, the arts flourished, and the empire grew dramatically.

Constantinople

Constantine moved the capital of the Roman Empire from Rome to the Greek city of Byzantium and renamed the city Constantinople. The new capital thrived. By the A.D. 500s, multicultural Constantinople had become one of the world's most advanced cities.

Constantinople's location was a major factor in the city's success. Located on a peninsula between the Black Sea and the Aegean Sea, the city's excellent harbors attracted fishing boats, trading ships, and warships. Because of its location at the crossroads of trade routes between Europe and Asia, Constantinople became the wealthiest part of the Roman Empire.

Constantinople was also easy to defend. Lying on a peninsula, the city was protected on three sides by the sea, and a large wall protected it on the fourth side. Later, a huge chain was strung across the city's harbor for greater protection. Surprise attacks were not easily carried out on Constantinople.

Reading HELPDESK

Taking Notes: *Listing*
Use a graphic organizer like this one to list reasons why the Byzantine Empire thrived.

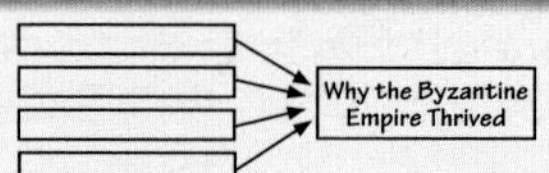

Content Vocabulary
- mosaics
- saints

What Cultural Influences Shaped the Byzantines?

Constantinople at first resembled other cities in the Roman Empire. The "New Rome," as it was called, had government buildings and palaces built in the Roman style. The city also had an oval arena called the Hippodrome (HIHP•uh•drohm) where chariot races and other events were held.

Rome influenced the political and social life of the Byzantine Empire. Emperors spoke Latin and enforced Roman laws. Many wealthy Roman families traveled east to the Byzantine Empire and lived in towns or on large farming estates. Similarly to how things were done in Rome, the government gave the empire's poor people free bread and entertainment shows.

Over time, the Roman influence on the Byzantine Empire faded, while Greek influence in the area increased. Most Byzantines spoke Greek, and Byzantine emperors and officials also began to speak Greek instead of Latin. The ideas of non-Greek peoples, like the Egyptians and the Slavs, also shaped Byzantine life. Still other customs came from Persia to the east. All of these cultures blended together to form the Byzantine civilization.

Between A.D. 500 and A.D. 1200, the Byzantines developed one of the world's most advanced civilizations. They preserved and passed on Greek culture and Roman law to other peoples. As you will learn, they also brought Christianity to people in Eastern Europe.

Sculptures of horses, such as the one above, greeted people who enjoyed chariot races at the Hippodrome.

▶ CRITICAL THINKING
Making Connections Why did Greek culture gradually influence the Byzantine Empire more than Roman culture?

☑ PROGRESS CHECK
Explaining Why was Constantinople important to the Byzantine Empire?

Build Vocabulary: *Word Origins*
The word *hippodrome* comes from the Greek words *hippos*, meaning "horse," and *dromos*, meaning "race" or "course."

BIOGRAPHY

Justinian I (A.D. 483–565)

Justinian's uncle, Justin, provided Justinian with an excellent education at a school in Byzantium. When Justin became emperor, he adopted Justinian and made him his chief advisor and, later, co-ruler. In A.D. 527, Justin died, and Justinian became emperor.

Empress Theodora (A.D. 500–548)

Theodora was a member of a lower social class. Justinian could not marry her: it was illegal for people of lower classes to marry nobles. Justinian's uncle Justin, who was the emperor, changed the law so that the couple could marry.

▶ CRITICAL THINKING
Making Inferences Why do you think there were laws preventing people from the lower classes from marrying nobles?

2 Justinian's Rule

GUIDING QUESTION *How did Emperor Justinian and Empress Theodora strengthen the Byzantine Empire?*

Justinian (juh•STIH•nee•uhn) ruled the Byzantine Empire at the height of its power. A skilled general and a strong leader, Justinian ruled from A.D. 527 until A.D. 565. He governed with supreme power and controlled the military and all of the **legal** decisions made within the empire. Many historians view Justinian as the greatest Byzantine emperor.

Who Was Theodora?

Justinian's wife, the empress Theodora (THEE•uh•DOHR•uh), was a beautiful, intelligent, and ambitious woman. She participated actively in government and helped Justinian choose government officials. Theodora helped Byzantine women win more legal rights. At her urging, Justinian changed Byzantine law so that a wife could own land. If a woman became a widow, her land would provide the income she needed to take care of her children.

Theodora showed her political wisdom during a crisis in A.D. 532. When angry taxpayers in Constantinople threatened the government, Justinian's advisers urged Justinian to flee the city. Theodora, however, told her husband to stay and fight. According to one Byzantine historian, Theodora told Justinian that she would rather die as an empress than escape and live as an outlaw:

PRIMARY SOURCE

> "May I never be separated from this purple [royal color], and may I not live that day on which those who meet me shall not address me as mistress. If, now, it is your wish to save yourself, O Emperor, there is no difficulty. For we have much money, and there is the sea, here the boats. However consider whether it will not come about after you have been saved that you would gladly exchange that safety for death. For as for myself, I approve a certain ancient saying that royalty is a good burial-shroud."
>
> —from "The Nika Riot," by Procopius

Taking Theodora's advice, Justinian stayed in the city and fought back. His army crushed the rebels. By doing this, Justinian was able to **restore** order and strengthen his power as emperor.

Reading HELPDESK

Academic Vocabulary
legal of or relating to the law
restore to bring back to an original state

Reading Strategy: *Listing*
Listing information you have read about helps you remember it. Create a bulleted list that shows the ways Theodora influenced or helped the Byzantine Empire.

Justinian's Legal Reforms

One of Justinian's lasting contributions to future civilizations was in the area of law. Shortly after he became emperor, Justinian realized that the empire's laws were disorganized and confusing. He ordered a group of legal scholars headed by Tribonian (truh•BOH•nee•uhn) to create a simpler and better code of laws.

The group's new legal code became known as the Justinian Code. The code helped officials and businesspeople better understand the empire's laws. Throughout the centuries, the Justinian Code has been the basis for the legal systems of almost every country in the Western world.

Byzantine Arts

Justinian, along with other Byzantine emperors, was interested in arts and architecture. The emperors ordered the construction of churches, forts, and government buildings throughout the Byzantine Empire. Among the hundreds of beautiful churches and palaces in Constantinople was the church called Hagia Sophia (HAH•jee•uh soh•FEE•uh), or "Holy Wisdom."

The dome of the Hagia Sophia towers more than 180 feet above the ground. For more than 1,000 years, the Hagia Sophia was the largest cathedral in the world. When the Ottoman Turks conquered Constantinople in A.D. 1453, the cathedral was converted to a mosque. Today, Hagia Sophia is a museum.

LESSON 3 • Day 1

ENGAGE

Analyzing Visuals Display a map of the United States from the Interactive World Atlas.

Ask: **What does this map show?** *(the United States)*

Ask students to locate New York City. 

Tell them that New York is a large city known for being a center of trade. AL ELL

Ask:

Before railroads, trucks, and airplanes, how do you think merchants in New York City sent and received products to trade? *(by ship)*

What characteristic do you think New York and Constantinople, also a center of trade in its time, might have in common? *(Students should note that both cities are, or were, located near bodies of water.)*

Next, ask students to describe a peninsula. *(a piece of land surrounded on three sides by water, connected to the mainland)* AL

Tell students that Constantinople had a great advantage being located on a peninsula. Tell them that, like New York City, Constantinople developed by benefiting from nearby physical features. These developments spurred economic growth.

TEACH & ASSESS

1 The New Rome

GUIDING QUESTION *How did the Byzantine Empire become rich and powerful?*

LECTURE SLIDE **Explaining** Show students the lecture slide displaying the reasons the Byzantine Empire thrived.

Ask:

Why was trade important to the Byzantine Empire? *(Students should discuss how trade brought wealth to the empire and exposed people to other cultures.)*

In their contact with other cultures, what did the Byzantines pass on to other people? *(Greek culture and Roman law)*

INTERACTIVE WORKSHEET

Geography and History Activity

Understanding Cause and Effect Have students locate the map of the Byzantine Empire in their textbooks. Ask students to identify the geographic characteristics of Constantinople. *(It is located on a peninsula between the Black Sea and the Mediterranean Sea; it connects two continents, Europe and Asia.)*

Next, have students explore the impact of geography on the culture of Constantinople. Organize students into groups of four to complete the Geography and History Activity about the Byzantine capital. Remind them to refer to the map of the Byzantine Empire as they complete the worksheet.

SLIDE SHOW **Speculating** Explain that emperors used wealth generated by trade to build large projects as a demonstration of their success and prosperity. Point to the Roman Colosseum as an example. Explain that the Byzantine emperors erected similar structures, such the Hippodrome of Constantinople.

Show students the slide show of the Hippodrome.

When you have finished,

ask:

What types of skills did the Romans need to create the Hippodrome? *(engineering and construction)*

Why might Constantine have chosen to build the Hippodrome instead of a church or some other kind of public building? *(to entertain the people; to provide "bread and circuses," or food and entertainment, as did Julius Caesar and the earlier Western Roman emperors)*

Have students think of a time they attended an outdoor sports event. Invite volunteers to speculate what the Byzantines would have experienced when they attended events in the Hippodrome. AL ELL

CLOSE & REFLECT

Making Connections Show the map of the United States again. Ask students to locate the city where they live. Have students describe the geographic factors that determined how and where their community developed.

Ask:

What is our community's major economic activity?

Is trade important to our community?

What physical features make trade easy or difficult?

Have students write a paragraph describing their city's economic success and how it has been influenced by geography. Have them share their paragraphs with the class. AL

LESSON 3 • Day 2

ENGAGE

Identifying Have students brainstorm a list of famous couples in history and describe what they accomplished. *(Examples might be Antony and Cleopatra or John and Abigail Adams.)*

Record their responses on the board. At the bottom of the list, add Justinian and Theodora.

Explain that Justinian and Theodora were a married couple who served as leaders of the Byzantine Empire. Tell students they will be learning more about this couple in this lesson.

TEACH & ASSESS

2 Justinian's Rule

GUIDING QUESTION *How did Emperor Justinian and Empress Theodora strengthen the Byzantine Empire?*

Comparing and Contrasting After students review the section "Justinian's Rule," have them debate this question: **Are laws needed to have a civilized society?**

Organize students into several paired groups, both pro and con, to debate this issue. Have each group choose a recorder to note the arguments for his or her team.

When student groups have debated the issue, discuss the question as a class. At the end of the discussion, ask students if the debate has changed the way they would answer the question. Ask volunteers to explain why they changed their opinion.

Drawing Conclusions Have students read the biographies of Justinian and Theodora and answer the question. Ask students to each write a sentence explaining what they think was the secret to the couple's success.

Answers for pages 360–363

P. 360 Taking Notes Constantinople's location; wide variety of cultural influences; great leaders such as Constantine and Justinian; the Justinian Code

P. 361 CRITICAL THINKING Roman influence faded, while Greek influence increased. Most Byzantines spoke Greek, and Roman rulers began to speak it.

P. 361 ☑ PROGRESS CHECK Constantinople became the center of political, economic, and social life in the Roman Empire.

P. 362 CRITICAL THINKING Students may say that the nobles probably wanted to preserve their power and not share it with members of the lower classes.

P. 362 Reading Strategy Sample answer:
- persuaded Justinian to make laws that helped women
- persuaded Justinian to stay and fight against rebels

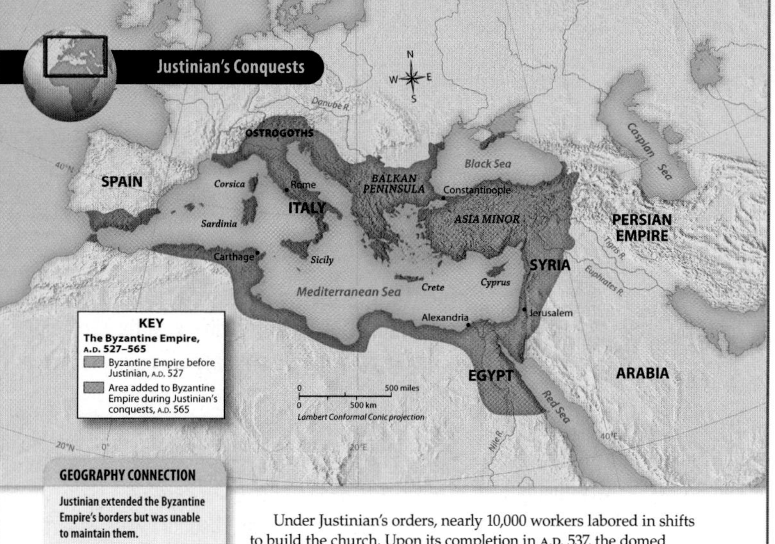

GEOGRAPHY CONNECTION

Justinian extended the Byzantine Empire's borders but was unable to maintain them.

1. **PLACE** How far west did the empire extend after Justinian's conquests?
2. **CRITICAL THINKING** *Inferring* Why might a cavalry be useful for defending this large empire?

Under Justinian's orders, nearly 10,000 workers labored in shifts to build the church. Upon its completion in A.D. 537, the domed church became the religious center of the Byzantine Empire. The interior of Hagia Sophia contains walls of polished marble and beautiful gold and silver ornaments. This unique building still stands in Istanbul today.

Numerous mosaics also decorated the interior walls of Hagia Sophia. **Mosaics** (moh•ZAY•ihks) are patterns or pictures made from small pieces of colored glass or stone. Popular in the Byzantine Empire, most mosaics showed figures of **saints**, or Christian holy people. Other mosaics, such as the one at the beginning of the chapter, honored Byzantine emperors.

In addition to the arts and architecture, Emperor Justinian was concerned about education. Learning was highly respected in the Byzantine culture. In Byzantine schools, boys studied religion, medicine, law, arithmetic, grammar, and other subjects. Some were schooled by private tutors. Girls did not generally attend schools and received any teaching at home.

Reading HELPDESK

mosaics motifs or images created by an arrangement of colored glass or stone

saints people considered holy by followers of the Christian faith

Military Conquests

Justinian wanted to restore the Roman Empire and bring back the glory of Rome. Led by a general named Belisarius (BEH•luh•SAR•ee•uhs), the Byzantine army was strengthened and reorganized. Instead of relying on foot soldiers, the new army used cavalry—soldiers mounted on horses. Byzantine cavalry wore armor and carried bows and lances, which were long spears.

Between A.D. 533 and A.D. 555, the Byzantine military conquered territories that were once part of the great Roman Empire. These territories included Italy and parts of Spain and northern Africa. They also defeated the Persians, which increased the security of the eastern borders of the empire. However, the conquests of Justinian's army were short-lived. During the mid-500s, a deadly disease known to historians as "Justinian's Plague" swept through Asia and Europe. The plague killed millions of people, including many men in Justinian's army. The loss of so many soldiers severely weakened the Byzantine Empire's ability to fight wars.

In addition, the Byzantines did not have the money to support an army large enough to defend against the Persians in the east and protect the lands in the west. Most of the western territories that Justinian conquered were lost after his death.

PROGRESS CHECK

Understanding Cause and Effect What effect did Theodora have on Justinian's rule?

In addition to body armor such as this, Byzantine cavalry soldiers also wore plumed helmets. Cavalry made the Byzantine army a formidable fighting force.

▶ **CRITICAL THINKING**
Explaining How did Belisarius strengthen the army of the Byzantine Empire?

The Art Archive/SuperStock

LESSON 3 REVIEW

Review Vocabulary

1. How were *saints* shown in *mosaics*?

Answer the Guiding Questions

2. ***Explaining*** How did Constantinople's location help it become a wealthy city?
3. ***Describing*** How did the advancements made by Greek and Roman civilizations influence the Byzantine Empire?
4. ***Identifying Cause and Effect*** What effect did the Justinian Code have on the Byzantine Empire?
5. ***Drawing Conclusions*** Why did the Byzantine military grow weaker?
6. **PERSUASIVE WRITING** Write a speech that Theodora might have given to Justinian to convince him to stay in Constantinople during the rebellion in A.D. 532.

NOTES

NOTES

LESSON 3 • Day 2 (cont.)

INTERACTIVE WHITEBOARD ACTIVITY

Comparing Have students refer to the section "Justinian's Rule" and complete the Interactive Whiteboard Activity comparing the characteristics and achievements of Justinian with those of Theodora.

When students have completed the Interactive Whiteboard Activity, have the class discuss the answers.

SLIDE SHOW **Identifying** Point out that it was Justinian who ordered the building of the Hagia Sophia. Show the slide show about the Hagia Sophia, and have students point out examples of a mosaic, an arch, and a dome.

Ask:

Have you seen any buildings as old as the Hagia Sophia that are still standing?

After students' respond, point out that even though earthquakes collapsed the Hagia Sophia's dome three times, each collapse took place hundreds of years apart. This allowed time for the dome to be rebuilt. AL ELL

Summarizing Have students create a graphic organizer such as web diagram or a fishbone diagram to list the successes of Justinian. When students have completed their graphic organizers, have several share their entries with the class. *(Sample answers may include simpler and better code of laws; construction of churches and government buildings; reformed army with new cavalry.)*

Ask:

What is Justinian most remembered for? *(Most students will probably say the creation of a simpler law code.)*

Assign the Lesson 3 Review as an in-class or as a homework activity.

CLOSE & REFLECT

Making Connections Ask students to identify leaders in their school, community, state, and nation. Guide students to identify their principal, mayor, governor, and president.

Ask students to choose one leader and write a paragraph that explains how that leader, like Justinian, has improved people's lives because of his or her service.

Have volunteers read their paragraphs to the class. Make connections between the traits of these leaders and those of Justinian. AL

BACKGROUND KNOWLEDGE

Justinian

Although modern historians view Justinian as a great emperor, he was not beloved in his own era.

Justinian relied upon advisers from outside the aristocracy. His selection of these advisers created tension with the Byzantine nobility.

This situation was worsened by Justinian's authoritarianism, which the nobility saw as undermining their authority.

Popular outrage against Justinian led to the Nika Riot in January of A.D. 532. It was during this rebellion that Theodora persuaded Justinian to stay in the city.

This period of unrest resulted in the burning of several important buildings, including the Hagia Sophia. The damage to Constantinople gave Justinian an opportunity for extensive rebuilding in the years that followed.

In the religious sphere, Justinian took a leading role in shaping church policy. As a firm defender of Christian Orthodoxy, he came into direct conflict with the Pope in Rome. This further strained relations between the western and eastern territories of his empire.

IF YOU HAVE MORE TIME . . .

Work in Groups to Make Time Lines About Roman and Byzantine Rulers

Sequencing On the whiteboard, list the Roman and Byzantine rulers that students have studied. List the names randomly or in alphabetical order.

Organize students into small groups. Have each group copy the list and work together to rearrange the names in chronological order.

Then, have students work in their groups to identify one key achievement of each ruler. Tell students to use this information to create an illustrated time line of the history of Roman civilization.

Students may need to refer to their textbooks or other reference materials to identify the appropriate dates for their time lines.

Explore the Region by Making Tourism Materials

Illustrating Show students examples of tourism posters and brochures. Explain that these documents are meant to encourage people to visit the places being shown.

Ask:

What is it about the posters and brochures that makes these places seem appealing? *(Students might note the use of bright colors, the photographs of sun and sand, the images of happy people, and so on.)*

Tell students they are going to create their own posters or brochures for the city of Constantinople during the era of the Byzantine Empire.

Work as a class to brainstorm images that students might use in their projects. *(Possible answers: Hagia Sophia, the Hippodrome, the Black and Mediterranean Seas, and so on)*

Then have students use this list of ideas to create their own tourism materials inviting people to visit Constantinople.

Answers for pages 364–365

P. 364 GEOGRAPHY CONNECTION

1. to southern Spain
2. CRITICAL THINKING Cavalry soldiers could travel quickly and defend large areas.

P. 365 CRITICAL THINKING He reorganized the army and used armored cavalry.

P. 365 ☑ PROGRESS CHECK Because of Theodora, Justinian gave women more legal rights. Theodora also strengthened his power by helping him stop a revolt.

LESSON 3 REVIEW

1. To make some mosaics, images of saints were created using small pieces of cut glass and stone.
2. Constantinople was located between the Black Sea and the Aegean Sea. It was at the crossroads between Asia and Europe, making it an important center for trade.
3. Rome influenced the political and social life of the Byzantine Empire. Emperors spoke Latin and enforced Roman laws. Architecture reflected the Roman style. Chariot races were held, and free bread and entertainment were provided for the poor, similar to how it had been in Rome. Over time, the Byzantine Empire became more heavily influenced by the Greeks. For example, emperors and officials began speaking Greek instead of Latin.
4. Justinian's Code organized laws more clearly and simplified them. Laws were more easily understood by officials and businesspeople.
5. Disease wiped out much of the empire's army. Also, the Byzantines did not have enough money to defend their eastern and western lands.
6. Speeches might include the argument that if Justinian fled, he would not like his new life, but if he stayed in Constantinople and faced his enemies, it would show that he was strong and fearless.

CHAPTER 12 Activities

Write your answers on a separate piece of paper.

1 Exploring the Essential Question
EXPOSITORY WRITING How would you describe the Romans compared to people who lived before them? Write a summary of what made the Romans a unique people. Think of the many ways they were different from the Greeks and other people who lived before them. Include what you think their strongest characteristic was and why.

2 21st Century Skills
DETERMINING CAUSE AND EFFECT Create a poster or other visual aid about the division of the Roman Empire in A.D. 395. Identify two causes and two effects of the split.

3 Thinking Like a Historian
DISTINGUISHING FACT FROM OPINION Review the primary source in Lesson 2, *Homiliarum in Ezechielem*, by Pope Gregory I. Decide which statements in the source are facts and which statements are opinions. List the statements of fact and the statements of opinion from the source in a chart like this one.

FACT	OPINION

4 GEOGRAPHY ACTIVITY

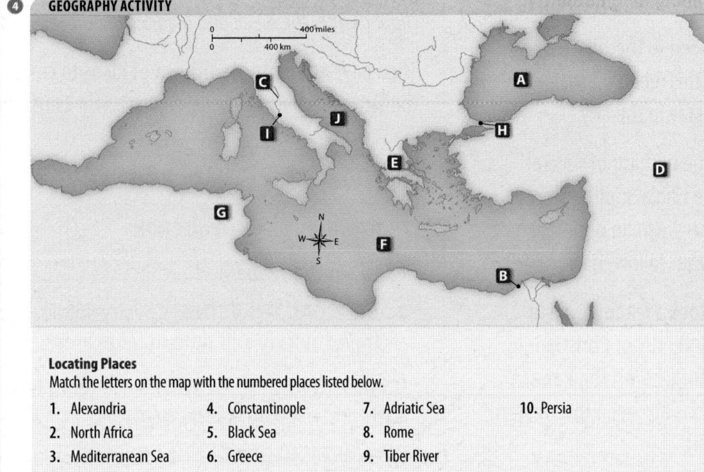

Locating Places
Match the letters on the map with the numbered places listed below.

1. Alexandria
2. North Africa
3. Mediterranean Sea
4. Constantinople
5. Black Sea
6. Greece
7. Adriatic Sea
8. Rome
9. Tiber River
10. Persia

CHAPTER 12 Assessment

REVIEW THE GUIDING QUESTIONS
Directions: Choose the best answer for each question.

1. Which is an example of Greek influence on Roman culture?
   A. arches and domes in Roman architecture
   B. Roman plays that told stories of military failures
   C. letter-like symbols in the Roman number system
   D. Roman statues that showed people's wrinkles and warts

2. Which is a true statement about the lives of Roman women?
   F. Roman women had the same rights as Roman men.
   G. Roman women did not participate in Roman society.
   H. Roman women had less power when Rome was an empire.
   I. Roman women had more freedom if their husbands were wealthy.

3. An increase in prices and a decline in the value of Roman money created
   A. reforms.
   B. inflation.
   C. food shortages.
   D. Germanic invasions.

4. Which of the following is a lasting cultural impact made by the Romans?
   F. the pyramids
   G. the canal lock system
   H. Buddhism
   I. the modern alphabet

5. As emperor, Justinian changed the legal system by
   A. creating a more organized code of laws.
   B. putting his wife, Theodora, in charge.
   C. taking away the rights of women.
   D. building new churches.

6. During the Byzantine Empire
   F. world trade expanded greatly.
   G. education was not considered important.
   H. Christianity was lost.
   I. the development of art and architecture stopped.

CHAPTER 12 Assessment *(continued)*

DBQ DOCUMENT-BASED QUESTIONS

Christian leader Jerome wrote this in a letter about attacks on Rome:

"Who would believe that Rome, victor over all the world would fall, that she would be to her people both the tomb [grave] and the womb [birthplace]."

—from The Epistles of St. Jerome, tr. Roland Bainton

7. **Drawing Conclusions** Which statement best summarizes what Jerome thinks about Rome before its fall?
   A. Jerome sees Rome as strong.
   B. Jerome sees a bright future for Rome.
   C. Jerome sees Rome as weak.
   D. Jerome sees that Rome is in danger.

8. **Comparing** Why does Jerome compare Rome to a womb [birthplace] and a tomb [grave] for its people?
   F. He has seen Rome on the decline from its beginning.
   G. There have been many births and deaths in Rome.
   H. The birth of Rome has meant the death of her people.
   I. The words *womb* and *tomb* represent a beginning and an end.

SHORT RESPONSE

"[The] Romans were proud of making their roads go straight even when this meant constructing long bridges over deep valleys or tunneling through solid rock mountains. . . . As the Roman Empire expanded . . . [t]hey helped the Romans . . . by enabling troops to be rushed to trouble spots . . . facilitated [made easier] long-distance trade and . . . sped up communication among the different regions."

—from *Daily Life in the Roman City* by Gregory Aldrete

9. What advantages did the system of roads provide to Romans?

10. What obstacles to building the network of roads did the Romans face?

EXTENDED RESPONSE

11. **Descriptive Writing** You are a citizen of Rome who recently moved to Constantinople. Write a letter to a friend in Rome about your new home. Explain the differences and similarities between the two cities.

Need Extra Help?

If You've Missed Question	1	2	3	4	5	6	7	8	9	10	11
Review Lesson	1	1	2	2	3	3	2	2	1	1	1, 3

NOTES

REFLECT, REVIEW, & REMEDIATE

INTERACTIVE WORKSHEET

Chapter Summary

Provide students with the Chapter Summary worksheet to help review the chapter and prepare for assessment.

Reviewing the Enduring Understanding

Review this chapter's Enduring Understanding with students:

- People, places, and ideas change over time.

INTERACTIVE WHITEBOARD On the board, have a student volunteer create a three-column chart. Use the first column to label the rows. Write "Roman Empire" at the top of the second column and "Byzantine Empire" at the top of the third. Then lead a discussion that allows students to recall features of daily life, the economy, and key events for each empire. Ask a student volunteer to note these features in the chart.

	Roman Empire	Byzantine Empire
Daily Life		
Economy		
Key Events		

ACTIVITIES ANSWERS

Exploring the Essential Question

1. Students should note that the lives of the Greeks were more self-contained. Their lives were spent mostly in conflict, either warring with other people or fighting among themselves over government or power. The Greeks were not as interested in interacting with the outside world as the Romans were. Once the Romans conquered a people, they allowed them to maintain their culture and way of life.

21st Century Skills

2. Student posters should indicate causes such as the size of the empire and the threats it faced, and effects such as the collapse and conquest of the Western Empire and the prosperity of the Eastern Empire.

Thinking Like a Historian

3. Facts might include: Cities are destroyed; fortifications are torn down to the ground; few inhabitants remain in the cities. Opinions might include: We see on all sides sorrows. What Rome herself, once deemed the Mistress of the World, has now become, we see—wasted away.

Locating Places

4. **1.** B, **2.** G, **3.** F, **4.** H, **5.** A, **6.** E, **7.** J, **8.** I, **9.** C, **10.** D

ASSESSMENT ANSWERS

Review the Guiding Questions

1. **C** The Romans created their own unique culture by using arches and domes in their architecture, writing plays about military failures, and creating sculptures of realistic-looking people. Thus, choice C, the use of letter-like symbols, is the correct answer.

2. **I** Roman women were not citizens and did not have full rights, but they participated in Roman society. When Rome was an empire, the wives of emperors began to exercise more power. Women's freedom was determined by the wealth and position of their husbands. Therefore, choice I is the correct answer.

3. **B** Reforms were a response to the increased prices and devalued money that created inflation, but they were not enough to end the food shortages that led to higher prices or to stop the foreign invasions that helped weaken the empire. Choice B is the correct answer.

4. **I** The Egyptians built the pyramids; canal lock systems were developed by other cultures; and Buddhism developed in the East. The Romans gave us the modern alphabet, choice I.

5. **A** Although Justinian listened to Theodora's advice, he never put her in charge. Justinian increased women's rights and improved Byzantine law by simplifying and reorganizing the legal system. Choice A is the correct answer.

6. **F** The location of Constantinople between Europe and Asia expanded world trade. Choice F is the correct answer.

Document-Based Questions

7. **A** Students might use the clue word *victor* to help them answer this question.

8. **I** Students should know the definitions of *womb* and *tomb*. If not, have them look up the words in the dictionary. Choice I is the correct answer.

Short Response

9. Student responses should include military control, trade, and communication. The roads signaled that an area belonged to the Roman Empire.

10. Roman engineers had to construct long bridges over deep valleys and tunnel through mountains of solid rock.

Extended Response

11. Students' letters should contain descriptive phrases indicating that Constantinople was a busy trading city. They should point out that, like Rome, it was the seat of power and had beautiful buildings and artworks. Unlike Rome, the economy was strong, and Constantinople was populated by a variety of people from many parts of the world, trading and living within the city.

ONLINE RESOURCES

networks

There's More Online!

- ☑ INTERACTIVE WORKSHEETS
- ☑ BIOGRAPHIES
- ☑ CHARTS/GRAPHS
- ☑ GAMES
- ☑ GRAPHIC ORGANIZERS
- ☑ IMAGES
- ☑ MAPS
- ☑ PRIMARY SOURCES
- ☑ SLIDE SHOWS
- ☑ TIME LINE
- ☑ LECTURE SLIDES
- ☑ INTERACTIVE WHITEBOARD ACTIVITIES
- ☑ ASSESSMENTS
- ☑ VIDEOS

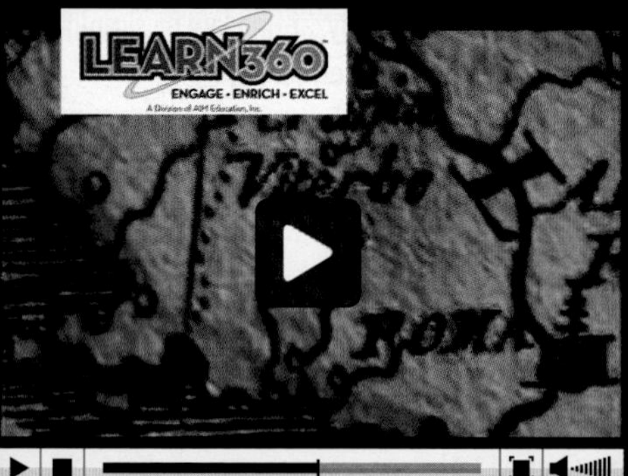

Christianity in Greece

The Development of Christianity in Ireland

Chapter **13**

The Rise of Christianity

Dear World History Teacher,

By the third century, a new religion—Christianity—was spreading throughout the Roman Empire. Christianity began among the followers of Jesus of Nazareth and slowly gained acceptance among people throughout the empire. Christianity was attractive to many people because of its promise of salvation, its similarity to previously established religions, and its universality as a religion for all, whether rich or poor, men or women, or Greek or Roman.

Beginning in the fourth century, Christianity became the official religion of the Roman Empire. After the collapse of the Roman Empire in the West, the Roman Catholic Church, as the Christian church was called, played a crucial role in the new Germanic kingdoms in Europe. Catholic monks and nuns converted many Germanic peoples to Christianity. The church developed an organized government under the leadership of the Bishop of Rome, who became known as the pope.

In the east, Christianity played an important role in the Byzantine Empire, which developed its own form of worship known as the Eastern Orthodox Church. By the eleventh century, Christianity had split into the Roman Catholic and Eastern Orthodox churches.

Jackson J. Spielvogel

More Media Resources

Current Events Online

Visit McGraw-Hill's current events Web site for high-interest news stories and activities for your students. Access the site through the Student or Teacher Center in **networks.**

Reading List

Grade 6 reading level:
Ancient Celts: Archaeology Unlocks the Secrets of the Celts' Past, by Jen Green

Grade 7 reading level:
Wonders and Miracles: A Passover Companion, by Eric A. Kimmel

Grade 8 reading level:
The Treasury of Saints and Martyrs, by Margaret Mulvihill

At the MOVIES

Watch portions of *The Gospel According to Saint Matthew*, a faithful retelling of Matthew's gospel by Italian filmmaker Pier Paolo Pasolini. Also watch clips from the Frontline documentary *From Jesus to Christ: The First Christians*, produced for PBS.

Discuss **Do documentaries convey different information about a topic than books?**

NOTE: Be sure to preview any clips to ensure they are age-appropriate.

Search for more videos online in the **networks** Resource Library.

CHAPTER 13 Planner

UNDERSTANDING BY DESIGN®

Enduring Understanding

- *People, places, and ideas change over time.*

Essential Questions

- *What are the characteristics of a leader?* • *How do religions develop?*

Students will know:

- *the message of Jesus and its connection to Jewish thought*
- *why Christianity spread in the Roman Empire*
- *the role Constantine played in the acceptance of Christianity in the Roman Empire*
- *the causes of the split of the Christian church into eastern and western branches*

Students will be able to:

- **synthesize** the geographic theme of movement and its importance to spreading Christianity in the Roman Empire
- **draw conclusions** about Christianity's expansion and eventual acceptance in the Roman Empire
- **organize** information graphically to record their understanding of the rise of Christianity
- **synthesize** what they have learned to come up with an essay topic on the subject of the rise and spread of Christianity
- **analyze** the split of the Christian church in an essay
- **discuss** their work with the class and read their essays aloud

Predictable Misunderstandings

Students may think:

- Jesus was not a Jew.
- Christianity was not shaped by politics or history.
- The Roman Empire never adopted Christianity.
- The Roman Catholic Church was the only Christian church in Europe.

Assessment Evidence

Performance Task

- Hands-On Chapter Project

Other Evidence

- Interactive Graphic Organizers
- 21st Century Skills Activity
- Primary Source Activity
- Geography and History Activity
- Economics of History Activity
- What Do You Think? questions
- Written paragraphs
- Lesson Reviews
- Responses to Interactive Whiteboard Activities
- Classroom discussion of Christianity's effect on the Roman Empire
- Drawing portraying a topic in early Christianity
- Brainstorming questions for an essay and writing the essay

Pacing Guide

Introducing the Chapter	1 day
Lesson 1 Early Christianity	1 day
Lesson 2 The Early Church	1 day
Lesson 3 A Christian Europe	1 day
Chapter Activities and Assessment	1 day
TOTAL TIME	**5 Days**

Differentiated Instruction

These lesson plans are written to address the needs of your On Level students. Discussion and activities that are well-suited to your Approaching Grade Level learners, Beyond Grade Level learners, as well as your English Language Learners, are coded as follows:

Approaching Grade Level

Beyond Grade Level

English Language Learner

NCSS Standards covered in "The Rise of Christianity"

Learners will understand:

1 CULTURE

4. That the beliefs, values, and behaviors of a culture form an integrated system that helps shape the activities and ways of life that define a culture

6. That culture may change in response to changing needs, concerns, social, political, and geographic conditions

2 TIME, CONTINUITY, AND CHANGE

6. The origins and influences of social, cultural, political, and economic systems

7. The contributions of key persons, groups, and events from the past and their influence on the present

3 PEOPLE, PLACES, AND ENVIRONMENTS

8. Factors that contribute to cooperation and conflict among peoples of the nation and world, including language, religion, and political beliefs

4 INDIVIDUAL DEVELOPMENT AND IDENTITY

3. How factors such as physical endowment, interests, capabilities, learning, motivation, personality, perception, and beliefs influence individual development and identity

4. How personal, social, cultural, and environmental factors contribute to the development and the growth of personal identity

5 INDIVIDUALS, GROUPS, AND INSTITUTIONS

3. Institutions are created to respond to changing individual and group needs

5. That groups and institutions change over time

6. That cultural diffusion occurs when groups migrate

8. That when two or more groups with differing norms and beliefs interact, accommodation or conflict may result

CHAPTER 13

Introducing the Chapter

(Student Edition p. 369)

The Story Matters . . .

Ask a volunteer to read "The Story Matters . . ." aloud, or read it aloud to the students. Then discuss what it might have been like to have lived in ancient Judaea during the lifetime of Jesus of Nazareth.

Ask:

Have you ever been inside a Christian church or listened to a priest or a minister speak to a group of people about religious matters? Have you seen programs on television or in a movie that depict the life of Jesus or explain how Christianity developed? Have a few students share their experiences.

Then ask:

What do you think are some connections between Judaism, the religion of the Jews, and Christianity? If Christianity began in ancient Galilee and Judaea, how do you think it became the worldwide religion it is today?

Tell the class that the beginning of Christianity 2,000 years ago can be well documented because of the many artifacts that have been found and the writings that have been preserved. Tell interested students that they can find more about the development of Christianity online.

ESSENTIAL QUESTIONS • *What are the characteristics of a leader?* • *How do religions develop?* • *How do new ideas change the way people live?*

networks *There's More Online* about the beginnings and development of Christianity.

CHAPTER 13

Lesson 1 *Early Christianity*

Lesson 2 *The Early Church*

Lesson 3 *A Christian Europe*

The Story Matters . . .

One of the chosen apostles of Jesus, Simon Peter of Galilee, was called "the rock" of the Christian church. He brought many followers to the Christian faith.

Soon after the death of Jesus, Peter, as he was called, became a leader of the early Christian church. He played an important role in spreading the teachings of Jesus and in contributing to the rise of Christianity. This painting imagines Peter as an older man.

◄ *This image of Peter was painted by the Greek artist El Greco around 1600. St. Peter's Basilica, or church, in the city of Rome, Italy is named in his honor.*

369

Introducing Place and Time

(Student Edition pp. 370–371)

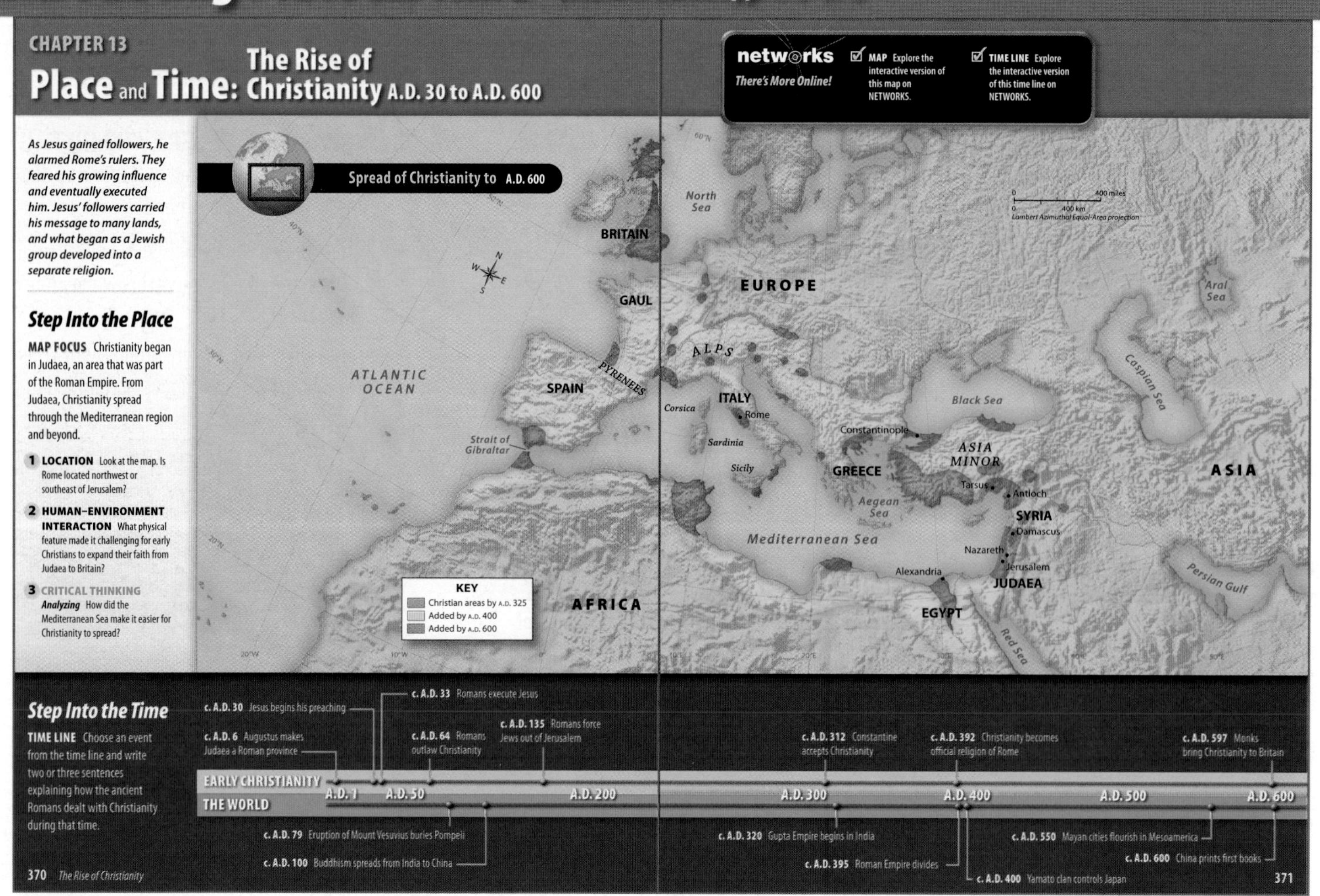
CHAPTER 13

Place and Time: The Rise of Christianity A.D. 30 to A.D. 600

As Jesus gained followers, he alarmed Rome's rulers. They feared his growing influence and eventually executed him. Jesus' followers carried his message to many lands, and what began as a Jewish group developed into a separate religion.

Step Into the Place

MAP FOCUS Christianity began in Judaea, an area that was part of the Roman Empire. From Judaea, Christianity spread through the Mediterranean region and beyond.

1 **LOCATION** Look at the map. Is Rome located northwest or southeast of Jerusalem?

2 **HUMAN-ENVIRONMENT INTERACTION** What physical feature made it challenging for early Christians to expand their faith from Judaea to Britain?

3 **CRITICAL THINKING** ***Analyzing*** How did the Mediterranean Sea make it easier for Christianity to spread?

networks *There's More Online!* **MAP** Explore the interactive version of this map on NETWORKS. **TIME LINE** Explore the interactive version of this time line on NETWORKS.

Step Into the Time

TIME LINE Choose an event from the time line and write two or three sentences explaining how the ancient Romans dealt with Christianity during that time.

370 *The Rise of Christianity*

371

Technology Extension

- Find an additional activity online that incorporates technology for this project.
- Visit the EdTechTeacher Web sites (included in the Technology Extension for this chapter) for more links, tutorials, and other resources.

Assessing Background Knowledge

INTERACTIVE WORKSHEET

What Do You Know? Activity

Have students complete the Anticipation Guide about the Rise of Christianity before they study the chapter. Direct students to read each statement. Then, in the "Before" column, check whether they agree or disagree with the statement. Next, take a class poll so you can tailor your lessons to focus on students' misconceptions.

After students complete the chapter, have them reread the statements and note in the "After" column whether they agree or disagree with the statement. Ask students who changed their responses to explain why they did so. *(Students should cite facts from the chapter to explain any changes in their views.)*

INTERACTIVE WORKSHEET

Guided Reading Activities

There is a Guided Reading Activity for each lesson in this chapter. You may wish to assign the Guided Reading Activity for Lesson 1 after introducing the chapter content.

Hands-On Chapter Project

Students will create blogs describing the characteristics and actions of early Christian leaders.

- Students will participate in a class discussion about the characteristics of religious leaders and the qualities that make them successful.
- Next, students will divide into small groups. Using worksheets and discussions as a guide, each group will plan their blogging project.
- Then, each group will research their time periods and religious leaders. Group members will take turns writing blog entries for each leader and responses to those blog entries.
- Students will share their blogs with the rest of the class.
- Finally, students will evaluate their research, presentation, and collaboration using an Assessment Rubric.

Visit **networks** online to see the full project and rubric.

Step Into the Place

Location Project the Interactive World Atlas on the whiteboard and project the Mediterranean region. Remind students that Christianity began in the Mediterranean region. Discuss with the class why the Roman Empire wanted to control this region and why the Mediterranean Sea was important to the spread of Christianity.

INTERACTIVE WHITEBOARD ACTIVITY At your interactive whiteboard, have student volunteers analyze the map showing the spread of Christianity and mark where they think geographical features might have helped or hindered the spread of Christianity. Next, project the Chapter Opener map on the whiteboard. As a class, discuss the Map Focus questions.

Step Into the Time

Making Inferences Have students review the time line for the chapter. Explain that they will be studying events from about A.D. 1 to A.D. 600.

Ask students: **Based on the information in the time line, what can you infer about what was happening in ancient Judaea beginning around A.D. 1?** *(The Romans governed the people who lived there, who were known as Jews and had their own religion. The Romans persecuted the Jews and later the Christians. Eventually, the Roman Empire accepted Christianity and made it the official religion of the empire.)*

Answers for pages 370–371

Step Into the Place

1. Rome is located northwest of Jerusalem.
2. the Mediterranean Sea
3. CRITICAL THINKING Answers may vary. Possible answers should include the fact that the Mediterranean Sea allowed followers of Jesus to travel by ship to many seaside cities and from there to travel inland to preach Jesus's message.

Step Into the Time

Sample answer for c. A.D. 33: The Romans crucified Jesus, and after his death they began to persecute his followers.

ONLINE RESOURCES

networks

Assign these interactive worksheets and quizzes from your Teacher Lesson Center. All resources are print-ready.

It's ALL Online!

Chapter 13 Resources

- ☑ Chapter Summary
- ☑ Vocabulary Builder
- ☑ What Do You Know?
- ☑ Hands-On Chapter Project

Lesson 1 Resources

- ☑ 21st Century Skills Activity
  Collaboration: Group Project
- ☑ Primary Source Activity
  Jesus and the Jewish Religion
- ☑ Interactive Guided Reading Activity
- ☑ Reading Essentials and Study Guide
- ☑ Online Self-Check Quiz

Lesson 2 Resources

- ☑ Geography and History Activity The Role of Geography in the Spread of Christianity
- ☑ Interactive Guided Reading Activity
- ☑ Reading Essentials and Study Guide
- ☑ Online Self-Check Quiz

Lesson 3 Resources

- ☑ Economics of History Activity
  The Economic Life of Christian Monasteries
- ☑ Interactive Guided Reading Activity
- ☑ Reading Essentials and Study Guide
- ☑ Online Self-Check Quiz

Assessment Resources

- ☑ Lesson Reviews
- ☑ Online Self-Check Quizzes
- ☑ Chapter Activities and Assessment
- ☑ Standardized Test Practice

Remediation Resources

- ☑ Reading Essentials and Study Guide
- ☑ Guided Reading Activities
- ☑ Online Self-Check Quizzes
- ☑ Chapter Summary

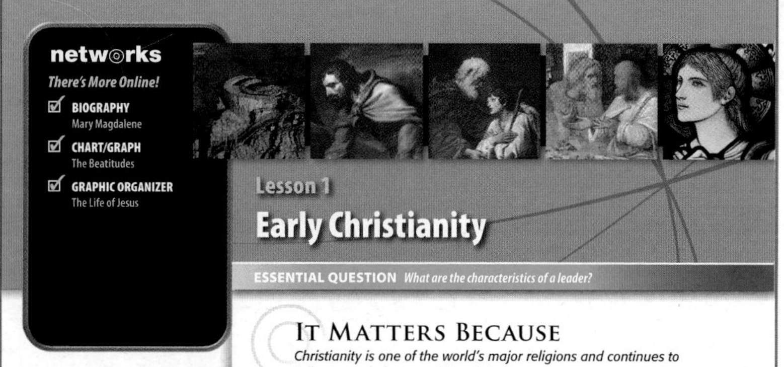

networks
There's More Online!
BIOGRAPHY
Mary Magdalene
CHART/GRAPH
The Beatitudes
GRAPHIC ORGANIZER
The Life of Jesus

Lesson 1

Early Christianity

ESSENTIAL QUESTION *What are the characteristics of a leader?*

It Matters Because

Christianity is one of the world's major religions and continues to influence people around the globe.

1 Judaism and Rome

GUIDING QUESTION *How did the Jews respond to Roman rule?*

The Romans allowed Judaism (JOO•dee•IH•zuhm) to be practiced throughout the empire. In Judaea and Galilee, however, Romans ruled the Jews with an iron hand. Many Jews hoped that God would send a deliverer to rescue them from Roman rule. They wanted the kingdom of Israel to be restored.

Control by Romans

The Romans had taken over Judah in 63 B.C., but they allowed Jewish kings to rule it. In A.D. 6, Augustus made Judah a Roman province and called it by the Roman name of Judaea (joo•DEE•uh). Augustus replaced the Jewish ruler with a Roman governor, called a procurator (PRAH•kyuh•RAY•tuhr). Judaea was now more tightly controlled by the Roman Empire.

The Jews disagreed among themselves over how to deal with the Romans. Some Jews wanted to avoid conflict with their rulers. They preferred to cooperate with them. Others limited their contact with Roman officials and continued to practice Jewish traditions. Some Jews completely ignored the Romans. They established communities in remote places, away from Roman rule. Jerusalem, however, remained their holy city.

Reading HELPDESK

Taking Notes: ***Identifying***

On a graphic organizer like this one, list three things we know about the life of Jesus.

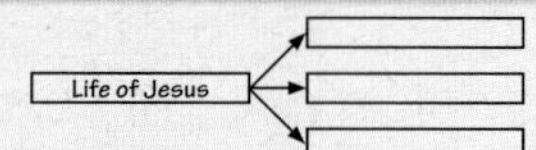

Content Vocabulary

- parable
- resurrection
- apostle
- salvation

Jewish Revolts

One group of Jews believed that they should fight the Romans for their freedom. These people, called Zealots (ZEH•luhtz), rebelled against Roman rule in A.D. 66. The Romans, however, brutally crushed the uprising. They destroyed the Jewish temple in Jerusalem and killed thousands of Jews.

The ruins of an ancient Jewish fortress called Masada (muh•SAH•duh) stand on a mountaintop in southeastern Israel. After Jerusalem fell to the Romans in A.D 70, about 1,000 Jewish defenders overtook the Masada fortress. For almost two years, these defenders held off an army of 15,000 Roman soldiers.

In A.D. 73, the Romans broke through the walls of the fortress but found only a few Jewish survivors—two women and five children. The others had taken their own lives rather than surrender to the Romans. The fortress is now recognized as a symbol of Jewish heroism.

The Jews organized another unsuccessful rebellion in A.D. 132. In response, the Romans forced all Jews to leave Jerusalem. The Romans then declared that no Jews could ever return to the city. Many Jews, mourning the loss of their city, established communities elsewhere.

By A.D. 700, the Jews had settled in regions as far west as Spain and as far east as Central Asia. In later centuries, they settled throughout Europe and the Americas.

An armed group of Jews captured this mountain fortress of Masada from the Romans. They defended it against a Roman army that outnumbered them 15 to one.

CRITICAL THINKING

Drawing Conclusions Why do you think the Jews wanted to control Masada?

BIOGRAPHY

Peter

Most of what we know about the disciple Peter comes from the Christian Bible. According to tradition, Peter deserted Jesus when Jesus was arrested in the garden outside Jerusalem. Later, Peter felt ashamed and regretted his lack of courage. In the years following the death of Jesus, Peter emerged as a respected leader of the earliest Christian community.

CRITICAL THINKING

Drawing Conclusions Why do you think Peter deserted Jesus when Jesus was arrested?

Although the Jews were scattered around the world, they kept their faith alive. They did this by studying and following their religious laws and traditions.

PROGRESS CHECK

Identifying Cause and Effect How did the A.D. 132 revolt affect the Jews of Judaea?

2 Jesus of Nazareth

GUIDING QUESTION *Why were the life and death of Jesus of Nazareth important to his followers?*

A few decades before the first Jewish revolt, a Jew named Jesus (JEE•zuhs) grew up in a small town called Nazareth (NA•zuh•ruhth) in Galilee (GA•luh•LEE), the region just north of Judaea. In about A.D. 30, Jesus began to travel throughout Galilee and Judaea, preaching to people about his ideas. A group of 12 close followers called disciples (dih•SY•puhlz) traveled with Jesus.

What Was the Message of Jesus?

According to the Christian Bible, Jesus preached that God was coming soon to rule the world. Jesus urged people to turn from their selfish ways and welcome the kingdom of heaven. In the excerpt below, Jesus calls on his followers to joyfully accept God's coming as a precious gift:

PRIMARY SOURCE

> "The kingdom of heaven is like a treasure buried in a field, which a person finds and hides again, and out of joy goes and sells all that he has and buys that field."
>
> —Matthew 13:54, *New American Bible*

Jesus preached that God **created** all people and loved them the way a father loves his children. Therefore, people should love God and one another. In this way, they would be obeying God.

The message of Jesus reinforced the Jewish teachings: "Love the Lord your God with all your heart and with all your soul and with all your mind and with all your strength" and "Love your neighbor as yourself."

The teachings of Jesus are summarized in his Sermon on the Mount. Jesus preached on a mountainside to a crowd of thousands.

Reading HELPDESK

Academic Vocabulary

create to bring into existence; to produce by a course of action

In it Jesus gave the people simple rules to live by called "The Beatitudes." He told people that it was not enough to follow religious laws. People had to love God and forgive others from the heart.

Jesus spoke using everyday language. He often preached using **parables** (PA•ruh•buhlz). These were stories about things his listeners could understand, using events from everyday life. They helped people **interpret**, or explain, the ideas Jesus taught.

In one parable, Jesus told of a Samaritan man who saw an injured traveler by the side of the road. Even though the injured man was not a Samaritan, the passerby helped him. In another parable, Jesus told the story of a father who forgave his son's mistakes. He welcomed his prodigal—or wasteful—son back into the family. Both parables taught that God is like the concerned Samaritan or the forgiving father. He loves people who have erred and will forgive them if they trust in him.

How Did Christianity Begin?

Jesus and his message sparked strong reactions from people. His followers spoke of times in which he healed the sick and performed other miracles. Stories about him were widely told.

INFOGRAPHIC — **THE BEATITUDES**

The *Beatitudes* are sayings or teachings intended to guide people. They are part of Jesus' Sermon on the Mount. The Sermon includes the Lord's Prayer and nine Beatitudes for leading a better life.

1. **DOCUMENT-BASED QUESTION** Jesus says the meek—or humble—shall inherit the Earth. What do you think he meant by this?
2. **CRITICAL THINKING** ***Making Generalizations*** Based on what Jesus says in the Beatitudes, what kind of people is he speaking to in his sermon?

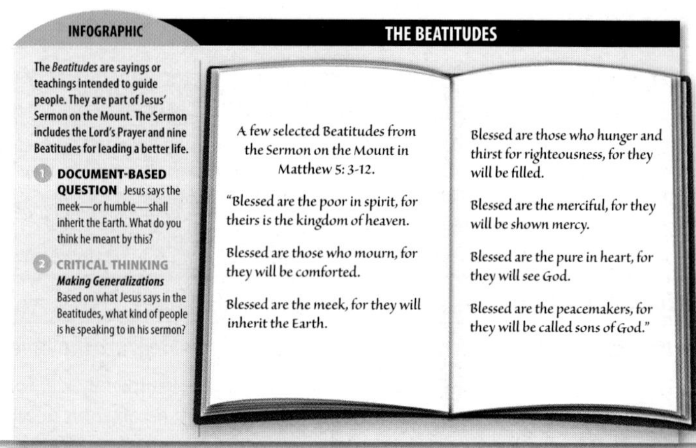

Blessed are those who mourn, for they will be comforted.

Blessed are the merciful, for they will be shown mercy.
Blessed are the pure in heart, for they will see God.
Blessed are the peacemakers, for they will be called sons of God."

parable a short story that teaches a principle about what is good behavior

Academic Vocabulary

interpret to explain the meaning of

LESSON 1

ENGAGE

SLIDE SHOW

Explaining Tell students that the core teachings of Jesus can be found in a Biblical passage called the Sermon on the Mount. Then present an interactive slide show depicting the Sermon on the Mount through the imaginations of various artists.

Tell students they will be learning about Christianity, including how it began and how it spread. This will include information on the life of Jesus, the connection between his teachings and Judaism, and the role of the apostles. AL 

TEACH & ASSESS

1 Judaism and Rome

GUIDING QUESTION *How did the Jews respond to Roman rule?*

LECTURE SLIDE

Discussing Discuss as a class the different ways in which the Jews related to Roman rule. *(Some Jews actively worked with the Romans. Others isolated themselves in their own communities. One group of Jews openly rebelled.)*

Show students the lecture slide on the zealots and their rebellions.

Ask:

What was the result of the Jewish rebellions? *(The Jewish rebellions failed to achieve their goal of driving out the Romans.)*

Why do you think these rebellions failed? *(Students might note the superior military strength of Rome and divisions among the Jewish community as reasons.)*

2 Jesus of Nazareth

GUIDING QUESTION *Why were the life and death of Jesus of Nazareth important to his followers?*

INTERACTIVE WORKSHEET

Comparing Explain to students that Jesus drew upon many ideas of the Jewish faith in his teachings. Assign the Primary Source Activity that draws connections between the teachings of Jesus and earlier Jewish writings.

INTERACTIVE WHITEBOARD

Making Inferences Remind students that Jesus used stories called parables to make it easier for his listeners to understand his ideas.

Ask:

Do you think people listened quietly to the stories and immediately understood the message they contained? Explain your answer. *(Possible response: Some people probably didn't agree with Jesus or wanted him to explain what he meant. They might have argued with him or among themselves about the meaning of a parable.)*

Tell students they will work in groups to create a modern version of a parable at the end of the lesson.

GRAPHIC ORGANIZER

Summarizing Have students complete the interactive graphic organizer on the life of Jesus to assess their understanding of the lesson so far. AL

3 Who Were the Apostles?

GUIDING QUESTION *How did early Christianity spread throughout the Roman Empire?*

LECTURE SLIDE

Identifying Show students the lecture slide defining the early apostles of Christianity.

Ask students:

How did the apostles spread the message of Jesus? *(They spoke to Jews in Judaea and Galilee before traveling to other parts of the Mediterranean region, carrying the message.)* AL

Have students complete the Lesson 1 Review.

CLOSE & REFLECT

INTERACTIVE WORKSHEET **Expressing** Have students work in groups to complete the 21st Century Skills Activity on creating a parable. Have student groups share their ideas for parables with the rest of the class. Encourage students within each group to divide tasks so they can each complete portions of the parable assignment as homework. BL

BACKGROUND KNOWLEDGE

The Apostle Peter

Information about Peter, an apostle of Jesus, is found in the New Testament. He is identified in the four Gospels, the Acts of the Apostles, the letters of Paul, and the two letters that bear his name. Peter was probably known by his Hebrew name Simeon or the Greek form of that name, Simon. During the time of Jesus, Peter lived in Capernaum, along the northwest coast of the Sea of Galilee. He and his brother Andrew were partners in the fishing industry.

In Matthew's Gospel account, when Jesus poses the question to his disciples about his identity, Simon declares that Jesus is the Son of God. Jesus gave Simon the title of Cephas, or Peter, which means "rock." Matthew continues to describe how Jesus would build his church upon the rock, or rather, upon Peter.

Answers for pages 372–375

P. 372 Taking Notes Jesus traveled throughout Galilee and Judaea, preaching to people; Roman rulers feared the growing influence of Jesus; Jesus was arrested, charged with treason, and executed.

P. 373 CRITICAL THINKING Answers should point out that the location of Masada in the mountains would give the Jews added protection from attack.

P. 374 CRITICAL THINKING Most likely Peter was afraid he would be arrested also.

P. 374 ☑ PROGRESS CHECK Roman authorities forced all Jews to leave the city of Jerusalem and told them they could never return.

P. 375 INFOGRAPHIC

1. Answers may vary. A plausible answer is that people who are meek will do a better job of caring for the Earth than those who are aggressive or warlike.
2. CRITICAL THINKING In the Beatitudes, Jesus seems to be addressing the powerless ("poor in spirit" and "meek") and the oppressed ("those who hunger and thirst for righteousness"). He also says those who are good on Earth will be rewarded after death.

The parables of the Good Samaritan (left) and the Prodigal Son (right) are shown here. In each case, one person is helping another.

▶ CRITICAL THINKING

Synthesizing What do you think of today when you hear that someone is a "good samaritan"?

Many believed he was the promised deliverer. Most Jews disagreed and did not follow Jesus. Roman rulers feared his preaching and growing influence and popularity. They viewed Jesus as a threat to law and order.

At the time of the Jewish holy days of Passover, there was growing tension between the Romans and the Jews. The Romans brought statues of the emperor into Jerusalem, the holy city of the Jews. Many Jews saw these statues as false idols and objected to their presence. The Jews had also grown weary of Roman rule and high taxes. Many Romans were angry because the Jews refused to worship statues of the Roman emperor.

In about A.D. 33, Jesus traveled to Jerusalem with his 12 disciples to celebrate the Jewish holy days of Passover. When he arrived in the city, an enthusiastic crowd greeted him as their promised deliverer. In an event known as the Last Supper, Jesus celebrated the Passover meal with his disciples.

Reading **HELP**DESK

Reading Strategy: *Paraphrasing*

Paraphrasing is restating what you read using your own words. Paraphrasing is a good way to check that you really understood what you read. As you finish reading a paragraph or a passage, ask yourself, "What is the main idea?" Then try to restate the main idea using your own words.

Betrayal of Jesus

After the meal, however, one of Jesus' closest followers betrayed him. Leaders in Jerusalem arrested Jesus to prevent trouble from erupting in the city. They may have charged Jesus with treason, or disloyalty to the government. He was questioned by the Roman governor and sentenced to death.

According to the Christian Bible, Jesus was crucified, or hung from a wooden cross, and died. Romans regularly crucified criminals and political rebels. The followers of Jesus were greatly saddened by his death. According to Christian belief, Jesus rose from the dead three days after his death and appeared to some of his disciples.

Early Christian writings state that Mary Magdalene, one of Jesus' followers, was the first to see him alive again. The message of Jesus' **resurrection** (REH•zuh•REHK•shuhn), or rising from the dead, led to the birth of Christianity. During this very early period, Christians were still one of the many groups that made up Judaism.

✔ PROGRESS CHECK

Explaining How did Jesus reinforce traditional Jewish teachings?

3 Who Were the Apostles?

GUIDING QUESTION *How did early Christianity spread throughout the Roman Empire?*

The early Christian leaders who spread the message of Jesus were called **apostles** (uh•PAH•suhlz). The apostles first spoke to the Jews in Judaea and Galilee. The apostles then traveled to other parts of the Mediterranean region. Small groups of Jews and non-Jews in the Greek-speaking cities of the eastern Mediterranean believed the message about Jesus.

Those who accepted Jesus and his teachings became known as "Christians" and referred to Jesus as "Jesus Christ." The word *Christ* comes from *Christos*, which is a Greek term that means "the anointed one."

The first Christians formed churches, or local groups for worship and teaching. Early Christians met in homes of men and women. At these gatherings, Christians prayed and studied the Hebrew Bible and early Christian writings. They also ate a meal similar to the Last Supper to remember the death and resurrection of Jesus.

BIOGRAPHY

Mary Magdalene

A practical, down-to-earth woman, Mary Magdalene went with Jesus during his travels throughout Galilee. Biblical accounts of the life of Jesus maintain that she was present during his crucifixion and burial. These accounts also say she and two other women went to his tomb a few days after he was placed there. Finding it empty, Mary hurried to tell the other followers. She then returned to the tomb with Peter, also a follower of Jesus.

▶ CRITICAL THINKING

Analyzing What risks did Mary Magdalene face by being loyal to Jesus?

resurrection the act of rising from the dead

apostle Christian leader chosen by Jesus to spread his message

At the end of the 1400s, the Italian artist Leonardo da Vinci created this famous painting of Jesus. Called *The Last Supper*, it was painted on a wall in Milan, Italy.

▶ CRITICAL THINKING

Analyzing What do you think is happening in this illustration of Jesus and his followers?

Early Christian Leaders

Apostles played an important part in the growth of Christianity. Peter and Paul were two important apostles in the early Christian church. Peter was a Jewish fisher from Galilee. He had known Jesus while he was alive and had been one of the 12 disciples Jesus had chosen to preach his message. According to Christian tradition, Peter helped set up a Christian church in Rome after the death of Jesus. Today, the center of the Catholic branch of Christianity is still located there.

Paul of Tarsus was another important Christian apostle. He was a well-educated Jew and a Roman citizen. He was raised as a loyal Roman who, as an adult, distrusted the Christians. Saul—his Hebrew name—at first tried to stop Christian ideas from spreading in Judaea and Galilee. The chief Jewish priest in Jerusalem then sent him to Damascus, a city in neighboring Syria. There, he was supposed to stop Christians in the city from spreading their ideas.

According to Christian belief, while he was traveling to Damascus in Syria, Paul saw a great light and heard the voice of Jesus. As a result of this encounter, Paul soon became a Christian and devoted his life to spreading the message of Jesus.

Reading **HELP**DESK

salvation the act of being saved from the effects of sin

Paul traveled throughout the eastern Mediterranean region and founded numerous Christian churches. Many of his important letters to churches in Rome, Greece, and Asia Minor are found in the Christian Bible.

Before becoming an apostle, Paul of Tarsus tried to stop the spread of Christian ideas. After he came to believe in Jesus, Paul became one of the most influential leaders of the early Christian movement.

▶ CRITICAL THINKING

Speculating Why do you think Paul at first tried to stop the spread of the message of Jesus?

What Are Basic Christian Beliefs?

The early Christians believed in one God, not the many gods of Rome. They believed that Jesus was the Son of God. They believed he had come to save people. By becoming Christians and by accepting Jesus and his teachings, people could gain **salvation** (sal•VAY•shuhn). They would be saved from their sins, or wrongdoings, and allowed to enter heaven. Like Jesus, people would be resurrected after death and join God in everlasting life.

Because of their faith in Jesus, Christians began to believe in God in a new way. Like the Jews, Christians believed in the God of Israel and studied the Hebrew Bible. However, they also believed in the Christian Trinity, which comes from a word meaning "three." In Christian belief, the Trinity refers to the three persons of God: the Father, Son, and Holy Spirit. These teachings became the basis of the Christian faith.

During the 100 years after Jesus' death, Christianity won followers throughout the world. The peace and order established by the Roman Empire gave people the ability to spread the Christian religion.

✔ PROGRESS CHECK

Identifying Why were the apostles important to early Christianity?

LESSON 1 REVIEW

Review Vocabulary

1. Why did Jesus preach using *parables*?
2. How did the *apostles* spread the message of Jesus?

Answer the Guiding Questions

3. ***Explaining*** How did Jewish traditions survive after A.D. 132?
4. ***Describing*** When Jesus said "love your neighbor as yourself," what was his message?
5. ***Contrasting*** How did some Jews differ in their beliefs about Jesus?
6. ***Explaining*** Why did Jesus have disciples?
7. **EXPOSITORY WRITING** In a paragraph, explain why there were growing tensions between the Romans and the early Christians.

LESSON 1 (cont.)

IF YOU HAVE MORE TIME . . .

Discuss the Message of Jesus

Making Connections Remind students that storytelling played an important role in the spread of Christianity during the first few centuries after Jesus's death.

First the apostles and then later generations of Christians told and retold the story of Jesus's life and death and the things he taught.

Ask: If Jesus were alive today, what are some ways in which his message might be shared with others? *(Possible response: He could have his own TV show or podcasts. His followers could create blogs or Web sites to publish his ideas and photos or videos of him teaching. He could appear on talk shows and give interviews to reporters.)*

Speculating Have students imagine that the story of Jesus of Nazareth takes place in the present.

Ask: What might Jesus think about the world we live in? How do you think people with authority might respond to Jesus today? *(Answers will vary. Students might speculate that Jesus would not be happy with the world today. His message of forgiveness, tolerance, and compassion for those in need might get him into trouble with powerful rulers.)*

Ask: Why did the Romans consider Jesus a dangerous person who had to be arrested? *(Possible response: They thought he had too much influence over people and might persuade people to rise up against Roman authority.)*

Ask: What other belief systems besides Christianity existed within the Roman Empire? *(The Jewish religion and the religions of the Romans were two other belief systems within the Roman Empire.)*

Take a Closer Look at Peter and Paul

Comparing and Contrasting Point out to students that two of the most important leaders of the early Christian church were Peter and Paul. Show students the interactive image with biographical background information on Paul.

Ask: What are some differences and similarities between Peter and Paul, two early Christian leaders? *(Peter was one of the original 12 followers of Jesus. Paul did not become a believer until after the death of Jesus. Peter was a fisher before becoming an apostle. Paul was an educated Jew and a Roman citizen. After the death of Jesus, Peter became a leader in the early church. Before his conversion to Christianity, Paul worked to prevent Christian beliefs from spreading.)*

To help students as they work through the lesson, read parts of the lesson aloud to them. This practice helps students learn about grammar and pronunciation. It also increases students' familiarity with book language. **AL** **ELL**

BACKGROUND KNOWLEDGE

Reading Strategies: Identifying Main Idea and Supporting Details

Trying to find the main idea of a passage is a difficult task—it requires the critical thinking skill of distinguishing between what is important and what is secondary.

Determining supporting details means locating the ideas or examples that extend the main idea or give additional information. Essentially, readers determine an author's purpose when they find main ideas in a selection. To do that, students need to use information about how a particular text is structured (for example, cause and effect, compare and contrast, problem and solution, chronological order) and combine that information with what they know about a topic, an idea, or an author.

Students should be reminded that the main idea of a paragraph is often found in the topic sentence; however, they will sometimes need to infer the main idea of a paragraph using prior knowledge and the information presented in the paragraph.

Teaching students to find the main idea and supporting details is helpful during and after reading. It helps students prepare to summarize. By activating prior knowledge and previewing the text before reading, students learn to anticipate what main ideas they will find.

Provide students with these techniques for determining main ideas and supporting details:

- Ask students to share prior knowledge about an author or a topic.
- Guide students to anticipate what might be important in a selection.
- Look at text structure to see how an author organizes ideas.
- Invite students to read one paragraph of text and model finding the main idea and supporting details.
- Ask questions while reading, such as: *What one idea are the sentences in this paragraph about? How does this idea fit in with what I know about the topic? About this author? About how the selection is organized? What sentences add information about this topic?*
- Remind students to look for headings, illustrations, captions, and other text features to help them determine the main idea.

Answers for pages 376–379

P. 376 CRITICAL THINKING A good samaritan is a person who helps someone who is in trouble. The term is often used to describe someone who helps a stranger.

P. 377 ☑ PROGRESS CHECK His message reinforced Jewish commandments to "Love the Lord your God with all your heart and with all your soul and with all your strength and with all your mind" and to "Love your neighbor as yourself."

P. 377 CRITICAL THINKING Mary could face shunning from other Jews and/or arrest by the Romans.

P. 378 CRITICAL THINKING Answers may vary. Possible answers include the following: Jesus and his followers are sharing the Passover meal somewhere in Jerusalem.

P. 379 CRITICAL THINKING Answers may vary. A possible response is that Paul thought followers of Jesus were not being faithful Jews.

P. 379 ☑ PROGRESS CHECK They were able to spread his message and the story of his resurrection throughout the Mediterranean region.

LESSON 1 REVIEW

1. Jesus used parables because they made it easier for people to understand his teachings.
2. Apostles spread the message of Jesus by traveling across the Mediterranean region setting up churches and telling people about Jesus.
3. Over a period of several centuries, Jews established communities outside of Jerusalem as far east as Central Asia and as far west as Spain. They kept their faith alive by studying and practicing their religious laws and traditions.
4. We should treat others the same way we want others to treat us: with respect, kindness, and even love.
5. Some Jews believed that Jesus was their promised deliverer. Most Jews did not believe this. They expected the deliverer to be a political leader who would liberate them from Roman rule.
6. Jesus needed disciples to spread his message after he was gone.
7. One reason for the growing tensions between the Romans and the early Christians was the fact that Christians refused to worship statues of the Roman gods. They also had grown tired of Roman rule and resented having to pay high taxes. Roman authorities, on the other hand, were wary of Jesus and his growing influence, which they feared might threaten law and order.

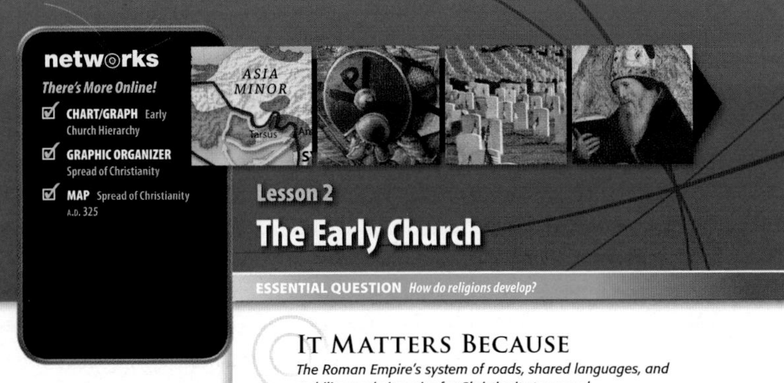

networks
There's More Online!
- CHART/GRAPH Early Church Hierarchy
- GRAPHIC ORGANIZER Spread of Christianity
- MAP Spread of Christianity A.D. 325

Lesson 2
The Early Church

ESSENTIAL QUESTION *How do religions develop?*

It Matters Because
The Roman Empire's system of roads, shared languages, and stability made it easier for Christianity to spread.

1 Christianity and the Empire
GUIDING QUESTION *How did Christianity change over time?*

As the apostles spread the message of Jesus, many people in the Mediterranean world became Christians. The Roman Empire contributed to this growth.

Christianity Spreads
Several factors helped Christianity spread throughout the empire. Areas controlled by the Romans were generally peaceful. Well-constructed roads meant Christians could easily travel from one **region** to another. Most people in the empire spoke Latin or Greek. This allowed Christians to communicate with them about the message of Jesus.

Another reason Christianity spread throughout the empire was that it had an attractive message. The official religion of Rome required people to honor the emperor and the state. This religion did not offer help to people when they experienced personal or economic problems. Christianity, however, provided comfort to people during difficult times. Christianity gave people hope that even if life was bad on Earth, there was the promise of a better afterlife.

Reading **HELP**DESK

Taking Notes: *Listing*
Use a graphic organizer like this one to list the major reasons that Christianity spread.

Reasons Christianity Spread
•
•
•
•

Content Vocabulary
- martyr
- hierarchy
- clergy
- doctrine
- gospel
- pope
- laity

Christianity also spread quickly throughout the empire because it provided its followers with security. Christians lived in **communities** where each member was responsible for taking care of the needs of others.

Why Did Romans Mistreat Christians?
As the number of Christians grew, some Romans believed that they were dangerous. They thought Christians were a threat to the empire. Romans expected everyone to worship the emperor as a god. The Christians, like the Jews, however, believed that only God could be worshipped. Christians criticized popular Roman festivals that honored the numerous Roman gods. Also, Christians did not support warfare as a way to resolve problems. As a result, they refused to serve in the Roman army. Furthermore, Christians buried their dead outside Rome in catacombs, or underground burial places. Christians could also meet there to hold memorial services.

GEOGRAPHY CONNECTION
Even though the Romans persecuted the Christians, the Christian religion continued to grow and spread its influence.
1. **LOCATION** What areas did Paul visit during his second journey?
2. **CRITICAL THINKING** *Speculating* What might have prevented Christianity from spreading to more places during its first three centuries?

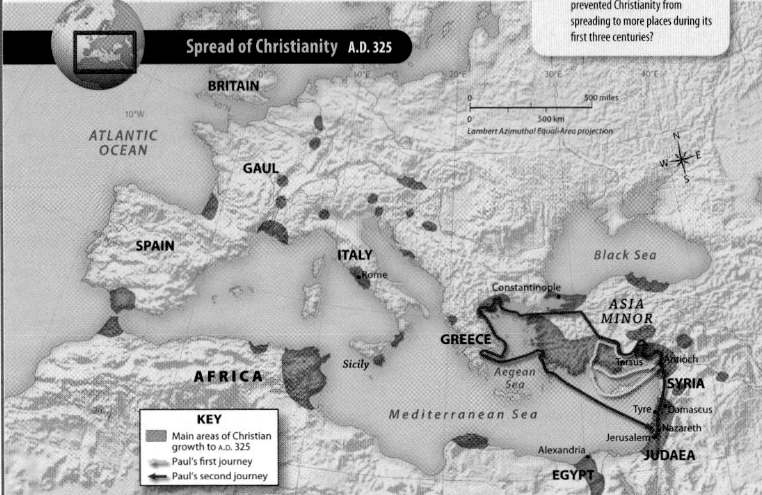

Academic Vocabulary
region a broad geographic area
community people living in a particular area; the area itself

THEN

During the early centuries of Christianity, the Roman Catacombs were used for burials and funeral meals. Today, cemeteries are still places where we go to honor our families, experience shared history, and reflect on the sacrifices of others.

NOW

▶ CRITICAL THINKING
Analyzing Why do you think early Christians buried their dead in hidden catacombs?

People who thought the Christians were dangerous believed that they should be punished. Some Romans blamed Christians for causing natural disasters. In A.D. 64, the emperor Nero falsely accused Christians of starting a fire that burned most of Rome. As a result, Christianity was outlawed.

Christians were often mistreated. They were arrested and beaten. Some Christians became **martyrs** (MAHR•tuhrz), or people who were willing to die rather than give up their beliefs. Despite the mistreatment, Christianity continued to flourish.

The Empire Accepts Christianity
In the early A.D. 300s, the emperor Diocletian carried out the last great persecution of Christians. But his attempt failed. Christianity had grown too strong to be destroyed by force.

In A.D. 312, the Roman emperor Constantine (KAHN•stuhn•TEEN) prepared to lead his **military** forces into battle. According to some early Christian writers, Constantine had a remarkable dream the night before the battle. In the dream he saw a flaming cross in the sky. Written beneath the cross were the Latin words that meant "In this sign you will conquer."

The next day, Constantine ordered his soldiers to paint the Christian cross on their battle shields. Constantine won the battle and believed the Christian God had helped him.

Constantine became a strong supporter of Christianity. In A.D. 313, he issued the Edict of Milan. This decree allowed all religious groups in the empire, including Christians, to practice their religions freely. Constantine attended religious meetings of Christian leaders and gave government aid to Christians. With the help of his mother, Helena (HEH•luh•nuh), he built Christian churches in Rome and Jerusalem. Christians were allowed to serve in government and were excused from paying taxes. They started to serve in the army.

One of Constantine's successors, the emperor Theodosius (THEE•uh•DOH•shuhs), banned Greek and Roman religions. In A.D. 392, he made Christianity the official religion of the Roman Empire.

PROGRESS CHECK
Evaluating How did Constantine support Christianity?

Reading **HELP**DESK

martyr a person who is willing to die for his or her beliefs

Academic Vocabulary
military relating to armed forces

Constantine led his troops to victory at the Battle of Milvian Bridge near Rome. This triumph led Constantine to convert to Christianity.

▶ CRITICAL THINKING
Analyzing Do you think the Romans could have destroyed Christianity if Constantine hadn't been converted? Explain.

2 Organizing the Church
GUIDING QUESTION *How did early Christians organize their church and explain their beliefs?*

As the number of Christians grew, the church had to become more organized to unite its followers. After the time of the apostles, separate Christian communities began to practice Christianity differently. In order to ensure one form of Christianity, early Christian leaders decided to clarify their beliefs by writing them down.

Church Leadership
Early Christians were familiar with how the Roman Empire was ruled. They used the empire as their model for organizing the church. Like the empire, the church came to be ruled by a **hierarchy** (HY•uh•RAHR•kee). A hierarchy is an organization with different levels of authority.

The **clergy** (KLUHR•jee), or church officials, were the leaders of the church. In the early church, only men were allowed to be members of the clergy. The role of the clergy was different from that of the **laity** (LAY•uh•tee), or regular church members. Although women were not allowed to serve in the clergy, they were members of the church. Women cared for sick and needy church members.

hierarchy an organization with different levels of authority
clergy church officials
laity regular church members

LESSON 2

ENGAGE

Making Connections Invite students to tell about any long car or bus trips they've taken.

Ask:

What were the roads like? Where did you stay? Did any problems arise along the way?

Inform students that the Romans built thousands of miles of roads that connected cities as well as border regions of the empire. These roads provided comfort and security, and they enabled people to travel long distances. Because of this network of roads, Christianity was able to spread fairly easily throughout the empire.

TEACH & ASSESS

1 Christianity and the Empire

GUIDING QUESTION *How did Christianity change over time?*

INTERACTIVE MAP **Analyzing Visuals** Show the interactive map "Spread of Christianity A.D. 325."

Then **ask** the following questions:

- **What does this map show?** *(The map shows the main areas of Christianity's growth to A.D. 325.)*
- **How far west had Christianity spread by A.D. 325?** *(Christianity had spread as far west as the southern coast of Spain and the northern coast of Africa.)*
- **How could Paul carry Jesus's message over such a great distance during his second journey?** *(The Roman system of roads meant he could easily travel from place to place.)*

GRAPHIC ORGANIZER **Organizing** Discuss as a class some of the reasons for the growth of Christianity. Then have students list the reasons for Christianity's appeal in the interactive graphic organizer.

(Sample answers: Promised a better life after death; Offered comfort during difficult times; Promised forgiveness for wrongdoing; Christian communities took care of their members.)

Summarizing Remind students that many Christians suffered under Roman rule.

Ask:

What were some of the reasons why the Romans persecuted the Christians? *(Christians would not worship the emperor; Christians criticized Roman games and festivals; Christians refused to serve in the Roman army; too many people were becoming Christians.)*

LECTURE SLIDE **Drawing Conclusions** Explain that over time the Roman Empire accepted Christianity and made it the empire's official religion. Show students the lecture slide on Constantine's support for Christianity.

Ask:

Why was Constantine's support of Christianity important? *(Constantine ended the persecution of Christians and allowed them to serve in government along with building churches and providing aid. These measures allowed Christianity to grow stronger and become more accepted by the Roman people.)*

INTERACTIVE WORKSHEET Assign the Geography and History Activity to assess student understanding of how Christianity spread. You might want to have students complete the activity as homework.

2 Organizing the Church

GUIDING QUESTION *How did early Christians organize their church and explain their beliefs?*

CHART **Discussing** Show students the interactive chart displaying the hierarchy of the early church.

Ask:

What was the difference between the roles of bishops and priests? *(Bishops had authority over more than one church and were responsible for determining Church doctrine. Priests were responsible for a single church and led daily worship.)*

LECTURE SLIDE **Explaining** Show students the lecture slide on the early writings of Christianity.

Ask:

How did these writings help Christianity become a unified religion? *(Answers may vary but should note that these writings became popular and influential, allowing many Christians to begin sharing the same beliefs about what it meant to be a Christian.)*

Have students complete the Lesson 2 Review.

CLOSE & REFLECT

Making Connections Note to students that Christianity has many active branches today. Add that in the second and third centuries A.D., Christianity was similarly diverse.

Ask:

What do you think are some of the issues that divided early Christians as they tried to organize themselves after Jesus' death? *(Possible response: Early Christians probably debated about which Jewish practices to keep and which to discard. They might also have differed about how to relate to the Romans and Roman political authority, how to explain certain Christian beliefs to critics, how the church should be organized, and who should have final authority in the church.)*

Answers for pages 380–383

P. 380 Taking Notes Because the Romans maintained peace and order over all the lands they ruled, Christians could easily travel safely from one region to another. Christianity had enormous appeal because it provided comfort to people and gave them hope for a better life after death. Christians helped those in need. Most people in the Roman Empire spoke Latin or Greek so Christians could easily communicate the message of Jesus.

P. 381 GEOGRAPHY CONNECTION

1. During his second journey, Paul traveled through Judaea, Syria, Asia Minor, and Greece.
2. CRITICAL THINKING Continued persecution of Christians, language barriers, and conflict with other religions are some of the factors that might have prevented Christianity from spreading to more places.

P. 382 CRITICAL THINKING By hiding burial places, early Christians could make sure they would not be disturbed.

P. 382 ☑ PROGRESS CHECK Constantine issued the Edict of Milan, which gave religious freedom to all religious groups in the empire, including Christians. He also gave financial aid to Christians and established Christian churches in Rome and Jerusalem.

P. 383 CRITICAL THINKING Answers may vary. A possible response is that the Christian movement had grown too strong and could not be stopped, even by the Romans.

EARLY CHURCH HIERARCHY

INFOGRAPHIC

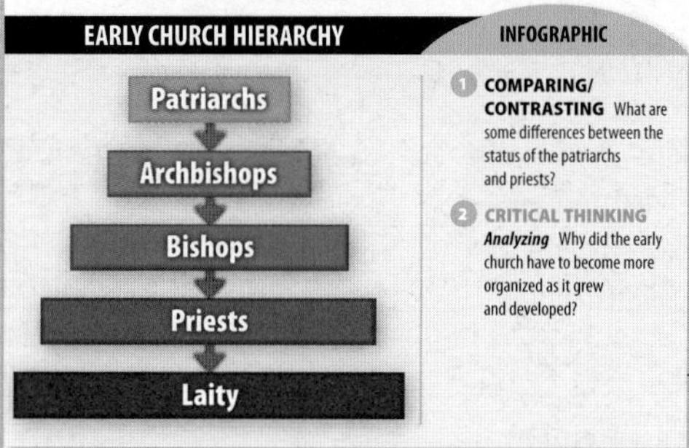

1. **COMPARING/ CONTRASTING** What are some differences between the status of the patriarchs and priests?
2. **CRITICAL THINKING** ***Analyzing*** Why did the early church have to become more organized as it grew and developed?

By A.D. 300, individual churches were headed by clergy called priests. Priests led worship services and managed local church activities. Clergy called bishops supervised the dioceses (DY•uh•suh•suhz), or several churches grouped together. Bishops explained Christian beliefs to other clergy and laity and managed regional church affairs. A bishop who was in charge of an entire region was known as an archbishop. The five leading archbishops—in charge of the cities of Rome, Constantinople, Alexandria, Antioch, and Jerusalem—were known as patriarchs (PAY•tree•AHRKS).

The bishops met together in councils to define the teachings of the Church. They wanted to make sure that Christians practiced the same beliefs. The decisions they reached at these councils were accepted as **doctrine** (DAHK•truhn), or official church teaching. The ideas that the bishops rejected were heresies (HER•uh•seez), or teachings that did not support the Christian faith.

What Writings Shaped Christianity?

Church leaders also preserved stories about Jesus and the writings of the apostles. Jesus did not write down what he said or did. His followers, however, wrote down and passed on what they remembered about him. By A.D. 300, four accounts of the life and teachings of Jesus were widely known. Christians believed that four apostles of Jesus—Matthew, Mark, Luke, and John—wrote these accounts.

Reading HELPDESK

doctrine official church teaching
gospel the accounts that apostles wrote of Jesus' life
pope the title given to the Bishop of Rome

Each account of Jesus' life was called a **gospel** (GAHS•puhl), which means "good news." Christians later included the four gospels with the writings of Paul and other early Christian leaders. Together, these works became known as the New Testament. The New Testament was added to the Greek version of the Jewish sacred writings, which Christians called the Old Testament. Together, these works formed the Christian Bible.

Other writings influenced the early church. Christian thinkers who explained church teachings became known as the Church Fathers. One of the most important Church Fathers was Augustine, a bishop in North Africa. In his writings, Augustine defended Christianity against its critics. Augustine wrote *The City of God*. This was one of the first history books written from the viewpoint of a Christian.

The Bishop of Rome

As the church grew, the bishop of Rome claimed power over the other bishops. He believed that he had received the authority of the apostle Peter. Also, his diocese was in Rome, the capital of the Roman Empire. By A.D. 600, people began to call the bishop of Rome by a special title—**pope** (POHP). The title is from a Latin word, *papa*, related to the word *pater*, meaning "father." Latin-speaking Christians in the western part of the empire accepted the pope as head of all the churches. The Latin churches as a group became known as the Roman Catholic Church. Greek-speaking Christians, however, would not accept the authority of the pope over them. Also claiming a link to the apostles, their churches became known as the Eastern Orthodox Church.

Augustine was one of the most important writers and thinkers in the history of Christianity. Even today, his books continue to inform and inspire.

▶ **CRITICAL THINKING**
Making Inferences Why do you think Augustine is remembered as one of the Church Fathers?

PROGRESS CHECK

Identifying What writings are included in the New Testament?

LESSON 2 REVIEW

Review Vocabulary

1. How did church *doctrine* help to unify early Christians?
2. How is the *pope* similar to and different from other bishops?

Answer the Guiding Questions

3. ***Identifying*** What were two main reasons Christianity spread during Roman times?
4. ***Describing*** Why were early Christians considered traitors to the Roman Empire?
5. ***Comparing*** Compare the responsibilities of a priest and a bishop in the early Christian church.
6. ***Making Inferences*** Why did bishops meet in councils?
7. **PERSONAL WRITING** Write a journal entry that Constantine might have written after the battle he believed God helped him win.

networks
There's More Online!
☑ **CHART/GRAPH** Cyrillic Alphabet
☑ **MAP** Spread of Christianity A.D. 325–1100

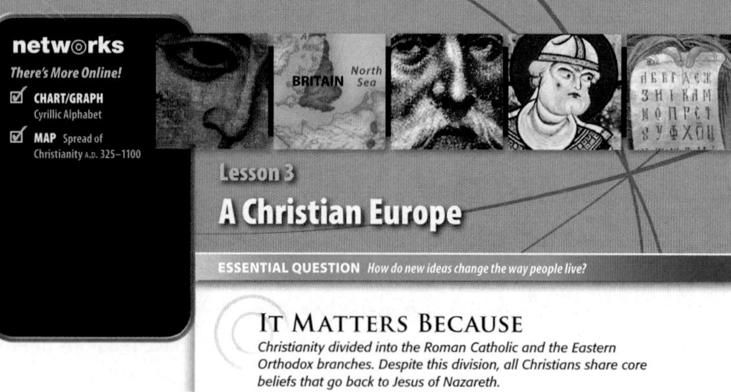

Lesson 3
A Christian Europe

ESSENTIAL QUESTION *How do new ideas change the way people live?*

IT MATTERS BECAUSE

Christianity divided into the Roman Catholic and the Eastern Orthodox branches. Despite this division, all Christians share core beliefs that go back to Jesus of Nazareth.

1 Two Christian Churches

GUIDING QUESTION *What issues divided the western and eastern Christian churches?*

The Roman Catholic Church was based in Rome, the capital of the Western Roman Empire. The church was led by the very powerful pope. As the Western Roman Empire declined, the Christian church of Rome survived. At the same time, the Roman Empire in the east, which soon became known as the Byzantine Empire, thrived. The Byzantines developed their own Christian church. Their church reflected their Greek heritage. This church became known as the Eastern Orthodox Church.

Byzantine Government and Religion

The emperor of the Byzantine Empire and the officials of the Eastern Orthodox Church worked closely together. The Byzantines believed their emperor was God's representative on Earth. Beginning in the A.D. 400s, emperors were crowned in a religious ceremony. They also took an oath to defend Eastern Orthodox Christianity. They believed it was their duty to unite the empire under one Christian faith. Thus, the emperors controlled the Eastern Orthodox Church. Emperors appointed church leaders and defined how people would worship. They also controlled the wealth of the church and helped settle disputes about church beliefs.

Reading HELPDESK

Taking Notes: *Listing*
Create a chart like this one and use it to list arguments for and against honoring icons.

Honoring Icons	
For	Against

Content Vocabulary
- **icon**
- **iconoclast**
- **excommunicate**
- **schism**
- **monastery**

What Are Icons?

Both Byzantine clergy and the Byzantine people discussed and often argued about religious matters. These arguments frequently became political issues and led to fights and riots.

In the A.D. 700s, a heated dispute about **icons** (EYE•KAWNZ) divided the Eastern Orthodox Church. Icons are paintings of Jesus, Mary (the mother of Jesus), and the saints, or Christian holy people. Many Byzantines **displayed** icons in their homes. They also covered the walls of their churches with them.

People who displayed icons claimed that these images symbolized the presence of God in their lives. They also believed that the images helped people understand Christian teachings. The thinker John of Damascus was the leading defender of icons.

Some Byzantines, however, did not approve of the use of icons. They thought it was a form of idol worship forbidden by God. In A.D. 726, Emperor Leo III ordered that all icons be removed from the churches. Government officials who carried out his orders were called **iconoclasts** (eye•KAH•nuh•KLASTS), or image breakers. Today, this word refers to someone who criticizes traditional beliefs or practices.

Most Byzantines, many church leaders, and even the pope in Rome disapproved of Emperor Leo's actions. The dispute over icons severely damaged the relationship between the Roman Catholic Church and the Eastern Orthodox Church. Over the next century, the argument became less heated, and icons were used once again. They are still important today.

This icon painted on wood shows the angel Gabriel. According to the Christian Bible, Gabriel was a messenger sent from God.

▶ **CRITICAL THINKING**
Explaining Why do you think some Byzantine people were against the use of icons?

The Great Split

Icons were only one of the issues that divided the eastern and western Christian churches. The most serious disagreement was about church authority. The pope claimed to be head of all Christian churches. He believed he was a successor, or person who follows another person, to Peter, disciple of Jesus. Peter was the first bishop of Rome. The Byzantines **rejected** the claim of the pope. They believed the patriarch of Constantinople and other bishops were equal to the pope.

icon a representation of an object of worship
iconoclast *originally:* a person who destroys icons; *today:* a person who criticizes traditional beliefs

Academic Vocabulary
display to place an object where people can view it
reject to refuse to accept

LESSON 2 (cont.)

IF YOU HAVE MORE TIME . . .

Complete a Brainstorming Activity About Hierarchy

Remind students that Christianity developed from small, informal gatherings in people's homes to a highly structured organization modeled on the Roman government.

Explain that church leaders eventually became part of a hierarchy. This meant that people in leadership positions at the top of the hierarchy had the most power. People with the least power were at the bottom. Remind students that the modern world has many examples of hierarchies.

As a class, brainstorm some examples of hierarchical organizations. Then, using a pyramid graphic organizer, have students name the various levels of authority in one of the organizations. *(Some types of hierarchical organizations include schools, the military, and the government.)* AL ELL

Answers for pages 384–385

P. 384 INFOGRAPHIC

1. Answers may vary but should point out that priests were responsible for just one church, but the patriarchs had power over all churches and made all the rules.
2. CRITICAL THINKING Answers may vary but should include something about the need to unify its followers.

P. 385 CRITICAL THINKING His writings helped define Christian beliefs and defended Christianity from its critics.

P. 385 ☑ PROGRESS CHECK The New Testament includes the four gospels and the writings of Paul and other early Christian leaders.

LESSON 2 REVIEW

1. Church doctrine helped make sure that Christians lived by the same beliefs.
2. The pope is the bishop of Rome and is also the leader of the other bishops.
3. Answers may vary. Good roads meant Christians could easily travel from one region to another to spread the word. Most people in the empire spoke Latin or Greek, which made it easier to communicate. Also, Christianity had a more attractive message than the official religion of Rome.
4. Some early Christians refused to serve in the Roman army and were seen as traitors.
5. Priests led worship services and managed local church activities. Bishops oversaw several churches instead of one and managed the affairs of these different churches.
6. Bishops met in councils to define the teachings of the church, deciding which particular beliefs were correct and which were wrong.
7. Answers may vary, but students' journal entries might include Constantine's expression of gratitude for the divine assistance he believed he had received. They might also include any changes Constantine expects to make (or promises God he will make) in his character or behavior now that he has become a Christian. Another possibility is for students to recall some of the highlights of the battle and of the specific ways in which God helped Constantine defeat the enemy.

Teaching *A Christian Europe*

(Student Edition pp. 386–391)

LESSON 3

ENGAGE

IMAGE **Previewing** Show students the image of Charlemagne as Holy Roman Emperor and read the accompanying text. Explain that the crowning of Charlemagne angered the leaders of the Byzantine Church because it favored the church leaders in Western Europe.

Tell students that this lesson explores some of the reasons early Christianity split into two main branches—the Roman Catholic Church and the Eastern Orthodox Church.

TEACH & ASSESS

1 Two Christian Churches

GUIDING QUESTION *What issues divided the western and eastern Christian churches?*

LECTURE SLIDE **Determining Cause and Effect** Show students the lecture slide listing the key issues that divided the early Christian church.

Ask:

Which of these disputes were about political issues? *(the relationship of church and government, refusal to defend Italy from invaders, pope crowning a Frankish king as emperor)*

Which ones were about religious issues? *(the use of icons, the authority of the pope versus the authority of the patriarch)*

GRAPHIC ORGANIZER **Contrasting** Show students the interactive graphic organizer that contrasts Byzantine reasons for and against the use of icons. Have student volunteers suggest reasons to place in each category, and then display the completed graphic organizer to the class.

(Reasons for the use of icons include: These images represent the presence of God in one's daily life; icons help people understand Christian teachings. Reasons against the use of icons include: Honoring icons is a form of idol worship, which is forbidden by God; icons distract Christians from thinking about spiritual matters.)

2 The Spread of Christianity

GUIDING QUESTION *How did Christianity spread across Europe?*

Theorizing Point out that the spread of Christianity took place before the invention of mass communications media like TV, radio, or the Internet, and when overland travel was slow and often dangerous.

Ask:

How do you think Christians were able to communicate their message to large numbers of people living in different parts of Europe and the British Isles? *(Answers will vary. Students might theorize that Christians set up churches or convinced local rulers to adopt Christianity as an official religion.)*

Answers for pages 386–387

P. 386 Taking Notes For: These images represent the presence of God in a person's or family's daily life; icons help people understand Christian teachings. Against: Honoring icons is a form of idol worship that is forbidden by God; icons distract Christians from thinking about spiritual matters.

P. 387 CRITICAL THINKING Answers may vary. A possible response is that some Byzantines might have thought icons were too much like images of the old Roman gods.

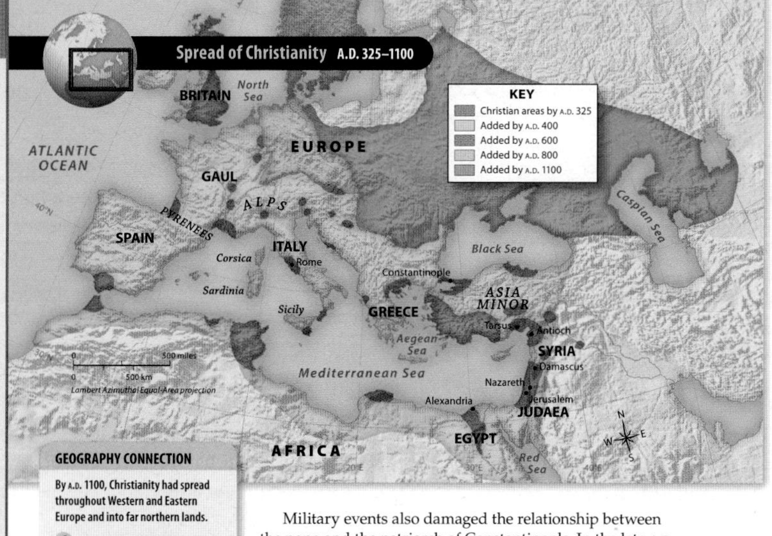

GEOGRAPHY CONNECTION

By A.D. 1100, Christianity had spread throughout Western and Eastern Europe and into far northern lands.

1. **UNDERSTANDING A MAP KEY** Which of these two areas became Christian first: Britain or Syria?
2. **CRITICAL THINKING** *Analyzing* Why do you think some areas took longer to convert to Christianity than others?

Military events also damaged the relationship between the pope and the patriarch of Constantinople. In the late A.D. 700s, Italy was invaded. The pope appealed to the Byzantine emperor for help, but the emperor refused. The pope then asked the Franks to help defend Rome. The Franks were a Germanic people that supported the pope as head of the Christian church.

The Franks successfully defended Italy against the invaders. To show his gratitude, the pope crowned the Frankish king, Charlemagne (SHAHR•luh•MAYN), emperor in A.D. 800. The pope's actions upset the Byzantines. They believed their ruler was the only Roman emperor.

The eastern and western churches also viewed their roles in government differently. In the Byzantine Empire, the emperor controlled both church and government. Byzantine church leaders supported the decisions of the emperor. In the West, the pope claimed he had religious and political authority over all of Europe. He often quarreled with kings about church and government affairs.

Reading **HELP**DESK

Finally, in A.D. 1054, after centuries of bitterness, the patriarch of Constantinople and the pope **excommunicated** (EHK•skuh•MYOO•nuh•KAY•tuhd) each other. To excommunicate means to declare that a person or group no longer belongs to the church. This created a **schism** (SIH•zuhm), or separation, between the two major churches of Christianity. The split between the Eastern Orthodox Church and the Roman Catholic Church still exists today.

PROGRESS CHECK

Identifying What issues divided the eastern and western Christian churches?

2 The Spread of Christianity

GUIDING QUESTION *How did Christianity spread across Europe?*

After the fall of the Western Roman Empire, people in many parts of Europe faced disorder and violence. Many looked to the Christian church for help. They hoped that Christianity would bring peace, order, and unity.

New Christian Communities

During the A.D. 300s, devout Christians in the Eastern Roman Empire formed religious communities called **monasteries** (MAH•nuh•STEHR•eez). In the monasteries, men called monks lived apart from the world. At the same time, they performed good deeds and modeled how Christians should live.

Christian women established religious communities of their own. These women were called nuns, and they lived in convents. During this time, one of the best known nuns was a Roman widow named Paula. In the early A.D. 400s, Paula helped a scholar named Jerome translate the Christian Bible into Latin.

The Greek bishop Basil (BAY•zuhl) created a list of rules for monks and nuns. Known as the Basilian (buh•ZIH•lee•uhn) Rule, this list told people how to live and pray in Eastern Orthodox monasteries and convents.

In the West, religious communities followed another set of regulations called the Benedictine Rule. An Italian monk named Benedict (BEH•nuh•DIHKT) wrote these rules about A.D. 529. Benedictines gave up material goods. They devoted their days to work and prayer. One of their major duties was to serve as missionaries. Missionaries teach their religion to those who are not followers.

Charlemagne believed his authority to rule came from God. Inspired by the teachings of St. Augustine, he considered both the spiritual and material needs of his subjects.

▶ CRITICAL THINKING

Explaining Why do you think Charlemagne, a Frankish king, defended Rome?

excommunicate to declare that a person or group is no longer a member of the church
schism a separation or division from a church
monastery a religious community

THE CYRILLIC ALPHABET

Cyrillic Letter	Written Name	English Sound
Б	beh	B
Г	gey	G
Ж	zheh	ZH
М	em	M
П	pey	P
С	ess	S
Ф	ef	F
Ч	cheh	CH

Cyril and Methodius quarreled with German church leaders who opposed the use of Slavic languages for preaching and worship. The Germans wanted only Latin to be used.

INFOGRAPHIC

Cyril, a Byzantine missionary, developed the Cyrillic alphabet, part of which is shown here. The original alphabet, based on Greek, had 43 letters.

1. **IDENTIFYING** Which Cyrillic letters make the same sounds as the letters "p" and "f" in the English alphabet?
2. **CRITICAL THINKING** *Applying* Why did Cyril create a new alphabet for people who spoke Slavic languages?

In addition, the Rule stated that monks were to welcome outsiders who were in need of food and shelter:

PRIMARY SOURCE

> "All guests who present themselves are to be welcomed as Christ, for he himself will say: I was a stranger and you welcomed me. . . . Once a guest has been announced, the superior and the brothers are to meet him with all the courtesy of love. . . . All humility [being humble] should be shown in addressing a guest on arrival or departure."
>
> —Benedictine Rule, Chapter 53: The Reception of Guests

Monks and nuns had important roles in Christian Europe. They helped the poor and ran hospitals and schools. They also helped preserve ancient Greek and Roman writings.

Christianity and the Slavs

The Byzantines wanted to bring their religion and culture to groups who lived north of their empire. Two brothers, Cyril (SIHR•uhl) and Methodius, were among the most dedicated Byzantine missionaries. Their mission was to deliver the Christian message to the Slavs, a people in Eastern Europe.

Cyril and Methodius believed that the Slavs would be more interested in Christianity if they heard about it in their own languages. About A.D. 863, Cyril invented an alphabet for the Slavic languages. It is known today as the Cyrillic (suh•RIH•lihk) alphabet in honor of its inventor. The Cyrillic alphabet was based on Greek letters. It is still used today by Russians, Ukrainians, Serbs, and Bulgarians.

Reading **HELP**DESK

Build Vocabulary: *Word Origins*

The English word *slave* comes from the word *Slav*. In the early Middle Ages, so many Slavic people were taken into slavery that their name came to be used for anyone who was treated as the property of another and forced to work.

Christianity in Western Europe

In Western Europe, Christian missionaries sought to convert the peoples of Britain and Ireland to Christianity. Roman soldiers were stationed there also. In the A.D. 300s, Roman soldiers left Britain to defend the empire against Germanic invaders.

Beginning in the A.D. 400s, Germanic tribes from present-day Germany and Denmark invaded much of Britain. Over time, these groups united to become known as the Anglo-Saxons. They built farming villages and founded several small kingdoms. Southern Britain soon became known as Angleland, or England. The people became known as the English.

In Britain, the Anglo-Saxons pushed aside the Celts (KEHLTS), the people already living there. Some Celts fled to remote, mountainous areas of Britain. Others crossed the sea to Ireland. In the A.D. 400s, a priest named Patrick brought Christianity to Ireland. He set up churches and monasteries where monks helped preserve Christian and Roman learning.

In A.D. 597, Pope Gregory I sent about 40 monks from Rome to bring Christianity to the Anglo-Saxons of Britain. They converted King Ethelbert of Kent to Christianity. Ethelbert allowed the missionaries to build a church in his capital city of Canterbury. In about 100 years, most of England had accepted the Christian faith. Monasteries were built throughout England. As in Ireland, they became centers of religion and culture.

Pope Gregory I is also known as Gregory the Great. A former monk, he was an excellent administrator. As pope, he continued to live as a monk and tried to bring about reforms in the church.

▶ CRITICAL THINKING

Analyzing How might Pope Gregory's background have affected the spread of Christianity?

PROGRESS CHECK

Analyzing Why were monasteries and convents important in Christian Europe?

LESSON 3 REVIEW

Review Vocabulary

1. Is an *iconoclast* someone who believes in using icons in worship or someone who opposes this practice?
2. When the early church underwent a *schism*, does that mean it changed its most important doctrines?

Answer the Guiding Questions

3. ***Comparing and Contrasting*** What different views of the role of the church in government did the Eastern and Western churches have?
4. ***Explaining*** What were monasteries and what purpose did they serve?
5. ***Identifying Cause and Effect*** How did the Cyrillic alphabet help the spread of Christianity?
6. ***Making Inferences*** Why do you think the Byzantine emperor refused to help the pope defend Rome from invaders?
7. **DESCRIPTIVE WRITING** Write a paragraph to describe what happened to Ireland once Patrick brought Christianity to its lands.

LESSON 3 (cont.)

MAP

Summarizing Remind students that the spread of Christianity across Europe and Britain took hundreds of years and was the result of many causes or factors. Show them the interactive map titled "Spread of Christianity A.D. 325–1100."

Ask:

What factors contributed to the spread of Christianity? *(Factors include the following: fall of the Western Roman Empire; people's need for peace, order, and unity; missionary work of monks and nuns; creation of the Cyrillic alphabet; monks sent to Britain; Patrick's missionary work in Ireland.)*

SLIDE SHOW

Identifying Show students the slide show on monasteries and monks. Have them identify the various roles played by monks and nuns in Christian Europe. *(Answers should include some or all of the following: Monks and nuns ran hospitals and schools, served the poor, preserved ancient Greek and Roman writings, and served as missionaries.)*

INTERACTIVE WORKSHEET

Analyzing Have students complete the Economics and History Activity on the economic life of monasteries.

Next, have students complete the Lesson 3 Review.

CLOSE & REFLECT

Synthesizing To allow students to synthesize and analyze what they have learned about the split in the Christian church, brainstorm a list of questions that might appear on a test.

Examples of such questions include:

- What was the role of Charlemagne in the split?
- Are icons a form of idol worship?
- Did the pope have the authority to crown Charlemagne emperor?

Have students form pairs or small groups. Assign one question from the list to each pair or group. Students will then answer their questions in the form of a short essay, which they can write in class or for homework.

Volunteers can read their essays aloud.

Answers for pages 388–391

P. 388 GEOGRAPHY CONNECTION

1. Syria became Christian before Britain.
2. CRITICAL THINKING Answers will vary. Christianity spread quickly around the Mediterranean, which provided transportation. Some far northern lands were separated from the mainland by water, while mountains cut off Eastern Europe.

P. 389 ☑ PROGRESS CHECK Three main issues divided the eastern and western churches. First, whether or not to worship using icons was an issue.

Another issue was the authority of the pope. Western churches believed the pope was the head of all Christian churches; the Byzantines claimed that the patriarch of Constantinople and other bishops were equal to the pope.

Finally, a third issue was the relationship of the church to the central government. In the East, the emperor controlled both church and government. In the West, the pope often quarreled with political leaders, including the European kings.

P. 389 CRITICAL THINKING Answers may vary. A possible response is that Charlemagne wanted the title of emperor in exchange for helping Pope Leo III.

P. 390 INFOGRAPHIC

1. The Cyrillic letters *pey* and *ef* sound like the English *p* and *f*.
2. CRITICAL THINKING By inventing a new alphabet, he and his brother Methodius were able to communicate the message of Jesus to Slavic peoples.

P. 391 CRITICAL THINKING One of the major duties of monks was to serve as missionaries. As a former monk, Pope Gregory would have been interested in spreading Christianity.

P. 391 ☑ PROGRESS CHECK Monasteries and convents were important in Christian Europe because monks and nuns helped the poor and ran hospitals and schools. They also preserved ancient Greek and Roman writings, and they spread their religion by serving as missionaries.

LESSON 3 REVIEW

1. An *iconoclast* is someone who opposes the use of icons in worship.
2. No; a schism is what happens when something divides or splits. The early church divided into western and eastern branches.
3. In eastern churches, church leaders usually supported the decisions of the emperor and recognized the emperor as having authority over the church and the government. In the West, the pope was not content to live under the authority of emperors or kings and often quarreled with political leaders.
4. Monasteries were religious communities where men called monks tried to live a purely Christian life away from the distractions of the world. Monks as well as nuns served as missionaries, helped those in need, and ran schools and hospitals.
5. The Cyrillic alphabet made it possible for Byzantine missionaries to bring their religion and culture to people living in Eastern Europe, including the Slavs.
6. Answers may vary but should point out that the Byzantines believed the head of the eastern church in Constantinople was equal to the pope in Rome. One possible inference from this is that the emperor wanted the pope to be defeated.
7. After Patrick arrived in Ireland, he converted many of the Irish to Christianity. These Irish Christians went on to set up monasteries and churches. Irish monks copied valuable manuscripts from Christian and Roman sources. Ireland eventually became a center of learning, where scholars, monks, and artists from Europe could come to study and work.

CHAPTER 13 Activities

Write your answers on a separate piece of paper.

❶ **Exploring the Essential Question**

CREATIVE WRITING Imagine you are Paul of Tarsus. You want to write your thoughts about how Christianity has developed and spread. You decide to do this in the form of a letter to church leaders. What part did you play in helping Christianity develop? What challenges did you personally face? Which accomplishments are you most proud of?

❷ **21st Century Skills**

ANALYZING IMAGES Create a presentation to compare and contrast Byzantine (Eastern Orthodox) churches and religious artifacts with Roman Catholic churches and religious artifacts. Use photos to show how Byzantine icons, for instance, are usually painted on flat surfaces. In Roman Catholic churches, however, religious symbols include more statues and other three-dimensional art works. Make sure you cite the source for your images. Present your findings to the class.

❸ **Thinking Like a Historian**

COMPARING AND CONTRASTING Create a diagram like the one shown here. Fill it in to identify the major differences and similarities between the eastern and western Christian churches.

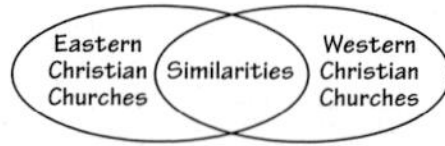

❹ **GEOGRAPHY ACTIVITY**

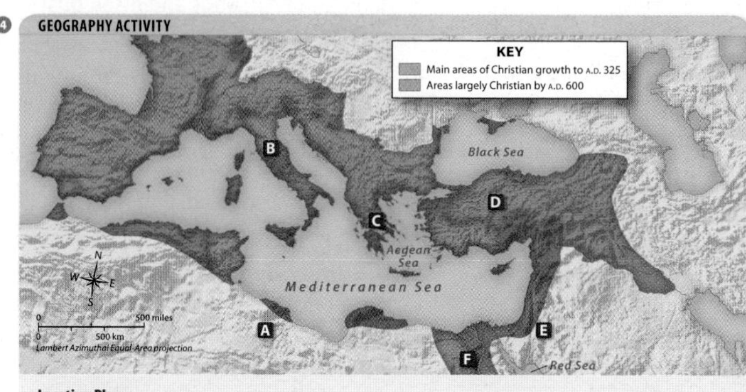

Locating Places

By A.D. 600, Christianity had spread to many parts of the known world as shown on the map. Match the letters on the map with the numbered places listed below.

1. North Africa
2. Judaea
3. Asia Minor
4. Italy
5. Egypt
6. Greece

CHAPTER 13 Assessment

REVIEW THE GUIDING QUESTIONS

Directions: Choose the best answer for each question.

❶ How did the Jews respond to Roman rule?

A. The Jews tried to be at peace with the Romans.
B. The Jews had mixed feelings about the Romans.
C. The Jews disliked everything about the Romans.
D. The Jews only wanted to please the Romans.

❷ Why were the life and death of Jesus important to his followers?

F. The followers of Jesus were able to profit from his life and death.
G. His life and death proved that Roman gods were inferior.
H. They inspired his followers to carry his message to other lands.
I. They made it easier for his followers to get along with the Romans.

❸ How did early Christianity spread throughout the Roman Empire?

A. Roman soldiers who believed in Jesus brought his message to others.
B. Jewish religious leaders traveled around the Mediterranean with stories of Jesus.
C. Christian leaders called apostles spread the message of Jesus.
D. Christian leaders forced other people to accept Christianity.

❹ How did Christianity change over time?

F. It switched from Latin to Greek as its official language.
G. It allowed church members to worship the old Roman gods.
H. It became less and less organized.
I. Christianity split into eastern and western churches.

❺ What issues divided the western and eastern Christian churches?

A. the authority of the pope and the use of icons
B. the failure of the Franks to help defend Rome from invaders
C. the dress code for important officials of the church
D. whether Latin or Greek should be spoken during church services

❻ How did Christianity continue to spread across Europe after the fall of the Western Roman Empire?

F. Christian missionaries traveled to different parts of Europe.
G. Christian monasteries converted people to Christianity.
H. Germanic tribes brought Christianity to Western Europe.
I. Saint Patrick spread Christianity across Europe.

CHAPTER 13 Assessment *(continued)*

DBQ DOCUMENT-BASED QUESTIONS

Drawing Conclusions Before becoming pope, Gregory I wrote this account of a monk who had not shared three gold coins with his fellow monks:

"When he was dead his body was not placed with the bodies of the brethren, but a grave was dug in the dung pit, and his body was flung down into it, and the three pieces of gold he had left were cast upon him, while all together cried, 'Thy money perish with thee!'"

—"Life in a Christian Monastery, ca. 585"

❼ Which statement best captures the attitude of Gregory toward monks who hold on to personal property?

A. They should be pitied for their selfishness.
B. They deserve to die alone, with no one to comfort them.
C. They must be treated with scorn, even when they are dead.
D. Their sins must be punished severely to keep others from sinning.

❽ **Inferring** What does Gregory's way of treating the dead monk reveal about life in an early Christian monastery?

F. Monks were expected to be cruel and hard-hearted.
G. Money was thought of as sinful and wicked.
H. Life was lived in common; all personal wealth was to be shared.
I. Monks paid a high price if they broke the rules.

SHORT RESPONSE

"Extremists among the Zealots turned to terrorism and assassination. . . . They frequented [went to] public places with hidden daggers to strike down persons friendly to Rome. . . . [A]t Masada in [A.D. 73] they committed suicide rather than surrender the fortress."

—Encyclopaedia Britannica, "Zealot," 2011

❾ Why do you think the Zealots were so against Roman rule?

❿ What effect do you think Zealot tactics had on other Jews and Romans?

EXTENDED RESPONSE

⓫ **Descriptive Writing** You are a young person who lives in Judaea during the time of Jesus' ministry. You have attended his Sermon on the Mount. Write a letter to your grandparents telling them about it.

Need Extra Help?

If You've Missed Question	❶	❷	❸	❹	❺	❻	❼	❽	❾	❿	⓫
Review Lesson	1	1	1	2	2	3	2	3	1	1	1

NOTES

REFLECT, REVIEW, & REMEDIATE

INTERACTIVE WORKSHEET

Chapter Summary

Provide students with the Chapter Summary worksheet to help review the chapter and prepare for assessment.

Reviewing the Enduring Understanding

Review this chapter's Enduring Understanding with students:

- People, places, and ideas change over time.

INTERACTIVE WHITEBOARD ACTIVITY On the interactive whiteboard, have a student volunteer create a two-column chart and write "Roman Catholic Church" in one column and "Eastern Orthodox Church" in the other. Then lead a discussion that allows students to compare and contrast the two churches according to how they related to political authority, how they viewed the authority of the pope, religious communities they established, and the role of missionaries. The student volunteer should note this information in the chart.

	Roman Catholic Church	Eastern Orthodox Church
Relationship with Political Authority		
Religious Communities		
Missionary Work		

ACTIVITIES ANSWERS

Exploring the Essential Question

1. Answers may vary. Responses might include an account of Paul's earlier opposition to Christianity and his later conversion. Students could also describe imagined accounts of Paul's many travels around the Mediterranean region, including sights he saw, people he met and how they responded to his message, and problems he had.

21st Century Skills

2. Students' slide show presentations will differ. However, the presentations should emphasize the stylistic differences between Byzantine and Roman Catholic Churches and their respective forms of religious art. Students' slides should be clear and engaging, and they should support the narration.

Thinking Like a Historian

3. Many eastern Christian churches approved of having icons, but western Christian churches, for the most part, did not approve of them. In the west, the pope believed he was the head of all Christian churches. The Byzantines strongly disagreed. They believed the patriarch of Constantinople and various bishops were the pope's equal. The eastern and western churches also disagreed about how the church should relate to political authority. Similarities between the two branches of Christianity include belief in Jesus as the Son of God, belief in his teachings, and the use of the Christian Bible, among other religious books.

Locating Places

4. **1.** A, **2.** E, **3.** D, **4.** B, **5.** F, **6.** C

ASSESSMENT ANSWERS

Review the Guiding Questions

1. **B** The text clearly states that some Jews wanted nothing to do with the Romans. Nothing in the text supports answer C. Some Jews left Jerusalem in order to avoid contact with Romans.

2. **H** The followers of Jesus were not interested in exploiting his fame. The life and death of Jesus had nothing to do with the Roman gods. After the death of Jesus, his followers were often mistreated by Roman authorities.

3. **C** Roman soldiers would have been deemed traitors if they had converted to Christianity. Many Jewish leaders did not believe that Jesus was the promised deliverer. The use of force would have been against the teaching of Jesus.

4. **I** Latin remained the official language of the Roman Catholic Church, although the Byzantine Church adopted Greek as its official language. The worship of any gods, except the Christian God, was forbidden and went against the teachings of Christianity. Christianity began with people worshiping in private homes and developed into a highly organized system with an official hierarchy.

5. **A** The Franks intervened to defend Rome from invaders. Answers C and D are incorrect because nothing in the text suggests that these were divisive issues.

6. **F** The apostles were mainly responsible for spreading the message of Jesus. People who joined monasteries were already Christian. Germanic tribes were not missionaries. They invaded Britain and conquered the people living there. The focus of Saint Patrick's missionary work was the land we now call Ireland.

Document-Based Questions

7. **D** The quoted passage does not speak of pity for the dead monk. Answers B and C are close, but they refer only to the punishment of the dead monk and not to the purpose behind this punishment.

8. **H** The quoted passage does not suggest that monks were expected to be cruel and hard-hearted. Answer G could be inferred, but the introduction to the quote states that the sin of the monk was the fact that he had not shared his wealth. I is close to the mark, but it is not necessarily true that monks would be severely punished for any misbehavior.

Short Response

9. Answers may vary but should at a minimum include some of the reasons why many Jews, not just Zealots, were opposed to Roman rule: Jews were expected to honor Roman gods; the Emperor Augustus made Judah a Roman province and replaced a Jewish king with a Roman governor; and the Romans treated the Jews cruelly.

10. Answers may vary. Because Zealots used violent means, students could infer that many Romans were afraid for their lives while also feeling angry. Some Jews might have secretly approved of the tactics used by Zealots, while others might have condemned the use of violence.

Extended Response

11. Answers may vary. Students might decide to focus on the Sermon on the Mount and include references to some of the beatitudes in the Sermon. They might also describe the setting in which they (as first-century Jews) first heard Jesus preach. Answers should explain what students have learned about Jesus' teachings.

ONLINE RESOURCES

networks

There's More Online!

- ☑ INTERACTIVE WORKSHEETS
- ☑ BIOGRAPHIES
- ☑ CHARTS/GRAPHS
- ☑ GAMES
- ☑ GRAPHIC ORGANIZERS
- ☑ IMAGES
- ☑ MAPS
- ☑ PRIMARY SOURCES
- ☑ SLIDE SHOWS
- ☑ TIME LINE
- ☑ LECTURE SLIDES
- ☑ INTERACTIVE WHITEBOARD ACTIVITIES
- ☑ ASSESSMENTS
- ☑ VIDEOS

Islamic World

Chapter 14

Islamic Civilization

Dear World History Teacher,

In the seventh century, a new religion called Islam arose in the Arabian peninsula and spread rapidly throughout the Middle East. Islam arose from the teachings of a man named Muhammad, and after Muhammad's death, his successors—known as caliphs—organized a great Arab expansion. Arabs moved westward, across North Africa and into Spain, and eastward into the Persian Empire, conquering Syria and Mesopotamia. Internal struggles, however, soon weakened the Arab Empire. The Umayyad dynasty, which began in A.D. 661, was replaced by the Abbasid dynasty in A.D. 750. The Abbasids were weakened by the Seljuk Turks and in 1258 fell to the Mongols.

By the end of the thirteenth century, the Arab Empire was no more, but it left a powerful legacy in Islam, which soon spread to other continents. Two powerful Muslim states—the Ottoman Empire in the Middle East and the Mogul Empire in India—rose during the early 1500s. The military and political talents of these empires helped protect much of the Muslim world.

Although Muslim Arabs absorbed much of the culture of the people they conquered, they also made advances of their own, especially in mathematics and the natural sciences. In literature and art, the Muslim world used Islamic ideals to create original works. Mosques from this period that remain standing today are visible symbols of the greatness of Islamic art and architecture.

Jackson J. Spielvogel

More Media Resources

Current Events Online

Visit McGraw-Hill's current events Web site for high-interest news stories and activities for your students. Access the site through the Student or Teacher Center in **networks.**

Reading List

Grade 6 reading level:
Salaam: A Muslim American Boy's Story,
by Tricia Brown

Grade 6 reading level:
Salaam: A Muslim American Boy's Story,
by Tricia Brown

Grade 7 reading level:
Mosque, by David Macaulay

Grade 8 reading level:
From the Rubaiyat—Selection from the poem,
by Omar Khayyam

Search for more videos online in the **networks** Resource Library.

CHAPTER 14 Planner

UNDERSTANDING BY DESIGN®

Enduring Understandings

- *People, places, and ideas change over time.* • *Religion can influence a society's beliefs and values.*

Essential Questions

- *How do religions develop?* • *How does religion shape society?*
- *How do new ideas change the way people live?*

Students will know:

- *how the physical geography of the Arabian peninsula influenced Arab civilization*
- *the message that Muhammad preached*
- *how Islam provides guidance to its followers*
- *how an empire was created with the spread of Islam*
- *how a split among Muslims led to a change in the Arab Empire*
- *the ways in which the Turks, Safavids, and Moguls ruled their empires*
- *what life was like in the Islamic world*
- *what contributions Muslims have made in mathematics, science, and the arts*

Students will be able to:

- **identify** key tenets of Islam
- **discuss** the significance of key components of Islam
- **identify** current-day countries in which Islam is a major religion
- **distinguish** the methods of how Islam was spread through various events and people
- **determine** how the Turks, Safavids, and Moguls incorporated Islam into their empires
- **discuss** the role that prayer plays in the lives of Muslims
- **identify** the contributions made by Muslims
- **explain** how discoveries and inventions affected the lives of Muslims

Predictable Misunderstandings

Students may think:

- All Muslims are violent extremists or terrorists.
- Islam was spread only by conquering armies.
- All Muslims are Arabs.

Assessment Evidence

Performance Task

- Hands-On Chapter Project

Other Evidence

- Class discussion answers
- Compare and Contrast activity
- Map activities
- Graphic organizer activities
- Written activities
- Economics of History Activity
- 21st Century Skills Activity
- Geography and History Activity
- Lesson Reviews
- Written paper to dispel misconception that all Muslims are Arabs
- Time line of Muslim contributions

Pacing Guide

Introducing the Chapter	1 day
Lesson 1 A New Faith	1 day
Lesson 2 The Spread of Islam	1 day
Lesson 3 Life in the Islamic World	1 day
Chapter Activities and Assessment	1 day
TOTAL TIME	**5 Days**

Differentiated Instruction

These lesson plans are written to address the needs of your On Level students. Discussion and activities that are well-suited to your Approaching Grade Level learners, Beyond Grade Level learners, as well as your English Language Learners are coded as follows:

AL **Approaching Grade Level**

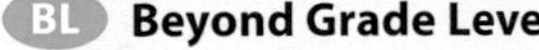
BL **Beyond Grade Level**

ELL **English Language Learner**

NCSS Standards covered in "Islamic Civilization"

Learners will understand:

1 CULTURE

4. That the beliefs, values, and behaviors of a culture form an integrated system that helps shape the activities and ways of life that define a culture

8. That language, behaviors, and beliefs of different cultures can both contribute to and pose barriers to cross-cultural understanding

2 TIME, CONTINUITY, AND CHANGE

7. The contributions of key persons, groups, and events from the past and their influence on the present

3 PEOPLE, PLACES, AND ENVIRONMENTS

8. Factors that contribute to cooperation and conflict among peoples of the nation and world, including language, religion, and political beliefs

4 INDIVIDUAL DEVELOPMENT AND IDENTITY

3. How factors such as physical endowment, interests, capabilities, learning, motivation, personality, perception, and beliefs influence individual development and identity

4. How personal, social, cultural, and environmental factors contribute to the development and the growth of personal identity

5 INDIVIDUALS, GROUPS, AND INSTITUTIONS

2. Concepts such as: mores, norms, status, role, socialization, ethnocentrism, cultural diffusion, competition, cooperation, conflict, race, ethnicity, and gender

6. That cultural diffusion occurs when groups migrate

9. That groups and institutions influence culture in a variety of ways

8 SCIENCE, TECHNOLOGY, AND SOCIETY

6. Values, beliefs, and attitudes that have been influenced by new scientific and technological knowledge (for example, invention of the printing press, conceptions of the universe, applications of atomic energy, and genetic discoveries)

CHAPTER 14 Introducing the Chapter

(Student Edition p. 395)

The Story Matters . . .

Ask a volunteer to read "The Story Matters . . ." aloud, or read it aloud to the class. Then discuss what it might have been like to be a young person living in the Islamic Empire when Osman took control of the land and government.

Ask:

Do changes in government affect students and how they live? Have a few students share their views.

Then ask:

Have you seen a change in government in your lifetime?

How did it affect you and how you live?

What events happened when the government changed?

Tell the class that the Islamic Empire was first ruled by various groups that included the Arabs, Persians, and Mongols. Later, it was ruled by Turkish people who called their empire the Ottoman Empire. Muslim accomplishments such as spreading the faith of Islam, the code of law developed by Ottoman ruler Suleiman I, and many advancements in science and medicine are well documented and tell us most of what we know about the Islamic Empire's culture and its history.

Islamic Civilization

A.D. 600 to A.D. 1629

ESSENTIAL QUESTIONS • *How do religions develop?* • *How do new ideas change the way people live?*

networks *There's More Online* about Islam and its impact on the world.

CHAPTER 14

Lesson 1 *A New Faith*

Lesson 2 *The Spread of Islam*

Lesson 3 *Life in the Islamic World*

The Story Matters . . .

In the 1300s, in the area now known as Turkey, a Muslim tribal chieftain named Osman gained power. He gradually took control of more lands and established the Ottoman Empire. The Ottoman Empire lasted for nearly six centuries and was ruled by Muslim leaders called sultans.

This painting of Suleiman II, sultan of the Ottoman Empire from 1687-1691, shows the elegant clothes worn by the sultan. The large turban, or headdress, indicates his status and position. For centuries, turbans were a part of dress throughout the Islamic world. An elaborate turban and richly decorated robes showed a person's high rank in society.

◄ *Portrait paintings of leaders such as Suleiman II are important historical artifacts that tell us about the cultures in which the leaders lived.*

Italian School/The Bridgeman Art Library/Getty Images

395

Introducing Place and Time (Student Edition pp. 396–397)

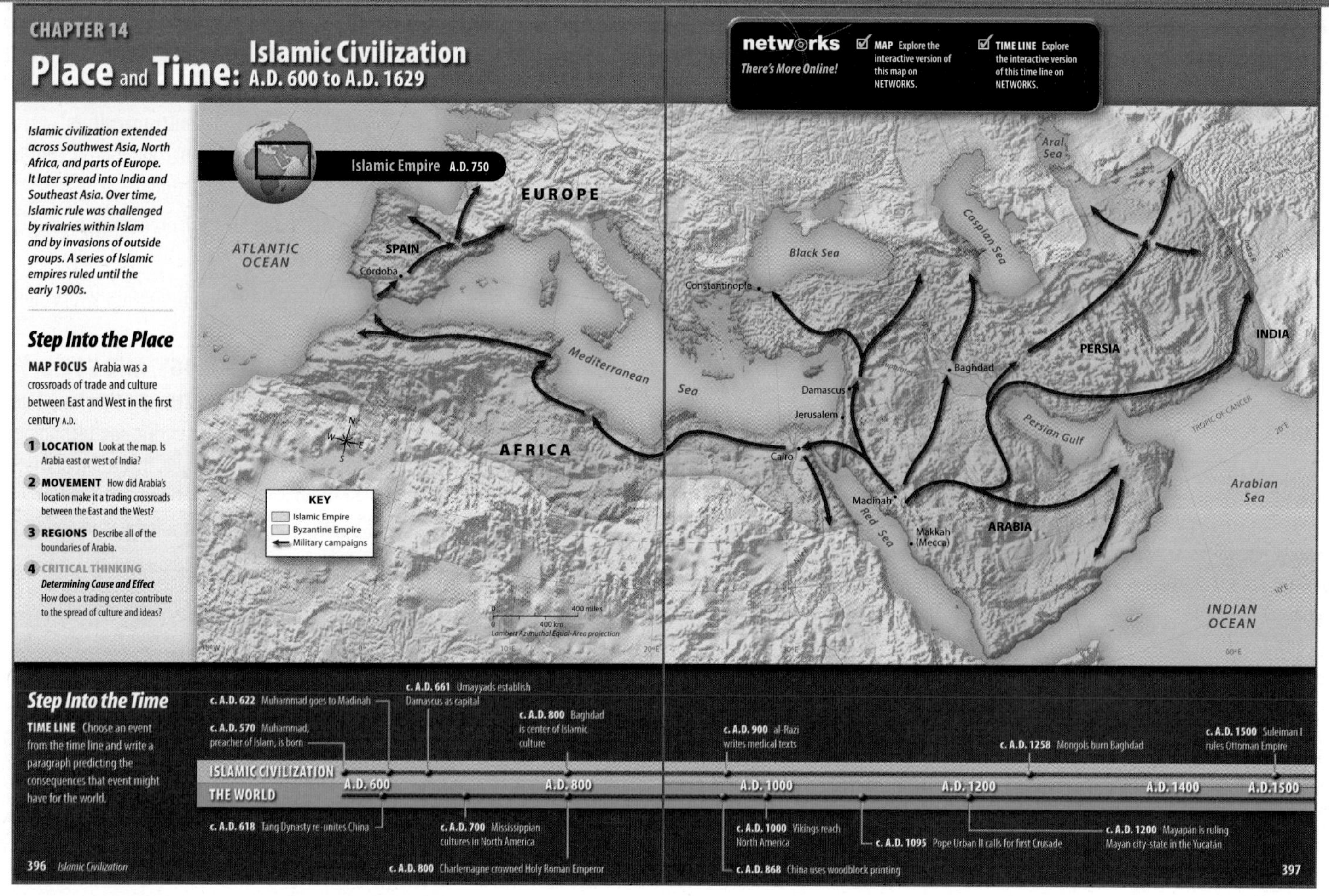

CHAPTER 14

Place and Time: Islamic Civilization A.D. 600 to A.D. 1629

Islamic civilization extended across Southwest Asia, North Africa, and parts of Europe. It later spread into India and Southeast Asia. Over time, Islamic rule was challenged by rivalries within Islam and by invasions of outside groups. A series of Islamic empires ruled until the early 1900s.

networks *There's More Online!* MAP Explore the interactive version of this map on NETWORKS. TIME LINE Explore the interactive version of this time line on NETWORKS.

Step Into the Place

MAP FOCUS Arabia was a crossroads of trade and culture between East and West in the first century A.D.

1. **LOCATION** Look at the map. Is Arabia east or west of India?
2. **MOVEMENT** How did Arabia's location make it a trading crossroads between the East and the West?
3. **REGIONS** Describe all of the boundaries of Arabia.
4. **CRITICAL THINKING** *Determining Cause and Effect* How does a trading center contribute to the spread of culture and ideas?

Step Into the Time

TIME LINE Choose an event from the time line and write a paragraph predicting the consequences that event might have for the world.

396 *Islamic Civilization*

397

Technology Extension

- Find an additional activity online that incorporates technology for this project.
- Visit the EdTechTeacher Web sites (included in the Technology Extension for this chapter) for more links, tutorials, and other resources.

Assessing Background Knowledge

INTERACTIVE WORKSHEET

What Do You Know? Activity

Have students complete the What Do You Know? Activity about Islamic civilization before they study the chapter. Direct students to read each statement and in the "Before" column and check whether they agree or disagree with the statement.

After students complete the chapter, have them reread the statements and note in the "After" column whether they agree or disagree with each statement. Ask students who changed their responses to explain why they did so. *(Students should cite facts from the chapter.)*

INTERACTIVE WORKSHEET

Guided Reading Activities

There is a Guided Reading Activity for each lesson in this chapter. You may wish to assign the Guided Reading Activity for Lesson 1 after introducing the chapter content.

Hands-On Chapter Project

Students will create an illustrated encyclopedia article about a topic related to Islamic civilization.

- Students will participate in a class discussion to review what they have learned about Islamic civilization.
- Then, students will divide into small groups, choose a topic, and research, write, and illustrate an article on that topic.
- Next, students will present their articles to the class.
- Finally, students will evaluate their research, presentation, and collaboration using an Assessment Rubric.

Visit **networks** online to see the full project and rubric.

ONLINE RESOURCES networks

Assign these interactive worksheets and quizzes from your Teacher Lesson Center. All resources are print-ready.

It's ALL Online!

Chapter 14 Resources

- ☑ Chapter Summary
- ☑ Vocabulary Builder
- ☑ What Do You Know?
- ☑ Hands-On Chapter Project

Lesson 1 Resources

- ☑ Interactive Graphic Organizer
- ☑ Geography and History Activity
Understanding Place: The Arabian Peninsula
- ☑ Guided Reading Activity
- ☑ Reading Essentials and Study Guide
- ☑ Online Self-Check Quiz

Lesson 2 Resources

- ☑ Interactive Graphic Organizer
- ☑ 21st Century Skills Activity
Sequence and Categorize Information
- ☑ Guided Reading Activity
- ☑ Reading Essentials and Study Guide
- ☑ Online Self-Check Quiz

Lesson 3 Resources

- ☑ Interactive Graphic Organizer
- ☑ Economics of History Activity
The Use of Credit in the Islamic Empire
- ☑ Guided Reading Activity
- ☑ Reading Essentials and Study Guide
- ☑ Online Self-Check Quiz

Assessment Resources

- ☑ Lesson Reviews
- ☑ Online Self-Check Quizzes
- ☑ Chapter Activities and Assessment
- ☑ Standardized Test Practice

Remediation Resources

- ☑ Reading Essentials and Study Guide
- ☑ Guided Reading Activities
- ☑ Online Self-Check Quizzes
- ☑ Chapter Summary

Step Into the Place

Location Discuss as a class how trade helped spread ideas and cultures, including Islam, between the East and the West.

Next, project the Chapter Opener map that displays the Islamic Empire in A.D. 750. Ask students what they know about life in Arabia at that time. Explain that trading was an important livelihood of people in Arabia.

Ask: What effect would that have on Arabian culture? *(Arabians would be exposed to many new ideas.)*

As a class, discuss the Map Focus questions.

Step Into the Time

Sequencing Have students review the time line for the chapter. Explain that they will be studying events from about A.D. 600 up to about A.D. 1500.

Ask: What are some events you already know about that happened during those years? *(Student answers might include that Europeans discovered cultures in North America.)*

Remind students to use the time lines in their books to help them think of other events that occurred during this time period.

Answers for pages 396–397

Step Into the Place

1. Arabia is west of India.
2. Arabia's location made it a connector between East and West through which trade routes often passed.
3. South of Arabia is the Arabian Sea. North of Arabia is the Mediterranean Sea. West of Arabia is the Red Sea bordered by Africa. East of Arabia is the Persian Gulf and Persia (Iran) and India.
4. CRITICAL THINKING People from many countries pass through a trading center. They share their ideas and values with the people they meet.

Step Into the Time

Students' answers will vary but will likely include the birth of Muhammad or the Vikings reaching North America.

networks
There's More Online!

- GRAPHIC ORGANIZER The Development of Islam
- DIAGRAM The Kaaba
- MAP Southwest Asia c. A.D. 600
- SLIDE SHOW
  - Lives of the Bedouin
  - Sacred Muslim Sites
- VIDEO

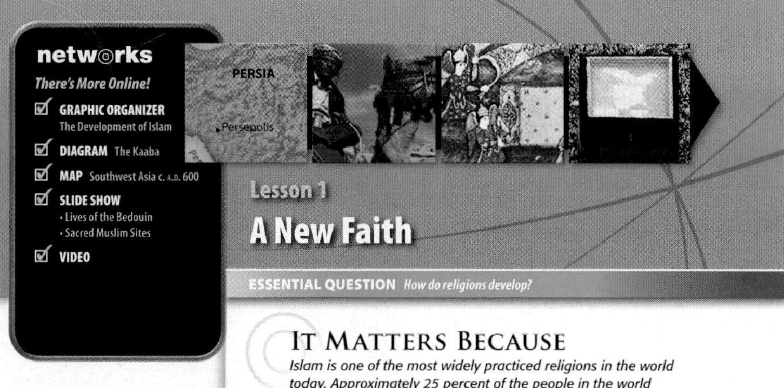

Lesson 1

A New Faith

ESSENTIAL QUESTION *How do religions develop?*

IT MATTERS BECAUSE

Islam is one of the most widely practiced religions in the world today. Approximately 25 percent of the people in the world are Muslim.

1 Arab Life

GUIDING QUESTION *How did physical geography influence the Arab way of life?*

Beginning in the A.D. 630s, people called Arabs created a new empire in Southwest Asia. The driving force behind their empire was the religion of **Islam** (IS•lahm). Within a century, Islam spread throughout parts of Asia, northern Africa, and Europe.

The Land of Arabia

The Arabian Peninsula, also called Arabia, is the homeland of the Arab people. It is also the center of Islam. Arabia is a huge wedge of land between the Red Sea and the Persian Gulf. Very dry plains and deserts cover most of the land. The desert heat can be intense. Summer temperatures can rise above 122° F (50° C). Water is available only at scattered springs and water holes. Such a spot is called an **oasis** (oh•AY•suhs). At an oasis, trees and other plants grow. Not all of Arabia is desert, however. There are mountains and valleys in the southwestern region. Enough rain falls in these locations for juniper and olive trees to grow.

In ancient times, the Arabian Peninsula was surrounded by many different civilizations. At various times, the Egyptian civilization was to the west, the Mesopotamian and Persian

Reading **HELP**DESK

Taking Notes: *Describing*

On a chart like this one, describe the importance of these places to the development of the religion of Islam.

The Development of Islam

Place	Importance
Arabia	
Makkah	
Madinah	

Content Vocabulary

- **Islam**
- **oasis**
- **sheikh**
- **caravan**
- **Quran**
- ***shari'ah***

Southwest Asia c. A.D. 600

Black Sea, CAUCASUS MTNS., Caspian Sea, Constantinople, ASIA MINOR, SYRIA, Mediterranean Sea, Damascus, Baghdad, PERSIA, Alexandria, Jerusalem, Persepolis, EGYPT, Persian Gulf, SAHARA, Red Sea, Yathrib, Makkah (Mecca), ARABIAN PENINSULA, YEMEN, Arabian Sea

KEY: Byzantine Empire; Persian Empire

Lambert Azimuthal Equal-Area projection

GEOGRAPHY CONNECTION

The prophet Muhammad brought the message of Islam to the people of Arabia.

1. **REGIONS** Which empire was located north and west of the Arabian Peninsula?
2. **PLACE** About how far is it from Makkah to Yathrib?
3. **CRITICAL THINKING** ***Analyzing*** How did Makkah's location make it a center for trade?

civilizations were to the north and east, and farther north were the civilizations of the Israelites, Greeks, and Romans. Long distances and the severe Arabian climate had kept these civilizations from invading the peninsula. This **isolation,** however, was not absolute, as trade brought some outside ideas and practices to the Arab civilization.

Life in the Desert

Long ago, many Arabs were nomads who herded animals and lived in tents. These nomads are called bedouin. The bedouin raised camels, goats, and sheep and traveled from oasis to oasis. The bedouin ate mainly fresh or dried dates and drank milk. On very special occasions they ate goat or sheep meat.

To survive the harsh desert climate, early Arabs formed tribes whose members were loyal to one another. The leader of each tribe was called a **sheikh** (SHAYK). Arab tribes raided other tribes to take camels and horses. Rival tribes battled one another over land and water.

Islam a religion based on the teachings of Muhammad
oasis a green area in a desert fed by underground water
sheikh the leader of an Arab tribe

Academic Vocabulary

isolation separation from other populated areas

Bedouins value the camel as a reliable carrier. Their wide, flat feet allow the camel to move very quickly across the dunes.

Can you imagine what a camel race might be like? The bedouin enjoyed camel and horse races and other games that improved their battle skills. In the evenings, they told stories around campfires. Poets wrote and recited poems about battles, camels, horses, and love. The lines below are about an Arab warrior and a battle he must fight. He describes his reliable camel.

PRIMARY SOURCE

> "My riding-camels are tractable [obedient],
> they go wherever I wish;
> while my intellect is my helper,
> and I drive it forward with a firm order."
>
> —from *The Poem of Antar*

Life in Towns

By the A.D. 500s, many Arab tribes had settled around oases or in fertile mountain valleys. They set up villages, farmed or raised animals, and traded goods. Merchants carried goods by camel across the desert to different markets. For protection against bedouin raids, some made journeys in **caravans** (KEHR•uh•vanz), or groups of traveling merchants and animals.

As trade grew, Arab merchants built towns along the trade routes in Arabia. The most important town was Makkah (MAH•kuh), also known as Mecca. Makkah was located about 50 miles (80 kilometers) inland from the Red Sea. The town became a crossroads of trade. Large caravans from southwestern Arabia passed through Makkah on their way to Syria and Mesopotamia. Some caravans traveled as far away as China.

Makkah was also an important religious site. In the center of the city was the Kaaba (KAH•buh). This was a low, block-like building surrounded by statues of Arabian gods and goddesses. The people of Arabia worshipped many deities, but the most important was Allah. They believed that Allah was the creator. Arabs believed that a large stone inside the Kaaba came from heaven. Many pilgrims, people who travel to a holy place, visited the Kaaba.

PROGRESS CHECK

Contrasting How did the lives of desert Arabs and town Arabs differ?

Reading **HELP**DESK

caravan a group of traveling merchants and animals

Reading Strategy: *Formulating Questions*

Asking questions can help you understand and remember what you read. Read about the life of Muhammad. On a separate sheet of paper, write down two or three questions that you would like answered.

Academic Vocabulary

authority power over thoughts, opinions, and behavior

2 Muhammad and His Message

GUIDING QUESTION *What message did Muhammad preach to the people of Arabia?*

Trade increased the contact between Arabs and other civilizations. Life in Arabia changed as people were exposed to new ideas. Arabs searched for ways to deal with these new challenges. Their search paved the way for the rise of Islam.

Who Was Muhammad?

The religion of Islam arose in the Arabian Peninsula in the A.D. 600s. Islam grew from the preachings of a man named Muhammad (moh•HAH•muhd). Muhammad was born into a merchant family in Makkah in A.D. 570. He was orphaned at the age of five or six. As a teenager, Muhammad worked as a caravan leader and eventually became a merchant.

Despite his success, Muhammad was troubled by many things he saw around him, including the greed of Makkah's wealthy citizens. He despised their dishonesty, neglect of the poor, and disregard for family life. Seeking guidance, he spent time alone praying in a cave outside the city.

Muslim tradition says that in A.D. 610, Muhammad had a vision in which a voice called him to preach Islam. Islam means "surrendering [to the will of Allah]." In the Arabic language, Allah is the word for "God." Three times the voice said, "Recite!" When Muhammad asked what he should recite, the voice said:

PRIMARY SOURCE

> "Recite in the name of your Lord Who created, created man from a clot of congealed [thickened] blood. Recite: and your Lord is Most Generous, Who taught by the pen, taught man what he did not know."
>
> —*Quran*, Surah 96:1-5

Muhammad returned to Makkah and began preaching. He told people that there was only Allah to worship, the one true God. He said they must destroy their statues of fake gods.

Muhammad also preached that people were equal in God's sight, and the rich should share their wealth with the poor. Everywhere he went, Muhammad preached that God valued good deeds. Muhammad urged people to prepare for the Day of Judgment, when God would punish evildoers and reward the just.

Muhammad's Opponents

The first people to become Muslims, or followers of Islam, were Muhammad's family members. Slowly, Muhammad won the support of the poor, who were attracted to his message of sharing. Most wealthy merchants and religious leaders, however, thought Muhammad was trying to destroy their **authority.**

BIOGRAPHY

Muhammad (A.D. 570–632)

The tomb of the prophet Muhammad is a holy place to Muslims. During Muhammad's lifetime, he was well known for fairly resolving disputes among his followers. According to Islamic tradition, when Muhammad was asked to resolve which tribe would have the honor to place the holy black stone in the corner of the rebuilt Kaaba, Muhammad put his cloak on the ground with the stone in the center and had each tribe lift a corner to bring the stone to the correct height to be placed in the Kaaba. Muhammad's legacy has made a major impact on the world.

► **CRITICAL THINKING**
Drawing Conclusions Why do you think Muhammad had each tribe carry his cloak with the holy black stone?

LESSON 1

ENGAGE

MAP **Analyzing Visuals** Show the Interactive Map of Southwest Asia in A.D. 600 on the whiteboard. Tell students that the Arabian peninsula was mostly a desert area that was a center of trading and the center of the Islamic faith.

Muhammad, the prophet of Islam, was born in Makkah. Have a student locate Makkah. ELL

Later in his life, Muhammad was accepted as a prophet of God by the people of Madinah. Have a student locate Madinah. ELL

Explaining Tell students that Makkah became an important trading town and religious site.

Ask:

What happens when people from different places meet and trade? *(They share their ideas and cultures.)*

TEACH & ASSESS

1 Arab Life

GUIDING QUESTION ***How did physical geography influence the Arab way of life?***

Describing Discuss as a class how geography affected life in Arabia.

Ask:

What three bodies of water surround the Arabian peninsula? *(the Arabian Sea, the Persian Gulf, and the Red Sea)*

Though Arabia is surrounded by water on three sides, what is most of the land like in Arabia? *(Most of the land in Arabia is hot, sandy desert.)*

Where were towns located in Arabia? *(Towns were settled where there was an oasis on a caravan route.)*

How did Makkah's geography make it a center of trade and religion? *(It was an oasis located just east of the Red Sea. Caravans passed through Makkah when traveling to the West or East.)*

How did the desert protect Makkah? *(The desert surrounding Makkah was hot and difficult to travel; that kept outside enemies from fighting battles to control Makkah.)*

What made Makkah an important religious center? *(The Kaaba, a religious site with statues of the Arabian gods and goddesses, was located in Makkah.)*

SLIDE SHOW **Making Connections** Have students think about how the physical features of the region might have affected the way Arabs lived and how they relied on one another. Invite them to draw on their own experiences such as a movie or television program about the desert they might have seen.

Show students the interactive slide show about bedouin life.

Ask:

What type of clothing did the bedouin wear? *(clothing that protected them from the sun and blowing sand)*

How did people living in the desert depend on one another? *(They formed tribes and were loyal to their tribal members.)*

How did the different tribes get along? *(Though the tribes helped one another, they also often battled each other.)*

Summarizing Using the information in the "Arab Life" section of the lesson, have the class summarize how Arabs lived in Arabia. *(Summaries may include information about the bedouin, tribal loyalties, caravans, and the formation of towns, including Makkah and its importance as a trading center and location of the Kaaba.)* AL

INTERACTIVE WORKSHEET

Geography and History Activity

Tell students that the way people live in the Arabian peninsula has changed over time. The people of Arabia once depended on trade for their livelihood, but today the economy of the peninsula depends on oil.

Assign the Geography and History worksheet as homework.

2 Muhammad and His Message

GUIDING QUESTION ***What message did Muhammad preach to the people of Arabia?***

SLIDE SHOW **Explaining** Review with students the main ideas that Muhammad preached. Show students the interactive slide show about sacred Muslim sites.

Ask:

Why is the Mosque of the Prophet important? *(It was built by the prophet Muhammad after his Hijrah to Madinah.)*

What is significant about the Dome of the Rock? *(It is sacred to Muslims and Jews.)*

3 Beliefs and Practices of Islam

GUIDING QUESTION ***How does Islam provide guidance to its followers?***

LECTURE SLIDE **Describing** Point out to students that all religions have traditions and ways of worshiping. Show students the lecture slide on the Five Pillars of Islam.

Ask:

Do other religions have similar guidelines for religious practice? What are they? *(Students may mention the Ten Commandments in Judaism and Christianity, the Eightfold Path in Buddhism, and so on.)*

Organize students into groups of five, and give each group a poster board or a large piece of butcher paper. Have each group create a graphic organizer or other visual representation of the Five Pillars of Islam. AL ELL

Have students complete the Lesson 1 Review.

Answers for pages 398–401

P. 398 Taking Notes Islam first spread in Arabia and, because it is a peninsula between Africa and western Asia, Islam spread west and east. Muhammad was born in Makkah and first preached Islam in Makkah. Fearing for their safety in Makkah, Muhammad and his followers fled to Madinah, and the people there received him as a prophet of God.

P. 399 GEOGRAPHY CONNECTION

1. the Byzantine Empire
2. about 200 miles (320 km)
3. CRITICAL THINKING Makkah's location gave it access to the trade routes that passed through the Red Sea. It also connected the trade routes that passed across the Arabian Desert with the Red Sea trade routes.

P. 400 ☑ PROGRESS CHECK Desert Arabs were nomads who traveled from oasis to oasis. Town Arabs were farmers or merchants. They stayed in one place.

P. 400 Reading Strategy Students may ask questions about Muhammad's personal life, such as the following: Was he married? Did he have children? What did Muhammad look like? How did he feel about being called to preach?

P. 401 CRITICAL THINKING Muhammad wanted to show that the tribes were all equal in status and honor.

Thousand of Muslim pilgrims surround the Kaaba in Makkah. A call to worship on special days draws thousands of people.

▶ CRITICAL THINKING

Making Inferences Why do you think the Muslim calendar begins with the year of the Hijrah?

In A.D. 622, Muhammad and his followers believed Makkah had become too dangerous. They moved to Yathrib (YA•thruhb). Muhammad's departure to Yathrib became known as the Hijrah (HIHJ•ruh). This Arabic word means "breaking off relationships." The year of the Hijrah later became the first year of the Muslim calendar. The people of Yathrib accepted Muhammad as God's prophet and their ruler. They renamed their city Madinah (mah•DEE•nah), which means "the city of the prophet."

The Islamic State

Muhammad was a skilled political and religious leader. He applied the laws he believed God had given him to all areas of life. He used these laws to settle disputes among the people. Muhammad also established the foundation for an Islamic state. The government of the state used its political power to uphold Islam. Muhammad required all Muslims to place loyalty to the Islamic state above loyalty to their tribes.

Muhammad formed an army to protect his new state. In a series of battles, Muhammad's soldiers regained Makkah and made it a holy city of Islam. The Muslims then began to expand into new areas. When Muhammad died in A.D. 632, the entire Arabian Peninsula was part of the Islamic state.

☑ PROGRESS CHECK

Analyzing Why did Makkah's merchants and religious leaders oppose Muhammad and his message?

Reading HELPDESK

Quran the holy book of Islam
shari'ah Islamic code of law

3 Beliefs and Practices of Islam

GUIDING QUESTION *How does Islam provide guidance to its followers?*

Islam shares some beliefs with Judaism and Christianity. Like Jews and Christians, Muslims are monotheists. Muslims believe in one all-powerful God who created the universe. They believe that God decides what is right and wrong.

Like Jews and Christians, Muslims believe that God spoke to people through prophets. For Muslims, these prophets include Adam, Abraham, Moses, Jesus, and Muhammad. In Islam, Muhammad is seen as the last and the greatest of the prophets.

The Quran

According to Muslim belief, Muhammad received messages from Allah for more than 20 years. These messages were not gathered into a written collection until after Muhammad died. This collection became the **Quran** (kuh•RAN), or holy book of Islam. Muslims believe the Quran is the written word of God. It contains accounts of events, teachings, and instructions.

For Muslims, the Quran provides guidelines for how to live. For example, the Quran instructs Muslims to be honest and treat others fairly. Muslims must respect their parents and be kind to their neighbors. The Quran forbids murder, lying, and stealing.

Islam stresses the need to obey the will of Allah. This means practicing acts of worship known as the Five Pillars of Islam. The Five Pillars are belief, prayer, charity, fasting, and pilgrimage.

Over centuries, Islamic scholars created a code of law called the ***shari'ah*** (shuh•REE•uh). *Shari'ah* is based on the Quran. According to *shari'ah*, Muslims may not gamble, eat pork, or drink alcoholic beverages. The *sunna* also guides Muslims. It is a set of customs based on Muhammad's words and deeds.

☑ PROGRESS CHECK

Evaluating Why is the Quran important in the daily life of Muslims?

Thinking Like a **HISTORIAN**

Using a Time Line

Many important events led Muhammad to establish Islam. Select three events from his life that you consider important to his founding of Islam. Sequence them on a time line, and present your time line to the class. Be sure to explain your choices in your presentation. For more information about time lines, read *What Does a Historian Do?*

LESSON 1 REVIEW

Review Vocabulary

1. Why would the people in a *caravan* be glad to see an *oasis*?

Answer the Guiding Questions

2. ***Determining Cause and Effect*** How did physical geography shape life in Arabia?
3. ***Explaining*** Why did Muhammad and his followers move to Madinah?
4. ***Describing*** What is the *shari'ah* and what is it based on?
5. **NARRATIVE WRITING** Imagine that you are a bedouin. Write a letter to a friend who lives in Makkah describing a day in your life.

networks
There's More Online!

- ☑ **BIOGRAPHY** Suleiman I
- ☑ **CHART/GRAPH** The Four Caliphs
- ☑ **GRAPHIC ORGANIZER** How Islam Spread
- ☑ **MAP**
  - Spread of Islam A.D. 632–750
  - Abbasid Empire A.D. 800
- ☑ **SLIDE SHOW** Islamic Architecture

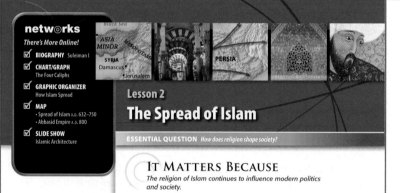

Lesson 2

The Spread of Islam

ESSENTIAL QUESTION *How does religion shape society?*

IT MATTERS BECAUSE

The religion of Islam continues to influence modern politics and society.

1 Founding an Empire

GUIDING QUESTION *How did the Arabs spread Islam and create an empire?*

When Muhammad died in A.D. 632, he left no instructions about who should be the next leader of Islam. Muslims knew that no person could take Muhammad's role as a prophet. They realized, however, that the Islamic state needed a strong leader to keep it united. A group of Muslim leaders chose a new type of leader called the **caliph** (KAY•luhf), or "successor."

The First Caliphs

The first four caliphs were close friends or relatives of Muhammad. The goal of the caliphs was to protect and spread Islam. Their military forces carried Islam beyond the Arabian Peninsula. Because the Muslim conquerors were Arab, the territory became known as the Arab Empire. By the 660s, the Arab Empire included all of southwest Asia and northeast Africa.

The Umayyads

Expansion continued under new caliphs known as the Umayyads (oo•MY•uhds). The Umayyads governed the Arab Empire from the city of Damascus (duh•MAS•kuhs) in Syria. They ruled from 661 to 750. Under the Umayyads, Muslim rule extended farther into Asia and Africa.

Reading HELPDESK

Taking Notes: Summarizing

On a diagram like this one, describe the ways in which the religion of Islam spread.

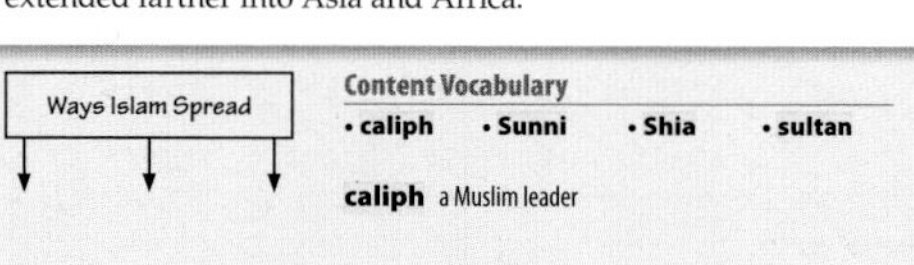

Content Vocabulary
- **caliph**
- **Sunni**
- **Shia**
- **sultan**

caliph a Muslim leader

A century after the death of Muhammad, Muslims had created a large and powerful empire. Arab soldiers were experienced horse riders and warriors, having raided rival tribes in the past. Now they used those same skills to fight large armies. In addition, Arab soldiers believed they had a religious duty to spread Islam.

The policies of their opponents also helped the Muslims. Byzantine and Persian rulers had tried to unite their peoples under an official religion. They often mistreated those who practiced other faiths. When Muslim armies attacked, many of these people were willing to accept Muslim rule.

After the Arabs gained control, they usually let conquered peoples practice their own religions. Islam teaches that Christians and Jews are "People of the Book," people who believe in one God and follow sacred writings. Therefore, many Muslims respect their beliefs and practices. As time passed, many of the conquered peoples in the Arab Empire became Muslims and learned the Arab language. The customs of the conquered peoples also influenced the Arab rulers. Eventually, the term *Arab* meant a speaker of Arabic, not a resident of Arabia.

Islamic Spain

Muslim warriors entered Spain from North Africa in the early 700s. They brought their religion, customs, and traditions. Spanish Muslims made the city of Córdoba a center of Islam.

Spain was home to many of Islam's greatest thinkers. Ibn Rushd (IH•buhn RUHSHT), also known as Averroës (uh•VEHR•uh•weez), practiced law and medicine in Córdoba.

GEOGRAPHY CONNECTION

After Muhammad's death, the territory of the Arab Empire expanded.

1. **MOVEMENT** What area of Europe came under Muslim control?
2. **PLACE** Describe the territories conquered by the Arabs by the year A.D. 661.
3. CRITICAL THINKING ***Making Connections*** Why do you think Muslim armies entered Europe from North Africa and not through Asia Minor?

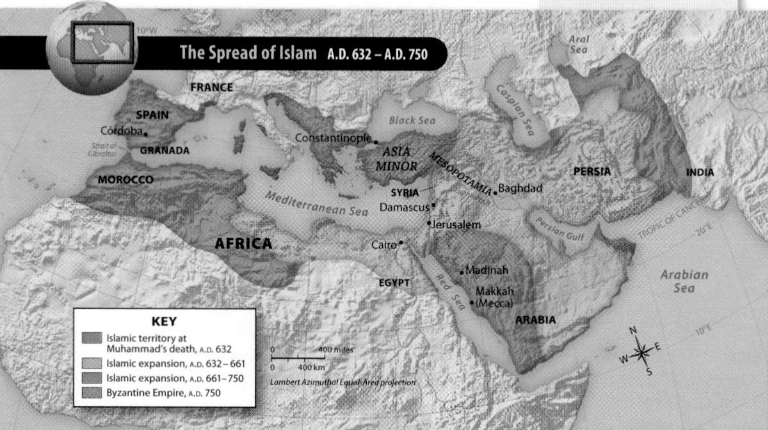

LESSON 1 (cont.)

CLOSE & REFLECT

Making Predictions Have students discuss how the spread of a religion can change the way of life. Ask students to predict how the spread of Islam changed the way of life in and around the Arabian peninsula.

Guide students to use what they already learned about the spread of Judaism, Christianity, Hinduism, and Buddhism, as well as their knowledge of Arabia, as the basis of their predictions.

Moderate a class discussion.

IF YOU HAVE MORE TIME . . .

Use Maps to Explore the Geography of the Arabian Peninsula

Locating Have students create or complete a map of the Arabian peninsula. You may choose to have students draw the map from scratch, or you may provide them with an outline map of the region. Provide students with atlases or other resources that include maps of the region. Tell students to label the waterways that surround the peninsula *(the Red Sea, the Arabian Sea, the Persian Gulf, the Mediterranean Sea)*. Then have students locate and label important cities, such as Makkah and Madinah. You may choose to include modern cities, such as Riyadh, and the borders of modern states. Students should also label important geographic features, such as the Rub' al-Khali *(the Empty Quarter)* in southern Arabia.

Have students use their maps as a basis for discussion about population distribution in the Arabian peninsula.

Answers for pages 402–403

P. 402 CRITICAL THINKING Students may say the Muslim calendar begins with the year of the Hijrah because the Hijrah marks the beginning of the Islamic state or the beginning of the spread of Islam outside of Makkah.

P. 402 ☑ PROGRESS CHECK Makkah's merchants and religious leaders thought Muhammad was trying to destroy their authority.

P. 403 ☑ PROGRESS CHECK The Quran provides guidelines on how to live.

LESSON 1 REVIEW

1. Caravans travel through the hot, dry desert, and an oasis is a place where water is available.
2. The terrain of the desert was extremely harsh, and it was necessary to join with others in groups in order to survive. The Arabs formed tribes in which people were loyal to one another and helped one another. Tribes are still important to the Arab way of life.
3. Muhammad and his followers moved to Madinah because they believed it was too dangerous for them to stay in Makkah.
4. The *shari'ah* is a code of law that provides Muslims with a set of practical laws for daily life. It is based on the Quran.
5. Students' letters should mention the bedouin way of living as well as the heat of the desert.

Teaching *The Spread of Islam* (Student Edition pp. 404–410)

LESSON 2

ENGAGE

MAP **Speculating** Project the world map from the Interactive World Atlas. Tell students that Islam spread from the Arabian peninsula to countries throughout the world.

Ask students to name a country that is not on the Arabian peninsula but where people follow Islam.

Have students brainstorm how Islam could have spread to so many places. Record their ideas on the whiteboard.

Tell students that in this lesson they are going to learn that the Arabs spread Islam and created an empire through teaching, trade, and conquest.

TEACH & ASSESS

1 Founding an Empire

GUIDING QUESTION *How did the Arabs spread Islam and create an empire?*

MAP **Describing** Display the map "The Spread of Islam, A.D. 632– A.D. 750." Discuss as a class what happened in Islam when Muhammad died.

Ask:

What happened to the empire when the Umayyads took control? *(They continued the expansion of the Arab Empire through conquest.)*

CHART **Comparing** Show students the interactive chart on the first four caliphs.

Ask:

What did the first four caliphs who ruled have in common? *(Each one was a close friend or relative of Muhammad.)*

What were two characteristics of their rules? *(They all wanted to protect and spread Islam. They all conquered lands beyond Arabia.)*

From what city did they rule the empire? *(Damascus, in Syria)* ELL

SLIDE SHOW **Explaining** Tell students that in the Arab Empire, people could practice their own religion, but many conquered peoples converted to Islam and learned Arabic.

Ask:

How did Muslim expansion into Spain affect the Jews and Christians who lived there? *(Jews and Christians were accepted and often studied medicine and philosophy with Muslims.)*

Show students the slide show "Muslim Architecture."

Ask:

What lasting impact did Islam have on Spanish culture? *(Many buildings, especially those in Córdoba, have features of Islamic architecture.)* BL

Answers for pages 404–405

P. 404 Taking Notes Teaching, Trade, and Conquest

P. 405 GEOGRAPHY CONNECTION

1. Spain came under Muslim control.
2. The territories are north, west, and east of Arab territory as of A.D. 632. They include the entire Arabian peninsula, Egypt, Mesopotamia, and Persia.
3. CRITICAL THINKING The Byzantine Empire blocked access to Europe through Asia Minor.

THE FIRST FOUR CALIPHS

	Abu Bakr	Umar	Uthman	Ali
Relationship to Muhammad	father-in-law	friend	son-in-law, member of the Umayyad family	first cousin, son-in-law
Career	merchant	merchant	merchant	soldier, writer
Years as Caliph	A.D. 632–634	A.D. 634–644	A.D. 644–656	A.D. 656–661
Achievements as Caliph	spread Islam to all of Arabia; restored peace after death of Muhammad; created code of conduct in war; compiled Quran verses	spread Islam to Syria, Egypt, and Persia; redesigned government; paid soldiers; held a census; made taxes more fair; built roads and canals; aided poor	spread Islam into Afghanistan and eastern Mediterranean; organized a navy; improved the government; built more roads, bridges, and canals; distributed text of the Quran	reformed tax collection and other government systems; spent most of caliphate battling Muawiya, the governor of Syria

CHART

1 **IDENTIFYING** Which caliph ruled the longest? Whose rule was the shortest?

2 CRITICAL THINKING
Contrasting How was Ali different from the other caliphs?

He is best known for his writings based on the works of the Greek philosopher Aristotle. Ibn Rushd's work influenced Christian and Jewish thinkers in Europe during the Middle Ages.

Muslims in Spain were generally tolerant, or accepting, of other cultures. In some schools, Muslims, Jews, and Christians studied medicine and philosophy together. In particular, the Jewish community in Córdoba flourished.

A Jewish scholar in Spain, Solomon ben Gabirol, wrote philosophy and poetry. His most famous book of philosophy, *The Well of Life*, shows the influence of the Greek philosophers. The book was translated from Arabic into Latin and influenced many philosophers in Christian Europe.

Another Jewish thinker called Moses Maimonides (my•MAHN•ih•deez) had to leave Spain at a very young age because it was conquered by an intolerant Muslim group. He later became a physician in the Muslim royal court in Egypt and wrote philosophy as well as a collection of Jewish laws.

Preachers and Traders

Muslim armies were not the only ones who spread Islam. Some Muslims used preaching to win followers to their religion. A group called Sufis (SOO•feez) won followers by teaching Islam.

Muslim merchants built trading posts throughout Southeast Asia and taught Islam to the people there. Today, the country of Indonesia (ihn•duh•NEE•zhuh) has more Muslims than any other nation in the world.

Reading **HELP**DESK

Some Muslim merchants crossed the Sahara to trade with powerful kingdoms in West Africa. In the 1300s, the West African city of Timbuktu (tihm•buhk•TOO) became a leading center of Muslim culture and learning.

PROGRESS CHECK

Explaining Why was the Arab military successful?

2 Division and Growth

GUIDING QUESTION *How did the Arab Empire change after the Umayyads?*

While Arab Muslims created an empire, rival groups within Islam argued about who had the right to succeed Muhammad as caliph. Muslims divided into two groups, the **Sunni** (SU•nee) and the **Shia** (SHEE•ah). This split still divides Muslims today. Most Muslims are Sunni. Shia Muslims, however, make up most of the populations in present-day Iran and Iraq.

The Shia believed that Ali, Muhammad's son-in-law, was his rightful heir. They also believed that all future caliphs had to be Ali's descendants. According to the Shia, the Umayyad caliphs in Damascus had no right to rule. The Sunni, who outnumbered the Shia, disagreed. They recognized the Umayyad caliphs as rightful rulers, though they did not always agree with their actions.

The Shia and the Sunni agreed on the major **principles** of Islam. They both believed that there was only one God. They also believed in the Quran as Islam's holy book and the Five Pillars of Islam. In other ways, the two groups developed different religious practices and customs.

A New Dynasty

During the 700s, opposition to the Umayyad caliphs grew. Many non-Arab Muslims were angry that Arab Muslims had the best jobs and paid lower taxes. Discontent was especially strong in Mesopotamia and Persia, where Shia Islam was popular.

About 750, the Shia Muslims rebelled and won support from other Muslims throughout the empire. They overthrew the Umayyads, and the Abbasid (uh•BA•suhd) dynasty came to power. Abbasid caliphs ruled the Arab Empire until 1258.

Muslim architecture can still be found in many parts of Spain today. The high interior arches, decorative columns, and brights colors are all details of Muslim design.

▶ CRITICAL THINKING
Drawing Conclusions Why was Spain home to many of Islam's great thinkers?

Sunni group of Muslims who accepted the rule of the Umayyad caliphs

Shia group of Muslims who believed the descendants of Ali should rule

Academic Vocabulary
principle an important law or belief

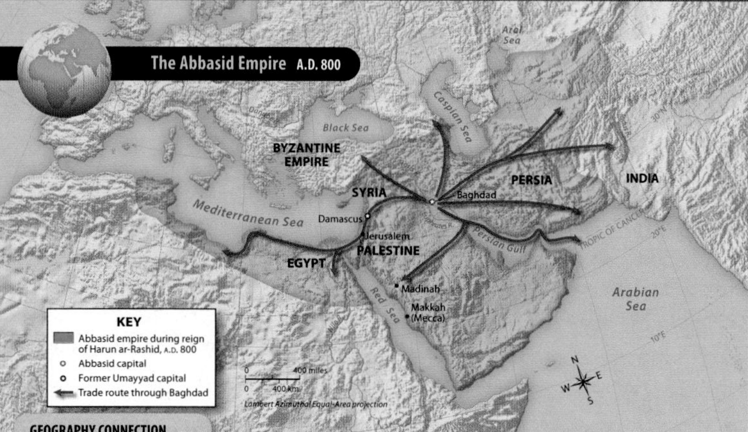

GEOGRAPHY CONNECTION

Baghdad became the capital of the Abbasid empire and an important center for trade.

1 **REGIONS** What blocked Abbasid expansion to the northwest?

2 CRITICAL THINKING
Evaluating Does Baghdad appear to be well located for trade? Explain.

The Abbasids focused on improving trade and **culture.** They made Baghdad (BAG•dad) their capital city. Baghdad's location along the Tigris River was on trade routes that connected the Mediterranean Sea to East Asia. By the 900s, Baghdad was one of the world's most beautiful and prosperous cities.

Under Abbasid rule, the Arab Empire enjoyed a golden age. The Abbasids appreciated Persian culture and brought many Persian influences into the Arab Empire.

Who are the Seljuk Turks?

The Abbasids developed a rich culture, but they could not hold their empire together. Over time, many territories broke free from Abbasid rule. In Egypt and Spain, the Muslims set up their own caliphs. Rival rulers took over much of Persia. By the 1000s, the Abbasids ruled little more than the area around Baghdad.

Around this time, the Seljuk Turks of central Asia began moving into Abbasid territory. The Seljuk Turks were nomads and great warriors. In 1055, the Seljuks seized Baghdad. They took control of the government and army but allowed the Abbasid caliph to manage religious matters. The Seljuk ruler called himself **sultan** (SUHL•tuhn), or "holder of power."

Reading **HELP**DESK

sultan Seljuk leader

Academic Vocabulary
culture the customs, art, science, and learning of a group of people

For 200 years, Seljuk sultans ruled with the Abbasid caliphs. Then, in the 1200s, people from central Asia, known as the Mongols, swept into the empire. In 1258 they stormed into Baghdad. There, the Mongols burned buildings and killed more than 50,000 people. This fierce attack brought an end to the Arab Empire.

PROGRESS CHECK

Comparing and Contrasting How did the Sunni and Shia differ? What beliefs did they share?

3 Three Muslim Empires

GUIDING QUESTION *How did the Turks, Safavids, and Moguls rule their empires?*

After the Arab Empire ended, other Muslim groups created their own empires. These empires included the Ottoman Empire based in what is now Turkey, the Safavid (sah•FAH•weed) Empire in Persia, and the Mogul Empire in India.

The Ottomans

During the late 1200s, Turkish clans settled part of Asia Minor. They called themselves Ottoman Turks, after their leader named Osman. The Ottomans conquered much of the Byzantine Empire. In 1453, the Ottoman ruler Mehmet II, known as "the Conqueror," seized the Byzantine capital, Constantinople. The Ottomans renamed the city Istanbul and made it their capital.

The Ottomans then pushed into southeastern Europe, Southwest Asia, and North Africa. The Ottomans controlled much of the Mediterranean region until the late 1500s.

The Ottoman leader was called a sultan, like the leader of the Seljuks. The most famous Ottoman sultan was Suleiman I (SOO•luh•mahn). He ruled during the 1500s. He was called "The Lawgiver" because he organized Ottoman laws. Suleiman also built many schools and mosques throughout the empire.

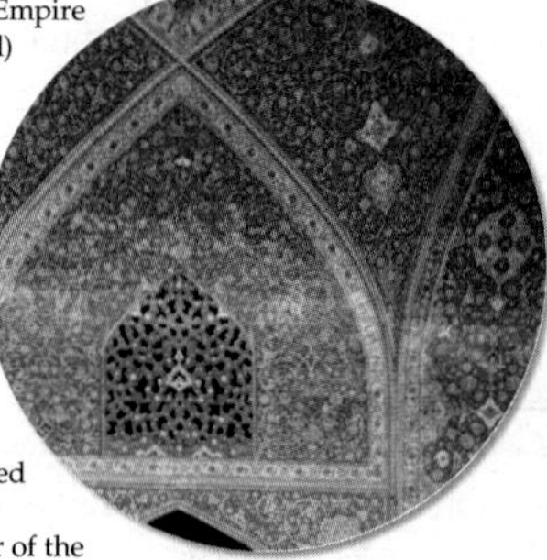

The Shah Mosque in Isafahan, Iran, shows traditional Muslim architecture. It is known for its internal design featuring mosaic tiles.

LESSON 2 (cont.)

Division and Growth

GUIDING QUESTION ***How did the Arab Empire change after the Umayyads?***

Listing Draw two columns on the board with the headings "Umayyads" and "Abbasids." Have students use information from their textbooks to provide details about each group for each column. *(Sample answers: Umayyads: ruled from Damascus; conquered new lands. Abbasids: ruled from Baghdad; improved trade and culture)* AL

LECTURE SLIDE **Explaining** Show students the lecture slide describing the Seljuk Turks and the Abbasid caliphate.

Ask:

Did the Seljuk Turks have more power, or did the Abbasids—who controlled religious matters—have more power? *(Some students might mention the idea that the Seljuk Turks held more power, but other students might say the Abbasids who controlled a religion that spread easily had more power.)*

What eventually happened to the joint rule of the empire? *(Another group, the Mongols from central Asia, burned Baghdad and ended the Arab Empire in 1258.)*

Three Muslim Empires

GUIDING QUESTION ***How did the Turks, Safavids, and Moguls rule their empires?***

LECTURE SLIDE **Making Inferences** Show students the lecture slide on the treatment of Muslims and non-Muslims in the Ottoman Empire.

Ask:

What special privileges did Muslims have in the Ottoman Empire? *(They were subject to their own laws. For example, they did not have to pay the special tax that non-Muslims paid.)*

Why do you think non-Muslims stayed in the Ottoman Empire? *(Students should note that the Ottoman Empire was large and included many different peoples. Conquered peoples most likely wanted to remain in their homes. The Ottomans also allowed religious freedom as long as non-Muslims paid taxes.)*

Do you think many people who lived in the Ottoman Empire chose to convert to Islam? Why? *(Some students might conclude that a number of people probably converted in order to enjoy the privileges that Muslims had. Other students might conclude that because non-Muslims had the freedom to practice their religion, they were less likely to convert to Islam.)*

INTERACTIVE WORKSHEET

21st Century Skills Activity

Sequencing Have students fill out the 21st Century Skills worksheet sequencing events in the Islamic Empire from 1000 to the late 1600s. Help students by **asking:**

Which group still ruled the Islamic Empire in 1000? *(the Arabs)*

Why is 1258 an important date in the Islamic Empire? *(It is when Baghdad fell and the Arabs lost control of the empire.)*

Remind students that three groups sequentially ruled the empire after Baghdad fell.

Explaining Have students write an essay that explains why all Muslims are not Arab. You may choose to have students write the essay for homework. Encourage students to share their essays with the class.

Have students complete the Lesson 2 Review.

CLOSE & REFLECT

Ask students why they think religion and government were so closely connected in Islamic countries. Have students give reasons for their ideas. Moderate the class discussion.

IF YOU HAVE MORE TIME . . .

Compare Shia and Sunni Beliefs Using a Chart

Have students make a chart that compares Shia beliefs about succession with Sunni beliefs about succession.

Ask:

How does this split in Islam still affect the world today? *(Answers may include that the split still influences events, such as wars, in the Muslim world and in international politics.)* BL

Discuss the Non-Arab Muslim Empires

Ask:

What faith did the Persian Safavids follow? *(They were Shia Muslims.)*

What faith did the Ottomans follow? *(They were Sunni Muslims.)*

Explain that this religious difference made the Safavids and the Ottomans enemies.

Ask:

What lasting legacy did the Safavids leave the Islamic world? *(Their language, Persian, spread widely. The language Urdu, which is spoken in Pakistan today, is partly based on Persian.)*

Describing Remind students that the Moguls were the third group to set up a Muslim empire. They swept into India riding elephants and horses.

Their best leader was Akbar, who let people worship as they pleased. After Akbar, Mogul leaders persecuted non-Muslims.

Ask:

How did the Mogul Empire grow weaker? *(Hindus and Sikhs rebelled against the Moguls. Then Europeans arrived and took over Mogul territory.)*

Analyzing Have students write an essay that analyzes the non-Arab Muslim empires—the Ottoman and Seljuk Turks, the Safavids, and the Moguls.

Ask students to assess the strengths and weaknesses of each group.

Encourage students to share their essays with the class.

Answers for pages 406–409

P. 406 CHART

1. Uthman's reign was the longest. Abu Bakr had the shortest reign.
2. CRITICAL THINKING Ali was a soldier and a writer rather than a merchant. He was also the first cousin of Muhammad.

P. 407 ☑ PROGRESS CHECK Arab soldiers were good riders and warriors. They applied the skills they had used on tribal raids to fight large armies. They believed they had a religious duty to spread Islam.

P. 407 CRITICAL THINKING Spain was home to many of Islam's great thinkers because the Muslim rulers of Spain created an atmosphere of religious tolerance where learning was encouraged.

P. 408 GEOGRAPHY CONNECTION

1. The Byzantine Empire blocked Abbasid expansion to the northwest.
2. CRITICAL THINKING Yes; Baghdad is centrally located and well positioned for the trade between Asia and the Mediterranean.

P. 409 ☑ PROGRESS CHECK The Sunni and Shia differed about who should lead Islam. They shared basic religious beliefs, such as the Five Pillars.

BIOGRAPHY

Suleiman I (1494–1566)

In 1520, at the age of 26, Suleiman I became the sultan of the Ottoman Empire. His reign is known as the Golden Age of the Ottoman Empire. He is often referred to as "Suleiman the Magnificent" or "The Lawgiver." He achieved many military successes and expanded the territory of the empire. Suleiman was responsible for the empire's greatest achievements in law, art, architecture, and literature.

▶ CRITICAL THINKING

Defending Why was Suleiman "magnificent"?

How Did the Ottomans Rule?

Because their empire was so large, the Ottomans ruled many peoples who practiced many religions. Islam was the empire's official religion, and Muslims enjoyed special privileges. The government passed different laws for non-Muslims. For example, non-Muslims had to pay a special tax. In return, they were free to practice their religion.

After Suleiman, the Ottoman Empire began to break down. It lost lands to the Europeans. Local rulers and conquered people broke away. The empire finally crumbled in the early 1900s.

The Safavids

In 1501, a Shia leader named Ismail proclaimed himself shah, or king, of Persia. Ismail founded the Safavid dynasty, which ruled Persia until the 1700s. During this period, Persian spread as a language of culture and trade. Urdu, a language spoken in Pakistan today, is partly based on Persian.

India's Mogul Empire

During the 1500s, the Moguls (MOH•guhlz) set up a Muslim empire in India. Under Akbar (AHK•bar), the Mogul empire prospered. He allowed people to practice their religions. After Akbar, Mogul rulers were less tolerant. They persecuted Hindus and Sikhs (SEEKS). Sikhs believe in one God and stress doing good deeds. Today, Sikhism is the world's fifth-largest religion.

During the late 1600s, Sikhs and Hindus rebelled against the Moguls. At the same time, Europeans arrived in India. Over time, the Moguls lost power, leaving the British in control.

☑ PROGRESS CHECK

Identifying What is Urdu?

LESSON 2 REVIEW

Review Vocabulary

1. How did the *Sunni* feel about the Umayyad *caliphs*?
2. In addition to the Seljuks, who else used the title *sultan*?

Answer the Guiding Questions

3. ***Identifying*** What area of Europe came under Muslim control at this time?
4. ***Describing*** What changes did Abbasid rulers bring to the world of Islam?
5. ***Determining Cause and Effect*** What effect did the burning of Baghdad in 1258 have on the Islamic Empire?
6. ***Explaining*** What led to the downfall of the Ottoman Empire?
7. **EXPOSITORY WRITING** Write a paragraph that compares how the Ottomans and Moguls each treated non-Muslims.

NOTES

NOTES

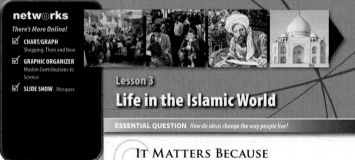

networks

There's More Online!

☑ **CHART/GRAPH** Shopping: Then and Now

☑ **GRAPHIC ORGANIZER** Muslim Contributions to Science

☑ **SLIDE SHOW** Mosques

Lesson 3

Life in the Islamic World

ESSENTIAL QUESTION *How do ideas change the way people live?*

IT MATTERS BECAUSE

Muslim advances in mathematics, business, science, architecture, and the arts helped to create our modern society.

1 Daily Life and Trade

GUIDING QUESTION ***How did people live and trade in the Islamic world?***

Muslim merchants controlled trade in much of Asia and Africa from the A.D. 700s until the 1400s. Their caravans traveled from Egypt and Mesopotamia to China. Their ships sailed the Indian Ocean to East Africa, India, and Southeast Asia. Muslim traders set out on their journeys with spices, cloth, glass, and carpets from their homelands. They traded these items for rubies from India, silk from China, and spices from Southeast Asia. They also traded for gold, ivory, and enslaved people from Africa. In addition, Muslim merchants sold crops such as sugar, rice, oranges, cherries, and cotton.

Why Were Muslim Traders Successful?

Muslim trade flourished for several reasons. Muslims spread the religion of Islam along with the Arabic language. As a result, Arabic became the language of business and trade in much of Asia and Africa. Muslim rulers also helped traders by providing them with coins to use for buying and selling goods. This was an easier trading method than bartering for goods.

Muslim merchants kept detailed records of their business dealings and their earnings. In time, these practices created a new industry—banking. Muslims respected merchants for their business skills and the wealth they created.

Reading HELPDESK

Taking Notes: *Organizing*

Draw a diagram like this one. Fill in details about Muslim contributions in the field of science.

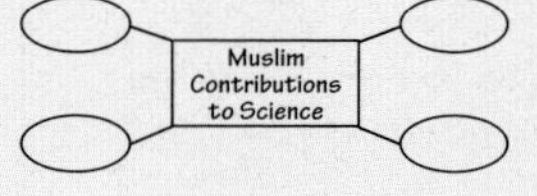

Content Vocabulary

- **mosque**
- **bazaar**
- **astrolabe**
- **minaret**

LESSON 2 (cont.)

BACKGROUND KNOWLEDGE

Sikhism

A teacher named Nanak founded Sikhism in the early 1500s in the Punjab region of India. Sikh religious leaders are called *gurus*. Sikh religious practice is based on the teachings of Nanak and the nine gurus who came after him.

Sikhs believe in one God and the equality of all human beings. Sikhism stresses doing good deeds such as caring for the less fortunate.

Today, Sikhism is the world's fifth-largest religion. It has 23 million followers around the world, but most Sikhs live in South Asia.

About 500,000 Sikhs live in the United States today.

Answers for page 410

P. 410 CRITICAL THINKING Suleiman was "magnificent" because he achieved military successes, expanded the territory of the Ottoman Empire, organized Ottoman law, and built many schools and mosques. His rule is considered the "Golden Age of the Ottoman Empire."

P. 410 ☑ PROGRESS CHECK Urdu is a language spoken in Pakistan that is based on the Persian language.

LESSON 2 REVIEW

1. The Sunni recognized the Umayyad caliphs as rightful rulers, although they sometimes disagreed with the caliphs' actions.
2. The Ottomans also called their rulers *sultans*.
3. Southwestern Europe and Spain came under Muslim control.
4. The Abbasids focused on improving trade and culture rather than conquering new lands.
5. The burning of Baghdad in 1258 marked the end of Arab leaders ruling the Islamic Empire.
6. After the rule of Suleiman I, the Ottoman Empire slowly declined. It lost territory to the Europeans. Conquered people rebelled and broke away from the empire. The Ottoman Empire dissolved in the early 1900s.
7. The Ottomans and the Moguls demonstrated some tolerance of non-Muslim groups. The Ottomans allowed non-Muslims to practice their religion if they paid a special tax, but Muslims were allowed special advantages. The Mogul leader Akbar also allowed people to practice their own religions. After Akbar, however, the Moguls were no longer tolerant of non-Muslims.

Teaching *Life in the Islamic World* (Student Edition pp. 411–415)

LESSON 3

ENGAGE

Identifying Divide the class into pairs. Explain that you are going to ask a question and each student will write down his or her answer. Then each student shares with a partner. After they have had time to compare answers, pairs will share their answers with the class.

Tell students that Muslims have made many contributions to the world in the fields of mathematics, science, medicine, and literature. Ask students to think of one thing Muslims have contributed to the world. Moderate a class discussion of Muslim contributions.

TEACH & ASSESS

1 Daily Life and Trade

GUIDING QUESTION *How did people live and trade in the Islamic world?*

Identifying Encourage students to identify reasons Muslims were so successful at trading. Record their answers in a list on the board. *(Answers: Most people spoke the same language—Arabic; Muslims developed a money system that eliminated bartering; Muslims kept records of their transactions, which later developed into a banking system.)*

CHART **Comparing and Contrasting** Remind students that a bazaar or marketplace for trading and shopping was and is today a feature in all Muslim cities. Have students work in pairs to compare and contrast an early city bazaar with a modern-day bazaar using the Shopping Then and Now activity in the Online Student Center. AL

SLIDE SHOW **Explaining** Tell students that in addition to a bazaar, all Muslim cities and towns had and today have a mosque.

Ask: **Besides being a house of worship, what else is located at a mosque?** *(Mosques are the location of schools and courts, and they are general centers of learning.)*

What are the most distinguishing features of a mosque? *(Minarets, wells, courtyards, and domes are common features of mosques.)*

Show students the slide show of mosques from around the world. AL ELL

Explaining Tell students that in the Islamic Empire, not all Muslims lived in cities and towns. Some lived in villages and farmed land.

Ask:

Who owned and controlled most of the land? *(Most of the land was owned and controlled by wealthy landowners.)*

How was Muslim society organized? *(It was based on wealth and power. Government leaders, large landowners, and wealthy merchants held the greatest power.)*

Answers for page 411

P. 411 Taking Notes Answers could be any four: Astronomers accurately described the sun eclipses and proved that the moon affects ocean tides. They perfected the astrolabe and used it to measure the size and distance around Earth. Muslim scientists developed the concepts of chemistry, and al-Razi was the first to label chemical substances as animal, vegetable, or mineral.

THEN

The word "bazaar" is Persian and refers to the public market district in a town. These ancient markets with many stalls and shops sold both local and imported goods from all over the world. They were the forerunners of modern shopping centers that we know today.

NOW

▶ CRITICAL THINKING

Evaluating What are the advantages of having a central marketplace?

Muslim Cities and Farms

Increased trade led to the growth of cities throughout the Islamic world. Makkah, Baghdad, Cairo (KY•roh), and Damascus were located on major trade routes. Muslim cities, however, were more than places of trade. They also became centers of government, education, and culture.

Muslim cities generally had narrow streets separating closely packed buildings. The main buildings were mosques and palaces. **Mosques** (MAHSKS) are Muslim houses of worship. They also served as schools, courts, and centers of learning.

Another important feature of every Muslim city was the **bazaar** (buh•ZAHR), or marketplace. Like shopping malls today, bazaars were full of shops and stalls where goods were sold. They were often covered to protect merchants and customers from the scorching sun. Nearby inns provided travelers a place to eat and rest.

Despite the importance of cities, most Muslims, however, lived in villages and farmed the land. The dry climate and the lack of rainfall, however, made farming difficult. Muslim farmers relied on irrigation to water their crops. They raised wheat, rice, beans, cucumbers, and melons in their fields. They planted orchards that provided almonds, apricots, figs, and olives. Farmers also grew flowers for use in perfume.

Some Muslim villagers owned small farms. Most of the productive land, however, was owned by wealthy landowners. They had large estates and hired farmers from nearby villages or used enslaved people to farm the land.

How was Muslim Society Organized?

People in the Muslim world were divided into social groups based on their power and wealth. Government leaders, landowners, and wealthy merchants held the greatest power. Below them were artisans, farmers, and workers. Enslaved people held no power.

As in other civilizations, slavery was common in Muslim lands. Many enslaved people were prisoners of war. Although they faced hardships, enslaved people had some rights under Islamic law. For example, mothers and young children could not be separated, and enslaved people could buy their freedom.

Men and women had separate roles in the Muslim world. Men were in charge of government, society, and business. Women managed their families and households.

Reading HELPDESK

mosque a Muslim house of worship

bazaar a marketplace

Women were also allowed to own property, invest in trade, and inherit wealth. Some upper-class women received an education and contributed to the arts.

PROGRESS CHECK

Explaining Why were Muslim merchants successful?

2 Muslim Contributions

GUIDING QUESTION *What were Muslim contributions in mathematics, science, and the arts?*

Arabic was the most widely spoken language in the Muslim world. The use of Arabic helped with the exchange of goods and ideas among the different Islamic peoples. For example, in A.D. 830 the Abbasid caliph Mamun (mah•MOON) founded the House of Wisdom in Baghdad. At this research center, Muslim, Jewish, and Christian thinkers translated Greek, Persian, and Indian works into Arabic.

From the 700s to the 1400s, scholars in Muslim lands preserved learning of the ancient world. Europeans had lost many ancient Greek writings. In Spain, however, Jewish and Muslim scholars translated some Greek writings into Arabic. When these Arabic translations were translated into Latin, western Europeans learned about ancient Greek thinkers.

Science and Mathematics

At the Baghdad observatory founded by Mamun, Muslim astronomers studied the skies. These studies helped them create mathematical models of the universe. They correctly described the sun's eclipses and proved that the moon affects ocean tides. They gave many stars names that are still used today.

Muslim astronomers improved the Greek **astrolabe** (AS•truh•layb). Sailors used this tool to determine their location at sea. Muslim scientists used the astrolabe to measure the distance around the Earth. Based on their measurements, they **confirmed** that the Earth is round.

Other Muslim scientists experimented with metals. As a result, Muslims are considered the founders of chemistry. One of the most famous Muslim chemists was al-Razi (ahl-RAH•zee). Al-Razi was the first scientist to label substances as animal, vegetable, or mineral. This type of labeling is still used today.

Connections to TODAY

Becoming a Doctor

Ancient Arab doctors had to attend medical school and pass a test before they could practice medicine. Today, doctors in the United States have similar requirements. To become a doctor, students must pass an exam to get into medical school and then complete four years of medical school. After completing those four years, medical students must pass another test to earn a license, or permit, to practice medicine. Without that license, they cannot be doctors.

Islamic civilization made important contributions to science, learning, and philosophy. This astrolabe advanced the Greek invention.

astrolabe a tool that helps sailors navigate by the positions of the stars

Academic Vocabulary

confirm to prove that something is true; to remove doubt

Omar Khayyam—known for his poetry—was also a mathematician, philosopher, and astronomer.

Muslims also made contributions in mathematics. The Persian scholar al-Khawarizmi (ahl-khwa•RIHZ•meh) invented algebra. He and the Arab scholar al-Kindi borrowed the symbols 0 through 9 from Hindu scholars. These numbers were passed on to Europeans. Today, they are known as "Arabic numerals."

Medicine

Muslims made important medical discoveries too. Arab doctors discovered that blood circulates, or moves, to and from the heart. They also diagnosed certain diseases. Al-Razi wrote a book identifying the differences between smallpox and measles.

Muslim doctors shared their knowledge by **publishing** their findings. The Persian doctor Ibn Sina (ih•buhn SEE•nuh) produced the *Canon of Medicine*, which described how diseases spread and analyzed hundreds of different medicines.

Unlike doctors in most other places, Arab doctors had to pass a test before they could practice medicine. The Arabs created the first medical schools and pharmacies. They also built medical clinics that gave care and medicine to the sick.

Literature

The Quran was the first and most important work written in Arabic. Muslims wrote non-religious literature as well. One of the best known works is *The Thousand and One Nights*, also called *The Arabian Nights*. It includes tales from India, Persia, and Arabia. Aladdin is one of the work's well-known characters.

Another Muslim, the Persian poet Omar Khayyam (OH•MAHR ky•YAHM), wrote the *Rubaiyat* (ROO•bee•aht). Many consider it one of the finest poems ever written. In a section of the poem, Khayyam describes the human being as a mystery:

PRIMARY SOURCE

“Man is a cup, his soul the wine therein,
Flesh is a pipe, spirit [give life to] the voice within;
O Khayyam, have you fathomed [figured out] what man is?
A magic lantern with a light therein!”

—from *The Rubaiyat* by Omar Khayyam, tr. E.H. Whinfield

Reading HELPDESK

minaret the tower of a mosque from which Muslims are called to prayer

Academic Vocabulary

publish to produce the work of an author, usually in print

Muslim scholars studied history. During the late 1300s, the Muslim historian Ibn Khaldun (IH•buhn KAL•DOON) looked for cause-and-effect relationships to explain historical events. He was one of the first historians to study how geography and climate shape human activities.

Art and Architecture

Muslims developed forms of art based on Islam and the different cultures of the Muslim world. Opposed to idol worship, Muslim leaders discouraged artists from creating images of living creatures. Instead, Muslim art included designs entwined with flowers, leaves, stars, and beautiful writing.

Muslim cities were known for their beautiful buildings. Mosques dominated the skylines of Baghdad, Damascus, Cairo, and Istanbul. The most prominent features of a mosque are its **minarets** (mih•nuh•REHTS). These are towers from which an announcer calls Muslims to prayer five times each day.

Islamic rulers lived in large palaces with central courtyards. To cool the courtyards, architects added porches, fountains, and pools. To provide protection, they surrounded the palaces with walls. One famous example of a Muslim palace is the Alhambra (al•HAM•bruh) in Granada (gruh•NAH•duh), Spain.

Another famous Muslim building is the Taj Mahal in Agra (AH•gruh), India. The Mogul ruler Shah Jahan built it as a tomb for his wife. The Taj Mahal is made of marble and precious stones and is considered one of the world's most beautiful buildings.

PROGRESS CHECK

Listing What achievements were made by Muslims in medicine?

It took Shah Jahan's workers and craftsmen more than 20 years to build the Taj Mahal.

▶ CRITICAL THINKING

Making Inferences What does the size and beauty of the Taj Mahal say about Shah Jahan's feelings for his wife?

LESSON 3 REVIEW

Review Vocabulary

1. Why is a *minaret* an important feature of a *mosque*?

Answer the Guiding Questions

2. ***Identifying*** What groups held the greatest power in Muslim society?
3. ***Explaining*** What did Muslim scientists discover once they improved the astrolabe?
4. ***Describing*** What are the defining features of Muslim art?
5. ***Summarizing*** Summarize the contributions that Muslim doctors made in the field of medicine.
6. **PERSUASIVE WRITING** What Islamic invention or development do you think has had the greatest effect on our world today? Explain your choice.

LESSON 3 (cont.)

LECTURE SLIDE **Analyzing** Show students the lecture slide comparing the roles of men and women in the Muslim world.

Then, lead a discussion with students about the role of women in Muslim society.

Ask:

What kind of role did women have in Muslim society?

How does this role compare to the roles of women in other cultures of this time period?

Moderate the discussion, and encourage students to give reasons and evidence for their opinions. *(Answers will vary but should reflect information in the chapter.)*

Muslim Contributions

GUIDING QUESTION ***What were Muslim contributions in mathematics, science, and the arts?***

INTERACTIVE WHITEBOARD ACTIVITY

Categorizing Students will categorize the many contributions Muslims have made. Using the Interactive Whiteboard Activity, have students identify Muslim contributions to science, architecture, art and literature, and economics. AL

Ask:

Can you think of any other contributions made by Muslims? *(Possible answers include the development of chemistry, the invention of algebra, and the discovery that the moon affects ocean tides.)*

INTERACTIVE WORKSHEET

Economics of History Activity

Explain that students will learn more about Muslim contributions to our modern banking system, including the use of checks and credit. Assign the Economics of History worksheet about banking for homework.

Have students complete the Lesson 3 Review.

CLOSE & REFLECT

LECTURE SLIDE **Discussing** Show students the lecture slide on major Muslim contributions. Discuss with students whether the contributions are evident today.

Ask:

Which contribution do you think is most important or has had the greatest impact?

Have students provide supporting details for their answers.

IF YOU HAVE MORE TIME . . .

Review Life in the Islamic World

Summarizing Have students work as a class to summarize what they have learned about life in the Islamic world. Ask each student to retell one important fact or idea from the lesson. Remind students that they should not repeat other students' facts and ideas. AL ELL

Explore the Importance of Education in the Islamic World

Describing Have students explore the role of education in the Islamic world.

Ask:

Mosques were used as schools. Why would education be important in the Islamic world? *(so Muslims could learn to read the* Quran*)*

Then, ask:

What do merchants need to know in order to do their job well? *(Possible responses include math, languages, and travel routes.)*

Challenge students to think about the connection between the ability to work as a merchant and education. Discuss what benefits there are to being a merchant. Prompt discussion by **asking:**

What might merchants do with their money if they became wealthy? *(donate it to a mosque, spend it on arts and architecture)* BL

Analyzing Point out to students that Muslim scholars translated many ancient Greek writings. Ask students to consider why this became so important, and encourage them to share their ideas with the class.

On the board, list the following: *Latin translations, ancient Greek writings, Arabic translations.* Have students explain the process by which the Greek writings were once again made available in Europe.

You may choose to have students draw a flowchart or other diagram to illustrate the sequence of events.

Create Time Lines to Understand Muslim Contributions

Sequencing Have students place in sequence on a time line the many Muslim contributions they learned about in this lesson. Discuss with students how these contributions influenced today's world.

Answers for pages 412–415

P. 412 CRITICAL THINKING The advantages of having a central marketplace include being able to one-stop shop (buy everything a person needs at the same place) and being able, as a merchant, to access the largest number of customers in one location.

P. 413 ☑ PROGRESS CHECK Muslim merchants were successful because they had support from Muslim rulers and kept detailed records.

P. 415 CRITICAL THINKING The size and beauty of the Taj Mahal indicate that Shah Jahan felt great affection and admiration for his wife.

P. 415 ☑ PROGRESS CHECK They discovered circulation of the blood and were able to diagnose certain diseases. Muslims also established medical schools and pharmacies and required doctors to pass a test in order to practice medicine.

LESSON 3 REVIEW

1. Minarets are towers on a mosque from which an announcer calls the people to prayer five times a day.
2. Government leaders, landowners, and wealthy merchants held the greatest power in Muslim society.
3. In measuring Earth with the astrolabe, Muslim astronomers discovered the world is round.
4. Muslim art does not show people or animals. It shows flowers, leaves, and stars, and it sometimes includes beautiful writing.
5. Muslim doctor al-Razi wrote a book identifying the differences between smallpox and measles. Ibn Sina, a Muslim doctor, produced the *Canon of Medicine*, a work that tried to summarize all the medical knowledge of the time. Other doctors discovered that blood circulates to and from the heart. Muslims also established medical schools and required doctors to pass a test in order to practice medicine.
6. Students should choose the Islamic invention or development they think is the most significant and back up their choice with reasons. Their reasons should explain the benefits to the world today.

Write your answers on a separate piece of paper.

1. **Exploring the Essential Question**
EXPOSITORY WRITING How does the spread of a religion change the way people live? Write an essay that discusses how the influence of Islam changed the way people lived throughout the Islamic Empire. Include the influence of Islam in daily life as well as in trade, government, and culture.

2. **21st Century Skills**
RECOGNIZE QUALITY SOURCES Using a computer word processing program, create a five-page report on the range of Islamic arts. Include arts that flourished in the Ottoman Empire during the reign of Suleiman I. Use primary source photos and information from reliable Internet sources such as the Metropolitan Museum of Art and national Turkish museums. Include secondary source information from encyclopedias.

3. **Thinking Like a Historian**
SEQUENCING EVENTS Create a time line. Place these four events in the correct order on the time line:
- Mongols burn Baghdad
- Abbasids replace the Umayyads
- Muhammad begins preaching
- Suleiman I rules the Ottoman Empire

4. **GEOGRAPHY ACTIVITY**

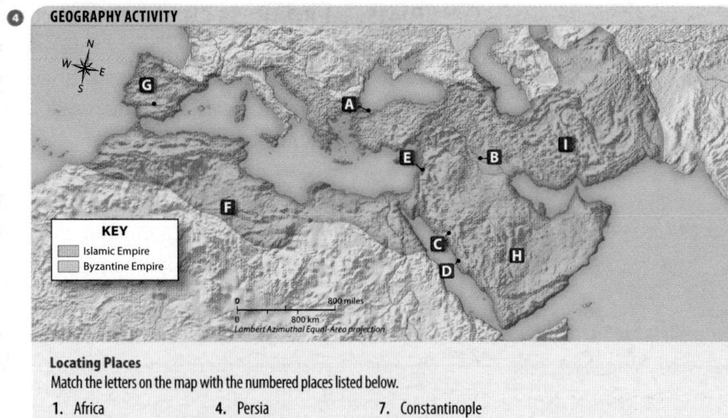

Locating Places
Match the letters on the map with the numbered places listed below.

1. Africa
2. Arabia
3. Spain
4. Persia
5. Makkah
6. Baghdad
7. Constantinople
8. Damascus
9. Madinah

REVIEW THE GUIDING QUESTIONS

1. The geography and climate that influenced the Arab way of life was
A. a tropical rain forest.
B. a cold and mountainous terrain.
C. a hot desert and dry plains.
D. a cool and rainy flat terrain.

2. What main source provides guidance to Islam's followers?
F. the Quran
G. teachings in the Bible
H. stories handed down by word-of-mouth
I. teachings in the Vedas

3. How did the Arab Empire change immediately after the Umayyads lost power?
A. The Mongols ruled and focused on education.
B. The Abbasids ruled and improved trade and culture.
C. The Romans ruled and built a large army.
D. The Safavids ruled and focused on religion.

4. How did the Ottomans rule an empire with many different people and religions?
F. Non-Muslims paid a special tax to practice their religions.
G. Everyone paid a freedom of religion tax.
H. No religious worship was allowed in the empire.
I. Muslims paid an extra tax to practice their religion.

5. How did trade spread throughout the Islamic world?
A. Muslim soldiers ran trading companies.
B. Throughout the Islamic Empire, Muslims built trading posts.
C. Traders in the Islamic Empire didn't have to pay taxes.
D. All schools in the empire taught trading skills.

6. What contributions did Muslims make to astronomy?
F. Muslim astronomers discovered the planet Mars.
G. Muslims proved that the moon affects ocean tides.
H. Muslim astronomers described the expanding universe.
I. Astronomers in the Islamic Empire tracked the Earth's orbit.

DBQ DOCUMENT-BASED QUESTIONS

Baghdad became a center of political and cultural power. A visitor, Yakut, describes the city after visiting it in A.D. 800.

"Baghdad formed two vast semi-circles on the right and left banks of the Tigris. . . . Baghdad was a veritable [true] City of Palaces, not made of stucco and mortar, but of [precious] marble."

—from *Readings in Ancient History,* edited by William Stearns Davis

7. **Summarizing** Which statement best summarizes Yakut's opinion about Baghdad?
A. Yakut is critical of Baghdad.
B. Yakut describes Baghdad as a small city on the Tigris River.
C. Yakut sees Baghdad as a poor city.
D. Yakut's description paints Baghdad as a splendid city of fine buildings.

8. **Comparing and Contrasting** Why does Yakut mention building materials?
F. All these materials were scarce throughout the Islamic Empire.
G. The building materials show how magnificent Baghdad was.
H. Stucco and mortar were unusual building materials.
I. Marble was a common building material throughout the Islamic Empire.

SHORT RESPONSE

"In the 7th century [600s] Persia fell to the conquering armies of Islam. ***Islamic*** *rule, under the* ***empire*** *of the caliphate, persisted for the next seven centuries. . . . Although Islam gave the Persians a wholly new religion and altered their way of living, Persian culture remained intact [unchanged]."*

—from "Islamic Dynasties" in *Encyclopedia Britannica Kids*

9. How did Islamic rule affect the Persians?

10. How did allowing Persian culture to remain unchanged strengthen the Islamic Empire?

EXTENDED RESPONSE

11. **Descriptive Writing** You are a merchant during the era of the Umayyads. You travel the empire buying and selling goods. Write a diary entry describing one of your travels.

Need Extra Help?

If You've Missed Question	1	2	3	4	5	6	7	8	9	10	11
Review Lesson	1	1	2	2	2	3	2	2	2	2	2

NOTES

REFLECT, REVIEW, & REMEDIATE

INTERACTIVE WORKSHEET

Chapter Summary

Provide students with the Chapter Summary worksheet to help review the chapter and prepare for assessment.

Reviewing the Enduring Understandings

Review this chapter's Enduring Understandings with students:

- People, places, and ideas change over time.
- Religion can influence a society's beliefs and values.

INTERACTIVE WHITEBOARD ACTIVITY Lead the class in a discussion of how Islam has provided change and unity to the Muslim world.

Ask: How did Islam change life on the Arabian peninsula? How did it change life in the countries that became part of Islamic empires? How did Islam become a source of unity? How did Islam change over time? What parts of Islam did not change?

Create a graphic organizer like the following in which to record student responses.

Changes Brought by Islam	Unifying Aspects of Islam

ACTIVITIES ANSWERS

Exploring the Essential Question

1. Students should note that religions often have a deep impact on culture and the way people live. They should compare life for the Arabs before Islam to life after people converted to Islam in categories such as daily life, trade, government, and overall culture. The development of Islam affected every aspect of people's lives.

21st Century Skills

2. Students should research carefully and use only reliable Internet sources in gathering photos and information for their reports on the development of the arts under the rule of Suleiman I. They should mention all of the arts that flourished but only focus on one or two. Students should be sure to cite references for their research.

Thinking Like a Historian

3. The time line should extend from A.D. 600 to 1600. The events should be placed on the time line in this order:
   - Muhammad begins preaching (A.D. 610)
   - Abbasids replace the Umayyads (A.D. 750)
   - Mongols burn Baghdad (1258)
   - Suleiman I rules the Ottoman Empire (1520–1566)

Locating Places

4. **1.** F, **2.** H, **3.** G, **4.** I, **5.** D, **6.** B, **7.** A, **8.** E, **9.** C

ASSESSMENT ANSWERS

Review the Guiding Questions

1. **C** Choice C is the correct answer. The geography and climate that influenced the Arab way of life included hot desert and dry plains. The area where Arabs lived was not a rain forest. It hardly rains in the desert and dry plains. It was not cold and mountainous like Viking countries, and although the geography was relatively flat, it was not cool and rainy.

2. **F** Choice F is the correct answer. The Quran, the holy book of Islam, is the primary teaching tool for the Islamic faith. Islam does not use the Christian Bible, and the Vedas are Hindu writings. Not all stories handed down by word-of-mouth are considered holy.

3. **B** Choice B is the correct answer. The Abbasids ruled the Arab Empire immediately after the Umayyads and focused on increasing trade and developing Arab culture. The Mongols did not rule until the 1200s. The Romans did not ever rule the Arab Empire, and the Safavids ruled after the Abbasids.

4. **F** Choice F is the correct answer. People in the Ottoman Empire were free to practice their own religion, but non-Muslims had to pay a special tax to do so.

5. **B** Choice B is the correct answer. Muslims increased trade throughout their empire by building trading posts in numerous places. Muslim soldiers did not operate trading companies wherever they were posted. Traders, like most people in the empire, had to pay taxes. Schools in the empire did not focus on teaching trading skills.

6. **G** Choice G is the correct answer. Muslim astronomers did not track Earth's orbit, describe the expanding universe, or discover the planet Mars. They proved that the moon affects ocean tides.

Document-Based Questions

7. **D** Choice D is the correct answer. Students should use the word *splendid* as a clue to help them answer this question.

8. **F** Choice F is the correct answer. Students should note that marble is a more beautiful building material than stucco and mortar. If they are unsure of the words and their meanings, have them look up the words in a dictionary.

Short Response

9. Islamic rule gave Persians a new religion and changed their way of living.

10. Answers should include that enabling the Persians to maintain their culture would make the Persian people more accepting of being part of the Islamic empire. The Persian people would be less rebellious.

Extended Response

11. Students' diary entries should include the geography of the upcoming trading trip and the method of travel. Students might want to estimate how long the trip will take as well as the sights they will see.

ONLINE RESOURCES
networks

There's More Online!

- ☑ INTERACTIVE WORKSHEETS
- ☑ BIOGRAPHIES
- ☑ CHARTS/GRAPHS
- ☑ GAMES
- ☑ GRAPHIC ORGANIZERS
- ☑ IMAGES
- ☑ MAPS
- ☑ PRIMARY SOURCES
- ☑ SLIDE SHOWS
- ☑ TIME LINE
- ☑ LECTURE SLIDES
- ☑ INTERACTIVE WHITEBOARD ACTIVITIES
- ☑ ASSESSMENTS
- ☑ VIDEOS

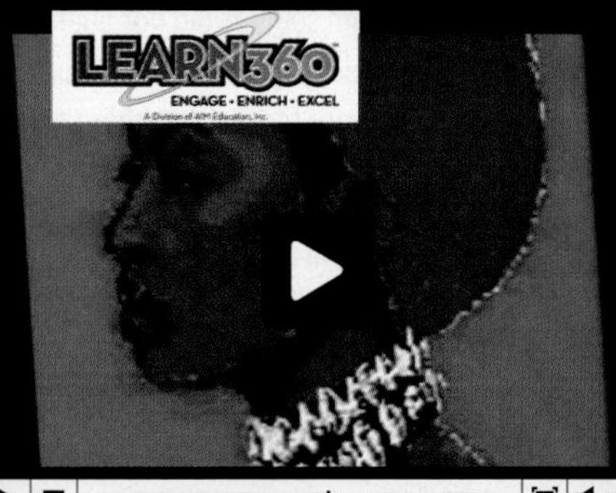

Great African Queens

History and Traditions of Mali

The History, Exploration, and Conquest of South America

Chapter 15 African Civilizations

Dear World History Teacher,

The mastery of agriculture gave rise to three early civilizations in Africa—Egypt, Kush, and Axum. Later, new states emerged in different parts of Africa, some of them strongly influenced by the spread of Islam. Ghana, Mali, and Songhai were three flourishing trade states in West Africa. Zimbabwe, which emerged around 1300, played an important role in the southern half of Africa.

Due to a lack of written records, we know little about early African society and culture. We do know, however, that the relationship between king and subjects was often less rigid in African society than in other civilizations. Family was the basic unit in African society. Religious beliefs focused on many gods, nature spirits, and the importance of ancestors. Africans produced a distinctive culture in wood carving, sculpture, music, and architecture.

In the fifteenth century, fleets from Portugal began to explore the coast of West Africa. At first their sponsors searched for gold and people to enslave, but as they expanded, their goal changed to domination of trade in the Indian Ocean as well. The demands of the Europeans would soon pose a threat to the peoples of Africa.

Jackson J. Spielvogel

More Media Resources

Current Events Online

Visit McGraw-Hill's current events Web site for high-interest news stories and activities for your students. Access the site through the Student or Teacher Center in **networks.**

At the 

Search for more videos online in the **networks** Resource Library.

Reading List

Grade 6 reading level:
A Pride of African Tales, by Donna L. Washington

Grade 7 reading level:
Africa for Kids: Exploring a Vibrant Continent, by Harvey Croze

Grade 8 reading level:
Time's Memory, by Julius Lester

CHAPTER 15 Planner

UNDERSTANDING BY DESIGN®

Enduring Understanding

- ***People, places, and ideas change over time.***

Essential Questions

- ***Why do people trade?*** • ***How does religion shape society?*** • ***How do religions develop?***

Students will know:

- *how Africa's geography influenced trade in the region*
- *what types of trade took place in Africa*
- *how the African economy was dependent on trade*
- *how Islam arrived in Africa*
- *how ideas spread through trade*
- *how African arts and music have influenced today's popular culture*
- *the economic reasons behind the slave trade*

Students will be able to:

- **analyze** how trade affected Africa's development
- **use** visuals to interpret information about trade and Africa
- **present** completed visuals to the class for evaluation
- **evaluate** a peer's work and informally compare and contrast it with their own
- **read** a map on the exchange of ideas with Africa via trade
- **analyze** how trade affects the exchange of ideas
- **demonstrate** understanding of Africa's influence on pop culture through classroom discussion
- **compare and contrast** primary source quotes on the slave trade
- **construct** an argument based on primary source quotes on the slave trade and information learned in the lesson

Predictable Misunderstandings

Students may think:

- Africa did not support many varied civilizations.
- European kingdoms grew larger and richer than African trading empires.
- The slave trade in Africa began with the arrival of the Europeans.

Assessment Evidence

Performance Task

- Hands-On Chapter Project

Other Evidence

- Responses to Interactive Whiteboard Activities
- Creation of an illustrated map
- Interactive Graphic Organizers
- 21st Century Skills Activities
- Economics in History Activity
- Geography and History Activity
- Responses to classroom discussions
- Lesson Reviews

Pacing Guide

Introducing the Chapter		1 day
Lesson 1	The Rise of African Civilizations	2 days
Lesson 2	African Governments and Religions	1 day
Lesson 3	African Society and Culture	1 day
	What Do You Think?	1 day
Chapter Activities and Assessment		1 day
TOTAL TIME		**7 Days**

Differentiated Instruction

These lesson plans are written to address the needs of your On Level students. Discussion and activities that are well-suited to your Approaching Grade Level learners, Beyond Grade Level learners, as well as your English Language Learners are coded as follows:

Approaching Grade Level

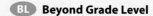

Beyond Grade Level

ELL **English Language Learner**

NCSS Standards covered in "African Civilizations"

Learners will understand:

1 CULTURE

1. "Culture" refers to the socially transmitted behaviors, beliefs, values, traditions, institutions, and ways of living together for a group of people

4. That the beliefs, values, and behaviors of a culture form an integrated system that helps shape the activities and ways of life that define a culture

2 TIME, CONTINUITY, AND CHANGE

6. The origins and influences of social, cultural, political, and economic systems

7. The contributions of key persons, groups, and events from the past and their influence on the present

9. The influences of social, geographic, economic, and cultural factors on the history of local areas, states, nations, and the world

3 PEOPLE, PLACES, AND ENVIRONMENTS

1. The theme of people, places, and environments involves the study of the relationships between human populations in different locations and geographic phenomena such as climate, vegetation, and natural resources

2. Concepts such as: location, region, place, migration, as well as human and physical systems

5. The concept of regions identifies links between people in different locations according to specific criteria (e.g., physical, economic, social, cultural, or religious)

6 POWER, AUTHORITY, AND GOVERNANCE

5. The ways in which governments meet the needs and wants of citizens, manage conflict, and establish order and society

7 PRODUCTION, DISTRIBUTION, AND CONSUMPTION

1. Individuals, government, and society experience scarcity because human wants and needs exceed what can be produced from available resources

3. The economic choices that people make have both present and future consequences

6. The economic gains that result from specialization and exchange as well as the trade-offs

7. How markets bring buyers and sellers together to exchange goods and services

CHAPTER 15

Introducing the Chapter

(Student Edition p. 419)

The Story Matters . . .

Ask a volunteer to read "The Story Matters . . ." aloud or read it aloud in class for the students. Discuss with students the circumstances that allowed the arts to flourish in Benin.

Ask:

What are some other early societies in which the arts held great importance? Have students share examples with which they are familiar, such as ancient Greece.

Then **ask:**

What can we learn about a culture by studying the works of art its people produce?

Lead the class in a discussion of this question. Guide students to recognize that works of art often reflect the daily lives, traditions, hopes, and concerns of a cultural group. As a result, these works can provide clues about how people lived in the past. Inform them that they can learn more about Benin and African culture online.

African Civilizations

400 B.C. to A.D. 1500

ESSENTIAL QUESTIONS • *Why do people trade?* • *How does religion shape society?* • *How do religions develop?*

There's More Online about the beginnings and development of culture, government, and religion in Africa.

CHAPTER 15

Lesson 1 *The Rise of African Civilizations*

Lesson 2 *Africa's Governments and Religions*

Lesson 3 *African Society and Culture*

The Story Matters . . .

Around A.D. 1400 the steamy rainforests of Africa were home to the kingdom of Benin. The region's steamy climate and fertile soil allowed farmers to grow surpluses of crops. Over time, communities and societies developed.

As a result, arts became very important in Benin. The kingdom became well known for the ivory and wood carvings its artists produced. An example is this rare pendant carved in ivory in honor of Queen Idia. Other artists worked with metals to produce realistic-looking masks. Today, this surviving art allows historians to learn more about the rich history and culture of early African civilizations.

◄ *The African kingdom of Benin became well known for the detailed works of its artists, such as this ivory carving.*

Peter Horree/Alamy

419

Introducing Place and Time (Student Edition pp. 420–421)

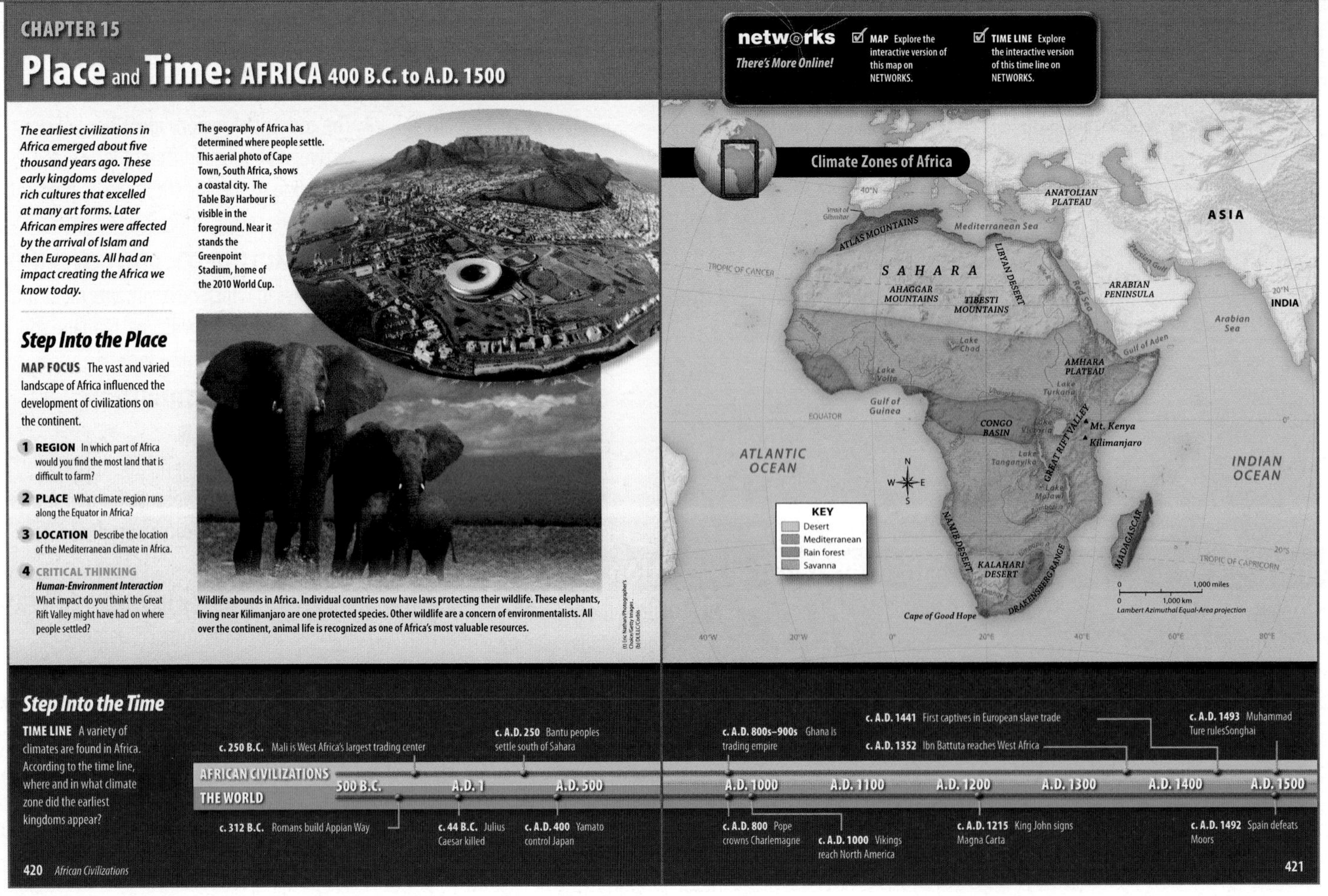

CHAPTER 15

Place and Time: AFRICA 400 B.C. to A.D. 1500

The earliest civilizations in Africa emerged about five thousand years ago. These early kingdoms developed rich cultures that excelled at many art forms. Later African empires were affected by the arrival of Islam and then Europeans. All had an impact creating the Africa we know today.

The geography of Africa has determined where people settle. This aerial photo of Cape Town, South Africa, shows a coastal city. The Table Bay Harbour is visible in the foreground. Near it stands the Greenpoint Stadium, home of the 2010 World Cup.

Step Into the Place

MAP FOCUS The vast and varied landscape of Africa influenced the development of civilizations on the continent.

1. **REGION** In which part of Africa would you find the most land that is difficult to farm?
2. **PLACE** What climate region runs along the Equator in Africa?
3. **LOCATION** Describe the location of the Mediterranean climate in Africa.
4. **CRITICAL THINKING** *Human-Environment Interaction* What impact do you think the Great Rift Valley might have had on where people settled?

Wildlife abounds in Africa. Individual countries now have laws protecting their wildlife. These elephants, living near Kilimanjaro are one protected species. Other wildlife are a concern of environmentalists. All over the continent, animal life is recognized as one of Africa's most valuable resources.

networks *There's More Online!* MAP Explore the interactive version of this map on NETWORKS. TIME LINE Explore the interactive version of this time line on NETWORKS.

Step Into the Time

TIME LINE A variety of climates are found in Africa. According to the time line, where and in what climate zone did the earliest kingdoms appear?

420 *African Civilizations*

421

Technology Extension

- Find an additional activity online that incorporates technology for this project.
- Visit the EdTechTeacher Web sites (included in the Technology Extension for this chapter) for more links, tutorials, and other resources.

Assessing Background Knowledge

INTERACTIVE WORKSHEET

What Do You Know? Activity

Have students complete the K-W-L chart for African civilizations before they study the chapter. Direct students to read each statement and then fill in the "What I Know" and "What I Want to Know" columns. Next, take a class poll so you can tailor your lessons to focus on any student misconceptions.

As students read the chapter, or after they complete it, have them fill in the "What I Learned" column. Ask students if they would change anything they wrote in the "What I Know" column. Ask students to explain why they would do so. *(Students should cite facts from the chapter that changed their answers.)*

INTERACTIVE WORKSHEET

Guided Reading Activities

You may wish to assign the Guided Reading Activity for Lesson 1 after introducing the chapter content.

Hands-On Chapter Project

Students will create an illustrated children's story about a topic related to African civilization.

- Students will participate in a class discussion to review what they have learned about African civilizations.
- Then, students will divide into small groups; choose a topic about an African region, river, or people; and plan how they will plot, write, and illustrate their story.
- Next, students will research, write, and illustrate their stories. Student groups will present their stories to the rest of the class.
- Finally, students will evaluate their research, presentation, and collaboration using an Assessment Rubric.

Visit **networks** online to see the full project and rubric.

Step Into the Place

Location Project the Interactive World Atlas on the whiteboard and project Africa. Direct students to take notice of the size of the continent, and point out important physical features. Discuss with students how Africa's location, size, and physical features might have influenced where people settled and traded.

At your interactive whiteboard, have student volunteers analyze the map of Africa and mark where they think trading empires might develop. Remind students to base their choices on their earlier observations about Africa's size and physical features. Ask each volunteer to explain his or her choice.

Next, project the Chapter Opener map on the whiteboard. As a class, discuss the Map Focus questions.

Step Into the Time

Making Inferences Have students review the time line for the chapter. Explain that they will be studying events from about 250 B.C. to A.D. 1500.

Ask students: **Based on the information listed in the time line, what can you infer about the history of African civilizations during the period shown on the time line?** *(Various empires were rising and falling in power.)*

Answers for pages 420–421

Step Into the Place

1. The northern part of Africa, covered in desert, would be the most difficult land to farm.
2. Rain forest and savannah climate regions run along the Equator in Africa.
3. The Mediterranean climate occurs in the far northern and the far southern portions of the continent.
4. CRITICAL THINKING The Great Rift Valley contains rivers and is accessible to the coast of the Indian Ocean. Because of this, it was a fertile and safe place to settle.

Step Into the Time

Answers will vary, but students should show understanding that the savanna and rain forest climate zones around central and west Africa were the birthplaces of the earliest kingdoms in Africa.

ONLINE RESOURCES

networks

Assign these interactive worksheets and quizzes from your Teacher Lesson Center. All resources are print-ready.

It's ALL Online!

Chapter 15 Resources

- ☑ Chapter Summary
- ☑ Vocabulary Builder
- ☑ What Do You Know?
- ☑ Hands-On Chapter Project

Lesson 1 Resources

- ☑ Interactive Graphic Organizer
- ☑ 21st Century Skills Activity
Information Literacy
- ☑ Geography and History Activity
Understanding Location
- ☑ Guided Reading Activity
- ☑ Reading Essentials and Study Guide
- ☑ Online Self-Check Quiz

Lesson 2 Resources

- ☑ Interactive Graphic Organizer
- ☑ Economics of History Activity
The Value of Gold
- ☑ Guided Reading Activity
- ☑ Reading Essentials and Study Guide
- ☑ Online Self-Check Quiz

Lesson 3 Resources

- ☑ Interactive Graphic Organizer
- ☑ 21st Century Skills Activity
Information and Communication Technologies
- ☑ Guided Reading Activity
- ☑ Reading Essentials and Study Guide
- ☑ Online Self-Check Quiz

Assessment Resources

- ☑ Lesson Reviews
- ☑ Online Self-Check Quizzes
- ☑ Chapter Activities and Assessment
- ☑ Standardized Test Practice

Remediation Resources

- ☑ Reading Essentials and Study Guide
- ☑ Guided Reading Activities
- ☑ Online Self-Check Quizzes
- ☑ Chapter Summary

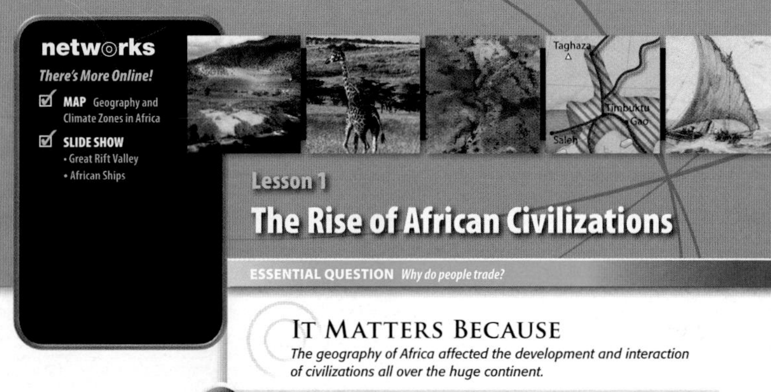

networks
There's More Online!
- MAP Geography and Climate Zones in Africa
- SLIDE SHOW
  - Great Rift Valley
  - African Ships

Lesson 1

The Rise of African Civilizations

ESSENTIAL QUESTION *Why do people trade?*

It Matters Because

The geography of Africa affected the development and interaction of civilizations all over the huge continent.

1 African Beginnings

GUIDING QUESTION *How did early peoples settle Africa?*

People have lived in Africa for a very long time. Scientists believe that the first humans appeared in eastern and southern Africa between 150,000 and 200,000 years ago. Early human groups in Africa lived as hunters and gatherers. These early peoples moved from place to place to hunt and gather food.

About seven or eight thousand years ago, hunters and gatherers in Africa began to settle in villages. They learned to tame animals and grow crops. Around 3000 B.C., as farming villages became more widespread and organized, Africa's first civilizations developed. These early civilizations were Egypt and Kush.

A Vast and Varied Landscape

The people of Africa found opportunities and challenges in the geography of the continent. First of all, Africa is very large in size. After Asia, Africa is the world's largest continent.

Most of Africa lies in the tropics. However, this enormous continent is made up of four distinct geographic zones.

Rain forests stretch along the Equator, which slices through the middle of the continent. These forests make up about 10 percent of Africa's land **area**. The rain forest zone gets heavy rainfall, and it is warm there all year long. The dense growth of

Reading HELPDESK

Taking Notes: *Identifying*

On a chart like this one, list the three major West African trading kingdoms. Then add one product that each kingdom traded.

West African Kingdom	Product

Content Vocabulary
- savanna
- griot
- plateau
- dhow

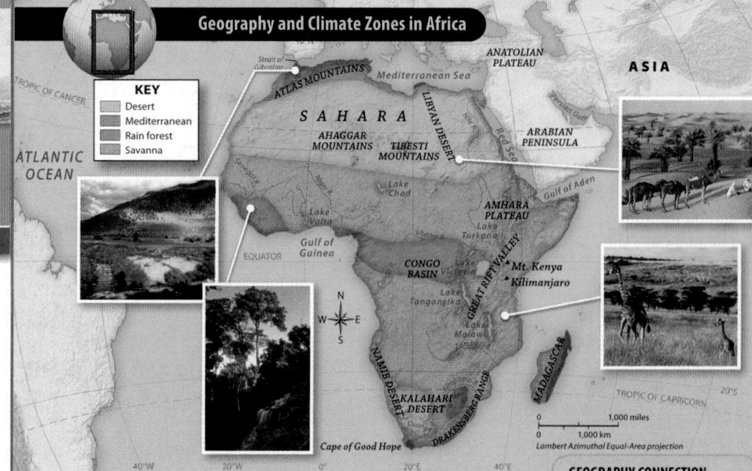

GEOGRAPHY CONNECTION

Differences in geographic features, such as climate, have had a strong influence on life in Africa's geographic zones.

1. **LOCATION** Which geographic feature covers most of East Africa?
2. **CRITICAL THINKING** ***Making Inferences*** How might the geographic zones of Africa have affected interaction between people from the northeastern and northwestern parts of the continent?

trees and plants in the rain forest can make farming difficult. Farmers, however, clear some of the forestland to grow root crops, such as yams.

Grasslands and Deserts

Vast grasslands make up the second zone. They stretch north and south of the rain forest. **Savannas** (suh•VAN•uhs) are tropical grasslands dotted with small trees and shrubs. These flat or rolling plains cover about 40 percent of Africa's land area. The savannas have high temperatures and uneven rains. However, they get enough rainfall for farming and herding. Farmers grow grains, such as millet and sorghum (SAWR•guhm). Herders raise cattle and other animals.

In northern Africa, the savannas connect with an area of even drier grasslands known as the Sahel (SA•hil). Plants that grow there provide barely enough food for people and animals. The people of the Sahel were traditionally hunters and herders.

savanna tropical grasslands dotted with small trees and shrubs

Academic Vocabulary

area the land included within a set of boundaries

Reading Strategy: *Contrasting*

When you contrast two things, you determine how they are different from each other. Read the information about savannas and the Sahel. On a separate sheet of paper, explain how these two areas differ.

COMPARING AFRICA TO THE U.S.

	Africa	United States
Size	11,667,159 square miles (30,217,894 sq. km)	3,794,085 square miles (9,826,680 sq. km)
Population Today	about 1.03 billion people	about 308 million people
Longest River	Nile River 4,160 miles (6,693 km)	Missouri River 2,565 miles (4,130 km)
Largest Desert	Sahara 3,500,000 square miles (9,065,000 sq. km)	Mojave 15,000 square miles (38,850 sq. km)

AFRICA

Encyclopaedia Britannica OnLine s.v., "Africa," http://www.britannica.com/EBchecked/topic/7924/Africa

INFOGRAPHIC

Many areas of Africa remain mostly unpopulated. Africa's population represents only about 10 percent of the world's total population.

1. **IDENTIFYING** What are the longest rivers in Africa and the United States?
2. **CRITICAL THINKING** ***Comparing and Contrasting*** How do Africa and the United States compare in size and population?

Deserts are Africa's third zone. They are found north and south of the grasslands. About 40 percent of the land in Africa is desert. The world's largest desert—the Sahara—stretches across much of North Africa. The Kalahari (KA•luh•HAHR•ee), another desert region, lies in southwestern Africa. For many years, the deserts limited travel and trade. People had to move along the coastline to avoid these vast seas of sand.

Small areas of mild climate—the Mediterranean—make up the fourth zone. These areas are found along the northern coast and southern tip of Africa. In these areas, **adequate** rainfall, warm temperatures, and fertile land produce abundant crops. This food surplus can support large populations.

Africa's Landforms and Rivers

Most of Africa is covered by a series of plateaus. A **plateau** (pla•TOH) is an area of high and mostly flat land. In East Africa, mountains, valleys, and lakes cross the plateau. Millions of years ago, movements of the Earth's crust created deep cuts in the surface of the plateau. This activity created the Great Rift Valley. In recent years, scientists have found some of the earliest human fossils in the Great Rift Valley.

Many large river systems are found in Africa. The civilizations of Egypt and Kush flourished along the banks of the Nile River in North Africa. The major river system in West Africa is found along the Niger (NY•juhr) River. Trade and farming led to the growth of villages and towns throughout the Niger River area.

Reading HELPDESK

plateau an area of high and mostly flat land

Academic Vocabulary

adequate enough to satisfy a need

transport to transfer or carry from one place to another

People living south of the Sahara also learned to make iron. This skill spread from East and Central Africa to West Africa. By 250 B.C., Djenné-jeno (jeh•NAY-JEH•noh) emerged as the largest trading center in West Africa. Its artisans produced iron tools, gold jewelry, copper goods, and pottery.

PROGRESS CHECK

Determining Cause and Effect How did Africa's climate zones affect people's ability to raise crops?

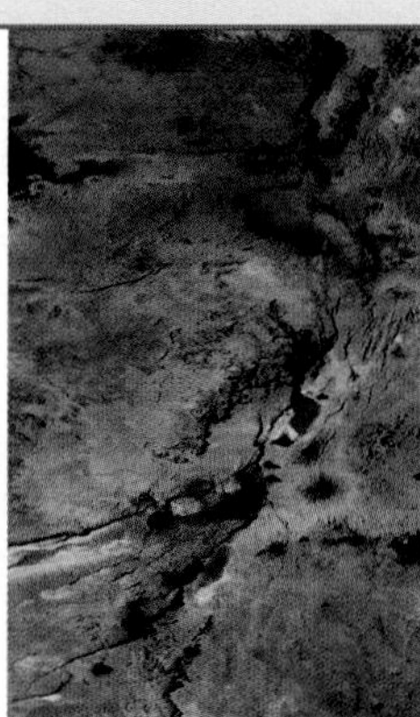

This satellite photo shows the Great Rift Valley, a deep crack in Earth's crust that is 6,000 miles (9,659 km) long. The valley began forming 20 million years ago.

2 Trading Empires in Africa

GUIDING QUESTION *How did trade develop in Africa?*

For thousands of years, the hot, dry Sahara isolated North Africa from the rest of the continent. Then, about 400 B.C., the Berber people of North Africa found ways to cross the Sahara to West Africa. Trade soon opened between the two regions.

How Did the Sahara Trade Develop?

For hundreds of years, the Berbers carried goods across the Sahara on donkeys and horses. The animals often did not survive the desert heat. The Romans introduced the central Asian camel in A.D. 200. The use of camels greatly changed trade in Africa. Camels are well suited for the desert. Their humps store fat for food, and they can travel for many days without water. The Berbers quickly adopted camels, both as a source of food and as a way to travel.

Berber traders formed caravans of many camels. These caravans crossed the Sahara between North Africa and West Africa. West African merchants sent gold mined in their region to towns bordering the Sahara. From there, caravans carried the gold northward. Some of this African gold reached Europe and Asia. Christian and Muslim rulers in these areas valued African gold.

Caravans from West Africa also carried ivory, spices, leather, and ostrich feathers. In addition, they **transported** enslaved people captured in wars. Merchants sent these captives to the Mediterranean area and Southwest Asia to serve as soldiers or servants.

PROGRESS CHECK

Explaining Why were camels essential for the Sahara trade?

3 West African Kingdoms

GUIDING QUESTION *Why did West African trading empires rise and fall?*

Caravans also headed from North Africa to West Africa. They transported cloth, weapons, horses, paper, and books. Once in West Africa, they traded for salt from mines in the Sahara.

LESSON 1 • Day 1

ENGAGE

MAP

Identifying Present to students the physical map of Africa. Direct them to identify some of the major physical features they see. If necessary, guide students to point out features such as the Sahara or the Nile River.

Ask:

How do you think these features might have affected trade in early Africa? *(Answers will vary, but students should draw reasonable inferences about the effects of major physical features on trade. For instance, students might suggest that rivers and oceans may have benefited trade, while other features, such as mountains and deserts, could have made trade more difficult.)* AL ELL

TEACH & ASSESS

1 African Beginnings

GUIDING QUESTION *How did early peoples settle Africa?*

LECTURE SLIDE

Interactive Whiteboard Activity

Identifying Show students the lecture slide on the geographic zones of Africa. Discuss the key differences among those zones.

Help students understand the important characteristics of these areas, as well as the differences between them.

Ask:

- **How did the land area covered by deserts compare to that covered by rain forests?** *(The land area covered by deserts was much larger than that covered by rain forests.)*
- **In which geographic zone could people raise many crops?** *(mild climate zone)*

SLIDE SHOW

Drawing Conclusions Direct students' attention to the information about plateaus and the Great Rift Valley in the section "Africa's Landforms and Rivers."

Then have students view the interactive slide show about the Great Rift Valley to learn more about this area.

Ask:

What does the information in the slide show suggest about the climate of the Great Rift Valley? *(Answers will vary but may include that in some areas of the Great Rift Valley, the climate allows plants and animals to survive. The slide show reveals many different kinds of animals living in this area.)* BL

INTERACTIVE WORKSHEET

Analyzing Visuals Display the Geography and History worksheet "Understanding Location: The Sahara."

Direct students' attention to the map of the Sahara. Have students work with a partner and study the map. Then, have them talk with their partners about what they notice about the map. Have students write their observations.

Next, as a whole-class activity, discuss each pair's observations. Finally, have students work with their partners to complete the worksheet.

2 Trading Empires in Africa

GUIDING QUESTION *How did trade develop in Africa?*

GRAPHIC ORGANIZER **Comparing** Present to students the interactive graphic organizer comparing the use of camels and horses for trade. Tell students they can use their responses to the questions above to complete the interactive Venn diagram featured in this activity.

INTERACTIVE WORKSHEET

Differentiating Display the 21st Century Skills worksheet "Information Literacy: Find Cardinal and Intermediate Directions."

Have more fluent readers take turns reading aloud the information about the skill. Ask other students to paraphrase this information to check for understanding. Then, have students work in pairs or small groups to complete the worksheet. ELL

CLOSE & REFLECT

Predicting Tell students to choose a major geographic feature of Africa described in the text, such as the Sahara, the Nile River, or the Sahel.

Instruct them to reflect on how this feature influenced settlement and trade in early Africa. Students should write one or two sentences analyzing their feature. Encourage volunteers to share their sentences with a partner.

Answers for pages 422–425

P. 422 Taking Notes Ghana: gold, salt; Mali: gold, salt; Songhai: gold, salt

P. 423 GEOGRAPHY CONNECTION

1. Savanna covers most of East Africa.
2. CRITICAL THINKING The difficulty of traveling across the desert zone probably would have limited interaction between people in these parts of Africa.

P. 423 Reading Strategy Savannas are tropical grasslands dotted with small trees and shrubs. They have high temperatures and uneven rains. However, savannas get enough rain to support farming and herding. The Sahel is drier than the savannas. It has different types of trees, thick shrubs, and grasses. These barely provide enough food for the people and animals that live there. For most of Africa's history, people living in this region were hunters and herders.

P. 424 INFOGRAPHIC

1. The longest river in Africa is the Nile River. The Missouri River system is the longest in the United States.
2. CRITICAL THINKING Africa is more than three times larger than the United States in size and in population.

P. 425 ☑ PROGRESS CHECK People could raise crops in Africa's rain forest, savanna, and mild climate zones. Growing crops was more difficult in the Sahel and desert zones.

P. 425 ☑ PROGRESS CHECK Camels could survive the harsh conditions of the desert with minimal food and water. Their feet were also well-suited to walking in the sand.

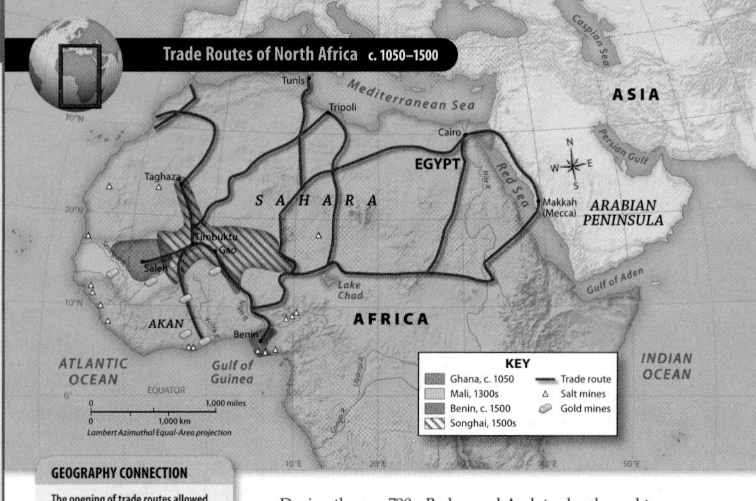

GEOGRAPHY CONNECTION

The opening of trade routes allowed the people of North Africa and West Africa to exchange products, such as gold and salt.

1. **LOCATION** What resource was found in the kingdom of Benin?
2. **CRITICAL THINKING** *Calculating* Use the map's scale to determine how many miles a caravan might travel along a route from Tunis to Benin.

During the A.D. 700s, Berber and Arab traders brought Islam to West Africa. They established ties with West African merchants, many of whom became Muslims.

The Saharan trade brought prosperity to West Africa. As a result of trade, the population grew, and powerful city-states emerged in the region. Eventually, rulers of these city-states began to build empires. From the A.D. 500s to the A.D. 1300s, these African empires were bigger than most European kingdoms in wealth and size.

How Did Ghana Begin?

Ghana (GAH•nuh) was the first great trading empire in West Africa. It rose to power during the A.D. 400s. The kingdom of Ghana was located in the Sudan. This area was mostly grassland, stretching across north central Africa. Fertile soil and iron tools helped the farmers of Ghana produce enough food.

Ghana was located between the Sahara salt mines and gold mines near the West African coastal rain forests. As a result, Ghana became an important crossroads of trade. From Ghana, trade

Reading HELPDESK

Reading in the Content Area

When reading primary source quotes, note any words or phrases in brackets. The use of brackets provides you with additional words that help clarify the meaning of the quote.

griot traditional storytellers

routes extended into North Africa and down the Niger River. They also linked to kingdoms in the Central African rain forest. Some routes reached all the way to Africa's eastern coast.

Traders interested in salt or gold had to pass through Ghana, which came at a price. Traders had no choice but to pay taxes to Ghana's kings. First, Ghana had iron ore and knew how to make iron weapons. Although Ghana owned no gold mines, it controlled the West Africans who did. Second, Ghana's kings had a well-trained army to enforce their wishes. Third, people were willing to pay any price for salt, a highly desired item used to flavor and preserve food. Berber traders wanted gold so they could buy goods from Arab countries and from Europe.

Abdullah Abu-Ubayd Al-Bakri (ehl•BEHK•ree), an Arab travelling writer in about A.D. 1067, described the way Ghana taxed merchants:

PRIMARY SOURCE

> "The king [of Ghana] exacts the right of one dinar [of gold] on each donkey-load of salt that enters his country, and two dinars of gold on each load of salt that goes out."
>
> —from *Ghana in 1067*

Ghana reached the height of its trading power in the A.D. 800s and 900s. Muslim Arabs and Berbers involved in the salt and gold trade brought Islam to Ghana.

Rise of Mali

During the A.D. 1100s, invaders from North Africa disrupted Ghana's trade, and the empire fell. As Ghana weakened, local groups separated to form new trading states in West Africa.

In the A.D. 1200s, a small state named Mali (MAH•lee) conquered Ghana. Mali created a new empire. West African **griots** (GREE•ohz), or storytellers, credit a great king for Mali's rise. His name was Sundiata Keita (sun•dee•AH•tuh KY•tuh)—the "Lion Prince." Sundiata ruled from 1230 to 1255. He united the people of Mali.

Sundiata conquered territory extending from the Atlantic coast inland to the trading city of Timbuktu (TIHM•BUHK•TOO). His conquests put Mali in control of the gold mines in West Africa. As a result, Mali built its wealth and power on the gold and salt trade.

How did Songhai Begin?

Mali weakened after the death of king Mansa Musa (MAHN•sah moo•SAH) in 1337. One of the states that eventually broke away from Mali's control was Songhai (SAWNG•eye). In 1464, Sunni Ali (sun•EE ah•LEE) became the ruler of Songhai. He seized control of Timbuktu. Sunni Ali used Songhai's location along the Niger River to extend his territory.

Thinking Like a **HISTORIAN**

Researching on the Internet

Ghana became the first great trading empire in West Africa. In the A.D. 800s and 900s, Ghana was at the height of its trading power. Use the Internet to find reliable sources about what life was like in Ghana during this period. Write two or three sentences that summarize your findings and present your summary to the class. For more information about using the Internet for research, read *What Does a Historian Do?*

This West African sculpture is of the Queen Mother of Benin. Benin had great rulers. By the mid-1500s, the kingdom of Benin stretched from the Niger River delta to what is now Lagos.

Werner Forman/Corbis

AFRICAN TRADING EMPIRES A.D. 100–1600

	East Africa	West Africa	West Africa	West Africa	SE Africa
Location	AXUM, Adulis	GHANA, Saleh	MALI, Timbuktu	SONGHAI, Gao	ZIMBABWE, Great Zimbabwe
Time Period	c. 100–1400	c. 400–1200	c. 1200–1450	c. 1000–1600	c. 700–1450
Goods Traded	ivory, frankincense, myrrh, enslaved people	iron products, animal products, salt, gold	salt, gold	salt, gold	gold, copper, ivory
Key Facts	King Ezana converted to Christianity; made it the official religion.	Taxes from traders passing through made Ghana rich.	King Mansa Musa built mosques and libraries.	Songhai gained control of West African trade by conquering Timbuktu.	King Mutota and Matope built huge empires.

INFOGRAPHIC

West African empires controlled trade for more than 1,000 years.

1. **IDENTIFYING** How long after the decline of Ghana did the Songhai Empire come to an end?
2. **CRITICAL THINKING** *Comparing and Contrasting* How were the goods traded by Ghana and Mali alike and different?

He took control of the river and then seized the salt mines. Songhai soon controlled the trade in salt from the Sahara and gold. By 1492, Songhai was the largest empire in West Africa. Invaders from North Africa ended the empire by A.D. 1600.

The West African kingdoms ruled the savannas. The rain forest, near the Equator, also had its own kingdoms. They included Benin, which arose in the Niger delta, and Kongo, which formed in the Congo River basin.

PROGRESS CHECK

Identifying What were two valuable products traded through Ghana?

4 East African Kingdoms

GUIDING QUESTION *How did trade affect the development of East African kingdoms?*

In ancient times, powerful kingdoms also arose in East Africa. The kingdom of Kush thrived on the Nile River for hundreds of years. One of Kush's neighbors was the kingdom of Axum (AHK•SOOM) on the Red Sea.

Axum benefited from its location on the Red Sea. It was an important stop on the trade route linking Africa, the Mediterranean, and India. Axum exported ivory, incense, and enslaved people. It imported cloth, metal goods, and olive oil.

Reading HELPDESK

dhow sailboat using wind-catching, triangular sails

Axum fought Kush for control of trade routes to inland Africa. Around A.D. 300, King Ezana (ay•ZAHN•uh) conquered Kush. In A.D. 334, Ezana made Christianity the official religion of Axum. Islam was introduced to Axum later. Both religions had a major impact on Axum and other trading states.

Coastal States

In the early A.D. 600s, Arab traders from the Arabian Peninsula had reached East Africa. They sailed to Africa in boats called **dhows** (dowz). In the A.D. 700s, many Arab Muslim traders settled along the Indian Ocean in East Africa. They shared goods and ideas with Africans living there. By the 1300s, a string of key trading ports extended down the East African coast. They included Mogadishu (MAH•guh•DIH•shoo), Kilwa, Mombasa (mahm•BAH•suh), and Zanzibar (ZAN•zuh•BAHR).

The Rise of Zimbabwe

The Indian Ocean trade reached far inland and led to the rise of wealthy states in Central and Southern Africa. These inland territories mined rich deposits of copper and gold. During the A.D. 900s, traders from the coastal cities of Africa began to trade with the inland states. The coastal traders brought silk, glass beads, carpets, and pottery. They traded for minerals, ivory, and coconut oil. They also obtained enslaved Africans for export to countries overseas.

An important trading state known as Zimbabwe (zihm • BAH • bway) arose in southeastern Africa. During the 1400s, this large empire reached from south of the Zambezi (zam•BEE•zee) River to the Indian Ocean.

PROGRESS CHECK

Explaining Why did Axum become a prosperous trading center?

A dhow usually had one or two sails. The bow, or front, of a dhow pointed sharply upward.

CRITICAL THINKING *Making Inferences* How do you think an invention such as the sails used on dhows might have benefited the Arab traders?

Mary Evans Picture Library

LESSON 1 REVIEW

Review Vocabulary

1. How is a *savanna* different from a *plateau*?

Answer the Guiding Questions

2. ***Explaining*** What are the four main geographic zones of Africa?
3. ***Identifying*** What role did the cities of Mogadishu and Mombasa play in the economic life of East Africa?
4. ***Naming*** What products did West Africans trade?
5. ***Describing*** What unique factors allowed the East African trading kingdoms to expand their trade?
6. **PERSONAL WRITING** You live in ancient West Africa. Your family is traveling to East Africa. In a personal journal, describe what you might experience when you arrive in East Africa. Tell about the people, land, and weather.

LESSON 1 • Day 2

ENGAGE

LECTURE SLIDE **Listing** Discuss the importance of caravans to trade in North Africa. Then ask students to make a list of trade goods that these caravans transported across the Sahara.

Next, compare their lists to the items shown on the lecture slide of Saharan trade goods. Their lists should include goods such as salt, gold, ivory, spices, leather, and ostrich feathers. Point out that caravans also included enslaved people who had been captured in wars.

Ask students to consider why these particular trade goods were carried. *(Students may note that many of these items had high value and low weight, such as spices and feathers. Others, such as salt, were needed for survival.)* AL

Tell students they will be learning about the importance of trade to the rise of empires in Africa.

TEACH & ASSESS

3 West African Kingdoms

GUIDING QUESTION *Why did West African trading empires rise and fall?*

Finding the Main Idea Refer students to the section titled "How Did Ghana Begin?" Point out to students that Ghana became the first great trading empire in West Africa.

Ask: **How did Ghana's location help it become a powerful trading empire?** *(Because Ghana was located between salt mines in the Sahara and gold mines near the West African rain forests, it became a crossroads of trade. Ghana's kings could tax traders passing through the kingdom. These taxes made Ghana wealthy.)* AL

INTERACTIVE WHITEBOARD ACTIVITY

Sequencing Direct students' attention to the section titled "West African Kingdoms," and have them complete the Interactive Whiteboard Activity on the changes that trade brought to West Africa.

Have students decide which of the effects in the item bank resulted from trade in West Africa. Help them place the effects they chose in the correct sequence on the chart. Remind students that trade did not affect only the economy of West Africa, but also areas such as government and culture.

Ask:

How do economic changes affect different areas of life today? *(Answers will vary, but students should make reasonable suggestions about the ways in which economic events can affect other areas of life. For instance, a student might suggest that economic changes can affect the course of an election.)* BL

4 East African Kingdoms

GUIDING QUESTION *How did trade affect the development of East African kingdoms?*

SLIDE SHOW

Speculating Tell students to refer to the section titled "Coastal States." Review with them the information about the role of Arab traders in the settlement and trade along the coast of East Africa.

Then, have students watch the interactive slide show on dhows and other ships. Invite students to study the slides and read the corresponding captions for each image.

Ask:

Why do you think it would have been important for Arab traders to be able to sail quickly? *(These traders took part in the Indian Ocean trade. From the coast of East Africa, they traveled great distances to trade in places such as India, Southeast Asia, and China.)* BL

Have students complete the Lesson 1 Review.

CLOSE & REFLECT

Illustrating

Ask students to sketch a rough outline map of Africa. Direct them to use the lesson content to shade in the areas in which West African trading empires, rain forest kingdoms, and coastal city-states were located.

Then, lead the class in a discussion of how best to summarize the trade that took place in each region.

Answers for pages 426–429

P. 426 GEOGRAPHY CONNECTION

1. Salt was found in the Sahara and Benin.
2. CRITICAL THINKING A caravan would travel about 2,000 miles (3,219 km) along a trade route on this journey.

P. 428 INFOGRAPHIC

1. about 400 years
2. CRITICAL THINKING Ghana and Mali traded salt and gold. However, Ghana also traded iron products and animal products.

P. 428 ☑ PROGRESS CHECK Salt and gold were the two most valuable products to be traded by way of Ghana.

P. 429 CRITICAL THINKING These sails might have helped the traders travel faster and more safely. This could have given them an advantage over other competing groups of traders.

P. 429 ☑ PROGRESS CHECK The location of Axum on the Red Sea made it an important trading center. It was located along a trade route connecting Africa, the Mediterranean world, and India.

LESSON 1 REVIEW

1. A savanna is a tropical grassland dotted with small trees and shrubs. A plateau is an area of high and mostly flat land.
2. The four main geographic zones of Africa are rain forests, grasslands, deserts, and small areas of mild climate along the northern coast and southern tip of the continent.
3. Mogadishu and Mombasa were trading posts that played key roles in East Africa's trade across the Indian Ocean.
4. West Africans traded products such as gold, ivory, spices, leather, and ostrich feathers with other nations.
5. The climate of the East African trading kingdoms allowed them to grow products to trade that could not be produced in the empires of West Africa.
6. Answers will vary but should accurately use information from the lesson to describe the landscape, people, and climate of East Africa.

networks
There's More Online!
- BIOGRAPHY Mansa Musa
- SLIDE SHOW Mosques in Africa
- GRAPHIC ORGANIZER Achievements of African Leaders
- VIDEO

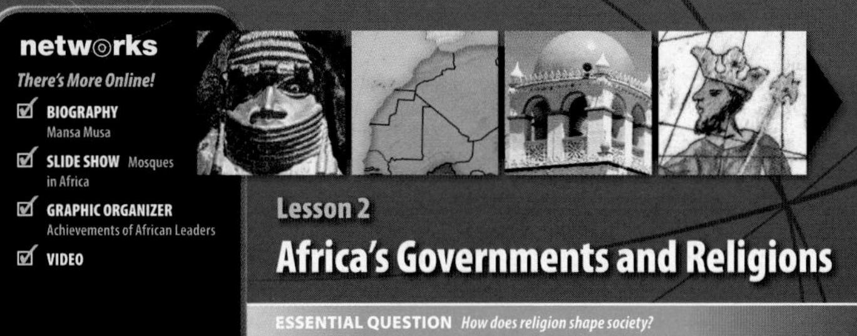

Lesson 2

Africa's Governments and Religions

ESSENTIAL QUESTION *How does religion shape society?*

It Matters Because

Ancient African societies showed the effects of government disputes, traditional religious beliefs, and Islam.

1 African Rulers and Society

GUIDING QUESTION *How did African rulers govern their territories?*

In most ancient societies, rulers were isolated from their subjects. In Africa south of the Sahara, the distance between kings and the common people was not as great. Often, African rulers would hold meetings to let their people voice complaints. In Ghana, drums called the people to the king. Anybody with a concern could address him. Before talking, subjects demonstrated their respect. They poured dust over their heads or fell to the ground. Next, they bowed and stated their business. Then they waited for their king's reply.

Kings and the People

Africans developed different ways to rule their territories. Powerful states, such as Ghana and Mali, favored strong central governments. Power rested with the rulers. They settled disputes, controlled trade, and defended the empire. They expected total loyalty from their people. Everyone benefited from the relationship. Merchants received favors from kings and paid the kings taxes in return. Local rulers held some power and gave the kings their support. This system allowed kingdoms to grow rich, control their lands, and keep the peace.

Reading **HELP**DESK

Taking Notes: *Organizing*

In a graphic organizer like this one, record at least one accomplishment of each of the leaders listed.

Leader	Accomplishments
Mansa Musa	
Muhammad Ture	
Askia Muhammad	

Content Vocabulary
- **clan**
- **Swahili**

What Was Ghana's Government Like?

The kings of Ghana were strong rulers who played active roles in running the kingdom with the help of ministers and advisors. As the empire grew, the kings divided their territory into provinces. Lesser kings often governed the provinces, which were made up of districts and governed by district chiefs. Each district was composed of villages belonging to the chief's **clan**. A clan is a group of people descended from the same ancestor.

Ghana's government had a **unique** method of transferring power from one ruler to another. "This is their custom and their habit," stated an Arab writer, "that the kingdom is inherited only by the son of the king's sister." In Arab lands, property was inherited by a man's sons. In Ghana, leadership passed to the king's nephew.

The Government of Mali

Mali had a government like that of Ghana, but on a grander scale. Mali had more territory, more people, and more trade. As a result, royal officials had more responsibilities.

Mali's kings controlled a strong central government. The empire was divided into provinces, like those of Ghana. However, the kings put generals in charge of these areas. Many people supported the generals, because the generals protected Mali from invaders. Also, the generals often came from the provinces they ruled.

Mansa Musa, Mali's most powerful king, won the loyalty of his subjects by giving them gold, property, and horses. He gave military heroes the "National Honor of the Trousers." As one Arab writer said:

This king of Benin was treated with respect by his subjects. This carving shows a public gathering.

▶ CRITICAL THINKING
Analyzing How does this carving show us that the people honored their king?

PRIMARY SOURCE

> "Whenever a hero adds to the lists of his exploits [adventures], the king gives him a pair of wide trousers. . . . [T]he greater the number of the knight's [soldier's] exploits, the bigger the size of his trousers."
>
> —from *Medieval West Africa: Views from Arab Scholars and Merchants*, excerpt by Ibn Fadl Allah al-'Umari

In Mali, only the king and his family could wear clothing that was sewn, like the clothes we wear today. Other people wore pieces of cloth wrapped around their bodies to form clothing. The trousers awarded to military heroes were truly a great honor.

clan a group of people descended from the same ancestor

Academic Vocabulary

unique one of a kind

The kings of Ghana taxed gold. This tax helped to control the amount of gold produced.

Government in Songhai

Songhai built on the political traditions of Ghana and Mali. It reached the height of its power under Muhammad Ture. A general and a devout Muslim, Muhammad Ture seized power in 1493 and created a new dynasty. He was a capable administrator who divided Songhai into provinces. A governor, a tax collector, a court of judges, and a trade inspector ran each province. Muhammad Ture **maintained** the peace and security of his empire with a navy and soldiers on horseback.

PROGRESS CHECK

Describing Why did many people in Mali support the generals who ruled the provinces?

2 Traditional African Religions

GUIDING QUESTION *How did traditional religions influence African life?*

Most African societies shared some common religious beliefs. One of these was a belief in a single creator god. Many groups, however, carried out their own religious practices. These practices differed from place to place. For example, the Yoruba lived in West Africa. They believed that their chief god sent his son from heaven in a canoe. The son then created the first humans. This religion was practiced by many of the enslaved people brought by Europeans to the Americas.

In some religions, the creator god was linked to a group of lesser gods. The Ashanti people of Ghana believed in a supreme god whose sons were lesser gods. Others held that the creator god had once lived on Earth but left in anger at human behavior. This god, however, was forgiving if people corrected their ways.

Even though Africans practiced different religions in different places, their beliefs served similar purposes. They provided rules for living and helped people honor their history and ancestors. Africans also relied on religion to protect them from harm and to **guarantee** success in life. A special group of people, called diviners, were believed to have the power to foretell events. Kings often hired diviners to guarantee good harvests and protect their kingdoms.

PROGRESS CHECK

Explaining What was the role of diviners in African religion?

Reading **HELP**DESK

Academic Vocabulary

maintain to keep in the same state
guarantee to promise
challenge to present with difficulties
convert to accept a new belief

Reading in the Content Area

When you interpret a pie chart, or pie graph, remember that each slice or wedge represents a part of the whole. That is, a slice may stand for a fraction or a percentage—a smaller part of the whole.

3 Islam Arrives in Africa

GUIDING QUESTION *How did Islam spread in Africa?*

Beginning in the A.D. 700s, traditional African religions were **challenged** by the arrival of Islam. Through trade, Berber and Arab merchants eventually introduced Muslim beliefs to West Africa. African rulers welcomed Muslim traders and allowed their people to **convert** to Islam. The rulers did not become Muslims themselves until the A.D. 1000s. By the end of the 1400s, much of the population south of the Sahara had converted to Islam.

Who Was Ibn Battuta?

Ibn Battuta (IH•buhn bat•TOO•tah) was a young Arab lawyer from Morocco. In 1325, he set out to see the Muslim world. He reached West Africa in 1352. There, he found that people had been following Islam for centuries. Yet not all West Africans were Muslims. People in rural areas still followed traditional African religions. Some rulers and traders accepted Islam only because it helped them trade with Muslim Arabs.

Ibn Battuta described in detail the people and places of West Africa. Some things amazed him. He was surprised that women did not cover their faces with a veil, as was the Muslim custom.

GEOGRAPHY CONNECTION

Today, people in Africa continue to practice a variety of religions.

1. **LOCATION** Which religion dominates the southern part of Africa?
2. **CRITICAL THINKING** *Analyzing* Use the graph to compare the percentages of Africans practicing traditional religions with those practicing Islam. How do they compare?

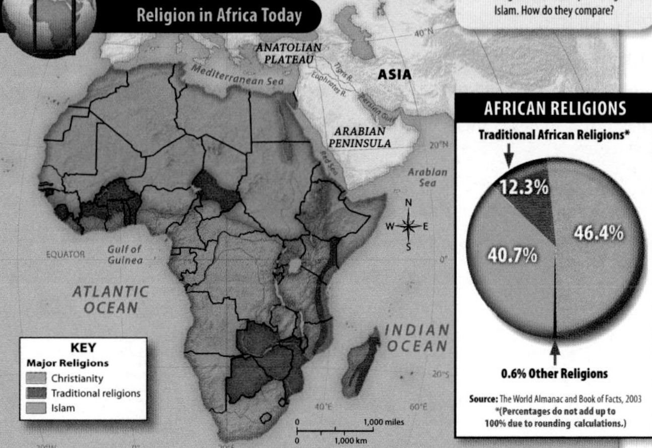

LESSON 2

ENGAGE

IMAGE **Analyzing Visuals** Present the interactive feature showing a carving of a king from Benin. Use the discussion question to prompt students' consideration of how this carving reflects the relationship between ruler and subjects that was previously discussed. Point out to students that the carving suggests this king is powerful but also has the respect and loyalty of his people.

TEACH & ASSESS

1 African Rulers and Society

GUIDING QUESTION ***How did African rulers govern their territories?***

Comparing and Contrasting Direct students' attention to the text about rulers' relationships with their subjects.

Ask:

- **How were African rulers' relationships with their subjects different from those of other rulers?** *(African rulers had closer relationships with common people than rulers in other civilizations.)* AL
- **How might this have helped these rulers govern more successfully?** *(By removing some of the distance between themselves and their subjects, African rulers may have won greater support from the people. This loyalty could have helped them govern more successfully.)* BL

Summarizing Divide the class into six groups. Assign two groups to each empire: Ghana, Mali, or Songhai. Have each group identify the key features of their empire's government and list those features on a poster, transparency, or other visual aid that can be presented to the class. Ask a volunteer from each group to share the group's visual aid.

After sharing information about the different empires in Africa, have students demonstrate their understanding using the graphic organizer.

GRAPHIC ORGANIZER **Identifying** Have students complete the graphic organizer about African leaders and their achievements.

INTERACTIVE WORKSHEET **Analyzing** Remind students that empires expand through trade, and that trade played an especially important role in the growth of African empires. Inform students that they should understand the role of economics in the growth of empires.

Display the Economics of History worksheet "The Value of Gold." Discuss which things are considered valuable (for example, gold, silver, money, diamonds, a college education). Then discuss why certain things are considered valuable and others are not. Point out that things can increase or decrease in value. Ask students for their ideas on why the value of something can change. Have students complete the worksheet for homework.

2 Traditional African Religions

GUIDING QUESTION ***How did traditional religions influence African life?***

LECTURE SLIDE **Explaining** Show students the lecture slide on traditional African religions. Note that although these religions varied from place to place, there were similarities.

Ask:

Why might traditional religion have been a comfort to Africans? *(It provided rules for living, and people believed it protected them from harm.)*

3 Islam Arrives in Africa

GUIDING QUESTION ***How did Islam spread in Africa?***

MAP AND GRAPH **Drawing Conclusions** Show students the interactive map and graph displaying the religions currently practiced in Africa.

Ask:

Where do most African Muslims live? *(in North Africa and along the eastern coast of Africa)* Ask students to recall what they learned in Lesson 1 about trade patterns in Africa.

Then ask:

How might trade have been tied to the spread of Islam? *(Students might suggest that many Muslim traders and merchants brought their religious beliefs with them to their new locations.)*

SLIDE SHOW **Analyzing Visuals** Present the slide show on African mosques to the class.

Ask:

Why do you think these mosques have different designs? *(Students might suggest that the mosques were built in different parts of Africa and reflect different combinations of Muslim and African culture.)* Explain that African and Muslim cultures blended across Africa in different ways. Tell students that in this lesson they will learn more about how such exchanges of cultures and ideas affected Africa.

Evaluating Have students read the section titled "Who Was Ibn Battuta?" Ask volunteers to identify some of the observations that Ibn Battuta made about Islam in West Africa. Remind students that Ibn Battuta traveled throughout the Muslim world recording his observations about the people and places he visited.

Ask: Why do you think writings such as those of Ibn Battuta are so valuable to historians? *(Answers will vary but may include that such writings provide historians with a firsthand account of a particular time in history. Observations such as the ones he made can give historians insight into a particular place or group of people.)* BL

Making Connections Refer students to the section titled "How Did Islam Develop in East Africa?" Point out that Ibn Battuta also visited East Africa.

Ask: What two meanings of the word *Swahili* had emerged in East Africa by 1331? *(By 1331, the word* Swahili *had come to describe the unique culture of East Africa's coast and the language spoken there.)* Point out to students that the Swahili culture and language combine African and Muslim cultures. Then have students identify some other familiar examples in which two cultures have blended to produce a new form of culture. *(Students may identify examples of cultural blending in a wide range of areas, including language, music, or food.)* Invite English language learners to identify words from their home languages that have been adopted into or taken on different meanings in English, or English words that have been adopted into their home language. ELL

Have students complete the Lesson 2 Review.

Answers for pages 430–433

P. 430 Taking Notes Musa—ruled Mali and developed it into one of the world's largest empires; devoted to Islam; built many libraries and mosques; made famous pilgrimage to Makkah; Ture—created new dynasty, divided nation into provinces; Muhammad—ruled Songhai and developed it into the largest empire in West Africa

P. 431 CRITICAL THINKING The way people are gathered around the king in this carving suggests that African kings were powerful and held the loyalty of their people. The two people fanning the king also show a measure of their respect.

P. 432 ☑ PROGRESS CHECK These generals protected the people from invaders. The generals also usually came from the province they ruled.

P. 432 ☑ PROGRESS CHECK Diviners were a special group of people who were believed to have the power to foretell events.

P. 433 GEOGRAPHY CONNECTION

1. Christianity dominates the southern part of Africa.
2. CRITICAL THINKING The percentage of Africans practicing traditional African religions is less than one-third of the percentage of Africans practicing Islam.

Muslim architecture, such as this mosque, demonstrates the lasting influence of Islam in Africa.

However, he did find that West African Muslims "zealously [eagerly] learned the Quran by heart" and faithfully performed their religious duties:

PRIMARY SOURCE

"On Fridays, if a man does not go early to the mosque [a Muslim place of worship], he cannot
find a corner to pray in, on account of the crowd.
It is a custom of theirs to send each man his boy
[to the mosque] with his prayer-mat; the boy spreads
it out for his master in a place befitting him [and remains on it] until
he comes to the mosque. Their prayer-mats are made of the leaves of a
tree resembling a date-palm, but without fruit."

—from *Travels in Asia and Africa*, by Ibn Battuta

The Journey of Mansa Musa

Ibn Battuta was impressed by Mansa Musa, Mali's most famous ruler. Mansa Musa let his subjects practice different religions. However, he was devoted to spreading Islam. Mansa Musa used his empire's wealth to build more mosques. In Timbuktu, Mansa Musa set up libraries with books from around the Muslim world.

In 1324, Mansa Musa increased the fame of Mali during a journey to Makkah (MAH•kuh). All Muslims are expected to travel to the Muslim holy city of Makkah. Mansa Musa made certain that people knew he was the ruler of a great empire.

Mansa Musa traveled in grand style. Eighty camels carried two tons of gold. Mansa Musa gave away so much gold to the poor on his journey that the price of gold fell. While in Makkah, Mansa Musa met scholars of Islam. He convinced them to return with him to Mali. They helped spread Islam in West Africa.

Islam in Songhai

Islam won followers among the Songhai people. Sunni Ali, the ruler, became a Muslim to keep the loyalty of merchants. After Sunni Ali died, his son refused to accept Islam. Muhammad Ture, a Songhai general, took over the government. With the backing of Muslim townspeople, he made himself king. He drove out Sunni Ali's family. He then took the name Askia.

Reading HELPDESK

Swahili the unique culture of Africa's East Coast and the language spoken there

Academic Vocabulary

survive to continue to function or prosper

Under Askia Muhammad (moo•HAH•muhd), the Songhai created the largest empire in West Africa's history. He ordered local courts to follow Muslim laws. He also made Timbuktu an important center of Islamic learning. Askia Muhammad set up a famous university and opened schools to teach the Quran.

The Songhai Empire **survived** disputes among royal family members. But it did not survive the guns of Moroccan invaders. This invasion in 1591 brought down the empire.

How Did Islam Develop in East Africa?

Islam spread slowly in East Africa. Islam arrived in the A.D. 700s, but the religion did not gain many followers until the 1100s and 1200s. A new society arose known as **Swahili** (swah•HEE•lee). It was based on a blend of African and Muslim cultures. The word Swahili comes from an Arabic word meaning "people of the coast." By 1331, however, it had come to mean both the culture of East Africa's coast and the language spoken there.

The African influences on the Swahili culture came from the cultures of Africa's interior. Muslim influences came from Arab and Persian settlers. The Swahili culture and language still thrive in Africa.

Islam's Effect on Africa

Islam had a far-reaching effect on much of Africa. Africans who accepted Islam adopted Islamic laws and ideas. They also were influenced by Islamic learning. Muslim schools introduced the Arabic language to their students. In addition, Islam influenced African art and its buildings. Muslim architects built beautiful mosques and palaces in Timbuktu and other cities.

☑ PROGRESS CHECK

Determining Cause and Effect What caused a unique brand of Islam to develop in Africa?

BIOGRAPHY

Mansa Musa (ruled 1312–1337)

Mansa Musa attracted the attention of many nations with his famous pilgrimage, or trip, to Makkah (Mecca). Countries in Europe, as well as kingdoms in North Africa and the Middle East, took notice. These nations hoped to trade with Mali and gain some of its wealth. Mansa Musa expanded his empire by capturing the cities of Gao (GAH•oh) and Timbuktu. During his reign, Mali was one of the world's largest empires. Mansa Musa once boasted that traveling from the empire's northern border to its southern border would take a year.

▶ CRITICAL THINKING

Identifying How did Mansa Musa's pilgrimage to Makkah benefit the kingdom of Mali?

LESSON 2 REVIEW

Review Vocabulary

1. What two meanings developed for the word *Swahili*?

Answer the Guiding Questions

2. ***Comparing*** What did all the early governments of African kingdoms have in common?
3. ***Explaining*** How did the leaders of Mali manage the grand scale of their government?
4. ***Describing*** What similar purposes did traditional African religions share?
5. ***Summarizing*** What did Ibn Battuta observe about the different religious groups in West Africa?
6. **EXPOSITORY WRITING** Write a brief paragraph in which you explain how Mansa Musa worked to spread Islam in West Africa.

networks
There's More Online!

☑ **BIOGRAPHY** Queen Nzinga
☑ **GRAPHIC ORGANIZER** African Culture
☑ **SLIDE SHOW** West African Art

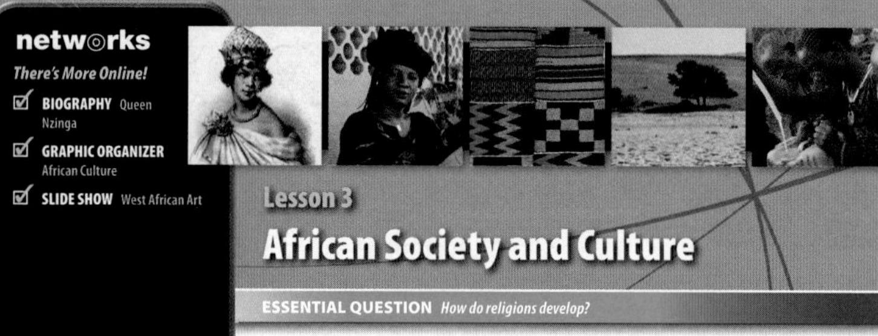

Lesson 3

African Society and Culture

ESSENTIAL QUESTION *How do religions develop?*

IT MATTERS BECAUSE

The people of early Africa formed complex societies with many common characteristics. They created artistic works that reflected their beliefs and built economies.

1 African Society

GUIDING QUESTION ***Why do people in different parts of Africa have similar traditions and cultures?***

In early Africa, most people lived in rural villages. Their homes consisted of small, round dwellings made of packed mud. Villagers generally were farmers. Africa's urban areas often began as villages with protective walls. These villages grew into larger **communities**. African towns and cities were centers of government and trade. Traders and artisans thrived in these communities. Artisans were skilled in metalworking, woodworking, pottery making, and other crafts.

Family Ties

The family formed the basis of African society. People often lived in **extended families**, or families made up of several generations. Extended families included parents, children, grandparents, and other relatives. These families ranged in size from a few individuals to hundreds of members.

Extended families were part of larger social groups known as lineage groups. Members of a lineage group could trace their family histories to a common ancestor. As in many other ancient societies, older members had more power than younger people. Members of a lineage group were expected to support and care for each other.

Bantu Migrations

Many of Africa's social practices are a result of migrations that began in West Africa about 3000 B.C. and lasted hundreds of years. The migrants, known as the Bantu (BAN•too), shared similar languages, cultures, and technologies. The Bantu migrated from West Africa to the south and east. They spread their farming and iron-working skills, along with their languages. Today, about 220 million Africans speak hundreds of Bantu languages.

Bantu villages were also **matrilineal** (ma•truh•LIH•nee•uhl). They traced their descent, or ancestry, through mothers, not fathers. When a woman married, however, she joined her husband's family. To make up for the loss, her family received presents from the husband's family. These gifts might include cattle, goats, cloth, or metal tools.

How Did African Children Learn?

In Africa's villages, education was the duty of both the family and other villagers. Children learned the history of their people and the basic skills they would need as adults.

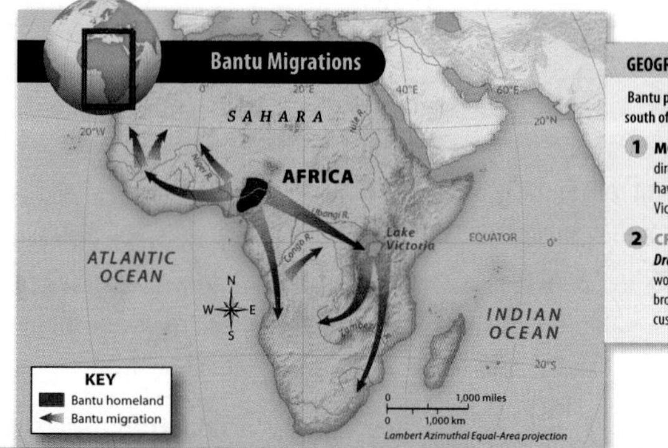

GEOGRAPHY CONNECTION

Bantu peoples settled most of Africa south of the Sahara by A.D. 300.

1. **MOVEMENT** In which direction would Bantu peoples have traveled to reach Lake Victoria from their homeland?
2. CRITICAL THINKING ***Drawing Conclusions*** Why would the Bantu migrations have brought common beliefs and customs to much of Africa?

Reading HELPDESK

Taking Notes: Finding the Main Idea

Use a chart like this one to record and organize important ideas about the different elements of African culture.

Cultural Element	Main Idea
Art	
Music and Dance	
Storytelling	

Content Vocabulary

- **extended family**
- **matrilineal**
- **oral history**
- **sugarcane**
- **spiritual**

extended family a family made up of several generations

matrilineal tracing family descent through mothers rather than fathers

Academic Vocabulary

community a large group with common values living in an area

LESSON 2 (cont.)

CLOSE & REFLECT

Making Connections Point out to students that the Swahili culture and language combine African and Muslim cultures. Lead students in a discussion of what the emergence of the Swahili culture suggests about the spread of Islam in Africa, as well as the influence of religious beliefs on African society.

Answers for pages 434–435

P. 435 CRITICAL THINKING Mansa Musa's pilgrimage to Makkah helped bring the kingdom to the attention of other nations. Because these nations wanted to gain access to the wealth displayed during Mansa Musa's pilgrimage, the pilgrimage helped Mali establish new trading connections.

P. 435 ☑ PROGRESS CHECK At times, the beliefs and practices of Islam contrasted with those of traditional African societies. As Africans adopted new ideas from Islam, they changed them to fit traditional ways. This blending caused a unique brand of Islam to develop in Africa.

LESSON 2 REVIEW

1. *Swahili* came to describe the unique culture of East Africa's coast and the language spoken there.
2. These kingdoms had strong central governments with powerful kings. However, the distance between the kings and the people of the kingdoms was not as great as in other societies.
3. Royal officials took on extra responsibilities in the government of Mali. The kings also divided the empire into provinces. They placed generals in charge of these provinces to help them govern there.
4. These religions provided rules for living and helped people stay connected to their history. Africans also believed these religions protected them from harm and guaranteed them success in life.
5. Upon his arrival in West Africa, Ibn Battuta observed that many people in rural areas continued to follow traditional African religions. He also observed that most Muslims in West Africa lived in the cities.
6. Sample response: Mansa Musa used his empire's wealth to build mosques. He also established libraries that housed books from across the Muslim world. During his pilgrimage to Makkah, he convinced many Muslim scholars to return with him to Mali and to help spread Islam in West Africa.

Teaching *African Society and Culture* (Student Edition pp. 436–441)

LESSON 3

ENGAGE

Making Connections Lead students in a discussion of their favorite styles of music. Encourage students to suggest a variety of styles, and compile a list of students' suggestions.

When this list is complete, inform students that many popular styles of music have developed from African music. These include ragtime, jazz, rock and roll, and rap.

Inform students that they will learn more about Africa's culture in this lesson. Explain that in addition to music, they will also learn about elements of African culture such as family and lineage groups, education, slavery, and arts. AL ELL

TEACH & ASSESS

African Society

GUIDING QUESTION *Why do people in different parts of Africa have similar traditions and cultures?*

LECTURE SLIDE **Explaining** Show students the lecture slide defining the term *extended family.* Point out that the family represented the basis of African society. **Ask:**

- **Who are members of your extended family?** *(Students should correctly identify several members of their extended families.)* AL
- **How do extended families differ from lineage groups?** *(A lineage group is a larger social group than an extended family. The members of a lineage group share a common ancestor.)* BL

SLIDE SHOW **Drawing Conclusions** Show students the slide show on Bantu migrations. Point out that these migrations had a significant impact on African history, though historians do not know what caused the Bantu to begin these migrations.

Ask: Why might historians be unable to determine the cause of the Bantu migrations? *(Answers will vary but may include that the Bantu might not have left any written records that could provide clues to the reasons for these migrations. There could also be few artifacts to help explain these migrations.)* BL

LECTURE SLIDE **Describing** Show students the lecture slide on children's education in Africa.

Ask: In what way were children especially valued in African families? *(African families especially valued children because they knew children guaranteed that the family would live on.)* Then, discuss with students how education in African villages reflected the importance placed on family and passing knowledge from generation to generation.

Answers for pages 436–437

P. 436 Taking Notes Art—Rock paintings were the earliest African art; Africans also made wooden masks and statues for religious ceremonies; they made fine metal and clay figures, and they wove cloth; Music/Dance—Music and dance were connected to everyday life; they were important to help ease the hard labors of daily life as well as to celebrate weddings and other milestones; Storytelling—Oral history played a vital role, as did griots, in passing down traditions and stories, especially of heroes.

P. 437 GEOGRAPHY CONNECTION

1. Bantu peoples would have traveled southeast to reach Lake Victoria from their homeland.
2. CRITICAL THINKING Bantu peoples traveled widely and settled throughout much of Africa during their migrations. By spreading their culture in the places they settled, they caused these beliefs to become common in many parts of the continent.

Some women in early Africa served as soldiers and political leaders. Queen Nzinga ruled in southern Africa.

▶ CRITICAL THINKING
Making Connections Why might European explorers have been surprised to observe women serving in these roles?

In West Africa, griots helped to teach the children. They vividly told their village's **oral history**. These stories were told and retold, and people passed them down from generation to generation. Many stories included a lesson about life. Lessons also were given through short proverbs. One Bantu proverb stated, "Patience is the mother of a beautiful child."

African Women

As in most other early societies, women in Africa acted mostly as wives and mothers. Men had more rights and supervised much of what women did. Visitors to Africa, however, noticed some exceptions. European explorers were amazed to learn that women served as soldiers in some African armies.

African women also served as rulers. In the A.D. 600s, Queen Dahia al-Kahina (dah•HEE•uh ahl•kah•HEE•nah) led an army against Arab invaders, who attacked her kingdom. Another woman ruler was Queen Nzinga (ehn•ZIHN•gah), who governed lands in southwestern Africa. She spent almost 30 years fighting Portuguese invaders and resisting the slave trade.

✓ PROGRESS CHECK

Describing What were families like in early Africa?

2 The Slave Trade

GUIDING QUESTION *How did the slave trade affect Africans?*

In 1441, a ship from the European nation of Portugal sailed down Africa's western coast. The ship captain's plan was to bring African captives back to Europe. During the voyage, the captain and crew seized 12 Africans—men, women, and boys. With its human cargo on board, the ship then sailed back to Portugal. These captives were the first Africans to be part of a slave trade that would involve millions of people.

How Was African Slavery Practiced?

Slavery was a common practice throughout the world. It had been practiced in Africa since ancient times. Bantu warriors raided nearby villages for captives to use as laborers, servants, or soldiers. Some were set free for a payment. Africans also enslaved their enemies and traded them for goods. The lives of enslaved Africans were hard, but they might win their freedom through work or by marrying a free person.

Reading **HELP**DESK

oral history stories passed down from generation to generation

sugarcane a grassy plant that is a natural source of sugar

Academic Vocabulary

contact interaction with other people

major great in rank or importance

The trade in humans grew as Africa's **contact** with the Muslim world increased. The Quran banned the enslavement of Muslims. Muslims, however, could enslave non-Muslims. Arab Muslim merchants, therefore, began to trade cotton and other goods for enslaved non-Muslim Africans.

When Europeans arrived in West Africa, a new market for enslaved Africans opened. Africans armed with European guns began raiding villages to seize captives to sell.

This colorful blanket is made from Kente cloth. Its name comes from an African word that means "basket."

The European Slave Trade

In 1444, a Portuguese ship brought 235 enslaved Africans to a dock in Portugal. An official of the royal court saw the Africans being taken off the vessel. He was moved to ask:

PRIMARY SOURCE

> "What heart could be so hard as not to [be] pierced with . . . feeling . . . ? For some kept their heads low, and their faces bathed in tears. . . . Others stood groaning . . . crying out loudly, as if asking [for] help. . . . others struck their faces. . . . But to increase their sufferings still more, . . . was it then needful to part fathers from sons, husbands from wives, brothers from brothers?"
>
> —from Gomes Eannes de Zurara, as quoted in *The Slave Trade* by Hugh Thomas

Portuguese merchants now sold humans. At first, most enslaved Africans worked as laborers in Portugal. Later, they were sent to the Atlantic islands of Madeira, the Azores, and Cape Verde. The Portuguese had settled these islands. The mild climate was ideal for growing **sugarcane** on plantations, or huge farms.

Harvesting sugarcane was hard work. Plantation owners could not pay high wages. Instead, they used enslaved Africans. Enslaved people received no wages. By 1500, Portugal had become the world's **major** supplier of sugar.

In the late 1400s, Europeans arrived in the Americas. They brought enslaved Africans across the Atlantic Ocean to grow sugar, tobacco, rice, and cotton.

✓ PROGRESS CHECK

Analyzing How did increased contact with other parts of the world affect the slave trade in Africa?

Griots, such as this woman, often accompany themselves on a stringed instrument called a kora.

▶ CRITICAL THINKING
Evaluating How might the tradition of oral storytelling have affected African stories over time?

The Slave Trade c. 1450–1800

KEY
Slave-gathering areas
Gold Coast
Ivory Coast
Slave Coast
Routes of slave traders

GEOGRAPHY CONNECTION

The slave trade carried enslaved Africans to different parts of the world.

1. **MOVEMENT** By what route is it likely a slave trader would have traveled from Mozambique to Brazil?
2. CRITICAL THINKING
Explaining What developments in world history might have caused the slave trade to grow during the time period shown here?

3 Culture in Africa

GUIDING QUESTION *Why were art forms important to Africans?*

Africans excelled in many art forms, including painting, weaving, woodcarving, poetry, dancing, and metalworking. These arts served a religious purpose. They also taught people the history of their communities.

Art in Africa

The earliest art forms in Africa were rock paintings. These paintings show the life of people in the area as they hunted animals, danced, and carried out everyday tasks.

African woodcarvers made masks and statues for religious ceremonies and teaching purposes. People believed the masks held spiritual powers. Clay and metal figures served **similar** purposes. Metalworkers in the West African region of Benin made beautiful bronze and iron statues of people and animals.

Reading **HELP**DESK

spiritual a gospel song

Academic Vocabulary

similar having characteristics in common

Reading Strategy: *Listing*

Making a list helps you organize facts presented while reading a passage. Make a list of the different types of art produced in early Africa.

Early African Music and Dance

Music and dance were connected to everyday African life. People used these arts to express their religious feelings. They also used the arts to help ease an everyday task, such as planting a field. Music and dance also had a vital role in community activities.

African music included group singing. In many African songs, a singer calls out a line, then other singers repeat it. Musical instruments, such as drums, whistles, horns, flutes, or banjos, were used to keep the beat in early African music.

Enslaved Africans relied on music to remind them of their homeland. In America, songs of hardship eventually developed into a type of music called the blues. Songs of religious faith and hopes for freedom became **spirituals**, or gospel songs. Over time, other forms of African-based music developed, such as ragtime, jazz, rock and roll, and, more recently, rap.

For many Africans, dance was a way to communicate with the spirits and express the life of a community. Lines of dancers swayed and clapped their hands. In the background, drummers sounded out the rhythm. Many African peoples had dance rituals that marked particular stages of life, such as when young boys or girls became adults.

African Storytelling

In addition to music and dance, Africans also kept alive their storytelling tradition. A few enslaved Africans escaped and shared their stories. Those who heard these stories retold them. They also retold popular stories that focused on the deeds of famous heroes.

✓ PROGRESS CHECK

Explaining What role did music and dance play in the everyday lives of early Africans?

Connections to TODAY

West African Music Today

West African music today rocks! Amadou and Miriam are a musical group from present-day Mali. In an unusual twist, both performers lost their eyesight at a young age. Eventually, they met at a school for the visually impaired. The duo first became well known in West Africa. They later grew in popularity in France before gaining worldwide acclaim. Their songs combine the music of West Africa with influences from rock and roll and the blues.

LESSON 3 REVIEW

Review Vocabulary

1. What made a Bantu village *matrilineal*?

Answer the Guiding Questions

2. ***Explaining*** How did the Bantu spread their language, culture, and technology throughout Africa?
3. ***Describing*** What roles did women play in early African society?
4. ***Identifying*** Which European nation established the slave trade between Africa and Europe?
5. ***Sequencing*** How did art in Africa change over time?
6. **PERSONAL WRITING** Describe your extended family. How might your extended family be similar to or different from extended families in early Africa?

LESSON 3 (cont.)

2 The Slave Trade

GUIDING QUESTION ***How did the slave trade affect Africans?***

Explaining Clarify for students that slavery did not begin with the arrival of the Europeans. Point out that slavery already existed in Africa and many other places throughout the world.

Ask:

How might enslaved people in Africa's slave trade gain their freedom? *(Enslaved Africans could be set free for a payment. They could also gain their freedom through hard work or by marrying free people.)*

3 Culture in Africa

GUIDING QUESTION ***Why were art forms important to Africans?***

Making Generalizations Help students locate the information about the purposes that African art forms served.

Ask:

In general, what two purposes did African art forms serve? *(These art forms connected people to the gods, spirits, and ancestors. They also helped teach people about their community's history and folktales when no written language had been developed.)* AL

Point out that African art forms also had more specific purposes. For instance, many enslaved Africans used music to remind them of their homelands.

Identifying Discuss with students the significance and purposes of the various African art forms.

Ask:

- **What were the earliest art forms in Africa?** *(rock paintings)*
- **What could historians learn from these works of art?** *(Historians could learn about the daily lives of the early people who created these rock paintings. The paintings show people taking part in everyday tasks such as hunting and dancing.)* BL

Making Connections Point out that, in Africa, dance served as a way to communicate with spirits and as a way to express the life of the community. Guide students to understand that many African groups held special dances to mark an important stage of life. Discuss with students examples of similar celebrations with which they are familiar. For instance, students might identify celebrations such as bar mitzvahs or quinceañeras.

SLIDE SHOW **Paraphrasing** Have students view the interactive slide show about African artwork. Have them study each slide and read its corresponding caption. Then ask a volunteer to paraphrase the caption. Repeat this process for each slide. ELL

GRAPHIC ORGANIZER **Finding the Main Idea** Review with students the Taking Notes interactive graphic organizer about African arts. Instruct students to draft a main idea statement for each cultural element shown.

Then direct them to work in small groups to compare and revise their main idea statements. When groups have completed their work, ask volunteers to share their final main idea statements.

INTERACTIVE WORKSHEET **Specifying** Display the 21st Century Skills worksheet "Information and Communication Technologies: Use Presentation Software." Have more fluent readers take turns reading aloud the information about the 21st Century Skill.

Ask other students to paraphrase this information to check for understanding. Then, have students work in pairs or small groups to complete the worksheet. Students may need to finish the worksheet as homework. ELL

Have students complete the Lesson 3 Review.

CLOSE & REFLECT

Making Inferences Review with students the lesson content describing the ways in which enslaved Africans relied on music to remind them of their homeland.

Lead students in a discussion about why people often turn to works of art or culture when facing difficult times or seeking comfort.

Answers for pages 438–441

P. 438 CRITICAL THINKING These explorers might have been surprised at these observations because few women in Europe served in politics or as soldiers.

P. 438 ☑ PROGRESS CHECK In early Africa, people often lived in extended families. Families formed the basis of African society.

P. 439 CRITICAL THINKING The tradition of oral storytelling might have caused these stories to change over time. Because the stories were not written down, storytellers may have gradually changed and adapted the stories as they retold them.

P. 439 ☑ PROGRESS CHECK The slave trade grew through increased contact with the Muslim world. Because Muslims could not enslave other Muslims, they began to trade goods for enslaved non-Muslim Africans. The arrival of Europeans in West Africa also opened a new market for the slave trade.

P. 440 GEOGRAPHY CONNECTION

1. A slave trader would be likely to sail around the southern tip of Africa before heading northwest across the Atlantic Ocean toward Brazil.
2. CRITICAL THINKING The increase in European exploration and settlement might have caused the slave trade to grow during this period.

P. 440 Reading Strategy Early African art included rock paintings, masks and statues for religious ceremonies, metal and clay figures, and woven cloth.

P. 441 ☑ PROGRESS CHECK Music and dance played a role in expressing the religious beliefs of Africans. These art forms also played a role in community events such as weddings, ceremonies, and rituals.

LESSON 3 REVIEW

1. Bantu villages were considered matrilineal because they traced their descent through mothers rather than fathers.
2. The Bantu traveled along Africa's waterways in small dugout canoes. They slowly spread across the continent. The Bantu would stop at a place to farm for a few years before moving on.
3. Women mostly acted as wives and mothers in African society. However, some women served as soldiers in African armies. Other women served as rulers.
4. Portugal established the slave trade between Africa and Europe.
5. The earliest forms of African art were rock paintings. In later centuries, artists made wood carvings and figures from clay and metal. By the 1200s and 1300s, metalworkers produced bronze and iron statues.
6. Answers will vary, but students should describe their extended families and use information from the lesson to identify potential similarities and differences with early African extended families.

What Do You Think?

Africa's Water Resources: Should Private Companies Control Them?

In ancient Africa, and today, the most precious natural resource is water. People worry about its availability. Many people cannot easily get clean water for daily use. Efforts are now underway to set up reliable water systems in Africa. Some local governments create their own water systems. Citizens are taxed according to their water use. Other governments cannot supply water. Then private companies agree to provide water to citizens for a fee. This system is known as *privatization*. Should control of water be left to governments or should private companies be allowed to control water?

Yes

PRIMARY SOURCE

"During the 1990s, it also became apparent [clear] that private participation could bring better oversight and management. The most detailed studies . . . concluded [found] that well designed private schemes [systems] have brought clear benefits–but not perfection. For example, in water, the most difficult sector, in cities as diverse as . . . Abidjan and Conakry service coverage has increased significantly. . . . Extended coverage tends to bring the biggest benefits to households with lower incomes, as they previously had to pay much more for the service by small informal vendors."

—Michael Klein, World Bank, Vice President for Private Sector Development and Infrastructure

During the dry seasons, some areas of Africa are completely without natural water. .

African governments are trying to find ways to provide clean drinking water for their people.

No

PRIMARY SOURCE

"Water is about life. The saying that 'water is life' cannot be more appropriate. Privatizing water is putting the lives of citizens in the hands of a corporate entity [business structure] that is accountable [responsible] only to its shareholders. Secondly, water is a human right and this means that any philosophy, scheme, or contract that has the potential to exclude [leave out] sections of the population from accessing water is not acceptable both in principal and in law. Privatization has that potential because the privateers are not charities: they are in for the profit. Price therefore becomes an important barrier to access by poor people. Water is the collective heritage of humanity and nature. . . . Water must remain a public good for the public interest."

—Rudolf Amenga-Etego, *Pambazuka News*

What Do You Think? DBQ

1. ***Describing*** What is privatization?
2. ***Identifying*** According to Michael Klein, where have private companies been most successful at providing water?

Critical Thinking

3. ***Analyzing*** What about Michael Klein's background would cause him to believe that privatization is the best solution?
4. ***Analyzing Information*** Why does Amenga-Etego mean when he says that "water is a human right. . ."?

Read to Write

5. ***Personal*** Write a paragraph describing your feelings about whether private companies have the right to make a profit by providing water to citizens.

NOTES

NOTES

ENGAGE

Analyzing

Show students the map of geography and climate zones in Africa. Point out the locations of major rivers and lakes. Have students identify the desert regions of Africa on the map. AL ELL

Remind students that the savanna climate zone covering much of Africa also receives uneven rainfall.

Ask:

How might the climate of Africa make accessing freshwater difficult? *(Students should note that much of Africa is desert where water is scarce and that the large savanna region does not receive a steady supply of rainfall.)*

TEACH & ASSESS

LECTURE SLIDE

Summarizing Ask students to think of the different ways in which they use water every day. *(Answers may include drinking, washing, and cooking.)*

Then show students the lecture slide and discuss the importance of access to clean water.

Ask:

Why is it important to have clean water? *(Using unclean water can cause deadly diseases and infections.)*

How would your daily life be different if you had to walk to collect water each day? If you could use only 1/20th the amount of water you normally use? *(Student answers will vary but should reflect an awareness of the challenges involved in using less water or spending more time and effort to collect it.)* BL

Defining

Make sure students understand the meaning of the term *privatization.* ELL

Explaining

Next, have students read the first excerpt. Discuss terms such as *oversight, management*, and *coverage* to make sure students understand the point being made.

Ask:

Why does the author think poor people would be better off buying water from a private company than a small vendor? *(He argues that a private company charges much less money for the water than a small vendor does.)*

Identifying Points of View

Have students read the second excerpt.

Ask:

What does the author mean when he says that "water is a human right"? *(The author is arguing that water is so essential to life that every human being should have a right to water so he or she can live.)*

Do you agree or disagree? Why? *(Student answers will vary, depending upon whether they think the need for things like food, water, and air can be considered rights.)*

IF YOU HAVE MORE TIME . . .

Practice a Reading Strategy

Analyzing Problems and Finding Solutions In both fiction and nonfiction, readers often need to identify a particular problem and find its solution. Certain stories are organized around a problem, or conflict, known as the plot and a series of events that lead to a solution, or resolution.

Informational texts and other expository materials may also ask readers to reflect on a problem or challenge. Sometimes writers provide solutions they think are logical and appropriate, and sometimes they ask readers to consider what steps or actions might work to solve a particular problem.

Helping students identify and analyze a problem in a selection enables them to see the complexity of an issue or an idea that a writer presents. Asking them to define, evaluate, or even determine a solution to a given problem gives students practice in thinking logically and systematically.

Students can use the following techniques for analyzing a problem and finding a solution:

- Ask students to identify through their reading the main problem in a passage or a selection.
- Ask students how that problem is defined. Does a person have a problem? Is the problem part of a task? Or is the problem the beginning of an explanation of a process?
- What logical steps or actions may be taken to solve the problem? Are possible or partial solutions presented? If so, what are they?
- What happens as a result of the steps or actions taken?
- What other actions may be taken to provide a more permanent solution?
- Ask students to evaluate why a solution did or did not work.
- How might they have solved the problem differently?

CLOSE & REFLECT

Expressing Review with students the key points from the excerpts and the class discussion. Then have students complete the document-based questions. They may complete the Read to Write question as homework.

Answers to *What Do You Think?*

1. Privatization is when private companies, rather than the government, provide services to people for a fee.
2. They have been most successful in providing water to cities.
3. Klein is the vice president of the World Bank private sector development division.
4. Amenga-Etego believes companies will exclude the poor because the companies will not make large enough profits in poor areas.
5. Paragraphs will vary but should include valid and logical arguments.

CHAPTER 15 Activities

Write your answers on a separate piece of paper.

1. **Exploring the Essential Question**
EXPOSITORY WRITING How would you explain the ways in which trade affected the history of early African civilizations? Write a short essay in which you consider the parts of these civilizations that were affected by trade. You may choose to focus on aspects such as the civilizations' growth, government, religion, or culture.

2. **21st Century Skills**
SUMMARIZING Write a paragraph summarizing what you have learned about one of the African civilizations discussed in this chapter. Your paragraph should describe why the civilization you chose is important in African and world history. It should also include significant events, people, and accomplishments related to this civilization.

3. **Thinking Like a Historian**
GEOGRAPHY AND CIVILIZATION Create a graphic organizer that lists at least three geographic features of Africa and explains their impact on the growth of civilizations there. For instance, you might write "Sahara" on the left side of your organizer. Then, on the opposite side, you could explain that for many years the Sahara limited travel and trade in Africa.

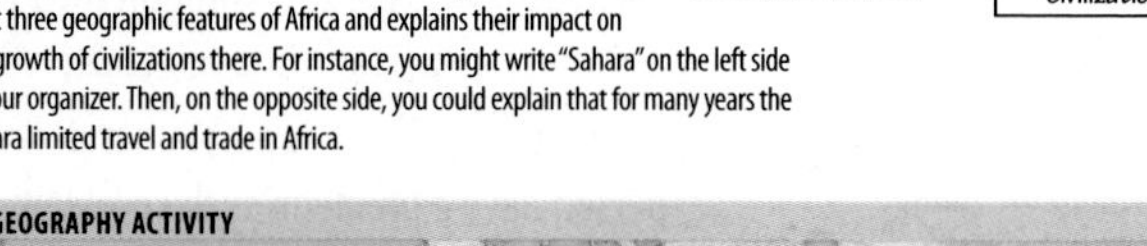

4. **GEOGRAPHY ACTIVITY**

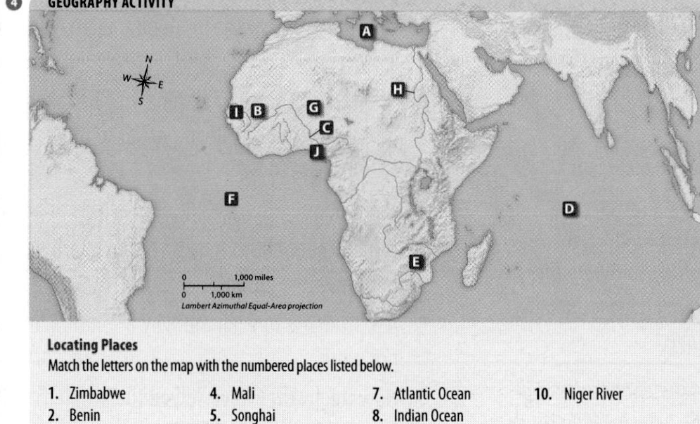

Locating Places
Match the letters on the map with the numbered places listed below.

1. Zimbabwe
2. Benin
3. Ghana
4. Mali
5. Songhai
6. Mediterranean Sea
7. Atlantic Ocean
8. Indian Ocean
9. Nile River
10. Niger River

CHAPTER 15 Assessment

REVIEW THE GUIDING QUESTIONS
Directions: Choose the best answer for each question.

1. About 40 percent of Africa's land area is covered by
   A. rain forests.
   B. plateaus.
   C. savannas.
   D. wetlands.

2. Which of the following conquered the declining empire of Ghana and created a new empire?
   F. Mali
   G. Songhai
   H. Benin
   I. Axum

3. Songhai reached the height of its power under the rule of
   A. Mansa Musa.
   B. Ibn Battuta.
   C. Sunni Ali.
   D. Muhammad Ture.

4. African and Muslim cultures blended to form the ______ culture.
   F. Mogadishu
   G. Moroccan
   H. Swahili
   I. Timbuktu

5. The migrations of which group brought common beliefs and practices to much of Africa?
   A. Kush
   B. Bantu
   C. Berbers
   D. Ashanti

6. Early Africans created art because
   F. it supported their beliefs.
   G. they had nothing else to do.
   H. the Sun god ordered them to.
   I. it was how they voted for a ruler.

CHAPTER 15 Assessment *(continued)*

DBQ DOCUMENT-BASED QUESTIONS

Ibn Battuta wrote during his travels in Mali that

"[The people of Mali] are careful to observe the hours of prayer, and assiduous [always dutiful] in attending them in congregations, and in bringing up their children to them."

—from *Travels in Asia and Africa, 1325–1354*

7. **Drawing Conclusions** Which statement best describes Ibn Battuta's impressions of the people of Mali?
   A. He praises their system for educating children.
   B. He criticizes the policies of the leaders of Mali.
   C. He criticizes the system of government used in Mali.
   D. He praises their devotion to their religious beliefs.

8. **Making Inferences** From the passage, you can infer that Ibn Battuta likely views the people of Mali with
   F. wonder.
   G. confusion.
   H. respect.
   I. jealousy.

SHORT RESPONSE

"Mansa Musa was a skilled organizer and administrator who built Mali into one of the world's largest empires of the time. The empire was significant in both size and wealth. Mansa Musa encouraged the growth of trade in the empire. He also strongly supported the arts and education in Mali. He ordered the construction of mosques [Islamic temples] and established a university for Islamic studies."

—**EncyclopediaBritannica Online,** "Musa."
http://www.britannica.com/EBchecked/topic/398420/Musa

9. How did Mansa Musa show his support for education in Mali?

10. What traits do you think made Mansa Musa a successful ruler?

EXTENDED RESPONSE

11. **Expository Writing** Write an essay in which you seek to explain the importance of the arts to early African society. What purposes did African art play in people's lives? How is the influence of early African art forms still felt today? Use details from the chapter to support your explanation.

Need Extra Help?

If You've Missed Question	1	2	3	4	5	6	7	8	9	10	11
Review Lesson	1	1	2	2	3	3	2	2	2	2	3

NOTES

REFLECT, REVIEW, & REMEDIATE

INTERACTIVE WORKSHEET

Chapter Summary

Provide students with the Chapter Summary worksheet to help review the chapter and prepare for assessment.

Reviewing the Enduring Understanding

Review this chapter's Enduring Understanding with students:

- People, places, and ideas change over time.

INTERACTIVE WHITEBOARD ACTIVITY Have a student volunteer write the heading "Effects of Trade in Africa" on the interactive whiteboard. Then, ask students to work in small groups to brainstorm a list of the ways in which trade brought changes to early African civilizations. Ask a representative from each group to write one or two of their ideas on the interactive whiteboard. When each group has recorded their responses, discuss with the class whether they agree or disagree with each response.

ACTIVITIES ANSWERS

Exploring the Essential Question

1. Students' essays will vary, but they should offer clear and accurate explanations of the ways in which trade affected various aspects of early African civilizations. For instance, they might point out that locations along trade routes helped empires such as Ghana expand, and the taxing of trade helped these civilizations become wealthy.

21st Century Skills

2. Students' paragraphs should provide an accurate overview of one of the civilizations discussed in the chapter. Paragraphs should give an overview of these civilizations' importance, as well as provide details about key events, historical figures, and achievements associated with the various civilizations.

Thinking Like a Historian

3. Answers will vary, but students should select several geographic features, such as rivers, valleys, and climate, and accurately explain how these features affected the growth of civilization in Africa.

Locating Places

4. **1.** E, **2.** J, **3.** B, **4.** I, **5.** G, **6.** A, **7.** F, **8.** D, **9.** H, **10.** C

ASSESSMENT ANSWERS

Review the Guiding Questions

1. **C** Choice C is correct. Rain forests are found in central Africa and cover only about 10 percent of its surface. Savannas cover about 40 percent of Africa's surface. Plateaus are found throughout much of Africa. The continent has few wetlands.

2. **F** Choice F is correct. Mali conquered the declining empire of Ghana and created a new empire in the 1200s. Songhai arose when the Mali Empire began to break up. Benin was a rain forest civilization in a different part of Africa. The kingdom of Axum became part of Ethiopia.

3. **D** Choice D is correct. Songhai reached the height of its power under Muhammad Ture. He seized power in 1493 and built a new dynasty. Mansa Musa was a king of Mali. Battuta was an Arab lawyer and traveler.

4. **H** Choice H is correct. African and Muslim cultures blended to form the Swahili culture in East Africa. Mogadishu was a trading port along the Indian Ocean. The Moroccans helped bring about the end of the Songhai Empire. Timbuktu was the capital of Mali.

5. **B** Choice B is correct. By A.D. 300, the migrations of the Bantu had led them to settle most of Africa south of the Sahara. These migrations allowed them to spread their culture throughout this region. Kush was a land bordering Egypt. The Berbers were nomadic people in North Africa. The Ashanti lived in Ghana.

6. **F** Choice F is correct. Early Africans created art as part of how they worshiped and supported their beliefs. It did not relate to their leadership selection.

Document-Based Questions

7. **D** Choice D is correct. Ibn Battuta praises the people of Mali for their devotion to Islam. The passage does not address any criticism of leaders, policies, or government. The passage mentions parents bringing children to religious services, but it does not address education.

8. **H** Choice H is correct. Ibn Battuta's appreciative description of the people's behavior suggests that he views them with respect. Nothing in the passage indicates that Battuta is in awe of the people or that he is confused by their behavior. The passage does not indicate envy on the part of Battuta.

Short Response

9. Mansa Musa demonstrated his support for education in Mali by establishing a university for the study of Islam.

10. Answers will vary, but students should point out the leadership characteristics of Mansa Musa, such as his skills as an organizer and administrator, and his support of arts and education.

Extended Response

11. Students' essays should explain the key role various African art forms played in early African society. Examples could include rock paintings, clothing, sculpture, dancing, and music. Students should also note the lasting impact of early African arts. For instance, they could point to the continued use of brightly colored cloth from West Africa. They could also discuss the development of African-based musical forms such as jazz, ragtime, rock and roll, and rap. Students should provide supporting details based on the chapter content.

ONLINE RESOURCES

networks

There's More Online!

- ☑ INTERACTIVE WORKSHEETS
- ☑ BIOGRAPHIES
- ☑ CHARTS/GRAPHS
- ☑ GAMES
- ☑ GRAPHIC ORGANIZERS
- ☑ IMAGES
- ☑ MAPS
- ☑ PRIMARY SOURCES
- ☑ SLIDE SHOWS
- ☑ TIME LINE
- ☑ LECTURE SLIDES
- ☑ INTERACTIVE WHITEBOARD ACTIVITIES
- ☑ ASSESSMENTS
- ☑ VIDEOS

Aztec, Maya, and Inca Civilizations

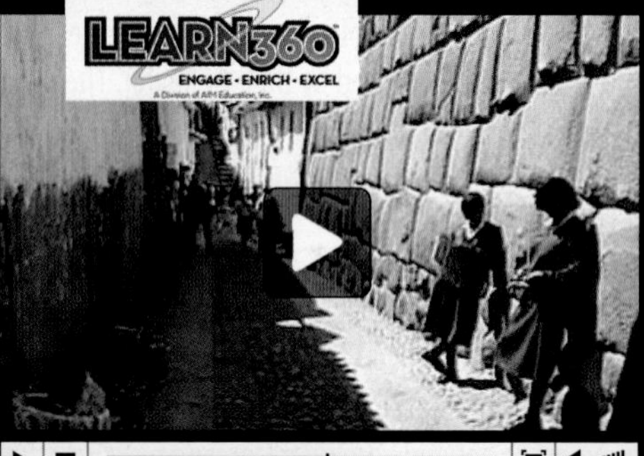

Peru: History

Chapter **16**

The Americas

Dear World History Teacher,

About 10,000 years ago, farming settlements began to appear in Mesoamerica. Soon organized communities along the Gulf of Mexico and in the central Andes began the long ascent toward civilization. The Maya and Aztec built elaborate cities that included pyramids, temples, and palaces. Maya civilization collapsed about A.D. 900, and the Aztec fell to Spanish invaders in the sixteenth century.

In the fifteenth century, another remarkable civilization—that of the Inca—flourished in South America. The Inca Empire was carefully planned and regulated, which is especially evident in the extensive network of roads that connected all parts of the empire. However, the Inca also fell to Spain, which possessed new, more effective weapons.

While the Maya, Aztec, and Inca were developing their civilizations, the peoples of North America were creating a remarkable number of different cultures. The Inuit, the Mound Builders, the Anasazi, the Plains people, and the Iroquois developed flourishing societies. These peoples settled and developed villages where land was easily farmed, or they led nomadic lives in search of food in less fertile areas. The native peoples of North America responded in their own unique ways to the different environmental conditions they faced.

All of these societies in the Americas developed in apparently total isolation from their counterparts elsewhere in the world. However, their cultural achievements were the equal of those achievements realized in other places.

Jackson J. Spielvogel

More Media Resources

Current Events Online

Visit McGraw-Hill's current events Web site for high-interest news stories and activities for your students. Access the site through the Student or Teacher Center in **networks.**

Reading List

Grade 6 reading level:
The Great Circle: A History of the First Nations,
by Neil Philip

Grade 7 reading level:
The Shaman's Nephew: A Life in the Far North,
by Simon Tookoome with Sheldon Oberman

Grade 8 reading level:
Who Came First? New Clues to Prehistoric Americans,
by Patricia Lauber

CHAPTER 16 Planner

UNDERSTANDING BY DESIGN®

Enduring Understandings

- *People, places, and ideas change over time.* • *Cultures are held together by shared beliefs and common practices and values.*

Essential Questions

- *How does geography affect the way people live?* • *What makes a culture unique?*

Students will know:

- *how geography defined the ways people settled in the Americas*
- *how early people arrived and settled in the Americas*
- *what role farming played in civilizations*
- *why the civilizations that developed in North America were so diverse*
- *how the Maya created their civilization in the rain forests of Mesoamerica*
- *how the Aztec built their society in central Mexico*
- *how the Inca organized their government and society*
- *how the different societies of North American peoples lived*

Students will be able to:

- **describe** how geography influenced migration from Asia to the Americas
- **show and explain** how early peoples arrived and settled in the Americas
- **compare** farming in the early civilizations of the Americas with farming in the early river valley civilizations
- **analyze** why farming was the basis of civilization
- **identify** aspects of culture from the Maya, Aztec, and Inca civilizations
- **describe** the cultures of the Maya, Aztec, and Inca civilizations
- **analyze** how the different societies of North American peoples lived
- **determine** whether a "typical" civilization existed in North America

Predictable Misunderstandings

Students may think:

- All early Americans lived as nomads.
- All early Americans lived in tepees.
- All early Americans spoke the same language and had the same traditions.

Assessment Evidence

Performance Task

- Hands-On Chapter Project

Other Evidence

- Responses to Interactive Whiteboard Activities
- Answers to discussion of how people migrated to the Americas
- Identification of geographic features that influenced where people settled
- Understanding of causes and effects of the growth of farming in the Americas
- Charting of the similarities and differences among native North Americans
- Answers to why farming was the anchor of a beginning civilization
- Answers to discussion of whether a "typical" Native American civilization existed
- Interactive Graphic Organizers
- Geography and History Activity
- 21st Century Skills Activity
- Written paragraphs
- Lesson Reviews

Pacing Guide

Introducing the Chapter	1 day
Lesson 1 The First Americans	1 day
Lesson 2 Life in the Americas	2 days
Chapter Activities and Assessment	1 day
TOTAL TIME	**5 Days**

Differentiated Instruction

These lesson plans are written to address the needs of your On Level students. Discussion and activities that are well-suited to your Approaching Grade Level learners, Beyond Grade Level learners, as well as your English Language Learners, are coded as follows:

Approaching Grade Level

Beyond Grade Level

English Language Learner

NCSS Standards covered in "The Americas"

Learners will understand:

1 CULTURE

1. "Culture" refers to the socially transmitted behaviors, beliefs, values, traditions, institutions, and ways of living together for a group of people
3. How culture influences the ways in which human groups solve the problems of daily living
4. That the beliefs, values, and behaviors of a culture form an integrated system that helps shape the activities and ways of life that define a culture
7. How people from different cultures develop different values and ways of interpreting experience

3 PEOPLE, PLACES, AND ENVIRONMENTS

1. The theme of people, places, and environments involves the study of the relationships between human populations in different locations and geographic phenomena such as climate, vegetation, and natural resources
2. Concepts such as: location, region, place, migration, as well as human and physical systems
4. The roles of different kinds of population centers in a region or nation
5. The concept of regions identifies links between people in different locations according to specific criteria (e.g., physical, economic, social, cultural, or religious)
7. Human modifications of the environment

Introducing the Chapter

(Student Edition p. 447)

The Story Matters . . .

After students have read "The Story Matters . . .," ask them why people long ago told stories to explain why things in nature happened. *(They didn't have scientific explanations for why things happened, but they wanted to understand their environment.)*

Ask:

If you don't understand why something happens, where do you expect to find the answer? On the Internet? In a textbook? Ask students where early Americans could look for answers to their questions. *(They might ask older people.)*

Then ask:

What topics might early people have known more about than you do? *(Students might say that early people probably knew more about hunting than they do. Early Americans knew more about agriculture and probably knew more about the stars than many of us do.)* Discuss with students who would have a harder time surviving in the other's world: an early American transported into our world or a contemporary student transported to the world of early Americans.

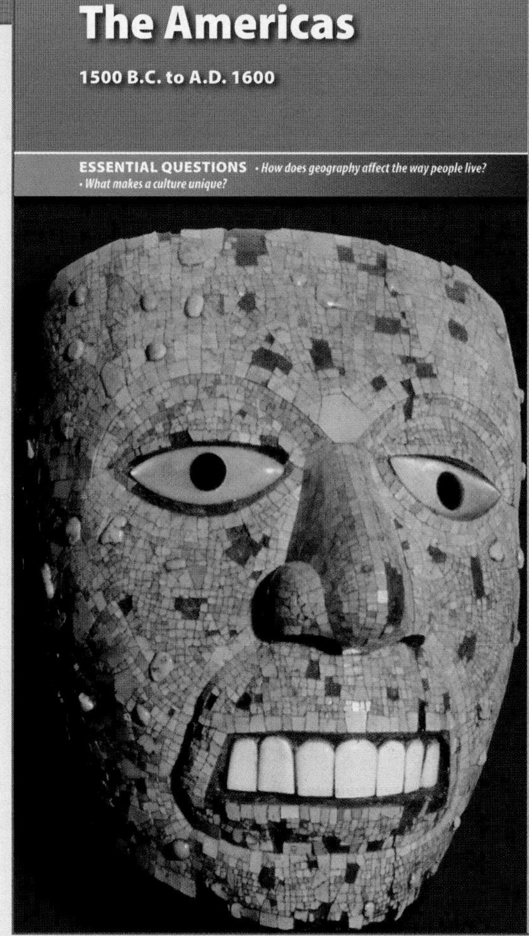

networks

There's More Online about the civilizations and customs of the Americas.

CHAPTER 16

Lesson 1 *The First Americans*

Lesson 2 *Life in the Americas*

The Story Matters . . .

Why do the seasons change? What causes thunder? Today, we look to science to answer these questions. Ancient people told stories.

The native people of Central America told a story to explain the origin of the sun. According to the legend, Nanahuatzin (nah • nah • WAHT • zeen), an Aztec god, had warts, or bumps, all over his face. At the time the world was created, Nanahuatzin threw himself into a great fire. Rather than dying in the flames, Nanahuatzin arose and became the sun.

This mask was made in Mexico about 600 years ago. Some historians believe it is a mask of Nanahuatzin. Other historians believe this represents Xiuhtecuhtli (zhee • ooh • tay • COOT • lee), the Aztec god of fire.

◄ *Xiuhtecuhtli was also known as "The Turquoise Lord." This mask is made of wood and covered with turquoise mosaic. The teeth are made from shells.*

Werner Forman/Art Resource, NY

447

Introducing Place and Time

(Student Edition pp. 448–449)

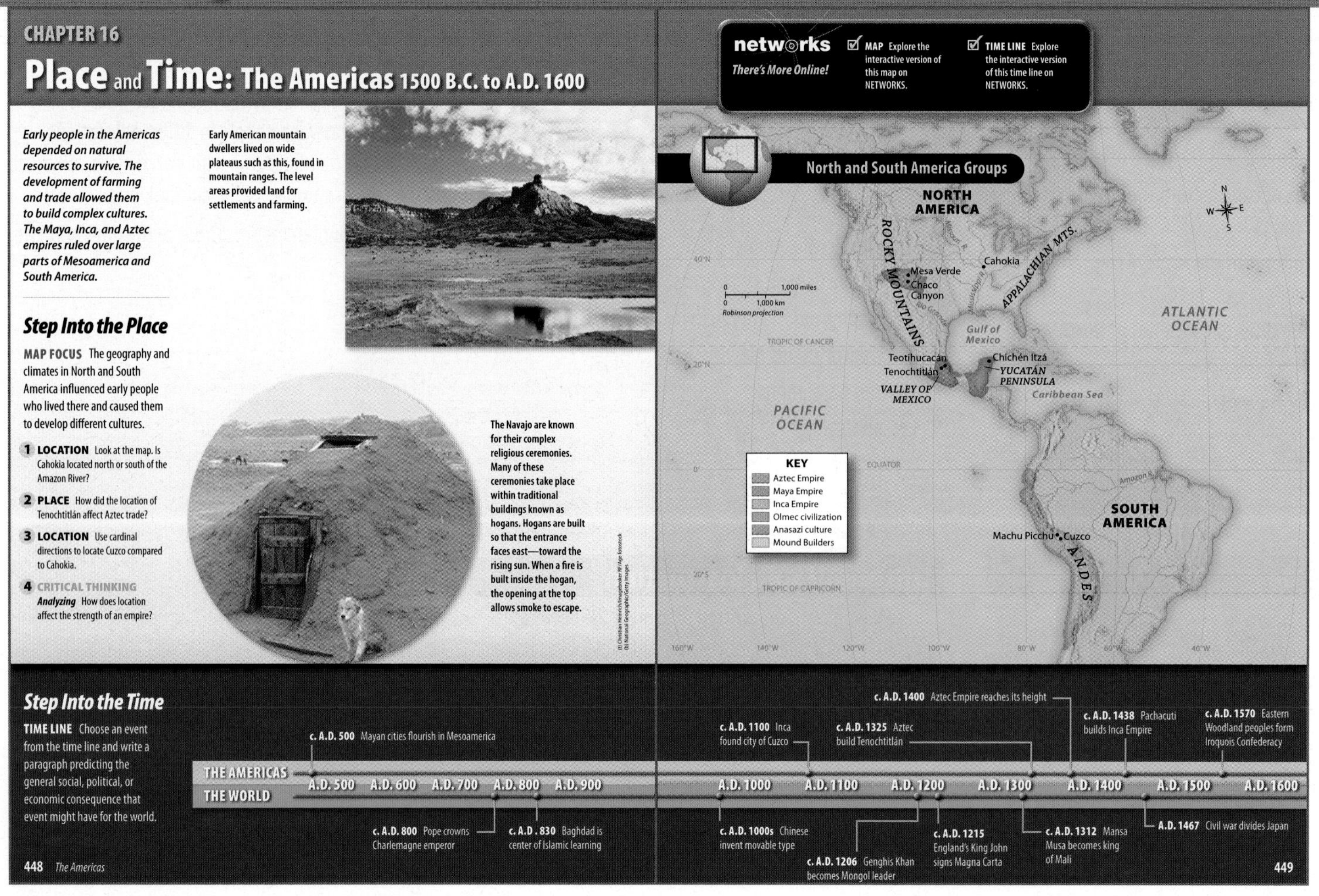
CHAPTER 16

Place and Time: The Americas 1500 B.C. to A.D. 1600

Early people in the Americas depended on natural resources to survive. The development of farming and trade allowed them to build complex cultures. The Maya, Inca, and Aztec empires ruled over large parts of Mesoamerica and South America.

Early American mountain dwellers lived on wide plateaus such as this, found in mountain ranges. The level areas provided land for settlements and farming.

The Navajo are known for their complex religious ceremonies. Many of these ceremonies take place within traditional buildings known as hogans. Hogans are built so that the entrance faces east—toward the rising sun. When a fire is built inside the hogan, the opening at the top allows smoke to escape.

Step Into the Place

MAP FOCUS The geography and climates in North and South America influenced early people who lived there and caused them to develop different cultures.

1. LOCATION Look at the map. Is Cahokia located north or south of the Amazon River?
2. PLACE How did the location of Tenochtitlán affect Aztec trade?
3. LOCATION Use cardinal directions to locate Cuzco compared to Cahokia.
4. CRITICAL THINKING *Analyzing* How does location affect the strength of an empire?

networks *There's More Online!* MAP Explore the interactive version of this map on NETWORKS. TIME LINE Explore the interactive version of this time line on NETWORKS.

Step Into the Time

TIME LINE Choose an event from the time line and write a paragraph predicting the general social, political, or economic consequence that event might have for the world.

448 *The Americas* 449

Technology Extension

- Find an additional activity online that incorporates technology for this project.
- Visit the EdTechTeacher Web sites (included in the Technology Extension for this chapter) for more links, tutorials, and other resources.

Assessing Background Knowledge

INTERACTIVE WORKSHEET

What Do You Know Activity

Have students complete the True or False activity about the Americas before they study the chapter. Direct students to read each statement and check whether they believe the statement is true or false. Then conduct a class poll to see how students answered so that you can tailor your lessons to focus on students' misconceptions.

After students have completed the lesson, have them reread the statements and determine if they were correct or incorrect about each one. Allow students to change their responses based on what they have learned in Chapter 16. Have students explain why they changed their answers.

INTERACTIVE WORKSHEET

Guided Reading Activities

There is a Guided Reading Activity for each lesson in this chapter. You may wish to assign the Guided Reading Activity for Lesson 1 after introducing the chapter content.

Hands-On Chapter Project

Students will write journal entries from the point of view of native peoples living in the Americas.

- Students will participate in a class discussion to review what they have learned about the native peoples and civilizations of the Americas.
- Then, students will discuss ideas for their journal entries and choose a group. After creating a plan, students will work individually to write journal entries.
- Students will share their journal entries with the rest of the class.
- Finally, students will evaluate their research, presentation, and collaboration using an Assessment Rubric.

Visit **networks** online to see the full project and rubric.

ONLINE RESOURCES

networks

Assign these interactive worksheets and quizzes from your Teacher Lesson Center. All resources are print-ready.

It's ALL Online!

Chapter 16 Resources

- ☑ Chapter Summary
- ☑ Vocabulary Builder
- ☑ What Do You Know?
- ☑ Hands-On Chapter Project

Lesson 1 Resources

- ☑ Geography and History Activity Migration
- ☑ Interactive Guided Reading Activity
- ☑ Reading Essentials and Study Guide
- ☑ Online Self-Check Quiz

Lesson 2 Resources

- ☑ 21st Century Skills Activity Compare and Contrast
- ☑ Interactive Guided Reading Activity
- ☑ Reading Essentials and Study Guide
- ☑ Online Self-Check Quiz

Assessment Resources

- ☑ Lesson Reviews
- ☑ Online Self-Check Quizzes
- ☑ Chapter Activities and Assessment
- ☑ Standardized Test Practice

Remediation Resources

- ☑ Reading Essentials and Study Guide
- ☑ Interactive Guided Reading Activities
- ☑ Online Self-Check Quizzes
- ☑ Chapter Summary

Step Into the Place

Movement Project the Chapter Opener map on the whiteboard. Ask students what they know about the climates and geography of the Americas. As you point to various geographic areas of the map, have students identify them. **Then ask:** **What native group covered a large area of mid-North America?** *(Olmec and Mound Builders)* Then point to areas on the map that have different geographical features. **Ask:** **What South American group lived in the mountains?** *(Inca)* Lead students to understand that the Americas form a vast region with many different climates and many different geographical features.

Step Into the Time

Drawing Conclusions Have students review the time line for the chapter.

Ask: **What was happening in the Americas around A.D. 500?** *(Maya cities in Mesoamerica were flourishing.)* Ask students to think about what they have studied about Europe at this time.

Ask: **What was happening in Europe around A.D. 500?** *(The Roman Empire fell, and the period known as the Early Middle Ages began.)*

Answers for pages 448–449

Step Into the Place

1. Cahokia is located north of the Amazon River.
2. The central location of Tenochtitlán allowed the Aztecs to use a web of trade routes that reached throughout Mexico.
3. Cuzco is south and east of Cahokia.
4. CRITICAL THINKING Answers will vary but should emphasize that access to water, trade routes, and natural resources can strengthen an empire.

Step Into the Time

Answers will vary depending upon the event chosen but should be based on facts and reasonable arguments.

networks
There's More Online!
GRAPHIC ORGANIZER Climates and Mountains
SLIDE SHOW Peoples of the Southwest
NORTH AMERICA

Lesson 1

The First Americans

ESSENTIAL QUESTION *How does geography affect the way people live?*

It Matters Because

Early people in the Americas built the beginnings of several civilizations.

1 Geography of the Americas

GUIDING QUESTION *How did geography shape the ways people settled in the Americas?*

About 15,000 years ago, prehistoric hunters left northeastern Asia and arrived in what is today Alaska. They are believed to be among the first people to settle the region called the Americas. Their descendants are called Native Americans. Over the centuries, Native American groups adopted different ways of life. Each group's way of life was based on local resources.

A Diverse Region

The Americas stretch north to south nearly 11,000 miles (almost 18,000 km). This vast region begins north at the Arctic Circle. It reaches south to Tierra del Fuego (tee•EHR•eh del FWAY•goh). Tierra del Fuego is a group of islands located off the coast of Chile and Argentina, at the southern tip of South America.

The four geographical areas of the Americas are North America, South America, Central America, and the Caribbean. North America and South America are both continents. The two continents make up most of the Americas. Central America is an **isthmus** (IHS•muhs), a narrow piece of land that connects two larger areas of land. East of Central America is the Caribbean Sea. A string of islands spreads across the Caribbean Sea to the Atlantic Ocean. As a group, these islands are known as the Caribbean.

Reading HELPDESK

Taking Notes: *Summarizing*

Use a chart like the one here to record the climates and mountain ranges of the four main areas of the Americas.

	Climate	Mountains
North America		
South America		
Central America		
Caribbean		

Content Vocabulary

- **isthmus**
- **maize**

isthmus a narrow piece of land linking two larger areas of land

Within the vast expanse of the Americas you can find many different geographic features and climates. North America lies north of the Equator and has climates that range from cold to tropical.

Central America and the Caribbean islands are also north of the Equator. South America extends both north and south of the Equator. Most of these areas have a warm, rainy climate. A broad range of plants grows in the three areas.

Towering Mountains

In the west, rugged mountain chains run nearly the entire length of the Americas. They separate coastal plains near the Pacific Ocean from broad eastern plains that sweep toward the Atlantic Ocean.

The Andes are the world's longest mountain system. These mountains stretch along the Pacific coast of South America. Valleys and plateaus (plah•TOES) lie between the mountain chains. Plateaus are large areas of raised land that have a flat surface.

The Rocky Mountains and the Pacific coastal ranges are in western North America. These mountains contain passes, or low areas. Even with these passes, overland travel across the mountains could be difficult.

In eastern North America, a range of mountains—the Appalachians—runs near the Atlantic coast. The Appalachians are lower than the Rockies and Pacific coastal ranges. Early Americans had no difficulty traveling over the Appalachians.

Mount McKinley is the tallest mountain in North America. It stands in Denali National Park, Alaska.

North America Physical

ROCKY MOUNTAINS, CANADIAN SHIELD, Hudson Bay, Great Lakes, CENTRAL LOWLAND, APPALACHIAN MTNS., COASTAL PLAIN, SIERRA MADRE OCCIDENTAL, SIERRA MADRE ORIENTAL, PACIFIC OCEAN, ATLANTIC OCEAN, Gulf of Mexico, Caribbean Sea, ARCTIC CIRCLE, TROPIC OF CANCER

Lambert Azimuthal Equal-Area projection

GEOGRAPHY CONNECTION

North America is the third-largest continent on Earth. It is mostly surrounded by water. Mountain ranges take up more than one third of the total land area.

1. **PLACE** Which mountain range is closest to where you live?
2. **CRITICAL THINKING** *Analyzing* What would have made travel across North America difficult for early Americans?

Rolling Plains

North America has many coastal and inland plains. The rolling grasslands of central North America are known as the Great Plains. The Great Plains have fertile soil for farming and raising cattle.

South America also has large areas of plains. In the northeast, the tropical Amazon Basin covers about 2.7 million square miles (7.0 million sq km). It is home to the world's largest rain forest.

Additional lowland plains are located north and south of the Amazon Basin. Tropical grasslands stretch across the northwest. Another area of plains called the Pampas lies in the south. The mild climate of the Pampas makes them a good place for growing grains. Many ranchers herd cattle there as well.

The land surrounding the Amazon is home to the greatest variety of plants on Earth. As many as 250 species of trees may grow in one acre of the Amazon River basin.

▶ CRITICAL THINKING
Analyzing How might early Americans have used the Amazon River?

Rushing Rivers

Large river systems drain the Americas. They begin in the mountain ranges and flow through interior plains to the oceans. Today, the many waterways of the Americas transport people, goods, and ideas.

In North America, the largest river system is the Mississippi. It flows 2,350 miles (3,782 km), from present-day Montana and Minnesota to the Gulf of Mexico. The Mississippi is the major waterway for the central part of North America.

The Amazon is South America's largest river system. It starts in the Andes and flows about 4,000 miles (6,437 km) to the Atlantic Ocean. The Amazon carries the highest **volume** of water of any river on Earth.

PROGRESS CHECK

Describing Which four separate areas make up the Americas?

Reading HELPDESK

Academic Vocabulary

volume amount included within limits
link to connect

2 Settling the Americas

GUIDING QUESTION *How did prehistoric people reach the Americas and form settlements?*

How did prehistoric people come to the Americas? Today, the Americas are not **linked** to the world's other landmasses, but they were long ago.

Reaching the Americas

Some scientists think that people walked across a land bridge from Asia into the Americas during the last Ice Age. Evidence of ancient tools and other artifacts reveals that these first Americans were hunters following herds of animals.

Other scientists argue that the first Americans arrived by boat. They passed by Alaska and sailed south along the Americas' Pacific coast. The travelers first explored coastal areas. They then journeyed inland where they set up campsites.

Once they arrived, the first Americans did not stay in one place. They moved south and east. They travelled in boats to islands in the Caribbean. In time, there were people living in different groups in North, Central, and South America.

Hunters and Gatherers

How did the first Americans survive? Historians believe it is likely that the first people in the Americas lived in small groups. These early Americans moved from place to place to find food.

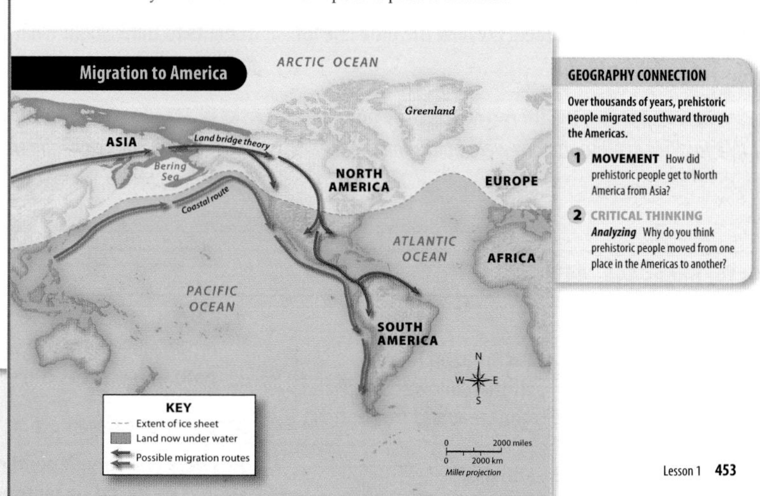

GEOGRAPHY CONNECTION

Over thousands of years, prehistoric people migrated southward through the Americas.

1. **MOVEMENT** How did prehistoric people get to North America from Asia?
2. **CRITICAL THINKING** *Analyzing* Why do you think prehistoric people moved from one place in the Americas to another?

LESSON 1

ENGAGE

MAP **Predicting** Show students the physical map of North America. Remind them that scientists believe humans settled from north to south.

Ask:

When do you think people first arrived in North America? *(If they do not know, tell students that the first people arrived in North America during the last Ice Age, about 15,000 to 20,000 years ago.)*

Ask:

How do you think people first got to North America? Write students' ideas on the board so you can return to them. Explain to students that they will be learning about the early peoples who settled the Americas. AL

TEACH & ASSESS

1 Geography of the Americas

GUIDING QUESTION *How did geography shape the ways people settled in the Americas?*

MAP **Analyzing Visuals** Show the map of the Americas on an interactive whiteboard. Have students locate geographical features marked on the map.

Ask students to locate the four geographical areas of the Americas: North America, Central America, South America, and the Caribbean. Have a volunteer circle these place names on the map.

Then ask students to locate the Andes, the Rocky Mountains, and the Appalachians, and have a volunteer circle these place names on the map. Next, have a student find and circle the Amazon River and the Mississippi River.

Ask:

How do you think these geographical features influenced where people settled? *(Students might say it is more likely that people first settled in river valleys and less likely that they settled in areas of high mountains.)*

2 Settling the Americas

GUIDING QUESTION *How did prehistoric people reach the Americas and form settlements?*

MAP **Summarizing** Show students the "Migration to America" map.

Ask:

According to the map, what are the two ways early people might have migrated to the Americas? *(over a land bridge between Asia and North America or by boat along the Pacific Coast of North America)*

Ask:

In the case of the migration of people to North America, what effect did geography have on history? *(The existence of a land bridge between Asia and North America made it easier for people to reach the Americas. Without the bridge, it might have taken much longer for people to settle in the Americas.)* Discuss the possible difficulties of the journey from Asia to North America.

Ask:

What do you think the journey from Asia to North America was like? What problems might early people have faced on the journey? *(Accept all reasonable responses.)* AL

INTERACTIVE WORKSHEET Present the Geography and History Activity, and have students work with a partner to complete it. BL

3 First American Societies

GUIDING QUESTION *How did farming make civilization possible in the Americas?*

INTERACTIVE WHITEBOARD ACTIVITY **Categorizing** Present the Interactive Whiteboard Activity "The Zapotec, Maya, and Teotihuacán." Have students drag and drop information about each group into the correct box. AL ELL

4 Early Cultures in North America

GUIDING QUESTION *Why did a large number of societies develop in North America?*

SLIDE SHOWS **Analyzing Visual Images** Present the slide show about the Mound Builders.

Then ask:

How were the Hohokam, the Anasazi, and the Mound Builders similar? *(They farmed and made impressive structures.)*

Ask:

How were they different? *(The Hohokam and the Anasazi lived in the Southwest and relied more on farming than the Mound Builders, who lived east of the Mississippi and were mainly hunters and gatherers.)*

Have students complete the Lesson 1 Review.

CLOSE & REFLECT

LECTURE SLIDE **Making Generalizations** Show students the lecture slide on how agriculture helped the development of early civilizations. Discuss with students the importance of agriculture to the early civilizations of the Americas. Note that farming spread throughout many regions.

Ask:

Where did farming begin in the Americas? *(Mesoamerica)*

Ask:

How did the introduction of farming change life for the peoples of the Americas? *(Farming allowed people to settle in one place, create more complex societies, and in some cases build cities.)*

Answers for pages 450–453

P. 450 Taking Notes

	Climate	Mountains
North America	cold to tropical	Rocky Mountains, Pacific coastal ranges, Appalachians
South America	warm, rainy	Andes
Central America	warm, rainy	
Caribbean	warm, rainy	

P. 451 GEOGRAPHY CONNECTION

1. Students should accurately identify the mountain range closest to their community.
2. High mountains, long distances, possible bad weather, and the need to cross wide rivers would have made travel across North America difficult.

P. 452 CRITICAL THINKING Early Americans might have used the Amazon River as a waterway for trade and transportation. They also might have used it as a source of freshwater and for fishing.

P. 452 ☑ PROGRESS CHECK The four geographical areas that make up the Americas are North America, South America, Central America, and the Caribbean.

P. 453 GEOGRAPHY CONNECTION

1. Prehistoric people took a land bridge from Asia to North America or used boats to travel down the coast of North America.
2. CRITICAL THINKING Students may mention the possibility that some places had harsh climates. They may also realize that some locations might have become overpopulated and could no longer support the people who lived there. Students might also mention a desire for adventure and curiosity about new places. Accept all reasonable responses.

Early Americans used corn in many forms. The corn grinding stone like this Anasazi tool developed out of necessity.

▶ CRITICAL THINKING

Predicting How do you think early Americans used ground corn?

Archaeologists have unearthed evidence of early American ways of life. This evidence includes heaps of shells, rounded grinding stones, and bone fishhooks.

Hunter-gatherers in the Americas used natural resources for food, clothing, and shelter. People living along seacoasts collected shellfish and snails. People who lived inland fished in rivers and gathered roots, nuts, and fruits in forests. Early Americans also hunted large animals, which provided meat, hides for clothing, and bones for tools.

The Beginnings of Agriculture

As the last Ice Age ended, the climate grew warmer. People in the Americas learned to plant the seeds of grains and other plants. The seeds would grow into crops that could be eaten. This activity became the start of farming in the Americas.

Farming began in Mesoamerica (meh•zoh•uh•MEHR•ih•kuh) 9,000 to 10,000 years ago. *Meso* comes from the Greek word for "middle." This region includes lands stretching from central Mexico to Costa Rica in Central America.

The geography of Mesoamerica was suited for farming. Much of the area had rich, volcanic soil and a mild climate. The first crops that early Americans grew included peppers, pumpkins, squash, gourds, beans, and potatoes. Corn, also known as **maize** (mayz), took longer to develop. However, it became the most important food in the Americas.

PROGRESS CHECK

Describing What were the first crops grown in the Americas?

3 First American Societies

GUIDING QUESTION *How did farming make civilization possible in the Americas?*

Growing and trading crops helped early Americans form more **complex** societies. The first American cultures emerged in Mesoamerica and along the western coast of South America.

Olmec Culture

About 1200 B.C., a people called the Olmec (OHL•mehk) built what may be the oldest culture in Mesoamerica. Based on farming and trade, the Olmecs lasted about 800 years.

Reading **HELP**DESK

maize corn

Academic Vocabulary

complex made up of many related parts

Civilizations of Mesoamerica

MEXICO

Lake Texcoco

Tula

Teotihuacán

Tenochtitlán

Tlaxcala

VALLEY OF MEXICO

Gulf of Mexico

La Venta

Chichén Itzá

YUCATÁN PENINSULA

Palenque

Tikal

Copán

PACIFIC OCEAN

0 300 miles

0 300 km

Bipolar Oblique projection

KEY

Olmec c. 500 B.C.

Maya c. A.D. 750

Toltec c. A.D. 1200

Aztec c. A.D. 1500

GEOGRAPHY CONNECTION

Mesoamerican societies developed in Mexico and Central America.

1 **PLACE** Which culture occupied the Yucatán Peninsula?

2 CRITICAL THINKING

Making Inferences The Olmec built a pyramid of clay and sand at La Venta. Why do you think they did not use stone?

The Olmec set up farms in the tropical lowlands along the Gulf of Mexico. They grew beans and produced salt. The Olmec traded with people living inland. They exchanged salt and beans for jade and obsidian, or volcanic glass. Olmec artisans used the jade for jewelry. They made sharp knives from the obsidian.

The Olmec created centers for religious ceremonies. In these areas, they built pyramids and other stone monuments.

First Planned Cities

About 400 B.C., the Olmec culture collapsed. A group of inland peoples rose to power in central Mexico. This group built one of the first planned cities in the Americas, Teotihuacán (tay•oh•tee•wuh•KAHN), or "Place of the Gods." It lasted from about A.D. 250 to A.D. 800. Around 120,000 to 200,000 people lived in Teotihuacán. Temples and palaces lined its main street, which led to the Pyramid of the Sun.

A people called the Zapotec (ZAH•poh•tehk) built farms and cities in south central Mexico. Their magnificent capital, Monte Albán (MON•teh AL•bahn), had a main square surrounded by stone temples, monuments, and tombs. In addition to farming, the Zapotec created pottery and traded with Teotihuacán and other places in Mesoamerica. The Zapotec developed a writing system based on hieroglyphs (HIGH•roh•glifz).

Another people called the Maya (MY•uh) prospered in the steamy rain forests of the Yucatán Peninsula (yoo•kuh•TAN). Like the Zapotec, the Maya traded throughout Mesoamerica. From their central location, the Maya spread into southern Mexico and Central America.

One of the things the Olmecs are most famous for is colossal heads made out of rock. Some were more than seven feet high. How they managed to get them to the sites where they remain to this day is unknown.

Teotihuacán and the Zapotec flourished between the A.D. 300s and A.D. 500s. Then, they declined. Historians are not sure why this happened. The causes for decline might have been a severe drought—a long period with little rainfall—or revolts by populations that had used up the natural resources of the area. Whatever the reason, the cities were **abandoned**.

Who Were the Toltec?

After the collapse of these cities, new groups rose to power in central Mexico. Most important were the Toltec (TOHL•tehk). The warlike Toltec conquered much of Mexico and northern Central America. Their empire reached the height of its power between A.D. 950 and A.D. 1150.

The Toltec grew crops of beans, maize, and pepper in irrigated fields. They also built pyramids and palaces. Toltec artisans introduced metalworking to Mesoamerica.

Around A.D. 1125, the Toltec Empire began to decline. Within a few decades, groups of invaders, including Aztec (AZ•tek) people, attacked and burned the Toltec city of Tollan (toh•lahn). For nearly 200 years, there was no ruling group in central Mexico. During the A.D. 1300s, the Aztec, a warrior people, gained control.

Early Cultures in South America

In South America, several different early civilizations thrived along the Pacific coast. One of the earliest of these, the Moche (MOH•cheh), developed around A.D. 100 in the dry coastal desert of Peru. The Moche built canals to bring water from rivers in the Andes foothills to their desert homeland. This enabled them to grow enough food to feed a large part of the region. Much about Moche culture is known from their arts and crafts.

In spite of everything they **achieved**, the Moche did not build an empire. The first empire in South America was built by another people called the Inca (IHNG•kuh). The Inca lived in the Andes mountain ranges of Peru. Their homeland was in the area of Cuzco (KOOS•koh). Cuzco was founded around A.D. 1100 and became the capital of the Inca Empire.

The story of the Moche culture is told through their artwork, such as this pottery figure of an alpaca.

▶ CRITICAL THINKING

Analyzing Visuals What can you tell about the Moche based on this example of art?

PROGRESS CHECK

Explaining Why did early American cultures decline?

Reading **HELP**DESK

Academic Vocabulary

abandon to leave, often because of danger

achieve to successfully complete a task; to gain something by working for it

Pueblo Bonito, located in present-day New Mexico, was a four-story sandstone village.

▶ CRITICAL THINKING

Analyzing Why do you think the ruins of this pueblo still remain?

4 Early Cultures in North America

GUIDING QUESTION *Why did a large number of societies develop in North America?*

North of Mesoamerica, other early Americans developed their own ways of living. Despite their cultural differences, many of these groups learned the same farming methods as their Mesoamerican neighbors. Farming spread to the American Southwest and then along the coasts and up the Mississippi, Missouri, and Ohio Rivers. As farming developed in these areas, so did new cultures.

Peoples of the Southwest

The scorching desert of what is now Arizona was home to the Hohokam (hoh•hoh•KAHM). About A.D. 300, the Hohokam planted gardens on lands between the Salt and Gila rivers. They dug hundreds of miles of irrigation canals to carry river water to their fields. They grew corn, cotton, beans, and squash. The Hohokam also made pottery, carved stone, and etched shells.

Another group called the Anasazi (ah•nuh•SAH•zee) lived about the same time as the Hohokam. The Anasazi settled in the canyons and cliffs of the Southwest. Like the Hohokam, they practiced farming. To water their crops, they gathered the water that ran off cliffs and sent it through canals to their fields.

The Anasazi built large stone dwellings that the Spanish explorers later called pueblos (PWEH•blohs). They also built dwellings in the walls of steep cliffs. Cliff dwellings were easy to defend and offered protection from winter weather.

The Anasazi and the Hohokam both prospered until the early A.D. 1000s. At that time, they faced droughts that killed their crops. The two groups eventually abandoned their settlements.

The Anasazi were skilled at making pottery and jewelry.

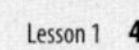

Build Vocabulary: *Prefixes*

Meso is a prefix that means "middle." Another, more common prefix meaning middle is "mid." *Midterm* is the middle of the school term. *Midway* is halfway between two places. What other words with the prefix *mid* can you think of?

LESSON 1 (cont.)

IF YOU HAVE MORE TIME . . .

Explore the Ways Geography Affects Cultures

Determining Cause and Effect

Point out to students that just as people debate whether biology determines destiny—especially for humans—people can also discuss whether geography determines the destiny of a group of people or a culture.

Ask:

Do you think geography determines what will happen to the people living in a particular region? How? Lead students in a discussion based on their answers to these questions.

Prompt students to make the connection between geography and human adaptation.

Ask:

Are people able to live in different climates? *(yes)* **Which?** *(Students might name any of the different geographic or climate zones, such as arctic, desert, Mediterranean, temperate, etc.)*

Explain that although some geographic locations are especially difficult to live in, such as in the arctic zone, humans can live nearly anywhere.

Ask: How is this possible? *(by building appropriate shelter, and if necessary, importing food, clothing, and other goods)*

Then, ask:

How do human adaptations lead to different cultures? *(Responses will vary. Students should express an understanding of what cultures are, how they develop and evolve, and what role geography plays in determining the characteristics of a culture. Require students to provide reasons and examples to support their positions.)*

Some students might want to look up on the Internet the research station at McMurdo, Antarctica, to illustrate how adaptation in extreme climates is possible. BL

Analyze the Effect of the Development of Agriculture in the Americas

Determining Cause and Effect Remind students that the reason something happens is called the cause. What happens as a result of the cause is the effect. Determining cause and effect means telling how or why one event caused another event to happen.

Ask:

What was one cause of the beginning of agriculture? *(When the last Ice Age ended, the climate warmed. People in the Americas learned to plant the seeds of grains and other plants.)*

Then ask:

What was the effect of agriculture in the Americas? *(Agriculture led to a surplus of goods, which increased trade. Increased trade led to the formation of settlements, which in turn led to the creation of complex civilizations.)*

Work with the class to create a cause-and-effect chain on the board.

Understand How People of the Americas Adapted to Their Environment

SLIDE SHOW **Analyzing Visual Images** Present the slide show about Native American groups, and discuss the images shown.

As the first photo is shown, **ask: What does this picture tell about how people adapt to their environment?** *(Students should point out details from the image of the Inuit, including the type of clothing and clues about the cold environment.)*

With the photo of the Hopi, **ask: How is building construction a good example of adaptation?** *(Not many trees grew where the Hopi lived to provide wood for buildings. Therefore, people used local materials like stone and mud bricks to build homes.)*

For the photo of the people of the Great Plains, **ask: What details in the image show how people adapted to life on the Great Plains?** *(Students should point out the nomadic lifestyle of the people and the portable construction of the buildings, the relatively mild climate based on the clothing and shelter, the horse used for transportation, and the tools made of materials that could be found on the plains.)*

Answers for pages 454–457

P. 454 CRITICAL THINKING Students might mention that ground corn, or cornmeal, could be used to make tortilla-like flatbread or it could be boiled to make mush.

P. 454 ☑ PROGRESS CHECK The first crops grown in the Americas included peppers, pumpkins, squash, gourds, beans, and potatoes.

P. 455 GEOGRAPHY CONNECTION

1. The Maya occupied the Yucatán Peninsula.
2. CRITICAL THINKING The Olmec probably used clay and sand because those materials were the most readily available to them. Stone had to be brought in from a long distance.

P. 456 CRITICAL THINKING Students might mention that the Moche used animals, in this case llamas, to carry goods.

P. 456 ☑ PROGRESS CHECK Though the exact reasons are unknown, early American cultures might have declined because of a drain on resources due to overpopulation, a long drought, destructive revolts, or invasions.

P. 457 CRITICAL THINKING The pueblo was built with strong materials and near cliffs for protection.

P. 457 Build Vocabulary Students might identify the words *midair* and *midday*.

The Mound Builders

East of the Mississippi River, another early American civilization arose. It began about 1000 B.C. and lasted until about A.D. 400. Its founders built huge mounds of earth that were used as tombs or for ceremonies. These constructions gave these people their name—Mound Builders.

The Great Serpent Mound, made by the Mound Builders, still exists in southern Ohio. This mound may have been used in religious ceremonies. Why do you think it was named the Great Serpent Mound?

Richard A. Cooke/CORBIS

The Mound Builders were mostly hunters and gatherers, but they began to practice farming. Two major groups made up the culture--the Adena people and the Hopewell. Scientists believe that the Mound Builders domesticated many wild plants, such as sunflowers, gourds, and barley. Corn became another popular crop after it was introduced to the region about A.D. 100.

Who Were the Mississippians?

By A.D. 700, a new people known as the Mississippians arose. Their name came from their location in the Mississippi River Valley. The Mississippians were able to produce enough corn, squash, and beans to become full-time farmers. They also built mounds and lived in cities.

Their largest city was Cahokia (kuh•HOH•kee•uh). It may have had 16,000 to 30,000 residents. Mississippian government was centered there between A.D. 850 and 1150. Cahokia was the site of the largest Mississippian mound. Cahokia and the Mississippian society collapsed during the A.D. 1200s.

PROGRESS CHECK

Explaining How were early Americans able to grow crops in desert areas of the Southwest?

LESSON 1 REVIEW

Review Vocabulary

1. Which main area of the Americas is an *isthmus*?
2. How did *maize* help early people in the Americas?

Answer the Guiding Questions

3. ***Summarizing*** How did prehistoric people reach the Americas?
4. ***Explaining*** Why was Cuzco significant to the Inca?
5. ***Comparing*** What did early societies in North America have in common?
6. **EXPOSITORY WRITING** Write a two-paragraph essay that describes the ways of life of the Olmec and the Toltec.

NOTES

NOTES

networks

There's More Online!

- GRAPHIC ORGANIZER Aztec Social Classes
- MAP People and Cultures of North America
- SLIDE SHOW
  - Native American Peoples
  - Tenochtitlán
- VIDEO

Lesson 2

Life in the Americas

ESSENTIAL QUESTION *What makes a culture unique?*

IT MATTERS BECAUSE

Long before the arrival of Europeans, people in the Americas created complex societies.

1 The Maya

GUIDING QUESTION *How did the Maya live in the rain forests of Mesoamerica?*

In A.D. 1839, archaeologists John Lloyd Stephens and Frederick Catherwood discovered an ancient city, hidden for centuries by vines and trees. The people who had built the city were called the Maya. These early Americans were the ancestors of the millions of Maya who live in present-day Mexico, Guatemala, Honduras, El Salvador, and Belize.

Maya Communities

About A.D. 300, the Maya developed a complex culture in parts of southern Mexico and Central America. The ancient Maya faced many challenges in the area that they settled, which was called Petén (peh•TEHN). Thick forests nearly blocked out sunlight. Stinging insects filled the air. Yet, the ancient Maya prospered.

Swamps and sinkholes gave the Maya a year-round source of water. A **sinkhole** is an area where the soil has collapsed into a hollow or depression. Sinkholes gave the Maya access to a network of underground rivers and streams.

The Maya began to develop a society. They worked together to clear forested areas. They planted fields of corn and other crops and built cities under government direction.

Reading HELPDESK

Taking Notes: Organizing

Use a pyramid like the one here to place the Aztec social classes in order. Begin at the top level of the pyramid and list classes from highest to lowest.

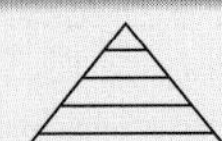

Content Vocabulary

- sinkhole
- hogan

LESSON 1 (cont.)

Compare Early Civilizations

Comparing and Contrasting Remind students that they have studied four early river valley civilizations.

Ask:

What early river valley civilizations have you learned about? *(Mesopotamia, Egypt, India, China)*

Create a two-column chart on the board. Label one column "Early River Valley Civilizations." Label the second column "First American Civilizations." Tell students they will use the chart to compare and contrast the early river valley civilizations with the first civilizations in the Americas.

As a class, brainstorm ways the two types of civilizations were alike and ways they were different. After they complete the chart as a class, have students write multi-paragraph essays comparing and contrasting the two kinds of civilizations. BL

Discuss the Role of Surplus in Trade

Begin the discussion by asking if students are familiar with games that use collectible or trading cards.

Ask:

What do you do when you have more than you want of one kind of card? *(Students probably will say they trade for a card they want.)*

Ask:

What does *surplus* mean? *(Students should understand that a surplus is more of something than is needed or wanted.)*

Then ask:

What do you think early farmers who grew more than they needed did with the extra? *(They traded the surplus for something they needed.)*

Lead students to understand that in order for trade to take place, someone must have more of a product than he or she needs.

Making Connections Help students make the connection that growing excess crops led to increased trade in the early Americas.

Answers for page 458

P. 458 The name of the mound reflects that it is shaped like a snake.

P. 458 ☑ PROGRESS CHECK Early Americans in desert areas of the Southwest dug irrigation canals to carry river water to their fields. They also collected water that ran off cliffs.

LESSON 1 REVIEW

1. Central America is an isthmus.
2. Maize became the most important food in the Americas.
3. People from Asia might have used a land bridge to cross into the Americas. Another theory suggests that the first Americans arrived by boat, passing Alaska and then sailing south along the Pacific coast.
4. Cuzco was the capital of the Inca Empire, the largest territory in the ancient Americas.
5. Many of these groups learned how to farm from their Mesoamerican neighbors. As farming developed, so did new cultures.
6. Answers will vary. Answers should identify the importance of farming and trade in the Olmec and Toltec civilizations.

Teaching *Life in the Americas* (Student Edition pp. 459–467)

LESSON 2 • Day 1

ENGAGE

MAPS **Analyzing** Discuss with students the four geographic regions of the Americas: North America, Central America, South America, and the Caribbean. Refer students to the chapter opener map so they can identify these four regions.

Then ask students to list mountain ranges and major rivers of the Americas. *(mountain ranges: the Andes, the Rocky Mountains, and the Appalachians; rivers: the Amazon River and the Mississippi River)*

Ask:

How do you think the geography and climate contributed to the creation of many unique cultures in the Americas? *(Student answers will vary depending upon their understanding of the many different geographic regions, such as far north, woodlands, desert, mountains, and so on, and the different climates inhabited by each culture.)*

Have students record their answers so they can refer to them at the end of the lesson.

TEACH & ASSESS

1 The Maya

GUIDING QUESTION *How did the Maya live in the rain forests of Mesoamerica?*

Analyzing Begin a discussion with students about how the Maya were able to create a civilization in the rain forests of Mesoamerica.

Ask:

What challenges did the Maya face in the rain forest? *(Thick forests blocked the sun. Lots of insects lived there.)*

Once students have identified the key challenges faced by the Maya,

Ask:

How did the Maya overcome these challenges? *(The Maya cleared the forests so they could plant crops and build cities.)*

LECTURE SLIDE **Identifying** Show students the structure of the Maya Empire from the lecture slide. Remind students that the Maya did not create a single, unified empire. Instead, they founded many independent city-states that shared cultural characteristics.

Ask:

What was Maya society like? *(Answers may include the following: Each Maya city-state was ruled by a king who claimed he was descended from the sun god. The city-states had strict class systems with nobles and priests at the top. Women played a significant role in Maya society.)*

Point out to students that the Maya are well known for their creation of complex calendars.

Ask:

Why were calendars important to the Maya? *(Maya priests studied the sun, moon, and stars to understand the plans of the gods. They used calendars to predict eclipses, schedule religious festivals, and decide when to plant and harvest crops.)*

Ask:

What were some of the significant achievements of the Maya? *(Answers may include developing calendars, creating mathematics, understanding and using the concept of zero, and developing a written language.)*

Answers for page 459

P. 459 Taking Notes The Aztec social classes, from highest to lowest, were the emperor, nobles, commoners, unskilled workers, and enslaved people.

Connections to TODAY

The Maya Today

Modern-day descendants of the Maya speak about 70 different languages. They typically live on farms and grow corn, beans, and squash. As weaving and spinning have become less common, most present-day Maya, especially women, wear traditional clothing made of cloth produced in a factory.

The Maya set up more than 50 independent city-states. The Maya city-states were connected by culture, political ties, and trade. However, they often fought each other for control of territory.

What Was Maya Society Like?

Each Maya city-state was ruled by a king, who claimed he was descended from the sun god. As god-kings, Maya rulers expected people to serve them. The greatest Maya king was Pacal II. He ruled the city-state of Palenque (puh•LENGH•KAY) for 67 years in the A.D. 600s. Pacal II built many structures considered to be some of the best examples of Maya architecture.

The Maya city-states had a strict class system. Nobles and priests assisted kings in governing the city-states. Below them were farmers, artisans, and hunters. People of this class paid taxes and worked on large building projects.

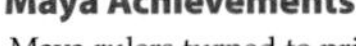

The Maya believed that the gods controlled everything that happened on Earth. Priests performed ceremonies to please the gods. These ceremonies sometimes included human sacrifice.

When the Maya fought battles, they wanted captives and they wanted land. When drought came and threatened their crops, Maya priests tried to please Chac (CHOCK), the god of rain, by offering the lives of their captives.

Women played a significant role in the Maya city-states. In the city-state of Calakmul (kah•lahk•MOOL), at least two women served as ruling queens. One of them may have helped to found the city.

Royal Maya women often married into royal families in other Maya city-states. This practice increased trade. It also helped form alliances—political agreements between people or states to work together.

Maya artists often portrayed Chac seated, waiting to receive the arrival of captives.

Maya Achievements

Maya rulers turned to priests for advice. The priests thought the gods revealed their plans through movements of the sun, moon, and stars. By watching the sky, the priests learned about astronomy.

They developed calendar systems to **predict** eclipses and to schedule religious festivals.

Reading HELPDESK

sinkhole a depression or hollow where soil has collapsed

Academic Vocabulary

predict to describe something that will happen in the future

In Maya society, a birth in the royal family called for a musical celebration, such as the one depicted above.

▶ CRITICAL THINKING

Making Inferences Priests were almost as powerful as kings. Why do you think the Maya so honored their priests?

They also used calendars to decide when to plant and harvest crops. The Maya had two major calendars. They used a 260-day calendar for religious events. They used a 365-day calendar for events related to the seasons and agriculture.

The Maya developed a system of mathematics. They invented a method of counting based on 20, and they used the concept of zero. They also developed a written language to record numbers and dates. Like the Zapotec, they used hieroglyphics. They carved hieroglyphics on stone monuments and used them in books.

About A.D. 900, the Maya culture collapsed. Historians do not know why this happened. Some evidence shows that conflict and warfare increased among city-states. Also, erosion and overuse of the soil may have caused a drop in food production. Too little food would have led to illnesses and starvation.

☑ PROGRESS CHECK

Explaining How were the Maya governed?

2 The Aztec

GUIDING QUESTION ***How did the Aztec establish their society in central Mexico?***

The Aztec came to power in Mesoamerica during the A.D. 1300s. The early Aztec were hunters and warriors. About A.D. 1200, they moved into central Mexico.

Rise of the Aztec

For many years, the Aztec had been searching for a home they believed had been promised to them by their sun god—the feathered serpent Quetzalcoatl (KWEHT•suhl•kuh•WAH•tuhl). In A.D. 1325, the Aztec took refuge on a swampy island in Lake Texcoco (tehs•KOH•koh). Although the land was hardly welcoming, the Aztec chose this site to be their new home.

Aztec priests declared that the gods demanded they build a great city upon this spot. Laborers worked around the clock. They built bridges to the mainland with soil dug from the lake bottom. Floating gardens dotted the surface of the lake. The wondrous city they built was Tenochtitlán (tay•nawch•teet•LAHN).

For the next 100 years, Aztec workers built temples, palaces, and homes in Tenochtitlán. The city eventually became the largest city in Mesoamerica. It was the center of a web of trade routes that reached throughout Mexico.

The Aztec **relied** on strong kings, or emperors, who claimed to be descended from the gods. A council of priests, nobles, and warriors usually named a new emperor from the ruling family. Council members wanted someone skilled in warfare who could lead troops into battle.

Montezuma I (MAHN•tuh•ZOO•muh) was perhaps the most powerful Aztec ruler. He governed from A.D. 1440 to A.D. 1469. Montezuma used his armies to expand the empire to the Gulf of Mexico. He also built temples, aqueducts, and roads.

By A.D. 1500, Aztec armies had conquered much of what is today Mexico. The new empire was a collection of partly independent territories governed by local leaders. The Aztec ruler supported these leaders in return for tribute—goods or money paid by conquered peoples to their conquerors.

This shield made of feathers most likely belonged to an Aztec emperor.

▶ CRITICAL THINKING

Analyzing What do you think the animal represented here is holding in its mouth?

Aztec Life

The emperor was at the top of Aztec society. There were four classes of people under the emperor. These were nobles, commoners, unskilled workers, and enslaved people. Most of the Aztec were commoners, who worked as farmers, artisans, or merchants.

From an early age, boys in Aztec society were taught to be warriors. Girls were trained to work at home, weave cloth, and prepare for motherhood. Although not equal to men, Aztec women could own and inherit property.

Priests played an important role in Aztec society. Some sacrificed captives to please the gods. Death was considered honorable. The Aztec believed that those sacrificed would be rewarded in the afterlife.

Aztec priests also worked to preserve the religion, history, and literature of their people. Priests recorded these in books that historians still refer to today. Like the Maya, the Aztec developed two different calendars. They used a religious calendar with 260 days to keep track of important ceremonies and festivals. They also had a 365-day calendar for everyday use and for marking the time for planting and harvesting crops.

Much of Mexico was not suited for farming. The Aztec overcame this difficulty by irrigating and fertilizing the land. Aztec crafts, as well as fruit, vegetables, and grain from Aztec farms, passed through markets and along trade routes. The trade in these goods and the tribute from conquered peoples helped make the Aztec Empire wealthy.

Reading HELPDESK

Academic Vocabulary

rely to depend on

☑ PROGRESS CHECK

Explaining Why did the Aztec develop two different calendars?

3 The Inca

GUIDING QUESTION ***How did the Inca organize their government and society?***

In the late A.D. 1300s, the Inca were only one of many groups that fought over scarce fertile land in the valleys of the Andes Mountains. From their capital of Cuzco, the Inca raided nearby groups and seized territory. Within 100 years, the Inca had created a powerful empire.

Inca Rulers

A series of strong emperors helped build the Inca Empire. Pachacuti (PAH•chah•KOO•tee) was the first of these rulers. In the A.D. 1430s, he launched a campaign of conquest. The two emperors who followed continued this expansion, building the largest empire in the Americas.

According to Aztec legend, in 1325 an eagle was seen atop a cactus with a snake in its mouth. This event fulfilled an Aztec prediction. As a result, this location became the capital of the Aztec Empire, Tenochtitlán.

LESSON 2 • Day 1 (cont.)

Explain to students that records such as calendars and samples of hieroglyphic writing have given us valuable information about the Maya and their way of life. AL

2 The Aztec

GUIDING QUESTION ***How did the Aztec establish their society in central Mexico?***

SLIDE SHOW **Analyzing Visuals** Present the digital slide show on the construction of Tenochtitlán. As students view the slides, note the size of the city and the types of buildings shown. Discuss with students what the construction of such a city tells us about the Aztec.

Ask:

What challenges did the Aztec overcome to build Tenochtitlán? *(Tenochtitlán was built on two small islands. The Aztec had to build artificial islands to allow the city to grow, as well as giant roads to connect it to the shore.)*

Ask:

What does studying the city of Tenochtitlán tell us about the Aztec? *(Answers may include the following: Religion was central to Aztec life; Aztec society had to be organized in order to build something so complex; the Aztec king was at the top of Aztec society. Accept other answers that are supported by the facts.)* BL

INTERACTIVE GRAPHIC ORGANIZER

Identifying Project the interactive graphic organizer for the class.

Ask volunteers to come up to the whiteboard and label each of the five Aztec social classes, from the highest rank to the lowest rank. *(These social classes from highest to lowest were the king, nobles, commoners, unskilled workers, and enslaved people.)* AL

Ask:

What role did priests play in Aztec society? *(They carried out sacrifices to the gods and recorded Aztec knowledge in books.)*

Comparing Use the graphic organizer and the question as a starting point for a class discussion that compares Aztec social classes with the class systems of other civilizations in general. Students should recognize that social structure is similar among many civilizations. BL

3 The Inca

GUIDING QUESTION ***How did the Inca organize their government and society?***

MAP **Making Inferences** Show students the interactive map of the Inca Empire linked to the image of the Inca leader Pachacuti. Note how the Inca Empire grew steadily in size over time, expanding to the north and south along the western coast of South America.

Ask:

Why do you think the Inca Empire spread in the way that it did? *(Students should note that the Andes and the Amazon jungle formed a natural barrier to eastern expansion, while the Pacific Ocean was a barrier to western expansion.)*

Summarizing

Ask:

How did Inca rulers hold their large empire together? *(They created a strong central government with tax bureaus, legal courts, and military posts. They required people to learn the Inca language and to work for the government.)*

Then discuss the geographic challenges the Inca had to overcome to build their civilization.

Ask:

How did the Inca overcome the challenges of living in the high mountains and coastal deserts? *(The Inca built a large network of roads, used terrace farming to overcome steep terrain, and took steps to irrigate and enrich the soil.)*

Comparing and Contrasting Return to the notes that students made about how the Maya, Aztec, and Inca adapted to their geographic surroundings. Then ask students to compare what they thought at the beginning of the class with what they have learned about each of these civilizations.

CLOSE & REFLECT

INTERACTIVE WORKSHEET

Comparing and Contrasting Present the 21st Century Skills Activity comparing and contrasting the traits of the Maya, Aztec, and Inca.

On the interactive whiteboard, create a Venn diagram similar to the one on the worksheet. After students have completed the activity, have a volunteer complete the Venn diagram on the interactive whiteboard.

LESSON 2 • Day 2

ENGAGE

Making Connections Discuss with students whether or not there was a "typical" Native American culture.

Ask:

What image do you think comes to many people's minds when they think of Native Americans? *(Students may mention the image of a horseback rider hunting buffalo on the Great Plains or a similar image.)*

Project a map of the United States. Have students locate where they live on the map.

Then ask:

Has anyone ever lived in or visited another part of the United States?

Have volunteers point out other places in the United States where they have lived or that they have visited. Have them describe the differences among the places named.

Ask:

- **How was the climate different?**
- **Were different kinds of geographic features located nearby?**
- **Were houses there different from houses here?**
- **What other kinds of differences have you noticed?**

Help students recognize how different geographic locations led to different ways of life. Then, use the maps to point out various locations where Native Americans lived. Make sure to include coastal regions and northern climates as well as the plains. Explain to students that although some Native American groups lived in the Great Plains, groups also lived throughout the continent.

Making Connections Students should understand that because they lived in different locations, there was no single, "typical" Native American culture.

Answers for pages 460–463

P. 461 CRITICAL THINKING Answers will vary. Students should mention that priests advised kings and conducted ceremonies to please the gods. These duties gave them power over the rulers as well as over the rest of the population.

P. 461 ☑ PROGRESS CHECK Each Maya city-state was ruled by a king. Nobles and priests assisted kings in governing the city-states.

P. 462 CRITICAL THINKING Answers will vary, but historians believe this shield shows a water beast, or a dragon, with a sacrificial knife in its mouth.

P. 463 ☑ PROGRESS CHECK The Aztec used a religious calendar to keep track of important ceremonies and festivals and another calendar for everyday use.

BIOGRAPHY

Pachacuti (ruled A.D. 1438–1471)

As emperor, Pachacuti concentrated on expanding the Inca Empire. When he wanted to conquer a kingdom, he first sent messengers to tell the local rulers all the benefits of being part of the Inca Empire. Pachacuti then asked the other rulers to join his empire. If they accepted willingly, they were treated with respect and given some rights. If they refused, the Inca attacked with brutal force.

▶ CRITICAL THINKING
Analyzing What do you think would be the advantages and disadvantages of joining the Inca Empire?

To hold the empire together, Inca rulers created a strong central government. They set up tax bureaus, legal courts, military posts, and other government offices. Inca emperors required people to learn Quechua (KEH•chuh•wuh), the language spoken by the Inca. People also had to work for the government for several weeks each year.

Inca Projects

The Inca had people work on projects such as a system of roads. When finished, these roads connected all parts of the empire. This large network helped the Inca overcome geographic barriers. The roads helped move soldiers, goods, and information quickly over the coastal deserts and high mountains.

The Inca also used irrigation and fertilizers to improve the soil. Inca engineers developed terrace farming. Terrace farming uses a series of wide steps built into a mountainside. Each step creates level farmland. Inca farmers grew potatoes and quinoa, a protein-rich grain. Government officials stored food when there were good harvests and **distributed** it when harvests were poor.

How Was Inca Society Organized?

The Inca believed their rulers had the protection of the sun god Inti (IHN•tee). As divine rulers, Inca emperors controlled the lives of their subjects. They owned all the land and set rules for growing crops and distributing food.

Below the emperor and his family were the head priest and the leading commander of the army. Next came regional army leaders. Below them were temple priests, local army commanders, and skilled workers. At the bottom were farmers, herders, and ordinary soldiers.

Like the Aztec Empire, the Inca Empire was built on war. All young men were required to serve in the army, which made it the largest and best armed military force in the region.

Culture of the Inca

The Inca believed in many gods. Unlike the Aztec, the Inca rarely sacrificed humans to honor their gods. They did, however, build large stone structures to please these dieties. They had no system of writing, no wheels, and no iron tools. Yet they built places like Machu Picchu (mah•choo PEE•choo), a retreat for Inca emperors. Constructed of white granite and thousands of feet high, Machu Picchu was located in the Andes.

Reading HELPDESK

Academic Vocabulary
distribute to hand out or deliver, especially to members of a group

Academic Vocabulary
temporary not permanent; lasting for a limited period

Building enormous structures like Machu Picchu required the Inca to develop a method for doing mathematics. The Inca used a **quipu** (KEE•poo), a rope with knotted cords of different lengths and colors. This was a useful tool for both mathematics and for record keeping.

The Inca were also skilled engineers. Inca workers fit stones so tightly together that they needed no mortar. Because the stone blocks could slide up and down during earthquakes, many Inca structures have survived.

The ruins of Machu Picchu draw thousands of visitors. Research suggests that this monument was used as a home for the royal family and as a center for celebrations.

✓ PROGRESS CHECK
Describing What building projects did the Inca carry out?

4 North American Peoples

GUIDING QUESTION *What were the societies of North American peoples like?*

By A.D. 1500, many different groups of Native Americans lived north of Mesoamerica. They spoke about 300 languages and called themselves by thousands of different names. As they spread across North America, these peoples adapted to the different environments.

How Did People Live in the Far North?

The first people to reach the far northern areas of North America called themselves the Inuit (IH•new•weht), which means "the people." The Inuit settled along the coasts of the tundra (TUN•drah) region, the treeless land south of the Arctic.

The Inuit adapted well to their cold environment. They used dogsleds on land and seal-skin kayaks (KEYE•ackz) at sea. In winter, they built homes from stone and blocks of earth. When they traveled, they built igloos, **temporary** homes made from cut blocks of hard-packed snow.

The Inuit were skilled hunters. They used spears made from animal antlers or tusks to hunt seals, walruses, caribou, and polar bears. Blubber, or fat, from seals and whales was a food that provided needed calories and furnished oil for lamps.

Visual Vocabulary
quipu a tool used in mathematics and as a system of historical record keeping. The quipu used knots to represent numbers and items.

People and Food Sources of North America c. 1300–1500

GEOGRAPHY CONNECTION

Certain groups lived in different North American regions. Depending on the geography of their region, North Americans found food in different ways.

1. **PLACE** What was the most common method for obtaining food on the Atlantic coast?
2. **CRITICAL THINKING** ***Analyzing*** Why do you think more groups did not live in the center of the California/Great Basin/Plateau?

West Coast Life

The Pacific coast of North America had a mild climate and reliable food sources. As a result, this was the most heavily populated region north of Mesoamerica.

In the Pacific Northwest, peoples such as the Tlingit (TLIHNG•kuht), Haida (HEYE•deh), and Chinook (shuh•NOOK) used cedar trees to build wooden houses and canoes. They hunted and fished for otters, seals, whales, and their main food—salmon.

More than 500 early American cultures thrived in the area that is now California, including the Chumash (choo•MASH), the Cahuilla (kuh•WEE•uh), and the Pomo (POH•moh).

In the Southwest, the Hopi (HOH•pee), the Acoma (AHK•eh•meh), and the Zuni (ZOO•nee) built apartment-like homes from sun-dried mud bricks called adobe (uh•DOH•bee). The Southwest peoples dug irrigation canals to bring water to their fields. Their major crops were corn, beans, squash, and melons. They developed a trade network that spread into Mesoamerica.

Reading HELPDESK

hogan a square wooden home

In the A.D. 1500s, two new groups—the Apache (uh•PAH•chee) and the Navajo (NAH•vah•hoe)—settled in the Southwest. The Apache and Navajo were hunters and gatherers. In time, the Navajo became farmers and settled in villages made up of square wooden homes called **hogans** (HOH•gahns). The Apache, however, remained hunters.

Life on the Great Plains

Native Americans living on the Great Plains were nomads. They set up temporary villages that lasted for only one or two growing seasons. Their homes were cone-shaped skin tents called tepees. Farming on the Great Plains was not easy. Peoples like the Mandan (MAHN•dahn) and Pawnee (paw•NEE), however, planted gardens in the fertile soil along rivers.

Plains women grew beans, corn, and squash. Before the arrival of the horse, men hunted by driving herds of antelope, deer, and buffalo over cliffs to their deaths. Plains peoples had many uses for the buffalo. They ate the meat, used the skins for clothing and tepees, and made tools from the bones.

How Did People Live in the Eastern Woodlands?

The land east of the Mississippi River was known as the Eastern Woodlands because of its dense forests. Farming was widely practiced in the southeast. The most important crops were corn, beans, and squash. In the cooler northeast, people depended more on hunting animals, such as deer, bear, rabbits, and beaver.

The people of the Eastern Woodlands formed complex societies with different kinds of governments. One plan was formed in the 1500s to end fighting among five groups. The Iroquois (IHR•uh•kwoy) Confederacy created the first constitution, or plan of government, in what is now the United States.

Thinking Like a HISTORIAN

Comparing and Contrasting

Early Americans adapted to the environments in which they settled. As a result, many different cultures and ways of life developed. As you read, note the similarities and differences among Native Americans living in the far north, the Pacific Coast, the Southwest, the Great Plains, and the Eastern Woodlands. Share your findings with the class. For more information on comparing and contrasting, read the chapter *What Does a Historian Do?*

✓ PROGRESS CHECK
Explaining Why did the Iroquois form a confederacy?

LESSON 2 REVIEW

Review Vocabulary

1. How did *sinkholes* help the Maya?
2. How did a *hogan* differ from a tepee?

Answer the Guiding Questions

3. ***Describing*** What role did Inca emperors play in the lives of their subjects?
4. ***Drawing Conclusions*** How did establishing a confederacy benefit Woodlands Native Americans?
5. ***Contrasting*** How did Native American groups on the Pacific Coast differ from those in the Southwest?
6. **NARRATIVE WRITING** Describe daily life in a Maya city-state from the point of view of a Maya priest.

LESSON 2 • Day 2 (cont.)

TEACH & ASSESS

North American Peoples

GUIDING QUESTION ***What were the societies of North American peoples like?***

LECTURE SLIDE **Analyzing** Show the different regions of North America from the lecture slide. Review the characteristics of the Native Americans living in different regions of North America.

SLIDE SHOW **Analyzing Visuals** Present the slide show about the Native Americans of North America.

After viewing each slide, **ask:**

- **What does this picture tell us about the people of this region?**
- **What does it tell us about their society?** *(Accept all reasonable answers that can be supported by reference to the picture.)* AL BL

MAP **Comparing** Show students the "People and Food Sources of North America" map. Note that North America is divided into different cultural regions. Explain that the Native Americans living in each of these regions often shared some cultural characteristics.

Use the map key showing the different ways in which Native American peoples gathered food as an example of some of the similarities shared by groups living in the same regions.

Analyzing Review the characteristics of the Native Americans living in different regions of North America.

Ask:

How did geography and climate shape the lifestyle of the Inuit? *(The Inuit lived in the cold Far North region, where farming was not possible. This forced them to rely on hunting and to learn to make tools from animals and shelter from stone, earth, and snow.)*

Comparing and Contrasting Guide the discussion to the West Coast and Southwest regions.

Ask:

How was life on the West Coast similar to and different from life in the Southwest? *(In the Pacific Northwest, people relied on plentiful fishing and forests for food and resources. The southern California areas had a climate more similar to the desert Southwest, where fishing was uncommon. In the Southwest, daily life was centered around agriculture, hunting, and gathering, depending on the culture group.)*

Identifying Move the discussion to the peoples who lived on the Great Plains.

Ask:

What animal was particularly important to the Plains peoples? Why? *(The buffalo was important to the Plains peoples because it provided them with meat for food, skins for clothing and tepees, and bones for tools.)*

Conclude the discussion of North American peoples with the people of the Eastern Woodlands region.

Ask:

What was special about the organization of the Iroquois? *(The Iroquois created a confederacy of five different peoples that had a constitution.)*

Identifying Stereotypes

Have students identify stereotypes about early Native Americans. Then, have them identify the facts they have learned in this chapter that dispel these stereotypes. BL

CLOSE & REFLECT

INTERACTIVE WHITEBOARD ACTIVITY

Thinking Like a Historian

Comparing and Contrasting Present the Interactive Whiteboard Activity comparing and contrasting the characteristics of the Native American peoples living in different regions. Have volunteers drag and drop the information to the column of the correct group of people. When students have completed the section, review the chart. AL

Have students complete the Lesson 2 Review as an in-class or a homework activity.

BACKGROUND KNOWLEDGE

Maya Myths in the *Popol Vuh*

The *Popol Vuh* was found in a Dominican monastery in the 1500s. It contains the first written account of Maya myths and is divided into four parts. The first part of the *Popol Vuh* describes the universe before Earth was created.

Humans do not appear until the third part. The first four men were made of corn dough and were known as the Quiche, or forefathers. Then, four women were created as wives for the men. They received their god, Tohil, who gave them fire. In return, however, Tohil required sacrifice. The last part tells how Tohil was victorious over Earth.

Answers for pages 464–467

P. 464 **CRITICAL THINKING** Students may answer that one advantage would be avoiding being attacked by the Inca. Other possible advantages would be gaining wealth and prestige by being part of a large empire. A disadvantage would be the loss of independence.

P. 465 **☑ PROGRESS CHECK** The Inca built a system of roads for trade and travel. They also built large works of stone, such as Machu Picchu, a retreat for Inca emperors.

P. 466 GEOGRAPHY CONNECTION

1. The most common method for obtaining food on the Atlantic coast was farming.
2. **CRITICAL THINKING** Students' answers will vary but may include that fish were more abundant along the Gulf of Mexico and in waters around Florida, or that the southern climate made it easier to fish throughout the year.

P. 467 **☑ PROGRESS CHECK** The Iroquois formed a confederacy to end fighting among five groups.

LESSON 2 REVIEW

1. Sinkholes connected the Maya with a huge network of underground rivers and streams and gave them a year-round source of water.
2. A hogan was a square, wooden home that was permanent; a tepee was a cone-shaped tent that was temporary.
3. Inca emperors controlled the lives of their subjects. They owned all the land and set rules for growing crops and distributing produce.
4. Answers will vary but should emphasize that federations connected several groups, promoting peace and protection.
5. Native Americans on the Pacific coast enjoyed a mild climate and reliable food sources. The Southwest peoples had to dig irrigation canals in order to water their fields and grow crops.
6. Students' writings should be consistent with lesson content describing Maya society.

CHAPTER 16 Activities

Write your answers on a separate piece of paper.

❶ **Exploring the Essential Question**
EXPOSITORY WRITING How did geography affect the societies and cultures that developed in the early Americas? Choose two early civilizations or cultures that developed in different parts of the Americas. Write an essay describing how each adapted to its environment. Describe their food, shelter, government, and religion.

❷ **21st Century Skills**
DEBATING Which society do you think had the greatest achievements—the Maya, the Aztec, or the Inca? Choose a culture and list its achievements as well as the reasons why those achievements are important. Then, debate the issue with a fellow classmate who chose a different culture.

❸ **Thinking Like a Historian**
SEQUENCING Create a time line like the one shown. Fill in significant events in the rise of the Aztecs.

A.D. 1200
Aztec move into central Mexico

❹ **GEOGRAPHY ACTIVITY**

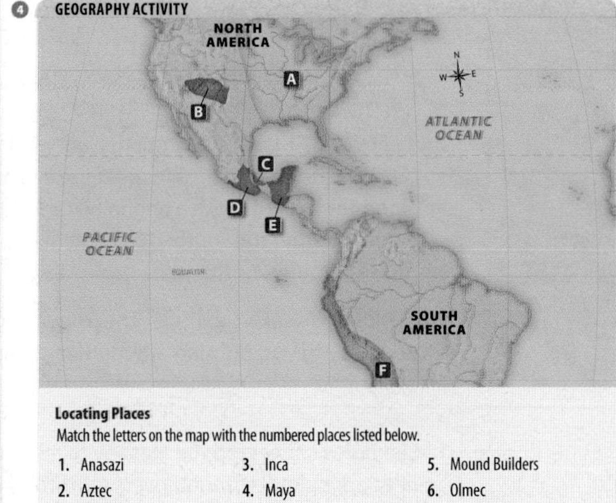

Locating Places
Match the letters on the map with the numbered places listed below.

1. Anasazi
2. Aztec
3. Inca
4. Maya
5. Mound Builders
6. Olmec

CHAPTER 16 Assessment

REVIEW THE GUIDING QUESTIONS
Directions: Choose the best answer for each question.

❶ Pueblo Bonito was an important trade or religious center for
A. the Inuit.
B. the Anasazi.
C. the Haida.
D. the Navajo.

❷ Which of the following is the major waterway for the central part of North America?
F. the Amazon River
G. the Hudson River
H. the Mississippi River
I. the Red River

❸ Which of the following represents an achievement made by the Maya?
A. calendar systems
B. floating gardens
C. quipu
D. terrace farming

❹ Native Americans living on the Great Plains
F. were part of the Iroquois League.
G. set up temporary villages.
H. hunted for walruses and caribou.
I. built homes from stone and blocks of earth.

❺ Which was the most important food in the Americas?
A. squash
B. potatoes
C. beans
D. corn

❻ Early Americans living in which of the following areas dug irrigation canals to carry river water to their fields?
F. the Southwest
G. the Pacific coast
H. the Great Plains
I. the Eastern Woodlands

CHAPTER 16 Assessment *(continued)*

DBQ DOCUMENT-BASED QUESTIONS

The author of the following creation myth of the Inca is unknown:

"Thus our imperial city . . . was divided into two halves: . . . [Upper] Cuzco was founded by our king and . . . [Lower] Cuzco by our queen . . . There existed only one single difference between them, . . . that the inhabitants of Upper-Cuzco were to be considered as the elders . . . [they] had been brought together by the male, and those below by the female element."

❼ **Analyzing** Which statement best describes how the imperial city was separated?
A. The citizens in Upper-Cuzco chose to be independent.
B. A council of elders decided to divide the city into four kingdoms.
C. Invaders captured the lower half of the city.
D. The king founded one half of the city and the queen founded the other.

❽ **Evaluating** Why were the inhabitants of Upper-Cuzco considered to be elders?
F. They were located to the north.
G. They had founded their city first.
H. Their city was founded by a male.
I. They had defeated the citizens of Lower-Cuzco.

SHORT RESPONSE

"Recently, archaeologists have studied the Maya in many new ways . . . A big breakthrough was learning to read Maya writing.

"Archaeologists also look at layers of dirt in lake bottoms to see how the land has changed. . . . They even dig through the Maya's trash.

"All this work has given scientists new ideas . . . A big one was that the Maya world probably had too many people . . . ."

—Guy Gugliotta, "Maya Mystery," *National Geographic* 2007

❾ Why do you think archaeologists think it is important to know about rain?

❿ What does it mean "the Maya world probably had too many people"?

⓫ **Descriptive Writing** You are an early American. Write a journal entry describing an encounter with a Native American people in one of the regions described in the chapter. How would you describe their daily life?

Need Extra Help?

If You've Missed Question	❶	❷	❸	❹	❺	❻	❼	❽	❾	❿	⓫
Review Lesson	1	1	2	2	1	1	2	2	2	2	1, 2

NOTES

REFLECT, REVIEW, & REMEDIATE

INTERACTIVE WORKSHEET

Chapter Summary

Provide students with the Chapter Summary worksheet to help review the chapter and prepare for assessment.

Reviewing the Enduring Understandings

Review this chapter's Enduring Understandings with students:
- People, places, and ideas change over time.
- Cultures are held together by shared beliefs and common practices and values.

INTERACTIVE WHITEBOARD ACTIVITY On the interactive whiteboard, have a student volunteer create a three-column chart. Write "Mesoamerica" in the first column, "Peru/Andes" in the second column, and "American Southwest" in the third column. Then have students come to the board and list the different Native American groups that lived in each area. Tell students to make sure they list the groups in chronological order according to when they lived in the area. When the chart is finished, ask students what generalizations they can make based on the information in the chart. *(The people who live in an area change over time.)*

Mesoamerica	Peru/Andes	American Southwest

ACTIVITIES ANSWERS

Exploring the Essential Question

1. Answers will vary. Students should note that early peoples in the Americas fished, hunted, and farmed, depending on the climate and natural resources available to them. They also built homes out of animal skins, trees, mud, or other resources that were easily accessible. These factors affected the civilizations that developed—from the gods they worshiped to the roles of their leaders.

21st Century Skills

2. Answers will vary. Students should support their choices with evidence from the text describing the achievements of their chosen civilization.

Thinking Like a Historian

3. Answers will vary but should include the following: Aztec begin to build Tenochtitlán (A.D. 1325), Montezuma becomes ruler (A.D. 1440), and Aztec armies conquer most of Mexico (A.D. 1500).

Locating Places

4. **1.** B, **2.** D, **3.** F, **4.** E, **5.** A, **6.** C

ASSESSMENT ANSWERS

Review the Guiding Questions

1. **B** The Anasazi built pueblos. The Inuit built their homes out of stone and turf or snow. The Haida used cedar trees to construct their homes. The Navajo lived in hogans.

2. **H** The Mississippi River is the major waterway for the central part of North America. The Amazon River flows in South America. The Hudson River flows from northeastern New York State to New York City. The Red River, a tributary of the Mississippi, flows from Texas to Louisiana, where it joins the Mississippi.

3. **A** The Maya developed a calendar for religious events and a calendar for events related to the seasons and agriculture. The Aztec created floating gardens. The Inca used the quipu and terrace farming.

4. **G** Native Americans living on the Great Plains were nomads, so they set up villages that lasted for one or two growing seasons. The Iroquois League was located in the Eastern Woodlands, not the Great Plains. The Inuit of the far north built homes from stones and blocks of earth and hunted caribou and walruses.

5. **D** Squash, potatoes, and beans were among the first crops grown in the Americas, but corn became the most important food in the Americas.

6. **F** Early Americans living in the scorching deserts of the Southwest dug irrigation canals to carry river water to their fields. Those living on the Pacific coast, on the Great Plains, or in the Eastern Woodlands did not experience the same irrigation problems.

Document-Based Questions

7. **D** Upper Cuzco was founded by the king, and Lower Cuzco was founded by the queen. Neither a council of elders nor invaders are mentioned in the myth. The citizens did not play a role in the separation.

8. **H** The inhabitants of Upper Cuzco were viewed as the elders because they had been brought together by a man. The myth does not mention the geography of the city, its founding dates, or any conflicts.

Short Response

9. Archaeologists probably want to know about rain to find out if the Maya experienced a drought. A drought could have caused the Maya to leave their cities.

10. When the author writes "the Maya world had too many people," he probably means more people lived there than the environment could support with the technology of the time. There might not have been enough land to grow enough food for a large number of people or enough water for all the people living there.

Extended Response

11. Answers will vary. Students' writings should be consistent with chapter content. Students should note characteristics such as how people got food, what sort of buildings they created, how they dressed, and what their beliefs were.

ONLINE RESOURCES

networks

There's More Online!

- INTERACTIVE WORKSHEETS
- BIOGRAPHIES
- CHARTS/GRAPHS
- GAMES
- GRAPHIC ORGANIZERS
- IMAGES
- MAPS
- PRIMARY SOURCES
- SLIDE SHOWS
- TIME LINE
- LECTURE SLIDES
- INTERACTIVE WHITEBOARD ACTIVITIES
- ASSESSMENTS
- VIDEOS

Ming Dynasty

Chinese History From the Grand Canal Waterway to Marco Polo

Marco Polo's Inspiration

Chinese History From the Ming Dynasty to the Three Gorges Dam

Chapter 17

Imperial China

Dear World History Teacher,

In China, 300 years of chaos followed the collapse of the Han dynasty. Eventually, during the Sui, Tang, and Song dynasties, Chinese civilization blossomed once again. Then, the Mongols overthrew the Song dynasty and established a new dynasty, the Yuan, in 1279. Mongol rulers adapted to the Chinese political system, but after Kublai Khan's death and then a series of weak rulers, an uprising overthrew the Mongols and resulted in the establishment of the Ming dynasty. It lasted nearly 300 years.

During the 1,000 years spanning these 5 dynasties, China's industrial and commercial sector grew considerably in size, complexity, and technological capacity. Meanwhile, in the countryside a flourishing agriculture bolstered China's economic prosperity. In addition, Chinese society achieved a level of stability and social tranquility that was the envy of observers from other lands, near and far. The civil service provided for a stable government bureaucracy and an avenue of upward mobility that was virtually unknown elsewhere in the world. At the same time, Ming China was still a predominantly agrarian society, with wealth based primarily on ownership of land. Commercial activities grew but remained under a high level of government regulation and by no means represented a major proportion of the national income.

China's achievements were unsurpassed throughout the world and made it a civilization that was the envy of its neighbors and of the world. It also influenced other states in the region, including Japan, Korea, and Vietnam.

Jackson J. Spielvogel

More Media Resources

Current Events Online

Visit McGraw-Hill's current events Web site for high-interest news stories and activities for your students. Access the site through the Student or Teacher Center in **networks.**

Reading List

Grade 6 reading level:
Chee-Lin: A Giraffe's Journey, by James Rumford

Grade 7 reading level:
The Kite Rider, by Geraldine McCaughrean

Grade 8 reading level:
Adventures of Marco Polo, by Russell Freedman

CHAPTER 17 Planner

UNDERSTANDING BY DESIGN®

Enduring Understandings

- *People, places, and ideas change over time.* • *Leaders can bring about change in a society.*

Essential Questions

- *How does geography influence the way people live?* • *How do new ideas change the way people live?* • *What are the characteristics of a leader?*

Students will know:

- *what improvements the Sui, Tang, and Song dynasties made to China*
- *accomplishments of the Tang and Song dynasties*
- *what life was like in the capital city of Changan*
- *why civil service examinations were important*
- *how China's economy changed under the Tang and Song dynasties*
- *the impact of technological advances developed during the Tang dynasty*
- *why the Tang and Song dynasties were a golden age*
- *how neo-Confucianism influenced Chinese government*
- *the extent of the Mongol conquest*
- *the traits and characteristics of the Mongols*
- *how Genghis Khan and Kublai Khan ruled China*
- *the effect of Mongol rule on China*
- *how the Ming dynasty restored China*
- *about the scope and purpose of Zheng He's travels*
- *about Chinese ships of exploration*
- *about a character from classic Chinese literature*
- *what an allegory is*

Students will be able to:

- **compare** concepts of leadership from imperial China with those of today
- **recognize** Chinese cultural artifacts
- **analyze** a map of Mongol conquests
- **evaluate** characteristics of leaders
- **determine** characteristics needed to rule a vast land
- **compare** ships from China with Columbus's ships
- **interpret** a map about China's exploration
- **analyze** the impact of neo-Confucian teachings
- **evaluate** the relationship between a culture's beliefs and its government
- **determine** the characteristics of an allegory
- **demonstrate** an understanding of allegory by completing a story

Predictable Misunderstandings

Students may think:

- China has always been an isolated culture with no contact with the outside world.
- Imperial China was less culturally and technologically advanced than Western Europe.

Assessment Evidence

Performance Task

- Hands-On Chapter Project

Other Evidence

- Research activity
- Participation in class discussions
- Written activities
- Interactive Whiteboard Activities
- Graphic Organizer activities
- Geography and History Activities
- Primary Sources Activity
- Economics of History Activity
- 21st Century Skills Activity
- Lesson Reviews
- The World's Literature questions

Pacing Guide

Introducing the Chapter	1 day
Lesson 1 China Reunites	2 days
Lesson 2 Chinese Society	1 day
Lesson 3 The Mongols in China	1 day
The World's Literature	1 day
Lesson 4 The Ming Dynasty	1 day
Chapter Activities and Assessment	1 day
TOTAL TIME	**8 Days**

Differentiated Instruction

These lesson plans are written to address the needs of your On Level students. Discussion and activities that are well-suited to your Approaching Grade Level learners, Beyond Grade Level learners, as well as your English Language Learners are coded as follows:

 **Approaching Grade Level**

 **Beyond Grade Level**

ELL **English Language Learner**

NCSS Standards covered in "Imperial China"

Learners will understand:

1 CULTURE

4. That the beliefs, values, and behaviors of a culture form an integrated system that helps shape the activities and ways of life that define a culture

6. That culture may change in response to changing needs, concerns, social, political, and geographic conditions

7. How people from different cultures develop different values and ways of interpreting experience

8. That language, behaviors, and beliefs of different cultures can both contribute to and pose barriers to cross-cultural understanding

2 TIME, CONTINUITY, AND CHANGE

5. Key historical periods and patterns of change within and across cultures (e.g., the rise and fall of ancient civilizations, the development of technology, the rise of modern nation-states, and the establishment and breakdown of colonial systems)

7. The contributions of key persons, groups, and events from the past and their influence on the present

3 PEOPLE, PLACES, AND ENVIRONMENTS

8. Factors that contribute to cooperation and conflict among peoples of the nation and world, including language, religion, and political beliefs

5 INDIVIDUALS, GROUPS, AND INSTITUTIONS

9. That groups and institutions influence culture in a variety of ways

7 PRODUCTION, DISTRIBUTION, AND CONSUMPTION

1. Individuals, government, and society experience scarcity because human wants and needs exceed what can be produced from available resources

8 SCIENCE, TECHNOLOGY, AND SOCIETY

2. Society often turns to science and technology to solve problems

4. Science and technology have had both positive and negative impacts upon individuals, societies, and the environment in the past and present

5. Science and technology have changed peoples' perceptions of the social and natural world, as well as their relationship to the land, economy and trade, their concept of security, and their major daily activities

CHAPTER 17

Introducing the Chapter

(Student Edition p. 471)

The Story Matters . . .

In class, read aloud "The Story Matters . . ." or ask a student volunteer to read it aloud. Make sure students understand the more advanced words in the passage, such as *ruthless, prosperity,* and *criticized.* Point out that the passage presents two opinions of Empress Wu. Have students identify the two opinions.

Ask: **Is one opinion supported by more evidence than the other?** *(Students might say that the positive opinion of Empress Wu is more strongly supported.)*

Point out to students how Empress Wu is remembered.

Ask: **Are all leaders remembered this way?** *(no)*

Why are some leaders remembered hundreds of years after their deaths but others are not? *(Some leaders accomplish great feats or cause lasting changes.)*

Invite volunteers to share their thoughts with the class.

Tell the class that the Chinese witnessed the rise and fall of five dynasties and several periods of civil war during the imperial period, which lasted more than 1,000 years. Yet with each new dynasty, China reunited itself, rebuilt its lands and economy, and rediscovered its culture and arts. Tell students they can explore Chinese arts and culture online.

Imperial China

A.D. 600 to 1644

ESSENTIAL QUESTIONS • *How does geography influence the way people live?* • *How do new ideas change the way people live?* • *What are the characteristics of a leader?*

networks

There's More Online about the lives and customs of people in Imperial China.

CHAPTER 17

Lesson 1 *China Reunites*

Lesson 2 *Chinese Society*

Lesson 3 *The Mongols in China*

Lesson 4 *The Ming Dynasty*

The Story Matters . . .

The year is A.D. 683, and the Chinese Emperor Gaozong (GOW • ZUNG) has died from a crippling stroke. Who will rule China? His empress steps in and takes control of the government. Empress Wu at first places her sons on the throne, although she holds the real power. Then, in 690, she seized the throne for herself. Wu would be the only woman ever to rule China as emperor. She governed China using ruthless methods. Yet she is remembered for achieving prosperity, being fair to the people, and improving government services. Her long career outlasted many government officials who criticized her. Wu ruled China until her death at age 80.

◄ *Empress Wu showed no mercy to her enemies and demanded absolute acceptance of her rulings.*

IMAGEMORE Co, Ltd./Getty Images

471

Introducing Place and Time (Student Edition pp. 472–473)

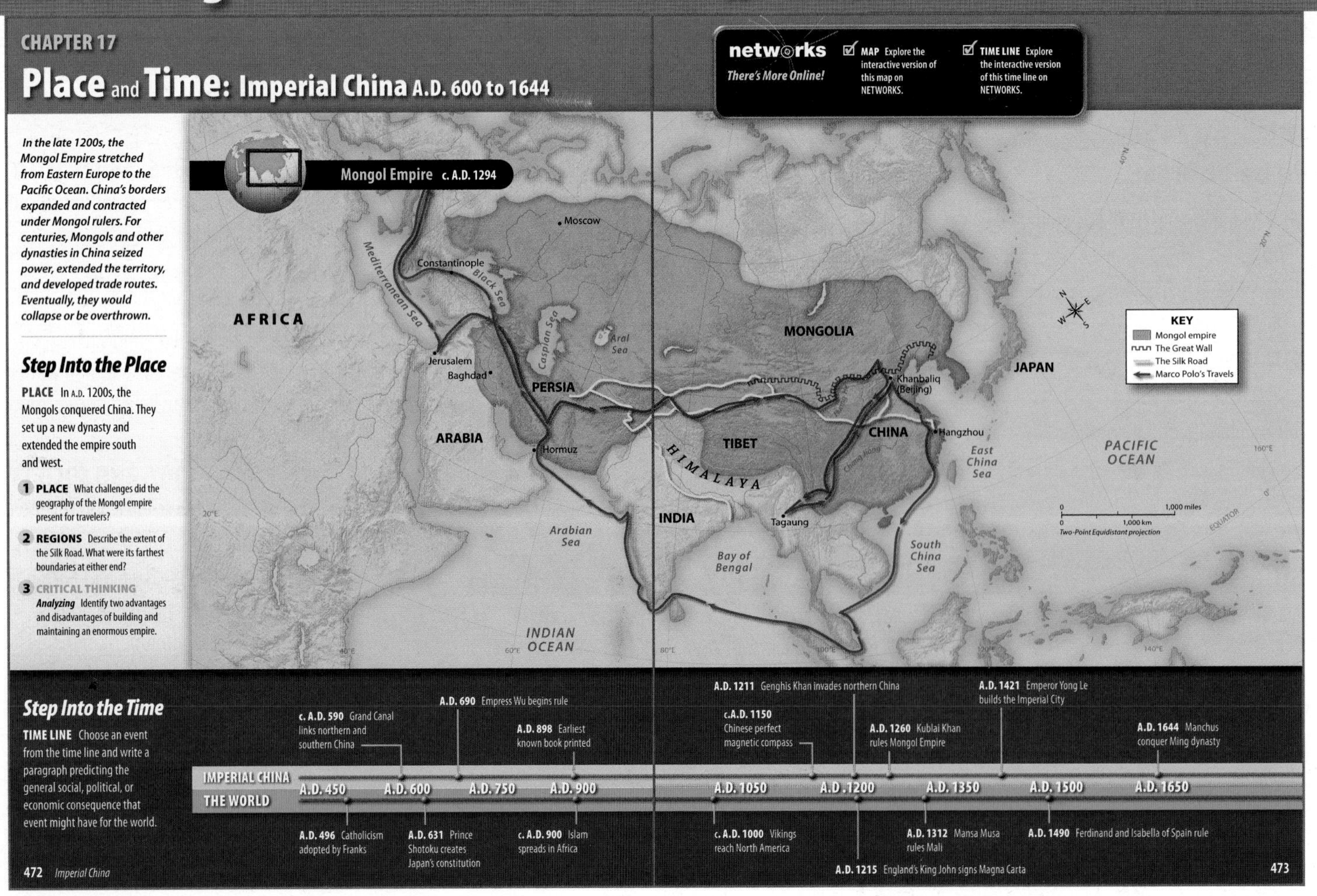

CHAPTER 17

Place and Time: Imperial China A.D. 600 to 1644

networks *There's More Online!* MAP Explore the interactive version of this map on NETWORKS. TIME LINE Explore the interactive version of this time line on NETWORKS.

In the late 1200s, the Mongol Empire stretched from Eastern Europe to the Pacific Ocean. China's borders expanded and contracted under Mongol rulers. For centuries, Mongols and other dynasties in China seized power, extended the territory, and developed trade routes. Eventually, they would collapse or be overthrown.

Step Into the Place

PLACE In A.D. 1200s, the Mongols conquered China. They set up a new dynasty and extended the empire south and west.

1. **PLACE** What challenges did the geography of the Mongol empire present for travelers?
2. **REGIONS** Describe the extent of the Silk Road. What were its farthest boundaries at either end?
3. **CRITICAL THINKING** *Analyzing* Identify two advantages and disadvantages of building and maintaining an enormous empire.

Step Into the Time

TIME LINE Choose an event from the time line and write a paragraph predicting the general social, political, or economic consequence that event might have for the world.

IMPERIAL CHINA

c. A.D. 590 Grand Canal links northern and southern China

A.D. 690 Empress Wu begins rule

A.D. 898 Earliest known book printed

c.A.D. 1150 Chinese perfect magnetic compass

A.D. 1211 Genghis Khan invades northern China

A.D. 1260 Kublai Khan rules Mongol Empire

A.D. 1421 Emperor Yong Le builds the Imperial City

A.D. 1644 Manchus conquer Ming dynasty

A.D. 450 A.D. 600 A.D. 750 A.D. 900 A.D. 1050 A.D. 1200 A.D. 1350 A.D. 1500 A.D. 1650

THE WORLD

A.D. 496 Catholicism adopted by Franks

A.D. 631 Prince Shotoku creates Japan's constitution

c. A.D. 900 Islam spreads in Africa

c. A.D. 1000 Vikings reach North America

A.D. 1215 England's King John signs Magna Carta

A.D. 1312 Mansa Musa rules Mali

A.D. 1490 Ferdinand and Isabella of Spain rule

472 *Imperial China*

473

Technology Extension

- Find an additional activity online that incorporates technology for this project.
- Visit the EdTechTeacher Web sites (included in the Technology Extension for this chapter) for more links, tutorials, and other resources.

Assessing Background Knowledge

INTERACTIVE WORKSHEET

What Do You Know? Activity

Have students review what they have already learned about ancient China by completing the What Do You Know? matching game. Direct students to cut out the cards and match each term to its definition. You may choose to have students work in pairs.

Once students have matched the cards, review with them the correct answers. Then have students mix up and match the cards again.

INTERACTIVE WORKSHEET

Guided Reading Activities

There is a Guided Reading Activity for each lesson in this chapter. You may wish to assign the Guided Reading Activity for Lesson 1 after introducing the chapter content.

Hands-On Chapter Project

Students will create an illustrated time line displaying key events and achievements of major Chinese dynasties of the period A.D. 581–1644.

- Students will participate in a class discussion to review what they have learned about the Sui, Tang, Song, Yuan, and Ming dynasties.
- Then, students will discuss research ideas and plan their projects before creating their time lines.
- Students will share their time lines with the rest of the class.
- Finally, students will evaluate their research, presentation, and collaboration using an Assessment Rubric.

Visit **networks** online to see the full project and rubric.

ONLINE RESOURCES

networks

Assign these interactive worksheets and quizzes from your Teacher Lesson Center. All resources are print-ready.

It's ALL Online!

CHAPTER 17 RESOURCES

- ☑ CHAPTER SUMMARY
- ☑ VOCABULARY BUILDER
- ☑ WHAT DO YOU KNOW?
- ☑ HANDS-ON CHAPTER PROJECT

Lesson 1 Resources

- ☑ INTERACTIVE GRAPHIC ORGANIZER
- ☑ GEOGRAPHY AND HISTORY ACTIVITY Understanding Location: Changan and Hangzhou
- ☑ GUIDED READING ACTIVITY
- ☑ READING ESSENTIALS AND STUDY GUIDE
- ☑ ONLINE SELF-CHECK QUIZ

Lesson 2 Resources

- ☑ INTERACTIVE GRAPHIC ORGANIZER
- ☑ ECONOMICS OF HISTORY Chinese Currency
- ☑ GUIDED READING ACTIVITY
- ☑ READING ESSENTIALS AND STUDY GUIDE
- ☑ ONLINE SELF-CHECK QUIZ

Lesson 3 Resources

- ☑ INTERACTIVE GRAPHIC ORGANIZER
- ☑ PRIMARY SOURCE ACTIVITY Two European Views of China During Mongol Rule
- ☑ GUIDED READING ACTIVITY
- ☑ READING ESSENTIALS AND STUDY GUIDE
- ☑ ONLINE SELF-CHECK QUIZ

Lesson 4 Resources

- ☑ INTERACTIVE GRAPHIC ORGANIZER
- ☑ GEOGRAPHY AND HISTORY ACTIVITY Sailing the Western Oceans: The Voyages of Zheng He
- ☑ 21ST CENTURY SKILLS ACTIVITY Creativity and Innovation: Identify Problems and Solutions
- ☑ GUIDED READING ACTIVITY
- ☑ READING ESSENTIALS AND STUDY GUIDE
- ☑ ONLINE SELF-CHECK QUIZ

ASSESSMENT RESOURCES

- ☑ LESSON REVIEWS
- ☑ ONLINE SELF-CHECK QUIZZES
- ☑ CHAPTER ACTIVITIES AND ASSESSMENT
- ☑ STANDARDIZED TEST PRACTICE

REMEDIATION RESOURCES

- ☑ READING ESSENTIALS AND STUDY GUIDE
- ☑ GUIDED READING ACTIVITIES
- ☑ ONLINE SELF-CHECK QUIZZES
- ☑ CHAPTER SUMMARY

Step Into the Place

Place Project the Chapter Opener map on the whiteboard and identify the boundaries of Mongol-ruled China. Point out that China's borders later began to shrink when the Mongols lost power. Challenge students to draw on their knowledge of history and geography to indicate the areas of Asia that were most likely always under Chinese rule. *(Students should indicate that the Chinese nearly always controlled the eastern part of the Asian continent, including the areas around Beijing, Changan, Guangzhou, and Hangzhou.)*

Next, as a class, discuss the Map Focus questions.

Step Into the Time

Formulating Questions Display the time line for the chapter. Explain that students will be studying events that took place between A.D. 590 and A.D. 1644.

Ask: **What questions do you have about events that occurred in imperial China?** *(Students might wonder why the Grand Canal was important, what the first printed book was about, and so on.)*

Write students' questions on the board so they are visible throughout instruction. Ask students to answer the questions as they progress through the chapter.

Answers for pages 472–473

Step Into the Place

1. The size of the region and the lack of waterways presented challenges for travelers.
2. The Silk Road extended from Persia in the west to the cities of Beijing and Hangzhou on China's east coast.
3. CRITICAL THINKING Advantages include access to large areas of land and unity among people for trade and travel. Disadvantages include difficulty of communicating and maintaining order. It is also difficult to defend such a large empire.

Step Into the Time

Students might predict that the magnetic compass helped people travel long distances.

networks
There's More Online!

- ☑ **BIOGRAPHY** Empress Wu
- ☑ **GRAPHIC ORGANIZER** Accomplishments of Three Dynasties
- ☑ **MAP**
  - Tang China c. A.D. 700
  - Song China c. A.D. 1200

Lesson 1

China Reunites

ESSENTIAL QUESTION *How does geography influence the way people live?*

It Matters Because

Ideas and innovations introduced during the Sui, Tang, and Song dynasties united China after centuries of chaos and helped it become a powerful empire.

1 China Rebuilds Its Empire

GUIDING QUESTION *How did China rebuild its empire after years of war?*

The Han dynasty of China came to an end in A.D. 220. For the next 300 years, China had no central government. The country collapsed into separate kingdoms, and the Chinese people suffered many hardships. Warlords—military leaders who rule local territories—fought each other. Meanwhile, groups of nomads attacked and captured parts of northern China.

While China faced these challenges at home, it lost control of the neighboring lands it had previously conquered. One of these lands was Korea (kuh•REE•uh), located on the Korean Peninsula to the northeast of China. The people of Korea decided to free themselves from Chinese rule and build their own civilization.

The Sui

China eventually became more unified. In A.D. 581, a Chinese general named Wendi (WHEHN•dee) declared himself emperor. He won many battles and set up a new dynasty called the Sui (SWAY). The Sui dynasty again unified China under the rule of emperors.

Reading HELPDESK

Taking Notes: *Identifying*

Use a chart like this one to list important events and accomplishments during each Chinese dynasty.

Sui	Tang	Song

Content Vocabulary

- **neo-Confucianism**

After Wendi died, his son Yangdi (YAHNG•dee) became emperor. Yangdi wanted to expand China's territory. He tried to regain lost lands. His army fought the Koreans, but it was badly defeated.

Within China, Yangdi had more success at expanding his dynasty. He wanted to bring back the glory of the Han dynasty. Yangdi repaired the Great Wall, which had fallen into ruins. He also rebuilt the magnificent Han capital city of Changan (CHAHNG•AHN).

Yangdi's most ambitious project was building the Grand Canal. This system of waterways connected China's two great rivers, the Huang He (HWAHNG HUH) (Yellow River) and the Chang Jiang (CHAHNG JYAHNG) (Yangtze River). The two rivers flowed east to west and were connected by the Grand Canal, which was built north to south. The Grand Canal made it easier to ship rice and other products between northern and southern China and united China's economy.

To rebuild China, Yangdi required help from the Chinese people. Farmers were forced to work on the Great Wall and the Grand Canal. They had to pay higher taxes to support these projects. Their taxes also paid for the emperor's luxurious way of life, which made the farmers angry. The farmers revolted and Yangdi was killed, bringing an end to the Sui dynasty.

Connections to TODAY

Three Gorges Dam

Construction of China's Three Gorges Dam began in 1994. Like the Grand Canal, the dam has had an effect on the Chinese economy. The dam controls flooding, produces electricity, and allows goods to be shipped inland. However, to create the dam, many towns were flooded. More than a million people lost their homes and farms, and historical and archaeological treasures were lost.

Tang China c. A.D. 700

MONGOLIA, ASIA, GOBI, Beijing, KOREAN PENINSULA, JAPAN, East China Sea, Changan, Luoyang, Hangzhou, TIBET, HIMALAYA, CHINA, Guangzhou, INDIA, Arabian Sea, Bay of Bengal, South China Sea, PACIFIC OCEAN

KEY: Tang dynasty; Grand Canal

GEOGRAPHY CONNECTION

The Tang dynasty lasted about 300 years.

1. **PLACE** What two cities were connected by the Grand Canal?
2. **CRITICAL THINKING** ***Determining Cause and Effect*** How might these cities have been affected by the building of the Grand Canal?

BIOGRAPHY

Empress Wu (A.D. 624–705)

Chinese ruler Empress Wu did not come from an upper-class family. As a young woman, she joined the emperor's court, where she used her intelligence to influence important people. Emperor Gaozong (GOW•ZUNG) declared her his empress, and she ruled China in his name during his many illnesses. After the death of Emperor Gaozong, Empress Wu's sons were rulers. In A.D. 690, Empress Wu overthrew her second son. Wu won the respect of the people because of her ability to rule and her determination to make China stronger.

▶ **CRITICAL THINKING**
Explaining How did Empress Wu gain a great deal of support from the people?

The Tang Dynasty

In A.D. 618, one of Yangdi's generals took over China. He made himself emperor and founded a new dynasty called the Tang (TAHNG). Unlike the short-lived Sui, the Tang dynasty lasted for nearly 300 years—from A.D. 618 to A.D. 907.

Tang rulers worked to **restore** a strong central government in China. They made many reforms, or changes, to improve the government. The most powerful Tang emperor was named Taizong (TY•DZUNG). He brought back the system of **civil** service examinations. Once again, government officials were selected based on how well they did on exams rather than on their family connections. Taizong also gave land to farmers and brought peace and order to the countryside.

During the late A.D. 600s, Empress Wu (WOO) ruled China. She was the only woman in Chinese history to rule the country on her own. Empress Wu was a powerful leader who added more officials to the government and strengthened the military.

Growth and Trade

Tang rulers worked to restore China's power in Asia. They expanded their rule westward to Tibet (tuh•BEHT), an area north of the Himalaya (HIH•muh•LAY•uh). The Chinese also took control of the Silk Road and northern Vietnam. They increased trade with other parts of Asia and forced neighboring states, such as Korea, to pay them tribute.

As trade increased, Chinese cities became wealthy. Changan, the Tang capital, grew to be the world's largest city. About one million people lived there. Visitors were impressed by its wide avenues and large market squares. Merchants in Changan sold goods from places as far away as India and Southwest Asia.

By the mid-A.D. 700s, however, the Tang faced growing challenges to their rule. Turkish nomads drove Tang armies out of central Asia and won control of the Silk Road. Because Chinese merchants could not use the Silk Road safely, trade and the economy suffered.

Revolts by Chinese farmers further weakened the Tang. In response, the Tang rulers hired Uighurs (WEE•GURZ), a Turkish-speaking people in the northwest, to fight for them. However, it was too late. Continued unrest led to the fall of the Tang rule in A.D. 907.

Reading HELPDESK

Academic Vocabulary

restore to bring something back to an earlier or better condition
civil relating to the state or government

CITY LIFE IN TANG CHINA

Musicians and dancers; Farmers selling goods; Civil service examinations; Print Shop; Making pottery

INFOGRAPHIC

Under the Tang, China grew wealthy. Its growing cities contained many shops and temples.

1. **DESCRIBING** What activities took place in the cities of Tang China?
2. **CRITICAL THINKING** ***Explaining*** How does producing a variety of goods make a country stronger?

The Song Dynasty

After the fall of the Tang, military leaders ruled China. Then in A.D. 960, one of the generals became emperor and founded the Song (SUNG) dynasty. The Song governed from A.D. 960 to A.D. 1279. During this time, the Chinese enjoyed economic prosperity and made many cultural achievements.

From the beginning, the Song emperors faced many challenges. They did not have enough military forces to protect their entire empire. In the north, groups of nomads took over parts of the country. For protection, the Song rulers moved their government south to the city of Hangzhou (HAHNG•JOH). Hangzhou was on the coast near the Chang Jiang delta.

☑ **PROGRESS CHECK**

Explaining How did the Grand Canal help China's economy?

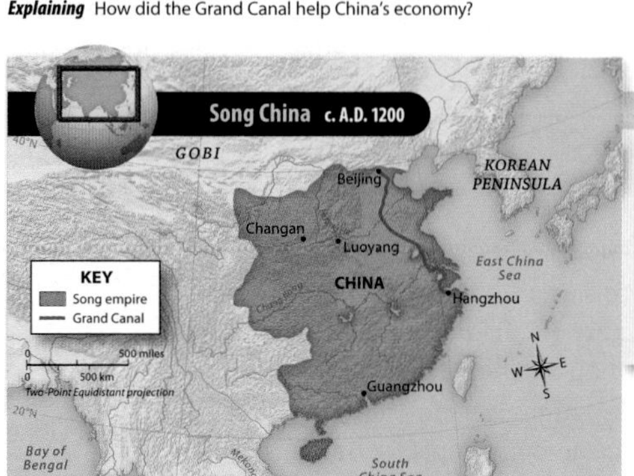

GEOGRAPHY CONNECTION

The Song dynasty moved the capital city from Changan to Hangzhou.

1. **LOCATION** About how far is the Korean Peninsula from the Song capital city of Hangzhou?
2. **CRITICAL THINKING** ***Comparing*** How did the size of Song China compare with the size of Tang China?

LESSON 1 • Day 1

ENGAGE

Describing Lead students in a discussion of what China must have been like after centuries of civil war. Lead students to understand that China had no centralized government and many Chinese were struggling to survive because farmlands, canals, and roads were in ruins. Explain that the Sui, Tang, and Song dynasties provided stability and peace in China.

Tell students that in this lesson they will be learning about the accomplishments of the Sui, Tang, and Song dynasties and the impact they had on China's land, economy, and population.

TEACH & ASSESS

1 China Rebuilds Its Empire

GUIDING QUESTION *How did China rebuild its empire after years of war?*

SLIDE SHOW **Analyzing Visuals** Show students the slide show of Tang art.

Ask:

What do you notice about these artifacts from the Tang dynasty? *(Students might notice the level of detail and the use of color in the artifacts.)* AL ELL

What skills and tools would have been needed to make these artifacts? *(Students might identify the need for precise cutting tools, paintbrushes, and metal stamps. They might also identify skills such as painting, carving, and sculpting.)*

INTERACTIVE WORKSHEET

Geography and History Activity

Summarizing For homework, have students view the map, read the text, and answer the questions about Changan and Hangzhou in the Geography and History Activity for Lesson 1. Afterward, ask students to summarize what they learned about the two capital cities.

2 Buddhism in China

GUIDING QUESTION *Why did Buddhism become popular in Tang China?*

LECTURE SLIDE **Identifying Points of View** Show students the lecture slide about Buddhism. Remind students that Buddhism teaches that the way to find the truth about the world is to give up all desires for things such as fame and money.

Ask:

- **Why did many Chinese become Buddhists?** *(Many had suffered during the civil wars before the Tang dynasty. They wanted a religion that would help ease their suffering.)*
- **Why do you think the Tang rulers at first encouraged the spread of Buddhism in China?** *(It provided people with comfort.)*
- **Why did China's rulers change their minds about Buddhism?** *(They saw it as a threat to Chinese traditions.)* AL

CLOSE & REFLECT

Discussing Lead students in a discussion about the effects of prosperity and economic growth on the city of Changan and imperial China. Guide students toward understanding that without the improvements to farming and the economy, Changan would not have been a thriving city.

IF YOU HAVE MORE TIME . . .

Explore Life in the City of Changan

Speculating Ask a volunteer to read aloud the paragraph about the city of Changan in the section "The Tang Dynasty." Direct students' attention to the illustration of city life in Tang China. Ask students to think of words to describe Changan during the Tang era. *(busy, thriving, growing, bustling, active)*

Formulating Questions Suggest that students think of questions about life in Changan that their textbook does not answer. Prompt students by **asking:**

- **What kind of houses did people live in?**
- **What foods did they eat?**
- **How did they dress?**
- **How did people entertain themselves?**
- **What kinds of schools did students go to?** BL

Have students form groups of three or four and decide on a question about life in Changan that they'd like to research. Provide in-class time for students to consult appropriate online sources.

Remind students to use only reliable sources in their research. Refer students back to the chapter *What Does a Historian Do?* for guidelines about determining the reliability of a source.

Instruct students to take notes so they can give brief presentations about their topics, with visual aids if possible. You may also choose to have students complete a bibliography of their research.

After the group presentations, lead the class in a short discussion.

Ask:

What was life like in Changan during the Tang dynasty?

Discussing Lead students in a discussion about the effects of prosperity and economic growth on the city of Changan and imperial China. Guide students toward understanding that without the improvements to farming and the economy, Changan would not have been a thriving city. AL

Answers for pages 474–477

P. 474 Taking Notes **Sui:** unified China, rebuilt Great Wall, built Grand Canal; **Tang:** civil service exams, expanded China's borders, Buddhism became popular, supported neo-Confucianism; **Song:** moved capital to Hangzhou, supported neo-Confucianism

P. 475 GEOGRAPHY CONNECTION

1. Beijing and Hangzhou
2. CRITICAL THINKING These cities could have seen population increases and economic growth.

P. 476 CRITICAL THINKING Empress Wu gained support from the people because she was an able ruler and she was determined to strengthen China.

P. 477 INFOGRAPHIC

1. printing, pottery making, selling of goods, shopping, test taking, entertainment
2. CRITICAL THINKING Producing a variety of goods makes a country stronger because it will have more goods to sell and it will be better able to survive the loss of a crop or some other struggle.

P. 477 ☑ PROGRESS CHECK The Grand Canal connected two important rivers that run east to west. It allowed trade and travelers to move north and south. As a result, China's economy improved because more goods could be sent throughout the Chinese empire.

P. 477 GEOGRAPHY CONNECTION

1. The Korean Peninsula is about 500 miles (805 km) from Hangzhou.
2. CRITICAL THINKING Song China was smaller than Tang China and did not extend as far to the north or west.

2 Buddhism in China

GUIDING QUESTION *Why did Buddhism become popular in Tang China?*

Traders and missionaries from India brought Buddhism to China during the A.D. 100s. At the time, the Han dynasty was in decline, and civil war soon broke out in China. Many people died from the fighting, hunger, and lack of shelter. Buddhism taught that people could escape suffering by following its teachings. As a result, many Chinese seeking peace and comfort became Buddhists.

How Did Tang Rulers View Buddhism?

Early Tang rulers did not practice Buddhism, but they did not interfere with its following in China. They approved the building of new Buddhist temples and shrines.

Many Chinese Buddhists joined religious communities called monasteries, where they lived, worked, and worshipped. The men in these communities were monks, and the women were nuns. Buddhist monks and nuns helped local people by running schools and providing food and shelter for travelers. Monks also served as bankers and provided medical care.

Although numerous Chinese became Buddhists, a large part of the population opposed the religion. Many believed that Buddhist temples and monasteries had grown too wealthy because of the donations they received. Others believed that monks and nuns weakened respect for family life because they were not allowed to marry.

Tang officials feared Buddhism's growing influence. They saw Buddhism as an enemy of China's Confucian (kuhn•FYOO•shuhn) traditions. Confucian traditions are customs related to the teachings of Confucius. In A.D. 845, the Tang government destroyed many Buddhist monasteries and temples. Buddhism in China never fully recovered from these attacks.

Buddhism in Korea

Korea broke free of Chinese rule when the Han dynasty fell in A.D. 220. For several hundred years afterward, Korea was divided into three distinct kingdoms.

In the A.D. 300s, Chinese Buddhists brought their religion to Korea. About A.D. 660, the three Korean kingdoms united to form one country. Because the new Korean government favored Buddhism, the religion attracted a large number of followers throughout Korea.

Reading **HELP**DESK

Reading Strategy: *Summarizing*

When you summarize, you restate important ideas in your own words. Read about how Tang rulers viewed Buddhism. On a separate sheet of paper, summarize what you read in one or two sentences.

Buddhism later spread from Korea to the nearby islands of Japan. In A.D. 552, a Korean king sent missionaries to the emperor of Japan. The missionaries brought Buddhist writings and a statue of the Buddha. They also brought a letter from the king meant to influence the emperor of Japan. As time passed, many people in Japan became Buddhists.

In a letter to the emperor, the Korean king wrote about Buddhism and its teachings:

PRIMARY SOURCE

> "This religion is the most excellent of all teachings. . . . It brings endless and immeasurable [countless] blessings . . . , even the attainment [achieving] of supreme enlightenment. . . . Moreover, the religion has come over to Korea far from India, and the peoples (in the countries between these two) are now ardent [eager] followers of its teaching."
>
> —from *Nihonji* (Chronicles of Japan)

✓ PROGRESS CHECK

Describing How did Buddhist monks and nuns help the Chinese?

This towering monument to the Buddha was carved in about A.D. 460 in the Yuan Kang caves of China.

▶ CRITICAL THINKING

Identifying Points of View Why might Buddhism appeal to people who had just experienced a civil war?

3 Revival of Confucian Ideas

GUIDING QUESTION *How did Confucian ideas shape China's government?*

Confucius believed that a good government depended on having wise leaders. The civil service examinations begun by Han rulers were based on Confucian **principles.** The exams helped provide China's government with well-educated, talented officials.

After the fall of the Han dynasty, China had no central government to give civil service examinations. Confucianism went into decline, and Buddhism won many followers with its message of escape from suffering. Tang and Song rulers worked to return Confucianism to the respected position it had held previously in Chinese society.

Neo-Confucianism

The Tang and Song dynasties backed a new understanding of Confucianism called **neo-Confucianism** (NEE•oh-kuhn•FYOO•shuhn•ih•zuhm). One reason this new Confucianism was created was to stop the growing influence of Buddhism. Neo-Confucianism taught that people should be concerned about this world as well as the afterlife. Followers were expected to be active in society and to help others. A Confucian thinker named Han Yü (HAHN YOO) lived from A.D. 768 to A.D. 824. He encouraged the Chinese to remain faithful to the Confucian teachings of their ancestors:

Confucius wrote about ethical and moral behavior, both by governments and individuals.

PRIMARY SOURCE

> "What were the teachings of our ancient kings? Universal love is called humanity. To practice this in the proper manner is called righteousness. To proceed according to these is called the Way. . . . They [ancestors] offered sacrifices to Heaven and the gods came to receive them. . . . What Way is this? I say: This is what I call the Way, and not what the Taoists [Daoists] and the Buddhists called the Way."
>
> —from *An Inquiry on The Way*, by Han Yü

This new form of Confucianism also included some Buddhist and Daoist beliefs. Chinese culture was developing and changing at this time. For many Chinese, Confucianism became more than a set of rules for good behavior. It became a religious tradition with beliefs about the spiritual world. Confucian thinkers taught that people would find peace of mind if they followed the teachings of Confucius.

Reading **HELP**DESK

neo-Confucianism a new form of the ideas of the philosopher Confucius; included Buddhist and Daoist beliefs

Academic Vocabulary

principle a basic truth or belief

The Civil Service

Tang and Song rulers saw neo-Confucianism and civil service examinations as a way to strengthen the government. They believed that a government run by educated people was less likely to become corrupt or weak.

The examinations tested candidates on their knowledge of Confucian writings. Only men were allowed to take the tests, and the examination system favored the rich. Few poor families could pay tutors to help their sons qualify for the tests.

Preparing for the tests was very difficult. At the age of four, boys began learning to write the characters of the Chinese language. Later, students had to memorize all the writings of Confucius. They had to recite the writings aloud. After years of preparing, the boys took the exams. Despite all the hard work, only one in five boys passed the tests. Those who did not pass usually found jobs teaching or helping government workers, but they were never given a government job.

Over the years, the examination system created a new class of leaders in China. This group was made up of scholar-officials. Strict rules set the scholar-officials apart from the rest of society. One rule was that the scholar-officials could not perform any job that required physical work. These scholar-officials influenced Chinese thought and government well into modern times.

✓ PROGRESS CHECK

Determining Cause and Effect How did the civil service examinations affect Chinese society?

Connections to **TODAY**

Civil Service Examinations

As in imperial China, most people who apply for government jobs in the United States must take a civil service examination. Before the late 1800s, most government posts in the U.S. were appointed. Many people were placed in important jobs because of their political connections.

LESSON 1 REVIEW

Review Vocabulary

1. How was *neo-Confucianism* different from Confucianism?

Answer the Guiding Questions

2. ***Describing*** What actions did the emperors of the Sui and Tang dynasty take to unify China?
3. ***Identifying*** How did Chinese farmers react to the changes made during the Sui and Tang dynasties?
4. ***Explaining*** Why did Buddhism become widely adopted in China?
5. ***Comparing and Contrasting*** How is Buddhism different from neo-Confucianism?
6. **PERSUASIVE WRITING** You are a young Chinese man who has just passed the civil service examination. You will be given a government job. What opinion are you likely to have about neo-Confucianism? Write a short persuasive letter in which you explain how neo-Confucianism will help or hurt your career.

LESSON 1 • Day 2

ENGAGE

Discussing Ask students with older family members or friends what they know about the process of applying for college or a job. If necessary, explain that most U.S. colleges require people to fill out forms, write essays, and take examinations like the SAT as part of the application process. Applicants study long hours and perfect their essays before submitting them. Then, they wait to hear if they have been accepted to the schools of their choice.

Tell students that during the Tang and Song dynasties, people who wanted to work for the government went through a similar process. They studied for years in order to take the civil service examination. Very few people passed the exam. Passing or not passing could affect a young person's entire career and life.

Tell students that in this lesson they will learn about the importance of Confucianism to the civil service examination.

TEACH & ASSESS

3 Revival of Confucian Ideas

GUIDING QUESTION *How did Confucian ideas shape China's government?*

LECTURE SLIDE **Explaining** Use the lecture slide to review the principles of Confucianism. Remind students that Confucianism is a system of beliefs introduced by the Chinese thinker Confucius. He taught that people needed to have a sense of duty to their family and community in order to bring peace to society.

Ask:

Why did China's rulers encourage Confucianism? *(Rulers thought that Confucius's teachings would help strengthen the government and focus people's attention on taking action to improve their lives now, rather than having them focus on the afterlife.)* AL

Do you think the civil service examinations were a good way to find candidates for important positions? Why or why not? *(Students might point out that the exams did a good job of identifying those who were intelligent and willing to work hard to study Confucian principles carefully.)*

GAME **Classifying** You may choose to have students review their knowledge of neo-Confucianism and the civil service exams by completing the true-false game for this lesson. AL

Have students complete the Lesson 1 Review.

CLOSE & REFLECT

Making Connections Ask students to draw connections between themselves and the young imperial Chinese who studied for the civil service examination.

Have volunteers explain why they would or would not want to take the civil service examination. Leave students with the impression that passing the examination was probably the most important act in a young Chinese man's life. Ask students to identify equally important events in a young person's life in this country today.

IF YOU HAVE MORE TIME . . .

Describe Life in Changan on Examination Day

Characterizing Have students write a short paper describing what examination day might have been like in Changan. In their papers, students should describe, from the point of view of someone taking the exam, the process of preparing for the civil service exam.

Students should explain why passing the examination was important to them and their families. Challenge students to include details about life in Changan that they have learned from their reading and research. Invite volunteers to read their papers aloud. BL

Compare Confucianism and Neo-Confucianism

Diagramming Have students refer to their textbooks to identify the main principles of Confucianism and neo-Confucianism. Students should refer to the earlier chapter about China to find information about Confucianism.

Draw a Venn diagram on the whiteboard. Label one circle *Confucianism* and the other *neo-Confucianism.* Have students sort their list of principles of each ideology and place them correctly in the diagram.

You may choose to have students complete this activity as a class, in pairs, or in small groups.

Answers for pages 478–481

P. 478 Reading Strategy At first, Tang rulers tolerated Buddhism. Later, they came to fear Buddhist influences so they destroyed Buddhist temples and shrines.

P. 479 ☑ PROGRESS CHECK Buddhist monks and nuns ran schools and provided food and shelter for travelers. The monks served as bankers and provided medical care.

P. 479 CRITICAL THINKING Answers may vary. Possible answer: Buddhism offers a path to peace and truth, which people who survived a civil war might find appealing.

P. 481 ☑ PROGRESS CHECK Tang and Song rulers used civil service examinations as the basis for hiring officials. The examinations evaluated a candidate's talent, not his social status. However, only the rich could afford to hire tutors to help their sons pass the exams.

LESSON 1 REVIEW

1. Neo-Confucianism added ideas from Buddhism and Daoism to the ideas of Confucius. Confucianism included only the ideas of Confucius.
2. The Sui emperors rebuilt the Great Wall and had the Grand Canal built to increase trade. The Tang emperors restored a strong central government and brought back civil service examinations. They also strengthened China's military forces.
3. Farmers were often angry about how they and their land were treated. Under the Sui, farmers grew angry about heavy taxes and having to build the Grand Canal. Under the Tang, farmers' revolts helped erode the power of the Tang dynasty.
4. Buddhism taught that people could escape suffering, and during hard times, many Chinese adopted this belief. The Chinese government allowed the spread of Buddhism because monks and nuns helped the poor and served society as teachers, bankers, and doctors.
5. Buddhism is about following steps in order to escape suffering in this world. Followers of neo-Confucianism believe it is important to be concerned about this world and to work to improve society and to help others.
6. Students' letters should be written from the point of view of a young Chinese man who has just passed the civil service exam. Letters should express and support an opinion about whether Confucianism will help or hurt a career in the civil service.

networks
There's More Online!
☑ GRAPHIC ORGANIZER Chinese Advancements
☑ SLIDE SHOW Silk-making

Lesson 2
Chinese Society

ESSENTIAL QUESTION *How do new ideas change the way people live?*

IT MATTERS BECAUSE
During the Tang and Song dynasties, the economy of China grew through trade and improvements in technology.

1 Economic Growth

GUIDING QUESTION *How did China's economy change under the Tang and Song dynasties?*

The fall of the Han dynasty in the A.D. 200s crippled the economy of China. Widespread fighting destroyed farms and cities. Farmers faced poor harvests. Artisans made fewer products, and merchants had fewer goods to trade. Under the Tang dynasty, China's economy recovered and even prospered.

Farming Improvements

After taking power in A.D. 618, the Tang gave more land to farmers. Farmers made many advances in farming these large land plots. They improved irrigation methods, which increased the growth of their crops. They developed new kinds of rice that grew well in poor soil. The new varieties of rice produced more rice per acre and resisted disease. Farmers also began to grow tea, which became a popular drink.

Because more food was available, China's population increased as well. People began to settle in new areas, which then developed into cities. Groups of farmers moved from the north to southern China. They grew abundant amounts of rice in the Chang Jiang valley.

Reading **HELP**DESK

Taking Notes: ***Categorizing***

Use a graphic organizer like the one here to identify Chinese advancements in the economy, technology, and the arts.

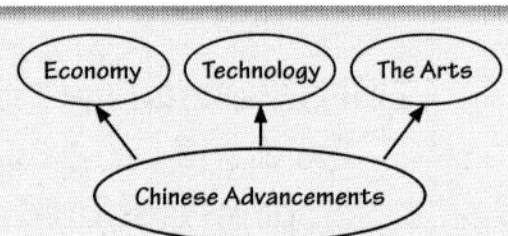

Content Vocabulary
- **porcelain** • **calligraphy**

Why Did China's Trade Grow?

Tang rulers built roads and waterways. As a result, travel within and outside of China became much easier. Chinese merchants increased trade with people in other parts of the world. After years of decline, the Silk Road reopened and thrived. Caravans traveled along it, carrying goods from China to other parts of Asia.

Silk fabric was one of the goods traded by the Chinese. Silk was in high demand in areas west of China. In addition, China traded other products, such as tea, steel, paper, and porcelain. **Porcelain** (POHR•suh•luhn) is made of fine clay that is baked at high temperatures. It is used to make dishes, vases, and other items. In return for Chinese products, countries sent goods such as gold, silver, precious stones, and fine woods to China.

Other trade routes were also opened. Roads connected China to other parts of Asia. In addition, the Tang opened new seaports along China's coast to increase trade.

☑ **PROGRESS CHECK**

Determining Cause and Effect How did advancements in farming affect China's population?

Silk worms spin cocoons made of raw silk thread. Workers then collect and unravel the valuable cocoons by hand.

▶ CRITICAL THINKING
Making Inferences Why do you think silk is still expensive today?

2 Technological Advances

GUIDING QUESTION *How did new inventions change China's society?*

During the Tang and Song dynasties, new discoveries and inventions brought change to Chinese society. In time, these technological advancements spread to other parts of the world.

Coal and Steel

Important changes took place in the use of fuels and metals. For most of their history, the Chinese burned wood to heat their homes and cook their food. By the A.D. 600s, less wood was available in China. The Chinese, however, discovered that coal could be used as a fuel. This discovery led to the development of a coal-mining industry.

porcelain a ceramic made of fine clay baked at very high temperatures

The Chinese used coal to heat furnaces to high temperatures. This process led to another discovery. When iron was produced in coal-heated furnaces, the melted iron mixed with carbon from the coal. This mixing created a new, stronger metal known today as steel.

The Chinese used steel to make many different products. They made armor, swords, and helmets for their armies. They also produced stoves, farm tools, and drills. Nails and sewing needles were made from steel as well.

The Invention of Printing

Paper had been invented during the time of the Han dynasty. Under the Tang, paper was produced in large amounts.

The manufacture of paper led to another important Chinese invention: a **method** for printing books. Before printing, books were copied by hand and were very expensive.

Chinese Buddhist monks began woodblock printing in the A.D. 600s. In woodblock printing, printers used a wooden block for each page they needed to print. They carved the page's Chinese characters into the block. Then they put ink on the block and pressed a piece of paper onto it. The printers rubbed the sheet of paper to **transfer** the Chinese characters onto the page. Each wooden block could be used to make thousands of copies.

The earliest known printed book dates from about A.D. 868. It is a Buddhist book called the *Diamond Sutra*. Even though woodblock printing was a major advancement, changes could not be made to a page once the wooden block was carved.

In the A.D. 1000s, a Chinese printer named Pi Sheng (PEE SHUHNG) solved this printing problem by inventing movable type. With movable type, each character is an individual piece. The pieces can be arranged to form sentences and used again and again. Pi Sheng made his pieces from clay and put them together to make book pages.

The Chinese invented movable type, which Europeans later used in the printing press. Books, magazines, newspapers, and other paper goods are still printed on presses, using techniques pioneered by the Chinese.

▶ CRITICAL THINKING
Speculating What physical skill would a block printer need to have?

Reading **HELP**DESK

Academic Vocabulary

method a way of doing something
transfer to copy from one surface to another by contact

Printing also led to the invention of paper currency. During the Tang dynasty, both rice production and trade greatly increased. Chinese traders needed more money to carry out business. The Chinese already produced copper coins, but they could not make enough coins to support the empire's economy.

In A.D. 1024, during the Song dynasty, the Chinese began to print the world's first paper money as a way to benefit traders. It still had the value of coin money, and it was lighter to carry. The use of paper money helped both the economy and cities to grow.

Gunpowder and Ships

Gunpowder was another Chinese invention created during the Tang dynasty. Gunpowder was used in explosives and weapons, such as the fire lance. This invention worked somewhat like a gun. It could shoot a mix of flames and objects a distance of 40 yards (36.6 m). The fire lance helped make China's army a powerful fighting force. The Chinese also used gunpowder to make fireworks.

Different Chinese inventions helped increase long-distance trade. The Chinese built large ships with rudders and sails, which helped with steering. About A.D. 1150, Chinese inventors perfected the magnetic compass. This compass helped Chinese sailors navigate their ships' locations and sail farther from land. As a result of these inventions, the Chinese were able to sail to Southeast Asia, India, and other places to the west.

Thinking Like a **HISTORIAN**

Drawing Conclusions

Historians have concluded that technological developments expanded China's power during the Tang dynasty. Identify one technological advancement of the Tang dynasty. Then draw a conclusion about how the advancement affected China's economy, culture, or government. Share your conclusions with the class. For more information about drawing conclusions, read *What Does a Historian Do?*

The Tang capital city of Changan had a population of about one million people at its peak. The royal palace, shown below, was surrounded by park lands. It is thought to be one of the largest palaces ever built.

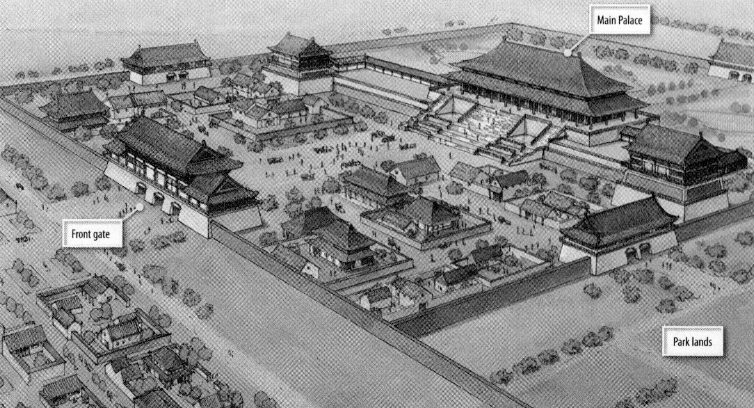

LESSON 2

ENGAGE

Analyzing Visuals Have students skim the lesson for illustrations of the following inventions: steel, movable type, gunpowder, paper money, and the navigational compass.

Allow students to meet with a partner to brainstorm what the inventions have in common. Explain that all the inventions were developed in China during the imperial period.

Tell students that in this lesson, they will learn how China's economy changed under the Tang dynasty and how important inventions were developed. They will also discover why the Tang and Song dynasties were a golden age of the arts, as well as a time of important economic growth and technological advances.

TEACH & ASSESS

1 Economic Growth

GUIDING QUESTION ***How did China's economy change under the Tang and Song dynasties?***

GRAPHIC ORGANIZER **Explaining** As a class, discuss how trade grew during the Tang dynasty. Point out that improving the roads and canals, reopening the Silk Road, and opening new trade routes and ports were crucial steps to increasing trade in China.

Then, have students work alone or in pairs to begin filling in the Taking Notes web diagram that appears on the first page of the lesson. Students will refer to the organizer later in this lesson.

INTERACTIVE WHITEBOARD ACTIVITY
Identifying To help students understand the area covered by China's trade routes, as well as the variety of goods shipped along them, have them complete the Interactive Whiteboard Activity "Traveling the Silk Road."

SLIDE SHOW **Synthesizing** Students may be interested in knowing how the imperial Chinese grew and made silk, one of the most important products traded during the Tang and Song dynasties. Show them the interactive slide show "Silk Making," and lead them to answer the class discussion question. AL

2 Technological Advances

GUIDING QUESTION ***How did new inventions change China's society?***

LECTURE SLIDE **Summarizing** Show the lecture slide that lists the technological advancements covered in the lesson.

Have students form small groups. Assign each group a technology from the list, and ask students to summarize the information about it in a sentence or two.

Ask each group to share its summary with the class by writing it on the board. Students may draw on details they recorded in their Taking Notes graphic organizer in the lesson opener.

Determining Cause and Effect After students summarize the importance of each new technology, ask them to think about the effects the technology had on life in China. Ask each small group from the previous activity to identify at least two effects of their technology.

Ask:

- **Why did coal become an important source of fuel?** *(After burning wood for centuries to cook food and heat homes, fewer trees were left to burn for fuel.)*
- **How did using steel to make weapons and tools improve life in China?** *(It made the army stronger and workers more efficient.)*
- **How did woodblock printing affect life in China?** *(It made the printing of books easier so ideas and information could spread throughout China.)*
- **Why was gunpowder an important invention?** *(It transformed the way wars were fought and gave the army more power.)*
- **What effect did improvements in shipbuilding and navigation have in China?** *(These improvements enabled Chinese ships to travel overseas for trade and exploration.)* AL

Assessing Lead students in a class discussion about which was the most important technological invention in China and why. Remind students to back up their answers with information from the lesson.

INTERACTIVE WORKSHEET
Economics of History Activity
Help students understand the impact of printed paper money on the Chinese economy by having students read and complete the Economics of History Activity as homework for this lesson.

3 Literature and the Arts

GUIDING QUESTION ***Why were the Tang and Song dynasties a golden age of literature and the arts?***

SLIDE SHOW **Expressing** Show students the slide with the poems of Li Bo. Read the poems aloud in an expressive voice. If necessary, read the poems more than once.

Then, ask students to respond to your reading orally or in a quickwrite. Have volunteers share their responses.

Ask:

- **What did you feel as you listened to the poems?**
- **What did you picture in your mind as I read the poems aloud?** AL

Guide students toward a generalization about imperial Chinese poetry based on their responses to the poems. *(Students should recognize that poetry of the time expressed appreciation of nature and a sadness at the shortness of life.)* AL

Challenge students who are interested in the poetry to find other examples of the writings of Li Bo and Du Fu. Ask students to read the samples to the class. BL

Making Inferences Refer students to the section titled "Landscape Painting."

Ask:

- **What do the landscape paintings tell you about the values and beliefs of the Chinese during the Tang and Song dynasties?** *(Students should suggest that peace, calm, nature, and beauty were important to the Chinese.)* BL

Answers for pages 482–485

P. 482 Taking Notes Economy: new kinds of rice, greater crop yields, increased trade on new roads and waterways, paper money; **Technology:** steel, woodblock printing, movable type, gunpowder, ships, magnetic compass; **The Arts:** poetry, landscape painting, porcelain

P. 483 CRITICAL THINKING Answers may vary. Possible answers: because the silk is so delicate that the process can't be done by machines, or silk is still expensive today because it is produced only by silkworms and is often still made by hand

P. 483 ☑ PROGRESS CHECK Farming advances led to larger crop yields. With more food available, China's population grew.

P. 484 CRITICAL THINKING Sample answer: A block printer would need to be able to carve wood.

In time, many of these Chinese inventions would have a great effect on Europe. For example, printing made it possible to publish books in large quantities. Gunpowder changed how wars were fought. The magnetic compass enabled Europeans to explore the world.

PROGRESS CHECK

Analyzing Why was the Chinese invention of printing important?

3 Literature and the Arts

GUIDING QUESTION *Why were the Tang and Song dynasties a golden age of literature and the arts?*

The Tang and Song dynasties were a golden age of Chinese culture. The invention of woodblock printing helped make literature more available and popular. Art, especially landscape painting, flourished during this period. Chinese rulers supported artists and writers. They invited them to live and work in the capital city of Changan.

According to legend, Li Bo drowned after reaching for the moon's reflection in the water beside his boat. He most likely died, poor and out of favor, in eastern China.

An Age of Poetry

The Tang dynasty is regarded as the great age of poetry in China. The best known Chinese writers of this time are poets. Chinese poets often expressed a Daoist appreciation of the world. They wrote about the beauty of nature, the changes of the seasons, and the joys of friendship. They also expressed sadness at the shortness of life.

Li Bo (LEE BWAW) was one of the most popular poets of the Tang dynasty. Known for leading a carefree life, Li Bo wrote poems about nature. His poem below is one of the best-known poems in China. For years, the Chinese have memorized it. Its title is "Alone Looking at the Mountain."

PRIMARY SOURCE

> ❝All the birds have flown up and gone;
> A lonely cloud floats leisurely by.
> We never tire of looking at each other—
> Only the mountain and I.❞
>
> —from "Alone Looking at the Mountain," by Li Bo

Reading HELPDESK

calligraphy artistic handwriting

Another favorite Tang poet was Du Fu (DOO FOO). He was a poor civil servant who faced many hardships. During Du Fu's lifetime, civil war raged throughout China. Food was scarce, and Du Fu nearly died of starvation. As a result, Du Fu often wrote about issues such as the problems of the poor, the unfairness of life, and the wastefulness of war. Du Fu wrote the poem below after an uprising left the capital city in ruins.

PRIMARY SOURCE

> ❝Behind those red gates
> meat and wine are left to spoil
> outside lie the bones
> of people who starved and froze.❞
>
> —from "Five Hundred Words About My Journey to Fengxian," by Du Fu

Landscape Painting

During the Song dynasty, many Chinese artists painted landscapes. However, they did not try to show the exact appearance of places. Instead they tried to portray the "idea" of mountains, lakes, and other scenes. They left empty spaces in their paintings on purpose. This style reflects the Daoist belief that a person cannot know the whole truth about something. Daoism is the belief that people should turn to nature and give up their worldly concerns.

This landscape (left)—painted in the 1100s—shows the Daoist love of nature. The lettering of the Chinese poems (right) is as delicate as the images in the art.

Daoism also influenced the way people are portrayed in landscape paintings. Humans are shown as very small figures in a natural landscape. The paintings express the idea that people are part of nature but do not control it. People are only one part of a much larger natural setting.

Chinese painters often wrote poems on their works. They used a brush and ink to write beautiful characters called **calligraphy** (kuh•LIH•gruh•fee).

Porcelain

During the Tang dynasty, Chinese artisans became skilled in making porcelain. As you may recall, porcelain is a ceramic made of fine clay baked at very high temperatures. Because porcelain later came from China to the West, people today sometimes call porcelain "china."

Porcelain can be made into figurines, vases, cups, and plates. An Arab traveler in A.D. 851 described Chinese porcelain:

PRIMARY SOURCE

> ❝There is in China a very fine clay from which are made vases having the transparency [clearness] of glass bottles; water in these vases is visible through them, and yet they are made of clay.❞
>
> —from *Account of Voyages Made by Arabs and Persians in India and China*

This bowl is Chinese porcelain. The word *porcelain* comes from French and Italian words for "shell," which the pottery resembles.

Methods for making porcelain spread to other parts of the world. They finally reached Europe in the A.D. 1700s.

PROGRESS CHECK

Identifying What themes did Chinese poets often write about?

LESSON 2 REVIEW

Review Vocabulary

1. What natural material do you need in order to make *porcelain*?
2. How is *calligraphy* similar to painting?

Answer the Guiding Questions

3. ***Describing*** How did the reopening of the Silk Road affect the economy and culture of China?
4. ***Explaining*** How did the printing of paper money help the economy of China?
5. ***Speculating*** Why did the rulers of the Tang and Song dynasties support the arts and literature?
6. ***Analyzing*** Which technological development had a greater impact on the Chinese empire—printing or gunpowder? Explain why.
7. **EXPOSITORY WRITING** You are an imperial scholar-official. Your job is to report to the emperor about changes taking place. Which technological, economic, or cultural development do you think the emperor should know about? Write a short report that describes an important development. Support your ideas with at least two reasons.

NOTES

LESSON 2 (cont.)

CLOSE & REFLECT

Summarizing Have students work in small groups to decide on the type of graphic organizer that would best help them identify and organize all the examples of China's cultural, technological, and economic advances during the Tang and Song dynasties. If necessary, ask leading questions to guide students. AL ELL

Have groups share their graphic organizers with the class. Ask students to explain their organizing principles and the information within the organizers.

Have students complete the Lesson 2 Review.

BACKGROUND KNOWLEDGE

How Gunpowder Works

Gunpowder consists of saltpeter (or potassium nitrate), sulfur, and carbon. Saltpeter makes up about 75 percent of the mixture. It produces oxygen when lit. This oxygen is needed to fuel fire. The sulfur and carbon are combustible. Together, the ingredients in gunpowder create enough of a contained explosion to quickly propel shot from a gun barrel.

Unfortunately, the carbon residue needs to be cleaned out of the barrel if the gun is to continue to shoot round balls with accuracy. Future improvements addressed this problem, but the basic formula developed by the Chinese is still effective.

IF YOU HAVE MORE TIME . . .

Explore Chinese Art

SLIDE SHOW **Describing** Review with students the Lesson 1 slide show images of Chinese art, pottery, and metalwork. In addition, show students examples of Chinese landscape paintings and calligraphy from the imperial period that you find online or in a book.

Point out how the objects' shapes were inspired by nature and the care with which the objects were crafted. If you show landscapes, be sure students recognize that nature is grand and humans are small.

Ask students these questions:

- **What words would you use to describe the objects?** *(detailed, intricate, polished)*
- **What do the objects tell you about how the Chinese felt about nature?** *(Nature was important; it inspired their art.)* AL

Practice Chinese-Style Poetry and Painting

Expressing Have students express their understanding of Chinese poetry by writing poems in the style of Li Bo or Du Fu. Ask volunteers to share their poems with the class.

If art supplies are readily available, you could also choose to have students create Chinese-style landscape paintings.

Explore How Advancements From Imperial China Are Used Today

LECTURE SLIDE **Making Connections** Show again the lecture slide that lists the technological advancements covered in the lesson. Have students form small groups. You may choose to have students re-form the groups from the Summarizing activity.

Assign each group one advancement from the list.

Ask: How is this advancement used today?

Have students conduct research to answer the question. Students should share the results of their research in written or oral form and provide a written bibliography of their sources.

Demonstrate Calligraphy in English

Applying Find calligraphy pens at a local craft or art supply store. Tell students that the letters of the English alphabet can also be written using calligraphy. Instead of brushes, special pens are used to create the fancy lettering.

Show students the calligraphy pens, pointing out the flat shape of the pens' tips. Explain that by holding the pen at an angle when you write, you can create lettering in English that is similar in style to Chinese calligraphy.

Following the directions on the pen package, write a word or two so students can see what English-language calligraphy looks like. *(Note: Calligraphy pens are usually not whiteboard-friendly so you will need to hang a piece of butcher paper or poster board on the whiteboard before writing.)*

If you have enough calligraphy pens to go around, you could have students practice calligraphy writing on their own, perhaps by writing their names or a short phrase.

Answers for pages 486–488

P. 486 ☑ PROGRESS CHECK The printing process made books readily available, which meant ideas could spread throughout China. The printing of paper money helped support China's growing economy.

P. 488 ☑ PROGRESS CHECK Chinese poets often wrote about themes of the beauty of nature, changes in seasons, the joys of friendship, and the shortness of life, as well as the problems of the poor and the wastefulness of war.

LESSON 2 REVIEW

1. You need fine clay in order to make porcelain.
2. Calligraphy and painting use brushes.
3. The reopening of the Silk Road made it easier for goods to travel between China and other parts of Asia. Because more goods were sold, the economy of China improved. Increased trade also meant that goods and ideas were exchanged with other places.
4. Because printed money was easier to make and carry than coins, more money became available for traders to use in business. As a result, the economy grew.
5. Students should suggest that the arts reflect the ideas and values of a culture. Rulers would have wanted poets and artists to create works that celebrated Chinese landscape, people, and beliefs.
6. Students may suggest that printing had a greater impact because printed books helped spread ideas and educate people. Others may suggest that gunpowder was more important because it gave the Chinese an advantage in war. Students should give clear reasons for their answers.
7. Students' reports should identify one development and give at least two reasons why it was important. For example, students might focus on the use of coal to make steel. They should explain that coal made it possible to form steel, an important material for crafting strong tools and weapons. The stronger tools and weapons allowed China's workers and soldiers to be more efficient.

NOTES

networks
There's More Online!
GRAPHIC ORGANIZER Mongols in China
VIDEO

Lesson 3

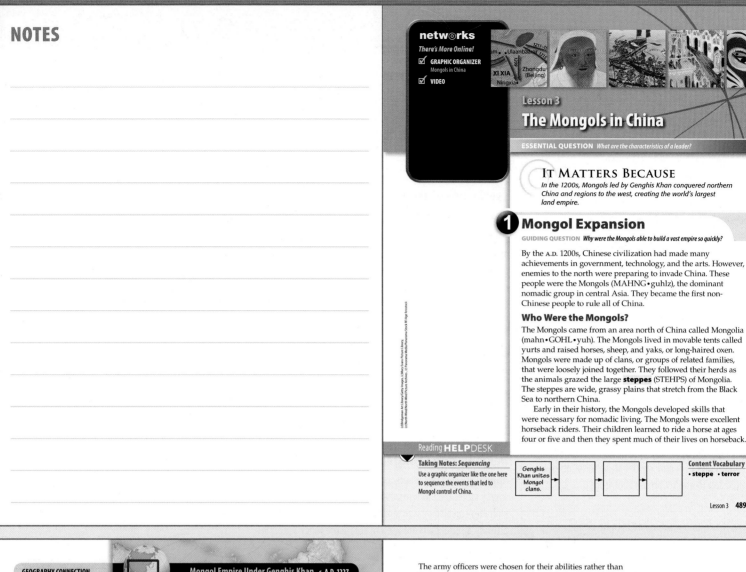

The Mongols in China

ESSENTIAL QUESTION *What are the characteristics of a leader?*

It Matters Because

In the 1200s, Mongols led by Genghis Khan conquered northern China and regions to the west, creating the world's largest land empire.

1 Mongol Expansion

GUIDING QUESTION *Why were the Mongols able to build a vast empire so quickly?*

By the A.D. 1200s, Chinese civilization had made many achievements in government, technology, and the arts. However, enemies to the north were preparing to invade China. These people were the Mongols (MAHNG•guhlz), the dominant nomadic group in central Asia. They became the first non-Chinese people to rule all of China.

Who Were the Mongols?

The Mongols came from an area north of China called Mongolia (mahn•GOHL•yuh). The Mongols lived in movable tents called yurts and raised horses, sheep, and yaks, or long-haired oxen. Mongols were made up of clans, or groups of related families, that were loosely joined together. They followed their herds as the animals grazed the large **steppes** (STEHPS) of Mongolia. The steppes are wide, grassy plains that stretch from the Black Sea to northern China.

Early in their history, the Mongols developed skills that were necessary for nomadic living. The Mongols were excellent horseback riders. Their children learned to ride a horse at ages four or five and then they spent much of their lives on horseback.

Reading HELPDESK

Taking Notes: ***Sequencing***

Use a graphic organizer like the one here to sequence the events that led to Mongol control of China.

Genghis Khan unites Mongol clans. → → →

Content Vocabulary
• steppe • terror

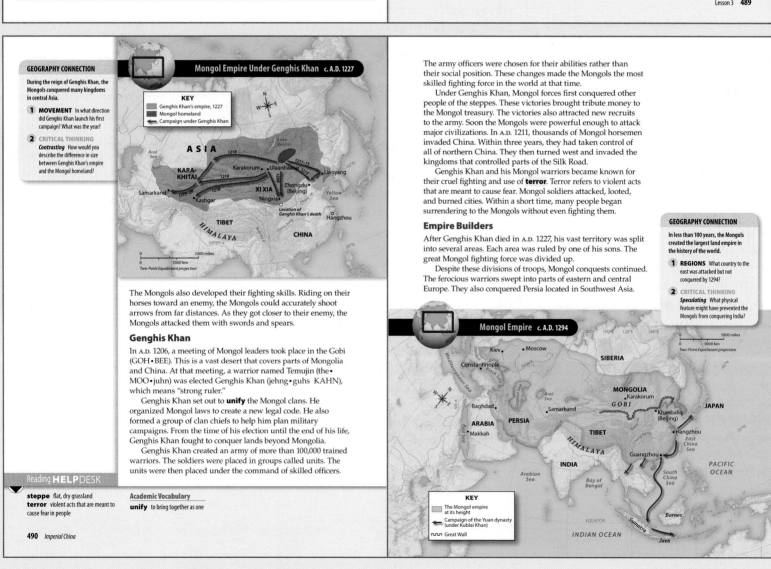

GEOGRAPHY CONNECTION

During the reign of Genghis Khan, the Mongols conquered many kingdoms in central Asia.

1. **MOVEMENT** In what direction did Genghis Khan launch his first campaign? What was the year?
2. **CRITICAL THINKING** ***Contrasting*** How would you describe the difference in size between Genghis Khan's empire and the Mongol homeland?

Mongol Empire Under Genghis Khan c. A.D. 1227

The Mongols also developed their fighting skills. Riding on their horses toward an enemy, the Mongols could accurately shoot arrows from far distances. As they got closer to their enemy, the Mongols attacked them with swords and spears.

Genghis Khan

In A.D. 1206, a meeting of Mongol leaders took place in the Gobi (GOH•BEE). This is a vast desert that covers parts of Mongolia and China. At that meeting, a warrior named Temujin (the•MOO•juhn) was elected Genghis Khan (jehng•guhs KAHN), which means "strong ruler."

Genghis Khan set out to **unify** the Mongol clans. He organized Mongol laws to create a new legal code. He also formed a group of clan chiefs to help him plan military campaigns. From the time of his election until the end of his life, Genghis Khan fought to conquer lands beyond Mongolia.

Genghis Khan created an army of more than 100,000 trained warriors. The soldiers were placed in groups called units. The units were then placed under the command of skilled officers.

Reading HELPDESK

steppe flat, dry grassland
terror violent acts that are meant to cause fear in people

Academic Vocabulary
unify to bring together as one

The army officers were chosen for their abilities rather than their social position. These changes made the Mongols the most skilled fighting force in the world at that time.

Under Genghis Khan, Mongol forces first conquered other people of the steppes. These victories brought tribute money to the Mongol treasury. The victories also attracted new recruits to the army. Soon the Mongols were powerful enough to attack major civilizations. In A.D. 1211, thousands of Mongol horsemen invaded China. Within three years, they had taken control of all of northern China. They then turned west and invaded the kingdoms that controlled parts of the Silk Road.

Genghis Khan and his Mongol warriors became known for their cruel fighting and use of **terror**. Terror refers to violent acts that are meant to cause fear. Mongol soldiers attacked, looted, and burned cities. Within a short time, many people began surrendering to the Mongols without even fighting them.

Empire Builders

After Genghis Khan died in A.D. 1227, his vast territory was split into several areas. Each area was ruled by one of his sons. The great Mongol fighting force was divided up.

Despite these divisions of troops, Mongol conquests continued. The ferocious warriors swept into parts of eastern and central Europe. They also conquered Persia located in Southwest Asia.

GEOGRAPHY CONNECTION

In less than 100 years, the Mongols created the largest land empire in the history of the world.

1. **REGIONS** What country to the east was attacked but not conquered by 1294?
2. **CRITICAL THINKING** ***Speculating*** What physical feature might have prevented the Mongols from conquering India?

Mongol Empire c. A.D. 1294

LESSON 3

ENGAGE

MAP **Identifying** Begin by showing students the interactive versions of the maps of the Mongol Empire. Point out that the territory in the Mongolian empire was acquired over a period of about 50 years, between 1206 and 1260.

Point out the major cities on the map. Explain that Khanbaliq is the site of China's modern capital, Beijing.

Ask students these questions:

- **In geographical terms, how did Genghis Khan expand the Mongol Empire?** *(He and his troops expanded the empire in nearly all directions, moving west, south, and southeast from the Mongol homeland.)*
- **Using geographical terms, how would you describe the Mongol Empire of Kublai Khan?** *(It extended from the Pacific Ocean in the east to eastern Europe in the west. It also extended from Siberia in the north to the Himalaya in the south. It covered almost all of Asia and parts of Europe.)*

Tell students that in this lesson they will learn how and why the Mongols were able to take over most of Asia in less than a century. They will also learn how the Mongols ruled the Chinese empire.

TEACH & ASSESS

1 Mongol Expansion

GUIDING QUESTION *Why were the Mongols able to build a vast empire so quickly?*

GRAPHIC ORGANIZER

Identifying Have students refer to the section "Mongol Expansion" to create and fill in a time line of events. Specifically, have them identify events that occurred in 1206, 1211, 1227, 1258, and 1260. Remind students to get details from their textbook. They may also use their time lines to help complete the Taking Notes activity in the lesson opener.

INTERACTIVE WHITEBOARD ACTIVITY

Have students use the information in the lesson to complete the Interactive Whiteboard Activity "Mongol Warriors." Students may work alone or in pairs.

2 Mongol Conquest of China

GUIDING QUESTION *How did the Mongols rule the Chinese?*

Analyzing Have students work in small groups to identify a graphic organizer that will best help them consider the "good" and "bad" leadership traits of the Mongols. Suggest that students create a T-chart, with one column labeled "Good Traits" and the other labeled "Bad Traits."

Remind students that the Mongols demonstrated certain leadership qualities during their drive to conquer, but they used a different set of skills to rule the empire. To help students, **ask:**

- **How did the Mongols get people to give up their lands?** *(They used terror; they were fierce fighters who burned and looted cities; they frightened people into giving up their lands.)*
- **What kind of rulers were they? How did they treat their subjects?** *(They were tolerant of different religions and admired by all cultures. They were peaceful rulers.)* AL ELL

Making Connections Ask students to compare the leadership traits of the Mongols to those of modern leaders they know about or have studied.

Ask:

Which of the Mongols' traits are desirable in a modern leader? Which are not? *(Students might point out that tolerance is a good trait, but using terror is not.)* BL

INTERACTIVE WORKSHEET

Primary Source Activity

Identifying Points of View Read aloud Polo's description of Khanbaliq in an expressive voice. Explain that Marco Polo's stories of imperial China provided many Europeans with their first glimpse of China and Chinese culture. To Europeans, Polo's tales of China would have sounded amazing.

Help students consider how outsiders viewed China during Mongol rule by having them complete the Primary Sources Activity for Lesson 3.

Ask:

Do you think the Europeans' tales of China's wealth were exaggerated or true? *(Students might suspect that some of the details were exaggerated, but the tone of respect and awe seems real.)*

Listing Have students identify the items that China traded with other parts of Asia and the West. Write their answers on the board. *(China exported tea, silk, porcelain, steel, gunpowder, and the compass; China imported silver, carpets, cotton, and spices.)*

Making Generalizations Ask students to make a generalization about China's trade during the Mongol era. *(It was thriving and widespread.)* ELL

Have students complete the Lesson 3 Review.

CLOSE & REFLECT

Making Connections Refer students back to the maps used in the Engage activity. Make sure they understand that the Mongol Empire was the largest land empire in history. Then have students review their lists of leadership traits. Lead students in a discussion of the traits that Mongol leaders would have relied on most while ruling such a vast empire.

Answers for pages 489–491

P. 489 Taking Notes Box #1 Genghis Khan unites Mongol clans. **Box #2** Mongols conquer northern China. **Box #3** Kublai Khan establishes capital at Khanbaliq. **Box #4** Kublai Khan conquers southern China.

P. 490 GEOGRAPHY CONNECTION

1. Genghis Khan launched his first campaign to the south in 1209.
2. CRITICAL THINKING Genghis Khan's empire is about nine times larger than the Mongol homeland.

P. 491 GEOGRAPHY CONNECTION

1. The Mongols attacked but could not conquer Japan.
2. CRITICAL THINKING The Himalaya might have prevented the Mongols from conquering India.

BIOGRAPHY

Genghis Khan (c. A.D. 1167–1227)

Genghis Khan's father, the Mongol chief Yisugei, named his son Temujin. According to folklore, Temujin had a large blood clot in his right hand, which meant he was destined to become a great warrior. In 1206, 40-year-old Temujin successfully took command of the Mongol forces in the Gobi. It is believed that he was inspired to rule because he grew up extremely poor, and his father was murdered by his enemies.

▶ CRITICAL THINKING

Determining Cause and Effect What about the personal life of Genghis Khan would have led him to want to rule?

In A.D. 1258, the Mongols captured the Muslim city of Baghdad. The Mongols then moved into Syria and Palestine to Egypt. The Muslim leaders of Egypt stopped the Mongol's advance in A.D. 1260.

All of these different areas formed a vast Mongol empire. Mongol rule stretched from the Pacific Ocean in the east to eastern Europe in the west and from Siberia in the north to the Himalaya in the south. The Mongols created the largest land empire in history.

The Mongols caused a great deal of damage to the lands they conquered, but they also brought stability. This stability encouraged trade and closer contact between Asia and Europe. Many of the great trade routes between Asia and Europe crossed Mongol lands. The Mongols grew wealthy because they taxed the products that were traded along these roads.

The Mongols admired the cultures they conquered, and sometimes they adopted their beliefs and customs. For example, the Mongols in Southwest Asia accepted Islam and adopted Arab, Persian, and Turkish ways.

The Mongols also learned from the Chinese. As they fought Chinese troops, the Mongols learned about gunpowder and its use as an explosive. They saw the Chinese use the fire lance, a weapon that the Chinese later developed into the gun and cannon. Adopting gunpowder and the fire lance from the Chinese, the Mongols became even more frightening to their opponents.

☑ PROGRESS CHECK

Determining Cause and Effect How were the Mongols influenced by their opponents?

2 Mongol Conquest of China

GUIDING QUESTION *How did the Mongols rule the Chinese?*

In A.D. 1260, the grandson of Genghis Khan, Kublai, became the new Mongol ruler. Kublai Khan (KOO•BLUH KAHN) continued the conquest of China that his grandfather had begun. In A.D. 1264, Kublai established his capital at Khanbaliq—the city of the khan—in northern China. Today, the modern city of Beijing (BAY•JIHNG) is located on the site of the former Mongol capital.

Bridgeman Art Library/Getty Images

Reading **HELP**DESK

Reading Strategy: *Predicting*

When you predict, you use clues in the text and your own knowledge to make an educated guess. Skim the headings in "Mongol Conquest of China." What do you think you will learn? Now read the passages. Were your predictions correct?

The Mongols invaded other areas after conquering China. Despite a fleet of warships built by the Koreans, the planned Mongol invasion of Japan ended in failure.

Mary Evans Picture Library

Mongols and Chinese

In 1271, Kublai Kahn decided he would control all of China. By A.D. 1279, Kublai Khan finished conquering southern China. He brought an end to the Song dynasty and declared himself emperor. Kublai Khan started the Yuan (YWAN) dynasty. The term *Yuan* means "beginning." The Yuan dynasty would last only about 100 years. Kublai Khan would rule for 30 of those years, until his death in A.D. 1294.

To keep tight control of these new lands, Kublai appointed Mongol leaders to top jobs in China. He also kept some Chinese officials in positions of power.

The Mongol culture was quite different from the Chinese culture. The Mongols had their own language, laws, and customs. These characteristics separated them from the Chinese people they ruled. Mongols lived apart from the Chinese and did not mix with them socially.

Government and Religion

In government affairs, the Yuan **regime** did not use civil service examinations as was previously done in China. Government jobs were open to non-Chinese people, including Mongols and Turks. However, the Yuan rulers respected Confucian writings and allowed Chinese scholar-officials to keep their posts.

This colored lithograph was taken from a manuscript that described Marco Polo's journeys. It shows him leaving Venice in 1338.

▶ CRITICAL THINKING

Explaining Why were Marco Polo's travels important to Europeans?

Like many Chinese, the Mongols in China practiced Buddhism, but they were respectful of other religions. For example, Kublai Khan encouraged Christians, Muslims, and Hindus from outside China to practice their faiths.

Under Mongol rule, China reached the height of its wealth and power. Foreigners were drawn to its capital city. Although they were foreigners, the Mongols gradually won the support of many Chinese people. Some Chinese appreciated the order and prosperity that the Mongols brought to the country. Foreign visitors were attracted to China and reached it by traveling along the Silk Road.

Marco Polo

One of the most famous European travelers to reach China was Marco Polo. He came from the city of Venice in Italy. Polo lived in the capital of Khanbaliq during the reign of Kublai Khan. He wrote his impressions of the magnificent appearance of this city:

North Wind/North Wind Picture Archives

Reading **HELP**DESK

Academic Vocabulary

regime rulers during a given period of time

PRIMARY SOURCE

> "The streets are so straight and wide that you can see right along them from end to end and from one gate to the other. And up and down the city there are beautiful palaces, and many great and fine hostelries [inns], and fine houses in great numbers."
>
> —from "Concerning the City of Cambaluc [Khanbaliq]" by Marco Polo

Kublai was fascinated by Marco Polo's stories about his journeys. For about 16 years, Polo was a privileged resident of China. Kublai sent him on trips all over the region to gather information and carry out business. For some of those years, Polo ruled the Chinese city of Yangzhou. When Polo returned to Italy, he wrote a book about his adventures.

Trade and Empire

The Mongol empire stretched from China to eastern Europe. As a result, Mongol China prospered from increased overland trade with many parts of the world. The Yuan dynasty also built ships and expanded seagoing trade. China traded tea, silk, and porcelain in exchange for goods such as silver, carpets, cotton, and spices. Muslims and Europeans also took Chinese discoveries back to their homelands.

Mongol armies advanced into Vietnam and northern Korea. The rulers of Korea, called the Koryo (koh•RY•oh), remained in power because they agreed to Mongol control. The Mongols forced thousands of Koreans to build warships. The Mongols used these ships in two attempts to invade Japan. Both voyages ended in failure when huge storms destroyed much of the fleet.

☑ PROGRESS CHECK

Describing What was Marco Polo's reaction to seeing China's cities?

LESSON 3 REVIEW

Review Vocabulary

1. If you were to visit the Mongolian *steppes*, what would you likely see?

Answer the Guiding Questions

2. ***Identifying*** Why did trading improve under Mongolian rule? Give examples of goods that were traded and how they were traded.
3. ***Analyzing*** How did the Mongols use terror in their conquests?
4. ***Summarizing*** How did the Chinese benefit from being ruled by the Mongols?
5. ***Evaluating*** Make a list of the leadership qualities of Genghis Khan and evaluate him as a leader.
6. **EXPOSITORY WRITING** Imagine that you are Genghis Khan. You are concerned about how your empire will be ruled after your death. Write a journal entry in which you record advice that you want your family members to follow.

LESSON 3 (cont.)

BACKGROUND KNOWLEDGE

How Big the Mongol Army Really Was

The Mongol army was usually described as quite large. In actuality, the Mongol army was often smaller than the armies they fought against. However, they used tactics to fool their enemies into thinking they had more soldiers than they did.

The Mongol army was almost entirely cavalry. A group of 10,000 soldiers was a common size. Each soldier had three extra horses, or remounts. The Mongols made straw dummies to sit on the remounts. Sometimes they had captives ride on the horses, or they used captives as infantry, leading them into new cities or towns ahead of the cavalry. With these tricks, an army of 10,000 Mongols could look like 50,000 soldiers.

IF YOU HAVE MORE TIME . . .

Discuss the Wealth of the Mongol Empire

Making Connections Look online or in books for images that show the wealth and style of the Mongol culture in China during the late thirteenth and early fourteenth centuries. Share these images with the class.

Explain that under Kublai Khan, China reached a new height of wealth and influence. Most of the Silk Road was now under Mongol protection, and trade flourished. In addition, Europeans and other outsiders traveled to China for the first time.

Ask:

Why is a place more likely to be enriched economically and culturally when its people regularly have contact with the outside world? *(Students should suggest that by trading ideas and goods with outsiders, a place and its people gain experiences and wealth.)*

Then, ask students to think about how empires, such as the Mongol Empire, display wealth. Write student responses on the board.

Next, direct the discussion to answer why empires display wealth. *(Student answers may vary, but they should recognize that power is often displayed through wealth.)*

Students might compare the Mongolian display of wealth with that of other cultures in the past or present. Have students draw on their knowledge of history and on their personal experiences to participate in the discussion. BL

Describe the Relationship Between the Mongols and the Chinese

Discussing Lead a class discussion of the relationship between the Mongols and the Chinese. Students should note how the Chinese influenced the Mongols (such as the Mongols' use of gunpowder and the fire lance) and how the Mongols treated the Chinese.

Lead students to understand that the Chinese and the Mongols seemed to respect each other even though they did not mix socially. Point out that the peace and prosperity the Mongols brought to China caused many Chinese to support the Mongol leaders. AL

Explore the Travels of Marco Polo by Writing Diary Entries

Illustrating Direct students back to the Chapter Opener map of the Mongol Empire in 1294. Have a student volunteer locate the route that Marco Polo took in his journeys.

Ask students to identify what Marco Polo might have seen during his travels. Students should draw on their knowledge from previous chapters when they speculate about Polo's experiences outside of China.

Have students write five diary entries from the perspective of Marco Polo or a member of Polo's entourage. Each entry should be at least one page in length and describe an experience in a different location along the route.

Students should include sensory details that bring the experience to life. They might need to conduct research to discover some of these relevant details.

Encourage students to include illustrations in their diaries, such as maps or drawings of animals, buildings, or people's clothing. Students also might want to create and decorate a cover for their diaries.

You might choose to have students share their diaries with the class. You may also choose to display students' diaries in the classroom.

Answers for pages 492–495

P. 492 CRITICAL THINKING Genghis Khan grew up poor, and his father was murdered. These experiences could have made Genghis Khan want the wealth and power that a ruler has.

P. 492 ☑ PROGRESS CHECK The Mongols sometimes adopted the technology and the customs of their opponents. For example, many Mongols accepted Islam and adopted Arab, Persian, and Turkish ways.

P. 492 Reading Strategy Students' predictions and reflections should demonstrate accurate comprehension of the section's heads and content.

P. 494 CRITICAL THINKING Marco Polo's travels were important to Europeans because he brought back stories and goods from China, the likes of which had not been seen before by Europeans. He helped spark interest in acquiring Asian goods.

P. 495 ☑ PROGRESS CHECK Marco Polo was amazed by the beauty and organization of Chinese cities.

LESSON 3 REVIEW

1. You would see wide-open, grassy areas.
2. Trade improved because the territories ruled by Mongols stretched from China to Eastern Europe. As a result, all trade routes were under one rule and would not be blocked by enemies. Examples of goods that were traded from other areas of Asia include silver, cotton, and spices. Tea, silk, and porcelain as well as gunpowder, steel, and compasses were sent from China to Europe and elsewhere.
3. Mongols used violence and destruction (looting, burning, and attacking cities) to terrorize enemies and force them to surrender.
4. Although the Mongols were fierce conquerors, they established stability and safe trade routes. They ruled as a separate class but allowed many Chinese scholar-officials to keep their government posts. They also allowed those they conquered to practice their faiths.
5. Students should note that Genghis Khan was disciplined, tough, organized, and willing to take risks. He understood the value of loyalty and appreciated people for their abilities, not for their family ties. Students should understand that he was an effective leader.
6. Students should write from the perspective of Genghis Khan by using the first-person pronoun to express his thoughts. Journal entries should include details that capture Khan's thoughts about conquering and ruling an empire. For example, as imagined by students, Khan might recommend using terror to conquer new lands and peoples.

Monkey

by Wu Cheng'en (c. A.D. 1505–1580)

Wu Cheng'en was a writer during the Ming Dynasty. He wrote stories in a language that most Chinese could read. His Monkey King stories are his most popular works. These stories describe Monkey King's encounters with gods, demons, fairies, and masters during his travels.

The Monkey King stories are allegories. They have a hidden meaning, such as a moral or a lesson. The characters, setting, and plot in an allegory are often symbols. As you read the excerpt, think about what Monkey symbolizes.

In the excerpt, the clever Monkey has been crowned king, but he is unhappy. He travels in search of someone who can teach him about the meaning of life. Monkey comes upon a teacher, the **Patriarch** (PAY • tree • AHRK), and his students. The Patriarch teaches Monkey some magical skills but warns Monkey to keep them secret. Later, Monkey joins the other students.

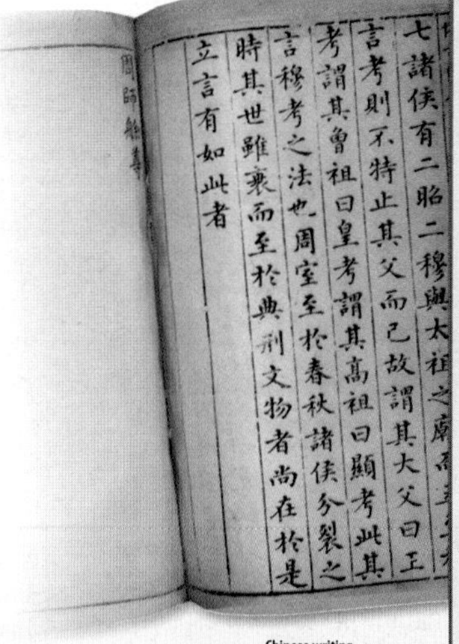

Chinese writing

> "If you saw someone turn into a tree, wouldn't you at once ask how it was done?"
>
> —from *Monkey: Folk Novel of China* by Wu Cheng'en

An actor playing the Monkey King searching for truth

PRIMARY SOURCE

The **disciples** (dih • SY • puhls) clapped and burst into loud applause. "Bravo, Monkey, bravo," they cried. There was such a **din** that the **Patriarch** came running out. . . . "Who's making all this noise?" he asked. . . . Monkey changed himself back into his true form and slipped in among the crowd, saying, "Reverend Master, we are doing lessons out here. I assure you there was no noise in particular." "You were all bawling," said the Patriarch angrily. "It didn't sound in the least like people studying. I want to know what you were doing here, shouting and laughing." "To tell the truth," said someone, "Monkey was showing us a **transformation** (TRANS • fuhr • MAY • SHUHN) just for fun. We told him to change into a pine tree, and he did it so well that we were all applauding him." . . . "Go away, all of you!" the Patriarch shouted. "And you, Monkey, come here! . . . Did you think I taught you [magic] in order that you might show off in front of other people? If you saw someone turn into a tree, wouldn't you at once ask how it was done? If others see you doing it, aren't they certain to ask you? If you are frightened to refuse, you will give the secret away; and if you refuse, you're very likely to be roughly handled. You're putting yourself in grave danger." "I'm terribly sorry," said Monkey. "I won't punish you," said the Patriarch, "but you can't stay here." Monkey burst into tears. "Where am I to go to?"

—From *Monkey: Folk Novel of China* by Wu Cheng'en

Vocabulary

disciples
students

din
loud noise

patriarch
an older male figure of authority, often within a religious community

transformation
a complete change

The mask of the adventurous Monkey King

Analyzing Literature DBQ

1. ***Describing*** What does Monkey do in front of the disciples?
2. ***Identifying Points of View*** Why is the Patriarch angry at Monkey after discovering what Monkey has done?
3. ***Synthesizing*** Do you agree with the Patriarch that showing off can lead to great danger? Why or why not?

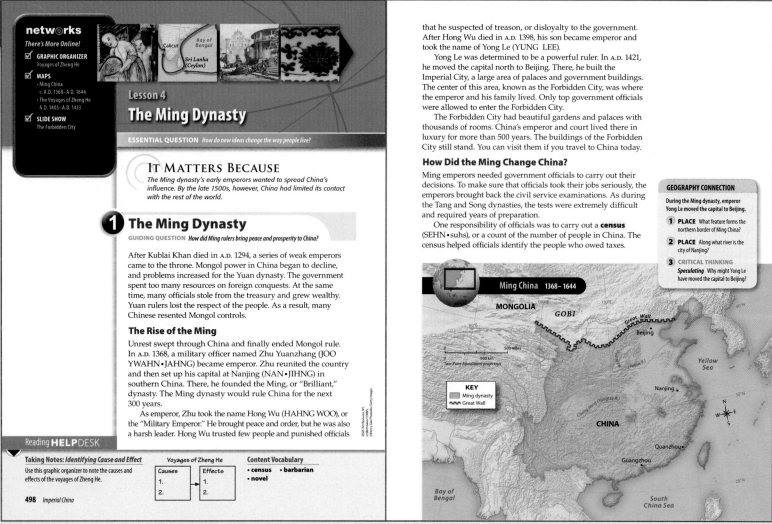

networks
There's More Online!

- GRAPHIC ORGANIZER
  Voyages of Zheng He
- MAPS
  - Ming China c. A.D. 1368–A.D. 1644
  - The Voyages of Zheng He A.D. 1405–A.D. 1433
- SLIDE SHOW
  The Forbidden City

Lesson 4

The Ming Dynasty

ESSENTIAL QUESTION *How do new ideas change the way people live?*

IT MATTERS BECAUSE

The Ming dynasty's early emperors wanted to spread China's influence. By the late 1500s, however, China had limited its contact with the rest of the world.

1 The Ming Dynasty

GUIDING QUESTION *How did Ming rulers bring peace and prosperity to China?*

After Kublai Khan died in A.D. 1294, a series of weak emperors came to the throne. Mongol power in China began to decline, and problems increased for the Yuan dynasty. The government spent too many resources on foreign conquests. At the same time, many officials stole from the treasury and grew wealthy. Yuan rulers lost the respect of the people. As a result, many Chinese resented Mongol controls.

The Rise of the Ming

Unrest swept through China and finally ended Mongol rule. In A.D. 1368, a military officer named Zhu Yuanzhang (JOO YWAHN • JAHNG) became emperor. Zhu reunited the country and then set up his capital at Nanjing (NAN • JIHNG) in southern China. There, he founded the Ming, or "Brilliant," dynasty. The Ming dynasty would rule China for the next 300 years.

As emperor, Zhu took the name Hong Wu (HAHNG WOO), or the "Military Emperor." He brought peace and order, but he was also a harsh leader. Hong Wu trusted few people and punished officials that he suspected of treason, or disloyalty to the government. After Hong Wu died in A.D. 1398, his son became emperor and took the name of Yong Le (YUNG LEE).

Yong Le was determined to be a powerful ruler. In A.D. 1421, he moved the capital north to Beijing. There, he built the Imperial City, a large area of palaces and government buildings. The center of this area, known as the Forbidden City, was where the emperor and his family lived. Only top government officials were allowed to enter the Forbidden City.

The Forbidden City had beautiful gardens and palaces with thousands of rooms. China's emperor and court lived there in luxury for more than 500 years. The buildings of the Forbidden City still stand. You can visit them if you travel to China today.

How Did the Ming Change China?

Ming emperors needed government officials to carry out their decisions. To make sure that officials took their jobs seriously, the emperors brought back the civil service examinations. As during the Tang and Song dynasties, the tests were extremely difficult and required years of preparation.

One responsibility of officials was to carry out a **census** (SEHN • suhs), or a count of the number of people in China. The census helped officials identify the people who owed taxes.

GEOGRAPHY CONNECTION

During the Ming dynasty, emperor Yong Le moved the capital to Beijing.

1. **PLACE** What feature forms the northern border of Ming China?
2. **PLACE** Along what river is the city of Nanjing?
3. **CRITICAL THINKING** *Speculating* Why might Yong Le have moved the capital to Beijing?

Ming China 1368–1644

0 500 miles
0 500 km
Two-Point Equidistant projection

KEY
Ming dynasty
Great Wall

Reading **HELP**DESK

Taking Notes: *Identifying Cause and Effect*
Use this graphic organizer to note the causes and effects of the voyages of Zheng He.

Voyages of Zheng He

Causes	Effects
1.	1.
2.	2.

Content Vocabulary
- census
- barbarian
- novel

ENGAGE

Explaining Check online or in a book for images of the Monkey King. Explain that the Monkey King is a mythical figure that was the subject of stories that were shared orally for centuries. In the 1500s, a Ming dynasty scholar-official named Wu Cheng'en-recorded them in a book.

Tell students that the stories are about a Buddhist monk who discovers the Monkey King while traveling through a desert in India. The Buddha has imprisoned the Monkey King under a rock. Even though the Monkey King has magical powers, he cannot escape without the monk's help. This is part of the Buddha's plan. The monk will now serve as the Monkey King's assistant while they undergo a series of dangerous quests.

Invite students to respond to the illustrations.

Ask: **What impression do you get of the Monkey King, based on the images?** *(The Monkey King likes bright colors and wears armor, like a soldier. He carries what looks like a weapon.)*

What characteristics do the images suggest the Monkey King possesses? *(Possible answers: He is intense and perhaps angry, but also playful. He is a fighter.)*

Tell students that in this lesson they will learn about allegories and read an excerpt from a Monkey King tale.

TEACH & ASSESS

LECTURE SLIDE **Classifying** Use the lecture slide to review the term *allegory*—a story in which the characters, settings, and events stand for or symbolize other ideas. Then ask students to brainstorm examples of allegories based on your definition. *(Students might recognize that the books* The Lion, the Witch and the Wardrobe *and* The Pilgrim's Progress, *the stories of Aesop's Fables, and the film* The Matrix *are allegories.)* Finally, tell them that the Monkey King story is also an allegory.

After students have read the excerpt, ask volunteers for evidence from the text that shows it is an allegory. Write students' responses on the board. *(Students should note that the Monkey King's magical powers, the lesson he learns at the end, and the fact that the Monkey King is not always what he seems suggest that the story is an allegory.)* Point out that allegories work on more than one level—a literal one and a symbolic one.

Challenge students to find the hidden or symbolic meaning of the story.

Ask: **What lesson might readers in imperial China have learned from the story?** *(Students should suggest that the point of the story is that people should not show off their talents or powers because others might misunderstand or become frightened or angry.)*

Have students write the next part of the story. Their writing should show what happens next to the Monkey King. It should also reflect students' understanding of what an allegory is. If students need help, have them work in groups to brainstorm what happens next in the story—where Monkey goes, whom he meets, and what other lessons he learns.

Challenge advanced learners to read more Monkey King stories and retell them in an entertaining and modern way. Students may also research the time period of the stories and provide relevant illustrations for them. BL

CLOSE & REFLECT

Ask volunteers to read aloud their story continuations. Ask the class to comment on the stories as allegories.

Answers to *Analyzing Literature* DBQ

1. He uses his powers to transform into a pine tree.
2. Monkey is showing off and putting himself in a dangerous situation.
3. Students' answers should suggest that there might be consequences for showing off. They should give an example from the excerpt. For instance, Monkey gained popularity by showing off but lost his home because the Patriarch was so angry and disappointed in him.

Teaching *The Ming Dynasty* (Student Edition pp. 498–503)

LESSON 4

ENGAGE

SLIDE SHOW **Describing** Show students images of the Forbidden City, which appear in the interactive slide show for Lesson 4.

Explain that the Forbidden City was where Ming emperors and their families lived. Ask students for their impressions of the buildings.

Ask:

What does the name of the city suggest about the Ming rulers? *(The city might have been off limits to anyone who was not important. The rulers kept themselves apart from the common people.)*

Tell students that in this lesson, they will learn how the Ming dynasty restored and changed China. They will also learn about the impact of sea voyages of exploration and trade on China and the reasons the government discontinued them.

TEACH & ASSESS

1 The Ming Dynasty

GUIDING QUESTION ***How did Ming rulers bring peace and prosperity to China?***

Summarizing Direct students' attention to "The Ming Dynasty" and **ask:**

- **What changes did the Ming rulers make?** *(They restored the civil service examination, carried out a census to collect taxes, rebuilt farms and canals, planted forests, paved roads, repaired the Grand Canal, and supported the silk industry.)*
- **What effect did these changes have on the population of China?** *(The changes made the government more effective and allowed farmers to grow and transport more food, so the population grew.)*

LECTURE SLIDE **Drawing Conclusions** Remind students that the civil service exams were based on Confucian teachings. Show them the lecture slide on Confucianism.

Ask:

How would following these principles affect the Chinese government? *(It would make the government run efficiently and thoughtfully; officials would be hard workers and strive to help others.)*

Answers for pages 498–499

P. 498 Taking Notes Causes: desire for trade and tribute; Chinese ship building
Effects: introduction of foreign elements; closing of borders

P. 499 GEOGRAPHY CONNECTION

1. The Great Wall forms the northern border of Ming China.
2. The city of Nanjing is along the Chang Jiang (Yangtze River).
3. CRITICAL THINKING Yong Le might have moved the capital to Beijing because Beijing was easier to defend or because it had been the capital under the Yuan (Mongol) dynasty.

The strong government of the early Ming emperors provided peace and security. As a result, the Chinese economy began to grow. Hong Wu rebuilt many canals and farms. He also ordered that new roads be paved and new forests planted. Agriculture thrived as farmers worked on the new lands and grew more crops.

Ming rulers also repaired and expanded the Grand Canal. This allowed merchants to ship rice and other products between southern and northern China. Chinese traders introduced new types of rice from Southeast Asia that grew faster. More food was available to the growing number of people living in cities.

The Ming also supported the silk industry. They encouraged farmers to start growing cotton and weaving cloth. For the first time, cotton became the cloth worn by most Chinese.

Arts and Literature

The arts flourished during the Ming dynasty. Newly wealthy merchants and artisans wanted entertainment and could afford to pay for printed books and trips to the theater. During the Ming period, Chinese writers produced **novels,** or long fictional stories. One of the most popular was *The Romance of the Three Kingdoms*. It described military rivalries at the end of the Han period. Many novels of the time were written in vernacular, or everyday language. Writers avoided formal language to tell their tales. Instead they tried to make their stories sound as if they had been told aloud by storytellers. Traditional Chinese dramas had been banned during the years of Mongol rule, but under the Ming they were restored to the stage. Actors in costumes performed stories of the day using words, music, dance, and symbolic gestures.

PROGRESS CHECK

Explaining What was the purpose of the Imperial City?

This painting from a Ming vase show
Chinese farm workers collecting te

2 Chinese Exploration

GUIDING QUESTION *How did Chinese contact with the outside world change during the Ming dynasty?*

Early Ming emperors wanted to know more about the world outside of China and to expand Chinese influence abroad. Ming emperors built a large fleet of ships to sail to other countries. The ships, known as junks, usually traveled along the coast of China. They could also sail on the open sea. Between A.D. 1405 and A.D. 1433, Ming emperors sent the Chinese fleet on seven overseas voyages. They wanted to trade with other kingdoms and demonstrate Chinese power. They also wanted to demand that weaker kingdoms pay tribute to China.

The leader of these journeys was a Chinese Muslim and court official named Zheng He (JUNG HUH). The voyages of Zheng He were quite impressive. On the first voyage, nearly 28,000 men sailed on 62 large ships and 250 smaller ships. The largest ship was over 440 feet (134 m) long. That was more than five times as long as the Santa María that Christopher Columbus sailed almost 90 years later.

Reading HELPDESK

census a count of the number of people in a country
novel a long fictional story

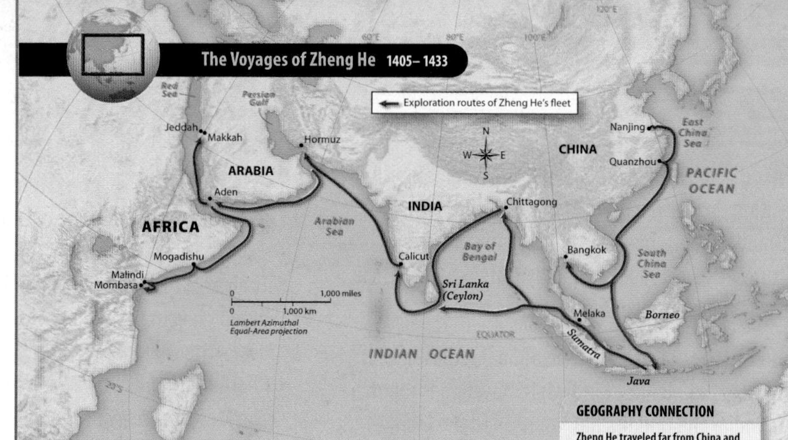

GEOGRAPHY CONNECTION

Zheng He traveled far from China and brought back many exotic items. He also spread Chinese culture.

1. **REGIONS** About how far is Nanjing from Chittagong?
2. **PLACE** Jeddah is on the coast of what body of water?
3. **CRITICAL THINKING** ***Making Connections*** Why were Zheng He's voyages important to the Chinese and other parts of the world?

The Travels of Zheng He

Zheng He took his first fleet to Southeast Asia. In later voyages, he reached the western coast of India and the city-states of East Africa. Zheng He wrote about his travels:

PRIMARY SOURCE

> "We have traversed [traveled] more than 100,000 li [30,000 mi. or 50,000 km] of immense water spaces and have beheld in the ocean huge waves like mountains rising sky-high, . . . and we have set eyes on barbarian [foreign] regions far away, hidden in a blue transparency of light vapours, [fog] while our sails, loftily unfurled like clouds, day and night continued their course, rapid like that of a star, traversing [crossing] those savage waves."
>
> —from tablet erected in Fujian, China by Zheng He

The Jesuits tried to convert the Chinese to Christianity. This image shows a Jesuit convent in China.

At the different ports he visited, Zheng He traded Chinese goods, such as silk, paper, and porcelain. He returned with items unknown in China. For example, Zheng He brought giraffes and other animals from Africa, which fascinated Emperor Yong Le. Yong Le placed them in his imperial zoo in Beijing. Zheng He also brought back visitors from the outside world, including representatives from South and Southeast Asia. The voyages of Zheng He encouraged Chinese merchants to settle in Southeast Asia and India. In these places, they traded goods and spread Chinese culture.

Despite these benefits, Chinese officials complained that the **ongoing** trips cost too much. They also said that these voyages would introduce unwanted foreign ideas. Some officials also believed that being a merchant was an unworthy and selfish occupation. A Confucian teaching said that people should place loyalty to society ahead of their own desires.

After Zheng He died in A.D. 1433, Confucian officials convinced the emperor to end the voyages. The fleet's ships were taken apart, and the construction of seagoing vessels was stopped. As a result, China's trade with other countries sharply declined. Within 50 years, the Chinese shipbuilding technology became outdated.

Arrival of Europeans

Ming China was not able to cut off all contacts with the rest of the world. In A.D. 1514, ships from the European country of Portugal (POHR•chih•GUHL) arrived off the coast of southern China. It was the first direct contact between China and Europe since the journeys of Marco Polo.

The Portuguese wanted to trade with China and **convert** the Chinese to Christianity. At the time, the Ming government paid little attention to the arrival of the Portuguese. China was a powerful civilization and did not feel threatened by outsiders. To the Chinese, the Europeans were **barbarians** (bahr•BEHR•ee•uhnz), or uncivilized people.

Reading HELPDESK

barbarian an uncivilized person

Academic Vocabulary
ongoing continuously moving forward
convert to bring from one belief to another

At first, local officials refused to trade with the Portuguese. The Chinese hoped the foreigners would give up and go home. By A.D. 1600, however, the Portuguese had built a trading post at the port of Macao (muh•KAU) in southern China. Portuguese ships carried goods between China and Japan. Trade between Europe and China, however, remained limited.

Despite limited contact, European ideas did reach China. Christian missionaries made the voyage to China on European merchant ships. Many of these missionaries were Jesuits, a group of Roman Catholic priests. The Jesuits were highly educated and hoped to establish Christian schools in China. Their knowledge of science impressed Chinese officials. However, the Jesuits did not convince many Chinese to accept Christianity.

The Fall of the Ming

After a long period of growth, the Ming dynasty began to weaken. Dishonest officials took over the country. They placed heavy taxes on farmers. The farmers objected to the taxes and began to revolt.

As law and order collapsed, a people—the Manchus—from the north prepared to invade a weakened China. Like the Chinese, the Manchus had been conquered by the Mongols. They had retreated to an area northeast of China's Great Wall, known today as Manchuria. The Manchus defeated the Chinese armies and captured Beijing. In A.D. 1644, they set up a new dynasty called the Qing (CHEENG) dynasty.

PROGRESS CHECK

Analyzing Why did Chinese officials oppose overseas voyages?

LESSON 4 REVIEW

Review Vocabulary

1. How would officials have taken a *census* of China's population?
2. Why did the Chinese consider Europeans to be *barbarians*?

Answer the Guiding Questions

3. ***Describing*** Describe the Imperial City and the Forbidden City.
4. ***Identifying*** How did the Ming dynasty change China?
5. ***Explaining*** Why did China's officials discourage the voyages of Zheng He?
6. ***Summarizing*** What effect did the arrival of the Jesuits have on the Chinese?
7. **PERSUASIVE WRITING** Imagine that you are Zheng He, and government officials have threatened to stop supporting your voyages. Write a letter to persuade officials to let you continue traveling. Give at least three reasons why you should be allowed to continue.

Chinese Exploration

GUIDING QUESTION *How did Chinese contact with the outside world change during the Ming dynasty?*

INTERACTIVE WORKSHEET

Geography and History Activity

Discussing In class, have students complete the Geography and History Activity for this lesson. Allow students to work in pairs to analyze the map, read the text, and answer the questions. Afterward, ask volunteers to summarize what they learned about the impact of Zheng He's voyages. They can also draw on what they learned from reading the lesson and filling in the Taking Notes graphic organizer in the lesson opener.

Summarizing Ask volunteers to summarize the objections that Confucian scholar-officials raised about Zheng He's voyages. *(They cost too much; they introduced foreign ideas; the wealth of traders was disrespectful of Confucian ideals.)* Point out that the Confucian scholar-officials eventually put a stop to overseas voyages.

INTERACTIVE WORKSHEET

21st Century Skills Activity

Analyzing To reinforce the point, have students work in class to complete the 21st Century Skills Activity. They will evaluate the government's decision to stop the voyages. Afterward, lead students in a discussion about whether the decision was the right one for China.

Ask:

Was it more important for China to be true to Confucian principles or to maintain connections with the rest of the world? *(Some students might say China was right to stick with Confucian principles because they were the foundation for China's greatness as an empire. Besides making merchants wealthy, Zheng He's voyages were not having a big impact on the world. Others may say that China, by cutting itself off from the rest of the world, might lose its place among the great empires of the world.)* BL

INTERACTIVE WHITEBOARD ACTIVITY

Identifying Allow students time to work in small groups to complete the Interactive Whiteboard Activities to identify the accomplishments of the dynasties of imperial China.

Have students complete the Lesson 4 Review.

CLOSE & REFLECT

Explaining Lead students in a discussion of how a society's beliefs affect the way its government operates. Ask students to draw examples from the lesson as well as from their understanding of U.S. politics and government.

IF YOU HAVE MORE TIME . . .

Explore the Technology of Zheng He's Voyages

Explaining Remind students about advances the Chinese made in shipbuilding (e.g., rudders and sails) and navigation (e.g., compasses). Explain that during the Ming dynasty, the Chinese continued to make progress in shipbuilding. Help students make the connection between Chinese shipbuilding and navigational skills during the Tang and Song dynasties and the voyages of Zheng He. Students should understand that the Chinese could not have built the enormous ships or navigated them for thousands of miles if they could not draw on the shipbuilding skills and knowledge of previous centuries.

Analyzing Locate online or in a book an illustration of a Chinese "Treasure Ship" from the Ming dynasty. Ask students to describe what they see. Explain that Ming emperors had these ships built in order to show China's power to the world.

Point out the description of Zheng He's fleet in the textbook. Tell students that these ships sailed tens of thousands of miles across the Indian Ocean between 1405 and 1433. Explain that they were far larger than the ships Christopher Columbus sailed only a few thousand miles across the Atlantic Ocean in 1492.

Ask:

Does this information change your perceptions of history? If so, how? *(Students may suggest that Columbus's ships and voyages seem less impressive now.)*

Discuss China's Contact With Europeans

Listing Have students review the section titled "Arrival of Europeans." Ask them to list the reasons the Portuguese wanted to establish contacts in China. *(They wanted to trade and to convert the Chinese to Christianity.)*

Ask:

- **How successful were the Portuguese in trading with and converting the Chinese?** *(They were not successful. They had limited trade and few converts.)*
- **Why do you think the Chinese did not welcome ideas brought by the Portuguese?** *(They thought the Portuguese were barbarians. They had their own traditions and did not see any reason to change.)*

Finally, invite volunteers to make a connection between the ending of Zheng He's voyages and China's reluctance to allow the Portuguese to trade and introduce Christianity. Students should recognize that China grew more isolated from the rest of the world during the Ming dynasty.

Answers for pages 500–503

P. 500 PROGRESS CHECK The Imperial City was the center of the government. The emperor and his family lived in its Forbidden City.

P. 501 GEOGRAPHY CONNECTION

1. Nanjing is about 1,750 miles (2,815 km) from Chittagong.
2. Jeddah is on the coast of the Red Sea.
3. CRITICAL THINKING Zheng He's voyages spread Chinese culture to other parts of the world and introduced foreign ideas to China. The voyages also helped increase trade between China and other parts of the world.

P. 503 PROGRESS CHECK Chinese officials thought the voyages were too expensive and that the trips would bring back unwanted foreign ideas to China. They also believed it was wrong for trading to benefit only the merchants instead of society as a whole.

LESSON 4 REVIEW

1. The officials would have counted the Chinese and recorded the numbers.
2. They thought the Europeans were uncivilized people.
3. The Imperial City was a large area filled with palaces and government buildings. At the center was the Forbidden City where the emperor and his family lived. Many beautiful gardens and huge palaces were built in the Forbidden City.
4. The Ming dynasty brought order to China by bringing back civil service examinations, conducting censuses, rebuilding canals and farms, paving roads, planting forests, supporting the silk industry, and repairing the Grand Canal. These efforts helped improve trade and the economy. More food was available, and the population began to grow.
5. Chinese officials were convinced that the sea voyages were too expensive and that too many foreign ideas were entering China. They also considered trading to be an unworthy—even selfish—occupation. Traders gained wealth for themselves and did not contribute to improving Chinese society.
6. The Jesuits had little effect beyond some trading. European Jesuits who hoped to convert the Chinese to Christianity had little success.
7. Students' letters should point out that sea voyages demonstrated Chinese power, extended China's influence, and added to the wealth and prestige of China through trade. The voyages also exposed China to the ideas, information, and technologies in other places. In addition, the sea voyages meant China could maintain a high level of shipbuilding and sailing skills. To lose those skills would weaken China's power and influence in the world.

CHAPTER 17 Activities

Write your answers on a separate piece of paper.

1. **Exploring the Essential Question**
   EXPOSITORY WRITING How would you describe imperial China's relations with other cultures through trade, travel, and war? Write an essay that summarizes how and why imperial China came into contact with groups outside its borders.

2. **21st Century Skills**
   SEQUENCE EVENTS Review the chapter and identify at least 10 important events that took place during imperial China. Try to vary the types of events, including military as well as cultural and civic developments. Then create a time line that shows the sequence of the events or developments and explains their importance. Use presentation software or art supplies to create a time line that includes images and text. Present your work to the class.

3. **Thinking Like a Historian**
   DRAWING CONCLUSIONS Think about the effects that an invention such as gunpowder had on imperial China. Then create a diagram like the one shown here. In the diagram, draw a conclusion about how that invention might have affected China.

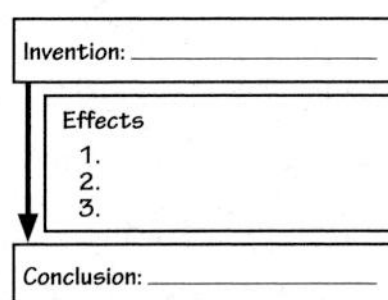

4. **GEOGRAPHY ACTIVITY**

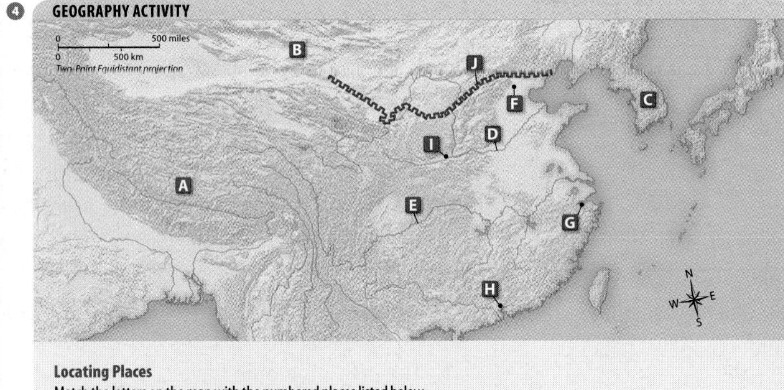

Locating Places
Match the letters on the map with the numbered places listed below.

1. Beijing
2. Hangzhou
3. Guangzhou
4. Changan
5. Great Wall
6. Tibet
7. Mongolia
8. Korean Peninsula
9. Huang He (Yellow River)
10. Chang Jiang (Yangtze River)

CHAPTER 17 Assessment

REVIEW THE GUIDING QUESTIONS
Directions: Choose the best answer for each question.

1. After years of war, what major construction project helped unify China during the Sui dynasty?
   A. the Forbidden City
   B. the Silk Road
   C. the Great Wall
   D. the Grand Canal

2. The Chinese rulers preferred Confucianism over Buddhism because it taught
   F. how to escape suffering.
   G. how to pass the civil service examination.
   H. the importance of being active in society.
   I. the use of terror in conquering enemies.

3. Which technological development immediately helped the Chinese economy during the Tang and Song dynasties?
   A. the use of coal for heating
   B. the printing process
   C. steel production
   D. shipbuilding

4. Which idea would poets write about during China's "golden age of the arts"?
   F. Nature is beautiful.
   G. The people are happy.
   H. The emperor is cruel.
   I. Life lasts too long.

5. Which of the following is the best description of the Mongols in China?
   A. disciplined fighters but lazy emperors
   B. fierce enemies but good rulers
   C. failed soldiers but respectful leaders
   D. loyal troops but selfish kings

6. What was the main reason Ming emperors sent ships overseas?
   F. to conquer new territories
   G. to demonstrate China's power
   H. to escape invading Manchus
   I. to share new technologies with the West

CHAPTER 17 Assessment *(continued)*

DBQ DOCUMENT-BASED QUESTIONS

John of Plano Carpini explained why the Mongols were skilled warriors.

"Their children begin as soon as they are two or three years old to ride and manage horses and to gallop on them, and they are given bows to suit their stature [size] and are taught to shoot; they are extremely agile [able to move quickly] and also intrepid [fearless]."

—from *History of the Mongols*, by John of Plano Carpini

7. **Drawing Conclusions** Which statement best summarizes why the Mongols were skilled soldiers?
   A. They believed that children should be free to play.
   B. They made children fight their battles for them.
   C. They taught their children to hate other people.
   D. They were trained to ride horses and fight at a young age.

8. **Inferring** What can you infer about the author's experiences with the Mongols?
   F. He read about them in a book.
   G. He was captured by the Mongols.
   H. He was a visitor to the Mongol empire.
   I. He was a Mongol fighter.

SHORT RESPONSE

"[Empress Wu] continued to eliminate [get rid of] potential rivals, even when these were her own relatives, but she governed the empire with great efficiency, . . . Her great ability as an administrator, her courage, decisive [able to make judgments quickly] character, and readiness to use ruthless [unforgiving] means . . . won her the respect, if not the love, of the court."

—from "Wuhou," *Encyclopedia Britannica*

9. According to the reading, how did Empress Wu treat her opponents?

10. Why did the empress win the respect of the court?

EXTENDED RESPONSE

11. **Expository Writing** You are studying for the civil service examination during the Tang dynasty. Write an essay to explain the examination and how it helps China. Tell why the examination is important to you and your family.

Need Extra Help?

If You've Missed Question	1	2	3	4	5	6	7	8	9	10	11
Review Lesson	1	1	2	2	3	4	3	3	1	1	1

NOTES

REFLECT, REVIEW, & REMEDIATE

INTERACTIVE WORKSHEET

Chapter Summary

Provide students with the Chapter Summary worksheet to help review the chapter and prepare for assessment.

Reviewing the Enduring Understandings

Review this chapter's Enduring Understandings with students:

- People, places, and ideas change over time.
- Leaders can bring about change in a society.

INTERACTIVE WHITEBOARD ACTIVITY On the interactive whiteboard, create a two-column chart. Label one column "Empress Wu" and the other "Kublai Khan." Then, lead the class in a discussion about how both leaders affected China's government, economy, and/or culture during their reigns. Write students' responses in the organizer. Challenge students to make a generalization about the impact of each ruler, based on their responses.

Empress Wu	Kublai Khan

ACTIVITIES ANSWERS

Exploring the Essential Question

1. Students' essays should suggest that China had positive and negative interactions with outsiders. When the Chinese were openly trading on the Silk Road during the Tang dynasty, China benefited because its goods, ideas, and influence were spread throughout the world. In return, China obtained goods and wealth. Even after China was invaded by the Mongols, the Chinese eventually experienced peace, order, and prosperity. Travelers such as the Italian Marco Polo visited and sent reports of China's greatness and inventions back to Europe. During the Ming dynasty, however, government officials became distrustful of the influence from outsiders. They stopped all sea voyages, and they tried to limit the influence of Europeans, such as Portuguese missionaries.

21st Century Skills

2. Students should select 10 events from the chapter that they consider important to the development of China during the imperial period. For example, they might select events such as the building of the Grand Canal, the restoration of the civil service examination, the invention of printing using movable type, the invasion of the Mongols, and the reading of novels. Students' time lines should clearly indicate the year in which the event happened. They should also provide a sentence or two that explains each event's significance. For example, the Grand Canal made it easier to transport goods to all areas of China.

Thinking Like a Historian

3. Students should select a technological invention discussed in the chapter, such as printing or gunpowder, and identify at least two effects of the invention. For example, printing allowed for the spread of Chinese ideas and the invention of paper currency. The conclusion that students may draw is that printing improved China's economy and communications.

Locating Places

4. **1.** F, **2.** G, **3.** H, **4.** I, **5.** J, **6.** A, **7.** B, **8.** C, **9.** D, **10.** E

ASSESSMENT ANSWERS

Review the Guiding Questions

1. **D** The Sui built the Grand Canal to connect two major rivers and make travel easier, thus unifying China. The Forbidden City was built by the Ming dynasty. The Great Wall was first built earlier in Chinese history. Thus, choice D is the correct answer.

2. **H** Leaders preferred Confucianism because it emphasized the importance of being active in this world. Buddhism taught people that they could escape suffering. Students had to understand Confucianism to pass the civil service examination, but the secret to passing was not among the principles. Confucianism emphasized living in harmony, not using terror. Choice H is the correct answer.

3. **B** Although the use of coal made the production of steel possible, it was printing paper money that gave an immediate boost to China's trade-based economy. Shipbuilding did not begin in earnest until the Ming dynasty. Therefore, choice B is the correct answer.

4. **F** Most poetry written during the "golden age" expressed the ideas that nature is beautiful and life is too short. Although poet Du Fu wrote about the hardships of the poor, no poet of the time would have criticized the emperor or complained that life was too long. Choice F is the correct answer.

5. **B** The Mongols used terror to conquer enemies and gain territory. However, they were organized and respectful rulers of the empire, who tolerated different faiths and encouraged trade and prosperity. They were successful and loyal soldiers but also good leaders. Thus, choice B is the correct answer.

6. **G** One of the main reasons Ming emperors dispatched ships was to extend China's influence—as well as increase trade and demand tribute from nearby regions. These were ways to demonstrate China's power. When the Ming dynasty collapsed, the Manchurians invaded Beijing; the emperor did not escape by ship. Choice G is the correct answer.

Document-Based Questions

7. **D** The details support the conclusion that the Mongols trained their children in riding and fighting skills from a very young age. The details do not suggest that Mongol children fought in battles or felt hatred. Mongol children might have been free to play, but they were taught skills while playing. Therefore, choice D is correct.

8. **H** Students should recall that Europeans like Marco Polo lived in China under the Mongols and would have observed Mongol traditions. A European was unlikely to be captured by Mongols or to be a Mongol fighter. It was also unlikely that there were many books about Mongols to read. Thus, choice H is correct.

Short Response

9. Empress Wu eliminated her opponents.

10. The empress was an effective ruler. She was efficient, decisive, brave, and willing to take action in order to rule China well.

Extended Response

11. Students should explain that the civil service examination is a written test that helps identify the most talented candidates for government jobs. The exam means that any good candidate, not just politically connected individuals, can obtain these jobs. These civil servants are more talented and suited for their jobs; therefore, the government benefits. Students should note that civil service positions are prestigious and provide a good source of income.

ONLINE RESOURCES

networks

There's More Online!

- ☑ INTERACTIVE WORKSHEETS
- ☑ BIOGRAPHIES
- ☑ CHARTS/GRAPHS
- ☑ GAMES
- ☑ GRAPHIC ORGANIZERS
- ☑ IMAGES
- ☑ MAPS
- ☑ PRIMARY SOURCES
- ☑ SLIDE SHOWS
- ☑ TIME LINE
- ☑ LECTURE SLIDES
- ☑ INTERACTIVE WHITEBOARD ACTIVITIES
- ☑ ASSESSMENTS
- ☑ VIDEOS

The Korean Landscape

East Asian Religions and Other Cultural Traditions

Religions of Southeast Asia

Chapter **18**

Civilizations of Korea, Japan, and Southeast Asia

Dear World History Teacher,

Situated at the crossroads of two oceans and two great civilizations, Southeast Asia has long served as a bridge linking peoples and cultures.

Korea and Japan, for example, borrowed liberally from Chinese culture. Though both countries expressed admiration and respect for China's achievement, they also sought to maintain their political independence. As an island nation, Japan was the most successful in protecting its political sovereignty and its cultural identity. Korea was compelled on various occasions to defend its independence through physical force. For Vietnam, years of conflict eventually led to Vietnam's conquest by China, ensuring that Chinese culture would profoundly affect the country.

China was not the only neighbor to influence Southeast Asia. Merchants and missionaries brought Indian influence to coastal areas along the Gulf of Thailand and elsewhere. Whatever the means, all the young states throughout the region were heavily affected by foreign ideas. And yet, the Southeast Asian peoples put their unique stamp on the ideas they adopted. The result was a region marked by cultural richness and diversity.

Jackson J. Spielvogel

More Media Resources

Current Events Online

Visit McGraw-Hill's current events Web site for high-interest news stories and activities for your students. Access the site through the Student or Teacher Center in **networks.**

Reading List

Grade 6 reading level:
Children of the Dragon: Selected Tales From Vietnam, by Sherry Garland

Grade 7 reading level:
Project Mulberry, by Linda Sue Park

Grade 8 reading level:
Cricket Never Does: A Collection of Haiku and Tanka, by Myra Cohn Livingston

At the MOVIES

Watch clips of films set in medieval Japan, such as *The Men Who Tread on the Tiger's Tail* (1945) NR, directed by Akira Kurosawa.

NOTE: Be sure to preview any clips to ensure they are age-appropriate.

Search for more videos online in the **networks** Resource Library.

CHAPTER 18 Planner

UNDERSTANDING BY DESIGN®

Enduring Understanding

- *People, places, and ideas change over time.*

Essential Questions

- *Why do people form governments?* • *How does geography influence the way people live?*
- *How do new ideas change the way people live?* • *What makes a culture unique?*

Students will know:

- *the reasons Korea is described as a bridge between China and Japan*
- *how Korea built a civilization*
- *how geography affected ways of life in Japan and Southeast Asia*
- *what caused military leaders to rise to power in Japan*
- *why powerful kingdoms and empires developed in Southeast Asia*

Students will be able to:

- **explain** why Korea is considered a bridge between China and Japan
- **describe** the ways in which Korea was influenced by China and Japan
- **explain** how geography shaped Japan's early society
- **discuss** why nature was important to the early Japanese
- **describe** how China influenced Japan during the Nara period
- **explain** how military leaders became powerful in Southeast Asia
- **explain** how and why culture flourished during the time of the shoguns
- **identify** and locate geographical features that affected settlement and early ways of life in Southeast Asia
- **explain** why powerful kingdoms and empires developed in Southeast Asia

Predictable Misunderstandings

Students may think:

- There is no difference between Korean culture and Chinese culture.
- Japan became a powerful nation only by going to war with its rivals.
- A shogun and a samurai are the same.
- No major religions other than Shinto are practiced in Southeast Asia.

Assessment Evidence

Performance Task

- Hands-On Chapter Project

Other Evidence

- Discussion answers to Korea as a bridge between China and Japan
- Identification of geographical features
- Answers from analyzing visuals
- Responses to Interactive Whiteboard Activities
- Geography and History Activity
- 21st Century Skills Activities
- Economics and History Activity
- Lesson Reviews
- Analysis paper on why the Shinto religion may be followed today
- Illustration of one area of Southeast Asia
- Discussion answers on how the area was influenced by cultures of India, China, and Islam

Pacing Guide

Introducing the Chapter	1 day
Lesson 1 Korea: History and Culture	1 day
Lesson 2 Early Japan	1 day
Lesson 3 Medieval Japan	2 days
Lesson 4 Southeast Asia: History and Culture	1 day
Chapter Activities and Assessment	1 day
TOTAL TIME	**7 Days**

Differentiated Instruction

These lesson plans are written to address the needs of your On Level students. Discussion and activities that are well-suited to your Approaching Grade Level learners, Beyond Grade Level learners, as well as your English Language Learners are coded as follows:

AL **Approaching Grade Level**

BL **Beyond Grade Level**

ELL **English Language Learner**

NCSS Standards covered in "Civilizations of Korea, Japan, and Southeast Asia"

Learners will understand:

1 CULTURE

1. "Culture" refers to the socially transmitted behaviors, beliefs, values, traditions, institutions, and ways of living together for a group of people
2. Concepts such as beliefs, values, institutions, cohesion, diversity, accommodation, adaption, assimilation, and dissonance
4. That the beliefs, values, and behaviors of a culture form an integrated system that helps shape the activities and ways of life that define a culture
5. How individuals learn the elements of their culture through interactions with others, and how individuals learn of other cultures through communication and study
7. How people from different cultures develop different values and ways of interpreting experience
8. That language, behaviors, and beliefs of different cultures can both contribute to and pose barriers to cross-cultural understanding

2 TIME, CONTINUITY, AND CHANGE

5. Key historical periods and patterns of change within and across cultures (e.g., the rise and fall of ancient civilizations, the development of technology, the rise of modern nation-states, and the establishment and breakdown of colonial systems)
6. The origins and influences of social, cultural, political, and economic systems
7. The contributions of key persons, groups, and events from the past and their influence on the present

3 PEOPLE, PLACES, AND ENVIRONMENTS

2. Concepts such as: location, region, place, migration, as well as human and physical systems
4. The roles of different kinds of population centers in a region or nation
5. The concept of regions identifies links between people in different locations according to specific criteria (e.g., physical, economic, social, cultural, or religious)
6. Patterns of demographic and political change, and cultural diffusion in the past and present (e.g., changing national boundaries, migration, and settlement, and the diffusion of and changes in customs and ideas)
8. Factors that contribute to cooperation and conflict among peoples of the nation and world, including language, religion, and political beliefs

5 INDIVIDUALS, GROUPS, AND INSTITUTIONS

6. That cultural diffusion occurs when groups migrate
7. That institutions may promote or undermine social conformity

CHAPTER 18

Introducing the Chapter

(Student Edition p. 507)

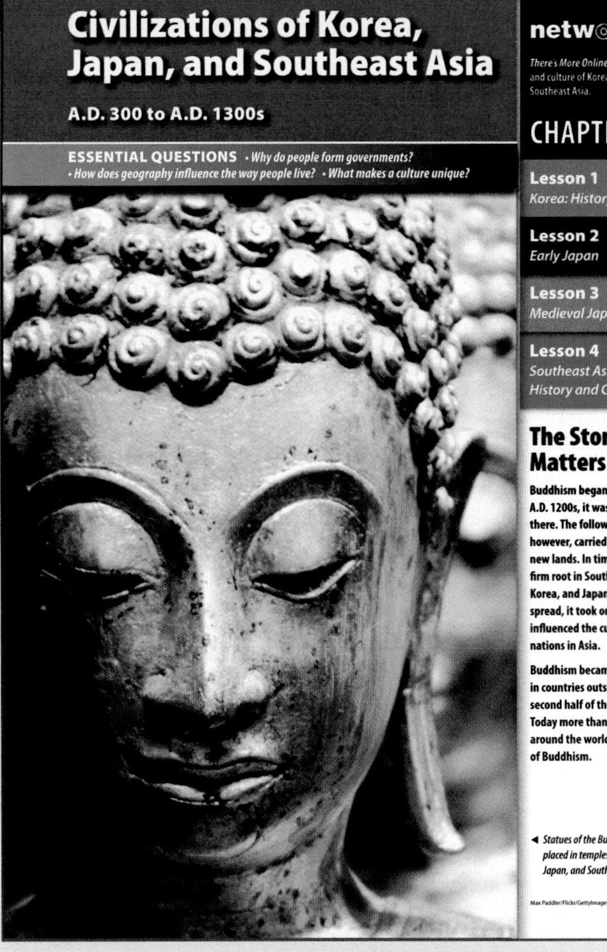

Civilizations of Korea, Japan, and Southeast Asia

A.D. 300 to A.D. 1300s

ESSENTIAL QUESTIONS • *Why do people form governments?* • *How does geography influence the way people live?* • *What makes a culture unique?*

networks *There's More Online* about the history and culture of Korea, Japan, and Southeast Asia.

CHAPTER 18

Lesson 1 *Korea: History and Culture*

Lesson 2 *Early Japan*

Lesson 3 *Medieval Japan*

Lesson 4 *Southeast Asia: History and Culture*

The Story Matters . . .

Buddhism began in India. By the A.D. 1200s, it was almost extinct there. The followers of the Buddha, however, carried his teachings to new lands. In time, Buddhism took firm root in Southeast Asia, China, Korea, and Japan. As Buddhism spread, it took on new forms and influenced the cultures of many nations in Asia.

Buddhism became more popular in countries outside of Asia in the second half of the twentieth century. Today more than 375 million people around the world practice some form of Buddhism.

◄ *Statues of the Buddha like this one were placed in temples throughout Korea, Japan, and Southeast Asia.*

Max Paddler/Flickr/Gettyimages

507

The Story Matters . . .

Read "The Story Matters . . ." aloud in class or ask a volunteer to read it aloud. Discuss with students the way in which Buddhism spread across Asia.

Ask:

Through which country did Buddhism pass as it made its way from China to Japan? *(Korea)*

Then ask:

In the past, how did geography affect the spread of news from different areas of the world? What is its effect today?

Lead the class in a discussion of this question. Point out that in modern times, we can learn about what is going on around us almost instantly, but before modern media, word traveled much more slowly. Encourage students to consider how different religions they have learned about might have spread before the age of modern communications.

Introducing Place and Time

(Student Edition pp. 508–509)

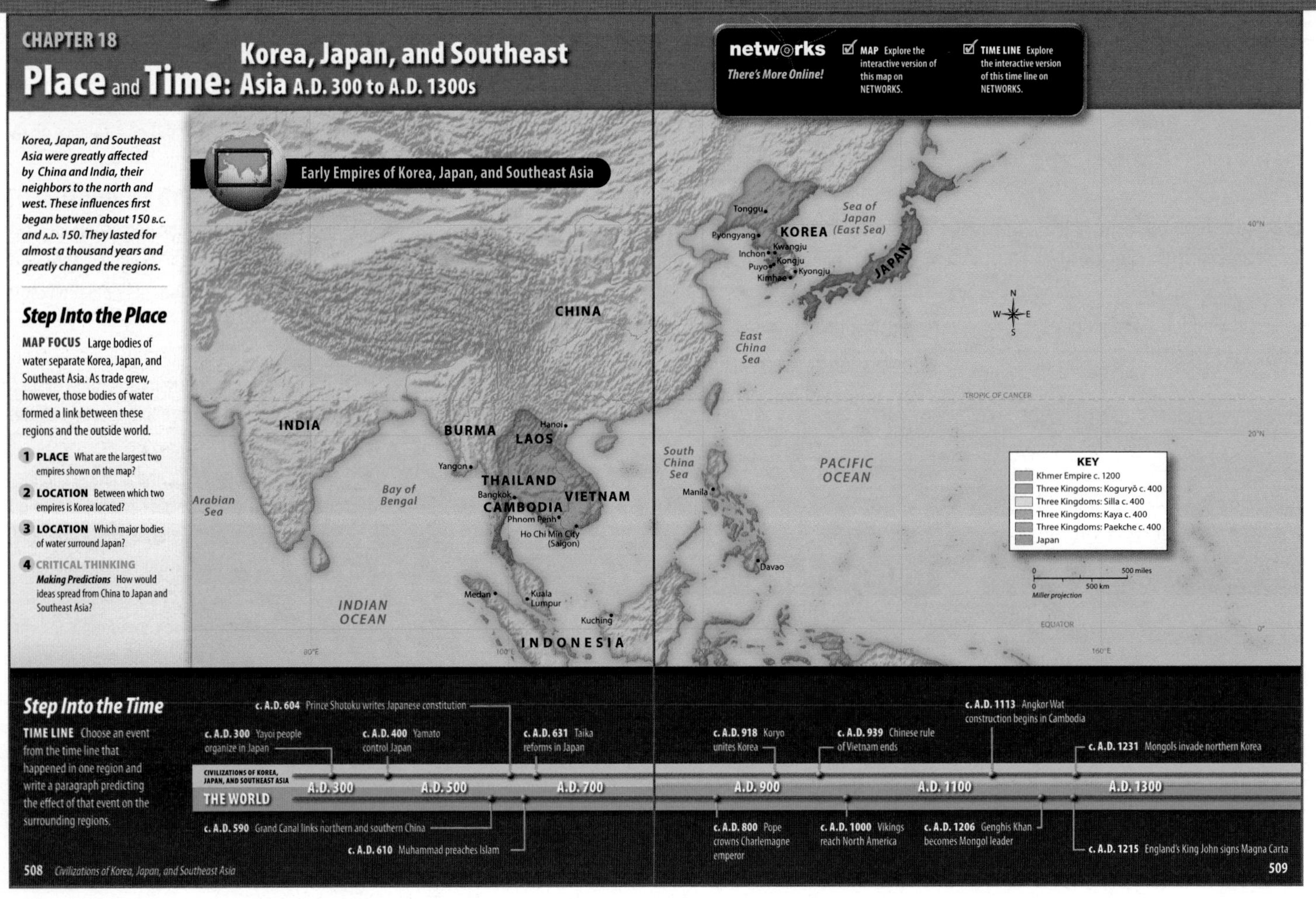

CHAPTER 18

Place and Time: Korea, Japan, and Southeast Asia A.D. 300 to A.D. 1300s

networks *There's More Online!* ☑ **MAP** Explore the interactive version of this map on NETWORKS. ☑ **TIME LINE** Explore the interactive version of this time line on NETWORKS.

Korea, Japan, and Southeast Asia were greatly affected by China and India, their neighbors to the north and west. These influences first began between about 150 B.C. and A.D. 150. They lasted for almost a thousand years and greatly changed the regions.

Step Into the Place

MAP FOCUS Large bodies of water separate Korea, Japan, and Southeast Asia. As trade grew, however, those bodies of water formed a link between these regions and the outside world.

1. **PLACE** What are the largest two empires shown on the map?
2. **LOCATION** Between which two empires is Korea located?
3. **LOCATION** Which major bodies of water surround Japan?
4. **CRITICAL THINKING** *Making Predictions* How would ideas spread from China to Japan and Southeast Asia?

Step Into the Time

TIME LINE Choose an event from the time line that happened in one region and write a paragraph predicting the effect of that event on the surrounding regions.

508 *Civilizations of Korea, Japan, and Southeast Asia*

509

Technology Extension

- Find an additional activity online that incorporates technology for this project.
- Visit the EdTechTeacher Web sites (included in the Technology Extension for this chapter) for more links, tutorials, and other resources.

Assessing Background Knowledge

INTERACTIVE WORKSHEET

What Do You Know? Activity

Have students complete the Anticipation Guide about the civilizations of Korea, Japan, and Southeast Asia before they study the chapter. Direct students to read each statement. Then have them write whether they agree or disagree with the statement. Next, read the sentences aloud and have students agree or disagree by a show of hands to better focus on any generalized misconceptions.

After students complete the chapter, have them reread the statements and write whether they now agree or disagree with each statement. Ask students who changed their responses to explain why they did so.

INTERACTIVE WORKSHEET

Guided Reading Activities

There is a Guided Reading Activity for each lesson in this chapter. You may wish to assign the Guided Reading Activity for Lesson 1 after introducing the chapter content.

Hands-On Chapter Project

Students will create travel itineraries for a trip to view the historical and geographic highlights of Korea, Japan, and Southeast Asia.

- Students will participate in a class discussion to review what they have learned about the ancient civilizations, cultures, and geography of Korea, Japan, and Southeast Asia.
- Then, students will divide into groups. Each group will use discussions and worksheets to plan their projects before creating their itineraries.
- Next, each group will complete its itinerary and share it with the rest of the class.
- Finally, students will evaluate their research, presentation, and collaboration using an Assessment Rubric.

Visit **networks** online to see the full project and rubric.

ONLINE RESOURCES

networks

Assign these interactive worksheets and quizzes from your Teacher Lesson Center. All resources are print-ready.

It's ALL Online!

CHAPTER 18 RESOURCES
- ☑ CHAPTER SUMMARY
- ☑ VOCABULARY BUILDER
- ☑ WHAT DO YOU KNOW?
- ☑ HANDS-ON CHAPTER PROJECT

Lesson 1 Resources
- ☑ INTERACTIVE GRAPHIC ORGANIZER
- ☑ GEOGRAPHY AND HISTORY ACTIVITY: Understanding Borders: Korea
- ☑ GUIDED READING ACTIVITY
- ☑ READING ESSENTIALS AND STUDY GUIDE
- ☑ ONLINE SELF-CHECK QUIZ

Lesson 2 Resources
- ☑ 21ST CENTURY SKILLS ACTIVITY Using Latitude and Longitude
- ☑ GUIDED READING ACTIVITY
- ☑ READING ESSENTIALS AND STUDY GUIDE
- ☑ ONLINE SELF-CHECK QUIZ

Lesson 3 Resources
- ☑ 21ST CENTURY SKILLS ACTIVITY Writing a Poem
- ☑ GUIDED READING ACTIVITY
- ☑ READING ESSENTIALS AND STUDY GUIDE
- ☑ ONLINE SELF-CHECK QUIZ

Lesson 4 Resources
- ☑ ECONOMICS OF HISTORY ACTIVITY The Rise of Angkor
- ☑ GUIDED READING ACTIVITY
- ☑ READING ESSENTIALS AND STUDY GUIDE
- ☑ ONLINE SELF-CHECK

ASSESSMENT RESOURCES
- ☑ LESSON REVIEWS
- ☑ ONLINE SELF-CHECK QUIZZES
- ☑ CHAPTER ACTIVITIES AND ASSESSMENT
- ☑ STANDARDIZED TEST PRACTICE

REMEDIATION RESOURCES
- ☑ READING ESSENTIALS AND STUDY GUIDE
- ☑ GUIDED READING ACTIVITIES
- ☑ ONLINE SELF-CHECK QUIZZES
- ☑ CHAPTER SUMMARY

Step Into the Place

Location Project the Interactive World Atlas on the interactive whiteboard and project the region of Korea, Japan, and Southeast Asia.

Discuss with students the geographical features of the region. Remind students that the region is made up of elongated peninsulas and many islands. Invite volunteers to suggest how trade was carried out among the many states.

INTERACTIVE WHITEBOARD ACTIVITY At your interactive whiteboard, have student volunteers analyze the map and locate strategic points for sea trade. Encourage them to consider why coastal cities were built where they were.

Next, project the Chapter Opener map on the interactive whiteboard. As a class, discuss the Map Focus questions.

Step Into the Time

Calculating Have students review the time line for the chapter. Explain that they will be studying events from about A.D. 300 to A.D. 1300.

Ask: According to the time line, how much time was there between when Genghis Kahn was chosen leader of the Mongols and the Mongols invaded Korea? *(about 25 years)*

Answers for pages 508–509

Step Into the Place

1. India and China
2. China and Japan
3. the Sea of Japan, the East China Sea, and the Pacific Ocean
4. CRITICAL THINKING through travel over land and by sea

Step Into the Time

Student answers will vary depending upon the event they choose.

networks
There's More Online!
☑ GRAPHIC ORGANIZER Shamans
☑ SLIDE SHOW Silla

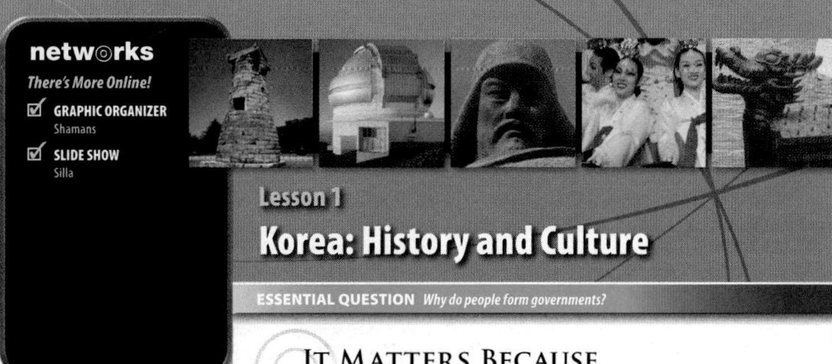

Lesson 1
Korea: History and Culture

ESSENTIAL QUESTION *Why do people form governments?*

It Matters Because
Located between two powerful civilizations—Japan and China—Korea has forged its own cultural identity over the centuries.

1 Location of Korea

GUIDING QUESTION *Why is Korea described as a bridge between China and Japan?*

Korea is slightly larger than the state of Minnesota. It lies on a mountainous peninsula in East Asia. The Korean Peninsula juts out to the southeast from northeastern China. It points toward the western tip of the islands of Japan.

Korea has been seen as a bridge between China and Japan. Being close to these two powerful Asian neighbors has greatly affected Korea's development. Throughout their long history, the people of Korea have adopted features of Chinese and Japanese civilizations. The Koreans have blended these features with their own traditions and created a unique civilization.

Early Koreans

Legend says that Tangun, the son of a bear and a god, founded the first Korean kingdom. Historians today believe that the first Koreans were nomads. They came to the peninsula from northern or central Asia. These groups were organized into tribes. The early Koreans lived in scattered villages with no central government. They grew rice and made tools and weapons of bronze. Later, they used iron to make these items.

Reading **HELP**DESK

Taking Notes: *Identifying*
Use a graphic organizer like this one to list details about the Silla kingdom and the two dynasties that followed it.

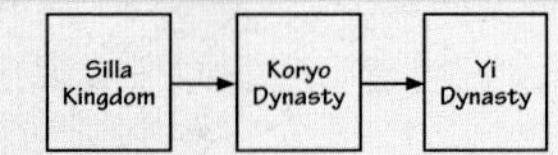

Content Vocabulary
• **shamanism**

Early Koreans believed in **shamanism** (SHAH•muh•nih•zuhm). They thought that certain people could communicate with spirits. These people, known as shamans, acted as a connection between humans and spirits. Many shamans were women. They carried out rituals—songs, dances, and chants—to convince the spirits to help people. Shamans were thought to have the ability to cure illnesses.

The Three Kingdoms

According to tradition, the earliest kingdom in Korea was founded in 2333 B.C. Historians know that the Chinese took over the northern part of the Korean Peninsula in 109 B.C. The Koreans drove them out in the A.D. 200s. Eventually, three kingdoms emerged: Koguryo (koh•goo•ryeoh) in the north, Paekche (payk•cheh) in the southwest, and Silla (sheel•lah) in the southeast. Historians call the years from about A.D. 300 to A.D. 700 the Three Kingdoms period.

Chinese culture spread from Koguryo to the other Korean kingdoms. The people of all three kingdoms used the Chinese writing system and adopted Buddhism and Confucianism.

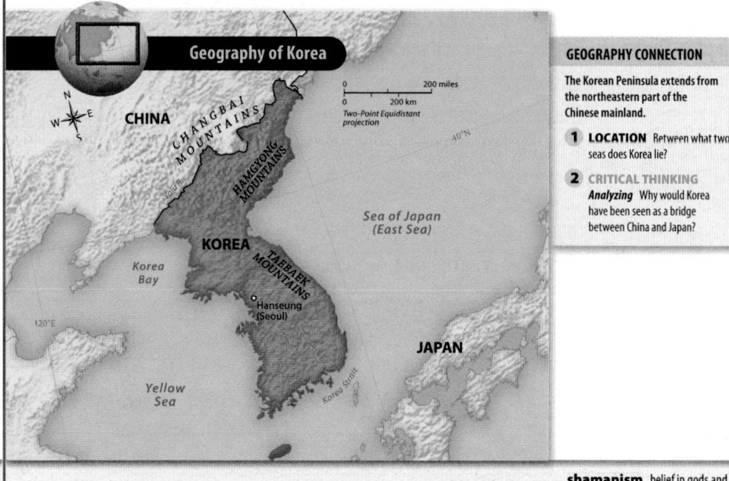

GEOGRAPHY CONNECTION
The Korean Peninsula extends from the northeastern part of the Chinese mainland.

1. **LOCATION** Between what two seas does Korea lie?
2. **CRITICAL THINKING** ***Analyzing*** Why would Korea have been seen as a bridge between China and Japan?

shamanism belief in gods and spirits

THEN

The early Koreans built this astronomical observatory during the Silla era. Today, observatories around the world use high-powered telescopes to give scientists the best view of stars, planets, and even far away galaxies.

NOW

▶ CRITICAL THINKING
Speculating How would ancient astronomers from Silla have observed the movement of stars and other objects compared to astronomers today?

They began using Buddhist sacred writings in Chinese translation. They applied Confucian principles to political life. Each Korean kingdom modeled its government on China's government. In addition, each kingdom was ruled by a powerful monarch with the help of scholarly officials and noble families.

During the Three Kingdoms period, influences from Japan also reached the Korean Peninsula. Paekche in the southwest was located closer to Japan than the other two Korean kingdoms. As a result, it developed trade with the Japanese. Japanese merchants, artisans, and scholars settled in Paekche and introduced elements of Japanese culture there.

Although the Koreans adapted many outside ideas and practices, they also made their own unique contributions. For example, in the A.D. 300s, Koguryo artists created enormous cave art paintings. In Silla, a queen built an astronomical observatory that still stands today. This stone structure is considered the oldest observatory in Asia.

The Silla Kingdom

Despite their close cultural ties, the three Korean kingdoms were hostile to each other. In the A.D. 500s and 600s, they fought wars for control of the Korean Peninsula. In one conflict during the A.D. 660s, the Tang dynasty of China sided with the Silla kingdom. With Chinese help, Silla conquered Paekche and Koguryo.

The rise of Silla brought a time of peace to Koreans as the Silla kings tried to create an ideal Buddhist kingdom. Society was made up of a few nobles at the top and a large group of farmers below. However, the government made some vital improvements. It gave land to farmers and helped build irrigation systems for rice fields. As a result, more food was produced, trade increased, and the economy prospered.

Silla kings also supported cultural advances. They wanted to employ educated people. To make that easier, they used an examination system to hire government officials. They also encouraged the arts, especially the building of many Buddhist temples. One temple was a nine-story wooden tower. This was perhaps the tallest structure in East Asia at the time. The printing of Buddhist sacred texts with wooden blocks was another Silla **achievement**.

☑ PROGRESS CHECK

Determining Cause and Effect How did outside influences affect early Korea?

Reading **HELP**DESK

Academic Vocabulary
achievement something gained by working for it

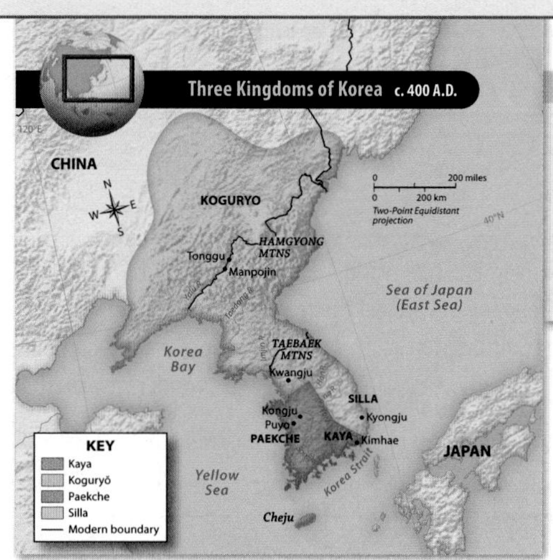

GEOGRAPHY CONNECTION
During the Three Kingdoms period (c. 400 A.D.), Koguryo, Paekche, and Silla were the three main powers.

1. **REGION** Which kingdom was the smallest?
2. **CRITICAL THINKING** ***Analyzing*** Why might Buddhism and Confucianism have reached Koguryo before they reached the other Korean kingdoms?

2 Korean Civilization

GUIDING QUESTION *How did Korea build a civilization?*

After years of conflict, the Silla kingdom finally collapsed. Nobles in the north fought each other for power. By A.D. 935, a general named Wang Kon (wahng•keon) had won out over these rivals. He became the first Korean ruler to unite the entire Korean Peninsula. Wang Kon also founded a new dynasty known as Koryo (KAW•ree•oh). The English word "Korea" comes from the term *Koryo.*

The Koryo Kingdom

Rulers of the Koryo kingdom followed the Chinese model of government that Silla had used. They were able to keep their territory united, and they remained in power for 400 years.

The Koryo rulers set up a code of laws. They also established a civil service system based on examinations. Under this leadership, Buddhism continued to grow and spread throughout the peninsula. Artisans developed movable metal type and produced the world's oldest book printed by this method.

Korean artisans also perfected the making of celadon pottery. This type of pottery is known for its green color and elegant shapes.

The Silla used a combination of military might and diplomacy to secure the kingdom.

LESSON 1

ENGAGE

MAP **Analyzing** Ask students to preview the text by looking at the geographic map of Korea. Tell students that China, Korea, and Japan have had a great influence on one another throughout history.

Ask:

Why do you think China influenced Korea before Japan did? *(The Chinese could enter Korea by land, but the Japanese had to access Korea by sea.)*

Tell students they will be learning more about the relationship between China and Korea, and how Korea acted as a "bridge" between China and Japan. They will also learn about the geography, history, and culture of the Korean civilization.

TEACH & ASSESS

1 Location of Korea

GUIDING QUESTION ***Why is Korea described as a bridge between China and Japan?***

INTERACTIVE WORKSHEET Have students complete the Geography and History worksheet on the borders of Korea.

Ask:

Why was the Yalu River significant? *(It provided fishing and a means of transportation, and it served as a natural border between China and Korea.)* AL

SLIDE SHOW **Determining Cause and Effect** Present the interactive feature on the Silla kingdom. Discuss with students how the rise of Silla affected the lives of Koreans.

Ask:

What were some of the key achievements of the Silla? *(The Silla drove out the Chinese, created a Buddhist kingdom, brought peace, increased food production, helped the economy prosper, and encouraged education and the arts.)*

2 Korean Civilization

GUIDING QUESTION ***How did Korea build a civilization?***

LECTURE SLIDE **Sequencing** Show students the lecture slide displaying how Korea changed from the time of the Silla kingdom to that of the Koryo kingdom.

Ask:

Who first united Korea? *(Wang Kon founded the Koryŏ dynasty, uniting Korea for the first time.)*

What led to the decline of the Koryo kingdom? *(The Mongols invaded Korea and forced the Koryo rulers to submit.)* AL

Comparing After reading about the fall of the Koryo kingdom, discuss with students how the people of Korea went from fighting against the Mongols from China to modeling their government on them.

Ask:

How were the Koryo and Yi governments similar to the Chinese government at the time? *(Each of these governments was ruled by a powerful monarch. Each also used a civil service system based on examinations to select scholarly officials to help run the government. The Yi also introduced the Chinese beliefs of neo-Confucianism to Korea.)*

Comparing Discuss with students the accomplishments of Sejong the Great during his rule. Point out that Sejong was a leader in science and technology. Explain that Sejong the Great was involved in producing globes that showed the position and motion of planets in the solar system.

Ask:

In what way was Sejong similar to the Silla queen Sondok? *(Both were interested in astronomy.)*

Explaining Extend the discussion about improved technology by discussing how a change in the alphabet would have impacted Korean society.

Ask:

How would an easier alphabet help Koreans? *(More Koreans would have been able to learn the simpler alphabet, and this would improve communications between leaders and people, as well as between citizens.)*

IMAGE **Drawing Conclusions** Present the interactive image on the hangul writing system. Discuss with students the writing systems of China, Korea, and Japan.

Ask:

Why might hangul have been easier to read than Japanese or Chinese? *(Possible answer: Japanese and Chinese required memorizing thousands of distinct characters. Hangul assigned a letter to each sound, reducing the amount of memorization needed.)* BL

Comparing and Contrasting Using the interactive whiteboard, create a three-column chart to compare and contrast the results of the Chinese, Mongol, and Japanese invasions of Korea.

Ask:

What happened when the Mongols invaded Korea? *(They seized control of the peninsula and brought much suffering to the Korean people before they were finally defeated.)*

What happened when the Japanese invaded Korea? *(The Koreans defeated the Japanese but suffered a great loss in land and lives.)*

What happened when the Chinese invaded Korea? *(Students should note that the Chinese invaded Korea more than once. At first, China controlled part of northern Korea. The Chinese later aided the Silla but were driven out. Finally, China's Manchu rulers invaded and forced the Yi dynasty to pay tribute.)* Have student volunteers write responses on the whiteboard.

Have students complete the Lesson 1 Review.

CLOSE & REFLECT

Drawing Conclusions Review the influences of China and Japan on Korea's development.

Ask students to consider whether foreign influences were more positive or negative for the Korean people. Discuss different answers to this question as a class. *(Students should note the hardships suffered by Koreans due to multiple foreign invasions as well as the political, technological, and cultural benefits that Korea received from contact with China and Japan.)*

Answers for pages 510–513

P. 510 Taking Notes Silla kingdom—built observatory; defeated other kingdoms to gain control of peninsula; time of peace and prosperity; opened up trade. Koryo dynasty—united Korean peninsula; lasted for about 400 years; increased spread of Buddhism; defeated by Mongols. Yi dynasty—defeated Mongols; lasted more than 500 years; influenced greatly by Chinese culture; greatest ruler was Sejong; did not support Buddhism; developed science and learning

P. 511 GEOGRAPHY CONNECTION

1. Korea lies between the Yellow Sea and the Sea of Japan.
2. CRITICAL THINKING Korea could be described as a bridge because it connects to northeastern China and points toward Japan.

P. 512 CRITICAL THINKING They would have had only the naked eye instead of telescopes.

P. 512 ☑ PROGRESS CHECK People adopted the Chinese writing system, adopted Buddhism and Confucianism, and applied the Chinese form of government.

P. 513 GEOGRAPHY CONNECTION

1. Silla
2. CRITICAL THINKING because Koguryo was physically closer to China

Like other Korean kingdoms before it, Koryo faced internal disorders and outside threats. The Mongols who had taken over China were the main outside danger. In A.D. 1231, the Mongols invaded the northern part of Korea. They forced the Koryo king and royal family to flee to an island near the present-day city of Seoul. After 25 years of struggle, the royal family surrendered.

To remain in power, the Koryo dynasty agreed to accept Mongol rule. The Mongols brought much suffering to the Korean people. They forced thousands of Korean peasants and artisans to build ships for the Mongol ruler Kublai Khan's attempted invasion of Japan.

Mongol power eventually declined, and so did the rule of the Koryo. In 1392, a Korean general named Yi Song-gye (YEE sung•jay) overthrew the Koryo and founded a new dynasty. The Korean people were once again in charge of their country.

The Yi Dynasty

The dynasty that Yi Song-gye founded became known as the Yi. It lasted for over 500 years. The Yi dynasty was one of the world's longest ruling families. Yi rulers set up their capital at Hanseong, the site of Seoul, the modern capital of South Korea.

From Hanseong, Yi rulers strengthened their rule of Korea. Yi rulers still made use of Chinese ideas and practices. They named neo-Confucianism the state philosophy. They opened schools to teach Chinese classics to civil service candidates. However, at the same time, they refused to support Buddhism. The religion declined during this period. Despite the influences from China, the Koreans kept their own traditions and unique identity.

One of the greatest Yi kings was Sejong. He ruled from 1394 to 1450. Sejong was interested in science and technology. He used bronze to invent the first instruments for measuring rain. As a result, Korea has the world's oldest record of rainfall. Sejong was also involved in producing water clocks, sundials, and globes. These globes showed the position and motion of planets in the solar system.

Sejong and his advisers worked to spread literacy, or the ability to read, among the Korean people. They made a great contribution by creating an alphabet called *hangul*. Chinese and Japanese use thousands of characters. Hangul is based on symbols that represent sounds. It uses one letter for each sound, similar to the English alphabet. Hangul is still the standard writing system in present-day Korea.

In the popular Korean fan dance, dancers in traditional robes hold brightly colored fans. They open and close and move the fans to make shapes of butterflies, flowers, and waves.

▶ CRITICAL THINKING
Drawing Conclusions Where do you think you would be most likely to see a traditional fan dance performance?

Ludovic Maisant/CORBIS

Reading HELPDESK

tribute payment to a ruler as a sign of submission or for protection

War and Technology

In 1592, Japanese forces attacked Korea. Their goal was to cross the Korean Peninsula and conquer China. With Chinese help, the Koreans stopped the Japanese attack on land. At sea, the Koreans were also successful because of a new Korean invention: the world's first iron-covered ships.

Before fighting the Japanese, a Korean general named Yi Sun-shin and a team of workers had produced several ships. The vessels were known as turtle ships. Their plated armor looked like turtle shells. They had cannons on all sides and rows of spikes to keep attackers from boarding. These well-protected ships had strong firepower. The general used them to carry out fierce attacks on the Japanese fleet and they were the clear winners.

The dragon's head at the bow of the turtle ships could launch cannon fire or flames.

▶ CRITICAL THINKING
Explaining How did technology change warfare?

Korean Struggles

Although the Koreans were able to defeat the Japanese, their victory came at a high price. The fighting on land had destroyed Korean farms, villages, and towns. The Japanese had killed or kidnapped many Korean farmers and workers.

In the early 1600s, while still recovering from Japan's invasion, the Koreans were attacked by the Chinese. China at this time was ruled by a foreign dynasty known as the Manchus. The Yi dynasty was forced to surrender. They had to pay **tribute** to China's Manchu rulers. Korea's relations with its powerful neighbor remained tense for many centuries.

Jo Yong-Hak/X90071/Reuters/Corbis

☑ PROGRESS CHECK
Explaining How did the building of turtle ships help the Koreans?

LESSON 1 REVIEW

Review Vocabulary

1. How was *shamanism* important to the Koreans?

Answer the Guiding Questions

2. ***Identifying*** What is the physical location of Korea, and how did its location affect China and Japan?
3. ***Summarizing*** What did the first Koryo rulers do to establish a lasting civilization?
4. ***Explaining*** Why was the period of Silla rule considered a time of peace?
5. ***Describing*** Describe the achievements of Sejong that led him to be called one of the greatest Yi kings.
6. **DESCRIPTIVE WRITING** Review the description of the Korean turtle ships. Write a letter to a friend describing the ships.

networks
There's More Online!
☑ GRAPHIC ORGANIZER China Influences Japanese Culture
☑ SLIDE SHOW Buddhist Temples

Heian-kyo (Kyoto) Mt. Fuji Nara Shikoku

Lesson 2
Early Japan

ESSENTIAL QUESTION *How does geography influence the way people live?*

IT MATTERS BECAUSE

Many of the characteristics of modern Japanese culture can be traced back to Shinto and to the samurai.

1 Geography and Settlement

GUIDING QUESTION ***How did geography shape Japan's early society?***

Japan (juh•PAN) lies to the east of Korea and China. Japan is an **archipelago** (ahr•kuh•PEH•luh•goh), or a chain of islands, that runs north to south in the Pacific Ocean. For centuries, most Japanese have lived on the four largest islands: Hokkaido (haw•KY•doh), Honshu (HAHN•shoo), Shikoku (shee•KOH•koo), and Kyushu (KYOO•shoo).

The islands of Japan are actually the tops of mountains that rise from the ocean floor. Earthquakes occur in Japan due to its position along an unstable part of the earth's crust. Because of the mountains, only a small amount of Japan's land can be farmed. Local armies have fought over this limited land for centuries.

Many Japanese turned to the sea to make a living. They built villages along the coast and fished. The Japanese also traveled by ship among their many islands. Still, the seas around Japan kept the Japanese **isolated**, or separated, from the rest of Asia. As a result, Japan developed a strongly independent civilization.

The First Settlers

The first people to settle in Japan probably came from northeastern Asia around 20,000 years ago. About 300 B.C., a new group of people, the Yayoi (YAH•yoy), brought farming to Japan and were the ancestors of the Japanese. They made pottery and grew rice and were skilled metalworkers. By A.D. 300, the Yayoi had organized themselves into clans, each headed by warrior chiefs. The clan's warrior chiefs protected the people.

Reading HELPDESK

Taking Notes: *Identifying*
Use a graphic organizer like the one here to show how Chinese culture influenced the early Japanese.

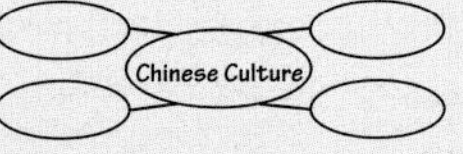

Content Vocabulary
- **archipelago**
- **animism**
- **constitution**

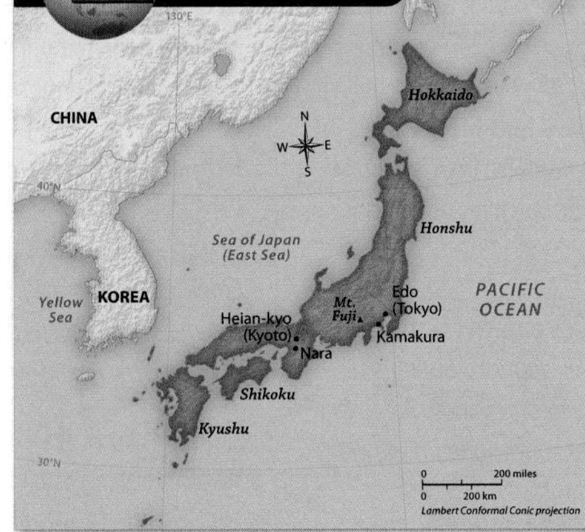

GEOGRAPHY CONNECTION

Japan lies just 110 miles (204 km) east of Korea.

1. **LOCATION** Between what two bodies of water does Japan lie?
2. CRITICAL THINKING ***Analyzing*** How did Japan's geography affect its relationships with its neighbors?

The Yamato

During the A.D. 500s, a clan called the Yamato (YAH•mah•taw) ruled most of Japan. Other clans had to give their loyalty to the Yamato chief. Yamato chiefs claimed that they were descended from a sun goddess who sent her grandson to rule over the people of Japan. Japanese legend states that a Yamato leader named Jimmu (jeem•moo) was the great-grandson of this goddess. This gave him the right to rule Japan. Jimmu took the title "emperor of heaven" and became the first emperor of Japan.

☑ PROGRESS CHECK
Identifying What skills did the Yayoi bring to Japan?

The skillfulness of the Yayoi people can be seen in their metalwork, such as this bronze bell.

archipelago an expanse of water with many scattered islands

Academic Vocabulary
isolate to set apart from others

LESSON 1 (cont.)

IF YOU HAVE MORE TIME . . .

Understand Changing Korean Leaders With a Time Line

Sequencing Write the names of each Korean dynasty on the board. Have students work in small groups to create a visual time line of the Korean rulers. For each entry on the time line, have students draw a picture and create a bulleted list of the characteristics of the rulers. Have them include details about the conflicts and progress that occurred during that ruler's reign.

After completing the time line, have each group present a summary of a single dynasty for the entire class.

Consider How Communication Helped and Hindered Koreans

Evaluating Have students read the passage about the hangul language. Then discuss the ways in which problems with communication created problems for the Korean people.

Ask:

How did poor communication with the Chinese cause problems for the Koreans? *(The Chinese language was difficult to learn, and many Koreans were illiterate until the hangul alphabet was invented. Improved literacy made it easier to communicate information among Koreans.)*

Answers for pages 514–515

P. 514 CRITICAL THINKING A traditional fan dance is probably performed at patriotic celebrations or special performances with great pageantry.

P. 515 CRITICAL THINKING The ironworking technology allowed warriors to have additional protection from harm.

P. 515 ☑ PROGRESS CHECK The ships were used to attack and defeat the Japanese fleet.

LESSON 1 REVIEW

1. Shamanism was the religion of early Koreans. The shaman asked favors of the spirits for people and also cured physical and mental illness.
2. Korea is located between China and Japan. It served as a link of culture and development between the two countries.
3. The Koryo rulers set up a code of laws. They introduced a civil service system based on examinations. They encouraged the growth of Buddhism. Among their many cultural achievements were the invention of movable metal type and the creation of celadon pottery.
4. Silla rulers tried to create an ideal Buddhist kingdom, improve society, and create greater economic opportunities through farming and trade.
5. Sejong stressed science, technology, and literacy. He spread a system of writing across Korea.
6. Answers should include several descriptive details such as the following: The turtle ship is covered in iron with oars and sails to allow movement.

Teaching *Early Japan* (Student Edition pp. 516–519)

LESSON 2

ENGAGE

MAP **Explaining** Project the map of Japan on the interactive whiteboard. Have a volunteer find Japan. Ask students to list the four main Japanese islands from north to south. *(Hokkaido, Honshu, Shikoku, Kyushu)* AL

Also have students locate the Pacific Ocean and the Sea of Japan.

Tell students they will be learning about the geography of Japan and how it influenced Japanese culture. They will also be learning about the first settlers in Japan and the development of religion in Japan.

TEACH & ASSESS

1 Geography and Settlement

GUIDING QUESTION *How did geography shape Japan's early society?*

Analyzing Discuss with students the topography of Japan.

Ask: **What effect did the mountainous terrain of Japan have on its early settlers?** *(They fought over the little farming land available and turned to the sea for food.)*

INTERACTIVE WORKSHEET Introduce students to the 21st Century Skills worksheet on using latitude and longitude. Assign the questions on the worksheet as homework.

Making Inferences Discuss the Yayoi people with students. Ask students why these people were significant.

Identifying Have students summarize the rise of the Yamato clans.

Ask: **What are historians certain of regarding the Yamato?** *(During the A.D. 500s, the Yamato grew strong enough to rule most of Japan. The other clans had to give their loyalty to the Yamato chief.)*

Ask: **Why was Jimmu an important Yamato figure?** *(He was the first emperor of Japan.)*

2 Shinto: Way of the Spirits

GUIDING QUESTION *Why did the early Japanese believe that nature was important?*

LECTURE SLIDE **Making Connections** Show students the lecture slide on Shinto. Discuss with students the effects of Shinto on Japanese customs and values.

Ask: **How did Shinto contribute to the early Japanese love of nature?** *(Possible answer: The early Japanese believed in nature spirits, so they wanted to honor them by showing them respect.)* **In what way did the Japanese honor the *kami*?** *(They worshiped at shrines where priests, dancers, and musicians performed rituals.)*

Answers for pages 516–517

P. 516 Taking Notes Answers should include government, Confucianism, Buddhism, Chinese art, philosophy, and medicine.

P. 517 GEOGRAPHY CONNECTION

1. the Sea of Japan and the Pacific Ocean
2. CRITICAL THINKING As an island nation, Japan was isolated from its neighbors, allowing it to develop its own civilization. At the same time, the seas provided opportunities for trade and other contact with its neighbors.

P. 517 ☑ PROGRESS CHECK They brought farming to Japan, especially the growing of rice in paddies. They also brought pottery making and metalworking.

Many Japanese still follow Shinto today and visit shrines such as the Kanda Myojin shrine in Tokyo. The design of this temple is similar to the temple built by Prince Shotoku hundreds of years before.

▶ CRITICAL THINKING

Explaining What about Shinto beliefs do you think appeals to modern people?

2 Shinto: Way of the Spirits

GUIDING QUESTION *Why did the early Japanese believe that nature was important?*

The early Japanese believed that humans, animals, plants, rocks, and rivers all have their own spirits. This idea is known as **animism** (A•nuh•mih•zuhm). People believed they could call on the *kami* (KAH•mih), or the nature spirits for help. To show respect to the *kami*, the Japanese worshipped at holy places.

Early Japanese beliefs developed into a religion called Shinto. The word *Shinto* means "way of the spirits." Shinto later became linked to Japan's rulers. Their duties included taking part in Shinto rituals to **ensure** the well-being of Japan.

The practice of Shinto affects the Japanese people today. It has contributed to the Japanese love of nature. It also has influenced their striving for simplicity, cleanliness, and good manners.

☑ PROGRESS CHECK

Explaining How did the Japanese show respect to the *kami*?

3 Prince Shotoku

GUIDING QUESTION *How did Prince Shotoku reform Japan's government?*

About A.D. 600, a Yamato prince named Shotoku (shoh•TOH•koo) ruled Japan on **behalf** of his aunt. He wanted to give Japan a strong, well-organized government, so Shotoku created a **constitution** (kahn•stuh•TOO•shuhn), or a plan of government. Shotoku's constitution stated that the emperor was an all-powerful ruler. The Japanese were expected to obey him. Specific rules in the constitution, based on the ideas of Confucius, stated how they should perform their duties.

Shotoku admired Chinese civilization and wanted the Japanese to learn from it. Officials and students studied Buddhism, as well as Chinese art, philosophy, and medicine.

After Shotoku's death, officials continued to use China as a model for Japan. In A.D. 646, the Yamato began the Taika (ty•kuh), or Great Change. Japan was divided into districts ruled by officials who reported to the emperor. All farmland was placed under the emperor's control. Clan leaders could oversee the farmers' work, but government officials now collected taxes. The Taika reforms created Japan's first strong central government.

☑ PROGRESS CHECK

Describing What was the goal of Shotoku's constitution?

Reading **HELP**DESK

animism belief in spirits that are outside of the body

constitution basic laws of a state that define the role of government and guarantee its obligation to the people

Academic Vocabulary

ensure to make sure; guarantee

behalf representing; in the place of

4 The Nara Period

GUIDING QUESTION *How did Chinese ways influence Japan during the Nara period?*

This grand statue of the Buddha stands in the Todaiji temple, which is one of the world's largest wooden buildings. This temple served as the major temple for Buddhism in Japan.

In the early A.D. 700s, Japanese emperors built a new capital city called Nara. It had broad streets, large public squares, Buddhist temples, and Shinto shrines. Nobles' families lived in large, Chinese-style homes. During the Nara period, the Japanese emperors ranked government officials into a hierarchy. However, they did not follow the Chinese practice of using examinations to hire officials. Instead, the emperor gave positions to nobles from powerful families. In return for their services, these officials received large farms. The emperor's control of the land gave him great power.

Buddhist teachings had reached Japan from Korea in the A.D. 500s. During the Nara period, Buddhism became powerful in Japan. In A.D. 770, a Buddhist monk tried to seize the throne. Shaken, the emperor decided to leave Nara for a new capital.

☑ PROGRESS CHECK

Explaining What was Nara?

LESSON 2 REVIEW

Review Vocabulary

1. How does a *constitution* benefit society?

Answer the Guiding Questions

2. ***Explaining*** Why was early society in Japan isolated?
3. ***Drawing Conclusions*** How did animism affect people's views about nature?
4. ***Identifying*** What was Prince Shotoku's main reform in government?
5. ***Contrasting*** How did the Japanese way of hiring officials differ from the Chinese during the Nara period?
6. **PERSUASIVE WRITING** You are a Japanese worker under Prince Shotoku's rule. Write a persuasive plea to Prince Shotoku asking him to change his new constitution to give workers more rights.

networks

There's More Online!

☑ **BIOGRAPHY**
- Minamoto Yoritomo
- Murasaki Shikibu c. A.D. 978–1014

☑ **CHART** Japanese Feudal Class System

☑ **SLIDE SHOW**
- Samurai
- Japanese Art

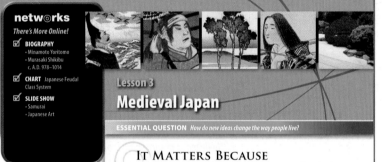

Lesson 3

Medieval Japan

ESSENTIAL QUESTION *How do new ideas change the way people live?*

IT MATTERS BECAUSE

Japanese society was transformed under the shoguns. The cultural influences from this time period still influence Japan and the world.

1 Samurai and Shoguns

GUIDING QUESTION *Why did military leaders rise to power in Japan?*

In A.D. 794, the emperor of Japan moved the capital from Nara to a new city called Heian-kyo (HAY•ahn kyoh). This city later became known as Kyoto (KYOH•toh). The city of Heian-kyo looked much like a major Chinese city.

Nobles Rise to Power

During the A.D. 800s, emperors continued to rule Japan, but their power greatly weakened. Why did this happen? After a period of strong emperors, a number of weak emperors came to the throne. Court officials known as regents governed for them. A regent is a person who rules for an emperor who is too young or too sick to govern.

The regents handled the city's day-to -day government, leaving the Japanese emperors to turn to learning and the arts. Emperors studied Buddhism or wrote poetry in their palace at Heian-kyo.

At the same time, other nobles took control in the outlying provinces of Japan. The government gave these nobles land in return for their support. It also let them stop paying taxes. It made the nobles responsible for governing the lands under their control. To pay for the local government, the nobles increased the taxes on the farmers working the land.

Reading **HELP**DESK

Taking Notes: *Showing Relationships*

Use a graphic organizer like the one here to show the relationship between daimyo and samurai.

Samurai → [ ] → [ ] → Daimyo

Content Vocabulary

- samurai
- shogun
- vassal
- feudalism
- guild
- sect
- martial art
- meditation

The Samurai and Their Code

The nobles gave land to warriors who agreed to fight for them. These warriors became known as **samurai** (SA•muh•ry). In battle, samurai fought on horseback with swords, daggers, and bows and arrows. They wore armor made of leather or steel scales and helmets with horns or crests.

A few Japanese women were outstanding warriors. Perhaps the most famous was Tomoe. She fought in the A.D. 1100s during a time of civil war in Japan. One account from the A.D. 1200s describes her:

PRIMARY SOURCE

> "[S]he was a fearless rider whom neither the fiercest horse nor the roughest ground could dismay, and so dexterously [skillfully] did she handle sword and bow that she was a match for a thousand warriors and fit to meet either god or devil. . . . and so in this last fight, when all the others had been slain or had fled, among the last seven there rode Tomoe."
>
> —from *Heike Monogatori (The Tale of Heike)*

The samurai were warriors in Japan who followed a very strict code of behavior known as Bushido.

▶ CRITICAL THINKING

Explaining Why did samurai agree to fight for a noble?

The word *samurai* means "to serve." The samurai lived by a strict code of conduct. This code was called Bushido (BU•shih•doh), or "the way of the warrior." It demanded that a samurai be loyal to his master. The samurai must also be brave and honorable. Samurai were not supposed to be concerned about riches. They viewed merchants as lacking in honor.

Bound to these principles, a samurai would rather die in battle than betray his master. He also did not want to suffer the disgrace of being captured in battle. The sense of loyalty that set apart the samurai lasted into modern times. During World War II, many Japanese soldiers fought to the death rather than accept defeat or capture. The Japanese have since turned away from the beliefs of the samurai.

Shoguns Assume Power

By the early 1100s, a period similar to the Middle Ages in Europe, noble families of Japan used their samurai armies to fight one another. They fought over land and to gain control of the emperor. In 1180, a civil war broke out between the two most powerful families: the Taira and the Minamoto. In a sea battle in 1185, the Taira were defeated. The commander of the Minamoto forces was Minamoto Yoritomo (mee•nah•MOH•toh yoh•ree•TOH•moh).

samurai a warrior who served a Japanese lord and lived by a strict code of loyalty

Prince Shotoku

GUIDING QUESTION ***How did Prince Shotoku reform Japan's government?***

IMAGE **Identifying** Present the interactive illustration on the zodiac calendar created by Prince Shotoku.

Ask: How is time measured on the calendar? *(Time is measured based on the movements of the sun and the moon.)* **How do animals play a part in the traditional zodiac calendar?** *(Animal zodiac signs are paired with specific repeating years.)*

The Nara Period

GUIDING QUESTION ***How did Chinese ways influence Japan during the Nara period?***

SLIDE SHOW, LECTURE SLIDE

Sequencing Discuss with students the rise of Buddhism in Japan. Show them the slide show on Buddhist temples. Then show students the lecture slide listing events involving Buddhism in Japan.

Ask students to order the events on a sequence of events chart. *(1. Buddhism comes to Japan from Korea; adopted first by nobles and government officials. 2. Buddhism gains acceptance among common people. 3. Power struggles erupt between supporters and opponents. 4. Buddhist monk tries to seize power. 5. Emperor abandons Nara.)* AL

Have students complete the Lesson 2 Review.

CLOSE & REFLECT

Contrasting Ask students to explain what they learned about Japan. Have them summarize the changes from early Japan up to the Nara period of Japan's history. Have them use their own words to summarize their reading. AL 

Answers for pages 518–519
P. 518 CRITICAL THINKING the respect for nature
P. 518 ☑ PROGRESS CHECK They worshiped at holy places.
P. 519 ☑ PROGRESS CHECK to give Japan a strong, well-organized government
P. 519 ☑ PROGRESS CHECK Nara was a new capital city built in the early A.D. 700s.

LESSON 2 REVIEW

1. A constitution offers a standard set of rules by which everyone in the country must live.
2. Japan is comprised of islands and was, therefore, largely isolated from other nations.
3. The early Japanese believed that all things in nature are alive. If humans, animals, plants, rocks, and rivers had their own spirits, they would gain importance and merit greater respect.
4. He wrote Japan's first constitution.
5. The Chinese used a system of examinations to hire officials. In Japan, officials were appointed by the emperor.
6. Writing should focus on the idea that actual freedoms for the people would lead to innovations or creativity. Students may discuss the negative reactions that many workers have to lack of control over their work.

Teaching *Medieval Japan*

(Student Edition pp. 520–527)

LESSON 3 • Day 1

ENGAGE

SLIDE SHOW **Making Inferences** Show students the slide show about the samurai. Discuss with students the weapons and armor used by the samurai.

Ask: Besides having the skills of a warrior, what else did a samurai need? *(Possible answer: To become a samurai, a person needed to have enough wealth to purchase the necessary weaponry.)*

Explain that Japan changed greatly with the rise of the samurai and shoguns. Tell students that in this section, they will learn how these military leaders rose to power and used their power.

TEACH & ASSESS

1 Samurai and Shoguns

GUIDING QUESTION ***Why did military leaders rise to power in Japan?***

Drawing Conclusions Discuss with students the rule of regents in Japan.

Ask: What were the advantages and disadvantages of regents ruling in Japan? *(Possible answer: Regents provided stable rule when an emperor was too young or sick, but regents didn't want to give up power when child emperors became adults.)*

Explaining Have students explain the code of Bushido in their own words.

Ask: Why did the samurai think merchants were lacking in honor? *(Merchants were concerned about riches, which samurai considered beneath their dignity.)*

IMAGE **Identifying** Present the interactive feature on the shoguns in Japan. Point out that the shoguns established a strict class system within Japanese society with the samurai at the top. This system lasted for about 700 years. The last of the class system set up by the shoguns was dismantled in 1868. Elicit students' questions to check their understanding of shoguns.

Ask: What was a shogunate? *(a military government in the Japanese Middle Ages)* AL

2 A Divided Japan

GUIDING QUESTION ***Why did Japan experience disunity from the 1300s to the 1500s?***

LECTURE SLIDE Show students the lecture slide on the emperor's rebellion in 1331 and the ensuing rise of the Ashikaga shogunate.

Ask: Why did so many samurai turn against the Kamakura shogun? *(The samurai wanted to be given more land.)*

CLOSE & REFLECT

INTERACTIVE WHITEBOARD ACTIVITY

Sequencing Use the Interactive Whiteboard Activity on feudal Japan to have students show what they have learned in the lesson by placing key events in Japanese history in their proper sequence. Lead a discussion about how the details about the samurai were different from students' original understanding of the samurai culture.

Answers for pages 520–521
P. 520 Taking Notes Daimyo gave land to samurai. Samurai gave an oath of loyalty to serve daimyo.
P. 521 CRITICAL THINKING Nobles gave land to the warriors who agreed to fight for them.

Minamoto Yoritomo, became the first shogun to rule Japan in 1185. One of his favorite pastimes was to release wild cranes on the beach near his castle. By this he believed he gained Buddhist merit.

▶ CRITICAL THINKING
Analyzing How did Minamoto Yoritomo come to power?

After Yoritomo won the civil war, the emperor feared that the Minamoto family would take the throne. To avoid this, he decided to reward Yoritomo to keep him loyal. In 1192, he gave Yoritomo the title of **shogun** (SHOH•guhn), or commander of the military forces.

This created two governments in Japan. The emperor remained in his palace at Heian-kyo with his advisers. He was Japan's official leader. Meanwhile, the shogun set up his own government in the small seaside town of Kamakura (kah•MAH•kuh•rah). This military government was known as a shogunate. For about the next 700 years, shoguns ran Japan's government.

Mongol Attacks

In the late 1200s, Japan was twice invaded by China's Mongol emperor. During both attempts, violent storms called typhoons destroyed many ships. The Mongols who made it to shore were defeated by the Japanese.

The victorious Japanese named the typhoons *kamikaze* (kah•mih•KAH•zee), or "divine wind," in honor of the spirits they believed had saved their islands. During World War II, Japanese pilots deliberately crashed their planes into enemy ships. They were named kamikaze pilots after the typhoons of the 1200s.

✓ PROGRESS CHECK

Identifying What is Bushido, and why was it important to the samurai?

2 A Divided Japan

GUIDING QUESTION *Why did Japan experience disunity from the 1300s to the 1500s?*

The Kamakura shogunate ruled Japan until 1333. At that time, a general named Ashikaga (ah•shee•KAH•gah) resisted the emperor and made himself shogun. A new government, the Ashikaga shogunate, began.

Asian Art & Archaeology, Inc./CORBIS

Reading HELPDESK

shogun a military governor who ruled Japan

Academic Vocabulary

labor work; the tasks that workers perform for pay

Reading Strategy: *Explaining*

Explaining means you give all the details of something. Why did the emperor make Minamoto Yoritomo shogun?

The Ashikaga shoguns turned out to be weak leaders. Uprisings swept Japan. The country soon divided into a number of small territories. These areas were headed by powerful military lords known as daimyo (DY•mee•oh).

The daimyo pledged to obey the emperor and the shogun. Still, they governed their lands as if they were independent states. To guard their lands, the daimyo used samurai warriors. They formed their own local armies.

Many samurai became **vassals** (VA•suhlz) of a daimyo. These samurai gave an oath of loyalty to their daimyo and pledged to serve him in battle. In return, each daimyo gave land to his samurai. This bond of loyalty between a lord and a vassal is known as **feudalism** (FYOO•duh•lih•zuhm). A similar form of feudalism existed in Europe between the fall of the Western Roman Empire and the early modern period.

With the collapse of central government, warriors battled one another throughout Japan. The violence finally ended the Ashikaga shogunate in 1567. By that time, only a few powerful daimyo were left. Each of these daimyo was eager to conquer his rivals—and rule all of Japan.

✓ PROGRESS CHECK

Analyzing Why did feudalism develop in Japan?

3 Society Under the Shoguns

GUIDING QUESTION *How were the Japanese affected by their country's growing wealth?*

Under the shoguns, Japan produced more goods and grew richer. However, only the emperor and his family, noble families of the emperor's court, and leading military officials enjoyed this wealth. A small but growing class of merchants and traders also benefited from Japan's prosperity. Most Japanese, however, were farmers who remained poor.

Farmers, Artisans, and Trade

For the most part, Japan's wealth came from the hard **labor** of its farmers. Some farmed their own land, but most lived and worked on the estates of the daimyo. Rice, wheat, millet, and barley were their chief crops. Life improved for Japan's farmers during the 1100s, despite their many hardships.

The collapse of a shogunate often led to a period of civil war. This daimyo is one of the powerful military lords that took control and governed.

▶ CRITICAL THINKING
Contrasting What was the difference between the shoguns and the daimyo?

Culver Pictures Inc./SuperStock

vassal a person under the protection of a lord to whom he has vowed loyalty

feudalism the system of service between a lord and the vassals who have sworn loyalty to the lord

In this painting, Japanese farmers are shown working their rice paddies.

▶ CRITICAL THINKING
Explaining How did improved irrigation practices help farmers?

A better irrigation process enabled them to plant more crops. This meant they could sell more food to the markets that were forming in the towns.

On the daimyo estates, other Japanese were producing a greater number of goods. Artisans made armor, weapons, and tools. These goods were sold by merchants in town markets throughout Japan. As trade increased, each region began to make certain goods that they were best at producing. These goods included pottery, paper, textiles, and lacquered ware.

Heian-kyo, now called Kyoto, developed into a major center of production. It also benefited from trade with Korea, China, and Southeast Asia. Japanese merchants traded wooden goods, sword blades, and copper for silk, dyes, pepper, books, and porcelain. More and more artisans and merchants began to live in Kyoto. They set up groups called **guilds** (GIHLDZ), or *za* in Japanese, to protect their jobs and increase their earnings.

Women in Shogun Japan

During the time of the shoguns, the typical Japanese family included grandparents, parents, and children in the same household. A man was head of the family. He had complete control over family members.

At the time of Prince Shotoku, wealthy Japanese women enjoyed a high standing in society. Several women were empresses, and women could own property. Wives who were abandoned could divorce and remarry. When Japan became a warrior society, upper-class women lost these freedoms.

In farming families, women had a greater say in choosing their husbands. However, they worked long hours in the fields. They also cooked, spun and wove cloth, and cared for their children. In the towns, the wives of artisans and merchants helped run the family businesses.

Despite the lack of freedom, some women were able to contribute to Japanese culture. These talented women gained fame as artists, writers, and entertainers.

✓ PROGRESS CHECK

Explaining Why did Japan's wealth increase under the rule of the shoguns?

Erich Lessing/Art Resource, NY

Reading HELPDESK

guild a group of merchants or craftspeople during medieval times

sect a religious group

martial arts sports that involve combat and self-defense

4 Religion and the Arts

GUIDING QUESTION *How did religion and the arts relate to each other under the shoguns?*

During the time of the shoguns, religion and the arts flourished in Japan. Many Japanese monks, artists, scribes, and traders visited China. This led to a borrowing of ideas and practices. Much of this borrowing from the Chinese exchange affected Japan in the areas of government and philosophy. The Chinese also influenced Japan's art, literature, science, and religion.

The Religions of Japan

Under the shoguns, religion influenced every part of daily life in Japan. Most Japanese came to believe in both Shinto and Buddhism. They worshipped at Shinto shrines and at Buddhist temples. To them, each religion met different needs. Shinto was concerned with daily life. It linked the Japanese to nature and their homeland. Buddhism promised spiritual rewards to the good. It prepared people for the life to come. In shogun Japan, religious ideas inspired many Japanese to write poems and plays and produce paintings. They also built shrines and temples.

Mahayana Buddhism, which teaches that the Buddha is a god, began in India and spread to China and Korea. By the time Buddhism reached Japan, it had formed into many different **sects** (SEHKTS), or small groups. One of the major sects in Japan was Zen. Buddhist monks brought Zen to Japan from China during the 1100s. Zen taught that people could find inner peace through self-control and a simple way of life. Followers of Zen disciplined their bodies through **martial arts** (MAHR•shuhl), or sports that involved combat and self-defense.

Zen Buddhists also practiced **meditation** (meh•duh•TAY•shuhn). A person who meditated sat cross-legged and motionless. The person tried to clear the mind of all worldly thoughts and desires. Meditation was considered a way for people to relax and find inner peace.

(l) Michael Maslan Historic Photographs/CORBIS, (r) B.S.P.I./CORBIS

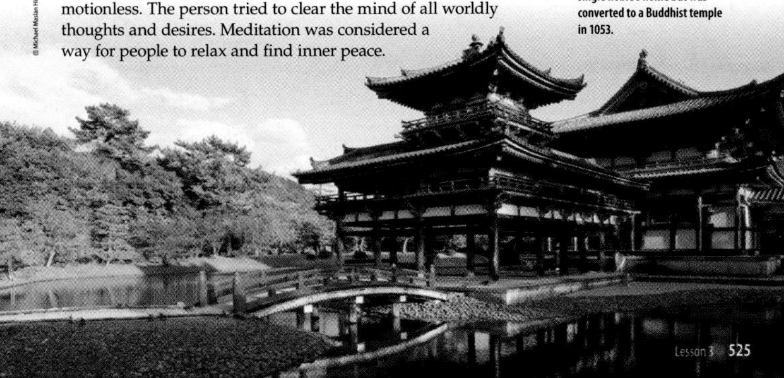

The Phoenix Hall was originally a single noble's home but was converted to a Buddhist temple in 1053.

LESSON 3 • Day 2

ENGAGE

Identifying Ask students to identify a beautiful church, synogogue, or other house of worship in your community. Have them explain what is beautiful about the building. Discuss how that the house of worship uses art in its architecture.

Ask:

What does art have to do with religion? *(Accept reasonable answers.)* Explain that in this part of the lesson, students will read about how the early religions of Japan cultivated artistic development.

Society Under the Shoguns

GUIDING QUESTION *How were the Japanese affected by their country's growing wealth?*

GRAPHIC ORGANIZER **Making Inferences** Present the graphic organizer showing the social structure of feudal Japan. Allow students time to read the information and ask questions to clarify their understanding.

Ask: How did the samurai help the daimyo stay in power? *(The samurai were warriors who served the daimyo and kept the other social groups in line.)* AL

Religion and the Arts

GUIDING QUESTION *How did religion and the arts relate to each other under the shoguns?*

SLIDE SHOW **Identifying** Present the interactive feature on Japanese art and architecture during the time of the shoguns. As you present each slide, ask students to describe what they notice. Encourage students to participate in the activity. Each student should provide at least one descriptive term. ELL

Ask:

What do the architecture and the art of Japan reveal about Japanese culture? *(Possible answer: their love of simplicity and beauty)*

Ask:

How do Japanese gardens compare or contrast with Western gardens? *(Japanese gardens are similar to Western gardens because they use plants, rocks, and water to create beauty. The gardens may differ in their use of raked rocks as a garden feature to represent water.)*

Have students complete the Lesson 3 Review.

CLOSE & REFLECT

INTERACTIVE WORKSHEET **Expressing** Students will use the art of tanka poems to show what they have learned in this lesson. Use the 21st Century Skills worksheet on writinq a tanka to review the structure of tanka poems with the class.

Ask:

How does the form of *tanka* differ from that of *haiku*? *(Tanka is an unrhymed poem of 5 lines. Haiku is a poem of 3 lines and 17 total syllables.)* Then assign the worksheet as homework. Encourage students to choose a subject from the lesson as the topic for their poems.

Discuss with the class some of the appropriate subjects from the lesson. For example, students might write about samurai, the code of bushido, or the art and architecture of Japan.

Remind students that they may use the images in the slide shows or their textbook for inspiration.

IF YOU HAVE MORE TIME . . .

Practice Researching Safely on the Internet

Determining Reliable Sources Looking for reliable online resources can be a challenge even for students who spend a lot of time with technology. Many articles are written authoritatively and intentionally disguise the authorship and publishing credentials. Moreover, conducting a search for a specific topic uncovers long lists of articles that include the mention of a particular topic.

However, understanding a few basic rules about Internet research will help students navigate their online travels.

- **Read the URL.** The letters at the end of a Web site name indicate an article's pedigree. The ending .gov indicates a government Web site. The ending .com indicates a company website. The ending .org indicates an organization, and the ending .edu indicates an educational institution.
- **Look for authorship.** An article written by a reputable author will include details about his or her academic credentials. An unsigned article should be considered carefully for its reliability.
- **Look for the updates.** A reputable Web site will indicate when the material has been updated. This information should be included in a bibliography reference.
- **Watch for bias.** The Internet has few safeguards that ensure accuracy. Anyone can publish their ideas, so many Web sites contain biased information or inaccurate interpretation of the facts. Students should use their critical thinking skills to decipher a bias in an online article. Facts in such articles should be further researched before they are considered accurate.
- **Use authoritative sources.** Most schools have implemented their own list of reliable Web sites, which may include such sources as Encyclopaedia Britannica, government Web sites, or Oxford Reference tools. Students will be most successful in their online research when they are given clear guidelines for acceptable research database sources.

Conducting Online Research Have students choose a topic from the lesson or chapter for a research project. Have them use the Internet to research their topic.

Suggest the following topics from Lesson 3:

- Japanese Samurai Warriors, Armor, Training, or Code of Honor
- The Shogun and His Rule
- Important Women in Japanese History
- The Japanese Practice of Shinto
- Zen Buddhism
- Basho and Haiku Poetry
- Japanese Noh Theater

Have students find three reliable online articles about their topic. Then have them summarize their research in a three-paragraph essay.

Answers for pages 522–525

P. 522 CRITICAL THINKING He defeated the Taira in the civil war and was then named shogun by the emperor.

P. 522 Reading Strategy to keep him loyal

P. 522 ☑ PROGRESS CHECK Bushido is a strict code of conduct. It set the standard for how a samurai must behave toward his master.

P. 523 CRITICAL THINKING The shoguns were military leaders in the emperor's army, and the daimyo were wealthy landowners with their own armies.

P. 523 ☑ PROGRESS CHECK Feudalism developed because the Ashikaga shoguns were weak leaders and could not keep Japan united. Japan soon divided into a feudalistic system with a number of small territories headed by daimyo.

P. 524 CRITICAL THINKING Improved irrigation helped farmers raise more crops with less labor.

P. 524 ☑ PROGRESS CHECK Under the shoguns, skilled workers in Japan produced more goods. When combined with improved roads and increased farm production, this led to greater trade. Greater trade meant greater wealth.

BIOGRAPHY

Murasaki Shikibu (c. A.D. 978–1014)

In addition to *The Tale of Genji*, Lady Murasaki Shikibu wrote a diary and more than 120 poems. Her father was a scholar and a governor, and he broke with tradition by educating his daughter Murasaki in Chinese language and literature. Her family was noble but not rich. While serving as a lady-in-waiting in the royal court, Murasaki began writing her novel based on observations of life around her.

▶ CRITICAL THINKING
Explaining How did Murasaki herself break from tradition?

Writing and Literature

During the A.D. 500s, the Japanese adopted China's writing system. They used Chinese picture characters that represented whole words. The Japanese and Chinese languages were very different, so the Japanese found it difficult to use these characters. Then, in the A.D. 800s, they added symbols that stood for sounds, much like the letters of an alphabet. Reading and writing became much easier.

The Japanese greatly admired calligraphy, or the art of writing beautifully. Every well-educated person was expected to practice it. Handwriting was believed to reveal much about a person's education, social standing, and character.

Under the shoguns, the Japanese wrote poems, stories, and plays. By the 1600s, a form of poetry called *haiku* (HY•koo) had emerged. A haiku consists of 3 lines of words with a total of 17 syllables. Haiku usually expresses a mood or feeling. The most noted writer of haiku was a man of samurai descent. Below are two of his most famous haiku.

PRIMARY SOURCE

First snow
falling
on the half-finished bridge.

A field of cotton—
As if the moon
had flowered.

—tr. by Robert Hass

Japan's first great prose literature was written around A.D. 1000 by women at the emperor's palace at Heian-kyo. Lady Murasaki Shikibu (mur•uh•SAH•kee shee•KEE•boo) wrote *The Tale of Genji*. This work describes the romances and adventures of a Japanese prince. Some people believe the work is the world's first novel, or long fictional story.

The Japanese also wrote plays. The oldest type of play is called Noh. Created during the 1300s, Noh plays developed out of religious dances and were used to teach Buddhist ideas. Many Noh plays are still performed in Japan today.

Architecture and Art

During the time of the shoguns, the Japanese adopted building and artistic ideas from China and Korea. They went on to develop their own styles. The architecture and art of Japan revealed the Japanese love of simplicity and beauty.

Reading HELPDESK

Visual Vocabulary
meditation mental exercise to reach a greater spiritual awareness

Shinto shrines were built in the Japanese style, usually as a simple wooden building, with one room and a rice straw roof. Often they were built near a sacred tree or rock.

Unlike Shinto shrines, Buddhist temples were built in the Chinese style. They had massive tiled roofs held up by thick, wooden pillars. Inside, the temples were richly decorated. They had many altars, paintings, and statues.

Around buildings, the Japanese created gardens that copied nature on a small scale. Carefully placed large rocks served as symbols of mountains, while raked sand gave the sense of water flowing. They might contain only a few plants. The gardens were built this way to create a feeling of peace and calmness.

Creative Artisans

To create beauty inside buildings, Japan's artisans made wooden statues, furniture, and household items. They used a shiny black or red coating called lacquer on many decorative and functional objects. Other Japanese artists learned to do landscape painting from the Chinese. Using ink or watercolors, they painted scenes of nature or battles on paper scrolls or on silk. Japanese nobles at the emperor's palace learned to fold paper to make decorative objects. This art of folding paper is called origami. Buddhist monks and the samurai turned tea drinking into a beautiful ceremony.

The larger rocks in the Japanese garden are symbols of mountains. The raked white stones represent flowing water.

☑ PROGRESS CHECK
Analyzing How did meditation play a part in Buddhism?

LESSON 3 REVIEW

Review Vocabulary

1. How did the *samurai* advisers serve the *shoguns*?

Answer the Guiding Questions

2. ***Determining Cause and Effect*** How did regents affect the rise to power of military leaders in Japan?
3. ***Determining Cause and Effect*** What caused Japanese disunity from the 1300s to the 1500s?
4. ***Identifying*** What groups of Japanese benefited the most from the increasing wealth in Japan?
5. ***Analyzing*** What effect did religion have on the arts during the time of the shoguns?
6. **NARRATIVE WRITING** Write a narrative in which you describe an encounter with a samurai in the 1300s. This samurai tells you about the code of Bushido. Be sure to include how the samurai dresses and acts.

networks
There's More Online!
☑ GRAPHIC ORGANIZER
Angkor Wat

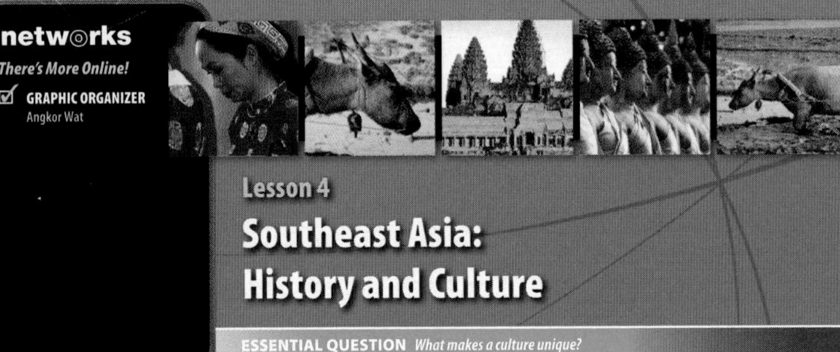

Lesson 4

Southeast Asia: History and Culture

ESSENTIAL QUESTION *What makes a culture unique?*

IT MATTERS BECAUSE

The varied cultures of Southeast Asia have been shaped by outside influences and, in turn, have shaped other cultures.

1 Early Civilization

GUIDING QUESTION ***How did geography affect settlement and early ways of life in Southeast Asia?***

China, Korea, and Japan were not alone in developing civilizations along Asia's Pacific coast. Farther south, other civilizations arose in a region known today as Southeast Asia. Southeast Asians developed their own traditions, though they were influenced by India, China, and Islam.

The Geography of Southeast Asia

Southeast Asia has two major parts. One is a mainland area made up of long, winding peninsulas. The other is a large archipelago, or chain of islands.

Mountain ranges cross mainland Southeast Asia, running north to south. Between the ranges are narrow river valleys and broad coastal deltas. These lowlands are rich in fertile soil. They became prosperous farming and trading centers and home to most mainland Southeast Asians.

South and east of the region's mainland are thousands of mountainous islands. Part of a geographical area known for being unstable, these islands hold many active **volcanoes**. These volcanoes provide rich soil for farming. Earthquakes affect the island peoples of Southeast Asia. One particular danger comes from **tsunamis** (soo•NAH•meez). A tsunami is a huge ocean wave caused by an underwater earthquake. Tsunamis usually strike coastal lowlands, killing many people and destroying buildings. This happened in Japan in 2011.

Sea trade and inland mountain barriers shaped Southeast Asia into a region of many ethnic groups, languages, and religions. As a result, Southeast Asia was never united under a single government. Instead, it was an area of separate territories.

Early Years

Early peoples in Southeast Asia grew rice, raised cattle and pigs, and made metal goods. These early people believed in animism, the idea that spirits exist in living and nonliving things. They practiced different rituals to honor their ancestors as well as animal and nature spirits.

Southeast Asia Today

GEOGRAPHY CONNECTION

Southeast Asia is made up of long peninsulas and a large archipelago, or chain of islands.

1. **LOCATION** Between which five countries is Laos located?
2. CRITICAL THINKING
Drawing Conclusions Looking at the map, why do you think a tsunami would be especially dangerous in this region?

Reading HELPDESK

Taking Notes: Identifying
Use a graphic organizer like this one to show what purposes the temple of Angkor Wat served.

Content Vocabulary
- volcano
- tsunami
- maritime

volcano a mountain that may release hot or melted rocks from inside the Earth
tsunami a huge ocean wave caused by an undersea earthquake

LESSON 3 • Day 2 (cont.)

IF YOU HAVE MORE TIME . . .

Analyze Zen Statements

Analyzing Explain to students that some Zen Buddhists meditate by thinking about paradoxical statements—that is, statements that seem inconsistent or even absurd. In Japan, these are known as koan (KOH-ahn).

Koan are not meant to be understood in an obvious way. The answer can only be discovered by intuition, or inner understanding, and not through rational thinking. Zen teachers might use koan to test the level of their students' understanding of Zen principles.

A famous collection of koans is known in the West as *The Gateless Gate*. One of the most well-known koan asks what the sound of one hand clapping is.

Researching Challenge students to research koan on the Internet and find examples. Have volunteers read these examples aloud.

Discussing Then, conduct a discussion to see what students think the answers might be to the koan they find. Remind students that it is not necessary to discover a correct answer, since the nature of koan is that the answers are hidden, if traditional answers exist at all. BL

Answers for pages 526–527

P. 526 CRITICAL THINKING She became a writer, something that few women of the time did because even upper-class women did not have a lot of freedom.

P. 527 ☑ PROGRESS CHECK Zen Buddhists practiced meditation to clear their minds and search for inner peace.

LESSON 3 REVIEW

1. They controlled Japan's countryside, kept law and order, and fought in the armies of the shoguns.
2. The regents refused to give up power when the emperors were old enough to rule. This caused a division of power. As the emperors grew weaker, more nobles assumed power over smaller holdings.
3. Central power declined, and Japan was divided into a number of smaller territories ruled by the daimyo.
4. Those who benefited the most were the emperor and his family, a number of noble families, leading military officials, and a small but growing class of merchants and traders.
5. In shogun Japan, a period similar to the Middle Ages in Europe, Shinto and Buddhist ideas inspired many Japanese people. They wrote poems and plays, produced paintings, and built shrines and temples.
6. Narratives should include the key elements of Bushido: loyalty, courage, and honor. They should also have descriptions of weapons, clothing, and so on.

Teaching *Southeast Asia: History and Culture* (Student Edition pp. 528–533)

LESSON 4

ENGAGE

IMAGE **Making Connections** Show students the interactive image of the Angkor Wat temple complex. Explain that the site displays evidence of Buddhist and Hindu influences.

Ask:

What does the design of Angkor Wat suggest about the cultures of Southeast Asia? *(Students should note that the temple complex represents a blend of cultures, suggesting that Southeast Asia was a place where different cultures met and exchanged ideas.)* BL

Explain to students that in this lesson they will learn about a number of different empires that rose and fell in Southeast Asia. They will see the similarities between these cultures as well as the aspects that made each culture unique.

TEACH & ASSESS

1 Early Civilization

GUIDING QUESTION *How did geography affect settlement and early ways of life in Southeast Asia?*

MAP **Identifying** Show students the map of Southeast Asia today. Have them identify key geographic features.

Ask:

What kind of landforms make up Indonesia? *(It is made up of a series of mountainous islands.)* ELL

Ask:

Why would the soil in the valleys and deltas be fertile? *(Rainwater would wash soil from the mountains down into the valleys. The rivers would carry silt to the deltas on the coast.)*

IMAGE **Analyzing Visuals** Present the interactive image showing a map of the Strait of Malacca.

Ask:

Why do you think the Strait of Malacca was important for shipping? *(Possible answer: It provided a shortcut between the Indian Ocean and the South China Sea.)*

Answers for pages 528–529

P. 528 Taking Notes Hindu temple; Buddhist temple; royal tomb; astronomical observatory

P. 529 GEOGRAPHY CONNECTION

1. Thailand, Cambodia, Vietnam, Myanmar, and China
2. CRITICAL THINKING A tsunami would be especially dangerous in this area because a tsunami would sweep over many small islands. Also, on a small island, there is little room for people to move inland to escape the danger.

Musicians from Vietnam perform traditional music using string and wind instruments.

Southeast Asians also developed their own forms of art. Artisans made a cloth of detailed patterns later called batik (buh•TEEK). Musicians played instruments including the *dan bau* (similar to a xylophone), the *dan day* (a type of guitar), and the *rammana* (a type of drum). Artists created a type of theater that used shadow puppets to tell stories. Performers holding long rods controlled the puppets behind a white screen, while audiences on the other side could see the puppets' moving shadows.

Outside Contacts

During the A.D. 100s, Hindu traders from India reached coastal areas of Southeast Asia. They set up a trading **network** that exchanged goods and ideas among the peoples of Southeast Asia, India, and the Middle East. As these contacts increased, the cultures of other civilizations spread throughout Southeast Asia. Over time, the people of the region blended Hindu and Chinese ways with their own traditions.

PROGRESS CHECK

Analyzing Why did outside influences have a powerful effect on early Southeast Asia?

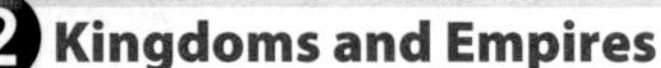

2 Kingdoms and Empires

GUIDING QUESTION *Why did powerful kingdoms and empires develop in Southeast Asia?*

From A.D. 500 to 1500, many kingdoms and empires thrived in Southeast Asia. States covering fertile inland areas drew their wealth from the land. States on the coast became **maritime** (MEHR•uh•tym), or seafaring, powers that controlled shipping.

Vietnam

Along the coast of the Indochinese Peninsula lies the present-day country of Vietnam. The ancient Viet were one of the first people in Southeast Asia to develop their own state and culture. During the 200s B.C., the Viet people ruled most of the Indochinese Peninsula.

During the early A.D. 900s, the Viet rebelled against China's weakened Tang dynasty. In A.D. 938, the Viet forces defeated a fleet of Chinese warships in the Battle of the Bach Dang River. The Viet had finally won independence.

Reading HELPDESK

maritime related to the sea or seafaring

Academic Vocabulary

network a system in which all parts are connected

style a distinctive form or type of something

The new state was modeled on the government of China and was known as Dai Viet, or Great Viet. Confucianism became its official religion. Viet emperors adopted Chinese court ceremonies. Just as in China, Viet government officials were selected through civil service examinations.

The Khmer Empire

West of Vietnam is the present-day country of Cambodia (kam•BOH•dee•uh). In ancient times, this region was the home of the Khmer (kuh•MEHR) people. During the A.D. 1100s, the Khmer founded an empire that covered much of mainland Southeast Asia. They became wealthy from growing rice.

Khmer kings based their rule on Hindu and Buddhist ideas from India. They increased their power by presenting themselves as god-kings to their people. A Chinese traveler once described the splendor, in dress and manner, of a Khmer king in about 1297:

PRIMARY SOURCE

> His crown of gold is high and pointed like those on the heads of the mighty gods. . . . His neck is hung with ropes of huge pearls; . . . his wrists and ankles are loaded with bracelets and on his fingers are rings of gold. . . . He goes barefoot—the soles of his feet, like the palms of his hands, are rouged [colored] with a red stuff. When he appears in public, he carries the Golden Sword.
>
> —from *A Record of Cambodia: The Land and Its People*, by Zhou Daguan, tr. by Peter Harris

Supported by Khmer kings, architects created a new **style** of building based on Indian and local designs. The most magnificent structure was Angkor Wat. It served as a religious temple, a royal tomb, and an astronomical observatory. Angkor Wat still stands today and attracts many visitors.

By the 1440s, building costs, high taxes, and internal revolts had weakened the Khmer Empire. In A.D. 1432, the Thai (TY), a neighboring Southeast Asian people, captured the capital city of Angkor. With this attack, the Khmer Empire faded into history.

Connections to TODAY

Saving Angkor Wat

Angkor Wat was overgrown by thick tropical plants and trees after its capture by the Thai in A.D. 1432. During the late 1900's the site was further damaged during various wars. Mostly, however, it suffered from neglect. In 1992, Angkor was named a UNESCO World Heritage site, a major step in protecting it for generations to come.

Angkor Wat, the largest religious structure in the world, is a temple complex built in Cambodia. Built in the 1100's, it took nearly 40 years to complete.

CRITICAL THINKING

Making Inferences Why do you think it took so long to build Angkor Wat?

Statues of the Buddha line a temple in Thailand. They are dressed in orange robes, which are the traditional garb for Buddhist monks.

CRITICAL THINKING

Drawing Conclusions How did Buddhist monks from India influence the Thai people?

The Thai

The earliest Thai settlements arose along the border of China. Between A.D. 700 and 1100, Thai groups moved southward. They set up a kingdom at Sukhothai (SOO•kah•TY) in what is today north central Thailand.

The Thai developed a writing system and made the kingdom a center of learning and the arts. Artisans from China taught the making of porcelain. Buddhist monks from India converted many Thai to Buddhism. The Thai were influenced by Hinduism in their political practices, dance, and literature.

About A.D. 1350 a new Thai kingdom known as Ayutthaya (ah•yoo•TY•uh) arose. Its capital city was located where the city of Bangkok, the present Thai capital, stands today.

The Ayutthaya kingdom lasted for about 400 years. At its height, it held control over large areas of Southeast Asia. The Thai region was an important center of Buddhist learning and culture. Its merchants traded in teak wood, salt, spices, and hides with China and neighboring Asian kingdoms.

Burma

West of the Thai kingdom, a people known as the Burmese developed a civilization. In A.D. 849, they set up a capital city called Pagan (pah•GAHN). During the next 200 years, Pagan became a major influence in the western part of Southeast Asia.

Reading HELPDESK

Academic Vocabulary

institution a custom or practice that many people accept and use

Reading Strategy: Determining Cause and Effect

Consider an event and what happens because of that event. What was the result of Khmer farmers building lakes, canals, and channels to irrigate their rice fields?

The city eventually became a center of Buddhist learning and culture. Like the Thai, the Burmese adopted Buddhism, as well as Indian political **institutions** and culture.

Attacks by the Mongols in the late 1200s weakened Pagan. To escape Mongol rule, many people in Burma moved south and built fortified towns along the rivers. Burmese culture was preserved, but the kingdom did not arise again until the 1500s.

The Malay States

On the Malay Peninsula and the islands of Indonesia, independent states developed around seaport cities. They traded porcelain, textiles, and silk, as well as Southeast Asian spices and wood.

Most of the people living on Southeast Asian islands were Malays. Despite common cultural ties, the Malays were divided into many separate communities by distance and trade rivalries. However, in the A.D. 700s, a Malay state arose on the islands of Java and Sumatra in present-day Indonesia. This state controlled the trade route passing through the Strait of Malacca.

Many Southeast Asian states continue to share common farming and trade ideas and practices.

Islam in Southeast Asia

Muslim Arab traders and missionaries settled coastal areas of Southeast Asia during the A.D. 800s. Eventually, many people in these places converted to Islam. The first major Islamic center was Melaka, a trading port on the Malay Peninsula.

From Melaka, Islam spread throughout the Indonesian islands. Bali was the only island to remain outside of Muslim influence. Even today, Bali keeps its Hindu religion and culture.

PROGRESS CHECK

Summarizing How did the culture of China affect Southeast Asian states?

LESSON 4 REVIEW

Review Vocabulary

1. Why do *maritime* workers live along a seacoast?

Answer the Guiding Questions

2. ***Identifying*** What separated early Southeast Asians?
3. ***Listing*** What were the most powerful kingdoms to develop on mainland Southeast Asia by A.D. 1500?
4. ***Contrasting*** Why did some Southeast Asian states rely mostly on trading while others relied on farming?
5. ***Explaining*** Why was Angkor Wat significant to the Khmer?
6. **DESCRIPTIVE WRITING** Look at the photograph of Angkor Wat. Then write a paragraph describing its appearance to someone who has never seen it before.

LESSON 4 (cont.)

Kingdoms and Empires

GUIDING QUESTION ***Why did powerful kingdoms and empires develop in Southeast Asia?***

INTERACTIVE WORKSHEET **Determining Cause and Effect** Show students the Economics of History worksheet on the rise and fall of the Khmer Empire. Have students complete the initial questions on the Khmer's rise to power; then assign the final questions as homework.

Identifying Discuss the significance of various religious beliefs on the peoples of Southeast Asia.

Ask:

What religion did the early peoples of Southeast Asia follow? *(animism)*

Which peoples adopted Buddhism as their main religion? *(The Thai and Burmese people became Buddhist. Buddhism was also important to the Khmer.)*

Where in the region was Islam practiced? *(primarily in the Malay Peninsula and the islands of Indonesia)* AL

INTERACTIVE WHITEBOARD ACTIVITY **Comparing and Contrasting** Create a three-column graphic organizer using the interactive whiteboard. Title the columns "India," "China," and "Arabia." Then hold a class discussion in which students identify key ways in which each of these outside cultures influenced Southeast Asia.

Ask:

What religions and other belief systems were introduced by each outside culture? *(India introduced Buddhism and Hinduism to the region, and later Islam. China introduced Confucian ideas. Arabia brought Islam to the Malay Peninsula.)* AL

Ask:

How did these outsiders influence government? *(India influenced the Funan and Sukhothai kingdoms. The Viet based their government on the Chinese examination-system model. States based on Islam formed in the Southeast Asian islands.)*

What role did trade play in spreading ideas? *(Indian merchants brought Hinduism and other ideas to Southeast Asia. Arabian merchants brought Islam to the Southeast Asian islands.)*

LECTURE SLIDE **Sequencing** Show students the lecture slide with a time line about the development of Thailand and Burma. Have a volunteer read aloud the details about each country. Discuss the similarities and differences that exist in the development of each country.

Have students complete the Lesson 4 Review.

CLOSE & REFLECT

Comparing and Contrasting Lead the class in a discussion of how Southeast Asian nations developed in the same ways and how they developed in distinct, or different, ways. Ask students to consider the influence of trade, conquest, and religion upon the region. BL

IF YOU HAVE MORE TIME . . .

Connect Reading and Writing Skills

Summarizing Information Ask students to consider the importance of geography in the rise of each political power in Southeast Asia including Vietnam, Cambodia, Thailand, Burma, Malay, and Indonesia. Share several techniques for summarizing information:

- Put the ideas you read into your own words. Have students retell the information they have just read.
- Use categories. Collapse examples and details into categories to create a general statement about the content.
- Avoid a string of facts. A good summary is a short version of the original, not a list of details.
- Revise and rewrite. After creating the first draft of a summary, rewrite it as a single paragraph, adding transition words, main idea sentences, and conclusions that make the summary complete.

Have students use these strategies when they summarize the importance of geography in determining how political power came about in Southeast Asia. AL ELL

Answers for pages 530–533

P. 530 ☑ PROGRESS CHECK Outside influences linked Southeast Asians with other parts of the world, thus influencing cultural elements such as forms of government and religion.

P. 531 CRITICAL THINKING Angkor Wat was so large that it likely took a long time because so many workers and materials were involved.

P. 532 CRITICAL THINKING The Buddhists from India converted many Thai to Buddhism.

P. 533 ☑ PROGRESS CHECK Answers should include that they affected government, architecture, and religion.

LESSON 4 REVIEW

1. It refers to the sea or to seafaring.
2. The vast mountain ranges and many seas separated the countries.
3. Dai Viet, Angkor, Sukhothai, Ayutthaya, Pagan, Srivijaya, Majapahit, Melaka
4. From A.D. 500 to 1500, the different states of Southeast Asia developed economies based on either farming or trade. States covering large inland areas drew their wealth from farming the land. Other smaller, coastal states became maritime, or seafaring, powers that controlled shipping and trade.
5. Angkor Wat served as a temple and a cultural center for many years; today, it attracts visitors from around the world.
6. Students should include vivid descriptive details, such as size and composition, color, location on the water, and how it reflects on the water.

CHAPTER 18 Activities

Write your answers on a separate sheet of paper.

❶ **Exploring the Essential Question**
EXPOSITORY WRITING Review the section about the first settlers in Japan. Then write a paragraph in which you discuss the Yayoi. How did they live? How were they organized? What kind of government did they have?

❷ **21st Century Skills**
USING LATITUDE AND LONGITUDE Many Southeast Asian countries are linked by water. Notice where the Equator falls in the region on the map below. Do research to find out what effect living on the Equator can have on the lives of the people of Southeast Asia. How might this latitude influence their economies and lifestyle. Share your finding with the class, using the map as part of your presentation.

❸ **Thinking Like a Historian**
UNDERSTANDING CAUSE AND EFFECT Create a diagram like the one to the right to identify what events caused shoguns to rise to power in Japan.

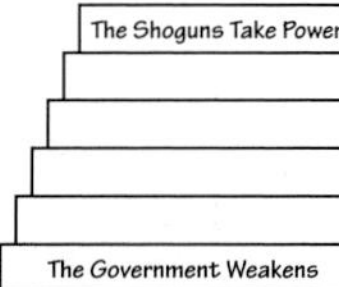

❹ **GEOGRAPHY ACTIVITY**

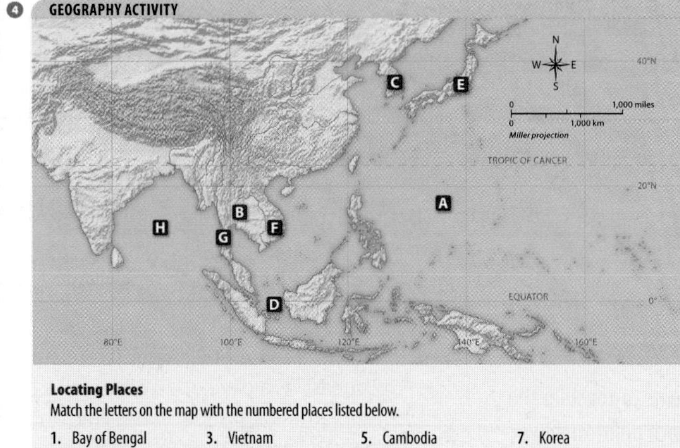

Locating Places
Match the letters on the map with the numbered places listed below.

1. Bay of Bengal
2. Pacific Ocean
3. Vietnam
4. Indonesia
5. Cambodia
6. Japan
7. Korea
8. Thailand

CHAPTER 18 Assessment

REVIEW THE GUIDING QUESTIONS
Directions: Choose the best answer for each question.

❶ Which group ruled Korea for 400 years?
A. the Koryo˘
B. the Silla
C. the Tang
D. the Confucians

❷ What is *hangul*?
F. an instrument for measuring rainfall
G. the standard writing system in present-day Korea
H. a globe that shows the position and motion of planets
I. a turtle ship

❸ Many samurai became
A. daimyo.
B. shoguns.
C. vassals.
D. Bushido.

❹ Why did the early Japanese turn to the sea for food?
F. They preferred fishing to farming.
G. There was little fertile land for farming.
H. The seas around Japan left them isolated.
I. Their crops were destroyed by volcanic eruptions.

❺ How did the Khmer Empire rulers increase their power?
A. They opened schools.
B. They built large temples.
C. They presented themselves as god-kings.
D. They traded goods with Hindu traders from India.

❻ Which city became a center of learning and trade in Burma?
F. Sukhothai
G. Pagan
H. Sumatra
I. Melaka

CHAPTER 18 Assessment *(continued)*

DBQ DOCUMENT-BASED QUESTIONS

A great Noh actor, explained how acting is mastered.

"As long as an actor is trying to imitate his teacher, he is still without mastery. . . . An actor may be said to be a master when, by means of his artistic powers, he quickly perfects the skills he has won through study and practice, and thus becomes one with the art itself."

—*The Book of the Way of the Highest Flower (Shikadō-Sho)*
by Seami Jūokubushū Hyōshaku

❼ **Analyzing** Which of the following best summarizes when actors become "masters"?
A. when they can imitate the teacher
B. when they begin to study and practice acting
C. when they learn artistic skills
D. when they become part of the art of acting

❽ **Comparing and Contrasting** What might a master actor and a samurai have in common?
F. Both were well paid.
G. Both worked for shoguns.
H. Both owned land.
I. Both practiced their skills to perfection.

SHORT RESPONSE

"During the Three Kingdoms , . . . power in all three of the kingdoms was held by those who lived in the capital and by the aristocratic families who dominated a very rigid and hereditary social status system. Members of the upper and lower classes were differentiated in almost every aspect of their lives, including clothing, food, housing, and occupation. . . . The lifestyle of the aristocracy was supported by slaves, who led miserable lives."

—May Connor, editor, *The Koreas*

❾ What factors differentiated members of the upper and lower classes?

❿ What privileges did aristocrats have that the lower class didn't have?

EXTENDED RESPONSE

⓫ **Expository Writing** Write a short essay in which you explain the concept of animism and its influence on the culture of the Japanese.

Need Extra Help?

If You've Missed Question	❶	❷	❸	❹	❺	❻	❼	❽	❾	❿	⓫
Review Lesson	1	1	3	2	3	4	3	2, 3	4	4	4

NOTES

REFLECT, REVIEW, & REMEDIATE

INTERACTIVE WORKSHEET

Chapter Summary

Provide students with the Chapter Summary worksheet to help review the chapter and prepare for assessment.

Reviewing the Enduring Understanding

Review this chapter's Enduring Understanding with students:

- People, places, and ideas change over time.

Guide students in small-group discussions about the ways in which the different Korean, Japanese, and Southeast Asian powers evolved over time. Help them see the interrelationships among the different states and empires and how control and influence shifted with the rise and fall of different powers.

INTERACTIVE WHITEBOARD ACTIVITY On the interactive whiteboard, have volunteers from each group list one key idea that they found necessary for founding and maintaining control of a specific government or dynasty in the region.

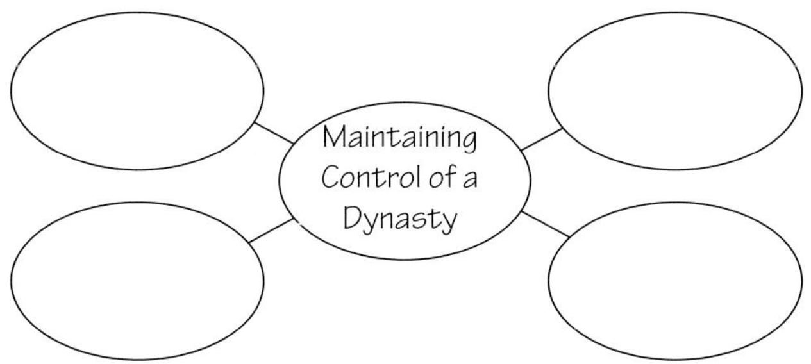

ACTIVITIES ANSWERS

Exploring the Essential Question

1. The early people hunted animals and gathered wild plants. They lived in pits dug into the ground. The Yayoi were farmers. They made pottery, iron tools, and bronze bells and weapons. They lived in clans headed by a small group of warriors.

21st Century Skills

2. Students may use the Internet, a wall map, or a globe to show the location of the countries of Southeast Asia in relation to the Equator. Presentations should include the effect of tropical rain forests on the types of crops grown and traded. They should also describe tropical-style housing and clothing.

Thinking Like a Historian

3. The Government Weakens—Regents Rule Japan—Nobles Take Control in Outlying Provinces—Nobles Form Their Own Armies—Civil War Breaks Out—Yoritomo Appointed Shogun by Emperor—The Shoguns Take Power

Locating Places

4. **1.** H, **2.** A, **3.** F, **4.** D, **5.** B, **6.** E, **7.** C, **8.** G

ASSESSMENT ANSWERS

Review the Guiding Questions

1. **A** The correct choice is A. The Koryo kingdom united Korea and held it for 400 years. The earlier rulers of the Silla kingdom and the Tang dynasty fell after conflict with other rulers. Confucian teaching was part of the cultural literacy of the time but not a ruling group.

2. **G** The correct choice is G. Hangul was developed under Sejong the Great and is the standard writing system in present-day Korea.

3. **C** The correct choice is C. Many samurai became vassals of a powerful lord called a daimyo. They pledged loyalty to the daimyo in return for land. Very few samurai would rise to the status of daimyo or shogun. Bushido was the warrior code of the samurai.

4. **G** The correct choice is G. Little fertile land was available for farming, so the Japanese turned to fishing to meet their food needs.

5. **C** The correct choice is C. The Khmer rulers led their people to believe they were god-kings. Although they built Angkor Wat as a large temple, this was not the primary way in which they gained power.

6. **F** The correct choice is F. Pagan became a major center of Buddhist learning and culture in Burma. Melaka was the first major Islamic center.

Document-Based Questions

7. **D** The correct choice is D. According to the passage, individuals become master actors when they have perfected the skills of acting through study and practice and thus become "one with the art itself."

8. **I** The correct choice is I. Both practiced their skills to perfection. For the actor, this means he or she does not imitate the teacher, but perfects the skills of acting; for the samurai, this means perfecting the skills of fighting.

Short Response

9. Students should clearly point out that upper- and lower-class members were differentiated by their clothing, food, housing, and occupation.

10. Aristocrats were permitted to marry according to their social class. Their lives were supported by slaves.

Extended Response

11. Students should explain that animism is the belief that all living things as well as nonliving things such as rocks and rivers have a spirit, called a *kami*. Believers in animism show respect to the kami by praying at shrines and temples. They ask the kami for help. Over time, belief in animism developed into Shintoism, a religion practiced by Japan's rulers who took part in Shinto rituals in order to ensure the well-being of the Japanese people. Today, Shintoism still affects the Japanese people, who have a deep love of nature.

ONLINE RESOURCES

networks

There's More Online!

- ☑ INTERACTIVE WORKSHEETS
- ☑ BIOGRAPHIES
- ☑ CHARTS/GRAPHS
- ☑ GAMES
- ☑ GRAPHIC ORGANIZERS
- ☑ IMAGES
- ☑ MAPS
- ☑ PRIMARY SOURCES
- ☑ SLIDE SHOWS
- ☑ TIME LINE
- ☑ LECTURE SLIDES
- ☑ INTERACTIVE WHITEBOARD ACTIVITIES
- ☑ ASSESSMENTS
- ☑ VIDEOS

Castle Design

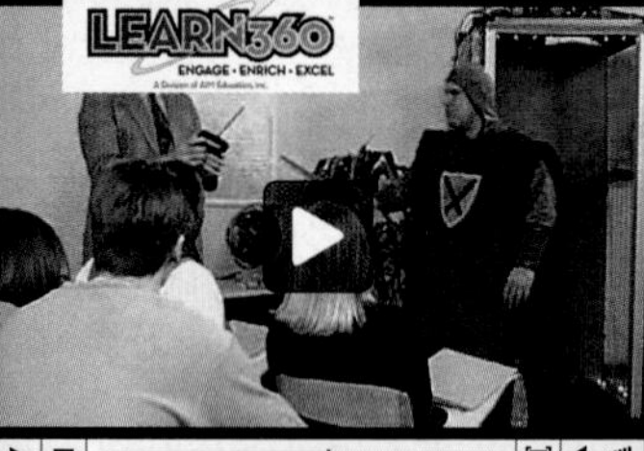

Feudalism, Lords, and Vassals

History of Austria in the Late Middle Ages

Chapter 19

Medieval Europe

Dear World History Teacher,

After the collapse of the Western Roman Empire and the formation of the Germanic states, a new European civilization slowly began to emerge during the Early Middle Ages. Charlemagne's crowning as Holy Roman emperor in A.D. 800 represented the blending of Roman, Germanic, and Christian ways to form a new European civilization.

After Charlemagne's empire collapsed, new political organizations, such as feudalism, began to develop in Europe. The feudal system put power into the hands of various ranks of nobles. The most powerful were the upper nobles, or lords who dominated the political, economic, and social life of Europe. Gradually, however, kings began to extend their power by bringing feudal territories under their direct control.

European civilization began to flourish in the Middle Ages with the rise of strong royal government, the expansion of towns and cities, and an improved economy. The Middle Ages also gave birth to an intellectual and spiritual revival that transformed European society. In the 1300s, however, Europe began to experience a devastating turn of events. The Black Death killed millions of people, and warfare was constant. Even the Catholic Church was not immune from the upheaval as several Church leaders fought over who was the rightful pope.

Jackson J. Spielvogel

More Media Resources

Current Events Online

Visit McGraw-Hill's current events Web site for high-interest news stories and activities for your students. Access the site through the Student or Teacher Center in **networks.**

Reading List

Grade 6 reading level:
The Travels of Benjamin of Tudela: Through Three Continents of the Twelfth Century, by Uri Shulevitz

Grade 7 reading level:
Eleanor of Aquitaine and the High Middle Ages, by Nancy Plain

Grade 8 reading level:
Good Masters! Good Ladies!: Voices from a Medieval Village, by Laura Amy Schlitz

At the MOVIES

Watch clips of popular culture films about medieval Europe, such as *Henry V*, *A Man for All Seasons*, *Becket*, or *The Adventures of Robin Hood*.

Ask: Do you think movies reflect what life was really like in the Middle Ages?

NOTE: Be sure to preview any clips to ensure they are age-appropriate.

Search for more videos online in the **networks** Resource Library.

CHAPTER 19 Planner

UNDERSTANDING BY DESIGN®

Enduring Understandings

- ***Religion can influence a society's beliefs and values.*** • ***Cultures are held together by shared beliefs and common practices and values.*** • ***Conflict can lead to change.***

Essential Questions

- ***Why does conflict develop?*** • ***What are the characteristics that define a culture?***
- ***How do governments change?*** • ***What is the role of religion in government?***

Students will know:

- *how the geography of Europe shaped the development of cultures*
- *the achievements of European kings and emperors*
- *the role of the Church in medieval Europe*
- *the power relationship between the Catholic Church and rulers in Europe*
- *what feudalism was and why it became an important social structure*
- *why the Magna Carta is important*
- *what the Crusades were and how they started*
- *about the Black Death and its effect on medieval life*
- *the conflicts experienced by the Catholic Church*
- *the effects of the Hundred Years' War and the Reconquista*

Students will be able to:

- **discuss and analyze** the balance of power between the pope and Charlemagne
- **draw conclusions** about Charlemagne's rule
- **explain** feudalism
- **compare and contrast** the lives of knights and peasants
- **analyze** why the Magna Carta was needed
- **explain** the causes and effects of the Crusades
- **discuss** changes that took place in the Mid to Late Middle Ages
- **analyze** the relationship between conformity and the Inquisition
- **read** a map about the spread of the plague
- **organize** information about problems during the Late Middle Ages
- **draw conclusions** about problems the Church faced
- **discuss** events that happened during the Late Middle Ages

Predictable Misunderstandings

Students may think:

- Society did not change during the Middle Ages.
- Feudalism is all about knights and castles, not everyday people.
- During the Crusades, one side was right and the other was wrong.

Assessment Evidence

Performance Task

- Hands-On Chapter Project

Other Evidence

- Geography and History Activity
- Primary Sources Activities
- 21st Century Skills Activity
- Economics of History Activity
- Responses to Interactive Whiteboard Activities
- Class discussions about the structure of the Church
- Class discussions about the relationship between the pope and the king
- Listing activity about the rights guaranteed by the Magna Carta
- Class discussion and written assignment about problems in the Church and society in the Late Middle Ages
- Lesson Reviews

Pacing Guide

Introducing the Chapter	1 day
Lesson 1 The Early Middle Ages	2 days
Lesson 2 Feudalism and the Rise of Towns	1 day
Lesson 3 Kingdoms and Crusades	2 days
Lesson 4 Culture and the Church	1 day
Lesson 5 The Late Middle Ages	1 day
Chapter Activities and Assessment	1 day
TOTAL TIME	**9 Days**

Differentiated Instruction

These lesson plans are written to address the needs of your On Level students. Discussion and activities that are well-suited to your Approaching Grade Level learners, Beyond Grade Level learners, as well as your English Language Learners, are coded as follows:

ELL English Language Learner

NCSS Standards covered in "Medieval Europe"

Learners will understand:

1 CULTURE

3. How culture influences the ways in which human groups solve the problems of daily living

4. That the beliefs, values, and behaviors of a culture form an integrated system that helps shape the activities and ways of life that define a culture

6. That culture may change in response to changing needs, concerns, social, political, and geographic conditions

2 TIME, CONTINUITY, AND CHANGE

6. The origins and influences of social, cultural, political, and economic systems

7. The contributions of key persons, groups, and events from the past and their influence on the present

8. The history of democratic ideals and principles, and how they are represented in documents, artifacts and symbols

9. The influences of social, geographic, economic, and cultural factors on the history of local areas, states, nations, and the world

3 PEOPLE, PLACES, AND ENVIRONMENTS

4. The roles of different kinds of population centers in a region or nation

5. The concept of regions identifies links between people in different locations according to specific criteria (e.g., physical, economic, social, cultural, or religious)

8. Factors that contribute to cooperation and conflict among peoples of the nation and world, including language, religion, and political beliefs

5 INDIVIDUALS, GROUPS, AND INSTITUTIONS

1. This theme helps us know how individuals are members of groups and institutions, and influence and shape those groups and institutions

5. That groups and institutions change over time

7. That institutions may promote or undermine social conformity

9. That groups and institutions influence culture in a variety of ways

6 POWER, AUTHORITY, AND GOVERNANCE

2. Fundamental ideas that are the foundation of American constitutional democracy (including those of the U.S. Constitution, popular sovereignty, the rule of law, separation of powers, checks and balances, minority rights, the separation of church and state, and Federalism)

3. Fundamental values of constitutional democracy (e.g., the common good, liberty, justice, equality, and individual dignity)

4. The ideologies and structures of political systems that differ from those of the United States

5. The ways in which governments meet the needs and wants of citizens, manage conflict, and establish order and society

7 PRODUCTION, DISTRIBUTION, AND CONSUMPTION

4. Economic incentives affect people's behavior and may be regulated by rules or laws

CHAPTER 19

Introducing the Chapter

(Student Edition p. 537)

The Story Matters . . .

Read "The Story Matters . . ." aloud in class or ask for a volunteer to read it aloud. Then lead students in a discussion about the qualities of a great leader. Tell students that Joan of Arc was an uneducated peasant girl who led an army against a powerful enemy.

Ask: **Would you have done what Joan of Arc did? Why or why not? Have a few students share their responses.**

Then ask: **Can you imagine what it was like for Joan of Arc––a young girl––to stand up to a grown man ready to fight? Is there a cause, idea, or other person you would stand up for? How difficult would that be?**

Tell the class that during the Middle Ages, the local lord and the Catholic Church were the two most important institutions in a person's life. Most people worked in the lord's fields or fought in his armies, and almost everyone attended church daily. The Church was responsible for caring for the sick and poor, keeping historical records, and preserving knowledge. The lords were responsible for maintaining political and social order, which they did for hundreds of years. Tell students they can learn more about the Middle Ages online.

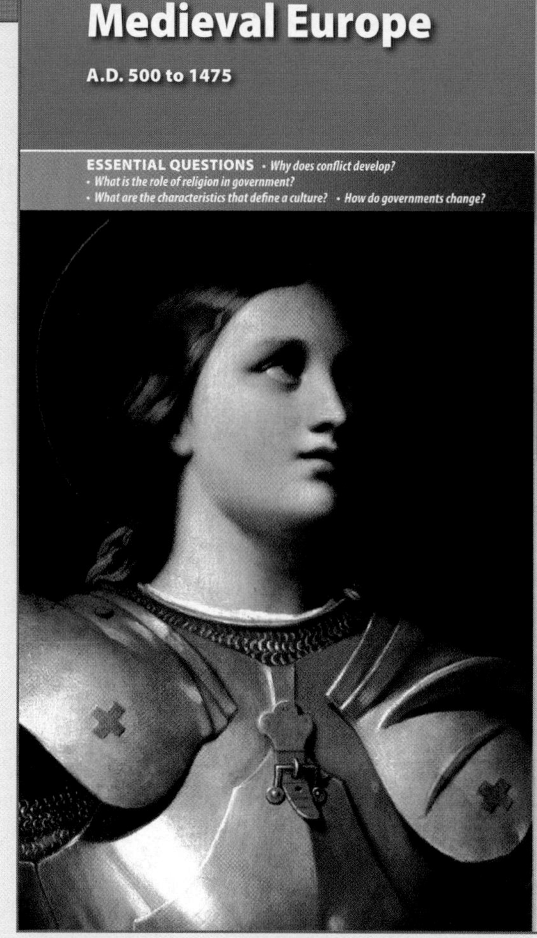

Medieval Europe

A.D. 500 to 1475

ESSENTIAL QUESTIONS · *Why does conflict develop?* · *What is the role of religion in government?* · *What are the characteristics that define a culture?* · *How do governments change?*

networks

There's More Online about the developing cultures of medieval Europe.

CHAPTER 19

Lesson 1 *The Early Middle Ages*

Lesson 2 *Feudalism and the Rise of Towns*

Lesson 3 *Kingdoms and Crusades*

Lesson 4 *Culture and the Church*

Lesson 5 *The Late Middle Ages*

The Story Matters . . .

Who would have predicted that a devout peasant girl, born in France in 1412, could help a prince become king? Yet Joan of Arc, shown in this painting, accomplished that for King Charles VII of France. She also helped defeat the English, whose armies occupied her native land.

The story of Joan of Arc reflects the history of medieval Europe in many ways. The Middle Ages was a time of struggle and conflict. It was also a period when the Catholic Church influenced almost every aspect of people's lives.

◄ *As a teenage girl in battle armor, Joan of Arc inspired the French army to defeat the English and rescue the French city of Orléans.*

Peter Willi/SuperStock/Getty Images

537

Introducing Place and Time (Student Edition pp. 538–539)

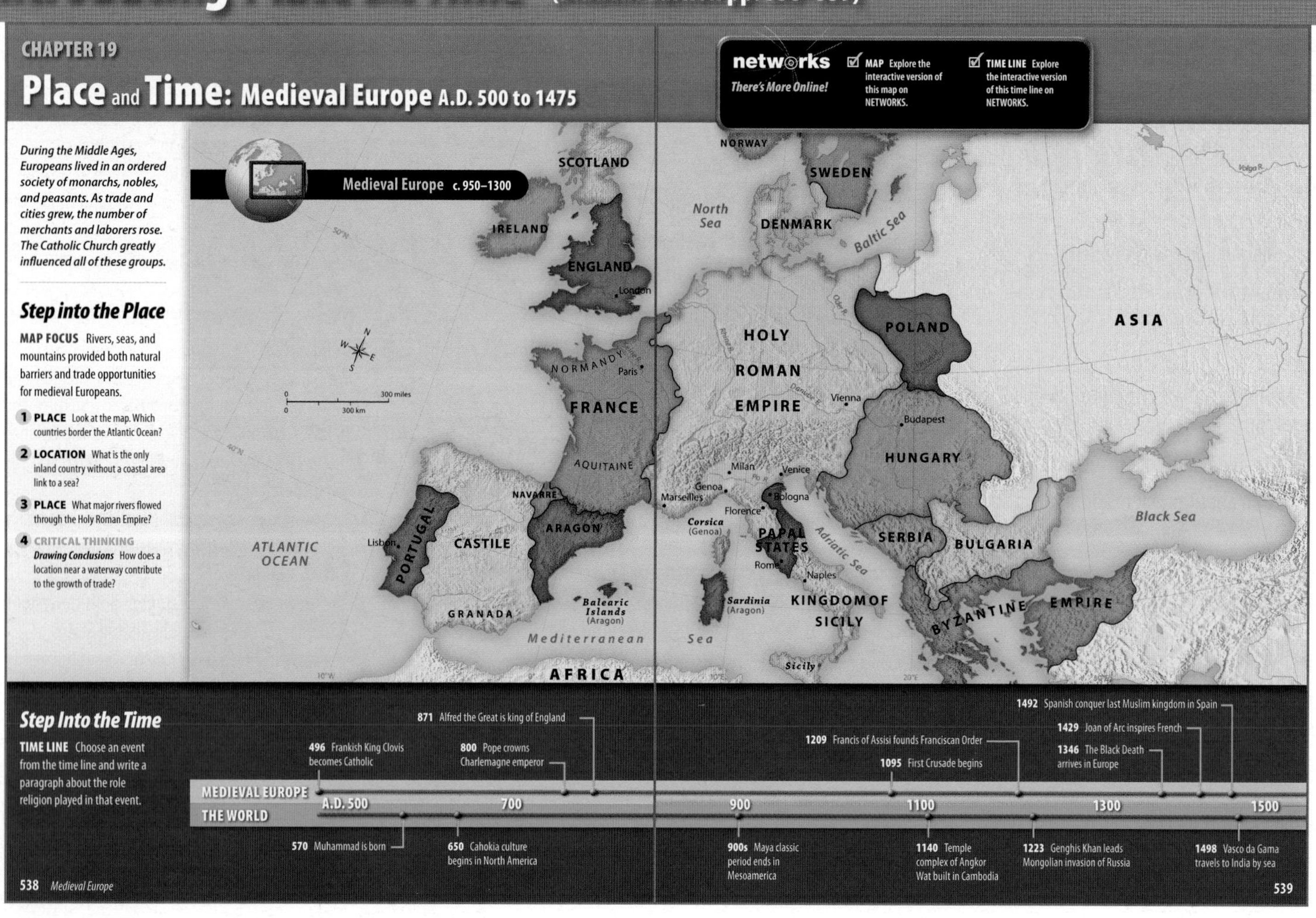

CHAPTER 19

Place and Time: Medieval Europe A.D. 500 to 1475

During the Middle Ages, Europeans lived in an ordered society of monarchs, nobles, and peasants. As trade and cities grew, the number of merchants and laborers rose. The Catholic Church greatly influenced all of these groups.

Step into the Place

MAP FOCUS Rivers, seas, and mountains provided both natural barriers and trade opportunities for medieval Europeans.

1. **PLACE** Look at the map. Which countries border the Atlantic Ocean?
2. **LOCATION** What is the only inland country without a coastal area link to a sea?
3. **PLACE** What major rivers flowed through the Holy Roman Empire?
4. **CRITICAL THINKING** *Drawing Conclusions* How does a location near a waterway contribute to the growth of trade?

networks *There's More Online!* ☑ **MAP** Explore the interactive version of this map on NETWORKS. ☑ **TIME LINE** Explore the interactive version of this time line on NETWORKS.

Step Into the Time

TIME LINE Choose an event from the time line and write a paragraph about the role religion played in that event.

MEDIEVAL EUROPE

- **496** Frankish King Clovis becomes Catholic
- **800** Pope crowns Charlemagne emperor
- **871** Alfred the Great is king of England
- **1095** First Crusade begins
- **1209** Francis of Assisi founds Franciscan Order
- **1346** The Black Death arrives in Europe
- **1429** Joan of Arc inspires French
- **1492** Spanish conquer last Muslim kingdom in Spain

A.D. 500 — 700 — 900 — 1100 — 1300 — 1500

THE WORLD

- **570** Muhammad is born
- **650** Cahokia culture begins in North America
- **900s** Maya classic period ends in Mesoamerica
- **1140** Temple complex of Angkor Wat built in Cambodia
- **1223** Genghis Khan leads Mongolian invasion of Russia
- **1498** Vasco da Gama travels to India by sea

538 *Medieval Europe*

539

Technology Extension
- Find an additional activity online that incorporates technology for this project.
- Visit the EdTechTeacher Web sites (included in the Technology Extension for this chapter) for more links, tutorials, and other resources.

Assessing Background Knowledge

INTERACTIVE WORKSHEET

What Do You Know? Activity

Have students complete the cloze activity before they study the chapter. Direct students to read each sentence in the paragraph and fill in the missing words as well as they can. Afterwards, ask students for their impressions of the Middle Ages. Write any misconceptions on the whiteboard. As students study the chapter and revise their ideas, erase the misconceptions. After students complete the chapter, have them read and complete the cloze activity again. Ask volunteers to read their answers aloud. Make note of and discuss any incorrect answers, which may indicate content that requires review.

INTERACTIVE WORKSHEET

Guided Reading Activities

You may wish to assign the Guided Reading Activity for Lesson 1 after introducing the chapter content.

Hands-On Chapter Project

Students will write a script about a day in the life of a lord, a vassal, a knight, or a peasant in medieval Europe.

- Students will participate in a class discussion to review what they have learned about medieval European society.
- Then, students will divide into groups. Each group will use discussions and worksheets to plan their projects before researching and creating their scripts.
- Next, each group will complete its script and share it with the rest of the class.
- Finally, students will evaluate their research, presentation, and collaboration using an Assessment Rubric.

Visit **networks** online to see the full project and rubric.

ONLINE RESOURCES

networks

Assign these interactive worksheets and quizzes from your Teacher Lesson Center. All resources are print-ready.

It's ALL Online!

CHAPTER 19 RESOURCES
- ☑ CHAPTER SUMMARY
- ☑ VOCABULARY BUILDER
- ☑ WHAT DO YOU KNOW?
- ☑ HANDS-ON CHAPTER PROJECT

Lesson 1 Resources
- ☑ INTERACTIVE GRAPHIC ORGANIZER
- ☑ GEOGRAPHY AND HISTORY ACTIVITY How Christianity United Europe
- ☑ INTERACTIVE GUIDED READING ACTIVITY
- ☑ READING ESSENTIALS AND STUDY GUIDE
- ☑ ONLINE SELF-CHECK QUIZ

Lesson 2 Resources
- ☑ INTERACTIVE GRAPHIC ORGANIZER
- ☑ PRIMARY SOURCE ACTIVITY The Lives of Peasants and Knights
- ☑ INTERACTIVE GUIDED READING ACTIVITY
- ☑ READING ESSENTIALS AND STUDY GUIDE
- ☑ ONLINE SELF-CHECK QUIZ

Lesson 3 Resources
- ☑ INTERACTIVE GRAPHIC ORGANIZER
- ☑ PRIMARY SOURCE ACTIVITY The First Crusade
- ☑ INTERACTIVE GUIDED READING ACTIVITY
- ☑ READING ESSENTIALS AND STUDY GUIDE
- ☑ ONLINE SELF-CHECK QUIZ

Lesson 4 Resources
- ☑ INTERACTIVE GRAPHIC ORGANIZER
- ☑ 21ST CENTURY SKILLS ACTIVITY Media Literacy
- ☑ INTERACTIVE GUIDED READING ACTIVITY
- ☑ READING ESSENTIALS AND STUDY GUIDE
- ☑ ONLINE SELF-CHECK QUIZ

Lesson 5 Resources
- ☑ INTERACTIVE GRAPHIC ORGANIZER
- ☑ ECONOMICS OF HISTORY ACTIVITY The Effects of the Black Death on Europe's Economy
- ☑ INTERACTIVE GUIDED READING ACTIVITY
- ☑ READING ESSENTIALS AND STUDY GUIDE
- ☑ ONLINE SELF-CHECK QUIZ

ASSESSMENT RESOURCES
- ☑ LESSON REVIEWS
- ☑ ONLINE SELF-CHECK QUIZZES
- ☑ CHAPTER ACTIVITIES AND ASSESSMENT
- ☑ STANDARDIZED TEST PRACTICE

REMEDIATION RESOURCES
- ☑ READING ESSENTIALS AND STUDY GUIDE
- ☑ GUIDED READING ACTIVITIES
- ☑ ONLINE SELF-CHECK QUIZZES
- ☑ CHAPTER SUMMARY

Step Into the Place

Location Project the Chapter Opener map of Europe on the whiteboard. Make sure students recognize that Europe is a peninsula. Review the meaning of the word, if necessary. Ask a volunteer to identify key geographical features, such as rivers, mountains, and seas. Discuss as a class possible effects of geography on a culture.

Encourage students to draw on prior knowledge. Have student volunteers analyze the map and circle regions that are set off by mountains or waterways. *(Britain, Ireland, France and Germany, Italy and the Mediterranean, Spain and Portugal, and Eastern Europe are separated from one another by mountains or waterways.)* As a class, discuss the Map Focus questions.

Step Into the Time

Making Generalizations Have students review the time line for the chapter. Explain that they will be studying events that occurred in Europe after the fall of the Western Roman Empire in A.D. 476 until the voyage of Christopher Columbus to the Americas in 1492.

Ask students: Based on the dates in the time line, how long did the Middle Ages last? *(about 1,000 years)*

As a class, complete the Step Into the Time activity and answer the question.

Answers for pages 538–539

Step Into the Place

1. Portugal, Spain, France, England, Scotland, and Ireland border the Atlantic Ocean.
2. Poland is the only inland country without access to a sea.
3. Rhine, Danube, Po, Oder
4. CRITICAL THINKING Goods can be moved easily to different places by boat.

Step Into the Time

Events that reflect the importance of religion are Charlemagne's coronation by the pope, the beginning of the First Crusade, the founding of the Franciscan Order, and the Spanish conquest of the Muslims.

networks
There's More Online!

- ☑ **BIOGRAPHY** Charlemagne (A.D. 742–814)
- ☑ **GRAPHIC ORGANIZER** Achievements of European Leaders
- ☑ **PRIMARY SOURCE** The Life of Charlemagne

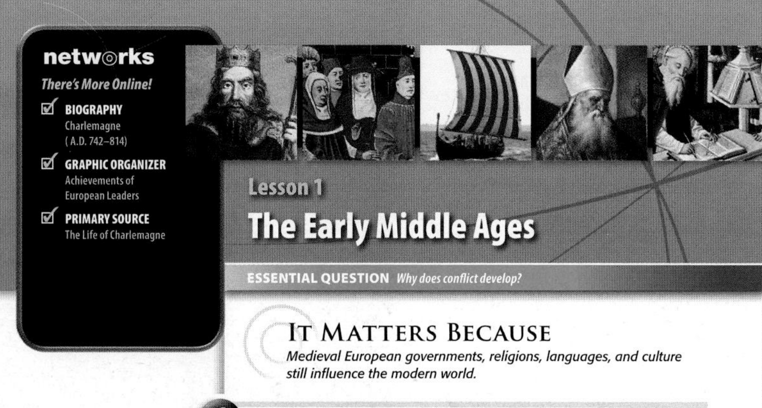

Lesson 1

The Early Middle Ages

ESSENTIAL QUESTION *Why does conflict develop?*

It Matters Because

Medieval European governments, religions, languages, and culture still influence the modern world.

1 Geography of Europe

GUIDING QUESTION *How did geography shape life in Europe after the fall of Rome?*

During the 400s, Germanic groups invaded the Western Roman Empire. In A.D. 476, these groups overthrew the last emperor in Rome and brought the Empire to an end. Europe then entered a new era called the Middle Ages, or medieval times. This was a 1,000-year period between ancient and modern times. During the Middle Ages, Western Europe was divided into many kingdoms, and Catholic Christianity strongly influenced society.

Physical geography shaped Europe's development. The continent of Europe is a huge peninsula, with many smaller peninsulas branching out from it. As a result, most land in Europe lies within 300 miles (483 km) of a seacoast. This encouraged trade and helped the European economy to grow.

Rivers and Seas

Rivers also played an important **role** in Europe's growth. Major rivers, such as the Rhine, Danube, Seine, and Po, flow from inland mountains into the oceans and seas surrounding the continent. These rivers are navigable, or wide and deep enough for ships to use. People and goods can sail easily from inland areas to the open sea and, from there, to other parts of the world.

Europe's seas and rivers provided protection as well as possibilities for trade. The English Channel, for example, separated the islands of Britain and Ireland from the rest of Europe. As a result, these people were far enough away to be largely safe from the many wars fought on Europe's mainland. They were able to develop their own governments and societies. In mainland Europe, wide rivers like the Rhine also kept groups of people separated. Because of this separation and isolation, many different cultures developed.

Europe also has many mountain ranges. In the southwest, the Pyrenees isolated what is now Spain and Portugal from the rest of Europe. In the middle of the continent, the Alps separated Italy from central Europe. The Carpathians cut off what is now Ukraine and Russia from southeast Europe. The mountains, like the rivers, made it difficult for one group to control all of Europe and encouraged the growth of independent territories.

☑ **PROGRESS CHECK**

Explaining Why were rivers important to the peoples of Europe?

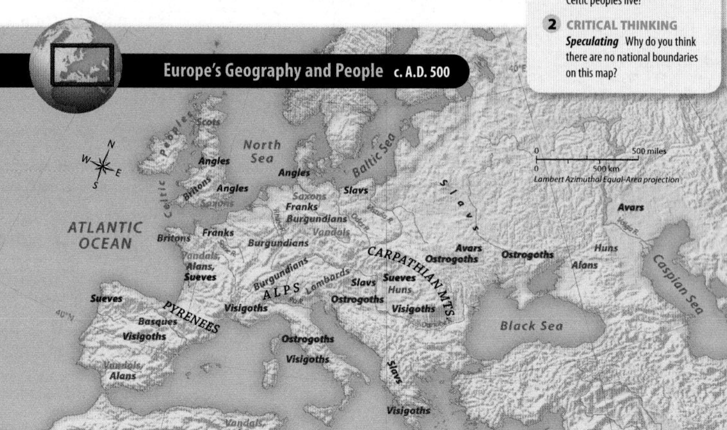

GEOGRAPHY CONNECTION

After the Western Roman Empire came to an end, many different peoples lived throughout Europe.

1. **LOCATION** Where did the Celtic peoples live?
2. **CRITICAL THINKING** ***Speculating*** Why do you think there are no national boundaries on this map?

Reading **HELP**DESK

Taking Notes: ***Identifying***

Choose four European leaders from this lesson. Use a diagram like this one to identify the achievements of each leader.

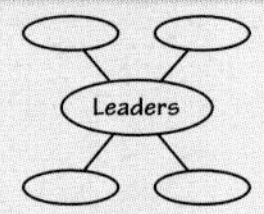

Content Vocabulary
- **fjord**
- **missionary**
- **concordat**

Academic Vocabulary

role something that plays a part in a process

2 Kingdoms in Western Europe

GUIDING QUESTION *How did Germanic groups build kingdoms in Western Europe?*

By A.D. 500, Western Europe had divided into many Germanic kingdoms. Germanic people in Italy and Spain adopted many Roman ways. People farther from Rome held on to more of their Germanic traditions.

Roman influence was even weaker in Britain. After Roman armies abandoned the area that is today England, Germanic groups known as Angles and Saxons settled there. In time, they became the Anglo-Saxons.

The Anglo-Saxons pushed aside earlier settlers known as the Celts (KEHLTS). Some Celts fled north and west, while others crossed the sea to Ireland. The Scottish, Welsh, and Irish peoples today are largely descended from the Celts.

The Franks in Europe

The Franks were the strongest Germanic group. They settled what is now France and western Germany. In 481, Clovis (KLOH•vuhs) became king of the Franks. Fifteen years later, he became the first Germanic ruler to accept Catholic Christianity. Before long, nearly all of the Franks became Catholic.

After Clovis died, Frankish kings lost much of their power. By 700, power had passed from kings to government officials known as mayors of the palace.

In 714, Charles Martel (mahr•TEHL), or "Charles the Hammer," became mayor of the palace. The pope, who was the head of the Catholic Church, gave Martel his support. Martel and the pope wanted to restore order and strengthen Catholic Christianity in the lands of the old Western Roman Empire.

Martel's first move was to halt the spread of Islam into Europe. By the early 700s, Muslims from North Africa had conquered Spain and entered France. In 732, Charles Martel defeated the Muslims at the Battle of Tours. This battle stopped the advance of Islam into Western Europe. It also ensured that Christianity would remain Western Europe's major religion.

After Charles Martel died, his son Pepin (PEH•puhn) became mayor of the palace. With the support and blessing of the pope, Pepin became king of the Franks. In return, Pepin was expected to help the pope. In 754, Pepin forced a Germanic group called the Lombards to leave Rome. He then gave the pope a large strip of Lombard land in Italy. These lands became known as the Papal States.

King Clovis won the support of Romans living in his kingdom when he accepted Christianity.

▶ **CRITICAL THINKING**
Speculating Why might the Romans in the kingdom have accepted Clovis more after he became a Christian?

Pope Leo III crowned Charlemagne "Emperor of the Romans."

▶ **CRITICAL THINKING**
Making Inferences Why was it important that the pope led the crowning ceremony?

The Emperor Charlemagne

After Pepin died in 768, his son Charles became king of the Franks. In the years that followed, Charles sent his armies into neighboring lands. He nearly doubled the size of his kingdom to include what is today Germany, France, northern Spain, and most of Italy.

By 800, Charles's kingdom had grown into an empire. For the first time since the fall of Rome, most Western Europeans were ruled by one government. His conquests won Charles the name of Charlemagne (SHAHR•luh•MAYN), or Charles the Great. A monk named Einhard described Charlemagne this way:

PRIMARY SOURCE

> "Charles was large and strong, and of lofty stature [height] … [his] nose a little long, hair fair, and face laughing and merry. … He used to wear the … Frankish dress—next [to] his skin a linen shirt and linen breeches [pants], and above these a tunic fringed with silk. … Over all he flung a blue cloak, and he always had a sword girt [fastened] about him."
>
> —from *The Life of Charlemagne*, by Einhard

Reading **HELP**DESK

Reading Strategy: ***Analyzing Primary Sources***

Why might Einhard—in his quote on the next page—have described Charlemagne's appearance in such positive terms?

LESSON 1 • Day 1

ENGAGE

Discussing Before you begin the discussion, ask students to brainstorm words or phrases that they associate with the Middle Ages. Lead the students in a discussion about why they associate certain words or phrases with the Middle Ages. Then have students scan the images and illustrations in their textbooks. Tell students to think of additional words that describe the images. Write their answers on the whiteboard. ELL

Tell students that in this lesson, they will learn how the geography of Europe shaped the development of its cultures during the Middle Ages.

TEACH & ASSESS

1 Geography of Europe

GUIDING QUESTION *How did geography shape life in Europe after the fall of Rome?*

MAP **Summarizing** Show students the interactive map "Europe's Geography and People."

Ask: How did geographical features affect the development of Europe during the Middle Ages? *(Mountains and rivers provided needed resources and protection that allowed different cultural groups to form. Rivers and seas provided transportation routes for trade and the development of a common European culture.)* AL

2 Kingdoms in Western Europe

GUIDING QUESTION *How did Germanic groups build kingdoms in Western Europe?*

GRAPHIC ORGANIZER **Identifying** Have students complete the graphic organizer that appears on the first page of the lesson. Ask volunteers to share their answers. If desired, you can have students enter responses on the interactive graphic organizer for the lesson. Also, make sure students have identified the key accomplishments of each ruler correctly. *(Answers may include the following: Clovis—won the support of Roman citizens living in his kingdom by becoming Catholic; Charles Martel—defeated Muslims at Tours; Charlemagne—crowned emperor by pope, encouraged education; Otto I of Germany—defeated Magyars, became emperor of Holy Roman Empire; Pope Gregory the Great—organized missionaries.)*

INTERACTIVE WHITEBOARD ACTIVITY **Summarizing** Have students complete the Interactive Whiteboard Activity for the lesson by sorting the descriptions of European leaders into the correct columns. If students have trouble sorting the facts, tell them to refer back to their notes and their graphic organizers. AL ELL

Ask: How did important kings like Clovis, Charlemagne, and Otto I affect European unity? *(Student answers will vary. They should note that Clovis helped spread Christianity, Charlemagne briefly united much of Western Europe in his empire, and Otto I helped unite the Germans and promote the power of the Holy Roman Empire.)* AL

CLOSE & REFLECT

Analyzing Discuss the following questions and answers with students to review the lesson:

- **What effect did geography have on the development of Europe during the Middle Ages?** *(It provided resources and isolated people, allowing them to develop their own cultures.)*
- **What effect did Germanic kings have on Europe's religion?** *(They helped spread Christianity in Western Europe.)*

BACKGROUND KNOWLEDGE

Charlemagne

A long historical debate has been waged over this question: Are the French or the Germans the true heirs of Charlemagne? His capital, Aachen, also known as *Aix-la-Chapelle* in French, sits just inside the German border near France, and German kings were crowned in the city's cathedral. On the other hand, the famous French military and political leader Napoleon called himself the successor of Charlemagne.

Ask students if they think Europe could be unified under a single leader like Charlemagne today. Have students describe why they believe such a unification would or would not work in modern Europe. *(Students might recognize that such a unification would be difficult to accomplish because Europe's national identities have become much stronger today.)*

The Celts

Many Americans are descendants of the Celtic peoples who were pushed into isolated areas of Great Britain by invading Angles and Saxons. Millions of Americans trace their roots to Ireland, Scotland, Wales, and parts of England where Celtic peoples lived.

Celtic tribes also lived on the fringes of the Roman Empire in Spain, France, Asia Minor, Switzerland, and other regions. Even older Celtic settlements have been discovered in Austria and Germany.

Saint Benedict of Nursia

The man most responsible for the creation of Christian monasteries in the West was Saint Benedict of Nursia (A.D. 480–547). Benedict was an Italian who was famous for his piety.

With a few followers, he founded a monastery south of Rome on a hilltop called Monte Cassino. This monastery became the source for the Benedictine Rule, a form of monastic life that has been the model for many Catholic institutions for 1,500 years.

Benedict stressed simplicity, learning, the importance of community, and the goal of helping others. Because his influence was so widespread, in 1964 Pope Paul VI named Benedict one of Europe's patron saints.

Answers for pages 540–543

P. 540 Taking Notes Answers may include the following: Clovis (won support of Roman citizens in his kingdom by becoming Catholic); Charles Martel (defeated Muslims at Tours); Charlemagne (crowned emperor by pope, encouraged education); Otto I of Germany (defeated Magyars, became emperor of Holy Roman Empire); Pope Gregory the Great (organized missionaries).

P. 541 ☑ PROGRESS CHECK Rivers provided protection and enabled many different cultures to develop.

P. 541 GEOGRAPHY CONNECTION

1. They lived on the islands off the west coast of Europe (Great Britain and Ireland).
2. CRITICAL THINKING Answers will vary, but students might say that no national boundaries exist because after the Western Roman Empire ended, so did national governments.

P. 542 CRITICAL THINKING They might have felt that he was now more like them than he was before.

P. 542 Reading Strategy Einhard understood that Charlemagne was a powerful king and wanted to flatter him.

P. 543 CRITICAL THINKING It was important because of the great authority and power that the Catholic Church held in medieval life.

Vikings sailed the northern seas in boats powered by oars and the wind. This longship is a replica of a Viking ship that carried explorers.

In 800, Charlemagne came to Rome and defended the pope against unruly Roman nobles. On Christmas day, Charlemagne was worshipping at the church of St. Peter in Rome. After the service, the pope placed a crown on Charlemagne's head and declared him the new Roman emperor. Charlemagne was pleased but also concerned. He did not want people to think the pope had the power to choose who was emperor.

Despite this concern, Charlemagne accepted his duties as emperor and worked to strengthen the empire. The central government, located in the capital of Aachen (AH•kuhn), was small. As a result, Charlemagne relied on local officials called counts to help him govern. The counts ran local affairs and raised armies for Charlemagne. Royal messengers went on inspections and told the emperor how the counts were doing.

Charlemagne wanted to advance learning in his kingdom. He had tried late in life to learn to write and wanted his people to be educated too. He **established** a school for the children of government officials. Students at the school studied religion, Latin, music, literature, and arithmetic.

Waves of Invaders

More than anything else, Charlemagne's forceful personality held the empire together. After Charlemagne died in 814, his empire did not last long. It was soon divided into three kingdoms.

These Frankish kingdoms were prey to outside attacks. In the 800s and 900s, waves of invaders swept across Europe. Muslims from North Africa raided France and Italy. Fierce nomads called Magyars from Hungary invaded eastern parts of France and Italy. Vikings launched raids from their homeland in Scandinavia (SKAN•duh•NAY•vee•uh).

Scandinavia is in northern Europe. Norway, Sweden, and Denmark are all part of modern Scandinavia. Much of Scandinavia has a long, jagged coastline. It has many **fjords** (fee•AWRDS), or narrow inlets of the sea. The fjords, surrounded by steep cliffs or slopes, were carved by glaciers long ago. The Viking people, known as Norsemen or "north men," lived in villages near the fjords.

Scandinavia has little farmland, so the Vikings had to depend on the sea for food and trade. They became skilled sailors and traveled in sturdy longboats. These boats could survive the rough Atlantic and also navigate shallow rivers.

Reading HELPDESK

fjord a narrow inlet of the sea between cliffs or steep slopes

Academic Vocabulary

establish to start; to bring into existence

In the 700s and 800s, the Vikings left their crowded homeland and carried out raids along Europe's coasts. The word *viking* comes from their word for raiding. The Vikings attacked villages and churches, seizing grain, animals, and other valuable items. They burned whatever they could not steal.

The Vikings were more than just raiders. They were also explorers and settlers. They sailed across the Atlantic, settled the islands of Greenland and Iceland, and even landed in North America. For a short time, Viking groups also lived in England. They founded the territory of Normandy in northwestern France and settled in parts of what are now Russia and Ukraine.

Formation of the Holy Roman Empire

Muslim, Magyar, and Viking invaders brought much suffering to Europe's people. Their attacks also weakened the Frankish kingdoms. By the 900s, the eastern Frankish kingdom, known as Germany, became a collection of small territories ruled by nobles. In 911, a group of these nobles sought to unite Germany by electing a king.

In 936, Duke Otto of Saxony was elected king of Germany. Otto became a powerful ruler. Germanic forces defeated the Magyars and freed the pope from the control of Roman nobles. To reward Otto, the pope crowned him emperor of the Romans in 962. Otto's territory became known as the Holy Roman Empire. It included most of present-day Germany and northern Italy.

GEOGRAPHY CONNECTION

During the Early Middle Ages, several different groups invaded and settled in Europe.

1. **MOVEMENT** Which groups of invaders traveled by sea?
2. **CRITICAL THINKING** ***Speculating*** Why might an army have found it more difficult to invade Italy than Hungary?

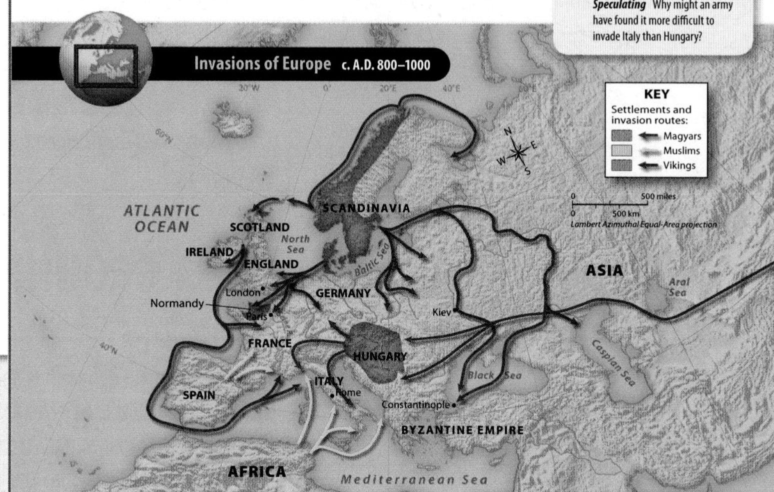

After Otto, two important emperors, Frederick I and Frederick II, tried to bring Germany and Italy under a strong central government during the 1100s and 1200s. The popes did not want the emperor to control them. They joined with Italy's cities to resist the emperors' forces. Ongoing conflict kept Germany and Italy from becoming united countries until the 1800s.

PROGRESS CHECK

Explaining What impact did the Battle of Tours have on European history?

3 The Church and Its Influence

GUIDING QUESTION *How did the Catholic Church influence life in early medieval Europe?*

The Roman Catholic Church played an important role in the growth of a new civilization in medieval Western Europe.

Christianity in Europe

At the time of Rome's fall, large areas of northwestern Europe practiced a variety of non-Christian religions. Ireland was different. In the 400s, a Christian priest named Patrick traveled to Ireland. There, Patrick spread Christianity and founded churches and monasteries, or religious houses.

Patrick inspired Pope Gregory I, or Gregory the Great, to spread Christianity. Gregory asked monks to become **missionaries** (MIH•shuh•NEHR•eez)—people who are sent out to teach their religion. In 597, Gregory sent 40 monks to Britain to teach Christianity. Other monks spread Christianity, so that by 1050, most Western Europeans had become Catholic Christians.

The Contributions of Monks and Nuns

Monks and monasteries provided schools and hospitals. They taught carpentry and weaving, and they developed improvements in farming. Many monks copied Christian writings as well as Roman and Greek works. They also made illuminations, which are manuscripts decorated with beautiful lettering and miniature religious paintings. These monks helped preserve knowledge of the classical and early Christian worlds.

Monks lived in communities headed by abbots (A•buhtz). Women called nuns lived in their own monasteries called convents. Convents were headed by abbesses (A•buhs•ihs).

This image shows Pope Gregory VII wearing his official vestments as head of the Church.

▶ CRITICAL THINKING

Drawing Conclusions Why do you think Pope Gregory VII wanted to stop kings from choosing Church officials?

Reading HELPDESK

missionaries people who are sent by a religious organization to spread the faith

concordat agreement between the pope and the ruler of a country

Church Authority

Many monasteries became wealthy. As their influence increased, abbots became active in political affairs. This caused disagreements. Kings wanted Church leaders to obey them. Popes, however, believed kings should obey the Church.

Elected pope in 1073, Gregory VII declared that only the pope had the power to appoint high-ranking Church officials. Pope Gregory's order angered Henry IV, the Holy Roman emperor. For many years, the Holy Roman emperor had chosen bishops in Germany. Henry insisted on naming his own bishops. Gregory then declared that Henry was no longer emperor and excommunicated him. This meant that he no longer had the rights of church membership and could not go to heaven.

When the German nobles supported the pope, Henry changed his mind. He traveled to Italy and begged the pope for forgiveness. Gregory forgave Henry, but the German nobles chose a new emperor. When Gregory accepted the new emperor, Henry seized Rome and named a new pope.

The struggle continued until 1122, when a new German king and a new pope agreed that only the pope could choose bishops, but only the king or emperor could give them government posts. This agreement, called the *Concordat of Worms*, was signed in the German city of Worms. A **concordat** (kuhn•KAWR•DAT) is an agreement between the pope and the ruler of a country.

In the days before printing presses, monks helped preserve knowledge by copying classical Greek and Roman writings as well as the Bible and other early Christian writings.

PROGRESS CHECK

Describing What major issue did kings and popes disagree on?

LESSON 1 REVIEW

Review Vocabulary

1. What is a *missionary* meant to do?
2. What natural process created the *fjords*?

Answer the Guiding Questions

3. ***Summarizing*** How did mountains and rivers make it difficult for one group to control all of Europe?
4. ***Explaining*** What happened in Britain after Roman armies abandoned the area during the 400s?
5. ***Identifying*** In what modern countries did the Franks settle?
6. ***Analyzing*** What did Charlemagne do to advance education?
7. ***Analyzing*** What role did monasteries play in medieval Europe?
8. **EXPOSITORY WRITING** Henry IV begged for the pope's forgiveness. If you were going to interview King Henry about this incident, what three questions would you ask him? Write your answer in a paragraph.

LESSON 1 • Day 2

ENGAGE

IMAGE **Analyzing Visuals** Show students the interactive image of the coronation of Charlemagne. Read the description of Charlemagne that accompanies the image.

Ask: **What does this image suggest about the connection between the Catholic Church and political rulers during the Middle Ages?** *(Students should note that the Church had a strong influence on political rulers such as kings.)*

Note that Christianity could be a source of conflict as well as unity during the Middle Ages. Tell students they will learn about the influence of geography, religion, and politics on medieval Europe.

B The Church and Its Influence

GUIDING QUESTION ***How did the Catholic Church influence life in early medieval Europe?***

INTERACTIVE WORKSHEET **Identifying** Reinforce the connection between geography and the spread of Christianity by introducing the Geography and History Activity to students. Guide them through the first few questions, and then have them complete the worksheet as homework.

LECTURE SLIDE **Explaining** Show students the lecture slide with the hierarchy of the Catholic Church.

Ask:
- **What were the pope's most important duties?** *(to crown kings or emperors, to appoint bishops)* AL
- **What did monks and nuns do?** *(Monks cared for the sick; taught people; provided shelter; and copied Christian, Roman, and Greek writings.)*
- **Why were abbots and bishops important?** *(Abbots and bishops were high-ranking officials who also served the king.)*

Discussing Introduce the conflict between Pope Gregory VII and the Holy Roman Emperor Henry IV as an example of disagreements between political and religious leaders.

Ask:
- **What was the source of the conflict?** *(The pope wanted to appoint the bishops, but Henry believed he had the power to appoint them.)*
- **What did the pope do to Henry?** *(The pope excommunicated Henry.)*
- **How did Henry respond?** *(First, Henry asked for forgiveness, and when he did not receive forgiveness, he went to war.)*

Have students complete the Lesson 1 Review.

CLOSE & REFLECT

Making Inferences Use the following question to prompt a discussion that reviews the lesson:

Ask: **How did the Church influence the Holy Roman emperors?** *(The pope crowned kings and fought for the right to appoint bishops and make political decisions.)*

Have students discuss why the Church had such an influence over the emperors. Discuss the role of religion in every-day life during the Middle Ages and how religion affected nearly every aspect of people's lives.

IF YOU HAVE MORE TIME . . .

Interview Historic Figures From the Middle Ages

Role-Playing Have students arrange a news interview show featuring important figures from this section. For example, students might "invite" Henry IV and Gregory VII to be interviewed by reporters, Clovis and Charles Martel might be invited to discuss their plans for the Frankish kingdom, or Charlemagne or Otto I could be interviewed about important issues facing their governments.

Have students assign roles, including a moderator and reporters as well as distinguished guests. Then have the groups present their programs for the class.

Discuss Cooperation and Conflict Between Church and State **Identifying Central Issues** Have students discuss these related questions.

Ask:
- **Why do political and religious rulers often cooperate, as did Charlemagne and the pope?** *(They might be working toward similar goals, or each might be gaining personally from the cooperation.)*
- **Why do they sometimes disagree, as did Gregory VII and Henry IV?** *(They might be competing for power and, therefore, be unwilling to compromise.)*
- **What issues do current political and religious leaders agree or disagree on?** *(Answers will vary. Leaders agree on improved education and disagree on the use of military action.)*

Explore the Effects of Conquerors on Britain Using a Graphic Organizer

Understanding Cause and Effect Ask students to make a diagram or a graphic organizer that shows cause-and-effect relationships related to the history of the Romans, Angles, Saxons, and Celts in Britain. *(Diagrams should reflect that the Roman influence on Britain was small; the Angles and Saxons invaded after the Romans left and pushed aside the Celts; the Celts fled to isolated regions.)* BL

Answers for pages 544–547

P. 545 GEOGRAPHY CONNECTION

1. Vikings and Muslims
2. CRITICAL THINKING Italy is a peninsula, surrounded on most sides by water and protected on the north by mountains; Hungary is inland and relatively protected by natural barriers.

P. 546 ☑ PROGRESS CHECK The defeat of the Muslims at Tours stopped the further advance of Islam into Western Europe. It also ensured that Christianity would remain Western Europe's major religion.

P. 546 CRITICAL THINKING The actions of the kings threatened to weaken the pope's authority as head of the Church.

P. 547 ☑ PROGRESS CHECK Kings wanted to appoint their own bishops, but popes used the power of excommunication to force kings to accept papal appointees.

LESSON 1 REVIEW

1. Missionaries are meant to go out and teach their religion.
2. Retreating glaciers carved the fjords along the coast of Scandinavia.
3. Mountains and rivers were natural barriers that separated different groups of people.
4. Soon after the Romans left Britain, the Angles and the Saxons, who were Germanic groups from Denmark and northern Germany, moved in and settled there.
5. They settled in what is now France and western Germany.
6. He set up a school for the children of government officials and put the English scholar Alcuin in charge of it.
7. Answers will vary. Possible answer: Monasteries provided schools and hospitals and helped preserve written knowledge. They also owned land and made goods, allowing many monasteries to grow wealthy and influence politics.
8. Answers will vary but should demonstrate students' recognition of the Church's powerful role in medieval Europe. The three questions they would ask should be included in their responses.

There's More Online!

☑ CHART/GRAPH
Pyramid of Classes

Lesson 2

Feudalism and the Rise of Towns

ESSENTIAL QUESTION *What are the characteristics that define a culture?*

It Matters Because

The organization of society in medieval Europe affected nearly every aspect of people's lives.

1 The Feudal Order

GUIDING QUESTION *How did Europeans try to bring order to their society after the fall of Charlemagne's empire?*

After the fall of Charlemagne's empire, strong governments collapsed in Western Europe. Kings lost much of their power. Local land-owning nobles became increasingly important in political affairs. They raised armies. They also collected taxes and imposed laws on the people living on their lands.

When invaders swept through Europe, people turned to the nobles for protection. Nobles governed and protected the people in return for services, such as fighting in a noble's army or farming the land. This led to a new political and social order known as **feudalism** (FYOO•duh•LIH•zuhm).

By 1000, Europe's kingdoms were divided into hundreds of feudal territories. Most of these territories were small. A noble's castle was the center of each territory.

Lords, Vassals, and Knights

Feudalism was based on ties of loyalty and duty among members of the nobility. Nobles were both lords and vassals. A lord was a high-ranking noble who had power over others. A **vassal** (VA•suhl) was a lower-ranking noble who served a lord. In return, the lord protected the vassal.

Reading HELPDESK

Taking Notes: ***Summarizing***

Use a cluster diagram like the one shown here to list important features of feudalism as a social system during the Middle Ages.

Content Vocabulary

- **feudalism**
- **knight**
- **chivalry**
- **vassal**
- **serf**
- **fief**
- **guild**

The tie binding a lord and his vassal was declared in a public ceremony. The vassal took an oath and placed his hands between those of his lord. Then the vassal swore:

PRIMARY SOURCE

> "Sir, I enter your homage [service] and faith and become your man by mouth and hands [that is, by taking the oath and placing his hands between those of the lord], and I swear and promise to keep faith and loyalty to you against all others."
>
> —from *A Source Book for Medieval History*, 1905

A vassal helped his lord in battle. In exchange for the vassal's **military** service, a lord gave his vassal land. The property granted to a vassal was known as a **fief** (FEEF).

Many lower-ranking vassals were known as **knights** (NYTS). They were armed warriors who fought on horseback. In early medieval times, warriors in Western Europe mostly fought on foot. In the 700s, knights began to use a foot piece called a stirrup. Stirrups allowed an armored warrior to sit on a horse and attack while he held a lance, or long, heavy spear.

Nobles and Knights in Medieval Society

During the Middle Ages, nobles were the most powerful people in Europe. Great lords had more land and wealth than ordinary knights. Yet, a shared belief in the feudal order united lords and knights in defending their society.

Knights followed the code of **chivalry** (SHIH•vuhl•ree). These rules stated that a knight was to be brave and obey his lord. A knight was also required to respect women of noble birth, honor the Church, and help people. Many of today's ideas about manners come from the **code** of chivalry.

Kings and queens
Lords and ladies
Knights
Peasants and serfs

feudalism political order; under feudalism, nobles governed and protected people in return for services

vassal a low-ranking noble under the protection of a feudal lord

fief a feudal estate belonging to a vassal

knight a mounted man-at-arms serving a lord

Academic Vocabulary

military relating to soldiers, arms, or war

Castles in the Middle Ages were designed to provide good defenses for their owners. For example, castles often occupied high ground. High towers at each corner gave soldiers the chance to drive attackers away.

Knights trained for war by fighting one another in tournaments, or special contests. The most popular event was the joust. Two knights on horseback carrying lances galloped toward each other and tried to knock each other off.

Nobles were often at war and away from their castles. In their absence, their wives or daughters ran the estates.

The castle was at the center of the estate. Every castle had two parts. The first was a motte (MAHT), or steep-sided hill. The second part was the bailey, an open space next to the motte. Both parts were encircled by high walls. The castle keep, its central building, was constructed on the motte.

In the basement of the keep, tools and food were stored. On the ground floor were kitchens and stables. Above these was a great hall. The lord held court and met visitors here.

☑ **PROGRESS CHECK**

Identifying What were the rules of behavior that knights followed?

Reading HELPDESK

chivalry the system, spirit, or customs of medieval knighthood

serf a member of the peasant class tied to the land and subject to the will of the landowner

Academic Vocabulary

code a system of principles or rules

2 The Medieval Manor

GUIDING QUESTION *How did most Europeans live and work during the Middle Ages?*

Nobles, knights, and peasants (or farmers) depended on the land for everything they needed. The lands of a fief consisted of manors. A manor was a farming community that a noble ran and peasants worked. It usually consisted of the noble's castle, the surrounding fields, and a peasant village.

Two Groups of Peasants

During the Middle Ages, the vast number of Europeans were peasants living and working on manors. There were two groups of peasants—freemen and serfs. Freemen paid the noble for the right to farm the land. They worked only on their own land and had rights under the law. They moved wherever and whenever they wished.

Most peasants, however, were **serfs** (SUHRFS). Serfs and their descendants were tied to the manor. They could not own property, move to another area, or marry without the noble's permission. Serfs were not enslaved, however. Nobles could not sell them or take away the land they farmed to support themselves. Nobles were also expected to protect their serfs.

Serfs worked long hours in the fields and did many services for the nobles. They spent three days of the week working the noble's land and the rest of the week farming their own. However, they had to give part of their own crops to the noble. They also had to pay him for the use of the village's mill, bread oven, and winepress.

It was not easy for serfs to gain their freedom. One way was to escape to the towns. If a serf was not caught and remained in a town for more than a year, he or she was considered free. By the end of the Middle Ages, serfs in many areas were allowed to buy their freedom.

The Lives of the Peasants

Peasants—both freemen and serfs—lived in villages clustered around an open area called a village green. Their homes were simple cottages. The poorest peasants lived in a single room.

Peasants worked year round. In late winter and spring, they planted crops of beans, peas, barley, and oats. In early summer, they weeded fields and sheared sheep. In late summer, they harvested grain. They also slaughtered livestock and salted the meat for winter storage. Many peasants tended small vegetable gardens.

Serfs had a busy life working in the fields growing the lord's crops and their own.

▶ **CRITICAL THINKING**

Differentiating What happened to the crops that serfs grew on their own land?

LESSON 2

ENGAGE

VIDEO **Describing** Show students the Lesson 2 video on castles. You can also provide images of medieval life that you find in books or on the Internet.

Ask:

- **What was life probably like for people in the Middle Ages?**
- **Would you have wanted to live in medieval Europe?**

Write students' responses on the whiteboard.

Then take a poll to see which students would like to have been a medieval knight and which students would like to have been a city merchant. Ask volunteers to explain their choices. Return to this poll at the end of the lesson to see if any students change their minds.

Tell students that in this lesson, they will learn about how most Europeans lived and worked during the Middle Ages.

TEACH & ASSESS

1 The Feudal Order

GUIDING QUESTION ***How did Europeans try to bring order to their society after the fall of Charlemagne's empire?***

LECTURE SLIDE **Determining Cause and Effect** Show students the lecture slide on feudalism. Write the word *causes* on the board.

Ask:

What were the causes of feudalism? *(the fall of Charlemagne's empire, the need for defense from enemies, the growing importance of local nobles)* ELL

Write the responses on the board. Discuss how feudalism improved life for Europeans.

Ask:

What benefits did feudalism provide for ordinary Europeans? *(It provided them with stability and protection from enemies.)*

GRAPH **Categorizing** Show students the diagram of the different social groups in the feudal system.

Ask:

Which group had the most power in the feudal system? Which group had the least? *(Students will note that kings and queens are at the top of the social pyramid. Peasants and serfs are at the bottom of feudal society.)* AL

GRAPHIC ORGANIZER **Diagramming** Allow students time to complete the cluster diagram on the first page of the lesson.

If desired, you can project the interactive graphic organizer on the whiteboard. Have student volunteers fill in the responses. *(Answers may include some of the following: ties of loyalty and duty; vassals and lords; fiefs; knights and code of chivalry; manorial system; serfs and freemen; nobles)*

2 The Medieval Manor

GUIDING QUESTION ***How did most Europeans live and work during the Middle Ages?***

Comparing and Contrasting Before discussing "The Medieval Manor," draw a T-chart on the whiteboard. Label one column "Knights" and the other "Peasants."

Ask:

What were the characteristics and duties of a knight? *(to serve his lord, to fight bravely, to follow the code of chivalry)*

SLIDE SHOW **Summarizing** Then show students the interactive slide show on manorial life. Now return to the table on the whiteboard.

Ask:

What were the duties of medieval peasants? *(to farm the nobles' land and maintain the manor)*

Point out that there were two kinds of peasants—serfs and freemen.

Ask:

How were freemen different from serfs? *(Freemen had rights and were not tied to the land. Serfs had to stay on the land and ask permission to move or get married. At first, serfs could not buy their freedom. This later changed.)* AL

INTERACTIVE WORKSHEET **Differentiating** Help students identify further similarities and differences between knights and peasants by completing the Primary Source Activity worksheet for Lesson 2. Students may complete the worksheet as homework if necessary.

3 The Growth of Towns and Cities

GUIDING QUESTION ***How did increased trade change life in medieval Europe?***

Comparing and Contrasting Have students prepare a class chart that compares and contrasts life in a medieval town with life on a manor.

Have students complete the Lesson 2 Review.

CLOSE & REFLECT

Analyzing Lead students in an oral discussion of life in a feudal society. Ask students to consider the answers they gave at the beginning of the lesson about whether they would want to have lived in medieval times. If they have changed their minds, ask them to explain why.

Make sure students use the lesson's vocabulary words in their answers. Review the meanings of vocabulary words, if necessary. ELL

Answers for pages 548–551

P. 548 Taking Notes Answers may include some of the following: ties of loyalty and duty; vassals and lords; fiefs; knights and code of chivalry; manorial system; serfs and freemen; nobles.

P. 550 ☑ PROGRESS CHECK A knight had to obey his lord, show bravery, respect women of noble birth, honor the Church, and help people. These rules were known as the code of chivalry.

P. 551 CRITICAL THINKING They gave part of the crops to the nobles and kept part for themselves.

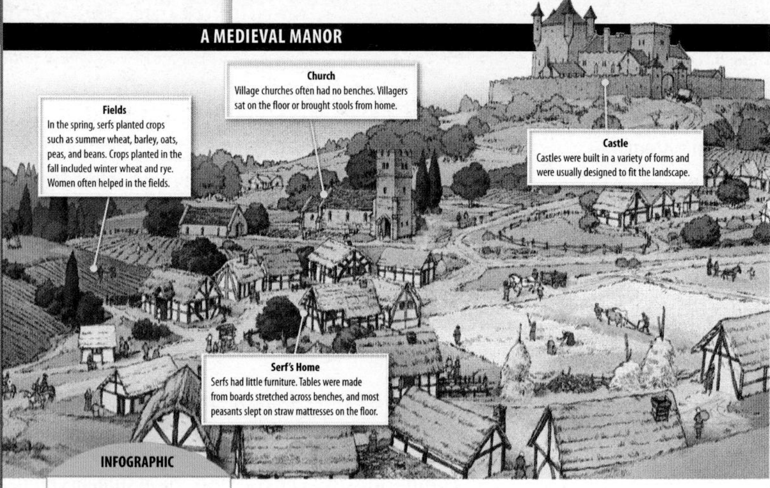

A MEDIEVAL MANOR
Church
Village churches often had no benches. Villagers sat on the floor or brought stools from home.
Fields
In the spring, serfs planted crops such as summer wheat, barley, oats, peas, and beans. Crops planted in the fall included winter wheat and rye. Women often helped in the fields.
Castle
Castles were built in a variety of forms and were usually designed to fit the landscape.
Serf's Home
Serfs had little furniture. Tables were made from boards stretched across benches, and most peasants slept on straw mattresses on the floor.
INFOGRAPHIC

A medieval manor had several parts. At the center was the lord's castle or fortified manor house. Peasants usually lived in a small village nearby. The village contained cottages, huts, barns, gardens, and perhaps a small church. The peasants grew crops in the fields around the village. Manors were found not only in western Europe, but were also common in Russia and Japan.

▶ CRITICAL THINKING

Explaining What were the four areas of a medieval manor?

During times of leisure, peasant life centered on the church and the village green. Peasants took a break from work and went to church on Sunday and Catholic feast days. Certain feast days were celebrated with singing and dancing on the green. Peasant men took part in sports such as wrestling and archery.

Besides working in the fields, peasant women raised children and prepared the family's food. They made dark, heavy bread, which peasants ate with vegetables, milk, nuts, and fruits. They also ate eggs and meat, washed down with ale.

Improvements in Farming

Manors usually produced only enough food to support the peasants and the lord's household. However, over time, Europeans developed new ways to increase the number of crops they could grow, as well as how much the crops produced.

One major improvement was a heavy wheeled plow with an iron blade. The new plow made deeper cuts in the dense clay soil. The heavier plow meant peasant farmers spent less time

Reading **HELP**DESK

Reading Strategy: *Analyzing*

When you analyze a passage you have read, you think about how the facts lead to main conclusions. Reread the section about the medieval manor looking for facts. Then analyze how the manor was beneficial to peasants.

in the fields. The horse collar was another important invention. The collar enabled a horse to pull a plow. Horses could pull plows faster than oxen could. This invention made it possible for peasants to produce more food.

Water and wind power also became important during the Middle Ages. Europe's rivers provided power for water mills to grind grain into flour. In places without rivers, windmills could be used for grinding grain, pumping water, and sawing wood.

Another improvement in agriculture was crop rotation. Peasants used three fields rather than two to keep the soil fertile. One field was planted in the fall, a second one in springtime, and the third field was left unplanted. With this system, only one-third of the land was left unused at a time, rather than one-half. More crops could be grown as a result. As food production increased, the population of Europe grew.

✓ PROGRESS CHECK

Comparing and Contrasting How did the lives of freemen and serfs differ?

3 The Growth of Towns and Cities

GUIDING QUESTION ***How did increased trade change life in medieval Europe?***

When the Roman Empire collapsed, trade throughout Europe sharply declined. Bridges and roads fell into ruin. Law and order largely disappeared. Most people spent their entire lives in the farming villages where they were born. They knew very little about the rest of the world.

By 1100, feudalism had made Europe safer. Nobles repaired roads, arrested bandits, and enforced the law. Meanwhile, new technology enabled people to produce more food and goods. Europe's population grew for the first time since the fall of Rome.

Peasants began to make cloth and metal products. Nobles also sought luxury items, such as sugar, spices, silks, and dyes. These goods came from the East.

As Europe became more feudalistic, towns and cities grew. Tall stone buildings lining narrow streets were similar in England and France. This street is still in use in Blesle, France.

Wealthy Trading Centers

As Europe's trade increased, towns grew larger. Several cities became wealthy from trade. The cities of Venice (VEH•nuhs), Pisa, and Genoa in Italy built fleets of trading ships. They became major trading centers. By 1200, these Italian cities controlled the profitable Mediterranean trade with the Byzantine Empire.

Trade was lively in medieval marketplaces with a variety of products for sale.

▶ CRITICAL THINKING

Analyzing Visuals What kinds of goods appear to be available at this market?

Meanwhile, Flanders—a region that is today part of Belgium—became a center of trade on Europe's northern coast. Towns in Flanders, such as Bruges and Ghent, were known for wool. Merchants from all over Western Europe traveled to these towns to trade their goods for woolen cloth.

Trade fairs were established in northern France. At these fairs, northern European merchants bartered their products. They traded furs, tin, honey, and wool for swords and cloth from northern Italy and silks, sugar, and spices from Asia.

As trade increased, merchants demanded payment in gold and silver coins. People again began using money to buy goods. Some merchants set up banks.

Government in Cities

The rise of trade and cities created a new middle class in medieval Europe. People in the middle class had some wealth as a result of their roles as merchants, bankers, or artisans. They became important leaders in the cities.

Eventually, medieval towns began to set up their own governments. Only males were considered citizens. In many cities, the citizens elected the members of a city council. These elected officials served as lawmakers and judges.

Under the feudal system, towns were often part of the territory belonging to a noble. As a result, nobles tried to control town affairs. Townspeople, however, disliked owing taxes and services to nobles. They wanted freedom to make their own

Reading **HELP**DESK

guild a group of merchants or craftspeople

laws. As their wealth increased, townspeople forced nobles to grant them basic rights. These included the right to buy and sell property and the freedom from having to serve in the army.

What Did Guilds Do?

Trade encouraged townspeople to produce many different kinds of products. Craftspeople organized **guilds**, or business groups. Each craft had its own guild.

Guilds controlled business and trade in a town. The guild set the price for a product or service. Guilds also set and enforced standards of quality for products.

In addition, guilds decided who could join a trade. An apprentice, or trainee, learned a trade from a master artisan who provided room and board but no wages. After completing this training, the apprentice became a journeyman who worked under a master for a daily wage.

Life in a Medieval City

Medieval cities were surrounded by stone walls. Inside the walls, stone public buildings and wooden houses were jammed close together. Candles and fireplaces were used for light and heat.

Towns could be unhealthy places. Wood and coal fires in people's homes and shops filled the air with ashes and smoke. Sewers were open, and there was little concern for cleanliness.

City women kept house, cared for children, and managed the family's money. Wives often helped their husbands in their trade, sometimes carrying on the trade after their husbands' deaths.

✓ PROGRESS CHECK

Analyzing How did guilds affect the way medieval townspeople made a living?

Thinking Like a **HISTORIAN**

Researching Using Internet Resources

One of England's earliest historians was Bede. Bede (A.D. 673–735) was an educated monk who lived in northern England. He wrote the *Ecclesiastical History of the English People*, using the Latin language. Use the Internet to find reliable copies or selections from Bede's history. Choose three facts you discover about English history and present them to your class. For more information about using sources, review *What Does a Historian Do?*

LESSON 2 REVIEW

Review Vocabulary

1. What was a *fief*?

Answer the Guiding Questions

2. ***Describing*** Draw a chart to show the major parts of a medieval manor.
3. ***Summarizing*** What impact did the code of chivalry have on knights during the Middle Ages?
4. ***Identifying Cause and Effect*** What explains the development of cities and towns during the Middle Ages?
5. ***Drawing Conclusions*** If you were a person in business in medieval Europe, why would membership in a guild be important to you?
6. **EXPOSITORY WRITING** What new inventions allowed people in Western Europe to grow more food during the Middle Ages? What was the result of this increase in food production?

LESSON 2 (cont.)

BACKGROUND KNOWLEDGE

Medieval Tournaments

One of the most famous activities of medieval knights was the tournament, a series of mock combats designed to showcase war skills. The earliest tournaments, probably held in France in the 1000s, featured a mock battle called a *melee* between two groups of knights.

The familiar joust, in which two riders charged each other and tried to knock an opponent off his horse with a long lance, came later.

By around 1300, steps were taken to prevent injury to the contestants, although serious injuries, and even death, sometimes occurred. In the 1500s, fighting on foot became popular, with knights striking each other across a barricade with swords and battle-axes.

Guilds

Guilds in the Middle Ages were of two basic types: merchant guilds and craft guilds. Merchant guilds arose first. They were associations of most or all merchants in a town, including retailers, wholesalers, and importers/exporters. In most towns, the guild charged an entrance fee for merchants to join. Merchant guilds also limited membership to the inhabitants of the town. Historians believe they might have begun as a means of protecting traveling peddlers from bandits. They gradually evolved into broader associations as trade became centralized in towns.

Craft guilds developed in response to the gradual division of labor. Individuals or family workshops that did similar work joined together to improve distribution, working conditions, and profits. Craft guild members were organized into three groups: masters (at the highest level), journeymen (middle level), and apprentices (beginners). Journeymen and apprentices underwent long periods of training. Once the craftsman could produce a work that met the approval of guild masters, he could gain membership in the guild.

IF YOU HAVE MORE TIME . . .

Discuss Loyalty in the Middle Ages

Comparing In the Middle Ages, people felt loyalty to their local lord or town. Countries and states as we know them did not really exist. Ask students to discuss their sense of loyalty and belonging to their community, state, and nation.

- **How are these different loyalties related?**
- **Does one always outweigh the others?**
- **In what circumstances might a local loyalty outweigh a broader one?**

If appropriate, remind students that during the American Civil War, most people felt a greater loyalty to their state or region than to the United States. Conclude by asking students to decide if local loyalties are a hindrance or a benefit to our sense of nationhood.

Take a Closer Look at the Feudal System

Interpreting Ask students what benefits feudalism provided for people at each of its levels. Have them offer suggestions regarding why those on the lower rungs generally accepted their roles.

Then ask them to name similar situations in which all parties benefit from an arrangement, even though it might not be ideal for all participants.

Hold a Class Debate on the Pros and Cons of Feudalism

Discussing Organize a class debate on whether the medieval institution of feudalism was good or bad. Form groups supporting each point of view. To support their arguments, have students find additional resources that discuss feudalism and its role in medieval society.

Students may use the library, the Internet, or other resources to find additional information about feudalism and serfdom.

After each group has compiled its research, have students present their group's viewpoint to the class. They should use their graphic organizers to help them in their presentations. Next, have the other group provide its opposing point of view.

Students might want to vote to decide which argument was more persuasive. BL

Make a Medieval Travelogue

Researching Ask groups of students to use the Internet and other resources to make a travelogue of medieval cityscapes. Have the groups use search engines to find photographs of European cities, towns, and villages that retain a medieval character.

Have them look for preserved buildings, such as shops, castles, and churches, and unchanged rural and agricultural landscapes. Suggest that they begin by looking at the Cotswold region and the city of York in England; Assisi, Italy; or Rothenberg in Germany.

Have the groups print information and photos of preserved places and prepare a bulletin board as their travelogue.

Answers for pages 552–555

P. 552 INFOGRAPHIC

CRITICAL THINKING the lord's castle, the peasant village, the fields, and the church

P. 552 READING STRATEGY The manor benefited peasants because they had enough to eat and were allowed to celebrate feast days and attend church.

P. 553 ☑ PROGRESS CHECK Freemen paid nobles for the right to farm their land and could move around as they wished. Serfs were tied to the manor. Freemen had legal rights, while the rights of serfs were restricted. Freemen and serfs were below the lord in the social order.

P. 554 CRITICAL THINKING mostly foodstuffs

P. 555 ☑ PROGRESS CHECK Guilds controlled all business and trade. They decided the price for products and services, set standards for quality, and established who could join a trade and the steps that a new tradesman had to follow.

LESSON 2 REVIEW

1. A fief was a property granted to a vassal by a lord.
2. Charts should show the lord's manor house or castle at the center of the manor, the nearby village populated by freemen and serfs, and the surrounding fields where crops were cultivated.
3. Chivalry had a great impact on knights because it was a code of behavior. For example, knights had to be brave, obey their lords, help people, respect women of noble birth, and honor the Church.
4. Growth in trade was the most important factor in the development of cities and towns during the Middle Ages. Increased trade allowed some townspeople to become wealthy and powerful enough to demand their rights from the nobles. Trade also was the reason many people left the farms to live and work in cities and towns.
5. Membership in a guild would be important because guilds, or trade and crafts associations, had a monopoly on the business of artisans and craftsmen. They controlled the setting of prices, the establishment of standards, and the rules by which apprentices were allowed to join the business.
6. Inventions included improved plows, the horse collar, and crop rotation. The effect of increased food production was growth in the population.

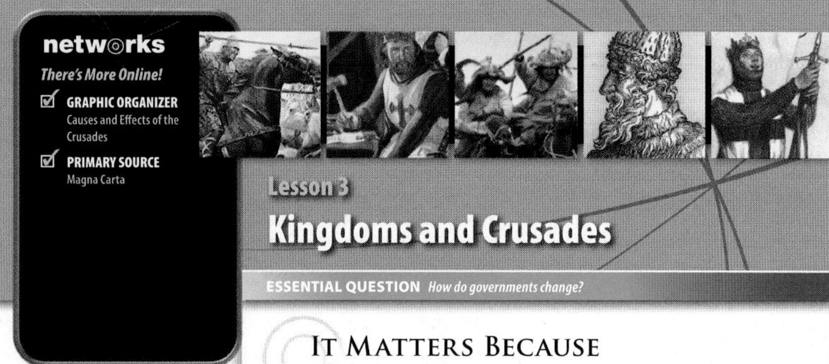

networks
There's More Online!
- GRAPHIC ORGANIZER: Causes and Effects of the Crusades
- PRIMARY SOURCE: Magna Carta

Lesson 3

Kingdoms and Crusades

ESSENTIAL QUESTION *How do governments change?*

It Matters Because

The development of law and government during the Middle Ages in Europe still affects us today.

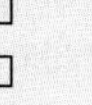

Royal Power in England

GUIDING QUESTION *How was the king's power strengthened and then limited in medieval England?*

In the late 800s, Vikings from Scandinavia attacked Britain, where the Anglo-Saxons had founded many small kingdoms. King Alfred of Wessex, later known as Alfred the Great, united the Anglo-Saxons and halted the Viking advance. The kingdom that Alfred united became known as "Angleland," or England.

Alfred ruled England from A.D. 871 to 899. Unfortunately for England, the Anglo-Saxon kings who followed Alfred were generally weak rulers.

William the Conqueror

In 1066, the last Anglo-Saxon king of England died without an heir. A noble named Harold Godwinson claimed the English throne. In France, a relative of the Anglo-Saxon kings, William, Duke of Normandy (NAWR•muhn•dee), said that he, not Harold, was the rightful king of England.

In the fall of 1066, William and his army of Norman knights landed in England. They defeated Harold and his foot soldiers at the Battle of Hastings. William was crowned king of England and became known as William the Conqueror.

Reading HELPDESK

Taking Notes: *Sequencing*
Complete a sequence diagram like this one to show the causes and effects of the Crusades.

Content Vocabulary
- grand jury
- trial jury

At first, the Anglo-Saxons resisted William's rule. To stop the Anglo-Saxon revolts, William seized the land of Anglo-Saxon nobles and divided it among his Norman knights.

William wanted to learn as much as possible about his new kingdom. To decide taxes, he carried out the first census since Roman times. Every person, and farm animal in England was counted and recorded in the *Domesday Book*.

The Normans who ruled England kept many Anglo-Saxon laws and practices. However, they also brought many customs from mainland Europe. Under William's rule, officials and nobles in England spoke French, the language of Normandy. They built castles, cathedrals, and monasteries in the Norman style. Anglo-Saxons learned new skills from Norman weavers and artisans. Yet, they still spoke their own Anglo-Saxon language, which later became English. As more and more Normans and Anglo-Saxons married, their customs merged into a new English culture.

Henry II

After the death of William, English kings further strengthened their power. From 1154 to 1189, King Henry II ruled England as well as most of Wales, and Ireland. He was also a feudal lord in France and Scotland. Some of the French lands belonged to his wife, Queen Eleanor of Aquitaine.

Henry set up a central royal court with lawyers and judges. Circuit judges, who traveled across the country to hear cases, brought the king's law to all parts of England.

At the Battle of Hastings, William the Conqueror led Norman knights on horseback as well as infantry to attack the English foot soldiers.

▶ CRITICAL THINKING
Identifying Points of View Why did William believe that he was the rightful king of England?

The courts created a body of common law, or law that was the same throughout the whole kingdom. Common law helped unite England by replacing laws that differed from place to place.

Henry also set up juries of citizens to settle disputes. Traveling circuit judges met with a **grand jury.** It decided if people should be accused of a crime. Next came a **trial jury** to decide whether a person was innocent or guilty.

The Magna Carta and Parliament

Henry's son John became king of England in 1199. King John increased taxes in England and punished his enemies without trials. English nobles began to rebel against the king.

In 1215, the nobles met with King John at Runnymede, a nearby meadow. There they forced John to put his seal on a **document** called the Magna Carta, or the Great Charter. The Magna Carta placed limits on the king's power. The king could collect taxes only if a group of nobles called the Great Council agreed.

The Magna Carta also forced the king to uphold the rights of freemen, including the right to fair trials by jury:

PRIMARY SOURCE

> "No free man shall be taken, imprisoned, disseised [seized], outlawed, banished [sent away], or in any way destroyed, nor will We proceed against or prosecute him, except by the lawful judgment of his peers [equals] and by the law of the land."
>
> —from the *Magna Carta*, 1215

King John signed the Magna Carta, a document that brought significant change to England.

The Magna Carta relied on the feudal idea that the king and his noble vassals both had certain rights and duties. Over time, however, the Magna Carta helped strengthen the idea that all people, regardless of rank, have rights, and that the power of government should be limited.

Edward I, king of England in the late 1200s, increased the authority of his council. This group of lords, church leaders, knights, and townspeople became known as Parliament (PAHR•luh•muhnt). Parliament came to be divided into two groups—an upper house and lower house. The growth of Parliament marked an important step toward representative government.

✓ PROGRESS CHECK

Explaining How did the common law help unite England?

Reading HELPDESK

grand jury a group of citizens that meets to decide whether people should be accused of a crime
trial jury a group of citizens that decides whether an accused person is innocent or guilty

Academic Vocabulary
document an original or official paper used as the basis or proof of something

Building Vocabulary: *Word Origins*
The English word *Parliament* comes from the French word *parler*, meaning to talk or converse. Parliament was where people could talk about problems or concerns facing the kingdom.

2 Monarchy in France

GUIDING QUESTION *How did the kings of France increase their power?*

In 843, Charlemagne's empire was split into three parts. The western part became the kingdom of France. In 987, the west Frankish nobles made Hugh Capet their king. Hugh began the Capetian (kuh•PEE•shuhn) dynasty of French kings. Capetian kings controlled only the area around Paris, the capital. Many French nobles had more power than the kings did. This began to change when Philip II became the king of France in 1180.

Philip worked to expand the French monarchy's wealth and power. At the beginning of Philip's reign, the king of England ruled feudal lands in western France. Philip fought wars against the English and gained some of these territories.

Philip IV wanted to raise taxes to pay for his wars. In 1302, he gained approval for this plan from representatives of the three estates, or classes, of French society. The first estate was the clergy, or priests. Nobles made up the second estate, and townspeople and peasants were the third estate. This meeting began the Estates-General, France's first parliament. The Estates-General never became as powerful as Parliament in England.

✓ PROGRESS CHECK

Comparing and Contrasting How was the Estates-General of France different from England's Parliament?

GEOGRAPHY CONNECTION

In 1160, Europe was divided into many small kingdoms and states.

1. **LOCATION** Which empire bordered Hungary to the south?
2. CRITICAL THINKING
   Analyzing What was the effect of having many small states ruled by French nobles?

LESSON 3 • Day 1

ENGAGE

MAP **Speculating** Project the map of medieval Europe on the whiteboard. Note for students how the continent is divided into many different kingdoms, states, and empires. Point out that medieval France and England were not countries with strong unified governments as they are today.

Ask:

What would life be like if no central government and no laws existed? Allow students one or two minutes to quickwrite a response. Ask volunteers to share their answers.

Make sure students understand how laws protect people. Laws guarantee that people with power do not take advantage of those with less power. AL

Tell students that in this lesson, they will learn about important political developments in Europe, particularly the ones that established rights and laws.

TEACH & ASSESS

Royal Power in England

GUIDING QUESTION ***How was the king's power strengthened and then limited in medieval England?***

LECTURE SLIDE **Listing** Show students the lecture slide on the kings of England. Ask students to work with a partner to create and complete a five-column chart on a sheet of paper. The chart should include a label for each king shown on the slide.

Ask pairs to work together to review the lesson for the key accomplishments of each leader and to write them in the chart. Ask volunteers to share their findings. Write answers on the whiteboard. If students need help,

ask:

- **Who united England?** *(Alfred)*
- **Which European noble conquered England in 1066?** *(William I)*
- **Which ruler developed a system of courts?** *(Henry II)*
- **Who agreed to give nobles more rights?** *(John)*
- **Who set up Parliament?** *(Edward I)*  

Determining Cause and Effect Explain that the Magna Carta placed limits on the English king's powers, and it forced the king to follow the same rules and laws as everyone else.

Ask:

How did the nobles get King John to sign the Magna Carta? *(They joined together. Together they had more power than the king.)*

How did the Magna Carta change the way kings ruled England? *(They had to respect the rights of freemen and obey laws. They could not rule by whim.)* AL

PRIMARY SOURCE **Comparing and Contrasting** Show students the primary source comparing the Magna Carta with the Bill of Rights in the U.S. Constitution. Read aloud or ask a student to read aloud each section of the table. ELL

Ask:

What do these documents say about religion? *(The Magna Carta says the English Church shall be free. The Bill of Rights says the government cannot create a state church, and it protects freedom of religion.)*

Ask:

What similar legal rights do they provide? *(Both require due process of law before a person can be convicted of a crime, ban unreasonable seizures of property, and prohibit excessive fines.)*

2 Monarchy in France

GUIDING QUESTION ***How did the kings of France increase their power?***

LECTURE SLIDE

Explaining Show students the lecture slide on the three estates of France. After discussing "Monarchy in France," **ask:**

What change in government did the Estates-General represent? *(It was France's first parliament and the country's first step toward representative government.)*

INTERACTIVE WHITEBOARD ACTIVITY

Sequencing Then have students complete the Monarchy in France Interactive Whiteboard Activity by placing events in the correct order in the sequence chart.

3 Eastern States of the Slavs

GUIDING QUESTION ***How did the cities of Kiev and Moscow become centers of powerful Slavic states?***

Identifying Have students refer to "Eastern States of the Slavs" in their textbooks.

Ask:

How did the Mongols help Moscow become a powerful city? *(The Slavs cooperated with Mongol control. As a result, the Mongols allowed Moscow to be built and gave its rulers special privileges to collect taxes and acquire land. Moscow was the crossroads of many trade routes and flourished as it grew.)*

CLOSE & REFLECT

Comparing and Contrasting Lead students in a discussion of the similarities and differences between the changes in government that took place in England, in France, and in the Eastern states. Ask them to consider who held power in each country and what rights the citizens of those countries possessed.

Answers for pages 556–559

P. 556 Taking Notes Answers may include some or all of the following: Byzantine Empire attacked by Turks → Pope agrees to help and calls for First Crusade → Pope promises salvation to those who die in battle → European Christians seize Jerusalem → Muslims conquer part of crusader states → Later crusades fail to recapture territory → Crusades result in a wider European worldview → Crusades help break down feudalism in Europe.

P. 557 CRITICAL THINKING The throne had been taken over by a nobleman, but William was related to the Anglo-Saxon kings.

P. 558 ☑ PROGRESS CHECK The law courts of King Henry II helped create a body of common law, which replaced laws that differed from place to place.

P. 559 GEOGRAPHY CONNECTION

1. The Byzantine Empire lies to the south of Hungary.
2. CRITICAL THINKING Many French nobles had more power than the kings did.

P. 559 ☑ PROGRESS CHECK France's Estates-General (made up of clergy, nobles, and townspeople and peasants) never became as powerful as England's Parliament did because the kings of France ruled with a firm hand.

3 Eastern States of the Slavs

GUIDING QUESTION *How did the cities of Kiev and Moscow become centers of powerful Slavic states?*

In Eastern Europe, people called the Slavs established villages and towns along the rivers of that region. The Slavs consisted of three important groups: the southern Slavs, the western Slavs, and the eastern Slavs.

The Rise of Kiev

In the 800s, the eastern Slavs began to expand the city of Kiev (KEE•EHF). The medieval state of Kievan Rus grew wealthy from its river trade with Scandinavia and the Byzantine Empire.

In 988, the Rus ruler, Vladimir, married the sister of the Byzantine emperor. Vladimir became an Eastern Orthodox Christian. Soon, priests from Constantinople came to teach the people of Kievan Rus religious rituals and the art of painting icons.

Mongol Invaders

About 1240, Mongol warriors from Central Asia conquered Kievan Rus. The Slavic city of Novgorod was the only major city to be spared attack by the Mongols. However, Novgorod's rulers had to pay tribute to the khan, the Mongol leader, and accept the Mongols as their rulers.

Although the Mongols spared Novgorod, the city faced attacks from the west by Germans and Swedes. In 1240, Novgorod forces led by a prince named Alexander Nevsky (NEHV•skee) defeated these invaders.

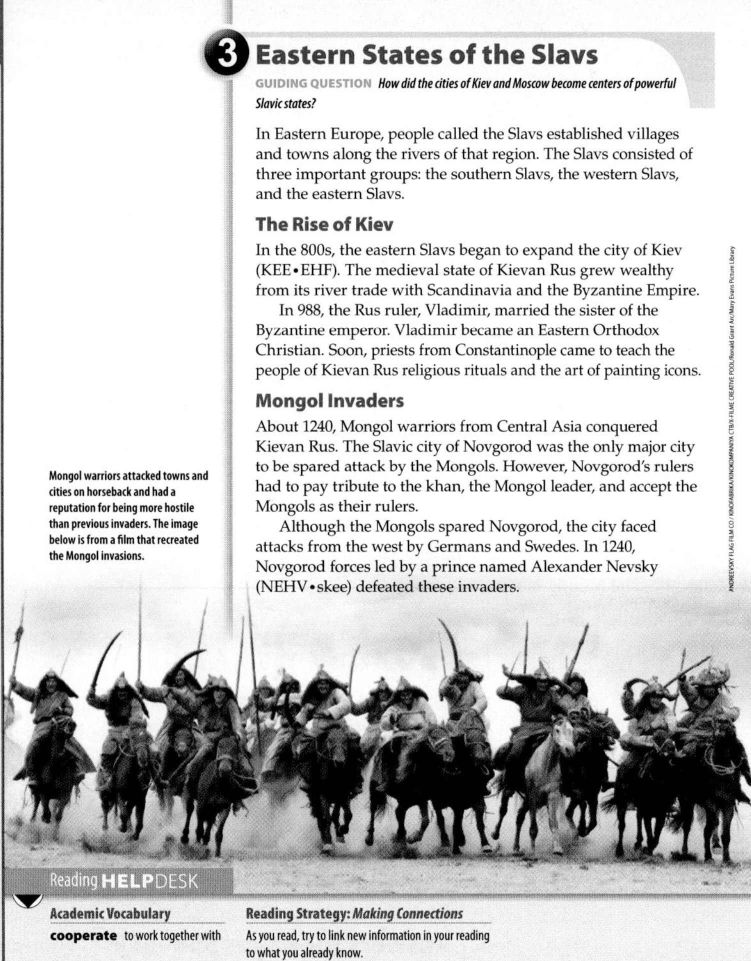

Mongol warriors attacked towns and cities on horseback and had a reputation for being more hostile than previous invaders. The image below is from a film that recreated the Mongol invasions.

Reading **HELP**DESK

Academic Vocabulary

cooperate to work together with

Reading Strategy: *Making Connections*

As you read, try to link new information in your reading to what you already know.

GEOGRAPHY CONNECTION

Like Kievan Rus, Moscow grew in power and wealth because of its location along trade routes.

1. **LOCATION** Use the scale on the map. About how far is Novgorod from Moscow?
2. **CRITICAL THINKING** *Analyzing Visuals* During which period did Moscow add the greatest amount of land to its territory?

The Importance of Moscow

During the period of Mongol rule, many Slavs moved north from Kiev and built settlements in the area that is now Russia. One new settlement was Moscow (MAHS•KOH). Moscow became a large city that prospered because it was at the crossroads of several major trade routes.

The rulers of Moscow learned to **cooperate** with the Mongols. In return, the Mongols gave them the right to collect taxes from other Slav territories. If a territory could not provide soldiers or tax money, Moscow's rulers took control of it. In this way, Moscow was able to gradually expand its territory.

Ivan III Becomes Czar

Ivan III became the ruler of Moscow in 1462. He married Sophia, a niece of the Byzantine emperor. Ivan adopted the lavish style of Byzantine rulers and was referred to as czar. The Russian word *czar,* like *Caesar* in Latin, means "emperor."

By 1480, Ivan III had finally driven the Mongols from Moscow and Russian territory. He turned next to the north and west to add territory. By then, the people of Moscow, now known as Russians, had made great strides toward establishing a huge empire.

Ivan III's reign focused on expanding the Russian empire. During his rule, the Russian territory tripled in size.

✓ PROGRESS CHECK

Determining Cause and Effect Why did the rulers of Moscow work with the Mongols?

The Crusades 1096–1204

KEY: Christian lands, c. 1100; Muslim lands, c. 1100; First Crusade, 1096–1099; Second Crusade, 1147–1149; Third Crusade, 1189–1192

GEOGRAPHY CONNECTION

This map shows that the crusaders came from all over Europe. It also shows the land and sea routes that they took to the Holy Land.

1. **MOVEMENT** On the First Crusade, how did the crusaders from Cologne reach the Holy Land? In what direction did they travel?
2. **CRITICAL THINKING** *Comparing* Which crusade involved the most travel: the First, the Second, or the Third?

4 European Crusaders

GUIDING QUESTION *Why did Western Europeans go on crusades?*

During the 1000s, the Byzantine Empire in the east came under attack. In 1071, an army of Muslim Turks defeated the Byzantines and seized control of most of the Byzantine lands in Asia Minor.

The Byzantine emperor asked Pope Urban II for military aid to save his Christian empire from Muslim forces. The pope agreed to help the Byzantines. He hoped that, in return, the Eastern Orthodox Church would again unite with the Roman Catholic Church and accept him as its religious leader.

In 1095, the pope asked Europe's nobles to begin a crusade, or holy war, against the Muslim Turks. He urged them to capture Jerusalem and free the Holy Land, where Jesus had lived, from the Muslims.

The Crusades Begin

Thousands of European soldiers on horseback and on foot headed east on the First Crusade. They reached Jerusalem in 1099. In a fierce battle with Muslims, they stormed the city.

Reading **HELP**DESK

Academic Vocabulary

accurate correct and free from errors

The crusaders conquered several regions. They set up four states controlled by Europe: the Kingdom of Jerusalem in the Holy Land, Edessa and Antioch in Asia Minor, and Tripoli in what is now Lebanon. These states were surrounded by Muslim territory. They depended on supplies from the Italian cities of Genoa, Pisa, and Venice.

Continued Conflicts

After Muslim forces retook Edessa, the Second Crusade began. This time, the Muslims easily defeated the Europeans. In 1174, led by a brilliant general named Saladin (SA•luh•DEEN), Muslims recaptured Jerusalem.

This action triggered the Third Crusade, which was also a failure. Throughout the 1200s, Europeans continued to organize crusades. They made few gains. By the end of the century, the Muslims had regained all the land conquered by the crusaders.

The Effects of the Crusades

The Crusades brought Western Europeans into contact with Byzantines and Muslims. As a result, Western Europeans gained new knowledge. In architecture, they learned how to build domes and create mosaics. They discovered how to build better ships and make more **accurate** maps. They also learned how to use the compass to tell direction. Wealthy people in Western Europe began to demand eastern goods such as spices, sugar, lemons, and silk.

The Crusades, however, weakened feudalism. Nobles who joined the Crusades sold their lands and freed their serfs. This reduced their power. Kings were able to build stronger central governments.

The Crusades lasted over a period of more than two hundred years. They caused bitter feelings between Christian Western Europe and the Islamic world.

Many Crusaders wore red crosses on their tunics to show they were risking their lives in support of Christianity and the pope.

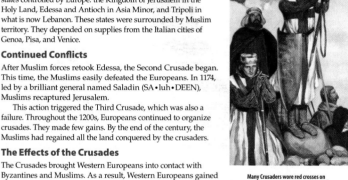

✓ PROGRESS CHECK

Determining Cause and Effect What was one way the Crusades changed Christian Europe?

LESSON 3 REVIEW

Review Vocabulary

1. How is a *grand jury* different from a *trial jury?*

Answer the Guiding Questions

2. ***Explaining*** How did the Magna Carta limit the power of the king of England?
3. ***Describing*** How did royal power in England progress from William to Henry II to John to Edward I?
4. ***Describing*** How did the cities of Kiev and Moscow become centers of powerful Slavic states?
5. ***Identifying Cause and Effect*** Why did Western Europeans go on Crusades?
6. **EXPOSITORY WRITING** Write a paragraph discussing how the Crusades affected feudalism.

LESSON 3 • Day 2

ENGAGE

SLIDE SHOW Provide students context by explaining that during the Middle Ages, people from every level of society went on pilgrimages, or journeys of faith. Pilgrims would travel from their homes in Europe to the Holy Land in the East. During the Middle Ages, many of these places were under Muslim control.

Note that conflicts between Christians and Muslim Turks led to the Crusades. Then show students the slide show for Lesson 3.

Ask:

What stands out to you about the Crusades after seeing the slides? *(Student answers may include that the Crusades were bloody and violent.)*

Tell students they will learn more about the causes and effects of the Crusades.

TEACH & ASSESS

European Crusaders

GUIDING QUESTION *Why did Western Europeans go on crusades?*

Identifying Points of View Ask a volunteer to read aloud the paragraph that contains Urban II's promise that "All who die . . . shall have immediate remission [forgiveness of sins]" in the Primary Source worksheet for Lesson 3. Then write *Europeans* and *Muslims* on the board.

Lead the class in a discussion about the Europeans' reasons for fighting. Then consider the Muslims' reasons for fighting the European crusaders.

Ask:

Why was each side fighting? *(Each side thought it was defending its religion. Both sides were also fighting over territory, including the Holy Land and the entire Byzantine Empire.)*

INTERACTIVE WORKSHEET

Have students work alone or in pairs to complete the Primary Source Activity for Lesson 3.

Afterwards, **ask: What generalization can you make about how the two sides in the holy wars viewed each other?** *(Each side thought the other was wrong. Anna Comnena thought the crusaders were rude. Pope Urban II believed the Muslims were "infidels," or nonbelievers.)*

GRAPHIC ORGANIZER

Determining Cause and Effect Have students complete the graphic organizer that appears on the first lesson page.

Then **ask:**

- **What were two causes of the Crusades?** *(Muslim Turks attacked Byzantium, and the emperor asked for help. Muslims would not allow Christians to visit sites in the Holy Land.)*
- **What were three effects of the Crusades?** *(Answers should include that Europeans gained a larger worldview, rediscovered lost knowledge, and began trading with the East. Also, feudalism broke down.)*

Have students complete the Lesson 3 Review.

CLOSE & REFLECT

Divide students into small groups. Assign each group an important person from the time of the Crusades, including Richard the Lionhearted, Eleanor of Aquitaine, Saladin, Godfrey of Bouillon, Anna Comnena, Urban II, Peter the Hermit, Louis IX, and Tancred de Hauteville. For homework, tell them to research their subjects in order to answer the following questions:

- **Who is your subject?**
- **When and where did he or she live?**
- **What was his or her connection to the Crusades?**
- **Why is your subject historically important?**

As homework, have students write a short biography of their subject based on their research. Advanced students should provide citations for their research. 

Students who need help should work in pairs or small groups to research and write their biographies.
AL ELL

Answers for pages 560–563

P. 561 GEOGRAPHY CONNECTION

1. Novgorod is about 300 miles (500 km) northwest of Moscow.
2. CRITICAL THINKING Moscow acquired the greatest amount of land in the period 1462–1505.

P. 561 ☑ PROGRESS CHECK because in return for their cooperation, the Mongols gave the rulers of Moscow the right to collect taxes from other Slav territories

P. 562 GEOGRAPHY CONNECTION

1. They traveled overland in a generally southeast direction.
2. CRITICAL THINKING The Third Crusade involved the most travel.

P. 563 ☑ PROGRESS CHECK Answers will vary. Possible answers: The split between Eastern and Western Christians became permanent. Western Europeans came into contact with cultured Byzantines and Muslims and developed a larger view of the world. They gained new knowledge of ancient texts and learned new building skills. The demand in Europe for luxury goods began to grow.

LESSON 3 REVIEW

1. A grand jury decides whether people should be accused of a crime. A trial jury decides whether an accused person is innocent or guilty.
2. In 1215, English nobles forced King John to sign the Magna Carta, which set limits on the king's power. It set limits on the king's ability to impose taxes and forced him to recognize the rights of the people.
3. William the Conqueror conquered England and created the *Domesday Book*; Henry II brought common law to England; John signed the Magna Carta; and Edward I established the English Parliament.
4. Kiev prospered from river trade between Scandinavia and the Byzantine Empire. Moscow was located at the crossroads of several major trade routes. In addition, Moscow cooperated with the Mongols, who gave the rulers of Moscow the right to collect taxes from other Slav territories.
5. The pope agreed to help the Byzantines. He urged Western Europeans to liberate Jerusalem from Muslim rule. He promised those who might die in battle that they would gain immediate forgiveness for their sins.
6. Essays should mention that the Crusades weakened feudalism. Nobles who joined the Crusades sold their lands, thereby reducing their power, which allowed kings to build stronger central governments.

networks
There's More Online!
- GRAPHIC ORGANIZER
  Organizing Information
  Medieval Life
- PRIMARY SOURCE
  The Song of Roland

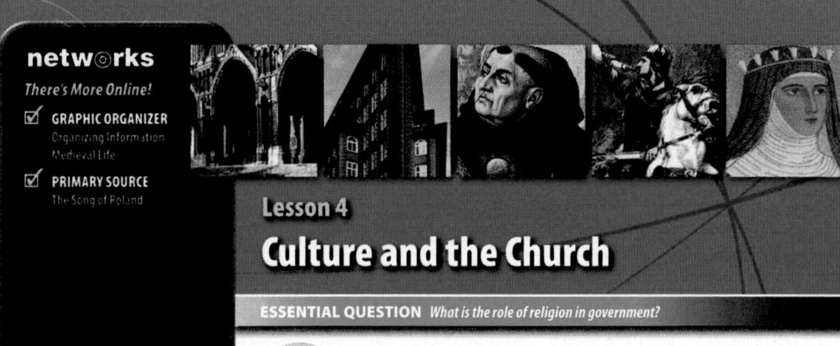

Lesson 4
Culture and the Church

ESSENTIAL QUESTION *What is the role of religion in government?*

IT MATTERS BECAUSE
Architecture, education, literature, and religion played very important roles in medieval life.

1 European Culture in the Middle Ages

GUIDING QUESTION *What types of learning and art developed during the Middle Ages?*

By the 1100s, the Crusades and the rise of strong governments made medieval Europeans more confident and **secure**. As a result, trade, banking, and businesses thrived. A better economy meant more money to spend on building and learning.

Styles in Architecture

In the 1000s and 1100s, Europeans began to construct many buildings. Because medieval society valued religion, many of the new buildings were churches and monasteries. Church leaders, wealthy merchants, and nobles supported the building of large churches called cathedrals. Soaring above the rooftops of medieval towns, cathedrals were built in either Romanesque (ROH•muh•NEHSK) or Gothic styles.

Early medieval churches were Romanesque, a style that combined the features of Roman and Byzantine buildings. Romanesque churches were rectangular buildings with long, rounded ceilings called barrel vaults. These ceilings were supported by heavy walls and thick pillars set close together. The churches' small windows let in little light.

Reading **HELP**DESK

Taking Notes: ***Organizing Information***
Use a table like the one shown here to list information about the parts of medieval life listed in the left-hand column.

Cathedrals	
Universities	
Theology	
Literature	
Religious Orders	

Content Vocabulary
- **mass**
- **heresy**
- **anti-Semitism**
- **theology**
- **scholasticism**
- **vernacular**

About 1150, builders began to construct churches in the Gothic style. They replaced Romanesque heavy walls with flying buttresses. These stone arches extended off the outside walls of the church and supported the weight of the building. They made it possible to build churches with thinner walls and large stained glass windows. Gothic churches were taller and had more space than Romanesque churches.

Colorful stained glass windows often presented scenes from the life and teachings of Jesus. They also let in sunlight, which symbolized the divine light of God.

Development of Universities

The universities of today trace their origins to the Middle Ages. Two of the first medieval universities were in Bologna (buh•LOH•nyuh), Italy, and Paris, France. Universities also were founded in England at Oxford and Cambridge. By 1500, Europe had 80 universities.

Groups of students and teachers created the first universities to educate scholars. Medieval university students studied grammar, public speaking, logic, arithmetic, geometry, music, and astronomy. Teachers read from a text and discussed it, while students took notes on small, portable chalkboards called slates. Students did not have books because books were rare before the European printing press was created in the 1400s.

To get a degree, students took oral exams after four to six years. They could earn a bachelor of arts and later a master of arts. In about ten more years, a student could earn a doctor's degree in law, medicine, or **theology** (thee•AH•luh•jee)—the study of religion and God. People with doctor's degrees were officially able to teach but could also pursue other careers. For example, the monk Roger Bacon turned from teaching theology to studying the natural world. His interest in using experiments to test ideas helped pave the way for the rise of modern science.

What is Scholasticism?

By 1100, a new way of thinking called **scholasticism** (skuh•LAS•tuh•SIH•zuhm) was changing the study of theology. Its followers wanted to show that ideas accepted on faith did not have to contradict ideas developed by reason. The first scholastic thinker was Anselm, who served as archbishop of Canterbury in England from 1093 to 1109. Anselm became known for his reasoning about the existence of God.

THEN

Advances in architecture enabled the French to build the great Gothic cathedral at Chartres. The Gothic style was revived in the 1700s. Today, architects still use this distinctive style of architecture. An example is this 1920s building in Hamburg, Germany.

NOW

▶ CRITICAL THINKING
Speculating Why do you think elements of the Gothic style might still be in use today?

theology the study of religious faith, practice, and experience
scholasticism a way of thinking that combined faith and reason

Academic Vocabulary
secure free from danger

Thomas Aquinas became one of the best-known scholars in the history of the Catholic Church.

▶ CRITICAL THINKING
Analyzing Visuals Why do you think Thomas Aquinas is shown with a church in one hand and a book in the other?

During the 1100s, the ideas of the ancient Greek philosopher Aristotle had a major influence on Europe. After the fall of Rome in the late 400s, Aristotle had been almost forgotten in Europe. Muslim libraries, however, had preserved copies of his books. In the 1100s, Muslim and Jewish scholars reintroduced Aristotle to Europe. The ancient philosopher's ideas disturbed some Christian thinkers. Aristotle used reason, rather than faith, to reach his conclusions.

In the 1200s, an Italian Dominican friar named Thomas Aquinas (uh•KWY•nuhs) became scholasticism's greatest thinker. His **goal** was to find agreement between Aristotle's teachings and Christian teachings. Aquinas taught that truths arrived at through reason could not conflict with truths arrived at through faith. Reason, unaided by faith, could discover truths about the physical universe but not spiritual truths.

Aquinas's major work was *Summa Theologica*, or a summary of knowledge on theology. In this book, Aquinas followed a logical order of scholarly investigation. First, he asked a question such as, "Does God exist?" Next, he quoted sources that offered opposing opinions and presented ways of reconciling these views. Finally, he drew his own conclusions.

In his writings about government, Thomas Aquinas stressed the concept of natural law. According to this idea, some laws have authority from human nature. Such laws do not have to be made by governments. Aquinas taught that natural law gives people certain basic rights. These include the right to live, to learn, to worship, and to marry. The ideas of Aquinas continue to influence human societies to the present day.

Language and Literature

In medieval times, Latin was the language of educated people, both for speaking and writing. Latin was also the language of the Church and of university teachers and scholars.

Besides Latin, each region in Europe had its own local language. People used this language, called the **vernacular** (vuhr•NA•kyuh•luhr), in everyday life. Among the vernacular languages in Europe were early versions of English, Italian, Spanish, French, and German.

Starting in the 1100s, writers created much new literature in the vernacular. Educated people became interested in this literature. One popular type of vernacular literature was troubadour (TROO•buh•DAWR) poetry. Troubadour poets often sang love poems, especially about the love of a knight for a lady.

Reading **HELP**DESK

vernacular the everyday spoken language of a region

Academic Vocabulary
goal something that a person works to achieve; aim

A second important type of vernacular literature was the heroic epic. Epics often tell the story of bold knights fighting in the service of kings and lords. *The Song of Roland* is an epic that was written in France about 1100. In this tale, a brave knight named Roland fights in the service of Charlemagne against the Muslims.

At a moment of crisis in the battle, Roland sounds his horn for Charlemagne to help him. For many the battle was over:

> "Roland looks up on the mountains and slopes,
> sees the French dead, so many good men fallen,
> and weeps for them, as a great warrior weeps:
>
> Barons, my lords, may God give you his grace,
> may he grant Paradise [heaven] to all your souls,
> make them lie down among the holy flowers.
> I never saw better vassals than you.
> All the years you've served me, and all the times,
> the mighty lands you conquered for Charles our King!"
>
> —from *The Song of Roland*

In this illustration from *The Song of Roland*, Roland is sounding his horn for Charlemagne to help him.

PROGRESS CHECK
Explaining Why was it important that literature was written in everyday language?

2 Religion Affected Society

GUIDING QUESTION *How did the Catholic Church affect the lives of medieval Europeans?*

During the Middle Ages, the Catholic Church became rich and powerful. Beginning in the 1000s, many Western Europeans became worried about the direction in which the Church was headed. They set out to return the Church to Christian ideals. They built more monasteries and formed new religious orders, or groups of priests, monks, and nuns.

New Religious Orders

One of the most important new orders was the Cistercian (sihs•TUHR•shuhn) order. It was founded in 1098 by monks who were unhappy with wealthy monasteries and wanted a simpler, more spiritual way of life. Cistercian monks worshipped, prayed, and farmed the land. They developed new farming methods. Bernard of Clairvaux (klehr•VOH) was a famous Cistercian monk.

LESSON 4

ENGAGE

SLIDE SHOW **Displaying** Show students the images of medieval churches, universities, and castles from the medieval architecture slide show for Lesson 4. Invite students to share their impressions.

Ask:

What words describe the buildings? *(Answers may include* large, brick *or* stone, heavy, massive, rounded *or* sharp-edged.*)* Use the structures to illustrate the point that change and innovation occurred during the Middle Ages, though often slowly compared to today. ELL

Tell students that in this lesson, they will learn how European ideas about architecture and education changed. They will also learn about new institutions within the Catholic Church and how they affected Europeans.

TEACH & ASSESS

European Culture in the Middle Ages

GUIDING QUESTION ***What types of learning and art developed during the Middle Ages?***

GRAPHIC ORGANIZER **Making Generalizations** Have students work alone or in pairs to complete the interactive graphic organizer that appears on the first page of the lesson.

Focus on the first four items in the organizer—cathedrals, universities, theology, and literature. Challenge students to make a generalization about medieval European culture. You might want to have students write their responses in the interactive graphic organizer. BL

If students need help, **ask:**

- **How did cathedrals change?** *(They became taller and more ornate and beautiful.)*
- **How did universities change medieval society?** *(More people could now go to school and become educated. They could learn professions.)*
- **How did people think differently about theology?** *(They began to use reason to understand their faith.)*
- **How did literature change?** *(Educated people began to write in the vernacular, as well as in Latin.)* AL

Students should understand that more people were becoming educated and able to express themselves during the 1000s and 1100s. Religion was an important concern of Europe's educated groups.

2 Religion Affected Society

GUIDING QUESTION ***How did the Catholic Church affect the lives of medieval Europeans?***

Evaluating Students should understand that the Church was a powerful institution. Its goal was to unify Europe as a Christian civilization or have everyone accept the Catholic Church's teachings. The Church tried to control Europe's rulers and had daily influence on ordinary people.

Ask:

- **On a scale of 1 to 10 (10 being highest), how important was the Church to Europe's peasants?** *(10)*
- **How important was the Church to Europe's rulers?** *(10)*
- **If the Church was so important, why did some people want to change it?** *(Some believed the Church had gotten too worldly, and they wanted to make it more spiritual again.)*
- **How did some people change the Church?** *(They started new religious orders.)* AL

LECTURE SLIDE **Discussing** Show students the lecture slide with the definitions of *heresy, anti-Semitism*, and *inquisition,* and review their meanings. ELL

Point out that the Church, while trying to unify Europe under Christianity, saw heretics (former believers) and, to a lesser extent, nonbelievers (Jews and Muslims) as a threat.

Ask:

Why was heresy a problem for the Church? *(Church leaders feared that if people stopped believing in Church teachings and became heretics, it would weaken the Church and endanger people's chances of getting into heaven.)*

GRAPHIC ORGANIZER **Drawing Conclusions** Show students the interactive graphic organizer on Church responses to heresy.

Ask:

What steps did the Church take to deal with heretics? *(It sent friars to preach. It also set up a court called the Inquisition to try heretics, or people suspected of heresy. Heretics could be excommunicated, sent to prison, or executed.)* Have volunteers fill in the blanks on the interactive graphic organizer with their answers.

Explain that people brought before the Inquisition did not have the rights that the accused have today. Thousands faced secret trials and suffered torture and punishment.

Ask:

What effect did Church policies have on Europe's non-Christian population? *(Church leaders actively persecuted Jews, and Christian mobs often attacked and killed Jewish people.)*

Have students complete the Lesson 4 Review.

CLOSE & REFLECT

INTERACTIVE WORKSHEET **Analyzing** To help students understand how vernacular literature reflected the values of the times, have them complete the 21st Century Skills Activity worksheet for Lesson 4 for homework. Make sure they understand that vernacular literature was likely to reach a wider audience than works written in Latin.

Answers for pages 564–567

P. 564 Taking Notes Answers may include the following points: Cathedrals (Gothic architecture: flying buttresses, stained-glass windows); Universities (Paris and Bologna, Oxford and Cambridge; degrees); Theology (Scholasticism, St. Thomas Aquinas, and Aristotle); Literature (vernacular, songs of troubadours, heroic epics); Religious Orders (Cistercians, Franciscans, Dominicans)

P. 565 CRITICAL THINKING Answers will vary but may include a sense of grandeur or history, and note that the high ceilings and large windows make spaces feel big and airy.

P. 566 CRITICAL THINKING He is probably shown this way because he found a way to reconcile truths arrived at through faith (represented by the Church) and through reason (represented by the book).

P. 567 ☑ PROGRESS CHECK Literature written in the vernacular could reach more people.

Bernard supported the Second Crusade, advised the pope, and took the side of the poor against the rich.

Between A.D. 1000 and 1200, many women joined female religious orders. Most of these women, called nuns, came from wealthy noble families. One famous nun of this period was Hildegard of Bingen. She was the abbess, or leader, of a convent in Germany and wrote music for the church. Most composers of church music at that time were men.

Hildegard of Bingen composed music for the Catholic Church at a time when most church music was written by men.

▶ CRITICAL THINKING

Making Inferences What advantages would medieval nuns have had over other women that would have enabled them to create music, literature, or art?

The Mission of Friars

Until the 1200s, most people in religious orders spent their time inside their monasteries in prayer or at work. They lived a simple life separate from the world. In the 1200s, several new religious orders were created. The men in these religious orders were called friars.

Friars were different from other monks. They left their monasteries and took Christianity to people in the towns. Friars preached, served as missionaries, and aided the poor. Friars could not own property or keep any personal wealth.

Two well-known orders of friars were the Franciscans (fran•SIHS•kuhns) and the Dominicans (duh•MIH•nih•kuhns). The Franciscan order was founded in 1209 by Francis of Assisi (uh•SIH•see). Franciscans were known for their cheerfulness and deep love of nature.

A Spanish monk named Dominic de Guzmán (DAH•muh•NIHK deh gooz•MAHN) started the Dominican order in 1216. Like the Franciscans, the Dominicans lived a life of poverty. Their chief goal was to defend the teachings of the Church.

The Role of Religion in Everyday Life

In medieval times, the Catholic Church affected almost every part of people's lives. On Sundays and holy days, most medieval Europeans gathered to attend **mass**, the Catholic worship service.

Medieval Christians also took part in church rituals called sacraments. The most important sacrament was Holy Communion during mass. People received bread and wine to remind them of the death of Jesus. Only clergy could give people the sacraments.

Saints also played an important role in the lives of medieval Christians. People prayed to the saints to ask for God's favor. Mary, the mother of Jesus, was the most honored of all the saints.

Reading **HELP**DESK

mass religious worship service for Catholic Christians
heresy ideas that go against church teachings
anti-Semitism hostility toward or discrimination against Jews

The Challenge of Heresy

Despite its power, the Church had to deal with **heresy** (HEHR•uh•see), or ideas that conflicted with church teaching. In the Middle Ages, heresy was regarded as a serious crime against the Church. In 1233, the pope set up a Church court called the Inquisition (IHN•kwuh•ZIH•shuhn). The Inquisition's task was to question and deal with people accused of heresy.

People who were found guilty by the Inquisition were allowed to confess their heresy and ask for forgiveness. Those who refused were excommunicated and punished. Punishment could mean going to prison, losing property, or being executed.

Anti-Semitism in the Middle Ages

In medieval Europe, Jews became scapegoats, or people blamed for other people's problems. Jews were often accused in times of trouble, such as famine, plague, or economic decline. Hostility toward Jews is called **anti-Semitism** (AN • tee • SEH • muh • TIH • zuhm).

In troubled times during the Middle Ages, anti-Semitism flared up. In towns and villages, Christians often discriminated against and even killed Jews. As a minority, Jews were often forced to live in separate neighborhoods called ghettos. Often, Jews were forbidden to own land and to practice certain trades.

Beginning in the 1100s, rulers in England, France, and central Europe even drove out their Jewish subjects. Many of these Jews settled in Eastern Europe, especially Poland. Over the centuries, the Jews of Eastern Europe developed thriving communities.

☑ PROGRESS CHECK

Explaining Why did Church officials set up the Inquisition?

LESSON 4 REVIEW

Review Vocabulary

1. What is *heresy*?

Answer the Guiding Questions

2. ***Contrasting*** Contrast the chief characteristics of Romanesque and Gothic architecture.
3. ***Comparing and Contrasting*** How were monks and friars similar? How did they differ from each other?
4. ***Analyzing*** Why did the writings and ideas of Aristotle disturb some medieval Christians?
5. ***Identifying*** During the Middle Ages, what were two popular types of vernacular literature? Briefly describe each type.
6. **EXPOSITORY WRITING** Write a brief announcement to attract students to a medieval university. In your announcement, include the location of the university, the subjects that students may study, and the degrees they can earn.

networks
There's More Online!
☑ BIOGRAPHY Joan of Arc
☑ CHART/GRAPH The Black Death

Lesson 5

The Late Middle Ages

ESSENTIAL QUESTION *How do governments change?*

IT MATTERS BECAUSE

During the Late Middle Ages, Europe experienced serious economic, political, and religious conflicts.

1 Famine and Plague

GUIDING QUESTION ***How did the Black Death affect Europe during the Late Middle Ages?***

Medieval Europe enjoyed prosperity and growth during the 1200s. Then, early in the next century, disaster struck. Extremely cold winters and rainy summers created miserable conditions. Crops rotted in the fields, and herds of livestock died from diseases. Soon, there was not enough food for Europe's growing population. The result was a great famine in northern Europe that lasted from about 1315 to 1322. During this time, many people died from starvation and epidemics.

The Plague Comes to Europe

The great famine was only the beginning of troubles. During the 1300s, a **plague** (PLAYG) spread from Asia across Europe. A plague is a disease that spreads quickly and kills large numbers of people. The Black Death, as the disease was known, was probably bubonic plague. This illness is caused by a type of bacteria spread by fleas. Rats carry the fleas. The Black Death probably began in central Asia and spread to other places through trade. It first broke out in China in the 1330s. Between 40 and 60 million people eventually died, nearly half of the Chinese population.

Trade between China, India, the Middle East, and Europe was greatly encouraged by the Mongols. Merchants used the Silk Road and other trade routes. Expanded trade also made it possible for the Black Death to spread quickly. More and more traders used the Silk Road and other routes linking Asia and Europe. As a result, rat-infested caravans and ships carried the disease from region to region. The plague then traveled to India and spread to Muslim territories.

In 1346, the Black Death reached the trading city of Caffa on the Black Sea. Italian ships carried the plague to the island of Sicily. From there, it spread to the Italian mainland and onto the continent of Europe. By the end of the 1340s, it had surfaced in France, Germany, and England. By 1351, the plague had reached Scandinavia, Eastern Europe, and Russia. Estimates of the dead in Europe between 1347 and 1351 range from 19 to 38 million people—nearly one out of every two Europeans.

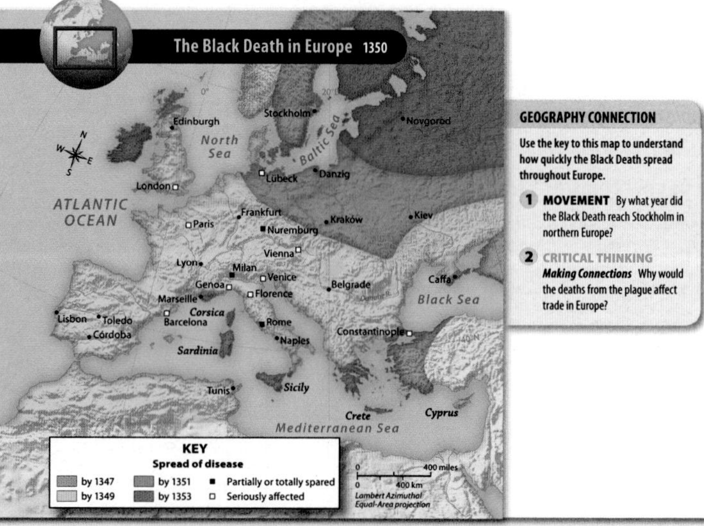

GEOGRAPHY CONNECTION

Use the key to this map to understand how quickly the Black Death spread throughout Europe.

1. **MOVEMENT** By what year did the Black Death reach Stockholm in northern Europe?
2. CRITICAL THINKING ***Making Connections*** Why would the deaths from the plague affect trade in Europe?

Reading **HELP**DESK

Taking Notes: *Summarizing*
Use a pie chart like the one shown to summarize the effects of the Black Death in Europe in the mid-1300s.

Content Vocabulary
• **plague** • **Reconquista**

plague a disease that spreads quickly and kills many people

LESSON 4 (cont.)

BACKGROUND KNOWLEDGE

Chartres Cathedral

One of the finest Gothic cathedrals is found in the French town of Chartres, southwest of Paris. Chartres Cathedral is recognized for the harmoniousness and quality of its architecture, stained glass, and sculpture.

One reason for the cathedral's cohesiveness is that much of the structure was completed in a span of 26 years, a remarkably short time for the construction of a cathedral.

Work on the present cathedral began in 1194, after the cathedral standing at the site burned down. The new cathedral used the façade and one of the towers from the burned church. This resulted in Chartres Cathedral's mismatched towers. The new tower is taller and much more ornate than the old one.

Answers for pages 568–569

P. 568 CRITICAL THINKING Nuns had more education than other women. They also came from wealthy families, who had greater access to luxuries like music and art.

P. 569 ☑ PROGRESS CHECK They set up the Inquisition to end heresy.

LESSON 4 REVIEW

1. Heresy is the belief in ideas that conflict with Church teaching.
2. Romanesque features were found on Roman and Byzantine buildings. Romanesque buildings were rectangular and had barrel-vault ceilings, heavy walls, thick pillars, and small windows. Gothic architecture featured flying buttresses, thinner walls, tall and slender pillars, pointed arches, and large windows of stained glass.
3. Both monks and friars helped the poor. Monks, however, lived in monasteries while friars took Christianity to people in the towns.
4. Aristotle's writings were disturbing because the ancient Greek philosopher seemed to rely on reason, rather than faith, to reach his conclusions.
5. Two popular types of vernacular literature were the songs of troubadours and heroic epics. Troubadour songs often centered on the love of a knight for a lady, while heroic epics told the story of brave knights fighting in the service of their king or lord.
6. Announcements should identify the university's location (for example, Paris, Bologna, or Oxford). Announcements may mention the following subjects: grammar, public speaking, logic, arithmetic, geometry, music, and astronomy. Degrees include a bachelor of arts, a master of arts, and a doctorate.

LESSON 5

ENGAGE

MAP **Making Generalizations** Display the interactive map of Asia that shows the spread of the Black Death.

Ask:

What generalization can you make about the spread of the Black Death? *(It was widespread. It affected much of Asia.)*

Discuss how the plague spread from place to place. Then tell students that the Black Death traveled from Asia to Europe, with devastating consequences.

Explain that in this lesson, they will learn about several catastrophes that medieval Europeans faced in the Late Middle Ages, including famine, plague, war, and conflicts within the Catholic Church.

TEACH & ASSESS

1 Famine and Plague

GUIDING QUESTION *How did the Black Death affect Europe during the Late Middle Ages?*

GRAPHIC ORGANIZER **Determining Cause and Effect** Have students work alone or in pairs to complete the interactive graphic organizer that appears on the first page of the lesson. Ask volunteers to list the effects of the plague that they identified.

LECTURE SLIDE Remind students that before the plague, much of Europe was affected by a severe famine. Show students the lecture slide defining *famine* and describing its causes. ELL

Ask:

What were the effects of the famine? *(People died of starvation and other diseases because they were weakened.)*

MAP **Identifying Cause and Effect** Show students the interactive map of the Black Death in Europe. As a class, identify all the countries that the plague affected. *(Ireland, England, Sweden, Russia, France, Spain, Germany, Italy, Eastern Europe, Turkey, northern Africa)* AL

Ask:

What happened to Europe's population as a result of the Black Death? *(Overall, the population of Europe was cut in half, with even greater percentages of people dying in some hard-hit areas and fewer in other places.)*

Answers for pages 570–571

P. 570 Taking Notes Answers may include the following: People did not know the causes of the plague, and many thought it was a punishment from God or the fault of the Jews; the economy was devastated and trade decreased; food prices fell sharply; the plague helped weaken the feudal system.

P. 571 GEOGRAPHY CONNECTION

1. It reached Stockholm by 1351.
2. CRITICAL THINKING So many people died during the plague that few people were left to buy or sell goods.

The Black Death inspired art and literature. This painting shows carts picking up those who had died to bury them quickly in mass graves.

▶ CRITICAL THINKING
Analyzing Visuals Why do you think the artist portrayed skeletons collecting the bodies of the dead?

Museo del Prado, Madrid, Spain/Giraudon, Paris/SuperStock

The Effects of the Plague

People at the time did not know why the plague had happened. Some people thought God was punishing them for their sins. Others blamed the Jews. For this reason, the Germans expelled many Jews from some of their cities.

The plague had an enormous effect on the **economy** of Europe. With so many deaths, trade declined. Wages rose steeply because of a high demand for workers. Fewer people, though, meant less demand for food, so food prices fell sharply.

Landlords now had to pay scarce workers more. Some peasants began to pay rent instead of providing services. Serfs gained more rights. Like the Crusades, the Black Death weakened feudalism.

✔ PROGRESS CHECK

Explaining How did the Black Death spread?

Reading **HELP**DESK

Academic Vocabulary

economy a country's system for the making, selling, and buying of goods and services

authority the power to influence or command thought, opinion, or behavior

2 Divisions in Religion and Politics

GUIDING QUESTION *How did disputes and wars change societies in Europe during the Late Middle Ages?*

In addition to the bubonic plague, conflict swept through Europe during the Late Middle Ages. Disputes in the Church reduced its **authority**. English and French kings battled over territory in the Hundred Years' War. Christians in the Iberian Peninsula fought to drive out the Muslims who had conquered land there.

Conflict in the Church

From 1378 to 1417, a dispute called the Great Schism (SIH • zuhm) deeply divided the Church. During this time, two and even three church leaders claimed to be the rightful pope. This caused great confusion and doubt throughout Western Europe. In 1417, a council of bishops met at the German city of Constance. It finally ended the Great Schism with the election of a pope that all church members could accept.

The Great Schism was only one challenge the Church faced during the Late Middle Ages. Powerful European kings questioned the authority of popes. The kings of England and France would soon go to war. Many people criticized the growing wealth and corruption of the clergy. Reform leaders emerged who called on church leaders to return to a more spiritual form of Christianity. These reformers included John Wycliffe in England and Jan Hus in the Holy Roman Empire.

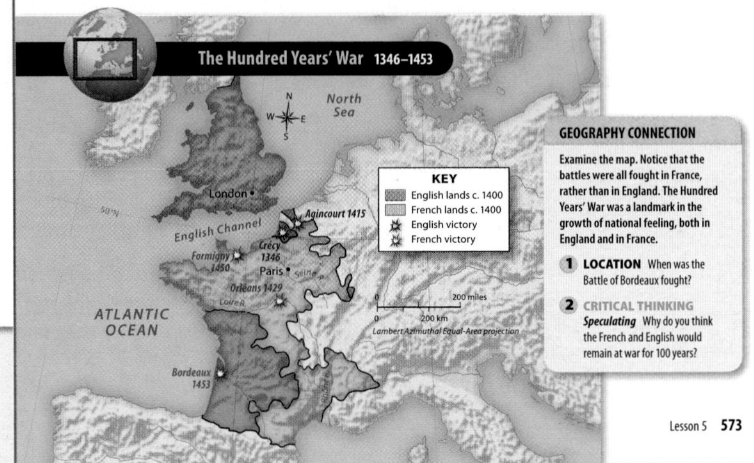

GEOGRAPHY CONNECTION

Examine the map. Notice that the battles were all fought in France, rather than in England. The Hundred Years' War was a landmark in the growth of national feeling, both in England and in France.

1 **LOCATION** When was the Battle of Bordeaux fought?

2 CRITICAL THINKING
Speculating Why do you think the French and English would remain at war for 100 years?

BIOGRAPHY

Joan of Arc (1412–1431)

Joan of Arc was born in the village of Domrémy in eastern France. She was the daughter of a tenant farmer. In her teens, Joan felt herself guided by the voices of three saints. Joan traveled from her native village in France to ask to fight for Charles, the crown prince. She faced examination by church authorities about her faith and the voices she heard. Convinced, they allowed Joan to take part in a battle against the English at the town of Orléans. The French victory there unified France and led to the coronation of Charles as king. However, Joan was captured later by the English, tried for heresy, and executed.

CRITICAL THINKING
Speculating Why do you think a teenage girl like Joan of Arc was able to inspire the French troops and lead them into battle?

The Hundred Years' War

Western Europe at this time was torn apart by political as well as religious disputes. For centuries, England's monarchs had ruled areas of France. France's kings, however, wanted to unite these lands with their kingdom. Then King Edward III of England declared himself king of France and invaded that country. The conflict that followed lasted over 100 years.

At first, the English were victorious—at Crécy (kray • SEE) in 1346 and Agincourt in 1415. The English had superior weapons: a longbow and an early form of the cannon. The longbow shot arrows that were able to pierce heavy armor at 300 yards (274 km). A French medieval writer described the effects of the longbow at Crécy:

PRIMARY SOURCE

> "Then the English archers stept forth one pace and let fly their arrows so wholly [together] and so thick, that it seemed snow. When the [French soldiers] felt the arrows piercing through heads, arms, and breasts, many of them cast down their cross-bows and did cut their strings and [retreated]."
>
> —from *The Chronicles of Froissart*, by Jean Froissart

Joan of Arc Aids the French

The French prince Charles wanted to take back French lands held by the English. In 1429, a 17-year-old French peasant girl named Joan came to his palace. Joan persuaded Charles to let her go with a French army to the city of Orléans. Joan's faith stirred the French soldiers. They defeated the English and freed the city.

Shortly after, with Joan at his side, Charles was crowned king. A few months later, however, the English army captured Joan. The English accused her of being a witch. Joan was burned at the stake for heresy. Later known as Joan of Arc, she became a French national hero and Catholic saint.

Joan's courage led the French to rally around their king. By 1453, French armies had driven the English out of most of France. Victory gave the French a new sense of loyalty to their country. French kings used that loyalty to strengthen their power.

The Hundred Years' War also affected the English. England's nobles were bitter about the loss of French lands. For the rest of the 1400s, they fought over who should be king in a civil war known as the Wars of Roses. The winner, Henry Tudor, became King Henry VII of England.

Stapleton Collection/Corbis

Reading **HELP**DESK

Reconquista the Christian "reconquest" of the Iberian Peninsula

Jews and Muslims in Spain

During the Middle Ages, Muslims ruled much of the Iberian Peninsula. Today, the Iberian Peninsula is made up of Spain and Portugal. Medieval Muslims in this area developed a rich culture. They set up schools and built beautiful mosques and palaces, such as the Alhambra in Granada.

The Christians drove out the Muslims in a struggle called the **Reconquista** (ray • kohn • KEES • tuh), or "reconquest." By 1250, there were three Christian kingdoms: Portugal, Castile, and Aragon. The only remaining Muslim kingdom was Granada. In 1469, Prince Ferdinand of Aragon married Princess Isabella of Castile. They united their kingdoms into one Catholic country called Spain.

Under Muslim rule, Iberian Jews had lived freely for the most part. As Christians gained control, they sometimes mistreated the Jews. In order to avoid persecution by Christians, many Jews became Christian. Ferdinand and Isabella, however, believed that some of the Jews secretly practiced Judaism. To force obedience to the Catholic Church, the rulers put the Spanish Inquisition into place.

The Spanish Inquisition tried and tortured thousands of people who were accused of being disloyal to the Catholic Church in Spain. In 1492, Ferdinand and Isabella ordered Jews to convert or leave Spain. Most Jews left to avoid the charge of heresy. After Spain conquered Granada in 1492, Muslims were given the same choice. Rather than convert to Catholicism, most Muslims left for North Africa.

✔ PROGRESS CHECK

Determining Cause and Effect How did Ferdinand and Isabella treat those of Muslim and Jewish faiths?

LESSON 5 REVIEW

Review Vocabulary

1. What is a *plague*?

Answer the Guiding Questions

2. ***Identifying*** After the Battle of Orléans, what happened to Joan of Arc?
3. ***Explaining*** How did the Black Death spread around the world?
4. ***Analyzing*** What was the major cause of the Hundred Years' War?
5. ***Explaining*** In what ways did the Muslims develop a rich culture in Spain and Portugal before they were forced out of those lands?
6. **PERSONAL WRITING** You are King Charles of France. A young girl, Joan of Arc, has told you she believes the saints want her to help save France. Write three questions that you might ask Joan of Arc to determine if she is fit for battle.

LESSON 5 (cont.)

LECTURE SLIDE **Making Connections** Show students the lecture slide displaying the population of the United States and of individual states. Have students consider the numbers of Europeans killed by the plague by **asking: Which states would have zero population if 19 to 38 million people died of the plague?** *(Student answers will vary depending upon the figures they are given.)*

INTERACTIVE WORKSHEET **Analyzing** Help reinforce students' understanding of the effects of the Black Death on Europe's economy by having them complete the Economics of History Activity for Lesson 5.

Divisions in Religion and Politics

GUIDING QUESTION ***How did disputes and wars change societies in Europe during the Late Middle Ages?***

Summarizing Have students work in pairs or small groups to devise a graphic organizer that best outlines three religious and political conflicts described in the lesson. Suggest that students create a three-column chart with the headings "Great Schism," "Hundred Years' War," and "Reconquista." Have students complete the graphic organizer by doing the following:

- **Briefly describe each conflict.** *(The Great Schism was an internal conflict of the Catholic Church. The Hundred Years' War was fought between England and France. The Reconquista was Spain's effort to drive out all Muslims.)* AL
- **Tell how each conflict was resolved.** *(A council of bishops ended the Great Schism by electing a single pope. The French eventually defeated the English and took over the lands whose ownership was disputed during the Hundred Years' War. By 1250, most Muslims had been driven out of Spain.)*
- **Identify one effect of each conflict.** *(The Great Schism hurt the authority of the Catholic Church. The Hundred Years' War strengthened the French monarchy by increasing patriotism. Spain became a predominantly Christian country.)* BL

Ask volunteers to share their answers with the class. Evaluate the answers as a class. Create a master graphic organizer on the board and write students' answers in it.

INTERACTIVE WHITEBOARD ACTIVITY Have students use what they have learned to complete the Interactive Whiteboard Activity for Lesson 5. Students should place events in the order in which they occurred. Then have students complete the Lesson 5 Review.

CLOSE & REFLECT

Discussing Have each student write a paragraph in which he or she states an opinion about the most important problem medieval Europeans faced during the Late Middle Ages. Students should include at least two reasons to support their answers. Ask volunteers to share their ideas with the class.

BACKGROUND KNOWLEDGE

The Black Death and a Nursery Rhyme

Many folklorists believe the popular nursery rhyme "Ring Around the Rosie" is about the plague. The first line refers to the round pink rash that is an early sign of the disease. Posies, or bouquets of flowers, were worn to disguise the terrible smell of the infection. The third line refers to the burning of infected corpses. Finally, almost everyone infected with the plague eventually died, or fell down.

IF YOU HAVE MORE TIME . . .

Speculate How New Weapons Affect War

Analyzing Information The English longbow had a crucial impact in the Hundred Years' War, allowing English archers to defeat a French feudal army with many mounted knights.

Ask students to think of new weapon developments that played an equally decisive role in other wars. *(Possible answers: the long spear of Alexander's Macedonians; tanks, submarines, or machine guns in World War I; the atomic bomb in World War II; the jet fighter in the Korean War; "smart" bombs in the Gulf War; drones in the Iraq War)*

Then have them speculate on what kinds of new weapons might have a similar impact in the future. BL

Answers for pages 572–575

P. 572 CRITICAL THINKING because so many people were dying of the plague that no one was left once it passed through a town

P. 572 ☑ PROGRESS CHECK Rats carrying fleas spread the plague. The fleas, in turn, carried a type of bacteria.

P. 573 GEOGRAPHY CONNECTION

1. 1453
2. CRITICAL THINKING Answers will vary but should include something about how neither France nor England wanted to give up their land claims.

P. 574 CRITICAL THINKING She had great faith, courage, and confidence.

P. 575 ☑ PROGRESS CHECK They pressured Muslims and Jews to convert to Christianity. Most refused and left Spain.

LESSON 5 REVIEW

1. A plague is a disease that spreads quickly and kills many people.
2. The English captured her, accused her of heresy, and then executed her. A subsequent investigation found her innocent of all the charges. Much later, she was declared a Catholic saint.
3. It originated in Asia and spread by rats along trade routes to Europe.
4. The war was caused by a dispute between England and France. The king of England laid claim to large areas of France, but the French wanted the English to leave France.
5. The Muslims built beautiful palaces and mosques, and they established schools.
6. Answers will vary but should reflect students' understanding of the Hundred Years' War and Joan of Arc's role in the conflict.

CHAPTER 19 Activities

Write your answers on a separate piece of paper.

1. **Exploring the Essential Question**
   EXPOSITORY WRITING How would you describe the influence of religion on life in medieval Europe? In a summary essay, identify and evaluate the relationships between the Church and the government, as well as the ways in which religion influenced everyday life.

2. **21st Century Skills**
   EVALUATING Consider the medieval order of feudalism. What strengths and weaknesses can you identify in feudalism? Do you think feudalism would work in modern society? Write your answer in a paragraph or two.

3. **Thinking Like a Historian**
   COMPARING Describe the equipment that students in present-day universities might use and compare it to the equipment available to students in medieval universities. In particular, compare the role books in university education then and now.

4. **GEOGRAPHY ACTIVITY**

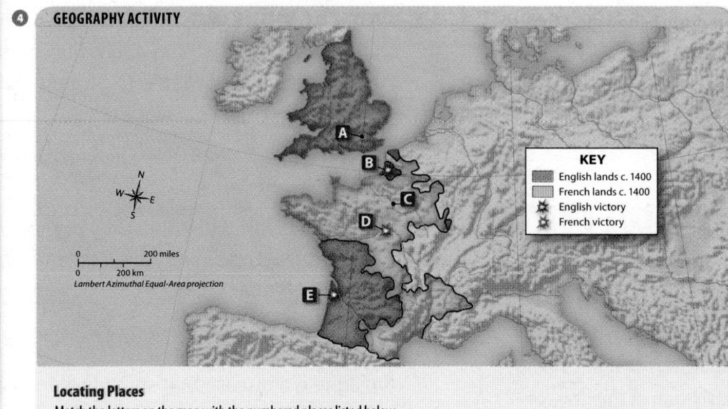

Locating Places

Match the letters on the map with the numbered places listed below.

1. Paris
2. Bordeaux
3. Orléans
4. London
5. Crécy

CHAPTER 19 Assessment

REVIEW THE GUIDING QUESTIONS

Directions: Choose the best answer for each question.

1. The Danube and the Po in Europe are which of the following?
   A. peninsulas
   B. mountain ranges
   C. rivers
   D. islands

2. In what way does the code of chivalry still affect people?
   F. It provided a model for starting a business.
   G. It formed the bases for our educational system.
   H. Many of our ideas about social manners are based on it.
   I. The code of chivalry did not have a lasting effect.

3. King Henry II of England used which of the following to increase his power?
   A. his serfs
   B. the pope
   C. courts of law
   D. the Magna Carta

4. "Flying buttresses" are related to which of the following?
   F. scholasticism
   G. vernacular language
   H. Romanesque architecture
   I. Gothic architecture

5. Why did Pope Urban II call for the First Crusade?
   A. He hoped to reunite the Church.
   B. He wanted to take over the Byzantine empire.
   C. He wanted to convert the Turks to Christianity.
   D. He was getting back at the Turks for an attack on Rome.

6. From which of these European countries were Jews expelled in 1492?
   F. Spain
   G. Italy
   H. England
   I. France

CHAPTER 19 Assessment *(continued)*

DBQ DOCUMENT-BASED QUESTIONS

Summarizing King Louis IX asked the following of his vassals:

> *"All vassals of the king are bound to appear before him when he shall summon [call] them, and to serve him at their own expense for forty days and forty nights, with as many knights as each one owes."*
>
> —King Louis IX, "Legal Rules for Military Service"

7. Which of the following best describes the obligations of the king's vassals?
   A. manorial system
   B. scholasticism
   C. feudalism
   D. guild system

8. **Making Inferences** Based on what you have learned about medieval Europe, which of the following best describes what would happen if the king needed vassals and knights for more than 40 days and nights?
   F. The vassals and knights would overthrow the king.
   G. The knights would rebel against the vassals.
   H. The vassals and knights would continue serving at the king's expense.
   I. The vassals and knights would withdraw to the manor.

SHORT RESPONSE

> *"A more lasting and serious consequence [of the plague] was the drastic reduction of the amount of land under cultivation [able to be farmed] due to the deaths of so many labourers. . . . The psychological effects of the Black Death were reflected . . . . by a preoccupation with death and the afterlife evinced [displayed] in poetry, sculpture, and painting."*
>
> —"Black Death," Encyclopaedia Britannica

9. According to the passage, what was one effect of the plague?

10. Why did the lack of labor have a negative effect on Europe?

EXTENDED RESPONSE

11. **Outlining a Reference Article** You have been asked to contribute to a reference article about the Middle Ages. You are responsible for these areas of medieval culture: architecture, literature, and education. Write an outline showing the specific facts and details you plan to cover in your article.

Need Extra Help?

If You've Missed Question	1	2	3	4	5	6	7	8	9	10	11
Review Lesson	1	2	3	4	3	5	2	2	3	5	5

NOTES

REFLECT, REVIEW, & REMEDIATE

INTERACTIVE WORKSHEET

Chapter Summary

Provide students with the Chapter Summary worksheet to help review the chapter and prepare for assessment.

Reviewing the Enduring Understandings

Review this chapter's Enduring Understandings with students:
- Religion can influence a society's beliefs and values.
- Cultures are held together by shared beliefs and common practices and values.
- Conflict can lead to change.

INTERACTIVE WHITEBOARD ACTIVITY On the interactive whiteboard, have a student volunteer create a two-column chart and write "The Church" in one column and "Feudalism" in the other. Then lead a discussion in which students explain how the Church and feudalism affected daily life, the economy, and key political events in Europe during the Middle Ages. The student volunteer should record answers in the chart.

	The Church	Feudalism
Daily Life		
Economy		
Political Events		

ACTIVITIES ANSWERS

Exploring the Essential Question

1. Essays should stress that religion had a major influence on almost everyone in medieval Europe, from kings to peasants. Kings and popes argued about who could appoint bishops; cities and towns built great churches and cathedrals; the clergy administered the sacraments; and religion was one of the main motivators of the Crusades.

21st Century Skills

2. Evaluations will vary. Students may mention that feudalism's strength was that the system valued virtues such as trust, loyalty, and bravery. It also involved a clear social hierarchy in which the nobles took care of the peasants in return for their service. Students might identify the following weaknesses: The nobles had all the power and wealth; the serfs were bound to the land; people in lower classes could not easily rise in society. Students might make a connection between how the medieval nobles took care of the peasants with the way modern governments provide social services for the poor or with how modern parents care for their children.

Thinking Like a Historian

3. Answers will vary, but students might mention that today's students have the use of computers and textbooks, but medieval students had only small, portable chalkboards. Without books, students had to rely on note taking and memorization far more than students do today.

Locating Places

4. **1.** C, **2.** E, **3.** D, **4.** A, **5.** B

ASSESSMENT ANSWERS

Review the Guiding Questions

1. **C** The Danube and the Po are rivers, not mountain ranges, peninsulas, or islands. Mountain ranges include the Pyrenees, the Alps, and the Carpathians; peninsulas include Spain and Italy; islands include England and Ireland.

2. **H** Chivalry is the knightly code of conduct. It had a lasting effect on most Western cultures and their belief systems today. It did not have an effect on business or education.

3. **C** Henry II increased his power using courts of law. Although Henry II had serfs, his peasant workers were not a source of increased power. Likewise, he did not rely on the pope, who was the head of the Catholic Church, or the Magna Carta, a document that limited the powers of the English king, to become more powerful.

4. **I** The flying buttress was a feature of Gothic architecture. Scholasticism was a philosophical worldview; the vernacular is everyday language; Romanesque architecture combined the features of Roman and Byzantine buildings.

5. **A** Urban II wanted to reunite the two Christian Churches. He did not want to take over the Byzantine Empire, convert the Turks to Christianity, or retaliate against the Turks.

6. **F** Jews were expelled in large numbers from Spain after Ferdinand and Isabella decided to make Roman Catholicism Spain's one religion. Jews were not expelled in large numbers from Italy, England, or France.

Document-Based Questions

7. **C** The relationship between king and vassal is part of the feudal system. The manorial system refers to the ways in which medieval communities grew crops and maintained a lifestyle centered on the manor. Scholasticism refers to a philosophical worldview. The guild system refers to organizations of craftspeople and artisans who controlled trade in medieval towns and cities.

8. **H** The fact that the king wrote down the rules for military service suggests that he intended to treat his vassals fairly by rewarding them for their service. It is unlikely that the vassals and knights would dare to rebel openly or overthrow the king or that the vassals and knights would become divided.

Short Response

9. The amount of farmland that could be cultivated was reduced substantially.

10. Without workers to work in the fields, the economy of Europe was greatly hurt.

Extended Response

11. Outlines will vary but may include the following: Architecture: construction of cathedrals and major features of the Romanesque and Gothic styles; Literature: use of the vernacular and major features of troubadour songs and heroic epics; Education: development of universities in cities such as Paris and Bologna, subjects and methods of study, examinations, and degrees.

ONLINE RESOURCES

networks

There's More Online!

- ☑ INTERACTIVE WORKSHEETS
- ☑ BIOGRAPHIES
- ☑ CHARTS/GRAPHS
- ☑ GAMES
- ☑ GRAPHIC ORGANIZERS
- ☑ IMAGES
- ☑ MAPS
- ☑ PRIMARY SOURCES
- ☑ SLIDE SHOWS
- ☑ TIME LINE
- ☑ LECTURE SLIDES
- ☑ INTERACTIVE WHITEBOARD ACTIVITIES
- ☑ ASSESSMENTS
- ☑ VIDEOS

Leonardo da Vinci

Henry V

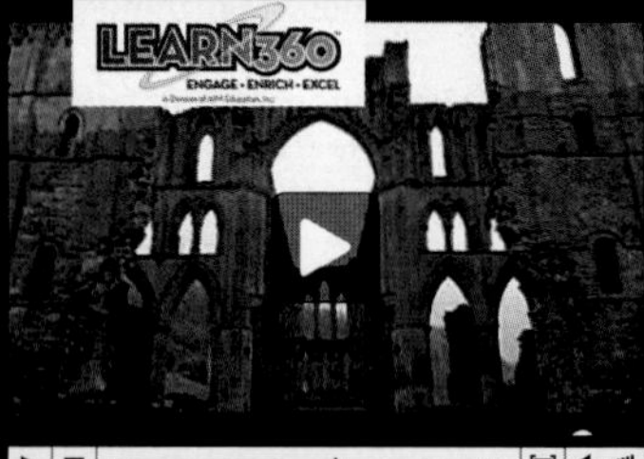

Britain Arises: England Defeats the Spanish Armada

Chapter **20**

Renaissance and Reformation

Dear World History Teacher,

Between 1350 and 1550, Italian intellectuals believed they were living in a new age based on a rebirth of the culture of the Greeks and Romans. The Renaissance, which began in Italy, was a period of transition. Some of the economic, political, and social trends that began in the High Middle Ages continued, but the new age ushered in changes as well. Intellectuals and artists proclaimed a new vision of humankind and raised fundamental questions about the value of the individual. Of course, the brilliant intellectual, cultural, and artistic accomplishments of the Renaissance were really products of and for the elite. The ideas of the Renaissance did not have a broad base among the masses of the people.

However, the Renaissance raised new questions about medieval traditions. In criticizing current religious practices, the humanists aroused fundamental issues about the Catholic Church. The intellectual revolution of the 1400s gave way to a religious reformation in the 1500s that touched the lives of all people in new and profound ways.

By challenging the Catholic Church's sale of indulgences, Martin Luther created a movement that quickly spread across Europe. Within a short time, new Protestant churches were attracting supporters all over Europe. Although seemingly helpless to stop the new churches, the Catholic Church also underwent a religious rebirth. By the mid-1500s, this religious division had produced two strong faiths—Calvinism and Catholicism—both prepared to fight for their beliefs. An age of religious passion would soon be followed by an age of religious warfare.

Jackson J. Spielvogel

More Media Resources

Current Events Online

Visit McGraw-Hill's current events Web site for high-interest news stories and activities for your students. Access the site through the Student or Teacher Center in **networks.**

Reading List

Grade 6 reading level:
Leonardo: Beautiful Dreamer, by Robert Byrd

Grade 7 reading level:
Elizabeth I, The Outcast Who Became England's Queen, by Simon Adams

Grade 8 reading level:
Around the World in 1500, by Virginia Schomp

CHAPTER 20 Planner

UNDERSTANDING BY DESIGN®

Enduring Understandings

- *The movement of people, goods, and ideas causes societies to change over time.*
- *People, places, and ideas change over time.* • *Religion can influence a society's beliefs and values.* • *Countries have relationships with each other.*

Essential Questions

- *How do people make economic choices?* • *How do new ideas change the way people live?*
- *How do religions develop?* • *How does conflict develop?*

Students will know:

- *why the city-states of Italy became centers of culture during the Renaissance*
- *how the city-states of Italy gained their power*
- *how Renaissance writers developed new ideas*
- *what methods Renaissance artists used to make their work natural and real*
- *how the Renaissance changed as it moved from Italy into northern Europe*
- *how the teachings of Protestant reformers shaped the western world*
- *how the Reformation influenced England and its American colonies*
- *how the Catholic Church responded to the spread of Protestantism*
- *how wars of religion affected Europe*

Students will be able to:

- **discuss** who ruled the city-states of Italy and how they achieved that power
- **analyze and identify** differences between a Middle Ages-style painting and a Renaissance-style painting
- **describe** humanism
- **analyze** a scene from a Shakespeare play
- **describe** who Shakespeare was and his influence on literature
- **explain** why the Church was pressured to reform
- **identify** the three main differences between Lutheranism and the Catholic Church
- **locate** European countries that were significant to the Reformation and explain why
- **describe** how the Reformation shaped England and its American colonies
- **analyze** which response by the Catholic Church was most effective
- **make connections** to present-day religious wars

Predictable Misunderstandings

Students may think:

- The Renaissance was only a period of time and not a way of thinking.
- Only painters, sculptors, and artists were a part of the Renaissance.
- There was only one Reformation.

Assessment Evidence

Performance Task

- Hands-On Chapter Project

Other Evidence

- Class discussion answers
- Class simulation participation
- Interactive Whiteboard Activity responses
- Brainstorming activity
- Geography and History Activity
- Economics of History Activities
- 21st Century Skills Activities
- Lesson Reviews
- Evaluation of class simulation
- Writing activities

Pacing Guide

Introducing the Chapter		1 day
Lesson 1	The Renaissance Begins	1 day
Lesson 2	New Ideas and Art	2 days
	The World's Literature	1 day
Lesson 3	The Reformation Begins	2 days
Lesson 4	Catholics and Protestants	2 days
Chapter Activities and Assessment		1 day
TOTAL TIME		**10 Days**

Differentiated Instruction

These lesson plans are written to address the needs of your On Level students. Discussion and activities that are well-suited to your Approaching Grade Level learners, Beyond Grade Level learners, as well as your English Language Learners are coded as follows:

 **Approaching Grade Level**

 **Beyond Grade Level**

 **English Language Learner**

NCSS Standards covered in "Renaissance and Reformation"

Learners will understand:

2 TIME, CONTINUITY, AND CHANGE

5. Key historical periods and patterns of change within and across cultures (e.g., the rise and fall of ancient civilizations, the development of technology, the rise of modern nation-states, and the establishment and breakdown of colonial systems)

7. The contributions of key persons, groups, and events from the past and their influence on the present

3 PEOPLE, PLACES, AND ENVIRONMENTS

4. The roles of different kinds of population centers in a region or nation

6. Patterns of demographic and political change, and cultural diffusion in the past and present (e.g., changing national boundaries, migration, and settlement, and the diffusion of and changes in customs and ideas)

8. Factors that contribute to cooperation and conflict among peoples of the nation and world, including language, religion, and political beliefs

5 INDIVIDUALS, GROUPS, AND INSTITUTIONS

5. That groups and institutions change over time

6. That cultural diffusion occurs when groups migrate

8. That when two or more groups with differing norms and beliefs interact, accommodation or conflict may result

7 PRODUCTION, DISTRIBUTION, AND CONSUMPTION

4. Economic incentives affect people's behavior and may be regulated by rules or laws

7. How markets bring buyers and sellers together to exchange goods and services

8 SCIENCE, TECHNOLOGY, AND SOCIETY

2. Society often turns to science and technology to solve problems

5. Science and technology have changed peoples' perceptions of the social and natural world, as well as their relationship to the land, economy and trade, their concept of security, and their major daily activities

6. Values, beliefs, and attitudes that have been influenced by new scientific and technological knowledge (e.g., invention of the printing press, conceptions of the universe, applications of atomic energy, and genetic discoveries)

CHAPTER 20

Introducing the Chapter

(Student Edition p. 579)

The Story Matters . . .

Read "The Story Matters . . ." aloud in class. Then discuss what it might have been like to live in Florence in the presence of so many famous artists and writers.

Ask: **What is a famous work of art that you have seen in pictures or in person?** Have a few students give examples.

Then ask: **What would it be like to live at the time artists were creating these works? What would it be like to see these works when they were new instead of hanging in museums?**

Tell the class that the citizens of Florence were surrounded by important art and artists because wealthy citizens paid for these works.

Ask: **What stadiums, museums, or parks in America are named for well-known people?** Have students give examples of buildings that are named for well-known people. *(Possible answers include the Getty Museum, Wrigley Field, Kennedy Space Center, and so on.)* Explain that these buildings are named for people who supported sports or the arts. These individuals are honored for their contributions by naming buildings after them. Tell students that modern examples of these contributors are like the Medicis of Florence during the Renaissance. The Medicis supported art and artists of their time. Similarly, people today support sports and a variety of art forms, such as music.

Renaissance and Reformation

1350 to 1650

ESSENTIAL QUESTIONS • *Why do people make economic choices?* • *How do new ideas change the way people live?* • *Why does conflict develop?*

networks *There's More Online* about life during the Renaissance and Reformation.

CHAPTER 20

Lesson 1 *The Renaissance Begins*

Lesson 2 *New Ideas and Art*

Lesson 3 *The Reformation Begins*

Lesson 4 *Catholics and Protestants*

The Story Matters . . .

The Renaissance was a brilliant flowering of European culture from the 1300s to 1600s. During this time, the city-state of Florence in Italy became the center of business, art, and learning. It attracted many artists who are still famous today, including Michelangelo and Leonardo da Vinci.

This image is from a Renaissance painting of the three wise men traveling to see the baby Jesus. The painting was made to decorate the palace of the powerful Medici family. The Medicis ruled Florence during the Renaissance. Lorenzo de' Medici was the model for the wise man shown here.

◄ *Benozzo Gozzoli painted "The Procession of the Magi" (1459) for the Medici family.*

Erich Lessing/Art Resource, NY

579

Introducing Place and Time

(Student Edition pp. 580–581)

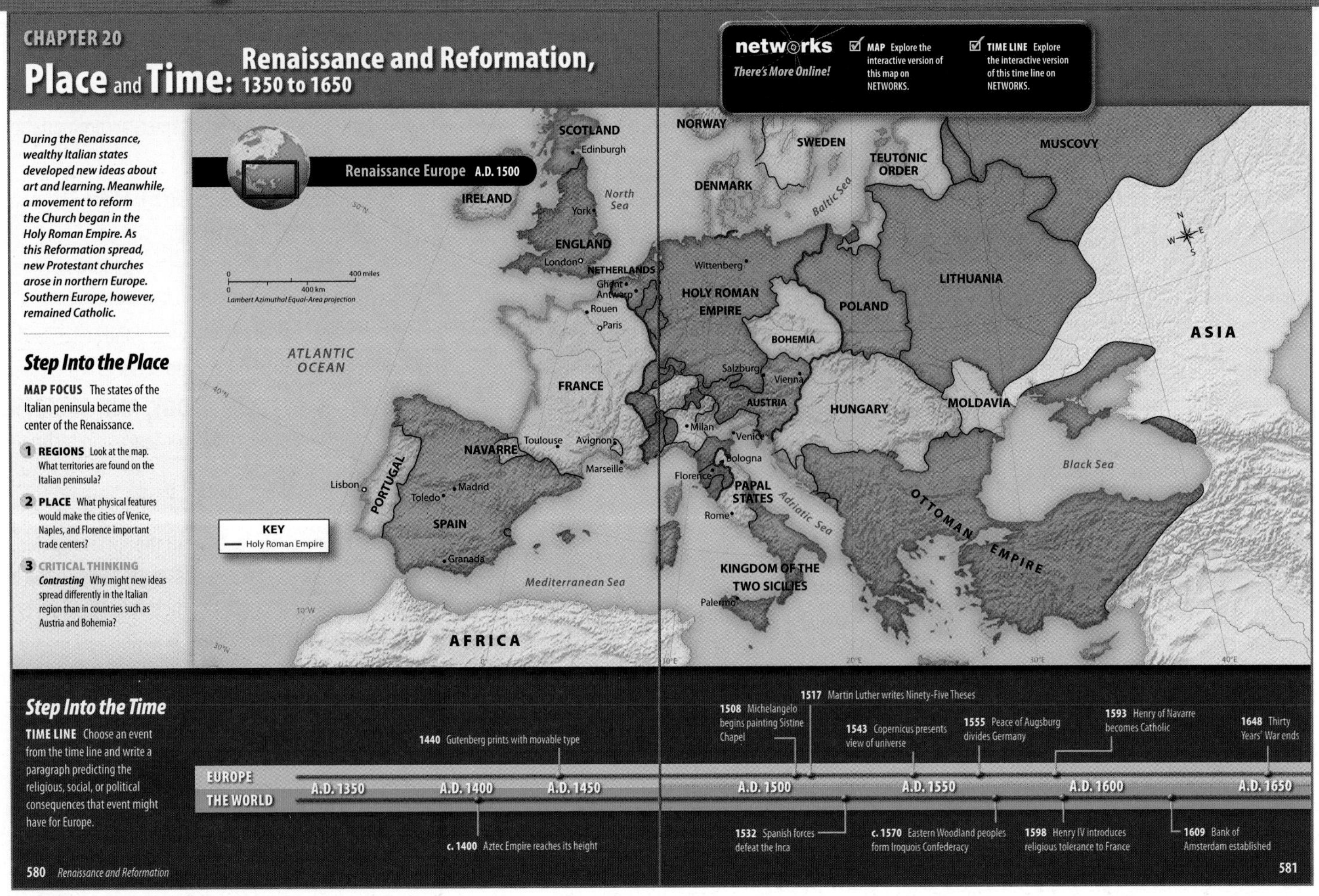

CHAPTER 20
Place and Time: Renaissance and Reformation, 1350 to 1650
networks There's More Online!
MAP Explore the interactive version of this map on NETWORKS.
TIME LINE Explore the interactive version of this time line on NETWORKS.
During the Renaissance, wealthy Italian states developed new ideas about art and learning. Meanwhile, a movement to reform the Church began in the Holy Roman Empire. As this Reformation spread, new Protestant churches arose in northern Europe. Southern Europe, however, remained Catholic.
Step Into the Place
MAP FOCUS The states of the Italian peninsula became the center of the Renaissance.
1 REGIONS Look at the map. What territories are found on the Italian peninsula?
2 PLACE What physical features would make the cities of Venice, Naples, and Florence important trade centers?
3 CRITICAL THINKING Contrasting Why might new ideas spread differently in the Italian region than in countries such as Austria and Bohemia?
Renaissance Europe A.D. 1500
KEY
Holy Roman Empire
Lambert Azimuthal Equal-Area projection
SCOTLAND
Edinburgh
IRELAND
North Sea
York
ENGLAND
London
NETHERLANDS
Ghent
Antwerp
Rouen
Paris
ATLANTIC OCEAN
FRANCE
NAVARRE
Toulouse
Avignon
Marseille
PORTUGAL
Lisbon
Toledo
Madrid
SPAIN
Granada
Mediterranean Sea
AFRICA
NORWAY
SWEDEN
DENMARK
Baltic Sea
TEUTONIC ORDER
MUSCOVY
Wittenberg
HOLY ROMAN EMPIRE
BOHEMIA
POLAND
LITHUANIA
Salzburg
Vienna
AUSTRIA
HUNGARY
MOLDAVIA
Milan
Venice
Bologna
Florence
PAPAL STATES
Rome
Adriatic Sea
KINGDOM OF THE TWO SICILIES
Palermo
OTTOMAN EMPIRE
Black Sea
ASIA
Step Into the Time
TIME LINE Choose an event from the time line and write a paragraph predicting the religious, social, or political consequences that event might have for Europe.
EUROPE
THE WORLD
A.D. 1350
A.D. 1400
A.D. 1450
A.D. 1500
A.D. 1550
A.D. 1600
A.D. 1650
1440 Gutenberg prints with movable type
1508 Michelangelo begins painting Sistine Chapel
1517 Martin Luther writes Ninety-Five Theses
1543 Copernicus presents view of universe
1555 Peace of Augsburg divides Germany
1593 Henry of Navarre becomes Catholic
1648 Thirty Years' War ends
c. 1400 Aztec Empire reaches its height
1532 Spanish forces defeat the Inca
c. 1570 Eastern Woodland peoples form Iroquois Confederacy
1598 Henry IV introduces religious tolerance to France
1609 Bank of Amsterdam established
580 Renaissance and Reformation
581

Technology Extension
- Find an additional activity online that incorporates technology for this project.
- Visit the EdTechTeacher Web sites (included in the Technology Extension for this chapter) for more links, tutorials, and other resources.

Assessing Background Knowledge

INTERACTIVE WORKSHEET

What Do You Know? Activity

Have students complete the What Do You Know? Four Square about the word *humanism* before they study the chapter. Explain that humanism was an important part of the Renaissance and the Reformation. Help students create a definition of the word by examining the word parts. Then, ask students to fill in the four squares with their best guesses.

After students have read the chapter, have them return to the Four Square and use what they learned in the chapter to add to or change their answers.

INTERACTIVE WORKSHEET

Guided Reading Activities

There is a Guided Reading Activity for each lesson in this chapter. You may wish to assign the Guided Reading Activity for Lesson 1 after introducing the chapter content.

Hands-On Chapter Project

Students will participate in an interview exercise with a partner in which they each get a chance to interview an important person from the Renaissance and be an interviewee.

- Students will participate in a class discussion to review what they have learned about important people of the Renaissance.
- Then, students will divide into pairs. Each pair will choose a Renaissance person to interview. They will use discussions and worksheets to help them prepare the questions and answers for their interview.
- Next, each pair will complete their interview questions and conduct the interview for the rest of the class.
- Finally, students will evaluate their research, presentation, and collaboration using an Assessment Rubric.

Visit **networks** online to see the full project and rubric.

Step Into the Place

MAP **Location** Project the Interactive World Atlas map of Europe. Have students point out the locations of countries they recognize or have heard of. Help students identify where major mountains, rivers, and oceans are located. You may also want to use the physical map of the world in the Reference Atlas.

Then project the chapter opener map of Renaissance Europe. Ask student to name any countries they recognize from the modern map. Point out some of the areas with different names. Explain that this is an historical map of the same area. Have them point out where physical characteristics are located. Tell them that as countries developed the borders they have today, these mountains, rivers, and oceans played an important part for determining those borders' locations.

Step Into the Time

Making Inferences Have students review the time line for the chapter. Explain that they will be studying events from about 1440 to 1648.

Ask: **Based on the information listed in the time line, what can you infer about what was happening in Europe around 1517?** *(Some people must have been dissatisfied with the Catholic Church. Martin Luther wrote Ninety-five Theses about how to change the Church.)*

Answers for pages 580–581

Step Into the Place

1. the Kingdom of the Two Sicilies, the Papal States, Florence, Bologna, Venice, and Milan
2. Venice, Naples, and Florence are located on the coast, which would allow for shipping.
3. CRITICAL THINKING Austria and Bohemia do not border the Mediterranean Sea. Ideas would not travel as quickly in those areas as they would in the Italian region because transportation and communication would be more difficult.

Step Into the Time

Answers will vary but may include Martin Luther's attempts to reform the Catholic Church, the Peace of Augsburg, and Henry of Navarre's need to change religion.

ONLINE RESOURCES

networks

Assign these interactive worksheets and quizzes from your Teacher Lesson Center. All resources are print-ready.

It's ALL Online!

Chapter 20 Resources
- Chapter Summary
- Vocabulary Builder
- What Do You Know?
- Hands-On Chapter Project

Lesson 1 Resources
- Interactive Graphic Organizer
- Economics of History Activity
  The Role of Guilds
- Guided Reading Activity
- Reading Essentials and Study Guide
- Online Self-Check Quiz

Lesson 2 Resources
- Interactive Graphic Organizer
- 21st Century Skills Activity
  Analyze Writing, Visuals, Communication
- Guided Reading Activity
- Reading Essentials and Study Guide
- Online Self-Check Quiz

Lesson 3 Resources
- Interactive Graphic Organizer
- 21st Century Skills Activity
  Determine Cause and Effect
- Guided Reading Activity
- Reading Essentials and Study Guide
- Online Self-Check Quiz

Lesson 4 Resources
- Interactive Graphic Organizer
- Primary Source Activity
  The Expulsion of the Jews From Spain
- Guided Reading Activity
- Reading Essentials and Study Guide
- Online Self-Check Quiz

Assessment Resources
- Lesson Reviews
- Online Self-Check Quizzes
- Chapter Activities and Assessment
- Standardized Test Practice

Remediation Resources
- Reading Essentials and Study Guide
- Guided Reading Activities
- Online Self-Check Quizzes
- Chapter Summary

networks
There's More Online!
- GRAPHIC ORGANIZER Wealth Grows in City-States
- MAP Italy, c. 1500
- SLIDE SHOW
  - Il Duomo
  - Venice

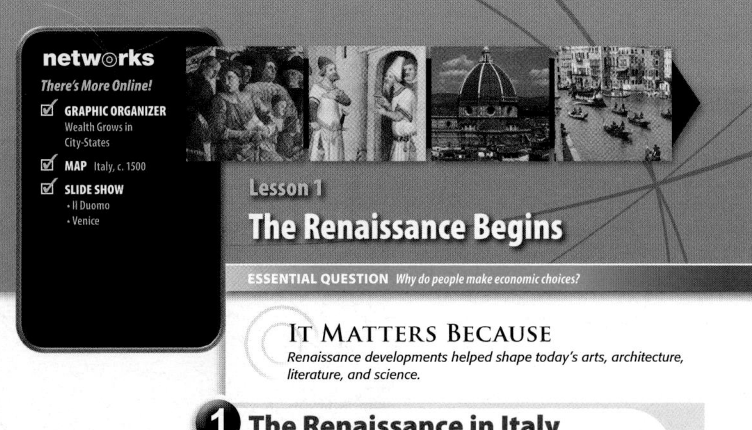

Lesson 1

The Renaissance Begins

ESSENTIAL QUESTION *Why do people make economic choices?*

It Matters Because

Renaissance developments helped shape today's arts, architecture, literature, and science.

1 The Renaissance in Italy

GUIDING QUESTION *Why did the states of Italy become leading centers of culture during the Renaissance?*

Between 1350 and 1650, ways of thinking changed greatly in Europe. As the Black Death eased, people became more confident about the future. Their interest in learning and the arts was renewed. This new interest in culture is called the **Renaissance** (reh•nuh•SAHNTZ), from the French word for "rebirth."

Rebirth of the Classics

The Renaissance sparked a renewed interest in ancient Greeks and Romans. European scholars improved their understanding of Greek and Latin languages, which they used to study ancient Greek and Roman writings.

Europeans also adopted many Greek and Roman ideas. They began to see that individual people could make a difference. They began to believe that people could change the world for the better.

During the Renaissance, most Europeans were still religious. However, they also began to value human efforts outside religion. As a result, people became more **secular** (SEH•kyuh•luhr). That is, they became more interested in worldly ideas and events, not just religious ones.

Reading **HELP**DESK

Taking Notes: *Identifying*
Use a chart like this one to show the reasons Italian states grew wealthy.

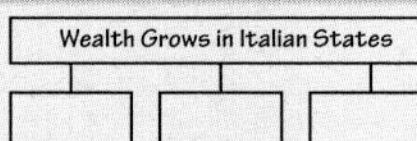

Content Vocabulary
- Renaissance
- secular
- urban
- mercenary
- diplomacy

The Renaissance is Born

The birthplace of the Renaissance was Italy, the heart of the old Roman Empire. The ruins and statues were familiar to Italians. Because of this, Italians readily turned to ancient examples to inspire them in their own artistic efforts.

Art also flourished because by the 1300s, Italian cities had become very wealthy. Their leading citizens could pay painters, sculptors, and architects to produce many new works.

The powerful states of Italy encouraged the Renaissance. The population of Italy was becoming more **urban** (UHR•buhn). That is, more people were living in cities than in the country. In other parts of Europe, most people still lived in rural areas, including the nobles who owned estates.

As a result of its city life, Italy began to develop a different society. Large city populations meant more discussion among people. Strong economies developed. It also meant more customers for artists and more money for a new kind of art.

GEOGRAPHY CONNECTION

Many Italian states prospered during the Renaissance.

1. **LOCATION** In which territory was Rome located?
2. **CRITICAL THINKING** *Drawing Conclusions* By what mode of transportation would you probably travel from Naples to Venice?

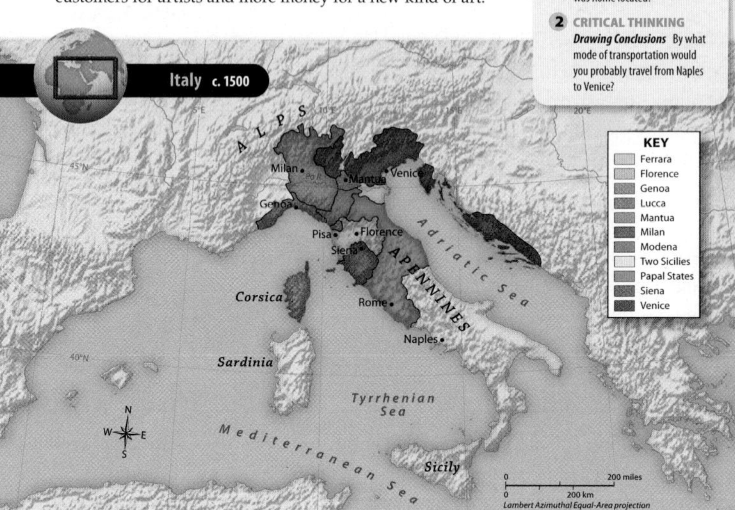

Renaissance a renewal or rebirth of interest in Greek and Roman arts
secular related to worldly things
urban having to do with a town or city

Like the city-states of ancient Greece, Renaissance Italy's urban society and scholars produced many great works of art and literature.

PROGRESS CHECK
Explaining Why did wealthy Italians support artists during the Renaissance?

2 The States of Italy

GUIDING QUESTION *How did Italy's states become wealthy and powerful?*

During the Middle Ages, Italy remained a collection of states, many of which were independent city-states. There were several reasons for this. The states of Italy did not want emperors and kings to rule them. In addition, the Catholic Church did not want a united Italy. It did not want a powerful emperor or king to control the pope.

The independent states in Italy were equally strong. They fought many wars and often took land from each other. However, no state was able to rule the others. Florence (FLAWR•uhntz), Venice (VEH•nuhs), Genoa (JEH•nuh•wuh), Milan (mih•LAN), and Rome were some of the most important cities of the Italian Renaissance. The Renaissance began in Italy because city life was stronger than in other parts of Europe.

Above all, Italy's states were independent because of their riches. They used their wealth to build large fleets of ships. They also hired mercenaries to fight in their armies. A **mercenary** (MUHR•suh•nehr•ee) is a full-time soldier who fights in an army for money. Wealthy merchants and bankers in Italy's states also loaned money to the kings of Europe. The kings left the states alone so they could borrow more money in the future.

The Gonzaga family ruled the Italian city-state of Mantua during the 1400s.

CRITICAL THINKING
Explaining Why was it possible for one family to become so powerful in Italy at this time?

Riches from Trade

The Italian states gained their wealth through trade. The long stretch of the Italian peninsula meant that many of the cities were port cities located on the coast.

Reading **HELP**DESK

mercenary a soldier who fights for money rather than loyalty to a country

The Italian peninsula was in the center of the Mediterranean world. The Byzantine and Ottoman Empires lay to the east, and Spain and France lay to the west. North Africa was only a short distance to the south. Italy's location made trade with these regions easier.

In eastern ports like Constantinople, Italian merchants bought Chinese silk and Indian spices from Byzantine, Turkish, and Arab merchants. The Italians sold these goods in Italy and Western Europe for very high prices. Italian merchants bought wool, wine, and glass in Western Europe and sold them in the Middle East. Meanwhile, Italian artisans bought raw materials and made goods to sell abroad for high prices.

An illustrated book written by a Florence merchant named Marco Polo made many Europeans excited about Asia and its wealth. He wrote about the riches he found there.

In addition to geography, two important events helped the Italians succeed in trade. One event was the Crusades. These conflicts brought Italian merchants into contact with Arab merchants in the Middle East. The second event was the Mongol conquests, which united much of Asia into one large trading network.

The Mongols protected trade along the Silk Road. This made it easier and cheaper for caravans to carry goods between China and the Middle East. As more silk and spices were sent from Asia, the price of these goods fell. More Europeans could pay for the luxuries, and demand for the goods increased.

Who Was Marco Polo?

In the 1270s, the merchant Marco Polo, his father, and his uncle left their home in Venice and traveled to China. Their goal was to meet Kublai Khan (KUH•bluh KAHN), the Mongol emperor of China.

When the Polo family reached the Khan's court, the emperor was amazed by the stories that Marco Polo told of his travels. Kublai sent Marco Polo on fact-finding trips all over China. Polo learned more about Asia than any other European. After returning to Europe, Polo wrote a book about his adventures. His stories about life in China amazed Europeans, who then wanted to buy Chinese goods.

Florence: A Renaissance City

The city of Florence was the first major center of the Renaissance. Its wealth and central location attracted many artists, sculptors, writers, and architects. Florence lay on the banks of the Arno River in central Italy. The city was surrounded by walls with tall towers for defense. Soaring above the city was the dome of its cathedral. A local architect, Filippo Brunelleschi (fih•LEEP•oh broon•ehl•EHS•kee), completed the dome in 1436. The dome is considered to be the greatest engineering achievement of the time.

LESSON 1

ENGAGE

SLIDE SHOW

Analyzing Visuals

Present the slide show of the cathedral of Santa Maria Del Fiore in Florence, Italy. Point out the doors by Lorenzo Ghiberti. Tell students that the doors are often called the Gates of Paradise and are made of gilded bronze. Explain that the doors contain reliefs of scenes from the Bible's Old Testament. Explain that some historians think the doors were the first ones to be built in the Renaissance style of architecture.

Ask:

How would you describe the style of Il Duomo? *(grand, formal, impressive)*

What is its most impressive feature? *(the large dome)*

What does the cathedral show about the people who built it? *(The people who built it had strong technical skills. They valued beauty and style.)* AL ELL

Tell students they will be studying how the architecture and methods of learning in Europe changed after the Middle Ages. Students will learn how the classic ideas of the Greeks and Romans influenced the artists and thinkers of Italy. They will learn about city life and how society developed in Italy. They will also find out how developments in Europe's economy and government helped bring about these changes.

TEACH & ASSESS

1 The Renaissance in Italy

GUIDING QUESTION *Why did the states of Italy become leading centers of culture during the Renaissance?*

MAP

Organizing

Review the map of Italy from the lesson to see how the region's geographic location could have helped launch the Renaissance.

Have students finish the sentence *"Because Italy has a long coastline, . . ."*. The answer should provide an "effect" that is logical for the "cause" statement provided.

GRAPHIC ORGANIZER

Determining Cause and Effect Display the cause-and-effect Taking Notes graphic organizer. Guide students to complete the graphic organizer with the causes and effects that stem from Italy's geographic location as a center of trade and commerce. Then have them think about how new ideas or technologies spread today, such as new computer technology, scientific discoveries, or fashion trends.

Ask:

What encourages the spread of this information? *(information from friends, from the Internet, or from books)*

How are ideas spread differently today than they were in the past? *(Ideas spread much more quickly today with the aid of computers and the Internet.)*

Then have students compare this information with their findings from the cause-and-effect graphic organizer.

2 The States of Italy

GUIDING QUESTION *How did Italy's states become wealthy and powerful?*

SLIDE SHOW

Analyzing Visuals

After reviewing this section with students, present the slide show of the city of Venice. Point out the images of the Piazza San Marco and descriptions of its details.

Ask:

What are the main features of the square? *(buildings, clock tower)*

How would you describe the buildings and bridges of Venice? *(The buildings and bridges are large and beautiful.)*

How did Venice adapt to its environment? *(Venice was built on a chain of islands. Rather than building roads, Venetians built canals and used boats for transportation.)* AL ELL

LECTURE SLIDE

Classifying

Show students the lecture slide identifying goods traded by the Italian city-states. Then ask students to classify some of the sources of the city-states' wealth.

Guide students by **asking:**

How important was the location of the city-states? *(Location was important because city-states were close to the sea and located in the center of the Mediterranean world.)*

Why was Venice an important link between Europe and Asia? *(Venetian merchants made trading contacts with eastern civilizations, and Venice had a large shipbuilding industry.)*

What types of merchants and artisans succeeded in the city-states? *(Answers may include bankers, cloth traders, and shipbuilders.)*

How did the city-states' wealth affect the arts? *(The wealth supported artists, architects, and writers and the city-states flourished with new buildings, sculptures, and books.)* BL

INTERACTIVE WORKSHEET

Summarizing Assign for homework the Economics of History Activity for this chapter, "The Role of Guilds." Be sure students understand the background information in the activity so they can answer the questions about the importance of guilds and trade in Renaissance city-states.

Answers for pages 582–585

P. 582 Taking Notes The following contributed to the growth of wealth in the Italian city-states: Italy's long coastline and many ports made it an ideal location for trade; the Crusades brought Italian merchants into contact with Arab merchants; the rise of the Mongol Empire united almost all of Asia into one trade network.

P. 583 GEOGRAPHY CONNECTION

1. Papal States
2. CRITICAL THINKING by horseback over land

P. 584 ☑ PROGRESS CHECK Wealthy Italians competed with one another to bring fame to their cities. By having artists in their cities, they could help bring fame to those cities.

P. 584 CRITICAL THINKING Wealth meant power in the Italian states. The Gonzaga family was extremely wealthy; thus, they had a lot of power.

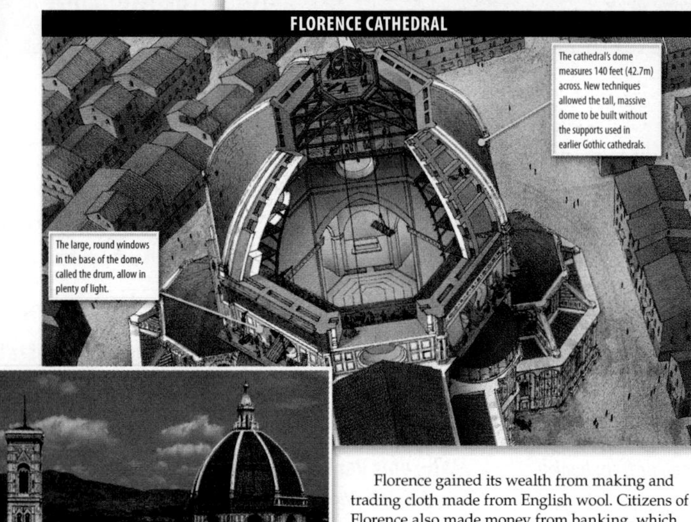

FLORENCE CATHEDRAL
The cathedral's dome measures 140 feet (42.7m) across. New techniques allowed the tall, massive dome to be built without the supports used in earlier Gothic cathedrals.
The large, round windows in the base of the dome, called the drum, allow in plenty of light.

The dome of the cathedral in Florence, Italy, became a symbol of the city. It was considered a great architectural design of its time.

▶ CRITICAL THINKING

Making Connections What earlier civilization was known for building domes?

Florence gained its wealth from making and trading cloth made from English wool. Citizens of Florence also made money from banking, which included lending money and charging interest. As goods poured into Italy from abroad, merchants had to determine the value of **currency,** or money, from different countries. Florentine bankers used the florin, the gold coin of Florence, to measure the value of other money. The city's wealthiest family, the Medici (MEH•duh•chee), owned the largest bank in Europe during the 1400s. The Medici had branch banks, or other offices, as far away as Flanders.

Venice: A City of Canals

Another leading Renaissance city was Venice. Located on the northern coast of the Adriatic Sea in eastern Italy, Venice was built on many small islands. Venetians drove long wooden poles into mud to support their buildings. Instead of paving roads, the Venetians built canals and used boats for transportation around the city. Even today, Venice's canals and waterways serve as streets.

alp images

Reading **HELP**DESK

diplomacy the practice of conducting negotiations between countries

Academic Vocabulary

currency money, in the form of coins or paper

complex complicated

During the Renaissance, Venice became an important link between Europe and Asia. Venetian merchants, such as Marco Polo, traveled abroad and made contacts with eastern civilizations. The city also was known as a major shipbuilding center. In a part of the city called the Arsenal, teams of workers built the wooden ships and also made the sails and oars.

☑ PROGRESS CHECK

Determining Cause and Effect How did the travels of Marco Polo affect Europeans?

3 A New Ruling Class

GUIDING QUESTION *Who controlled the states of Italy?*

Wealthy merchants and bankers in the Italian city-states formed a new kind of leadership. Before the Renaissance, nobles in Europe gained their wealth from land, not trade.

In Italy, old noble families moved from the country to the cities. They became urban nobles. They formed ties of business and friendship with wealthy merchants.

Meanwhile, merchants began to adopt the customs of the nobles. Soon, the sons and daughters of nobles and rich merchants were marrying each other. These new families became the upper class of the city-states.

Who Ruled Italian City-States?

Many Italian city-states began as republics. A republic is a government in which power comes from its citizens. However, not all people in an Italian city-state were citizens. Citizenship belonged only to merchants and artisans.

In ancient Rome, power was often given to a dictator during a war or revolt. A dictator was a ruler who had absolute power. In many cases, the Italian city-states relied on a single powerful individual to run the government. Some of these leaders ruled harshly, using force to keep control. Others used a more gentle approach. To win support, these rulers improved city services.

In Venice, the ruler was the duke, or doge (DOHJ). He officially ran the city, but a council of wealthy merchants held the real power. This council passed laws and elected the doge.

In Florence, the powerful Medici family controlled the government for many years. Lorenzo de' Medici governed Florence from 1469 to 1492. He used his wealth to support artists, architects, and writers. As a result of Florence's prosperity and fame, Lorenzo was known as "the Magnificent."

Philippe Michel/Age fotostock

Thinking Like a HISTORIAN

Drawing Conclusions

During the Renaissance, Venice's canals were avenues of transportation. The famous Grand Canal formed a large "S" shape winding through the city. Lining the canal were the homes of wealthy merchants. Many of these still stand today. Compare Venice with other Italian Renaissance cities. Then draw a conclusion about Renaissance Italy. For more information about drawing conclusions, read the chapter *What Does a Historian Do?*

The Venetians cut canals through the swampy land around the city's original islands. Today, gondolas—long, narrow boats—still carry people along these canals.

Keeping the Peace

Political affairs in Italy were **complex,** or complicated. Within each state, rulers had to put down revolts by the poor. They also had to prevent other wealthy people and city leaders from seizing control. At the same time, the rulers had to keep good relations with bordering states.

To deal with the neighboring states, the Italians developed **diplomacy** (duh•PLOH•muh•see). Diplomacy is the art of making agreements with other countries. Italians worked to be sure that no single state had enough power to threaten the others.

How could a ruler keep his hold on power in the Italian states? Niccolò Machiavelli (nee•koh•LOH mah•kee•uh•VEH•lee), a diplomat in Florence, tried to answer this question. In 1513, he wrote *The Prince*, a book that took a critical look at politics in Renaissance Italy. In this work, Machiavelli stated that rulers should do whatever was necessary to keep power and protect their city, even if they had to lie and kill. Machiavelli gave leaders the following advice:

Lorenzo de' Medici had enough power to rule Florence by himself. He chose, however, to govern with the help of assemblies that represented the people of his city-state.

▶ CRITICAL THINKING

Theorizing Through what means do you think de' Medici would settle a dispute between nobles?

PRIMARY SOURCE

> "Upon this a question arises: whether it is better to be loved than feared or feared than loved? It may be answered that one should wish to be both, but, because it is difficult to unite them in one person, it is much safer to be feared than loved."
>
> —from *The Prince*, by Niccolò Machiavelli

Today when we say someone is being "Machiavellian," we mean that person is cunning or acting without a conscience.

Scala/Art Resource, NY

☑ PROGRESS CHECK

Analyzing Why did the Italian states develop diplomacy?

LESSON 1 REVIEW

Review Vocabulary

1. What elements of Renaissance culture show *secular* ideas?
2. How could a focus on *diplomacy* have helped the states of Italy?

Answer the Guiding Questions

3. ***Explaining*** Why would ideas about art and culture develop faster in the city than in the countryside?
4. ***Identifying*** What was one reason Italian trade grew during the Renaissance?
5. ***Differentiating*** How were urban nobles different from nobles who lived in the country?
6. **EXPOSITORY WRITING** Why did Renaissance ideas arise in the 1300s? Explain your answer in the form of a short essay.

NOTES

LESSON 1 (cont.)

A New Ruling Class

GUIDING QUESTION *Who controlled the states of Italy?*

LECTURE SLIDE

Identifying Central Issues Discuss as a class the development of business and trade. Remind students that trade made people wealthier while, at the same time, it helped increase people's knowledge of other parts of the world.

Ask: **How would an active trading business help a city grow?** *(Students might say that trading would encourage people to move to cities. Trading would also encourage the growth of new ideas.)*

Show students the lecture slide defining the term *republic.* ELL

Then have students describe the wealthy leaders of city-states.

Ask: **Who controlled trade in the city-states?** *(urban nobles, wealthy merchants)*

How could the leaders of city-states govern their regions? *(Some individual leaders used force; others won the support of citizens by providing city services, arts, and entertainment.)* BL

Predicting

Ask students the following questions:

What was the role of the doge in Venice? *(He ruled the city, although a council of merchants had the real power.)*

What might happen to a doge if he did not follow the wishes of the council of merchants? *(Students might say that the merchants would replace the doge with someone who supported them.)*

Why was it important for the Italians to develop diplomacy? *(Students might say that Italians needed to make sure the city-states contributed equally and that no city-state became more powerful than the others. Italy was also close to other countries and had to keep good relations with bordering countries.)*

Have students complete the Lesson 1 Review.

BACKGROUND KNOWLEDGE

Why the Renaissance Began in Italy

Numerous factors contributed to the fact that the Renaissance began in Italy. These factors included, but were not limited to:

- Italy was the center of the Roman Empire.
- Italy's cities had become wealthy and could afford to pay artists to produce new works.
- Italy was divided into smaller city-states that competed with one another to have artists make their city-state famous.
- Many people lived in cities in Italy, which allowed for a greater sharing of ideas.

A Summary of Italian Renaissance Cities

Florence

Florence was the first major center of the Renaissance. Located in the center of the Italian peninsula, it became a major trading post and made a great deal of wealth from the woolen cloth trade. The symbol of this city was its beautiful domed cathedral.

Venice

Venice was a city of canals. Its location in Italy made it a crucial city that linked Europe and Asia. This made Venice a center of trade and commerce and, in turn, a place where Renaissance ideas thrived. Marco Polo was from Venice, and the items that he brought back to Italy from China made Italians interested in exploring other parts of the world.

Genoa

The city of Genoa was a major port city in Italy. Being a center of trade, it became a center of Renaissance ideas. Genoa was also a powerful city in that it had gained control of Corsica and Sardinia following the Crusades. These colonial claims helped increase the wealth of Genoa.

Rome

The city of Rome was home to some of the greatest masterpieces that came from Renaissance artists: Michelangelo's painting on the ceiling of the Sistine Chapel as well as his *Pietá* in St. Peter's Cathedral; Raphael's *The School of Athens* in the Vatican; and Donato Bramante's architectural designs for St. Peter's to list a few.

CLOSE & REFLECT

Synthesize Ask students to identify the strengths of the Italian city-states and why they were successful. Student responses should summarize the lesson.

Answers for pages 586–588

P. 586 CRITICAL THINKING Muslim civilization

P. 587 ☑ PROGRESS CHECK The stories about China made Europeans want to buy the Chinese goods that Marco Polo described.

P. 588 CRITICAL THINKING Students might say that de' Medici would have used his money to bring opposing sides together and help settle disputes between nobles.

P. 588 ☑ PROGRESS CHECK Italian states developed diplomacy to keep power balanced and to avoid conflicts.

LESSON 1 REVIEW

1. The Renaissance focus on trade, diplomacy, and art provides examples of secular ideas.
2. A focus on diplomacy helped city-states form alliances and avoid wars, which would have improved the safety of people in city-states.
3. People in the city had more people to discuss ideas with than people who lived in rural areas. In addition, cities had wealth, which they could use to develop and support art and culture.
4. Italian trade grew during the Renaissance because people were becoming more aware of other countries' goods and were more open to trying different things than they were before the Renaissance.
5. Urban nobles were merchants who earned their money through trade. Nobles who lived in the country made their money from land, and they once thought of themselves as better than merchants.
6. Answers will vary but should include the idea that the rise of city-states and their wealth allowed the Renaissance to develop in Italy.

NOTES

networks *There's More Online!*
- GRAPHIC ORGANIZER Renaissance Art
- SLIDE SHOW
  - Leonardo da Vinci
  - Gutenberg Press and Type
- VIDEO

Lesson 2

New Ideas and Art

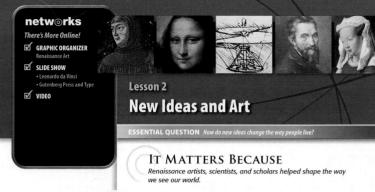

ESSENTIAL QUESTION *How do new ideas change the way people live?*

It Matters Because

Renaissance artists, scientists, and scholars helped shape the way we see our world.

1 Renaissance Humanism

GUIDING QUESTION *How did Renaissance writers rely on the past to develop new ideas?*

In the 1300s and 1400s, European scholars developed a new way of understanding the world called **humanism.** It was based on ancient Greek and Roman ideas. Humanists, as these scholars were called, gave importance to the individual and to human society. They wanted to gain knowledge through reason, not just through religious faith. Humanism encouraged people to be active in their cities and to develop their talents.

Discovering Ancient Works

In the 1300s, Italian scholars began to study ancient Roman and Greek works. For most of the Middle Ages, Western Europeans knew little about these writings. During the Crusades, however, they came into contact with the Middle East. Arab Muslim scholars there and in Spain knew the classic Greek and Roman writings. They passed on their knowledge to the Western Europeans. Byzantine scholars also brought classical works to Italy.

One famous humanist scholar was Petrarch (PEE•trahrk). Francesco Petrarch lived in Italy during the 1300s. He studied Roman writers such as Cicero (SIH•suh•roh) and wrote biographies of famous Romans.

Reading **HELP**DESK

Taking Notes: *Describing*

Create a word web to list examples of Renaissance art. For each type of art, describe how it reflects Renaissance ideas.

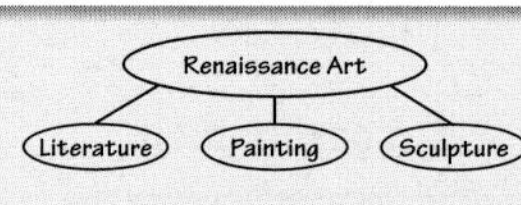

Content Vocabulary
- **humanism**

Petrarch traveled to different monasteries to find old Latin manuscripts. Scholars throughout Europe followed Petrarch's example. In time, new libraries were built to hold the newly found manuscripts. The largest of these libraries was at the Vatican, the home of the pope in Rome.

Italians also began to value the ancient buildings and statues all around them. Throughout Rome, workers removed dirt and rubble from damaged columns and statues. Artists then eagerly studied the proportion of ancient works. For example, artists compared the length of a statue's arms to its height. They believed this comparison could tell them why the statue looked perfect.

A New Literature

In addition to studying the classics, humanists in Italy and other parts of Europe made important achievements of their own. One of their contributions was new forms of literature.

During the Renaissance, educated Europeans wrote in the classical Latin used in ancient Rome. However, they also began writing in the vernacular, the everyday language people spoke in a region. Vernacular languages included Italian, French, and German. For example, Petrarch used Italian to write sonnets, or short poems, which expressed his love for a woman who died from the Black Death. Many more people could read works written in the vernacular instead of in Latin.

In the early 1300s, a poet from Florence named Dante Alighieri (DAHN•tay ah•lee•GYEHR•ee) wrote *The Divine Comedy*. It is known as one of the world's greatest poems. Written in the vernacular, it tells of a person's journey from hell to heaven. The poem describes the horrible punishments for different sins.

The English writer Geoffrey Chaucer (CHAW•suhr) also wrote popular vernacular literature. Chaucer wrote his famous work *The Canterbury* (KAN•tuhr•behr•ree) *Tales* in English. *The Canterbury Tales* is a collection of stories told by pilgrims on a religious journey to the town of Canterbury, England. In this work, Chaucer portrayed the entire **range** of English society. His work shows both nobles at the top of society and the poor at the bottom. The English we speak today comes from the form of English that Chaucer used in his writing.

Petrarch has been called the father of Italian Renaissance humanism.

Reading **HELP**DESK

humanism belief in the worth of the individual and that reason is a path to knowledge

Academic Vocabulary

range the limits between which something can change or differ

Gutenberg's Printing Press

The printing press helped spread humanist ideas throughout Europe. In the early 1450s, a German printer named Johannes Gutenberg (yoh•HAHN•uhs GOO•tuhn•buhrg) developed a printing press that used movable metal type. This new press held individual carved letters that could be arranged to form words and then could be used again. As a result, books could be quickly printed by machine rather than slowly written by hand.

The Chinese had already invented movable type. However, their written language had so many characters that the movable type system did not work well. For Europeans, the printing press was a great advance. It was easy to use with linen paper, another invention from China.

Gutenberg's printing press made many more books available to people. Its invention came at a time when many townspeople were learning to read and think for themselves. Scholars could read each other's works and discuss their ideas, often in letters. Ideas developed and spread more quickly than ever before in Europe.

In 1455, Gutenberg produced the first European printed book, the Christian Bible, on the new press. Soon, many books became available in Europe. In fact, more books were printed in the first 50 years of printing than were written by hand in the entire history of the world up to 1450. Half of the 40,000 books published by the year 1500 were religious works such as the Christian Bible or prayer books.

Gutenberg produced bibles on this printing press. Today, there are five complete original Gutenberg Bibles in the United States.

What Effect Did Humanism Have on Society?

Humanist scholars were curious about such subjects as biology, medicine, and astronomy. Scholars' study of mathematics helped them in many areas of knowledge.

One of the leading Renaissance scientists was also a great artist, Leonardo da Vinci (lee•uh•NAHR•doh duh VIHN•chee). Da Vinci cut open dead bodies to learn more about the human body. He studied fossils to understand Earth's early history. Da Vinci was also an inventor and an engineer.

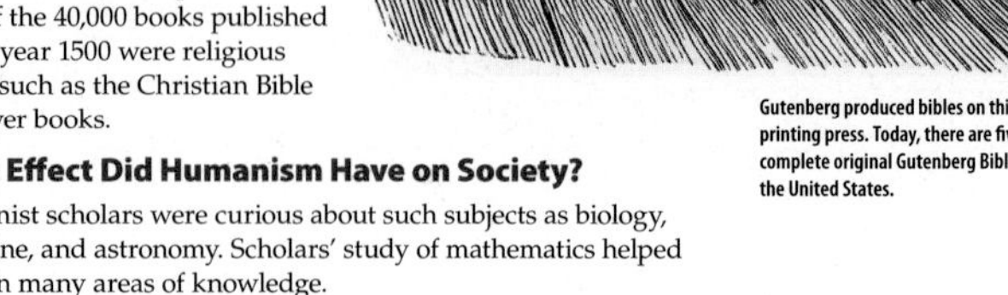

LESSON 2 • Day 1

ENGAGE

Comparing and Contrasting

In a Think-Pair-Share activity, have students write down some of the differences between the art of the Middle Ages and the art of the Renaissance. If possible, show students a painting from the Middle Ages next to one from the Renaissance and have them compare the different styles of painting.

Ask:

How did art change during the Renaissance? *(Answers should include that art became more realistic and natural in appearance.)* AL ELL

Tell students they will be learning some of the reasons Renaissance artists and writers began to change the methods they used to show and describe the world around them.

TEACH & ASSESS

1 Renaissance Humanism

GUIDING QUESTION ***How did Renaissance writers rely on the past to develop new ideas?***

INTERACTIVE WORKSHEET

Evaluating

Show students the 21st Century Skills worksheet for this lesson. Write on the board the bulleted ideas about humanism that are below. Tell students to review these ideas when they begin the worksheet. They may complete the worksheet as a homework assignment.

- Renaissance artists and writers used humanist ideas about art, culture, and education in creating their works.
- Petrarch was a Renaissance writer who used the ideas of ancient Romans.
- Renaissance writers and artists believed that the ideas of individuals were important. AL

SLIDE SHOW

Explaining

Show students the slide show on Gutenberg's printing press.

Ask:

How did the printing press help spread humanism throughout Europe? *(The printing press made it easier and faster to print books, which helped spread humanist ideas.)*

2 Italy's Renaissance Artists

GUIDING QUESTION ***How did Renaissance artists learn to make their art look natural and real?***

LECTURE SLIDE

Analyzing

Show students the lecture slide defining the terms *perspective* and *chiaroscuro.* ELL

Ask:

How did these techniques help Renaissance artists improve their paintings? *(Perspective allowed artists to give paintings a three-dimensional look. Chiaroscuro softened edges by using light and shadow, making paintings more dramatic.)*

LECTURE SLIDE

Listing

Show students the lecture slide listing Italian Renaissance artists.

Ask:

What subjects were all three artists famous for painting? *(All three painted religious subjects. Da Vinci painted the Last Supper, Michelangelo painted the Sistine Chapel, and Raphael painted the Virgin Mary.)*

CLOSE AND REFLECT

Identifying Points of View

To summarize, ask students to discuss how someone from the Middle Ages might view art and literature from ancient Rome. Then, compare that opinion to one of a person who lived during the Renaissance.

IF YOU HAVE MORE TIME . . .

Research a Renaissance Artist

Have students choose a Renaissance artist and work in groups to research that artist. Students should research the artist's background, where he or she lived and worked, what types of medium the artist worked in, and what some of the artist's most important works are. Ask each group to include visual aids in their research.

As they conduct their research, have students discuss the following questions within their groups:

Why was this person an important Renaissance artist? *(Students might note that the artist's style was inherently that of the Renaissance, either in its subject matter or in the use of materials.)*

What made the artist fit into the style of the Renaissance? *(Students may respond that the artist had a humanist style or that he or she wrote or painted in a way that was unique to the Renaissance style.)*

Did the artist collaborate or work with any other Renaissance artists? *(Student answers will vary depending on the artist they choose.)*

What was the artist's most important work? *(Student answers will vary depending on the artist they choose.)*

Why are the artist's works still valued today by people around the world? *(Student answers will vary, but they might say that the works of a particular artist are timeless and can still be appreciated because they are such excellent examples of a certain style of writing or painting.)*

How did this artist's work influence other artists? *(Student answers will vary depending on the artist they choose.)*

Have groups prepare presentations and take turns sharing information on their artist with the class. Students should include pictures of the artist's works in their presentation.

Encourage groups to use a computer and slide show presentation software to organize their research. Then, groups can use the software during their presentation to the class. BL

Answers for pages 589–591

P. 589 Taking Notes Literature—can be written in the vernacular; **Painting**—can show realistic-looking people; **Sculpture**—artists studied human body

The *Mona Lisa* by Leonardo da Vinci is one of the most famous paintings from the Renaissance. It hangs today in the *Louvre*, a museum in Paris.

▶ CRITICAL THINKING
Speculating Why do you think people have been so fascinated by Mona Lisa's smile?

Most of what we know about da Vinci comes from his notebooks. Da Vinci filled the pages of his notebooks with notes and sketches of his scientific and artistic projects. These drawings often pictured parachutes, flying machines, and other mechanical inventions far ahead of his time.

✓ PROGRESS CHECK

Explaining How did Gutenberg's printing press bring change to Europe?

2 Italy's Renaissance Artists

GUIDING QUESTION *How did Renaissance artists learn to make their art look natural and real?*

In Renaissance Italy, wealthy families and church leaders appreciated beautiful buildings and works of art. They hired talented people to construct beautiful buildings and to fill them with artwork. The pope funded works of art to decorate the Vatican, his headquarters in Rome.

Renaissance builders and artists carefully studied ancient Greek and Roman art, science, and mathematics. They also expressed the new humanist ideas. As one artist declared, human beings were "the center and measure of all things."

What New Styles Did Artists Develop?

Renaissance art was very different from medieval art. Artistic works of the Renaissance tried to show what people really looked like. They also tried to reveal people's feelings. An artist from Florence named Giotto (JAH•toh) was the first to show this change in the early 1300s. His series of wall paintings showed the life of Francis of Assisi. The paintings used gestures and facial expressions to reveal people's emotions.

Renaissance painters also used new methods that brought life, color, and action to their works. The most important was **perspective** (puhr•SPEHK•tihv), a way of showing people and things as they appear at different distances. Artists in the past had tried to use perspective, but Renaissance artists such as Leonardo da Vinci perfected it. Perspective, as used by these artists, gave paintings a realistic, three-dimensional look.

Renaissance artists studied the human body to learn how to draw it accurately. They began to experiment with light, color, and shade. To make their paintings more realistic, artists used

Reading **HELP**DESK

Academic Vocabulary

perspective a way of drawing to show the relationship of objects in a drawing to give the look of depth or distance

a technique called chiaroscuro (kee•ahr•uh•SKYUR•oh). Chiaroscuro used light and shadows instead of stiff outlines to separate objects. In Italian, *chiaro* means "clear or light," and *oscuro* means "dark." Chiaroscuro created drama and emotion.

Many Renaissance artists painted on fresh wet plaster with watercolor paint. A painting done this way is called a fresco (FREHS•koh), which means "fresh" in Italian. Frescoes were painted in churches all over Italy.

Da Vinci was a great innovator. His drawing of a helicopter was very advanced for his time and he is credited with having the first idea for a vehicle that could fly vertically.

Who Were Leading Renaissance Artists?

The period between 1490 and 1520 was the golden age of Italian Renaissance painting. Three of the most famous artists were Leonardo da Vinci, Michelangelo Buonarroti (MY•kuh•LAN•juh•loh bwah•nah•RAH•tee) and Raphael Sanzio (rah•feye•EHL SAHN•zee•oh).

Leonardo da Vinci was born in Florence. He is known for the *Mona Lisa*, a portrait of a young noblewoman. He gave her a smile that makes the viewer wonder what she is thinking. Da Vinci also painted *The Last Supper*, a wall painting of Jesus and his disciples. In this work, da Vinci showed human emotions through the way in which the apostles hold their heads or sit in relation to Jesus.

Another great Renaissance artist was Michelangelo. He began his career as a sculptor in Florence. In 1508, Pope Julius II hired Michelangelo to work at the Vatican. There, Michelangelo painted the ceiling of the Sistine Chapel with scenes from the Bible. These paintings are still famous today. A noted Renaissance biographer praised Michelangelo:

PRIMARY SOURCE

> The work [Sistine Chapel ceiling] has been, indeed, a light of our art, illuminating the world which had been so many centuries in darkness. Oh, truly happy age, and oh, blessed artists, who at such a fountain can purge [remove] away the dark films from your eyes. Give thanks to Heaven, and imitate Michael Angelo [Michelangelo] in all things.
>
> —from *Lives of the Artists* by Giorgio Vasari

All of Michelangelo's painted figures were like sculptures. They had muscular bodies that showed life and power. This scene of the creation of Adam appears on the ceiling of the Sistine Chapel in Rome.

BIOGRAPHY

Michelangelo Buonarroti (1475–1564)

As a young artist, Michelangelo received support from Lorenzo de' Medici, the ruler of Florence. When he saw the young man's talent, de' Medici let Michelangelo study his collection of ancient Roman statues. One of Michelangelo's first large sculptures was inspired by these statues. Michelangelo's most famous works, however, were based on Bible stories, such as "David and Goliath." He made his 13-foot-tall marble statue of David seem calm, yet ready for action. Most of Michelangelo's sculptures suggested strong but controlled emotions.

▶ CRITICAL THINKING
Assessing How important was the de' Medici family to Michelangelo?

Like Michelangelo, the artist Raphael worked at the Vatican. He painted many frescoes for the palace of the pope. Perhaps his best-known fresco, the *School of Athens*, shows Greek philosophers. People also admired his paintings of Mary, the mother of Jesus. These works were done in bright colors and showed the Renaissance ideals of grace and beauty.

Renaissance women had few roles independent of men. Some women, though, contributed to the arts. These women were either the daughters of artists or the children of nobles. The most celebrated female artist was Artemisia Gentileschi (ahr•teh•MIHZ•ee•uh jehn•tih•LEHS•kee). She was one of the first women to paint major historical and religious scenes.

✓ PROGRESS CHECK

Describing What is the technique of chiaroscuro?

3 The Northern Renaissance

GUIDING QUESTION *How did the Renaissance change as it moved from Italy into northern Europe?*

During the late 1400s, the Renaissance spread from Italy to northern Europe. War, trade, travel, and the printing press all spread humanist ideas. The people of northern Europe eagerly accepted Italian Renaissance style but changed it to suit their own tastes and needs.

Northern European Painters

The term "Northern Renaissance" refers to the cultural changes in what is today Belgium, the Netherlands, Luxembourg, and Germany. Like Italian artists, northern artists wanted more realism in their works. However, they used different methods to achieve it.

Northern artists began painting in oils rather than using water-based paints. Oils provided richer colors and allowed changes to be made on the painted canvas. Artists also used oils to show small surface details, such as the gold trim on a robe.

The Flemish painter Jan van Eyck (YAHN van EYEK) was skilled in using oils. One of his best-known paintings is *The Arnolfini* (ahr•nuhl•FEE•nee) *Portrait*. It shows a newly married couple standing together in a formal room. Van Eyck showed every fold in their richly colored clothes and every detail of the ceiling lamp above them.

Reading **HELP**DESK

Reading Strategy: Finding the Main Idea

Finding the main idea of a passage will help you understand what the passage is about. Read about the northern European painters. On a separate sheet of paper, write the main idea of that passage in your own words.

Albrecht Dürer (AHL•brehkt DYUR•uhr) of Germany was another important artist of the Northern Renaissance. His work blended Italian Renaissance methods and medieval German traditions. Dürer was skilled in showing perspective and fine detail. He is best known for his engravings. An engraving is produced from an image carved on metal, wood, or stone. Ink is placed on the surface, and then the image is printed on paper.

Dürer's *Four Horsemen of the Apocalypse* (uh•PAH•kuh•lihpz) is an outstanding example of a woodcut, a print made from carved wood. His work shows four fierce riders who announce the end of the world.

The richly detailed objects in this van Eyck painting reflect the lives of the people portrayed, a merchant and his wife.

▶ CRITICAL THINKING
Analyzing Visuals What does this painting tell you about the lives of the people in it?

England's Theaters

The Renaissance reached its height in England during the rule of Elizabeth I in the late 1500s. The people of Renaissance England were especially fond of plays. About 1580, the first theaters in England were built. Their stages stood in the open air. Some wealthy people sat under a roof or covering. Admission was only one or two cents, so even the poor could attend. The poor stood in a large open area.

English playwrights, or authors of plays, wrote about people's strengths, weaknesses, and emotions. The greatest English playwright of that time was William Shakespeare (SHAYK•spihr). Shakespeare wrote all kinds of plays: histories, comedies, and tragedies. He drew ideas for his plays from the histories of England and ancient Rome. His plays often included Italian scenes, characters, and plots. Many of his plays were about loyalty, family, friendship, or justice. Some of Shakespeare's most famous works are *Hamlet*, *Macbeth*, *Romeo and Juliet*, and *Henry V*.

✓ PROGRESS CHECK

Comparing and Contrasting How did northern Renaissance painters differ from Italian Renaissance painters?

LESSON 2 REVIEW

Review Vocabulary

1. How could *humanism* help people solve problems?

Answer the Guiding Questions

2. ***Explaining*** How were Renaissance scholars able to study ancient texts?
3. ***Determining Cause and Effect*** How did Gutenberg's printing press contribute to the spread of the ideas of scholars?
4. ***Making Inferences*** How might Renaissance scientific advances have helped artists to make more realistic art?
5. ***Contrasting*** How did Renaissance ideas influence northern and southern European art differently?
6. **EXPOSITORY WRITING** How do you think ancient Greek and Roman ideas have affected how people learn, relate, or think about their place in the world? Explain your answer in a short paragraph.

LESSON 2 • Day 2

ENGAGE

IMAGE

Making Generalizations

Tell students you will show them an example of Renaissance art from a northern European country. Then display Jan van Eyck's *The Arnolfini Portrait*.

Explain that he was a Flemish artist, meaning he was from Flanders, an area that is now Belgium and the Netherlands. Ask students to point out some of the small details in the painting.

Ask:

What art material, or medium, allowed van Eyck to paint such small details? *(He worked in oil paints. Because the paint is thick and dries slowly, an artist can paint small details.)* BL

Tell students that in this lesson, they will learn more about Northern Renaissance artists and writers, including Shakespeare.

The Northern Renaissance

GUIDING QUESTION *How did the Renaissance change as it moved from Italy into Northern Europe?*

IMAGE

Making Generalizations Have students refer to the section "Northern European Painters" in their textbooks. Next, have students examine German artist Albrecht Dürer's *Four Horsemen of the Apocalypse*.

Ask:

What details does the woodcut include about the horsemen and their victims? *(The horsemen look angry; one is very thin, as if he were starving. The woodcut shows the reactions of people being trampled by the horses.)* AL 

Then ask:

Review the images of the art by van Eyck and Dürer. Based on these examples, what generalizations can you make about the artists of the Northern Renaissance? *(In general, the artists included small details that reflected their time and place. They featured ordinary people and subjects, even when they depicted extraordinary events, like the apocalypse.)*

Analyzing

Provide students with information about Shakespeare's background. Explain that Shakespeare was an enormously successful playwright in London, England. Shakespeare wrote plays about history, tragedies, and romance, as well as sonnets. In 1609 Shakespeare published his 154 sonnets. Remind students that a sonnet is a poem that expresses an idea or a sentiment in 14 lines with iambic pentameter. Play the audio clip of the Shakespearian sonnet.

Ask:

According to the sonnet, what usually happens to beauty? *(It fades over time.)*

How is the beauty of the person to whom the sonnet is addressed different? *(It will never fade, even after that person dies, as long as it is remembered in the words of the sonnet.)* BL

IMAGE

Describing Present students with the short selection from *Romeo and Juliet* from the interactive image of the Globe Theater.

Ask:

What happens in this scene? *(Students may say that Romeo and Juliet declare their love for one another.)*

What helped you understand what was happening in the play? *(Students may say that gestures, vocal inflection, or facial expression helped their understanding.)*

Have students complete the Lesson 2 Review.

CLOSE & REFLECT

Making Inferences

Discuss with students some of the ways in which Shakespeare's plays have been adapted and retold in modern times. Note that many films and stories have been based on the ideas in famous plays such as *Romeo and Juliet* or *Hamlet*.

Ask:

Why do you think Shakespeare's works continue to be popular? *(Possible answers include: They are about universal themes, such as love, fear, jealousy, and family relationships; the words are eloquent, and many familiar expressions come from his work; the comedies are funny; and popular actors continue to appear in them.)*

Answers for pages 592–595

P. 592 ☑ PROGRESS CHECK The printing press made books available to many people and allowed ideas to spread more rapidly.

P. 592 CRITICAL THINKING Students might note that the *Mona Lisa's* smile is mysterious and makes the viewer wonder what she was thinking as her portrait was painted.

P. 594 ☑ PROGRESS CHECK Chiaroscuro uses light and shadow, rather than stiff outlines, to separate objects in a painting.

P. 594 CRITICAL THINKING The Medici's support of Michelangelo helped the young artist develop his talents.

P. 594 **Reading Strategy** Student answers should accurately summarize the section on Northern European painters.

P. 595 CRITICAL THINKING that the people were wealthy

P. 595 ☑ PROGRESS CHECK Northern Renaissance painters painted in oils rather than in watercolors.

LESSON 2 REVIEW

1. Humanism helped people solve their problems using reason and logic.
2. Muslim scholars had access to ancient writings. Renaissance scholars from the West visited Muslim libraries to see these writings from ancient Greece and Rome.
3. The printing press made many more books available to many more people. Scholars could read each other's works and spread ideas much faster than before.
4. Artists who learned more about the human body and how it worked would have been able to depict people more accurately and realistically.
5. Northern Europeans painted in oils rather than in water-based paint. Southern Europeans based their art on ancient Greek and Roman models.
6. Answers will vary but should include the idea that humanism, which was based on ancient Greek and Roman ideas, encouraged people to use reason and knowledge to think for themselves as individuals. Humanism encouraged people to take responsibility for themselves and help their communities work for change.

Henry V

by William Shakespeare

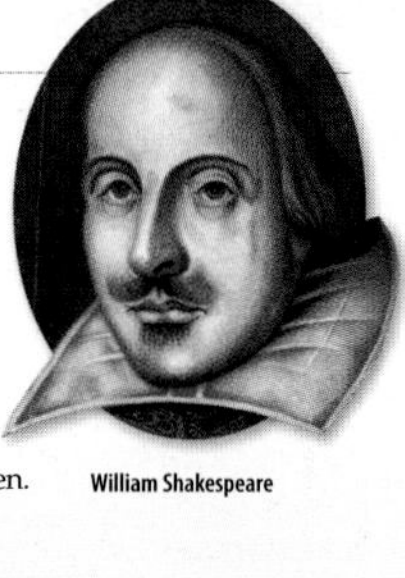
William Shakespeare

William Shakespeare, the greatest English playwright, was enormously successful. His theater company, the King's Men, employed London's best actor and playwright—Shakespeare himself.

Shakespeare's plays included histories of several British kings. In writing *Henry V*, Shakespeare drew on histories of the real King Henry V, who invaded France in 1415. The play *Henry V* tells how a small English army faces a much larger French force. Against all odds, the outnumbered Englishmen win.

Henry V is most famous for the king's uplifting speech to his men. Tired and outnumbered, the soldiers think they will be defeated in the next day's battle. Henry encourages them by describing their bravery, and how they will be remembered.

Henry V:
We few, we happy few, we band of brothers;
For he to-day that sheds his blood with me
Shall be my brother.

—From *Henry V*, Act IV, Scene iii, by William Shakespeare

The Globe theater was home to Shakespeare's acting troupe and was where Shakespeare's plays were presented. The theater could hold about 3,000 people, either standing or sitting. The flag on its roof signaled the type of play being presented: black for tragedies, white for comedies, and red for history plays.

PRIMARY SOURCE

Henry V:

“This day is called the feast of Crispian:
He that outlives this day, and comes safe home,
Will stand a tip-toe when the day is named,
And **rouse** him at the name of Crispian.

He that shall live this day, and see old age,
Will yearly on the **vigil** feast his neighbors,
And say 'To-morrow is Saint Crispian:'
Then will he strip his sleeve and show his scars.
And say 'These wounds I had on Crispin's day.'

Old men forget: yet all shall be forgot,
But he'll remember with advantages
What **feats** he did that day: then shall our names.
Familiar in his mouth as household words
Harry the king, Bedford and Exeter,
Warwick and Talbot, Salisbury and Gloucester,[1]
Be in their flowing cups freshly remember'd.

This story shall the good man teach his son;
And Crispin Crispian shall ne'er go by,
From this day to the ending of the world,
But we in it shall be remember'd;
We few, we happy few, we band of brothers;
For he to-day that sheds his blood with me
Shall be my brother; be he ne'er so **vile**,
This day shall gentle his condition:
And gentlemen in England now a-bed
Shall think themselves **accursed** they were not here,
And hold their manhoods cheap whiles any speaks
That fought with us upon Saint Crispin's day.”

—From William Shakespeare's *Henry V*, Act IV, Scene iii

[1] Bedford, Exeter, Warwick, Talbot, Salisbury, and Gloucester were noblemen in Henry's army.

Vocabulary
rouse to stir up or excite
vigil the night before a religious feast
feats achievements, successes
vile morally low
accursed doomed, miserable

Analyzing Literature DBQ

1. ***Analyzing*** What is the purpose of King Henry's speech to his soldiers? What words show this purpose?
2. ***Interpreting*** What does the king mean when he says, “For he to-day that sheds his blood with me / Shall be my brother; . . .”?
3. ***Assessing*** Would the king's speech persuade men to face death in battle? Why or why not?

networks
There's More Online!
- GRAPHIC ORGANIZER Reasons for the Reformation
- MAP Holy Roman Empire, 1520
- CHART/GRAPH
  - Martin Luther and the Reformation
  - Sale of Indulgences

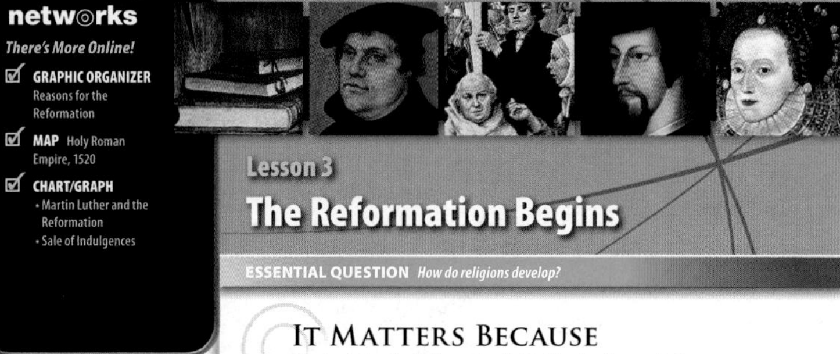

Lesson 3

The Reformation Begins

ESSENTIAL QUESTION *How do religions develop?*

IT MATTERS BECAUSE

Events during the Reformation led to the development of new Christian churches that still exist today.

1 Early Calls for Reform

GUIDING QUESTION *Why was the Church under pressure to reform itself?*

Many educated Europeans were influenced by Renaissance humanism. They began to criticize the wealth and power of the Catholic Church. In 1517, a German monk named Martin Luther questioned the authority of the Church.

At first, Luther only wanted to reform the Catholic Church. This is why these events are called the **Reformation** (reh•fuhr•MAY•shuhn). The Reformation, however, produced a new form of Christianity called Protestantism (PRAH•tuhs•tuhnt•ih•zuhm). By 1600, many Protestant churches had risen in Europe.

John Wycliffe Speaks Out

As early as the 1300s, many Europeans knew that the Catholic Church faced problems. Church officials had grown wealthy by collecting taxes. Some bishops acted like kings by building palaces and providing jobs for their relatives. Yet, in many villages, priests could barely read. In addition, churches began offering indulgences. An **indulgence** (ihn•DUHL•juhntz) was a certificate issued by the church. The certificate granted a pardon for a person's sins. Church members who performed “good works,” such as giving money to build a church, could receive this pardon.

People were angry about the Church's focus on money. They also began to question the authority of the Church. Many years before, disputes within the Catholic Church had led to more than one leader claiming to be the rightful pope. Since then, respect for the pope had declined. In the 1370s, an English priest named John Wycliffe (WIH•klihf) preached that Christians needed only to recognize Jesus as head of the Church, not the pope.

Wycliffe also claimed that all religious truth came from the Christian Bible. He wanted everyone to read the Bible, so he translated many passages from Latin into English for his followers to use. After Wycliffe died, his followers finished the translation, creating the first Christian Bible in English.

Who Was Erasmus?

Renaissance humanism led to a new movement called Christian humanism. Christian humanists were loyal Catholics who wanted to restore the simple faith of the early Church. They believed that humanist learning and Bible study were the best ways to improve the church.

The best known Christian humanist was Desiderius Erasmus (DEHS•ih•DIHR•ee•uhs ih•RAZ•muhs). Erasmus believed that people should use their reason to become better Christians. He said that it was not enough to participate in religious activities like going to church on Sunday. He believed it was more important that Christians be good in their everyday lives. By improving themselves, they would be able to reform the Church and society.

In 1509, Erasmus wrote a book called *Praise of Folly*. In this work, he used humor to criticize Church corruption. He especially attacked the wealth of Renaissance popes. He said the popes were so concerned with luxury and pleasure that they no longer practiced Christianity.

Erasmus entered a monastery early in his life. His studies led him to criticize the wealth and power of Church leaders.

PROGRESS CHECK

Explaining What were the goals of the Christian humanists?

Reading HELPDESK

Taking Notes: *Determining Cause and Effect*
Use a diagram like this one to list some of the reasons for the Reformation.

Reasons for the Reformation

Content Vocabulary
- **Reformation**
- **indulgence**
- **predestination**
- **annul**

Reformation a religious movement that produced a new form of Christianity known as Protestantism
indulgence a pardon, or forgiveness, of a sin

ENGAGE

Making Connections **Ask:** **What is a live performance that you have seen?** *(Students may share examples of theater, music, comedy, or skits performed in class.)* Share an example of a performance you have seen that was especially moving or funny.

Tell students they will be learning about a great playwright who attracted huge audiences to see his plays performed live.

INTERACTIVE WHITEBOARD On your interactive whiteboard, project the Interactive Time Line from the Chapter Opener.

Ask: **What was going on at about the time Shakespeare was writing?** *(King Henry IV of France was becoming Catholic to win the loyalty of the French people.)* **Based on what you have read so far, what war(s) might Shakespeare have known about as he wrote this play?** *(Shakespeare would have known that France was having a war between Protestants and Catholics.)* BL

TEACH & ASSESS

Analyzing Write the following term on the board: *monologue.* Tell students that the excerpt they are reading is a *monologue,* which is a long speech spoken by a single person.

Ask: **Do you think Henry was the only actor on the stage when he gave this speech?** *(No; he is addressing other people.)*

As a class, identify what Henry says his soldiers will do on Crispin's Day in the future. *(They will stand "tip-toe"; they will show their scars.)*

Ask: **Why does the king tell his soldiers what they will do in the future?** *(He is telling them they will survive the battle and win. He is telling them they will be heroes in the future because of their victory.)* BL

Read aloud the passage beginning "Familiar in his mouth as household words."

Ask: **What do you think the king is doing as he speaks the names of the English nobles?** *(He might be pointing to them on the stage. He might be nodding at them and encouraging them.)*

Read aloud the last four lines of King Henry's speech.

Ask: **Who does King Henry say are the people who are "accursed"?** *(the people who are not fighting with him and his men)* **Why will they "hold their manhoods cheap"?** *(The men who fight with King Henry will be remembered by history as great heroes. The men who miss this battle will never receive such high honors.)*

Have students complete the Analyzing Literature questions.

CLOSE & REFLECT

Summarizing To summarize, ask students to explain why they think King Henry's speech would appeal to his men. *(Answers will vary but may include that the men would be encouraged when Henry says they are a "band of brothers." After Henry reminds them of their close ties, they will fight harder to help and protect one another.)*

Answers to *Analyzing Literature* DBQ

1. King Henry wants to raise his soldiers' spirits and encourage them to fight. Phrases such as "we in it shall be remember'd; We few, we happy few, we band of brothers" promise soldiers that their bravery will be remembered and respected.
2. King Henry says the men who fight with him are noble, even though they might be peasants. He honors all the men who fight with him and says their bravery overcomes their humble status.
3. The king's speech is persuasive and stirring. Students might say that it appeals to men's sense of honor and would move them to fight for their country.

Teaching *The Reformation Begins* (Student Edition pp. 598–605)

LESSON 3 • Day 1

ENGAGE

Discussing

Have students think about people and groups who act as leaders in our society.

Ask:

What do we expect of these leaders? *(that they will be fair, that they will set good examples, and so on)*

Explain to students that for centuries, the Catholic Church played the most important leadership role in Europe.

Tell students they will be learning about what conditions led people in the Reformation to challenge the authority of the Catholic Church.

TEACH & ASSESS

Early Calls for Reform

GUIDING QUESTION *Why was the Church under pressure to reform itself?*

LECTURE SLIDE

Defining

Show students the lecture slide defining the terms *Reformation* and *indulgence.* ELL

Ask:

What was the Catholic Church like in the 1500s? *(rich, powerful)*

Why were many people angry with the Church? *(People believed the Church's focus on money and power in the 1500s meant they were not acting like good religious leaders.)* AL

INTERACTIVE WHITEBOARD ACTIVITY

Making Generalizations

Refer students to the section "Early Calls for Reform." Point out to students the number of reformers who were interested in translating the Bible. Work with the class to complete the Interactive Whiteboard Activity identifying details about Martin Luther, John Wycliffe, and Erasmus.

Ask:

Which reformers wanted to translate the Bible into other languages? *(Wycliffe translated it into English; Erasmus wanted translations in vernacular languages.)*

IMAGES

Making Generalizations Show students the interactive images of reformers John Wycliffe and Erasmus. After they have clicked the text to see the images, **ask:**

What generalization can you make about why reformers thought Christians should be able to read the Bible for themselves? *(In general, reformers thought that Christians should be able to read their key religious document without having another person interpret it for them.)* BL

Answers for pages 598–599

P. 598 **Taking Notes** Answers may include: Martin Luther's Ninety-five Theses; the Church's focus on money; Luther's excommunication.

P. 599 ☑ PROGRESS CHECK Christian humanists wanted to reform the Catholic Church. Some wanted to make the Bible available to people in the vernacular language.

2 Luther's Reformation

GUIDING QUESTION *How did Luther's reforms lead to a new form of Christianity?*

Martin Luther's family wanted him to become a lawyer, but he decided on a career in the church.

During the early 1500s, Martin Luther supported the cause of Church reform. Opposed by the pope, Luther broke away from many Catholic teachings. His rebellion led to a religious revolution that changed Europe.

Who was Martin Luther?

Born in 1483, Martin Luther became a monk and faithfully followed Church teachings and practices. However, he still worried about the fate of his soul. His concern about reaching heaven was not surprising. He had seen epidemics, famine, and war.

Luther's doubts grew after he visited Rome. He was shocked to find priests there made fun of Catholic rituals. They disobeyed Church rules. Some of them could not read the Bible. How could these disrespectful priests help people get to heaven?

Back in Wittenberg (VIH•tuhn•buhrg), Germany, Luther searched for answers. The Church taught that a person needed both faith and good works to go to heaven. His experiences in Rome caused Luther to question church policy.

In 1517, Luther became even angrier at Church leaders. Pope Leo X needed money to rebuild St. Peter's Basilica, a large church in Rome. To get that money, he sent monks out to sell indulgences. Local church leaders had offered, and even sold, indulgences for many years. Now the Pope was selling them, too. How could Church leaders put a price on God's forgiveness? Luther thought the Church had moved too far away from the Bible in what they were teaching.

Luther prepared a list of 95 arguments against the indulgences. He sent the list to his bishop. Some accounts say that Luther also nailed them to the door of Wittenberg Cathedral. The list became known as the Ninety-Five Theses. Thousands of copies were printed and read all across Germany.

A New Church

Luther began to openly attack other Catholic beliefs. He said that popes could make mistakes. He argued that the only true guide to religious truth was the Bible, which all Christians had a right to read. Finally, he stated that all Christians could confess their sins directly to God without the help of a priest.

Reading **HELP**DESK

Reading Strategy: *Activating Prior Knowledge*

Martin Luther was concerned with salvation. You learned about the idea of salvation in an earlier chapter. What does the word *salvation* mean?

Pope Leo X believed that Luther was dangerous. In 1521, he excommunicated Luther. A person who is excommunicated can no longer belong to the church. Then, a diet, or council, of German princes met in the city of Worms. The princes wanted Luther to change his ideas. Luther refused:

PRIMARY SOURCE

> "Unless I am convinced by Scripture and plain reason—I do not accept the authority of the popes and councils, for they have contradicted [spoken against] each other—my conscience is captive [loyal] to the Word of God. I cannot and will not recant [take back] anything for to go against conscience is neither right nor safe. God help me. Amen."
>
> —from Martin Luther's speech at the Diet of Worms, 1521

Luther's ideas eventually led to the creation of the first Protestant church, known as Lutheranism (LOO•thuh•ruhn•ihzm). The new church was based on three main ideas. The first idea is that faith in Jesus, not good works, brings someone a place in heaven. The second is that the Bible is the final source for truth about God. Finally, Lutheranism said that the church was made up of all its believers, not just the clergy.

Revolts in Germany

Lutheranism gave rural peasants in Germany hope for a better life. During the 1520s, the peasants suffered as a result of poor crops and high taxes paid to noble landowners. The peasants thought that if Luther could rebel against the pope, then they could stand up to greedy nobles.

Huge revolts swept Germany. The peasants looked to Luther for support. At first, Luther agreed with their cause. In his sermons, Luther criticized nobles for their mistreatment of the peasants. However, Luther also feared violence. He told the peasants that God had set the government above them and they must obey it. The nobles soon defeated the peasants.

In this painting, indulgences are being sold at a village market.

Rulers and Lutheranism

In the past, the Catholic Church could stop the spread of ideas that it opposed. Why was it unable to stop Protestantism in the 1500s? One reason is that Protestantism had the support of some European rulers. These rulers believed that they could increase their power by supporting Protestantism against the Catholic Church. The Lutheran movement became closely tied to politics.

GEOGRAPHY CONNECTION

In 1520, the Holy Roman Emperor ruled over a large part of Europe.

1. **REGIONS** What are some of the areas that made up the Holy Roman Empire?
2. CRITICAL THINKING *Drawing Conclusions* Why would it have been difficult for one ruler to control the Holy Roman Empire?

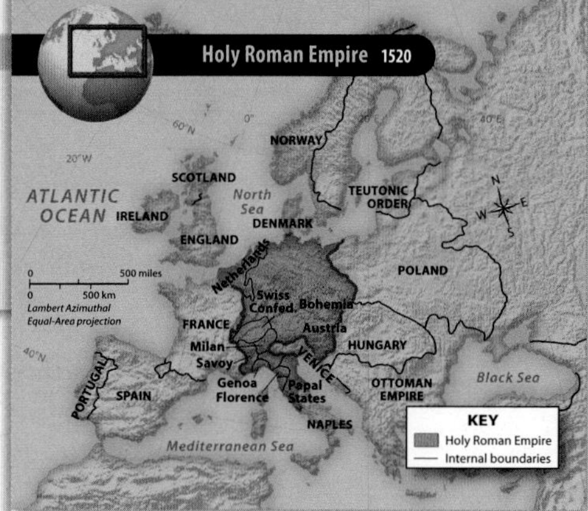

The Holy Roman Empire was Catholic and covered much of central Europe. It included about 300 German states. In 1519, Charles V became the Holy Roman Emperor. He also ruled Spain, the Netherlands, parts of Italy, and territories in the Americas.

Local German rulers worried about the growing power of Charles V. They wanted to keep their independence. Many of these leaders became Lutherans. By doing so, their states also became Lutheran. After breaking with the Catholic Church, these rulers took over Catholic lands in their territories. Now they, and not the Catholic Church, would earn income from those lands.

When rulers adopted Lutheranism, taxes no longer flowed to the pope in Rome. Rulers could **impose** their own church taxes and keep the money for themselves. This made Lutheran rulers stronger and the Catholic Church weaker.

In order to regain control of these lands, Charles V went to war with the Lutheran rulers. However, he was not able to defeat them. In 1555, an agreement known as the Peace of Augsburg (AUGHZ•buhrg) ended the fighting. Under its terms, each German ruler—whether Catholic or Lutheran—could decide

Reading **HELP**DESK

predestination a religious belief that God has already decided who will go to heaven and who will not

Academic Vocabulary

impose to establish by force or authority

the religion of his people. The Peace of Augsburg allowed the division of Germany into a Protestant north and a Catholic south. This division remains to this day.

☑ PROGRESS CHECK

Determining Cause and Effect How did the Ninety-Five Theses affect the Catholic Church in Germany?

3 The Reformation Spreads

GUIDING QUESTION *How did the teachings of Protestant reformers shape the western world?*

As the Reformation spread, different forms of Protestantism developed. Soon after Lutheranism began in Germany, many people in nearby Switzerland accepted Protestant ideas. They set up new reformed churches.

Who Was John Calvin?

John Calvin was born in France in 1509. Known for his sharp mind, Calvin studied law, humanism, and religion in Paris. He was especially interested in religion. He got up early and stayed up late to read books about it. The more Calvin read, the more he was convinced that Luther was right.

Eventually, Calvin fled from Paris because it became too dangerous to talk about Protestantism. He finally found safety in Geneva (juh•NEE•vuh), Switzerland. There, his powerful preaching convinced many people to follow him.

What Is Calvinism?

As he studied the Bible, Calvin developed his own ideas. He agreed with Luther that faith alone brought salvation, but he added other ideas. Calvin's main idea was that God decides the final outcome of all events in the universe. Therefore, God has already chosen who will go to heaven and who will not. This belief is called **predestination** (pree•dehs•tuh•NAY•shuhn).

Most of Calvin's followers believed that they were among the people who would be saved. To prove it, they worked hard, behaved well, and obeyed the laws of their towns. In this way, Calvinism became a powerful tool in society. It encouraged people to work hard at their business and watch their behavior.

Another idea of Calvinism is that church members, not kings or bishops, should choose the clergy. This idea influenced people in England, Scotland, and the Netherlands. Because of Calvinism, people began to think that they could elect government leaders.

The writings of John Calvin helped Europeans accept Protestantism.

▶ CRITICAL THINKING

Explaining Why would followers of Calvin work to live a good life, even though they believed that God had already decided their fate?

☑ PROGRESS CHECK

Analyzing How did Calvinism influence ideas about government?

LESSON 3 • Day 1 (cont.)

2 Luther's Reformation

GUIDING QUESTION ***How did Luther's reforms lead to a new form of Christianity?***

INTERACTIVE WORKSHEET

Determining Cause and Effect

Have students analyze the causes and effects of Martin Luther's call for reforms of the Catholic Church. Organize students into groups of four. Then have them complete the 21st Century Skills Activity for this lesson.

CHART

Determining Cause and Effect

When students have completed the worksheet, ask them to complete the interactive chart about Martin Luther and the Protestant Reformation.

Ask:

What did Luther believe about salvation? *(Salvation could not be bought or sold, and all people needed salvation.)*

What did Catholic Church leaders do that caused Luther to become angry? *(He was angry because the Catholic Church was abusing power, selling indulgences, and not getting rid of corrupt priests.)*

What did Luther do as a result of his beliefs? *(posted the Ninety-five Theses, argued against the practices of the Catholic Church, helped start the Reformation)*

CLOSE & REFLECT

Finding the Main Idea

Have students list three main ideas that set Lutheranism apart from the Catholic Church. *(Faith in Jesus, not good works, brings salvation; the Bible is the source of truth about God; the Church is made up of all believers, not just clergy.)*

Answers for pages 600–603

P. 600 Reading Strategy Salvation means the act of being saved from the effects of sin.

P. 602 GEOGRAPHY CONNECTION

1. Austria, Bohemia, Netherlands, Swiss Confederation, states in northern Italy
2. **CRITICAL THINKING** It was large and contained many different ethnic groups.

P. 603 ☑ **PROGRESS CHECK** The Ninety-Five Theses began the Reformation, which led many people to leave the Catholic Church in Germany and begin Protestant churches.

P. 603 CRITICAL THINKING Students may answer that because people didn't know what fate God had decided for them, they assumed they were among those who would be saved. Thus, they behaved well and obeyed the laws.

P. 603 ☑ **PROGRESS CHECK** Because of Calvinism, people thought of electing government officials and that government leaders should not control the church.

Teaching *The Reformation Begins* (cont.) (Student Edition pp. 598–605)

LESSON 3 • Day 2

ENGAGE

MAP **Identifying** Show students the map of the Holy Roman Empire. Have students locate Switzerland and England on the map. Then tell students that the German states were located in the part of the Holy Roman Empire north of Switzerland and east of the Netherlands.

Ask students to explain the significance of each of those countries as they relate to the Reformation. *(Lutheranism began in Germany; Calvinism began in Switzerland; Puritanism began in England.)*

Then ask:

In what part of Europe are these countries located? *(northern Europe)*

How was England different politically from Germany or Switzerland? *(England was not part of the Holy Roman Empire.)* ELL AL

Tell students they will be learning about the spread of the Reformation through Europe and its effects on the Catholic Church and the Holy Roman Empire.

TEACH & ASSESS

3 The Reformation Spreads

GUIDING QUESTION ***How did the teachings of Protestant reformers shape the western world?***

IMAGE **Contrasting** Show students the interactive image of John Calvin. Read aloud the accompanying text. Review the meaning of the term *predestination* with students. ELL

Then ask: What did Calvin believe about salvation? *(Only a select few, chosen by God, would receive salvation. Nothing could be done to change who would receive salvation.)*

How does this view contrast with the beliefs of Martin Luther? *(Luther believed that salvation was available to all people.)* AL

Assessing Refer students to the section "The Reformation Spreads." Then discuss as a class how people throughout Europe and North America got their ideas about the Reformation.

Ask: Why was Switzerland important in the development of the Reformation? *(Answers will vary, but students might say that Calvin developed his ideas in Switzerland, making the country a center of Reformation influence.)*

Comparing and Contrasting Have students create a chart with columns titled "Luther," "Calvin," and "Henry VIII." Then have them summarize the reasons each of these leaders protested against the Catholic Church.

Ask: How were Henry VIII's reasons for protesting different from the reasons of Luther or Calvin? *(Henry wanted to annul his marriage, so his reason was more selfish, or worldly, than those of Luther or Calvin.)*

4 The Reformation in England

GUIDING QUESTION ***How did the Reformation shape England and later its American colonies?***

LECTURE SLIDE **Identifying Points of View** Show students the lecture slide on English rulers and the religion they practiced.

Ask: During this time, what could have happened to people in England who practiced a religion that was different than their ruler's religion? *(They could be punished or killed.)* Remind students how frequently England's rulers changed during this time.

Ask: How did the change of rulers affect religion in England? *(The country's religion changed every time the monarch changed. Henry made the country Anglican. Mary made it Catholic. Elizabeth made it Anglican again.)* AL

4 The Reformation in England

GUIDING QUESTION *How did the Reformation shape England and later its American colonies?*

The Reformation reached England about 10 years after it began in central Europe. In England, religious change at first did not come from church officials or the people. It started as a political quarrel between the king and the pope. Religious beliefs did not play a part until much later.

The Break with Rome

Henry VIII ruled England from 1509 to 1547. He belonged to the Tudor family. Henry wanted to keep the Tudors on the throne. However, he had no son to follow him. Catherine, the first of Henry's six wives, had children. Only one of her children, Mary, survived.

As Catherine grew older, Henry feared she could not have any more children. At the same time, he had fallen in love with Anne Boleyn (buh•LIHN), a young noblewoman. Henry asked the pope to **annul,** or declare invalid, his marriage to Catherine so that he could marry Anne. The Catholic Church did not allow divorce. If the pope granted an annulment, it would be as if Henry and Catherine had never married.

The pope refused Henry's request. Catherine was the daughter of King Ferdinand and Queen Isabella of Spain. Her nephew was Charles V, the Holy Roman Emperor. The pope did not want to anger Catherine's important family.

Henry had the Archbishop of Canterbury—the highest church official in England—end his marriage to Catherine. Henry then married Anne Boleyn. In response, the pope excommunicated Henry. Henry fought back. In 1534, he had Parliament pass the Act of Supremacy. The act made the king head of the new Church of England.

Henry ordered all bishops and priests in England to accept the Act of Supremacy. Some who refused were killed. Henry seized the land of the Catholic Church in England and gave some of it to his nobles. Giving the nobles this property made sure they remained loyal to Henry and his church.

Henry VIII challenged the Church to solve his own problems in England.

▶ CRITICAL THINKING

Explaining Why did the Pope refuse Henry's request to undo his marriage to Catherine?

Reading **HELP**DESK

annul to declare invalid

Academic Vocabulary

restore to bring back

Who Was Bloody Mary?

The Church of England became known as the Anglican (AYN•glih•kuhn) Church. After Henry's death, the Anglican Church accepted some Protestant ideas, but it kept most Catholic rituals. Many English Catholics wanted more. They supported Henry's Catholic daughter Mary when she became queen.

As queen, Mary **restored** the Catholic Church in England and arrested Protestants who opposed her. More than 300 Protestants were burned at the stake. The English were horrified and turned against their queen, calling her "Bloody Mary."

Mary died in 1558. Her half-sister Elizabeth, the Protestant daughter of Henry VIII and Anne Boleyn, took the throne as Queen Elizabeth I. She restored the Anglican Church. Elizabeth became one of the greatest rulers in English history.

Elizabeth I succeeded her half-sister Mary as queen and halted the persecution of English Protestants.

Calvinism in England

Most English people were pleased with the Anglican Church. Some Protestants, however, had become Calvinists. These people became known as Puritans because they wanted to purify, or cleanse, the Anglican Church of Catholic ways. Puritan groups often refused to accept the authority of Anglican bishops.

Queen Elizabeth I tolerated the Puritans. When James I became king in 1603, however, the Puritans faced opposition. James believed that the Puritans threatened his power. He and later his son, King Charles I, closed Puritan churches and imprisoned Puritan leaders. Many Puritans left England and settled in North America to practice their religion freely.

PROGRESS CHECK

Explaining Why did Henry VIII seize Catholic Church lands in England?

LESSON 3 REVIEW

Review Vocabulary

1. Why did Martin Luther want the *Reformation* of the Catholic Church?
2. Why did the pope want to sell *indulgences*?

Answer the Guiding Questions

3. ***Identifying*** Why did many Europeans criticize the Catholic Church at the time of the Reformation?
4. ***Generalizing*** What three types of reforms did Luther want for the Catholic Church?
5. ***Making Inferences*** Why was Germany's split between Protestants in the north and Catholics in the south important?
6. ***Determining Cause and Effect*** How did John Calvin's ideas take root in the American colonies?
7. **PERSUASIVE WRITING** Which argument for religious reform might be convincing to a priest, pope, or king? Choose one idea for reform and support it with evidence. Write a persuasive paragraph to one of these people that defends your idea.

networks

There's More Online!

- CHART/GRAPH De' Medici Family Tree
- GRAPHIC ORGANIZER
  - Reform in the Catholic Church
  - Effects from the Council of Trent
- MAP Religion in Europe, c. 1600

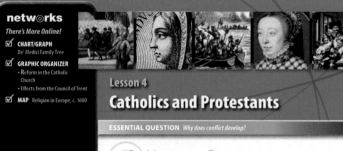

Lesson 4

Catholics and Protestants

ESSENTIAL QUESTION *Why does conflict develop?*

IT MATTERS BECAUSE

The struggle between Catholics and Protestants during the Reformation shaped the churches that we know today.

1 The Catholic Reformation

GUIDING QUESTION *How did the Catholic Church respond to the spread of Protestantism?*

In the 1500s and 1600s, Catholics set out to improve their Church and to stop the spread of Protestant ideas. This effort was known as the Catholic Reformation. It helped the Church regain some of the areas in Europe it had lost to Protestantism.

Catholic Reforms

Catholics were dedicated to fighting Protestantism. They also knew they needed to reform their Church. Pope Paul III called a council of bishops. The council met at different times between 1545 and 1563 at Trent, Italy.

The Council of Trent supported Catholic beliefs that had been challenged by the Protestants. However, it ended many Church abuses, such as the sale of indulgences. The Council also ordered bishops and priests to follow strict rules of behavior. The Church set up seminaries to train new priests. A **seminary** (SEH•muh•nehr•ee) is a special school for training and educating priests.

The Church also set out to win followers and to strengthen the spiritual life of Catholics. In 1540, Pope Paul III recognized a new order of priests, the Society of Jesus, known as the Jesuits. They taught and preached in an effort to bring Protestants back to the Catholic faith.

Reading **HELP**DESK

Taking Notes: *Determining Cause and Effect*

Use a diagram like this one to show the results of the Catholic Church's attempts at reform.

Reform in the Catholic Church

Content Vocabulary

- **seminary**
- **heresy**

The man who founded the Jesuits was a Spanish noble, Ignatius (ihg•NAY•shuhs) of Loyola (loy•OH•luh). He was a soldier whose life changed when he was wounded in battle. While recovering, he read about the lives of the saints. Ignatius decided he would be a soldier for Jesus and the Church.

The Spanish nun Teresa of Avila (AH•vih•luh) was another reformer. Teresa founded an order of nuns and opened new convents throughout Spain. Teresa became known for her spiritual writings that rank among the classics of Christian writing.

Ferdinand and Isabella united the separate kingdoms of Aragon and Castile into the country of Spain.

Catholic Spain

Protestant ideas never became very popular in Spain. Still, when religious conflict began to divide Europe, Spain was affected. Spanish rulers distrusted Protestant countries and their own Protestant citizens.

When Luther called for reform in 1517, Spain was a united country. King Ferdinand of Aragon and Queen Isabella of Castile had married and joined their two kingdoms in 1469. They wanted to unite Spain and make all of their subjects be Catholic.

In the late 1400s, many Muslims lived in Spain. Muslims had ruled much of Spain during the Middle Ages. Under Muslim rule, Christians and Jews paid special taxes and had limited rights, but they were able to practice their religions. Muslims and non-Muslims lived in relative peace. This time period was a golden age for Jews in Spain.

This age of religious harmony ended under Ferdinand and Isabella. Spain's rulers pressured Jews and Muslims to convert to Catholicism. But even those who converted were not safe. Spanish officials suspected them of secretly practicing their old religions. To ensure that their orders were being carried out, Ferdinand and Isabella began the Spanish Inquisition.

Spanish Inquisition

The Spanish Inquisition was a religious court. It was similar to the one that the Catholic Church had set up earlier in Europe to root out **heresy** (HEHR•uh•see), or beliefs that opposed Church teaching.

The Council of Trent is considered one of the most important councils in the history of the Catholic Church.

▶ CRITICAL THINKING

Identifying What do you think was the most important decision of the Council?

seminary a school for religious training

heresy a religious belief that contradicts what the church says is true

LESSON 3 • Day 2 (cont.)

What do you think it would have been like to live in England when the official religion changed so often? *(scary, uncertain)*

How did religious disagreements in England affect the founding of the American colonies? *(Puritans who were persecuted in England founded some of the first English colonies in North America.)*

Have students complete the Lesson 3 Review.

CLOSE & REFLECT

Making Connections Discuss with students how reformers of the 1500s and 1600s changed well-established religious practices. Then, ask students to think of other examples in ancient or modern times in which people started a movement to change a part of society. *(Answers will vary but may include the following: Gandhi challenged the use of violence to achieve a goal; Martin Luther King, Jr., challenged assumptions about racial inequalities; Susan B. Anthony challenged attitudes about women in the United States.)* BL

BACKGROUND KNOWLEDGE

Erasmus of Rotterdam

Desidarius Erasmus was a Dutch scholar and priest. He studied the Bible and early Christian writings for inspiration. He improved Greek and Latin translations of the New Testament. One of his goals was to translate the Bible into the vernacular language, or the language of ordinary people. He wanted farmers and workers as well as nobles to be able to read the Bible.

Henry VIII

Henry VIII enjoyed sports, music, and literature, but he was also demanding and ruthless. He imprisoned and executed bishops and nobles for disagreeing with him. Henry married six times. He divorced his first wife (Catherine of Aragon, mother of Mary I) and beheaded his second wife (Anne Boleyn, mother of Elizabeth I). His third wife (Jane Seymour), mother of his only son Edward, died from complications of childbirth. Henry divorced his fourth wife (Anne of Cleves) and beheaded his fifth wife (Katherine Howard). Henry died while married to his last wife, Katherine Parr.

Answers for pages 604–605

P. 604 CRITICAL THINKING because the Catholic Church did not allow divorce

P. 605 ☑ PROGRESS CHECK Henry seized the lands to gain the support of his nobles for the Church of England.

LESSON 3 REVIEW

1. Luther thought the Catholic Church was corrupt.
2. The pope wanted to sell indulgences to raise money to rebuild St. Peter's Basilica in Rome.
3. The Catholic Church angered its members by focusing on money and thereby losing its moral authority.
4. Luther wanted the Church to declare that it could make mistakes, stop selling indulgences, and take responsibility from priests and give it to Church members.
5. The split of Protestants and Catholics divided the continent and let rulers use religion to make their kingdoms stronger.
6. Some of John Calvin's followers wanted to "purify" the Anglican church. Because they did not accept the church's authority, many of these Puritans moved to the American colonies.
7. Students should support their ideas with different reformers' arguments and their own opinions.

Teaching *Catholics and Protestants* (Student Edition pp. 606–611)

LESSON 4 • Day 1

ENGAGE

Making Connections

In a Think-Pair-Share activity, have students brainstorm a list of reasons people in Europe left the Catholic Church. *(Answers may include the Church's corruption and focus on money.)*

Ask:

What would you do if you were a leader in the Catholic Church? How would you respond to the spread of Protestantism?

Tell students that in this lesson, they will learn how the Catholic Church responded to calls for reform and how the Church responded to other religions. AL

TEACH & ASSESS

The Catholic Reformation

GUIDING QUESTION *How did the Catholic Church respond to the spread of Protestantism?*

GRAPHIC ORGANIZER

Problem Solving

Discuss as a class how the Catholic Church lost members and influence to the Protestant church.

As a class, complete the Effects of the Council of Trent graphic organizer. Guide students to identify how the Council of Trent responded to the spread of Protestantism and developed institutions that helped the Catholic Church regain its authority and membership.

Ask:

How did the Council of Trent help the Catholic Church respond to Protestantism? *(It made changes within the Catholic Church.)* Then use the information under "Catholic Reforms" to help students complete the graphic organizer.

INTERACTIVE WORKSHEET

Assign the Primary Source Activity as homework to help students understand religious conflicts in Spain. BL

MAP

Analyzing Visuals

Show students the map displaying religions in Europe in 1600. Have students identify which countries are Protestant and which are Catholic. Then lead a class discussion about why religion could influence a country's government.

Ask: How might a religion compete with a country's government for wealth and power? Tell students that during this time period, rulers of countries used religion to unite and control their people.

CLOSE AND REFLECT

Comparing and Contrasting

Have students compare and contrast the reform methods developed by the Council of Trent with those of the rulers of Spain.

Ask: Which method do you think was most effective in stopping the spread of Protestantism? *(Students may say that the Spanish Inquisition was most effective because it made people fear for their lives.)*

Answers for pages 606–607

P. 606 Taking Notes Answers may include Council of Trent: set of strict rules for priests' behavior, made Catholic beliefs clear, set up seminaries; Society of Jesuits founded: fought heresy, taught, preached

P. 607 CRITICAL THINKING Possible answer: The most important decision made by the Council of Trent was to make Catholic beliefs clear because it helped people understand what the Catholic Church preached.

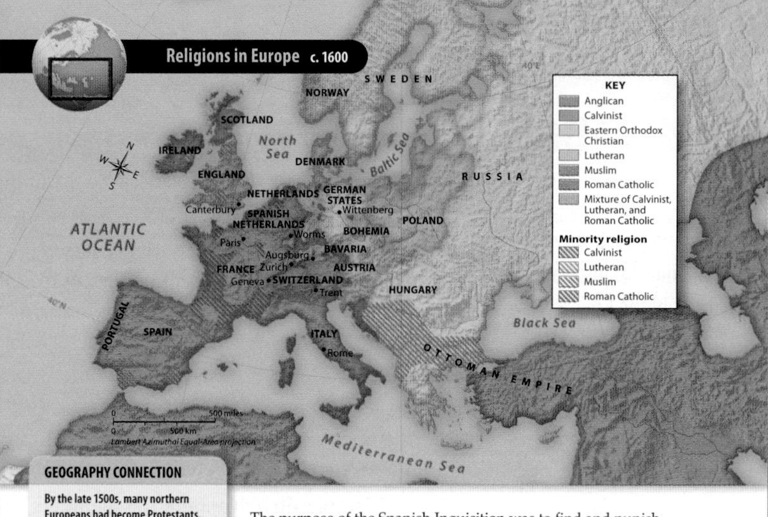

GEOGRAPHY CONNECTION

By the late 1500s, many northern Europeans had become Protestants, and most southern Europeans had remained Catholic.

1. **PLACE** Which areas of Europe became mostly Calvinist?
2. **CRITICAL THINKING** ***Making Inferences*** Where in Europe was religious conflict most likely to take place?

The purpose of the Spanish Inquisition was to find and punish those guilty of heresy. Torture was used to force people to confess their guilt. The head of the Spanish Inquisition was Tomás de Torquemada (tawr • kay • MAH • duh). Even the pope could not stop him from eventually executing about 2,000 Spaniards.

In 1492, the Spanish monarchs ordered all Jews to become Catholic or leave the country. Ten years later, they gave Muslims the same order. Many people left in response to these orders.

Despite strong Church and government controls, literature and the arts flourished in Catholic Spain. The writer Miguel de Cervantes (mih • GEHL day suhr • VAHN • tehz) wrote the novel *Don Quixote* (dahn kee • HOH • tee), about a comical knight and his peasant servant. A Greek artist whom the Spanish called El Greco (ehl GREH • koh) painted religious figures with very long bodies, parts of which stretched beyond normal size.

PROGRESS CHECK

Explaining What was the goal of the Spanish Inquisition?

Reading HELPDESK

Academic Vocabulary

unify to join; to make into one group

2 Religious Wars

GUIDING QUESTION *How did wars of religion affect Europe?*

By the mid-1500s, most northern Europeans were Protestant, and most southern Europeans were Catholic. European monarchs had used religion to help **unify,** or unite, their people and to build powerful nations. The kings and queens of Europe expected their subjects to practice the religion of their ruler. People who did not join the churches of their monarchs were persecuted, or treated cruelly and unjustly. This led to bitterness among people of different faiths. Differences in religion led to wars between countries. Toward the end of the 1500s, Europe entered a period of religious wars that lasted until about 1650.

The Spanish Armada

Under the rule of Queen Elizabeth I, England became the leading Protestant power in Europe. At that time, Spain was the leading Catholic power. The Spanish king was Philip II, the son of Charles V and the great-grandson of Ferdinand and Isabella. King Philip at first supported Elizabeth as England's queen, against the wishes of the pope. However, during the 1560s, the Protestant Dutch rebelled against Spanish rule. Elizabeth helped the Dutch by letting Englishmen attack Spanish ships. Philip decided to get revenge against Elizabeth by invading England.

A combination of bad decisions by the Spanish, faster English ships, and stormy weather sank the Spanish Armada.

In 1588, Philip sent a huge fleet known as the Spanish Armada (ahr • MAH • duh) to England. To block the invasion, the English knew they had to make the Spanish ships break their formation. Their chance came when the Spanish fleet entered the English Channel, the narrow body of water between England and Europe. The huge Spanish ships had many guns, but they were hard to steer. The smaller English ships moved much more quickly in the tight channel. Their attacks forced the Armada to retreat. A great storm later broke up the mighty Spanish navy. The English throne was saved, and the English celebrated their victory.

Although Spain was still a powerful nation, England had shown that it could defend itself. The English gained respect throughout Europe as defenders of the Protestant faith.

BIOGRAPHY

Catherine de' Medici (1519–1589)

The powerful de' Medici family was led by strong Italian men and women. Catherine de' Medici was a firm supporter of the arts. She promoted Renaissance ideas when she wed Prince Henry of France. She took Italian artists, dancers, musicians, and writers with her to the French court. Catherine supported the arts in France, also. She added to the royal library and sponsored a dance and theater presentation that is thought to be the first ballet performance.

▶ **CRITICAL THINKING**

Speculating How might the French people have felt about having Catherine de' Medici as their queen?

Religious Conflict in France

While England and Spain became rivals, a religious conflict divided France. During the 1500s, most people in France were Catholic. However, many wealthy people in France became Protestants. These Protestants, who were called Huguenots (HYU • guh • nahtz), followed the teachings of John Calvin.

Many French nobles wanted to weaken the king, Henry II. The Huguenot nobles especially wanted the king weak so they could practice their religion freely. At the same time, Henry II wanted to build a strong central government.

Henry died in 1559, and his son Francis II died the next year. As a result, Charles, the younger brother of Francis, became king of France at the age of 10. Because Charles was too young to rule, his mother, Catherine de' Medici, ruled for him. She was the daughter of Lorenzo de' Medici, the powerful Italian leader of Florence.

Influential Rulers

Catherine was determined to keep the French kingdom strong for her son. When a civil war broke out, Catherine tried to keep the peace by supporting both Huguenots and Catholics. But in 1572, she allowed Catholic nobles to kill the leading Huguenots in Paris. Catholics in other parts of France also revolted. They formed mobs that killed Protestants and burned their homes. Many Protestants fled the country. The few who stayed were led by the Huguenot prince, Henry of Navarre (nuh • VAHR). Henry was a member of the powerful Bourbon family. He was in line for the throne of France.

In 1589, Henry of Navarre became King Henry IV of France. He wanted to gain the loyalty of the people. Because most French people were still Catholic, Henry decided to convert to Catholicism. According to tradition, he said that Paris, the French capital, was "worth a [Catholic] mass." Henry meant that being king of France was more important than being Protestant.

As king, Henry worked to end the fighting between Catholics and Protestants in France. In 1598, he issued an edict, or order, while visiting the city of Nantes. The Edict of Nantes said Catholicism was the official religion of France. However, it also allowed Huguenots to worship freely.

Reading HELPDESK

The Thirty Years' War

The most violent religious war of the Reformation period was fought in the Holy Roman Empire in the early 1600s. The war began in Bohemia, today known as the Czech Republic. Protestant nobles in Bohemia rebelled against their Catholic king. When other Protestant rulers in Germany joined the rebels, the war spread across the empire.

The Thirty Years' War began when Protestant nobles threw two government officials out a window. The officials represented the Catholic Holy Roman Emperor.

The conflict grew into the Thirty Years' War that lasted from 1618 to 1648. Sweden and Denmark sent troops to help the Protestants. Spain and the Holy Roman Emperor supported the Catholics. Although France was Catholic, it wanted to gain power over neighboring states, so it entered the war on the Protestant side. As France fought against other Catholic countries, the war became a struggle for territory and wealth, not just religion.

The German people suffered great hardships during the war. A city official described the effects of the fighting on the German city of Magdeburg (MAHG • duh • burk):

PRIMARY SOURCE

> "Thus in a single day this noble and famous city, the pride of the whole country, went up in fire and smoke; and the remnant [remainder] of its citizens, with their wives and children, were taken prisoners and driven away by the enemy with a noise of weeping and wailing that could be heard from afar."
>
> —Otto von Guericke, from "Destruction of Magdeburg in 1631"

Finally, in 1643, the Holy Roman Emperor asked for peace. In 1648, the warring nations signed the Peace of Westphalia (wehst • FAYL • yuh). This treaty ended the conflict. The war had weakened Spain and the Holy Roman Empire, while France emerged as a stronger nation.

PROGRESS CHECK

Analyzing Why was the Edict of Nantes important in the history of France?

LESSON 4 REVIEW

Review Vocabulary

1. What kind of training might a priest receive in a *seminary*?

Answer the Guiding Questions

2. ***Identifying*** Who were the Jesuits?
3. ***Making Inferences*** How did the spread of Protestantism in Europe threaten the Catholic Church?
4. ***Explaining*** Why did France fight against Catholic countries in the Thirty Years' War?
5. **PERSONAL WRITING** You are visiting France and have friends who are both Catholic and Huguenot. Write a letter to a friend explaining the difficulties between the two religions and how the Edict of Nantes changes the situation.

LESSON 4 • Day 2

ENGAGE

Identifying

Have students use a two-column graphic organizer to brainstorm reasons why people or countries might fight a war. Then ask students how many of those reasons could involve religious differences. Write this information on the graphic organizer.

Religious Wars

GUIDING QUESTION *How did wars of religion affect Europe?*

LECTURE SLIDE

Analyzing

Show students the lecture slide identifying the causes of the Thirty Years' War. Point out the role of France, a Catholic nation, which sided with Protestants in the Thirty Years' War.

Ask:

Why would you expect France to side with the Catholics? *(France's king and most of its subjects were Catholic.)* AL

What does the outcome of the war show about France's decision? *(France was a stronger country after the war, so its decision was a good one.)*

What does France's decision to side with the Protestants indicate about why countries go to war? *(Answers may include that money and power can be more important than religion.)*

IMAGE

Making Generalizations

Show students the interactive image of Henry of Navarre, and read the section on the Edict of Nantes to the class.

Ask:

How could the Edict of Nantes offer an example for how countries could avoid religious conflicts? *(Answers may include that the Edict of Nantes allowed Protestants to practice their religion in a Catholic country and so showed religious tolerance. Students may say that policies of tolerance can help countries avoid religious conflicts.)*

Have students complete the Lesson 4 Review.

CLOSE & REFLECT

Summarizing

Have students work in pairs or trios to summarize the changes in Europe as a result of the Catholic Reformation and the wars of religion. You may choose to have students create visual summaries, written summaries, or oral summaries.

IF YOU HAVE MORE TIME . . .

Create Time Lines About Religion and Conflict

Making Connections

Review with students the various conflicts that came about because of religion during the 1500s and 1600s. Ask students to think about why religion might cause such wars to happen.

Have students work in pairs to discuss the various religious reasons countries would go to war. Have them discuss some of the conflicts we see around the world today that are fueled by people with diverse religious beliefs.

Have students create a time line that shows the different conflicts that occurred during the 1500s and 1600s over religion. Have them write on the time line the reasons behind these conflicts.

BACKGROUND KNOWLEDGE

Queen Elizabeth I

Elizabeth I became queen of England upon the death of her half-sister Mary in 1558. Elizabeth's father, Henry VIII, became a leading figure in the Reformation in England when the Catholic Church excommunicated him in 1534. As a result, Elizabeth became a Protestant and brought her religion with her when she took the throne from her Catholic sister.

Elizabeth's religion was ever-present during her reign. As the primary Protestant power in the world, she encountered conflicts with the primary Catholic power, Spain. The English navy's famous defeat of the powerful Spanish Armada spoke to her abilities as a ruler as well as to her commitment to Protestantism.

Answers for pages 608–611

P. 608 GEOGRAPHY CONNECTION

1. Switzerland, Scotland
2. CRITICAL THINKING where there was a mixture of groups

P. 608 ☑ PROGRESS CHECK The goal of the Spanish Inquisition was to identify and punish those people who were guilty of heresy.

P. 610 CRITICAL THINKING They would have liked having her as their queen because she supported so many Renaissance ideas.

P. 611 ☑ PROGRESS CHECK The Edict declared Catholicism the country's official religion, but it gave Protestants the right to worship freely.

LESSON 4 REVIEW

1. A priest might learn about Catholic Church rules and policy, might study the Bible, or might learn biblical languages.
2. The Jesuits were a new order of priests recognized by the pope in 1540. They taught, preached, and won followers for the Catholic faith.
3. Protestants were leaving the Catholic Church. The Church was losing influence, members, and power.
4. France was a Catholic country, but it saw the war as a struggle for territory and power, not just religious beliefs.
5. Student responses should provide details about conflicts between Protestants and Catholics in France. Their responses should show an understanding of how the Edict of Nantes gave Protestants religious freedom in France.

CHAPTER 20 Activities

Write your answers on a separate piece of paper.

1 Exploring the Essential Question
DESCRIPTIVE WRITING How would you describe Renaissance ideas about humanism to a medieval person who knows nothing about them? Write a descriptive essay to explain humanism to a medieval person. Describe how these ideas will change this person's life.

2 21st Century Skills
ANALYZING IMAGES Create a PowerPoint™ presentation that highlights art of the Renaissance. Use photos of the artwork from important artists such as Michelangelo and Leonardo da Vinci and point out important details in the artwork. Share your presentation with the class.

3 Thinking Like a Historian
SEQUENCING The Reformation of the Catholic Church was an important development in Europe's history. Create a time line that shows important events that led to the Reformation of the Catholic Church.

4 GEOGRAPHY ACTIVITY

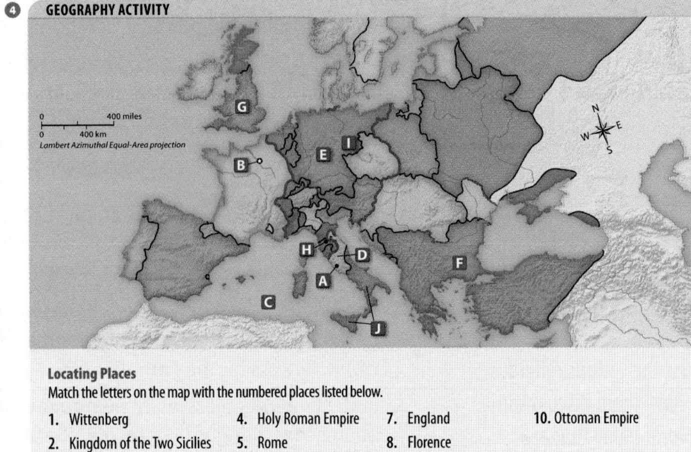

Locating Places
Match the letters on the map with the numbered places listed below.

1. Wittenberg
2. Kingdom of the Two Sicilies
3. Papal States
4. Holy Roman Empire
5. Rome
6. Paris
7. England
8. Florence
9. Mediterranean Sea
10. Ottoman Empire

CHAPTER 20 Assessment

REVIEW THE GUIDING QUESTIONS
Directions: Choose the best answer for each question.

1. The leaders of the city-states of Italy were
   A. landowners.
   B. merchants.
   C. bishops.
   D. artists.

2. The technique of *perspective* allowed Renaissance artists to
   F. place their work in cathedrals.
   G. charge more for their art.
   H. show details in their work.
   I. add dimension and depth to their art.

3. Why did people such as Erasmus criticize the Catholic Church?
   A. They thought Church leaders were too concerned with money.
   B. They wanted Church services to be conducted in the vernacular.
   C. They thought indulgences should be more affordable.
   D. They wanted priests to provide an education to all children.

4. Martin Luther believed that the Bible was
   F. less important than the words of the pope.
   G. equally important as the words of the pope.
   H. the best source of religious truth.
   I. the worst source of religious truth.

5. The Catholic Church responded to the spread of Protestantism by
   A. selling more indulgences.
   B. allowing divorces.
   C. setting up seminaries.
   D. banning the Jesuits.

6. In order to unite their kingdom, Queen Isabella and King Ferdinand
   F. supported Protestant ideas for reform.
   G. required their subjects to practice Catholicism.
   H. protected Jews and Muslims from abuse.
   I. increased religious freedom for all believers.

CHAPTER 20 Assessment *(continued)*

DBQ DOCUMENT-BASED QUESTIONS

7. **Summarizing** Martin Luther's Ninety-Five Theses included the following:

   21. Therefore those [supporters] of indulgences are in error, who say that by the pope's indulgences a man is freed from every penalty, ...

   36. Every truly repentant Christian has a right to full remission of penalty [forgiveness] and guilt, even without letters of pardon.

   —from "Disputation of Doctor Martin Luther on the Power and Efficacy of Indulgences," by Martin Luther, 1517

   Which statement best summarizes Martin Luther's opinion?
   A. Christians can be forgiven without indulgences.
   B. Letters of pardon may be given by mistake.
   C. All true Christians may receive letters of pardon.
   D. Only the pope's indulgences are effective.

8. **Making Inferences** What do Luther's statements imply about forgiveness?
   F. A pope can forgive only certain sins.
   G. Forgiveness is available to all sinners.
   H. Sinners should ask a priest for forgiveness.
   I. All sinners will receive letters of pardon if they ask.

SHORT RESPONSE

" 'I would not believe a land could have been so despoiled [looted] had I not seen it with my own eyes,' reported the Swedish general Mortaigne ... Marburg, which had been occupied 11 times, had lost half its population by 1648. When ... imperial troops finally sacked [raided] ... Magdeburg in 1631, it is estimated that only 5,000 of its 30,000 inhabitants survived ..."

—from *Europe's Tragedy: A History of the Thirty Years' War*, by Peter H. Wilson

9. How did the Thirty Years' War affect the people of Marburg?

10. What does the statement from the Swedish general add to the description?

EXTENDED RESPONSE

11. **Descriptive Writing** You live in a village where people oppose the sale of indulgences. Write a letter to a friend in Rome and describe how people in your village feel about indulgences.

Need Extra Help?

If You've Missed Question	1	2	3	4	5	6	7	8	9	10	11
Review Lesson	1	2	3	3	4	4	3	3	4	4	3, 4

NOTES

REFLECT, REVIEW, & REMEDIATE

INTERACTIVE WORKSHEET

Chapter Summary

Provide students with the Chapter Summary worksheet to help review the chapter and prepare for assessment.

Reviewing the Enduring Understandings

Review this chapter's Enduring Understandings with students:

- The movement of people, goods, and ideas causes societies to change over time.
- People, places, and ideas change over time.
- Religion can influence a society's beliefs and values.
- Countries have relationships with each other.

INTERACTIVE WHITEBOARD ACTIVITY On the interactive whiteboard, have student volunteers create a two-column chart and write "Renaissance" in one column and "Reformation" in the other. Then lead a discussion that allows students to recall features and key events for each transformation. Student volunteers should record answers in the chart.

Renaissance	Reformation

ACTIVITIES ANSWERS

Exploring the Essential Question

1. Descriptive essays should include treatment of how humanism will change medieval people's understanding of reason and logic. Essays also should include information about developments in art, literature, and science.

21st Century Skills

2. Student presentations should include representative images of artists discussed in the chapter, such as Michelangelo, da Vinci, or van Eyck. Presentations should point out examples of Renaissance style, such as the depiction of human emotion or the realistic depiction of the human body. Students should identify details, such as perspective, that are discussed in the chapter.

Thinking Like a Historian

3. Time lines may include the following information:
1370s Wycliffe calls for reform of Catholic Church
1509 Erasmus's *Praise of Folly* criticizes Catholic Church leaders
1517 Luther writes Ninety-five Theses
1521 Luther is excommunicated from Catholic Church
1555 Peace of Augsburg allows rulers to decide the religion of their people

Locating Places

4. **1.** I, **2.** J, **3.** D, **4.** E, **5.** A, **6.** B, **7.** G, **8.** H, **9.** C, **10.** F

ASSESSMENT ANSWERS

Review the Guiding Questions

1. **B** The correct choice is B. The leaders of Italian city-states in the Renaissance were urban traders and bankers. Landowners were city leaders during the Middle Ages. Church leaders such as bishops focused on religious issues, not leading city-states. Leaders hired artists, but artists were not city leaders.

2. **I** The correct choice is I. Perspective could make artwork look three-dimensional. The technique, therefore, made Renaissance art appear more natural and realistic.

3. **A** The correct choice is A. Reformers were angry that the Catholic Church sold indulgences to make money. The money was used to build a cathedral, not for charity or education. The Catholic Church spent money for artwork, but nothing indicates that people objected to art.

4. **H** The correct choice is H. Martin Luther argued that the people should have access to the Bible and learn about its beliefs for themselves. He believed that people should be able to get their information from the Bible themselves without going through ministers.

5. **C** The correct choice is C. The Catholic Church established seminaries to improve the education of priests. Better-educated priests who could read, write, and preach well would help the Catholics win back people who had joined the Protestant church. It ended the practice of selling indulgences and made stricter rules for priests. The Jesuit order was another type of Catholic reform.

6. **G** The correct choice is G. The Spanish monarchy removed or punished residents who did not practice Catholicism. They rejected the beliefs of Protestants, Jews, and Muslims.

Document-Based Questions

7. **A** The correct choice is A. Luther says that Christians are forgiven if they ask for forgiveness. They do not need to ask a priest for indulgences or letters of pardon.

8. **G** The correct choice is G. Martin Luther thinks that anyone can be forgiven if he or she is truly sorry. He does not think people need to ask a pope or a priest for forgiveness.

Short Response

9. During the Thirty Years' War, many people in Marburg were killed, and their property was stolen or destroyed.

10. The statement from the Swedish general adds authority to the description. The general has seen war and destruction before, yet he finds the condition of northern Germany worse than any battlefield he has witnessed.

Extended Response

11. Students' responses should define and describe indulgences. Letters should show an understanding of how the indulgences raise money for the Catholic Church and why people object to selling forgiveness to the wealthy.

ONLINE RESOURCES

networks

There's More Online!

- INTERACTIVE WORKSHEETS
- BIOGRAPHIES
- CHARTS/GRAPHS
- GAMES
- GRAPHIC ORGANIZERS
- IMAGES
- MAPS
- PRIMARY SOURCES
- SLIDE SHOWS
- TIME LINE
- LECTURE SLIDES
- INTERACTIVE WHITEBOARD ACTIVITIES
- ASSESSMENTS
- VIDEOS

Journey to the New World: Christopher Columbus

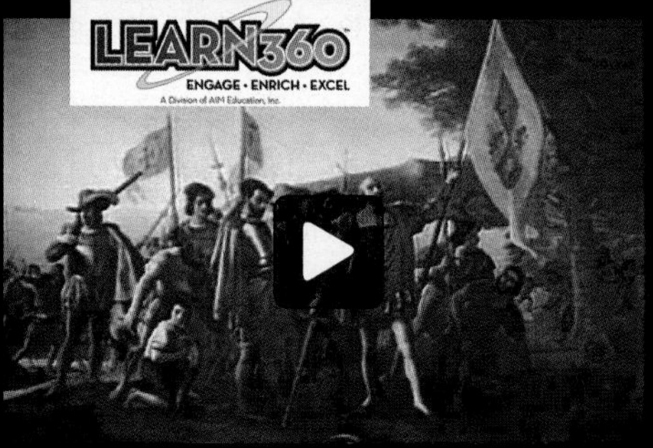

Hernan Cortés

Age of Discovery: English, French, and Dutch Explorations

Chapter **21**

Age of Exploration and Trade

Dear World History Teacher,

At the end of the fifteenth century, Europeans sailed out into the world. Portuguese ships ventured southward along the West African coast in the mid-1400s, bringing back gold and enslaved Africans.

The goal of the Portuguese Empire was trade because its population was too small to establish large colonies. However, Spain had greater resources, and the process of European expansion accelerated with the voyages of Christopher Columbus to the Americas and Vasco de Gama to the Indian Ocean in the 1490s. Spanish conquistadors overthrew the Aztec and Inca Empires. Spain created two major supervisory territories in present-day New Mexico and Peru that subjected the native populations to Spanish control. Soon a number of other European peoples had joined in the process of expansion. By the end of the 1700s, they had created a global trade network dominated by Western ships and Western power.

The European age of exploration changed the shape of the world. In some areas, such as the Americas and the Spice Islands in Asia, that exploration led to the destruction of indigenous civilizations and the establishment of European colonies. In others—such as Africa, India, and mainland Southeast Asia—it left native regimes intact but had a strong impact on local societies and regional trade patterns.

Jackson J. Spielvogel

More Media Resources

Current Events Online

Visit McGraw-Hill's current events Web site for high-interest news stories and activities for your students. Access the site through the Student or Teacher Center in **networks.**

Reading List

Grade 6 reading level:
Step Into the . . . Aztec and Maya Worlds, by Fiona MacDonald

Grade 7 reading level:
If You Were There in 1492, by Barbara Brenner

Grade 8 reading level:
Ferdinand Magellan and the Discovery of the World Ocean, by Rebecca Stefoff

At the MOVIES

Watch clips of popular culture films about Christopher Columbus, such as *Christopher Columbus: The Discovery* and *1492: Conquest of Paradise.* You can also view documentaries about the exploration of America, such as *The Explorers: The Spanish in America.*

Then discuss: Can fictional movies capture historical events accurately?

NOTE: Be sure to preview any clips to ensure they are age-appropriate.

Search for more videos online in the **networks** Resource Library.

CHAPTER 21 Planner

UNDERSTANDING BY DESIGN®

Enduring Understanding

- *The movement of people, goods, and ideas causes societies to change over time.*

Essential Questions

- *How does technology change the way people live?* • *Why do civilizations rise and fall?*
- *Why do people make economic choices?*

Students will know:

- *where Europeans explored*
- *where Europeans established colonies*
- *how the Columbian Exchange affected Europe and the Americas*
- *how economics influenced exploration*
- *key features of the commercial revolution*

Students will be able to:

- **read** a map of the world at 1400
- **understand** why goods from Asia were a catalyst for exploration
- **understand** a map depicting Cortés's exploration
- **analyze** primary source text on Cortés in the Americas
- **analyze** Europe's cultural dominance as exhibited through colonization
- **draw conclusions** about the advancements in economics that occurred due to trade and colonization
- **recognize** cause-and-effect relationships pertaining to trade and exploration
- **make** a connection between history and economics by analyzing trade and exploration

Predictable Misunderstandings

Students may think:

- Indigenous peoples had no influence on Europeans.
- The reasons for colonization were simple.
- The wealth that Europeans accumulated through colonization was not extraordinary.
- Mesoamerican civilizations were not very advanced.

Assessment Evidence

Performance Task

- Hands-On Chapter Project

Other Evidence

- Lesson Reviews
- Day-in-the life writing assignment
- Writing activity on why the Spanish conquered the Aztec and the Inca
- Answers to identifying the steps in creating an empire
- Graphic organizer activities
- Responses to Interactive Map discussion
- Economics of History Activities
- Geography and History Activity
- Primary Source Activity
- Discussion answers about why Europeans explored the world
- Answers from analyzing visuals
- Interactive Whiteboard Activity responses
- Brainstorming activity
- Answers to student activities

Pacing Guide

Introducing the Chapter	1 day
Lesson 1 The Age of Exploration	1 day
Lesson 2 Spain's Conquests in the Americas	1 day
Lesson 3 Exploration and Worldwide Trade	2 days
Chapter Activities and Assessment	1 day
TOTAL TIME	**6 Days**

Differentiated Instruction

These lesson plans are written to address the needs of your On Level students. Discussion and activities that are well-suited to your Approaching Grade Level learners, Beyond Grade Level learners, as well as your English Language Learners are coded as follows:

AL **Approaching Grade Level**

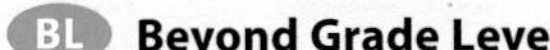

BL **Beyond Grade Level**

ELL **English Language Learner**

NCSS Standards covered in "Age of Exploration and Trade"

Learners will understand:

2 TIME, CONTINUITY, AND CHANGE

5. Key historical periods and patterns of change within and across cultures (e.g., the rise and fall of ancient civilizations, the development of technology, the rise of modern nation-states, and the establishment and breakdown of colonial systems)

7. The contributions of key persons, groups, and events from the past and their influence on the present

3 PEOPLE, PLACES, AND ENVIRONMENTS

4. The roles of different kinds of population centers in a region or nation

5 INDIVIDUALS, GROUPS, AND INSTITUTIONS

6. That cultural diffusion occurs when groups migrate

8. That when two or more groups with differing norms and beliefs interact, accommodation or conflict may result

7 PRODUCTION, DISTRIBUTION, AND CONSUMPTION

1. Individuals, government, and society experience scarcity because human wants and needs exceed what can be produced from available resources

3. The economic choices that people make have both present and future consequences

5. That banks and other financial institutions channel funds from savers to borrowers and investors

6. The economic gains that result from specialization and exchange as well as the trade-offs

7. How markets bring buyers and sellers together to exchange goods and services

8 SCIENCE, TECHNOLOGY, AND SOCIETY

2. Society often turns to science and technology to solve problems

5. Science and technology have changed peoples' perceptions of the social and natural world, as well as their relationship to the land, economy and trade, their concept of security, and their major daily activities

CHAPTER 21

Introducing the Chapter

(Student Edition p. 615)

The Story Matters . . .

Read "The Story Matters . . ." aloud in class or ask for a volunteer to read it aloud. Then discuss with students what it might have been like to be a crew member on one of Columbus's ships.

Ask: **How would you feel trusting your captain to sail off across an ocean without knowing if you were ever going to find land?** Have a few students share their opinions and feelings.

Then ask: **Would you be willing to climb into a spaceship today that might be a one-way voyage to Mars?** Have students explain how they would cope with that possibility.

Tell the class that Christopher Columbus believed until his death that he had found Asia, not a continent between Europe and Asia. Later in life, Columbus lived in Spain in disgrace for his failure as a colonial governor. Nonetheless, he was a wealthy man because of the gold he brought back to Europe. Although he was the first European to publicize the new route he found, he was one of many adventurers who took up the challenge of expanding Europe's awareness of the world. Tell students that they can read online about the conditions Columbus and other explorers faced.

Age of Exploration and Trade

1400 to 1700

ESSENTIAL QUESTIONS • How does technology change the way people live? • Why do civilizations rise and fall? • Why do people make economic choices?

networks

There's More Online about how civilizations changed during the Age of Exploration and Trade.

CHAPTER 21

Lesson 1 The Age of Exploration

Lesson 2 Spain's Conquests in the Americas

Lesson 3 Exploration and Worldwide Trade

The Story Matters . . .

Christopher Columbus lived in Genoa, Italy. He joined the Portuguese merchant marine and became a sailor. On trading voyages to Africa, he learned about navigation and wind currents. Columbus believed that if he sailed west, he would eventually reach Asia. He tried to convince various European rulers to help him test his idea.

Finally, Queen Isabella of Spain decided that Columbus could win glory and wealth for Spain. She and her husband Ferdinand supplied money for his voyage. When Columbus reached the Americas in 1492, he believed he had reached Asia. Instead, Columbus had opened up the Americas to Europeans.

◄ The first voyage of Columbus in 1492 resulted in dramatic changes throughout the Americas, Europe, and the world.

The Granger Collection, NYC. All rights reserved Joseph Walter

615

Introducing Place and Time (Student Edition pp. 616–617)

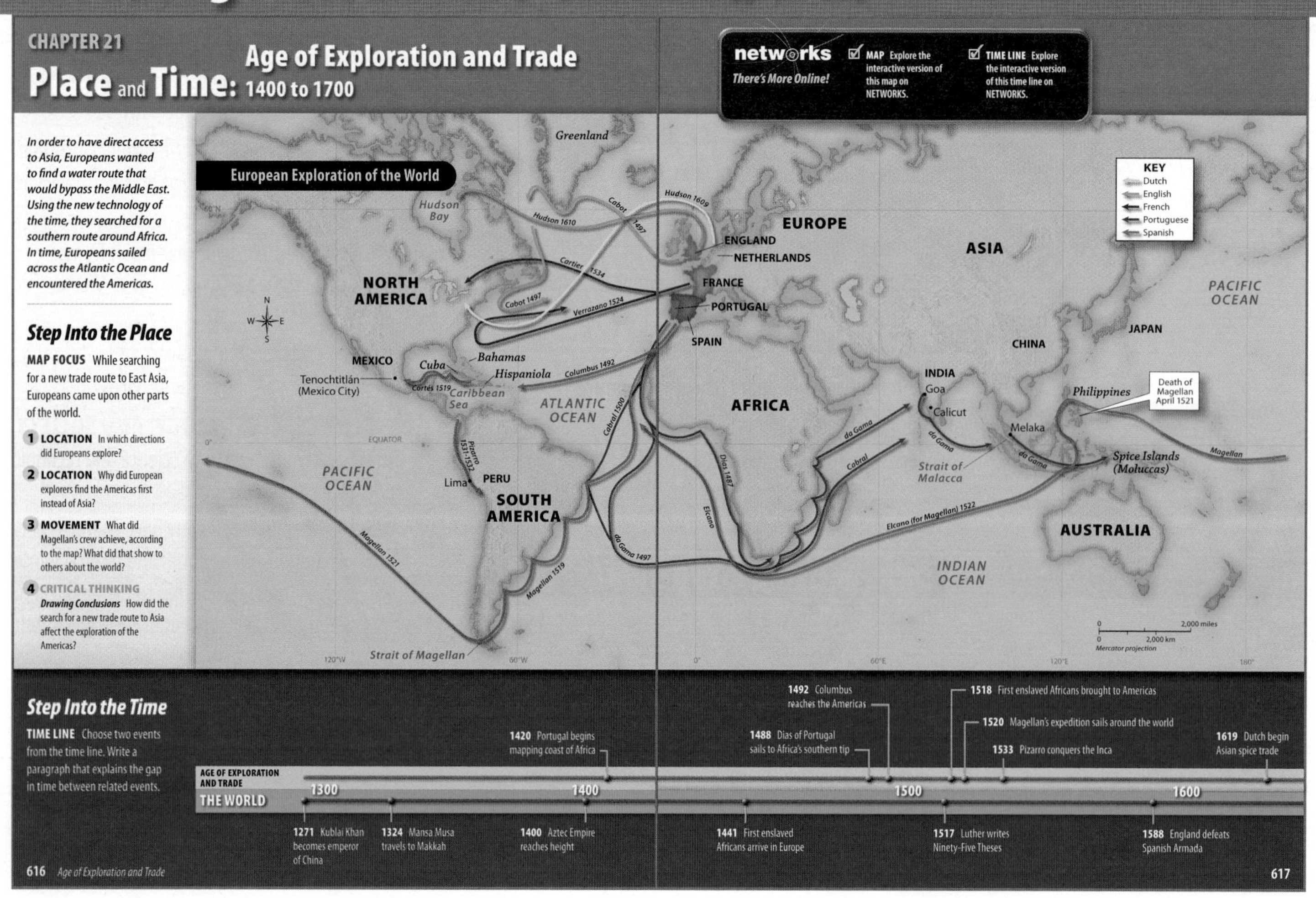

CHAPTER 21

Place and Time: 1400 to 1700

Age of Exploration and Trade

networks There's More Online!

MAP Explore the interactive version of this map on NETWORKS.

TIME LINE Explore the interactive version of this time line on NETWORKS.

In order to have direct access to Asia, Europeans wanted to find a water route that would bypass the Middle East. Using the new technology of the time, they searched for a southern route around Africa. In time, Europeans sailed across the Atlantic Ocean and encountered the Americas.

Step Into the Place

MAP FOCUS While searching for a new trade route to East Asia, Europeans came upon other parts of the world.

1 LOCATION In which directions did Europeans explore?

2 LOCATION Why did European explorers find the Americas first instead of Asia?

3 MOVEMENT What did Magellan's crew achieve, according to the map? What did that show to others about the world?

4 CRITICAL THINKING *Drawing Conclusions* How did the search for a new trade route to Asia affect the exploration of the Americas?

Step Into the Time

TIME LINE Choose two events from the time line. Write a paragraph that explains the gap in time between related events.

AGE OF EXPLORATION AND TRADE

1420 Portugal begins mapping coast of Africa

1488 Dias of Portugal sails to Africa's southern tip

1492 Columbus reaches the Americas

1518 First enslaved Africans brought to Americas

1520 Magellan's expedition sails around the world

1533 Pizarro conquers the Inca

1619 Dutch begin Asian spice trade

1300 1400 1500 1600

THE WORLD

1271 Kublai Khan becomes emperor of China

1324 Mansa Musa travels to Makkah

1400 Aztec Empire reaches height

1441 First enslaved Africans arrive in Europe

1517 Luther writes Ninety-Five Theses

1588 England defeats Spanish Armada

616 Age of Exploration and Trade

617

Technology Extension

- Find an additional activity online that incorporates technology for this project.
- Visit the EdTechTeacher Web sites (included in the Technology Extension for this chapter) for more links, tutorials, and other resources.

Assessing Background Knowledge

INTERACTIVE WORKSHEET

What Do You Know? Activity

Have students complete the What Do You Know? activity before they study the chapter.

Have students consider what they have already learned about explorers and the lands they encountered. **Ask: What were explorers looking for?** *(adventure, wealth, glory)* **What tools and technology would explorers need to be successful?** *(ships, maps, weapons, navigational equipment)* Tell students they will be learning about explorers who came to the Americas, including why they made the journey and what happened as a result. When students have finished the chapter, have them update their web diagrams with what they have learned.

INTERACTIVE WORKSHEET

Guided Reading Activities

There is a Guided Reading Activity for each lesson in this chapter. You may wish to assign the Guided Reading Activity for Lesson 1 after introducing the chapter content.

Hands-On Chapter Project

Students will create a poster and display honoring the achievements of a famous explorer.

- Students will participate in a class discussion to review what they have learned about famous explorers and the Age of Exploration.
- Then, students will choose an explorer to research. Working independently, each student will plan, research, and create his or her poster and display.
- Next, each student will present his or her poster and display to the class as part of the Hall of Explorers.
- Finally, students will evaluate their research, content, and presentation using an Assessment Rubric.

Visit **networks** online to see the full project and rubric.

ONLINE RESOURCES

networks

Assign these interactive worksheets and quizzes from your Teacher Lesson Center. All resources are print-ready.

It's ALL Online!

Chapter 21 Resources

- ☑ Chapter Summary
- ☑ Vocabulary Builder
- ☑ What Do You Know?
- ☑ Hands-On Chapter Project

Lesson 1 Resources

- ☑ Interactive Graphic Organizer
- ☑ Geography and History Understanding Location: Europeans and the Known World
- ☑ Guided Reading Activity
- ☑ Reading Essentials and Study Guide
- ☑ Online Self-Check Quiz

Lesson 2 Resources

- ☑ Primary Source Activity Cortés Arrives in Tenochtitlán
- ☑ Guided Reading Activity
- ☑ Economics of History Activity Quipu and Incan Society
- ☑ Reading Essentials and Study Guide
- ☑ Online Self-Check Quiz

Lesson 3 Resources

- ☑ Economics of History Activity The Columbian Exchange
- ☑ Guided Reading Activity
- ☑ Reading Essentials and Study Guide
- ☑ Online Self-Check Quiz

Assessment Resources

- ☑ Lesson Reviews
- ☑ Online Self-Check Quizzes
- ☑ Chapter Activities and Assessment
- ☑ Standardized Test Practice

Remediation Resources

- ☑ Reading Essentials and Study Guide
- ☑ Guided Reading Activities
- ☑ Online Self-Check Quizzes
- ☑ Chapter Summary

Step Into the Place

Location Project the chapter map. Students should notice that each route is a different color. Point out that each of these colors represents the country that funded the exploration and claimed the lands that each explorer discovered. Ask student volunteers to answer each of these questions using the whiteboard.

- Which country sponsored the most explorations?
- Which country's route covered the most distance?
- Which countries led expeditions that entered the interior of North America?

Then have students answer and discuss the Map Focus questions.

Step Into the Time

Sequencing Have students review the time line for the chapter. Explain that during this short period, Europe went from almost no detailed knowledge of the world to a much more accurate understanding.

Ask students: Why would Columbus's voyage sailing west across the Atlantic Ocean be the opposite of Portuguese sailors sailing south around the tip of Africa? *(The Portuguese sailed east to find China. Columbus sailed west to find China.)*

Elicit understanding that one exploration led to another.

Answers for pages 616–617

Step Into the Place

1. They sailed south, east, and west.
2. They didn't know the Americas existed, but they landed there while sailing west to Asia.
3. They proved that a water route can be used to travel around the world. It showed that the world is round.
4. CRITICAL THINKING As explorers traveled the continents' rivers and bays, they explored the interior of the Americas and eventually reached the Pacific Ocean.

Step Into the Time

Answers will vary, but students might suggest reasons for the time gaps that include new technology, better maps, an increase in competition between nations, and so on.

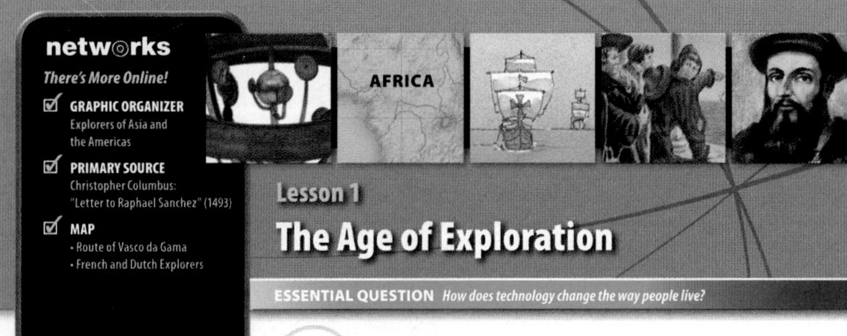

networks
There's More Online!
- ☑ **GRAPHIC ORGANIZER** Explorers of Asia and the Americas
- ☑ **PRIMARY SOURCE** Christopher Columbus: "Letter to Raphael Sanchez" (1493)
- ☑ **MAP**
  - Route of Vasco da Gama
  - French and Dutch Explorers

Lesson 1
The Age of Exploration

ESSENTIAL QUESTION *How does technology change the way people live?*

IT MATTERS BECAUSE

The demand for goods from Asia as well as advances in technology helped start Europe's age of exploration.

1 Europe Gets Ready to Explore

GUIDING QUESTION *Why did Europeans begin to explore the world?*

In the 1400s and 1500s, Europeans gradually gained control of the Americas and parts of Asia. Many events came together to create the right time for **overseas** exploration.

Search for Trade Routes

During the Middle Ages, Europeans began to buy silks, spices, and other luxury goods from Asia. Spices, such as pepper, cinnamon, and nutmeg were in great demand. Europeans used spices to preserve and flavor food, and for perfumes, cosmetics, and medicine.

A network of merchants controlled trade from Asia to Europe. Chinese and Indian traders sent spices by caravan over the Silk Road and other routes to the eastern Mediterranean region. From there, Arab and Byzantine traders shipped the spices to Europe. The Arabs earned huge profits selling luxury goods to Italian merchants. The Italians then sold the products to other Europeans.

Political changes eventually disrupted this trading network. However, merchants knew that if they could get goods directly and cheaply, they could make more profits. Also, if Europeans could reach Asia by sea, then they would not have to travel overland through the Middle East.

Reading HELPDESK

Taking Notes: ***Identifying***

Use a diagram like the one shown here to list the different Europeans who explored Asia and the Americas.

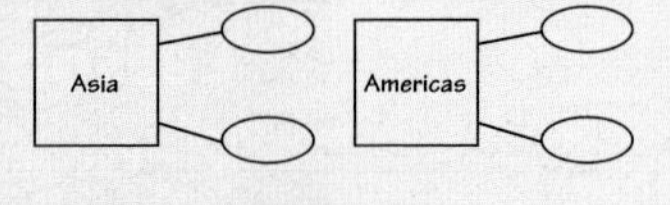

Content Vocabulary
- **circumnavigate**
- **conquistadors**

Technology and Exploration

By the 1400s, a number of technological inventions became available to European explorers. These inventions helped them navigate vast oceans. Europeans learned about the astrolabe (AS•truh•layb) and the compass from the Arabs. The astrolabe was an ancient Greek instrument that was used to find latitude. Sailors used the compass to help determine the direction in which they were sailing.

European mapmakers also improved their skills. During the late Middle Ages, most educated Europeans were aware that the earth was round. The only maps that were available, however, were of Europe and the Mediterranean region. That changed during the Renaissance when people began to study ancient maps and books.

Europeans rediscovered the work of Ptolemy (TAH•luh•mee), a Greek geographer. Ptolemy had drawn maps of the world for his book, *Geography*. He recorded the latitude and longitude of over 8,000 locations. With the invention of the printing press, accurate maps became readily available to sailors and explorers.

European mapmakers also learned about the Indian Ocean by studying the works of the Arab geographer al-Idrisi (ehl-ah•DREE•see). Many Europeans concluded that sailing around Africa was the best way to get to Asia.

In addition, shipbuilders improved ships by using triangular sails developed by Arab traders. With these sails and other improvements, ships could now go in nearly every direction no matter where the wind blew.

Rise of Strong Kingdoms

Even with new sailing skills and tools, exploration was still expensive and dangerous. But by the 1400s, the rise of towns and trade had strengthened Europe's governments. By the end of the 1400s, four strong kingdoms had emerged in Europe: Portugal, Spain, France, and England. All of these kingdoms had ports on the Atlantic Ocean—and all were eager to find a sea route to Asia.

☑ **PROGRESS CHECK**

Explaining How did new technology make it possible for Europeans to make long ocean voyages?

THEN

An astrolabe was made of brass or iron. It had discs with star maps and coordinate lines that rotated around a pin. The pin was in the position of the North Star. Today, navigation systems still look to the heavens. Computers use the positions of satellites in space to help drivers, pilots, sailors, and hikers know exactly where on Earth they are.

NOW

▶ **CRITICAL THINKING**
Contrasting What do you think are some of the differences between using an astrolabe and using a computerized system?

Academic Vocabulary

overseas across the ocean or sea

GEOGRAPHY CONNECTION

Vasco da Gama followed the coastline of Africa to reach India.

1. **LOCATION** What is the southernmost point that da Gama reached?
2. **CRITICAL THINKING** ***Cause and Effect*** Why would sailors take a longer route along the coastline instead of the shortest distance between two points?

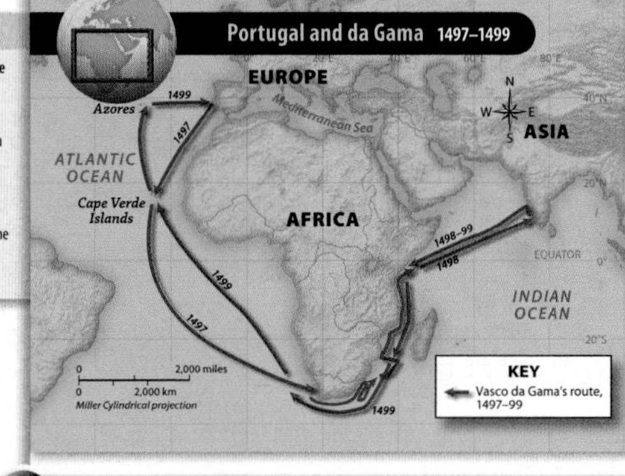

2 Early Voyages of Discovery

GUIDING QUESTION *Which leaders were responsible for European exploration of the world?*

During the early 1400s, England and France were still at war with each other, and Spain was still fighting the Muslims. This let Portugal take the lead in exploring new trade routes to Asia.

Portugal Leads the Way

Prince Henry of Portugal became known as "Henry the Navigator," even though he had never made an ocean voyage. Henry was eager for Portugal to explore the world, and he paid for many voyages of exploration. About 1420, Henry's adventurers sailed along Africa's west coast, mapping its features. They **obtained** gold from trade with African kingdoms. The explorers also traveled west into the Atlantic Ocean, where they seized the Azores (AY•zawrz), Madeira (muh•DIHR•uh), and Cape Verde (VUHRD) islands.

In 1488, the Portuguese explorer Bartolomeu Dias (bahr•tuh•luh•MEH•uh DEE•ahsh) sailed to the southern tip of Africa. Nine years later, Vasco da Gama (VAHS•koh dah GAM•uh) rounded the tip of Africa and landed on India's southwest coast. Europeans had at last found a water route to Asia.

During Prince Henry's lifetime, Portuguese sailors explored only about half of the west coast of Africa. Through Henry's efforts, other rulers knew that trade—and gold—could finance further exploration.

▶ **CRITICAL THINKING**
Drawing Conclusions How did Prince Henry contribute to European exploration?

Reading HELPDESK

Academic Vocabulary

obtain to take possession of

The First Voyage of Columbus

While the Portuguese explored Africa's western coast, an Italian navigator named Christopher Columbus formed a bold plan to reach Asia. He would sail west across the Atlantic Ocean.

For years, Columbus had tried to convince various European rulers to pay for a voyage of exploration. Finally, in 1492, Ferdinand and Isabella of Spain agreed to support him. Earlier that year, the Spanish monarchs had defeated the Muslims in Spain. They were now able to pay for voyages seeking new trade routes.

In August 1492, Columbus sailed west from Spain with three ships: the Santa María, the Niña, and the Pinta. As the weeks passed without sight of land, the sailors grew frightened. They wanted Columbus to sail back to Europe. Finally, the expedition sighted land. Columbus and his crew went ashore on San Salvador (sahn SAHL•vuh•dawr), an island in the Caribbean Sea.

Columbus claimed the island of San Salvador for Spain. He then traveled farther west in the Caribbean Sea. Eventually, his ships reached and explored the islands of Cuba and Hispaniola (hihs•puh•NYOH•luh). Today, the countries of Haiti and the Dominican Republic are located on the island of Hispaniola. Columbus began trading with the Taino (TEYE•noh) people.

INFOGRAPHIC

Columbus's flagship, the Santa María, was larger and slower than the other two ships on the voyage.

1. **TIME** What do the details of the ship reveal about the skills sailors at this time would need?
2. **CRITICAL THINKING** ***Making Generalizations*** Make a generalization about the hardships the crew probably faced on the long journey.

THE SANTA MARÍA

LESSON 1

ENGAGE

IMAGE **Analyzing Visuals** Show students the interactive image of Columbus meeting with the Taino people. Note that this was the first contact between the two cultures.

Ask:

What differences between European and Taino technology are suggested by this image? *(Students should note that the Europeans have metal weapons and armor. They may also note that the Europeans had the sailing technology to travel to the Taino, but the Taino lacked these technologies.)*

Explain to students that Columbus was part of the age of exploration, in which Europeans traveled around the world.

Ask:

Why do you think Europeans wanted to travel to distant lands? *(Students may answer that Europeans wanted to trade for rare goods, to form colonies, or to gain knowledge.)*

What changes might this exploration have caused? *(Student answers will vary. They may suggest that Europe could have grown wealthy, that new ideas would be spread, or that conquered peoples would suffer.)*

In this lesson, students will learn why Europeans began exploring and how profoundly this changed Europe as well as the rest of the world. Later, they will return to their answers above in order to predict how worldwide trade and exploration affected different civilizations, including Europe.

TEACH & ASSESS

1 Europe Gets Ready to Explore

GUIDING QUESTION ***Why did Europeans begin to explore the world?***

Determining Cause and Effect Draw a cause-and-effect diagram on the whiteboard. Label the effect as "Europeans begin voyages of exploration." Have the class use information from their textbooks to provide the causes. *(the loss of the Silk Road, a desire for luxury goods, improved technology, the desire to spread Christianity, a desire for wealth, strong central governments)*

IMAGE **Explaining** Show students the interactive image of the *Santa Maria*.

Ask:

Why were improvements in ship technology important? *(They made it possible for explorers to sail greater distances.)* AL

GRAPHIC ORGANIZER **Describing** Discuss as a class why it took great daring to sail around Africa and across the Atlantic Ocean. Have students describe what was known of the world at the time. Then have students work alone or in pairs to complete the Taking Notes interactive graphic organizer. Ask volunteers to share their organizers with the class. If necessary, review the routes taken by the explorers discussed in the lesson. AL

INTERACTIVE WORKSHEET

Explaining Ask: What would explorers need to know in order to complete a successful journey? *(how to sail, direction of winds and tides, geography)* Point out that explorers needed to have an idea of what the world looked like so they could establish directions of travel and destinations. As knowledge of world geography increased, the ability to travel the world became easier. Ask students to keep this in mind as they complete the Geography and History Activity for this lesson. Assign the worksheet for homework.

2 Early Voyages of Discovery

GUIDING QUESTION ***Which leaders were responsible for European exploration of the world?***

LECTURE SLIDE **Analyzing** Show students the lecture slide discussing Portugal's explorations. Use the key to measure how far the explorers traveled to get to India.

SLIDE SHOW **Describing Ask: Which European country was the first to begin voyages of exploration?** *(Portugal)* **Who was responsible for this?** *(Prince Henry the Navigator)* Use the map from the chapter and the lecture slide to illustrate the location of the first territories of the Portuguese Empire: the Azores, the Madeira, and the Cape Verde islands. Then, show students the slide show about the Madeira islands.

Ask:

What evidence of European culture do you see in Madeira? *(a cathedral and other buildings with European-style architecture)*

IMAGE **Explaining** Show students the biography of Magellan as well as the interactive image on GPS technology.

Ask: How did technology help people learn about the world in Magellan's day, and how does it help in modern times? *(Magellan used modern technology of the time to find his way around the world. Today we use GPS technology to help us find our way around streets and towns.)*

Have students complete the Lesson 1 Review.

Answers for pages 618–621

P. 618 Taking Notes Answers may vary. Sample answer: Asia: Vasco da Gama, Ferdinand Magellan; Americas: Christopher Columbus, Ferdinand Magellan

P. 619 CRITICAL THINKING Answers may vary but could include: An astrolabe requires more skill to use, computers are more reliable, astrolabes don't need batteries or power, and computers work during the daytime.

P. 619 ☑ PROGRESS CHECK Precise maps, new navigational equipment, and sturdy ships enabled Europeans to undertake long-distance voyages that were impossible before.

P. 620 GEOGRAPHY CONNECTION

1. the southern tip of Africa
2. CRITICAL THINKING They tried to avoid the unknown and use the coastline as a guide.

P. 620 CRITICAL THINKING Prince Henry paid for voyages of exploration and led other countries to begin exploring as well.

P. 621 INFOGRAPHIC

1. Sailors needed to be able to climb and be strong to lift sails.
2. CRITICAL THINKING The crew probably faced hardships of bad weather and crowded conditions.

The Taino were the island's Native American people. Columbus returned to Spain with colorful parrots, some gold and spices, and several Taino as proof of his discovery.

Columbus, however, believed that he had been exploring the coast of Asia. He never realized that he had actually arrived in the Americas. It was not until 1502 that another Italian explorer, Amerigo Vespucci (ahm•uh•REE•goh veh•SPOO•chee), became convinced that Columbus had discovered a "new world." In 1507, early map makers labeled what is now the South American continent with the name *America*. Later, the name was applied to North America as well.

Spanish Conquerors

Columbus's success pleased the Spanish monarchs. Eager investors urgently, or quickly, organized a second return voyage. Columbus set out again in 1493. On this voyage, he took soldiers with him to conquer the people of these new lands. In November, the Spanish landed on Hispaniola.

For the first time, the Taino saw the **conquistadors** (kahn•KEES•tuh•dawrz), the soldier-explorers that Spain sent to the Americas. The Taino became frightened by what they witnessed. Men in armor rode on powerful horses, with snarling dogs running alongside them. In a display of might, the soldiers fired guns that shot out flames and lead balls. The conquistadors claimed Hispaniola for Spain, and then they enslaved the Taino.

In 1494, Spain and Portugal signed the Treaty of Tordesillas (tawr•day•SEE•yahs). This agreement divided South America between Spain and Portugal.

Amerigo Vespucci, explorer of the Americas, is believed to have influenced the naming of these lands with his name.

Voyage of Magellan

During the 1500s, Spain continued to explore the Americas, but it was still interested in finding a western route to Asia. In 1518, Spain hired Ferdinand Magellan (muh•JEH•luhn) for an exploration voyage. Sailing west from Spain, Magellan's **primary** goal was to sail around the Americas and then on to Asia.

Magellan traveled along South America's eastern coast, searching for a route to Asia. Near the southern tip of the continent, he reached a narrow water passage that is now called the Strait of Magellan. After passing through the stormy strait, the expedition entered a vast sea. It was so peaceful that Magellan named the sea the Pacific Ocean.

Reading HELPDESK

conquistadors Spanish soldiers who conquered people in other lands
circumnavigate to go completely around something, such as the world

Academic Vocabulary
primary most important; first

Magellan then sailed west. Water and food ran out, and the crew had to eat leather, sawdust, and rats. Some sailors died. Finally, after four months at sea, the expedition reached the present-day Philippines. There, Magellan was killed in a battle between local groups. The remaining crew members continued west across the Indian Ocean, around Africa, and back to Spain. They became the first known people to **circumnavigate** (suhr•kuhm•NAV•uh•GAYT), or sail around, the world.

Early French and English Explorers

The Portuguese successes led England and France to begin their own overseas exploration. In 1497, Englishman John Cabot (KA•buht) explored the North American coasts of Newfoundland and Nova Scotia. He was unsuccessful in finding a waterway to Asia.

In 1524, France sent Giovanni da Verrazano (joh•VAH•nee dah ver•uh•ZAH•noh) to find a northern route to Asia. Verrazano explored and mapped much of the eastern coast of North America, but he did not find a route to Asia. In 1534, the French navigator Jacques Cartier (ZHAHK kahr•TYAY) sailed inland along the St. Lawrence River to present-day Montreal. Cartier claimed much of eastern Canada for France.

After these early expeditions, France and England had to focus their attention on religious conflicts and civil wars in their own countries. By the early 1600s, these countries renewed their overseas explorations. This time, the French and English began to establish their own settlements in the Americas. Since most of Spain and Portugal's territories were in South America, Mexico, and the Caribbean, France and England began to establish colonies in North America.

PROGRESS CHECK

Sequencing Why was it important for the explorers of the Americas to use information they learned from earlier explorers?

Thinking Like a HISTORIAN

Predicting Consequences

Columbus was almost out of supplies when he reached land. Research how Columbus planned for his trip. What supplies did he take, and why? Then think about how his trip would be different today. What supplies would he take with him on a modern first voyage? Use library and Internet resources for your research. Then report your findings and predictions to your class. For more information about making predictions, read the chapter *What Does a Historian Do?*

Magellan, sailing for Spain, did not live to complete his voyage around the world.

LESSON 1 REVIEW

Review Vocabulary

1. How might sailors *circumnavigate* an island?

Answer the Guiding Questions

2. ***Identifying*** Which European leaders most encouraged exploration of the world?
3. ***Explaining*** What prevented Europeans from exploring the world sooner, during the Middle Ages?
4. ***Differentiating*** Why did Portugal begin exploring before France, England, or Spain did?
5. ***Contrasting*** How did the second voyage of Columbus differ from the first?
6. **CREATIVE WRITING** The crew of Magellan's voyage became the first people to sail all the way around the world. You are a crew member. Write a diary entry expressing your feelings after sailing around the world.

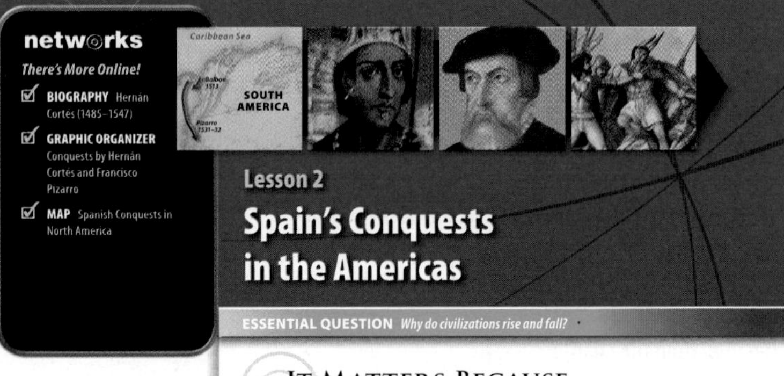

networks
There's More Online!
BIOGRAPHY Hernán Cortés (1485–1547)
GRAPHIC ORGANIZER Conquests by Hernán Cortés and Francisco Pizarro
MAP Spanish Conquests in North America
SOUTH AMERICA

Lesson 2

Spain's Conquests in the Americas

ESSENTIAL QUESTION *Why do civilizations rise and fall?*

IT MATTERS BECAUSE

The Spanish conquest of Central and South America remains a dominant influence in the cultures and customs of these areas.

1 The Spanish Conquer Mexico

GUIDING QUESTION *How did Spain conquer Mexico?*

The voyages of Christopher Columbus inspired many poor Spanish nobles to become conquistadors. Their goal was to travel to the Americas and seek wealth. Nineteen-year-old Hernán Cortés (ehr•NAHN kawr•TEHZ) was one of these nobles. In 1504, he sailed to Hispaniola. Eleven years later, he took part in Spain's invasion of Cuba.

Cortés Arrives in Mexico

While Cortés was in Cuba, he heard stories of Mexico's riches and the powerful Aztec Empire. In 1519, Cortés traveled to Mexico in search of gold and glory. He arrived near present-day Veracruz (vehr•uh•KROOZ) with about 508 soldiers, 100 sailors, 16 horses, and 14 cannons. How could such a small army expect to defeat the mighty Aztec?

Cortés used his army's guns and horses to frighten Native Americans. In a display of power, he forced thousands of them to surrender. Cortés also **relied** on a Maya woman named Malintzin (mah•LIHNT•suhn) for information about the Aztec.

Reading HELPDESK

Taking Notes: *Summarizing*

Use a chart like this one to describe the methods used by Hernán Cortés and Francisco Pizarro to conquer the people of Central and South America.

Hernán Cortés	Francisco Pizarro

Content Vocabulary
- **allies**
- **ambush**
- **smallpox**
- **hostage**

Spanish Explorations 1500-1600

NORTH AMERICA, PACIFIC OCEAN, ATLANTIC OCEAN, Caribbean Sea, SOUTH AMERICA, Santa Fe, St. Augustine, Tenochtitlán (Mexico City), De Soto 1539–42, Cabeza de Vaca 1528–36, Coronado 1540–42, Cabrillo 1542–43, Narváez 1528, Ponce De León 1513, Cortés 1519, Balboa 1513, Pizarro 1531–32

KEY: Spanish exploration

0 1,000 miles; 0 1,000 km; Lambert Azimuthal Equal-Area projection

GEOGRAPHY CONNECTION

Spanish conquistadors explored during the 1500s.

1. **LOCATION** What is the northernmost point the Spanish explorers reached?
2. **CRITICAL THINKING** ***Cause and Effect*** What part of the world was affected by the Spanish conquests the most?

Malintzin spoke with Cortés through a Spanish translator who knew Mayan. She told Cortés that many people in her land resented the Aztec rulers. One reason for their anger was the Aztec practice of human sacrifices. Most often to please their gods, the Aztec killed people whom they had captured in war. Malintzin believed that people who were conquered by the Aztec would help Cortés. Malintzin helped Cortés find **allies** (AL•leyes), or other groups willing to battle the Aztec.

Finally, another factor that helped Cortés defeat the Aztec was an invisible ally—germs that carried diseases such as the measles and **smallpox**. These diseases would eventually kill more Aztec people than Spanish weapons would.

Cortés Defeats the Aztec

The Spanish traveled hundreds of miles inland to reach Tenochtitlán (TAY•NAWCH•teet•LAHN), the Aztec capital. Messengers reported their every move to the Aztec ruler, Montezuma II (MAHN•tuh•ZOO•muh). The Aztec believed in a light-skinned god named Quetzalcoatl (KWEHT•zuhl•kuh•WAH•tuhl). According to Aztec legend, this god, who opposed the practice of human sacrifice, had sailed away long ago but had promised to return someday to reclaim his land.

Montezuma II was the ninth Aztec emperor to rule the region of present-day Mexico.

allies those who support each other for some common purpose
smallpox a disease that causes a high fever and often death

Academic Vocabulary
rely to depend on; to count on for help

LESSON 1 (cont.)

CLOSE & REFLECT

Predicting As a class, brainstorm a list of predictions that answer this question: **How did making contact with other lands and civilizations change Europeans and the cultures they contacted?**

Guide the discussion so students consider the possibilities of conquest, cultural exchange, and the exchange of plants and animals. Write responses on the board. If students need help, remind them to look at the list of goods that were traded between Asia and Europe.

Review how people in each place suddenly could get things they needed. These were items they never had before, and they became things that changed their lives.

BACKGROUND KNOWLEDGE

Lasting Effects of Spanish and French Exploration on American Culture

Spain and France established relatively few settlements in North America, especially compared with Britain. Despite this, the Spanish and the French had a large impact on American culture. In the Southwest especially, many geographic names come from the Spanish language. St. Augustine, Florida; Sante Fe, New Mexico; and San Diego, California were Spanish settlements. The names of several different plants in the region come from Spanish as well. Other examples of Spanish influence, including, art, literature, music, and food, have been a part of the culture of the region for centuries.

For example, two of the most recognizable symbols of the American West, the horse and cattle, come from Spain. Rodeos, too, originated in Spanish culture. Examples from architecture include adobe and stucco building materials, tile roofs, and curved archways.

Communities from St. Paul, Minnesota, through St. Louis, Missouri, and then south to New Orleans, Louisiana, include remnants of the French presence in America. They show, for example, a French influence in language and architecture. The cuisine of the region includes unmistakably French-inspired dishes such as baked goods like croissants, and dishes with sauces, or etouffe.

Answers for pages 622–623

P. 623 ☑ PROGRESS CHECK The Western world was explored in steps, going farther because it started with what was already known.

LESSON 1 REVIEW

1. Sailors would circumnavigate an island by sailing all the way around it until they returned to where they started.
2. Prince Henry the Navigator, Christopher Columbus, Ferdinand and Isabella of Spain, Bartolomeu Dias, Vasco da Gama, and Ferdinand Magellan
3. A lack of central governments with wealth and power kept them from exploring.
4. France and England were at war, and Spain was still fighting the Muslims. This allowed Portugal under Prince Henry to explore first.
5. The first voyage was an exploration; the second was to conquer the lands he had discovered.
6. Answers will vary, but students should note that Magellan was trying to find a passage through the Americas and then go on to Asia. His crew would be excited and proud that they had accomplished something no one had ever done before. They also would be exhausted and extremely homesick.

Teaching *Spain's Conquests in the Americas* (Student Edition pp. 624–627)

LESSON 2

ENGAGE

LECTURE SLIDE **Discussing** Show students the lecture slide with the quote from Bartolomé de Las Casas, noting that it was recorded in 1542. Explain that it was written by a Spanish observer, talking about the Spanish conquistadors and the Native Americans. Help students with any difficult passages or vocabulary in the quote. Then ask students to comment on this observation. ELL

Ask: Why do you think the Spanish treated the Native Americans in the way described? *(Answers will vary, but students may say that the Spanish didn't consider Native Americans to be their equals.)*

How did the Spaniards' desire to find gold and other wealth lead to their poor treatment of Native Americans? *(Students may say that the Spanish thought any land or people they discovered could be used to make them rich.)* BL

Tell students that in this lesson they will learn how Spanish exploration of the Americas began with Columbus but evolved into conquest of the Native Americans and the destruction of the native empires of the Aztec and the Inca.

TEACH & ASSESS

1 The Spanish Conquer Mexico

GUIDING QUESTION *How did Spain conquer Mexico?*

MAP **Identifying** Show students the map of Spanish exploration in the Americas. Have student volunteers identify the location of the territories conquered by Hernán Cortés *(Mexico)* and Francisco Pizarro *(Peru).*

2 Spain Conquers Peru

GUIDING QUESTION *How did Spanish conquistadors conquer the Inca?*

GRAPHIC ORGANIZER **Listing** Have students work alone or in pairs to complete the graphic organizer listing the ways Cortés and Pizarro defeated the Aztec and Inca Empires, respectively.

Ask: What factors helped Cortés in Mexico in 1521 and Pizarro in Peru in 1533 seize control of much larger forces? *(help from other Native Americans, the perception that Cortés was a returning god, disease, guns and horses, attacking the Native Americans first, and not being taken seriously)* Have students set aside their answers. They will return to them later in the lesson. AL

Answers for pages 624–625

P. 624 Taking Notes Answers may include:
Hernán Cortés —1. used his army's guns and horses to impress and frighten Native Americans, 2. relied on a Mayan woman named Malintzin to supply information about the Aztec, 3. took advantage of diseases weakening the Aztec, 4. attacked first and took Montezuma hostage;
Francisco Pizarro—1. shot at Inca villagers and raided their storehouses, 2. used support from Native Americans who were hostile to Atahualpa, 3. took Atahualpa hostage, 4. failed to honor a deal to release Atahualpa for gold, 5. sentenced Atahualpa to death for crimes and installed a new ruler he controlled

P. 625 GEOGRAPHY CONNECTION

1. Explorers reached almost the line of 40 degrees N latitude, north of present-day Santa Fe, New Mexico.
2. CRITICAL THINKING The areas that are modern-day Mexico, Florida, and northern South America were most affected by the Spanish conquests.

BIOGRAPHY

Hernán Cortés (1485–1547)

Assigned to lead troops in Mexico, Hernán Cortés forced his men to exercise and be disciplined. His well-trained forces acted quickly allowing Cortés to use their small numbers to outmaneuver a much larger Aztec force. He had also burned his ships so his men knew they had only one option—victory. After conquering Mexico, Cortés left in 1524 to explore Honduras. His two-year absence led to chaos in Mexico and ruined his reputation in Spain. He died in 1540, in debt and haunted by scandals.

▶ CRITICAL THINKING

Making Inferences What does it tell you about Cortés that he continued exploring even though he had conquered a great nation?

Montezuma was afraid Cortés was this god returning home. He was afraid to attack the Spanish right away. As Cortés marched closer, Montezuma changed his mind and decided to ambush the Spanish troops. Cortés, however, had already learned about the planned **ambush**.

In November 1519, Cortés took control of the Aztec capital. To prevent an Aztec uprising, Cortés took Montezuma **hostage** (HAHS•tihj), or prisoner. He then ordered the Aztec to stop sacrificing people.

Cortés's orders angered the Aztec, who planned a rebellion. Fighting broke out, and the Spanish killed thousands of Aztec. However, there were far more Aztec, and Cortés had to fight his way out of the city. The Spanish took refuge in the nearby hills.

While Cortés prepared a second attack, smallpox broke out in Tenochtitlán. Many Aztec died of the disease, and the remaining Aztec could not fight off the Spanish and their allies. In June 1521, the Spanish destroyed the Aztec capital.

☑ PROGRESS CHECK

Explaining Why did the Aztec allow Cortés to remain in their lands?

2 Spain Conquers Peru

GUIDING QUESTION *How did Spanish conquistadors conquer the Inca?*

Like Cortés, Vasco Núñez de Balboa (VAHS•koh NOON•yays day bal•BOH•uh) also sailed to the Americas. In 1513, he led a band of soldiers across the mountains of present-day Panama to look for a golden empire.

Balboa found a sea, known today as the Pacific Ocean, but he never found the golden empire he was looking for. A jealous Spanish official in Panama falsely charged Balboa with treason and had him beheaded.

Francisco Pizarro (fruhn•SIHS•koh puh•ZAHR•oh) had served as one of Balboa's soldiers. After Balboa was executed, Pizarro continued the search for gold. Even though Pizarro could not even write his own name, he knew how to fight. He longed to find the empire that Balboa had sought.

Pizarro Meets the Inca

The Inca ruled the empire that Balboa and Pizarro wanted to conquer. By the 1530s, the powerful Inca Empire had become **considerably** weaker. Despite their weaknesses, the Inca did not fear Pizarro and his troops. Pizarro had only 168 soldiers, one cannon, and 27 horses compared to the Inca army's 30,000 warriors. Still, Pizarro and his small army moved to attack the Inca homeland. In late 1532, Pizarro decided on a bold plan.

Reading HELPDESK

ambush a surprise attack
hostage someone held against his or her will in exchange for something

Academic Vocabulary
considerable large in size, quantity, or quality
global involving the entire Earth

The Inca Fall

Spanish messengers invited the Inca ruler Atahualpa (ah•tuh•WAHL•puh) to meet with Pizarro. Atahualpa agreed and came to the meeting with just 4,000 unarmed bodyguards. At their meeting, Pizarro demanded that Atahualpa give up his gods. The emperor laughed at this, and Pizarro ordered an attack. The Spanish fired into the unarmed Inca crowd. Pizarro dragged Atahualpa from the battlefield.

Atahualpa tried to buy his freedom. He offered Pizarro an entire room full of gold and silver. Pizarro immediately accepted Atahualpa's offer. Atahualpa had his people bring Pizarro the precious metals. Pizarro, however, did not set Atahualpa free. Instead, he charged the emperor with plotting a rebellion, worshipping false gods, and other crimes. In 1533, a military court found the emperor guilty and sentenced him to death.

Pizarro betrayed Atahualpa. He set his soldiers to attack the Inca bodyguards.

The Spanish king rewarded Pizarro by making him governor of Peru. Pizarro chose a new emperor for the Inca, who had to follow Pizarro's orders. Still, the Spanish could not gain complete control of the Inca Empire. Even after Pizarro died in 1541, the Spanish were still fighting Inca rebels. Nonetheless, the conquest of Peru opened most of South America to Spanish rule. Spain would create the world's first **global** empire.

☑ PROGRESS CHECK

Evaluating How successful were the efforts of Atahualpa to free himself from Pizarro?

LESSON 2 REVIEW

Review Vocabulary

1. How did Pizarro's act of taking Atahualpa *hostage* force the Inca to do what Pizarro wanted?

Answer the Guiding Questions

2. ***Describing*** Describe the troops and weapons that Hernán Cortés brought to Mexico.
3. ***Explaining*** What factors helped Cortés defeat the Aztec?
4. ***Differentiating*** How were the methods used by Cortés and Pizarro to conquer Native Americans different?
5. ***Inferring*** Why might Núñez de Balboa have believed that his expedition in Panama was a failure?
6. **EXPOSITORY WRITING** Why do you think the Spanish conquered the Aztec and the Inca instead of trading with them for gold and other resources? Write a paragraph that explains your reasons.

networks
There's More Online!

☑ GRAPHIC ORGANIZER
Crops and Workers in Three Colonies

☑ MAP
• European Trade in Asia
• Columbia Exchange

Lesson 3

Exploration and Worldwide Trade

ESSENTIAL QUESTION *Why do people make economic choices?*

IT MATTERS BECAUSE

European nations established colonies that produced great wealth, changing the Americas and other conquered lands forever.

1 Settling the Americas

GUIDING QUESTION *How did European nations build empires in the Americas?*

The Treaty of Tordesillas divided the Americas between Spain and Portugal. Other nations, however, did not accept this treaty. The Netherlands, France, and England soon joined Spain and Portugal in a race to gain wealth in new lands and to spread Christianity.

The Americas were the primary region where Europeans explored and established settlements. In the 1500s, the Spanish and the Portuguese had built empires in the Americas. Beginning in the 1600s, the French, English, and Dutch also began to establish their own settlements.

Spain's American Empire

By the 1600s, Spain's empire in the Americas had grown to include parts of North America and much of South America. The islands in the Caribbean Sea were also a part of this empire. Spanish rulers sent royal officials called viceroys to govern local areas. Councils of Spanish settlers also advised the viceroys.

The Spanish rulers set two goals for the colonists of their American empire: to bring wealth back to Spain and to convert Native Americans to Christianity. Spanish settlers grew crops of sugarcane on large farms known as **plantations** (plan•TAY•shuns).

Reading HELPDESK

Taking Notes: *Listing*

Use a diagram like the one here to list the crops or products and the type of workers found in each colony.

	Spanish Colonies	Portuguese Colonies	English Colonies
Crops or products			
Workers			

Content Vocabulary
• plantations • commerce
• cash crops • entrepreneur
• mercantilism • cottage industry

Landowners also operated gold and silver mines. At the same time, Spanish priests established missions, or religious communities, to teach Christianity to the Native Americans.

Spain permitted its settlers to use Native American labor to work the plantations. The Spanish, however, enslaved and mistreated the Native Americans. Also, the Spanish settlers unknowingly brought contagious diseases with them. Millions of Native Americans died from illness during the first 50 years of the arrival of Europeans. As the number of Native Americans declined, more laborers were needed. To solve this problem, the Spanish brought over enslaved Africans to work on the plantations and in the mines. In time, this mingling of Europeans, Native Americans, and Africans gave rise to a new **culture**.

Portuguese Brazil

In 1500, the Portuguese explorer Pedro Álvares Cabral (PAY•droh AHL•vahr•ihs kuh•BRAHL) arrived in the region of South America that is now Brazil. He claimed this territory for Portugal. Settlers in Brazil grew **cash crops** such as sugarcane, tobacco, coffee, and cotton. A cash crop is a crop that is grown in large quantities to be sold for profit. With the help of enslaved Africans, Brazil became one of Portugal's most profitable overseas territories.

The French in North America

The fur trade was one of the main reasons the French settled in North America. By the 1600s, beaver fur was very popular in Europe. The French hoped they would become wealthy if they set up fur trading posts in North America. In 1608, French merchants hired explorer Samuel de Champlain (sham•PLAYN) to help them obtain furs in New France, which today is much of Eastern Canada. Champlain set up a trading post named Quebec (kwih•BEHK). Quebec became the capital of New France.

Sugarcane is a tall grassy plant. Its pulpy fibers are processed to create sugar as a final product.

plantation a large estate or farm that used enslaved people or hired workers to grow and harvest crops
cash crops crops grown in large amounts to be sold for profit

Academic Vocabulary
culture the customs, learning, and art of a civilization

LESSON 2 (cont.)

VIDEO, INTERACTIVE WORKSHEET

Analyzing Show students the video clip on Cortés and his conquest of the Aztec. Then assign the Primary Source Activity about the arrival of Cortés in Tenochtitlán. Help students understand the meaning of any unfamiliar words in the sources, particularly the letter from Cortés to Charles V. Have students work in pairs or small groups to complete the worksheet.

Then **ask:** **Why did the Aztec welcome Cortés at first?** *(They believed he was a god.)* **How did Cortés act toward the statues of the Aztec gods?** *(He knocked them down and destroyed them.)* AL

INTERACTIVE WORKSHEET Assign the Economics of History Activity about the Inca and quipu for homework.

INTERACTIVE WHITEBOARD ACTIVITY

Matching Have students work alone or in pairs to complete the Interactive Whiteboard Activity. Have students use the definitions and other details in their textbooks to assist them in matching each description with the proper people. AL ELL

Have students complete the Lesson 2 Review.

CLOSE & REFLECT

Summarizing As a class, look back to the answers given earlier for how Cortés and Pizarro were able to defeat much larger Native American forces. Have volunteers summarize their previous answers and reconsider them now that the lesson is completed. *(Possible summary: Cortés and Pizarro tricked Montezuma and Atahualpa in order to imprison them and put them to death, leaving the Aztec and Inca without their leaders. They also got help from other Native Americans; Cortés was thought to be a returning god; disease weakened the Native Americans; they frightened people who had never seen guns and horses; they also attacked the Native Americans first; and Pizarro, particularly, was not seen as a threat.)* AL

Answers for pages 626–627

P. 626 CRITICAL THINKING His skills and interests lay in conquest and exploration, not in safer pursuits like administration, politics, or retirement.

P. 626 ☑ PROGRESS CHECK They believed he might be a returning god, and they were afraid to anger him.

P. 627 ☑ PROGRESS CHECK Atahualpa was not successful. When he tried to buy his freedom, Pizarro took his gold and then killed Atahualpa anyway.

LESSON 2 REVIEW

1. Pizarro threatened his hostage Atahualpa with harm. This forced the Inca to do what Pizarro wanted out of fear that he would harm their emperor.
2. He commanded about 508 soldiers, 100 sailors, 16 horses, and 14 cannons.
3. He had the help of a local woman translator, diseases that killed the Aztec, and the Aztec believing he was a returning light-skinned god.
4. Pizarro had fewer men and benefited from the Inca not thinking he was dangerous. Cortés attacked the Aztec first and used local translators.
5. He wanted to find a great empire filled with gold, but he found only the Pacific Ocean instead.
6. Answers will vary, but students might note that the Spanish were outnumbered, wanted to control the new lands they found and take the wealth for themselves, and forced the leaders of the Native Americans to give up their gods.

Teaching *Exploration and Worldwide Trade* (Student Edition pp. 628–635)

LESSON 3 • Day 1

ENGAGE

Analyzing Visuals Show students a map of European colonies in the Americas, such as the English colonies in North America or the Spanish colonies in North and South America.

Guide students toward understanding that after exploration and conquest, making money from the colonies was the next goal of European nations.

Tell students that in this lesson they will be learning about how the colonies became moneymaking ventures for the Europeans. They will also learn about economic systems that used the areas the Europeans set up as colonies.

TEACH & ASSESS

1 Settling the Americas

GUIDING QUESTION *How did European nations build empires in the Americas?*

GRAPHIC ORGANIZER

Comparing and Contrasting Have students use the graphic organizer comparing the Spanish, Portuguese, and English colonies. Students can expand the chart by adding French, English, and Dutch colonies as well.

Ask:

- **What similarities do you notice among these different colonies?** *(They grew similar crops, such as sugarcane and tobacco, and they used Native Americans and enslaved Africans as workers.)*
- **What did the French find in their colonies that was as valuable as gold or silver?** *(beaver and animal furs)*
- **How did the Dutch differ from other Europeans?** *(The Dutch made their money from trade as opposed to other Europeans, who made their money from establishing colonies where they could produce raw materials for other markets.)* AL

INTERACTIVE WHITEBOARD ACTIVITY **Sequencing** Review the explorers mentioned in the lesson. Use a map to identify the region explored by each voyage. Then show students the Interactive Whiteboard Activity. Ask volunteers to match the name of the explorer to the voyage. Extend the activity by having students put the explorations in order from earliest to latest. Point out that each voyage used information that was learned in a previous voyage.

Ask:

How did these later explorers help other European countries establish colonies? *(They explored different areas of the Americas.)* AL

Answers for pages 628–629

P. 628 Taking Notes Spanish Colonies: sugarcane, gold, silver; Native Americans, enslaved Africans. Portuguese Colonies: sugarcane, tobacco, coffee, cotton; Native Americans, enslaved Africans. English Colonies: tobacco; enslaved Africans

IMPORTANT EUROPEAN EXPLORERS

Christopher Columbus	Vasco da Gama	Ferdinand Magellan	Jacques Cartier	Henry Hudson
Voyages: 1492, 1493, 1498, 1502	**Voyage:** 1497–1499	**Voyage:** 1519–1522	**Voyages:** 1534, 1535, 1541	**Voyages:** 1607, 1608, 1609, 1610
First European to sail west searching for a water route to Asia	First European to sail around the south of Africa and reach India	Led the first expedition to sail completely around the world	Explored the St. Lawrence River	Explored the Hudson River and Hudson Bay

INFOGRAPHIC

For more than a hundred years, explorers searched for new trade routes.

1. **TIME** Who was the earliest European explorer?
2. **CRITICAL THINKING** ***Cause and Effect*** Which explorer gave his name to an important American river?

During the 1660s, the French king began sending political and military officials to rule New France. Jesuit and other Catholic missionaries also arrived. They taught Christianity to the Native Americans. The Native Americans called the Jesuits "Black Robes" because of the black clothes they wore.

From Quebec, French explorers, fur trappers, and missionaries spread out into the central part of New France. In 1673, the explorers Jacques Marquette (mar•KET) and Louis Joliet (joh•lee•EHT) reached the Mississippi River. Just nine years later, the French explorer La Salle (luh SAL) traveled south along the Mississippi to the Gulf of Mexico. He named the region Louisiana in honor of King Louis XIV. Like the Portuguese settlers, the French used enslaved Africans to work the fields.

England's Colonies in North America

During the early 1600s, England started to establish its own settlements in North America. The English government was interested in the natural **resources** from overseas territories.

English settlers sailed to North America for many reasons. Groups of merchants created settlements for trade. Others fled to North America to find religious freedom. Economic troubles in England also helped speed the growth of English settlements.

Reading HELPDESK

Academic Vocabulary

resource a ready supply of something valuable

Reading Strategy: *Identifying Cause and Effect*

As you read, look for key words to help you identify cause and effect, such as "because" and "since." Read about the English colonies in North America. What were the conditions—causes—that sent settlers to the New World?

In 1606, a group of English merchants and nobles formed the Virginia Company. North America's first permanent English settlement was founded with the Virginia Company's support in 1607. The founders named it Jamestown after King James I. It was the first settlement in the new territory called Virginia.

At first, the early settlers in Virginia could barely find enough food to survive. During the winters, many of them starved to death. Others were killed in clashes with Native Americans.

In the early years, the merchants and nobles who invested in the settlement did not make any money. Jamestown needed to develop an economic activity in order to become profitable. Settlers discovered that tobacco grew well in Virginia.

Connections to TODAY

Blending Languages

Spanish and Portuguese settlers brought their languages to the Americas. Over time, Native Americans combined elements of Spanish and Portuguese with their own languages. Native American words such as "chocolate" and "coyote—words that we still use today—migrated into Spanish and later English. Another term--Hispanic--was originally used to describe a Spanish person in the Americas.

Crops to Sell

Tobacco was very popular in Europe in the 1600s. Soon, the English settlers were producing and shipping it back to England in large amounts. Tobacco became the first cash crop of the English settlements. Eventually, it was grown on large plantations that needed many workers. Once again, enslaved Africans were brought in to work the land.

Encouraged by its success in Virginia, England continued to establish settlements in North America that produced cash crops. South Carolina, for example, began growing rice and indigo, a dye-producing plant. The English established sugarcane plantations on Caribbean islands, such as Jamaica. Enslaved African people worked the lands on English plantations, as they did on French and Portuguese plantations.

Dutch Traders

Another European country, the Netherlands, was interested in overseas exploration and settlement. The Netherlands won its independence from Spain in the late 1500s. Its people, known as the Dutch, believed that trade was key to their survival.

The 1600s were a golden age for the Netherlands. Dutch ships were efficient. Compared with ships from other European countries, Dutch ships could transport more goods and be operated by smaller crews.

Dutch trading ships sailed to the southern tip of Africa to the islands of Southeast Asia and soon set out for North America. An English navigator named Henry Hudson claimed land for the Dutch along the Atlantic coast of North America. In 1621, Dutch traders established settlements in the Americas, including one on Manhattan Island that they called New Amsterdam. Today, this region is part of New York City.

King James I (top) approved the creation of the Virginia Company. In 1619, the company created the House of Burgesses, America's first legislature. This seal is the king's official stamp put on important documents.

Time & Life Pictures/Getty Images

PROGRESS CHECK

Summarizing Why did European colonists bring enslaved Africans to their plantations in the Americas?

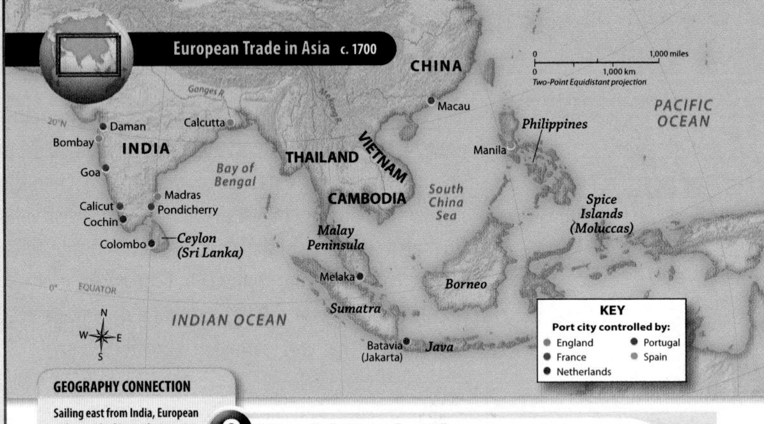

GEOGRAPHY CONNECTION

Sailing east from India, European sailors pushed into other areas of Asia.

1. **PLACE** Which countries had trading posts on the South China Sea?
2. **CRITICAL THINKING** ***Cause and Effect*** Why would the port cities shown on this map develop differently over time as compared to other cities in Asia?

2 World Trade Changes

GUIDING QUESTION ***How did Europe's merchants change the world trade system?***

As Europeans created empires, profitable trade developed between their homelands and their overseas settlements. As a result, Europe's economy expanded. By the 1600s, European nations were competing for markets and trade goods.

What Is Mercantilism?

Spain and Portugal took advantage of the gold and silver they gained from their empires. Other European countries wanted to do the same. This led to the theory of **mercantilism** (MUHR•kuhn•TEE•lih•zuhm). The key idea of mercantilism is that a country's power depends on its wealth. Countries can increase their wealth by owning more gold and silver. What is the best way for a country to get more gold and silver? According to mercantilism, a country must export, or sell to other countries, more goods than it imports, or buys from other countries.

According to mercantilism, countries should establish colonies. A colony is a settlement of people living in a territory controlled by their home country. Colonists provide raw materials that are not found or made in the home country.

Reading HELPDESK

mercantilism an economic theory that depends on a greater amount of exports than imports in order to increase a country's supply of gold and silver

These materials are then shipped to the home country. In the home country, the raw materials are used to manufacture goods so that the home country does not have to buy these goods from other countries.

Europeans established trading posts and colonies in Asia and North America. By the end of the 1500s, Spain had a colony in the Philippines. In the 1600s, English and French merchants arrived in India. They began trading with the people there. In 1619, the Dutch built a fort on the island of Java, in what is now Indonesia. The Dutch became so powerful that they pushed the Portuguese out of the spice trade.

Guns and powerful ships helped Europeans defeat Arab fleets and Indian armies. Across Asia, Europeans forced local rulers to open their lands to trade. The arrival of the Europeans in Japan caused a dramatic change in that society. A new Japanese shogun used European-made guns and cannons to dominate his enemies. He was finally able to defeat the feudal lords and the daimyo and reunite Japan.

Creating Joint-Stock Companies

Europeans found that paying for overseas trading voyages was expensive. In the 1600s, however, Europeans developed new business **methods**. Historians call this the Commercial Revolution. **Commerce** (KAH•muhrs) is the buying and selling of goods in large amounts over long distances.

This type of commerce needed large amounts of money in order to be profitable. So, a new type of businessperson called an **entrepreneur** (AHN•truh•pruh•NUHR) emerged. Entrepreneurs **invest**, or put money into a project. Their goal is to make money from the success of the project.

As overseas trade increased in the 1600s, many projects were too large for one entrepreneur to pay for. If a voyage failed, for example, that individual would lose everything. As a result, groups of entrepreneurs began to form joint-stock companies. A joint-stock company is a business in which many people can invest. Groups or individuals, called investors, buy shares in the company. These shares are called stocks. By owning stock, investors would share the expenses, the risks—and the profits.

Henry Hudson lands in North America ready to establish trade with Native Americans. He was sent by the Netherlands to find a Northwest Passage to Asia.

CRITICAL THINKING

Speculating What do you think Native Americans thought of Hudson and his crew?

Bettmann/CORBIS

commerce an exchange of goods; business

entrepreneur one who organizes, pays for, and takes on the risk of setting up a business

Academic Vocabulary

method a way of doing something; a process or procedure

invest to give money to a company in exchange for a return, or profit, on the money

LESSON 3 • Day 1 (cont.)

World Trade Changes

GUIDING QUESTION ***How did Europe's merchants change the world trade system?***

Determining Cause and Effect Have students meet in small groups to plan and complete a graphic organizer of their own design that demonstrates the concept of mercantilism between European nations and their colonies. Have students show their graphic organizer on the whiteboard.

Ask: **How will you best show imports and exports between a colony and its European mother country?** *(Students may suggest arrows moving to and from boxes showing the colony and the mother country.)*

How can you show a country gaining wealth and power by exporting or selling more than it imports? *(Students may suggest showing symbols for money or goods as well as power.)*

Why would you need to add other boxes or circles to show other countries and their colonies? *(Students might realize that to show a country increasing its wealth and power as well as what it imports and buys from other countries, these countries have to be shown.)*

Have students experiment with different ways of showing this interchange among colonies, countries, and other countries they deal with. Allow volunteers to present their graphic organizers and use them to explain the theory of mercantilism. BL

LECTURE SLIDE

Synthesizing Show students the lecture slide that compares mercantilism, joint-stock companies, and cottage industries. Ask a volunteer to read each paragraph from the slide. Then have students synthesize the information and explain each business arrangement in their own words. ELL

SLIDE SHOW

Making Generalizations Challenge students to make a generalization about how entrepreneurs tried to reduce the risk of losing money. Students should note how joint-stock companies shared this risk. They should also discuss how cottage industries allowed for smaller operations. This involved less risk for that investment as well.

Ask: **Why did entrepreneurs create these different ways to invest in producing or trading goods?** *(Students may say they were trying to lower their risk.)* Challenge students to be as specific as possible. Show students the slide show about cottage industries.

Have them interpret the slides and explain the process of setting up a cottage industry. They can also use examples like the Virginia Company when discussing joint-stock companies. Be sure students understand the meaning of these terms. AL ELL

CLOSE & REFLECT

Summarizing Lead students in a discussion of how trade led to a variety of new business models.

Ask: **How did peasants benefit from the new types of businesses that developed as a result of worldwide trade?** *(Peasants could make a living by working on a trade from their homes. It gave them economic independence.)*

LESSON 3 • Day 2

ENGAGE

Listing Point out that many products and ideas became part of American culture as a result of an exchange of goods that happened during the age of exploration. This period was called the Columbian Exchange.

Ask students to review their textbooks under the section titled "A Global Exchange." Then, have them call out foods that came to America through the Columbian Exchange. Write their suggestions on the whiteboard. *(Possible answers include: chocolate, coffee, sugarcane, bananas, citrus fruits, wheat, oats, rice, horses, cattle, etc.)*

Then, have students suggest what dishes Americans like to eat that may not be possible had the Columbian Exchange not taken place. *(Possible answers include: chocolate cake, breakfast cereals, orange juice, hamburgers, sugar-sweetened desserts, wheat bread, etc.)* ELL

3 A Global Exchange

GUIDING QUESTION ***How did trade change the world?***

Defining Ask students to define the Columbian Exchange. *(the purposeful and accidental flow of goods and ideas between Europe and the Americas during the Age of Exploration)*

Ask: **Why is this flow of goods and ideas called the Columbian Exchange?** *(It is named after Christopher Columbus.)*

Summarize Lead students in a discussion of the following question: **How did the Columbian Exchange permanently change the cultures of Europe and the Americas?**

Guide students to understand that a new crop or a fruit or an animal that hasn't existed in that place before can meet a need or be used in a way that was not possible before.

Use the horse as an example. The Americas had other domesticated animals, and the horse was only of limited use in many places in the Americas. When it was brought from Spain to the Americas, it made a significant difference to Native Americans living on the Great Plains. The horse turned small tribes of Native Americans into powerful hunters and warriors.

INTERACTIVE WORKSHEET **Summarizing** Assign the Economics of History Activity about the Columbian Exchange as homework.

Have students complete the Lesson 3 Review.

CLOSE & REFLECT

Applying Lead students in a discussion of the following question about contact between Europe and the places explorers and conquerors encountered.

Ask: **Who do you think benefited more from the contact between the Americas and European nations? Why?** *(Answers will vary. Students may argue that Europeans gained many beneficial plants and animals from the Americas, as well as treasure. Or they may note that the Europeans transformed the people and cultures of the Americas.)*

Answers for pages 630–633

P. 630 INFOGRAPHIC

1. Christopher Columbus
2. Henry Hudson

P. 630 Reading Strategy Answers will vary but could include: Merchants wanted trade; religious freedom; economic troubles; forced off their farms; wanted to own their own lands.

P. 631 ☑ PROGRESS CHECK Disease had reduced the number of Native Americans who were available to work, so enslaved Africans were brought in to do the labor on these plantations, which required large numbers of workers.

P. 632 GEOGRAPHY CONNECTION

1. Spain and Portugal
2. CRITICAL THINKING The port cities would be affected by foreign influences from European trading. Goods and economic forces would change the development of the ports.

P. 633 CRITICAL THINKING Student answers will vary but could include they were frightening; perhaps gods or heavenly spirits.

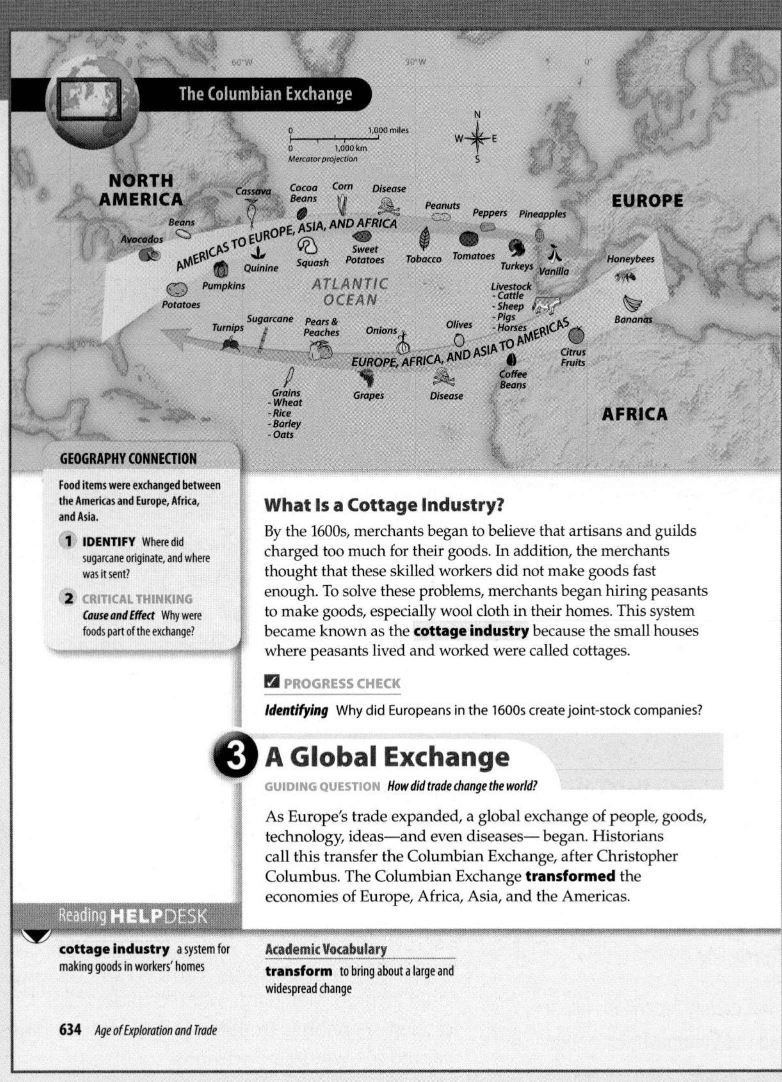

GEOGRAPHY CONNECTION

Food items were exchanged between the Americas and Europe, Africa, and Asia.

1 **IDENTIFY** Where did sugarcane originate, and where was it sent?

2 **CRITICAL THINKING** ***Cause and Effect*** Why were foods part of the exchange?

What Is a Cottage Industry?

By the 1600s, merchants began to believe that artisans and guilds charged too much for their goods. In addition, the merchants thought that these skilled workers did not make goods fast enough. To solve these problems, merchants began hiring peasants to make goods, especially wool cloth in their homes. This system became known as the **cottage industry** because the small houses where peasants lived and worked were called cottages.

PROGRESS CHECK

Identifying Why did Europeans in the 1600s create joint-stock companies?

3 A Global Exchange

GUIDING QUESTION *How did trade change the world?*

As Europe's trade expanded, a global exchange of people, goods, technology, ideas—and even diseases— began. Historians call this transfer the Columbian Exchange, after Christopher Columbus. The Columbian Exchange **transformed** the economies of Europe, Africa, Asia, and the Americas.

Reading HELPDESK

cottage industry a system for making goods in workers' homes

Academic Vocabulary

transform to bring about a large and widespread change

Merchants introduced foods from the Americas to Europeans. Two of the most important crops were corn and potatoes. In Europe, these crops became essential to daily life. Corn was used to feed livestock, producing larger, healthier animals. This resulted in more meat, leather, and wool. Potatoes helped Europeans feed more people from their land.

Europeans acquired other foods from Native Americans, such as squash, beans, and tomatoes. Tomatoes greatly changed cooking in Italy, where tomato sauces became widely used. Chocolate was a popular food from Central America. By mixing chocolate with milk and sugar, Europeans made candy.

American settlers planted many European and Asian grains, such as wheat, oats, barley, rye, and rice. Coffee and tropical fruits, such as bananas, were brought to the Americas as well. Eventually, coffee and banana farms employed thousands of workers in Central America and South America.

Explorers and settlers also brought pigs, sheep, cattle, chickens, and horses to the Americas. Raising chickens changed the diet of many people in Central and South America.

The lives of Native Americans on the Great Plains changed when they acquired horses. Horses provided a faster way to travel. As a result, Native Americans became more efficient at hunting buffalo for food and at fighting enemies.

Europeans obtained sugarcane from Asia and began growing it in the Caribbean. This caused a migration, or movement of people. To plant and harvest the sugarcane, over time Europeans enslaved millions of Africans and moved them to the Americas.

In addition to slavery, the Columbian Exchange spread diseases from one area to another. When Europeans arrived in America, they were carrying viruses that were new to Native Americans. These diseases were deadly and eventually killed millions.

Bananas—a huge cash crop—grow on plantations in tropical locations such as Central America.

PROGRESS CHECK

Evaluating Was the Columbian Exchange a benefit or a problem for the Americas?

LESSON 3 REVIEW

Review Vocabulary

1. How does *mercantilism* benefit the homeland more than the colony?

Answer the Guiding Questions

2. ***Explaining*** Why was growing tobacco an important boost to help colonists trade?
3. ***Identifying*** Which group was brought in to replace Native American workers in American colonies?
4. ***Explaining*** Who receives the benefits and profits from a joint-stock company?
5. ***Identifying*** What was the Columbian Exchange?
6. **CREATIVE WRITING** Write a paragraph describing how either Europeans or Native Americans might have reacted when they first tasted foods from another continent. Consider how chocolate, tomatoes, peanuts, and bananas must have puzzled people who were eating it for the first time.

NOTES

NOTES

LESSON 3 • Day 2 (cont.)

IF YOU HAVE MORE TIME . . .

Teach Cause and Effect

Review the content about the Columbian Exchange, and point out that the movement of goods and the results of this movement were caused by many factors. The Exchange also had many long-term effects. Use the episode in history to reinforce the skills of understanding cause and effect.

Many students struggle to connect how events in history are connected to one another. They miss the subtle causes, and they do not understand the larger effects of small events. Therefore, begin the discussion with a definition of the terms *cause* and *effect*. Give an example such as the following: A settler arrives in the Americas. He is hungry. He eats the food that grows in the Americas. When he returns to Europe, he takes some of this new food with him. Farmers in Europe begin to cultivate new foods.

Ask:

- **What caused the settler to try new foods?** *(He was hungry.)*
- **What was the effect of taking the foods back to Europe?** *(European farmers began to plant the new food.)*

Identify Cause-and-Effect Signal Words

Because it is more difficult to identify cause and effect outside of clear, classroom-staged activities, offer students a list of words that signal a cause-and-effect relationship.

- *because*
- *so*
- *therefore*
- *as a result*
- *due to*

Explain that students should look for these words in their reading to identify causes and effects. They should also use these words in their writing to show cause-and-effect relationships.

Have students break into pairs and practice using these signal words in a sentence about the Columbian Exchange. Invite volunteers to share their sentences with the class. Then, as a class, identify the cause and effect in each sentence. Elicit understanding that the signal words clarify the cause-and-effect relationship the writer is expressing.

Use Graphic Organizers to Show Cause and Effect

Explain to students that a graphic organizer might make it easier to visualize cause-and-effect relationships. Draw two large circles on the board. Draw an arrow between the circles. Label one circle "Cause." Label the second circle "Effect." Using one of the student-generated sentences as an example, fill in the graphic organizer, dividing the information into a cause and an effect.

Next, draw a more complex cause-and-effect organizer on the board with a string of circles linked together by arrows. Explain how this arrangement is used to show a string of causes and effects, one leading to the next. Use the following example to demonstrate the organizer.

Explorers first tasted chocolate when they conquered the Aztec people. The explorers took the chocolate drink to Europe. The bitter flavor was too strong for Europeans, so they combined it with sugar. As a result, many Europeans began drinking a hot chocolate beverage. Today, chocolate is one of the most popular candies.

Point out that all cause-and-effect relationships are not linear. Instead, there are often many causes that lead to a single effect. Draw a third organizer on the board consisting of several circles (the causes) pointing at one larger circle (the effect).

Likewise, in some cases, one cause might lead to several effects. Draw an organizer on the board in which one central circle (cause) points outward and toward several smaller circles (effects).

Arrange students into small groups, and have students come up with examples from the chapter or from real life that could fit into the organizers; for example, several factors that led to a war, the many effects of climate change, etc. BL

To better grasp the concept of cause and effect, have students connect the idea to their own lives. For example have them list several causes that led to a single event. Likewise, have them list several effects that resulted from a single cause, such as several effects of staying up late at night. AL ELL

Answers for pages 634–635

P. 634 ☑ PROGRESS CHECK Joint-stock companies were a way for European businesses to increase the amount of money they had to invest in new ventures and decrease the risk of losing money. Investors bought shares in the business; the business used this money to buy or make new goods cheaply; from the sale of these goods at higher prices, the company hoped to make a profit, which was shared with the investors.

P. 634 GEOGRAPHY CONNECTION

1. Sugarcane came from Europe, Africa, and Asia to the Americas.
2. CRITICAL THINKING They were either unique to one place or there was a demand for them in the place where they were sent.

P. 635 ☑ PROGRESS CHECK Answers will vary, but students should discuss the devastation of Native American peoples from disease and how this made it easier for Europeans to conquer them. These ideas should be compared to the benefits introduced by Europeans.

LESSON 3 REVIEW

1. The colony's purpose is to provide raw materials for manufacturing in the homeland. The majority of the profits are earned in the homeland, which is the purpose of mercantilism.
2. By trading items such as tobacco that had value in Europe, colonists provided income that supported the colonies in much the same way that mining gold and silver justified the expenses of establishing colonies elsewhere.
3. Enslaved Africans were brought in to work when the number of Native Americans declined.
4. stockholders
5. It was an interchange of goods, ideas, people, and diseases between Europe and the Americas.
6. Answers will vary, but students should describe how this exposure to something new would delight and perplex someone from a culture that had never experienced it before.

CHAPTER 21 Activities

Write your answers on a separate piece of paper.

1 Exploring the Essential Question
EXPOSITORY WRITING When different cultures share technologies, the interchange can affect the lives of people on different continents. Write an expository essay about how sailing technologies led to changes in Europe and in the Americas.

2 21st Century Skills
CREATING A BLOG Create a blog to share your thoughts on exploration. Discuss your observations about the positive and negative effects of the first encounters between Europeans and Native Americans. To encourage an exchange of ideas with other bloggers, ask discussion questions about how these two civilizations saw their contact in very different ways. Your questions should require bloggers to support their opinions with examples.

3 Thinking Like a Historian
MAKING CONNECTIONS Create a diagram like the one shown here that traces the progress of European explorations. Start with the first attempts to seek a route to Asia by going around Africa to eventually sailing around the world.

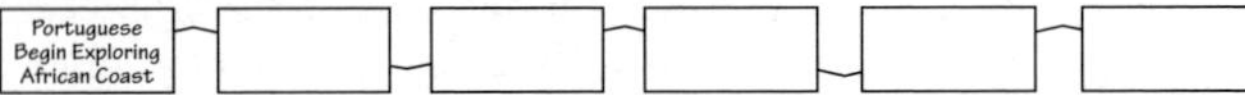

4 GEOGRAPHY ACTIVITY

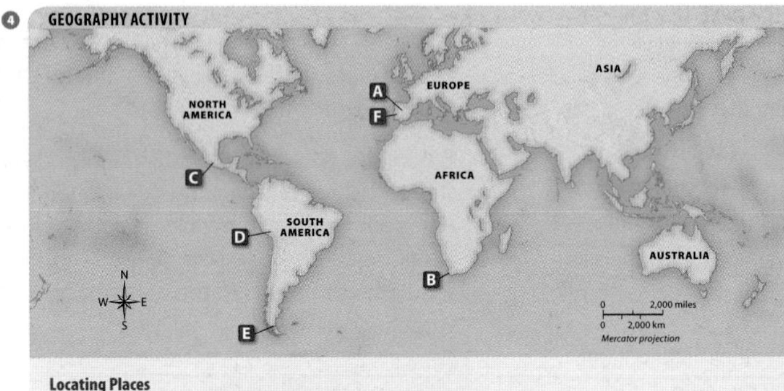

Locating Places
Match the letters on the map with the numbered places listed below.

1. Portugal
2. Aztec Empire
3. Inca Empire
4. Spain
5. Cape of Good Hope
6. Straights of Magellan

CHAPTER 21 Assessment

REVIEW THE GUIDING QUESTIONS
Directions: Choose the best answer for each question.

1 Europeans wanted to find a water route to Asia because
A. the Italians cut off the flow of goods from Asia.
B. the Ottoman Turks made spices less expensive.
C. the Mongols lost power and overland trade was disrupted.
D. the lack of road repairs blocked the Silk Road.

2 Which advancement made by the Greeks did the Europeans adopt for overseas exploration?
F. Ptolemy's maps
G. triangular sails
H. the astrolabe
I. the compass

3 Who first tried to help the Europeans to find a water route to Asia?
A. Vasco da Gama
B. Ferdinand of Spain
C. Hernán Cortés
D. Henry the Navigator

4 Which of the following helped Europeans the most in conquering Native Americans?
F. diseases
G. gold
H. improved ships
I. horses

5 Europeans used enslaved Africans to
A. expand their conquering armies.
B. explore unknown lands.
C. work on farms in their colonies.
D. form joint-stock companies.

6 The key idea behind the concept of mercantilism is that countries
F. did not need colonies.
G. wanted to export more goods.
H. wanted to import more goods.
I. no longer needed entrepreneurs.

CHAPTER 21 Assessment *(continued)*

DBQ DOCUMENT-BASED QUESTIONS

Drawing Conclusions Columbus wrote about meeting Native Americans:

"Thus they bartered [traded], like idiots, cotton and gold for fragments of bows, glasses, bottles, and jars; which I forbad[e] as being unjust, and myself gave them many beautiful . . . articles which I had brought with me, taking nothing from them in return; I did this in order that . . . I might induce [persuade] them to take an interest in . . . delivering to us such things as they possessed in abundance, but which we greatly needed."

—Christopher Columbus, letter to Raphael Sanchez, March 14, 1493

7 Why did Columbus prevent his soldiers from trading items of little value with Native Americans?
A. to get more gold for himself
B. to encourage open and fair trading
C. to prevent any interchange between them
D. to avoid wasting their valuables on useless things

8 **Making Inferences** What were the "things as they possessed in abundance" which Columbus mentions?
F. bows and glasses
G. beautiful articles Columbus had brought
H. fragments of bottles and jars
I. gold and cotton

SHORT RESPONSE
Write your answers on a separate piece of paper.

"There are all kinds of green vegetables, . . . fruits, . . . honey and wax from bees . . . .Different kinds of cotton thread of all colors in skeins [loose balls] are exposed for sale in one quarter of the market, which has the appearance of the silk-market at Granada; . . . everything that can be found throughout the whole country is sold in the markets."

—from *The Second Letter to Charles V, 1520*, by Hernan Cortés

9 What can you tell about the economy of the Aztec empire from this description by Cortés?

10 What comparison does Cortés make to Granada, Spain?

EXTENDED RESPONSE

11 **Descriptive Writing** Write a paragraph about how the Columbian Exchange presented advantages and disadvantages for Native Americans and Europeans.

Need Extra Help?

If You've Missed Question	1	2	3	4	5	6	7	8	9	10	11
Review Lesson	1	1	1	2	2	3	1	1	2	2	3

NOTES

REFLECT, REVIEW, & REMEDIATE

INTERACTIVE WORKSHEET

Chapter Summary

Provide students with the Chapter Summary worksheet to help review the chapter and prepare for assessment.

Reviewing the Enduring Understanding

Review this chapter's Enduring Understanding with students:

- The movement of people, goods, and ideas causes societies to change over time.

Lead a discussion that allows students to recall the science and technology that changed people's lives in this chapter. Remind students how Europeans and the civilizations they encountered affected each other. Conclude by having volunteers cite how people, goods, and ideas were moved, and what changes they brought.

INTERACTIVE WHITEBOARD ACTIVITY Then have students divide into debate teams. Their topic will be "Should the Europeans have conquered and occupied the Americas or merely traded and shared goods and ideas?" Have students argue both sides of the issue. Provide a Pros and Cons graphic organizer to help record their ideas. Students' debates should consider alternatives to what actually did occur. Students could also debate whether the Native Americans should have tried to conquer Europe in the same way that Europeans took over the Americas. Lastly, students should propose how a more peaceful and creative interchange could have occurred between these very different civilizations, one of trade and cultural exchange, as well as mutual respect.

Pros	Cons

ACTIVITIES ANSWERS

Exploring the Essential Question

1. Students' essays should correctly identify the technology that came from Arabic traders (astrolabe, triangular sails, ancient maps) and explain how this exchange fueled a larger exchange once the European explorers used these tools to extend their travels to unknown places. Students may discuss how the secondary exchange that occurred after Europeans began trading with and conquering other civilizations was a benefit as well as a detriment to both parties.

21st Century Skills

2. Students should have a blog format or a bulletin board forum that clearly presents their opinions and observations and states how they feel about the positive and negative aspects of the interchange between cultures. Discussion questions should provoke reader reaction by offering differing viewpoints of the exchange but also require those making a response to support their opinions with examples.

Thinking Like a Historian

3. Graphic organizers should identify in sequence the various stages in the exploration of the world: Portuguese sail around Africa; Columbus sails to the Americas; Balboa discovers Pacific Ocean; French and Dutch explore North America; Magellan sails to Asia and back to Portugal.

Locating Places

4. Students should correctly locate the named places as follows:
1. F, **2.** C, **3.** D, **4.** A, **5.** B, **6.** E

ASSESSMENT ANSWERS

Review the Guiding Questions

1. **C** The correct choice is C. When the Mongol Empire collapsed, local rulers could no longer protect people trading along the Silk Road. The Ottoman Turks took control of the spice trade with Europe and made Asian goods much more expensive. The Italians did not cut off the flow of goods from Asia, nor were road repairs related to the closing of the Silk Road.

2. **F** The correct choice is F. Ptolemy, a Greek, had prepared maps of the known world that European explorers used to venture into oceans and areas they knew little about. Triangular sails, the astrolabe, the compass, and the caravel were not Greek inventions.

3. **D** The correct choice is D. Henry the Navigator brought the finest minds of his time to advance the science of exploration. Although he wasn't an explorer himself, he helped Portugal begin the first explorations of Africa as a way to find a new route to Asia.

4. **F** The correct choice is F. The diseases the Europeans carried unintentionally caused vast loss of life in the Americas and weakened the empires there, allowing Europeans to take over. Caravels were useful for traveling to the Americas, and horses were useful in warfare, but they were less important factors. Many Europeans came to the Americas seeking gold.

5. **C** The correct choice is C. Europeans brought enslaved Africans to their colonies to replace Native Americans who had been killed by disease as well as by the Spanish conquest. Enslaved Africans were not employed as soldiers, explorers, or company investors.

6. **G** The correct choice is G. Countries need to export more goods than they import under the theory of mercantilism. They acquire raw goods cheaply from their colonies and convert these to manufactured goods, which they sell to obtain wealth and power. If they had to purchase raw materials at high prices, they would not profit as much by converting them into products.

Document-Based Questions

7. **B** The correct choice is B. Columbus wanted the Native Americans to trade with the Spanish so they could get goods and raw materials to bring back to Europe. He was not trying to protect his soldiers as much as he was preserving a relationship with the locals. B is the best answer.

8. **I** The correct choice is I. Europeans wanted products like cotton and gold that were valuable to them but were abundant or less expensive to the Native Americans.

Short Response

9. The description makes it clear that the Aztec Empire had a strong economy and a wide variety of goods for sale. The city was thriving with activity.

10. In the excerpt, the Aztec markets are compared to the silk market in Granada.

Extended Response

11. Students' descriptive writing should provide details about how having new foods, guns, domestic animals, and fresh ideas would benefit Native Americans. They should also note how disease, being conquered, and being forced to work as enslaved people ruined the world they once knew.

ONLINE RESOURCES
networks

There's More Online!

- INTERACTIVE WORKSHEETS
- BIOGRAPHIES
- CHARTS/GRAPHS
- GAMES
- GRAPHIC ORGANIZERS
- IMAGES
- MAPS
- PRIMARY SOURCES
- SLIDE SHOWS
- TIME LINE
- LECTURE SLIDES
- INTERACTIVE WHITEBOARD ACTIVITIES
- ASSESSMENTS
- VIDEOS

Planetary Motion: Kepler's Three Laws

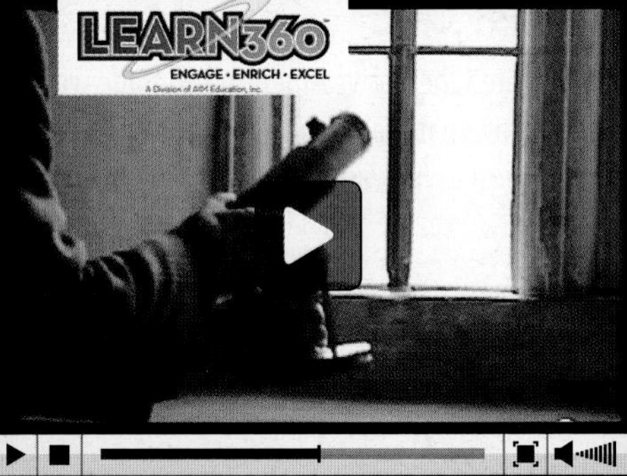

Reason and the Age o f Enlightenment

Chapter 22

The Scientific Revolution and the Enlightenment

Dear World History Teacher,

The Scientific Revolution was a major turning point in modern civilization. During the Scientific Revolution, the Western world overthrew the medieval, Ptolemaic worldview and arrived at a new conception of the universe: the sun at the center, the planets as material bodies revolving around the sun in elliptical orbits, and an infinite rather than a finite world. The work of Bacon and Descartes left Europeans with the separation of mind and matter and the belief that by using only reason, they could in fact understand and dominate the world of nature. The development of a scientific method furthered the work of scientists.

Highly influenced by the new worldview created by the Scientific Revolution, the philosophers of the eighteenth century hoped they could create a new society by using reason to discover the natural laws that governed it. They believed education could create better human beings and a better human society. They created the new "sciences of man": economics, politics, and education. Together, the Scientific Revolution of the seventeenth century and the Enlightenment of the eighteenth century made up an intellectual revolution that laid the foundations for a modern worldview based on rationalism and secularism.

Jackson J. Spielvogel

More Media Resources

Current Events Online

Visit McGraw-Hill's current events Web site for high-interest news stories and activities for your students. Access the site through the Student or Teacher Center in **networks.**

Reading List

Grade 6 reading level:
Isaac Newton and Physics for Kids, by Kerrie Logan Hollihan

Grade 7 reading level:
Catherine, The Great Journey, Russia, 1743, by Kristiana Gregory

Grade 8 reading level:
1000 Inventions and Discoveries, by Roger Bridgman

At the MOVIES

Watch clips of movies about the Scientific Revolution, such as *Galileo*, and the documentaries *Genius: Galileo* and *Sir Isaac Newton: The Gravity of Genius*. For the Enlightenment, have students watch the movie *Leonard Bernstein's Candide* and the documentary *Catherine the Great*.

Discuss: Have students compare the fictional movie about Galileo with the documentary about him. **Which version did they like better? Which version did they think was more accurate?**

NOTE: Be sure to preview any clips to ensure they are age-appropriate.

Search for more videos online in the **networks** Resource Library.

CHAPTER 22 Planner

UNDERSTANDING BY DESIGN®

Enduring Understandings

- *Science and technology can change people's lives.* • *The value that society places on individual rights is often reflected in that society's government.*

Essential Questions

- *How do new ideas change the way people live?* • *How do governments change?*

Students will know:

- *the Scientific Revolution generated much new knowledge*
- *the scientific method represented a new way of studying the world*
- *the Enlightenment influenced ideas about human rights and government*

Students will be able to:

- **describe** how science was practiced in ancient and medieval times
- **compare and contrast** the theories of Ptolemy and Copernicus
- **identify** how planets are held in orbit, according to Newton
- **explain** why Descartes believed that mathematics is the source of scientific truth
- **identify** who developed the heliocentric theory
- **summarize** how the ancient Greeks studied nature
- **explain** what instrument made the discovery of bacteria possible
- **define** the scientific method
- **compare and contrast** the ideas of Hobbes and Locke
- **describe** the importance of Diderot's *Encyclopedia*
- **explain** how Frederick the Great influenced the Enlightenment
- **identify** which absolute monarch freed the serfs
- **describe** the type of government that John Locke supported
- **explain** why Voltaire criticized the Roman Catholic Church

Predictable Misunderstandings

Students may think:

- Most people knew that Earth revolved around the sun before Copernicus.
- Most important scientific discoveries are recent.
- The English fought a war to gain democratic reforms.
- The monarchs in Europe were against any democratic reforms.

Assessment Evidence

Performance Task

- Hands-On Chapter Project

Other Evidence

- Responses to Interactive Whiteboard Activities
- Class discussion answers about the life and discoveries of Isaac Newton
- Organizing the steps in the scientific method
- Comparing and contrasting primary sources of Hobbes and Locke
- 21st Century Skills Activity
- Primary Source Activity
- Interactive Graphic Organizers
- What Do You Think? questions
- Written paragraphs
- Lesson Reviews

Pacing Guide

Introducing the Chapter	1 day
Lesson 1 The Scientific Revolution	2 days
Lesson 2 The Enlightenment	1 day
Chapter Activities and Assessment	1 day
TOTAL TIME	**5 Days**

Differentiated Instruction

These lesson plans are written to address the needs of your On Level students. Discussion and activities that are well-suited to your Approaching Grade Level learners, Beyond Grade Level learners, as well as your English Language Learners are coded as follows:

Approaching Grade Level

Beyond Grade Level

ELL **English Language Learner**

NCSS Standards covered in "The Scientific Revolution and the Enlightenment"

Learners will understand:

2 TIME, CONTINUITY, AND CHANGE

5. Key historical periods and patterns of change within and across cultures (e.g., the rise and fall of ancient civilizations, the development of technology, the rise of modern nation-states, and the establishment and breakdown of colonial systems)

6. The origins and influences of social, cultural, political, and economic systems;

7. The contributions of key persons, groups, and events from the past and their influence on the present

8. The history of democratic ideals and principles, and how they are represented in documents, artifacts and symbols

4 INDIVIDUAL DEVELOPMENT AND IDENTITY

1. The study of individual development and identity helps us know that individuals change physically, cognitively, and emotionally over time

5. That individuals' choices influence identity and development

6 POWER, AUTHORITY, AND GOVERNANCE

2. Fundamental ideas that are the foundation of American constitutional democracy (including those of the U.S. Constitution, popular sovereignty, the rule of law, separation of powers, checks and balances, minority rights, the separation of church and state, and Federalism)

3. Fundamental values of constitutional democracy (e.g., the common good, liberty, justice, equality, and individual dignity)

4. The ideologies and structures of political systems that differ from those of the United States

5. The ways in which governments meet the needs and wants of citizens, manage conflict, and establish order and society

8 SCIENCE, TECHNOLOGY, AND SOCIETY

1. Science is a result of empirical study of the natural world, and technology is the application of knowledge to accomplish tasks

2. Society often turns to science and technology to solve problems

4. Science and technology have had both positive and negative impacts upon individuals, societies, and the environment in the past and present

5. Science and technology have changed peoples' perceptions of the social and natural world, as well as their relationship to the land, economy and trade, their concept of security, and their major daily activities

6. Values, beliefs, and attitudes that have been influenced by new scientific and technological knowledge (e.g., invention of the printing press, conceptions of the universe, applications of atomic energy, and genetic discoveries)

8. Science and technology sometimes create ethical issues that test our standards and values

CHAPTER 22

Introducing the Chapter

(Student Edition p. 639)

The Story Matters . . .

Read "The Story Matters . . ." aloud in class. Alternately, ask a volunteer to read it aloud. Then discuss what it might have been like to have lived in Russia during the time of Catherine the Great.

Ask: **Who are some kings and queens that are living today? Have you seen any television shows or news reports about these monarchs?** Have a few students share their thoughts.

Then ask: **Why do you think some countries still have kings and queens? Do you think these monarchs have a great deal of power?**

Tell the class that during the Scientific Revolution and the Enlightenment, most of the countries in Europe were ruled by monarchs. Tell interested students that they can find more online about Catherine the Great and other monarchs of the 1600s and 1700s.

The Scientific Revolution and the Enlightenment

1500 to 1800

ESSENTIAL QUESTIONS • *How do new ideas change the way people live?* • *How do governments change?*

networks

There's More Online about the developments that led to the Scientific Revolution and the Enlightenment.

CHAPTER 22

Lesson 1
The Scientific Revolution

Lesson 2
The Enlightenment

The Story Matters . . .

Catherine the Great ruled Russia from 1762 to 1796. Catherine was born a German princess, but at the age of fifteen she married Russian Grand Duke Peter. Soon her husband became the emperor of Russia. Peter, however, was a weak leader. In contrast, Catherine was intelligent and also ambitious. She wanted to rule Russia herself. She used military support to remove her husband from the throne. Soon afterward, he was assassinated.

As empress, Catherine the Great made Russia into a world power. She could be a harsh ruler, especially toward the peasants whom she made serfs. However, she also supported advances in the sciences and culture. Indeed, new ideas were sweeping across most of Europe. Many of them, however, challenged the idea of monarchy.

◀ *Catherine II of Russia became known as Catherine the Great because she expanded her country's borders. This portrait hangs in the Museum of History in Moscow, Russia.*

The Art Archive/CORBIS

639

Introducing Place and Time (Student Edition pp. 640–641)

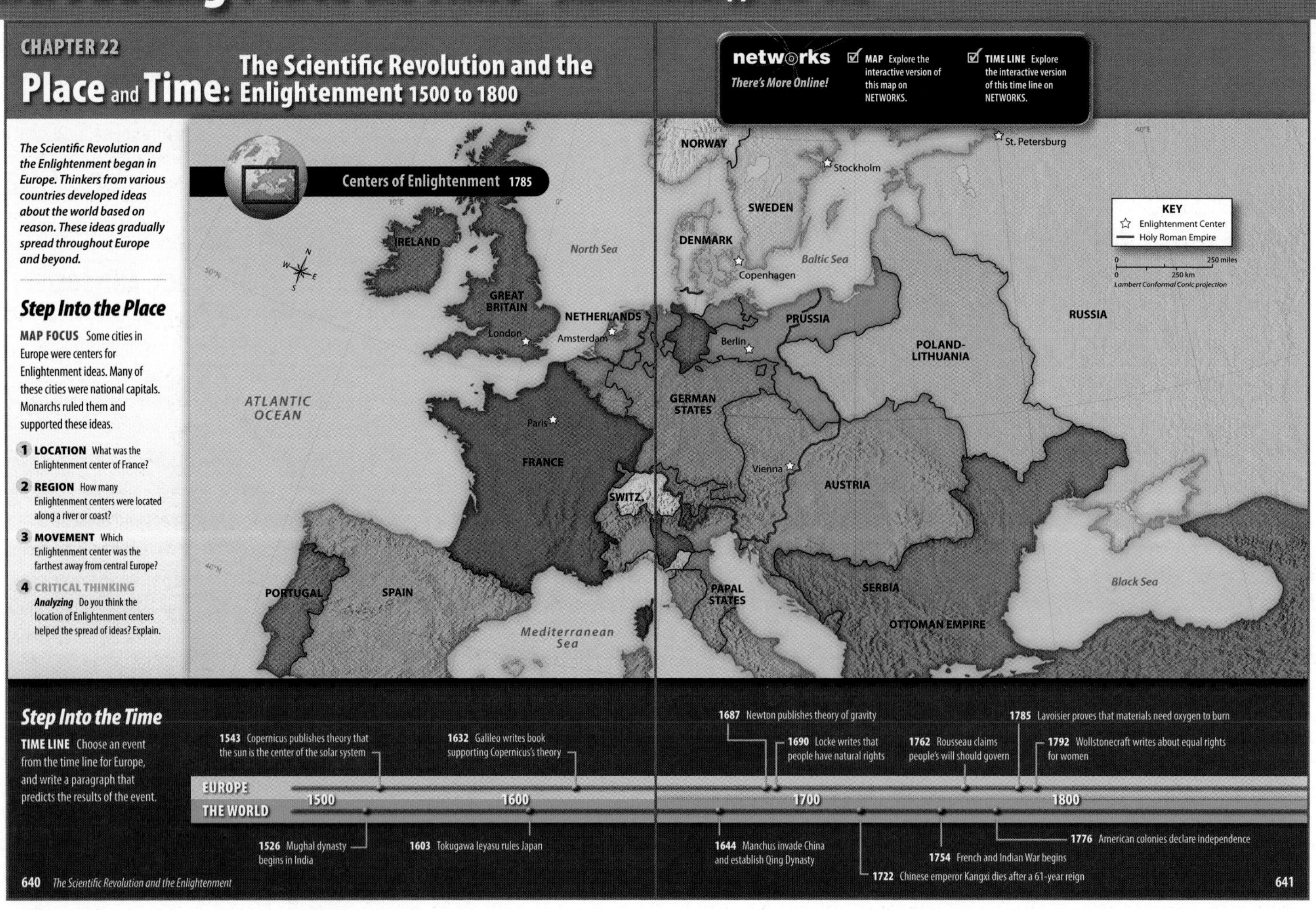

CHAPTER 22

Place and Time: The Scientific Revolution and the Enlightenment 1500 to 1800

networks *There's More Online!*

☑ MAP Explore the interactive version of this map on NETWORKS.

☑ TIME LINE Explore the interactive version of this time line on NETWORKS.

The Scientific Revolution and the Enlightenment began in Europe. Thinkers from various countries developed ideas about the world based on reason. These ideas gradually spread throughout Europe and beyond.

Step Into the Place

MAP FOCUS Some cities in Europe were centers for Enlightenment ideas. Many of these cities were national capitals. Monarchs ruled them and supported these ideas.

1. **LOCATION** What was the Enlightenment center of France?
2. **REGION** How many Enlightenment centers were located along a river or coast?
3. **MOVEMENT** Which Enlightenment center was the farthest away from central Europe?
4. **CRITICAL THINKING** *Analyzing* Do you think the location of Enlightenment centers helped the spread of ideas? Explain.

Step Into the Time

TIME LINE Choose an event from the time line for Europe, and write a paragraph that predicts the results of the event.

640 *The Scientific Revolution and the Enlightenment*

641

Technology Extension

- Find an additional activity online that incorporates technology for this project.
- Visit the EdTechTeacher Web sites (included in the Technology Extension for this chapter) for more links, tutorials, and other resources.

Assessing Background Knowledge

INTERACTIVE WORKSHEET

What Do You Know? Activity

Have students complete the cloze activity about the Enlightenment before they study the chapter. Direct students to read the paragraphs on the worksheet. Then, have them fill in each blank with the term from the box that they think is correct. Next, take a poll for each blank to see how many students filled it in correctly. You can use this information to tailor your lessons to focus on students' misconceptions.

After students complete the chapter, have them reread the paragraphs and note which blanks they filled in correctly and which blanks they filled in incorrectly. Ask students who changed their responses to explain why they did so. *(Students should cite facts from the chapter.)*

INTERACTIVE WORKSHEET

Guided Reading Activities

You may wish to assign the Guided Reading Activity for Lesson 1 after introducing the chapter content.

Hands-On Chapter Project

Students will create a newspaper article describing an important scientist and discovery of the Scientific Revolution.

- Students will participate in a class discussion to review what they have learned about scientists and discoveries of the Scientific Revolution.
- Then, students will divide into small groups. Each group will choose a scientist and a discovery. Students will use worksheets and discussions to help them plan, research, and write their newspaper articles.
- Next, each group will present their newspaper article to the class.
- Finally, students will evaluate their research, content, and presentation using an Assessment Rubric.

Visit **networks** online to see the full project and rubric.

ONLINE RESOURCES

networks

Assign these interactive worksheets and quizzes from your Teacher Lesson Center. All resources are print-ready.

It's ALL Online!

CHAPTER 22 RESOURCES

- ☑ CHAPTER SUMMARY
- ☑ VOCABULARY BUILDER
- ☑ WHAT DO YOU KNOW?
- ☑ HANDS-ON CHAPTER PROJECT

Lesson 1 Resources

- ☑ 21ST CENTURY SKILLS ACTIVITY
  Write a Résumé
- ☑ INTERACTIVE GUIDED READING ACTIVITY
- ☑ READING ESSENTIALS AND STUDY GUIDE
- ☑ ONLINE SELF-CHECK QUIZ

Lesson 2 Resources

- ☑ PRIMARY SOURCE ACTIVITY
  The Ideas of Hobbes and Locke
- ☑ INTERACTIVE GUIDED READING ACTIVITY
- ☑ READING ESSENTIALS AND STUDY GUIDE
- ☑ ONLINE SELF-CHECK QUIZ

ASSESSMENT RESOURCES

- ☑ LESSON REVIEWS
- ☑ ONLINE SELF-CHECK QUIZZES
- ☑ CHAPTER ACTIVITIES AND ASSESSMENT
- ☑ STANDARDIZED TEST PRACTICE

REMEDIATION RESOURCES

- ☑ READING ESSENTIALS AND STUDY GUIDE
- ☑ GUIDED READING ACTIVITIES
- ☑ ONLINE SELF-CHECK QUIZZES
- ☑ CHAPTER SUMMARY

Step Into the Place

Location Project the Interactive World Atlas on the whiteboard and project Europe. Remind students about the countries in Europe they already have studied in the chapter on the Renaissance. Discuss with the class how the locations of England, France, Germany, and Italy gave them access to the spread of ideas.

INTERACTIVE WHITEBOARD ACTIVITY Have volunteers analyze the map of Europe and mark where they think new ideas about science and government might have started.

Next, project the Chapter Opener map on the whiteboard. As a class, discuss the Map Focus questions.

Step Into the Time

Making Inferences Have students review the time line for the chapter. Explain that they will be studying events in Europe from about 1500 to 1800.

Ask: **Based on the information in the time line, what can you infer about what was happening in Europe beginning around the 1500s?** *(Copernicus, Galileo, and Newton developed new ideas about the universe. Locke and Rousseau came up with new ideas about the nature of man. Wollstonecraft stressed that women should have equal rights with men. Lavoisier proved that materials need oxygen to burn.)*

Answers for pages 640–641

Step Into the Place

1. Paris was the Enlightenment center of France.
2. Six Enlightenment centers were located either along the coast of the Baltic Sea or along a river.
3. St. Petersburg was the Enlightenment center that was the farthest away from Central Europe.
4. CRITICAL THINKING Answers will vary. Because many Enlightenment centers were located along waterways, people could easily spread ideas by ship to other lands.

Step Into the Time

Answers will vary but should demonstrate awareness of the level of scientific knowledge in Europe before the Enlightenment.

networks
There's More Online!
- ☑ **BIOGRAPHY** Galileo (1564–1642)
- ☑ **CHART/GRAPH**
  - Hindu-Arabic Numbers/Roman Numerals
  - Scientific Revolution
  - Scientific Method

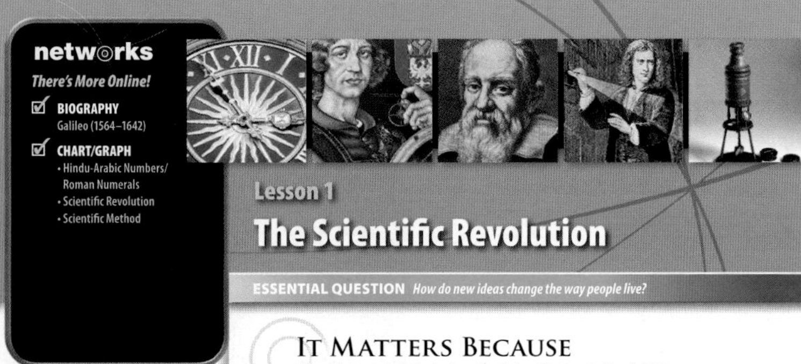

Lesson 1

The Scientific Revolution

ESSENTIAL QUESTION *How do new ideas change the way people live?*

It Matters Because

The advances made during the Scientific Revolution laid the groundwork for modern science.

1 Early Science

GUIDING QUESTION *How were the scientific ideas of early thinkers passed on to later generations?*

During the Renaissance and the Age of Exploration, people developed new ways to learn about nature. However, humans have always shown an interest in the world around them. Thousands of years ago, people began watching plants and animals grow. Activities such as these represented the beginnings of science. Science is any organized study of the physical world. Scientists study the physical world to determine how things work.

The First Scientists

The people of ancient civilizations developed science to solve problems. They used mathematics to keep records. People who studied the movement of the stars developed astronomy. This science helped people keep time and decide when to plant crops.

The ancient Greeks developed a large amount of scientific information. They believed that reason was a way to analyze nature. Their studies helped them develop theories. A **theory** is an explanation for how or why something happens. Theories are based on what people can observe about a thing or event. A theory may be incorrect, but it seems to explain the facts.

Reading HELPDESK

Taking Notes: *Categorizing*

Use a chart like this one to categorize the main advances of the Scientific Revolution concerning the universe or the human body.

Scientific Advances

Universe	Human Body

Content Vocabulary
- **geocentric**
- **Scientific Revolution**
- **heliocentric**

The ancient Greeks and Romans made many scientific advances. The Greek philosopher Aristotle (A•ruh•STAH•tuhl), for example, gathered facts about plants and animals. He then classified living things by arranging them into groups based on their similarities and differences. However, classical thinkers did not conduct scientific experiments. That means they did not test new ideas to find out whether they were true. Instead, they based their conclusions on "common sense," which led to many false beliefs. For instance, during Roman times, the Egyptian-born astronomer Ptolemy (TAH•luh•mee) stated that the sun and the planets moved around the Earth. His **geocentric** (JEE•oh•SEHN•trihk), or Earth-centered, theory was accepted in Europe for more than 1,400 years.

In today's world, we use Indian-Arabic numbers. However, during the Middle Ages in Europe, Roman numerals were more common. The chart at the bottom of this page compares the two number systems.

▶ CRITICAL THINKING
Making Inferences How would the number 7 be written using Roman numerals?

Indian-Arabic Numbers	Roman Numerals
1	I
2	II
3	III
4	IV
5	V
6	VI
7	VII
8	VIII
9	IX
10	X
50	L
100	C
1,000	M

Medieval Science

During the Middle Ages, most Europeans were interested in religious ideas. Few people were interested in studying nature. Their ideas about science were based mostly on ancient classical writings. They did not think it was necessary to research the facts and draw their own conclusions. Many of the classical writings were poorly preserved. As people wrote out copies of the old texts, they sometimes made errors that changed the information.

At the same time, Arabs and Jews in the Islamic empire preserved Greek and Roman science. They copied many Greek and Roman works into Arabic. They also came into contact with the Indian system of numbers that is used today. This system of numbers is now called Indian-Arabic.

Arab and Jewish scientists made their own advances in mathematics, astronomy, and medicine. Even with these achievements, scientists in the Islamic world did not conduct experiments.

During the 1100s, European thinkers began to have more contact with Islamic peoples. As a result, they gained a renewed interest in science. Europeans began to read copies of Islamic works in Latin. After the Indian-Arabic system of numbers reached Europe, people adopted it in place of Roman numerals.

Content Vocabulary
- **ellipses**
- **gravity**
- **elements**
- **rationalism**
- **scientific method**

geocentric an earth-centered theory; having or relating to the earth as the center

Academic Vocabulary

theory an explanation for how or why something happens

Thomas Aquinas (uh•KWY•nuhs) and other Christian thinkers showed that Christianity and reason could work together. Also, Europeans began building new universities. In these schools, teachers and students helped the growth of science.

Beginning in the 1400s, voyages of exploration added to scientific knowledge in Europe. Europeans began to create better charts and maps. These tools helped explorers reach different parts of the world. As more of the world was explored, people learned new information about the size of oceans and continents. Scientists gathered data about diseases, animals, and plants and organized the new information.

Gradually, scientific knowledge **expanded** in Europe. As this happened, a new understanding of the natural world developed.

☑ PROGRESS CHECK

Describing How was science practiced in ancient and medieval times?

2 New Ideas About the Universe

GUIDING QUESTION *Why did European ideas about the universe change during the 1500s and 1600s?*

In the 1500s, Europeans began to think differently about science. They began to realize that scientists had to use mathematics and experiments to make advances. This new way of thinking led to the **Scientific Revolution**. This revolution changed how Europeans understood science and how they searched for knowledge. The Scientific Revolution first affected astronomy, the science that studies the planets and stars of the universe. New discoveries in this field began to change European thinking about the universe. They challenged the traditional idea that God had made the Earth as the center of the universe.

Copernicus and Ptolemy

Nicolaus Copernicus (koh•PUHR•nih•kuhs) was a Polish astronomer. In 1491, he began his career at a university in Poland. A year later, Columbus reached the Americas. Like Columbus, Copernicus challenged old beliefs held by Europeans.

In 1543, Copernicus wrote a book called *On the Revolutions of the Heavenly Spheres*. He disagreed with Ptolemy's theory that the Earth was the center of the universe. Copernicus developed a **heliocentric** (HEE•lee•oh•SEHN•trihk), or sun-centered, theory of the universe. Copernicus believed that the sun was the center of the universe. Earth and the other planets followed a circular path around the sun.

Copernicus's theory disagreed with church teachings. As a result, publication of his book was delayed. He reportedly did not receive the first copy until he was dying.

Reading HELPDESK

Scientific Revolution a period from the 1500s to the 1700s in which many scientific advances changed people's traditional beliefs

heliocentric having or relating to the sun as the center

ellipses ovals shapes

Academic Vocabulary

expand to increase in number, volume, or scope

A NEW VIEW OF THE UNIVERSE

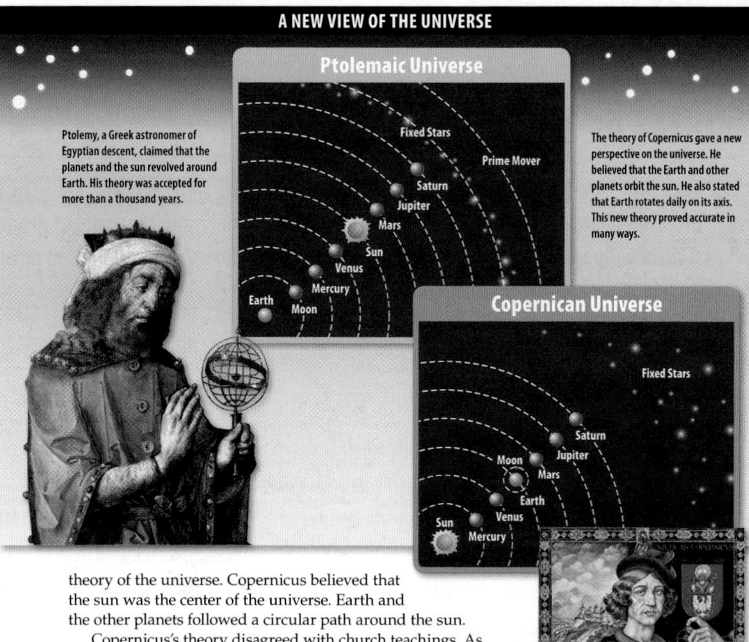

Ptolemy, a Greek astronomer of Egyptian descent, claimed that the planets and the sun revolved around Earth. His theory was accepted for more than a thousand years.

The theory of Copernicus gave a new perspective on the universe. He believed that the Earth and other planets orbit the sun. He also stated that Earth rotates daily on its axis. This new theory proved accurate in many ways.

▶ CRITICAL THINKING
Analyzing Study the diagrams. How did the theory of Copernicus differ from the theory of Ptolemy?

Kepler's Ideas About Planets

A German astronomer named Johannes Kepler (KEH•pluhr) made more advances. He used mathematics to support Copernicus's theory that the planets revolve around the sun. His findings also made corrections to the theory. Kepler added the idea that the planets move in oval paths called **ellipses** (ih•LIHP•seez) instead of the circular paths in Copernicus's theory.

Also, Kepler stated that planets do not always travel at the same speed. Instead, they move faster as they approach the sun and slower as they move away from it. Kepler's theory provided a simpler explanation for the movements of the planets. In addition, it marked the beginning of modern astronomy.

LESSON 1 • Day 1

ENGAGE

SLIDE SHOW Show students the interactive slide show about Sir Isaac Newton. Students will see some of Newton's contributions and have a sense of his personality. Explain to students that Newton was just one of many important scientists who helped develop the ideas that scientists still use today.

Point out to students that much of our modern technology relies on scientific concepts that were developed over time. Tell students that in this Lesson they will be learning about the development of scientific thought, with an emphasis on advances made in Europe.

TEACH & ASSESS

Early Science

GUIDING QUESTION ***How were the scientific ideas of early thinkers passed on to later generations?***

Finding the Main Idea Hold a class discussion to review the contributions made by early philosophers. AL

Ask:

What were some of the key advances made by the Greeks? *(They used reason to study nature and develop theories. Aristotle classified living things. Ptolemy advanced the geocentric theory in astronomy.)*

Why were the Greeks important to later scientists? *(Greek ideas influenced Arab and Jewish scholars and were later rediscovered by Europeans, encouraging the development of new scientific ideas.)*

What were some of the issues with medieval science? *(There was not a big focus on science during the Middle Ages. People were focused more on religious ideas. Also, scientific texts were poorly preserved and contained many errors as people copied them down.)*

How did contact with Islamic peoples help science grow in Europe during the Middle Ages? *(As a result of contact with Islamic peoples, Europeans gained a renewed interest in science.)*

2 New Ideas About the Universe

GUIDING QUESTION ***Why did European ideas about the universe change during the 1500s and 1600s?***

LECTURE SLIDE **Making Predictions** Show students the lecture slide listing the scientific advances of Copernicus, Kepler, and Galileo.

Ask:

How do you think the advances of Copernicus, Kepler, and Galileo influenced later scientists? *(Answers will vary, but students might mention that Newton probably supported a heliocentric view of the universe because of the advances made by previous scientists. Also, later scientists probably used experiments like Galileo.)*

Record their answers on the whiteboard using a chart.

INTERACTIVE WORKSHEET **Write a Résumé** Tell students that they will be writing a résumé for Isaac Newton. Then, assign students the 21st Century Skills Activity on writing a résumé. Guide students through the introduction to the format of a résumé to make sure they understand the goal of the assignment. AL ELL

CLOSE & REFLECT

Formulating Questions Review the accomplishments of the scientists discussed in "New Ideas About the Universe." Ask students to write down a single scientific question that they would like to ask one of these scientists. Allow students to share some of these questions with the class.

BACKGROUND KNOWLEDGE

Distinction Between Astronomy and Astrology

Clarify the distinction between the term *astronomy*, the scientific study of bodies in space, and the term *astrology*, the nonscientific study of the motions of celestial bodies in the belief that they influence human affairs. Explain that although astrology and horoscopes can be fun, they are not based on science.

Kepler's Other Discoveries

Johannes Kepler also made the first modern discoveries in another important field. He was the pioneer in the study of how the human eye works. He explained the function of the pupil, which lets light into the eye, and how light is focused on the retina.

His understanding of the optical characteristics of the eye also explained for the first time how eyeglasses, already in use for three centuries, helped people see better. The glass lens refocused the light image correctly on the retina.

Galileo and the Moons

When Galileo used a telescope to study the heavens, he made some startling discoveries. The moon's surface was rough and uneven, not smooth. He also saw four moons around Jupiter. In addition, he found more stars in the sky than people could see without a telescope.

How Small Is Small?

Anton van Leeuwenhoek's microscope, the first of its kind, was a single-lens instrument. Its maximum magnification power was only about 300 times. However, it enabled him to see bacteria that were 2 to 3 millionths of a meter long. Subsequent microscopes used electron beams, which allowed a magnification of 250,000 times. Even more recent microscopes use high-frequency sound waves. The latest microscope, called a scanning tunneling microscope, measures variations in an electric current. It is so powerful that it allows scientists to see the movement of individual atoms.

Newton's Influences

When Isaac Newton arrived at the University of Cambridge in 1661, he found that outmoded ideas of science held sway. The new ideas of Copernicus, Kepler, and Galileo had made no impression on the faculty. Aristotle was considered the most important source, even though he had been dead for more than 17 centuries. Even as a student, however, Newton believed in searching further than ancient sources for understanding.

Answers for pages 642–645

P. 642 Taking Notes Universe: Copernicus forms the heliocentric theory of the universe; Kepler refines Copernicus's view of the universe; Galileo supports the heliocentric view of the universe; **Human Body:** Vesalius describes the internal structure of the human body; Hooke discovers cells; van Leeuwenhoek discovers bacteria

P. 643 CRITICAL THINKING The number 7 would be written as VII using Roman numerals.

P. 644 ☑ PROGRESS CHECK During ancient and medieval times, science was practiced by using "common sense." This method did not involve experimentation.

P. 645 CRITICAL THINKING Copernicus believed that Earth and other planets orbited the sun, which was contrary to Ptolemy's view that the sun revolved around Earth.

BIOGRAPHY

Galileo (1564–1642)

In 1632, Galileo, an Italian, published his ideas. Soon afterward, Catholic Church officials banned his book. They believed that the Christian Bible taught that the Earth was the center of the universe. Galileo's theory disagreed and stated the Earth revolved around the sun. Because of this, Galileo was ordered to stand trial for heresy. He was also forced to withdraw many of his statements.

▶ CRITICAL THINKING

Explaining Why did the Catholic Church want to stop the spread of Galileo's ideas?

Galileo's Achievements

An Italian scientist named Galileo Galilei (GA•luh•LEE•oh GA•luh•LY) made the next great discovery in the Scientific Revolution. He believed that conducting experiments was the correct way to achieve new scientific knowledge. His studies caused him to disagree with some long-held ideas. For example, Aristotle had thought that heavy objects fall to the ground faster than objects that weigh less. Galileo's experiments proved that was not correct. Objects fall at the same speed no matter what they weigh.

Galileo also believed that scientific instruments could help people better explore the natural world. He heard about an early telescope and designed one of his own. With the telescope, Galileo found evidence that supported Copernicus's theory that Earth revolves around the sun.

Galileo also improved the making of clocks. One day, Galileo was watching an overhead lamp swing back and forth from a cathedral ceiling. He timed each swing and discovered that all of the swings took the same amount of time. Galileo used this idea to make a clock that had a swinging pendulum. The pendulum made the clock more accurate.

Galileo also developed new scientific instruments. In 1593, he invented a water thermometer. People could now measure changes in temperature. An assistant of Galileo then built the first barometer, an instrument that measures air pressure.

☑ PROGRESS CHECK

Comparing and Contrasting How did Galileo go about making scientific discoveries?

3 New Scientific Advances

GUIDING QUESTION *Which discoveries did scientists make during the 1600s and 1700s?*

During the 1600s and 1700s, scientists built on the advances of Copernicus, Kepler, and Galileo. These scientists made advances in medicine, astronomy, and physics.

Newton's Universe

Isaac Newton was an English mathematician. According to tradition, Newton was sitting in his garden one day when he saw an apple fall to the ground. The apple's fall led him to the idea of **gravity**. Gravity is the pull of the Earth or other bodies in space on objects that are on or near them.

In 1687, Newton published a book called *Principia*. This was one of the most important books in the history of modern science. In *Principia*, Newton gave his laws, or well-tested theories, about the motion of objects on Earth and in space. The most important was the law of gravitation. It states that the force of gravity holds the solar system together. It does this by keeping the sun and the planets in their orbits. Newton's ideas greatly influenced the thinking of other scientists.

Reading HELPDESK

gravity the attraction that the Earth has on an object on or near its surface

Stock Montage/Archive Photos/Getty Images

Isaac Newton analyzed rays of light. His experiments showed that light is made up of a wide band of colors called a spectrum.

▶ CRITICAL THINKING

Speculating Do you think Aristotle's scientific method could have been used to discover the spectrum? Explain your answer.

North Wind Picture Archives

Studying the Human Body

Many changes were made in medicine during the 1500s and 1600s. Since ancient times, the teachings of the Greek physician Galen had influenced European doctors. Galen wanted to study the human body, but he was not allowed to dissect, or cut open, dead human bodies. So, he dissected animals instead.

In the 1500s, the Flemish doctor Andreas Vesalius (vuh•SAY•lee•uhs) advanced medical research. He began dissecting dead human bodies. In 1543, he published *On the Structure of the Human Body*. In it, Vesalius described the internal structure of the human body. His account challenged many of Galen's ideas.

THE SCIENTIFIC REVOLUTION — INFOGRAPHIC

Scientist	Nation	Discoveries
Nicolaus Copernicus (1473–1543)	Poland	Earth orbits the Sun; Earth rotates on its axis
Galileo Galilei (1564–1642)	Italy	other planets have moons
Johannes Kepler (1571–1630)	Germany	planets have elliptical orbits
William Harvey (1578–1657)	England	heart pumps blood
Robert Hooke (1635–1703)	England	cells
Robert Boyle (1627–1691)	Ireland	matter is made up of elements
Isaac Newton (1642–1727)	England	gravity; laws of motion; calculus
Antoine Lavoisier (1743–1794)	France	how materials burn

During the Scientific Revolution, scientists made discoveries in many fields, such as astronomy and medicine. For example, William Harvey discovered that the heart pumps blood.

▶ CRITICAL THINKING

Comparing What other scientists worked with the same subject matter as Galileo?

Early microscopes (left) were used to discover information about items too small to see, like bacteria and cells. Early telescopes (below) were used to learn about larger things in space, like planets and stars.

Other advances in medicine took place. In the early 1600s, an English scientist named Robert Hooke began using a microscope. He soon discovered cells, which are the smallest units of living matter. Then the Dutch merchant Antonie van Leeuwenhoek (LAY•vuhn•huk) improved the microscope by using more powerful lenses. He used this microscope to discover tiny organisms later called bacteria (bak•TIHR•ee•uh).

In the mid-1600s, the Irish scientist Robert Boyle proved that all matter is made up of **elements**. Elements are basic materials that cannot be broken down into simpler parts.

During the 1700s, European scientists discovered gases such as hydrogen, carbon dioxide, and oxygen. By 1783, Antoine Lavoisier (AN•twahn luh•WAH•zee•AY) of France proved that materials need oxygen in order to burn. Marie Lavoisier, also a scientist, made contributions to her husband's work.

☑ PROGRESS CHECK

Identifying According to Newton, how are the planets held in orbit?

4 The Triumph of Reason

GUIDING QUESTION *How did Europeans of the 1600s and 1700s develop new ways of gaining knowledge?*

European thinkers soon began to apply the ideas of science to human society. These thinkers believed science revealed the natural laws of the universe. By using reason, people could study these laws and use them to solve many human problems.

Descartes and Pascal

France became a major center of scientific thought. In 1637, the French René Descartes (reh•NAY day•KAHRT) wrote a book called *Discourse on Method*. In this book, Descartes studied the problem of knowing what is true. To find truth, he decided to ignore everything he had learned and start over. However, one fact seemed to be beyond doubt. This fact was his own existence. To summarize this idea, Descartes wrote the phrase, "I think, therefore I am."

In his work, Descartes claimed that mathematics is the source of scientific truth. In mathematics, he said, the answers are always true. His reasoning was that mathematics begins with simple principles. It then uses logic, or reason, to move to more complex truths. Descartes is viewed as the founder of modern **rationalism** (RASH•uh•nuh•LIH•zuhm). This is the belief that reason is the main source of knowledge.

During the 1600s, another French thinker Blaise Pascal (blehz pa•SKAL) studied science. At the age of 19, he invented a calculating machine. Pascal believed that reason and scientific ideas based on experiments could solve many practical problems. However, Pascal was also a religious man. He believed that the solutions to moral problems and spiritual truth could come only from faith in Christian teachings.

(l) SSPL/Getty Images, (b) SSPL/Science Museum/Getty Images

Reading HELPDESK

element a substance that consists of atoms of only one kind

rationalism the belief that reason and experience must be present for the solution of problems

scientific method the steps for an orderly search for knowledge

Academic Vocabulary

generation the time span between the birth of parents and the birth of their children

What Is the Scientific Method?

In the 1600s, the English thinker Francis Bacon influenced scientific thought. He believed that unproven ideas from earlier **generations** should be put aside. Bacon believed that to find the truth, you had to first find and examine the facts.

He developed the scientific method. This method is an orderly way of collecting and analyzing evidence. Its basic principles are still used in scientific research today.

The **scientific method** consists of several steps. First, scientists observe facts. Then, they try to find a hypothesis (hy•PAH•thuh•suhs), or an explanation of the facts. Scientists conduct experiments to test the hypothesis. These tests are done under all types of conditions. Repeated experiments may show that the hypothesis is true. Then it is considered a scientific law.

The Scientific Method
Observe some aspect of the universe.
Hypothesize about what you observed.
Predict something based on your hypothesis.
Test your predictions through experiments and observations.
Modify hypothesis in light of results.

The scientific method involves five steps. These steps build on each other.

▶ CRITICAL THINKING

Conjecturing Do you think scientists often have to do the fifth step? Explain.

☑ PROGRESS CHECK

Explaining Why did Descartes believe that mathematics is the source of scientific truth?

LESSON 1 REVIEW

Review Vocabulary

1. How is *rationalism* used in the *scientific method*?

Answer the Guiding Questions

2. ***Identifying*** What was the heliocentric theory and who developed it?
3. ***Summarizing*** How did the ancient Greeks study nature?
4. ***Explaining*** What instrument made the discovery of bacteria possible? Explain.
5. ***Defining*** What is the scientific method?
6. **PERSUASIVE WRITING** During the Scientific Revolution, advances were made in many scientific fields. Choose the step forward that you think is the most significant and explain your choice.

LESSON 1 • Day 2

ENGAGE

Analyzing Tell students that they will be learning about the scientific method. Then, illustrate the concept by presenting the example of water evaporating. Ask the following question.

How would you prove that water evaporates? *(Answers will vary. Students might say they would experiment by placing a measured amount of water in a dish and remeasuring the quantity in the dish after time passes.)*

Have a class discussion about this question. Record their answers on the interactive whiteboard.

New Scientific Advances

GUIDING QUESTION *Which discoveries did scientists make during the 1600s and 1700s?*

The Triumph of Reason

GUIDING QUESTION *How did Europeans of the 1600s and 1700s develop new ways of gaining knowledge?*

GRAPHIC ORGANIZER **Organizing** Review the steps involved in the scientific method. Then have students complete the Interactive Whiteboard Activity about the scientific method.

Ask:

Is it necessary to do the steps of the scientific method in a certain order? Explain. *(Yes; the steps build on each other. Doing one step out of order would not be logical. For example, a person could not hypothesize about what is observed without observing something first.)*

Ask:

What is the goal of the scientific method? *(The scientific method is a means of carefully gathering data about the universe and using that data to form theories about how and why the universe looks and works as it does.)*

Ask:

Do you think following the scientific method always results in finding the truth? *(Answers will vary. Some students will recognize that test results might be faulty because of a limited sample being tested or because of a limitation of the hypothesis.)*

INTERACTIVE WHITEBOARD ACTIVITY

Summarizing Show students the Interactive Whiteboard Activity on Bacon, Descartes, Newton, Copernicus, and Boyle. Have them identify the key accomplishments of each thinker.

Have students complete the Lesson 1 Review.

CLOSE & REFLECT

Summarizing Review with students some of the key discoveries discussed in the lesson. Then conduct a debate about which discovery is the greatest. Have students form groups of four. Assign each group a discovery from the lesson.

Tell each group to discuss why its discovery is the greatest and to write down at least two reasons. Ask students to re-form into groups based on their opinions.

Which discovery do students respond to the most, or are the groups evenly distributed? Did the discussion affect anyone's choice? Then, have the students consider the effects these discoveries have had on people's lives. Students can use the whiteboard chart to record their reasons.

IF YOU HAVE MORE TIME . . .

Evaluate Branches of Science

Examining Have students choose which of the three branches of science—mathematics, astronomy, or medicine—was the most critical for ancient people and why. Then ask students to decide the same question for people today. Have them support their choices with reasons.

Analyze Charts

Making Connections Ptolemy and Copernicus were limited by the complexity of their observations, as illustrated in the charts in Lesson 1.

Ask:

What things that exist in our solar system are missing from one or both charts? Why do you think these men did not include these objects in their schemes? *(Uranus, Neptune, Pluto, the asteroids, other planets' moons, comets; they probably could not see them accurately with the tools they had.)*

Summarize Discoveries

Identifying Have pairs of students construct graphic organizers that show the order of the scientists discussed in this lesson. Beside each scientist's name, pairs should write a summary of the discoveries of each scientist. AL ELL

Present a Talk Show on Descartes

Discussing Was Descartes correct when he stated that reason is the chief source of knowledge? What might other people have said about Descartes's idea? Ask a group of students to write, rehearse, and present a TV talk show featuring Descartes and some other individuals as guests. Have each student playing a figure research what that person might have said about rationalism and other ways of arriving at truth. Choose one student to play the host, and ask the players to leave time for "audience" questions.

Answers for pages 646–649

P. 646 CRITICAL THINKING Galileo's ideas disagreed with the Catholic Church's view of the universe. Because of this, the Church felt threatened by Galileo. The Church might have feared that an increasing number of people would disagree with Church teachings.

P. 646 ☑ PROGRESS CHECK Galileo believed that conducting experiments was the correct way to go about making scientific discoveries.

P. 647 CRITICAL THINKING No; Aristotle's method was based on using "common sense." If a person just observes light, "common sense" tells the person that light is not made of many colors, because this fact is not easily seen with simple observation.

P. 647 INFOGRAPHIC

CRITICAL THINKING Copernicus and Kepler worked with the same subject matter as Galileo.

P. 648 ☑ PROGRESS CHECK According to Newton, the planets are held in orbit by gravity.

P. 649 CRITICAL THINKING Yes; it is probably difficult to have predictions that are entirely accurate. Repeated experiments will most likely show some flaws in the prediction. As a result, the hypothesis will need to be modified.

P. 649 ☑ PROGRESS CHECK Mathematics uses reason or logic to move from simple truths to more complex truths. This process makes mathematics accurate. Because of this, Descartes believed that the mathematical process works well for science.

LESSON 1 REVIEW

1. The scientific method involves a series of steps. Reason and experimentation are used to move from one step to another. The use of reason is called rationalism.
2. Copernicus developed the heliocentric theory, which states that the sun is the center of the universe.
3. The ancient Greeks used reason to study nature. They then developed theories based on their studies. However, they did not use experimentation.
4. The microscope magnified tiny materials, making it possible to see organisms such as bacteria.
5. The scientific method is an orderly way of collecting and analyzing evidence.
6. Answers will vary but should be supported by facts and logical arguments.

networks
There's More Online!
- ☑ **MAP** Growth of Prussia and Austria
- ☑ **PRIMARY SOURCE**
  - Montesquieu
  - Wollstonecraft

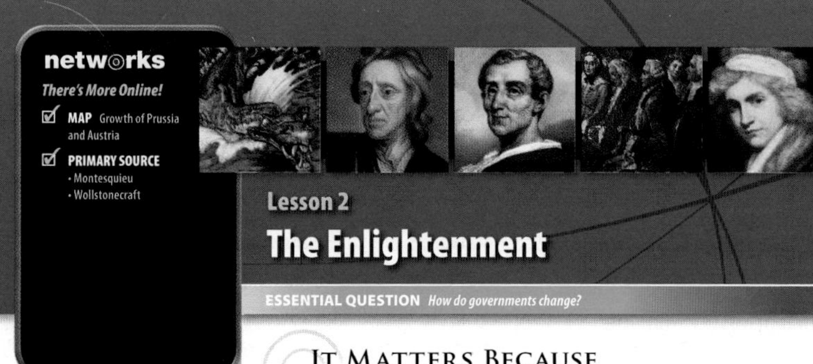

Lesson 2

The Enlightenment

ESSENTIAL QUESTION *How do governments change?*

It Matters Because

The ideas of the Enlightenment have strongly influenced the government and society of the United States and many other nations.

1 Reason and Politics

GUIDING QUESTION *How did European thinkers apply scientific ideas to government?*

During the 1700s, European thinkers were impressed by advances in science. They believed that reason could discover the scientific laws that shaped human behavior. Once these laws were understood, thinkers believed, people could use the laws to improve society.

The Scientific Revolution stressed the use of reason to solve problems. Before this period, people often relied on faith or tradition as guides. However, in the 1700s, many educated Europeans began to break away from tradition. They viewed reason as a "light" that uncovered error and showed the path to truth. As a result, the 1700s became known as the **Age of Enlightenment**.

During the Enlightenment, political thinkers tried to use reason to improve government. They claimed that there was a natural law, or a law that applied to everyone and could be understood by reason. This natural law was the key to making government work properly. As early as the 1600s, two English thinkers used natural law to develop very different ideas about government. The two men were Thomas Hobbes and John Locke.

Reading HELPDESK

Taking Notes: ***Identifying***
On a chart like this one, list the main thinkers of the Enlightenment and a major idea for each one.

Thinker	Idea

Content Vocabulary
- **Age of Enlightenment**
- **absolutism**
- **Glorious Revolution**
- **constitutional monarchy**
- **social contract**
- **separation of powers**

Who Was Thomas Hobbes?

English writer Thomas Hobbes wrote about England's government and society. At the time, England was torn apart by conflict. King Charles I wanted absolute power. Parliament, however, demanded a greater role in governing. The king's supporters fought those who supported Parliament.

Parliament already had some control over the king. In the 1620s, Parliament had forced Charles to sign the Petition of Right. It said the king could not tax the people without Parliament's approval. Also, he could not imprison anyone without a just reason. The Petition also stated that the king could not declare a state of emergency unless the country was at war.

Charles, however, ignored the Petition. His differences with Parliament led to civil war. The fighting finally forced Parliament's supporters to execute Charles. This event shocked Thomas Hobbes, who supported the monarchy.

In Hobbes's *Leviathan*, a sea serpent like the one below, represents the powerful ruler necessary to running the most effective type of government—an absolute monarchy.

▶ **CRITICAL THINKING**
Analyzing How does the image of a serpent help make Hobbes's point about government?

Hobbes' Beliefs

In 1651, Hobbes wrote a book called *Leviathan*. In this work, Hobbes argued that natural law made absolute monarchy the best form of government. According to Hobbes, humans were naturally violent and selfish. They could not be trusted to make wise decisions on their own. Left to themselves, people would make life "nasty, brutish, and short."

Therefore, Hobbes said, people needed to obey a government that had the power of a leviathan (luh•VY•uh•thuhn), or sea monster. To Hobbes, this meant the rule of a powerful king, because only a strong ruler could give people direction. Under this ruler, people had to remain loyal. This political theory of Hobbes became known as **absolutism** (AB•suh•LOO•tih•zuhm), since it supported a ruler with absolute, or total, power.

Age of Enlightenment the time period in the 1700s during which many Europeans began to break away from tradition and rethink political and social norms

absolutism political system in which a ruler has total power

John Locke wrote about many subjects, including education and religion. His ideas contributed to the U.S. Declaration of Independence.

▶ **CRITICAL THINKING**
Making Inferences Would Locke have supported freedom of religion? Explain.

Locke and the Glorious Revolution

Another English thinker, John Locke, believed differently. He used natural law to support citizens' rights. He said the government had to answer to the people. During Locke's life, another English king, James II, wanted to be a strong ruler. Parliament again was opposed to the king's wishes. When civil war threatened in 1688, James fled the country. Parliament then asked Mary, the king's daughter, and her husband, William, to take the throne. This event became known as the "**Glorious Revolution**."

The Glorious Revolution eventually turned England into a **constitutional monarchy.** This is a form of government in which written laws limit the powers of the monarch. In return for the English throne, William and Mary agreed to a Bill of Rights. This document required William and Mary to obey Parliament's laws. The Bill of Rights also **guaranteed** all English people basic rights. For example, people had the right to a fair trial by jury and the right to freedom from cruel punishment for a crime.

In 1690, John Locke wrote a book called *Two Treatises of Government*. His book explained many of the ideas of the Glorious Revolution. Locke stated that government should be based on natural law and natural rights. These rights included the right to life, the right to liberty, and the right to own property.

Locke believed that the purpose of government was to protect people's rights. He said that all governments were based on a **social contract.** This is an agreement between the people and their leaders. If rulers took away people's natural rights, the people had a right to rebel and set up a new government.

Montesquieu and Government

After the Glorious Revolution, many thinkers in France admired the government of England. They liked it better than the absolute monarchy that ruled France. In 1748, a French thinker, Baron Montesquieu (mahn•tuhs•KYOO), published a book called *The Spirit of the Laws*.

In this book, Montesquieu stated that England had the best government. He liked English government because it had a separation of powers. **Separation of powers** means that power should be equally divided among the branches of government: legislative, executive, and judicial. The legislative branch makes the laws. The executive branch enforces the laws. The judicial branch interprets the laws and makes judgments when the laws are broken. By separating these powers, government could not become too powerful and threaten people's rights. As Montesquieu explained in the case of judges:

PRIMARY SOURCE

> "Again, there is no liberty, if the power of judging be not separated from the legislative and executive powers. Were it joined with the legislative, the life and liberty of the subject would be exposed to arbitrary [unreasonable] control, for the judge would be then the legislator. Were it joined to the executive power, the judge might behave with all the violence of an oppressor [cruel dictator]."
>
> —from *The Spirit of the Laws*, 1748

Montesquieu believed in the rights of individuals. His work influenced the writing of the constitutions of many countries, including the United States Constitution.

☑ **PROGRESS CHECK**
Comparing and Contrasting How did Hobbes and Locke differ in their ideas about government and the people?

Baron Montesquieu traveled through Europe and compared governments. He wrote his conclusions in *The Spirit of Laws*.

▶ **CRITICAL THINKING**
Drawing Conclusions Why did so many scholars respect Montesquieu's ideas?

2 The Philosophes of France

GUIDING QUESTION *How did French thinkers influence Europe during the Enlightenment?*

During the 1700s, France became the most active center of the Enlightenment. Thinkers in France and elsewhere became known by the French name *philosophe* (FEE•luh•ZAWF), which means "philosopher." Most philosophes were writers, teachers, and journalists who often discussed and debated new ideas at gatherings. These gatherings were held in the homes of wealthy citizens.

Philosophes wanted to use reason to improve society. They attacked superstition, or unreasoned beliefs, and disagreed with religious leaders who opposed new scientific discoveries. Philosophes believed in freedom of speech and claimed that each person had the right to liberty. Their ideas spread across Europe.

Reading HELPDESK

Glorious Revolution the overthrow of King James II of England

constitutional monarchy a political system in which a king or queen rules according to a constitution

social contract an agreement between the people and their government

separation of powers a government structure that has three distinct branches: legislative, executive, and judicial

Academic Vocabulary

guarantee to make sure or certain; promise

LESSON 2

ENGAGE

Predicting Review the introduction to the section "Reason and Politics." Tell students that thinkers during the Enlightenment started to use reason to determine the best type of government.

Ask: What type of government do you think these thinkers decided was the best? Explain. *(Answers will vary. Students might say the thinkers decided democracy was the best, because it is reasonable to give people a say in the government.)*

Ask: Do you think different thinkers came up with different ideas about the best type of government? *(Answers will vary. Some students might say that using reason will cause thinkers to decide on similar governments. Others will say that people think differently about what is reasonable, so the type of government they decide on could also be different.)* Use the interactive whiteboard to record answers. AL

TEACH & ASSESS

1 Reason and Politics

GUIDING QUESTION *How did European thinkers apply scientific ideas to government?*

Evaluating Remind students that scientists based their conclusions on evidence. During the Enlightenment, thinkers adopted this approach.

Ask: Do you think Hobbes had evidence to support his conclusion about the best government? *(Answers will vary. Some students might say yes. He saw people constantly fighting each other in wars and in other ways, so he concluded that people are basically selfish.)*

Comparing and Contrasting Ask students to compare and contrast the Glorious Revolution and the American Revolution.

Ask: How are the Glorious Revolution and the American Revolution different? *(They happened in different countries; they happened in different time periods; the American Revolution involved a war, but the Glorious Revolution did not; the American Revolution did away with monarchy, but the Glorious Revolution kept the monarchy.)*

Ask: How were these two revolutions similar? *(Both established more liberty for the people; both resulted in a government with a separation of powers.)*

Defining Review with students the definition of *constitutional monarchy.* ELL

Ask: How did the constitutional monarchy guarantee more freedom for the British people? *(It required the British monarchs to obey Parliament's laws; it gave people the right to a fair trial by jury; it gave people freedom from cruel punishment for a crime.)* List student responses on the interactive whiteboard.

INTERACTIVE WORKSHEET **Comparing and Contrasting** Tell students that Hobbes and Locke used reason to develop different ideas about government. Complete the Primary Source Activity as a class to help students understand the differences between the ideas of Hobbes and Locke.

INTERACTIVE WHITEBOARD ACTIVITY **Identifying** Ask students to consider the accomplishments of Hobbes, Locke, and Montesquieu. Ask them to use the interactive whiteboard to identify some of the key accomplishments for each philosopher by dragging the correct achievement beneath each one. AL

2 The Philosophes of France

GUIDING QUESTION *How did French thinkers influence Europe during the Enlightenment?*

LECTURE SLIDE **Defining** Show students the lecture slide defining the term *philosophes* and explaining their basic beliefs. ELL

Identifying Then **ask:**

- **Who were three of the key French thinkers of the Enlightenment?** *(Voltaire, Diderot, and Rousseau)*
- **What were they most famous for writing?** *(Voltaire wrote novels, plays, and essays and supported freedom of religion. Diderot compiled a huge encyclopedia of knowledge. Rousseau wrote* The Social Contract.*)* AL

3 Absolute Monarchs

GUIDING QUESTION *How did European monarchs model their countries on Enlightenment ideas?*

LECTURE SLIDE **Summarizing** Show students the lecture slide listing key absolute monarchs of Europe during the Enlightenment.

Ask:

- **Which of these rulers tried to make reforms that were influenced by Enlightenment ideas?** *(Frederick the Great, Maria Theresa, Joseph II, Peter the Great, and Catherine the Great)*
- **What are some of the reforms they supported?** *(Student answers may include improved government, religious tolerance, freedom of speech, and freeing serfs.)*

Have students complete the Lesson 2 Review.

CLOSE & REFLECT

Moderate a class discussion on the views of the political philosophers of the Enlightenment that they have studied. Ask students to choose the philosopher whose political ideas they believe are best supported by evidence and argument. Allow students to explain their choices and reasoning.

Answers for pages 650–653

P. 650 Taking Notes Answers may vary but may include any of the following: Hobbes—developed the absolutism theory; Locke—thought government should be based on natural laws; Montesquieu—believed in the separation of powers for governments; Voltaire—had many criticisms of traditional beliefs; Diderot—supported religious freedom in a 28-volume encyclopedia; Wollstonecraft—supported equality for women; Rousseau—thought government should be based on a social contract.

P. 651 CRITICAL THINKING The image of a serpent makes Hobbes's point by showing that an effective ruler needed to have the strength and power of a serpent.

P. 652 CRITICAL THINKING Yes, Locke claimed that people had a natural right to liberty. This implies that he thought people should have the freedom to choose their own religion.

P. 653 ☑ PROGRESS CHECK Hobbes thought a government should be ruled by an absolute monarch. Locke believed that government should serve the people by protecting their rights.

P. 653 CRITICAL THINKING Answers may vary, but responses should focus on the idea that Montesquieu wanted to compare the strengths and weaknesses of various governments before deciding which type was best.

Voltaire had opinions that caused a large amount of controversy. He was jailed for his viewpoints in France's Bastille prison.

During the Enlightenment, wealthy people held gatherings to discuss the ideas of the day. Here a group reads and discusses the works of Voltaire.

Who Was Voltaire?

In 1694, François-Marie Arouet (ahr•WEH) was born to a middle-class family in France. He became one of the greatest thinkers of the Enlightenment. Called just Voltaire (vohl•TAR), he wrote novels, plays, and essays that brought him wealth and fame.

Voltaire opposed the government favoring one religion and forbidding others. He thought people should be free to choose their own beliefs. He often criticized the Roman Catholic Church for keeping knowledge from people in order to maintain the Church's power.

Voltaire was a supporter of deism (DEE•ih•zuhm), a religious belief based on reason. Followers of deism believed that God created the universe and set it in motion. God then allowed the universe to run itself by natural law.

Diderot's *Encyclopedia*

The French thinker Denis Diderot (duh•NEE dee•DROH) was also committed to spreading Enlightenment ideas. In the late 1700s, he produced a large, 28-volume encyclopedia that took him about 20 years to complete. The Encyclopedia covered a wide range of topics including religion, government,

(t) Giraudon/Art Resource, NY; (b) Réunion des Musées Nationaux/Art Resource, NY

Reading **HELP**DESK

Reading Strategy: *Analyzing Primary Sources*

How does Mary Wollstonecraft think the advancement of women will affect men? What part in the quote on the next page supports your answer?

the sciences, history, and the arts. The philosophes used it as a weapon in their fight against traditional ways. Many articles supported freedom of religion. Others called for changes to make society fairer for all people.

Women and the Enlightenment

Prior to the Enlightenment, women did not have equal rights with men. By the 1700s, a small number of women began to call for such rights. In 1792, the English writer Mary Wollstonecraft (WUL•stuhn•KRAFT) wrote a book called *A Vindication of the Rights of Woman*. In it, she states that women should have the same rights as men. Many consider Wollstonecraft to be the founder of the women's movement.

PRIMARY SOURCE

> "In short, . . . reason and experience convince me that the only method of leading women to fulfil their peculiar [specific] duties, is to free them from all restraint [control] by allowing them to participate in the inherent [basic] rights of mankind."
>
> —from *A Vindication of the Rights of Woman*, by Mary Wollstonecraft, 1792

Connections to **TODAY**

Women's Rights Around the World

Mary Wollstonecraft published *A Vindication of the Rights of Women* in 1792. Today, many organizations still work to advance and protect the social and political equality of women. In 2010, the United Nations voted unanimously to set up UN Women, an organization to promote gender equality around the world. UN Women is based in New York City.

Who was Rousseau?

A Swiss thinker named Jean-Jacques Rousseau (roo•SOH) questioned Enlightenment ideas. In 1762 he published a book of political ideas called *The Social Contract*. This book states that government rests on the will of the people and is based on a social contract. This is an agreement in which everyone in a society accepts being governed by the general will. That is, what society as a whole wants should be law.

✓ **PROGRESS CHECK**

Describing What was Diderot's *Encyclopedia* ?

3 Absolute Monarchs

GUIDING QUESTION ***How did European monarchs model their countries on Enlightenment ideas?***

During the Enlightenment, thinkers called for controls on government. However, most of Europe was ruled by kings and queens who claimed to rule by divine right, or the will of God. Some absolute rulers used Enlightenment ideas to improve their societies—but they refused to give up any of their powers.

Who was France's Sun King?

During the 1600s and 1700s, France was one of Europe's most powerful nations. In 1643, Louis XIV, called the Sun King, came to the throne. He built the grand Versailles (vuhr•SY) palace. There, he staged large ceremonies to celebrate his power.

Mary Wollstonecraft thought that women should have equal rights in education, the workplace, and political life.

▶ CRITICAL THINKING

Explaining How did Mary Wollstonecraft support her argument for women's equality?

(t) Tate Gallery, London/Art Resource, NY

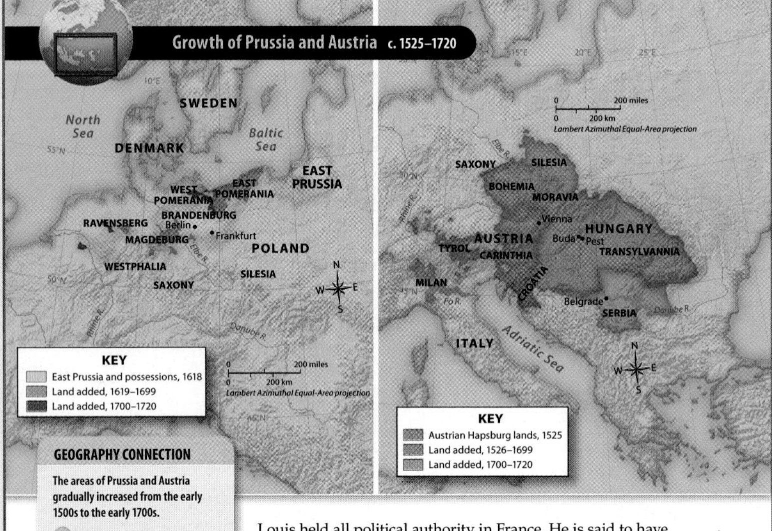

GEOGRAPHY CONNECTION

The areas of Prussia and Austria gradually increased from the early 1500s to the early 1700s.

1. **REGION** During which time period did Austria add the most territory?
2. CRITICAL THINKING ***Analyzing Visuals*** Which state had better access to the sea—Prussia or Austria? Explain.

Louis held all political authority in France. He is said to have boasted, "I am the State." Louis's army won wars that expanded the area of France. These conflicts, though, cost the country a large amount of money and soldiers. The king's constant wars and spending weakened France and the monarchy.

German Rulers

Germany consisted of many territories during the 1600s and 1700s. The two most powerful German states were Prussia and Austria. The most famous Prussian ruler was Frederick II, also called Frederick the Great. He ruled Prussia from 1740 to 1786. Frederick strengthened the army and fought wars to gain new lands for Prussia.

Although Frederick was an absolute monarch, he saw himself as "first servant of the state." He therefore dedicated himself to the good of his people. Frederick permitted more freedom of speech and religious tolerance.

Reading **HELP**DESK

Academic Vocabulary

military relating to the armed forces, such as the army, navy, and the air force

The other German state, Austria, was ruled by the Hapsburg family. In 1740, a Hapsburg princess named Maria Theresa became the ruler of Austria. She introduced reforms. She set up schools and tried to improve the living conditions of the serfs, people who worked under the harsh rule of landowners.

After Maria Theresa died in 1780, her son, Joseph II, became ruler. He carried her reforms even further. He freed the serfs and made land taxes equal for nobles and farmers. The nobles opposed his reforms. As a result, Joseph was forced to back down.

Russia's Reforming Czars

East of Austria, the vast empire of Russia was ruled by czars. One of the most powerful czars was Peter I, also known as Peter the Great. Peter tried to make Russia a strong European power. He began reforms to help the government run more smoothly. Peter also improved Russia's **military** and created a navy.

Peter wanted Russia to have access to the Baltic Sea, but Sweden controlled the land. Peter went to war with Sweden in a conflict lasting 21 years. Russia won in 1721. Just three years after the war started, Peter founded the city of St. Petersburg (PEE•tuhrz•BUHRG). By 1712, this city was the Russian capital.

After Peter died, a series of weak monarchs governed Russia. Then, in 1762, a German princess named Catherine came to the throne. Catherine II expanded Russia's territory and became known as Catherine the Great. She supported the ideas of the Enlightenment and wanted to free the serfs. However, a serf revolt changed her mind. In the end, Catherine allowed the nobles to treat the serfs as they pleased.

In 1787, Catherine the Great and Joseph II traveled together through Southern Russia. An artist commemorated their trip with this oil painting.

▶ CRITICAL THINKING

Comparing What social reforms did both Joseph II and Catherine II seek for their countries?

Heritage Images/Corbis

✓ **PROGRESS CHECK**

Explaining How was Frederick the Great influenced by the Enlightenment?

LESSON 2 REVIEW

Review Vocabulary

1. How did the *Glorious Revolution* lead to a *constitutional monarchy* in England?

Answer the Guiding Questions

2. ***Identifying*** Which monarch freed the serfs?
3. ***Summarizing*** What did the *Encyclopedia* created by Diderot contain?
4. ***Describing*** What type of government did John Locke support?
5. ***Explaining*** Why did Voltaire criticize the Roman Catholic Church?
6. **PERSUASIVE WRITING** You are an Enlightenment thinker who opposes the views of Thomas Hobbes. Write a short letter to Hobbes that explains to him why you disagree with his ideas about government.

LESSON 2 (cont.)

IF YOU HAVE MORE TIME . . .

Take a Closer Look at Voltaire

Speculating Voltaire visited and wrote to many of the monarchs and leaders of Europe, including Frederick the Great of Prussia, Catherine the Great of Russia, and the English parliamentary leaders Bolingbroke and Walpole. Ask students what they think these leaders might have gained from their contact with Voltaire. Also ask if students think that today's politicians can learn from philosophers and writers. Why or why not?

Discuss Nature vs. Nurture

Drawing Conclusions Tell students that John Locke believed that when people were born, their minds were a "blank slate," or in Latin, *tabula rasa*. He believed this blank slate was filled by their experiences. Ask students to evaluate this claim. Be sure the discussion includes the effects of nature, or genetic background, and those of nurture, or life experiences that shape us.

Ask: Do you agree with Locke that nurture is more important? Do you believe that some of what we are is affected by our nature? *(Answers will vary but should include supporting proof.)* BL

Compare and Contrast Encyclopedias

Evaluating Ask students how Diderot's *Encyclopedia* differs from and is similar to a modern one. *(Different: Diderot's* Encyclopedia *had a point of view and a "message"; Similar: It covers a wide range of topics.)*

Consider Human Nature

Identifying Remind students of Rousseau's belief that people are naturally good. Ask students to list characteristics of a "good" person. *(Possible answers include: trustworthiness, loyalty, courage, honesty, etc.)* Then, ask students if they agree with Rousseau that people are essentially good. AL ELL

Conduct a Panel Discussion on Natural Law

Discussing Ask a group of students to research and prepare a panel discussion on the subject of natural law. Have them address questions, such as:

- What is natural law?
- Where does it come from?
- How is the idea used today?
- How do we know what natural laws are?
- How do we use natural law?

Remind the panel members to leave time for questions after the discussion. BL

BACKGROUND KNOWLEDGE

Locke and Education

Locke's ideas about education, like his ideas about government and human nature, have also proven to be influential. In his 1693 book *Some Thoughts Concerning Education* and in other works, Locke describes his ideal education. It makes the learning of virtue more important than the acquisition of knowledge. As in his other works, Locke made experience the greatest teacher. Ask students to discuss Locke's ranking of virtue over knowledge. Is learning to do the right thing more important in education than knowledge?

Wollstonecraft's Social Circle

Mary Wollstonecraft was at the center of liberal and radical thought in the late 1700s. Her friends included Thomas Paine, author of *Common Sense*, and the writer William Godwin, whom she married. Their daughter also became famous. Mary Wollstonecraft Shelley was the author of *Frankenstein*.

The Origins of England's Constitutional Monarchy

The Glorious Revolution of 1688 marked the beginning of England's constitutional monarchy. James II, who gained the throne in 1685, immediately alienated most of the English people with his absolutism and favoring of Catholicism. When his wife gave birth to a son, who was a Catholic and the heir to the throne, English parliamentary leaders feared a continuation of pro-Catholic and absolutist policies.

To avoid this, they asked William and his wife, Mary, to take the throne in replacement, as long as they accepted the parliamentary checks on royal power. As a result, the king could no longer suspend laws, nor could a Catholic become king.

Peter the Great—A Great Traveler

When he was a young ruler, Peter the Great realized that his knowledge of the Western world, like that of most Russians, was limited. In order to correct his ignorance, Peter undertook a grand tour of Western Europe. Traveling under a false name, Peter spent much of his time studying shipbuilding. He worked for several months in Dutch and English shipyards. He hoped his knowledge would help Russia create a great navy. While in England, Peter also went to weapons arsenals, museums, factories, schools, and even to Parliament. He returned to Russia a year and a half later, better prepared to transform the huge, developing country into a modern nation.

Answers for pages 654–657

P. 654 Reading Strategy She thinks men will also become better and wise: "Make them free, and they will quickly become wise and virtuous, as men become more so; for the improvement must be mutual."

P. 655 ☑ **PROGRESS CHECK** It was a 28-volume encyclopedia that helped spread ideas about freedom of religion and making society fairer throughout Europe.

P. 655 CRITICAL THINKING Women possess the same capacity for reason as men, so they should have the same rights as men.

P. 656 GEOGRAPHY CONNECTION

1. Austria acquired the most land from 1526 to 1699.
2. **CRITICAL THINKING** A large part of Prussia bordered the Baltic Sea, but only a small part of Austria bordered the Adriatic Sea. Prussia had better access to the sea.

P. 657 CRITICAL THINKING They both wanted to free the serfs.

P. 657 ☑ **PROGRESS CHECK** Frederick permitted more freedom of speech and religious tolerance.

LESSON 2 REVIEW

1. King James II of England was overthrown. Then the throne was offered to William and Mary under the condition that they allow their powers to be limited. William and Mary accepted the terms. This change of power is referred to as the Glorious Revolution. The result of this revolution was a new form of government called a constitutional monarchy.
2. Joseph II freed the serfs.
3. It contained 28 volumes with articles that covered religion, government, sciences, history, and the arts. Many of the articles in it called for religious freedom and a fairer society.
4. Locke supported a government based on a social contract between the government and its people. According to this contract, the government protects the rights of the people.
5. Voltaire criticized the Roman Catholic Church for keeping knowledge from the people to maintain its power.
6. Answers will vary but should be supported by logic and demonstrate an understanding of Hobbes's view of government—that natural law supported monarchy, and that monarchy would protect people from their selfish, violent nature. The letter should stress the importance of the rights of the people and the need for a government to support these rights.

CHAPTER 22 Activities

Write your answers on a separate piece of paper.

1. **Exploring the Essential Questions**
EXPOSITORY WRITING How did governments in Europe change during the 1600s and 1700s? Write a summary essay about how they changed during this period. Think about various Enlightenment ideas that influenced the formation of governments. Include the effects these ideas had on government structure and on rulers.

2. **21st Century Skills**
COMMUNICATION Create a presentation that explains the contributions of Galileo to the world of science. What do you think was his most important new idea? Do further research on the Internet. Write a short summary of Galileo's most important contribution to science. Include any diagrams or charts that will help support your argument. In your presentation, have the class ask you questions that require you to defend your opinion about Galileo.

3. **Thinking Like a Historian**
COMPARING AND CONTRASTING Create a diagram like the one on the right to compare and contrast the ideas and lives of Thomas Hobbes and John Locke.

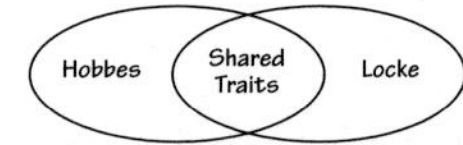

4. **GEOGRAPHY ACTIVITY**

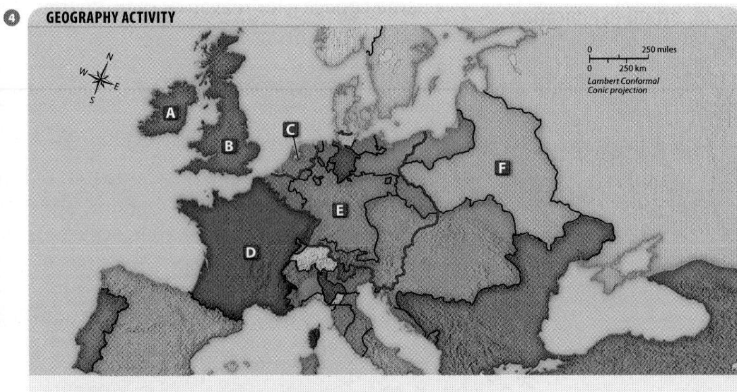

LOCATING PEOPLE
Match the scientists and thinkers listed below with their countries.

1. Voltaire
2. Copernicus
3. Locke
4. Kepler
5. Leeuwenhoek
6. Boyle

CHAPTER 22 Assessment

REVIEW THE GUIDING QUESTIONS
Directions: Choose the best answer for each question.

1. Which of the following best summarizes the ideas of Copernicus?
A. The sun orbits the Earth.
B. The Earth orbits the sun.
C. The stars orbit the Earth.
D. The moon orbits the sun.

2. Which of the following discoveries did Antoine Lavoisier make?
F. Matter needs oxygen to burn.
G. Matter is made up of elements.
H. Living matter contains cells.
I. Matter on Earth obeys the laws of gravity.

3. Descartes summarized his philosophy with the phrase
A. "I am, therefore I think."
B. "I think, therefore I am."
C. "I am, therefore I have faith."
D. "I have faith, therefore I am."

4. The theory of Montesquieu was called separation of powers because it separated government
F. into two branches, both with equal power.
G. into two branches, with the judiciary being the more powerful.
H. into three branches, all with equal power.
I. into three branches, with the judiciary being the most powerful.

5. Which of the following best summarizes the ideas of Rousseau?
A. Reason is what people should rely on.
B. People are naturally bad.
C. The right to rule rests with a monarch.
D. People should pay more attention to their feelings.

6. During his reign, Frederick II
F. thought about freeing the serfs.
G. allowed freedom of speech and religion.
H. built the palace of Versailles.
I. made land taxes equal for nobles and farmers.

CHAPTER 22 Assessment *(continued)*

DBQ DOCUMENT-BASED QUESTIONS

Drawing Conclusions This excerpt was published by John Locke in 1690.

"To understand political power aright … we must consider what estate all [people] are naturally in, and that is, a state of perfect freedom …, within the bounds of the law of Nature. …

A state also of equality, wherein all the power and jurisdiction [enforcement of laws] is reciprocal [shared], no one having more than another."

—from *The Second Treatise of Government*, by John Locke

7. Which statement do you think Locke would agree with?
A. All people have freedom to do what they want.
B. All people should enforce laws.
C. All people should have equal wealth.
D. All people should have few possessions.

8. **Finding the Main Idea** Which of the following is the main idea of the excerpt?
F. People will naturally form democracies.
G. People must obey the laws of nature.
H. People are in a natural state of freedom and equality.
I. People have the freedom to learn about nature.

SHORT RESPONSE

"A sovereign [ruler] is not elevated to his high position … that he may live in lazy luxury. … The sovereign is the first servant of the state. He is well paid in order that he may sustain the dignity of his office, but one demands that he work efficiently for the good of the state,…"

—from the *Political Testament*, by Frederick II (the Great) of Prussia

9. What does Frederick mean when he says a ruler should be "the first servant of the state?"

10. What would Frederick think of a king who acted foolish in public?

EXTENDED RESPONSE

11. **Descriptive Writing** Write a description of a meeting in which Voltaire, Jean-Jacques Rousseau, and Mary Wollstonecraft discuss and argue their viewpoints. Include dialogue.

Need Extra Help?

If You've Missed Question	1	2	3	4	5	6	7	8	9	10	11
Review Lesson	1	1	1	2	2	2	2	2	1	1	2

NOTES

REFLECT, REVIEW, & REMEDIATE

INTERACTIVE WORKSHEET

Chapter Summary

Provide students with the Chapter Summary worksheet to help review the chapter and prepare for assessment.

Reviewing the Enduring Understandings

Review this chapter's Enduring Understandings with students:

- Science and technology can change people's lives.
- The value that society places on individual rights is often reflected in that society's government.

INTERACTIVE WHITEBOARD ACTIVITY On the interactive whiteboard, have a student volunteer create a two-column chart and write "Changes to European Society" as the title for both columns. Below this, have the volunteer write "Science" in one column and "Government" in the other. Then lead a discussion that allows students to recall ways that the science and government of Europe changed during the Scientific Revolution and the Enlightenment. The student volunteer should record these features in the chart.

Changes to European Society	
Science	Government

ACTIVITIES ANSWERS

Exploring the Essential Question

1. Answers will vary, but students' answers should demonstrate an understanding of the ideas of Hobbes, Locke, Montesquieu, Diderot, and Rousseau and how these ideas affected the formation of a constitutional monarchy in England. They should also address the reforms attempted by other rulers in Europe.

21st Century Skills

2. Presentations will vary but should demonstrate an understanding of Galileo's view of the universe and provide reasons for this view. Students should also use a diagram to show a heliocentric universe.

Thinking Like a Historian

3. Hobbes: He thought government should have an absolute ruler. He did not trust the people to rule themselves. He thought people did not have the right to rebel against their ruler.

   Shared Traits: Both lived in England; both lived during the Enlightenment; both thought about politics.

   Locke: He thought people had natural rights. He thought the power of the monarch should be limited. He thought government should be based on a social contract, in which the government agrees to protect the rights of the people. He thought the people had the right to overthrow an unjust ruler.

Locating People

4. **1.** D, **2.** F, **3.** B, **4.** E, **5.** C, **6.** A

ASSESSMENT ANSWERS

Review the Guiding Questions

1. **B** Earth orbits the sun. The sun does not orbit anything. The stars do not orbit Earth, and the moon does not orbit the sun.
2. **F** Lavoisier showed that matter needs oxygen to burn. Robert Boyle proved that all matter is made up of elements. Robert Hooke showed that all living matter contains cells. Isaac Newton realized that matter on Earth obeys the laws of gravity.
3. **B** Descartes stated, "I think, therefore I am." He did not believe that "I am, therefore I think," "I am, therefore I have faith," or "I have faith, therefore I am." His beliefs had nothing to do with faith.
4. **H** Montesquieu wrote that the best form of government involved a split into three, not two, separate branches—executive, legislative, and judicial. None of the three branches was given more power than the other two.
5. **D** Rousseau believed people should pay more attention to their feelings and rely less on reason. He also thought people were naturally good. He did not think that the right to rule rested with a monarch.
6. **G** Frederick II allowed freedom of speech and religion. Catherine II thought about freeing the serfs. Louis XIV built the palace of Versailles. Joseph II made land taxes equal for nobles and farmers.

Document-Based Questions

7. **A** Locke is supporting the idea that all men have freedom. He is not stating that all men should enforce laws. Also, he is not saying they should have equal wealth. In addition, he is not telling people to have limited possessions.
8. **H** The excerpt does not state that people must obey the laws of nature. Also, it does not claim that people will naturally form democracies. In addition, it is not specifically saying that people have the freedom to learn about nature.

Short Response

9. He meant that he is not only a ruler, but also a citizen who needs to obey the laws as other citizens do. He must set a good example for his citizens in order to be a just and effective ruler.
10. He would think that the king was not setting the proper example for his people and that it was inappropriate for the king to act so undignified.

Extended Response

11. Student responses should include dialogue for Voltaire, Rousseau, and Wollstonecraft. This dialogue should clearly present the ideas of each thinker and the reasons for these ideas. Also, a general description of the meeting should be included.

ONLINE RESOURCES

networks

There's More Online!

- INTERACTIVE WORKSHEETS
- BIOGRAPHIES
- CHARTS/GRAPHS
- GAMES
- GRAPHIC ORGANIZERS
- IMAGES
- MAPS
- PRIMARY SOURCES
- SLIDE SHOWS
- TIME LINE
- LECTURE SLIDES
- INTERACTIVE WHITEBOARD ACTIVITIES
- ASSESSMENTS
- VIDEOS

Making a Revolution

Napoleon's Early Military Career

The Industrial Revolution

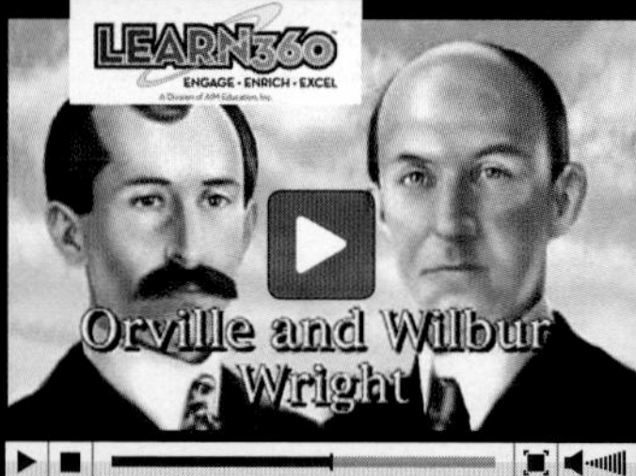

The Wright Brothers

Chapter **23**

Political and Industrial Revolutions

Dear World History Teacher,

The revolutionary era of the late eighteenth century brought dramatic changes. Revolutions, beginning in North America and continuing in France, produced movements in which the people, not individuals, became the source of political power. The revolutions were also based on the principles of liberty and equality. *Liberty* meant, in theory, freedom from arbitrary power and the freedom to think, write, and worship as one chose. *Equality* meant equality in rights, although it did not include equality between men and women.

In 1815 a conservative order was reestablished in Europe that the great powers worked to maintain. However, waves of revolution, brought about by the French Revolution and the Industrial Revolution, showed that nationalism and liberalism were still alive and active.

Between 1850 and 1871, the nation-state became the focus of people's loyalty. Wars were fought to create unified nation-states, while reforms served to strengthen them. Liberal nationalists believed unified states would preserve individual rights and lead to a community of European peoples. Instead, the nationalism of the late nineteenth century divided people, as evident when states competed bitterly against each other.

Jackson J. Spielvogel

More Media Resources

Current Events Online

Visit McGraw-Hill's current events Web site for high-interest news stories and activities for your students. Access the site through the Student or Teacher Center in **networks.**

Reading List

Grade 6 reading level:
Odd Boy Out: Young Albert Einstein, by Don Brown

Grade 7 reading level:
Something Out of Nothing: Marie Curie and Radium, by Carla Killough McClafferty

Grade 8 reading level:
The Real Revolution: The Global Story of American Independence, by Marc Aronson

At the MOVIES

Watch clips of popular culture films about the French Revolution, such as *Marie Antoinette: A Film by David Grubin* (PBS Paramount).

Discuss: **How did the royalty of the era perceive the revolution differently from the people of France?**

NOTE: Be sure to preview any clips to ensure they are age-appropriate.

Search for more videos online in the **networks** Resource Library.

CHAPTER 23 Planner

UNDERSTANDING BY DESIGN®

Enduring Understandings

- *Conflict can lead to change.* • *The social sciences help us understand history.*
- *The movement of people, goods, and ideas causes societies to change over time.*
- *Science and technology can change people's lives.*

Essential Questions

- *Why does conflict develop?* • *Why is history important?* • *How do governments change?*
- *How does technology change the way people live?* • *How do new ideas change the way people live?*

Students will know:

- *why the American colonies revolted against Britain*
- *the ideas that shaped the Declaration of Independence and the U.S. Constitution*
- *why France revolted against its monarchy*
- *how Napoleon became the leader of France*
- *the effects of nationalism on Europe*
- *the causes and effects of the American Civil War*
- *the advancements made during the Industrial Revolution and their impact on society*
- *the ideas of liberalism and socialism*
- *the art movements of romanticism, realism, and modernism*
- *scientific advancements of the late nineteenth and early twentieth centuries*

Students will be able to:

- **analyze** the role of economics in the American Revolution
- **draw conclusions** about the reasons for the American Revolution
- **recall** the reasons for the French Revolution
- **analyze** the influence of the American Revolution
- **explain** how Napoleon rose to power
- **evaluate** why the French rebelled against monarchy and then later accepted Napoleon's dictatorship
- **distinguish** between *nation* and *state*
- **describe** changes in Europe due to nationalism
- **organize** information about the politics in Europe
- **describe** westward expansion of the United States
- **compare** pre- and post-Industrial Revolution society
- **compare and contrast** liberalism and socialism
- **recognize** works of different art movements
- **research** a nineteenth-century scientist

Predictable Misunderstandings

Students may think:

- The American Revolution had no influence on political change in Europe.
- The Magna Carta and the English Bill of Rights had no impact on the United States.
- The Industrial Revolution began in the United States.

Assessment Evidence

Performance Task

- Hands-On Chapter Project

Other Evidence

- Interactive Graphic Organizers
- Economics of History Activities
- 21st Century Skills Activities
- Geography and History Activity
- Responses to Interactive Whiteboard Activities
- Lesson Reviews
- Participation in class discussion and debates
- Essay about nationalism
- Participation in class simulation
- Research projects

Pacing Guide

Introducing the Chapter	1 day
Lesson 1 The American Revolution	2 days
Lesson 2 The French Revolution and Napoleon	1 day
What Do You Think?	1 day
Lesson 3 Nationalism and Nation-States	2 days
Lesson 4 The Industrial Revolution	1 day
Lesson 5 Society and Industry	2 days
Chapter Activities and Assessment	1 day
TOTAL TIME	**11 Days**

Differentiated Instruction

These lesson plans are written to address the needs of your On Level students. Discussion and activities that are well-suited to your Approaching Grade Level learners, Beyond Grade Level learners, as well as your English Language Learners are coded as follows:

AL **Approaching Grade Level**

BL **Beyond Grade Level**

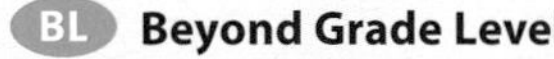

ELL **English Language Learner**

NCSS Standards covered in "Political and Industrial Revolutions"

Learners will understand:

2 TIME, CONTINUITY, AND CHANGE

5. Key historical periods and patterns of change within and across cultures (e.g., the rise and fall of ancient civilizations, the development of technology, the rise of modern nation-states, and the establishment and breakdown of colonial systems)
7. The contributions of key persons, groups, and events from the past and their influence on the present

3 PEOPLE, PLACES, AND ENVIRONMENTS

4. The roles of different kinds of population centers in a region or nation
6. Patterns of demographic and political change, and cultural diffusion in the past and present (e.g., changing national boundaries, migration, and settlement, and the diffusion of and changes in customs and ideas)
7. Human modifications of the environment
8. Factors that contribute to cooperation and conflict among peoples of the nation and world, including language, religion, and political beliefs

5 INDIVIDUALS, GROUPS, AND INSTITUTIONS

4. That ways in which young people are socialized include similarities as well as differences across cultures
5. That groups and institutions change over time
6. That cultural diffusion occurs when groups migrate
7. That institutions may promote or undermine social conformity
8. That when two or more groups with differing norms and beliefs interact, accommodation or conflict may result

6 POWER, AUTHORITY, AND GOVERNANCE

1. Rights are guaranteed in the U.S. Constitution, the supreme law of the land
2. Fundamental ideas that are the foundation of American constitutional democracy (including those of the U.S. Constitution, popular sovereignty, the rule of law, separation of powers, checks and balances, minority rights, the separation of church and state, and Federalism)
3. Fundamental values of constitutional democracy (e.g., the common good, liberty, justice, equality, and individual dignity)
5. The ways in which governments meet the needs and wants of citizens, manage conflict, and establish order and society

7 PRODUCTION, DISTRIBUTION, AND CONSUMPTION

1. Individuals, government, and society experience scarcity because human wants and needs exceed what can be produced from available resources
2. How choices involve trading off the expected value of one opportunity gained against the expected value of the best alternative
3. The economic choices that people make have both present and future consequences
4. Economic incentives affect people's behavior and may be regulated by rules or laws
6. The economic gains that result from specialization and exchange as well as the trade-offs

8 SCIENCE, TECHNOLOGY, AND SOCIETY

1. Science is a result of empirical study of the natural world, and technology is the application of knowledge to accomplish tasks
2. Society often turns to science and technology to solve problems
3. Our lives today are media and technology dependent
4. Science and technology have had both positive and negative impacts upon individuals, societies, and the environment in the past and present
5. Science and technology have changed peoples' perceptions of the social and natural world, as well as their relationship to the land, economy and trade, their concept of security, and their major daily activities
6. Values, beliefs, and attitudes that have been influenced by new scientific and technological knowledge (e.g., invention of the printing press, conceptions of the universe, applications of atomic energy, and genetic discoveries)
8. Science and technology sometimes create ethical issues that test our standards and values
9. The need for laws and policies to govern scientific and technological applications

CHAPTER 23

Introducing the Chapter

(Student Edition p. 661)

The Story Matters . . .

Read "The Story Matters . . ." aloud in class. Then, tell students that this episode took place during a revolution in France.

Ask: **The text says the revolution will lead to great joy and great tragedy. Based on the details of the paragraph, what is the great joy? What tragedy do you predict will occur as a result of the revolt?** Have students use the details from the paragraph to make their predictions.

Then ask:

Why do you think the artist sees commoners as interesting artistic subjects?

What message is the artist sending about life during this time period?

How is this message sad, happy, or troubling?

Tell students that some artists wanted to show the world as it truly was. They painted scenes of real life and real people, such as in this painting. Explain that students will learn more about the artistic movements that emerged during the periods of revolution covered in this chapter.

networks

There's More Online about how revolutions changed Europe and the United States.

CHAPTER 23

The Story Matters . . .

The people of France have risen up. They have stormed prisons, seized property, and set nobles on the run. In Paris, the capital, crowds fill the streets, thrilled with their power. Yet, problems remain. The poor are hungrier than ever. It may be a long time before there will be work to do or safe places to set up markets. As you read this chapter, note how revolution can lead to great joy and great tragedy.

◄ *French artist Jacques Louis David became famous for his paintings about the French Revolution. He painted ordinary people, such as this poor woman of Paris, and leaders, such as the Emperor Napoleon.*

661

Introducing Place and Time

(Student Edition pp. 662–663)

CHAPTER 23

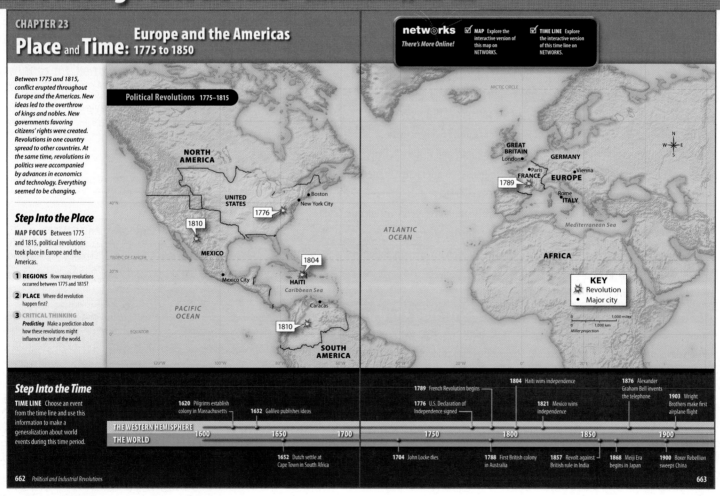

Place and Time: Europe and the Americas 1775 to 1850

networks *There's More Online!*

☑ **MAP** Explore the interactive version of this map on NETWORKS.

☑ **TIME LINE** Explore the interactive version of this time line on NETWORKS.

Between 1775 and 1815, conflict erupted throughout Europe and the Americas. New ideas led to the overthrow of kings and nobles. New governments favoring citizens' rights were created. Revolutions in one country spread to other countries. At the same time, revolutions in politics were accompanied by advances in economics and technology. Everything seemed to be changing.

Step Into the Place

MAP FOCUS Between 1775 and 1815, political revolutions took place in Europe and the Americas.

1. **REGIONS** How many revolutions occurred between 1775 and 1815?
2. **PLACE** Where did revolution happen first?
3. **CRITICAL THINKING** *Predicting* Make a prediction about how these revolutions might influence the rest of the world.

Political Revolutions 1775–1815

NORTH AMERICA
UNITED STATES
Boston
New York City
1776
1810
MEXICO
Mexico City
1804
HAITI
Caribbean Sea
Caracas
1810
SOUTH AMERICA
PACIFIC OCEAN
ATLANTIC OCEAN
ARCTIC CIRCLE
TROPIC OF CANCER
EQUATOR
GREAT BRITAIN
London
GERMANY
Paris
FRANCE
1789
Vienna
EUROPE
Rome
ITALY
Mediterranean Sea
AFRICA

KEY
Revolution
Major city

0 1,000 miles
0 1,000 km
Miller projection

Step Into the Time

TIME LINE Choose an event from the time line and use this information to make a generalization about world events during this time period.

THE WESTERN HEMISPHERE

- **1620** Pilgrims establish colony in Massachusetts
- **1632** Galileo publishes ideas
- **1776** U.S. Declaration of Independence signed
- **1789** French Revolution begins
- **1804** Haiti wins independence
- **1821** Mexico wins independence
- **1876** Alexander Graham Bell invents the telephone
- **1903** Wright Brothers make first airplane flight

1600 1650 1700 1750 1800 1850 1900

THE WORLD

- **1652** Dutch settle at Cape Town in South Africa
- **1704** John Locke dies
- **1788** First British colony in Australia
- **1857** Revolt against British rule in India
- **1868** Meiji Era begins in Japan
- **1900** Boxer Rebellion sweeps China

662 *Political and Industrial Revolutions*

663

Technology Extension

- Find an additional activity online that incorporates technology for this project.
- Visit the EdTechTeacher Web sites (included in the Technology Extension for this chapter) for more links, tutorials, and other resources.

Assessing Background Knowledge

INTERACTIVE WORKSHEET

What Do You Know? Activity

Have students complete the What Do You Know? KWL Chart about the American, French, and Industrial Revolutions. Encourage them to include any details they might know about the subjects. Then brainstorm meaningful questions about each subject.

After students complete the chapter content, have them return to the questions. Discuss whether the questions were answered. Have students complete the chart and research any unanswered questions.

INTERACTIVE WORKSHEET

Guided Reading Activities

There is a Guided Reading Activity for each lesson in this chapter. You may wish to assign the Guided Reading Activity for Lesson 1 after introducing the chapter content.

Hands-On Chapter Project

Students will create a political cartoon that expresses a point of view about one of the events that took place during the political revolutions of the nineteenth century.

- Students will participate in a class discussion to review what they have learned about events such as the Boston Tea Party, the Stamp Act, the signing of the Declaration of Independence, or Napoleon's exile to Elba.
- Then, students will divide into small groups. Each group will choose an event and create a political cartoon for that event. Students will use worksheets and discussions to help them plan their cartoons.
- Next, each group will present their political cartoons to the class.
- Finally, students will evaluate their research, content, and presentation using an Assessment Rubric.

Visit **networks** online to see the full project and rubric.

Step Into the Place

INTERACTIVE WHITEBOARD ACTIVITY

Place Use the whiteboard to project the Chapter Opener map. Have students explore the political revolutions that occurred from 1775 to 1815. Encourage students to think about the impact on the world of the many revolutions within this 40-year time period.

Remind students that communication was slow during the late 1700s and that news of a revolt might have taken months to travel between continents. Explain that in spite of slow communications, the early revolutions inspired the later ones.

Step Into the Time

Evaluating Have students review the time line for the chapter. Point out the events that represent a revolution. Have students identify the nations in which the revolutions took place. Have them evaluate how many years passed between each major revolution.

Ask: **Which events on the time line are probably part of the Industrial Revolution?** *(1876—Alexander Graham Bell invents the telephone; 1903—Wright Brothers make first airplane flight)*

Answers for pages 662–663

Step Into the Place

1. five
2. United States (1776)
3. CRITICAL THINKING Possible answers: These revolutions might frighten the rest of the Western Hemisphere. These revolutions might inspire revolutions in other parts of the Western Hemisphere.

Step Into the Time

Students may say this was a time period of great change.

ONLINE RESOURCES

networks

Assign these interactive worksheets and quizzes from your Teacher Lesson Center. All resources are print-ready.

It's ALL Online!

CHAPTER 23 RESOURCES

- ☑ Chapter Summary
- ☑ Vocabulary Builder
- ☑ What Do You Know?
- ☑ Hands-On Chapter Project

Lesson 1 Resources

- ☑ Interactive Graphic Organizer
- ☑ Economics of History
  Tariffs in the American Colonies
- ☑ Guided Reading Activity
- ☑ Reading Essentials and Study Guide
- ☑ Online Self-Check Quiz

Lesson 2 Resources

- ☑ Interactive Graphic Organizer
- ☑ 21st Century Skills Activity Citizenship
- ☑ Guided Reading Activity
- ☑ Reading Essentials and Study Guide
- ☑ Online Self-Check Quiz

Lesson 3 Resources

- ☑ Interactive Graphic Organizer
- ☑ Geography and History Activity
  Crossing the Andes
- ☑ Guided Reading Activity
- ☑ Reading Essentials and Study Guide
- ☑ Online Self-Check Quiz

Lesson 4 Resources

- ☑ Interactive Graphic Organizer
- ☑ 21st Century Skills
  Research on the Internet
- ☑ Guided Reading Activity
- ☑ Reading Essentials and Study Guide
- ☑ Online Self-Check Quiz

Lesson 5 Resources

- ☑ Interactive Graphic Organizer
- ☑ Economics of History
  Specialization and the Industrial Revolution
- ☑ Guided Reading Activity
- ☑ Reading Essentials and Study Guide
- ☑ Online Self-Check Quiz

Assessment Resources

- ☑ Lesson Reviews
- ☑ Online Self-Check Quizzes
- ☑ Chapter Activities and Assessment
- ☑ Standardized Test Practice

Remediation Resources

- ☑ Reading Essentials and Study Guide
- ☑ Guided Reading Activities
- ☑ Online Self-Check Quizzes
- ☑ Chapter Summary

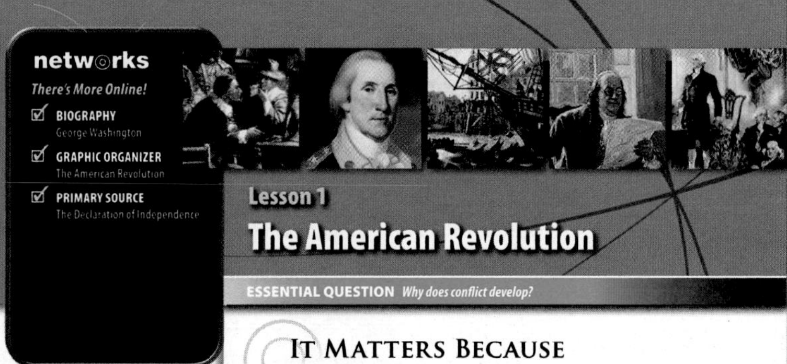

networks
There's More Online!
- ☑ BIOGRAPHY — George Washington
- ☑ GRAPHIC ORGANIZER — The American Revolution
- ☑ PRIMARY SOURCE — The Declaration of Independence

Lesson 1

The American Revolution

ESSENTIAL QUESTION *Why does conflict develop?*

It Matters Because

The American Revolution guaranteed the freedoms we still have in America today. When we learn about the difficult struggle to gain independence, we value and protect our freedoms.

1 Britain's American Colonies

GUIDING QUESTION ***Why did England found colonies in North America?***

The first permanent English colony in North America was set up by the Virginia Company in the area that is now Virginia. The company owners wanted riches and planned to make money from the colony. People who wanted religious freedom, such as the Puritans, established other colonies in North America.

During the early 1600s, Puritans in England were **persecuted** (PUR•seh•kyoo•tehd) for their beliefs. When a group is persecuted, its members are punished and made to suffer. People sometimes persecute others because of religious differences.

In 1620, a group of Puritans known as the Pilgrims left Britain for America so they could worship freely. They sailed across the Atlantic Ocean in a ship called the *Mayflower* and landed in what is today the state of Massachusetts. Their settlement was called Plymouth.

Founding Colonies

The success of Plymouth may have influenced other Puritans to come to America. In 1630, about 1,000 Puritans founded the Massachusetts Bay Colony. Others soon followed. By the mid-1640s, more than 20,000 Puritans had settled in America.

Reading **HELP**DESK

Taking Notes: ***Cause and Effect***

As you read, keep track of the events on a cause-and-effect chart. For each event, note what happened as a result of the event.

The American Revolution

Cause	Effect
Puritans were persecuted.	
The Stamp Act	
The Articles of Confederation	

Other people seeking religious freedom set up colonies elsewhere along the Atlantic coast. For example, English Catholics founded Maryland in 1634. The Quakers, a religious group that had also been persecuted in England, established Pennsylvania in 1680.

When the first English settlers arrived in North America, they came into contact with Native Americans. At first the two groups lived peacefully. The English learned Native American farming skills. Settlers began eating local foods, such as corn and beans. As more English settlers arrived, however, the relationship worsened. Native Americans often died of diseases brought by the English or in battles with the settlers over land.

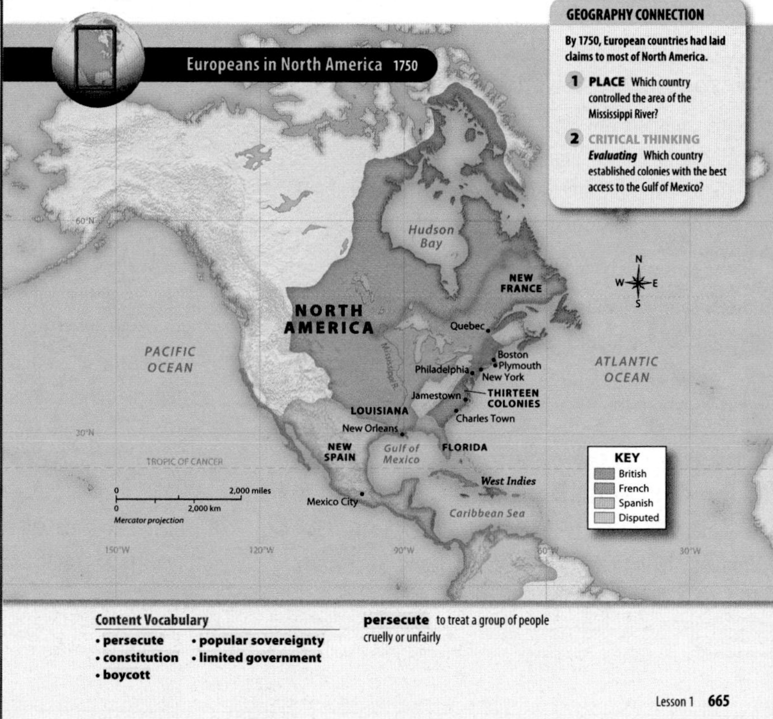

GEOGRAPHY CONNECTION

By 1750, European countries had laid claims to most of North America.

1. **PLACE** Which country controlled the area of the Mississippi River?
2. **CRITICAL THINKING** ***Evaluating*** Which country established colonies with the best access to the Gulf of Mexico?

Content Vocabulary
- persecute
- constitution
- boycott
- popular sovereignty
- limited government

persecute to treat a group of people cruelly or unfairly

By the early 1700s, the English had thirteen colonies along the Atlantic coast of North America. Settlers in northern colonies found a cool or moderate climate and rocky soil. The land was more suitable for smaller farms than the warmer, more fertile southern colonies. In the South, large plantations worked by enslaved African people grew crops for export.

In 1620, before stepping off the Mayflower ship, the Pilgrims signed the Mayflower Compact. The Mayflower Compact was a document that called for the signers to follow any laws that would be established.

Self-Government in the Colonies

Self-government began early in England's American colonies. To attract more settlers, the Virginia Company gave colonists in Virginia the right to elect burgesses, or representatives. The elected burgesses formed the first House of Burgesses, modeled on England's Parliament. The House of Burgesses first met in 1619.

The House of Burgesses set an example of representative government, or a government in which people elect representatives to make laws. Other colonies soon set up their own legislatures.

The Puritans in Massachusetts also wanted to govern themselves. Before leaving the *Mayflower*, the Pilgrims signed an agreement called the Mayflower Compact. They agreed that they would choose their own leaders and make their own laws:

PRIMARY SOURCE

> We, whose names are underwritten . . .Having undertaken for the glory of God, and Advancement of the Christian Faith . . . a Voyage to plant [a] colony . . . do . . . enact, constitute, and frame, such just and equal Laws . . . as shall be thought most meet [acceptable] and convenient for the general good of the Colony . . . .
>
> —from the *Mayflower Compact*

Over the years, most of the English colonies developed **constitutions,** or written plans of government. These **documents** let the colonists elect assemblies and protected their rights.

☑ **PROGRESS CHECK**

Explaining What steps did the colonists take to govern themselves?

Reading **HELP**DESK

constitution a document that describes how a country will be governed and guarantees people certain rights

Academic Vocabulary

document a piece of writing

boycott to protest by refusing to do something

2 Road to Revolt

GUIDING QUESTION ***How did conflict develop between Britain and its American colonies?***

During the 1700s, many changes came to England and its colonies. In 1707, England united with Scotland to form Britain. The term *British* came to mean both the English and the Scots. Meanwhile, the colonies came to depend on Britain for trade and defense.

Trade and the Colonies

The American colonies shipped their raw materials to Britain. In return, they received British manufactured products as well as tea and spices from Asia. To control this trade, Britain passed the Navigation Acts. Under these laws, the colonists had to sell their products to Britain even if they could get a better price elsewhere. Any goods bought from other countries had to go to Britain first and be taxed before going to the Americas.

The colonists at first accepted the trade laws because Britain was a guaranteed buyer of their raw materials. Later, as the colonies grew, colonists wanted to produce their own manufactured goods. They also wanted to sell their products elsewhere if they could get higher prices. Many colonial merchants began smuggling goods in and out of the colonies. Smuggling is shipping products without paying taxes or getting government permission.

Britain Tightens Its Controls

Between 1756 and 1763, Britain and France fought a war for control of North America. When Britain won, it gained nearly all of France's North American empire. The conflict, however, left Britain deeply in debt. Desperate for money, the British made plans to tax the American colonists and tighten trade rules.

In 1765, Parliament passed the Stamp Act, which taxed newspapers and other printed material. These items had to bear a stamp showing that the tax was paid. The colonists were outraged. They responded by boycotting British goods. **Boycotting** is refusing to buy specific products in protest.

Finally, nine colonies sent delegates to a Stamp Act Congress in New York City. The Congress declared that Parliament could not tax the colonies because the colonies did not have representatives in Parliament. The colonists united under the slogan, "No taxation without representation!" They believed that only colonial legislatures had the right to tax them. The British government backed down for a while, but it still needed money. In 1767, Parliament placed taxes on glass, lead, paper, paint, and tea.

George Washington at first tried to peacefully settle the Americans' differences with Britain. What do you think changed his mind about going to war?

LESSON 1 • Day 1

ENGAGE

Describing Write the word *pilgrim* on the board. Remind students that although the term has broad usage, students are to think about it in relation to American history.

Ask: What do you think of when I say the word *pilgrim*? *(Possible answers: Thanksgiving, Plymouth Rock, black and white clothing, the* Mayflower*)*

Write answers on the board. Tell students they will learn how the first English settlers served as role models in many ways for generations to come. AL ELL

TEACH & ASSESS

Britain's American Colonies

GUIDING QUESTION *Why did England found colonies in North America?*

LECTURE SLIDE **Identifying Points of View** Show students the lecture slide with the excerpt from the Mayflower Compact. Invite a volunteer to read the excerpt to the class.

Ask:

Why did the Puritans create such a document? *(They wanted to govern themselves, and a written document was the best way to start doing that.)*

Why do you think it is important for a group of people to be led by a written list of rules? *(When all people in a group agree to live by the rules of one document, the group is likely to get along.)*

Explain that the Mayflower Compact and the U.S. Declaration of Independence have some similarities. Help students identify some of those similarities.

Road to Revolt

GUIDING QUESTION *How did conflict develop between Britain and its American colonies?*

Identifying Central Issues Write the slogan "No taxation without representation" on the board. Ask volunteers to define the words in the slogan.

Ask:

Who used the slogan? *(the colonists)*

What does it mean? *(It means the colonists wanted to participate in the decisions about who and what would be taxed. They wanted a say in the process.)*

Confirm that students understand the importance of taxes in supporting society. Students should evaluate, however, whether the colonists' demand is reasonable. Have students create a list of reasons to demonstrate their understanding of whether the demand was fair.

INTERACTIVE WORKSHEET

Economics of History Activity

Evaluating Have students complete the Economics of History worksheet in class. Tell students they will learn how governments use tariffs to control trade. It will also help them understand why the colonists objected to Britain's effort to control trade. If students are unable to complete the worksheet in class, assign the remaining as homework.

CLOSE & REFLECT

Review with students why the colonists set out to form their own country and govern themselves. Then, ask students to think about the role economics had on the causes of the American Revolution. Make sure students understand the purposes of taxes and tarriffs. Then, explain to students that the Declaration of Independence was written by Thomas Jefferson, and it is the document that proclaimed America's freedom from British rule.

The following provides support for the next lesson.

BACKGROUND KNOWLEDGE

The Declaration of Independence

When writing the Declaration of Independence, Thomas Jefferson drew on historical as well as contemporary ideas. The Declaration drew from earlier English documents, such as the Magna Carta and the English Bill of Rights. Both documents established the idea that government powers have limits. They also say that rulers have to obey the laws and treat citizens fairly.

The document also cited newer ideas from the Enlightenment, most significantly the ideas of English philosopher John Locke. Locke stated that all people are born with certain natural rights: the rights to life, liberty, and property. Jefferson borrowed this idea but changed the list of inalienable rights to life, liberty, and the pursuit of happiness.

Locke also believed in the concept of a social contract. According to Locke, this contract was an agreement between the people and their government stating that the government would protect the people's rights. If the government failed to do so and it violated the social contract, the people had the right and the responsibility to overthrow that government and replace it with leadership that would abide by the social contract. This argument formed the crux of the Declaration of Independence: King George III had abused the rights of the colonists; therefore, the colonists were obliged to rebel against him.

IF YOU HAVE MORE TIME . . .

Debate the Reasons for American Independence

Defending Point out the moment in the text when the colonial leaders decided to declare their independence from Britain.

Ask:

Were the colonists justified in revolting against British rule? *(Accept reasonable answers.)*

Divide the class into two groups. On the board, have one group list the reasons for independence and the other group list the reasons against it.

Students should refer to these lists during an informal debate about whether the American Revolution was justified.

Answers for pages 664–667

P. 664 Taking Notes Possible answers include: **Row 1:** Colonists settle in North America, balancing self-government with British rule; **Row 2:** Conflict between Britain and colonists escalates, leading to acts of rebellion such as the Boston Tea Party and, eventually, war; **Row 3:** The nation's leaders agree to form a new Constitution based on a federal model, with a stronger central government.

P. 665 GEOGRAPHY CONNECTION

1. France controlled the area of the Mississippi River.
2. CRITICAL THINKING Spain established colonies with the best access to the Gulf of Mexico.

P. 666 ☑ PROGRESS CHECK The colonists wrote constitutions, and they elected their own representatives to organize the colonies.

P. 667 Students might say that the fighting at Lexington and Concord changed George Washington's mind or that he was convinced by the arguments of those who were for independence, such as Samuel Adams.

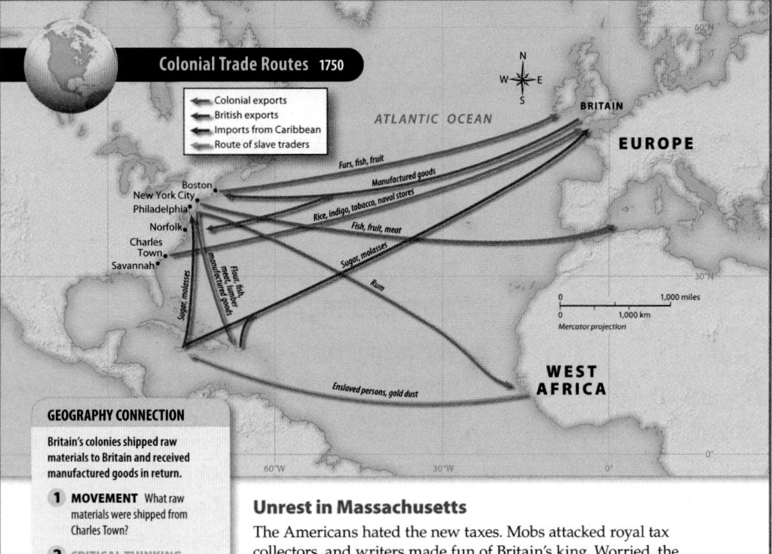

GEOGRAPHY CONNECTION

Britain's colonies shipped raw materials to Britain and received manufactured goods in return.

1. **MOVEMENT** What raw materials were shipped from Charles Town?
2. **CRITICAL THINKING** *Explaining* Why were exports from the Southern islands so valuable?

Unrest in Massachusetts

The Americans hated the new taxes. Mobs attacked royal tax collectors, and writers made fun of Britain's king. Worried, the British sent troops to Boston, Massachusetts, where the strongest protests had taken place.

In March 1770, British troops and American colonists clashed. A Boston crowd threw snowballs at British soldiers. The soldiers fired their weapons. Five people were killed. The event became known as the Boston Massacre. In response, Parliament repealed, or canceled, all of the taxes except the one on tea.

In 1773, Parliament passed the Tea Act. It allowed the British East India Company to ship tea to the colonies without paying the tax that American tea merchants had to pay. This allowed the company to sell its tea very cheaply and threatened to drive the American tea merchants out of business.

In Boston, angry colonists decided to take action. A group of protesters disguised themselves as Native Americans. They boarded British ships in Boston Harbor and dumped their tea into the water. This event is known as the Boston Tea Party.

Reading **HELP**DESK

To punish the colonists, Parliament passed laws that shut down Boston Harbor and placed Massachusetts under military control. It also required colonists to house and feed British soldiers. The colonists called these laws the Intolerable Acts, or laws they could not accept. The Acts made the colonies realize that they had to work together to defend their liberties. In September 1774, delegates from twelve colonies met in Philadelphia at the First Continental Congress. They demanded that the Intolerable Acts be repealed. Colonial leaders, however, could not agree about what to do. Some, such as George Washington of Virginia, hoped to settle the dispute with Britain. Others, like Samuel Adams of Massachusetts and Patrick Henry of Virginia, wanted the colonies to declare independence.

PROGRESS CHECK

Identifying Cause and Effect What were the Intolerable Acts? How did the colonists respond to them?

3 A War for Independence

GUIDING QUESTION ***How did war between Britain and the American colonies lead to the rise of a new nation—the United States of America?***

While colonial leaders debated, fighting began in Massachusetts. British soldiers set out to destroy colonial weapons being stored in the town of Concord. On April 19, 1775, they met armed colonists at Lexington and fought the first battle of the American Revolution.

News of the conflict spread throughout the colonies. In May 1775, the Second Continental Congress met in Philadelphia. It created an army with George Washington as commander. The Congress, however, tried one last time to settle differences with the British. Members sent an appeal to King George III, but he refused to listen.

Over 100 people, mostly young artisans and laborers, took part in the Boston Tea Party. Nearly 45 tons of tea—about equal in value to a million dollars today—were tossed into Boston Harbor.

CRITICAL THINKING
Explaining Why did the protesters dress up as Native Americans?

Benjamin Franklin, John Adams, and Thomas Jefferson worked together to write the Declaration of Independence.

CRITICAL THINKING
Speculating Why do you think Americans needed an official document to declare independence?

More and more Americans began to think that independence was the only answer. In January 1776, in a pamphlet called *Common Sense*, writer Thomas Paine called on the colonists to break away from Britain.

The Declaration of Independence

On July 4, 1776, the Congress issued the Declaration of Independence. Written by Thomas Jefferson of Virginia, the Declaration stated that the colonies were separating from Britain and forming a new nation—the United States of America.

In the Declaration, Jefferson explained why the Americans were creating a new nation. He referred to John Locke's idea that people can overthrow a government that ignores their rights. The Declaration stated that "all men are created equal" and have certain God-given rights. King George III had violated colonists' rights, and so the colonists had the right to rebel.

An American Victory

The Declaration turned the conflict into a war for independence. The struggle was long and bitter. The American Continental Army had fewer and less-disciplined soldiers than the British. However, they had a skilled general in Washington. The British had the disadvantage of trying to fight a war a long way from home. Also, they had to conquer the whole country to win. The Americans only had to hold out until the British accepted defeat.

The turning point came in October 1777 when the Americans won the Battle of Saratoga in New York. France, Britain's old enemy, realized that the colonists might win and agreed to help the Americans.

The final victory came in 1781 at the Battle of Yorktown in Virginia. American and French forces surrounded and trapped the British. The British surrendered. Peace talks began, and two years later, the Treaty of Paris ended the war. Britain finally accepted American independence.

The United States Constitution

The United States at first was a confederation, or a loose union of independent states. Its plan of government was called the Articles of Confederation. The Articles created a national government, but the states held most powers. It soon became clear that the Articles were too weak to deal with the new nation's problems.

To change the Articles, 55 delegates met in Philadelphia in 1787. They decided instead to write a constitution for an entirely new national government. The new United States Constitution set up a **federal** system, which divided powers between the national government and the states. The delegates divided power in the national government between executive, legislative, and judicial branches. A system called checks and balances enabled each branch to limit the powers of the other branches.

The Constitution made the United States a republic with an elected president. In 1789, George Washington was elected the first president of the United States. That same year, a Bill of Rights was added to the Constitution. The Bill of Rights guaranteed certain rights to citizens that the government could not violate. These rights included freedom of religion, speech, and press, and the right to trial by jury.

The U.S. Constitution was shaped by Enlightenment principles. One of these is **popular sovereignty**, or the idea that government receives its powers from the people. Another principle is **limited government**, or the idea that a government may use only those powers given to it by the people.

Reading **HELP**DESK

popular sovereignty the idea that government is created by the people and must act according to people's wishes

limited government a government whose powers are restricted through laws or a document such as a constitution

Academic Vocabulary

federal referring to an organized union of states under one government

The American leaders who met in Philadelphia in 1787 and wrote the U.S. Constitution were some of the nation's best political minds. What sort of government did the Constitution create?

PROGRESS CHECK

Explaining What kind of government did the Americans set up after the American Revolution?

LESSON 1 REVIEW

Review Vocabulary

1. Use the words *persecute* and *boycott* in a sentence about the American colonies.
2. What is meant by *popular sovereignty* and why was it important?

Answer the Guiding Questions

3. ***Evaluating*** Why did the success of the Pilgrims influence others to settle in the Americas?
4. ***Making Connections*** What types of British laws did American colonists protest the most?
5. ***Drawing Conclusions*** Why do you think it was important for the authors of the Constitution to create a Bill of Rights?
6. **PERSUASIVE WRITING** Write a short essay from the viewpoint of Thomas Paine in which you try to persuade American colonists to declare independence from Britain.

LESSON 1 • Day 2

ENGAGE

Predicting Prompt students to recall that the colonists were angry about the increase in taxes by the British government. **Ask:** **What do you predict will happen after the American leaders announce their Declaration of Independence?** *(A war will break out.)*

A War for Independence

GUIDING QUESTION ***How did war between Britain and the American colonies lead to the rise of a new nation—the United States of America?***

LECTURE SLIDE **Determining Cause and Effect** Show students the lecture slide listing key events of the Revolutionary War.

Draw a cause-and-effect graphic organizer on the board, and have students evaluate the following important developments.

Ask:

What was the immediate cause of the first battle of the war? *(The British set out to destroy colonial weapons in Concord, Massachusetts. This led to the first battle, which was fought in nearby Lexington.)*

What was the effect of the first battle? *(The Second Continental Congress met and organized an army. It also sent an appeal to the king to settle their differences.)*

What was the effect of the French presence in the war? *(The French helped the Americans corner the British troops in Yorktown, New York, until the British surrendered.)* BL

Summarizing Hold a class discussion with students about the challenges that faced the Patriots and the British during the Revolutionary War.

Have students list advantages and disadvantages for each side on the board. *(The following are possible answers. Patriots: Advantages include fighting on home soil, fighting for a cause they believed in, willingness to use nontraditional tactics in battle; disadvantages include having a smaller and weaker army and navy.*

British: Advantages include having a much stronger military; disadvantages include having to fight far from Britain, needing to defeat the opposition in many different colonies, and facing foreign allies of America.)

Then ask:

Could the American forces have defeated the British without foreign help? *(Student answers will vary but should be based upon an understanding of the lesson content.)*

INTERACTIVE WHITEBOARD ACTIVITY

Identifying Central Issues Present the Interactive Whiteboard Activity about the Bill of Rights. Allow students time to complete the matching activity. For each item on the list, have students identify why the colonists would have believed that such a right was important to include.

Ask: **What experiences had the colonists just lived through that might have led them to include such an item in the Bill of Rights?** *(Accept reasonable answers that speculate about each item.)*

Have students complete the Lesson 1 Review.

CLOSE & REFLECT

Present to students examples of a time line; a basic, two-column table; and a cause-and-effect chart. Then, have students pick which type of graphic organizer they would like to use to summarize what they have learned about the American Revolution.

Students can complete the organizers in pairs, or group students by the type they chose. When finished, display the different organizers, and compare and contrast each type's effectiveness at presenting the information in the Lesson.

IF YOU HAVE MORE TIME . . .

Use Posters to Reinforce Key Concepts

Illustrating Guide the class to identify key turning points from the lesson such as the establishment of Puritan colonies, protests against the Stamp Act, and the writing of the Declaration of Independence. Write these events on the whiteboard.

Organize students into pairs or trios. Assign, or allow each group to choose, one turning point from the class list. Have each group create a poster illustrating that event. For example, the group assigned the establishment of Puritan colonies might choose to design a poster that invites settlers to enjoy the benefits of the new colonies.

Once the posters are completed, display them on a wall or a window in random order. Then have students help you rearrange them in correct chronological order. AL ELL

BACKGROUND KNOWLEDGE

The U.S. Constitution

Like the Declaration, the Constitution draws upon the ideas of the social contract and natural rights. The first line of the document ("We the People of the United States of America . . .") makes it plain that the people are the source of government power. The Bill of Rights enforces the idea that all people are guaranteed certain rights. The Constitution also draws upon other Enlightenment ideals, such as Montesquieu's separation of powers. Although the Founders might have agreed on the broad principles of the Constitution, many heated arguments occurred over the details. Larger states wanted to make sure they had power proportionate to their size. Smaller states wanted to make sure they had power equal to that of the larger states. In the end, a compromise was reached: a bicameral (two-house) legislature.

Answers for pages 668–671

P. 668 GEOGRAPHY CONNECTION

1. Rice, indigo, and tobacco were shipped from Charles Town.
2. CRITICAL THINKING because they could not be found in Europe

P. 669 ☑ PROGRESS CHECK The Intolerable Acts was the name given by the colonists to a series of laws imposed by the British and designed to punish the colonists. In response, the colonists agreed to work together to protect their rights. The colonists' displeasure with the Acts led to the First Continental Congress.

P. 669 CRITICAL THINKING Protesters dressed up as Native Americans to disguise their identities and to make the British think Native Americans were responsible for the Tea Party.

P. 670 CRITICAL THINKING so that they would be taken seriously by the British crown

P. 671 The Constitution set up a representative government.

P. 671 ☑ PROGRESS CHECK After the American Revolution, the Americans set up a national government under the Articles of Confederation. This confederation, or loose union of states, gave most power to the states.

LESSON 1 REVIEW

1. Sample answer: American colonists felt persecuted by British tax policies, so they boycotted British goods.
2. Popular sovereignty is the idea that government receives its powers from the people. It is significant because it determines the source of power in a government: the people.
3. The success of the Pilgrims set an example for other groups seeking religious freedom, such as the Quakers and the Catholics.
4. The colonists protested the most against British laws that restricted colonial businesses or impacted the colonial economy.
5. The Bill of Rights spelled out the laws held by the citizens of the nation that could not be taken away by the national government.
6. Essays should include a coherent argument in favor of declaring independence. Examples and concrete details should be included to support the argument.

networks
There's More Online!

- ☑ GRAPHIC ORGANIZER
  Time Line
- ☑ MAP
  Napoleon's Empire
- ☑ SLIDE SHOW
  - The Estates General
  - The Bastille
- ☑ VIDEO

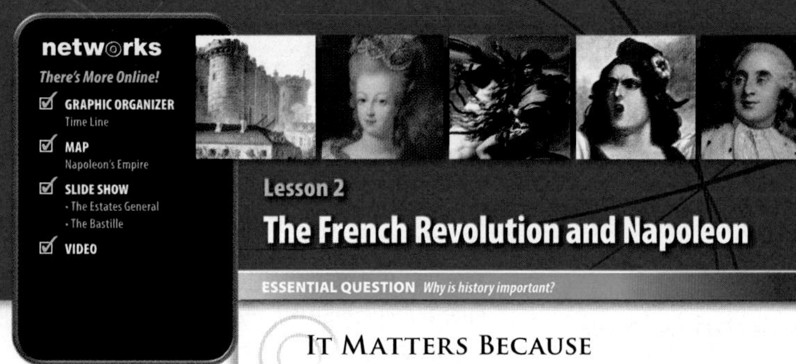

Lesson 2

The French Revolution and Napoleon

ESSENTIAL QUESTION *Why is history important?*

IT MATTERS BECAUSE

The French Revolution drew on some of the ideas of the American Revolution.

1 The Revolution Begins

GUIDING QUESTION *Why did revolution break out in France?*

The American Revolution had an immediate effect on many people in France. They also wanted political changes based on the ideas of freedom and equality. The French Revolution began in 1789. It dramatically changed France and all of Europe.

The Causes of the French Revolution

In the 1700s, France was one of the most powerful countries in Europe. French kings ruled with absolute power. Nobles lived in great wealth and enjoyed many privileges. Most of France's people, however, were poor. They had little education and struggled to make a living.

The French people were divided into three **estates,** or classes. This system determined a person's legal rights and social standing. It also created great inequality in French society.

The First Estate was the Catholic clergy, or church officials. They did not pay taxes, and they received money from church lands. The Second Estate was the nobles. They held the highest posts in the military and in government. Like the clergy, the nobles paid no taxes. They lived in luxury at the king's court or in their country houses surrounded by large areas of land.

Reading HELPDESK

Taking Notes: *Sequencing*

As you read, use a time line to keep track of when events happened. Note the date and a word or two about the event.

1780 1800 1820

Content Vocabulary

- **estate**
- **bourgeoisie**
- **coup d'etat**

Everyone else in France belonged to the Third Estate. At the top of this group were members of the middle class, known as the **bourgeoisie** (burzh•wah•ZEE). Merchants, bankers, doctors, lawyers, and teachers were members of the bourgeoisie. Next were the city workers—artisans, day laborers, and servants. At the bottom were the peasants, who made up more than 80 percent of the French people. Although the members of the Third Estate paid taxes to the king, they had no voice in governing the country.

As the middle class learned more about Enlightenment ideas, they began to resent the privileges of the nobles and clergy. An Englishman traveling in France discovered how **widespread** the unrest had become:

PRIMARY SOURCE

> ❝Walking up a long hill . . . I was joined by a poor woman who complained of the times, and that it was a sad country; . . . she said her husband had but a morsel [small piece] of land, one cow, and a poor little horse, yet they had [42 lbs.] of wheat and three chickens to pay as rent to one [lord], and [4 lbs.] of oats, one chicken, and 1s. [a coin] to pay to another, besides very heavy tallies [land taxes] and other taxes.❞
>
> —from *Travels*, by Arthur Young, 1789

The National Assembly

In 1788, food shortages and rising prices caused great discontent throughout France. At the same time, the French government was almost bankrupt because of costly wars and rising expenses for the court of King Louis XVI (LOO•ee). French banks became reluctant to lend money to the government. The king, desperate for funds, asked the nobles and clergy to pay taxes. When these groups refused, Louis called a meeting of the country's legislature, the Estates-General. This group was made up of representatives from all three estates. If the Estates-General agreed, Louis could impose new taxes.

In the Estates-General, the nobles and clergy refused to give up their privileges, including not paying taxes. Frustrated, the delegates of the Third Estate decided to meet separately. They formed a new group—the National Assembly—and agreed not to break up until they wrote a constitution for France.

The people of Paris celebrated this victory, but they worried that the king's troops would shut down the National Assembly. They got ready to fight. On July 14, 1789, a large crowd stormed a prison called the Bastille (ba•STEEL).

THE THREE ESTATES IN PREREVOLUTIONARY FRANCE

Population

98.0% Third Estate: Commoners
0.5% First Estate: Clergy
1.5% Second Estate: Nobility

Land Ownership

65% Third Estate: Commoners
10% First Estate: Clergy
25% Second Estate: Nobility

Taxation

100% Third Estate: Commoners

Ninety-eight of every 100 people in France were members of the Third Estate.

▶ CRITICAL THINKING
Drawing Conclusions Upon which estate in France did the government depend for its income?

estate a social class in France before the French Revolution
bourgeoisie the middle class in France

Academic Vocabulary

widespread frequent in many places; common

Connections to TODAY

Political Left and Right

When the National Assembly met in 1789, those who supported far-reaching political changes sat on the left side of the meeting room. The people who favored little or no change sat on the right side. Today we still use the terms *left* and *right* to describe these two political viewpoints.

News of the fall of the Bastille spread to the countryside, where the peasants rose up against the nobles. To satisfy the people, the National Assembly ended the privileges of the clergy and nobles. It also issued the Declaration of the Rights of Man and the Citizen. Based on Enlightenment ideas, the declaration stated that the government's powers came from the people, not the king. All people, it said, were equal under the law.

In 1791, the National Assembly made France a constitutional monarchy. France was to be ruled by an elected legislature. Louis, however, refused to accept these changes and tried to flee Paris. As Europe's kings threatened to crush France's revolution, some leaders in Paris pushed for greater change. In 1792, they set up a new government called the National Convention.

☑ PROGRESS CHECK

Identifying What political reforms did the National Assembly adopt?

2 A Republic in France

GUIDING QUESTION *How did supporters of France's revolution enforce their reforms?*

The National Convention ended the monarchy and made France a republic. It wrote a new constitution giving the vote to every man, whether or not he owned property. Meanwhile, two groups fought for control of the Convention. One group, called Girondists, believed the revolution had gone far enough. The other group, known as Jacobins, favored more **radical** change. The Jacobins finally won and took power.

The people of Paris demonstrated against the king by violently attacking the hated Bastille prison. Today, the French celebrate the day of attack—July 14—as Bastille Day, their national holiday. Why do you think the French celebrate a day of violence?

Reading HELPDESK

Academic Vocabulary

radical extreme or far-reaching

Toward the Future

In late 1792, the National Convention put King Louis XVI on trial and found him guilty of aiding France's enemies. A month later, Louis was beheaded on the guillotine (GEE•oh•teen)—a new machine designed to quickly execute people.

Louis's execution alarmed Europe's ruling monarchs. The rulers of Austria and Prussia were already at war with France. In early 1793, Britain, Spain, the Netherlands, and Sardinia joined them in battle against France's revolutionary army.

As the threat of foreign invasions rose, many French people rushed to defend the revolution. The people of Paris were dedicated supporters, shopkeepers, artisans, and workers who saw themselves as heroes and heroines and demanded respect from the upper classes. They addressed each other as "citizen" or "citizeness" rather than "mister" or "madame."

The Reign of Terror

Despite widespread support, the revolution had many enemies within France. To deal with growing unrest, the National Convention set up the Committee of Public Safety to run the country. The Committee took harsh steps against anyone they felt opposed the revolution. Revolutionary courts sentenced to death by guillotine anyone believed to be disloyal. This included Girondists, clergy, nobles, and even women and children. To blend in, wealthy people adopted the simple clothing of the lower classes. About 40,000 people died, including Queen Marie Antoinette. This period, from July 1793 to July 1794, became known as the Reign of Terror.

During this time, the Committee came under the control of a lawyer named Maximilien Robespierre (mak•see•meel•ya ROHBZ•pyehr). Robespierre wanted to create a "Republic of Virtue." By this he meant a democratic society made up of good citizens. Under Robespierre's lead, the Committee opened new schools, taught the peasants new farming skills, and worked to keep prices under control. Robespierre even created a new national religion that worshipped a "Supreme Being." This attempt to replace France's traditional Catholic faith, however, did not last.

With France facing pressure from foreign invasions, the Committee decided to raise a new army. All single men between the ages of 18 and 25 were required to join this new army.

BIOGRAPHY

Marie Antoinette (1755–1793)

As the wife of King Louis XVI, Queen Marie Antoinette ruled over a court of luxury. Her many expenses were partly to blame for France's large debt. As problems and debts mounted, many French people turned against her. Public anger rose when the queen was claimed to have said, "Let them eat cake!" in response to the cry that the peasants had no bread. Later, during the Revolution, Louis and Marie Antoinette tried to flee to Austria, where the queen's brother ruled. They did not get far. Soldiers arrested the royal couple and returned them to Paris. In August 1792, the queen was held in prison until she was executed more than a year later.

▶ CRITICAL THINKING
Speculating Would Marie Antoinette have been treated differently if she had not fled Paris?

LESSON 2

ENGAGE

ategorizing Write the word *bourgeoisie* on the board. ave students brainstorm a list of jobs they would like to old when they are grown. ELL

fter writing these jobs on the board, cross out any overnment jobs or jobs in the church. Tell students that the emaining workers would be considered part of the rench bourgeoisie.

xplain that students will learn how the bourgeoisie solved ome of their problems in this lesson.

TEACH & ASSESS

The Revolution Begins

UIDING QUESTION *Why did revolution break out n France?*

SLIDE SHOW **Differentiating** Show students the slide how describing the membership of the three estates f France.

hen draw a triple Venn diagram on the board labeled with ach of the three estates in French society.

Ask:

What were the three estates? *(The clergy were the First Estate, the nobles were the Second Estate, and the commoners were the Third Estate.)*

How were they different? *(The nobles and the clergy did not pay taxes and had higher status than the commoners.)*

How were they alike? *(All were part of French society.)*

A Republic in France

GUIDING QUESTION *How did supporters of France's revolution enforce their reforms?*

Expressing Review the section titled "The Reign of Terror." Hold a brief debate to argue for and against the following statement: *Robespierre was justified in enforcing his violent laws during the Reign of Terror.*

Have students take a position and justify it with their opinions and with facts from the textbook.

INTERACTIVE WORKSHEET

21st Century Skills Activity

Evaluating Explain to students that the nobles and monarchy of France were not meeting the needs of their people, which led to a bloody revolt and the downfall of the government. Assign the 21st Century Skills worksheet on citizenship for homework. Tell students that they will think about the relationship between the government and the people of a nation.

3 Napoleon Leads France

GUIDING QUESTION *How was Napoleon able to take over France's government?*

LECTURE SLIDE **Defining** Show students the lecture slide defining the term *coup d'etat.* ELL

Ask:

What group did Napoleon overthrow? *(the Directory)*

What title did he take? *(First Consul)* 

LECTURE SLIDE **Summarizing** Show students the lecture slide summarizing the key changes that Napoleon made when he took office.

Ask:

What was the Napoleonic Code? *(a new legal system based on Enlightenment ideas)*

What key event happened in 1804? *(Napoleon crowned himself emperor.)*

4 The Creation of an Empire

GUIDING QUESTION *How did Napoleon build and then lose an empire?*

INTERACTIVE WHITEBOARD ACTIVITY

Sequencing Show students the time line covering the periods in France's revolution. Have them place the events of the revolution in order.

Assessing Have students review their textbook's discussion of the reign of Napoleon. Point out that Napoleon's rule has been interpreted differently over time. Make a two-column chart on the board with "Pro" as the title of the first column head and "Con" as the title of the second column.

Ask: What were the pros and cons of Napoleon's leadership of France? *(Pros: new schools, new legal system, peaceful relationship with the church; Cons: limited freedom of press and speech, fought bloody wars to expand the empire)*

Comparing and Contrasting Have students compare life in France before the revolution to life in France under Napoleon.

Ask:

What were the goals of the French Revolution? *(equality, better lives for the Third Estate)*

Did life under Napoleon include these things? *(to some extent)*

Based on their understanding of the goals and effects of the French Revolution, have students decide if the revolution was a success.

Have students complete the Lesson 2 Review.

Answers for pages 672–675

P. 672 Taking Notes
1789 French Revolution Begins
1791 National Assembly makes France a constitutional monarchy; Marie Antoinette imprisoned
1792 Louis XVI executed
1793 Reign of Terror begins
1794 Reign of Terror ends; the Directory is created
1799 Napoleon takes power in coup d'etat
1804 Empire of Napoleon established

P. 673 CRITICAL THINKING the Third Estate

P. 674 ☑ PROGRESS CHECK The National Assembly issued the Declaration of the Rights of Man, which guaranteed freedom of speech, the press, and religion, and protected against unjust arrest and punishment.

P. 674 The French celebrate a day of violence because it marks the start of their revolution.

P. 675 CRITICAL THINKING Students might say that Marie Antoinette probably would not have been treated any differently if she had stayed in Paris. As queen, she was the symbol of the monarchy, and the people of France were angry at the monarchy. Also, the rumor that she told people to eat cake probably made the French even angrier with her.

With this new force of almost a million soldiers, France halted the threat from abroad. Revolutionary generals gained confidence from their military victories. They soon became important in French politics.

With the republic out of danger, people in France wanted to end the Reign of Terror. Robespierre lost his influence, and his enemies ordered him to be executed without trial. Wealthy middle-class leaders then came to power.

France's new leaders tried to follow more moderate policies. They wrote a new constitution that allowed only men with property to vote. In 1795, a five-man council known as the Directory was created to run the country. The Directory, however, was unable to handle food shortages, rising prices, government bankruptcy, and attacks by other countries. By 1799, the Directory had lost much support. The French people began to look for a strong leader who could restore order.

The guillotine was designed by Dr. Joseph Guillotine to make executions quick and more humane. Instead, the guillotine came to represent harshness and fear during the French Revolution.

PROGRESS CHECK

Identifying What was the Reign of Terror?

3 Napoleon Leads France

GUIDING QUESTION *How was Napoleon able to take over France's government?*

As the Directory weakened at home, the French army won victories in the war with Europe's monarchies. One battle front was in Italy, where the French were fighting against Austrian troops. In those battles, a young French general captured public attention. His name was Napoleon Bonaparte (nuh•POH•lee•uhn BOH•nuh•pahrt).

Born on the Mediterranean island of Corsica in 1769, Napoleon Bonaparte went to military school and became an officer. He supported the revolution. His great talent for military work helped him rise to the rank of general by the time he was 24 years old. After his successes in Italy, Napoleon attacked the British in Egypt in 1799. While in Egypt, he heard of the political troubles back home. He immediately returned to France. There, he opposed the Directory and took part in a **coup d'etat** (koo day • TAH). This is when a group seeking power uses force to suddenly replace top government officials. Napoleon took the title of First Consul and became the strong leader many French people believed they needed.

Reading **HELP**DESK

coup d'etat a change of government in which a new group of leaders seize power by force

676 *Political and Industrial Revolutions*

Napoleon quickly reorganized the government to strengthen his control. He changed France's finances and tax system. He appointed local officials and created many new schools. In addition, he created a new legal system known as the Napoleonic Code. This code of laws was based on Enlightenment ideas. Finally, Napoleon established a more peaceful relationship with the Catholic Church, which had opposed the revolution.

Napoleon did not carry out all of the French Revolution's ideas. People were equal under the law, but freedom of speech and the press were restricted. A new class of nobles was created, based on ability rather than wealth or family. Then, in 1804, Napoleon crowned himself emperor, and France became an empire. Now his dream could be fulfilled.

PROGRESS CHECK

Explaining How did Napoleon strengthen his control after becoming First Consul?

This famous portrait of Napoleon shows him riding to battle. It was painted by Jacques-Louis David.

▶ CRITICAL THINKING

Analyzing How did the artist show that Napoleon was a powerful leader?

4 The Creation of an Empire

GUIDING QUESTION *How did Napoleon build and then lose an empire?*

Napoleon wanted to do more than govern France. He wanted to build a great empire. Beginning in 1803, Napoleon won a number of military battles that helped him reach his goal. By 1807, Napoleon controlled an empire that stretched across Europe from the Atlantic Ocean to Russia.

Many different territories were part of Napoleon's empire. Napoleon directly ruled France and parts of Germany and Italy. He named relatives to govern other lands in his empire, such as Spain and the Netherlands. Outside the empire, independent countries, such as Prussia, Austria, and Sweden, were forced to ally with France.

Two forces, however, helped to bring Napoleon's empire to an end. One was nationalism, or the desire of a people for self-rule. The nations conquered by Napoleon's army rejected his rule and the French practices forced on them. The other force was the combined strength of Britain and Russia working against him.

Napoleon Meets Defeat

Napoleon hoped to cross the English Channel and invade Britain. He never achieved this goal. A major French defeat took place off the coast of Spain. There, in 1805, the British admiral Lord Horatio Nelson defeated the French navy in the Battle of Trafalgar.

Lesson 2 677

Napoleon's Empire

GEOGRAPHY CONNECTION

From 1807 to 1812, Napoleon controlled a large part of Europe.

1. **PLACE** About how far south did Napoleon's empire extend by 1812?
2. CRITICAL THINKING ***Theorizing*** What geographic feature of Britain might explain why the British navy was able to defeat Napoleon's attempts at invasion?

After Trafalgar, Napoleon decided to strike at Britain's economic lifeline—trade. In a plan called the Continental System, Napoleon forbade the countries in his empire to trade with Britain. However, the Continental System was difficult to enforce and finally proved unsuccessful.

Napoleon next decided to invade Russia. He organized the Grand Army, a force of about 600,000 soldiers from all over Europe. Napoleon led the Grand Army into Russia in the summer of 1812. Except for one battle, the Russians refused to fight. Instead, they drew Napoleon's army deeper into Russia. When the harsh Russian winter arrived, Napoleon's soldiers were unprepared, helpless, and far from home. Their retreat proved to be a disaster. Fewer than 100,000 soldiers returned alive.

France's enemies then captured Napoleon and exiled him to Elba, an island off the coast of Italy. Napoleon escaped and returned to France in the spring of 1815. He easily won public support and assembled his old army. At Waterloo in Belgium, an international force led by Britain's Duke of Wellington finally defeated Napoleon. This time, Napoleon was sent to the island of St. Helena in the southern Atlantic Ocean, where he died in 1821.

Reading **HELP**DESK

Academic Vocabulary

overseas across an ocean

678 *Political and Industrial Revolutions*

What Was the Congress of Vienna?

In September 1814, European leaders gathered in Vienna, Austria. Their goal was to return peace and stability to Europe. This meeting, called the Congress of Vienna, was led by Austria's foreign minister, Klemens von Metternich (MEH•tuhr•nihk).

Metternich and the other leaders were conservative. That is, they opposed changes that threatened traditional ways. Today, conservatives in the U.S. believe in traditional ways but also support self-rule. European conservatives of the early 1800s supported powerful monarchies. They opposed individual liberties and the right of self-rule. Hoping to crush revolutionary ideas, the conservative leaders at the Congress restored the royal families who had ruled in Europe before Napoleon.

European leaders at Vienna also redrew Europe's borders. France lost the lands won by Napoleon. It also had to pay other countries for war damages. At the same time, Russia, Prussia, Austria, and Great Britain expanded in size. Russia increased its share of Poland, Prussia gained more German lands, and Austria acquired territory in Italy. Adding to its **overseas** empire, Britain won colonies in Asia, Africa, and the Caribbean.

The Congress above all wanted to create a balance of power, or equal strength among their countries. They hoped that such a balance would prevent any one nation from controlling Europe. To keep the peace, the leaders agreed to meet from time to time. These meetings were called the Concert of Europe.

Austria's foreign minister Klemens Von Metternich led the Congress of Vienna. This was a gathering of European leaders who shared the goal of returning Europe to a time of unity and stability.

PROGRESS CHECK

Analyzing Why did the Congress of Vienna support rule by powerful monarchs?

LESSON 2 REVIEW

Review Vocabulary

1. Use the word *bourgeoisie* in a sentence about the Third Estate in French society.
2. Explain how a *coup d'etat* is different from an election.

Answer the Guiding Questions

3. ***Differentiating*** What were the three estates in France before the revolution, and how were their tax responsibilities different?
4. ***Assessing*** What was the result of Napoleon's invasion of Russia in 1812?
5. ***Evaluating*** What happened at the Battle of Trafalgar, and why was it significant?
6. **EXPOSITORY WRITING** Explain the results of the Congress of Vienna in a short paragraph.

Lesson 2 679

LESSON 2 (cont.)

CLOSE & REFLECT

Evaluating Ask students to discuss whether Napoleon's rule was good or bad for the nation of France.

Then ask students to consider whether Napoleon's rule was good or bad for Europe as a whole. *(Accept answers that are well supported by evidence.)*

BACKGROUND KNOWLEDGE

The Guillotine

Along with the Bastille, the guillotine remains one of the enduring symbols of the French Revolution. In 1789 a member of the National Assembly named Dr. Joseph-Ignace Guillotin proposed sweeping legal reform. Among the tenants of his reform bill were the ideas that death as punishment for a crime should be without torture and that the best way to achieve this kind of painless death was by decapitation by machine. At the time of the proposal, such a machine did not exist. The National Assembly did not take action on Dr. Guillotin's proposal for two years, but his idea was dubbed the "guillotine."

The guillotine was born of noble principles. It was meant to fulfill the Enlightenment ideals of individual dignity and humanitarianism, as well as the revolutionary ideal of equality. Before the French Revolution, a person's social status determined his or her punishment. Commoners were subjected to more brutal forms of punishment than nobles, but all punishments included some element of torture. With the guillotine, all convicts would suffer the same punishment: a quick, humane death.

The actual machine was designed by Dr. Antoine Louis and built by a man named Tobias Schmidt. It was tested on animals and corpses before its first public use in 1792.

The Reign of Terror transformed the symbolism of the guillotine. Thousands of often innocent people were beheaded by the machine. At times, the guillotine resembled an assembly line of death. The bloodshed turned a symbol of equality and dignity into a symbol of fear and power run amok.

France continued to use the guillotine as a form of capital punishment into the twentieth century. However, executions were conducted privately, behind prison walls, rather than in public. The last execution by guillotine in France was in 1977. Four years later, France abolished the death penalty.

IF YOU HAVE MORE TIME . . .

Compare Historic Documents

Finding the Main Ideas Provide students with extended excerpts of the Declaration of the Rights of Man, the Declaration of Independence, and the U.S. Constitution. Read each excerpt to the class while they follow along, or have more advanced students read them aloud. BL 

On the board, list the key concepts and ideas from each excerpt.

Have students then organize the items listed on the board into a Venn diagram. The diagram should have three circles, one for each document and overlapping in the center. You may choose to complete the diagram as a class or have the students work in pairs or small groups to complete the graphic organizer on their own.

Use Drama to Illustrate the Differences Among the Three Estates

Simulating Organize the class into five groups. Assign each group one of the following social classes: nobles, clergy, bourgeoisie, urban workers, peasants. Have each group discuss among themselves the lifestyle of their social class before the French Revolution. Tell students to consider how each social group earned a living, what their living conditions were like, and their role in taxation.

Then, tell students that they have been called to represent their social class at the meeting of the Estates General. Have each group create a list of demands for the meeting.

Bring the whole class together as the Estates General. Ask each group to choose a spokesperson to present the group's demands. Moderate as the class debates the items on each list.

To debrief, help students notice similarities among the demands of the bourgeoisie, the urban workers, and the peasants and between the nobles and the clergy. AL

Ask:

Could these groups ever have come to an agreement? *(Students will likely say no, because their interests were too different and their demands were too far apart.)*

Answers for pages 676–679

P. 676 ☑ PROGRESS CHECK The Reign of Terror was the period after the French Revolution in which harsh steps were used to end unrest within France. Anyone believed to be disloyal to the revolution was sentenced to death by revolutionary courts. This period lasted from July 1793 to July 1794.

P. 677 ☑ PROGRESS CHECK Napoleon reorganized the government, created many new schools, and appointed local officials. He reorganized the country's finances and tax system. He created a new legal system and made peace with the Catholic Church.

P. 677 CRITICAL THINKING Napoleon is in uniform and riding a horse. He is pointing forward as if to say "Let's go." Students might notice the disproportionate scale of the image, such as Napoleon being bigger than his horse and as big as the mountain.

P. 678 GEOGRAPHY CONNECTION

1. His empire extended to the south of Rome.
2. Great Britain is made up of islands. Islands require a strong navy for protection from invasion.

P. 679 ☑ PROGRESS CHECK At the Congress of Vienna, Europe's leaders wanted to return to traditional ways and a firm social order. They wanted royal families to return to power. In this way, their own power would increase and the power of the lower classes would decrease.

LESSON 2 REVIEW

1. The bourgeoisie was part of the Third Estate and included merchants, bankers, lawyers, and teachers.
2. A *coup d'etat* is a change of government by force. An election is peaceful.
3. The three estates were the clergy, the nobles, and a group made up of the bourgeoisie, urban workers, and peasants. The nobles and clergy did not pay taxes, so the remaining group, which comprised the largest part of the population, had the burden of the cost of governing the nation.
4. Napoleon's invasion of Russia was a disaster because he was not prepared for the harsh Russian winter.
5. Napoleon was defeated by Lord Nelson of Britain, whose forces defeated the French navy. It was significant because it weakened Napoleon's power in Europe.
6. Paragraphs should explain how the Congress of Vienna redrew the borders of European nations, created a balance of power in Europe, and created regular meetings called the Concert of Europe.

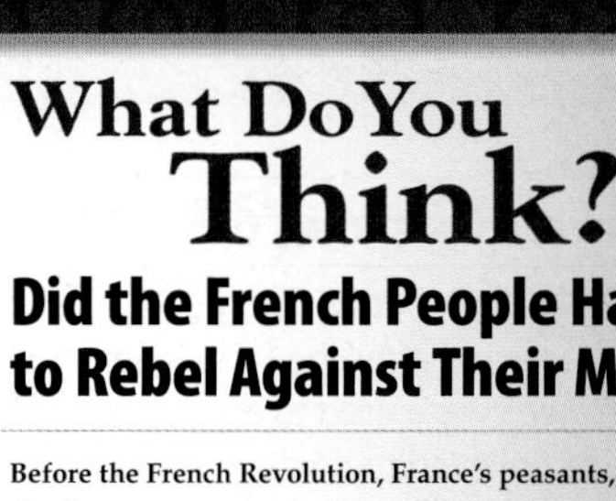

What Do You Think?

Did the French People Have Cause to Rebel Against Their Monarchy?

Before the French Revolution, France's peasants, workers, and shopkeepers expressed anger about their lack of political and social rights. The officials of King Louis XVI believed that the lower classes neglected their duties and were disloyal to the government that protected them.

Yes

PRIMARY SOURCE

"The nobility enjoys and owns everything, and would like to free itself from everything. However, if the nobility commands the army, the Third Estate makes it up. If nobility pours a drop of blood, the Third Estate [common people] spreads rivers of it. The nobility empties the royal treasury, the Third Estate fills it up. Finally, the Third Estate pays everything and does not enjoy anything."

—from *1789: The French Have Their Say*, by Pierre Goubert and Michel Denis

The woman in the painting represents the Third Estate. She wears the colors of the Revolution—red, white, and blue—and carries a torch of freedom.

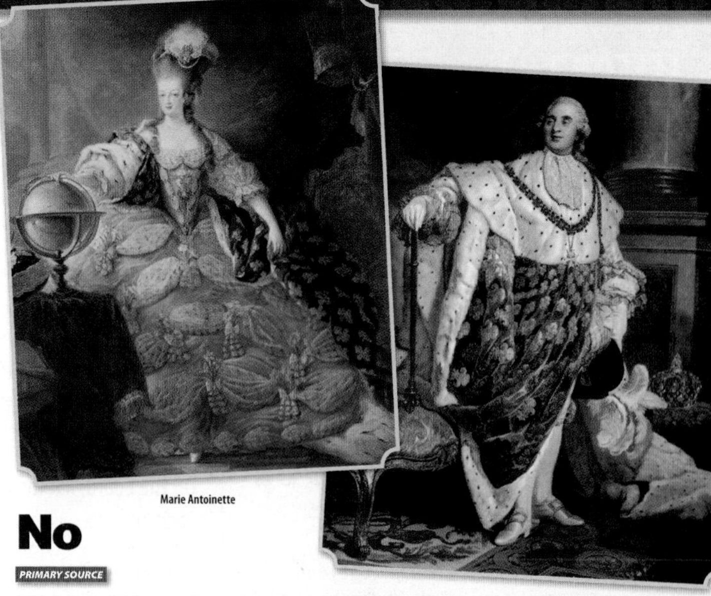

Marie Antoinette

King Louis XVI

No

PRIMARY SOURCE

"[The] districts [of the country] are made up of a certain number of towns and villages, which are in turn inhabited by families. To them belong the lands which yield products, provide for the livelihood of the inhabitants, and furnish the revenues [money] from which salaries are paid to those without land and taxes are levied to meet public expenditures....

Families themselves scarcely know that they depend on this state, of which they form a part: ... They consider the ... taxes required for the maintenance of public order as nothing but the law of the strongest; and they see no other reason to obey than their powerlessness to resist. As a result, everyone seeks to cheat the authorities and to pass social obligations on to his neighbors."

—from *The Works of Turgot*, ed. by Gustave Schelle

What Do You Think? DBQ

1. ***Explaining*** What were conditions like for the Third Estate in France before the Revolution?
2. ***Identifying Central Issues*** What was the position of the ruling class on taxes? Do you think its attitude was fair or unfair? Why?
3. ***Making Inferences*** Who does the Third Estate think enjoys the benefits from government money? Why?

networks
There's More Online!
- GRAPHIC ORGANIZER Uprisings and Outcomes
- MAP The Rise of Italy and Germany
- PRIMARY SOURCE *Blood and Iron*

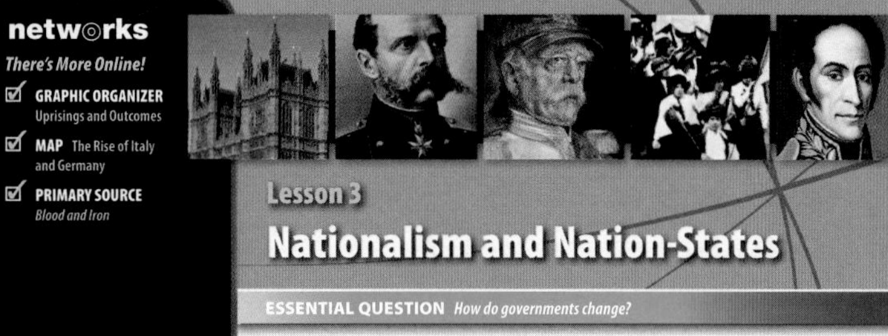

Lesson 3

Nationalism and Nation-States

ESSENTIAL QUESTION *How do governments change?*

IT MATTERS BECAUSE

The demands of peasants and workers can make changes in a nation's government.

1 Nationalism and Reform

GUIDING QUESTION *What political ideas shaped Europe during the 1800s and early 1900s?*

Nationalism means the desire of people with the same history, language, and customs for self-rule. During the 1800s, nationalism, along with demands for political reform, led to dramatic and far-reaching changes in Europe and the Americas.

Political Reform in Britain

While war and revolution raged in most of Europe, change came peacefully to Britain. In the early 1800s, nobles ran Britain's government, and the middle and working classes could not vote. Groups having no voice in government began demanding change. In 1832, the British government passed a law that gave voting rights to most middle-class men. New and growing cities gained more seats in Parliament.

As industry continued to grow, dissatisfied workers began to speak out and protest for additional rights. Workers still did not have the right to vote and felt they were being unfairly represented by the government. In 1838, supporters of the working class, known as Chartists, demanded a fully democratic Parliament and reforms, including the vote for all men. They sent a petition to Parliament, stating:

PRIMARY SOURCE

"May it please your Honourable House ... to use your utmost endeavors [efforts] ... to have a law passed, granting to every male of lawful age, sane mind, and unconvicted of crime, the right of voting for members of Parliament; and directing all future elections ... to be in the way of secret ballot; ...."

—from *The Life and Struggles of William Lovett*

The government would not accept the Chartists' demands. By the late 1800s, however, Britain's leaders were willing to make some changes. William Gladstone led the Liberal Party, which was supported by many middle-class voters. After Gladstone became prime minister in 1868, he had Parliament grant the vote to many rural workers and reorganize districts to give more equal representation.

Benjamin Disraeli, the leader of the Conservative Party, was Gladstone's main rival. Disraeli worked to maintain British traditions but cautiously adopted reforms. In 1867, Disraeli's Conservative government gave the vote to many urban workers.

In 1900, a new political group—the Labour Party—formed. It claimed to represent the working class. Labour Party supporters backed a Liberal government elected in 1906. Liberal and Labour members of Parliament tried to improve workers' lives. They passed laws that provided workers with retirement pensions, a minimum wage, unemployment aid, and health insurance.

In the early 1900s, British women known as suffragettes pushed for women to have the right to vote. They marched in protest and went on hunger strikes. In 1918, Parliament gave women over the age of 30 the right to vote. Ten years later, it gave the vote to all women over age 21.

Irish Demands for Self-Rule

During the 1800s, Britain had difficulty ruling its neighbor, Ireland. British and Irish Protestants owned most of Ireland's wealth. Yet, most Irish people were Catholic and poor. By 1830, their protests had won them the right to vote and to sit in Britain's Parliament. Still, British leaders refused to grant the Irish their main goal—self-rule.

The Palace at Westminster, which includes London's famous Big Ben, also houses the British Parliament. In 1870, the two houses of Parliament—House of Lords and House of Commons—established headquarters there.

Reading HELPDESK

Taking Notes: *Organizing*
As you read about the uprisings in each country, keep a list of the nations and the events of each revolt. Write down the outcome in each case.

Country	Uprising and Its Outcome

Content Vocabulary
- nationalism
- abolitionism
- guerrilla warfare
- kaiser

nationalism the desire of people with the same customs and beliefs for self-rule

Build Vocabulary: *The Suffix –ism*
Throughout this chapter, you will read many words with the suffix *–ism*. The suffix *–ism* means "belief in." Nationalism, for example, can mean "belief in nations."

Teaching *What Do You Think?*

(Student Edition pp. 680–681)

ENGAGE

Analyzing Tell students that this feature deals with the relationship between governments and citizens.

Ask:

Do you think government leaders should get paid more than other people?

Do you think those in government should have more luxurious lifestyles?

Do you think all citizens should pay taxes or only some citizens? *(Students should show some understanding of the complexity of the relationship between citizens and their government leaders.)*

TEACH & ASSESS

Summarizing Review challenging words in each passage with students. Then have volunteers summarize the main argument made by each author.

Ask:

What government services does the public official believe the citizens are not aware of? *(maintaining public order)*

Why does he think the king cannot enforce his tax laws by using force? *(He believes the king would be seen as a brute if he enforced the tax laws and that it would cause war to break out.)*

Defending Hold a debate over the issue of how the government should tax its citizens. Split the class into two groups, and assign a position on the issue to each group.

Then have students prepare their arguments. Encourage them to use details from their reading, examples from other periods of history, or their own experiences to support their positions.

Finally, allow each side to make an opening statement, ask a question of the other side, and present a closing statement that supports its position.

Complete the lesson by having students complete the questions at the end of the feature.

CLOSE & REFLECT

Making Connections Point out that the debate over who should pay taxes and how much they should pay continues today. Point out that some taxes are charged on goods, such as the taxes you pay when you buy a TV or a book at the bookstore.

Have students reflect on whether the French citizens would object to these taxes as well, or if the French citizens' objections had more to do with who had to pay taxes and who did not.

Answers to *What Do You Think?* DBQ

1. The members of the Third Estate were the laborers, and they supported the lifestyle of the nobles and the monarchy. They did not enjoy the same privileges as the other two estates.
2. The ruling class argued that the people of the state received services from the state and should pay for them. Students might agree with this idea, or they might disagree and say everyone, including the ruling class, needs to pay a fair share.
3. The Third Estate believes the nobility benefits the most from government money. The passage, for example, says "the nobility empties the royal treasury; the Third Estate fills it up." Before the revolution, the nobility had special privileges that exempted them from paying taxes. The government was built on taxes paid by the Third Estate.

Teaching *Nationalism and Nation-States*

(Student Edition pp. 682–689)

LESSON 3 • Day 1

ENGAGE

Defining Write the word *nationalism* on the board. Have volunteers define the term. *(nationalism: an attitude of common identity of people and desire for self-determination)* 

Next, discuss examples of nationalism that students have already learned about.

Ask: How were the American colonies and France changed by feelings of nationalism? *(Nationalism contributed to the American colonies' fight for independence and to France's revolution and support for Napoleon.)*

Tell students that in this lesson they will be learning about the effects of nationalism around the world.

TEACH & ASSESS

Nationalism and Reform

GUIDING QUESTION *What political ideas shaped Europe during the 1800s and early 1900s?*

LECTURE SLIDE **Summarizing** Show students the lecture slide listing the political reforms that took place in Britain.

Ask: How did these reforms affect voting rights in Britain? *(The right to vote was gradually expanded by the reforms, first expanding the vote to middle-class and rural men and finally giving women the vote.)*

Evaluating Ask students to consider how each set of political reforms that the British government passed might have made it easier to enact later reforms. During the class discussion, note that as more people in Britain were allowed to vote, it became easier for them to express their concerns in Parliament. *(Students should note that as the British workers and middle class were able to elect politicians to represent their interests, it would have become easier for new reforms to be brought up in and passed by Parliament.)*

2 New Nations in Europe

GUIDING QUESTION *Why did new nations arise in Europe during the mid-1800s?*

INTERACTIVE WHITEBOARD ACTIVITY **Determining Cause and Effect** Have students review the series of events in the formation of Germany and Italy. Create a cause-and-effect chart on the whiteboard, and have small groups of students complete it with details from the text.

Ask:

What convinced the German kingdoms to join the nation under Bismarck? *(Prussia was rich and powerful. It defeated Denmark, Austria, and France. The German kingdoms wanted to avoid war with Bismarck.)*

What conflict led to the south of Italy joining with the north? *(Piedmont used its friendship with Britain and France to force Austria out of northern Italy.)* BL

After completing the chart, ensure that students understand how nationalism played a role in the way the nations united.

Answers for pages 682–683

P. 682 Taking Notes Possible answers: Britain: gave more people the right to vote; France: elected Louis Napoleon, became an empire again, and then returned to being a republic; Germany: became a united country; Italy: became a united country; Haiti: became independent

Irish hatred of British rule increased when a severe famine hit Ireland in the 1840s. The British government did not send enough aid. At least one million Irish died of starvation and disease. Millions more left for the United States and other lands.

After this tragedy, pressure rose for Irish home rule, or Ireland's right to its own legislature to handle Irish affairs. Gladstone tried to pass home rule, but Parliament did not support him. Many British and Irish Protestants opposed home rule, fearing it would lead to Irish independence.

After defeat in the Austro-Prussian War, Russian ruler Czar Alexander II introduced reforms in hopes of making Russia the strongest country in Europe.

Political Changes in France

In 1848, nationalist and reforming revolts swept Europe. Most of them failed, but revolution was somewhat successful in France. There, King Louis-Philippe was overthrown and a republic declared. Louis Napoleon, nephew of Napoleon Bonaparte, soon was elected president and later emperor. Under Napoleon III, France enjoyed prosperity, but its government was not democratic.

In 1870, Napoleon III declared war on Prussia, the most powerful German state. Prussia won, and Napoleon's government fell. France faced civil war when workers took control of Paris. The upper-class government sent troops to crush the workers. By 1875, France was again a republic. However, distrust between upper classes and workers remained strong.

Monarchies in Austria and Russia

During the late 1800s, monarchs in Austria and Russia tried to block reform. However, bitter defeats in war forced both empires to make some changes.

In 1867, Austria made a deal with the Hungarians, who were part of the Austrian Empire. Hungary became a separate kingdom linked to Austria, called Austria-Hungary. The Hungarians were satisfied, but other national groups were not. Their demands for self-rule increased.

In Russia, defeat in war made Czar Alexander II realize that his country was far behind other European powers. He decided to build factories and improve farming. In 1861, Alexander freed the serfs—peasants tied to the land, which they farmed for landlords. The peasants did not get enough land, however, and they remained discontented.

PROGRESS CHECK

Inferring Why might the people of France have voted for Louis Napoleon?

Chris Hellier/CORBIS

Reading **HELP**DESK

guerrilla warfare a form of war in which soldiers make surprise attacks on the enemy

Reading Strategy: *Activating Prior Knowledge*

You read about Napoleon Bonaparte in the previous lesson. Who was he? What did he do?

2 New Nations in Europe

GUIDING QUESTION *Why did new nations arise in Europe during the mid-1800s?*

In the early 1800s, Germany and Italy as we know them today did not exist. They were made up of many territories. After 1850, their peoples began to form united countries.

How Did Italy Unite?

In 1848, Austria controlled most of Italy's small territories. In the north, the kingdom of Piedmont was independent. Piedmont's rulers were King Victor Emmanuel and the prime minister, Camillo di Cavour (kah•MEEL•loh dee kuh•VUR). Both leaders wanted to unite all of Italy into one nation.

In 1854, Piedmont sided with Britain and France in a war with Russia. In return for Piedmont's support, France helped Piedmont drive Austria out of Italy in 1859. Piedmont's victory was the first step toward uniting Italy. Soon, other parts of northern Italy overthrew their rulers and united with Piedmont.

At the same time, nationalist leader Giuseppe Garibaldi (joo•ZEHP•pay gar•uh•BAWL•dee) led uprisings in southern Italy. In 1860, his forces gained control of the island of Sicily. Garibaldi was skilled in **guerrilla warfare** (guh•RIH•luh WAWR•fehr), a type of fighting in which soldiers make surprise attacks on the enemy. Garibaldi's army won Italy's mainland. People in the south then voted to join a united Italy.

GEOGRAPHY CONNECTION

Both Italy and Germany unified their nations in the mid-1800s.

1 **PLACE** What was the effect of adding the North German Confederation to Prussia?

2 CRITICAL THINKING

Drawing Conclusions How did nationalism influence the rise of Italy?

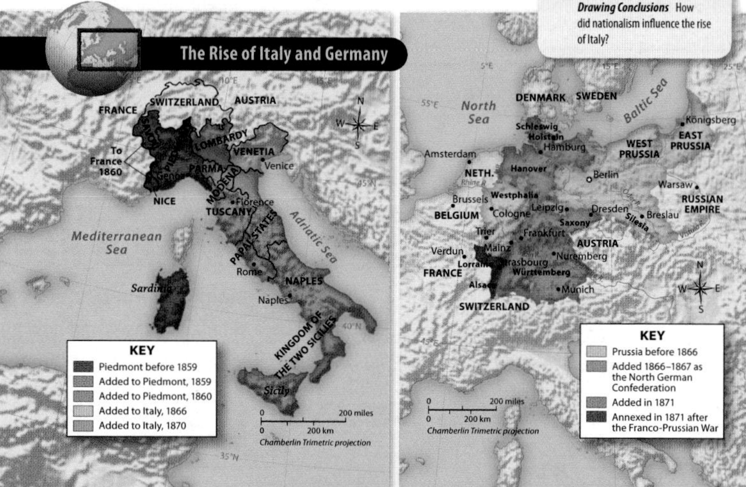

In 1861, Italy became a constitutional monarchy. Two areas remained outside the new kingdom. One was Rome, and the other was Venice. By 1870, wars had brought both areas into Italy.

Otto von Bismarck was a firm leader. He decided to govern with an iron fist rather than win people over with speeches.

CRITICAL THINKING

Analyzing How did Bismarck's "iron fist" make him a successful prime minister?

A New German Empire

During the mid-1800s, nationalism grew stronger in the German states. Many people wanted a united Germany under a strong monarchy. They gained Prussia's support. In 1862, Prussia's King William I named Otto von Bismarck (AHT•oh fawn BIHZ•mahrk) as his prime minister.

Bismarck was a deeply conservative Junker (YUN•kuhr), or wealthy landowner. He vowed to govern Prussia by "blood and iron" rather than by votes and speeches. Bismarck quickly strengthened Prussia's army. He used the army to defeat Denmark, Austria, and France. As a result of Bismarck's victories, other German states agreed to unite with Prussia. On January 18, 1871, William was proclaimed **kaiser** (KY•zuhr), or emperor, of a united Germany.

PROGRESS CHECK

Explaining What role did Bismarck play in uniting Germany?

3 Growth of the United States

GUIDING QUESTION *How did the United States change during the 1800s?*

Nationalism helped shape the United States during the 1800s. The country's size steadily grew. Many Americans believed that their nation was destined to be rich and powerful.

Westward Expansion

During the 1800s, the United States pushed westward. Many Americans came to believe in "Manifest Destiny," the idea that their country should stretch from the Atlantic Ocean to the Pacific Ocean.

In 1845, the United States annexed Texas, which had declared independence from Mexico. This led to war between the United States and Mexico. The United States won in 1848 and gained the area that today includes California and several other western states.

Settlers set up farms, **founded** communities, and created states in the new lands. The westward drive, however, brought suffering—loss of land, culture, and life—to Native Americans.

Imagno/Hulton Archive/Getty Images

Reading **HELP**DESK

kaiser emperor of Germany

abolitionism movement to end slavery

Academic Vocabulary

found to establish; to bring into being

U.S. Expansion 1783–1898

KEY

Territory gained by the United States

- Original 13 states
- Gained 1783
- Gained 1795
- Gained 1803
- Gained 1818
- Gained 1819
- Gained 1842
- Gained 1845
- Gained 1846
- Gained 1848
- Gained 1853
- Gained 1867
- Gained 1898

PACIFIC OCEAN

ATLANTIC OCEAN

Gulf of Mexico

GEOGRAPHY CONNECTION

Because of continued expansion, the United States reached across the middle of the North American continent by 1848.

1 **LOCATION** What present-day state was gained in 1819?

2 CRITICAL THINKING

Theorizing Why might Americans have wanted the country to expand all the way to the Pacific Coast?

The American Civil War

Over time, the Northern and Southern states developed different ways of life. The South had an agricultural economy based on raising cotton. Cotton growing depended on the labor of enslaved African Americans. In the North, industries created a manufacturing economy. Some Northerners believed in **abolitionism** (a•buh•LIH•shuhn•ih•zuhm), a movement to end slavery.

The disagreement over slavery grew more heated. In 1860, Abraham Lincoln, an opponent of slavery, was elected president. Southern states feared that he would end slavery. Eleven states seceded, or left, the United States. They formed the Confederate States of America. Fighting erupted between this group and the United States in April 1861. The American Civil War had begun.

The North had more people and more industries than the South. In spite of this, skilled military leaders such as Robert E. Lee led Confederate forces to many early victories. Later, the North threw all of its resources against the South. The conflict ended in a Northern victory. More than 600,000 Americans died in the war.

The North's victory reunited the country. Millions of African Americans were freed from slavery and became citizens. Factories, railroads, and cities were built at increasing speeds. Millions of immigrants from Europe and Asia contributed to the country's growth during the late 1800s.

LESSON 3 • Day 1 (cont.)

Growth of the United States

GUIDING QUESTION *How did the United States change during the 1800s?*

MAP **Analyzing Visuals** Show students the map of westward expansion in the United States. Note the territories possessed by the United States before 1867. Then help students identify the states shown on the map that became part of the Union and the Confederacy during the Civil War.

Hold a class discussion about the role westward expansion helped play in causing a conflict between the North and the South. Make sure students understand the different views on slavery in the North and the South. *(Students should note that as the United States expanded to the west, northern and southern states began to argue over whether new states formed from western territories would allow slavery.)*

CLOSE & REFLECT

Analyzing Have students discuss whether they believe nationalism is a positive force for change or whether it can be harmful, and if so, how. Encourage students to support their opinions with facts from the text.

IF YOU HAVE MORE TIME . . .

Explain the Difference Between a Nation and a State

Defining Write the words *nation* and *state* on the board. Help students define each term. *(nation: an attitude of common identity of people and a desire for self-determination; state: a government and institutions that run a country or other political entity)*

Ask: **Is it possible to be a nation and not be a state?** *(yes)*

Challenge students to give an example. *(Students may cite modern examples such as the Kurds in Southwest Asia or Tibetans in China or historical examples such as the Irish in the United Kingdom.)* BL

Ask: **Is it possible to be a state and not be a nation?** *(probably not)*

Can a state be made up of many nations? *(yes)*

What challenges does that present? *(forming a common identity, finding common goals, and so on)*

Answers for pages 684–685

P. 684 ☑ PROGRESS CHECK The people of France might have thought that his name reminded them of Napoleon Bonaparte, and they hoped Louis Napoleon would be like his uncle.

P. 684 Reading Strategy Napoleon Bonaparte was a general who became emperor of France. He established a French empire, reformed French law, and restored order after the chaos of the French Revolution.

P. 685 GEOGRAPHY CONNECTION

1. Adding the North German Confederation unified two separate areas of Prussia.
2. CRITICAL THINKING Answers will vary, but students should show understanding of the concept of nationalism and that the various parts of Italy joined together during a period when nationalism was part of the culture.

LESSON 3 • Day 2

ENGAGE

Speculating Write the words *Manifest Destiny* on the board. Ask volunteers to define the words. Explain that some of the early leaders of the United States had the idea that the country should reach from the Atlantic to the Pacific—it was our Manifest Destiny.

Tell students that many believed this would never happen. They believed that the continent was too big and that the United States would never reach this enormous size.

Ask: **What kind of power do you think this idea had on the way people thought of the country?** *(made people proud, united, feeling part of a great country)*

Growth of the United States

GUIDING QUESTION *How did the United States change during the 1800s?*

INTERACTIVE WHITEBOARD ACTIVITY

Contrasting Present the Interactive Whiteboard Activity about the northern and southern states at the outbreak of the American Civil War. Have students drag and drop each characteristic of the group into the correct area.

Ask: **How did the differences between the states contribute to the outcome of the war?** *(The more industrialized North was able to supply its troops better than the South could supply its troops.)* AL

4 Independence in Latin America

GUIDING QUESTION *How did the countries of Latin America win independence?*

MAP **Identifying** Show students the map titled "New Nations in Latin America."

Ask: **Which leader helped Colombia, Bolivia, and Venezuela gain independence?** *(Simón Bolívar)* **From which European country did most Latin American nations gain their independence?** *(Spain)* AL

INTERACTIVE WORKSHEET

Geography and History Activity

Analyzing For homework, assign the Geography and History Activity about Simón Bolívar's decision to cross the Andes Mountains. Preview the activity by explaining to students that geography played a role in many revolutions and wars for independence.

Ask: **How did geography help the American colonists win their war against Britain?** *(They knew the land better. They didn't have to wait for supplies and more troops to travel across the ocean.)*

How did geography hurt Napoleon's war against Russia? *(Russia was too far away from France for Napoleon's supply lines to work.)*

Tell students that geography was also important in the South American wars for independence.

Have students complete the Lesson 3 Review.

Answers for pages 686–687

P. 686 CRITICAL THINKING Bismarck's "iron fist" made him a successful prime minister because he was willing to do what was necessary to make his country strong and to achieve his goals.

P. 686 ☑ PROGRESS CHECK Bismarck fought against the neighboring countries to form a united Germany.

P. 687 GEOGRAPHY CONNECTION

1. The present-day state of Florida was gained in 1819.
2. CRITICAL THINKING Answers will vary but may include national pride, to protect their borders, greed, and to seek new trading ports.

Women suffragists marched in Washington D.C. the day before President Woodrow Wilson's inauguration in 1913. Though Wilson did not support woman suffrage at first, in the years following he helped pass the Nineteenth Amendment, which gave all women the right to vote.

America Rebounds

During the 1800s, the United States became more democratic. President Andrew Jackson's election in 1828 was called a victory for the "common people." It was made possible by the spread of voting rights to almost all adult white men.

In the 1800s, women also began to demand equality. Women suffragists fought hard for the right to vote. Finally, in 1920, the Nineteenth Amendment to the Constitution was ratified, or approved. This guaranteed women in all states the right to vote.

✔ **PROGRESS CHECK**

Comparing and Contrasting How were the economies of the North and the South different before the American Civil War?

4 Independence in Latin America

GUIDING QUESTION *How did the countries of Latin America win independence?*

During the 1700s, Spain and Portugal did not face serious challenges to their rule in Latin America. In the early 1800s, the situation changed. Latin Americans, inspired by the American and French revolutions, wanted independence.

Winning Independence

The first successful revolt against European rule took place in Haiti, an island territory in the Caribbean Sea. There, Toussaint L'Ouverture (TOO•sahn LOO•vehr•toor) led enslaved Africans in a revolt that **eventually** threw off French rule in 1804.

People in the Spanish colonies of Latin America were also ready to revolt. In Mexico in 1810, two Catholic priests, Miguel Hidalgo and José María Morelos, urged Mexican peasants to fight for freedom. Mexico finally won its independence in 1821.

Reading **HELP**DESK

Academic Vocabulary

eventual finally, after some time

In 1823, Central America declared its independence from Mexico. During the next decade, it divided into the republics of Guatemala, Honduras, Nicaragua, El Salvador, and Costa Rica.

In the northern part of South America, a wealthy military leader named Simón Bolívar (see•MAWN boh•LEE•vahr) started a revolt in 1810. Bolívar's forces finally crushed the Spanish at the 1819 Battle of Boyacá in Colombia. It took another 20 years, but Bolívar won freedom for the present-day countries of Venezuela, Colombia, Bolivia, Ecuador, Peru, and Panama.

As Bolívar fought in the north, a soldier named José de San Martín (hoh•SAY day san mahr•TEEN) led the struggle in the south. In 1817, San Martín led his army from Argentina across the Andes Mountains into Chile. The crossing was difficult, but San Martín took the Spanish by surprise. A few years later, San Martín and Bolívar together defeated the Spanish in Peru.

Many places have been named after Simón Bolívar to honor his revolutionary spirit, including the South American nation of Bolivia.

Challenges to Growth

Latin Americans wanted their new countries to become stable and prosperous. Their hopes, however, were not realized and these new countries faced many challenges. Political parties quarreled over the role of the Catholic Church. Border disagreements led to wars between countries. Tensions developed between rich and poor.

✔ **PROGRESS CHECK**

Contrasting How did Haiti's revolution differ from those of other Latin American countries?

LESSON 3 REVIEW

Review Vocabulary

1. Use the following terms in a sentence about revolutions in South America: *guerrilla warfare, nationalism.*

Answer the Guiding Questions

2. ***Comparing*** How were the political reforms that took place in Britain similar to the reforms that took place in France?
3. ***Evaluating*** How did nationalism play a part in the rise of Italy and Germany?
4. ***Determining Cause and Effect*** How did the expansion of settlers in the United States affect Native Americans?
5. ***Identifying Points of View*** Why were Americans divided over abolitionism?
6. ***Assessing*** What factors led to continued discontent after Latin American countries had won their freedom?
7. **EXPOSITORY WRITING** Write a short essay in which you explain how José de San Martín and Simón Bolívar changed life in South America.

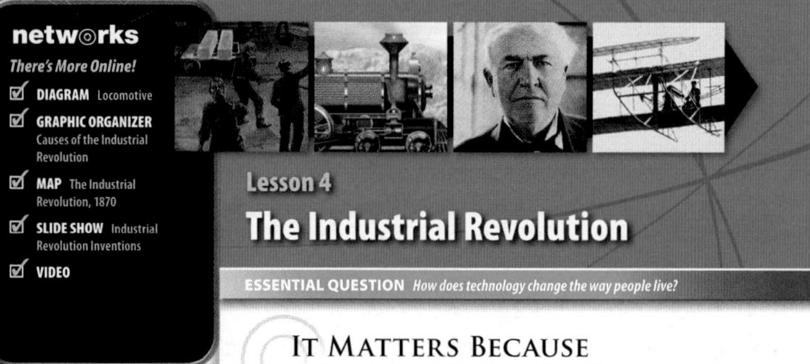

networks
There's More Online!
DIAGRAM Locomotive
GRAPHIC ORGANIZER Causes of the Industrial Revolution
MAP The Industrial Revolution, 1870
SLIDE SHOW Industrial Revolution Inventions
VIDEO

Lesson 4

The Industrial Revolution

ESSENTIAL QUESTION *How does technology change the way people live?*

IT MATTERS BECAUSE

Small steps in industrial development led to big changes over time.

1 Birth of Industry

GUIDING QUESTION *Why did the Industrial Revolution begin in Britain?*

While political change affected much of Europe and the Americas, a new economic system known as **industrialism** began in Britain. There, people began to use machines to do work that had been performed by animals or humans. Over the next 200 years, industrialism affected life so dramatically that historians call the changes it brought the Industrial Revolution.

Before the rise of industrialism, most people lived in small farming villages. Cloth was made by village people working in their homes. Merchants went from cottage to cottage, bringing the workers raw wool and cotton. The workers used hand-powered wheels to spin the wool and cotton into thread. They worked on looms to weave the thread into cloth. The merchants then sold the finished cloth for the highest possible price.

The Industrial Revolution began in the woven cloth, or textile, industry. Merchants could make a great deal of money from textiles, so they began to look for ways to produce cloth better and faster. By the 1700s, changes in Britain made this possible.

What Caused the Industrial Revolution?

Britain led the way in the Industrial Revolution for many reasons. One important reason was a change in the way British landowners used their land. For hundreds of years, landowners rented land to villagers, who divided it into strips. Different families worked different strips of land. In addition, villagers could keep livestock on public lands.

In the 1700s, new enclosure laws allowed landowners to combine and fence off the strips and public lands. This created large farms where the same crop could be grown on large areas. This meant larger harvests and greater profits. Often the landowners used the land as pasture for sheep. The landowners could then sell wool to the textile industry.

Successful farming provided landowners with more money to spend. Many chose to invest, or put money into new businesses. Money invested in businesses is called capital. A growing middle class of merchants and shopkeepers also began to invest capital in new industries.

Reading **HELP**DESK

Taking Notes: Sequencing

Use a diagram like the one shown here to list events that led to the Industrial Revolution.

Cause	Effect
	The Industrial Revolution

Content Vocabulary
- **industrialism**
- **corporation**

GEOGRAPHY CONNECTION

The Industrial Revolution spread throughout Europe in the 1800s.

1. **HUMAN-ENVIRONMENT INTERACTION** In what areas do most of the coal mining and ironworking symbols appear?
2. CRITICAL THINKING ***Making Generalizations*** What generalization can you make about the location of railroads and manufacturing and industrial areas?

Industrial Revolution 1870

KEY
- Manufacturing and industrial area
- • Major industrial center
- Major railways by 1870

Industry:
- Coal mining
- Ironworking
- Textile production

industrialism an economic system where machines do work that was once performed by animals or humans

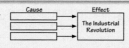

Teaching *Nationalism and Nation-States* (cont.) (Student Edition pp. 682–689)

LESSON 3 • Day 2 (cont.)

CLOSE & REFLECT

Explaining Have students write a one-page essay defining *nationalism*. Tell them to provide at least three examples that illustrate the effects of nationalism on Europe and the Americas in the 1800s and 1900s.

IF YOU HAVE MORE TIME . . .

Role-Play to Learn About the Leaders of Latin American Revolutions

Identifying Work with the class to generate a list of leaders of Latin American independence movements, such as Touissaint L'Ouverture, Miguel Hidalgo, and Simón Bolívar. Students should refer to their textbooks as needed.

Describing Assign each student one leader from the list. Allow time for students to research their assigned leaders. Tell students to look not only for details about the lives of the leaders, but also for clues about the leaders' personalities.

When students have completed their research, have them write a one- to two-page memoir from the viewpoint of their assigned leader. The memoir should reflect on the leader's proudest achievements and show the leader's personality 

Ask volunteers to read their memoirs to the class. ELL

Answers for pages 688–689

P. 688 ☑ PROGRESS CHECK Before the Civil War, the economy of the North depended on industry and small farms. The economy of the South was agricultural and depended on the labor of enslaved Africans.

P. 689 ☑ PROGRESS CHECK Haiti's revolution was led by enslaved Africans against French rule. The other Latin American revolutions were led by priests or wealthy soldiers against Spanish rule.

LESSON 3 REVIEW

1. Sentences should show understanding that a feeling of nationalism led to fighting, much of which was guerrilla warfare.
2. The political reforms in Britain and France were similar because they were driven by feelings of nationalism.
3. In both countries, nationalists wanted to unite their regions under one ruling government.
4. Native Americans suffered from loss of their land, their culture, and their lives.
5. Abolitionists believed that slavery should be ended. Those against ending slavery depended on enslaved Africans for the agricultural economy.
6. Political parties in Latin America quarreled over the role of the Catholic Church in society. Individual countries went to war over boundary disputes. Tensions developed between rich and poor.
7. Students should understand that the two revolutionaries, Simón Bolívar and José de San Martín, led revolutions that caused the overthrow of the Spanish colonial government in South America.

Teaching *The Industrial Revolution* (Student Edition pp. 690–695)

LESSON 4

ENGAGE

SLIDE SHOW

Making Connections Show students the slide show on the inventions of the textile industry. Have volunteers read the captions that appear when the image is activated. Explain that these machines were astonishing modern inventions in their day.

Have students respond to the images by listing and describing inventions that have changed how people work today.

Then ask students to consider how these inventions affect society and business.

Compare these changes to some of the changes described in the slide show. For example, new technologies made production more efficient, but many workers were afraid that the new machines would put them out of work.

Ask students to evaluate whether technology is helpful or harmful in their lives. *(Student answers will vary, but most are likely to say technological changes benefit their lives in many different areas.)* AL ELL

TEACH & ASSESS

1 Birth of Industry

GUIDING QUESTION *Why did the Industrial Revolution begin in Britain?*

GRAPHIC ORGANIZER

Determining Cause and Effect Show students the interactive graphic organizer on the causes of the Industrial Revolution. Have student volunteers provide causes based on their reading and list these causes on the whiteboard.

LECTURE SLIDE

Applying Show the lecture slide that explains the difference between factories and cottage industries.

To illustrate the difference between factory work and cottage industry, have students divide into two groups. One group will be the cottage industry group. The other will be the factory group.

Provide simple instructions for creating a paper airplane.

The members of the cottage industry group each get the instructions, and each individual makes airplanes. They can modify the design or decorate the airplanes any way they want. Meanwhile, the factory team chooses a boss who positions the team in a line with each member creating one fold or performing one action per the instructions. The team makes airplanes on an assembly line. ELL

Answers for pages 690–691

P. 690 Taking Notes enclosure laws; changes in farming; entrepreneurship

P. 691 GEOGRAPHY CONNECTION

1. The northern part of Western Europe is home to more coal mining and ironworks operations.
2. CRITICAL THINKING The railroads appear more frequently in the industrial and manufacturing areas.

Henry Bessemer invented the first method of mass-producing steel. This process revolutionized the development of industry and machinery.

Stock Montage/Archive Photos/Getty Images

Increased Population

Still another cause of the Industrial Revolution was the growing workforce. Britain's population grew rapidly in the 1700s. People now had more and better food. They were healthier, lived longer, and had larger families. At the same time, changes in farming helped increase the supply of industrial workers. New machines, such as the steel plow, meant that farms needed fewer workers. Workers forced off the land often went to work in new industries.

Britain's rich supply of natural resources also helped in the rise of industry. The country had fine harbors and a large network of rivers that flowed year-round. Britain's earliest cotton mills were powered by the flow of river water. Britain also had large supplies of coal and iron. Coal, which replaced wood as a fuel, helped to run machines. Iron was used to build machinery.

Inventors Make Advances

In the late 1700s, cloth merchants were looking for new ways to increase production. A textile weaver named James Hargreaves (HAHR•greevz) invented a machine called a spinning jenny that could spin cotton into thread very quickly. Richard Arkwright developed a way to power a spinning machine with water. Edmund Cartwright created a new powered loom. This machine could weave the thread into cloth as fast as the spinning machines produced it.

As industry developed, machines required more power than water could provide. Steam power answered this need. In 1769, the Scottish mathematician James Watt **designed** a steam engine that could power the new machines. Steam soon replaced water as the major source of power.

As the need for machines grew, iron was needed to make machine parts. In 1753, Henry Cort discovered a way to use coal to turn iron ore into pure iron. As a result, iron production grew. Coal mining became a major industry. In 1856, Henry Bessemer, an engineer, invented a less costly way to make large amounts of iron into steel. Steel was excellent for making machinery, because it was stronger than iron. Soon mining towns and steel centers grew in areas with supplies of iron ore and coal.

Reading **HELP**DESK

Academic Vocabulary

design to skillfully plan or create something

A LOCOMOTIVE

INFOGRAPHIC

The steam-powered locomotive made trains the fastest way to travel during much of the 1800s.

1. **IDENTIFYING** What natural resource was used to power the locomotive?
2. **CRITICAL THINKING** ***Assessing*** In addition to speed, what other advantages did a locomotive provide?

Factories and Railroads

Faster modes of transportation and new business successes fueled enormous economic growth. In 1807, Robert Fulton, an American inventor, developed a boat powered by a steam engine.

Then came the railroad—the biggest improvement in land transportation. By the mid-1800s, trains pulled by steam-powered locomotives were faster and cheaper than any other kind of transportation. Railroads soon connected major cities all across Europe. They completely changed the amount of time and money spent on the transport of goods to market. Trains carried raw materials and finished goods, as well as passengers, faster than horses.

Ambitious entrepreneurs, or people who took risks to start businesses, set up and ran Britain's growing industries. They created industries by bringing together capital, labor, and new industrial inventions. Their efforts led to the building of factories, the major centers of the Industrial Revolution.

Why did factories develop? Machines became too large and expensive for home use. Workers and machines were brought together in one place in factories, working under managers. Workers could share skills. Factories provided a better organized and less costly way to produce large amounts of goods.

Edison's electric light bulb took about two years to develop and allowed people to use electric lighting in their homes and businesses. How would nighttime be different in your city without this invention?

akg-images/The Image Works

One British writer described the changes brought by factory organization, especially in weaving cloth:

PRIMARY SOURCE

> "In 1818, there were in Manchester, Stockport, Middleton, . . .and their vicinities, fourteen factories, containing about two thousand Looms. In 1821, there were in the same neighbourhoods thirty-two factories, containing five thousand seven hundred and thirty-two Looms. Since 1821, their number has still farther increased, and there are at present not less than ten thousand Steam Looms at work in Great Britain."
>
> —from *Compendious History of the Cotton Manufacture* by Richard Guest

As the Industrial Revolution developed, entrepreneurs looked for different ways to raise money. One way was to form a partnership in which two or more people owned the business and pooled their own money. Another way was to create a **corporation** (kor•puh•RAY•shuhn). A corporation raises money by selling shares, or partial ownership, in the company to investors. Creating a corporation allowed entrepreneurs to have the capital to build large factories with hundreds of workers.

PROGRESS CHECK

Understanding Cause and Effect How did successful farming and a growing population influence the Industrial Revolution in Britain?

2 Growth of Industry

GUIDING QUESTION *How did new inventions help advance the growth of industry?*

Britain's early start in the Industrial Revolution made it the richest and most productive country in the world. To protect this dominant position, Parliament passed laws restricting the flow of ideas, machines, and skilled workers out of the country. Despite these laws, many inventors and entrepreneurs left Britain. They carried their industrial knowledge with them. As a result, the Industrial Revolution soon spread to other areas.

Reading **HELP**DESK

corporation a type of company that sells shares in the company to investors

Reading Strategy: *Comparing and Contrasting*

When you compare and contrast, you look for similarities and differences between two things as you read. Read the section about the growth of industry in Britain and America. Note one or two similarities between the two countries. Then identify one difference.

Industry Grows in Europe and America

The Industrial Revolution spread from Britain to other European countries. European governments helped build factories, railroads, canals, and roads. The Industrial Revolution also took hold in the United States. British investors and American engineers built factories and ironworks in New England.

Like Britain, the United States had many natural resources. Americans quickly built roads and canals across the vast nation. Fulton's steamboats provided transportation on inland waterways. Railroads soon crisscrossed the country.

New Scientific Advances

During the 1800s, inventors found many ways to use electricity. In the 1830s, Samuel Morse developed the telegraph. It sent coded messages through wires. Soon telegraph lines linked most European and North American cities.

Alexander Graham Bell developed the telephone in 1876. The telephone used tiny electrical wires to carry sound. For the first time, telephones allowed people to speak to each other over long distances. Finally, in 1895, Guglielmo Marconi put together a wireless telegraph, which was later developed into the radio.

Inventors found more ways to use electric power. In 1877, Thomas Edison developed the light bulb. As demand for electricity rose, investors in Europe and the United States funded the first power plants. These were powered by coal or oil.

Major breakthroughs also took place in transportation. In the 1880s, Rudolf Diesel and Gottlieb Daimler invented internal combustion engines. These engines produced power in autos by burning oil-based fuels. In 1903, Orville and Wilbur Wright successfully tested the world's first airplane.

Hulton Archive/Getty Images

PROGRESS CHECK

Identifying How did electricity change communications?

BIOGRAPHY

The Wright Brothers
(Wilbur Wright 1867–1912; Orville Wright 1871–1948)

The brothers Orville and Wilbur Wright were bicycle mechanics. They also were fascinated with the idea of human flight. It took them years of study to develop a flying machine. In their local library, they researched everything they could find on the subject of flight. Finally, when they could learn no more from other experts, they began experimenting with their own airplane models. The brothers eventually built a flying machine that would support a human being. Their research and experiments formed the basis of the modern airplane industry.

CRITICAL THINKING

Theorizing How would the Wright Brothers' knowledge of bicycles have helped them build an airplane?

LESSON 4 REVIEW

Review Vocabulary

1. How does a *corporation* raise money?
2. Write a sentence to explain how *industrialism* changed the lives of workers.

Answering the Guiding Questions

3. ***Finding the Main Idea*** Why do historians consider this time of industrial development a revolution?
4. ***Determining Cause and Effect*** What inventions had an effect on the textile industry?
5. ***Analyzing*** Why were the telegraph and telephone important inventions at this time?
6. **EXPOSITORY WRITING** Explain how the Industrial Revolution spread from Britain to other places in the world.

LESSON 4 (cont.)

Have students work for a set period of time. Then compare the number and quality of the airplanes that were made by each group. AL

Ask: **What were the advantages and disadvantages of each method?** *(Factory groups produced a higher quantity with more consistency, although the factory airplanes might not have been as unique or as high in quality as those produced by the cottage industry group.)*

Allow students a predesignated period of time for flying the airplanes after the lesson.

INTERACTIVE WORKSHEET

21st Century Skills Activity

Evaluating Explain to students that the Industrial Revolution was not the end of technological progress. Point out that many people would say that we are currently in the age of a digital revolution in which information is available digitally at the click of a button.

Assign the 21st Century Skills worksheet on conducting Internet research for homework. Tell students they will choose a topic from the worksheet and use the Internet to begin researching the topic.

Remind students to use reliable sources. Refer them to the chapter *What Does a Historian Do?* for guidelines for determining the reliability of sources.

Growth of Industry

GUIDING QUESTION ***How did new inventions help advance the growth of industry?***

Organizing Have students work in small groups to make a list of the new inventions of the Industrial Revolution. Combine the lists into a single class list.

Then circle those inventions that are still vital to industry today, such as coal and steel manufacturing.

Ask: **Why do you think the other inventions are not as important today?** *(Some inventions have been replaced by more efficient machines that perform the same function.)*

Discussing Tell students that the American textile industry is credited to Samuel Slater, who violated the English laws against exporting information about textile factories when he disguised himself as a farmer and sailed to New York. Slater had worked in textile factories and had completely memorized the plans for building and managing a mill. Once in New York, Slater sold his knowledge to Moses Brown, a Quaker merchant in Pawtucket, Rhode Island. Together they built the first successful, water-powered textile mill in America.

Ask students to consider whether Slater did the right thing in breaking the English laws. Hold a class discussion about the fairness of the English laws and the benefits of spreading the Industrial Revolution.

Have students complete the Lesson 4 Review.

CLOSE & REFLECT

Evaluating Review the key advancements made during the Industrial Revolution. Note to the class that some of these advancements involved new types of machines, while others involved new ways of organizing workers.

Ask: **What were the most important advancements in the Industrial Revolution?** *(Students may suggest individual inventions or processes, such as the assembly line.)* Encourage students to explain their choice and to support it with facts and details from the text. AL

BACKGROUND KNOWLEDGE

Child Labor During the Industrial Revolution

The Industrial Revolution created a huge demand for child labor. Children were needed in the factories to help maintain the machines, but they were also needed for other odd jobs that were unique to the new urban environment. In addition to working in factories and mines, children could earn money as rat catchers or chimney sweeps. Sometimes children would be paid for collecting dog and horse droppings. These droppings would often be sold to local tanneries for use in curing hides to make leather.

Living Conditions and the Spread of Disease

The crowded, unclean living conditions of the working class were a breeding ground for diseases. Cholera, which had a 50 percent death rate, spread through contaminated water. Typhus, which was caused by lice, was also common in crowded, dirty living quarters. The most common disease of the era was tuberculosis. In 1838 it caused one out of every six deaths in Britain.

Most houses did not have indoor plumbing. In Haworth, England, for example, a government inspector found a street where 24 houses shared the same toilet. On another street, 8 families shared a toilet. The inspector found that waste from the toilets was leaking into the town's drinking water. Nor was there regular garbage collection. Instead, people threw their garbage out their windows and onto the street, where it would pile up, rot, and breed diseases.

The inspector's discovery in Haworth and a study by John Snow that traced a cholera outbreak to a single water pump led to a crusade to ensure that people had clean drinking water. Other public health policies soon followed. A common belief of the era was that illness was caused by bad smells. As a result, efforts were made to clean up the garbage rotting garbage on the streets. Cleaning up the garbage removed many disease-causing germs.

Answers for pages 692–695

P. 693 INFOGRAPHIC

1. The locomotive was powered by steam, which was created by burning coal.
2. CRITICAL THINKING In addition to speed, the locomotive could move larger quantities of goods over longer distances than a horse or a human being could. Locomotives also allowed goods to be moved farther inland, which was an advantage over using boats.

P. 694 Without the invention of the light bulb, people could not drive at night. They would have to use fires, torches, and candles to see by, which means they could do less at night and would be more likely to cause a house fire.

P. 694 ☑ PROGRESS CHECK Successful farming meant people ate better and were healthier. Because people were living longer, there were enough people to provide a workforce for factories.

P. 694 Reading Strategy Similarities: abundant natural resources, access to waterways. Difference: The United States is much larger than Britain, so it had to build more roads, canals, and railways.

P. 695 CRITICAL THINKING The Wright Brothers' knowledge of bicycles would have helped them build an airplane because it gave them an understanding of how to build things that move and how physics works.

P. 695 ☑ PROGRESS CHECK The telegraph, the telephone, and later the radio were advances in communications that used electricity.

LESSON 4 REVIEW

1. A corporation raises money by selling shares in the company to investors.
2. Because of industrialism, workers moved from working on farms to working in factories.
3. Industry affected life so dramatically that historians call the changes it brought the Industrial Revolution.
4. Inventions such as the spinning jenny and the industrial loom changed the textile industry.
5. The telegraph and the telephone were important inventions because they allowed people who were separated by great distances to communicate much faster.
6. Students should show an understanding that information about building machines and mechanizing factories spread as entrepreneurs moved to new countries and as nations encouraged the growth of industry.

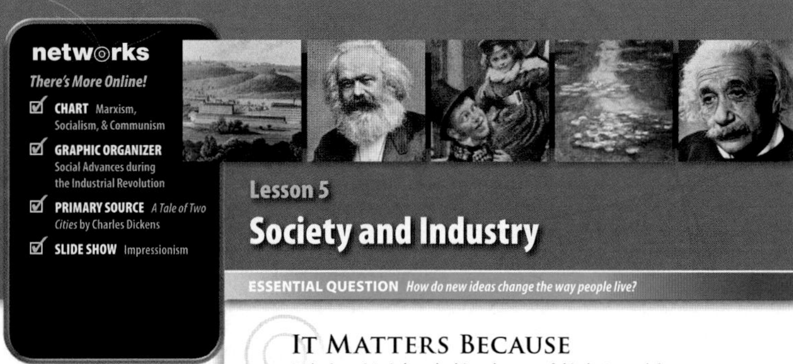

networks
There's More Online!
- CHART Marxism, Socialism, & Communism
- GRAPHIC ORGANIZER Social Advances during the Industrial Revolution
- PRIMARY SOURCE *A Tale of Two Cities* by Charles Dickens
- SLIDE SHOW Impressionism

Lesson 5
Society and Industry

ESSENTIAL QUESTION *How do new ideas change the way people live?*

It Matters Because
Today's society is largely driven by powerful industry and the movement of goods around the world.

1 A New Society

GUIDING QUESTION *How did industry change society in Europe and North America during the 1800s and early 1900s?*

By the 1860s, the Industrial Revolution brought sweeping changes to Europe and North America. During the next 100 years, industrialism also changed other regions of the world.

The Growth of Cities

One important change was the rapid growth in the population of cities. **Urbanization** (uhr•buh•nuh•ZAY•shuhn) is the movement of people from the countryside to cities. A nation is urbanized when many of its people live in cities.

Why did cities grow so rapidly? Farms were using more machines. This meant there were fewer jobs for farm workers. To find employment, many rural workers headed to nearby cities. They hoped to find jobs in the new factories.

A New Industrial Society

Before the rise of industry, there were fewer job opportunities. The Industrial Age, however, brought new jobs and a new way of life. The middle class grew as more people took advantage of these new opportunities.

Industrial growth expanded not just the size of the middle class, but also its power and wealth. The middle class had once been made up of a small number of bankers, lawyers, doctors, and merchants. Now it included the successful owners of factories, mines, and railroads. Professional workers such as clerks, managers, and teachers added to the growing number.

Industrial growth also created a much larger working class. The members of this group were people who labored in the factories and mines. Their lives were often hard, and they had few of the luxuries enjoyed by the new middle class.

Working-Class Families

Entire working-class families—children as well as adults—had to work to make enough money to live. Working conditions ranged from barely acceptable to dreadful. Workers did the same tasks over and over again. People worked up to 16 hours a day, 6 days a week. Factories and mines were hot and dirty. Diseases spread quickly. The machinery often was unsafe. As a result, many workers lost fingers, limbs, or even their lives.

Living conditions in the cities were often miserable. However, rural workers continued to look for urban factory jobs. Despite low pay and long hours, most city workers had more money than when they lived in the country. Cities also offered many leisure-time opportunities. These included parks, sports, libraries, and education.

As time passed, working conditions improved. Workers organized to demand changes. Middle-class reformers tried to better the lives of workers. As a result, factories were made safer. Working hours for women and children were reduced. New laws were passed that reduced pollution and unclean food and water in the cities.

City life was often hard, but it was usually better than life as a farm worker. Often several families lived together and shared what they had.

▶ CRITICAL THINKING
Analyzing Why did people living in cities face hardships?

Women's Lives

During the 1800s, women of all classes had fewer legal rights than men. It was believed that a woman's place was in the home. At this time, women worked to improve their position and find new roles. Women found jobs in businesses and in government service. There were also more opportunities for education.

Reading HELPDESK

Taking Notes: *Explaining*
Use a web diagram like this one to list ways that the Industrial Revolution affected society.

Social Advances during the Industrial Revolution

Content Vocabulary
- urbanization
- liberalism
- utilitarianism
- socialism
- proletariat
- labor union

urbanization the increase in the proportion of people living in cities rather than rural areas

For its time, New Lanark, Scotland was a socially progressive industrial community. Workers here enjoyed better than average conditions.

▶ CRITICAL THINKING
Explaining How did industrialization improve the lives of the working class?

Women began to demand equal rights with men. In the United States, Britain, and other countries, women challenged the long-standing idea that politics was a man's world. They demanded the rights to vote and to hold public office.

PROGRESS CHECK
Describing What were working conditions like for early industrial workers?

2 Industrialization Changes Political Ideas

GUIDING QUESTION *What new political ideas arose as a result of industrial society?*

The Industrial Revolution brought many changes, both good and bad. Starting in the early 1800s, people looked for ways to solve the problems that industry had created. They developed different ideas to address these concerns.

What Is Liberalism?

One of these new ideas was **liberalism.** Liberalism is a political philosophy based on the ideas of the Enlightenment and the French Revolution.

Liberals in the 1800s believed that all people have individual rights. These include equality under the law and freedom of speech and the press. Liberals also believed that government power should be limited by written constitutions. They felt that elected legislatures should make the laws. Most liberals believed that only men who owned property should be allowed to vote.

The new middle class adopted liberalism. Middle class businesspeople believed that government should not interfere with business or society. British economist Adam Smith supported this idea. In a book called *The Wealth of Nations*, Smith wrote that government should stay out of the economy and let businesses compete. This idea was known as "laissez-faire," a French word meaning "to let be."

Two other liberal thinkers in Britain, however, believed that government should step in to make society better. Jeremy Bentham (BEHN•thuhm) and John Stuart Mill promoted an idea known as **utilitarianism** (yoo•tih•luh•TEHR•ee•uh•nih•zuhm). As utilitarians, Bentham and Mill believed society should promote the greatest happiness for the most people. They supported ideas like full rights for women and improved health services. They also promoted better education.

What Is Socialism?

Not all thinkers in the 1800s agreed with the ideas of liberalism. Some supported an idea known as **socialism.** Socialists believed that the people should own and control all factories, land, capital, and raw materials. They believed that the government should manage these means of production for the people. In this way, wealth could be distributed equally among all citizens.

Some early socialists set up communities where workers could share equally in the profits. Robert Owen, a wealthy British factory owner, was one of these socialists. Owen believed that if people **cooperated,** they could create a better society.

In 1800, Owen made the Scottish mill town of New Lanark into a model industrial community. He did not turn the mill over to the workers. However, he did greatly improve living and working conditions.

The Socialism of Karl Marx

Other socialists thought Owen's work was impractical. They believed it would do little to change society. One of these socialists was Karl Marx.

Marx believed that history was a continual struggle between social classes. According to Marx, the ruling class controlled production. They also held on to most of the wealth. The working class were the actual makers of goods, therefore they should share in the profits. However, they were not paid enough.

Karl Marx believed in equality and a classless society. He also supported a government controlled by the workers. Why might Marx have been thought of as a rebel?

Reading HELPDESK

liberalism a political philosophy based on the Enlightenment ideas of equality and individual rights

utilitarianism the idea that society should promote the greatest happiness for the largest number of people

socialism the idea that the means of production should be owned and controlled by the people, through their government

Academic Vocabulary
cooperate to work together for the good of all

LESSON 5 • Day 1

ENGAGE

SLIDE SHOW **Analyzing Visuals** Show students the slide show on working conditions in the textile mills.

Ask: **Would you want to work under these conditions?**

Explain that the Industrial Revolution brought many changes to society. Some changes were positive, and others were negative.

Tell students that in this lesson they will learn more about how the Industrial Revolution changed people's daily lives, as well as ideas about politics, art, and science.

TEACH & ASSESS

A New Society

GUIDING QUESTION ***How did industry change society in Europe and North America during the 1800s and early 1900s?***

Comparing and Contrasting Ask students to compare and contrast the effects of the Industrial Revolution on middle class and professional workers and industrial workers who labored in factories and mines.

Create a Venn diagram on the board to help students organize the answers they provide during class discussion. *(Students should note that the Industrial Revolution led to the growth of the middle class and the number of industrial workers. However, working conditions and pay were much better for the middle class than for the majority of the working class.)*

Then ask students to compare how conditions for these two groups changed over time. *(In class discussion, students should note that middle-class reformers and organized workers both pushed for changes that improved working conditions in factories and living conditions in the cities.)*

INTERACTIVE WORKSHEET

Economics of History Activity

Evaluating Point out that the successful industries during the Industrial Revolution were those that found ways to use machines that completed a single task at a time. For homework, assign the worksheet Economics of History: Specialization and the Industrial Revolution.

2 Industrialization Changes Political Ideas

GUIDING QUESTION ***What new political ideas arose as a result of industrial society?***

LECTURE SLIDE

Comparing and Contrasting Show students the lecture slide defining *liberalism*, *utilitarianism*, and *socialism*.

Ask students to compare and contrast the views of these different theories about how society should operate. *(Students should note that utilitarianism and liberalism supported the idea of individual rights. However, liberals argued for little or no government involvement in the economy, utilitarians argued for government involvement to improve society, and socialists argued that the government should play a major role in running the economy.)*

IMAGE Then present the image on the work of Robert Owen, who built a factory in New Lanark, Scotland, as an early example of socialism.

CHART **Analyzing** Show students the Interactive Chart that compares Marxism, socialism, and communism. Have students read the chart.

Then, as a class, create a Venn diagram on the board. Have volunteers suggest information to include in each part of the diagram. BL

CLOSE & REFLECT

Have students discuss whether they believe the Industrial Revolution had a positive or a negative impact on society.

Ask: **Were the changes mostly positive or negative?** *(Possible answer: The changes were mostly positive because they brought about an improvement in people's lives.)*

IF YOU HAVE MORE TIME . . .

Use a Graphic Organizer to Illustrate the Ideas of Karl Marx

Sequencing Students often struggle to grasp the tenets of Marxism. Help them by drawing a sequence chart on the whiteboard. The chart should have four boxes. AL

In the first box, write "Society is divided into haves and have-nots." Ask students to explain who the haves and have-nots are. *(The haves are the people who have wealth and power, such as government leaders and factory owners. The have-nots are the people without wealth and power, such as industrial workers.)*

In the second box, write "Industrialization makes the gap between the haves and the have-nots even bigger."

In box three, write "The have-nots rebel and overthrow the haves."

In the fourth box, write "The have-nots create a new society without social classes. Everyone shares wealth and power equally."

Ask: **Is this outcome a realistic possibility? Why or why not?** *(Students will likely say this outcome is not realistic because people are too competitive and usually want more than what their neighbor has.)*

Research Social Issues of the Industrial Revolution

Discovering Divide students into small groups, and assign to each group a topic related to the social issues of the Industrial Revolution. Topics may include working women, child labor, factory conditions, new inventions, or labor unions.

Have each group research to find a primary source quote about their topic. Have volunteers share their primary sources with the class.

Answers for pages 696–699

P. 696 Taking Notes workers moved from the farm to cities, women found new opportunities, the arts blossomed in new directions, scientific discovery advanced medicine.

P. 697 CRITICAL THINKING People living in cities faced hardships because they lived in crowded areas and worked long hours for low pay.

P. 698 CRITICAL THINKING Industrialization improved the lives of the working class by leading to reforms such as expanded voting rights, safer working conditions, and better treatment of workers.

P. 698 ☑ PROGRESS CHECK Working conditions were unhealthful, with long hours and polluted air and water. However, factory work paid higher wages than farm labor.

P. 699 Karl Marx might have been considered a rebel because his socialist theories proposed overthrowing the current industrial system.

Marx stated that eventually the working class, which he called the **proletariat** (proh•luh•TEHR•ee•uht), would revolt and create a communist society. Under communism, social classes would end. People would be equal and share the wealth.

Marx's ideas, later called Marxism, were very influential. His ideas were the basic principles of socialist political parties in Germany, Britain, and other countries. These socialist parties encouraged government control of industry. However, instead of calling for revolution, many of these parties adopted the democratic process. Their supporters elected representatives to national legislatures, where they worked to pass laws that helped workers.

The growth of labor unions was another response to the horrors of factory life. A **labor union** is an organization of workers who unite to improve working conditions. Union leaders used strikes, or work stoppages, to force owners to bargain with the unions. One woman who worked in a textile mill wrote about a strike led by factory women in the 1830s:

The realistic characters in Charles Dickens's novels such as *Oliver Twist* and *Great Expectations* were the everyday people of England. This painting shows a scene from Dickens' *A Christmas Carol.*

PRIMARY SOURCE

> "The mills were shut down, and the girls ... listened to incendiary [angry] speeches from some early labor reformers. One of the girls stood on a pump, and gave vent [release] to the feelings of her companions in a neat speech, declaring that it was their duty to resist all attempts at cutting down wages.... [The] event caused ... consternation [dismay]."
>
> —from "Early Factory Labor in New England" by Harriet H. Robinson

PROGRESS CHECK

Describing What did Adam Smith believe about government and business?

3 Revolution in the Arts

GUIDING QUESTION *How did artists and writers describe the new industrial society?*

The growth of industry also sparked new movements in art, literature, and music. The often ugly appearance of industrial society caused some artists to turn away from it. Others, however, chose to portray it.

Reading **HELP**DESK

proletariat the working class

labor union an organization of those employed who work together to improve wages and working conditions

Academic Vocabulary

symbol something that stands for or suggests something else

What Is Romanticism?

By the late 1700s, artists and writers known as the romantics began to react against the Enlightenment's stress on order and reason. Their movement, called romanticism, valued feelings and the imagination as the best way to find the truth.

Poets, such as Britain's William Wordsworth and Germany's Johann von Goethe (yoh•HAHN fawn GUH•tuh), chose nature, the past, and the unusual as their subjects. They wrote poems to express their inner feelings. Romantic painters, such as Eugène Delacroix (yoo•JEEN deh•luh•KWAH) of France, chose historical or legendary subjects. Their paintings were meant to stir the emotions. The first great romantic musician was Ludwig van Beethoven (LOOD•wihg vahn BAY•toh•vuhn). This German composer's music expressed strong emotions.

Beethoven remains one of Germany's most famous composers. At age 49, Beethoven was completely deaf but continued to compose music. This sculpture stands in his honor in Bonn, Germany.

What is Realism?

By the mid-1800s, some artists and writers began to reject the romantic emphasis on feelings. Known as the realists, they wanted to portray life as it actually was.

Novelists like Britain's Charles Dickens, France's Honoré de Balzac (AHN•uh•ray day BAWL•zak), and Russia's Leo Tolstoy focused on ordinary people in everyday settings. Painters like France's Gustave Courbet (GUS•tahv kur•BAY) and Honoré Daumier (AHN•uh•ray doh•MYAY) also portrayed life in the city and countryside.

Dawn of Modernism

The late 1800s saw the rise of modernism. Modernist artists and writers experimented with new subjects and styles. One group of modernists studied social problems of the day.

Novelists such as Émile Zola of France and American Theodore Dreiser explored issues such as crime, alcoholism, and women's rights. Norwegian Henrik Ibsen also dealt with social issues in his plays. Another modernist group took a different approach. Symbolist artists and writers believed that the outer world was a reflection of an individual's inner reality. They studied dreams and **symbols** and used them in their works.

The soft sunlight sparkles off the water in Claude Monet's impressionist painting.

BIOGRAPHY

Albert Einstein (1879–1955)

Albert Einstein was born in Germany in 1879. He struggled to do well at school and had trouble finding work after graduation. After attending technical school, Einstein worked as a clerk in a government office. The job was simple for him, and it left him plenty of time to pursue his interest in physics. Einstein's research earned him a job as a professor at a university. When Hitler came to power in Germany, Einstein moved to the United States and continued his work in physics. His ideas about the physical universe eventually led to the development of the atomic bomb and the nuclear reactor.

▶ CRITICAL THINKING

Making Inferences Why might Einstein have struggled to find work after graduation?

During the 1870s, a group of artists developed a style called impressionism. The impressionists were interested in color and the effects of light on outdoor subjects. The French impressionists included Claude Monet (moh•NAY), Pierre-Auguste Renoir (REN•wahr), and Edgar Degas (duh•GAH). Mary Cassatt of the United States was also a famous impressionist painter. Composers, led by France's Claude Debussy, created impressionist music. They layered sound upon sound to create a dreamy, shimmering effect.

PROGRESS CHECK

Describing What did the romantics emphasize in their works?

4 The New Science

GUIDING QUESTION *What advances made in science in the mid-1800s have transformed life today?*

During the 1800s, scientists expanded knowledge about life and the universe. Their work also led to medical advances that cured deadly diseases and lengthened life spans.

The Diversity of Life

During the 1800s, many people wondered why the world has so many kinds of plants and animals. Charles Darwin set out to find an answer. His research led him to develop a theory of evolution: plants and animals change very slowly over time.

In a book called *On the Origin of Species,* Darwin stated that plant and animal populations increase faster than the food supply. As a result, they are constantly struggling to survive. Those that survive are better adapted to their environment. They produce offspring that have the same successful characteristics.

Darwin believed that humans evolved, or developed, from animal species. His ideas were controversial. Some people believed that his theory contradicted the biblical story of creation. Others believed it opened the door to a world without moral values. Many people, however, accepted Darwin's theory.

In the 1860s, Gregor Mendel discovered how characteristics were passed to the next generation. From his studies of pea plants, Mendel concluded that offspring receive their traits from their parents. He developed rules to explain what traits parents pass on. Today, Mendel is known as the father of genetics.

Reading **HELP**DESK

Reading Strategy: *Making Inferences*

As you read, you can put together clues to gain information the author doesn't tell you directly. This is called making inferences. Read about Jenner and Pasteur. Make an inference about what it would have been like for someone who became sick in the early 1800s.

What Did Pasteur Discover?

During the 1800s, scientists made advances that gave people longer, healthier lives. One of the first breakthroughs was the discovery of vaccines. In 1796, Edward Jenner noticed that workers who caught a disease called cowpox never caught the deadly smallpox. Jenner found that vaccinating people with cowpox made them immune, or resistant, to smallpox.

About 50 years later, Louis Pasteur learned why Jenner's vaccination worked. In the 1850s, Pasteur discovered bacteria, or germs. He proved that they cause infectious diseases. Pasteur also showed that killing bacteria prevented many diseases.

The discovery of anesthesia, or pain-deadening drugs, was another great step forward. It enabled patients to sleep through their operations. British surgeon Joseph Lister provided another advance. He developed ways to sterilize medical instruments. Before Lister, many patients died after surgery due to infection.

Darwin's observations led him to develop his theory of natural selection. This is the idea that the animals best adapted to their environment would multiply. Poorly adapted members of a species would die off.

Einstein and Physics

New ideas also changed the way people understood the world. Expanding the work of Galileo and Newton, scientists developed the atomic theory. This is the idea that all matter is made up of tiny particles called atoms.

Albert Einstein then overturned long-held ideas about the universe. His theory of relativity stated that space and time could not be measured in an absolute sense. Instead, they depended on the relative motion of bodies in space. For example, the speed of two trains appears differently to people on the station platform than it does to passengers on the train.

PROGRESS CHECK

Explaining How did Louis Pasteur extend the work of Edward Jenner?

LESSON 5 REVIEW

Review Vocabulary

1. Use the word *socialism* in a sentence about working conditions in the Industrial Revolution.
2. Explain the significance of *urbanization* in the context of the Industrial Revolution.

Answer the Guiding Questions

3. ***Determining Cause and Effect*** How did the lives of women change during the Industrial Revolution?
4. ***Analyzing*** What effect did labor unions have on the working conditions in factories?
5. ***Contrasting*** How were the realists different from the romantics?
6. ***Assessing*** What was the importance of Gregor Mendel's work?
7. **PERSONAL WRITING** Choose a style of art from the lesson. In a paragraph, describe your personal reaction to that style.

LESSON 5 • Day 2

ENGAGE

SLIDE SHOW **Interpreting** Show students the slide show about Claude Monet's impressionist paintings. Point out that the famous paintings in the slide show were significant for their use of color and outdoor subjects.

Ask:

What emotions do the paintings make the viewer feel? *(Possible answers: peacefulness, gentleness, appreciation of nature or the outdoors)* AL ELL

Revolution in the Arts

GUIDING QUESTION ***How did artists and writers describe the new industrial society?***

LECTURE SLIDE **Recognizing** Point out that Monet was just one painter from the impressionist movement and that impressionism was just one artistic movement among many from the period.

Show students the lecture slide listing the definitions of *romanticism*, *realism*, *modernism*, and *impressionism*.

Use encyclopedias or other in-class reference materials to display examples of these artistic movements.

Ask: **How are these movements unique?** *(Answers should reflect information from the text.)*

Analyzing

Remind students that modernist writers such as Émile Zola and Henrik Ibsen wrote about realistic issues that face people in their everyday lives. If available, have students read excerpts from some of their works to show examples of their use of realism.

Ask:

How did modernist novels and stories compare to earlier novels and stories? *(Modern novelists studied social problems of the day, such as crime, alcoholism, and women's rights. Earlier works did not deal with such issues.)*

How do you think people reacted when they first read realistic works? *(Possible answer: At first, people were shocked by what they read because it was so different from anything else they had read before. But once they got into the stories, they could identify with the issues that the characters had.)*

The New Science

GUIDING QUESTION ***What advances made in science in the mid-1800s have transformed life today?***

Synthesizing Have students choose a scientist from their reading, such as Charles Darwin, Gregor Mendel, Edward Jenner, Louis Pasteur, Joseph Lister, or Albert Einstein.

Have them use research materials to compile a brief biography about the scientist they chose. Biographies should include name, important dates, contribution to science, and impact of the scientific discovery on society.

Stipulate that each biography should include at least one detail that is not mentioned in the text.

Have students share their biographical research with the class.

Evaluating

In addition to the biographies, have students form small groups and discuss their chosen scientist. Groups should evaluate the scientist's impact on society. Then, have the members of the group choose the one scientist they believe has made the greatest impact. BL

Have students complete the Lesson 5 Review.

CLOSE & REFLECT

Ask volunteers to tell how artistic movements impact society and how the impact of art on society is different from the impact of science.

IF YOU HAVE MORE TIME . . .

Work in Groups to Summarize the Lesson

Comprehending Organize the class into four groups. Assign each group one section from the lesson: A New Society, Industrialization Changes Political Ideas, Revolution in the Arts, and The New Science.

Have each group write a one-paragraph summary of their section. You may also choose to have students summarize the lesson visually, such as with a graphic organizer. AL

When each group has completed their summaries, ask them to present their summaries to the class.

Explore Artists and Their Work

Researching Students will expand their knowledge of different artistic movements by creating presentations that focus on a movement from the lesson and sharing with the class. Refer to the lecture slide for this lesson for the names of the art movements.

Form students into four groups, and assign one movement to each group. Ask them to conduct further research on their topic. Groups should list artists that are associated with their movement. Then, ask groups to choose at least four artists from their list to research further. They should provide short biographies of each artist and include examples of his or her work. Students might present their research using slide show software. BL

Answers for pages 700–703

P. 700 ☑ PROGRESS CHECK Smith believed that if government stayed out of the economy and let businesses compete, prosperity and a better society would result.

P. 702 ☑ PROGRESS CHECK The romantics valued feelings and the imagination as the best way to find truth. Their work focused on subjects that were meant to stir the emotions, not the intellect.

P. 702 CRITICAL THINKING Einstein might have struggled to find work after graduation because he did not do well in school.

P. 702 **Reading Strategy** It was dangerous to become sick in the early 1800s because doctors did not know much about the cause or spread of diseases.

P. 703 ☑ PROGRESS CHECK Louis Pasteur discovered the reason that Jenner's research was correct. He discovered bacteria, which were the basis of Jenner's successful vaccine.

LESSON 5 REVIEW

1. The horrid working conditions of the Industrial Revolution led some leaders to look for a better way of governing called socialism, in which the people of a nation share the wealth equally.
2. Urbanization occurred as a result of the Industrial Revolution. Cities grew when workers moved there from the countryside to get factory jobs.
3. Women began to work outside the home. They earned higher wages and had more opportunities for education.
4. Labor unions forced owners to bargain with union members for better working conditions.
5. The realists examined industrialized society closely, while the romantics turned away from it.
6. Gregor Mendel conducted experiments that proved traits are passed from one generation to the next.
7. Answers will vary, but students should identify an artistic style and recognize how it appeals to them on a personal level.

CHAPTER 23 Activities

Write your answers on a separate piece of paper.

1. **Exploring the Essential Question**
   EXPOSITORY WRITING How do new ideas change the way people live? Write an essay that explains how inventions in the textile industry led to changes in the way British people lived in the nineteenth century.

2. **21st Century Skills**
   BUILD A WEB SITE Plan a Web site with a home page and three linking pages on either the French Revolution or the American Revolution. On the page, identify the important events you will include, the documents you will link to, and the images that will help tell the story. On your home page, set up a logical list of categories to help a visitor navigate your pages.

3. **Thinking Like a Historian**
   IDENTIFYING POINTS OF VIEW Think about the views of a nineteenth century person who believed in liberalism and one who believed in socialism. Using a Venn diagram compare and contrast the viewpoints of these two belief systems.

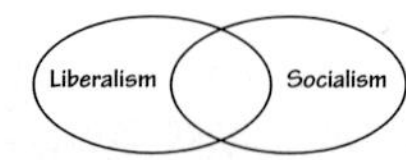

4. **GEOGRAPHY ACTIVITY**

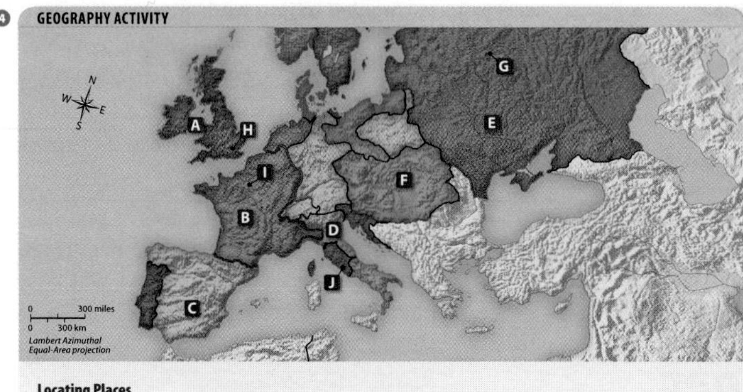

Locating Places
Match the letters on the map with the numbered places listed below.

1. Britain
2. France
3. Spain
4. Kingdom of Italy
5. Russian Empire
6. Austrian Empire
7. Moscow
8. London
9. Paris
10. Rome

CHAPTER 23 Assessment

Directions: Choose the best answer for each question.

1. The slogan "No taxation without representation" is associated with which revolution?
   A. the French Revolution
   B. the Revolution in Haiti
   C. the Industrial Revolution
   D. the American Revolution

2. Why was the Napoleonic Code created?
   F. Napoleon wanted to control his military leaders.
   G. The Catholic Church demanded that Napoleon create the code.
   H. Napoleon created the code of laws to control the people of France.
   I. Napoleon created it when he planned to rule all of Europe.

3. Which two men led the South American fight for independence?
   A. Miguel Hidalgo and José María Morelos
   B. Simón Bolívar and José de San Martín
   C. Toussaint L'Ouverture and Giuseppe Garibaldi
   D. Camillo di Cavour and Otto von Bismarck

4. What was Manifest Destiny?
   F. the idea that America should hold all lands from east to west on the North American continent
   G. the idea that industry should grow fastest in the north
   H. the idea that enslaved Africans should be free
   I. the idea that all people should be represented by a fair government

5. Why do historians call the period of industrialization the "Industrial Revolution"?
   A. because it was bloody and terrible
   B. because it dramatically changed life in many places
   C. because it led to the overthrow of leaders
   D. because it stopped scientific advances

6. Which of the following best describes a laissez-faire approach to government?
   F. Government should stay out of the way and let businesses compete.
   G. Federal government should have more control than states.
   H. Businesses should have more control of laws than government.
   I. Business is better able to run a government.

CHAPTER 23 Assessment *(continued)*

DBQ DOCUMENT-BASED QUESTIONS

Drawing Conclusions Charles Darwin sums up his research on how animals in nature survive.

"It is not the strongest of the species [group] that survives, nor the most intelligent that survives. It is the one that is the most adaptable to change."
—from *Psyography: Charles Darwin* by Shayla Porter

7. According to Darwin's theory, which species are the most likely to survive?
   A. the strongest
   B. the most intelligent
   C. the least intelligent
   D. the most adaptable to change

8. **Analyzing** According to Darwin, which of the following is correct?
   F. The ability to change is not as important as being strong.
   G. The ability to change is not as important as being intelligent.
   H. The ability to change is as important as being strong and intelligent.
   I. The ability to change is more important than being strong or intelligent.

SHORT RESPONSE

9. In one or two sentences, describe the working conditions shown in the image of the textile factory in England during the Industrial Revolution.

10. Explain what Karl Marx would say about these conditions.

EXTENDED RESPONSE

11. **Persuasive Writing** You have read Thomas Paine's *Common Sense* and you know American colonists who object to the Intolerable Acts. But the choice to declare independence from England will mean bitter war. Write a letter to the editor in which you take a position on whether the American colonies should declare their independence from England.

Need Extra Help?

If You've Missed Question	1	2	3	4	5	6	7	8	9	10	11
Review Lesson	1	2	3	3	4	5	5	5	4	5	1

NOTES

REFLECT, REVIEW, & REMEDIATE

INTERACTIVE WORKSHEET

Chapter Summary

Provide students with the Chapter Summary worksheet to help review the chapter and prepare for assessment.

Reviewing the Enduring Understandings

Review this chapter's Enduring Understandings with students:

- Conflict can lead to change.
- The social sciences help us understand history.
- The movement of people, goods, and ideas causes societies to change over time.
- Science and technology can change people's lives.

INTERACTIVE WHITEBOARD ACTIVITY Divide the class into four groups. Assign each group one of the Enduring Understandings for this chapter. Have each group list examples of each understanding from this chapter. Then have the groups record their examples on the interactive whiteboard. Discuss and add information as needed. Challenge more advanced students to make connections between their group's examples and the world today.

Enduring Understanding	Example from Chapter

ACTIVITIES ANSWERS

Exploring the Essential Question

1. Answers may include the concept that ideas can spark people to take actions that change the world. Inventions such as the spinning jenny led to a change in the way British people lived.

21st Century Skills

2. Student plans should show logical connections and appropriate examples of two or more revolutions discussed in the chapter. Plans should also demonstrate an understanding of how Web pages are designed and navigated.

Thinking Like a Historian

3. Graphic organizers should contain information indicating that liberals and socialists wanted reform. Liberals, however, wanted limited reform and for government to stay away from businesses. Socialists wanted broad reforms and for government to take over the means of production from businesses.

Locating Places

4. **1.** A, **2.** B, **3.** C, **4.** D, **5.** E, **6.** F, **7.** G, **8.** H, **9.** I, **10.** J

ASSESSMENT ANSWERS

Review the Guiding Questions

1. **D** The correct choice is D. This slogan was associated with the American Revolution. Colonists in North America objected to being taxed by King George III without a chance to represent themselves in Parliament. The slogan of the French Revolution involved liberty for the masses. The Industrial Revolution was not involved with taxation, and the revolution in Haiti was fought to get rid of a colonial power.

2. **H** The correct choice is H. Napoleon made many changes in France as consul and later as emperor. One such change was to create the Napoleonic Code—a code of laws to enforce the rules of his empire. As emperor, Napoleon did not take orders from the Catholic Church, and he had other means of controlling his military leaders.

3. **B** The correct choice is B. Símon Bolívar and José de San Martín led the movements for South American independence. Miguel Hidalgo and José María Morelos sparked the revolution in Mexico. Toussaint L'Ouverture led the Haitian revolution. Giuseppe Garibaldi and Camillo di Cavour united Italy, and Otto von Bismarck united Germany.

4. **F** The correct choice is F. As the United States expanded into the Louisiana Territory, Florida, California, and the Oregon Territory, many people began to believe that U.S. occupation of all the lands from east to west was destined to occur. Although many reformers worked on freeing enslaved Africans or on policies of fair government and growth of industry, Manifest Destiny involved the simple concept of the U.S. right to expand from coast to coast.

5. **B** The correct choice is B. The Industrial Revolution changed the way people worked, lived, communicated, and enjoyed their culture. The changes were so profound that historians think of this period as revolutionary. The Industrial Revolution was neither bloody nor terrible. It did not overthrow any government leaders. The revolution was a result of scientific advances rather than the stopping of those advances.

6. **F** The correct choice is F. Adam Smith believed government should stay out of the economy and let businesses compete and that this system would lead to prosperity and a better society. The concept did not involve a business takeover of government or allow businesses to make new laws. The idea that the federal government should have more control than states was the opposite of laissez-faire policies.

Document-Based Questions

7. **D** The correct choice is D. The most adaptable species can find ways to survive even when their habitats change or when other influences impact their lives. Darwin saw how strong creatures, as well as those with great or little intelligence, were equally likely to become extinct, while those that could adapt were likely to survive changes in their environment.

8. **I** The correct choice is I. Darwin's quote makes it clear that the ability to change is more important in determining which creatures will survive. This ability is more important than being strong or intelligent.

Short Response

9. Answers should use details and descriptive language to describe the features of the image. They should recognize dangerous working conditions and note the presence of women and children in the factory.

10. Karl Marx believed that such working conditions would cause workers to rebel and overthrow the ruling class. The workers would then create a communist society based on equality.

Extended Response

11. Students' editorials should make a convincing argument for or against declaring independence from England. They should include specific details and a clear call to action.

GLOSSARY/GLOSARIO

NOTE Page numbers listed below refer to the page numbers shown on the reduced student edition pages.

- Content vocabulary words are words that relate to world history content.
- Words that have an asterisk (*) are academic vocabulary. They help you understand your school subjects.
- All vocabulary words are **boldfaced** or **highlighted in yellow** in your textbook.

ENGLISH — A — ESPAÑOL

ENGLISH	ESPAÑOL
***abandon** to leave and not return; to leave, often because of danger (p. 252; p. 456)	***abandonar** salir y no regresar; dejar, con frecuencia debido al peligro (pág. 252; pág. 456)
abolitionism movement to end slavery (p. 687)	**abolicionismo** movimiento para poner fin a la esclavitud (pág. 687)
absolutism a political system in which a ruler has total power (p. 651)	**absolutismo** sistema político en el cual un gobernante tiene poder total (pág. 651)
***accompany** to go with someone as a companion (p. 200)	***acompañar** ir con alguien como compañero (pág. 200)
***accurate** free from errors; in agreement with truth (p. 239; pp. 562–563)	***exacto** sin errores; que se ajusta a la verdad (pág. 239; págs. 562–563)
accursed doomed, miserable (p. 597)	**maldito** condenado, miserable (pág. 597)
***achieve** to succeed; to gain something as the result of work; to successfully complete a task (p. 187; p. 456)	***lograr** tener éxito; obtener algo como resultado del trabajo; completar una tarea con éxito (pág. 187; pág. 456)
***achievement** something gained by working for it (p. 512)	***logro** algo que se obtiene trabajando por ello (pág. 512)
***acquire** to get possession of something; to get as one's own (p. 124; p. 310)	***adquirir** tomar posesión de algo; tomar como propio (pág. 124; pág. 310)
acupuncture an originally Chinese practice of inserting fine needles through the skin at specific points to treat disease or relieve pain (pp. 296–297)	**acupuntura** práctica originaria de la China que consiste en insertar agujas delgadas a través de la piel en puntos específicos para tratar una enfermedad o aliviar el dolor (págs. 296–297)
***adequate** enough for a particular requirement (p. 424)	***adecuado** suficiente para un requisito en particular (pág. 424)
***administer** to be lawfully in charge of (p. 342)	***administrar** estar legalmente a cargo (pág. 342)
***affect** influence; to cause a change (p. 179)	***afectar** influir; ocasionar un cambio (pág. 179)
agora a gathering place; marketplace in ancient Greece (p. 180)	**ágora** sitio de reunión; plaza de la Grecia antigua (pág. 180)
allies those who support each other for some common purpose (pp. 624–625)	**aliados** quienes se apoyan entre sí para un propósito en común (págs. 624–625)
alphabet a set of letters or other characters used to write a language (pp. 144–145)	**abecedario** conjunto de letras o de otros caracteres usados en la lengua escrita (págs. 144–145)

ambush a surprise attack (p. 626)	**emboscada** ataque sorpresivo (pág. 626)
anatomy the study of the body's structure (p. 344)	**anatomía** estudio de la estructura del cuerpo (pág. 344)
ancestor a person that someone is descended from (p. 282)	**ancestro** persona de la cual alguien desciende (pág. 282)
animism belief in spirits that are outside of the body (p. 518)	**animismo** creencia en espíritus que están fuera del cuerpo (pág. 518)
annul to declare invalid (p. 604)	**anular** declarar inválido (pág. 604)
anthropology the study of human culture and how it develops over time (pp. 8–9)	**antropología** estudio de la cultura humana y su desarrollo a lo largo del tiempo (págs. 8–9)
anti-Semitism hostility toward or discrimination against Jews (pp. 568–569)	**antisemitismo** hostilidad o discriminación hacia los judíos (págs. 568–569)
apostle Christian leader chosen by Jesus to spread his message (pp. 377)	**apóstol** líder cristiano elegido por Jesús para difundir su mensaje (pág. 377)
archaeology the study of objects to learn about past human life (p. 8)	**arqueología** estudio de objetos para conocer el pasado de la vida humana (pág. 8)
archipelago many scattered islands surrounded by an expanse of water (pp. 516–517)	**archipiélago** muchas islas dispersas rodeadas por una extensión de agua (págs. 516–517)
***area** the land included within a set of boundaries (pp. 422–423)	***área** terreno incluido dentro de un conjunto de límites (págs. 422–423)
aristocrat a member of an upper class of society, usually made up of hereditary nobility (p. 282)	**aristócrata** miembro de la clase alta de la sociedad o de la nobleza, por lo general formada por la nobleza hereditaria (pág. 282)
artifact an object made by people (pp. 8–9)	**artefacto** objeto elaborado por las personas (págs. 8–9)
***assume** to take for granted to be true (p. 316)	***suponer** dar por hecho que algo es cierto (pág. 316)
astrolabe a tool that helps sailors navigate using the positions of the stars (p. 413)	**astrolabio** instrumento que ayuda a los marineros a navegar mediante la ubicación de las estrellas (pág. 413)
astronomer a person who studies planets and stars (p. 92)	**astrónomo** persona que estudia los planetas y las estrellas (pág. 92)
***authority** the right or power to give orders, make decisions, or control people; power over thoughts, opinions, and behavior (p. 125; pp. 400–401; pp. 572–573)	***autoridad** derecho o facultad de dar órdenes, tomar decisiones o controlar a las personas; poder sobre los pensamientos, las opiniones y el comportamiento (pág. 125; págs. 400-401; págs. 572–573)
***available** ready to be used (p. 56)	***disponible** listo para usarse (pág. 56)
***awareness** the state of having understanding or knowledge (p. 32)	***conciencia** tener comprensión o conocimiento (pág. 32)

B

barbarians uncivilized people (p. 502)

bárbaros personas no civilizadas (pág. 502)

bard someone who writes or performs epic poems or stories about heroes and their deeds (p. 178)

bardo alguien que escribe o relata poemas épicos o historias sobre héroes y sus hazañas (pág. 178)

barter to trade by exchanging one good or service for another; to exchange goods without using money (p. 42)

hacer trueque comerciar intercambiando un bien o servicio por otro; intercambiar productos sin usar dinero (pág. 42)

bazaar a marketplace (p. 412)

bazar mercado (pág. 412)

***behalf** representing; in the place of (p. 518)

***en nombre** en representación; en lugar de (pág. 518)

***benefit** to receive help; to gain (p. 310)

***beneficiarse** recibir ayuda; obtener (pág. 310)

Bhagavad Gita a section of the Indian epic *The Mahabharata* (p. 269)

Bhagavad Gita sección de la epopeya india el Mahabharata (pág. 269)

bias an unreasoned, emotional judgment about people or events (p. 12)

parcialidad juicio emotivo o que no tiene fundamento racional acerca de personas o eventos (pág. 12)

bourgeoisie the middle class in France (p. 673)

burguesía clase media francesa (pág. 673)

boycott to protest by refusing to do something (pp. 666–667)

boicotear protestar negándose a hacer algo (págs. 666–667)

Brahman the universal spirit worshiped by Hindus (pp. 257–258)

Brahmán espíritu universal adorado por los hindúes (págs. 257–258)

Bronze Age the period in ancient human culture when people began to make and use bronze (p. 67)

Edad del Bronce periodo de la cultura humana antigua en el cual las personas comenzaron a fabricar y usar el bronce (pág. 67)

Buddhism a religion founded in ancient India by the religious teacher the Buddha (p. 260)

budismo religión fundada en la antigua India por el maestro religioso Buda (pág. 260)

bureaucracy a group of non-elected government officials (p. 284)

burocracia grupo de funcionarios del gobierno que no son elegidos (pág. 284)

bureaucrat a government official (p. 109)

burócrata funcionario del gobierno (pág. 109)

C

caliph a Muslim leader (p. 404)

califa líder musulmán (pág. 404)

***calligraphy** artistic handwriting (p.486; p. 488)

***caligrafía** letra artística (pág. 486; pág. 488)

***capable** able, competent (p. 331)

***capaz** hábil, competente (pág. 331)

capital money and goods used to help people make or do things (pp. 38–39)

capital dinero y bienes usados para ayudar a las personas a hacer cosas (págs. 38–39)

caravan a group of merchants traveling together for safety, usually with a large number of camels; a group of traveling merchants and animals (p. 92; p. 400)

caravana grupo de mercaderes que viajan juntos por seguridad, usualmente con un gran número de camellos; grupo de mercaderes y animales que viajan (pág. 92; pág. 400)

cardinal directions north, south, east, and west (p. 35)

puntos cardinales norte, sur, este y oeste (pág. 35)

cash crops crops grown in large amounts to be sold for profit (p. 629)

cultivo comercial cultivo producido en grandes cantidades para venderlo y obtener ganancias (pág. 629)

caste an Indian social class whose members are restricted in the jobs they may take and in their association with others (p. 254; p. 256)

casta clase social de la India a cuyos miembros se les restringen los trabajos que pueden desempeñar y su relación con miembros de otras castas (pág. 254; pág. 256)

cataract a waterfall or rapids in a river (p. 102)

catarata cascada o rápidos de un río (pág. 102)

cavalry part of an army in which the soldiers ride horses (p. 232)

caballería división de un ejército en la cual los soldados montan a caballo (pág. 232)

censor an official who watches others for correct behavior (p. 293)

censor funcionario que vigila el correcto comportamiento de otros (pág. 293)

census a count of the number of people in a country (pp. 499–500)

censo conteo del número de personas de un país (págs. 499–500)

***challenge** to invite the start of a competition; to present with difficulties (p. 130; pp. 432–433)

***desafiar** invitar para que se dé inicio a una competencia; presentarse con dificultades (pág. 130; págs. 432–433)

***channel** a straight or narrow sea between two land masses; a canal; narrow body of water between two land masses (p. 196; p. 280)

***canal** mar recto o estrecho que se encuentra entre dos masas continentales; masa de agua estrecha que se encuentra entre dos masas continentales (pág. 196; pág. 280)

checks and balances a system in which each branch of government limits the power of another branch (pp. 44–45)

equilibrio de poderes sistema en el cual cada rama del gobierno limita el poder de otra (págs. 44–45)

chivalry the system, spirit, or customs of medieval knighthood (pp. 549–550)

caballerosidad sistema, espíritu o costumbres de los caballeros medievales (págs. 549–550)

choropleth a special-purpose map that uses color to show population density (p. 36)

mapa de coropletas mapa temático que mediante colores muestra la densidad de población (pág. 36)

circumference the outer border of a circle; the measurement of that border (p. 239)

circunferencia borde externo de un círculo; medida de ese borde (pág. 239)

circumnavigate to go completely around something, such as the world (pp. 622–623)

circunnavegar rodear por completo algo, como por ejemplo el mundo (págs. 622–623)

city-state a city that governs itself and its surrounding territory (pp. 78–79)

ciudad-Estado ciudad que se gobierna a sí misma y el territorio que la rodea (págs. 78–79)

civic duty the idea that citizens have a responsibility to help their country (p. 315)

deber cívico idea según la cual los ciudadanos tienen la responsabilidad de ayudar a su país (pág. 315)

***civil** of or relating to citizens; relating to the state or government (p. 324; p. 476)

***civil** relativo a los ciudadanos; relativo al Estado o al Gobierno (pág. 324; pág. 476)

civil service the administrative service of a government (p. 294)

clan a group of people descended from the same ancestor (p. 431)

clergy church officials (p. 383)

***code** a set of official rules; a system of principles or rules (p. 87; pp. 549–550)

collapse to break down; to lose effectiveness (p. 194)

colony a group of people living in a new territory who have ties to their homeland; a new territory (p. 179)

comedy a play or film that tells a humorous story (p. 217)

command economy an economic system in which a central government decides what goods will be made and who will receive them (p. 40)

commandment a rule that God wanted the Israelites to follow (p. 143)

commerce an exchange of goods; business (p. 633)

***commit** to carry out or do (p. 261)

***communicate** to share information with someone; to exchange knowledge or information (p. 58; p. 156)

***community** a group of people with common interests and values living in an area; people living in a particular area; an area (p. 157; pp. 174–175; p. 238; p. 381; pp. 436–437)

***complex** having many parts, details, or ideas; made up of many related parts; complicated (pp. 90–91; p. 454; p. 586; p. 588)

***conclude** to reach an understanding; to make a decision (p. 176)

conclusion a decision reached after examining evidence (p. 14)

concordat agreement between the pope and the ruler of a country (pp. 546–547)

***confirm** to prove that something is true; to remove doubt (p. 413)

***conflict** a battle or war; a fight or disagreement; a fight or battle (p. 203; pp. 218–219)

servicio civil servicio administrativo de un gobierno (pág. 294)

clan grupo de personas que descienden el mismo ancestro (pág. 431)

clero funcionarios de la Iglesia (pág. 383)

***código** conjunto de leyes oficiales; sistema de principios o reglas (pág. 87; págs. 549–550)

colapsar derrumbarse; perder efectividad (pág. 194)

colonia grupo de personas que viven en un nuevo territorio y mantienen vínculos con su tierra natal; territorio nuevo (pág. 179)

comedia obra de teatro o película que cuenta una historia humorística (pág. 217)

economía planificada sistema económico en el cual un gobierno central decide qué bienes se producirán y quién los recibirá (pág. 40)

mandamiento regla que Dios quería que los israelitas cumplieran (pág. 143)

comercio intercambio de bienes; negocio (pág. 633)

***cometer** llevar a cabo o hacer (pág. 261)

***comunicar** compartir información con alguien; intercambiar conocimientos o información (pág. 58; pág. 156)

***comunidad** grupo de personas con intereses y valores comunes que viven en un área; personas que viven en un área en particular; un área (pág. 157; págs. 174–175; pág. 238; pág. 381; págs. 436–437)

***complejo** que tiene muchas partes, detalles o ideas; que consta de muchas partes relacionadas (págs. 90–91; pág. 454; pág. 586; pág. 588)

***concluir** llegar a un acuerdo; tomar una decisión (pág. 176)

conclusión decisión que se toma luego de examinar evidencias (pág. 14)

concordato acuerdo entre el papa y el gobernante de un país (págs. 546–547)

***confirmar** demostrar que algo es verdadero; despejar dudas (pág. 413)

***conflicto** batalla o guerra; lucha o desacuerdo; lucha o batalla (pág. 203; págs. 218–219)

Confucianism a system of beliefs based on the teachings of Confucius (pp. 286–287)	**confucianismo** sistema de creencias basado en las enseñanzas de Confucio (págs. 286–287)
conquistadors Spanish soldiers who conquered people in other lands (p. 622)	**conquistadores** soldados españoles que conquistaron pueblos en otras tierras (pág. 622)
***consider** to give careful thought (pp. 183–184)	***considerar** pensar detenidamente (págs. 183–184)
***considerable** large in size, quantity, or quality (p. 626)	***considerable** de gran tamaño, cantidad o calidad (pág. 626)
***consist** to be made up of (p. 80)	***constar** estar formado de (pág. 80)
***constant** always happening (p. 58)	***constante** que siempre sucede (pág. 58)
constitution basic laws of a state that define the role of government and guarantee its obligation to the people; a document that describes how a country will be governed and guarantees people certain rights (p. 518; p. 666)	**constitución** leyes básicas de un Estado que definen la función del Gobierno y garantizan su obligación con el pueblo; documento que describe cómo será gobernado un país y garantiza a las personas algunos derechos (pág. 518; pág. 666)
constitutional monarchy a political system in which the head of state is a king or queen who rules according to a constitution (p. 652)	**monarquía constitucional** sistema político en el cual el jefe de Estado es un rey o una reina que gobierna de acuerdo con una Constitución (pág. 652)
***construct** to build by putting parts together; to build; to create (pp. 56–57; p. 115; p. 188; pp. 214–215)	***construir** formar uniendo las partes; edificar; crear (págs. 56-57; pág. 115; pág. 188; págs. 214–215)
consul head of a government, usually with a limited term in office (p. 313)	**cónsul** jefe de un gobierno, por lo general durante un tiempo limitado en el cargo (pág. 313)
***contact** communication or connection; interaction with other people (p. 344; pp. 438–439)	***contacto** comunicación o conexión; interacción con otras personas (pág. 344; págs. 438–439)
***contrast** the act of comparing by looking at differences (p. 330)	***contrastar** acción de comparar observando diferencias (pág. 330)
***contribute** to give or donate something (p. 269)	***contribuir** dar o donar algo (pág. 269)
***convert** to accept a new belief; to bring from one belief to another (pp. 432–433; p. 502)	***convertir** (se) aceptar una nueva creencia; llevar de una creencia a otra (págs. 432–433; pág. 502)
***cooperate** to work together for the good of all (pp. 560–561; pp. 698–699)	***cooperar** trabajar juntos para el bien de todos (págs. 560–561; págs. 698–699)
***cooperation** working together (p. 163)	***cooperación** trabajar juntos (pág. 163)
corporation a type of company that sells shares in the company to investors (p. 694)	**sociedad anónima** tipo de compañía que vende acciones en la compañía a inversionistas (pág. 694)
cottage industry making goods in workers' homes (p. 634)	**industria casera** fabricación de bienes en casa de los trabajadores (pág. 634)
coup d 'etat a change of government in which a new group of leaders seize power by force (p. 676)	**golpe de Estado** cambio de gobierno en el cual un nuevo grupo de líderes se hace al poder por medio de la fuerza (pág. 676)

covenant an agreement with God (p. 142)

alianza acuerdo con Dios (pág. 142)

***create** to make or produce something; to bring something into existence; to produce by a course of action (pp. 230–231; p. 374)

***crear** hacer o producir algo; hacer que algo exista; producir mediante una serie de acciones (págs. 230-231; pág. 374)

credentials something that gives confidence that a person is qualified for a task (p. 19)

credenciales algo que brinda confianza con respecto a las cualificaciones de una persona para una tarea (pág. 19)

***crucial** important or significant (p. 110)

***crucial** importante o relevante (pág. 110)

***culture** the set of beliefs, behaviors, and traits shared by a group of people (pp. 36–37; pp. 140–141; p. 408; p. 629)

***cultura** conjunto de creencias, comportamientos y características que comparte un grupo de personas (págs. 36–37; págs. 140–141; pág. 408; pág. 629)

cuneiform writing developed by the Sumerians that used wedge-shaped marks made in soft clay (p. 82)

cuneiforme sistema de escritura desarrollado por los sumerios que consta de marcas en forma de cuña hechas sobre arcilla blanda (pág. 82)

***currency** something, such as coins or paper money, that is used as a medium of exchange; money in the form of coins or paper (p. 293; p. 586)

***moneda** algo que se usa como medio de intercambio, como las monedas o el papel moneda; dinero en forma de o monedas billetes (pág. 293; pág. 586)

D

Dao Chinese system of beliefs which describes the way a person must rule (pp. 284–285)

Tao sistema chino de creencias que describe la manera en que una persona debe gobernar (págs. 284–285)

Daoism a Chinese philosophy concerned with obtaining long life and living in harmony with nature (p. 288)

taoísmo filosofía china que se interesa en la forma de obtener larga vida y vivir en armonía con la naturaleza (pág. 288)

***data** information, usually facts and figures (p. 20)

***datos** información, por lo general hechos y cifras (pág. 20)

***decade** a group or set of 10; period of 10 years (p. 5; p. 202)

***década** grupo o conjunto de diez; periodo de diez años (pág. 5; pág. 202)

***decline** to become weaker; to move toward a weaker condition (pp. 126–127; p. 177; p. 268)

***decaer** debilitarse; moverse hacia una condición de mayor fragilidad (págs. 126–127; pág. 177; pág. 268)

delta a fan-shaped area of silt near where a river flows into the sea (p. 102)

delta área cenagosa en forma de abanico cercana al punto donde un río desemboca en el mar (pág. 102)

demand the amount of something that a consumer wants to buy (p. 39)

demanda cantidad de algo que los consumidores quieren comprar (pág. 39)

democracy a government by the people (p. 184)

democracia gobierno del pueblo (pág. 184)

descendant future member of a family (p. 349)

descendiente miembro futuro de una familia (pág. 349)

***design** to skillfully plan or create something (p. 692)

***diseñar** planear o crear algo con destreza (pág. 692)

***despite** in spite of; regardless of (p. 222)

***a pesar de** pese a que, sin tener en cuenta (pág. 222)

***devote** to give one's time, effort, or attention earnestly (p. 309)	***dedicar** brindar tiempo, esfuerzo o atención sinceramente (pág. 309)
***devotion** dedication, a strong commitment (p. 163)	***devoción** dedicación, compromiso sólido (pág. 163)
dharma a person's personal duty, based on the individual's place in society (pp. 258–259)	**darma** deber individual de una persona, de acuerdo con su lugar en la sociedad (págs. 258–259)
dhow sailboat using wind-catching, triangular sails (pp. 428–429)	**dhow** velero que usa velas triangulares para atrapar el viento (págs. 428–429)
Diaspora groups of Jews living outside of the Jewish homeland (pp. 160–161)	**diáspora** grupos de judíos que viven fuera de su territorio natal (págs. 160–161)
dictator a person with absolute power to rule (p. 314)	**dictador** persona con poder absoluto para gobernar (pág. 314)
din loud noise (p. 497)	**bulla** ruido alto (pág. 497)
diplomacy conducting negotiations between countries (p. 586; p. 588)	**diplomacia** realizar negociaciones entre países (pág. 586; pág. 588)
direct democracy a form of democracy in which all citizens can participate firsthand in the decision-making process (pp. 198–199)	**democracia directa** forma de democracia en la cual todos los ciudadanos pueden participar directamente en el proceso de toma de decisiones (págs. 198–199)
disciple student (p. 497)	**discípulo** estudiante (pág. 497)
***display** to place an object where people can view it (p. 387)	***exponer** colocar un objeto donde las personas puedan verlo (pág. 387)
***distort** to twist out of shape or change the size of (pp. 30–31)	***distorsionar** deformar o cambiar el tamaño de algo (págs. 30–31)
***distribute** to divide into shares and deliver the shares to different people; to give or deliver to members of a group (p. 109; p. 330; p. 464)	***distribuir** dividir en partes y repartirlas entre diferentes personas; dar o repartir a los miembros de un grupo (pág. 109; pág. 330; pág. 464)
doctrine official church teaching (p. 384)	**doctrina** enseñanza oficial de la Iglesia (pág. 384)
***document** an official paper used as proof or support of something; an original or official paper used as the basis or proof of something; a piece of writing (p. 166; p. 558; p. 666)	***documento** texto oficial que se usa como prueba o respaldo de algo; papel original u oficial que se usa como base o prueba de algo; escrito (pág. 166; pág. 558; pág. 666)
domesticate to adapt an animal to live with humans for the advantage of the humans (pp. 62–63)	**domesticar** adaptar a un animal para que viva con los seres humanos para provecho de estos (págs. 62–63)
***dominate** control or influence something or someone (pp. 174 – 175)	***dominar** controlar o ejercer influencia sobre algo o alguien (págs. 174–175)
downtrodden people who are poor or suffering (p. 349)	**oprimidos** personas pobres o que están sufriendo (pág. 349)
drama a story written in the form of a play (p. 217)	**drama** historia escrita en forma de obra de teatro (pág. 217)
dynasty a line of rulers from one family (pp. 106–107)	**dinastía** línea de gobernantes de una familia (págs. 106–107)

E

***economic** the system in a country that involves making, buying, and selling goods (p. 176)

***económico** sistema de un país que implica la elaboración, compra y venta de productos (pág. 176)

***economy** the system of economic life in an area or country; an economy deals with the making, buying, or selling of goods and services (p. 64; p. 572)

***economía** sistema de la vida económica en un área o un país; la economía se relaciona con la elaboración, compra y venta de productos o servicios (pág. 64; pág. 572)

.edu the ending of an Internet URL of a Web site for an educational institution (p. 20)

.edu parte final del URL (por sus siglas en inglés) del sitio web de una institución educativa (pág. 20)

elements substances that consist of atoms of only one kind (p. 648)

elementos sustancias formadas por átomos de un solo tipo (pág. 648)

ellipses shapes like stretched circles; ovals (pp. 644–645)

elipses figuras semejantes a círculos estirados; óvalos (págs. 644–645)

embalming the process of treating a body to prevent it from decaying (p. 111)

embalsamamiento proceso que consiste en tratar un cuerpo para evitar que se descomponga (pág. 111)

embrace to hug someone (p. 85)

abrazar estrechar entre los brazos a alguien (pág. 85)

***emerge** to come into being or become known (p. 252; pp. 278–279)

***surgir** llegar a ser o darse a conocer (pág. 252; págs. 278–279)

***emphasize** attach a sense of importance to something; express the importance of something (p. 203)

***poner énfasis** dar importancia a algo; expresar la importancia de algo (pág. 203)

empire a large territory or group of many territories governed by one ruler (pp. 86–87)

imperio gran territorio o grupo de muchos territorios a cargo de un gobernante (págs. 86–87)

***enable** to make possible (p. 326)

***permitir** hacer posible (pág. 326)

***ensure** to make certain or make sure of (pp. 146–147; p. 518)

***asegurar** tener certeza o garantizar (págs. 146–147; pág. 518)

entrepreneur one who organizes, pays for, and takes on the risk of setting up a business (p. 633)

empresario persona que organiza, paga y asume el riesgo de establecer un negocio (pág. 633)

entrepreneurship the act of running a business and taking on the risks of that business (pp. 38–39)

espíritu empresarial acción de dirigir un negocio y asumir los riesgos de ese negocio (págs. 38–39)

envoy a government representative to another country (p. 123)

enviado representante de un gobierno ante otro país (pág. 123)

ephor a high-ranked government official in Sparta who was elected by the council of elders (p. 186)

éforo funcionario del gobierno de alto rango en Esparta a quien elegía el consejo de ancianos (pág. 186)

epic a long poem that records the deeds of a legendary or real hero (pp. 82–83)

epopeya poema largo que registra las hazañas de un héroe legendario o real (págs. 82–83)

Epicureanism the philosophy of Epicurus, stating that the purpose of life is to look for happiness and peace (p. 238)

epicureísmo filosofía instaurada por Epicuro, la cual afirmaba que el propósito de la vida es la búsqueda de la felicidad y la paz (pág. 238)

era a large division of time (p. 5)	**era** gran división de tiempo (pág. 5)
***establish** to start; to bring into existence (p. 544)	***establecer** iniciar; hacer que exista (pág. 544)
estate a social class in France before the French Revolution (pp. 672–673)	**estado** una de las clases sociales en Francia antes de la Revolución francesa (págs. 672–673)
***estimate** to determine an approximate value, size, or nature of something (p. 262)	***estimar** determinar el valor, el tamaño o la naturaleza aproximados de algo (pág. 262)
***eventual** taking place at an unnamed later time; later; final or ultimate; (p. 266; p. 308; p. 688)	***final** que ocurre en un tiempo futuro indeterminado; posterior o último (pág. 266; pág. 308; pág. 688)
evidence something that shows proof or an indication that something is true (pp. 10–11)	**evidencia** algo que proporciona pruebas o indicios de que algo es cierto (págs. 10–11)
excommunicate to declare that a person or group is no longer a member of the church (p. 389)	**excomulgar** declarar que una persona o un grupo ya no son miembros de la Iglesia (pág. 389)
executive branch the part of government that enforces laws (pp. 44–45)	**poder ejecutivo** rama del gobierno que hace cumplir las leyes (págs. 44–45)
extended family a family made up of several generations (pp. 436–437)	**familia extendida** familia compuesta por varias generaciones (págs. 436–437)
Exodus the departure of the Israelites out of slavery in Egypt (p. 142)	**éxodo** salida de los israelitas de Egipto que puso fin a su esclavitud (pág. 142)
exile a forced absence from one's home or country (pp. 152–153)	**exilio** ausencia obligada del propio hogar o país (págs. 152–153)
***expand** to enlarge; to spread out; to increase the number, volume, or scope (p. 162; pp. 352–353; p. 644)	***expandir** agrandar; extender; aumentar el número, el volumen o el alcance (pág. 162; págs. 352–353; pág. 644)
***expert** a skilled person who has mastered a subject (p. 41)	***experto** persona cualificada que domina una materia (pág. 41)
export a good that is sent from one country to another in trade (p. 42)	**exportación** producto enviado de un país a otro para comercializarlo (pág. 42)
***extract** to remove by a physical or chemical process (p. 145)	***extraer** eliminar mediante un proceso físico o químico (pág. 145)

F

fable a story meant to teach a lesson (p. 216)	**fábula** historia que busca enseñar una lección (pág. 216)
feat achievement, success (p. 597)	**hazaña** logro, éxito (pág. 597)
***federal** referring to an organized union of states under one government (pp. 670–671)	***federal** relativo a una unión organizada de estados bajo un gobierno (págs. 670–671)
federal system a government which divides power between central and state governments (pp. 44–45)	**sistema federal** gobierno en el cual el poder está dividido entre el gobierno central y los gobiernos estatales (págs. 44–45)

feudalism the system of service between a lord and the vassals who have sworn loyalty to the lord; political order; under feudalism, nobles governed and protected people in return for services (p. 523; pp. 548–549)

feudalismo sistema de servicio entre un señor y los vasallos que le han jurado lealtad; orden político; en el feudalismo, los nobles gobernaban y protegían a las personas a cambio de sus servicios (pág. 523; págs. 548–549)

fief a feudal estate belonging to a vassal (p. 549)

feudo propiedad feudal perteneciente a un vasallo (pág. 549)

filial piety the responsibility of children to respect, obey, and care for their parents (pp. 290–291)

piedad filial responsabilidad que tienen los hijos de respetar, obedecer y cuidar a sus padres (págs. 290–291)

***finite** limited; having boundaries (p. 14)

***finito** limitado; que tiene límites (pág. 14)

fjord a narrow inlet of the sea between cliffs or steep slopes (p. 544)

fiordo entrada estrecha del mar entre acantilados o pendientes empinadas (pág. 544)

***focus** to place all of one's attention on something (p. 260)

***enfocar** poner toda la atención en algo (pág. 260)

fossil plant or animal remains that have been preserved from an earlier time (pp. 8–9)

fósil restos vegetales o animales que se han preservado desde una época anterior (págs. 8–9)

***found** to create or set up something such as a city; to set up or establish; established or took the first steps in building; (p. 6; p.151; p. 307; p. 686)

***fundar** crear o instituir algo, como una ciudad; establecer o formar; establecer o dar los primeros pasos en la construcción (pág. 6; pág. 151; pág. 307; pág. 686)

G

***generation** a group of individuals born and living at the same time; the time span between the birth of parents and the birth of their children (p. 295; pp. 648–649)

***generación** grupo de individuos que nacen y viven en la misma época; periodo de tiempo entre el nacimiento de los padres y el nacimiento de sus hijos (pág. 295; págs. 648–649)

geocentric an Earth-centered theory; having or relating to the Earth as the center (p. 643)

geocéntrico teoría centrada en la Tierra; que tiene o se relaciona con la Tierra como el centro (pág. 643)

gladiator in ancient Rome, a person who fought people or animals for public entertainment (p. 341)

gladiador en la antigua Roma, alguien que se enfrentaba a una persona o a un animal para entretener al público (pág. 341)

***global** involving the entire Earth (pp. 626–627)

***global** que implica toda la Tierra (págs. 626–627)

globalization the growth in free trade between countries (pp. 42–43)

globalización crecimiento del libre comercio entre los países (págs. 42–43)

Glorious Revolution the overthrow of King James II of England (p. 652)

Revolución Gloriosa derrocamiento del rey Jacobo II de Inglaterra (pág. 652)

***goal** something that a person works to achieve; aim (p. 566)

***meta** algo que una persona se esfuerza por alcanzar; objetivo (pág. 566)

gospel the accounts that apostles wrote of Jesus' life (pp. 384–385)

evangelio relato que los apóstoles escribieron sobre la vida de Jesús (págs. 384–385)

.gov the ending of a URL of a government Web site (p. 20)

.gov parte final del URL (por sus siglas en inglés) de un sitio web del gobierno (pág. 20)

grand jury a group of citizens that meets to decide whether people should be accused of a crime (p. 558)

gran jurado grupo de ciudadanos que se reúne para decidir si se debe acusar a una persona de un crimen (pág. 558)

gravity the attraction that the Earth or another celestial body has on an object on or near its surface (pp. 646–647)

gravedad atracción que la Tierra u otro cuerpo celeste ejerce sobre un objeto que se encuentra en su superficie o cerca de esta (págs. 646–647)

griot traditional storyteller (pp. 426–427)

griot narrador tradicional (págs. 426–427)

guarantee to promise (p. 432)

garantizar prometer (pág. 432)

***guarantee** something that is assured or certain (pp. 652–653)

***garantía** algo que se asegura o es cierto (págs. 652–653)

guerrilla warfare a form of war in which soldiers make surprise attacks on the enemy (pp. 684–685)

guerra de guerrillas forma de guerra en la cual los soldados lanzan ataques sorpresivos al enemigo (págs. 684–685)

guild a group of merchants or craftsmen during medieval times; a group of merchants or craftspeople (p. 524; pp. 554–555)

gremio grupo de mercaderes o artesanos durante la Edad Media; grupo de mercaderes o artesanos (pág. 524; págs. 554–555)

guru a teacher (p. 254; p. 256)

gurú maestro (pág. 254; pág. 256)

H

heliocentric having or relating to the sun as the center of the solar system (p. 644)

heliocéntrico que tiene o se relaciona con el Sol como centro del sistema solar (pág. 644)

Hellenistic Era the time period following the death of Alexander during which Greek culture spread through the known world (pp. 234–235)

Época helenística periodo posterior a la muerte de Alejandro, durante el cual la cultura griega se difundió por todo el mundo conocido (págs. 234–235)

helot enslaved person in ancient Sparta (p. 185)

ilota persona esclavizada de la antigua Esparta (pág. 185)

hemisphere a "half sphere," used to refer to one-half of the globe when divided into North and South or East and West (p. 29)

hemisferio "media esfera"; término usado para referirse a la mitad del planeta al dividirlo en Norte y Sur, o en Este y Oeste (pág. 29)

hereditary having title or possession by reason of birth (p. 284)

hereditario que tiene el título o la posesión debido a su nacimiento (pág. 284)

heresy ideas that go against Church teachings; a religious belief that contradicts what the Church says is true (pp. 568–569; p. 607)

herejía ideas que van en contra de las enseñanzas de la Iglesia; creencia religiosa que contradice lo que la Iglesia dice que es cierto (págs. 568-569; pág. 607)

***hierarchy** an organization with different levels of authority; a classification into ranks (p. 383; pp. 518–519)

***jerarquía** organización con diferentes niveles de autoridad; clasificación en categorías (pág. 383; págs. 518–519)

hieroglyphics a writing system made up of a combination of pictures and sound symbols (p. 105)

jeroglíficos sistema de escritura formado por una combinación de imágenes y símbolos que representan sonidos (pág. 105)

Hinduism a major religion that developed in ancient India (pp. 257–258)

hinduismo religión de gran importancia que se desarrolló en la antigua India (págs. 257–258)

Hippocratic Oath a set of promises about patient care that new doctors make when they start practicing medicine (pp. 226–227)

Juramento Hipocrático conjunto de promesas acerca del cuidado de los pacientes que los nuevos médicos hacen cuando empiezan a ejercer su profesión (págs. 226–227)

hogan a square wooden home of Native Americans (pp. 466–467)

hogan casa cuadrada de madera (págs. 466–467)

hostage someone held against his or her will in exchange for something (p. 626)

rehén alguien retenido en contra de su voluntad a cambio de algo (pág. 626)

humanism an emphasis on worldly concerns; belief in the worth of the individual and that reason is the path to knowledge (pp. 589–590)

humanismo énfasis en las preocupaciones terrenales; creencia de que la razón es el camino al conocimiento, y en el valor del individuo (págs. 589–590)

I

Ice Age a time when glaciers covered much of the land (p. 60)

Era de Hielo tiempo en el cual los glaciares cubrían la mayor parte de la Tierra (pág. 60)

icon a representation of an object of worship (p. 387)

ícono representación de un objeto de adoración (pág. 387)

iconoclast originally: a person who destroys icons; today: a person who criticizes traditional beliefs (p. 387)

iconoclasta originalmente, persona que destruye íconos; hoy, persona que critica las creencias tradicionales (pág. 387)

ideograph a symbol in a writing system that represents a thing or idea (p. 282)

ideograma símbolo en un sistema escrito que representa un objeto o una idea (pág. 282)

import a good brought into a country from another country (p. 42)

importación producto que entra a un país procedente de otro (pág. 42)

***impose** to establish by force or authority (p. 602)

***imponer** establecer mediante la fuerza o la autoridad (pág. 602)

incense a material that produces a pleasant smell when burned (p. 123)

incienso material que produce un aroma agradable al quemarlo (pág. 123)

***individual** a single human being; human being; person (pp. 40–41; p. 223; p. 287)

***individuo** un solo ser humano; ser humano; persona (págs. 40–41; pág. 223; pág. 287)

indulgence a pardon, or forgiveness, of a sin (pp. 598–599)

indulgencia perdón, o exoneración, de un pecado (págs. 598–599)

industrialism an economic system where machines do work that was once performed by animals or humans (pp. 690–691)

industrialismo sistema económico en el cual las máquinas realizan el trabajo que antes realizaban los animales o las personas (págs. 690–691)

inflation a continued rise in prices or the supply of money; a period of rapidly increasing prices (p. 41)

inflación aumento continuo de los precios o de la oferta de dinero; periodo de rápido aumento de los precios (pág. 41)

***innovation** the introduction of something new (pp. 316–317)

***innovación** introducción de algo nuevo (págs. 316–317)

***inspect** to look over carefully (p. 329)

***inspeccionar** examinar de una manera cuidadosa (pág. 329)

institution a custom or practice that many people accept and use (pp. 532–533)	**institución** costumbre o práctica que muchas personas aceptan y usan (págs. 532–533)
***integral** essential, necessary (pp. 4–5)	***integral** esencial, necesario (págs. 4-5)
***intensify** to become stronger (pp. 316–317)	***intensificar** hacerse más fuerte (págs. 316-317)
***interpret** to explain the meaning of (p. 375)	***interpretar** explicar el significado de algo (pág. 375)
***interpretation** an explanation of the meaning of something (pp. 14–15)	***interpretación** explicación del significado de algo (págs. 14–15)
***invest** to give money to a company in exchange for a return, or profit, on the money; to put money in new businesses or other money-making projects (p. 633; p. 691)	***invertir** dar dinero a una compañía a cambio de rendimientos, o ganancias, sobre el dinero; colocar dinero en nuevas empresas y otros proyectos lucrativos (pág. 633; pág. 691)
***investigate** to observe or study by examining closely and questioning systematically (pp. 224–225)	***investigar** observar o estudiar examinando detenidamente y formulando preguntas de manera sistemática (págs. 224–225)
***involve** to include (p. 307)	***involucrar** incluir (pág. 307)
irrigation a system that supplies dry land with water through ditches, pipes, or streams (p. 77)	**irrigación** sistema que abastece de agua los terrenos secos mediante zanjas, tuberías o corrientes (pág. 77)
Islam a religion based on the teachings of Muhammad (pp. 398–399)	**islam** religión basada en las enseñanzas de Mahoma (págs. 398–399)
***isolate** to separate from others; to separate from other populated areas; to set apart from others (p. 102; p. 399; pp. 516–517)	***aislar** separar de otros; separar de otras áreas pobladas; apartar de otros (pág. 102; pág. 399; págs. 516–517)
***issue** a concern or problem that has not yet been solved (p. 46)	***asunto** inquietud o problema que aún no se ha resuelto (pág. 46)
isthmus a narrow piece of land linking two larger areas of land (p. 450)	**istmo** porción estrecha de tierra que une dos áreas más grandes de tierra (pág. 450)

J

Jainism a religion of ancient India that does not believe in a supreme being, but emphasizes nonviolence and respect for all living things (p. 263)	**jainismo** religión de la antigua India que no cree en un ser supremo sino que enfatiza en la no violencia y el respeto a todos los seres vivos (pág. 263)
judicial branch part of government that interprets laws (p. 45)	**poder judicial** rama del gobierno que interpreta las leyes (pág. 45)
***jury** a group of people sworn to make a decision in a legal case (pp. 45–46)	***jurado** grupo de personas que prestan juramento para tomar una decisión en un caso legal (págs. 45–46)

K

kaiser emperor of Germany (p. 686)	**káiser** emperador de Alemania (pág. 686)

karma a force that decides the form that people will be reborn into in their next lives (pp. 258–259)

karma fuerza que decide la forma en que las personas renacerán en sus próximas vidas (págs. 258–259)

knight a mounted man-at-arms serving a feudal superior (p. 549)

caballero hombre armado que cabalga y sirve a un superior feudal (pág. 549)

kosher prepared according to Jewish dietary law (p. 158)

kosher preparado de acuerdo con la ley judía sobre la alimentación (pág. 158)

L

***labor** the ability of people to do work; work; the tasks that workers perform (pp. 38–39; pp. 112–113; pp. 522–523)

***mano de obra** capacidad de las personas para trabajar; tareas que los trabajadores realizan (págs. 38–39; págs. 112–113; págs. 522–523)

labor union an organization of those employed who work together to improve wages and working conditions (p. 700)

sindicato organización de empleados que trabajan juntos para mejorar sus salarios y condiciones laborales (pág. 700)

laity regular church members (p. 383)

laicado miembros regulares de la Iglesia (pág. 383)

language family a group of similar languages (p. 253)

familia lingüística grupo de idiomas semejantes (pág. 253)

latifundia large farming estates (p. 321)

latifundios propiedades agrícolas de gran tamaño (pág. 321)

latitude imaginary lines that circle the Earth parallel to the Equator (p. 30)

latitud líneas imaginarias que rodean la Tierra en dirección paralela al ecuador (pág. 30)

***legal** of or relating to the law (p. 362)

***legal** relativo a la ley (pág. 362)

legalism a Chinese philosophy that stressed the importance of laws (p. 289)

***legalismo** filosofía china que resaltaba la importancia de las leyes (pág. 289)

legion large groups of Roman soldiers (p. 310)

legion grupos numerosos de soldados romanos (pág. 310)

legislative branch the part of government that passes laws (pp. 44–45)

poder legislativo rama del gobierno que aprueba las leyes (págs.44–45)

***legislature** a group of people who make the laws (p. 313)

***asamblea legislativa** grupo de personas que hace las leyes (pág. 313)

liberalism a political philosophy based on the Enlightenment ideas of equality and individual rights (p. 698)

liberalismo filosofía política basada en la Ilustración y en las ideas de igualdad y derechos individuales (pág. 698)

limited government a government whose powers are restricted through laws or a constitution (pp. 670–671)

gobierno limitado gobierno cuyos poderes los restringen las leyes o la constitución (págs. 670–671)

***link** a connecting element or factor; to connect; to join (p. 298; pp. 452–453)

***vínculo** elemento o factor que conecta; el término en inglés "link" también significa "conectar"; "unir" (pág. 298; págs. 452–453)

***locate** set up in a particular place (p. 65)

***localizarse** establecerse en un lugar en particular (pág. 65)

Glossary/Glosario

longitude imaginary lines that circle the Earth from the North Pole to the South Pole, measuring distance east or west of the Prime Meridian (p. 30)

longitud líneas imaginarias que rodean la Tierra desde el Polo Norte hasta el Polo Sur, que mide la distancia al este o al oeste del meridiano principal (pág. 30)

M

***maintain** to keep in the same state (p. 432)

***mantener** conservar en el mismo estado (pág. 432)

maize corn (p. 454)

maíz elote (pág . 454)

Mandate of Heaven the belief that the Chinese king's right to rule came from the gods (p. 284)

mandato divino creencia de que el derecho de gobernar del emperador chino venía de los dioses (pág. 284)

***manual** involving physical effort; work done by hand (p. 118; p. 254; p. 256)

***manual** que implica esfuerzo físico; trabajo elaborado a mano (pág. 118; pág. 254; pág. 256)

maritime related to the sea or seafaring (p. 530)

marítimo relacionado con el mar o los marineros (pág. 530)

martial arts sports that involve combat and self-defense (pp. 524–525)

artes marciales deportes que implican combate y defensa personal (págs. 524–525)

martyr a person who is willing to die for his or her beliefs (p. 382)

mártir persona dispuesta a morir por sus creencias (pág. 382)

mass religious worship service for Catholic Christians (p. 568)

misa culto religioso de los cristianos católicos (pág. 568)

matrilineal tracing descent through mothers rather than fathers (p. 437)

matrilineal linaje que se traza teniendo en cuenta la línea materna, no la paterna (pág. 437)

***medical** relating to the practice of medicine (p. 344)

***médico** relativo al ejercicio de la medicina (p. 344)

***meditate** to focus one's thoughts to gain a higher level of spiritual awareness (p. 260)

***meditar** enfocar los pensamientos para alcanzar un nivel más elevado de conciencia espiritual (pág. 260)

mercantilism an economic theory that depends on a greater amount of exports than imports in order to increase a country's supply of gold and silver (p. 632)

mercantilismo teoría económica que depende de una mayor cantidad de exportaciones que de importaciones para aumentar la oferta de oro y plata de un país (pág. 632)

mercenary a soldier who fights for money rather than loyalty to a country (p. 584)

mercenario soldado que combate por dinero y no por lealtad a un país (pág. 584)

***method** a way of doing something; a procedure or process (p. 56; p. 239; p. 484; p. 633)

***método** manera de hacer algo; procedimiento o proceso (pág. 56; pág. 239; pág. 484; pág. 633)

***migrate** to move from one place to another (p. 252)

***migrar** desplazarse de un lugar a otro (pág. 252)

migration the movement of people from one place to settle in another place (p. 36)

migración desplazamiento de personas de un lugar a otro (pág. 36)

***military** of or relating to soldiers, arms, or war; relating to the armed forces (p. 87; p. 185; p. 281; p. 549; pp. 656–657)

***militar** relativo a los soldados, las armas o la guerra; relativo a las fuerzas armadas (pág. 87; pág. 185; pág. 281; pág. 549; págs. 656–657)

minaret the tower of a mosque from which Muslims are called to pray (pp. 414–415)

alminar torre de una mezquita desde la cual se convoca a los musulmanes a orar (págs. 414–415)

missionaries people who are sent by a religious organization to spread the faith (p. 546)

misioneros personas enviadas por una organización religiosa a difundir la fe (pág. 546)

monarchy a government whose ruler, a king or queen, inherits the position from a parent (p. 68)

monarquía gobierno cuyo jefe, un rey o una reina, hereda el cargo de uno de sus padres (pág. 68)

monastery a religious community (p. 389)

monasterio comunidad religiosa (pág. 389)

monotheism a belief in one God (pp. 140–141)

monoteísmo creencia en un solo Dios (págs. 140–141)

monsoon seasonal wind, especially in the Indian Ocean and southern Asia (p. 249)

monzón viento estacional, especialmente en el océano Índico y el sur de Asia (pág. 249)

mosaics motifs or images created by an arrangement of colored glass or stone (p. 364)

mosaicos motivos o imágenes creadas con vidrios o piedras de colores (pág. 364)

mosque a Muslim house of worship (p. 412)

mezquita casa musulmana de culto (pág. 412)

myth a traditional story that explains the practices or beliefs of a people or something in the natural world (pp. 212–213)

mito historia tradicional que explica las prácticas o creencias de un pueblo, o algo en el mundo natural (págs. 212–213)

N

nationalism the desire of people with the same customs and beliefs for self-rule (pp. 682–683)

nacionalismo deseo de autogobierno de las personas con las mismas costumbres y creencias (págs. 682–683)

neo-Confucianism a new form of the ideas of the philosopher Confucius; included Buddhist and Daoist beliefs (p. 480)

neoconfucianismo nueva forma de las ideas del filósofo Confucio; incluía las creencias budistas y taoístas (pág. 480)

Neolithic Age relating to the latest period of the Stone Age (pp. 62–63)

Era Neolítica relativo al último periodo de la Edad de Piedra (págs. 62–63)

***network** a connected group or system; a system where all parts are connected (p. 297; p. 530)

***red** grupo o sistema conectado; sistema donde todas las partes están conectadas (pág. 297; pág. 530)

nirvana in Buddhism, a state of perfect happiness and peace (p. 261)

nirvana en el Budismo, estado de felicidad y paz perfecta (pág. 261)

nomads people who move from place to place as a group to find food (pp. 54–55)

nómadas personas que viajan de un lugar a otro en búsqueda de alimento (págs. 54–55)

novel a long fictional story (p. 500)

novela historia de ficción larga (pág. 500)

O

oasis a green area in a desert fed by underground water (pp. 398–399)

oasis área verde en el desierto que se alimenta de agua subterránea (págs. 398–399)

obstacle something that stands in the way (p. 85)

obstáculo algo que se interpone en el camino (pág. 85)

***obtain** to gain something through a planned effort; to acquire or receive something; to take possession of (p. 118; p. 191; p. 620)	***obtener** conseguir algo mediante un esfuerzo planificado; adquirir o recibir algo; tomar posesión de (pág. 118; pág. 191; pág. 620)
***occur** to happen (p. 308)	***ocurrir** suceder (pág. 308)
ode a lyric poem that expresses strong emotions about life (pp. 346–347)	**oda** poema lírico que expresa fuertes emociones acerca de la vida (págs. 346–347)
oligarchy a government in which a small group has control (p. 184)	**oligarquía** gobierno en el cual un grupo pequeño tiene control (pág. 184)
ongoing continuously moving forward (p. 502)	**en curso** que se mueve continuamente hacia delante (pág. 502)
opportunity cost what is given up, such as time or money, to make or buy something (p. 40)	**costo de oportunidad** lo que se entrega, como tiempo o dinero, para hacer o comprar algo (pág. 40)
oracle a sacred shrine where a priest or priestess spoke for a god or goddess (p. 214)	**oráculo** templo sagrado donde un sacerdote o una sacerdotisa hablaba en nombre de un dios o una diosa (pág. 214)
oral history stories passed down from generation to generation (p. 438)	**historia oral** historias transmitidas de generación en generación (pág. 438)
oral tradition the custom of passing along stories by speech (pp. 216–217)	**tradición oral** costumbre de transmitir historias verbalmente (págs. 216–217)
orator a public speaker (p. 349)	**orador** persona que habla en público (pág. 349)
.org the ending of an Internet URL for an organization (p. 20)	**.org** parte final del URL (por sus siglas en inglés) de una organización (pág. 20)
***overseas** across the ocean or sea (pp. 618–619; pp. 678–679)	***ultramar** cruzando el océano o el mar (págs. 618–619; págs. 678–679)

P

Paleolithic relating to the earliest period of the Stone Age (pp. 54–55)	**Paleolítico** relativo al periodo más antiguo de la Edad de Piedra (págs. 54–55)
paleontology the study of fossils (pp. 8–9)	**paleontología** estudio de los fósiles (págs. 8–9)
papyrus a reed plant that grows wild along the Nile River (pp. 104–105)	**papiro** planta hueca que crecía a lo largo del río Nilo (págs. 104–105)
parable a short story that teaches moral lesson (p. 375)	**parábola** historia corta que enseña una lección moral (pág. 375)
***parallel** moving or lying in the same direction and the same distance apart (p. 77)	***paralelo** que se mueve o se extiende en la misma dirección y a la misma distancia (pág. 77)
***participate** to take part (p. 356)	***participar** tomar parte (pág. 356)

patriarch an older male figure of authority, often within a religious community (p. 497)

patriarca figura masculina de edad mayor que representa la autoridad, con frecuencia dentro de una comunidad religiosa (pág. 497)

patricians the ruling class of ancient Rome (pp. 312–313)

patricios clase gobernante de la antigua Roma (págs. 312–313)

Pax Romana Roman peace (pp. 328–329)

Pax Romana paz romana (págs. 328–329)

peninsula a piece of land nearly surrounded by water (pp. 174–175)

península espacio de tierra casi completamente rodeado por agua (págs. 174–175)

***period** a division of time that is shorter than an era (p. 150)

***periodo** división de tiempo más corta que una era (pág. 150)

persecute to treat a group of people cruelly or unfairly (pp. 664–665)

perseguir tratar a un grupo de personas de manera cruel o injusta (págs. 664–665)

***perspective** a way of showing the relationship between objects in a drawing to give the look of depth or distance (p. 592)

***perspectiva** modo de mostrar la relación entre los objetos en un dibujo para dar un aspecto de profundidad o distancia (pág. 592)

phalanx a group of armed foot soldiers in ancient Greece arranged close together in rows (p. 182)

falange grupo de infantería armada en la Grecia antigua que se organizaba en filas muy cerradas (pág.182)

pharaoh ruler of ancient Egypt (pp. 108–109)

faraón emperador del antiguo Egipto (págs. 108–109)

philosopher a person who searches for wisdom or enlightenment (p. 199)

filósofo persona que busca la sabiduría o la iluminación (pág. 199)

***philosophy** the study of the basic ideas about society, education, and right and wrong; basic beliefs, concepts, and attitudes (pp. 286–287; p. 344)

***filosofía** estudio de las ideas básicas sobre la sociedad, la educación y el bien y el mal; creencias, conceptos y actitudes básicas (págs. 286–287; pág. 344)

physical map a map that shows land and water features (p. 34)

mapa físico mapa que muestra los accidentes geográficos terrestres y marítimos (pág. 34)

pictograph a symbol in a writing system based on pictures (p. 282)

pictograma símbolo usado en un sistema de escritura que se basa en imágenes (pág. 282)

pilgrim a person who travels to holy sites (p. 268)

peregrino persona que viaja a lugares santos (pág. 268)

plagiarize to present someone's work as your own without giving that person credit (pp. 20–21)

plagiar presentar el trabajo de otra persona como propio sin darle ningún crédito a esa persona (págs. 20–21)

plague a disease that spreads quickly and kills many people (p. 570)

plaga enfermedad que se extiende rápidamente y mata a muchas personas (pág. 570)

plane geometry a branch of mathematics centered around measurement and relationships of points, lines, angles, and surfaces of figures on a plane (p. 240)

geometría plana rama de las matemáticas que estudia las medidas, las propiedades y las relaciones entre los puntos, las rectas, los ángulos y las superficies de las figuras en un plano (pág. 240)

plantation a large estate or farm that used enslaved people or hired workers to grow and harvest crops (pp. 628–629)

plantación gran propiedad o granja en la cual los esclavos o personas contratadas cultivaban y recolectaban las cosechas (págs. 628–629)

plateau an area of high and mostly flat land (p. 424)	**meseta** área alta y en su mayoría plana (pág. 424)
plebeians ordinary citizens in ancient Rome (pp. 312–313)	**plebeyos** ciudadanos comunes en la Roma antigua (págs. 312–313)
point of view a personal attitude about people or life (p. 12)	**punto de vista** actitud personal acerca de la vida o las personas (pág. 12)
polis a Greek city-state (p. 180)	**polis** ciudad-Estado griega (pág. 180)
political map a map that shows the names and borders of countries (p. 34)	**mapa político** mapa que muestra los nombres y las fronteras de los países (pág. 34)
polytheism a belief in more than one god (pp. 78–79)	**politeísmo** creencia en uno o más dioses (págs. 78–79)
pope the title given to the Bishop of Rome (pp. 384–385)	**papa** título dado al obispo de Roma (págs. 384–385)
popular sovereignty the idea that government is created by the people and must act according to people's wishes (pp. 670–671)	**soberanía popular** la idea de que el gobierno es creado por el pueblo y debe actuar de acuerdo con sus deseos (págs. 670–671)
porcelain a ceramic made of fine clay baked at very high temperatures (p. 483)	**porcelana** cerámica elaborada con arcilla fina cocida a temperaturas muy elevadas (pág. 483)
praetors Roman government officials who interpreted the law and judged (p. 313)	**pretores** funcionarios del gobierno romano que interpretaban la ley y actuaban como jueces (pág. 313)
***precise** exact (p. 6)	***preciso** exacto (pág. 6)
predestination a religious belief that God has already decided who will go to heaven and who will not (pp. 602–603)	**predestinación** creencia religiosa según la cual Dios ya ha decidido quién irá al Cielo y quién no (págs. 602–603)
***predict** to describe something that will happen in the future (p. 460)	***predecir** describir algo que sucederá en el futuro (pág. 460)
***primary** most important; first (p. 622)	***principal** lo más importante; primero (pág. 622)
primary source firsthand evidence of an event in history (pp. 10–11)	**fuente primaria** evidencia de primera mano de un hecho histórico (págs. 10–11)
***principle** an important law or belief; rules or a code of conduct (p. 407; p. 480)	***principio** ley o creencia importante; reglas o código de conducta (pág. 407; pág. 480)
proconsul a governor (p. 329)	**procónsul** gobernador (pág. 329)
***professional** relating to a type of job that usually requires training and practice (p. 322)	***profesional** relativo a un tipo de trabajo que por lo general exige capacitación y práctica (pág. 322)
projection a way of showing the round Earth on a flat map (pp. 30–31)	**proyección** manera de mostrar la forma redonda de la Tierra sobre un planisferio (págs. 30–31)
proletariat the working class (p. 700)	**proletariado** clase obrera (pág. 700)
***promote** to encourage the doing of something (pp. 266–267)	***promover** estimular la realización de algo (págs. 266–267)

prophet a messenger sent by God to share God's word with people (pp. 140–141)

profeta mensajero enviado por Dios para compartir su palabra con las personas (págs. 140–141)

***protect** to defend from trouble or harm (pp. 342–343)

***proteger** defender de problemas o daños (págs. 342-343)

proverb a wise saying (p. 150)

proverbio refrán sabio (pág. 150)

province a territory governed as a political district of a country or empire (p. 88)

provincia territorio gobernado como distrito político de un país o imperio (pág. 88)

psalm a sacred song or poem used in worship (p. 149)

salmo canción o poema sagrado que se usa en el culto (pág. 149)

***publish** to produce the work of an author, usually in print (p. 414)

***publicar** producir la obra de un autor, por lo general de manera impresa (pág. 414)

***pursue** to follow in order to capture or defeat (pp. 232–233)

***perseguir** seguir para capturar o derrotar (págs. 232–233)

pyramid great stone tomb for an Egyptian pharaoh (pp. 112–113)

pirámide gran tumba de piedra para los faraones egipcios (págs. 112–113)

Q

quipu a tool with a system of knots used for mathematics (p. 465)

quipu instrumento con un sistema de nudos usado para las matemáticas (pág. 465)

Quran the holy book of Islam (pp. 402–403)

Corán libro sagrado del islam (págs. 402–403)

R

rabbi the official leader of a Jewish congregation (p. 166)

rabino líder oficial de una congregación judía (pág. 166)

***radical** extreme or far-reaching (pp .674–675)

***radical** extremo o de largo alcance (págs. 674–675)

raja an Indian prince (p. 254)

rajá príncipe indio (pág. 254)

***range** the limits between which something can change or differ (p. 590)

***intervalo** límites entre los cuales algo puede cambiar o diferir (pág. 590)

rationalism the belief that reason and experience must be present for the solution of problems (pp. 648–649)

racionalismo creencia en que la razón y la experiencia son necesarias para la solución de problemas (págs. 648–649)

recession a period of slow economic growth or decline (p. 41)

recesión periodo de crecimiento económico lento o descendente (pág. 41)

Reconquista the Christian effort to take back the Iberian Peninsula (pp. 574–575)

Reconquista esfuerzo cristiano por recuperar la Península Ibérica (págs. 574–575)

Reformation a religious movement that created a new form of Christianity known as Protestantism (pp. 598–599)

***Reforma** movimiento religioso que creó una nueva forma de cristianismo conocida como protestantismo (págs. 598–599)

reforms changes to bring about improvement (p. 352)

reformas cambios para obtener mejoras (pág. 352)

***regime** rulers during a given period of time (pp. 493–494)	***régimen** gobernantes durante un periodo determinado (págs. 493–494)
***region** a broad geographic area (p. 90; pp. 380–381)	***región** área geográfica amplia (pág. 90; págs. 380–381)
reincarnation the rebirth of the soul (p. 258)	**reencarnación** renacimiento del alma (pág. 258)
***reinforce** to strengthen (p. 352)	***reforzar** fortalecer (pág. 352)
***reject** to refuse to accept or consider (p. 221; p. 387)	***rechazar** negarse a aceptar o considerar (pág. 221; pág. 387)
***reluctantly** hesitantly or unwillingly (p. 315)	***a regañadientes** con vacilación o de mala gana (pág. 315)
***rely** to depend on someone or something; to be dependent; to count on for help (pp. 128–129; p. 281; p. 462; pp. 624–625)	***confiar** depender de alguien o de algo; ser dependiente; contar con la ayuda de alguien (págs. 128–129; pág. 281; pág. 462; págs. 624-625)
Renaissance a renewal or rebirth of interest in Greek and Roman arts (pp. 582–583)	**Renacimiento** renacer del interés en las artes griegas y romanas (págs. 582–583)
representative democracy a form of democracy in which citizens elect officials to govern on their behalf (pp. 198–199)	**democracia representativa** forma de democracia en la cual los ciudadanos eligen a los funcionarios para que gobiernen en su nombre (págs. 198–199)
representative government government in which citizens elect officials who administer its policies (pp. 44–45)	**gobierno representativo** gobierno en el cual los ciudadanos eligen a los funcionarios que administran sus políticas (págs. 44–45)
republic a form of government in which citizens elect their leaders (p. 310)	**república** forma de gobierno en la cual los ciudadanos eligen a sus líderes (pág. 310)
***reside** to be present continuously or have a home in a particular place; to live (p. 111; p. 252)	***residir** estar presente de manera continua o tener un hogar en un lugar determinado; vivir (pág. 111; pág. 252)
***resource** something that is useful; a ready supply of something valuable (pp. 38–39; p. 630)	***recurso** algo que es útil; una provisión constante de algo valioso (págs. 38–39; pág. 630)
***restore** to bring something back to an original state; to bring something back to an earlier or better condition (p. 362; p. 476; pp. 604–605)	***restaurar** volver a dejar algo en su estado original; volver a dejar algo en una condición anterior o mejor (pág. 362; pág. 476; págs. 604–605)
resurrection the act of rising from the dead (p. 377)	**resurrección** acción de levantarse de entre los muertos (pág. 377)
***reveal** to make information public; to tell a secret; to make known (p. 221)	***revelar** hacer pública una información; contar un secreto; dar a conocer (pág. 221)
rhetoric the art of public speaking and debate (p. 221)	**retórica** arte de hablar y debatir en público (pág. 221)
ritual words or actions that are part of a religious ceremony (p. 213)	**ritual** palabras o acciones que forman parte de una ceremonia religiosa (pág. 213)
***role** the function or part an individual fills in society; something that plays a part in the process (p. 116; pp. 540–541)	***rol** función o papel que un individuo cumple en la sociedad; algo que desempeña un papel en el proceso (pág. 116; págs. 540–541)

rouse to stir up or excite (p. 597)

despertar provocar o suscitar (pág. 597)

S

Sabbath a weekly day of worship and rest (pp. 154–155)

sabbat día semanal de culto y descanso (págs. 154–155)

saints people considered holy by followers of the Christian faith (p. 364)

santos personas que los seguidores de la fe cristiana consideran sagradas (pág. 364)

salvation the act of being saved from the effects of sin (pp. 378–379)

salvación acción de salvarse de los efectos del pecado (págs. 378–379)

samurai a warrior who served a Japanese lord and lived by a strict code of loyalty (p. 521)

samurái guerrero que servía a un señor japonés y vivía de acuerdo con un estricto código de lealtad (pág. 521)

Sanskrit the first written language of India (p. 254)

sánscrito primera lengua escrita de la India (pág. 254)

satrap the governor of a province in ancient Persia (p. 191)

sátrapa gobernador de una provincia en la antigua Persia (pág. 191)

satrapy the territory governed by an official known as a satrap (p. 191)

satrapía territorio gobernado por un funcionario llamado sátrapa (pág. 191)

satire verse or prose that pokes fun at human weakness (pp. 346–347)

sátira verso o prosa que se burla de la debilidad humana (págs. 346–347)

savanna a flat grassland, sometimes with scattered trees, in a tropical or subtropical region (pp. 128–129; p. 423)

sabana pradera llana en una región tropical o subtropical, algunas veces con árboles dispersos (págs. 128-129; pág. 423)

scale a measuring line that shows the distances on a map (p. 35)

escala línea de medición que muestra las distancias en un mapa (pág. 35)

scarcity the lack of a resource (p. 40)

escasez falta de un recurso (pág. 40)

schism a separation or division from a church (p. 389)

cisma separación o división de una Iglesia (pág. 389)

scholarly concerned with academic learning or research (p. 14)

erudito relacionado con el aprendizaje académico o la investigación (pág. 14)

scholasticism a way of thinking that combined faith and reason (p. 565)

escolasticismo forma de pensar que combinaba la fe y la razón (pág. 565)

scientific method the steps for an orderly search for knowledge (pp. 648–649)

método científico pasos para una búsqueda de conocimiento ordenada (págs. 648–649)

Scientific Revolution a period from the 1500s to the 1700s in which many scientific advances changed people's traditional beliefs about science (p. 644)

revolución científica periodo entre los siglos XVI y XVIII en el cual muchos avances científicos cambiaron las creencias tradicionales de las personas sobre la ciencia (pág. 644)

scribe a person who copies or writes out documents; often a record keeper (p. 82)

escriba persona que copia o escribe documentos; con frecuencia, quien lleva los archivos (pág. 82)

scroll a long document made from pieces of parchment sewn together (p. 155)

rollo documento largo elaborado con pedazos de pergamino unidos (pág. 155)

secondary source a document or written work created after an event (p. 11)	**fuente secundaria** documento o trabajo que se escribe después de que ocurre un evento (pág. 11)
sect a religious group (pp. 524–525)	**secta** grupo religioso (págs. 524–525)
secular related to worldly things (pp. 582–583)	**secular** relacionado con las cosas terrenales (págs. 582–583)
***secure** free from danger (pp. 564–565)	***seguro** libre de peligro (págs. 564–565)
***seek** to look for or try to achieve; to search for (pp. 45–46; p. 237)	***buscar** indagar o tratar de alcanzar; investigar (págs. 45–46; pág. 237)
seminary a school for religious training (pp. 606–607)	**seminario** escuela para la formación religiosa (págs. 606–607)
separation of powers the division of power among the branches of government; a government structure that has three distinct branches: legislative, executive, and judicial (pp. 44–45; pp. 652–653)	**separación de poderes** división del poder entre las ramas del gobierno; estructura de gobierno que tiene tres ramas distintas: legislativa, ejecutiva y judicial (págs. 44–45; págs. 652–653)
serf a member of the peasant class tied to the land and subject to the will of the landowner (pp. 550–551)	**siervo** miembro de la clase campesina atado a la tierra y sujeto a la voluntad del terrateniente (págs. 550–551)
shadoof a bucket attached to a long pole used to transfer river water to storage basins (p. 104)	**cigoñal** cubeta atada a una pértiga larga que se usa para pasar agua del río a vasijas de almacenamiento (pág. 104)
shamanism belief in gods, demons, and spirits (p. 511)	**chamanismo** creencia en dioses, demonios y espíritus (pág. 511)
shari'ah Islamic code of law (pp. 402–403)	***sharia*** código jurídico islámico (págs. 402–403)
Shia group of Muslims who believed the descendants of Ali should rule (p. 407)	**chiíta** grupo musulmán que creía que los descendientes de Alá debían gobernar (pág. 407)
sheikh the leader of an Arab tribe (p. 399)	**jeque** líder de una tribu árabe (pág. 399)
shogun a military governor who ruled Japan (p. 522)	**sogún** gobernante militar que reinaba en Japón (pág. 522)
shrine a place where people worship (p. 66)	**templo** lugar donde la gente rinde culto (pág. 66)
silt fine particles of fertile soil (p. 77)	**limo** partículas finas de suelo fértil (pág. 77)
***similar** having things in common; having characteristics in common (p. 287; p. 440)	***similar** que tiene cosas en común; que tiene características en común (pág. 287; pág. 440)
sinkhole a depression or hollow where soil has collapsed (pp. 459–460)	**sumidero** depresión u hoyo donde el suelo ha colapsado (págs. 459–460)
smallpox a disease that causes a high fever and often death (p. 625)	**viruela** enfermedad que produce fiebre alta y con frecuencia, la muerte (pág. 625)
smith craftsperson who works with metal (p. 349)	**herrero** artesano que trabaja los metales (pág. 349)
***social class** a group of people who are at a similar cultural, economic, or educational level (p. 289)	***clase social** grupo de personas con un nivel cultural, económico o educativo similar (pág. 289)

Socratic method philosophical method of questioning to gain truth (p. 221)

método socrático método filosófico que consiste en hacer preguntas para conocer la verdad (pág. 221)

social contract an agreement between the people and their government (p. 652)

contrato social acuerdo entre el pueblo y su gobierno (pág. 652)

socialism the means of production are owned and controlled by the people, through their government (pp. 698–699)

socialismo medios de producción de propiedad de las personas y controlados por ellas a través de su gobierno (págs. 698–699)

solid geometry a branch of mathematics about measurement and relationships of points, lines, angles, surfaces, and solids in three-dimensional space (p. 240)

geometría sólida rama de las matemáticas que estudia las medidas, las propiedades y las relaciones entre los puntos, las líneas, los ángulos, las superficies y los sólidos en el espacio tridimensional (pág. 240)

Sophists Greek teachers of philosophy, reasoning, and public speaking (p. 221)

sofistas maestros griegos de filosofía, razonamiento y retórica (pág. 221)

***source** a document or reference work (pp. 10–11)

***fuente** documento u obra de referencia (págs. 10–11)

special-purpose map a map that shows themes or patterns such as climate, natural resources, or population (pp. 34–35)

mapa temático mapa que muestra temas o patrones como el clima, los recursos naturales o la población (págs. 34–35)

specialization the act of training for a particular job (p. 66)

especialización acción de capacitarse para un trabajo específico (pág. 66)

species a class of individuals with similar physical characteristics (pp. 8–9)

especie clase de individuos con características físicas semejantes (págs. 8–9)

spiritual a gospel song (pp. 440–441)

espiritual canción de música gospel (págs. 440–441)

***stability** the condition of being steady and unchanging (p. 186)

***estabilidad** cualidad de estar fijo o ser inalterable (pág. 186)

***status** a person's rank compared to others (pp. 258–259)

***estatus** posición de una persona en comparación con otras (págs. 258–259)

steppe flat, dry grassland (pp. 489–490)

estepa sabana plana y seca (págs. 489–490)

Stoicism the philosophy of the Stoics who believed that people should not try to feel joy or sadness (p. 238)

estoicismo filosofía de los estoicos, quienes creían que las personas no debían tratar de sentir alegría ni tristeza (pág. 238)

***stress** to focus on or emphasize (p. 701)

***destacar** enfocarse o poner énfasis en algo (pág. 701)

***structure** a building or other built object (p. 270)

***estructura** edificio u otro tipo de construcción (pág. 270)

stupa a Buddhist shrine, usually dome-shaped (pp. 266–267)

estupa templo budista, por lo general en forma de domo (págs. 266–267)

stutter an uneven repetition of sounds and words (p. 85)

tartamudeo repetición irregular de sonidos y palabras (pág. 85)

***style** a distinctive form or type of something (pp. 218–219; pp. 530–531)

***estilo** forma o tipo característicos de algo (págs. 218–219; págs. 530–531)

subcontinent a large landmass that is smaller than a continent (pp. 248–249)

subcontinente gran masa continental más pequeña que un continente (págs. 248–249)

***successor** one that comes after (p. 332)	***sucesor** persona que sucede a otra (pág. 332)
***sufficient** enough (p. 202)	***suficiente** bastante (pág. 202)
sugarcane a grassy plant that is a natural source of sugar (pp. 438–439)	**caña de azúcar** planta herbácea que es una fuente natural de azúcar (págs. 438–439)
sultan Seljuk leader (p. 408)	**sultán** líder seléucida (pág. 408)
Sunni group of Muslims who accepted the rule of the Umayyad caliphs (p. 407)	**sunita** grupo musulmán que solo acepta el mandato de los califas Umayyad (pág. 407)
supply the amount of a good or service that a producer wants to sell (p. 39)	**oferta** cantidad de un producto o servicio que un productor quiere vender (pág. 39)
surplus an amount that is left over after a need has been met (p. 78)	**excedente** cantidad que queda luego de satisfacer una necesidad (pág. 78)
***survive** to continue to live; to live through a dangerous event; to continue to function or prosper (p. 152; pp. 434–435)	***sobrevivir** seguir viviendo; vivir luego de haber tenido una experiencia peligrosa; continuar funcionando o prosperar (pág. 152; págs. 434–435)
Swahili the unique culture of Africa's East Coast and the language spoken there (pp. 434–435)	**swahili** cultura exclusiva de la costa este de África y lengua que se habla allí (págs. 434–435)
***symbol** a sign or image that stands for something else; something that stands for or suggests something else (p. 35; p. 701)	***símbolo** signo o imagen que representa otra cosa; algo que representa o sugiere algo más (pág. 35; pág. 701)
synagogue a Jewish house of worship (pp. 154–155)	**sinagoga** casa judía de culto (págs. 154–155)
systematic agriculture the organized growing of food on a regular schedule (pp. 62–63)	**agricultura sistemática** cultivo organizado de alimentos de acuerdo con un calendario habitual (págs. 62–63)

T

***technology** the use of advanced methods to solve problems; an ability gained by the practical use of knowledge (pp. 38–39; p. 56)	***tecnología** uso de métodos avanzados para solucionar problemas habilidad obtenida mediante el uso práctico del conocimiento (págs. 38–39; pág. 56)
***temporary** not permanent; lasting for a limited period (pp. 464–465)	***temporal** que no es permanente; que dura un periodo limitado (págs. 464–465)
tenant farmer a farmer who works land owned by someone else and pays rent in cash or as a share of the crop (p. 295)	**agricultor arrendatario** agricultor que trabaja la tierra que pertenece a otro y le paga una renta ya sea en efectivo o con parte de sus cosechas (pág. 295)
***tensions** opposition between individuals or groups; stress (p. 164)	***tensiones** oposición entre individuos o grupos; presión (pág. 164)
terror violent acts that are meant to cause fear in people (pp. 490–491)	**terror** actos violentos que buscan atemorizar a las personas (págs. 490–491)

***text** words written down in a particular form, such as a book (p. 254)

***texto** palabras escritas en un formato específico, como un libro (pág. 254)

textile woven cloth (pp. 132–133)

textil tela tejida (págs. 132–133)

***theme** a topic that is studied or a special quality that connects ideas (p. 32)

***tema** materia que se estudia o cualidad especial que conecta ideas (pág. 32)

theocracy a government of religious leader(s) (pp. 108–109)

teocracia gobierno de uno o más líderes religiosos (págs. 108–109)

theology the study of religious faith, practice, and experience (p. 565)

teología estudio de la fe, la práctica y la experiencia religiosas (pág. 565)

***theory** an explanation of how or why something happens (pp. 642–643)

***teoría** explicación de cómo o por qué sucede algo (págs. 642–643)

Torah teachings that Moses received from God; later became the first part of the Hebrew Bible (p. 143)

Tora enseñanza que recibió Moisés de Dios; llegó a ser la primera parte de la Biblia hebrea (pág. 143)

***tradition** a custom, or way of life, passed down from generation to generation (pp. 154–155)

***tradición** costumbre, o forma de vida, que se transmite de una generación a otra (págs. 154–155)

traditional economy an economic system in which custom decides what people do, make, buy, and sell (p. 40)

economía tradicional sistema económico en el cual la costumbre decide lo que las personas hacen, producen, compran y venden (pág. 40)

tragedy a play or film in which characters fail to overcome serious problems (p. 217)

tragedia obra de teatro o película en la cual los personajes no pueden superar problemas graves (pág. 217)

***transfer** to copy from one surface to another by contact (p. 484)

***transferir** copiar de una superficie a otra por contacto (pág. 484)

***transform** to change the structure of; to bring about a large and widespread change (p. 322; p. 634)

***transformar** cambiar la estructura; provocar un cambio grande y generalizado (pág. 322; pág. 634)

transformation a complete change (p. 497)

transformación cambio total (pág. 497)

transport to transfer or carry from one place to another (pp. 424–425)

***transportar** transferir o llevar de un lugar a otro (págs. 424–425)

trial jury a group of citizens that decides whether an accused person is innocent or guilty (p. 558)

jurado grupo de ciudadanos que decide si un acusado es inocente o culpable (pág. 558)

tribe a social group made up of families or clans (p. 142)

tribu grupo social conformado por familias o clanes (pág. 142)

tribune an elected Roman official who protects the rights of ordinary citizens (p. 313)

tribuno funcionario romano elegido que protege los derechos de los ciudadanos comunes (pág. 313)

tribute payment made to a ruler or state as a sign of surrender; payment to a ruler as a sign of submission or for protection (p. 88; pp. 514–515)

tributo pago hecho a un gobernante o Estado en señal de rendición; pago a un gobernante como señal de sumisión o para obtener protección (pág. 88; págs. 514–515)

triumvirate three rulers who share equal political power (p. 323)

triunvirato tres gobernantes que comparten el mismo poder político (pág. 323)

tsunami a huge ocean wave caused by an undersea earthquake (p. 529)

tsunami enorme ola oceánica causada por un sismo subacuático (pág. 529)

tyrant an absolute ruler unrestrained by law; harsh ruler (pp. 183–184; p. 719)

tirano gobernante absoluto que actúa sin control por parte de la ley; gobernante cruel (págs. 183–184; pág. 719)

U

***unify** to bring together in one unit; to join; to make into one group (pp. 106–107; pp. 292–293; pp. 608–609)

***unificar** juntar en una unidad; unir; formar un grupo (págs. 106–107; págs. 292–293; págs. 608–609)

***unique** one of a kind; different from all others (pp. 100–101; p. 431)

***exclusivo** único en su clase; diferente de los demás (págs. 100–101; pág. 431)

urban having to do with a town or city rather than a rural area (p. 583)

urbano relativo a un pueblo o una ciudad, no a un área rural (pág. 583)

urbanization the increase in the proportion of people living in cities rather than rural areas (pp. 696–697)

urbanización aumento en la proporción de personas que viven en las ciudades y no en áreas rurales (págs. 696–697)

utilitarianism belief that society should provide the greatest happiness for the largest number of people (p. 699)

utilitarismo creencia de que la sociedad debe brindar la mayor felicidad al mayor número de personas (pág. 699)

URL the abbreviation for uniform resource locator; the address of an online resource (p. 20)

URL abreviatura de uniform resource locator (localizador uniforme de recursos); dirección de un recurso en línea (pág. 20)

V

vassal a person under the protection of a lord to whom he has vowed loyalty; a low-ranking noble under the protection of a feudal lord (p. 523; pp. 548–549)

vasallo persona bajo la protección de un señor a quien ha jurado lealtad; noble de baja categoría bajo la protección de un señor feudal (pág. 523; págs. 548–549)

vault a curved ceiling made of arches (p. 345)

bóveda techo curvo compuesto por arcos (pág. 345)

Vedas ancient sacred writings of India (p. 254)

Vedas antiguos escritos sagrados de la India (pág. 254)

vernacular the everyday spoken language of a region (p. 566)

vernácula lengua hablada en una región (pág. 566)

***version** a different form or edition; a translation of the Bible (p. 161)

***versión** formato o edición diferentes; traducción de la Biblia (pág. 161)

veto to reject (p. 313)

vetar rechazar (pág. 313)

vigil the night before a religious feast (p. 597)

vigilia la noche anterior a una fiesta religiosa (pág. 597)

vile morally low (p. 597)

vil de baja moral (pág. 597)

***violate** to disobey or break a rule or law (pp. 20–21)

***violar** desobedecer o incumplir una regla o ley (págs. 20-21)

volcano a mountain that releases hot or melted rocks from inside the Earth (pp. 528–529)

volcán montaña que libera rocas calientes o fundidas desde el interior de la Tierra (págs. 528–529)

***volume** amount included within limits (p. 452)

***volumen** cantidad incluida dentro de los límites (pág. 452)

***voluntarily** by choice or free will; willingly (p. 231)

***voluntariamente** por elección o voluntad propia, con gusto (pág. 231)

W

warlord a military commander exercising civil power by force, usually in a limited area (p. 281)

caudillo comandante militar que ejerce el poder civil por la fuerza, usualmente en un área limitada (pág. 281)

widespread frequent in many places, common (p. 673)

***generalizado** frecuente en muchos lugares, común (pág. 673)

Z

ziggurat a pyramid-shaped structure with a temple at the top (p. 80)

zigurat estructura en forma de pirámide, en cuya punta se encuentra un templo (pág. 80)

Zoroastrianism a Persian religion based on the belief of one god (p. 192)

zoroastrismo religión persa que se basaba en la creencia en un dios (pág. 192)

INDEX

NOTE Page numbers listed below refer to the page numbers shown on the reduced student edition pages.

The following abbreviations are used in the index: *m=map, c=chart, p=photograph or picture, g=graph, crt=cartoon, ptg=painting, q=quote*

Index

Index

Index

Index

Index

Index

Index

Index

Index

Index

Index

Index

Index

Index

Index